Autodesk Fusion Black Book (V 2701.1.18) Part II

By
Gaurav Verma
Matt Weber
(CADCAMCAE Works)

ISBN # 978-1-77459-205-2

DEDICATION

To teachers, who make it possible to disseminate knowledge
to enlighten the young and curious minds
of our future generations

To students, who are the future of the world

THANKS

To my friends and colleagues

To my family for their love and support

Table of Contents

Chapter 13 : Sculpting-2

Chapter 14 : Mesh Design

Chapter 15 : Manufacturing

Chapter 16 : Generating Milling Toolpaths - 1

Chapter 17 : Generating Milling Toolpaths - 2

Chapter 18 : Generating Turning and Cutting Toolpaths

Chapter 19 : Probing, Additive Manufacturing, and Miscellaneous CAM Tools

Chapter 20 : Introduction to Simulation in Fusion

Chapter 21 : Simulation Studies in Fusion

Chapter 22 : Sheetmetal Design

Chapter 23 : Generative Design

Part I of this book covers

Preface

Autodesk Fusion is a product of Autodesk Inc. Fusion is the first of its kind software which combine 3D CAD, CAM, and CAE tool in single package. It connects your entire product development process in a single cloud-based platform that works on both Mac and PC. In CAD environment, you can create the model with parametric designing and dimensioning. The CAD environment is equally applicable for assembly design. The CAE environment facilitates to analysis the model under real-world load conditions. Once the model is as per your requirement then generate the NC program using the CAM environment.

The **Autodesk Fusion Black Book** (V 2701.1.18) is 9th edition of our series on Autodesk Fusion. The book is updated on Autodesk Fusion Student Version 2701.1.18 which is March, 2026 version of software. With lots of features and thorough review, we present a book to help professionals as well as beginners in creating some of the most complex solid models. The book follows a step by step methodology. In this book, we have tried to give real-world examples with real challenges in designing. We have tried to reduce the gap between educational use of Autodesk Fusion and industrial use of Autodesk Fusion. This edition of book, includes latest topics on Sketching, 3D Part Designing, Assembly Design, Sculpting, Mesh Design, CAM, Simulation, Sheetmetal, 3D printing, Manufacturing, and many other topics. Latest enhancements of the software have been added in this edition. The book covers almost all the information required by a learner to master the Autodesk Fusion. The book starts with sketching and ends at advanced topics like Manufacturing, Simulation, and Generative Design. Some of the salient features of this book are :

In-Depth explanation of concepts

Every new topic of this book starts with the explanation of the basic concepts. In this way, the user becomes capable of relating the things with real world.

Topics Covered

Every chapter starts with a list of topics being covered in that chapter. In this way, the user can easy find the topic of his/her interest easily.

Instruction through illustration

The instructions to perform any action are provided by maximum number of illustrations so that the user can perform the actions discussed in the book easily and effectively. There are about **2450** small and large illustrations that make the learning process effective.

Tutorial point of view

At the end of concept's explanation, the tutorial make the understanding of users firm and long lasting. Almost each chapter of the book has tutorials that are real world projects. Moreover most of the tools in this book are discussed in the form of tutorials.

Project

Free projects and exercises are provided to students for practicing.

For Faculty

If you are a faculty member, then you can ask for video tutorials on any of the topic, exercise, tutorial, or concept. As faculty, you can register on our website to get electronic desk copies of our latest books, self-assessment, and solution of practical. Faculty resources are available in the **Faculty Member** page of our website (**www.cadcamcaeworks.com**) once you login. Note that faculty registration approval is manual and it may take two days for approval before you can access the faculty website.

Formatting Conventions Used in the Text

All the key terms like name of button, tool, drop-down etc. are kept bold.

Free Resources

Link to the resources used in this book are provided to the users via email. To get the resources, mail us at ***cadcamcaeworks@gmail.com*** with your contact information. With your contact record with us, you will be provided latest updates and informations regarding various technologies. The format to write us mail for resources is as follows:

Subject of E-mail as ***Application for resources of ________ book***.
Also, given your information like
Name:
Course pursuing/Profession:
E-mail ID:

Note: We respect your privacy and value it. If you do not want to give your personal informations then you can ask for resources without giving your information.

About Authors

The author of this book, Gaurav Verma, has authored and assisted in more than 17 titles in CAD/CAM/CAE which are already available in market. He has authored **Autodesk Fusion PCB Black Book** for working on electronics design. He has authored **AutoCAD Electrical Black Books** which are available in both **English** and **Russian** language. He has also authored books on various modules of Creo Parametric and SolidWorks. He has provided consultant services to many industries in US, Greece, Canada, and UK. He has assisted in preparing many Government aided skill development programs. He has been speaker for Autodesk University. He has assisted in preparing AutoCAD Electrical course for Autodesk Design Academy. He has worked on Sheetmetal, Forging, Machining, and Casting designs in Design and Development departments of various manufacturing firms.

For Any query or suggestion

If you have any query or suggestion, please let us know by mailing us on ***cadcamcaeworks@gmail.com***. Your valuable constructive suggestions will be incorporated in our books.

Page left blank intentionally

Chapter 12

Sculpting

Topics Covered

The major topics covered in this chapter are:

- ***Introduction to Sculpting***
- ***Box***
- ***Plane***
- ***Cylinder***
- ***Sphere***
- ***Torus***
- ***Quadball***
- ***Pipe***
- ***Face***
- ***Extrude***
- ***Revolve***
- ***Edit Form and Edit By Curve Tool***
- ***Insert Edge and Insert Point***
- ***Subdivide and Bridge***
- ***Merge Edge***
- ***Fill Hole***
- ***Erase and Fill***
- ***Weld Vertices and Unweld Edges***
- ***Crease and Uncrease***
- ***Bevel Edges and Slide Edges***
- ***Smooth and Cylindrify***
- ***Pull and Flatten***
- ***Straighten and Interpolate***
- ***Match and Thicken***
- ***Freeze and UnFreeze***

INTRODUCTION

Sculpting is a workspace that offers tools to push, pull, grab, or pinch objects to modify their shapes. In this chapter, you will learn various commands and tools of **FORM** mode which are used to create or modify the object.

OPENING THE FORM MODE

The components or parts created in Form mode can be easily converted to solid bodies. Form mode is used to create sculpt features using free flow modifications of model surfaces. This mode is available in **DESIGN** workspace. The procedure to activate this mode is discussed next.

- Click on the **DESIGN** option from the **Change Workspace** drop-down in the **Toolbar**. The **DESIGN** workspace will be displayed in **Autodesk Fusion** window.
- Click on the **Create Form** tool from **CREATE** drop-down in the **Toolbar**; refer to Figure-1. The **FORM** mode will be displayed with the updated **Toolbar**; refer to Figure-2.

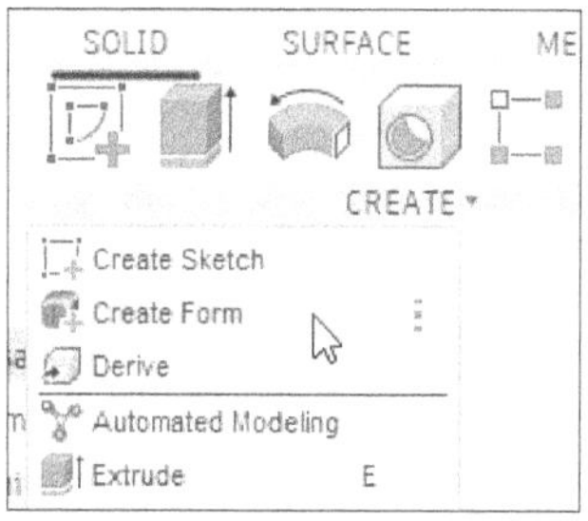

Figure-1. Create Form tool

Figure-2. Form Mode

CREATION TOOLS

In this section, we will discuss the creation tools used to create form (also called sculpt).

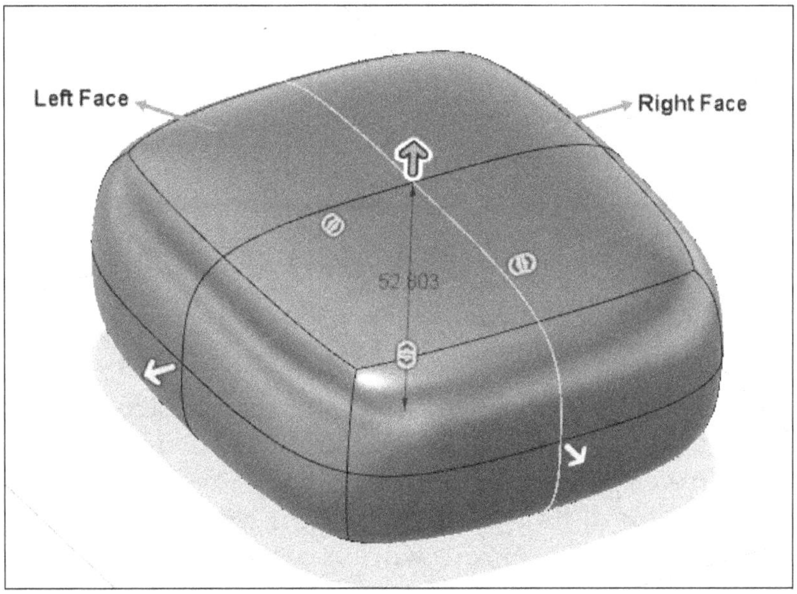

Figure-8. Width Symmetry

- Select the **Height Symmetry** check box if you want to apply mirror symmetry between upper and lower faces of sculpt object; refer to Figure-9.

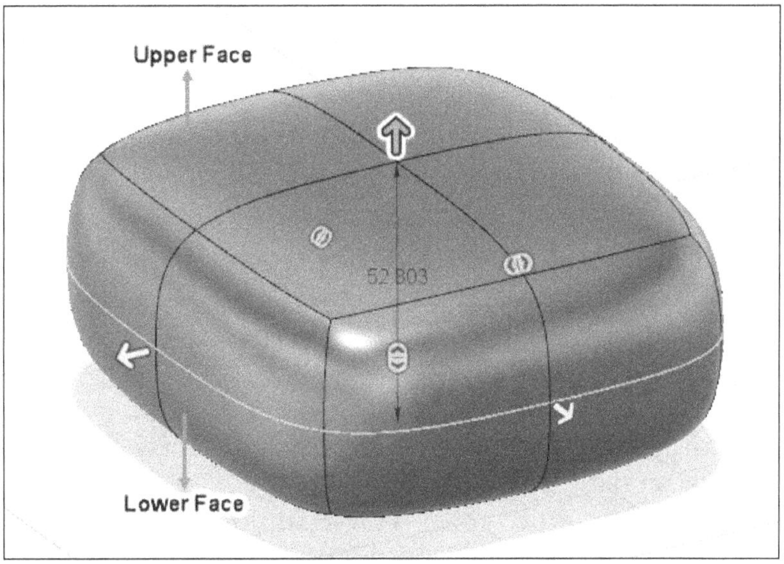

Figure-9. Height Symmetry

- Specify desired parameters in **Direction** drop-down as discussed earlier in **DESIGN Workspace**.
- Note that you can also change shape of box by using the drag handles. After specifying the parameters, click on **OK** button from **BOX** dialog box to complete the process.

Plane

The **Plane** tool is used to create T-Spline plane. The procedure to use this tool is discussed next.

- Click on the **Plane** tool from **CREATE** drop-down; refer to Figure-10. The **PLANE** dialog box will be displayed; refer to Figure-11.

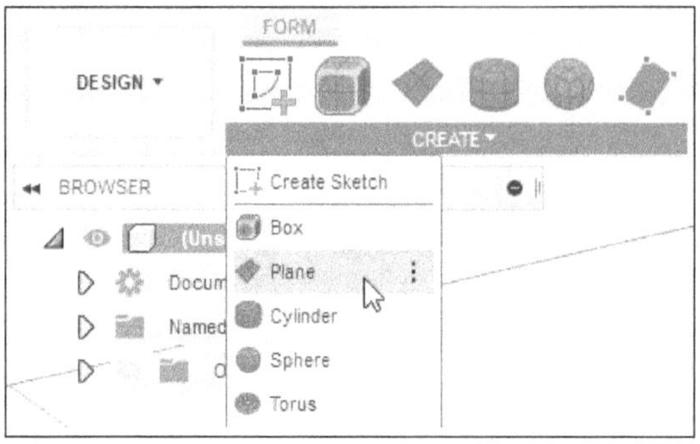

Figure-10. Plane tool

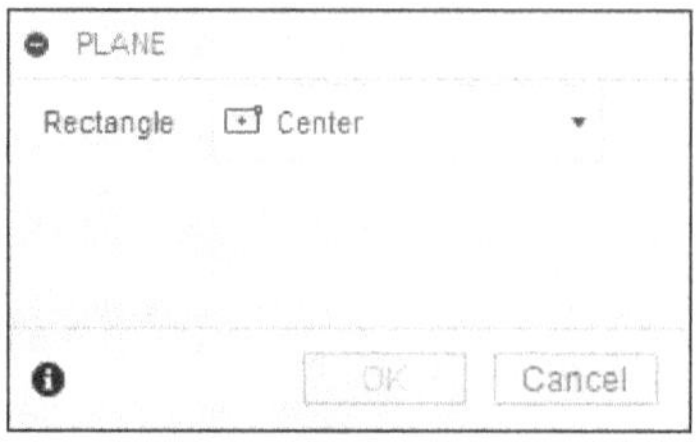

Figure-11. PLANE dialog box

- The options of **Rectangle** drop-down in **PLANE** dialog box are same as discussed earlier in last section.
- Click on the screen to specify the center point.
- Type desired dimension of length and width in respective input boxes and click on the screen. The preview of plane will be displayed along with updated **PLANE** dialog box; refer to Figure-12.

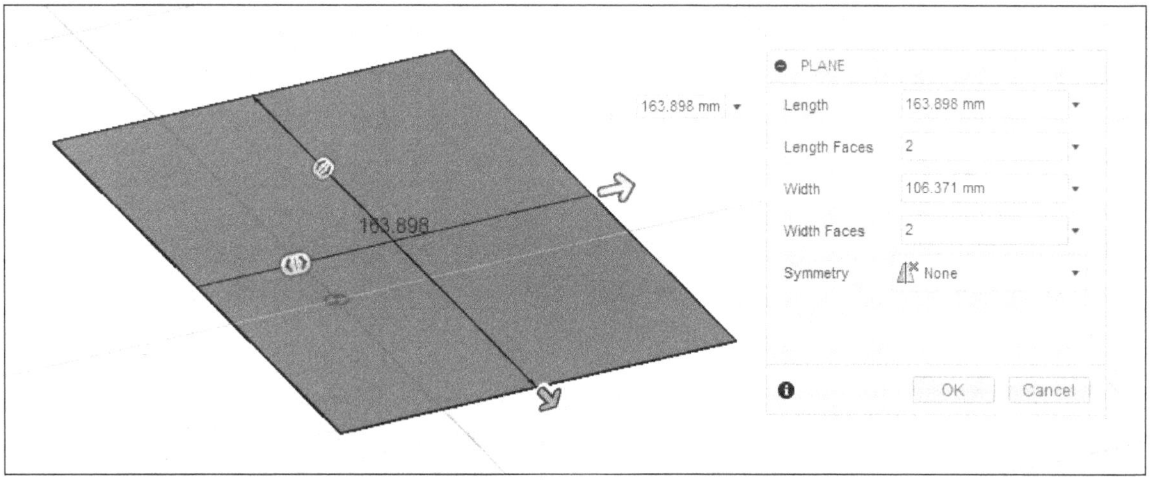

Figure-12. Updated PLANE dialog box

- If you want to change the length of plane then click in the **Length** edit box and enter desired value or use drag handles.
- Click in the **Length Faces** edit box of **PLANE** dialog box and enter the number of faces in which surface of plane will be divided along the length.
- If you want to change the width of plane then click on the **Width** edit box and enter desired value.
- Click in the **Width Faces** edit box of **PLANE** dialog box and enter the number of faces in which surface of plane will be divided along the width.
- After specifying the parameters, click on the **OK** button from **PLANE** dialog box to complete the process of creating plane. The plane will be displayed; refer to Figure-13.

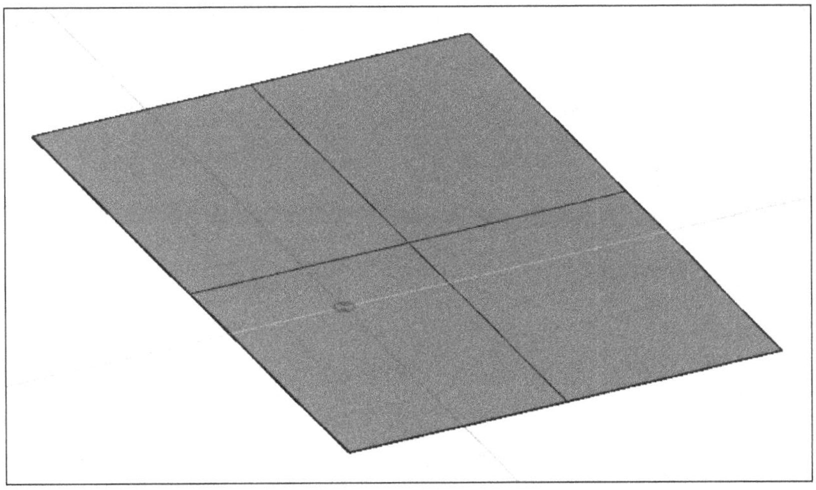

Figure-13. Plane created

Cylinder

The **Cylinder** tool is used to create a cylindrical body by defining diameter and depth. The procedure to use this tool is discussed next.

- Click on the **Cylinder** tool from **CREATE** drop-down; refer to Figure-14. The **CYLINDER** dialog box will be displayed; refer to Figure-15.

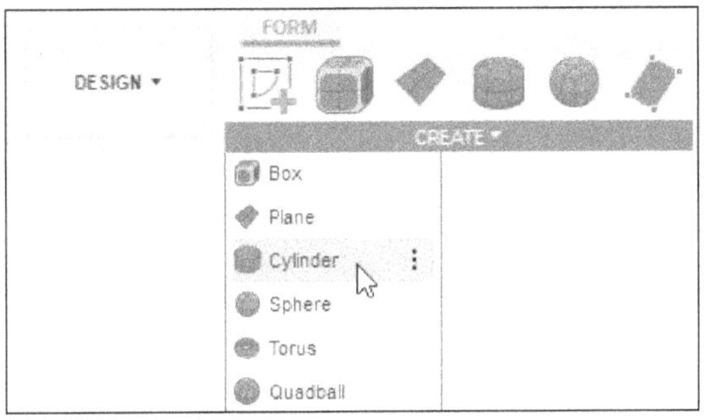

Figure-14. Cylinder tool

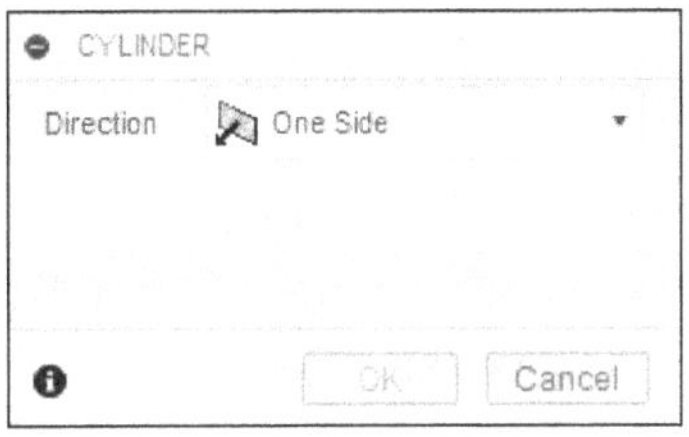

Figure-15. CYLINDER dialog box

- You need to select the base plane or face to create the cylinder. Click on the plane to select.
- Click on the screen to specify the center point and enter desired radius of cylinder; refer to Figure-16.

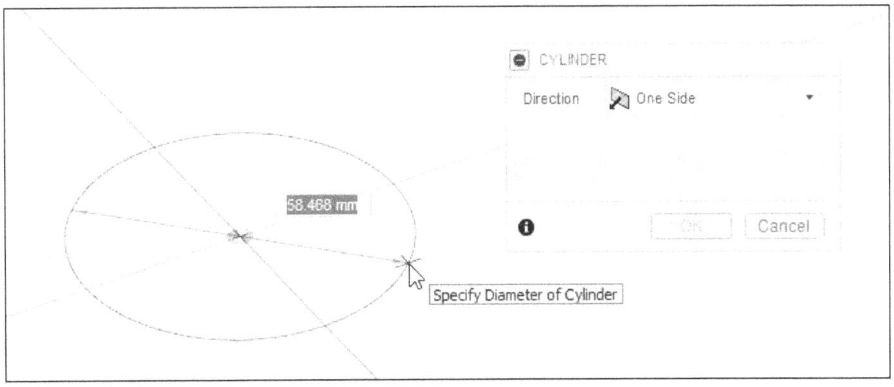

Figure-16. Creating circle for cylinder

- After specifying the diameter, click on the screen. The preview of cylinder will be displayed along with updated **CYLINDER** dialog box; refer to Figure-17.

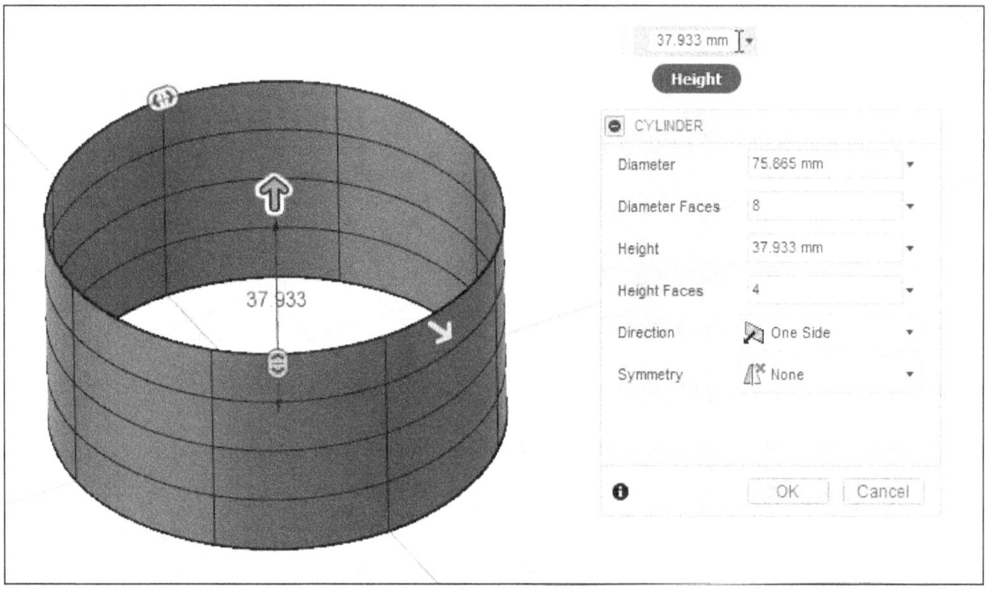

Figure-17. Updated CYLINDER dialog box

- If you want to change the diameter of cylinder then click on the **Diameter** edit box of **CYLINDER** dialog box and enter desired diameter.
- Click in the **Diameter Faces** edit box and enter the number of faces in which the round surface of cylinder will be divided.
- Click in the **Height** edit box and enter desired value of height of cylinder.
- Click in the **Height Faces** edit box and enter the number of faces in which height of cylinder will be divided along the height.
- The options in the **Direction** drop-down have been discussed earlier.
- Select **Circular** option from **Symmetry** drop-down if you want to apply circular symmetry between the faces of sculpt object.
- Click on the **Symmetric Faces** edit box and enter desired value of circular symmetry on round surface.
- After specifying the parameters, click on the **OK** button from **CYLINDER** dialog box to complete the process.

Sphere

The **Sphere** tool is used to create a T-Spline sphere. The procedure to use this tool is discussed next.

- Click on the **Sphere** tool from **CREATE** drop-down; refer to Figure-18. The **SPHERE** dialog box will be displayed; refer to Figure-19.

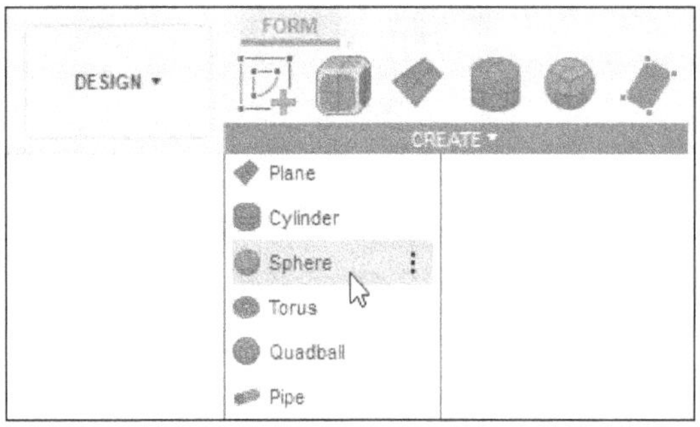

Figure-18. Sphere tool

Figure-19. SPHERE dialog box

- You are asked to select the base plane to create the sphere. Click on the plane/ face where you want to place the sphere.

- You are asked to specify centerpoint of the sphere. Click on desired location to specify the center point. The preview of sphere will be displayed along with updated **SPHERE** dialog box; refer to Figure-20.

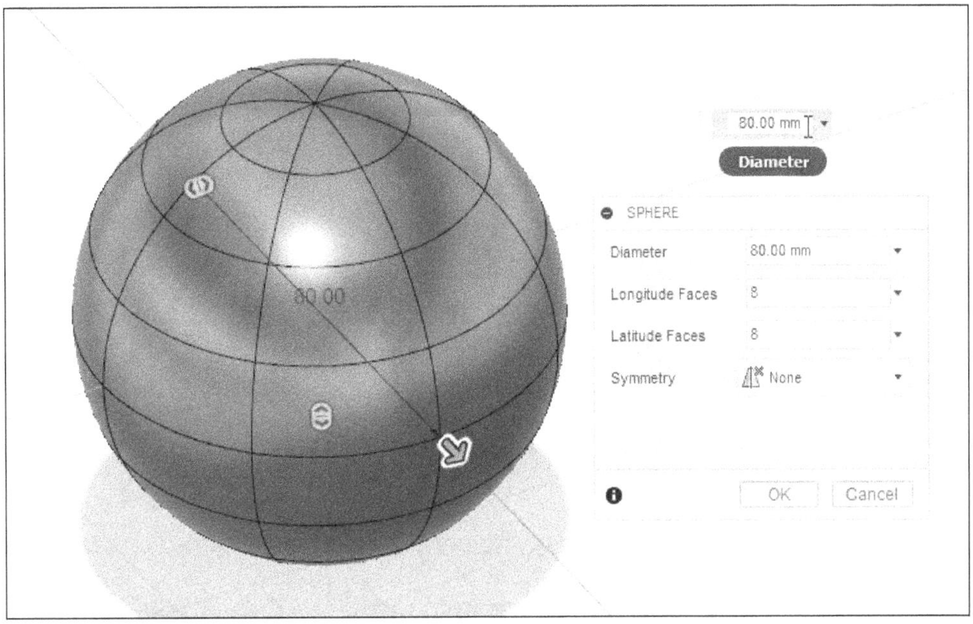

Figure-20. Updated SPHERE dialog box

- Click in the **Diameter** edit box and enter desired value of sphere diameter.
- Click in the **Longitude Faces** edit box and enter desired number of faces displayed on longitude of sphere.
- Click in the **Latitude Faces** edit box and enter desired number of faces displayed on latitude of sphere.
- The options of **Symmetry** drop-down have been discussed earlier in **Box** and **Cylinder** tools.
- After specifying the parameters, click on the **OK** button from **SPHERE** dialog box to complete the process.

Torus

The **Torus** tool is used to create a T-Spline torus. The procedure to use this tool is discussed next.

- Click on the **Torus** tool from **CREATE** drop-down; refer to Figure-21. The **TORUS** dialog box will be displayed; refer to Figure-22.

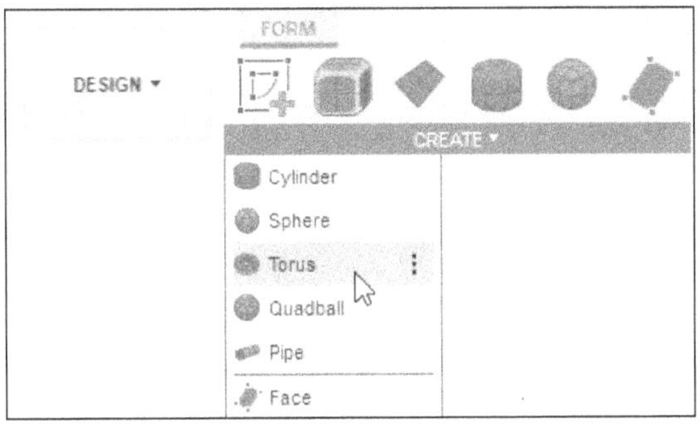

Figure-21. Torus tool

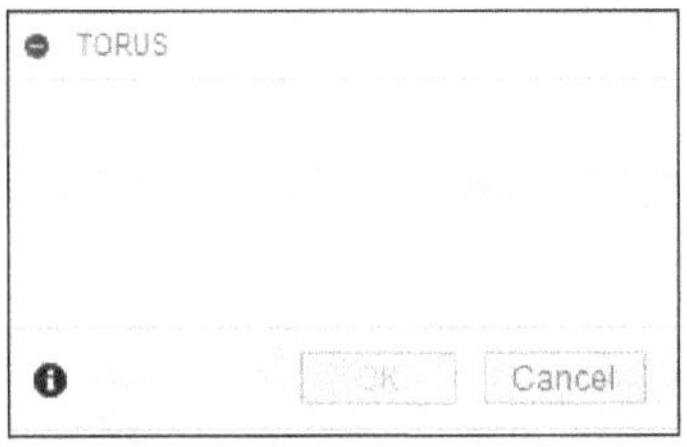

Figure-22. TORUS dialog box

- You need to select the base plane to create the torus. Click on the screen to select.

- Click on the screen to specify the center point and enter desired diameter of torus in the input box. The preview of torus will be displayed along with updated **TORUS** dialog box; refer to Figure-23.

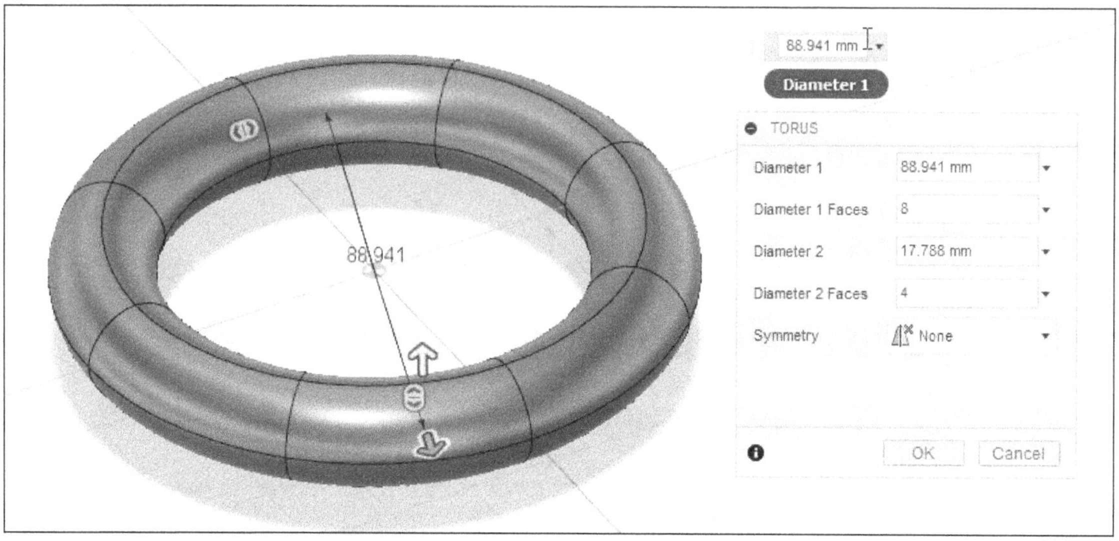

Figure-23. Updated TORUS dialog box

- Click in the **Diameter 1** edit box of **TORUS** dialog box and enter desired value of diameter for center circle of torus.
- Click in the **Diameter 1 Faces** edit box and enter the number of faces in which round torus will be divided horizontally.
- Click in the **Diameter 2** edit box and enter the diameter of torus tube.
- Click in the **Diameter 2 Faces** edit box and enter the number of faces in which round torus will be divided vertically.
- After specifying the parameters, click on the **OK** button from **TORUS** dialog box.

Quadball

The **Quadball** tool is used to create a T-Spline quadball. The procedure to use this tool is discussed next.

- Click on the **Quadball** tool from **CREATE** drop-down; refer to Figure-24. The **QUADBALL** dialog box will be displayed; refer to Figure-25.

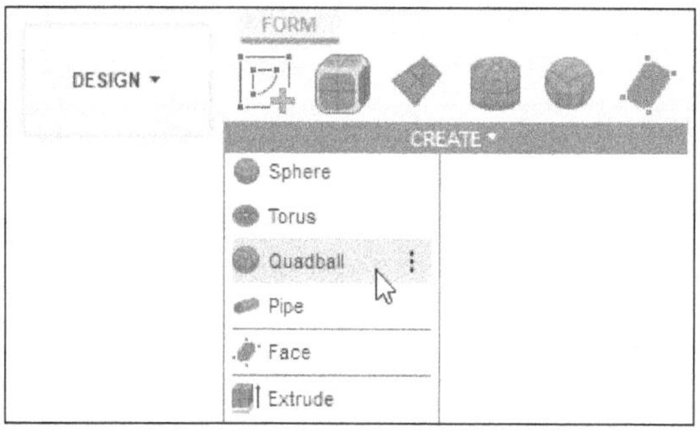

Figure-24. Quadball tool

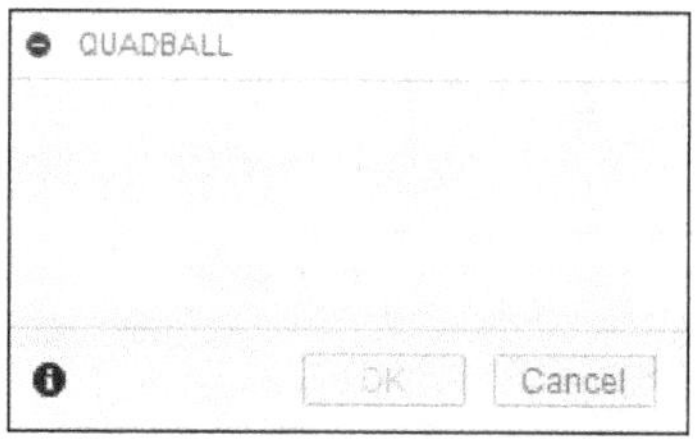

Figure-25. QUADBALL dialog box

- You need to select the base plane to create the quadball. Click on desired face/ plane to select.
- Click on the screen to specify the center point. The preview of quadball will be displayed along with updated **QUADBALL** dialog box; refer to Figure-26.

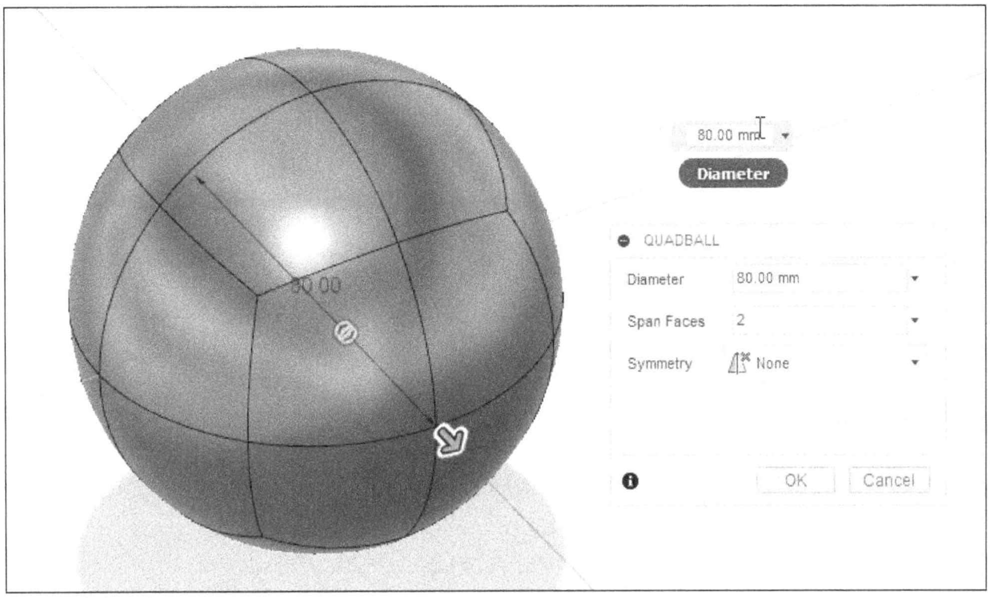

Figure-26. Updated QUADBALL dialog box

- Click in the **Diameter** edit box and enter desired value of quadball diameter.
- Click in the **Span Faces** edit box and enter the number of faces in which quadball will be divided.
- The options of **Symmetry** and **Operation** drop-down were discussed earlier.
- After specifying the parameters, click on **OK** button from **QUADBALL** dialog box. The quadball will be displayed; refer to Figure-27.

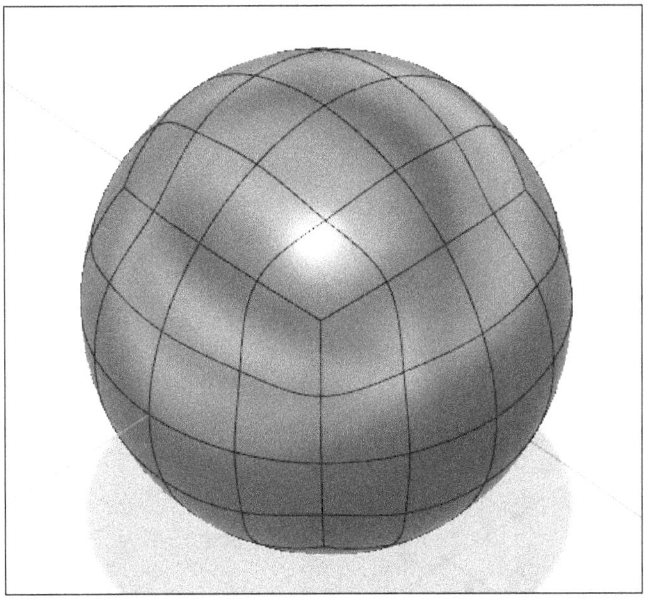

Figure-27. Quadball created with 4 span faces

Pipe

The **Pipe** tool is used to create complex pipe based on selected sketch. The procedure to use this tool is discussed next.

- Click on the **Pipe** tool from **CREATE** drop-down; refer to Figure-28. The **PIPE** dialog box will be displayed; refer to Figure-29.

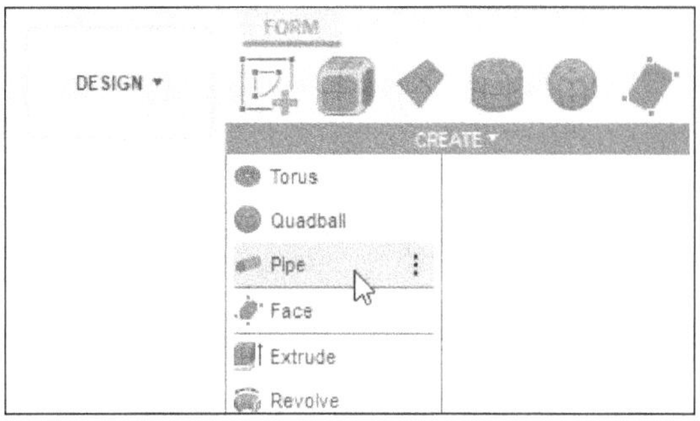

Figure-28. Pipe tool

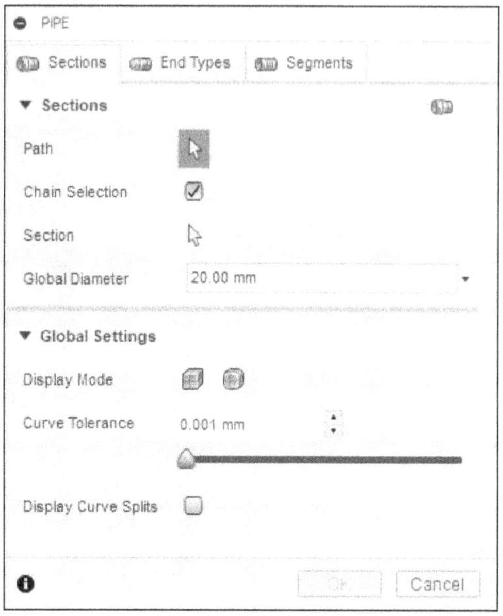

Figure-29. PIPE dialog box

- The **Path** selection button is active by default. Click on the path to select. You can select sketch lines/curves or edges of the model. You can also use window selection to create pipe.
- Select the **Chain selection** check box if you want to select the nearby geometries in chain while selecting the one.
- On selection of sketch, the preview of pipe will be displayed; refer to Figure-30.

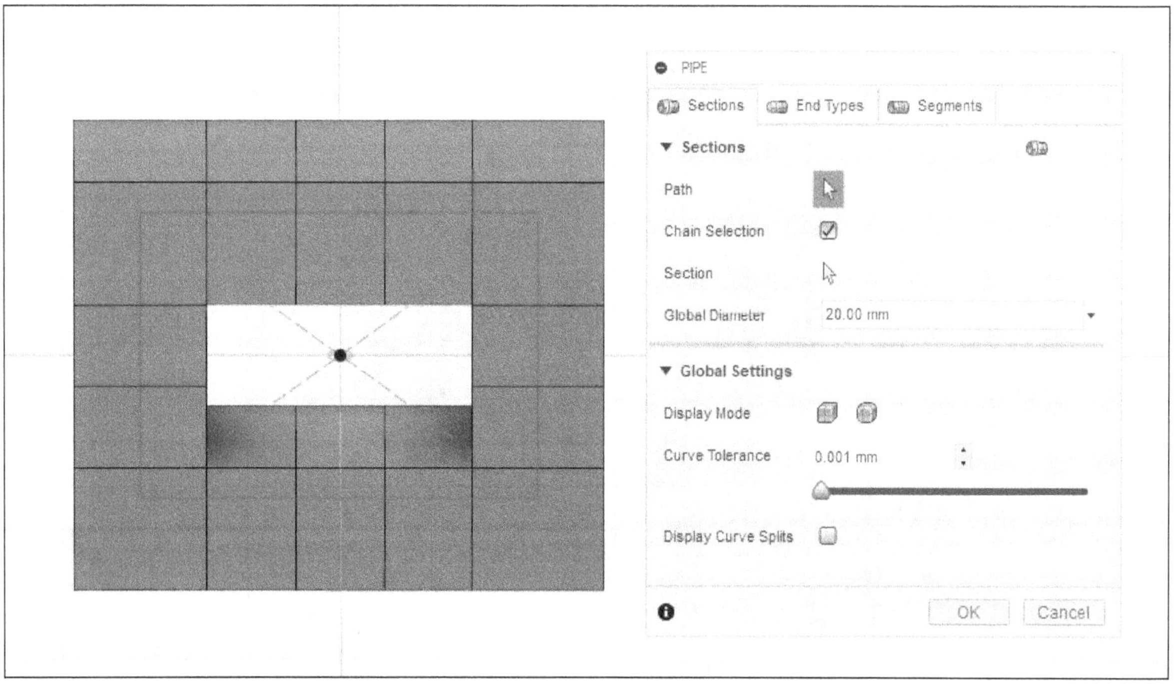

Figure-30. Preview of Pipe

- Click on the **Section** button of **Sections** tab if you want to modify the sections of pipe. On selecting the button, the sections of pipe will be displayed; refer to Figure-31.

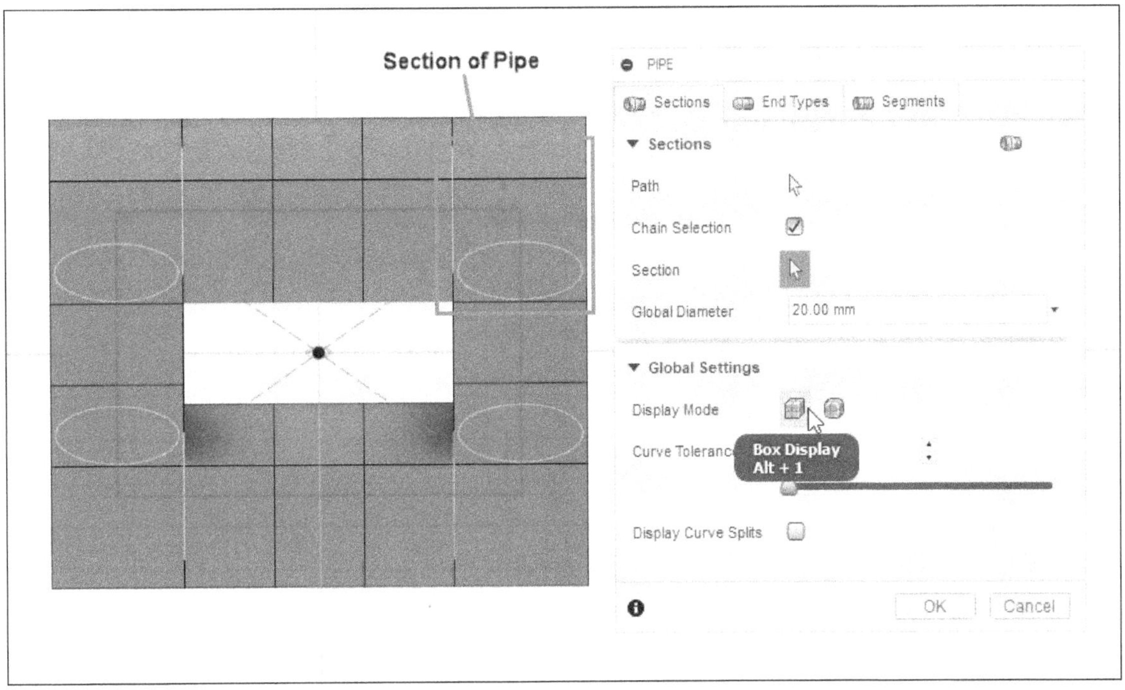

Figure-31. Sections of pipe

- Click on desired section to change the diameter, angle, and position.
- Click on the **Diameter** edit box and enter desired value of particular section diameter; refer to Figure-32.

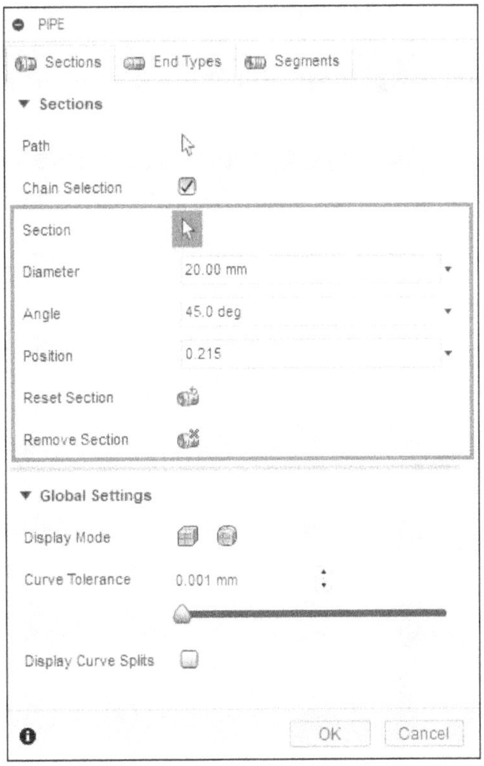

Figure-32. Section options in PIPE dialog box

- Similarly, specify the value of **Angle** and **Position** in their respective edit boxes as desired. You can also move the arrow displayed on the selected section to specify the value.
- Click on the **Reset Section** button to reset all the changed value of sections.
- Click on the **Remove Section** button to remove the selected section.

- Click on **Box Display** button of **Display Mode** section from **Global Settings** area to display the rectangular T-Spline pipe of the selected sketch.
- Select **Smooth Display** button of **Display Mode** section from **Global Settings** area to display a smooth circular pipe; refer to Figure-33.

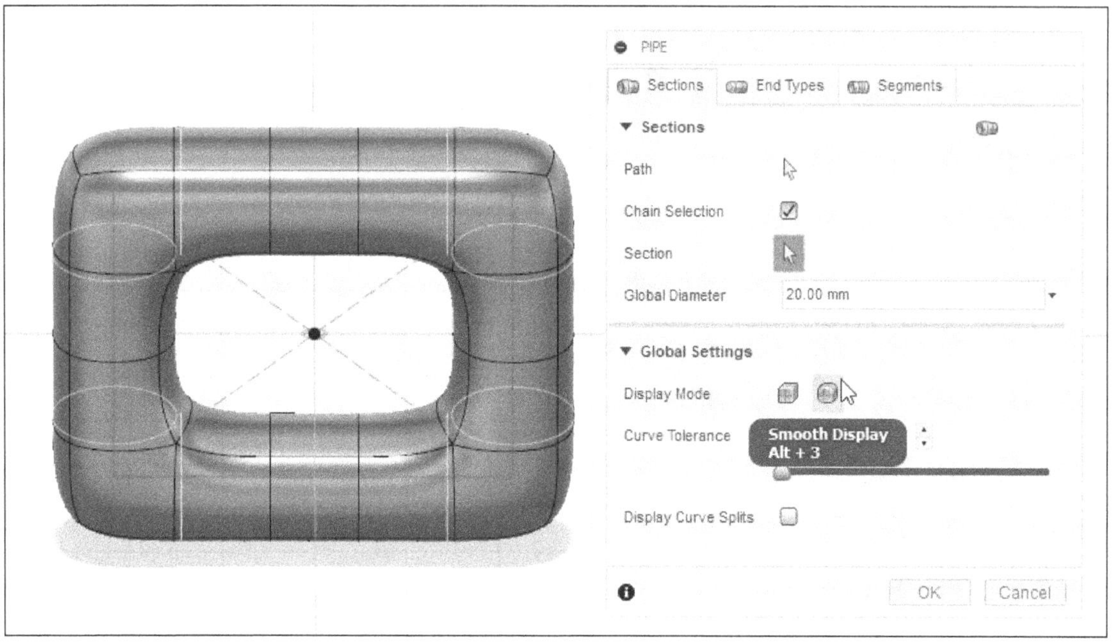

Figure-33. Smooth pipe

- Click in the **Curve Tolerance** edit box and enter the value of pipe tolerance. You can also set the tolerance by adjusting the **Curve Tolerance** slider.
- Select the **Display Curve Splits** check box if you want to see the curve splits of pipe.
- Click on the **End Types** tab in the dialog box. The **Handle** selection button of **End Types** tab is active by default and you are asked to select the end handle of pipe to modify its shape.
- Select desired end handle from the model. Select **Open** option from **End Type** drop-down of **End Types** tab if you want to keep all the ends of pipe open; refer to Figure-34.

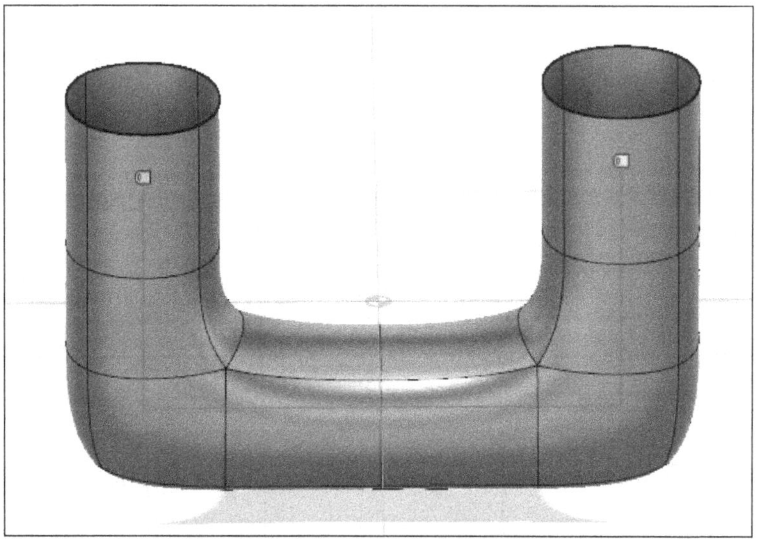

Figure-34. Open End Type

- Select **Square** option from **End Type** drop-down of **End Types** tab if you want to close all the ends of pipe in square like structure; refer to Figure-35.

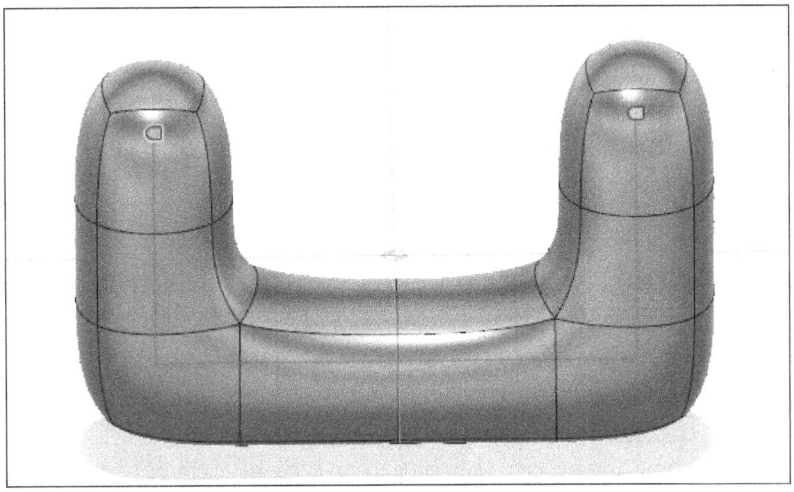

Figure-35. Square End Type

- Select **Spike** option from **End Type** drop-down of **End Types** tab if you want to close all the ends of pipe in spike like structure; refer to Figure-36.

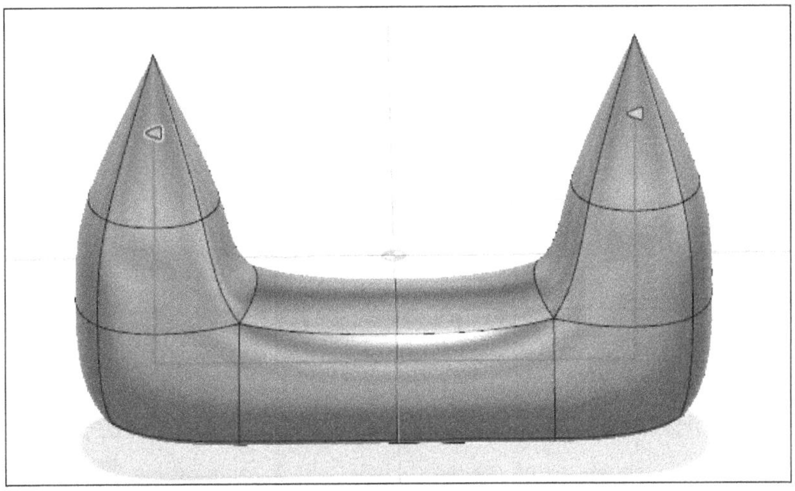

Figure-36. Spike End Type

- Click on the **Segments** tab in the dialog box. The **Segment** selection button of **Segments** tab is active by default.
- Move the **Density** slider to increase or decrease the density of pipe segment.
- After specifying the parameters, click on the **OK** button from **PIPE** dialog box to complete the process.

Face

The **Face** tool is used to create individual faces. The procedure to use this tool is discussed next.

- Click on the **Face** tool from **CREATE** drop-down; refer to Figure-37. The **FACE** dialog box will be displayed; refer to Figure-38.

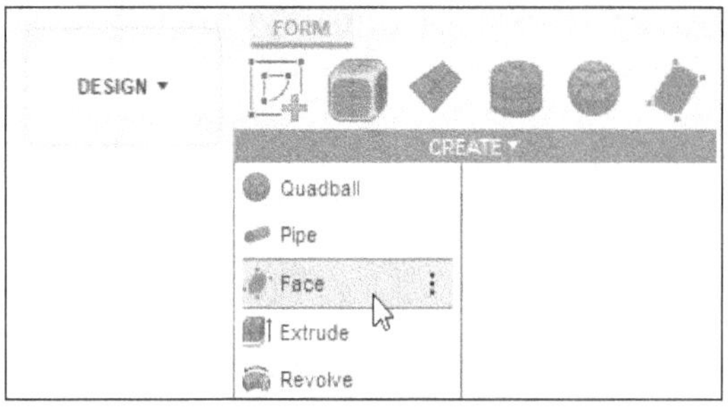

Figure-37. Face tool

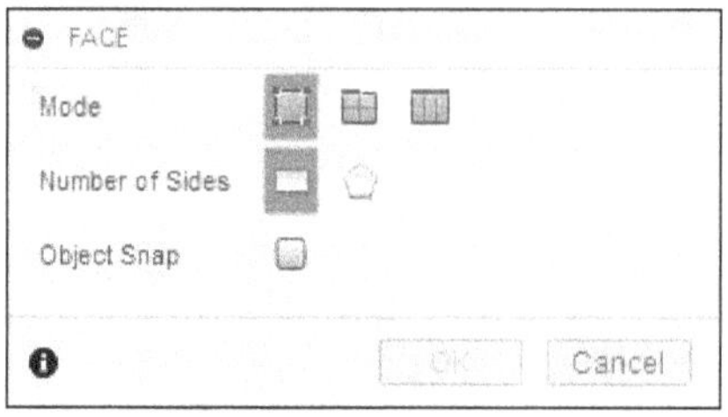

Figure-38. FACE dialog box

Creating Face using Simple button

- Select **Simple** button from **Mode** section of **FACE** dialog box if you want to create a simple face by selecting four vertices on a specific plane.
- On selecting the **Simple** button, you need to select plane for creating the face. Click to select the plane.
- Now, specify the four corner on the plane as desired; refer to Figure-39.

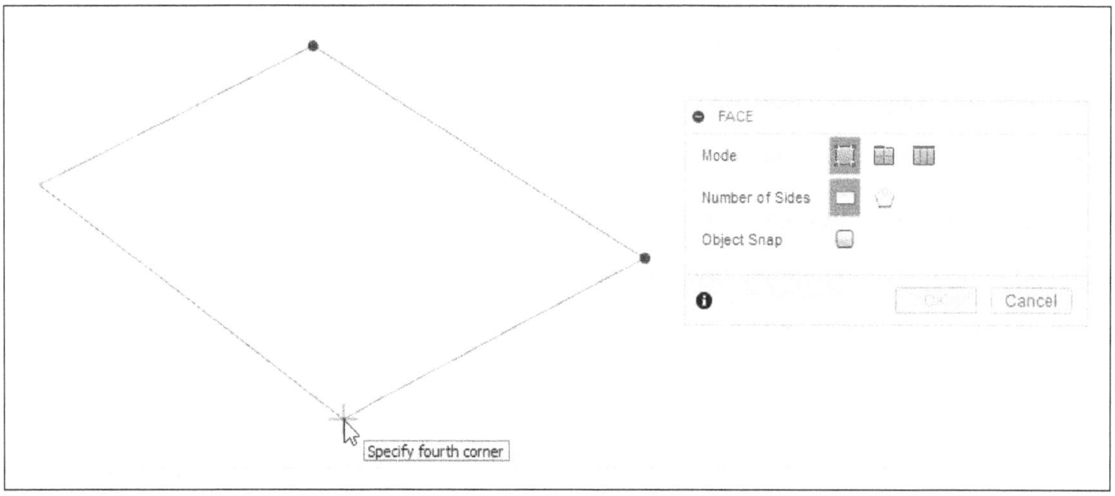

Figure-39. Specifying corners for creating face

- On selecting the fourth corner, the face will be created; refer to Figure-40.

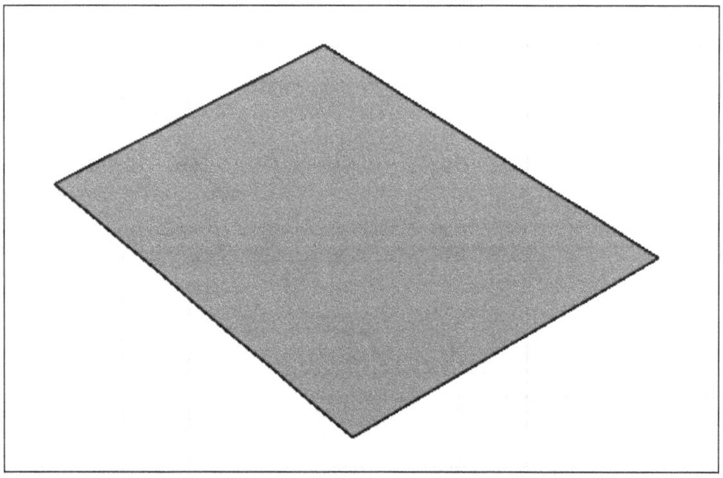

Figure-40. Face created

Creating Face using Edge button

The **Edge** button is used to create a face by selecting an edge. The procedure is discussed next.

- Select the **Edge** button from **Mode** section of **FACE** dialog box. You need to select the edge of an object.
- Now, you need to select the plane on which you want to create a face. Click to select the plane.
- Click on the screen to specify third and fourth corner.
- On creating fourth corner, the face will be created; refer to Figure-41.

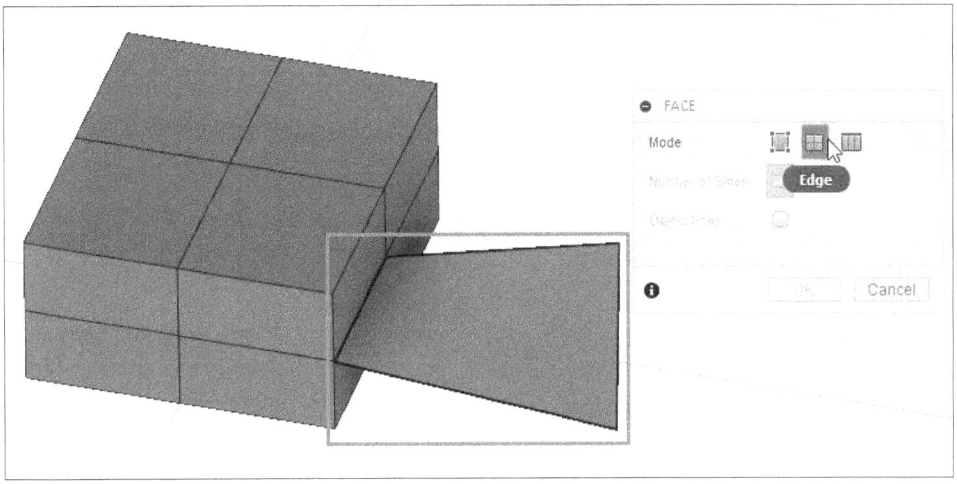

Figure-41. Face created by Edge button

Creating Chain of Faces using Edges

The **Chain** button is used to create multiple faces continuously. The procedure is discussed next.

- Select the **Chain** button from **Mode** section of **FACE** dialog box. You will be asked to select an edge for creating face.
- Select desired edge. Now, you need to select the plane on which you want to create a face. Click to select the plane.
- Specify third and fourth corner to create first face; refer to Figure-42.

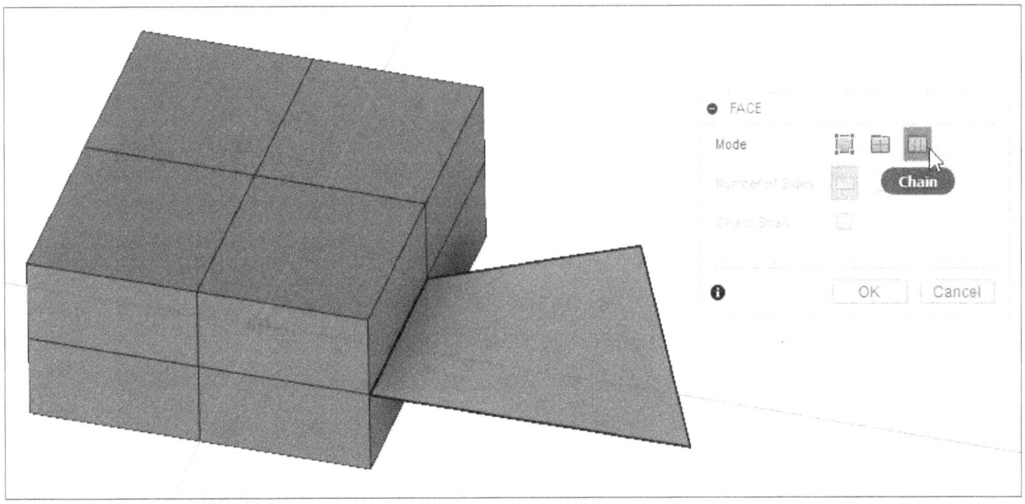

Figure-42. First face created

- After creating first face, specify third and fourth corner to create second face.
- On creating second face, click on the screen to create next faces as desired; refer to Figure-43.

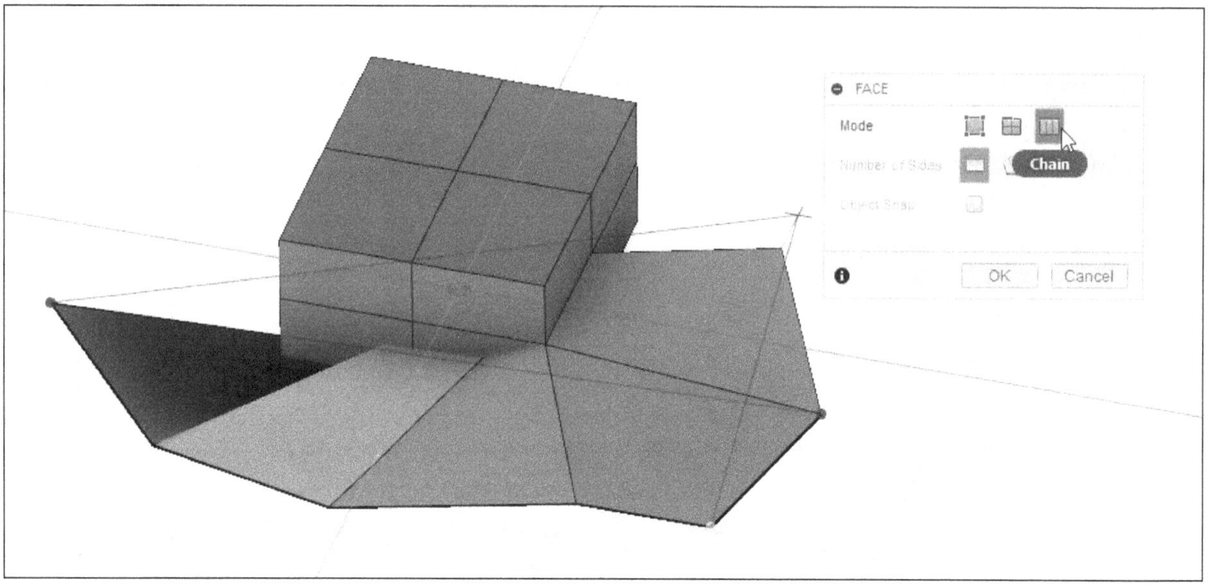

Figure-43. Multiple faces created using Chain Mode

- After creating desired number of faces, click on the **OK** button from **FACE** dialog box to complete the process.

Extrude

The **Extrude** tool is used to extrude the selected sketch up to desired depth or height. The procedure to use this tool is discussed next.

- Click on the **Extrude** tool from **CREATE** drop-down; refer to Figure-44. The **EXTRUDE** dialog box will be displayed; refer to Figure-45.

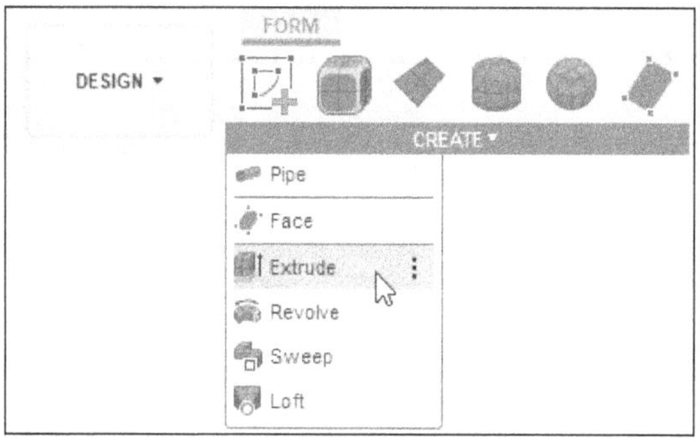

Figure-44. Extrude tool

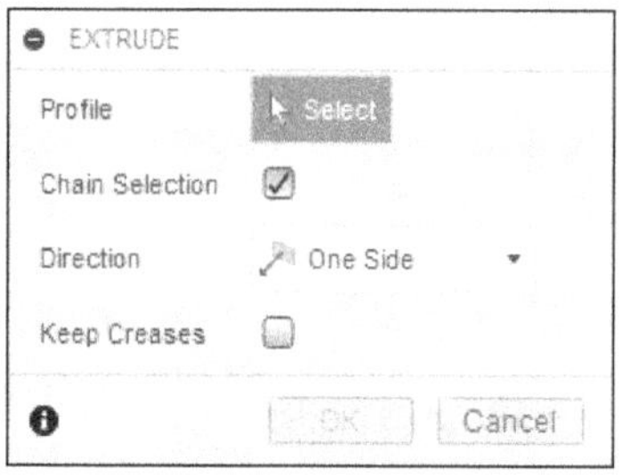

Figure-45. EXTRUDE dialog box

- The **Select** button of **Profile** section in **EXTRUDE** dialog box is active by default. You are asked to select the sketch for extrude. On selecting the sketch; the updated **EXTRUDE** dialog box will be displayed; refer to Figure-46.

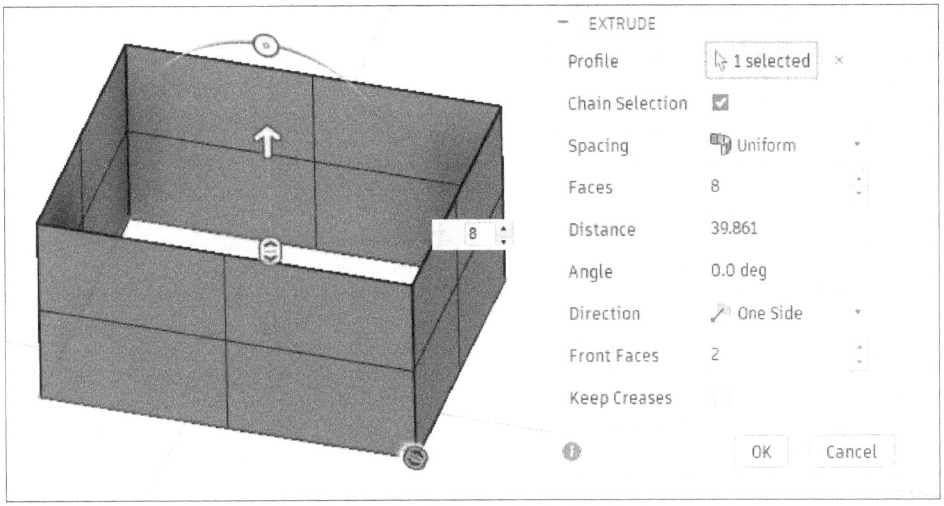

Figure-46. Updated EXTRUDE dialog box

- Select the **Chain Selection** check box if you want to select the nearby geometries.
- Select **Uniform** option from **Spacing** drop-down if you want to position the faces evenly around the profile.
- Select **Curvature** option from **Spacing** drop-down if you want to position the faces based on the curvature of the profile. The more the curvature area, more the faces.
- Click in the **Faces** edit box and enter desired number of faces in which curvature of extruded sketch will be divided.
- Click in the **Distance** edit box and enter the distance for extrusion.
- Click in the **Angle** edit box and enter desired angle of extrusion.
- Click in the **Front Faces** edit box and enter desired number of faces in which surface of extrude will be divided along the height.
- Select the **Keep Crease** check box from **EXTRUDE** dialog box if you want to keep the crease at merged edges.
- After specifying the parameters, click on the **OK** button from **EXTRUDE** dialog box to complete the extrusion process. Note that you can also select face of any other sculpt body to extrude but some of the options in this dialog box will not be available in that case.

Revolve

The **Revolve** tool is used to create a revolve feature by sweeping selected sketch around selected axis. The procedure to use this tool is discussed next.

- Click on the **Revolve** tool from **CREATE** drop-down; refer to Figure-47. The **REVOLVE** dialog box will be displayed; refer to Figure-48.

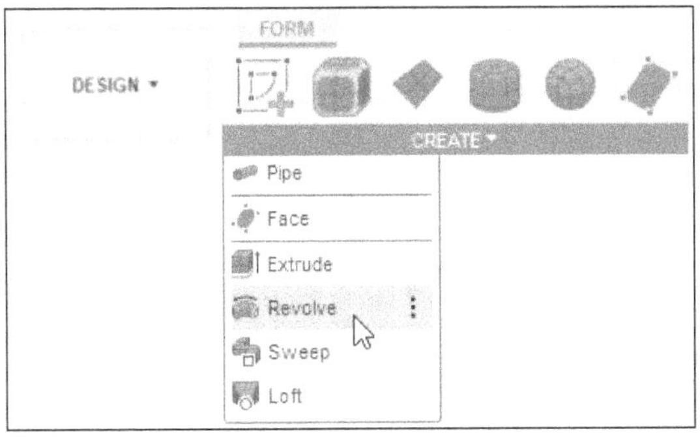

Figure-47. Revolve tool

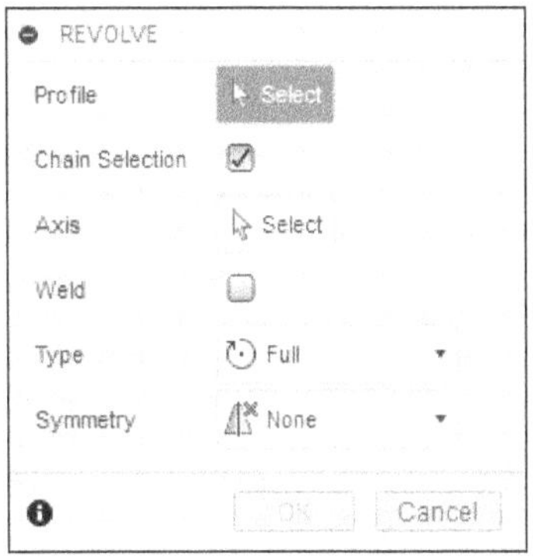

Figure-48. REVOLVE dialog box

- The **Select** button of **Profile** section in **REVOLVE** dialog box is active by default. Click on the sketch to apply revolve feature.
- Click on **Select** button of **Axis** section and select the axis of rotation of sketch; refer to Figure-49.

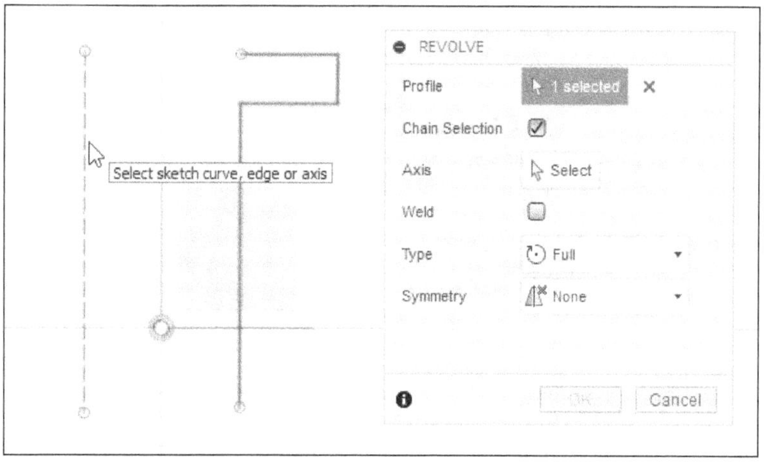

Figure-49. Selection of axis for sketch

- On selecting the axis, the preview of revolve feature will be displayed along with updated **REVOLVE** dialog box; refer to Figure-50.

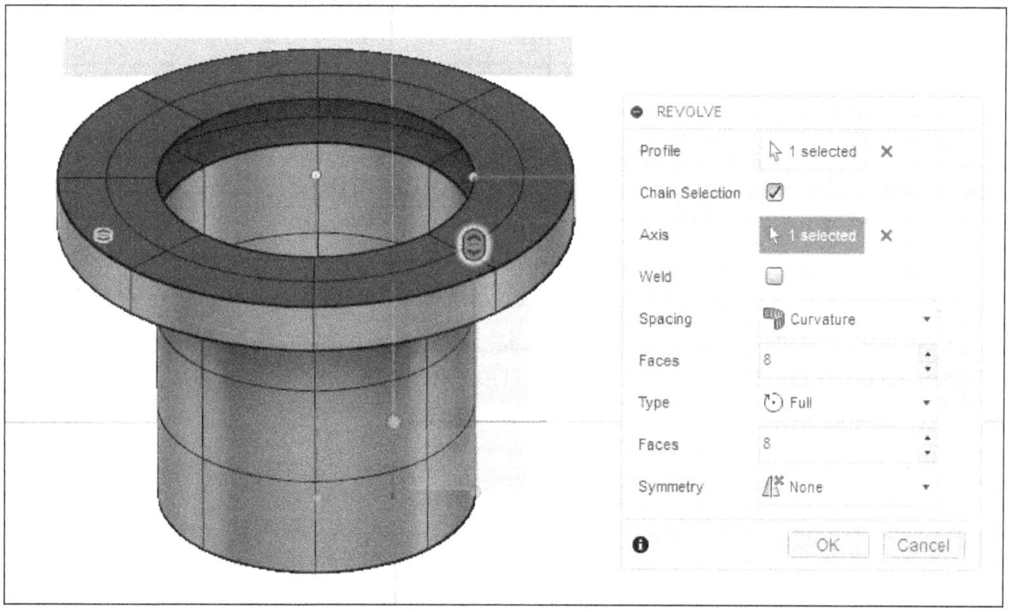

Figure-50. Updated REVOLVE dialog box

- Click in the **Faces** edit box below **Spacing** section and enter desired number of faces in which curvature of revolved sketch will be divided along flat faces; refer to Figure-51.

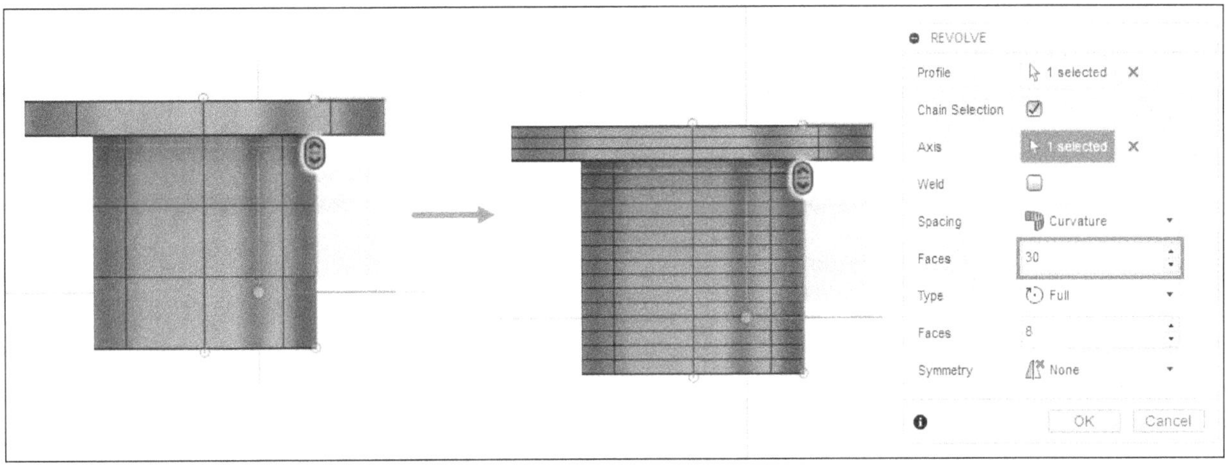

Figure-51. Entering the value of first faces option

- Click in the **Faces** edit box below **Type** section and enter desired number of faces in which curvature of revolved sketch will be divided along round faces; refer to Figure-52.

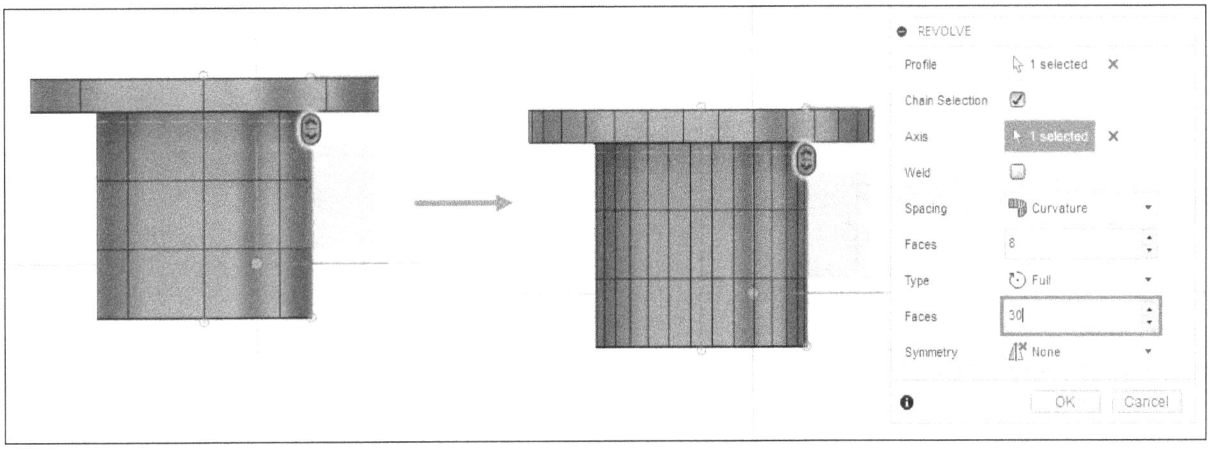

Figure-52. Entering the value of second faces option

- After specifying the parameters, click on the **OK** button from **REVOLVE** dialog box to complete the process.

Similarly, you can use other tools of **CREATE** drop-down as discussed in **DESIGN Workspace**.

MODIFYING TOOLS

Till now, you have learned about various tools to create the sculpt object. In this section, you will learn various tools for modifying the sculpt object.

Edit Form

The **Edit Form** tool is used to move, scale, or rotate selected geometry. The procedure to use this tool is discussed next.

- Click on the **Edit Form** tool from **MODIFY** drop-down; refer to Figure-53. The **EDIT FORM** dialog box will be displayed; refer to Figure-54.

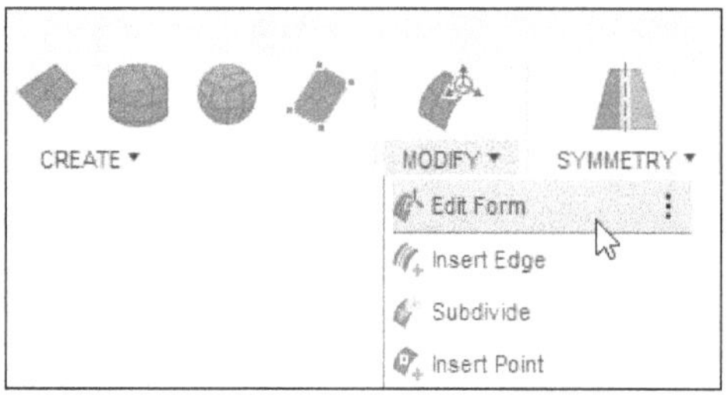

Figure-53. Edit Form tool

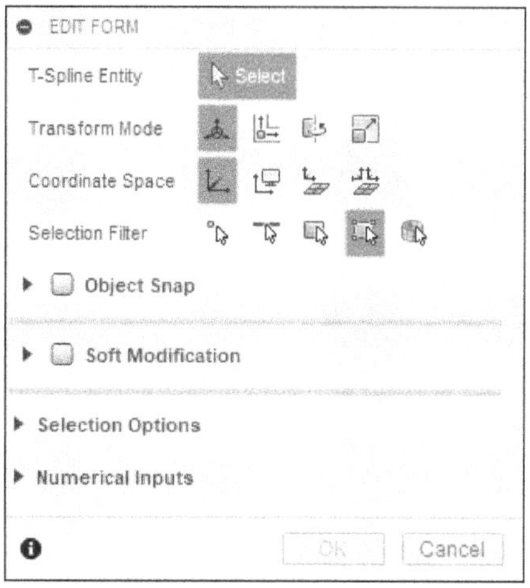

Figure-54. EDIT FORM dialog box

- The **Select** button of **T-Spline Entity** section is active by default. Click on any face of the sculpt object to edit.
- Select **Multi** button from **Transform Mode** section to edit the face with the help of 3D Manipulator; refer to Figure-55.

Figure-55. Multi manipulator

- Select the **Translation** button from **Transform Mode** section to edit the face with the help of translation manipulator; refer to Figure-56.

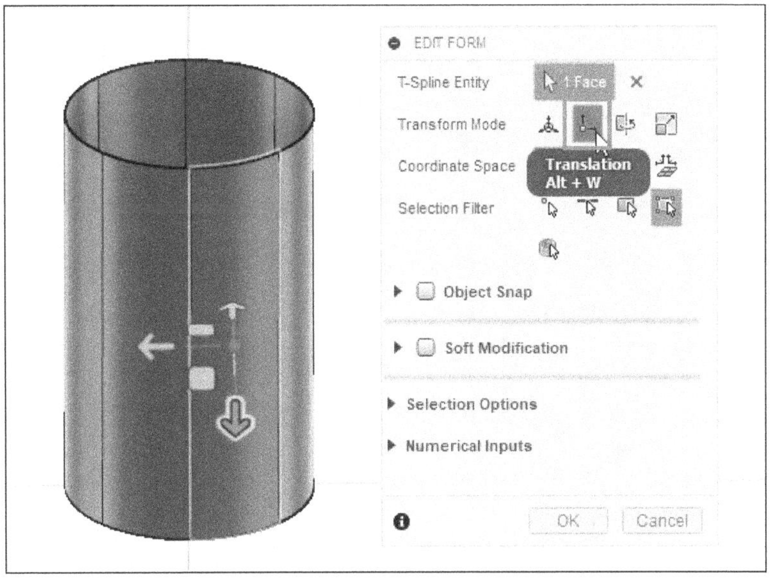

Figure-56. Translation manipulator

- Select **Rotation** button from **Transform Mode** section to edit the face with the help of rotation manipulator; refer to Figure-57.

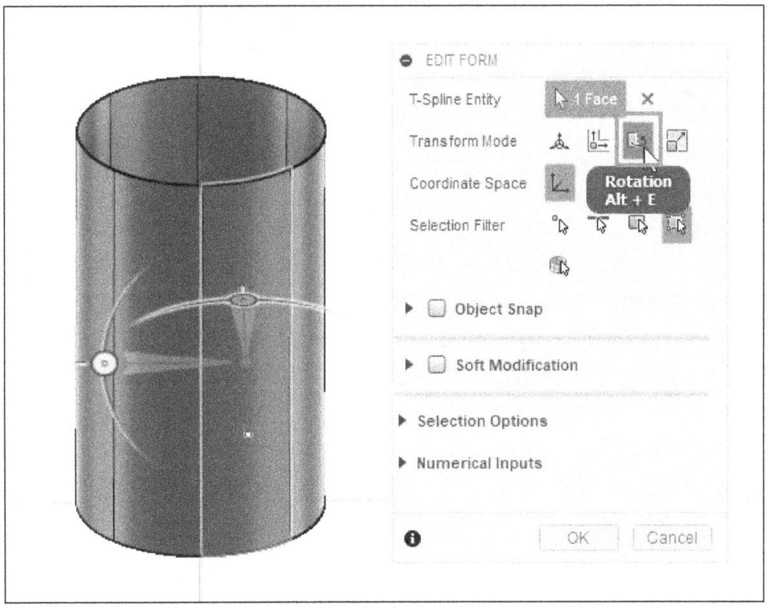

Figure-57. Rotation manipulator

- Select **Scale** button from **Transform Mode** section to edit the face with the help of scale manipulator; refer to Figure-58.

Figure-58. Scale manipulator

- Select the **World Space** button from **Coordinate Space** section to orient the manipulator relative to the origin of model.
- Select the **View Space** button from **Coordinate Space** section to orient the manipulator relative to the current view of model.
- Select the **Selection Space** button from **Coordinate Space** section to orient the manipulator relative to the selected face.
- Select the **Local Per Entity** button from **Coordinate Space** section to orient the manipulator relative to the selected object.
- Select **Vertex** button from **Selection Filter** section to select the vertex of object for editing purpose. On selecting this button, only vertices will available for selection.
- Select **Edge** button from **Selection Filter** section to select the edge of object. On selecting this button, only edges of object will be available for selection.
- Select **Face** button from **Selection Filter** section to select the face of object. On selecting this button, only faces of object will be available for selection.
- Select **All** button from **Selection Filter** section to select the edge, vertex, or face from an object. On selecting this button, edge, vertex, and face will available for selection.
- Select **Body** button from **Selection Filter** section to select the body for editing.
- Select the **Object Snap** check box and specify desired value in the **Offset** edit box to specify the limit within which the selected vertex can move.

Soft Modification

Select the **Soft Modification** check box if you want to control the influence of changes on the surrounding area of object. On selecting the check box, the updated **EDIT FORM** dialog box will be displayed; refer to Figure-59.

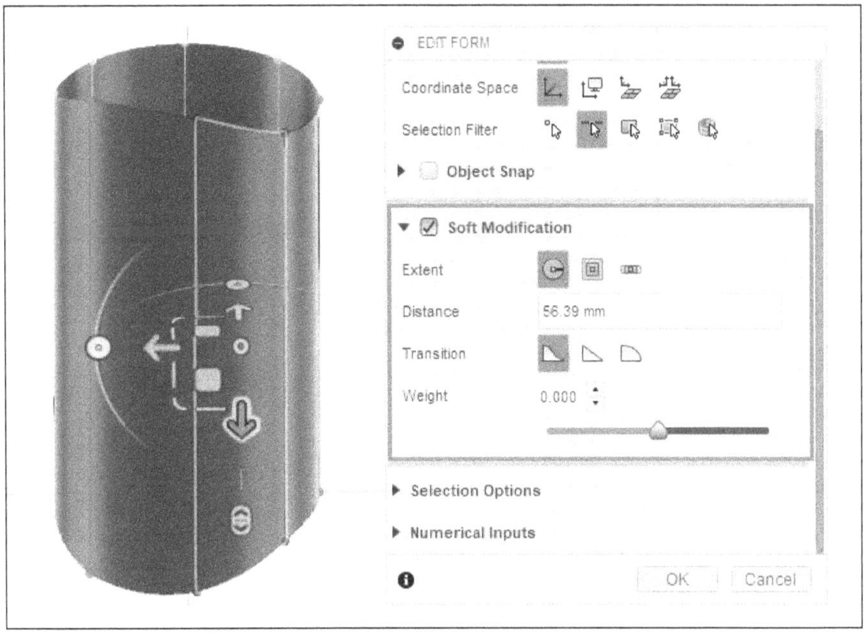

Figure-59. Updated EDIT FORM dialog box

- When selected, the vertices of body is visually represented with red and white vertices highlighting that can be adjusted with the gradient slider.
- Select **Distance** button from **Extent** section to specify the distance in the **Distance** edit box for controlling the influence of round region. With the help of vertices displayed on object, you can control the amount of change they undergo and the shape of the affected region.
- Select **Face Count** button from **Extent** section to specify the number of faces far from selected object.
- Select **Rectangular Face Count** button from **Extent** section to specify the number of width and length faces.
- Select desired shape of the affected region from **Transition** section.
- Click in the **Weight** edit box and enter the value of amount of influence applied in the affected region. The value of weight will be in between -1 to 1. You can also adjust the value of weight by moving the **Weight** slider.

Selection Options

- Click on the **Selection Options** node from **EDIT FORM** dialog box. The options of **Selection Options** node will be displayed; refer to Figure-60.

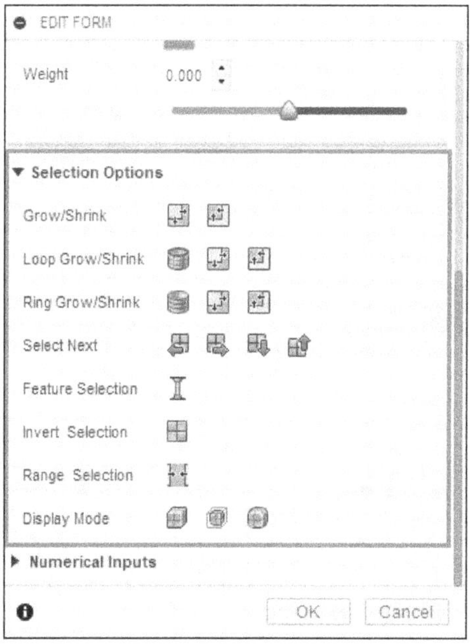

Figure-60. Selection Options

- The **Grow/Shrink** section is used to contract and expand the selected region.
- The **Loop Grow/Shrink** section is used to expand and contract the selected loop for the current location.
- The **Ring Grow/Shrink** section is used to expand and contract the ring after selecting the adjacent edge of the selected edge.
- The **Select Next** options are used to move the selected vertex, edge, or face to the next adjacent object. The movement to adjacent faces is based upon the current camera position.
- The **Feature Selection** button is used to select all the faces of a strut or a hole.
- The **Invert Selection** button is used for reverse the selection. It means all the selected object will be deselected and deselected will be selected.
- The **Range Selection** button is used to select all the faces between two selected faces.
- The **Display Mode** section is used to select **Box display**, **Control Frame display**, and **Smooth Display** mode for the object.

Numerical Inputs

- Click on the **Numerical Inputs** node from **EDIT FORM** dialog box to enter the numerical value of various parameters, refer to Figure-61.

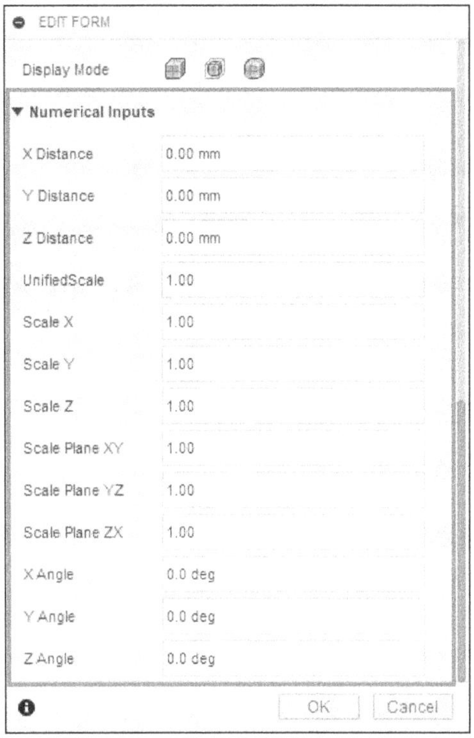

Figure-61. Numerical Inputs

- After specifying the various parameters, click on **OK** button from **EDIT FORM** dialog box to complete the process.

Edit By Curve

The **Edit By Curve** tool is used to manipulate T-Spline edges using a driving curve. The procedure to use this tool is discussed next.

- Click on the **Edit By Curve** tool from **MODIFY** drop-down; refer to Figure-62. The **EDIT BY CURVE** dialog box will be displayed; refer to Figure-63.

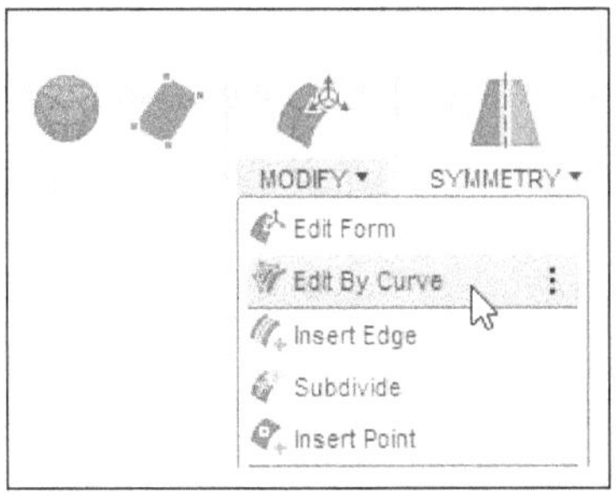

Figure-62. Edit By Curve tool

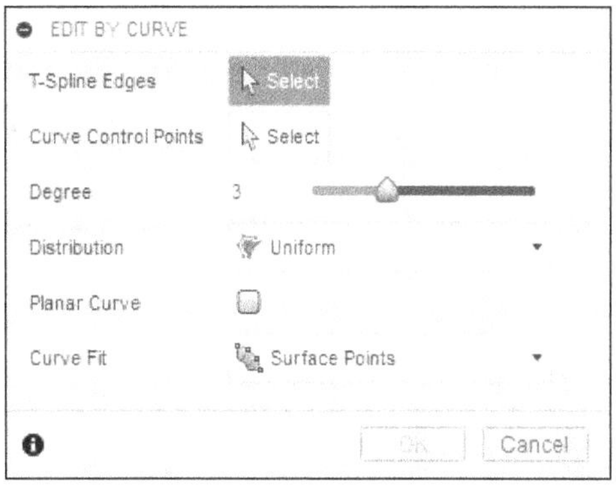

Figure-63. EDIT BY CURVE dialog box

- The **Select** button of **T-Spline Edges** section is active by default. Click on the edges from T-Spline body to be used for modification; refer to Figure-64.

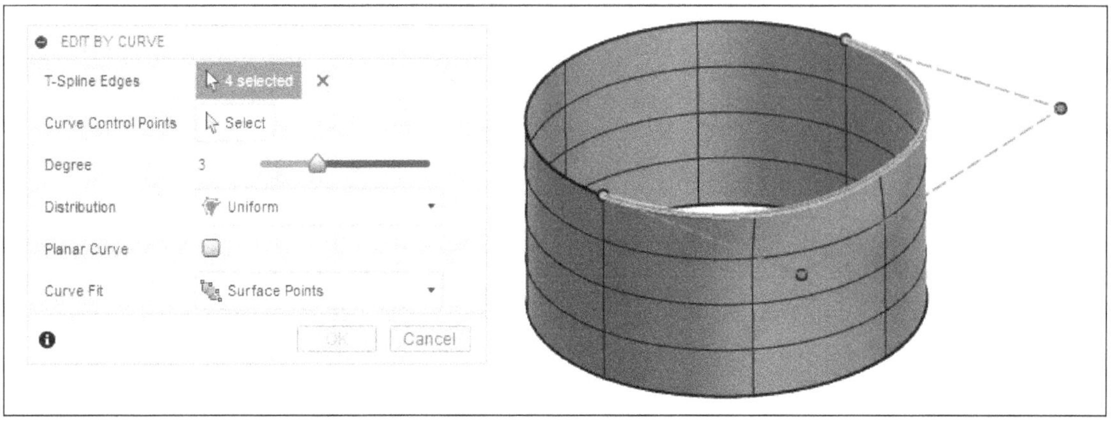

Figure-64. Selecting the T Spline edges

- Click on **Select** button of **Curve Control Points** section of the dialog box and select the points to be used for editing on earlier selected curve; refer to Figure-65. The handles to modify select point will be displayed.

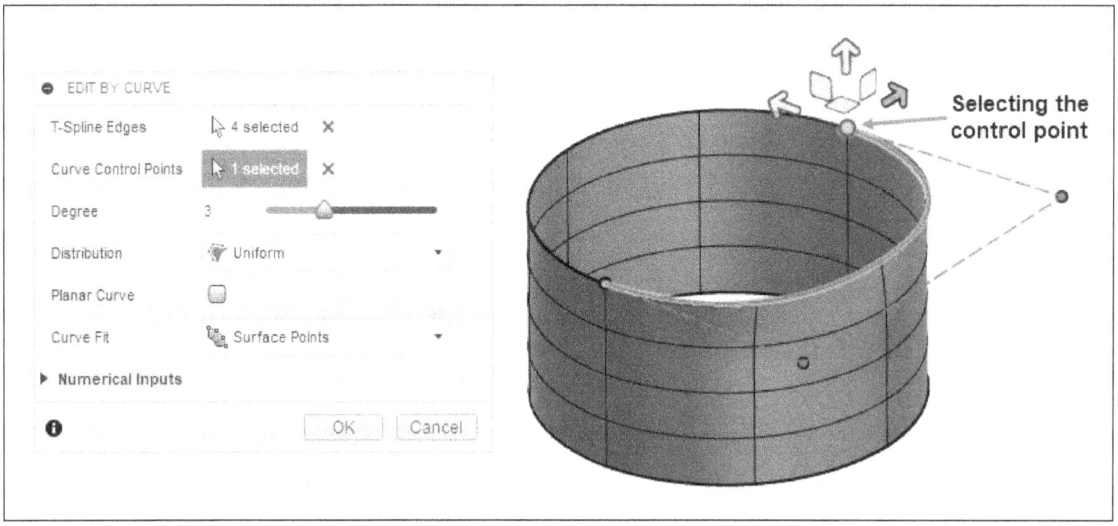

Figure-65. Selecting the curve control points

- Specify desired value in **Degree** edit box or specify the degree value by sliding the **Degree** slider to use 1-7 degrees of control on the driving curve. This will generate specified number of control points on the curve.
- Select **Uniform** option from **Distribution** drop-down to distribute control points uniformly along curve.
- Select **Edge Length** option from **Distribution** drop-down to distribute control points in proportion to lengths of T-Spline edges.
- Select **Planar Curve** check box to restrict modification of driving curves in best fit plane; refer to Figure-66.

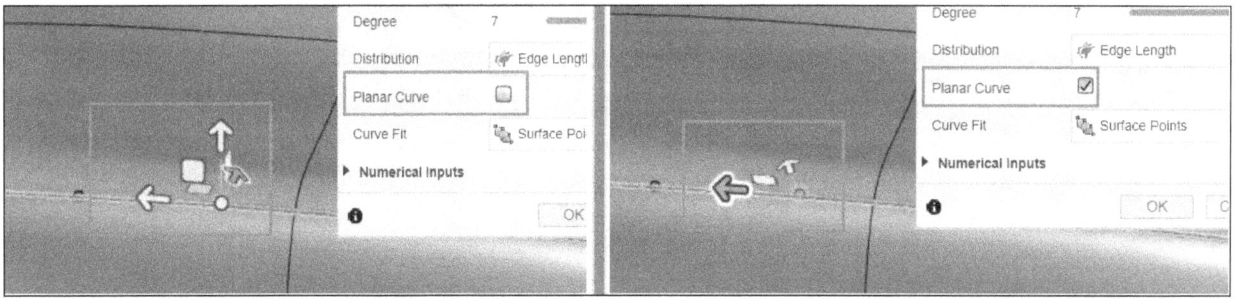

Figure-66. Effect of Planar Curve check box

- Select the **Surface Points** option from **Curve Fit** drop-down to fit vertices on smooth surface to driving curve.
- Select the **Control Points** option from **Curve Fit** drop-down to fit control points of selected edges to driving curve.
- Expand the **Numerical Inputs** node and specify numerical values of various parameters or use the distance, planar, scale, and rotation manipulator handles in the canvas to adjust the control points; refer to Figure-67.

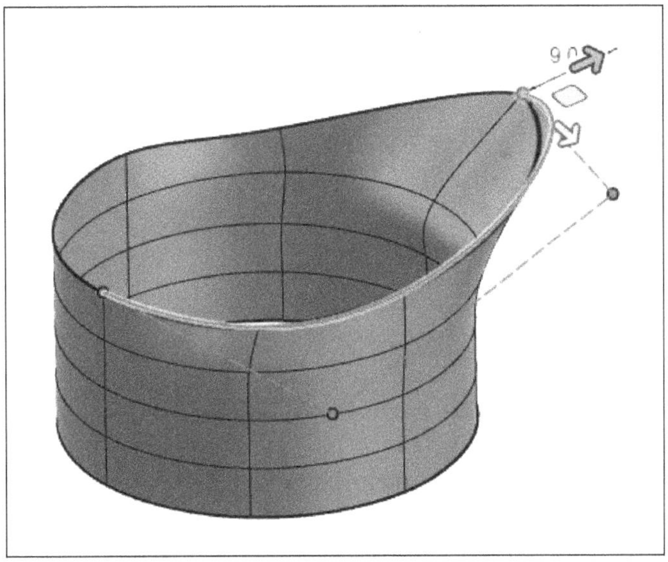

Figure-67. Adjusting the control points using manipulator

- After specifying desired parameters, click on the **OK** button from **EDIT BY CURVE** dialog box to complete the process.

Insert Edge

The **Insert Edge** tool is used to insert an edge at a specified distance from the selected edge. The procedure to use this tool is discussed next.

- Click on the **Insert Edge** tool from **MODIFY** drop-down; refer to Figure-68. The **INSERT EDGE** dialog box will be displayed; refer to Figure-69.

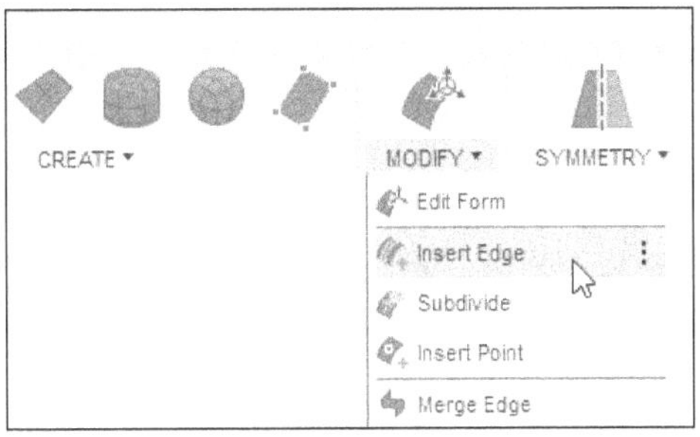

Figure-68. Insert Edge tool

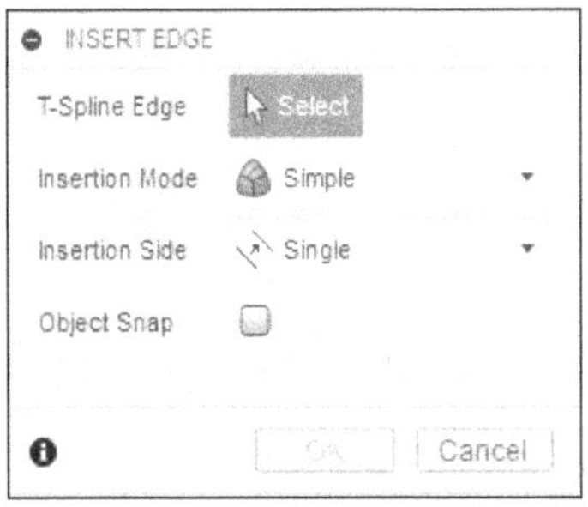

Figure-69. INSERT EDGE dialog box

- The **Select** button of **T-Spline Edge** section is active by default. Click on the edge from model to select. The preview of inserted edge will be displayed in green color; refer to Figure-70.

Figure-70. Preview of inserted edge

- Select **Simple** option from **Insertion Mode** drop-down if you do not want to move any point but may be it change the surface shape.
- Select **Exact** option from **Insertion Mode** drop-down to maintain the exact surface shape by adding points.
- Select **Single** option from **Insertion Side** drop-down to insert the edge in only one side to the selected edge.
- Select **Both** option from **Insertion Side** drop-down to insert the edge on both side to the selected edge.
- Click in the **Insert Location** edit box and enter the value of location for inserting the edge. The value of **Insert Location** lies between 0 to 1.
- Select the **Object Snap** check box to move the new vertices to the closest point. These vertices can snap to solid, surface, and mesh bodies.
- Click in the **Offset** edit box and enter desired value.
- After specifying the parameters, click on the **OK** button from **INSERT EDGE** dialog box to complete the process.

Subdivide

The **Subdivide** tool is used to divide selected face in four or more faces. The procedure to use this tool is discussed next.

- Click on **Subdivide** tool from **MODIFY** drop-down; refer to Figure-71. The **SUBDIVIDE** dialog box will be displayed; refer to Figure-72.

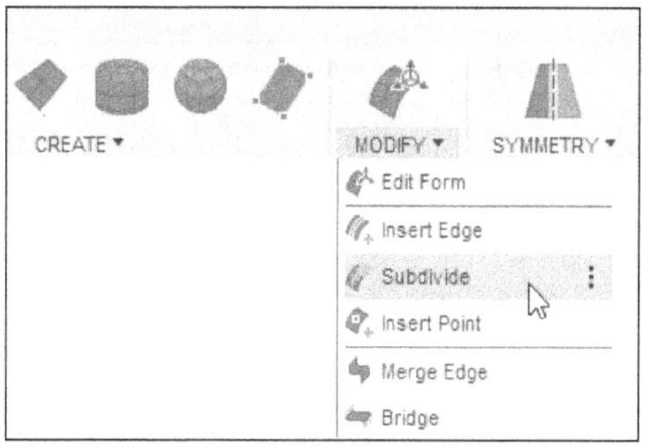

Figure-71. Subdivide tool

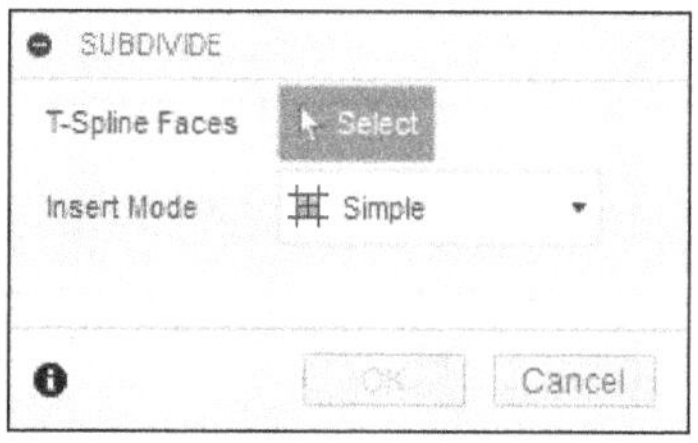

Figure-72. SUBDIVIDE dialog box

- The **Select** button of **T-Spline Faces** section is active by default. Click on the face from model to select. Selected face will be divided into four face; refer to Figure-73.

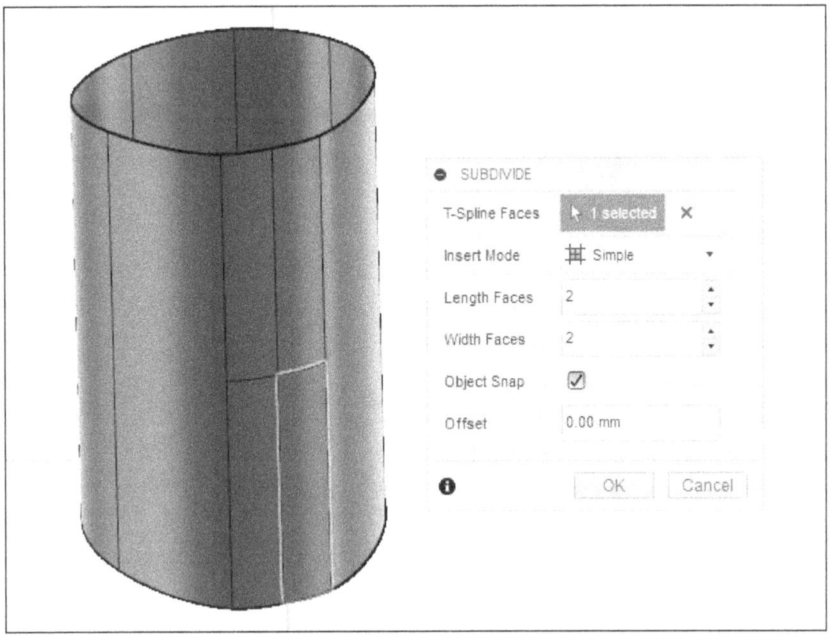

Figure-73. Selected face subdivided

- Select **Simple** option from **Insert Mode** drop-down to add the minimum number of control points to the subdivided face.
- Select **Exact** option from **Insert Mode** drop-down if you do not want to change the surface body and maintain the extra shape control points are added.
- Select the **Object Snap** check box to move the new vertices to the closest point. These vertices can snap to solid, surface, and mesh bodies.
- Click in the **Offset** edit box and enter desired value.
- After specifying the parameters, click on the **OK** button from **SUBDIVIDE** dialog box to complete the process.

Insert Point

The **Insert Point** tool is used to insert control points at the selected locations. The procedure to use this tool is discussed next.

- Click on the **Insert Point** tool from **MODIFY** drop-down; refer to Figure-74. The **INSERT POINT** dialog box will be displayed; refer to Figure-75.

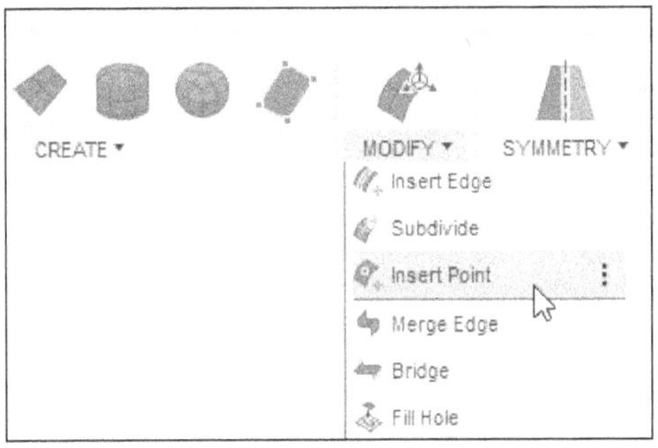

Figure-74. Insert Point tool

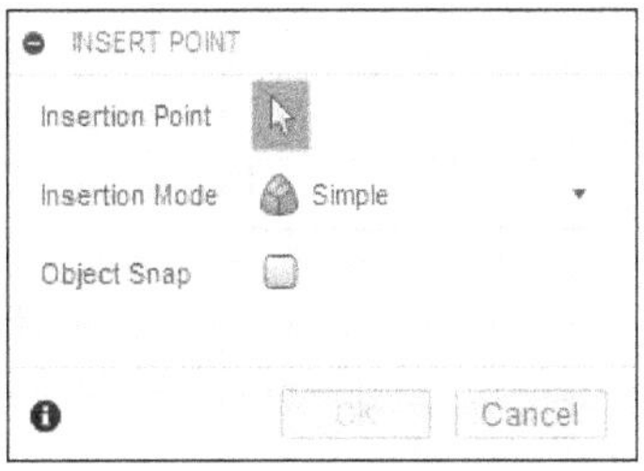

Figure-75. INSERT POINT dialog box

- The **Insertion Point** selection button is active by default. You need to click on the edge of the model to insert point; refer to Figure-76.

Figure-76. Inserting point

- The options of **Insertion Mode** and **Object Snap** were discussed earlier in this book.
- After specifying the parameters, click on the **OK** button from **INSERT POINT** dialog box to complete the process.

Merge Edge

The **Merge Edge** tool is used to connect two bodies by joining their edges. The procedure to use this tool is discussed next.

- Click on the **Merge Edge** tool from **MODIFY** drop-down; refer to Figure-77. The **MERGE EDGE** dialog box will be displayed; refer to Figure-78.

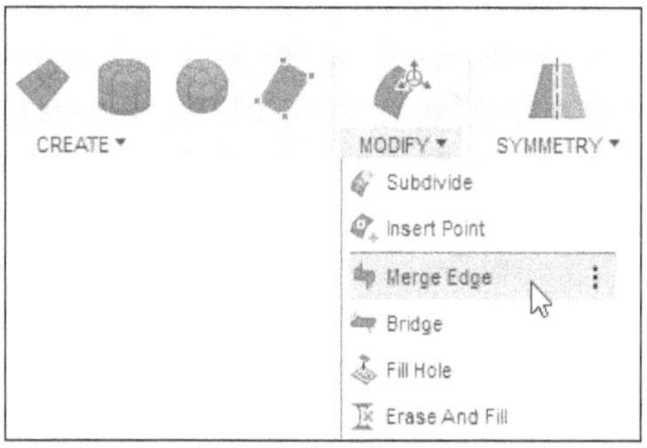

Figure-77. Merge Edge tool

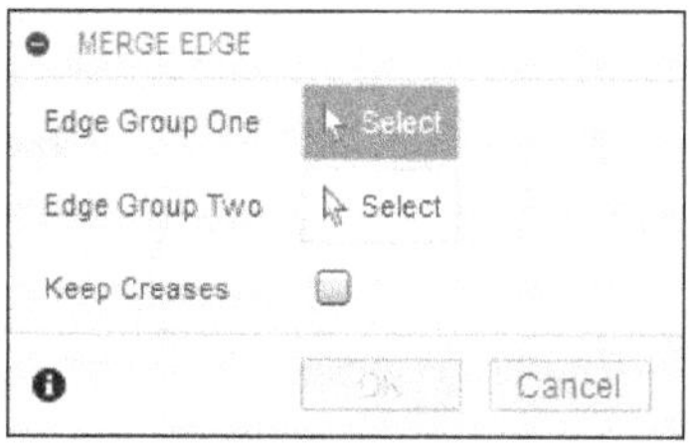

Figure-78. MERGE EDGE dialog box

- The **Select** button of **Edge Group One** section is active by default. You need to select the edges or boundaries of a body.
- Click on the **Select** button of **Edge Group Two** section and select the boundary of other group; refer to Figure-79.

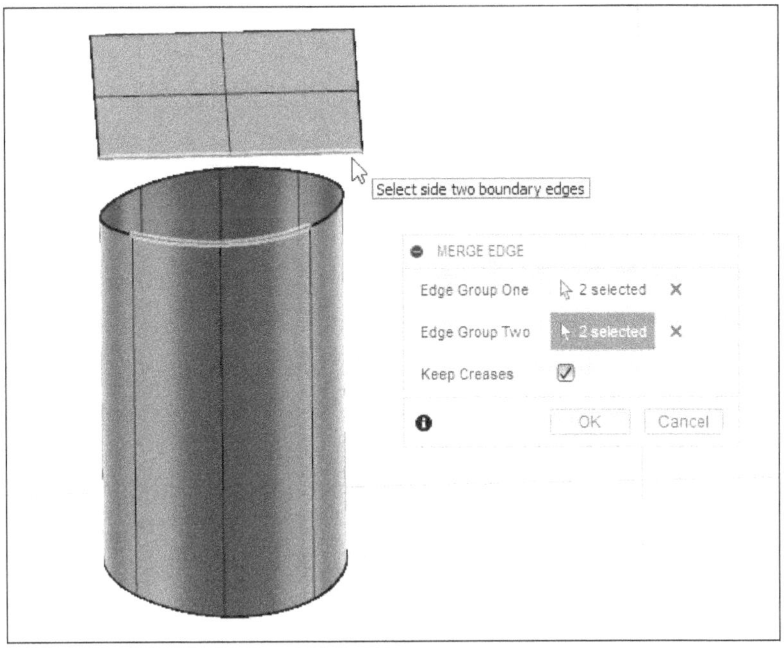

Figure-79. Selecting edges to merge

- Double-click on the edge of a face to select the adjacent edges also.
- Select the **Keep Creases** check box from **MERGE EDGE** dialog box to keep the crease at the merged edges.
- After specifying the parameters, click on the **OK** button from **MERGE EDGE** dialog box to complete the process; refer to Figure-80.

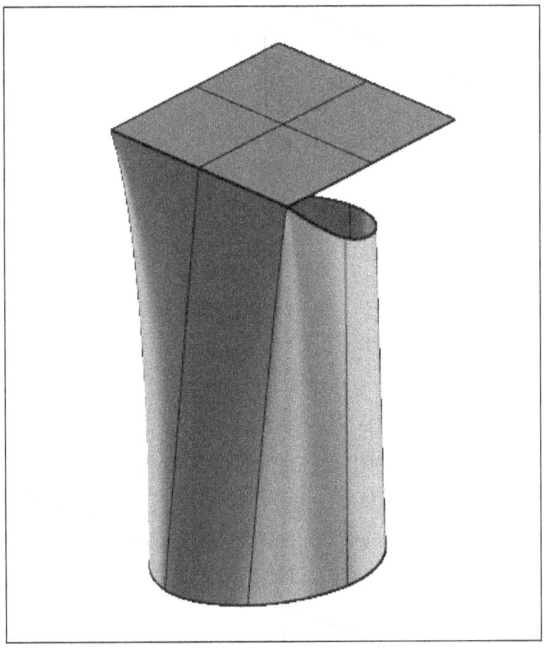

Figure-80. Edges merged

Bridge

The **Bridge** tool is used to connect two bodies by adding their intermediate faces. The procedure to use this tool is discussed next.

- Click on the **Bridge** tool from **MODIFY** drop-down; refer to Figure-81. The **BRIDGE** dialog box will be displayed; refer to Figure-82.

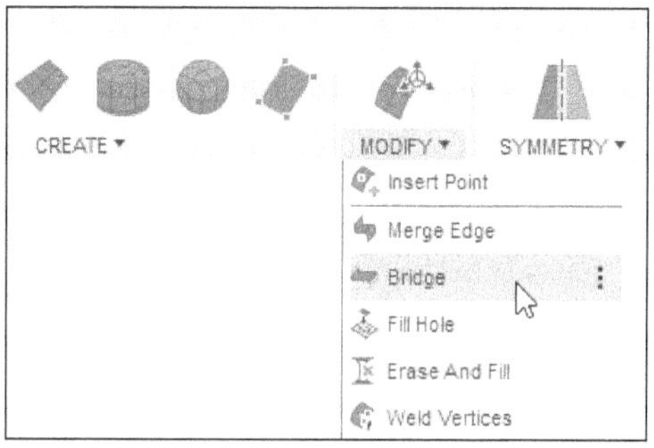

Figure-81. Bridge tool

Figure-82. BRIDGE dialog box

- Click on the **Side One** button from **BRIDGE** dialog box and select desired faces.
- Click on the **Side Two** button from **BRIDGE** dialog box and select the faces from the model to join.
- Click on the **Follow Curve** button from **BRIDGE** dialog box and select a curve for the bridge to follow.
- Select the **Preview** check box to display a mesh preview of the bridge from the selected faces; refer to Figure-83.

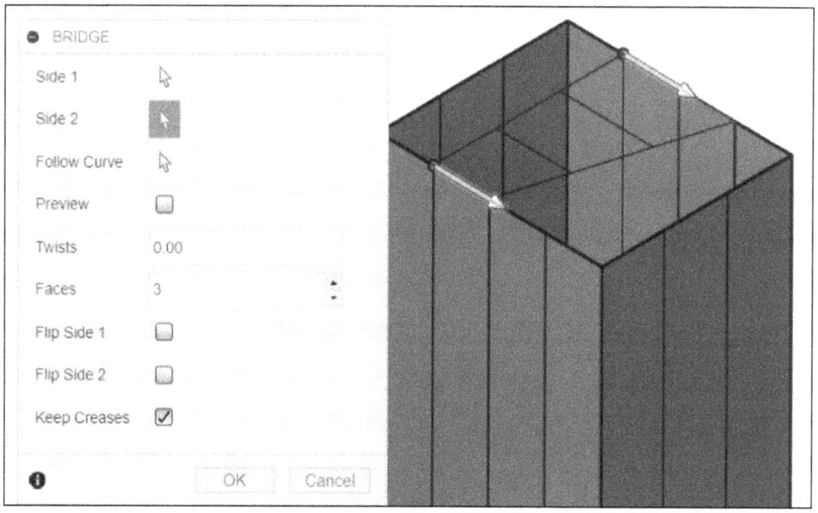

Figure-83. Preview of bridge

- Click in the **Twists** edit box and specify the number of rotation of bridge between two selected different faces (side one and side two).
- Click in the **Faces** edit box and specify the number of faces created between two selected sides.
- Select the **Flip Side 1** check box to flip the bridge direction of side one.
- Select the **Flip Side 2** check box to flip the bridge direction of side two.
- Select the **Keep Creases** check box from **BRIDGE** dialog box to keep the crease at the merged edges.
- After specifying the parameters, click on the **OK** button from **BRIDGE** dialog box to complete the process; refer to Figure-84.

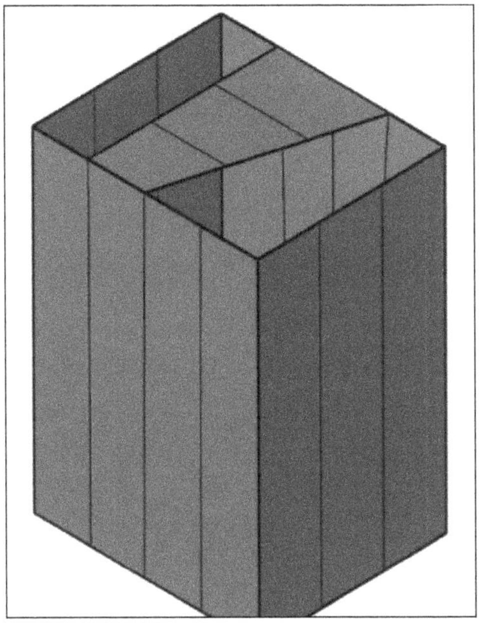

Figure-84. Bridge created

Fill Hole

The **Fill Hole** tool is used to close the opening of a T-Spline model. The procedure to use this tool is discussed next.

- Click on the **Fill Hole** tool from **MODIFY** drop-down; refer to Figure-85. The **FILL HOLE** dialog box will be displayed; refer to Figure-86.

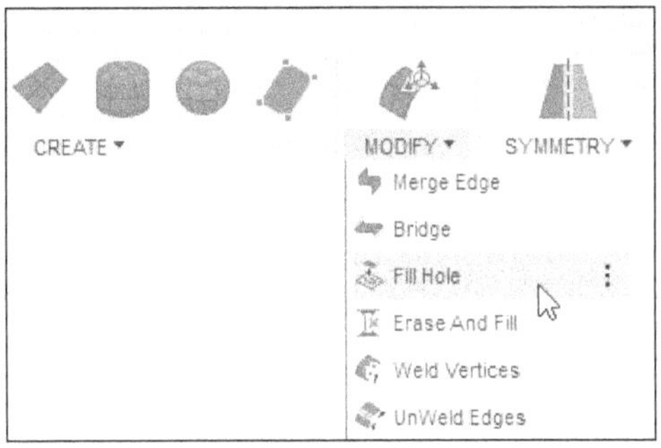

Figure-85. Fill Hole tool

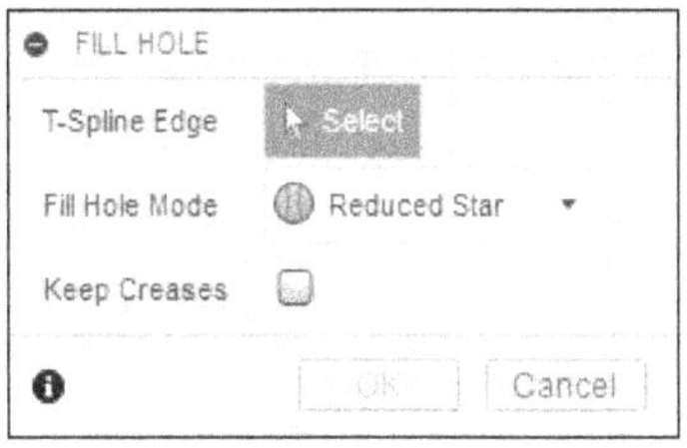

Figure-86. FILL HOLE dialog box

- The **Select** button of **T-Spline Edge** section is active by default. Click on the edge of hole to select. A preview will be displayed; refer to Figure-87.

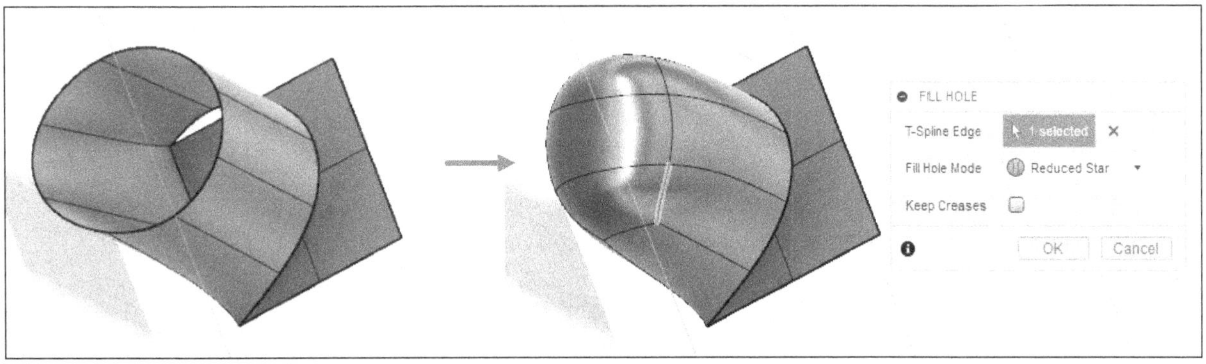

Figure-87. Preview of fill hole

- Select **Reduced Star** option from **Fill Hole Mode** drop-down to fill the hole by adding minimum number of star points of face.

- Select **Fill Star** option from **Fill Hole Mode** drop-down to fill the hole using single face. Due to this option, the star points will created at each vertex; refer to Figure-88.

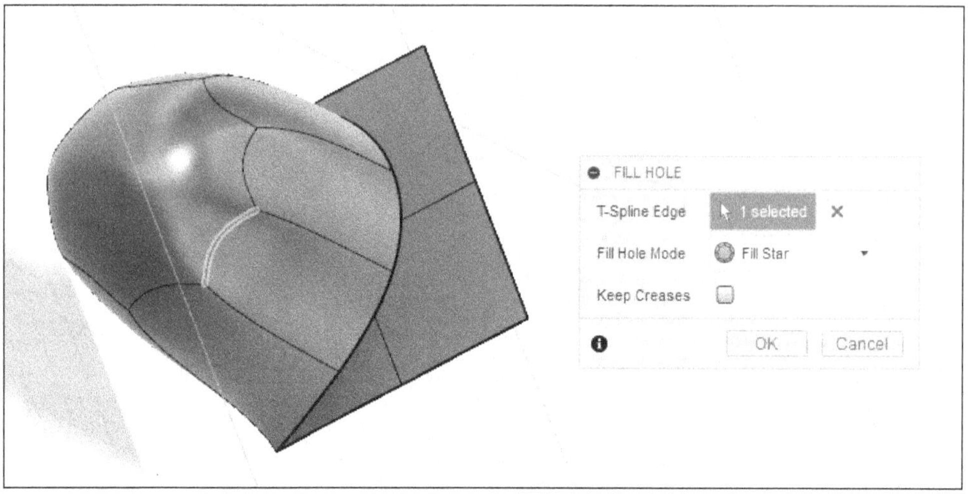

Figure-88. Fill Star option

- Select **Collapse** option from **Fill Hole Mode** drop-down to fill the hole by collapsing all the vertices of selected edge to the center point of hole face; refer to Figure-89.

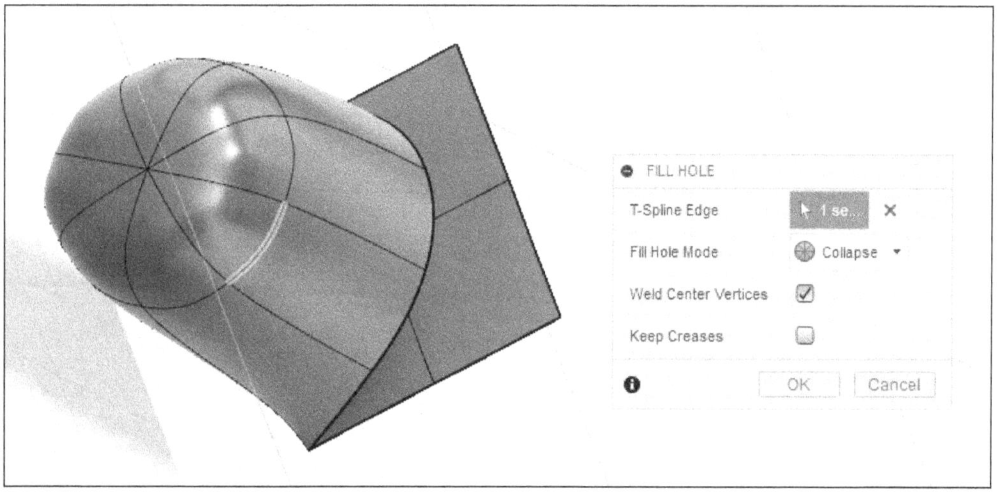

Figure-89. Collapse option

- Select the **Weld Center Vertices** check box from **FILL HOLE** dialog box to weld the vertices at the center of hole face. The **Weld Center Vertices** option is available when **Collapse** option is selected in the **Fill Hole Mode** drop-down.
- After specifying the parameters, click on the **OK** button from **FILL HOLE** dialog box to complete the process.

Erase And Fill

The **Erase And Fill** tool is used to delete a part of T-Spline geometry and fill new gaps with faces. The procedure to use this tool is discussed next.

- Click on the **Erase And Fill** tool from **MODIFY** drop-down; refer to Figure-90. The **ERASE AND FILL** dialog box will be displayed; refer to Figure-91.

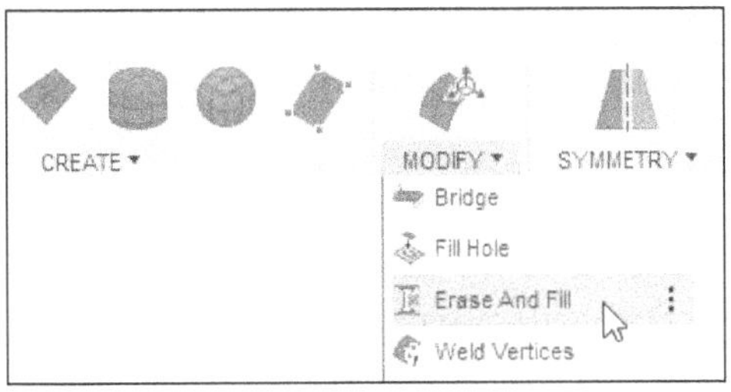

Figure-90. Erase And Fill tool

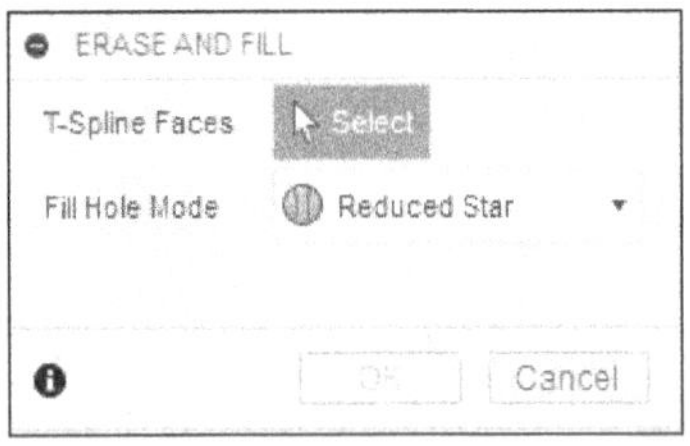

Figure-91. ERASE AND FILL dialog box

- The **Select** button of **T-Spline Faces** section is active by default. Select the faces to be erased and filled; refer to Figure-92.

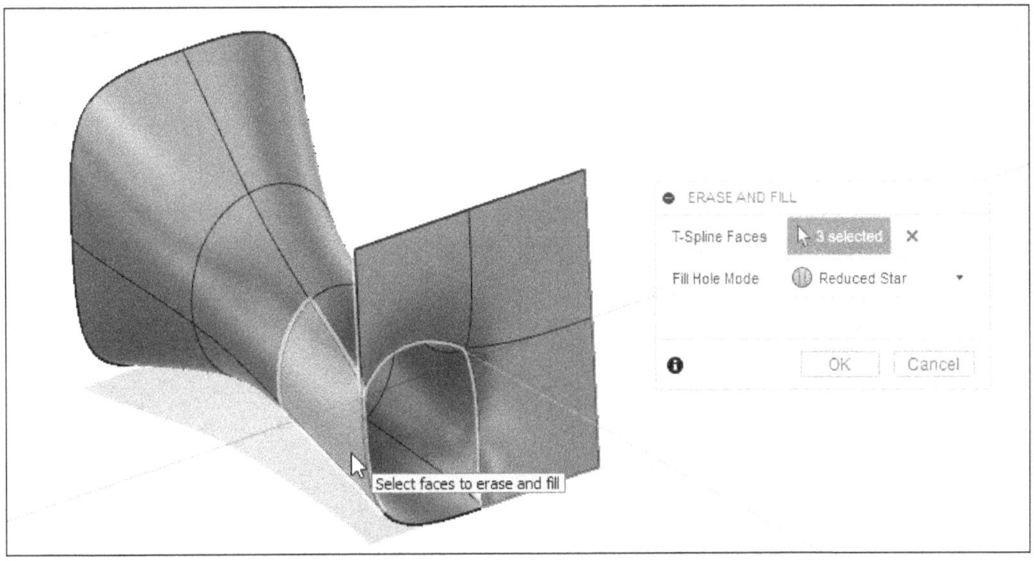

Figure-92. Selection of faces to erase and fill

- Select **Reduced Star** option from **Fill Hole Mode** drop-down to create the faces using minimum number of star points.
- Select **Fill Star** option from **Fill Hole Mode** drop-down to fill the hole with a single face. This tool creates star points at each vertex.
- After specifying the parameters, click on the **OK** button from **ERASE AND FILL** dialog box to complete the process; refer to Figure-93.

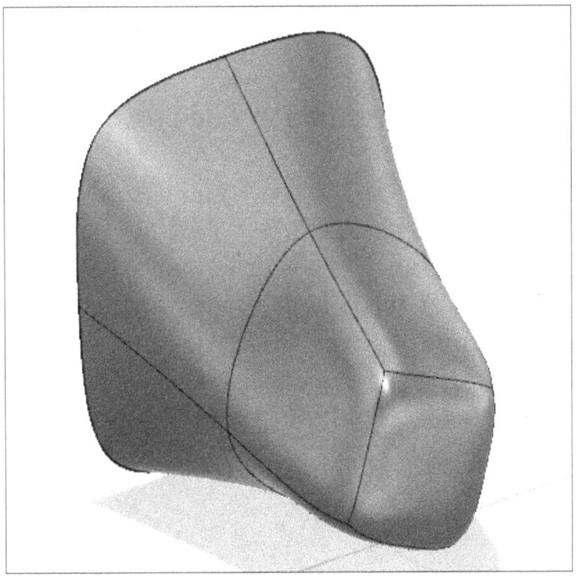

Figure-93. Faces erased and filled

Weld Vertices

The **Weld Vertices** tool is used to join two vertices into single vertex. The procedure to use this tool is discussed next.

- Click on the **Weld Vertices** tool from **MODIFY** drop-down; refer to Figure-94. The **WELD VERTICES** dialog box will be displayed; refer to Figure-95.

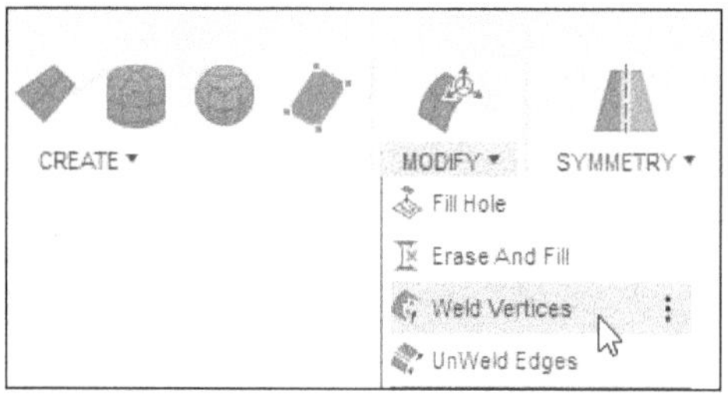

Figure-94. Weld Vertices tool

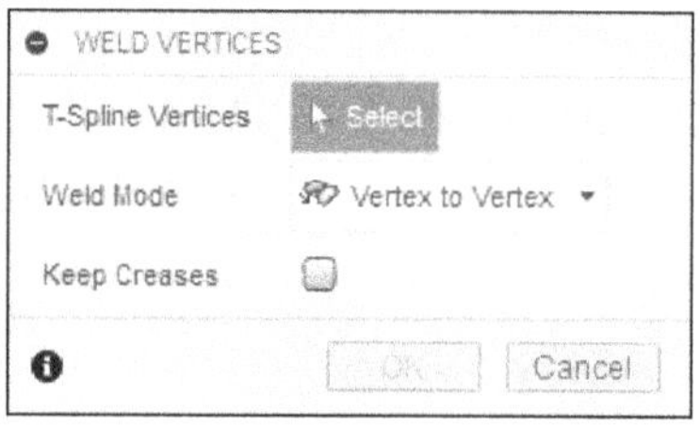

Figure-95. WELD VERTICES dialog box

- The **Select** button of **T-Spline Vertices** section is active by default. Click on the vertices to join together; refer to Figure-96.

Figure-96. Selecting vertices

- Select **Vertex to Vertex** option from **Weld Mode** drop-down to move the first vertex to the second vertex.
- Select **Vertex to Midpoint** option from **Weld Mode** drop-down to move the two vertices to the midpoint of the selections.
- Select **Weld to Tolerance** option from **Weld Mode** drop-down to weld all the visible and invisible vertices together with in a specified tolerance.
- Click in the **Weld Tolerance** edit box and enter the value of tolerance as required.
- After specifying the parameters, click on the **OK** button from **WELD VERTICES** dialog box to complete the process; refer to Figure-97.

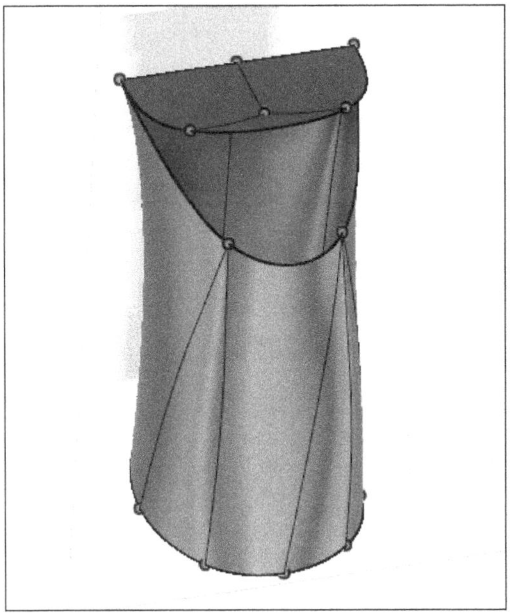

Figure-97. Vertices welded

UnWeld Edges

The **UnWeld Edges** tool is used to detach an edge or loop. The procedure to use this tool is discussed next.

- Click on the **UnWeld Edges** tool from **MODIFY** drop-down; refer to Figure-98. The **UNWELD EDGES** dialog box will be displayed; refer to Figure-99.

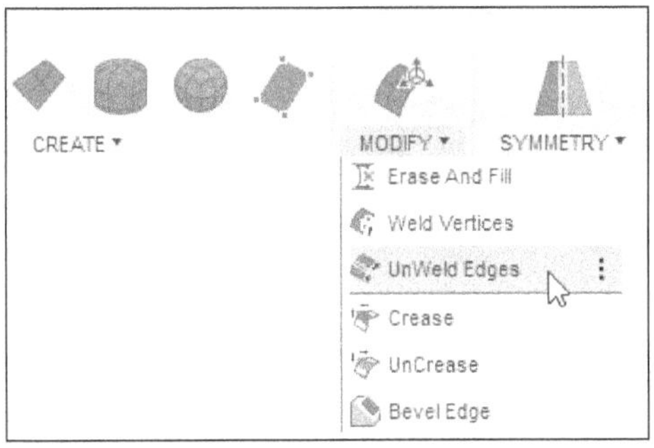

Figure-98. UnWeld Edges tool

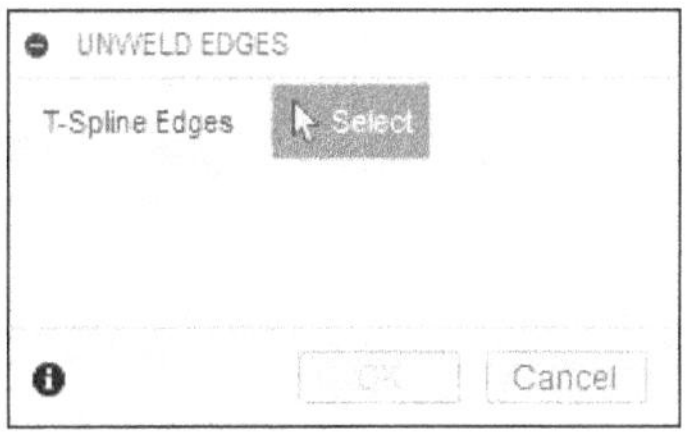

Figure-99. UNWELD EDGES dialog box

- The **Select** button of **T-Spline Edges** section is active by default. Click on the edge or loop to select; refer to Figure-100. Double-click on the edge to select the loop.

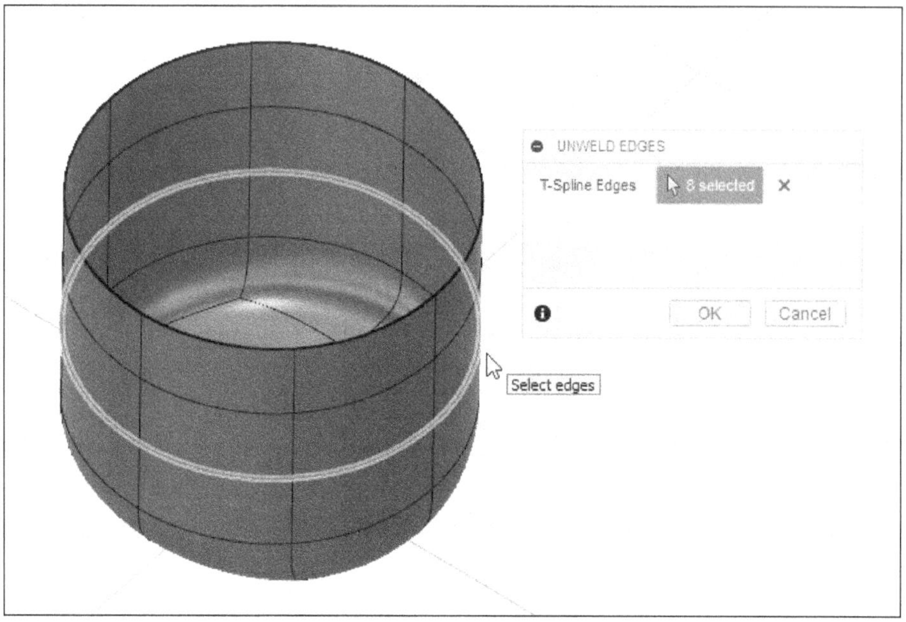

Figure-100. Selecting loop

- After selecting the edge or loop, click on the **OK** button from **UNWELDED EDGES** dialog box to complete the process; refer to Figure-101.

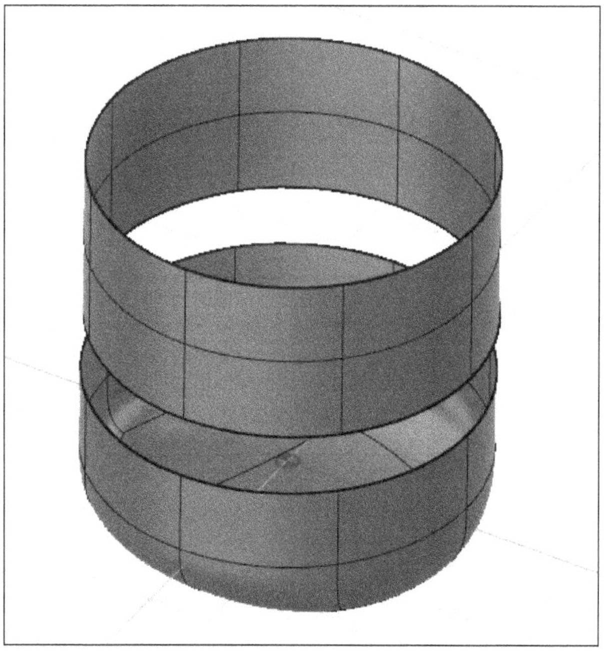

Figure-101. Edges unwelded

Crease

The **Crease** tool is used to add a sharp crease on the selected T-Spline body. The procedure to use this tool is discussed next.

- Click on the **Crease** tool from **MODIFY** drop-down; refer to Figure-102. The **CREASE** dialog box will be displayed; refer to Figure-103.

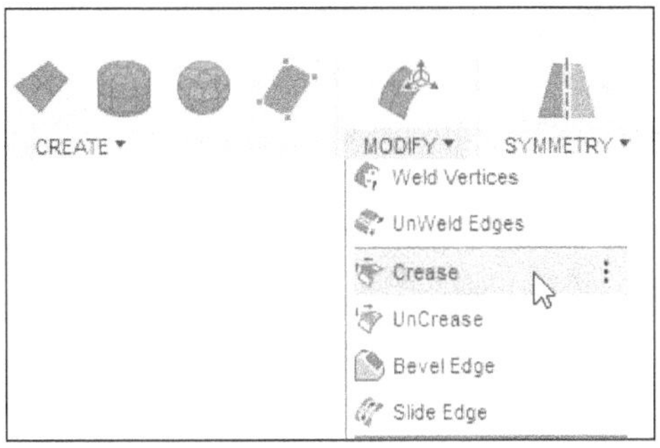

Figure-102. Crease tool

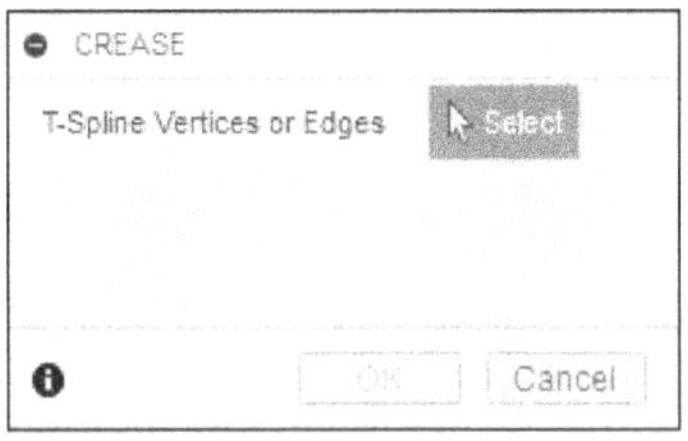

Figure-103. CREASE dialog box

- The **Select** button of **T-Spline Vertices or Edges** section is active by default. Click to select the edge. You can also use window selection to select multiple edges; refer to Figure-104.

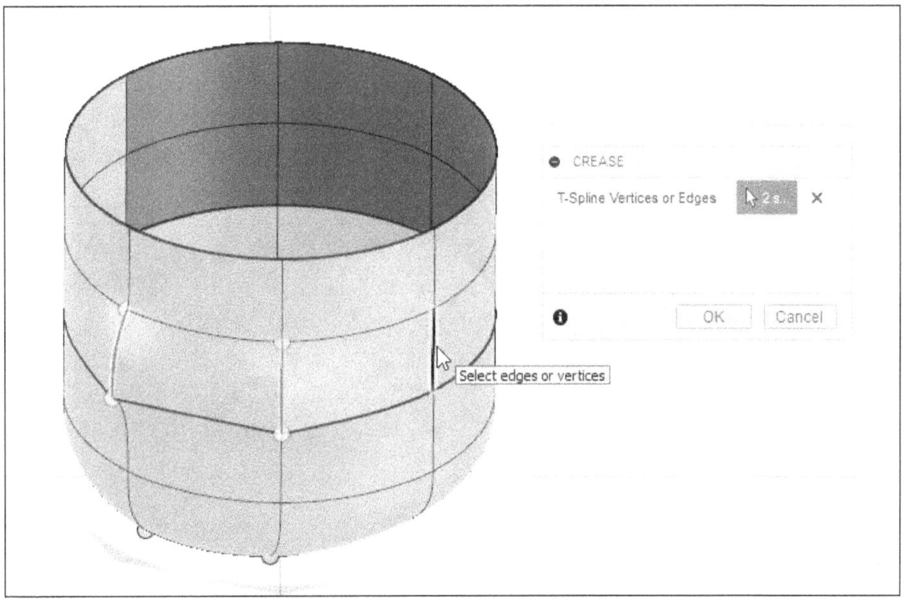

Figure-104. Selection of edges for crease

- After selection of edges for crease, click on **OK** button from **CREASE** dialog box. The selected edges will be converted into creased edges; refer to Figure-105.

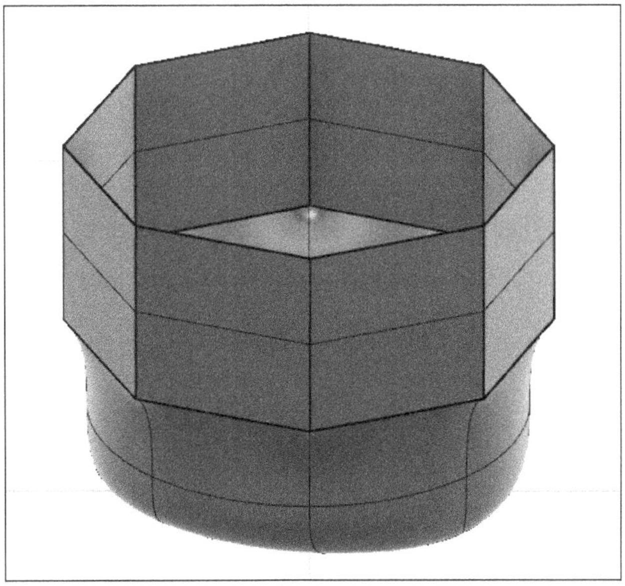

Figure-105. Edges creased

UnCrease

The **UnCrease** tool is used to remove crease from the selected body, edge, or vertex. The procedure to use this tool is discussed next.

- Click on the **UnCrease** tool from **MODIFY** drop-down; refer to Figure-106. The **UNCREASE** dialog box will be displayed; refer to Figure-107.

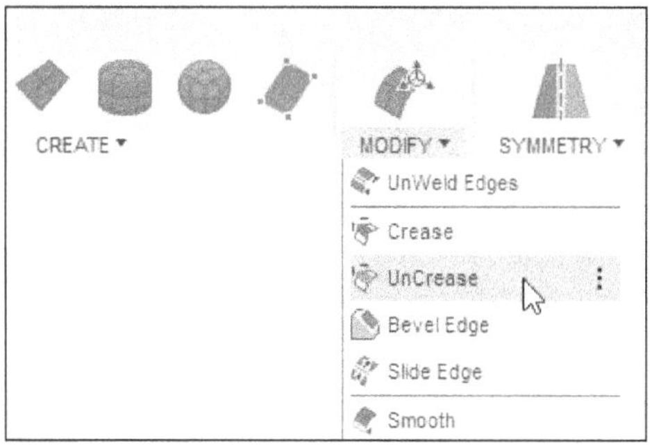

Figure-106. UnCrease tool

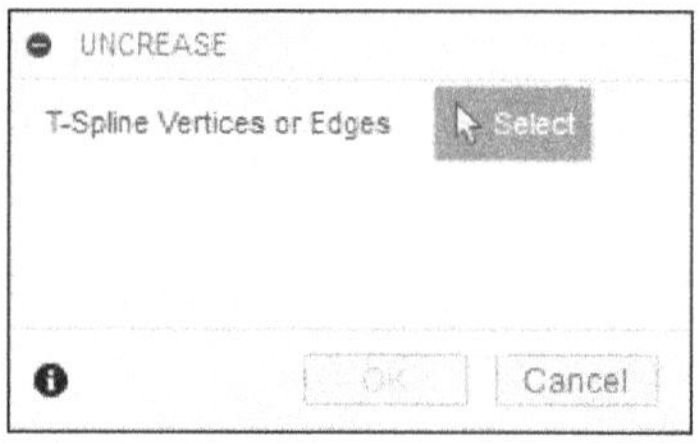

Figure-107. UNCREASE dialog box

- The **Select** button of **T-Spline Vertices or Edges** section is active by default. Click to select the edge. You can also use window selection to select multiple edges; refer to Figure-108.

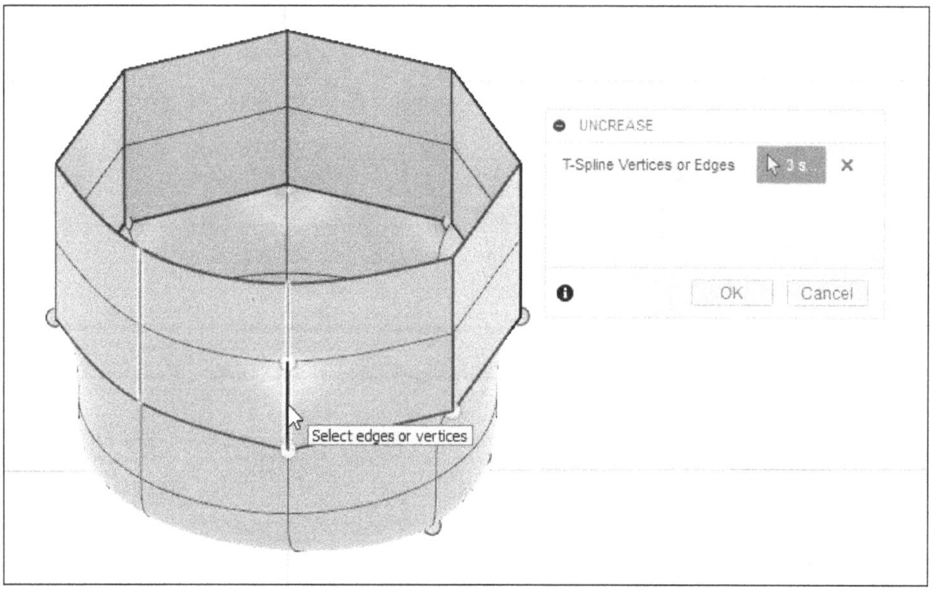

Figure-108. Selection of edges for uncrease

- After selection of edges for uncrease, click on **OK** button from **UNCREASE** dialog box to complete the process; refer to Figure-109.

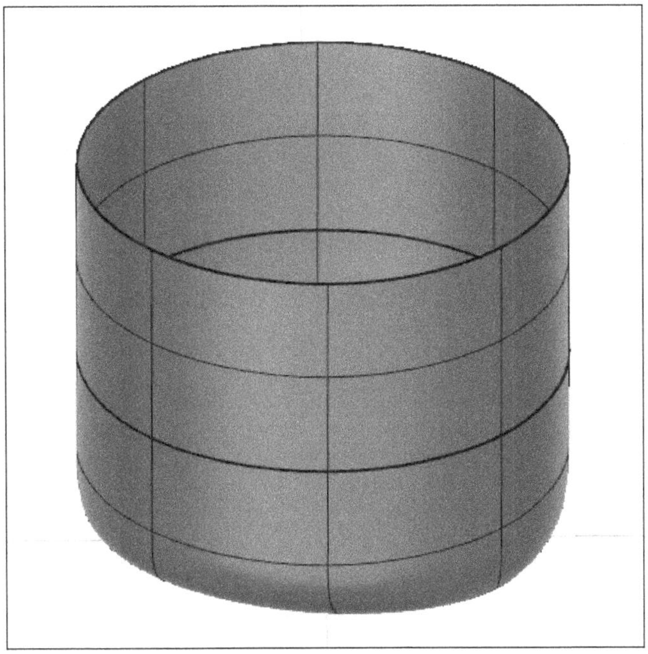

Figure-109. Edges uncreased

Bevel Edge

The **Bevel Edge** tool is used to flatten the area of body by selecting a specific edge. The procedure to use this tool is discussed next.

- Click on the **Bevel Edge** tool from **MODIFY** drop-down; refer to Figure-110. The **BEVEL EDGE** dialog box will be displayed; refer to Figure-111.

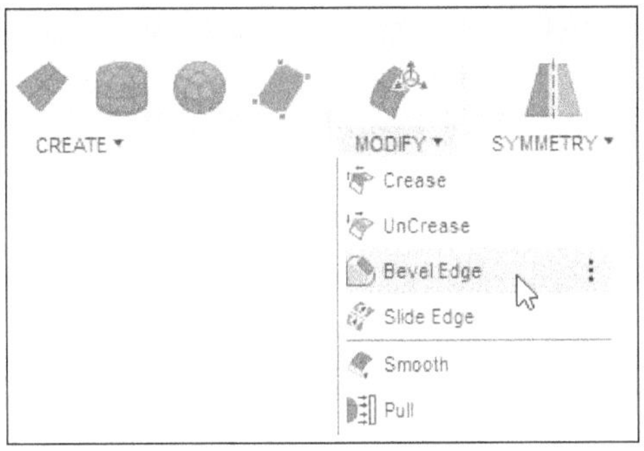

Figure-110. Bevel Edge tool

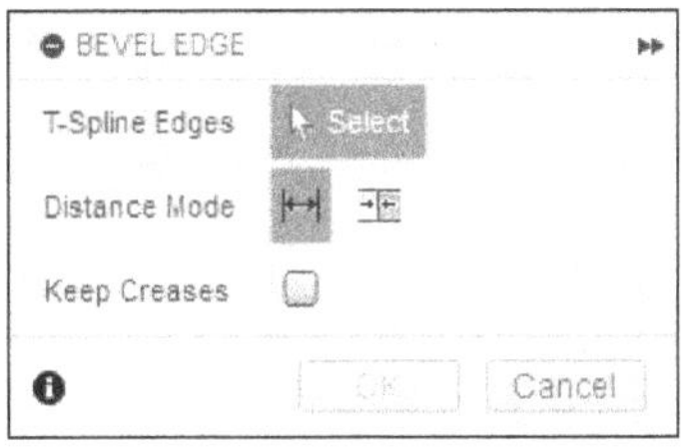

Figure-111. BEVEL EDGE dialog box

- The **Select** button of **T-Spline Edge** section is active by default. Click on the edge of a body to select; refer to Figure-112.

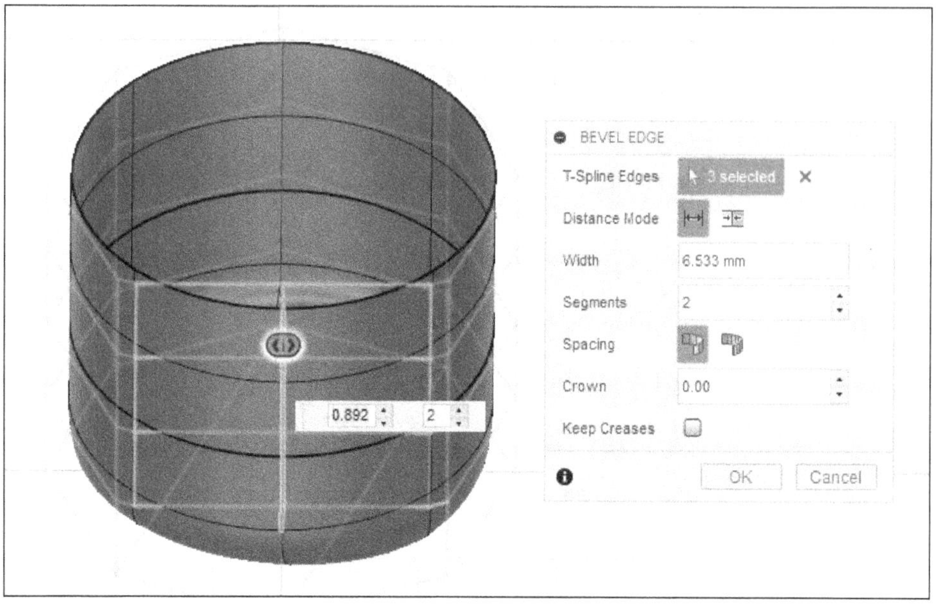

Figure-112. Selection of edges for bevel edge

- Select **Bevel Width** option from **Distance Mode** area and specify desired bevel width in the **Width** edit box to create a bevel with sides of equal distance. Select **Relative Offset** option and specify desired offset ratio of the outer edges relative to the original edge in the **Offset Ratio** edit box.
- Click in the **Segments** edit box and enter desired number of faces to be inserted in between new edges.
- Select **Uniform** option from **Spacing** area to create segments equally spaced across the bevel. Select **Parametric** option to create segments parametrically spaced along the bevel.
- Specify desired value between **0** and **2** in the **Crown** edit box to create a rounded bevel, specify value **0** in the edit box for a flat bevel, and specify value **2** in the edit box for a sharp bevel.
- After specifying desired parameters, click on **OK** button from the dialog box. The selected edge will be flattened; refer to Figure-113.

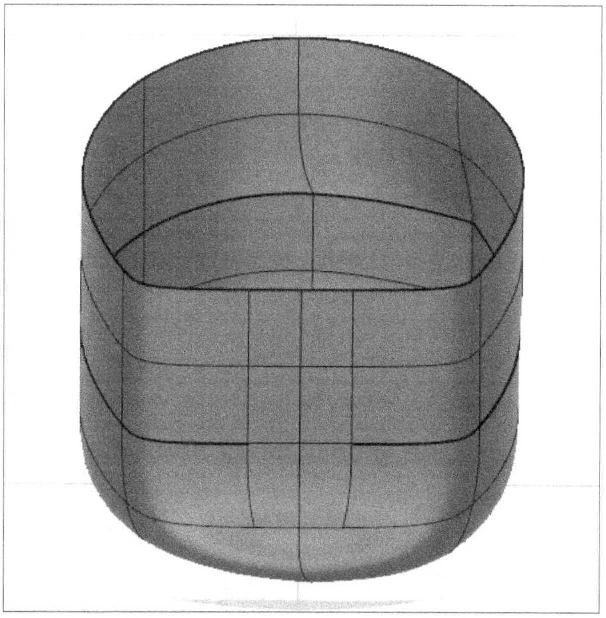

Figure-113. Bevel edge created

Slide Edge

The **Slide Edge** tool is used to move two edges closer together or farther apart. The procedure to use this tool is discussed next.

- Click on the **Slide Edge** tool from **MODIFY** drop-down; refer to Figure-114. The **SLIDE EDGE** dialog box will be displayed; refer to Figure-115.

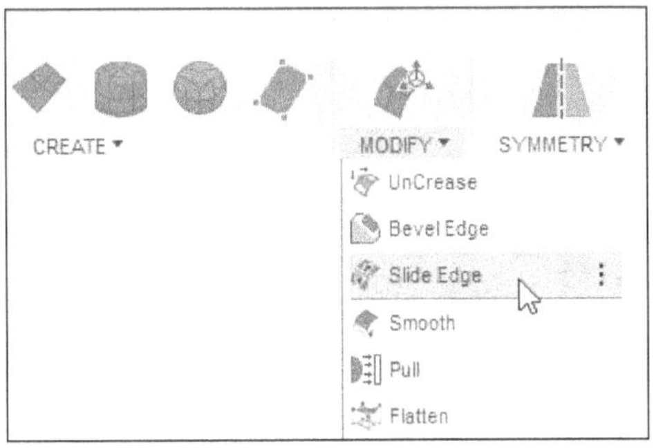

Figure-114. Slide Edge tool

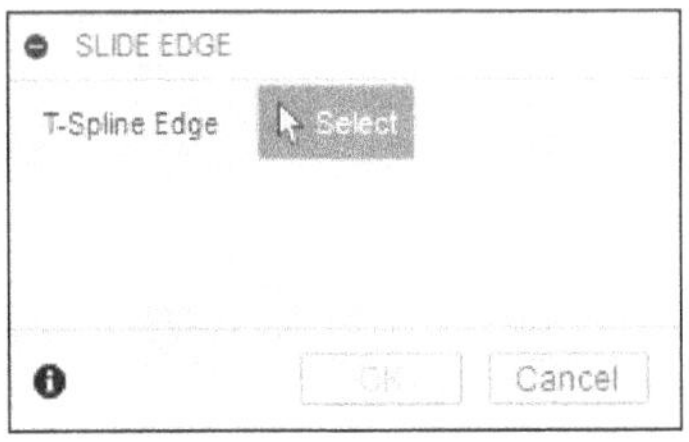

Figure-115. SLIDE EDGE dialog box

- The **Select** button of **T-Spline Edge** section is active by default. Click on the edge of a body to select; refer to Figure-116.

Figure-116. Selection of edges for slide edge

- Click in the **Slide Location** edit box and enter the value to position the new edge in decimal percentage. You can also set the value of **Slide Location** option by moving the manipulator displayed on the selected edge.
- After specifying the parameters, click on the **OK** button from **SLIDE EDGE** dialog box. The slide edge will be created; refer to Figure-117.

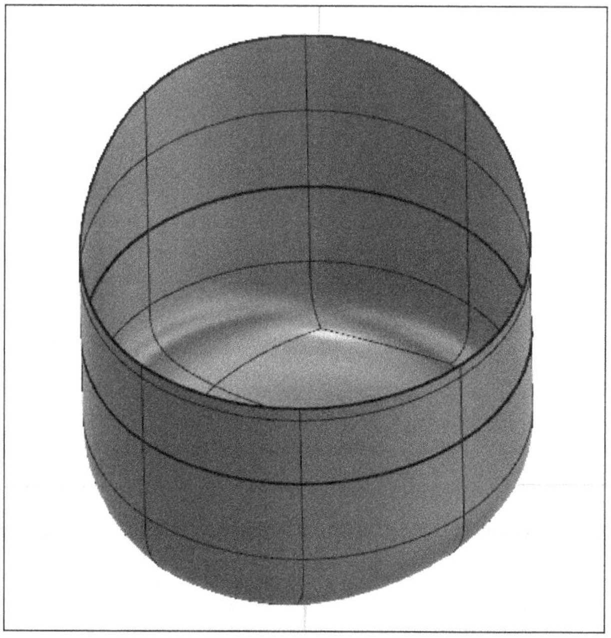

Figure-117. Slide edge created

Smooth

The **Smooth** tool is used to smooth an area of the T-Spline geometry by selecting desired faces. The procedure to use this tool is discussed next.

- Click on the **Smooth** tool from **MODIFY** drop-down; refer to Figure-118. The **SMOOTH** dialog box will be displayed; refer to Figure-119.

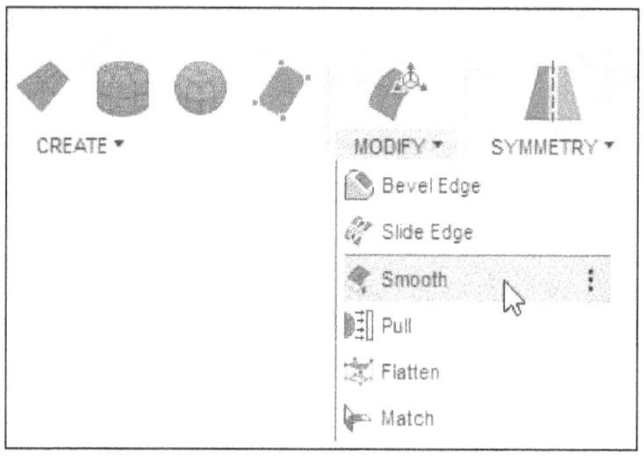

Figure-118. Smooth tool

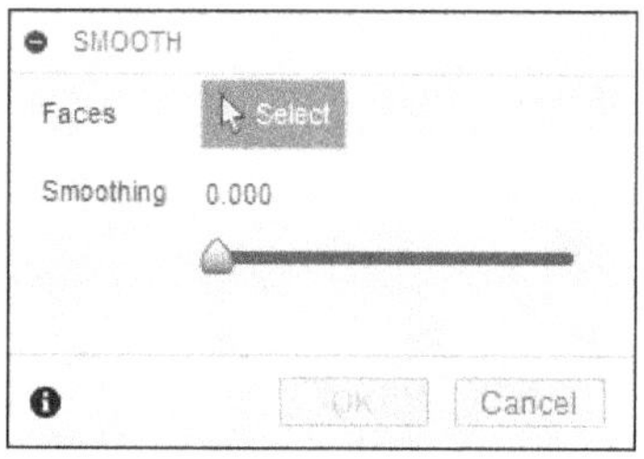

Figure-119. SMOOTH dialog box

- The **Select** button of **Faces** section is active by default. Select the faces around desired area; refer to Figure-120.

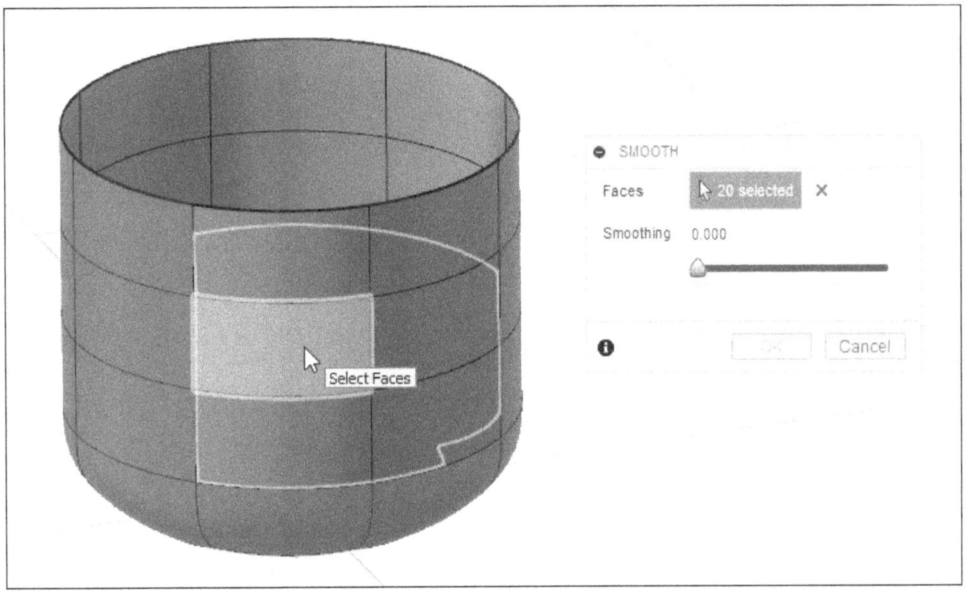

Figure-120. Selection of faces for smoothing

- Click in the **Smoothing** edit box and enter the value of smoothing rate from 0 to 1. You can also set the value of **Smoothing** option by moving the slider.
- After specifying the parameters, click on the **OK** button from **SMOOTH** dialog box to complete the process; refer to Figure-121.

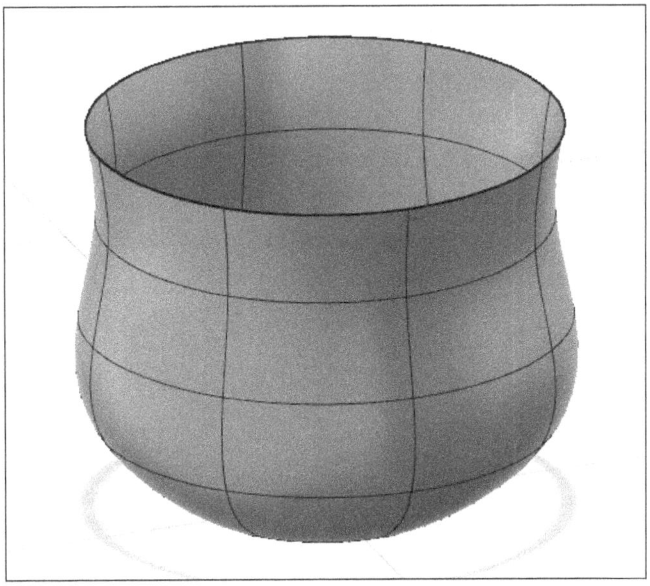

Figure-121. Faces smoothen

Cylindrify

The **Cylindrify** tool is used to form uneven T-Spline geometry into a smooth cylindrical shape. The procedure to use this tool is discussed next.

- Click on the **Cylindrify** tool from **MODIFY** drop-down; refer to Figure-122. The **CYLINDRIFY** dialog box will be displayed; refer to Figure-123.

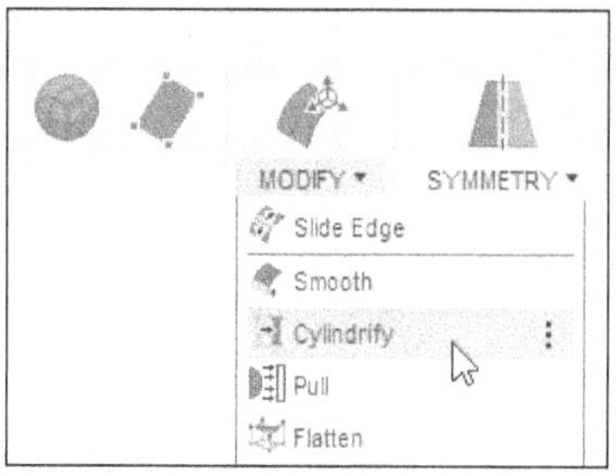

Figure-122. Cylindrify tool

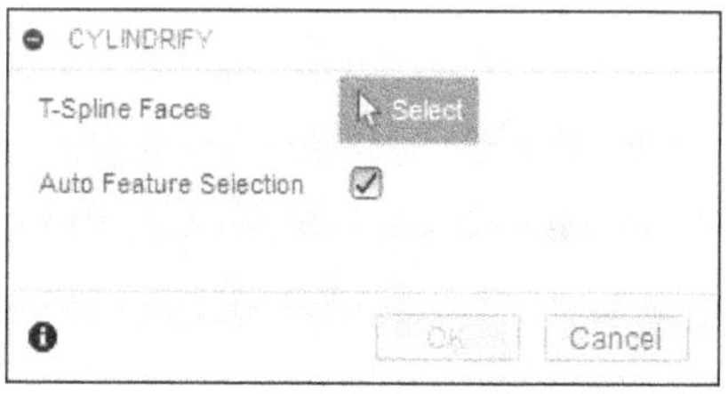

Figure-123. CYLINDRIFY dialog box

- The **Select** button of **T-Spline Faces** section is active by default. Select the faces around desired area; refer to Figure-124.

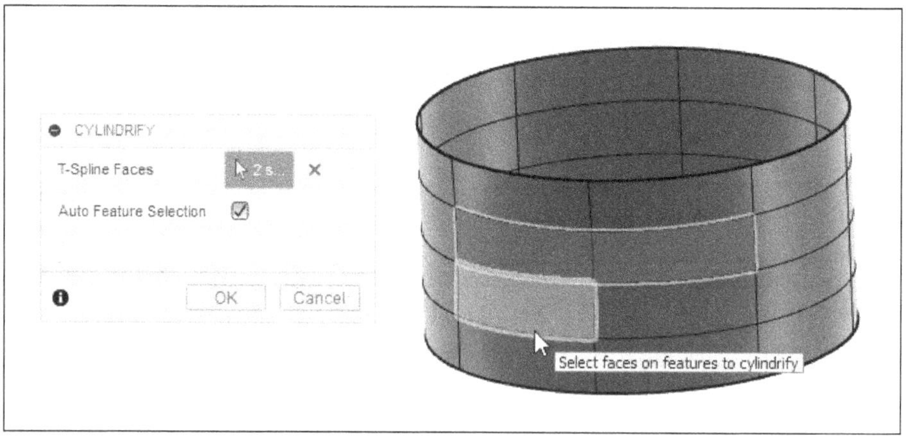

Figure-124. Selection of faces to cylindrify

- Select **Auto Feature Selection** check box to automatically select and preview entire features.
- After specifying the parameters, click on the **OK** button from the **CYLINDRIFY** dialog box to complete the process; refer to Figure-125.

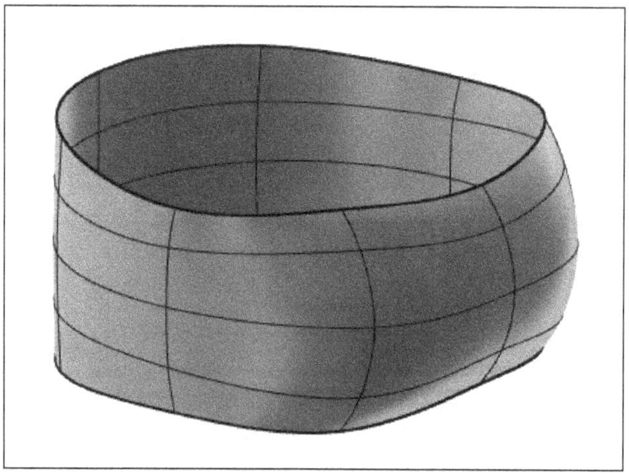

Figure-125. Faces cylindrified

Pull

The **Pull** tool is used for moving the selected vertices to the target body. The procedure to use this tool is discussed next.

- Click on the **Pull** tool from **MODIFY** drop-down; refer to Figure-126. The **PULL** dialog box will be displayed; refer to Figure-127.

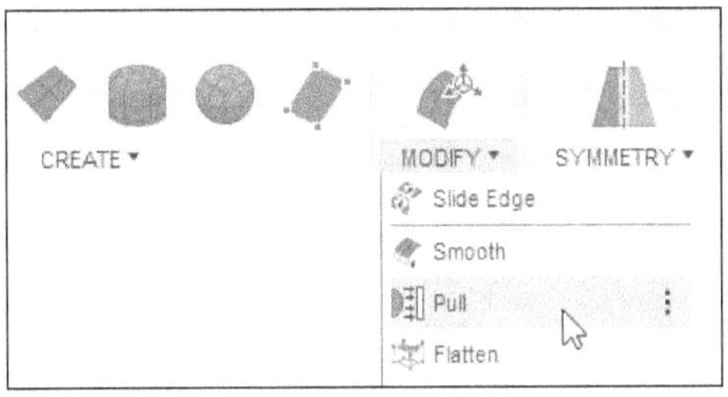

Figure-126. Pull tool

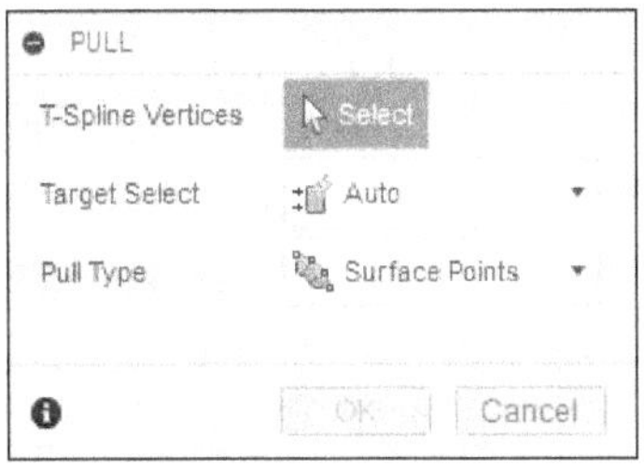

Figure-127. PULL dialog box

- The **Select** button of the **T-Spline Vertices** section is active by default. You need to click on the specific vertex to pull the vertex up to the targeted body; refer to Figure-128.

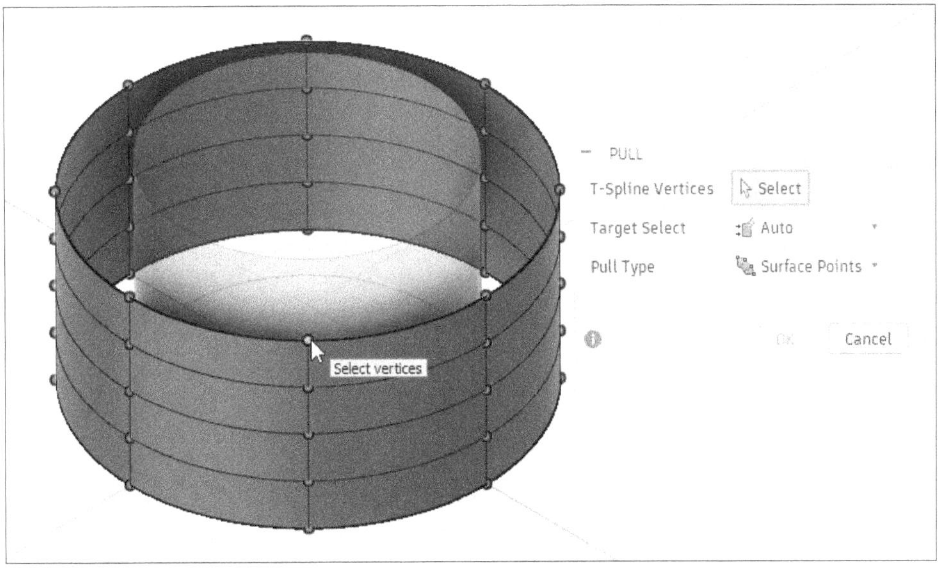

Figure-128. Pulling the vertex

- Select **Auto** option from **Target Select** drop-down to automatically pull the selected vertex.
- Select the **Select Targets** option from **Target Select** drop-down to manually select the target body. The updated **PULL** dialog box will be displayed; refer to Figure-129.

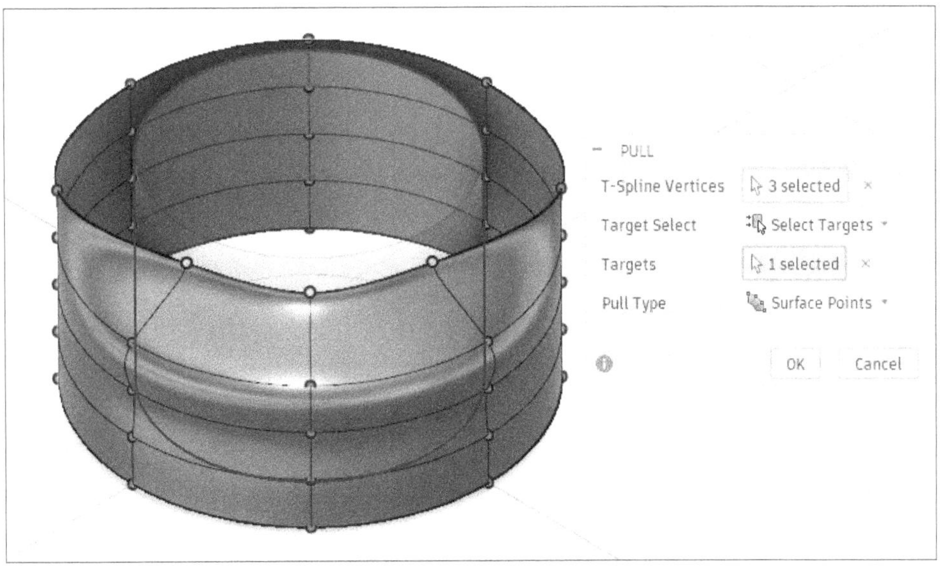

Figure-129. Updated PULL dialog box

- The **Select** button of **Targets** section is active by default. You need to click on the target body to pull the selected vertex.
- Select **Surface Points** option from **Pull Type** drop-down to move the surface points to the target body.
- Select **Control Points** option from **Pull Type** drop-down to move the control points to the target body.
- After specifying the parameters, click on the **OK** button from **PULL** dialog box to complete the process.

Flatten

The **Flatten** tool is used for moving the selected control point to the plane for flatten the selected surface. The procedure to use this tool is discussed next.

- Click on the **Flatten** tool from **MODIFY** drop-down; refer to Figure-130. The **FLATTEN** dialog box will be displayed; refer to Figure-131.

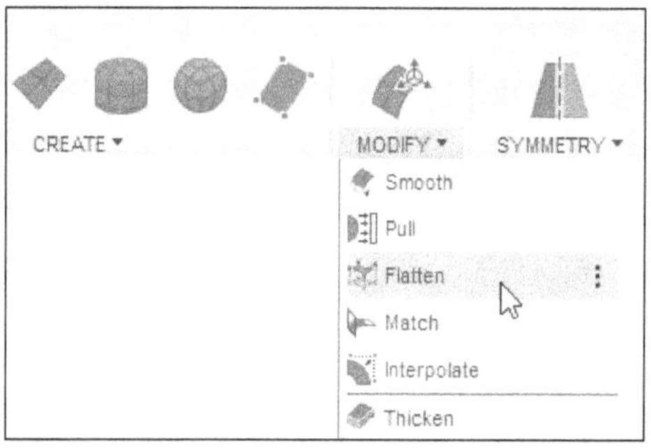

Figure-130. Flatten tool

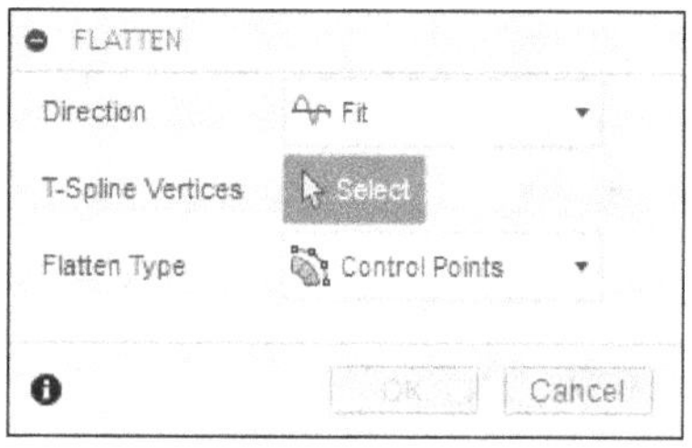

Figure-131. FLATTEN dialog box

- The **Select** button of **T-Spline Vertices** section is active by default. Select the vertices of the face which you want to flatten; refer to Figure-132.

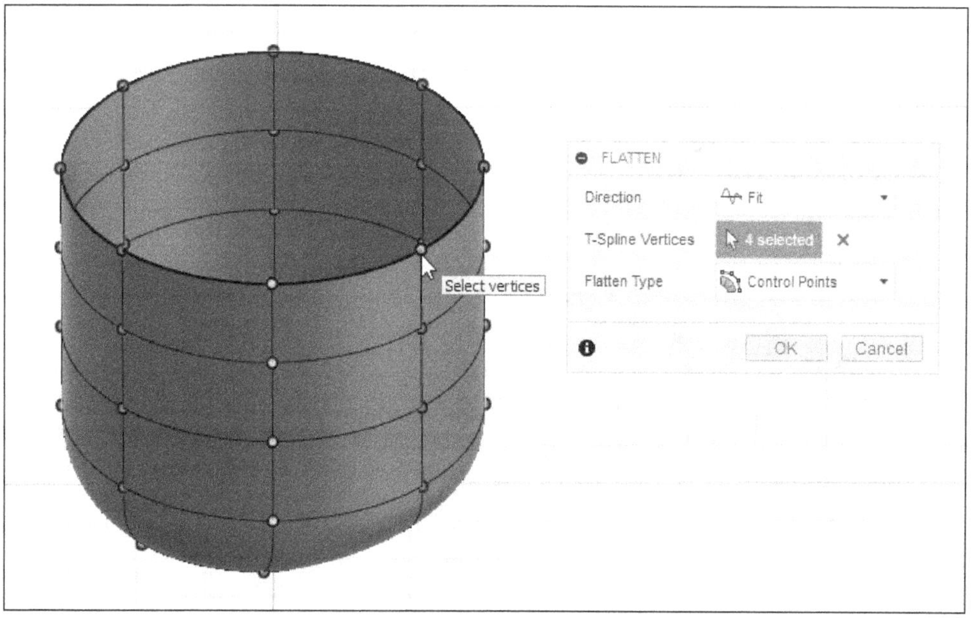

Figure-132. Selecting vertices for flatten surface

- On selecting all the vertices, the preview of flatten surface will be displayed; refer to Figure-133.

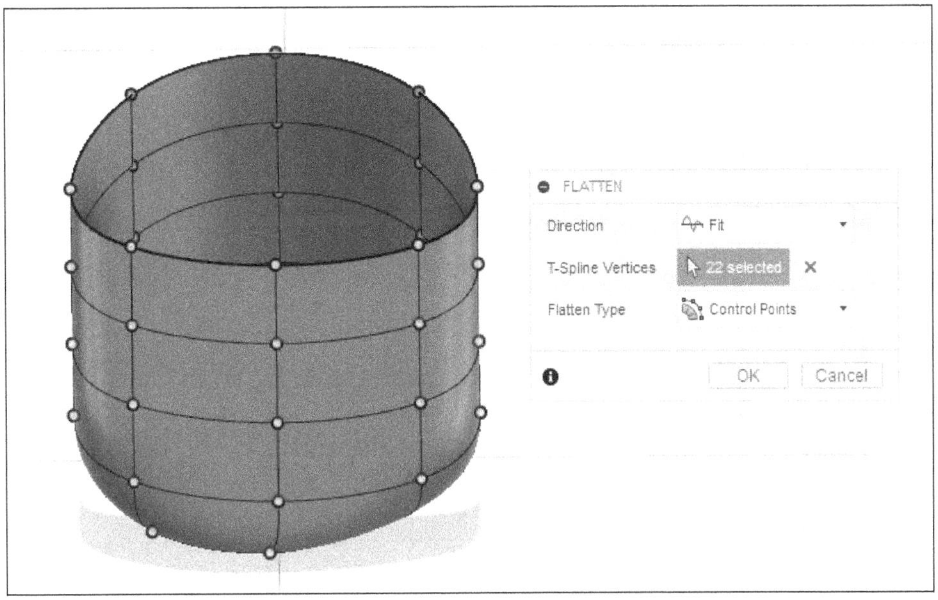

Figure-133. Preview of flatten surface

- Select **Fit** option from **Direction** drop-down to select the best fit plane for flatten the selected surface.
- Select the **Select Plane** option from **Direction** drop-down to manually select the plane to flatten all control points. You are required to select the plane.
- Select the **Select Parallel Plane** option from **Direction** drop-down to move the control points to the selected parallel plane. You are required to select the plane.
- Select desired option from the **Flatten Type** drop-down as discussed earlier in this chapter.
- After specifying the parameters, click on the **OK** button from **FLATTEN** dialog box to complete the process.

Straighten

The **Straighten** tool is used to align vertices of a T-Spline body into best fit line, existing line, or a line through two selected points. The procedure to use this tool is discussed next.

- Click on the **Straighten** tool from **MODIFY** drop-down; refer to Figure-134. The **STRAIGHTEN** dialog box will be displayed; refer to Figure-135.

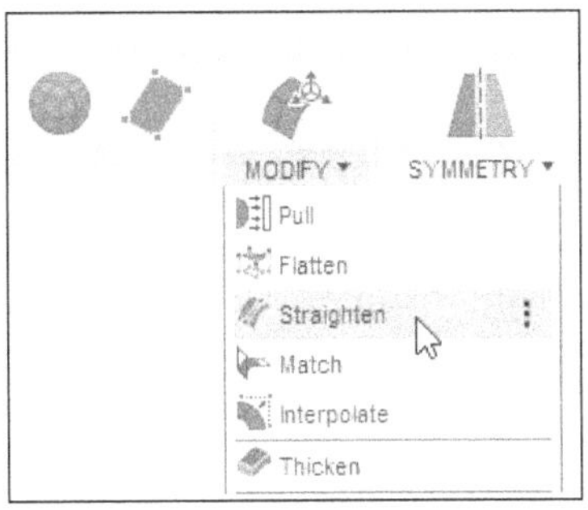

Figure-134. Straighten tool

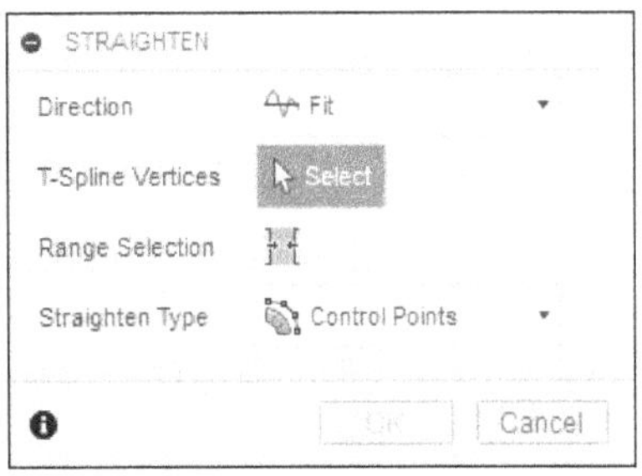

Figure-135. STRAIGHTEN dialog box

- The **Select** button of **T-Spline Vertices** section is active by default. Select the vertices of the face which you want to straighten; refer to Figure-136.

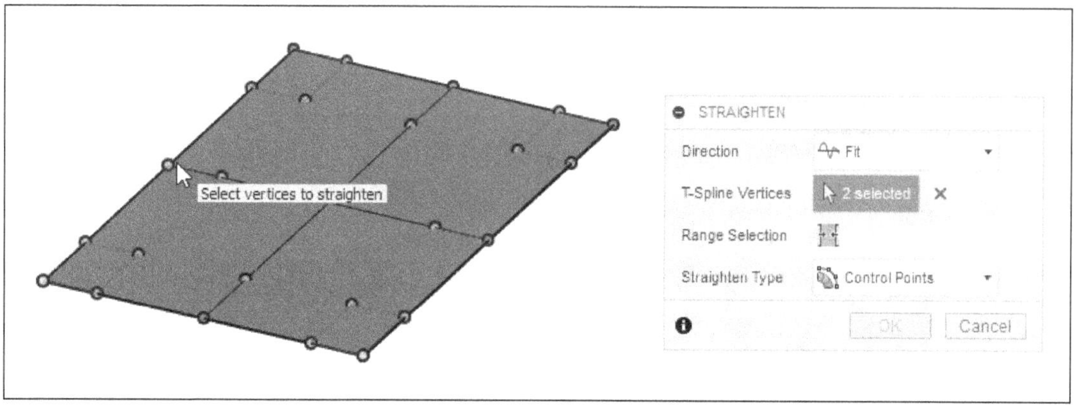

Figure-136. Selecting vertices for straighten surface

- On selecting all the vertices, the preview of straighten surface will be displayed; refer to Figure-137.

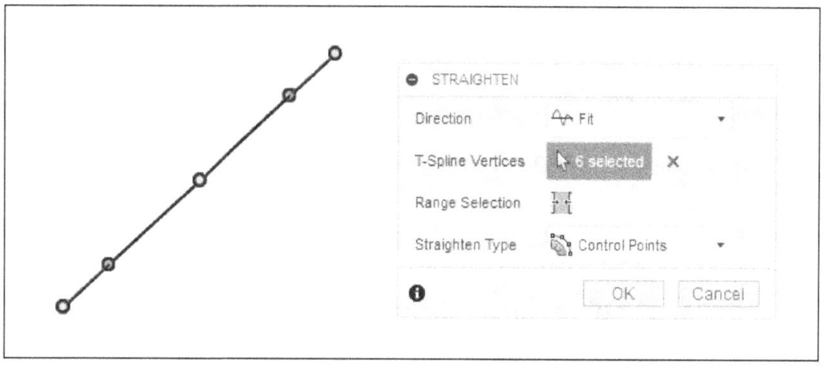

Figure-137. Preview of straighten surface

- Select **Fit** option from **Direction** drop-down to select the best fit plane for flatten the selected surface.
- Select the **Select Line** option from **Direction** drop-down to manually select the lines to straighten all control points. You are required to select the line.
- Select the **Select Parallel Line** option from **Direction** drop-down to select the parallel lines to straighten the control points. You are required to select the line.
- Select the **Select Two Points** option from **Direction** drop-down to select two points to define a line to straighten control points. You are required to select two points.
- Click on the **Range Selection** button to select all vertices or tangency handles between two selected vertices or tangency handles in the same row.
- Select desired option from **Straighten Type** drop-down which have been discussed earlier.
- After specifying the parameters, click on the **OK** button from **STRAIGHTEN** dialog box to complete the process.

Match

The **Match** tool is used to align selected T-Spline edge with a sketch, face, or edge. The procedure to use this tool is discussed next.

- Click on the **Match** tool from **MODIFY** drop-down; refer to Figure-138. The **MATCH** dialog box will be displayed; refer to Figure-139.

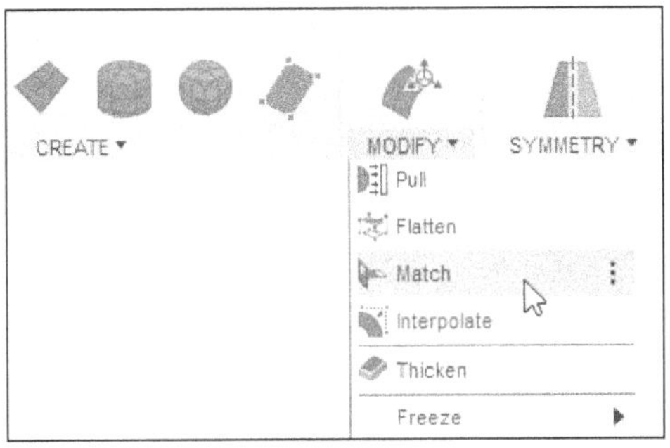

Figure-138. Match tool

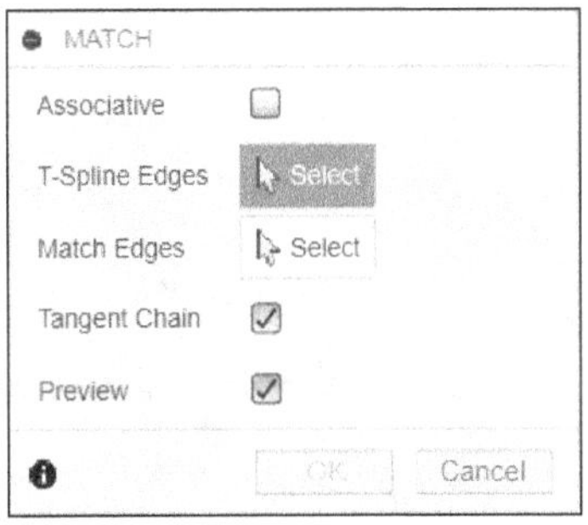

Figure-139. MATCH dialog box

- The **Select** button of **T-Spline Edges** section is active by default. You need to select the edge of model to be matched with sketch section. You can also select the loop by double clicking on the edge; refer to Figure-140.

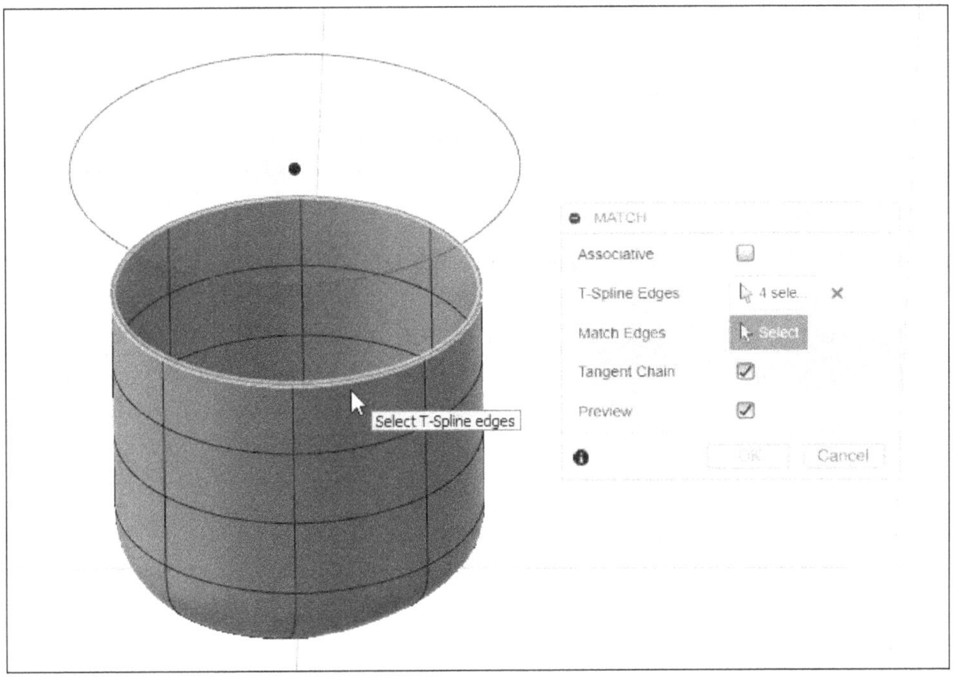

Figure-140. Selecting loop for match

- Click on the **Select** button of **Match Edges** section and select the target edge or sketch.
- Select the **Tangent Chain** check box to automatically select tangent chain geometries.
- On selecting, the preview of alignment will be displayed along with updated **MATCH** dialog box; refer to Figure-141.

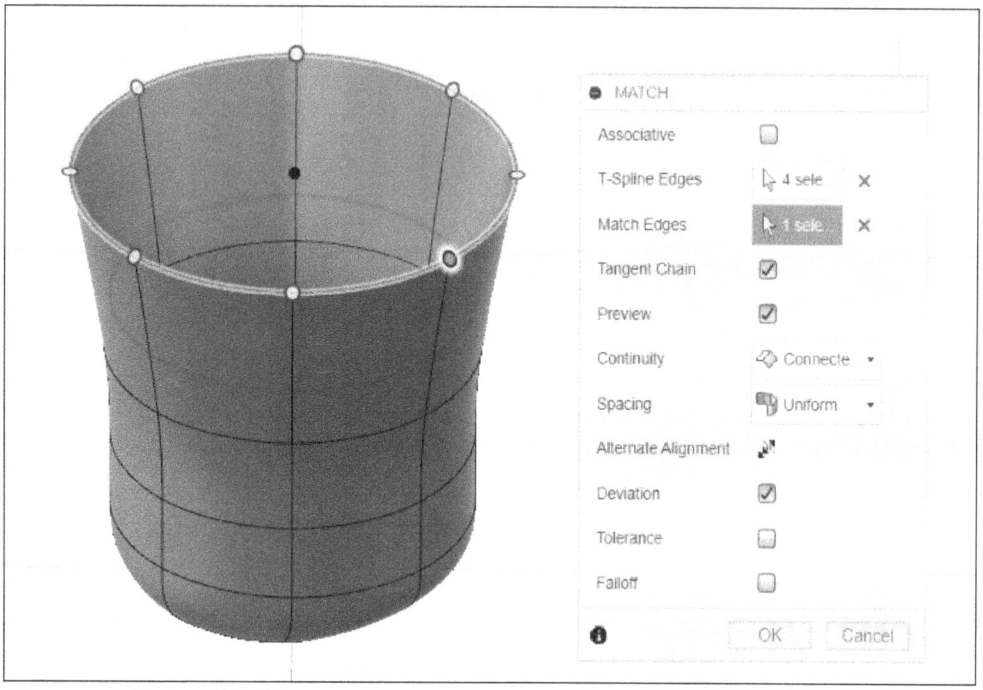

Figure-141. Updated MATCH dialog box

- Select the **Associative** check box to make feature associated with selected sketch section/solid/surface edges. If this check box is selected then match feature will be updated automatically based on changes in the sketch selected for matching.
- Click on the **Alternate Alignment** button from **MATCH** dialog box to flip the direction of alignment; refer to Figure-142.

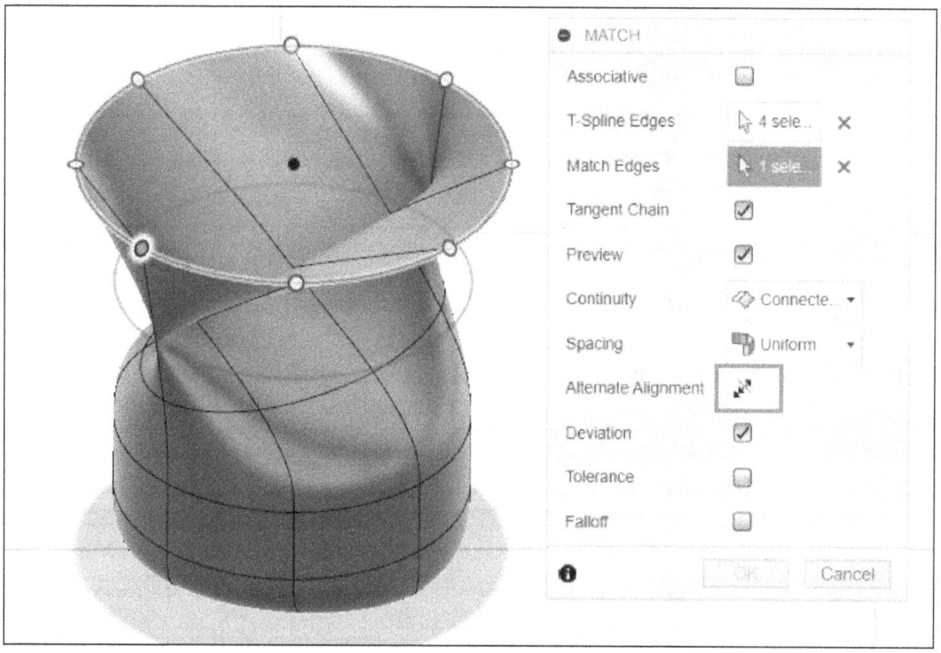

Figure-142. Flipped direction of alignment

- Select the **Deviation** check box from **Tolerance** node to display the amount and location of maximum deviation.
- Select the **Tolerance** check box from **Tolerance** node to specifies the value of how close the T-Spline edges need to be to the target edge.
- Select the **Falloff** check box from **MATCH** dialog box to determine the range of surface affected by the match.

- Click in the **Falloff Distance** edit box displayed on selecting the **Falloff** check box and enter the value of surface affected by the match.
- After specifying the parameters, click on the **OK** button from **MATCH** dialog box to complete the process.

Interpolate

The **Interpolate** tool is used to move the T-Spline control points or surface points for improving fitting. The procedure to use this tool is discussed next.

- Click on the **Interpolate** tool from **MODIFY** drop-down; refer to Figure-143. The **INTERPOLATE** dialog box will be displayed; refer to Figure-144.

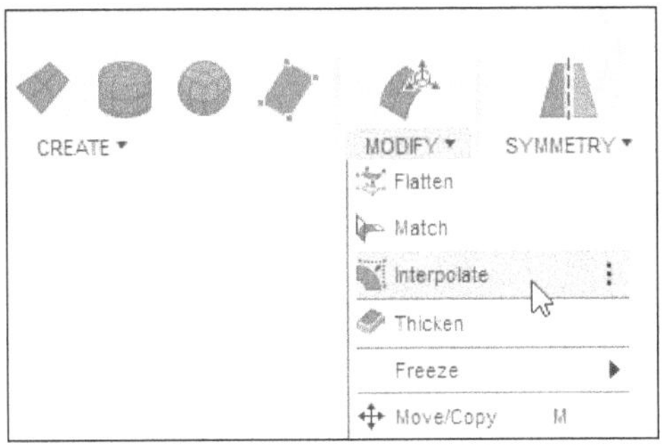

Figure-143. Interpolate tool

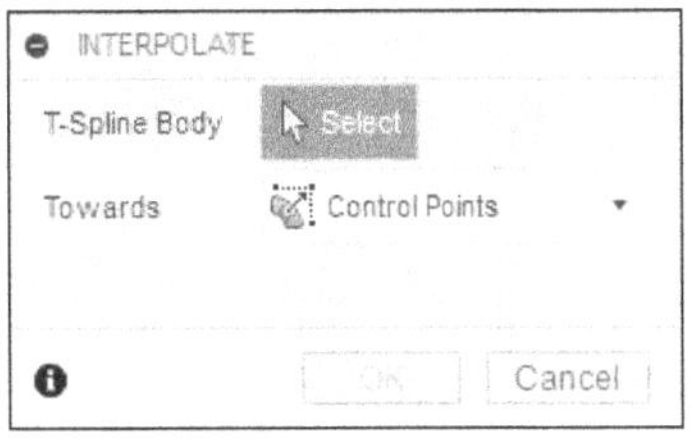

Figure-144. INTERPOLATE dialog box

- The **Select** button of **T-Spline Body** section is active by default. Click on the body to select; refer to Figure-145.

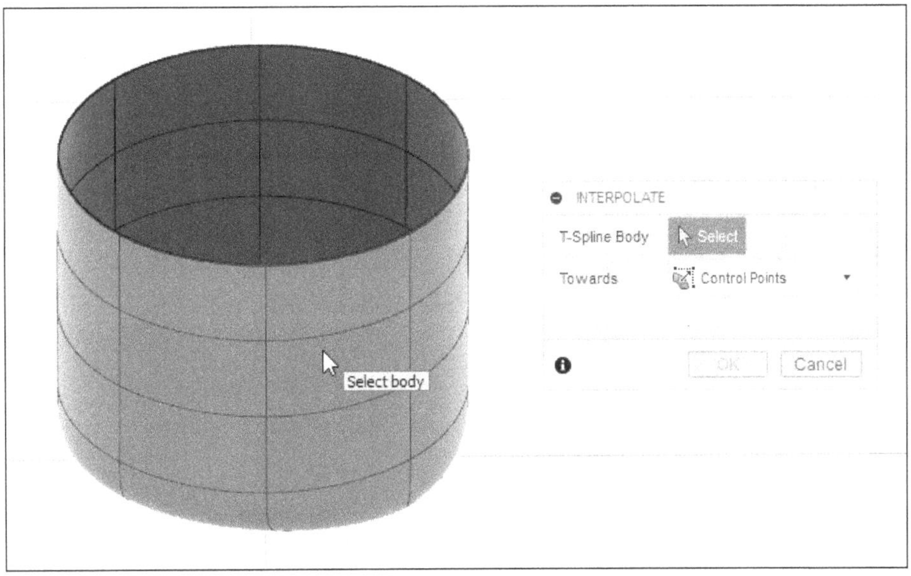

Figure-145. Selecting the body

- On selecting the body, preview will be displayed; refer to Figure-146.

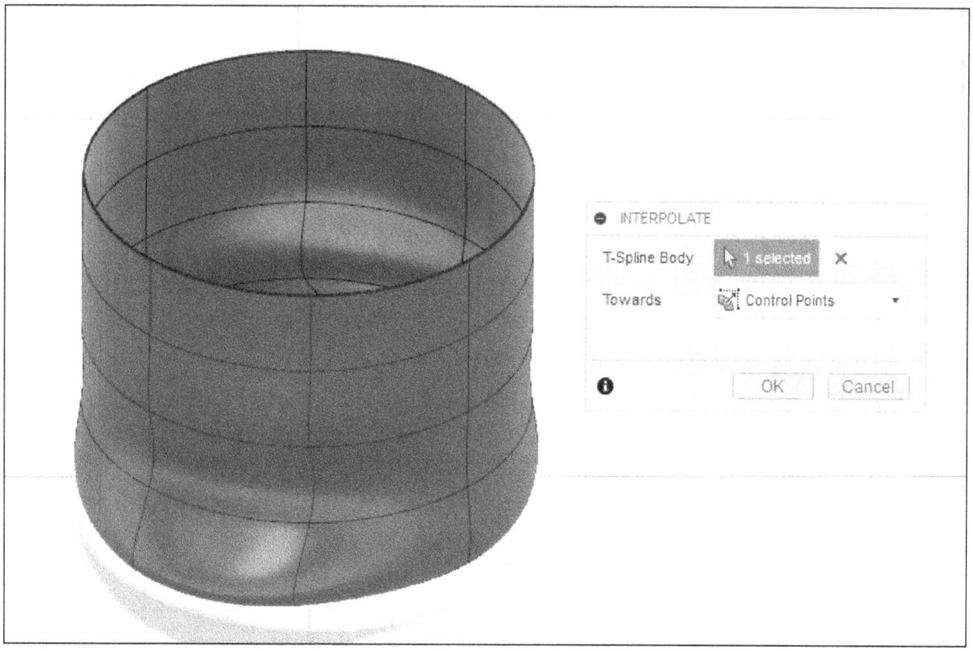

Figure-146. Preview of Interpolate

- Select **Surface Points** option from **Towards** drop-down to move the control points towards the surface.
- Select **Control Points** option from **Towards** drop-down if you want to fit the surface through existing control points.
- After specifying the parameters, click on the **OK** button from **INTERPOLATE** dialog box to complete the process.

Thicken

The **Thicken** tool is used to apply thickness to the sculpt faces. The procedure to use this tool is discussed next.

- Click on the **Thicken** tool from **MODIFY** drop-down; refer to Figure-147. The **THICKEN** dialog box will be displayed; refer to Figure-148.

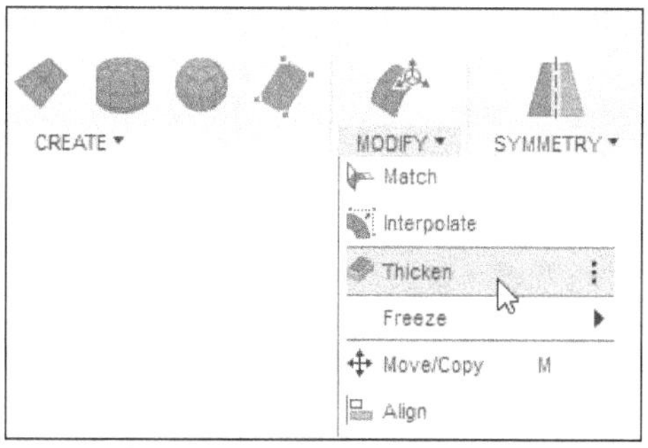

Figure-147. Thicken tool

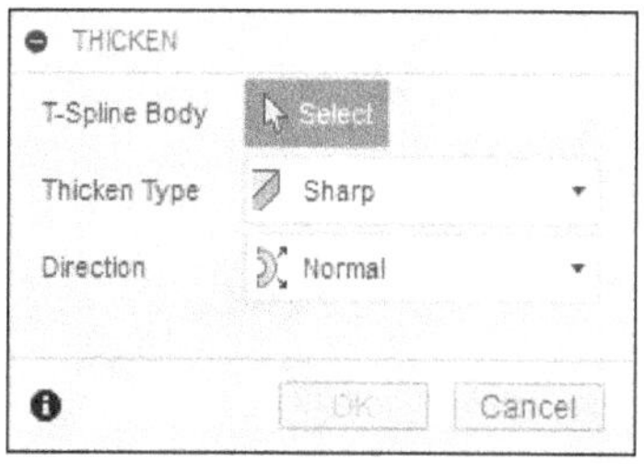

Figure-148. THICKEN dialog box

- The **Select** button of **T-Spline Body** section is active by default. Click on the body to select. The updated **THICKEN** dialog box will be displayed.
- Click in the **Thickness** edit box and enter desired thickness. You can also move the arrow displaying on the selected model to adjust the thickness; refer to Figure-149.

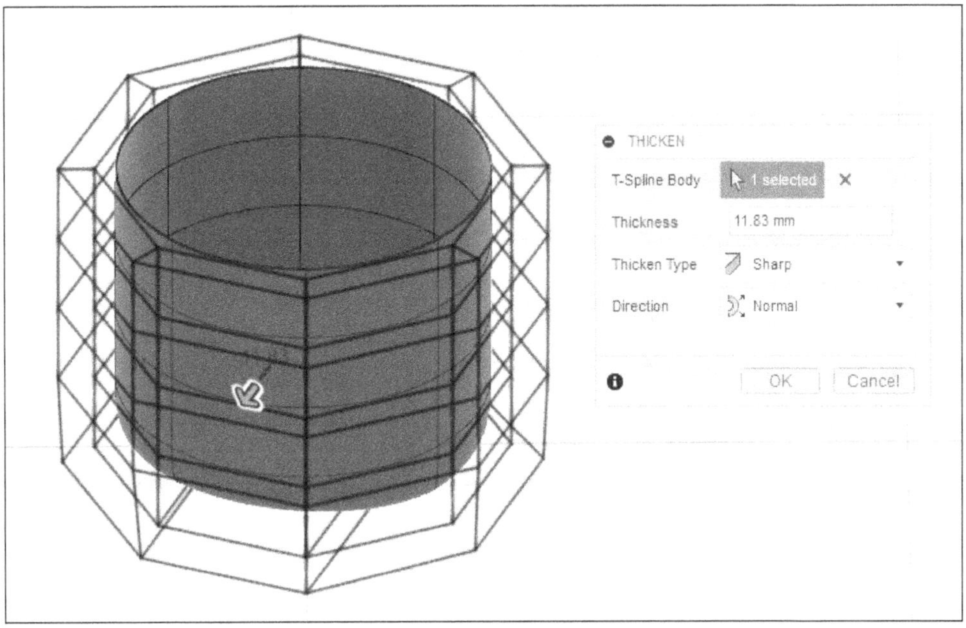

Figure-149. Updated THICKEN dialog box

- Select the **Sharp** button from **Thicken Type** drop-down to connect the surface with the straight face.
- Select the **Soft** button from **Thicken Type** drop-down to connect the surface with the round face.
- Select the **No Edge** button from **Thicken Type** drop-down to not connect the surfaces.
- Select **Normal** button from **Direction** drop-down to create a new surface perpendicular to the selected surface.
- Select **Axis** button from **Direction** drop-down to create a new surface perpendicular to a selected axis.
- After specifying the parameters, click on the **OK** button from **THICKEN** dialog box. Thickness will be applied to the model; refer to Figure-150.

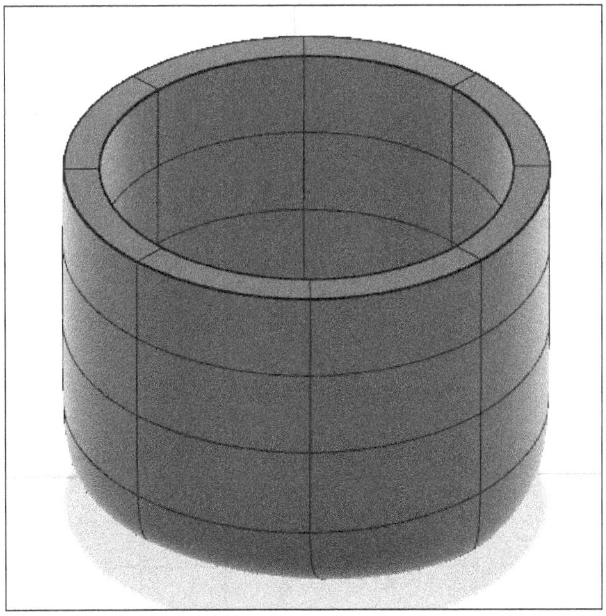

Figure-150. Surface thickened

Freeze

The **Freeze** tool is used to freeze the selected edges or faces to prevent changes. The procedure to use this tool is discussed next.

- Click on the **Freeze** tool from **Freeze** cascading menu in the **MODIFY** drop-down; refer to Figure-151. The **FREEZE** dialog box will be displayed; refer to Figure-152.

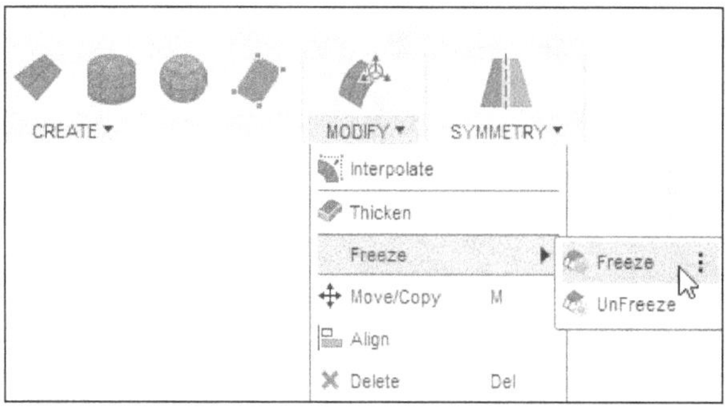

Figure-151. Freeze tool

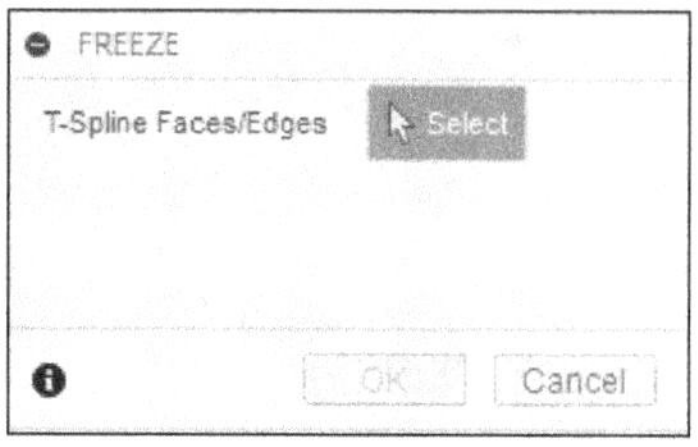

Figure-152. FREEZE dialog box

- The **Select** button of **T-Spline Faces/Edges** section is active by default. Click on the edges/ faces to select; refer to Figure-153.

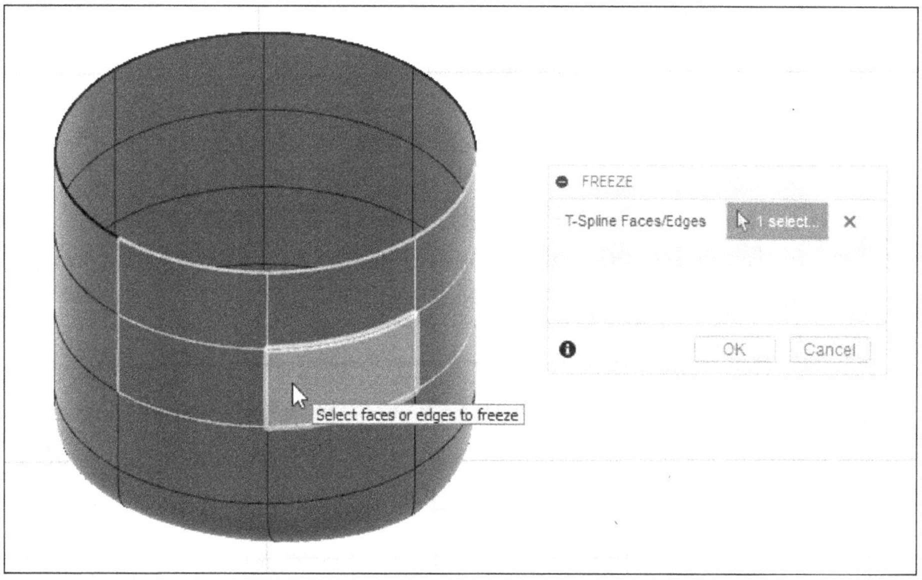

Figure-153. Selection of faces and edges to freeze

- After selection of edges, click on the **OK** button from **FREEZE** dialog box. The selected edges or faces will be frozen; refer to Figure-154.

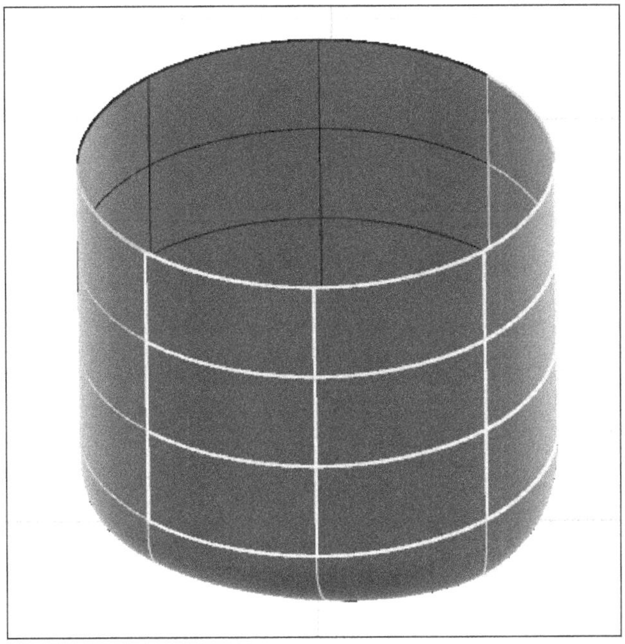

Figure-154. Faces frozen

UnFreeze

The **UnFreeze** tool is used to unfreeze the frozen edges of faces. The procedure to use this tool is discussed next.

- Click on the **UnFreeze** tool of **Freeze** cascading menu from **MODIFY** drop-down; refer to Figure-155. The **UNFREEZE** dialog box will be displayed; refer to Figure-156.

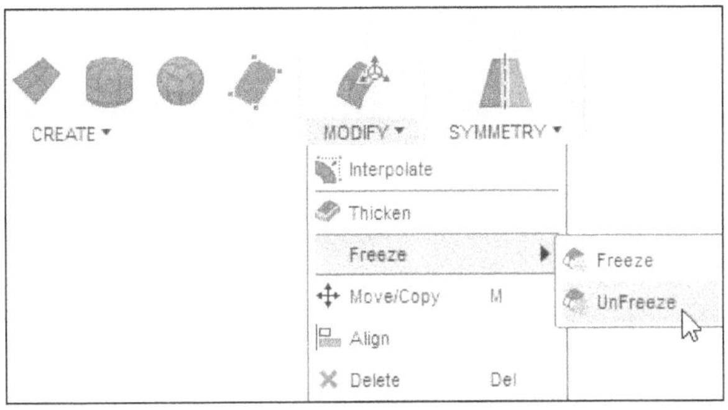

Figure-155. UnFreeze tool

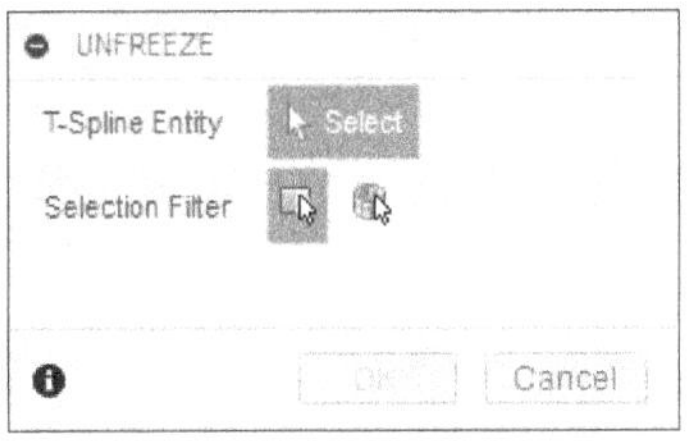

Figure-156. UNFREEZE dialog box

- The **Select** button of **T-Spline Entity** section is active by default.
- Select **Face/Edge** option from **Selection Filter** area to select faces or edges to be unfreeze and select **Body** option to select desired body to be unfreeze. In our case, we selected **Face/Edge** option.
- Click on the edges/faces to unfreeze; refer to Figure-157.

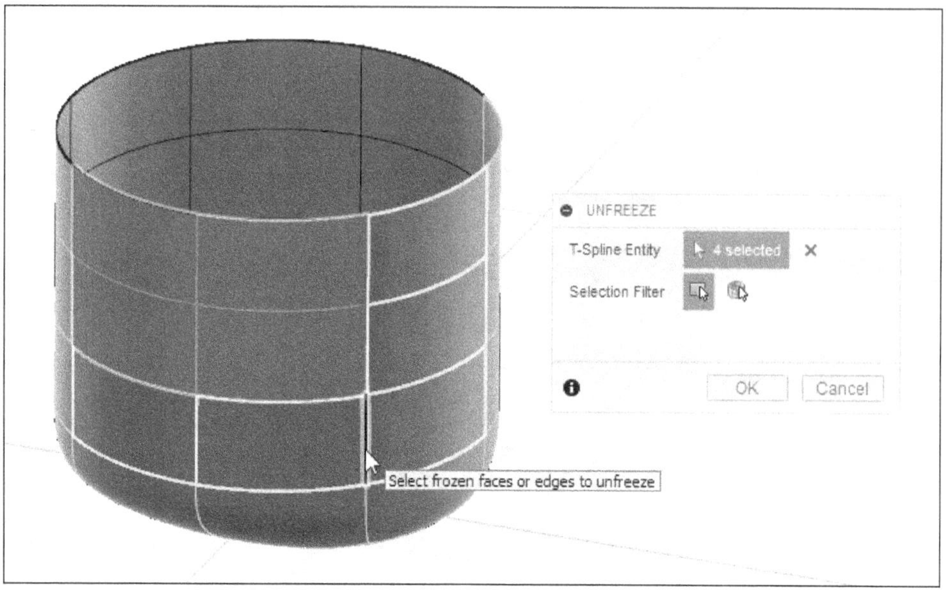

Figure-157. Selection of faces and edges to unfreeze

- After selecting, click on the **OK** button from **UNFREEZE** dialog box. The frozen edges will be unfreeze; refer to Figure-158.

Figure-158. Faces and edges unfroze

PRACTICAL

In this practical, you will create the model shown in Figure-159.

Figure-159. Model for Practical 1

Creating Sketch

- Open the **FORM** mode as discussed earlier.
- Click on the **Create Sketch** tool from **CREATE** drop-down in the **Toolbar** and select a plane on which you want to create sketch.
- Click on the **Center Rectangle** tool of **Rectangle** cascading menu from **CREATE** drop-down and create a rectangle as shown in Figure-160.

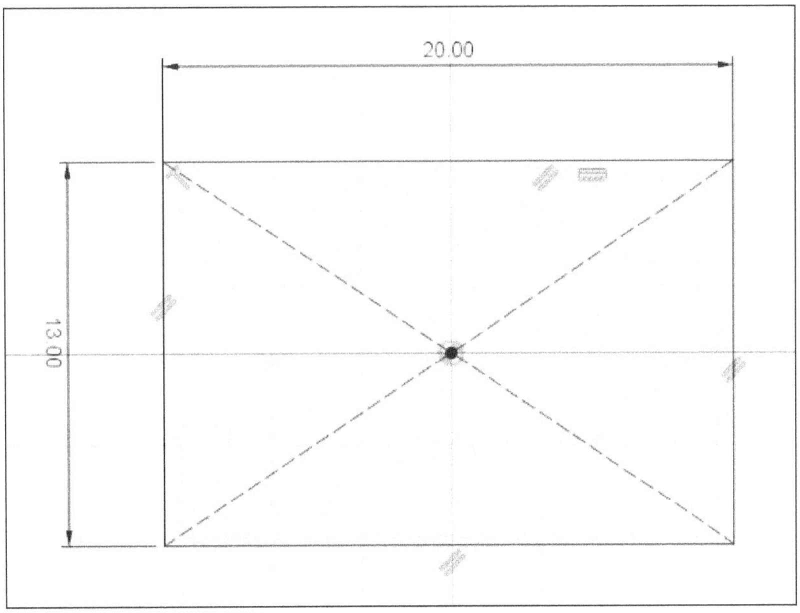

Figure-160. Creating first sketch

- Click on the **Fillet** tool of **MODIFY** drop-down from **Toolbar** and apply the fillet of **3** as shown in Figure-161.

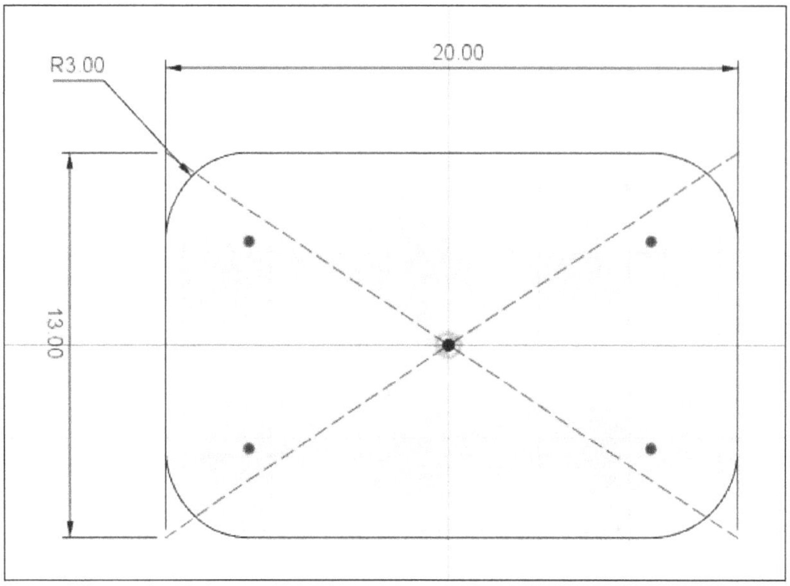

Figure-161. Applying the Fillet

- Click on the **Finish Sketch** button from **Toolbar** to exit the sketch.

Creating plane

- Click on the **Offset Plane** tool from **CONSTRUCT** drop-down in the **Toolbar**. The **CONSTRUCTION GEOMETRY** dialog box will be displayed.
- The **Select** button of **Plane** section is active by default. You need to select the recently created sketch plane as reference; refer to Figure-162.

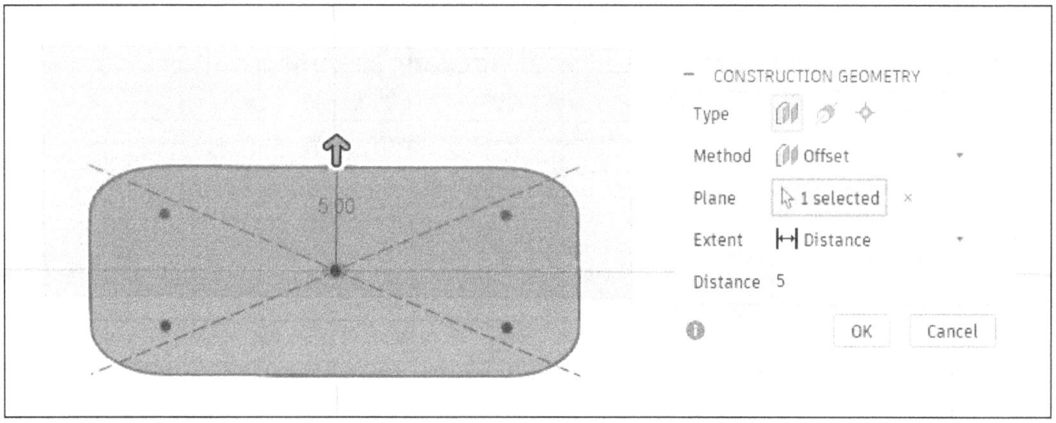

Figure-162. Creating offset plane1

- Click in the **Distance** edit box of **CONSTRUCTION GEOMETRY** dialog box and enter the value as **5**.
- After specifying the parameters, click on the **OK** button from **CONSTRUCTION GEOMETRY** dialog box. The plane will be created and displayed above the first sketch.

Creating second sketch

- Click on the **Create Sketch** tool from **CREATE** drop-down in the **Toolbar** and select the recently created plane as reference to create sketch.
- Click on the **Center Rectangle** tool from **Rectangle** cascading menu in the **CREATE** drop-down and create a sketch as shown in Figure-163.

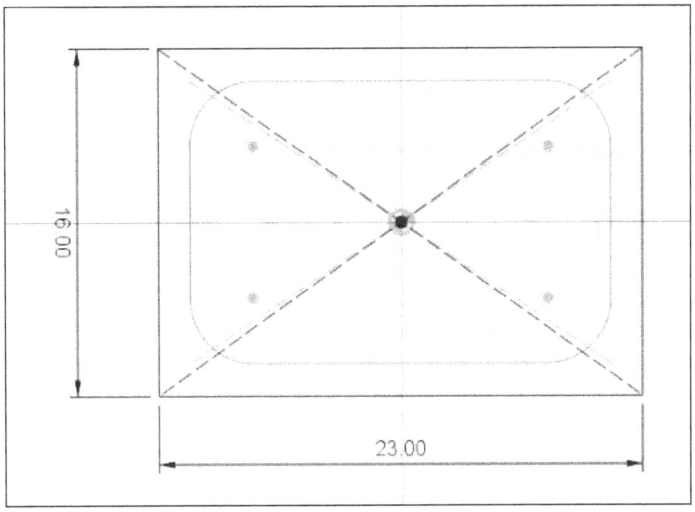

Figure-163. Creating second sketch

- Click on the **Fillet** tool of **MODIFY** drop-down from **Toolbar** and apply the fillet of **4** as shown in Figure-164.

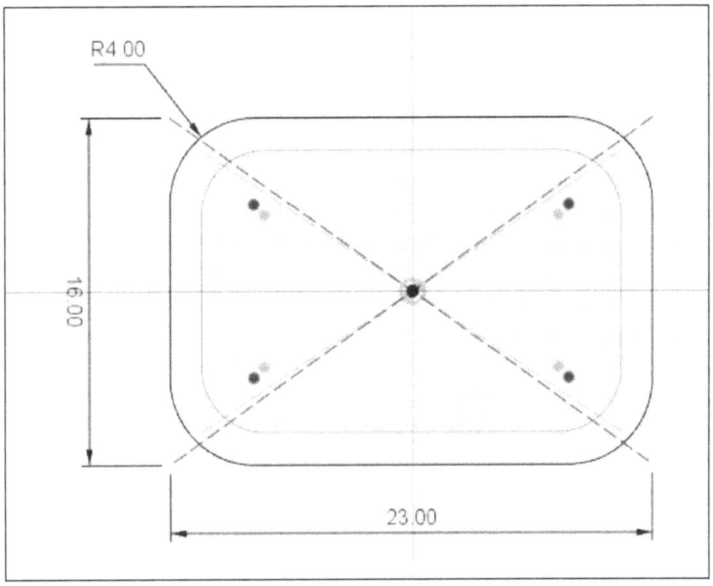

Figure-164. Applying fillet in second sketch

- Click on the **Finish Sketch** button from **Toolbar** to exit the sketch.

Creating Loft Feature

- Click on the **Loft** tool of **CREATE** drop-down from **Toolbar**. The **LOFT** dialog box will be displayed.
- Click on the **Chain Selection** check box of **LOFT** dialog box to select the edges in chain.
- Select the first and second created sketch to select in **Profiles** section; refer to Figure-165.

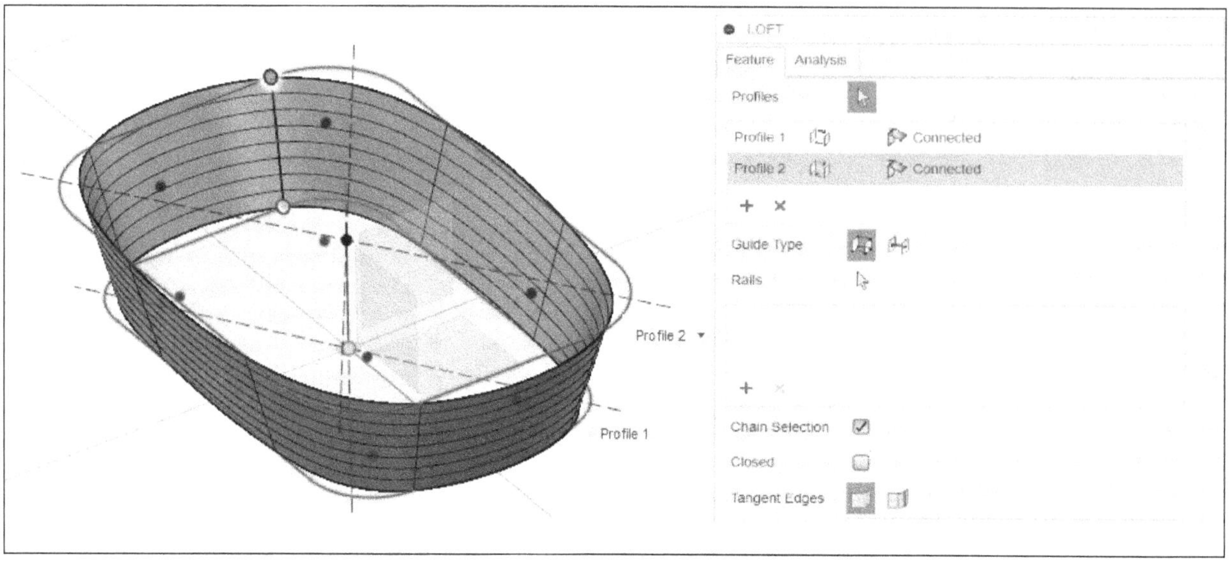

Figure-165. Selection of profiles for loft

- After specifying the parameters displayed on above figure, click on the **OK** button from **LOFT** dialog box.

Applying Fill Hole

- Click on the **Fill Hole** tool of **MODIFY** drop-down from **Toolbar**. The **FILL HOLE** dialog box will be displayed.
- Select the edge from the model as displayed; refer to Figure-166.

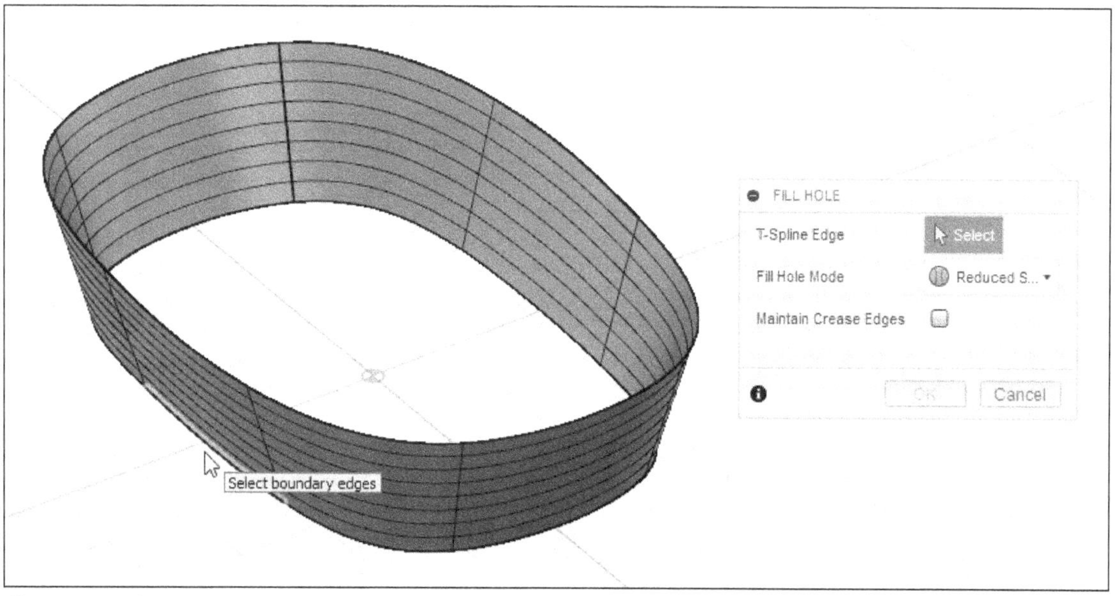

Figure-166. Selecting the edge for fill hole

- The selected hole will be filled.
- Click on the **PIPE** tool of **CREATE** drop-down from **Toolbar**. The **PIPE** dialog box will be displayed.
- Click on the edges of model as shown in figure to select as a path for pipe; refer to Figure-167.

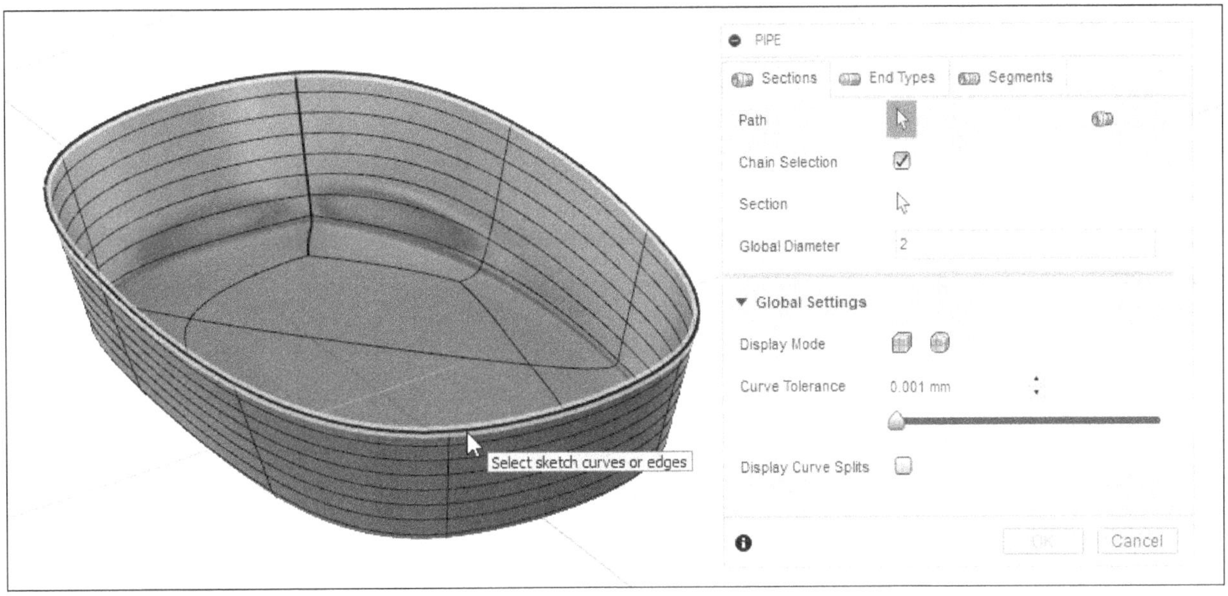

Figure-167. Selecting path for pipe

- Click on the **Smooth Display** button of **Display Mode** section in **Global Settings** area from **Sections** tab of **PIPE** dialog box and enter the parameters as displayed in above figure.
- After specifying the parameters, the model will be displayed as shown in Figure-168.

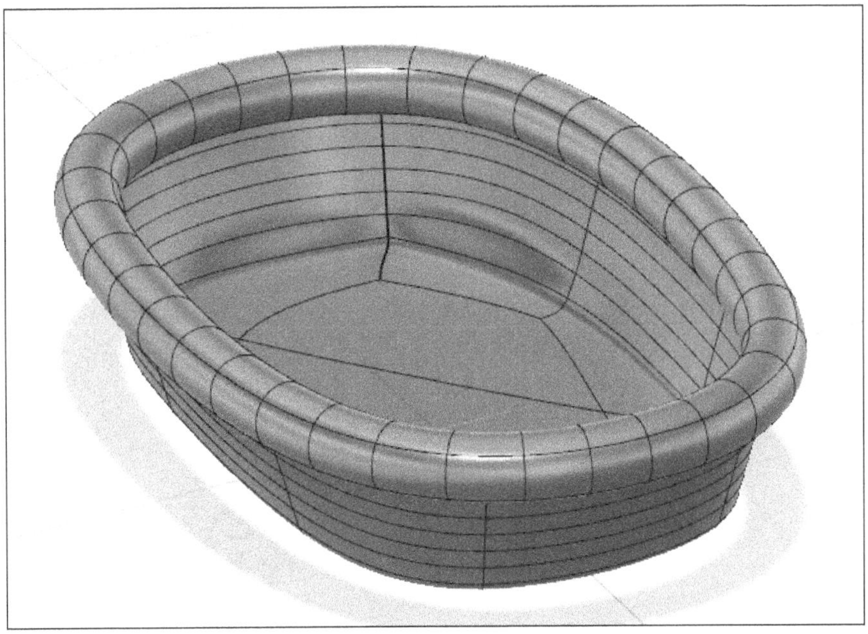

Figure-168. Practical 1 created

Practice 1

Create a wooden tool as displayed in Figure-169 and Figure-170. As a primitive structure, use the Sculpt cylinder.

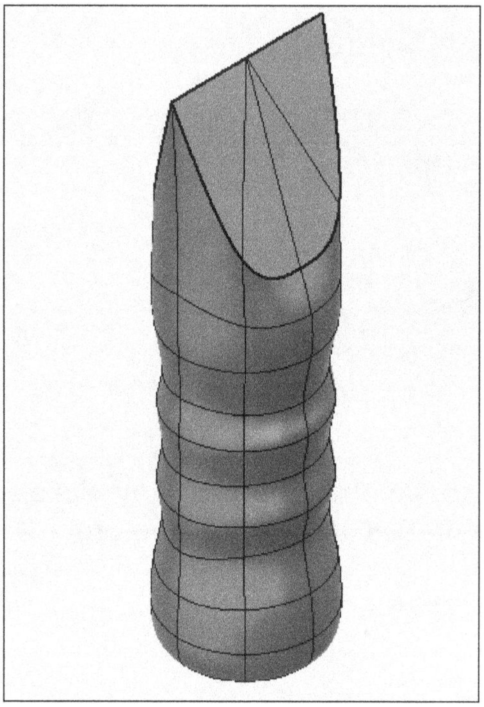

Figure-169. First view of Practice 1

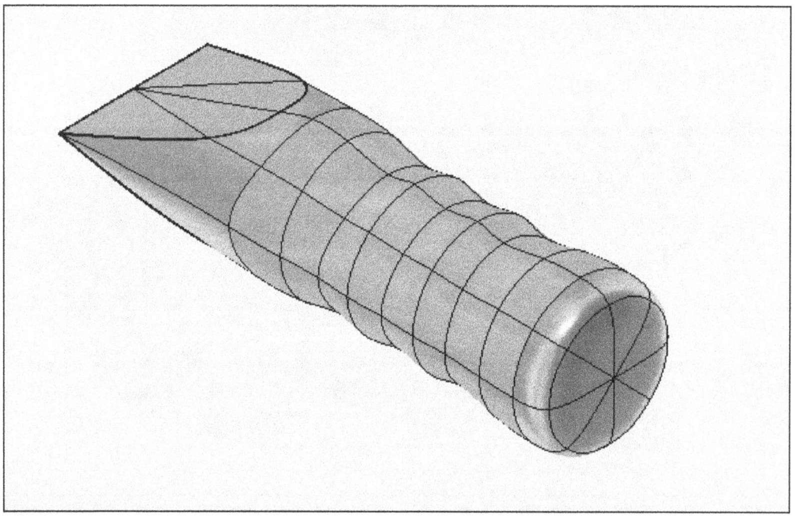

Figure-170. Second view of Practice 1

Practice 2

Create the model as shown in Figure-171 and Figure-172 by using the tools of **FORM** mode.

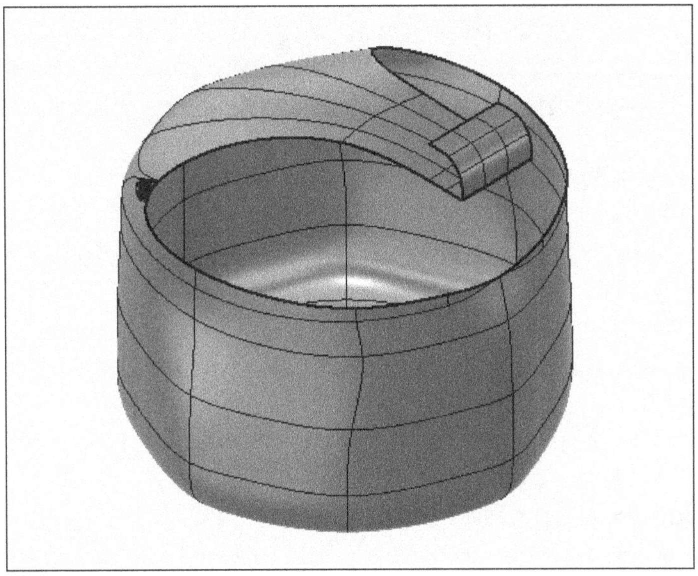

Figure-171. First view of Practice 2

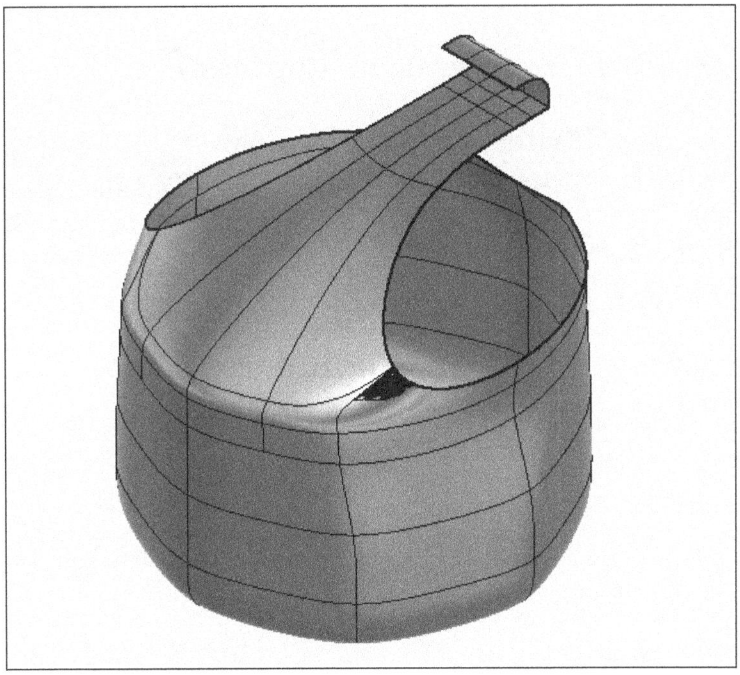

Figure-172. Second view of Practice 2

SELF ASSESSMENT

Q1. What is Sculpting?

Q2. Select the .... check box if you want to see the curve splits of pipe.

Q3. The .... button is used to create multiple faces continuously.

Q4. What is the use of **Edit Form** tool?

Q5. The **Feature** selection button is used to select all the faces of a selected hole. (T/F)

Q6. The **Merge Edge** tool is used to connect two bodies by joining their edges. (T/F)

Q7. What is the primary purpose of the Form mode in Autodesk Fusion?

A. To create solid bodies using Boolean operations
B. To sculpt features using free-flow modifications of model surfaces
C. To assemble multiple components in a design
D. To simulate mechanical movements

Q8. How can you access the Form mode in Autodesk Fusion?

A. By clicking on the MODIFY tool from the Toolbar
B. By selecting DESIGN workspace and then clicking on Create Form tool from CREATE drop-down
C. By switching to the MANUFACTURE workspace and selecting Form mode
D. By activating the SIMULATION workspace and choosing Form mode

Q9. What option should you select from the Rectangle drop-down to create a center rectangle while using the Box tool?

A. 2-Point
B. 3-Point
C. Center
D. Tangent

Q10. In the Box tool, what is the purpose of the Length Faces edit box?

A. To specify the total length of the box
B. To set the number of faces dividing the surface along the box's length
C. To determine the symmetry of the box along its length
D. To create the box's height

Q11. Which symmetry option should be selected to apply mirror symmetry between upper and lower faces of a box?

A. Width Symmetry
B. Height Symmetry
C. Length Symmetry
D. Center Symmetry

Q12. What is the first step to create a cylinder in Autodesk Fusion?

A. Select the CYLINDER dialog box
B. Specify the cylinder's diameter
C. Select the base plane or face
D. Enter the cylinder's height

Q13. Which dialog box option allows you to divide the height of a cylinder into multiple faces?

A. Height
B. Diameter Faces
C. Height Faces
D. Symmetry

Q14. What tool is used to create a smooth circular pipe in Autodesk Fusion?

A. Box Display button
B. Smooth Display button
C. Curve Tolerance slider
D. Display Curve Splits check box

Q15. In the Pipe tool, what is the purpose of the End Types tab?

A. To define the density of the pipe segments
B. To modify the shape of the pipe ends
C. To select the sketch path
D. To reset the parameters of the pipe

Q16. Which tool is used to create a T-Spline quadball in Autodesk Fusion?

A. Sphere tool
B. Torus tool
C. Quadball tool
D. Pipe tool

Q17: What is the function of the Face tool in the CREATE drop-down?

A. To modify geometry
B. To create individual faces
C. To extrude sketches
D. To insert edges

Q18: Which button in the FACE dialog box allows the creation of a simple face by selecting four vertices?

A. Chain
B. Edge
C. Simple
D. Plane

Q19: What must be selected first when using the Edge button in the FACE dialog box?

A. Plane
B. Vertex
C. Edge of an object
D. Axis

Q20: What does the Chain button in the FACE dialog box allow you to do?

A. Create a single face
B. Create multiple faces continuously
C. Insert edges
D. Modify geometry

Q21: What is the purpose of the Extrude tool in the CREATE drop-down?

A. To move, scale, or rotate geometry
B. To create faces
C. To extrude a selected sketch to a specific depth or height
D. To create a revolve feature

Q22: Which option in the Spacing drop-down positions faces based on the curvature of a profile?

A. Uniform
B. Distance
C. Curvature
D. Angle

Q23: In the REVOLVE dialog box, what must be selected as the axis of rotation?

A. Vertex
B. Face
C. Plane
D. Sketch

Q24: Which tool allows the modification of geometry by moving, scaling, or rotating it?

A. Edit By Curve
B. Edit Form
C. Insert Edge
D. Revolve

Q25: What does the Soft Modification check box do in the EDIT FORM dialog box?

A. Allows control over changes to surrounding areas of an object
B. Deletes selected faces
C. Creates faces from selected vertices
D. Rotates the geometry

Q26: Which button in the EDIT FORM dialog box restricts modification to a plane?

A. Coordinate Space
B. Local Per Entity
C. Planar Curve
D. Selection Filter

Q27: What does the Insert Edge tool allow you to do?

A. Insert an edge at a specific distance from a selected edge
B. Add vertices to a plane
C. Create a face from a selected edge
D. Extrude a sketch

Q28: What option in the Insertion Mode drop-down maintains the exact surface shape by adding points?

A. Simple
B. Exact
C. Single
D. Both

Q29. What is the primary function of the Subdivide tool?

A. To join two edges
B. To divide a face into four or more faces
C. To move vertices closer together
D. To create a mesh preview

Q30. Which option in the Insert Mode drop-down of the Subdivide tool is used to maintain the extra shape of a surface body?

A. Simple
B. Reduced Star
C. Exact
D. Fill Star

Q31. What does the Object Snap check box do in the Subdivide tool?

A. Moves new vertices to the closest point
B. Divides the face into eight parts
C. Creates a sharp crease on edges
D. Deletes unwanted vertices

Q32. Which button is active by default when using the Insert Point tool?

A. Edge Group One
B. Insertion Point
C. T-Spline Faces
D. Slide Location

Q33. What is the function of the Merge Edge tool?

A. To join two vertices
B. To connect two bodies by joining their edges
C. To delete a part of the T-Spline geometry
D. To move edges closer or farther apart

Q34. Which checkbox in the Merge Edge dialog box allows retaining the crease at merged edges?

A. Flip Side
B. Preview
C. Keep Creases
D. Exact

Q35. The Bridge tool is used to:

A. Fill a hole in the T-Spline model
B. Connect two bodies by adding intermediate faces
C. Weld vertices together
D. Move edges closer together

Q36. Which option in the Fill Hole tool adds the minimum number of star points?

A. Fill Star
B. Collapse
C. Reduced Star
D. Weld Center Vertices

Q37. What does the Weld Vertices tool do when the Vertex to Midpoint option is selected?

A. Moves the first vertex to the second vertex
B. Moves both vertices to the midpoint
C. Joins all visible vertices within a tolerance
D. Deletes unwanted vertices

Q38. Which tool is used to detach an edge or loop?

A. Subdivide
B. UnWeld Edges
C. Crease
D. Bridge

Q39. What is the main function of the Crease tool?

A. To divide faces into smaller parts
B. To add a sharp crease on the edges
C. To weld vertices together
D. To flatten the area of a body

Q40. The Bevel Edge tool uses which button to specify a distance for creating a bevel with equal sides?

A. Slide Location
B. Bevel Width
C. Offset Ratio
D. Uniform

Q41. Which option in the Slide Edge tool determines the new edge position in decimal percentage?

A. Bevel Width
B. Uniform
C. Slide Location
D. Relative Offset

Q42. What is the purpose of the Smooth tool in T-Spline geometry?

A. To form a smooth cylindrical shape
B. To smooth an area by selecting desired faces
C. To align selected edges with a sketch
D. To apply thickness to sculpt faces

Q43. How is the smoothing rate specified in the Smooth tool?

A. By selecting control points
B. By moving a slider or entering a value between 0 and 1
C. By selecting Auto Feature Selection
D. By choosing a fit plane

Q44. Which tool is used to form uneven T-Spline geometry into a cylindrical shape?

A. Smooth
B. Cylindrify
C. Pull
D. Flatten

Q45. What is the default active button in the Cylindrify tool dialog box?

A. Select T-Spline Faces
B. Select Auto Feature Selection
C. Select Target Body
D. Select Smoothing Rate

Q46. What does the Pull tool primarily do?

A. Pull vertices to the target body
B. Flatten control points to a plane
C. Align edges with a sketch
D. Smooth uneven surfaces

Q47. Which option in the Pull tool allows manual selection of a target body?

A. Auto
B. Select Targets
C. Surface Points
D. Control Points

Q48. What is the main purpose of the Flatten tool?

A. To align vertices to a line
B. To flatten control points to a plane
C. To thicken sculpt faces
D. To freeze selected edges

Q49. Which option in the Flatten tool automatically selects the best fit plane?

A. Select Parallel Plane
B. Fit
C. Select Plane
D. Flatten Type

Q50. The Straighten tool aligns vertices into which options?

A. A plane
B. A cylinder
C. A best fit line, existing line, or a line through two points
D. A thickened surface

Chapter 13

Sculpting-2

Topics Covered

The major topics covered in this chapter are:

- ***Mirror Internal***
- ***Mirror Duplicate***
- ***Circular Internal***
- ***Circular Duplicate***
- ***Clear Symmetry***
- ***Isolate Symmetry***
- ***Display Mode***
- ***Repair Body***
- ***Make Uniform***
- ***Convert Tools***

INTRODUCTION

In the last chapter, we have learned to create and modify the sculpt object by using various tools. In this chapter, we will discuss the symmetry and utilities tool used in **FORM** mode.

SYMMETRY TOOLS

Symmetry tools are used to create symmetric copies of the selected sculpt features in the **FORM Mode**. These tools are discussed next.

Mirror - Internal

The **Mirror - Internal** tool is used to create an internal mirror symmetry in the T-Spline body on selecting an edge, face, and vertex. The procedure to use this tool is discussed next.

- Click on the **Mirror - Internal** tool from **SYMMETRY** drop-down; refer to Figure-1. The **MIRROR - INTERNAL** dialog box will be displayed; refer to Figure-2.

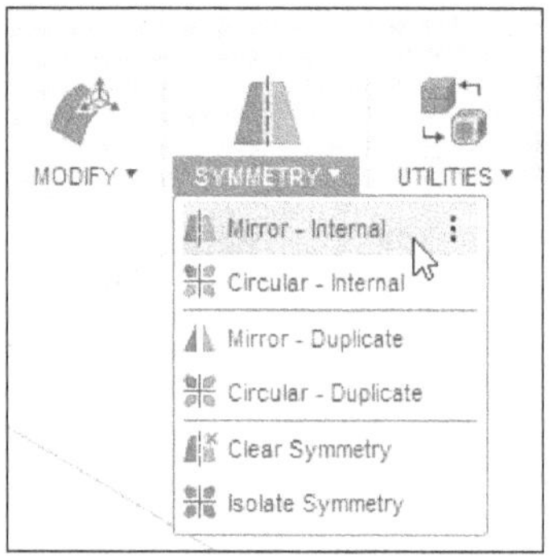

Figure-1. Mirror - Internal tool

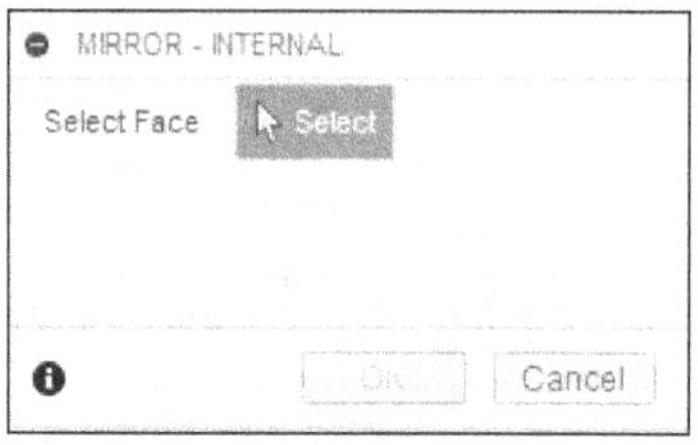

Figure-2. MIRROR- INTERNAL dialog box

- The **Select** button of **Select Face** section is active by default. Click on the face from master side; refer to Figure-3.

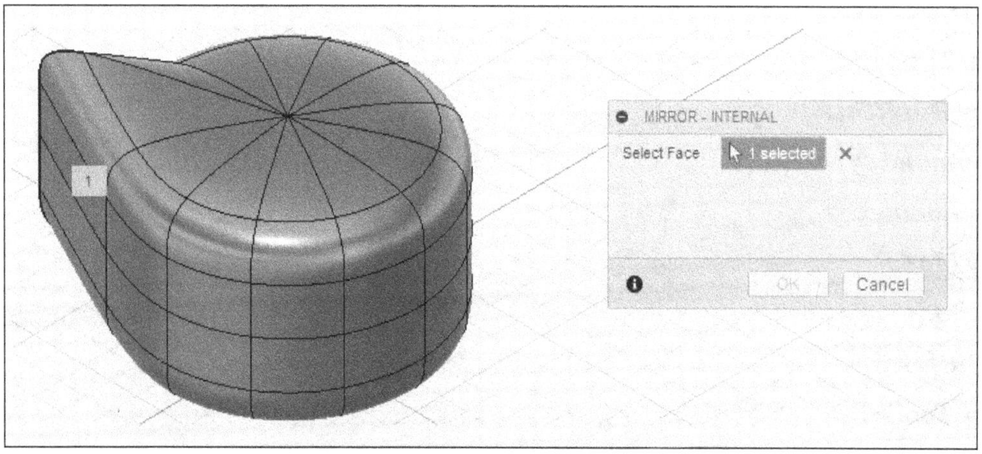

Figure-3. Selecting face on master side

- Click on the face to be made mirror symmetric. Note that if you select two consecutive faces then they will act as mirror references for two sides; refer to Figure-4. You can also select opposite side faces to be used as mirror. The preview of mirror will be displayed; refer to Figure-5.

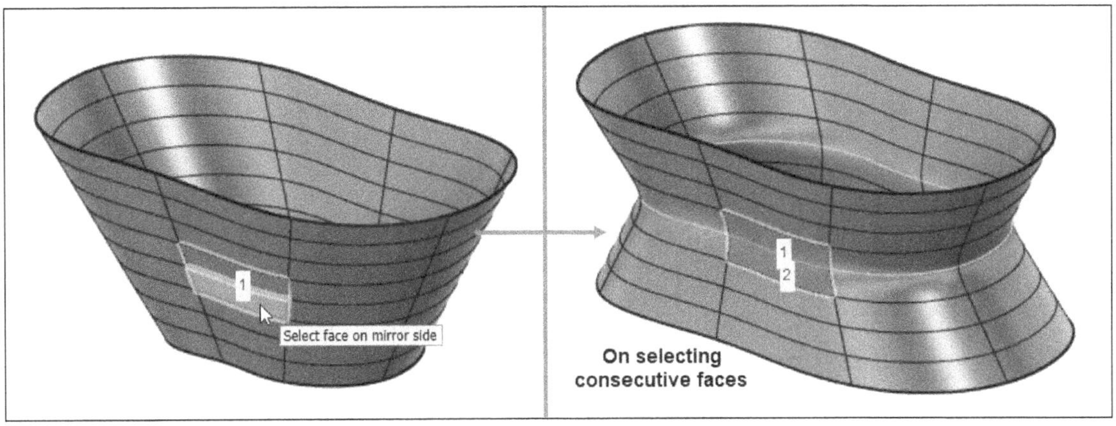

Figure-4. Internal mirror with consecutive faces

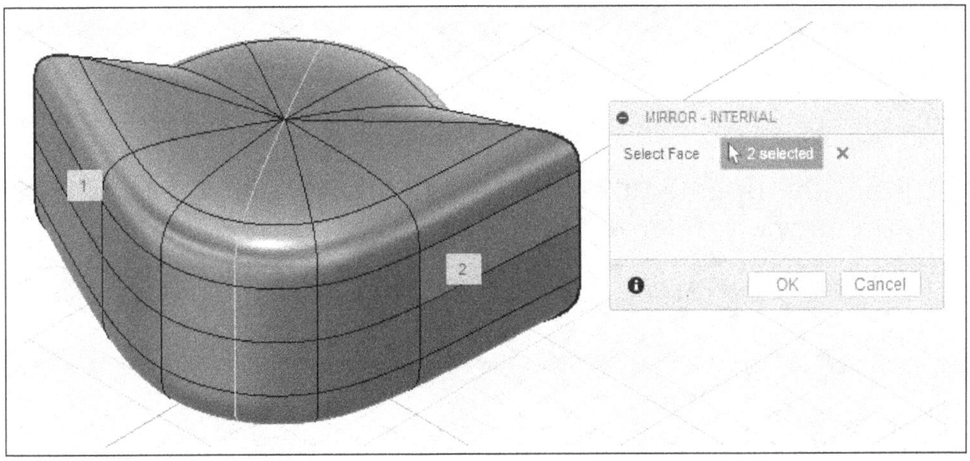

Figure-5. Preview of mirror

- If the preview of mirror symmetry is as required then click on the **OK** button from **MIRROR - INTERNAL** dialog box to complete the process.

Circular - Internal

The **Circular - Internal** tool is used to create an internal circular symmetry based on selected face, edge, or vertex. The procedure to use this tool is discussed next.

- Click on the **Circular - Internal** tool from **SYMMETRY** drop-down; refer to Figure-6. The **CIRCULAR - INTERNAL** dialog box will be displayed; refer to Figure-7.

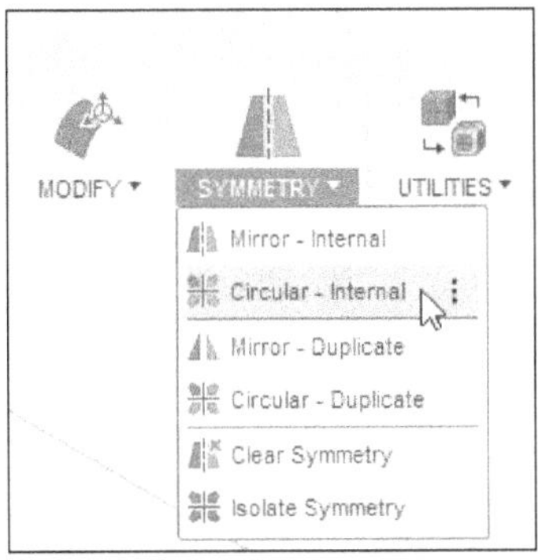

Figure-6. Circular- Internal tool

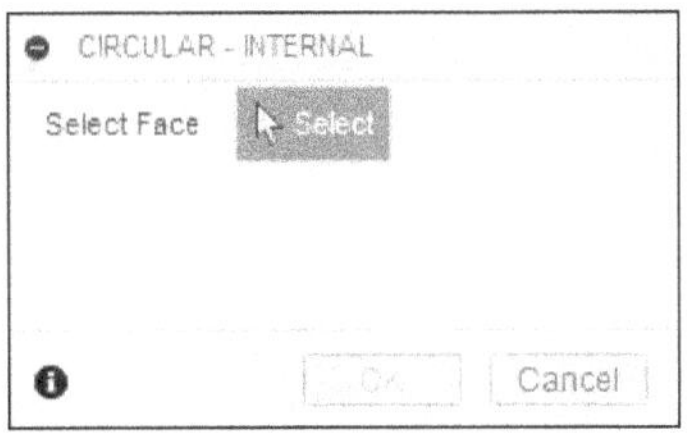

Figure-7. CIRCULAR- INTERNAL dialog box

- The **Select** button of **Select Face** section is active by default. Click on the face to select for symmetry; refer to Figure-8.

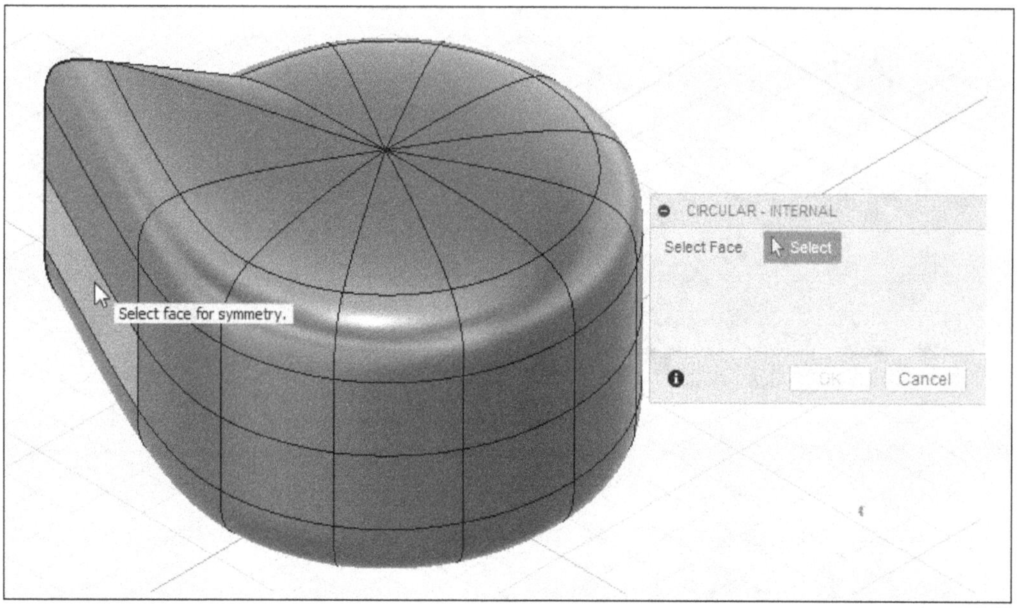

Figure-8. Selecting face for symmetry

- After selecting, the updated **CIRCULAR - INTERNAL** dialog box will be displayed along with the preview; refer to Figure-9.

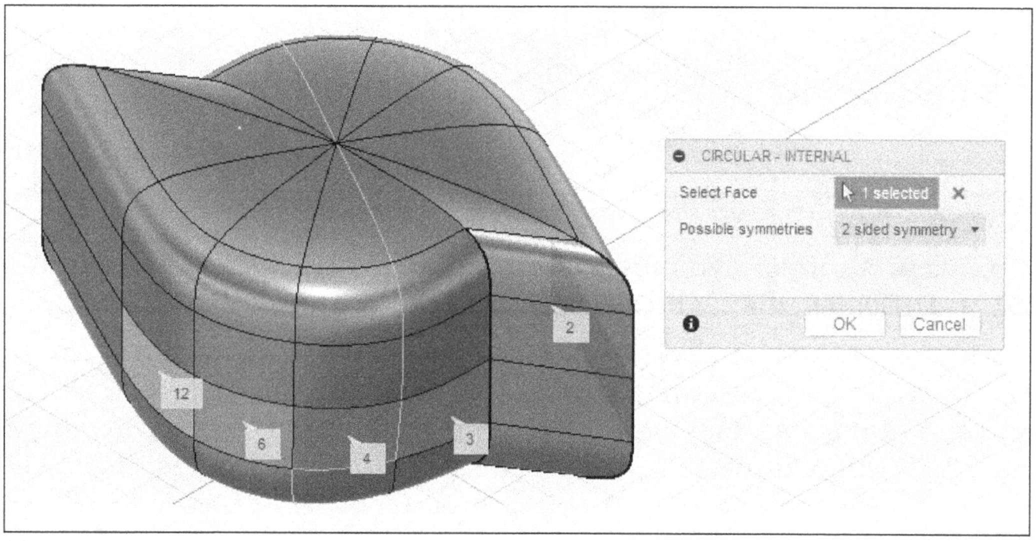

Figure-9. Updated CIRCULAR INTERNAL dialog box

- Select desired option from **Possible symmetries** drop-down to define number of symmetric sections and click on the **OK** button from **CIRCULAR - INTERNAL** dialog box to complete the process; refer to Figure-10 and Figure-11.

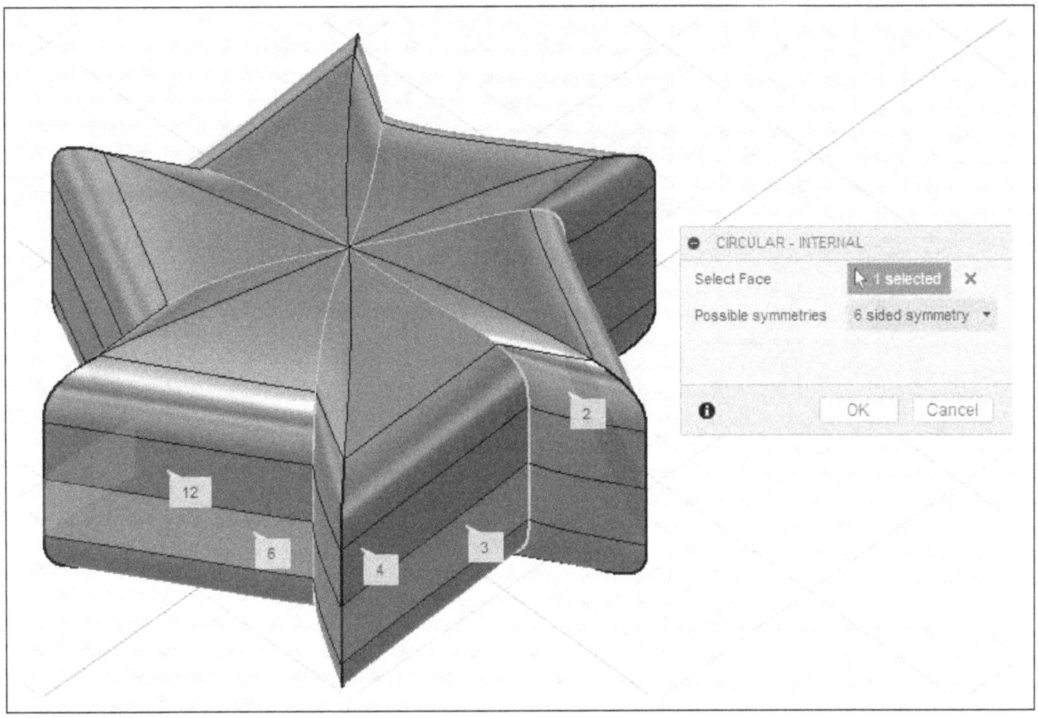

Figure-10. 6-sided circular symmetry created

Figure-11. Circular symmetry internal

Mirror - Duplicate

The **Mirror - Duplicate** tool is used to create a new T-Spline body or surface based on the selected plane or face. The procedure to use this tool is discussed next.

- Click on the **Mirror - Duplicate** tool from **SYMMETRY** drop-down; refer to Figure-12. The **MIRROR - DUPLICATE** dialog box will be displayed; refer to Figure-13.

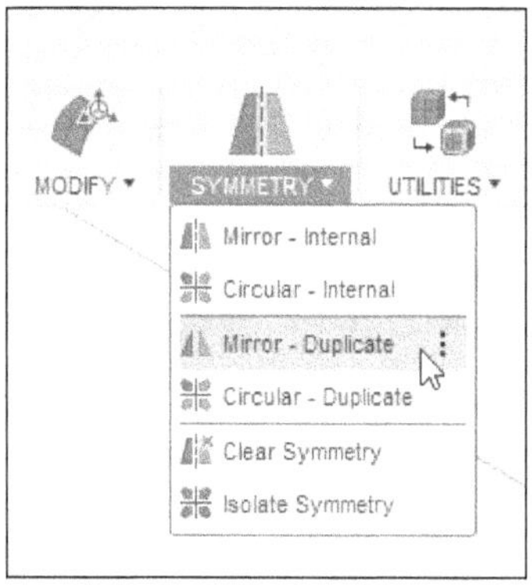

Figure-12. Mirror- Duplicate tool

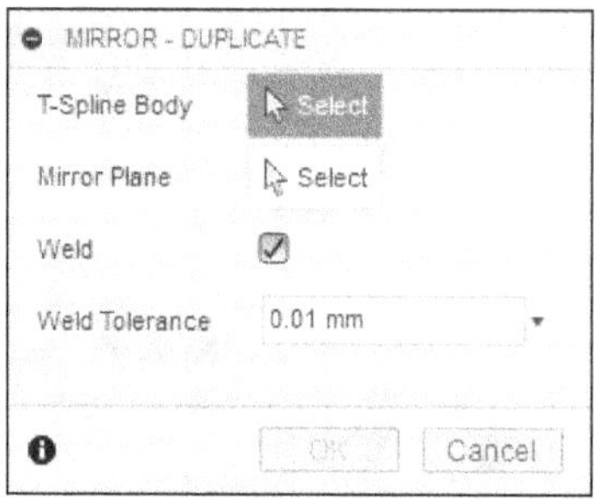

Figure-13. MIRROR- DUPLICATE dialog box

- The **Select** button of **T-Spline Body** section is active by default. Click on the sculpt body whose mirror copy is to be created; refer to Figure-14.

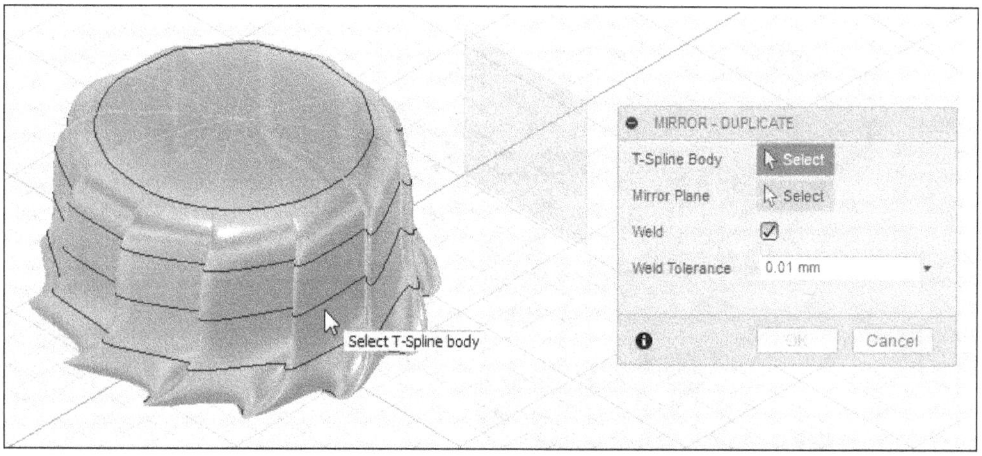

Figure-14. Selection of body for mirror

- Now, click on the **Select** button of **Mirror Plane** section and select desired plane to mirror the selected body. The preview of mirror will be displayed; refer to Figure-15.

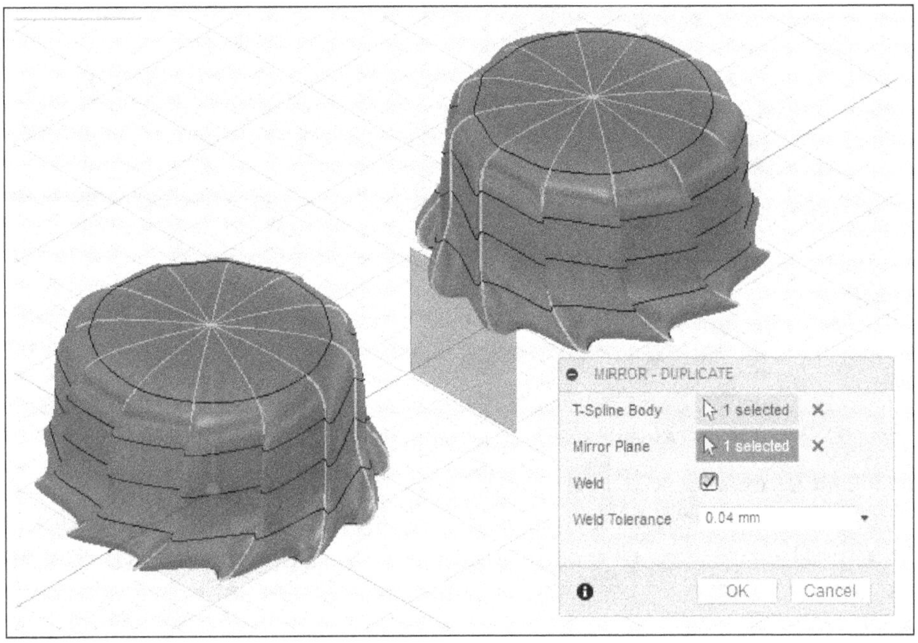

Figure-15. Preview of mirror-duplicate

- Select the **Weld** check box from **MIRROR - DUPLICATE** dialog box to weld the symmetric edges together.
- Click in the **Weld Tolerance** edit box and enter desired value of tolerance.
- After specifying the parameters, click on the **OK** button from **MIRROR - DUPLICATE** dialog box to complete the process.

Circular - Duplicate

The **Circular - Duplicate** tool is used to create circular symmetric copies of the selected body around an axis. The procedure to use this tool is discussed next.

- Click on the **Circular - Duplicate** tool from **SYMMETRY** drop-down; refer to Figure-16. The **CIRCULAR - DUPLICATE** dialog box will be displayed; refer to Figure-17.

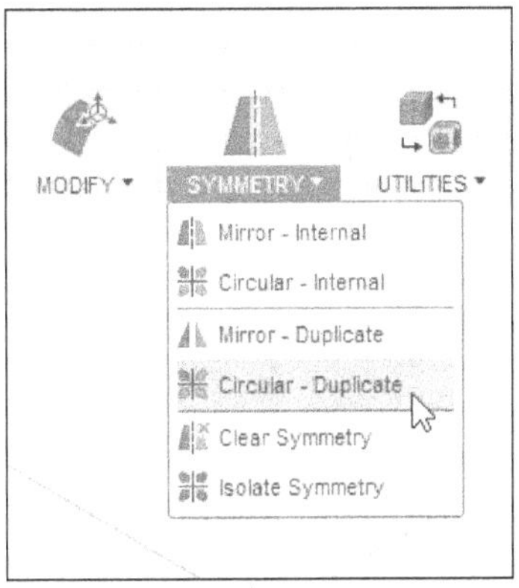

Figure-16. Circular- Duplicate tool

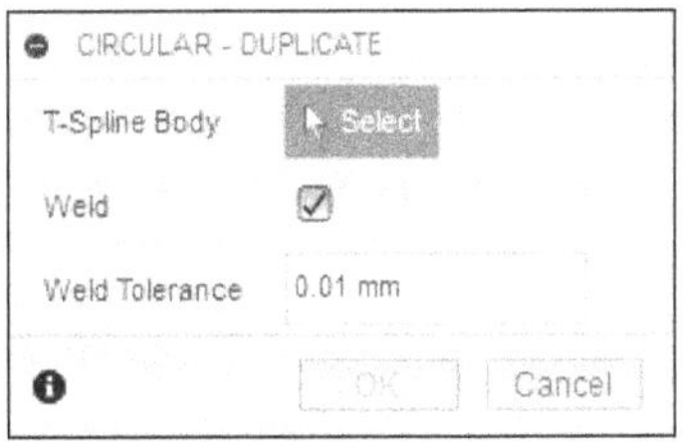

Figure-17. CIRCULAR-DUPLICATE dialog box

- The **Select** button of **T-Spline Body** section is active by default. Click on the body from canvas to select.
- Click to select the axis; refer to Figure-18.

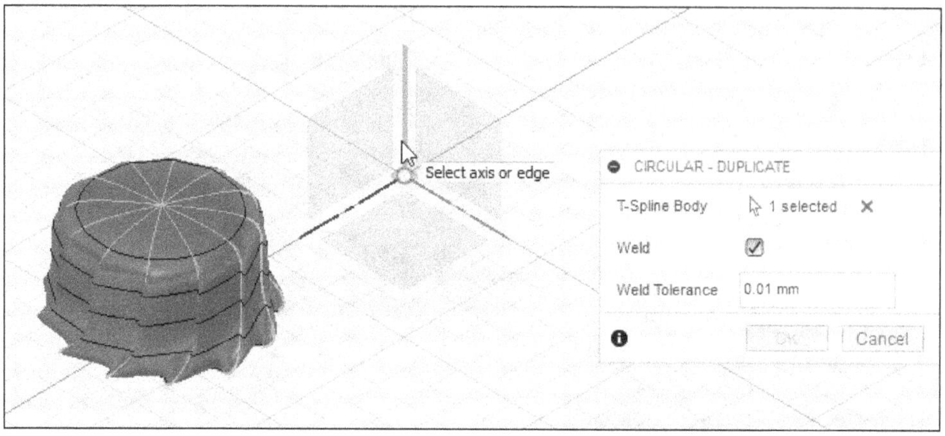

Figure-18. Selecting the axis for rotation

- Select the **Weld** check box if required to make the copies single body.
- Click in the **Quantity** edit box and enter desired number of duplicate copies you want to create; the preview of duplicate copies will be displayed; refer to Figure-19.

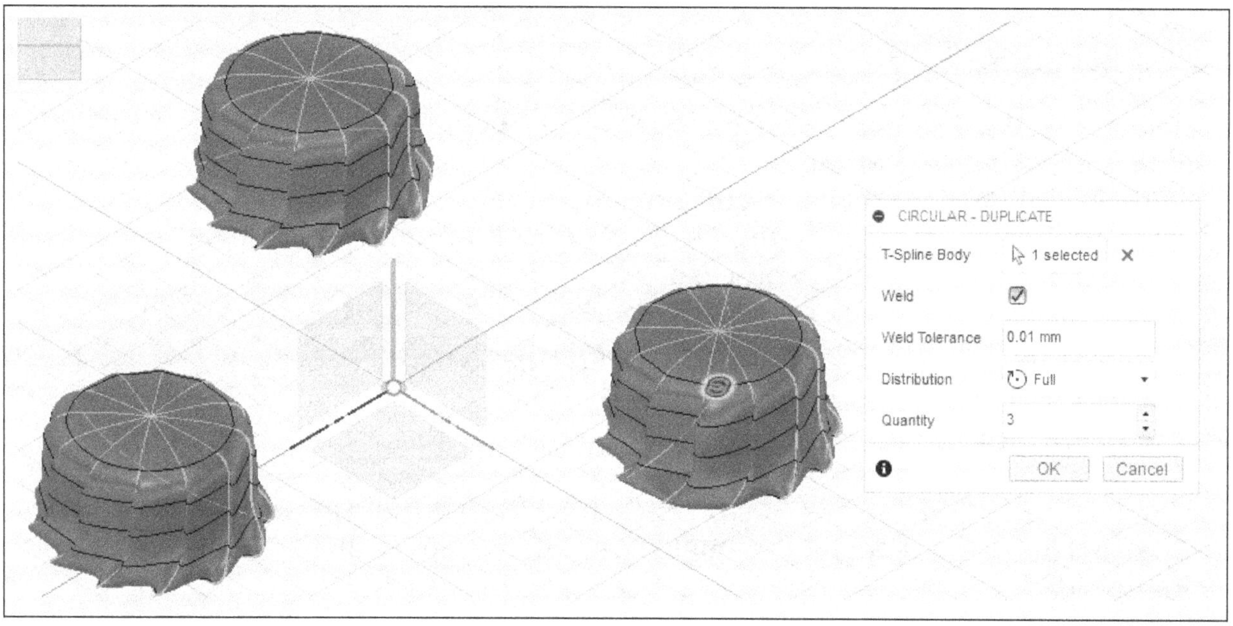

Figure-19. Preview of duplicate copies

- After specifying the parameters, click on the **OK** button from **CIRCULAR -DUPLICATE** dialog box to complete the process.

Clear Symmetry

The **Clear Symmetry** tool is used to delete the symmetry created earlier on the body. The procedure to use this tool is discussed next.

- Click on the **Clear Symmetry** tool from **SYMMETRY** drop-down; refer to Figure-20. The **CLEAR SYMMETRY** dialog box will be displayed; refer to Figure-21.

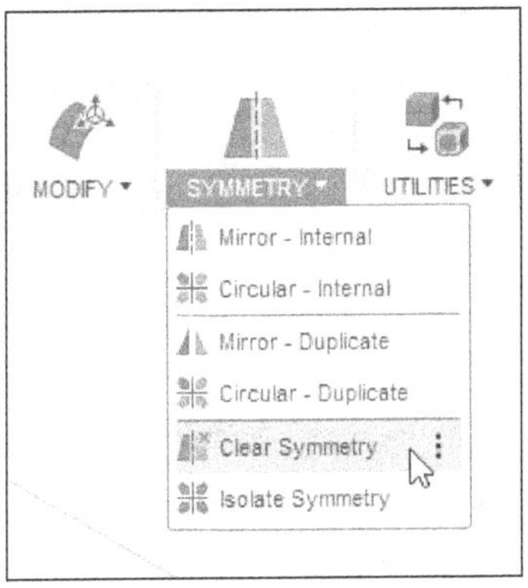

Figure-20. Clear Symmetry tool

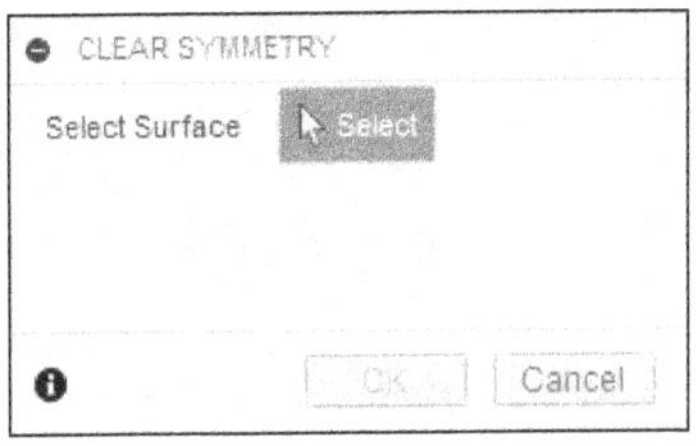

Figure-21. CLEAR SYMMETRY dialog box

- The **Select** button of **Select Surface** section is active by default. Click on the symmetry bodies for removing the symmetry constraint; refer to Figure-22.

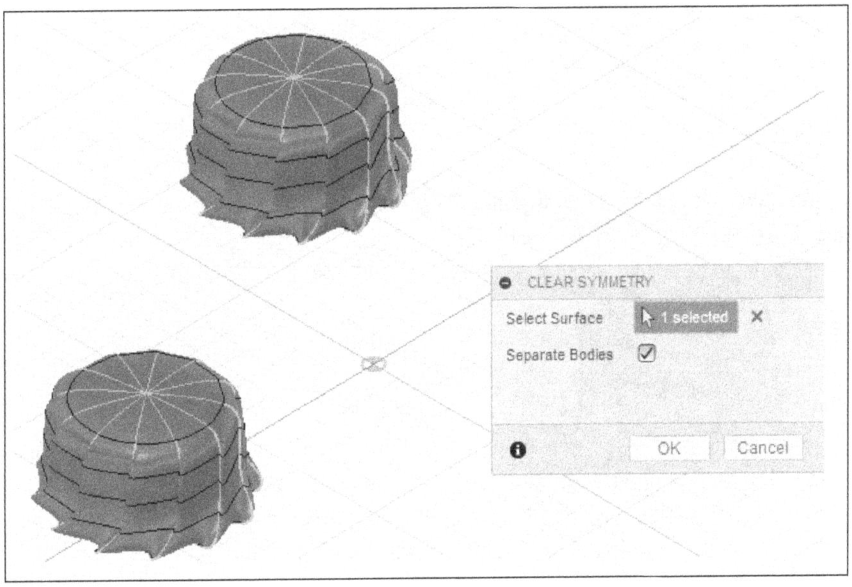

Figure-22. Selecting bodies for clearing symmetry

- Select the **Separate Bodies** check box to create new bodies for disjointed surface.
- After specifying the parameters, click on the **OK** button from **CLEAR SYMMETRY** check box to complete the process; refer to Figure-23.

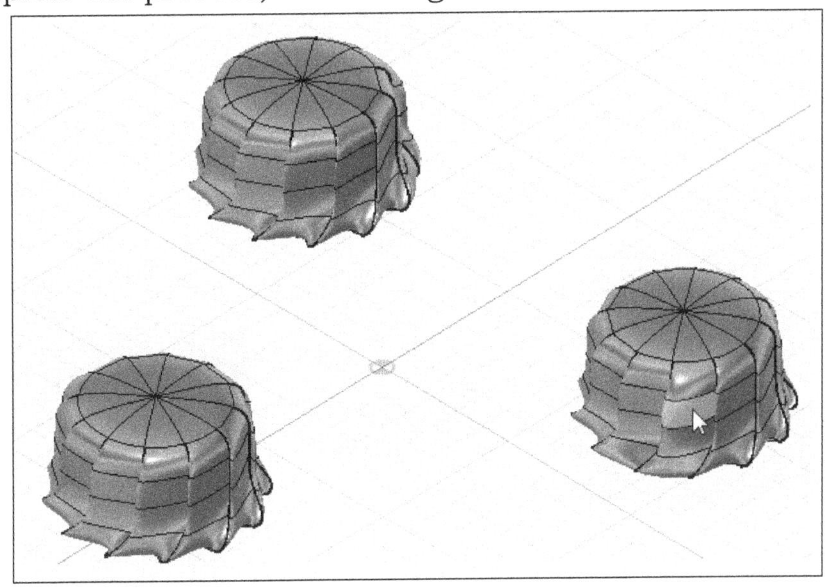

Figure-23. Deleted symmetry from bodies

Isolate Symmetry

The **Isolate Symmetry** tool is used to remove the symmetry condition from the selected face, edge, or vertex but the selected geometry will still symmetric to the other duplicate bodies. The procedure to use this tool is discussed next.

- Click on the **Isolate Symmetry** tool from **SYMMETRY** drop-down; refer to Figure-24. The **ISOLATE SYMMETRY** dialog box will be displayed; refer to Figure-25.

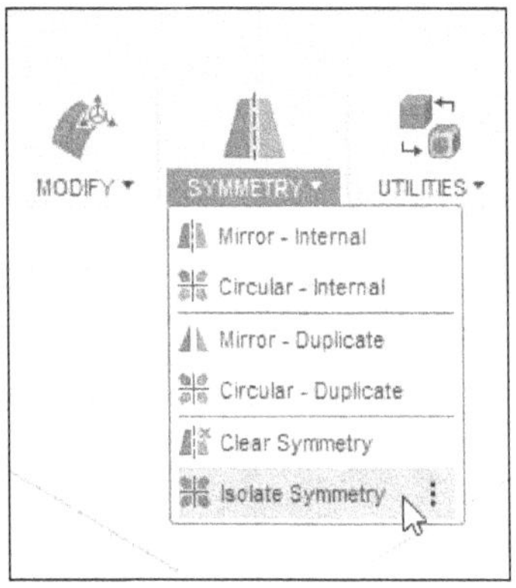

Figure-24. Isolate Symmetry tool

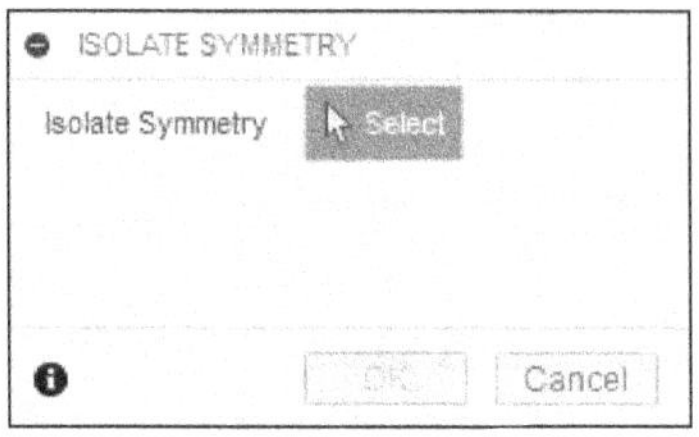

Figure-25. ISOLATE SYMMETRY dialog box

- The **Select** button of **Isolate Symmetry** section is active by default. Click on the symmetry to select; refer to Figure-26.

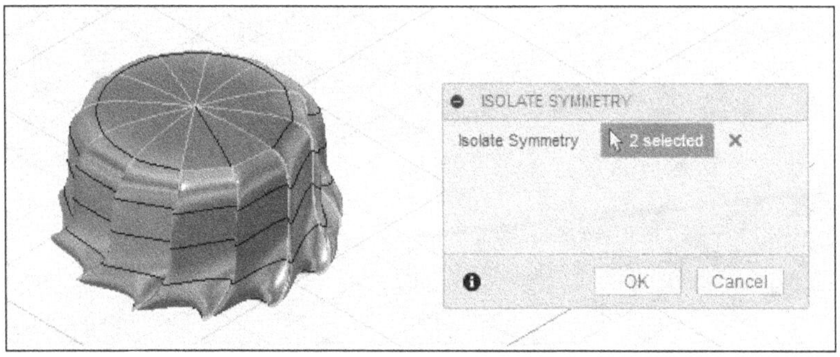

Figure-26. Selecting faces

- After specifying the parameters, click on the **OK** button from **ISOLATE SYMMETRY** dialog box to complete the process.
- If you edit or modify the isolated face, the symmetry faces will modified accordingly; refer to Figure-27.

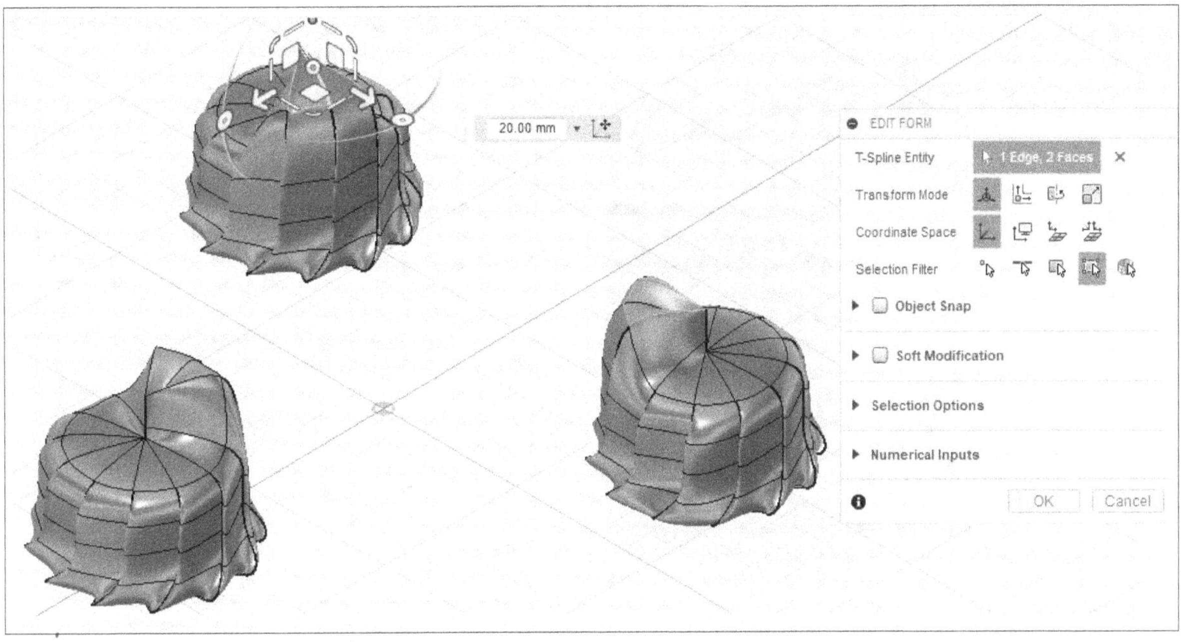

Figure-27. Modifying the selected face

UTILITIES

Till now, you have learned about various symmetric tool. In this section, you will learn about various utility tools used in **FORM Mode**.

Display Mode

The **Display Mode** tool is used to switches the view of selected body to box or smooth display. The procedure to use this tool is discussed next.

- Click on the **Display Mode** tool from **UTILITIES** drop-down; refer to Figure-28. The **DISPLAY MODE** dialog box will be displayed; refer to Figure-29.

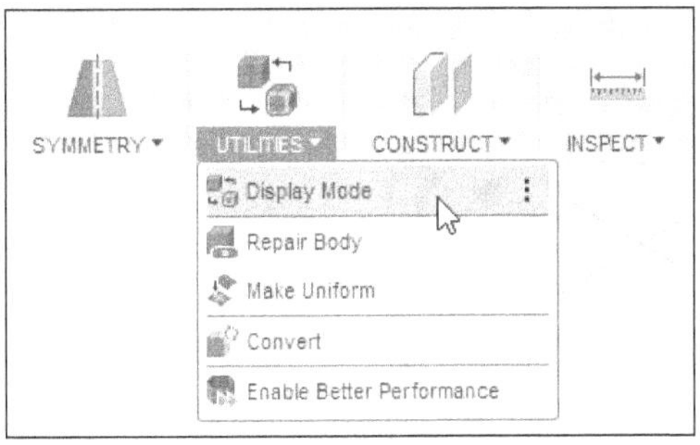

Figure-28. Display Mode tool

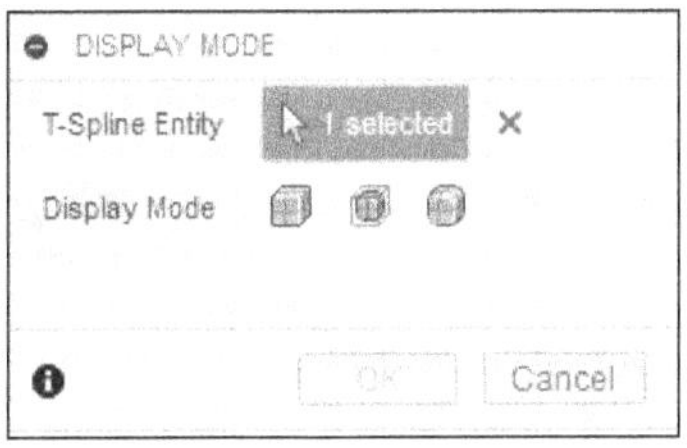

Figure-29. DISPLAY MODE dialog box

- The **Select** button of **T-Spline Entity** section is active by default. You need to select the face, edge, body, or vertex. You can also use window selection for selecting the whole geometry; refer to Figure-30.

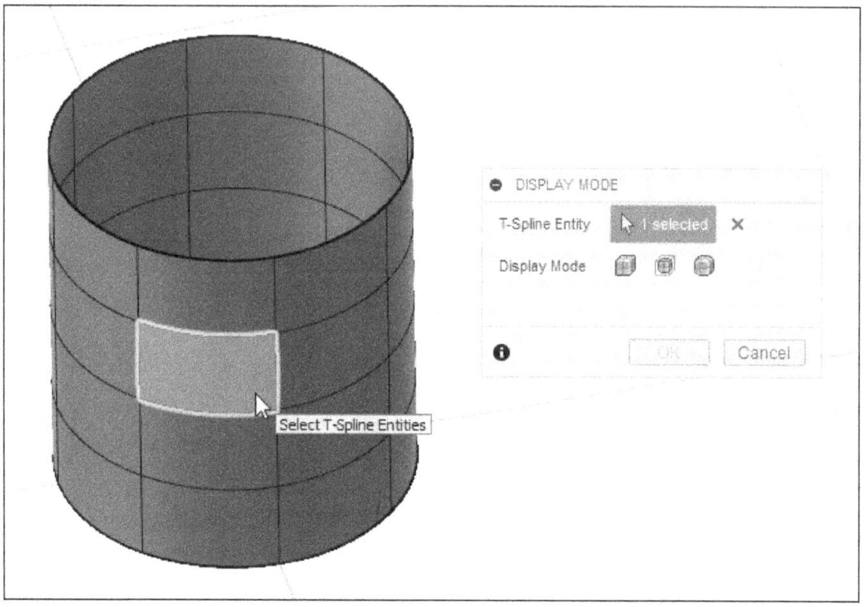

Figure-30. Selecting the face

- Select **Box Display** button from **Display Mode** section to display the control points of the T-Spline body.
- Select **Control Frame Display** button from **Display Mode** section to display the rounded frame body with the control frame around it.
- Select **Smooth Display** button from **Display Mode** section to display the rounded shape of the T-Spline body.
- After selecting the required display, click on the **OK** button from **DISPLAY MODE** dialog box to complete the process; refer to Figure-31.

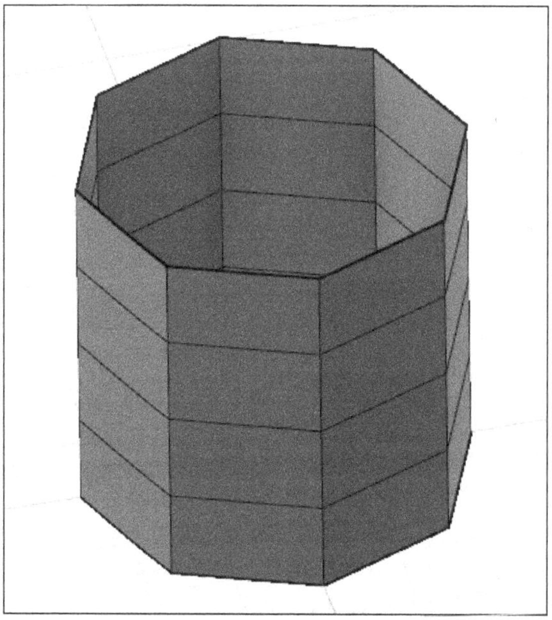

Figure-31. Box display mode created

Repair Body

The **Repair Body** tool is used for displaying the information about the mesh of sculpt body. This tool also repairs error star points and error T points. The procedure to use this tool is discussed next.

- Click on the **Repair Body** tool from **UTILITIES** drop-down; refer to Figure-32. The **REPAIR BODY** dialog box will be displayed; refer to Figure-33.

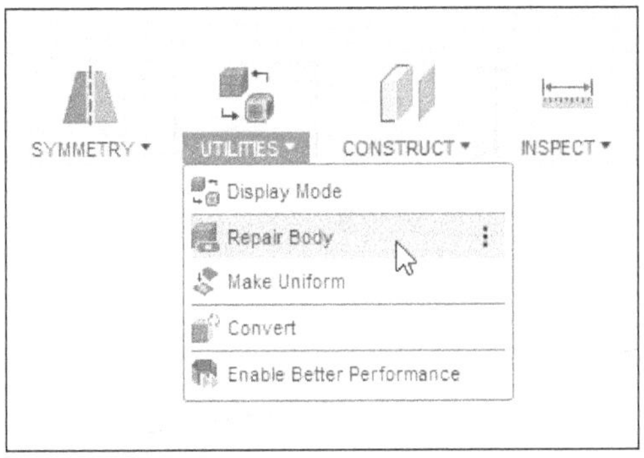

Figure-32. Repair Body tool

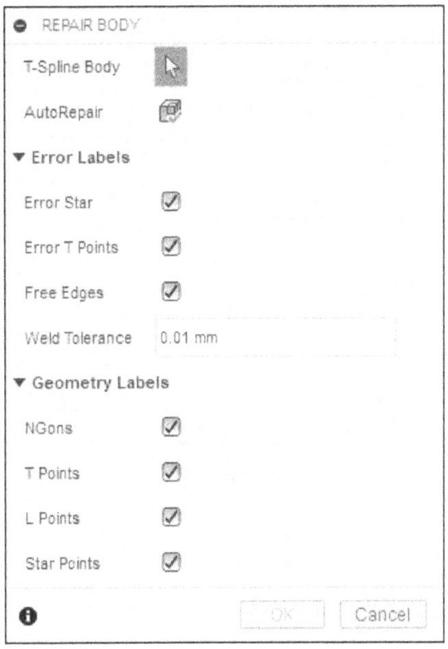

Figure-33. REPAIR BODY dialog box

- The **Select** button of **T-Spline Body** section is active by default. Click on the body to select.
- Click on the **AutoRepair** button from **REPAIR BODY** dialog box to repair error star points, error T points, and free edges.
- Select the **Error Star** check box of **Error Labels** section to display a red star on star points with an error.
- Select **Error T Points** check box of **Error Labels** section to display a red T on T point with an error.
- Select **Free Edges** check box to highlight the open edges on the body.
- Click in the **Weld Tolerance** edit box and specify the distance between edges to weld when using **AutoRepair** button.
- Select the **NGons** check box from **Geometry Labels** section to display the NGons with the number of edges on the selected model. NGons are faces with less than or more than 4 edges.
- Select the **T Points** check box to display a yellow T on T points of model.
- Select the **L Points** check box to display a yellow L on L Points of the selected model.
- Select the **Star Points** check box to display a yellow star on star points of model.
- After specifying the parameters, click on the **OK** button from **REPAIR BODY** dialog box to complete the process.

Make Uniform

The **Make Uniform** tool is used to create uniform surface of the selected body. This tool is used for making all the knots interval of selected body uniform. The procedure to use this tool is discussed next.

- Click on the **Make Uniform** tool from **UTILITIES** drop-down; refer to Figure-34. The **MAKE UNIFORM** dialog box will be displayed; refer to Figure-35.

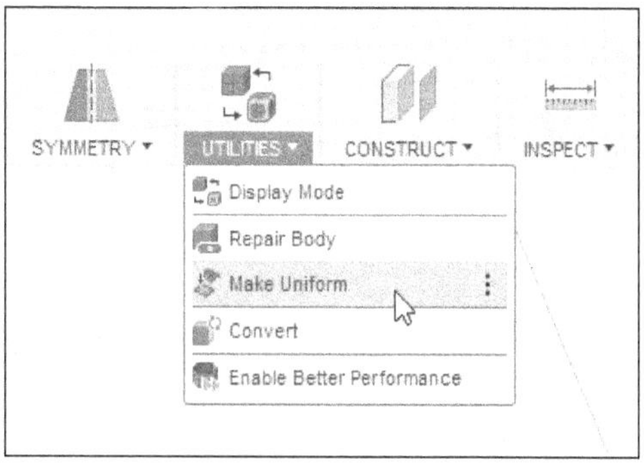

Figure-34. Make Uniform tool

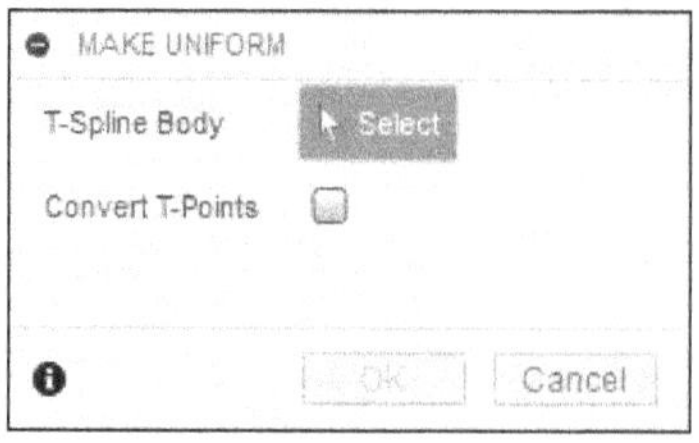

Figure-35. MAKE UNIFORM dialog box

- The **Select** button of **T-Spline Body** section is active by default. Click on the body to select to select the T-Spline body.
- Select **Convert T-Points** check box to convert all T-Points to star points.
- After specifying the parameters, click on the **OK** button. The body will be modified.

Convert

The **Convert** tool is used to convert a sculpt object into other forms. The type of created body depends on selected body. The procedure to use this tool is discussed next.

- Click on the **Convert** tool from **UTILITIES** drop-down; refer to Figure-36. The **CONVERT** dialog box will be displayed; refer to Figure-37.

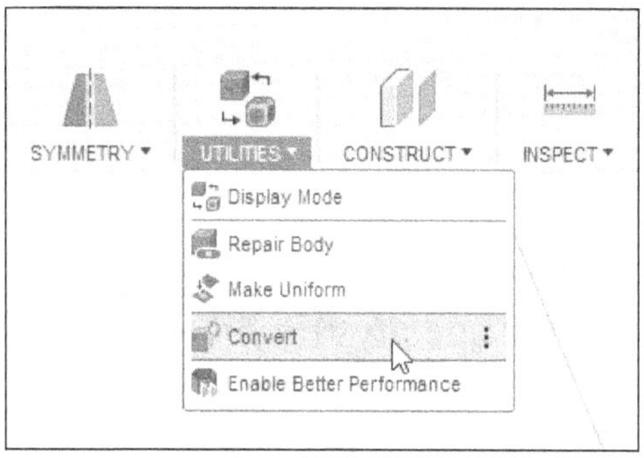

Figure-36. Convert tool

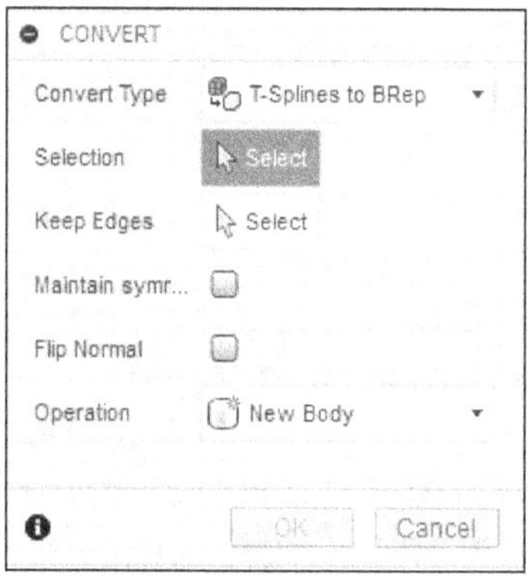

Figure-37. CONVERT dialog box

- Select **T-Splines to BRep** option from **Convert Type** drop-down to convert a T-Spline body into solid body.
- Select **BRep Face to T-Splines** option from **Convert Type** drop-down to convert a surface/face into sculpt.
- Select **Quad Mesh to T-Splines** option from **Convert Type** drop-down to convert a mesh body to a T-Spline body (sculpt).
- In our case, we are converting a T-Spline body to a solid body. The **Select** button of **Selection** section is active by default. Click on the sculpt body to convert; refer to Figure-38.

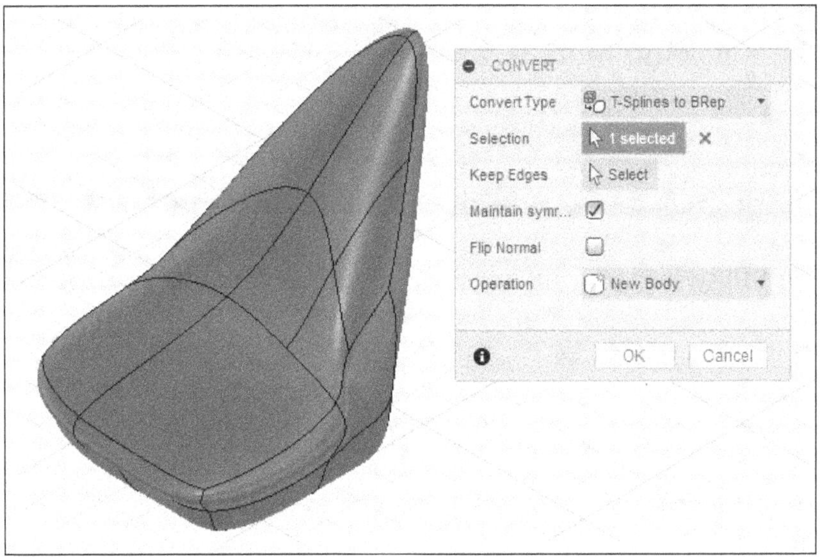

Figure-38. Selection of body to convert

- Click on the **Select** button from **Keep Edges** section and select required edges to maintain the selected edges in converted body.
- Select the **Maintain symmetry** check box from **CONVERT** dialog box to maintain the symmetry of T-Spline body after conversion.
- Select the **Flip Normal** check box to change the normal direction of selected bodies.
- After specifying the parameters, click on the **OK** button from **CONVERT** dialog box; refer to Figure-39. The converted body will be displayed in **DESIGN Workspace**.

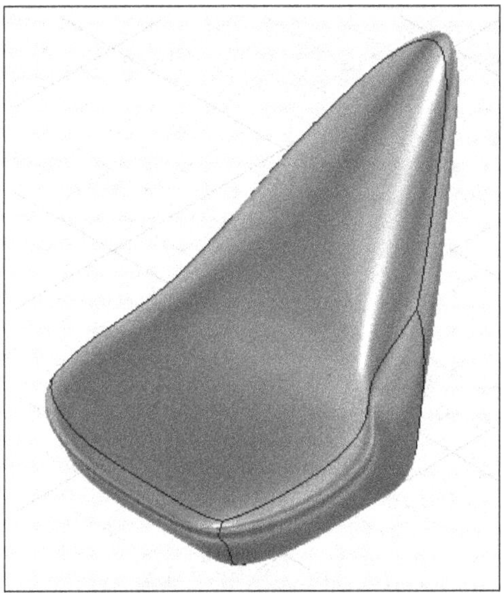

Figure-39. Converted body

Enable Better Performance

The **Enable Better Performance** tool is used to toggle between better performance or better display. The better display shows the bodies at highest quality and better performance calculates modification by applying G0 conditions at star points.

SELF ASSESSMENT

Q1. Which of the following tools is used to replicate changes made in one side of sculpt body to another side?

a. Mirror - Duplicate
b. Mirror - Internal
c. Isolate Symmetry
d. Circular - Internal

Q2. Which of the following tool is used to create replica of sculpt body with respect to a plane?

a. Mirror - Duplicate
b. Mirror - Internal
c. Isolate Symmetry
d. Circular - Internal

Q3. Which of the following tool is used to create symmetrical copies of selected sculpt body about an axis?

a. Mirror - Duplicate
b. Mirror - Internal
c. Circular Duplicate
d. Circular - Internal

Q4. Which of the following tool is used to remove symmetric conditions applied selected faces of sculpt body?

a. Clear Symmetry
b. Make Uniform
c. Isolate Symmetry
d. Erase and Fill

Q5. Which of the following tool is used to check geometry labels of sculpt mesh like L points, T points, and Star points?

a. Display Mode
b. Repair Body
c. Make Uniform
d. Enable Better Performance

Q6. What is the purpose of the Mirror - Internal tool?

A. To create an external mirror symmetry.
B. To create an internal mirror symmetry.
C. To create circular symmetry.
D. To duplicate T-Spline bodies.

Q7. Which tool is used to create internal circular symmetry?

A. Mirror - Internal
B. Circular - Internal
C. Mirror - Duplicate
D. Circular - Duplicate

Q8. What is the function of the Weld checkbox in the Mirror - Duplicate tool?

A. To create circular symmetry.
B. To weld the symmetric edges together.
C. To delete symmetry.
D. To isolate symmetry.

Q9. Which tool allows you to create circular symmetric copies around an axis?

A. Circular - Internal
B. Circular - Duplicate
C. Mirror - Internal
D. Mirror - Duplicate

Q10. What does the Clear Symmetry tool do?

A. Deletes the symmetry and creates new bodies.
B. Repairs symmetry errors.
C. Isolates symmetry conditions.
D. Creates circular symmetric copies.

Q11. What is a feature of the Isolate Symmetry tool?

A. Removes the symmetry condition while keeping the geometry symmetric.
B. Deletes symmetry constraints entirely.
C. Creates circular symmetry.
D. Repairs error star points.

Q12. Which display mode shows the control points of a T-Spline body?

A. Box Display
B. Control Frame Display
C. Smooth Display
D. Highlight Display

Q13. What does the Repair Body tool NOT do?

A. Highlight NGons with the number of edges.
B. Convert T-Points to star points.
C. Display red stars on error star points.
D. Repair free edges.

Q14. What is the function of the Make Uniform tool?

A. To delete symmetry.
B. To make all knot intervals uniform.
C. To isolate symmetry conditions.
D. To repair error T-points.

Q15. Which Convert Type option is used to convert a surface/face into a sculpt?

A. T-Splines to BRep
B. Quad Mesh to T-Splines
C. BRep Face to T-Splines
D. Solid Body to Sculpt

Q16. What is the default active section when using the Mirror - Internal tool?

A. Select Edge
B. Select Face
C. Select Vertex
D. Select Plane

Q17. How does the Circular - Internal tool preview the symmetry?

A. By showing the axis of rotation.
B. By highlighting the selected face.
C. By displaying a preview of symmetric sections.
D. By creating new bodies directly.

Q18. What happens when the Weld Tolerance value is specified in the Mirror - Duplicate tool?

A. Symmetric edges are ignored.
B. Symmetric edges are joined within the tolerance range.
C. Symmetry is deleted.
D. Mirror symmetry is isolated.

Q19. What does the Separate Bodies checkbox in the Clear Symmetry tool do?

A. Combines disjointed surfaces.
B. Creates new bodies for disjointed surfaces.
C. Deletes symmetry conditions.
D. Highlights the symmetric sections.

Q20. Which of the following tools repairs free edges and error star points?

A. Repair Body
B. Clear Symmetry
C. Isolate Symmetry
D. Make Uniform

Q21. What type of symmetry does the Isolate Symmetry tool remove?

A. Mirror symmetry
B. Circular symmetry
C. Symmetry condition for selected geometry
D. Symmetry condition for entire bodies

Q22. Which Display Mode option shows a rounded frame with the control frame around it?

A. Box Display
B. Smooth Display
C. Control Frame Display
D. Highlight Display

Q23. What does the NGons checkbox in the Repair Body tool display?

A. Red stars on error points
B. Free edges of the body
C. Faces with less than or more than four edges
D. Symmetry conditions

Q24. What is the purpose of the Convert tool's Maintain Symmetry checkbox?

A. To remove symmetry from the converted body.
B. To weld symmetric edges together.
C. To keep symmetry after conversion.
D. To display symmetry errors.

Q25. What happens if the Enable Better Performance tool is set to better display?

A. Modifications are calculated using G0 conditions.
B. The bodies are displayed at the highest quality.
C. T-Points are converted to star points.
D. Symmetry conditions are removed.

Q26. What is the primary function of the Mirror - Internal tool?

A. To create external symmetry in the T-Spline body.
B. To create an internal mirror symmetry within the T-Spline body.
C. To duplicate a T-Spline body.
D. To remove symmetry from the body.

Q27. When using the Circular - Internal tool, what determines the number of symmetric sections?

A. The selected axis.
B. The Possible Symmetries drop-down.
C. The face selected.
D. The Weld check box.

Q28. Which tool is used to create circular symmetric copies of the selected body around an axis?

A. Circular - Internal
B. Mirror - Duplicate
C. Circular - Duplicate
D. Clear Symmetry

Q29. What happens if you select the Weld check box in the Circular - Duplicate tool?

A. Separate bodies are created for duplicates.
B. The symmetry condition is isolated.
C. The copies are combined into a single body.
D. The preview of symmetry is disabled.

Q30. What is the purpose of the AutoRepair button in the Repair Body tool?

A. To convert T-points to star points.
B. To repair error star points, error T points, and free edges.
C. To isolate symmetry conditions.
D. To delete NGons.

Q31. In the Display Mode tool, which option highlights the control points of the T-Spline body?

A. Smooth Display
B. Box Display
C. Control Frame Display
D. Symmetry Display

Q32. Which tool is used to create uniform knot intervals on a T-Spline body?

A. Repair Body
B. Make Uniform
C. Convert
D. Clear Symmetry

Q33. What happens when you select the Convert T-Points checkbox in the Make Uniform tool?

A. All T-Points are repaired.
B. All T-Points are converted to star points.
C. The T-Spline body is converted into a solid body.
D. Symmetry is removed from T-Points.

Q34. Which option in the Convert tool changes a T-Spline body into a solid body?

A. Quad Mesh to T-Splines
B. BRep Face to T-Splines
C. T-Splines to BRep
D. Solid Body to Sculpt

Q35. What does the Flip Normal check box in the Convert tool do?

A. Maintains symmetry after conversion.
B. Converts solid bodies into sculpt bodies.
C. Changes the normal direction of selected bodies.
D. Converts NGons into T-Points.

FOR STUDENT NOTES

Chapter 14

Mesh Design

Topics Covered

The major topics covered in this chapter are:

- ***Introduction to Mesh Workspace***
- ***Insert Mesh***
- ***BRep to Mesh***
- ***Remesh***
- ***Reduce***
- ***Make Closed Mesh***
- ***Erase and Fill***
- ***Smooth***
- ***Plane Cut***
- ***Reverse Normal***
- ***Delete Faces***
- ***Separate and Merge Bodies***
- ***Face Groups***

INTRODUCTION

A mesh model consists of vertices, edges, and faces that use polygonal representation, including triangles and quadrilaterals, to define a 3D shape. Mesh models has no mass properties but they can be used as frame reference to create solid model with mass properties. Working with mesh model allows to use manipulation techniques that are not available in solid modeling like applying crease, split, smoothness level, and so on. Note that 3D printers use mesh model to create the 3D print.

OPENING THE MESH WORKSPACE

The tools to create mesh objects are available in the **MESH** tab of **Ribbon** in **DESIGN** workspace; refer to Figure-1.

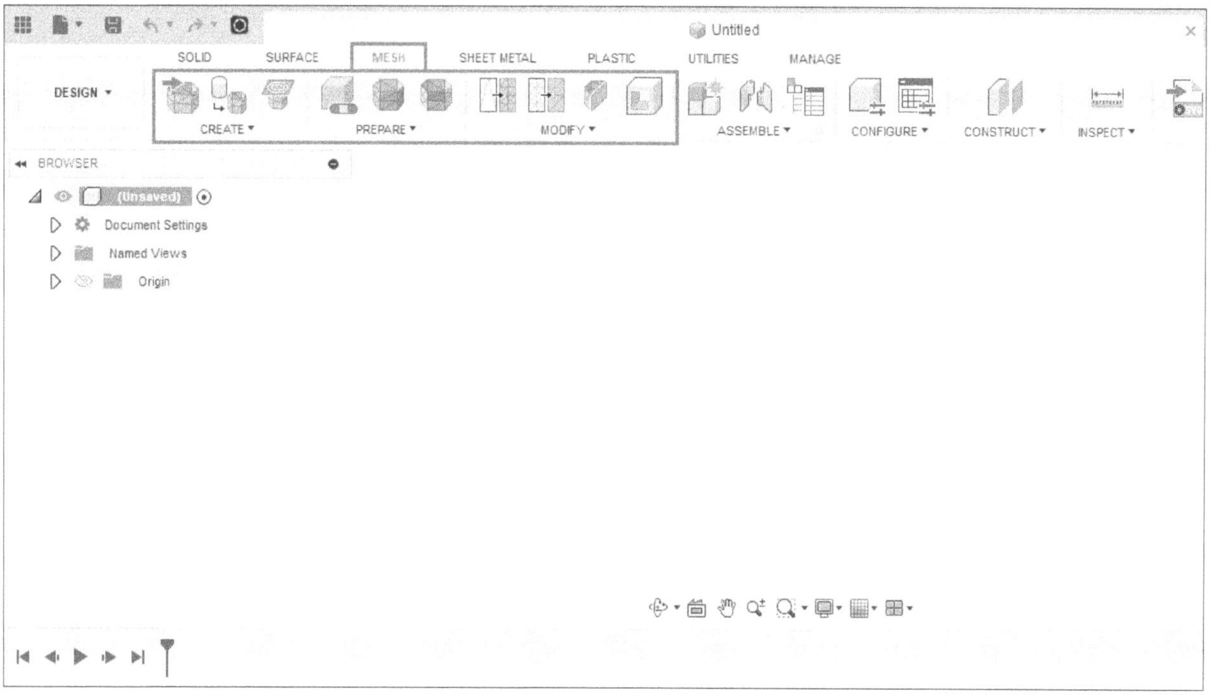

Figure-1. MESH tab in Ribbon

INSERTING FILE

After activating Mesh tools, the next step is to import a mesh model or convert an existing solid to mesh model. In this section, you will learn to insert selected file into Mesh workspace and convert a solid model to mesh model.

Insert Mesh

The **Insert Mesh** tool is used for inserting a .OBJ or .STL mesh file into current design. The procedure to use this tool is discussed next.

- Click on the **Insert Mesh** tool from **CREATE** drop-down; refer to Figure-2. The **Insert** dialog box will be displayed; refer to Figure-3.

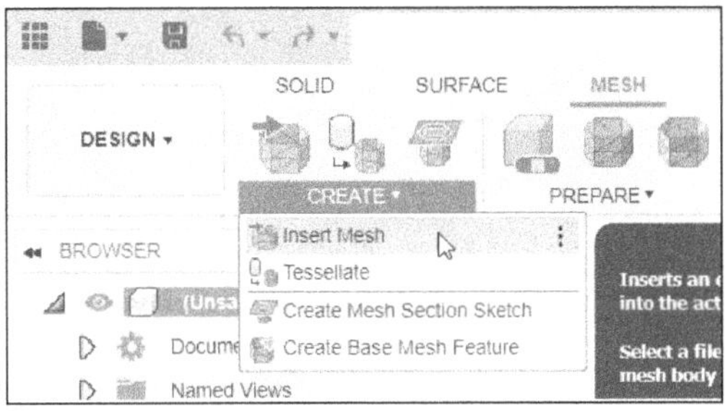

Figure-2. Insert Mesh tool

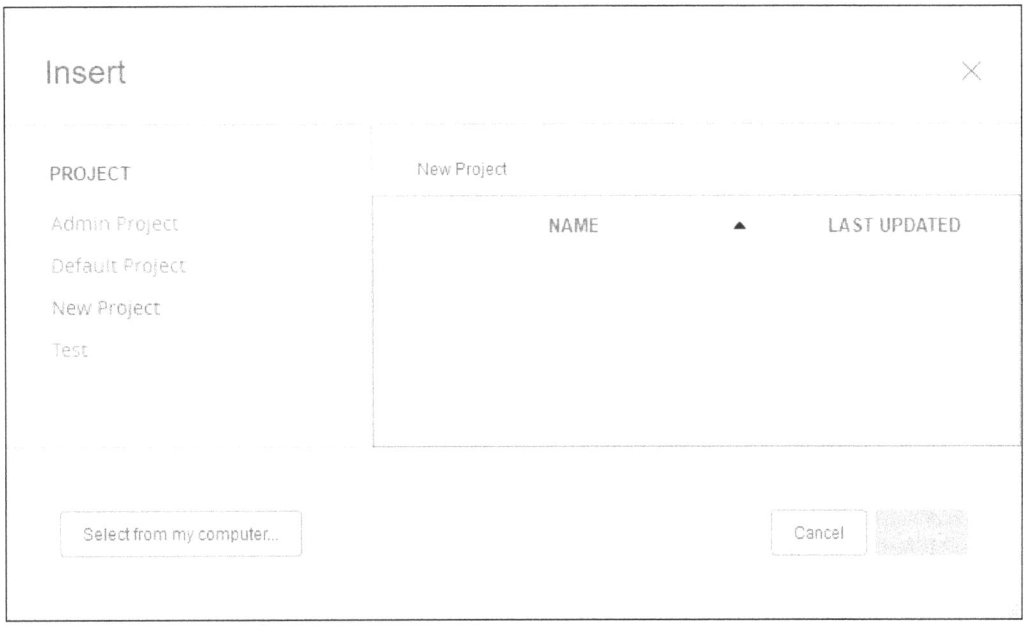

Figure-3. Insert dialog box

- Select desired file and click on the **Select** button or click on the **Select from my computer** button. The updated **Insert** dialog box will be displayed; refer to Figure-4.

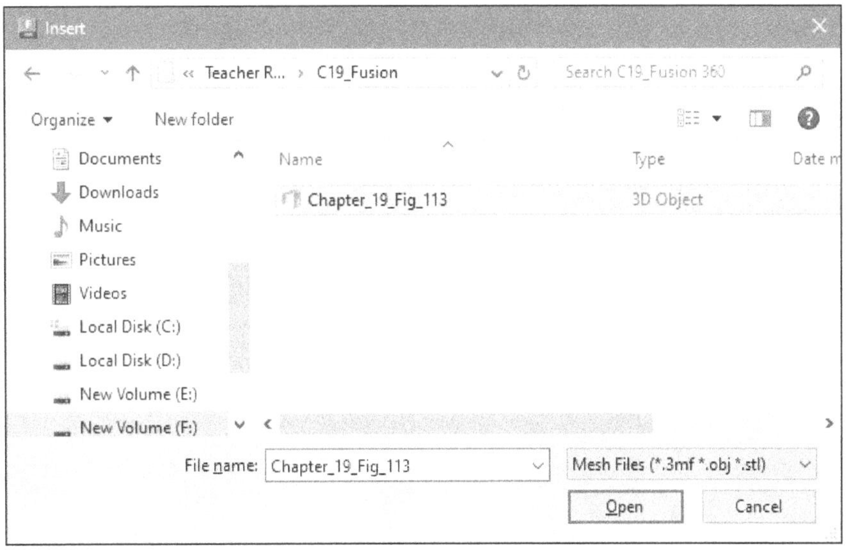

Figure-4. Updated Insert dialog box

- Select desired file and click on the **Open** button. The selected file will be displayed in the **MESH** workspace and the **INSERT MESH** dialog box will be displayed; refer to Figure-5.

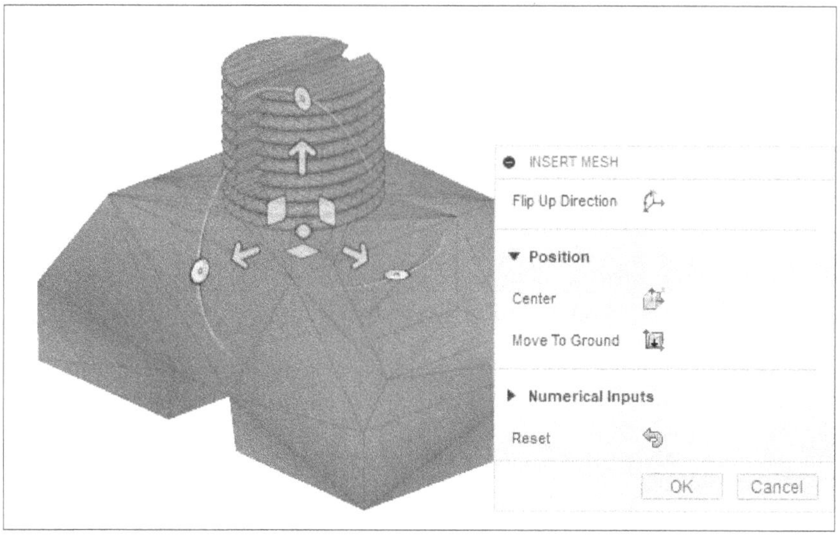

Figure-5. Model with INSERT MESH dialog box

- Set desired orientation of model and then click on the **OK** button from the dialog box to insert the mesh. You can also use the handles displayed on model to modify orientation of mesh model.

Tessellate (BRep to Mesh)

The **Tessellate** tool is used to convert the selected solid body into mesh body. A BRep (Boundary representation) method is the one in which object is defined by its boundary limits. In Solid modeling and CAD, Solids and surfaces are generally created by BRep method. Sometimes, solids and surfaces are collectively called BRep. The procedure to use this tool is discussed next.

- Make sure you have a solid/surface model created in **DESIGN** workspace or open a model and then switch to **MESH Workspace** to convert the body to mesh body.
- Click on the **Tessellate** tool from **CREATE** drop-down; refer to Figure-6. The **TESSELLATE** dialog box will be displayed; refer to Figure-7.

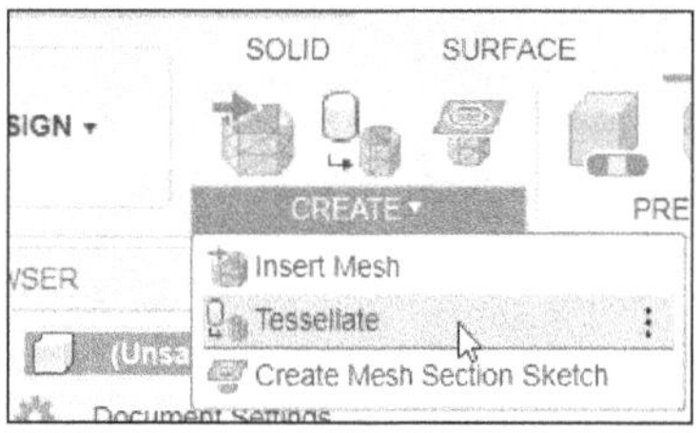

Figure-6. Tessellate tool

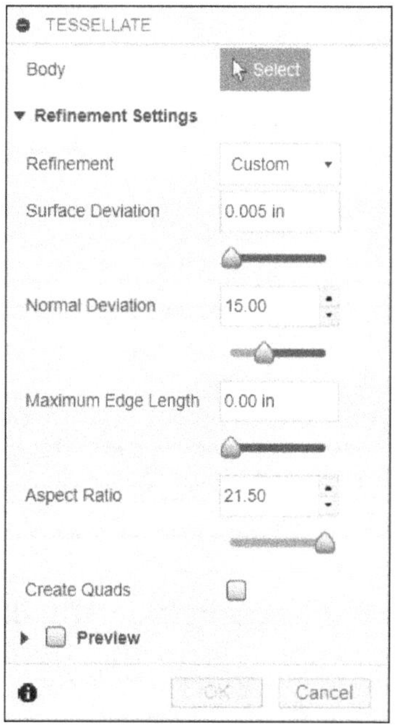

Figure-7. TESSELLATE dialog box

- The **Select** button of **Body** section is active by default. Click on the body to be converted to mesh; refer to Figure-8.

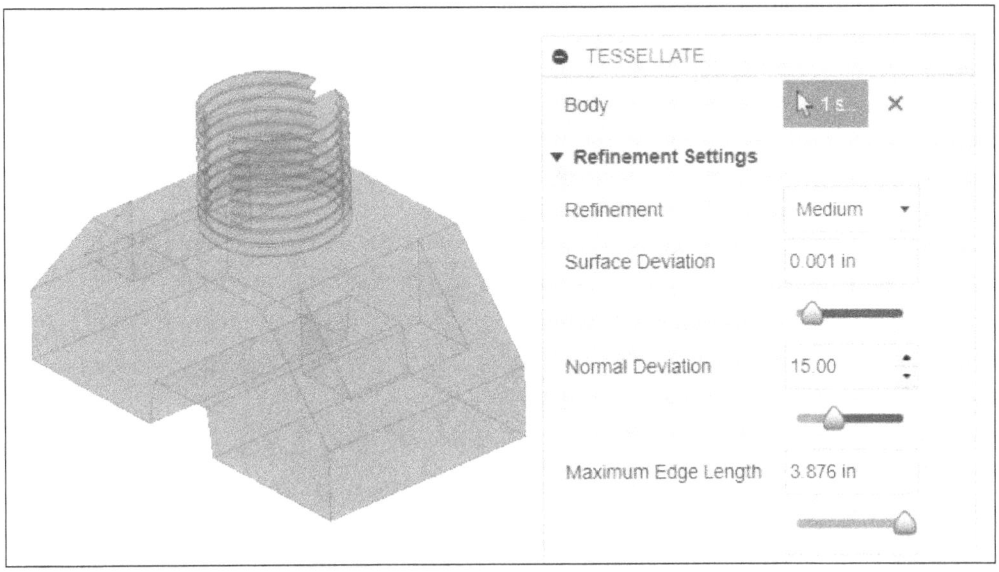

Figure-8. Selecting a body

- Select the **Preview** check box under **Preview** node from the dialog box to display the preview of mesh body of the selected solid body. The preview of mesh body will be displayed along with **Number of Triangles**; refer to Figure-9.

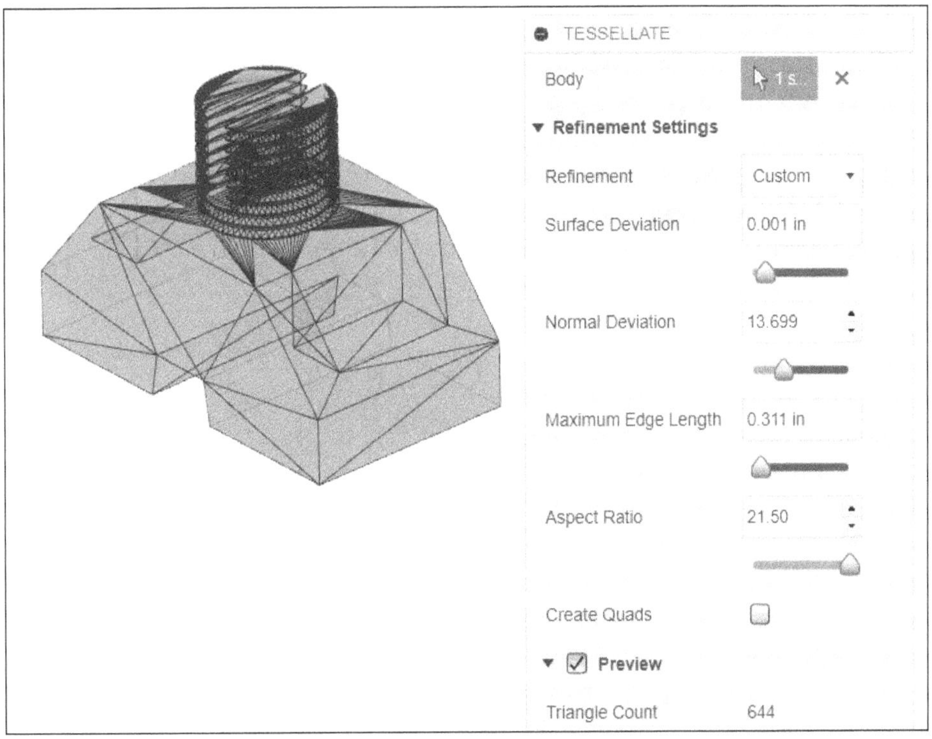

Figure-9. Preview of mesh body

- Select the **High**, **Medium**, or **Low** option from **Refinement** drop-down to set the refinement of mesh body automatically.
- If you want to set the refinement manually then click on the **Custom** option from **Refinement** drop-down.
- Move the **Surface Deviation**, **Normal Deviation**, **Maximum Edge Length**, and **Aspect Ratio** sliders to set the respective values.

- Select the **Create Quads** check box to create rectangular facets in place of triangular facets.
- After specifying the parameters in dialog box, click on the **OK** button from dialog box to complete the process; refer to Figure-10.

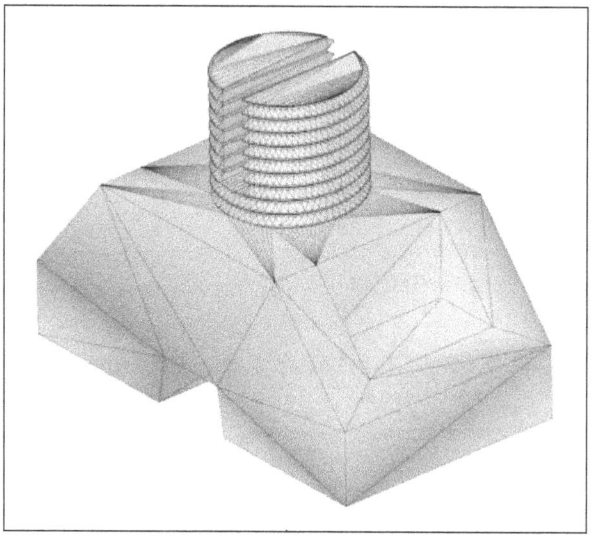

Figure-10. Created mesh body

Creating Mesh Section Sketch

The **Create Mesh Section Sketch** tool is used to create sketch generated by intersection of a plane and mesh body. The generated sketch is boundary of mesh body intersecting with the plane. The procedure to use this tool is given next.

- Click on the **Create Mesh Section Sketch** tool from the **CREATE** drop-down in the **MESH** tab of the **Ribbon**. The **CREATE MESH SECTION SKETCH** dialog box will be displayed; refer to Figure-11.

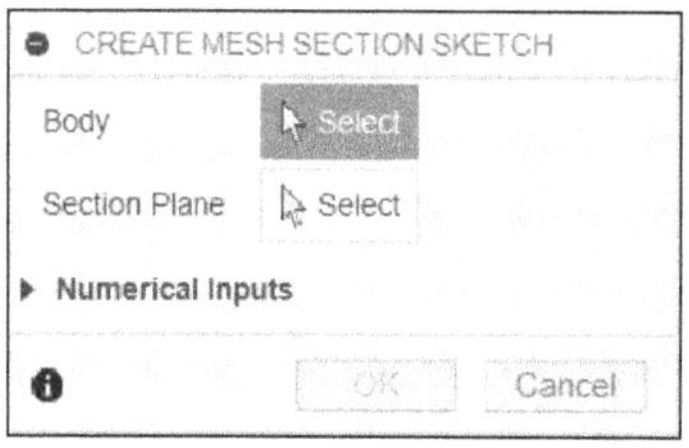

Figure-11. CREATE MESH SECTION SKETCH dialog box

- Select the mesh body whose intersection boundaries are to be generated in a sketch.
- Click on the **Select** button for **Section Plane** section from the dialog box and select the intersecting plane. Preview of mesh section sketch will be displayed; refer to Figure-12.

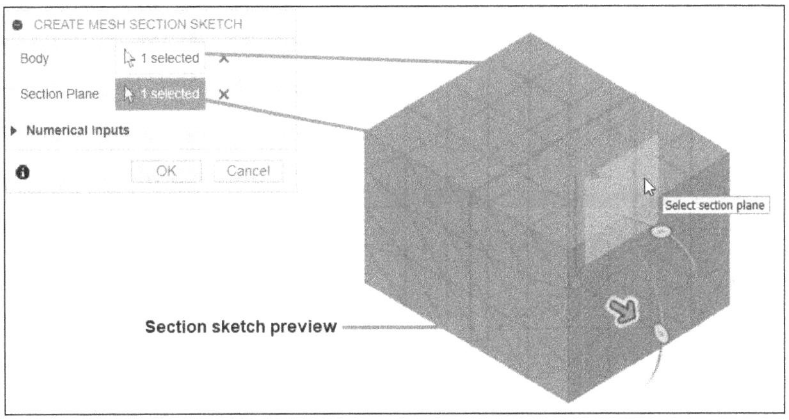

Figure-12. Preview of section sketch

- Using the dynamic arrows displayed on model, you can offset the section sketch at desired distance in direction normal to the plane.
- Click on the **OK** button from the dialog box to create the section sketch.

Creating Base Mesh Feature

The **Create Base Mesh Feature** tool is used to create empty mesh feature that can be later modified as required. The procedure to use this tool is given next.

- Click on the **Create Base Mesh Feature** tool from the **CREATE** drop-down in the **MESH** tab of **Ribbon**. The **DIRECT MESH EDITING** toolbar will be displayed in **Ribbon**; refer to Figure-13. You will learn about these tools later in this chapter.

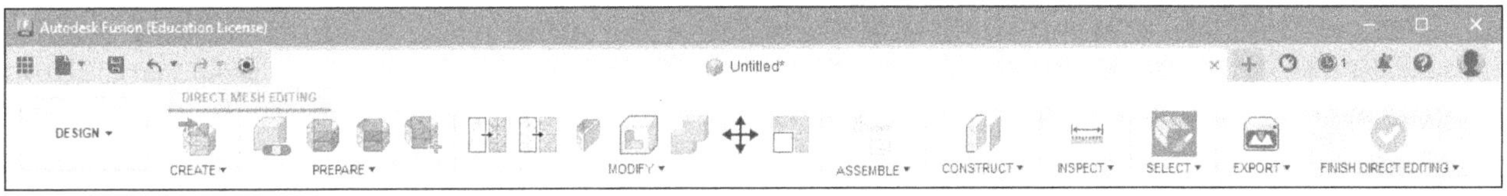

Figure-13. Direct Mesh Editing Toolbar

MESH PREPARATION TOOLS

The tools in **PREPARE** drop-down of **Ribbon** are used to repair the model imported from non-native CAD files; refer to Figure-14. The tools in this drop-down are discussed next.

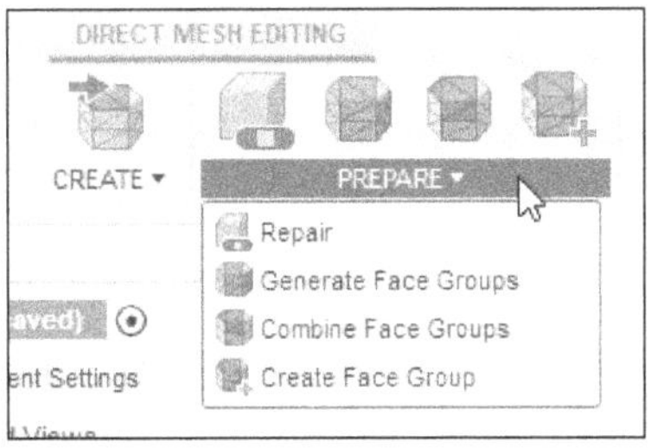

Figure-14. PREPARE drop-down

Repairing Mesh Body

The **Repair** tool is used to perform various repairing operations on imported mesh body like stitching/removing sections of mesh, closing holes, performing wrap, and rebuild. The procedure to use this tool is given next.

- Click on the **Repair** tool from **PREPARE** drop-down in the **Ribbon** after importing the mesh body. The **REPAIR** dialog box will be displayed; refer to Figure-15.

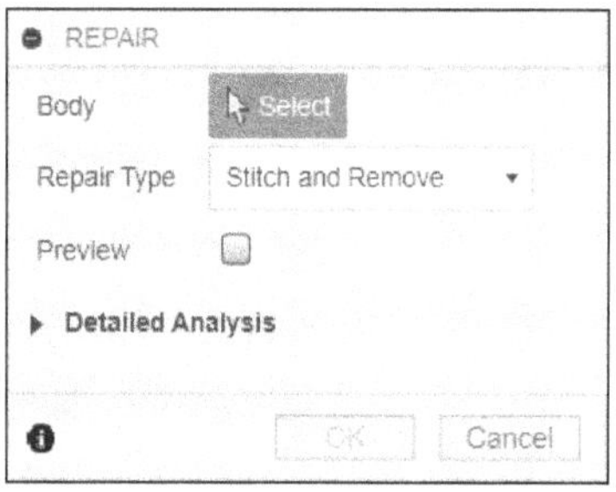

Figure-15. REPAIR dialog box

- Select the mesh body to be repaired from the graphics area.
- Select the **Close Holes** option from the **Repair Type** drop-down to close all the holes in the mesh body. Select the **Stitch and Remove** option from the drop-down to stitch the triangles in mesh within allowed tolerance and remove double triangles, degenerated faces, and tiny shells. Select the **Wrap** option from the drop-down to perform all the modifications generated by **Stitch and Remove** option and also apply wrap on the surface of mesh while removing internal structures. Select the **Rebuild** option to reconstruct the mesh body based on inputs from imported mesh structure. There are four rebuild types available in the **Rebuild Type** drop-down on selecting **Rebuild** option which are **Adaptive**, **Fast**, **Accurate**, and **Blocky**. Select the **Adaptive** option to rebuild the mesh body with an adaptive volume structure. Select the **Fast** option to speed up rebuilding on the cost of accuracy. Select the **Accurate** option to perform accurate replica of mesh body. Select the **Blocky** option to create mesh body in small blocks. You can set the density of rebuilt mesh by using the **Density** slider displayed below the drop-down; refer to Figure-16. Select the **Preserve edges** check box to perform fast rebuilding while preserving sharp edges of the mesh body. The **Close Holes** and **Stitch and Remove** options are faster in repairing mesh body. If they cannot get you desired finish in mesh body then you should use the other options of the drop-down.

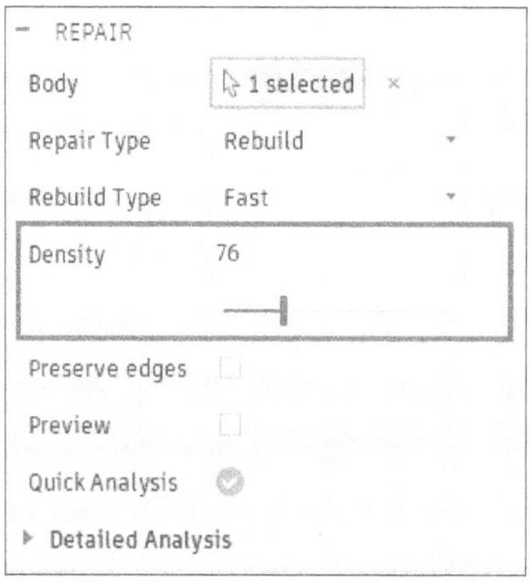

Figure-16. Density slider

- Select the **Preview** check box to check preview of modifications in the graphics area.
- After setting desired parameters, expand the **Detailed Analysis** node in the dialog box. The options in dialog box will be displayed as shown in Figure-17.

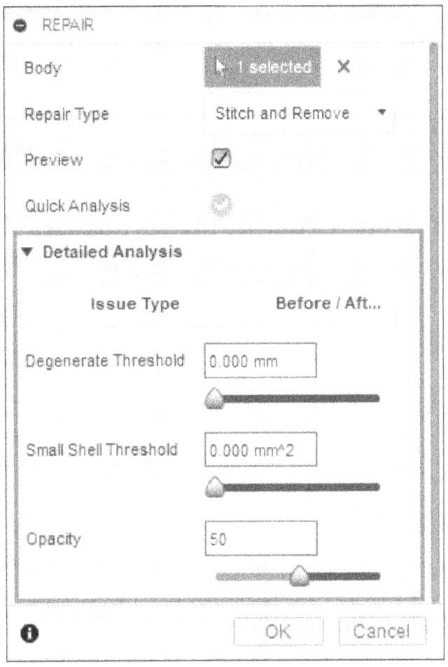

Figure-17. Detailed Analysis options

- Set desired parameters in **Detailed Analysis** section to check the model after rebuilding.
- After setting desired parameters, click on the **OK** button from the dialog box to create the mesh repaired body.

Generating Face Groups

The **Generate Face Groups** tool is used to automatically generate face groups based on their normal angles from the imported mesh body. The procedure to use this tool is given next.

- Click on the **Generate Face Groups** tool from the **PREPARE** drop-down in the **Ribbon**. The **GENERATE FACE GROUPS** dialog box will be displayed; refer to Figure-18.

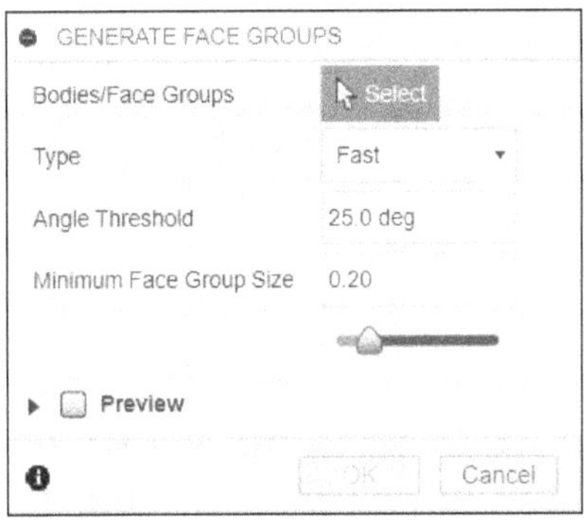

Figure-18. GENERATE FACE GROUPS dialog box

- Select faces of the mesh body to be modified.
- Select the **Fast** option from **Type** drop-down to generate face groups faster while compromising at accuracy. Select the **Accurate** option to generate face groups accurately.
- Set the maximum limit of angle variation within which faces will be created in same group.
- Set desired value in **Minimum Face Group Size** edit box to define size in percentage of mesh body size which defines minimum size of a face group.

- Select the **Preview** check box to see preview of face groups and click on the **OK** button to perform operation.

Combining Face Groups

The **Combine Face Groups** tool is used to combine two or more face groups to form single face group. On selecting this tool from the **PREPARE** drop-down in **Ribbon**, the **COMBINE FACE GROUPS** dialog box is displayed; refer to Figure-19. Select different face groups from the mesh body in graphics area and click on the **OK** button. The same face group will be applied to selected faces; refer to Figure-20.

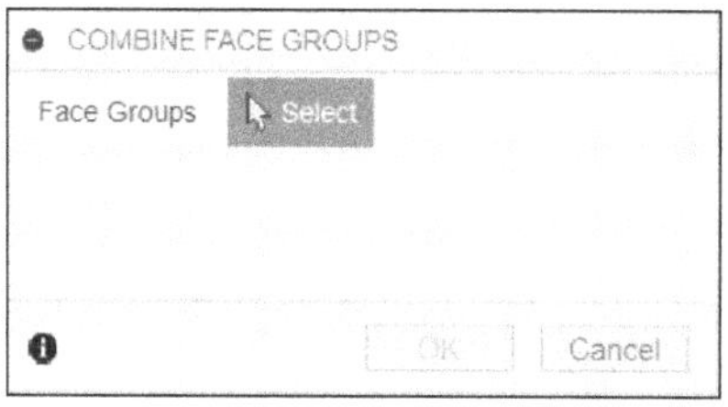

Figure-19. COMBINE FACE GROUPS dialog box

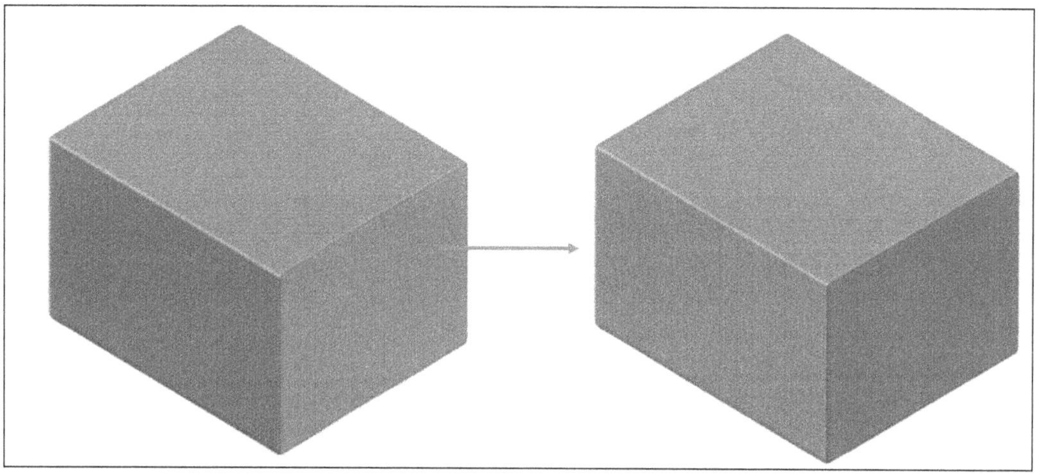

Figure-20. Combining face groups

MODIFICATION TOOLS

In this section, we will discuss various tools which are used to modify the mesh body.

Remesh

The **Remesh** tool is used to refine selected mesh faces or body to form regular-shaped triangular faces. Note that in FEM, there can be different shaped elements in a mesh like tetrahedra, hexahedra, and so on. The procedure to use this tool is discussed next.

- Click on the **Remesh** tool from **MODIFY** drop-down; refer to Figure-21. The **REMESH** dialog box will be displayed; refer to Figure-22.

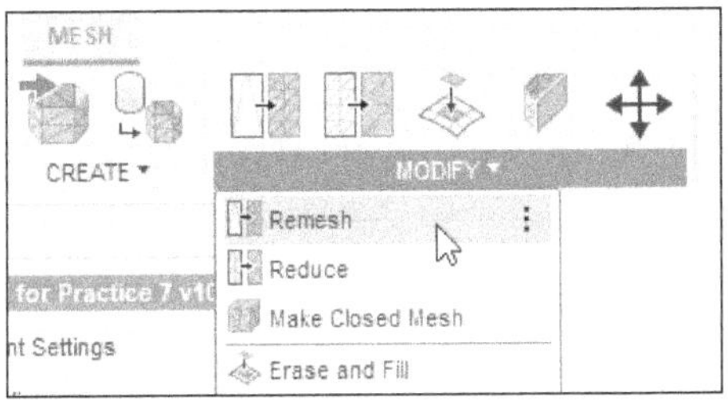

Figure-21. Remesh tool

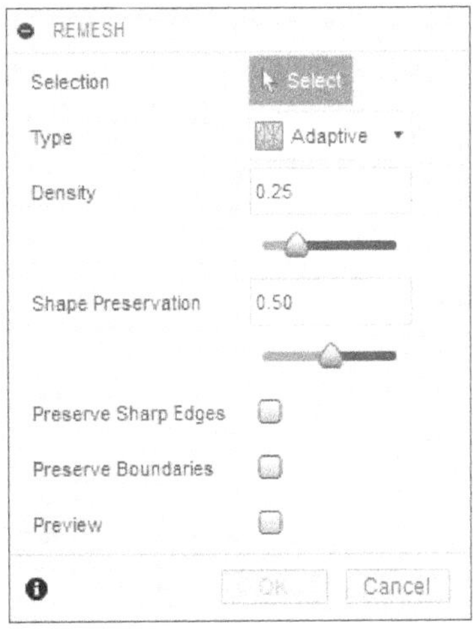

Figure-22. REMESH dialog box

- The **Select** button of **Selection** section is active by default. Click on the faces to select. You can also drag the cursor to select multiple faces.
- Select **Uniform** option from **Type** drop-down for creating the similar size face on the entire selection. This option is used for keeping the face sizes even.
- Select **Adaptive** option from **Type** drop-down for smaller faces in the region of high detail and larger faces in the region of low detail. This option is used for preserving details on the selected model.
- Click in the **Density** edit box and enter desired value of density. You can also specify the value of density by moving the **Density** slider from **REMESH** dialog box; refer to Figure-23. It controls the number of faces created.

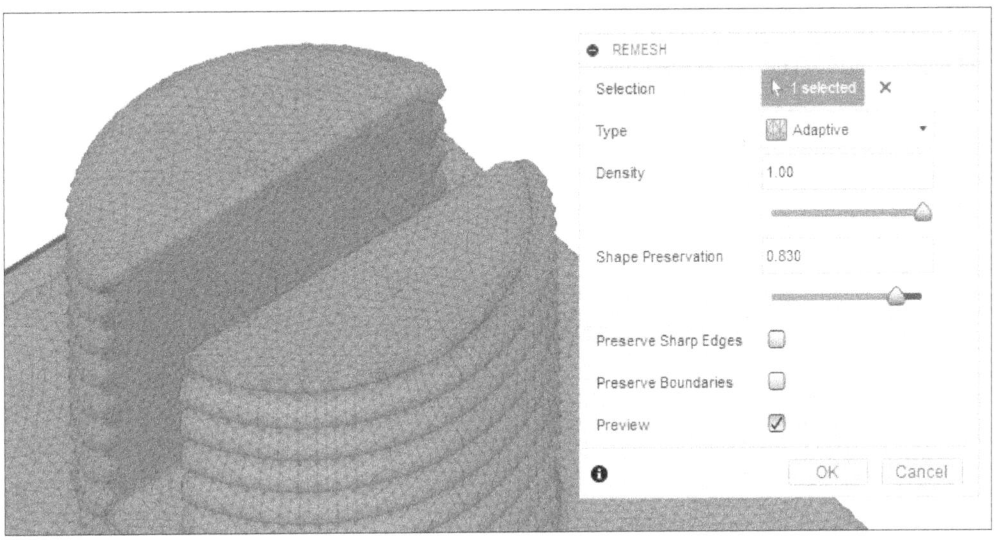

Figure-23. Specifying density

- Click in the **Shape Preservation** edit box and enter the value. You can also specify the value by moving the **Shape Preservation** slider. The value of **Shape Preservation** lies between 0 to 1. Note that this option will be available if you have selected **Adaptive** option from the **Type** drop-down in dialog box.
- Select the **Preserve Sharp Edges** check box from **REMESH** dialog box to preserve the sharp edges from the input mesh.
- Select the **Preserve Boundaries** check box from **REMESH** dialog box to make sure that any open boundaries of the selected model do not change shape. This option is useful if you have two separate bodies meeting at open boundaries that you wish to merge later.

- Select the **Preview** check box to view the mesh preview, before it is created.
- After specifying the parameters, click on the **OK** button from **REMESH** dialog box. The created mesh body will be displayed; refer to Figure-24.

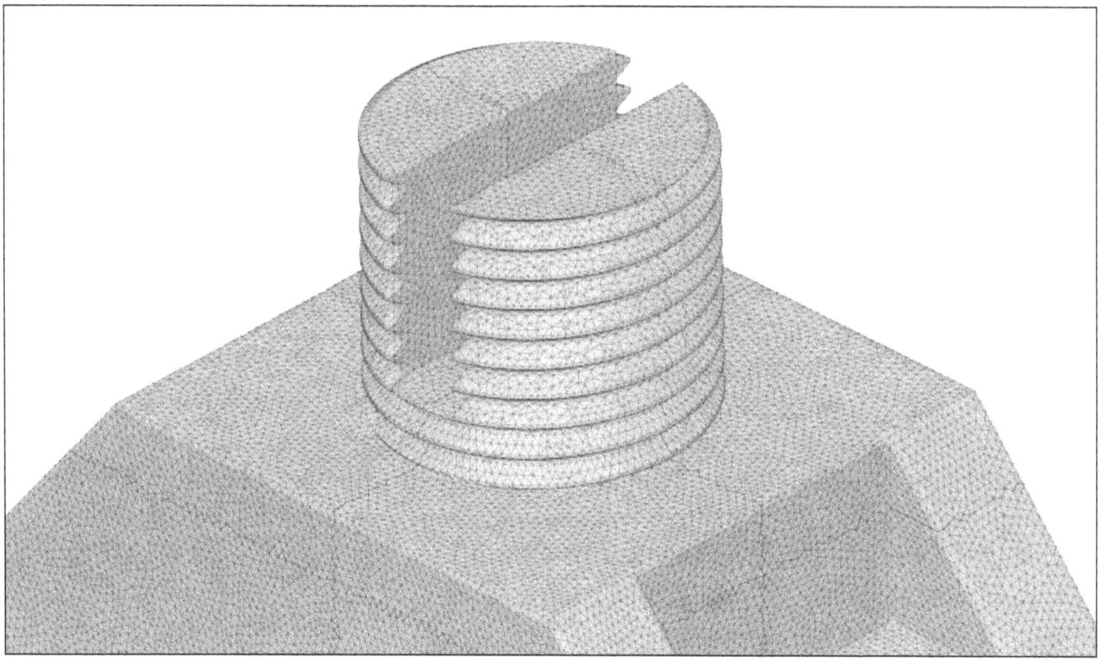

Figure-24. Created mesh body

Reduce

The **Reduce** tool is used to reduce the number of faces on your model while trying to maintain its shape. The procedure to use this tool is discussed next.

- Click on the **Reduce** tool from **MODIFY** drop-down; refer to Figure-25. The **REDUCE** dialog box will be displayed; refer to Figure-26.

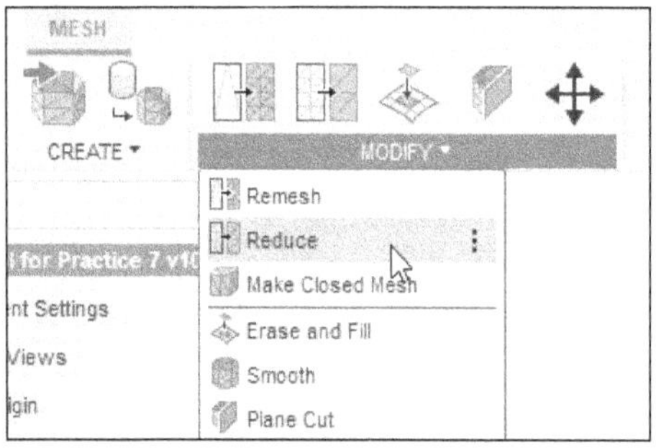

Figure-25. Reduce tool

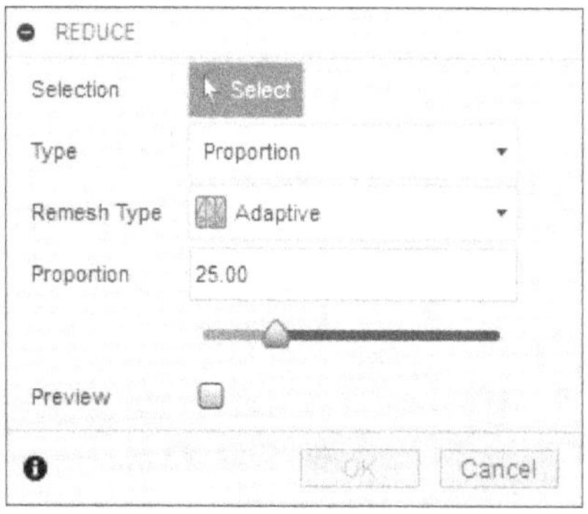

Figure-26. REDUCE dialog box

- The **Select** button of **Selection** section is active by default. Click on the mesh body from the **BROWSER** or select faces of mesh.
- Select the **Tolerance** option from the **Type** drop-down to merge faces within maximum deviation from original mesh shape. After selecting this option, move the **Tolerance** slider to define maximum deviation from original mesh body; refer to Figure-27.

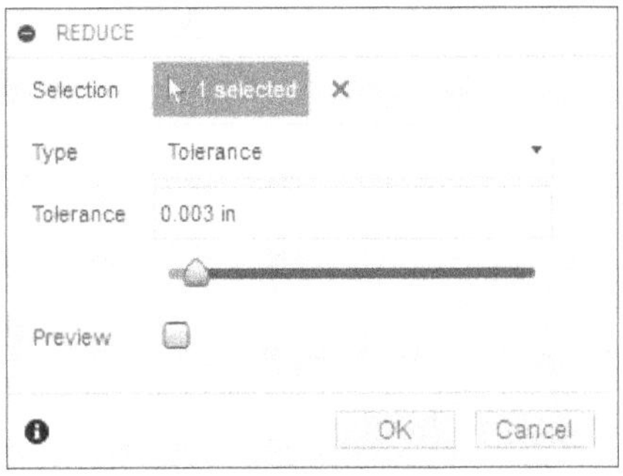

Figure-27. Reducing mesh using tolerance slider

- Select the **Proportion** option from the **Type** drop-down to reduce mesh faces by percentage specified in the **Proportion** edit box. Move the slider to increase or decrease the proportion value by which mesh will be reduced; refer to Figure-28.
- Select the **Adaptive** option to remesh adaptively and select the **Uniform** option to uniformly reduce the faces.

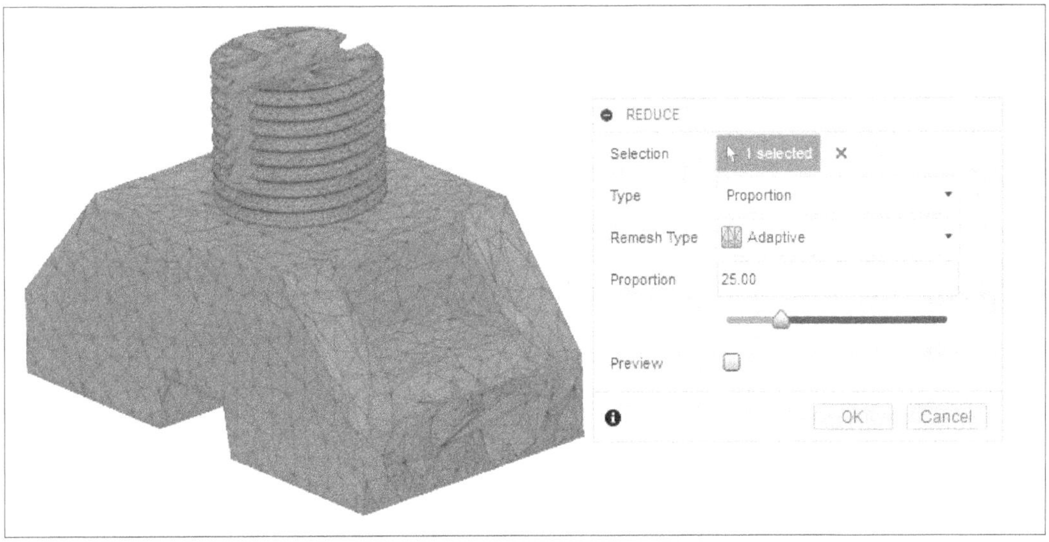

Figure-28. Adjusting the density of mesh body

- Select the **Face Count** option from the **Type** drop-down to reduce specified number of faces from the model; refer to Figure-29.

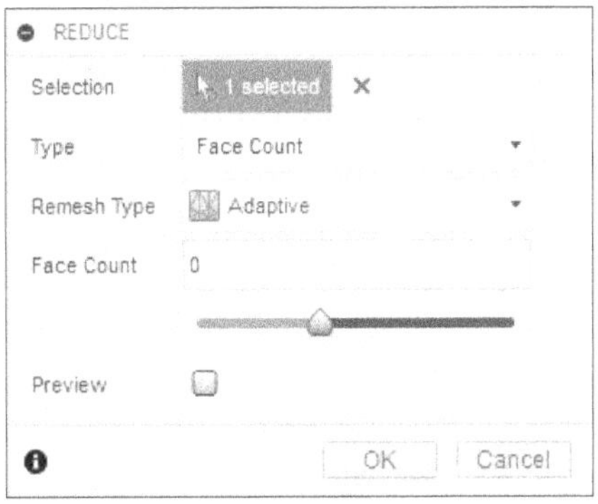

Figure-29. Reducing by face count

- Select the **Preview** check box to view the mesh preview, before it is created.
- After specifying the parameter, click on the **OK** button from the **REDUCE** dialog box. The mesh body will be created; refer to Figure-30.

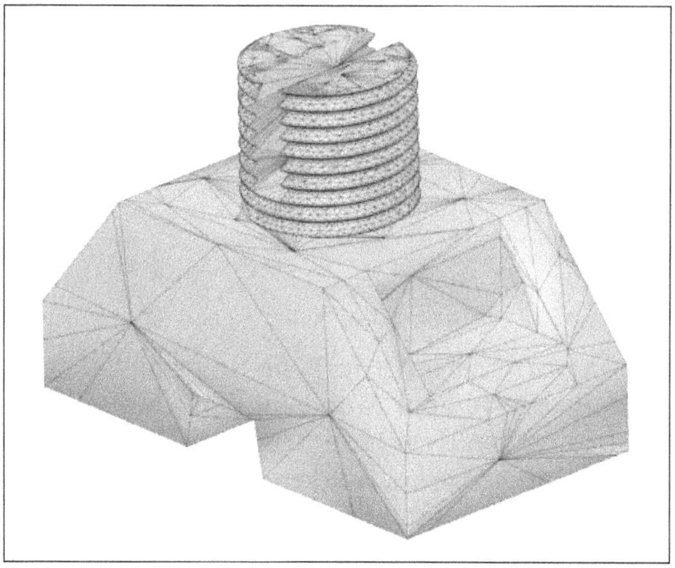

Figure-30. Created mesh body after Reduce tool

Plane Cut

The **Plane Cut** tool is used to cut the selected mesh body using a plane/face/surface. The procedure to use this tool is discussed next.

- Click on the **Plane Cut** tool from **MODIFY** drop-down; refer to Figure-31. The **PLANE CUT** dialog box will be displayed; refer to Figure-32.

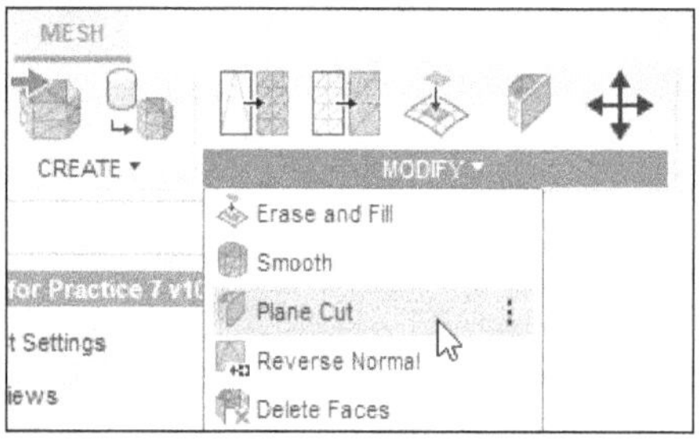

Figure-31. Plane Cut tool

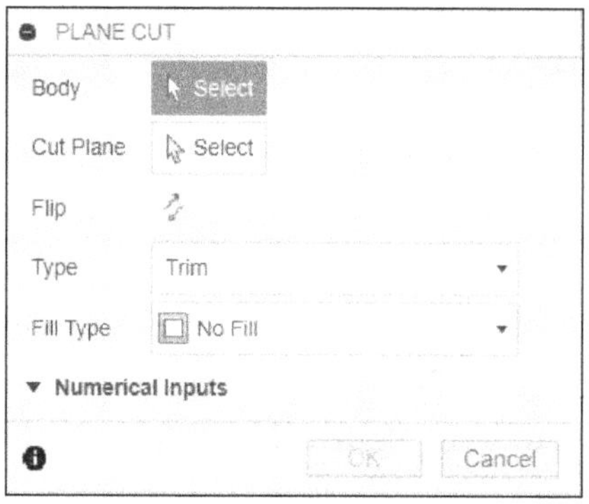

Figure-32. PLANE CUT dialog box

- The **Select** button of **Body** section is active by default. Click on the body to select. You will be asked to select cut plane.
- Select desired plane to be used as cutting plane. The manipulator will be displayed on the selected body; refer to Figure-33.

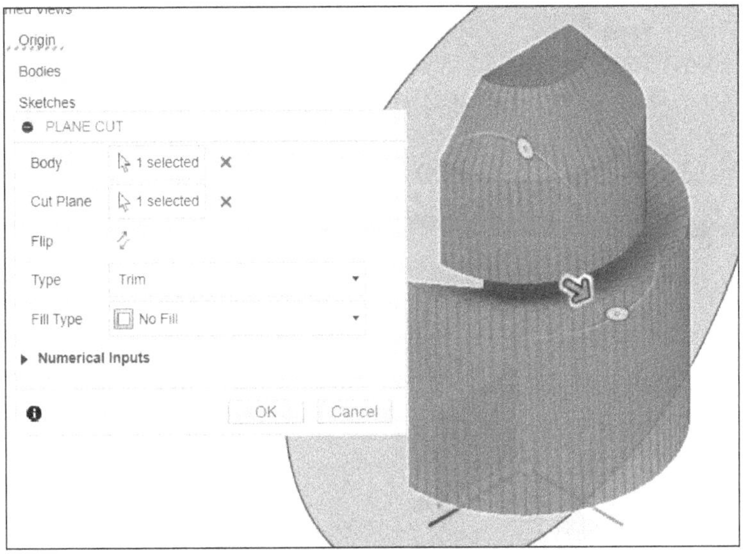

Figure-33. Manipulator displayed on the selected body

- Move the manipulator at desired location to split the body.
- Click on the **Flip** button from **PLANE CUT** dialog box to flip the direction of split.
- Select **Trim** option from **Type** drop-down to split the body into two sides and removes one of the sides.
- Select **Split Body** option from **Type** drop-down to split the body to create two separate mesh body.
- Select **Split Faces** option from **Type** drop-down to split the faces that intersect the plane but keep the body intact. This option will create a new face group on one side of the split.
- Select **No Fill** option from **Fill Type** drop-down if you want to leave open boundary at the cut.
- Select **Uniform** option from **Fill Type** drop-down if you want to fill the hole with new faces of regular shape.
- Select **Minimal** option from **Fill Type** drop-down if you want to fill the hole with minimal number of possible faces.
- Click on the **Numerical Inputs** node from **PLANE CUT** dialog box to manually enter the value of manipulator in respective edit box.
- After specifying the parameters, click on the **OK** button from **PLANE CUT** dialog box to split the model. The model will be displayed; refer to Figure-34.

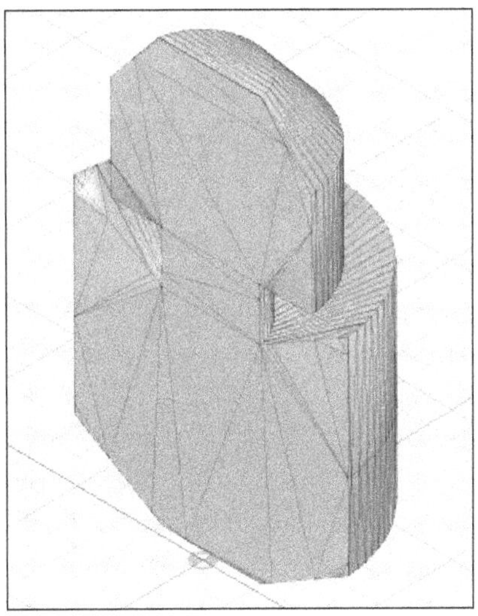

Figure-34. Split model

Shell

The **Shell** tool is used to scoop out material from mesh body and apply thickness. The procedure to use this tool is given next.

- Click on the **Shell** tool from the **MODIFY** drop-down in the **MESH** tab of the **Ribbon**. The **SHELL** dialog box will be displayed; refer to Figure-35 and you will be asked to select the body.

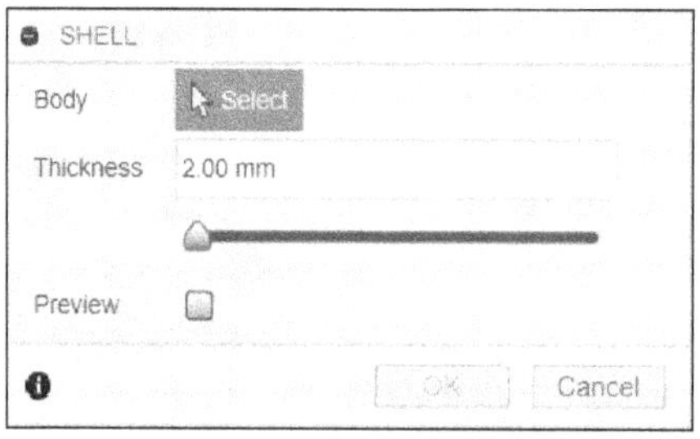

Figure-35. SHELL dialog box

- Select the body from graphics area and set desired thickness of model in the **Thickness** edit box.
- Select the **Preview** check box to check the preview of shell feature while setting parameters.
- Click on the **OK** button from the dialog box to apply shell operation.

Combining Mesh Bodies

The **Combine** tool is used to perform boolean operations on mesh bodies. The procedure to use this tool is given next.

- Click on the **Combine** tool from the **MODIFY** drop-down in the **MESH** tab of the **Ribbon**. The **COMBINE** dialog box will be displayed; refer to Figure-36.

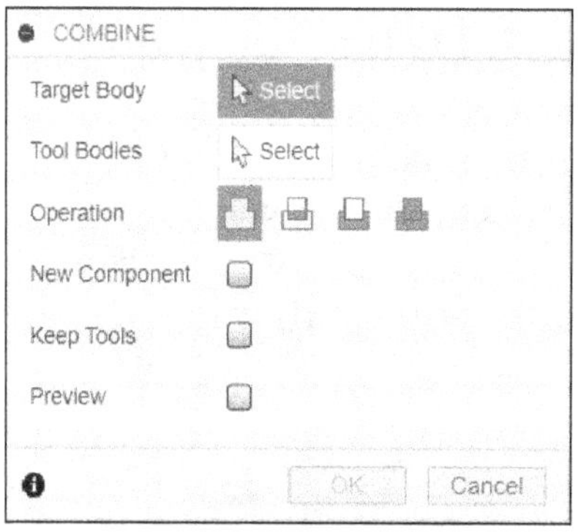

Figure-36. COMBINE dialog box

- Select the target body and then tool bodies from the graphics area; refer to Figure-37.

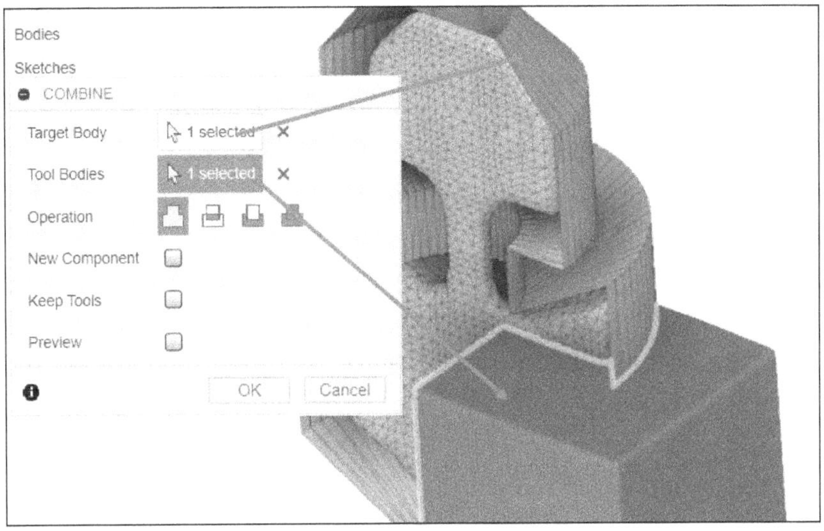

Figure-37. Bodies selected for combining

- Select the **Join** button from **Operation** section in the dialog box to combine bodies into a single mesh body. Select the **Intersect** button from dialog box to create common of two mesh bodies. Select the **Cut** button from dialog box to remove tool bodies from target body. Select the **Merge** button to combine two bodies and remove extra portion of two bodies.
- Select the **New Component** check box to create a new mesh body based on Combine operation.
- Select the **Keep Tools** check box to keep original bodies after performing combine operation.
- Select the **Preview** check box to check preview of combined mesh body while performing modifications.
- After setting desired parameters, click on the **OK** button to perform operation.

Smooth

The **Smooth** tool is used to smooth out uneven regions on the mesh. The procedure to use this tool is discussed next.

- Click on the **Smooth** tool from **MODIFY** drop-down; refer to Figure-38. The **SMOOTH** dialog box will be displayed; refer to Figure-39.

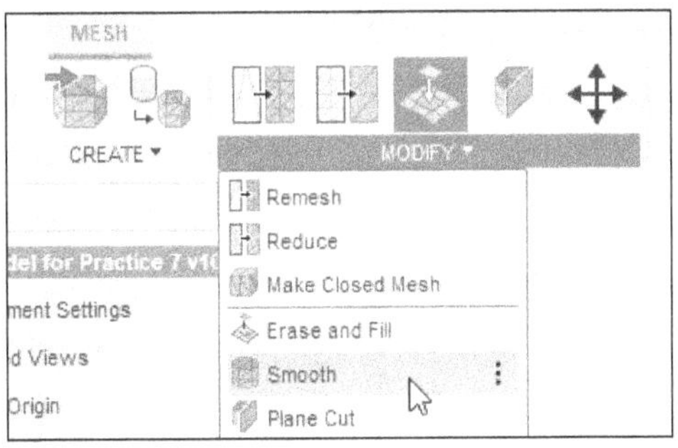

Figure-38. Smooth tool

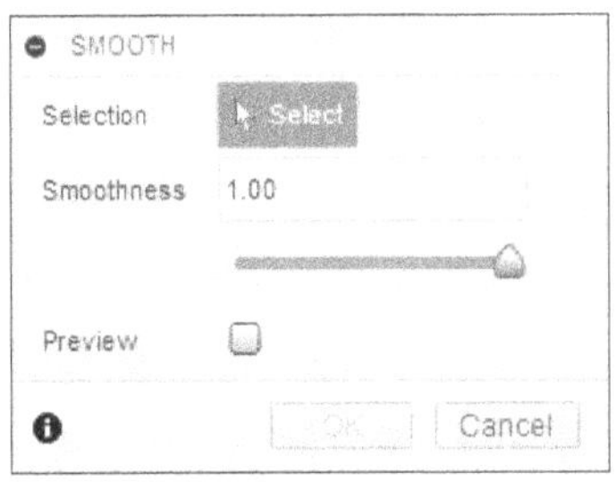

Figure-39. SMOOTH dialog box

- The **Select** button of **Selection** section is active by default. Click on the body to select; refer to Figure-40.

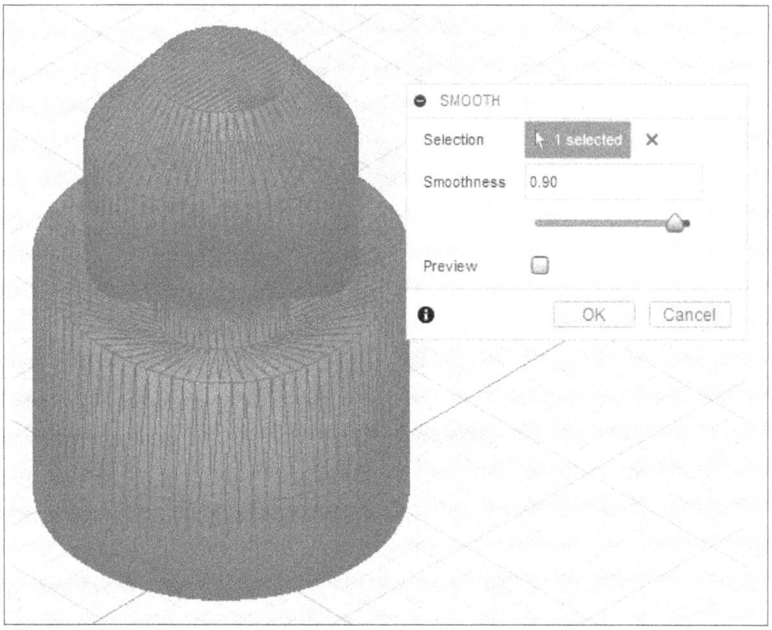

Figure-40. Selecting Mesh body for smooth

- Click in the **Smoothness** edit box and enter desired value for smoothing of mesh body. You can also move the **Smoothness** slider to specify the smoothing value.
- After specifying the parameters, click on the **OK** button from **SMOOTH** dialog box. The mesh body will be displayed; refer to Figure-41.

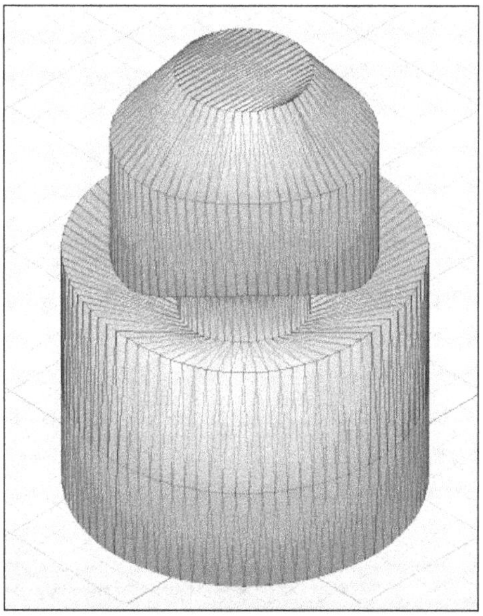

Figure-41. Smoothened mesh body

Reverse Normal

The **Reverse Normal** tool is used to flip the normal direction of the selected face. The procedure to use this tool is discussed next.

- Click on the **Reverse Normal** tool from **MODIFY** drop-down; refer to Figure-42. The **REVERSE NORMAL** dialog box will be displayed; refer to Figure-43.

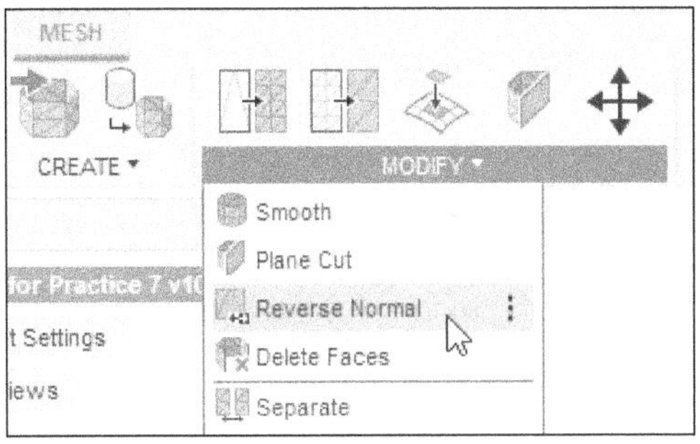

Figure-42. Reverse Normal tool

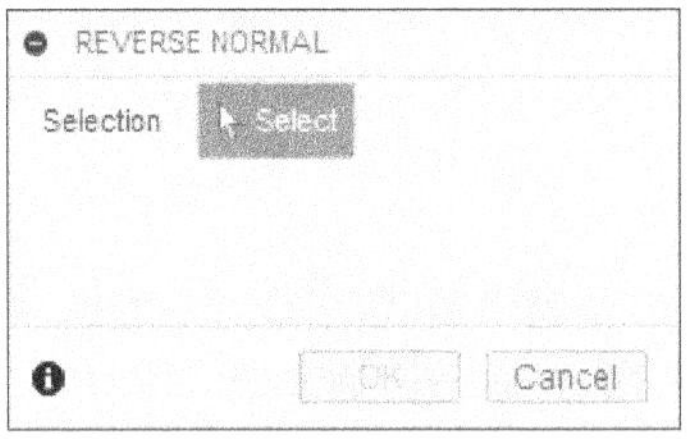

Figure-43. REVERSE NORMAL dialog box

- The **Select** button of **Selection** section is active by default. Click on the face of mesh body to select; refer to Figure-44.

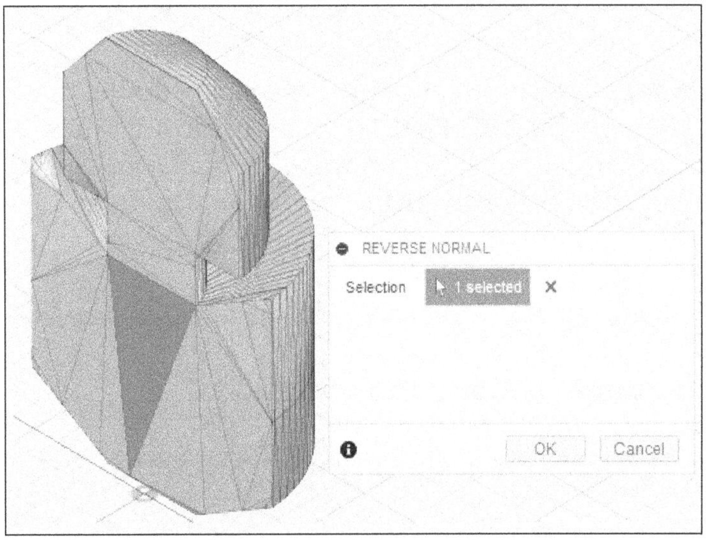

Figure-44. Selecting face for mesh body

- You can also select multiple faces by clicking on them.
- After selecting required faces, click on the **OK** button from **REVERSE NORMAL** dialog box. The normal direction of selected face will be flipped; refer to Figure-45.

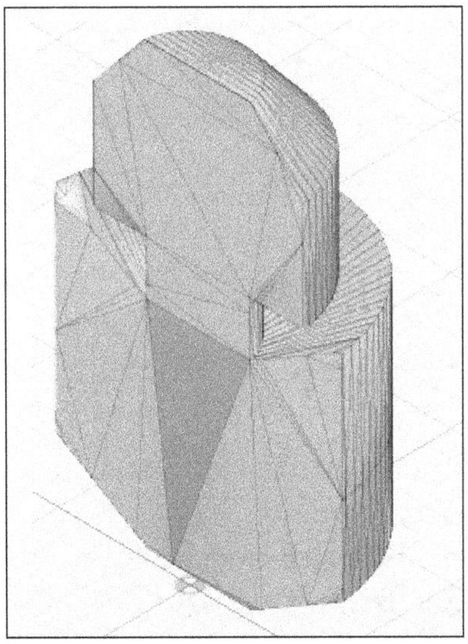

Figure-45. Applied reverse normal on selected face

Separating Mesh into Independent Bodies

The **Separate** tool is used to create mesh bodies using selected regions. The procedure to use this tool is given next.

- Click on the **Separate** tool from **MODIFY** drop-down in the **MESH** tab of the **Ribbon**. The **SEPARATE** dialog box will be displayed; refer to Figure-46.

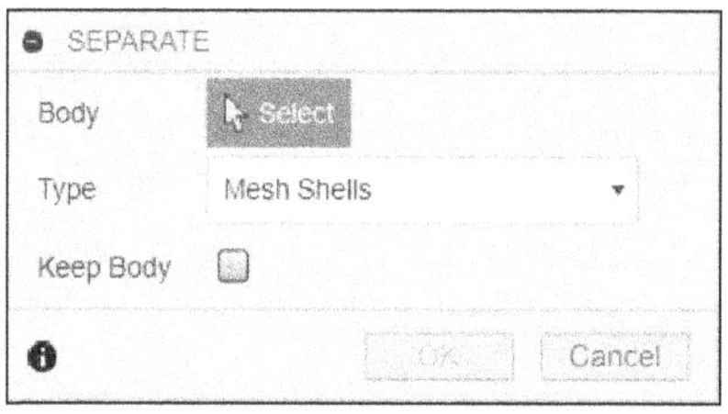

Figure-46. SEPARATE dialog box

- Select the **Mesh Shells** option from the **Type** drop-down to select the mesh shell to be separated. Select the **All Face Groups** option from the **Type** drop-down to select all the face groups to create separate mesh bodies. Select the **Select Face Groups** option from the model to individually select faces for converting them to individual mesh bodies. Select the **Multiple Bodies** check box to create multiple mesh bodies.
- Select the **Keep Body** check box to keep original mesh body after performing operation.
- Click on the **OK** button to perform the operation.

The **Move/Copy** tool in **MODIFY** drop-down works the same way as discussed earlier in the book.

Scaling Mesh

The **Scale Mesh** tool is used to increase/decrease the size of mesh by specified scale factor. The procedure to use this tool is given next.

- Click on the **Scale Mesh** tool from the **MODIFY** drop-down in **MESH** tab of the **Ribbon**. The **SCALE MESH** dialog box will be displayed; refer to Figure-47.

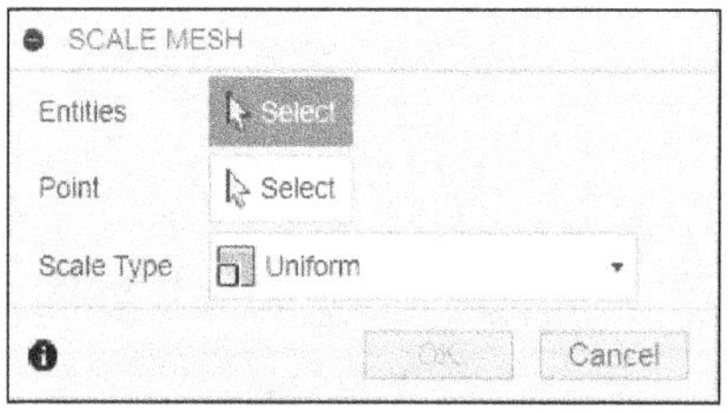

Figure-47. SCALE MESH dialog box

- Select the body at desired location. By default, the centroid of body will be used as reference point for scaling.
- Click on the **Select** button of **Point** section and select desired point to be used as reference for scaling; refer to Figure-48.

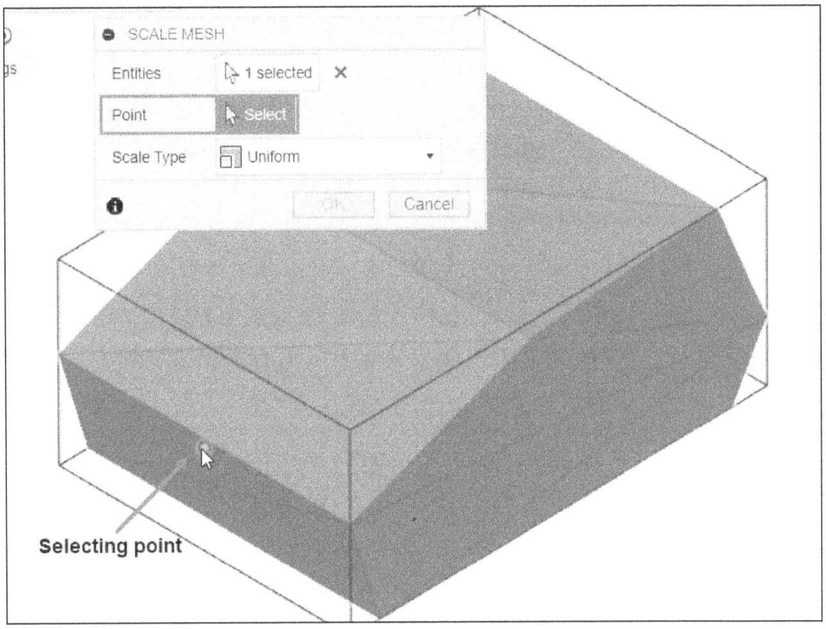

Figure-48. Selecting reference point

- Select the **Uniform** option from the **Scale Type** drop-down to uniformly increase/decrease the size of mesh body in all directions and specify desired scale factor in **Scale Factor** edit box. Specify **2** in edit box to double the size and **0.5** to half the size of mesh body.
- Select the **Non Uniform** option from the **Scale Type** drop-down to specify different scale factors for different directions. On selecting this option, the **X Scale**, **Y Scale**, and **Z Scale** edit boxes will be displayed. Specify desired values in each edit box.
- Click on the **OK** button to apply scaling.

Converting Mesh to Solid

The **Convert Mesh** tool is used to convert selected mesh body to a solid body. The procedure to use this tool is given next.

- Click on the **Convert Mesh** tool from the **MODIFY** drop-down in **MESH** tab of the **Ribbon**. The **CONVERT MESH** dialog box will be displayed; refer to Figure-49.

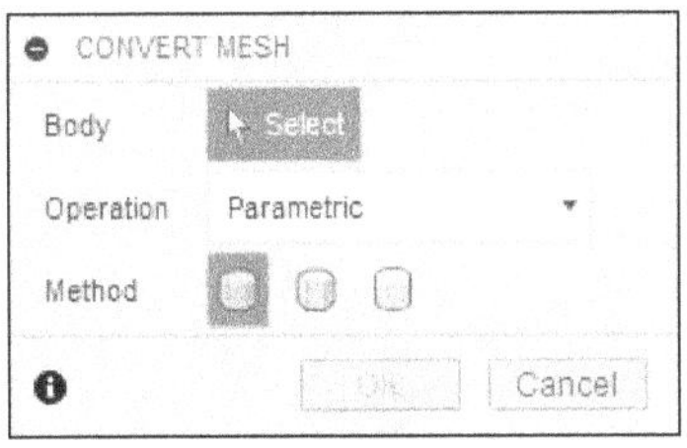

Figure-49. CONVERT MESH dialog box

- Select the mesh body to be converted to solid from graphics area.
- Select the **Parametric** option from **Operation** drop-down if you want to keep parametric relationship of model upstream. It means the history will be kept after converting the model to solid. Select the **Base Feature** option from drop-down to convert the model to a base feature or T-spline solid and model history before the conversion point will be lost.

- Select the **Faceted** button from **Method** section to convert each individual face of mesh to individual face of solid. Select the **Prismatic** button from dialog box to merge faces in same prismatic plane to single face. Select the **Organic** button from dialog box to convert the mesh body to a T-spline form body and open the Form editing environment. Note that the **Organic** option is part of **Product Design Extension** so you need to activate the extension first.
- After setting desired parameters, click on the **OK** button from the dialog box.

DIRECT EDITING MODE

The **Direct Edit** tool is used to modify a mesh body directly without recording changes in parametric history of model. The procedure to use this tool is given next.

- Click on the **Direct Edit** tool from the **MODIFY** drop-down in the **MESH** tab of the **Ribbon**. The **DIRECT EDIT** dialog box will be displayed; refer to Figure-50.

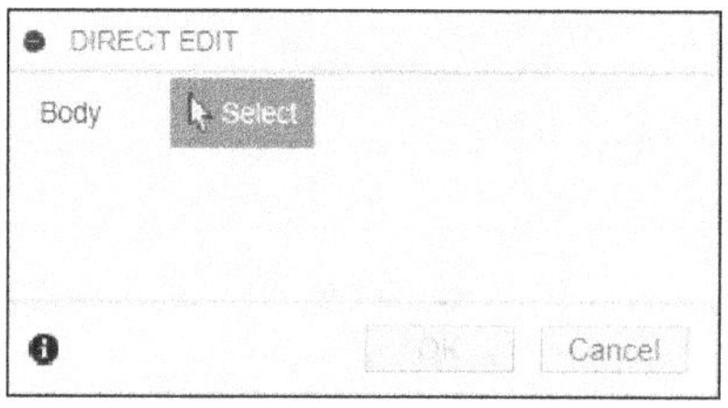

Figure-50. DIRECT EDIT dialog box

- Select the mesh body to be modified and click on the **OK** button from the dialog box. The **DIRECTION MESH EDITING** environment will be activated with **MESH SELECTION PALETTE** dialog box displayed in graphics area; refer to Figure-51.

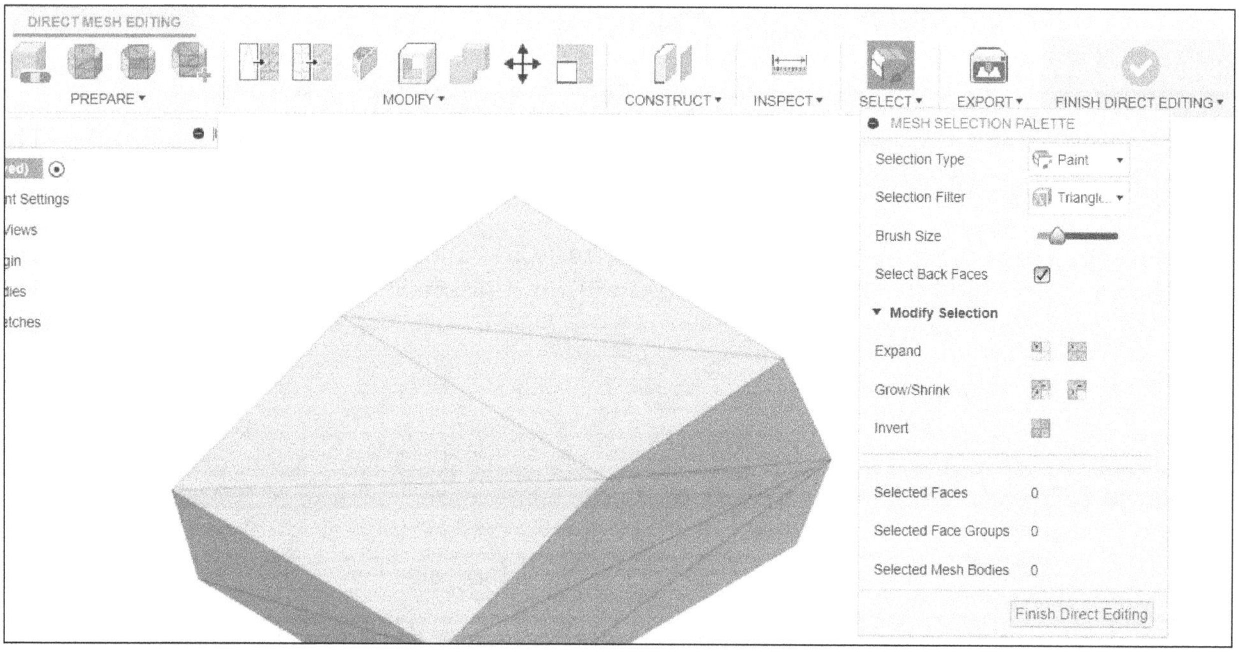

Figure-51. Direct Mesh Editing environment

- Set desired brush size using the **Brush Size** slider in **MESH SELECTION PALETTE** to define the range within which entities will be selected near the cursor when selecting.

- Select the faces of model to be modified and you can perform the direction editing operations as discussed earlier. Most of the operations are same in direct editing as discussed earlier. The tools which are not common are discussed next. After performing direct editing operations, click on the **Finish Direct Editing** tool from the **Ribbon** to exit.

Deleting Faces

- Select the faces of mesh from the graphics area to be deleted and click on the **Delete** tool from **MODIFY** drop-down in **DIRECT MESH EDITING** tab of the **Ribbon**; refer to Figure-52. The faces will be deleted; refer to Figure-53.

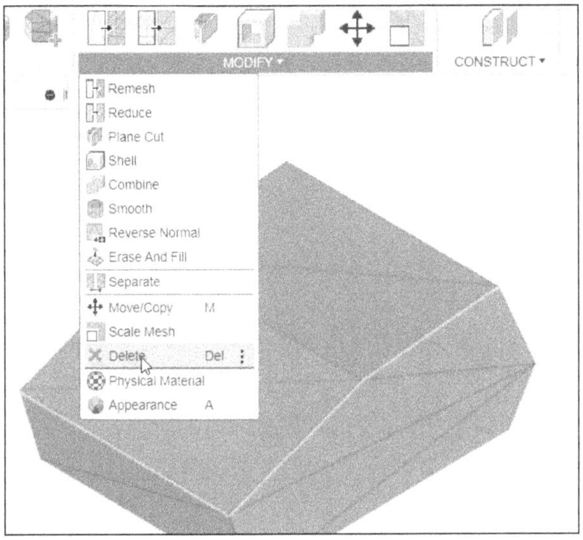

Figure-52. Delete Faces tool

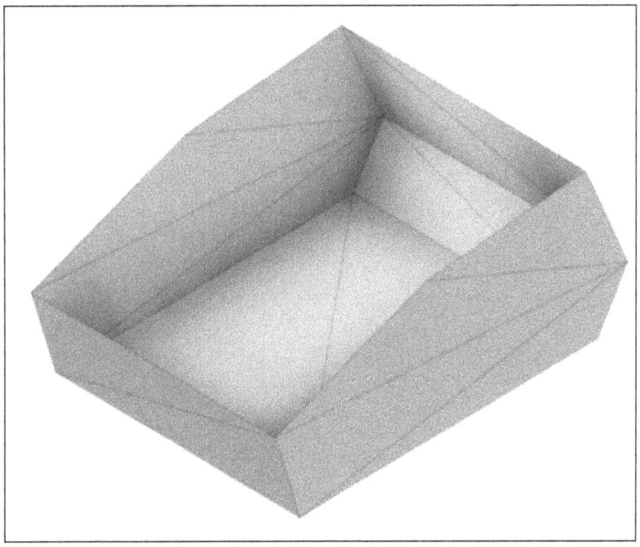

Figure-53. After deleting faces

You can also delete the selected faces by pressing **DELETE** key from keyboard.

Create Face Group

The **Create Face Group** tool is used to create a new face group from selected set of faces. The procedure to use this tool is discussed next.

- Click on the **Create Face Group** tool from **PREPARE** drop-down in **DIRECT MESH EDITING** tab of the **Ribbon**; refer to Figure-54. The **CREATE FACE GROUP** dialog box will be displayed; refer to Figure-55.

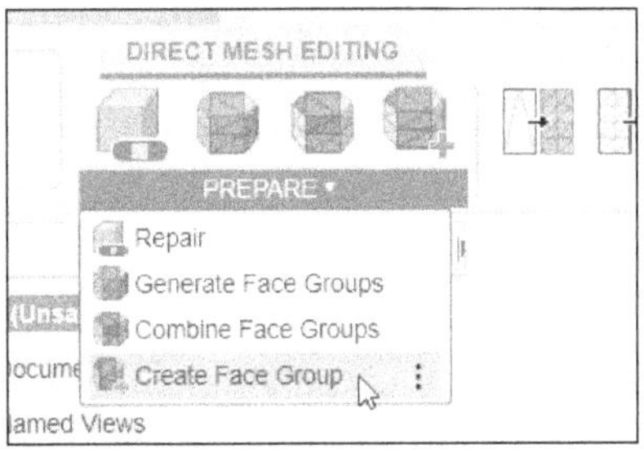

Figure-54. Create Face Group tool

Figure-55. CREATE FACE GROUP dialog box

- The **Select** button of **Faces** section is active by default. Click on desired faces to select; refer to Figure-56.
- After selection of required faces, click on the **OK** button from **CREATE FACE GROUP** dialog box. The created face group will be displayed; refer to Figure-57.

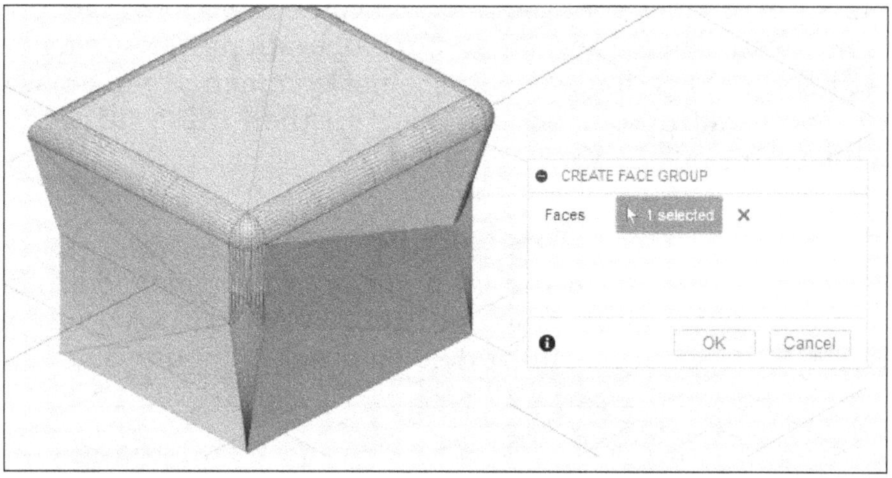

Figure-56. Selection of faces for creating face group

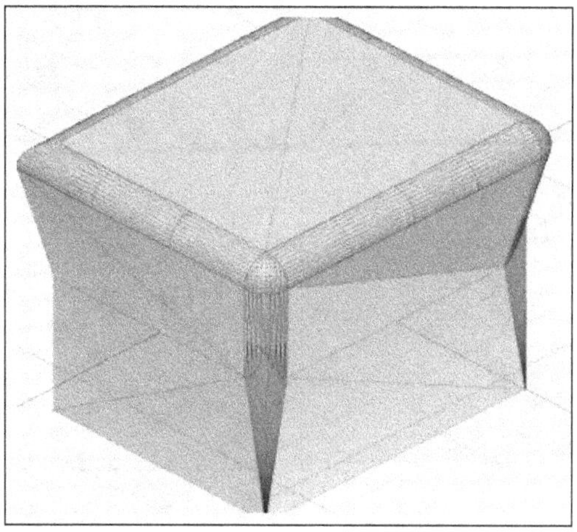

Figure-57. Created face group

Erase and Fill

The **Erase and Fill** tool is used to fill a hole or heal regions or defects on a mesh body. The procedure to use this tool is discussed next.

- Select the boundary of hole/cut in the mesh or select the complete mesh model to be filled or healed; refer to Figure-58.

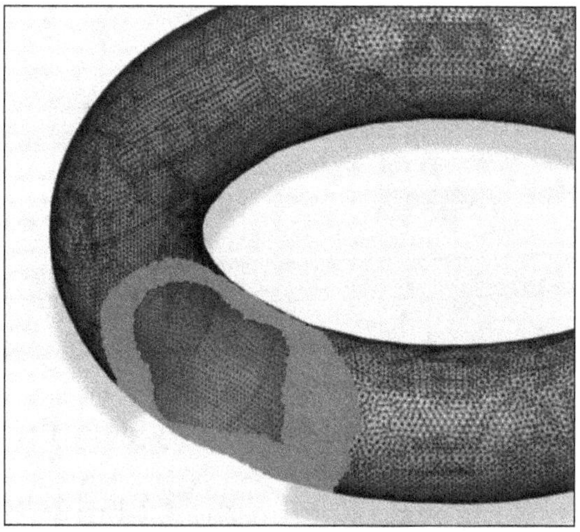

Figure-58. Boundary of cut selected for healing

- Click on the **Erase and Fill** tool from **MODIFY** drop-down in the **Toolbar**; refer to Figure-59. The **ERASE AND FILL** dialog box will be displayed along with preview of fill feature; refer to Figure-60.

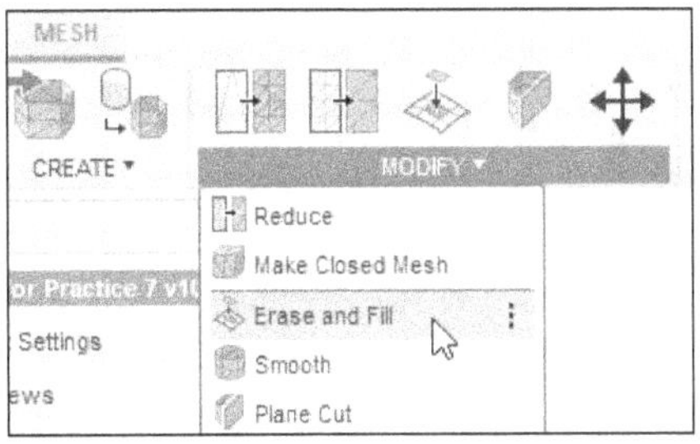

Figure-59. Erase and Fill tool

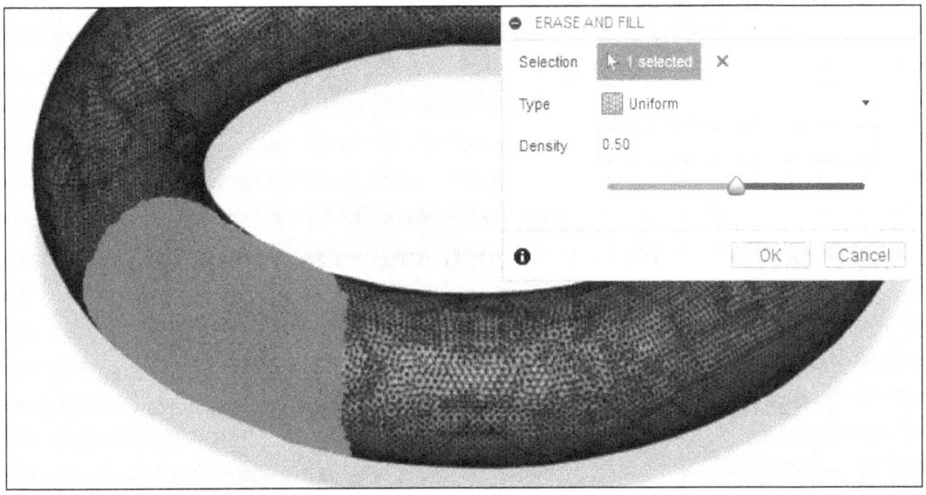

Figure-60. ERASE AND FILL dialog box

- Select **Uniform** option from **Type** drop-down to fill the selected region with regular shaped triangles. This option gives the smoothest and most reliable results.
- Select **Minimal** option from **Type** drop-down to use the minimum number of faces to fill the selected hole.
- (For **Uniform** option) Click in the **Density** edit box and enter desired value. You can also specify the value of density by moving the **Density** slider.
- (For **Smooth** option) Click in the **Scale** edit box and enter the weight mesh after filling. You can also specify the weight by moving the **Scale** slider. Note that weight defines the maximum deviation of new fill face from surrounding faces.
- After specifying the parameters, click on the **OK** button from **ERASE AND FILL** dialog box. The filled hole will be displayed; refer to Figure-61.

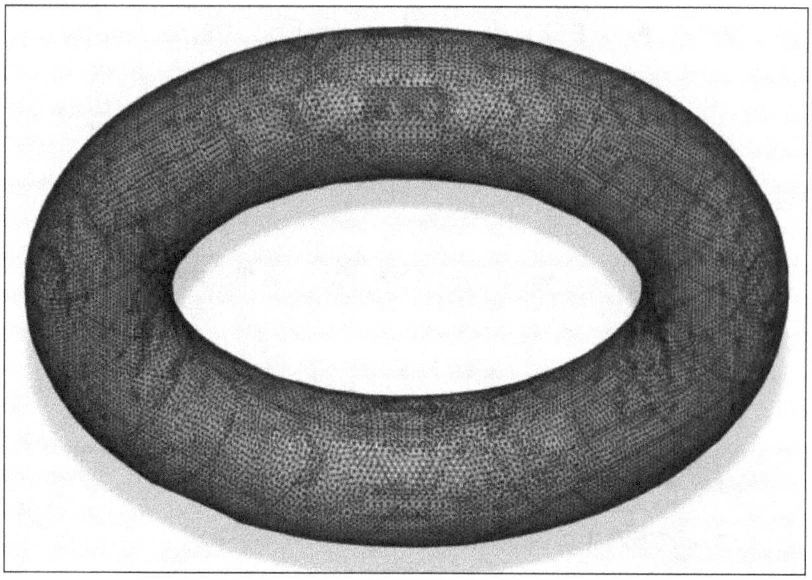

Figure-61. Filled hole

Mesh Align

The **Mesh Align** tool is used to align a mesh face to a plane with one transformation. The procedure to use this tool is discussed next.

- Click on the **Mesh Align** tool from **MODIFY** drop-down in the **Toolbar**; refer to Figure-62. The **MESH ALIGN** dialog box will be displayed; refer to Figure-63.

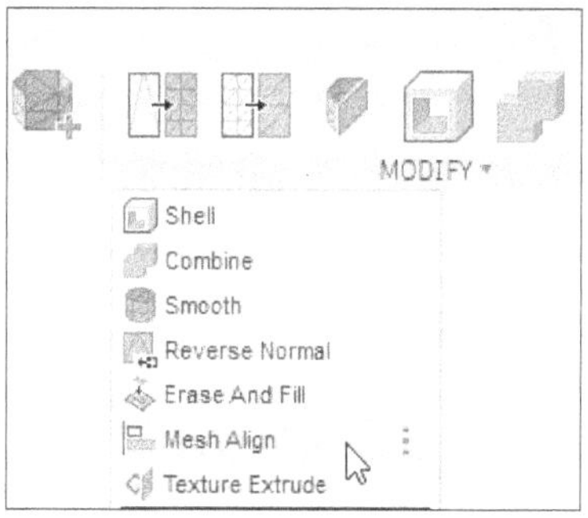

Figure-62. Mesh Align tool

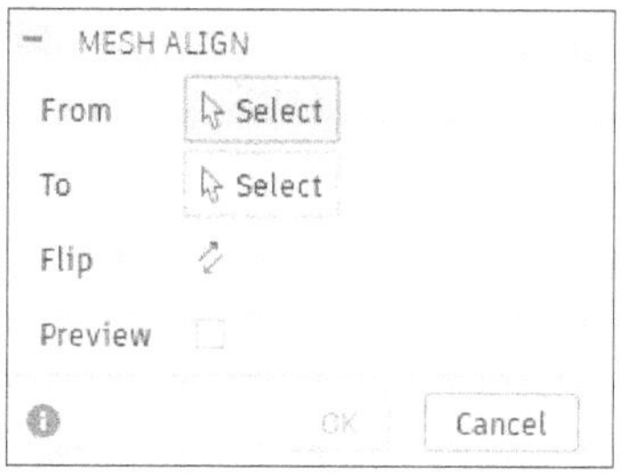

Figure-63. MESH ALIGN dialog box

- The **Select** button of **From** section is active by default. Select desired face on the mesh body to be aligned; refer to Figure-64.

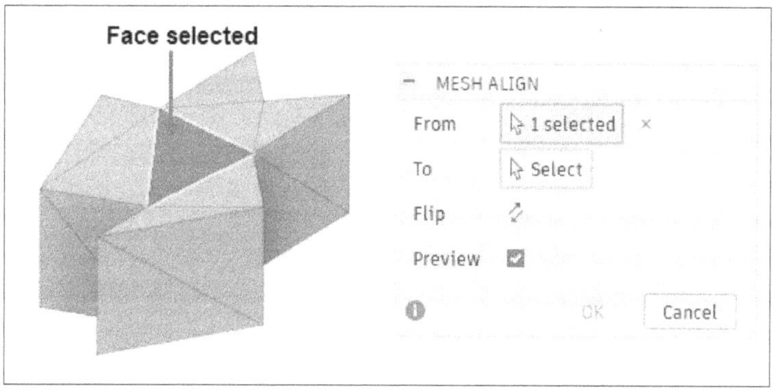

Figure-64. Face selected on mesh body

- Click on the **Select** button of **To** section and select desired plane to which the body to be aligned; refer to Figure-65.

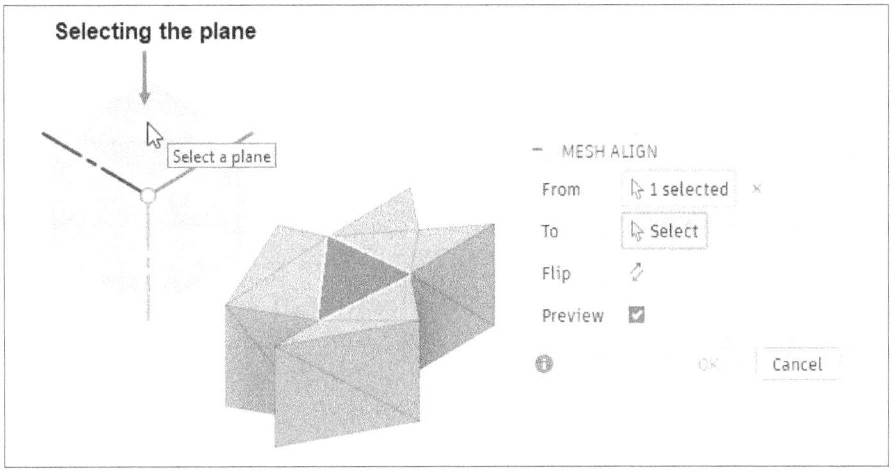

Figure-65. Selecting the plane

- Select the **Flip** button to flip the aligned body.
- Select the **Preview** check box to display the preview of aligned mesh body.
- On selecting the plane, the preview of aligned mesh body will be displayed; refer to Figure-66.

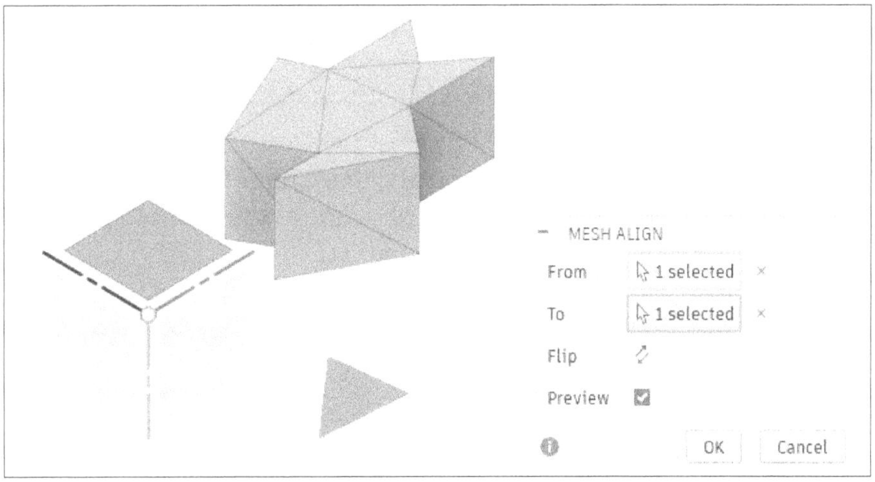

Figure-66. Preview of mesh body alignment

- Click on **OK** button to complete the alignment procedure of mesh body.

Texture Extrude

The **Texture Extrude** tool is used to apply an image as texture on a mesh body in Fusion. This tool is available in commercial version of software. The procedure to use this tool is discussed next.

- Click on the **Texture Extrude** tool from **MODIFY** drop-down in the **Toolbar**; refer to Figure-67. The **TEXTURE EXTRUDE** dialog box will be displayed; refer to Figure-68.

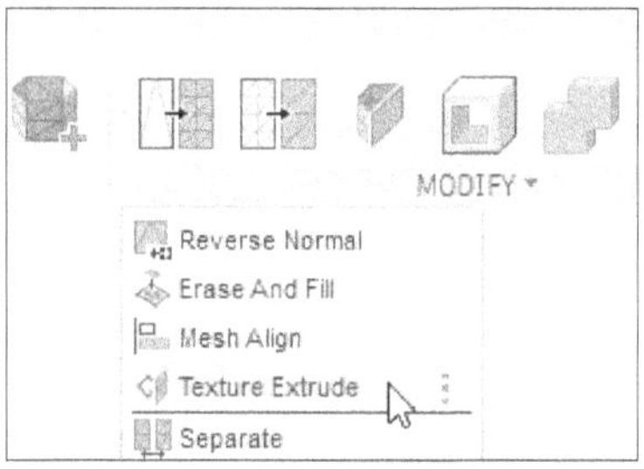

Figure-67. Texture Extrude tool

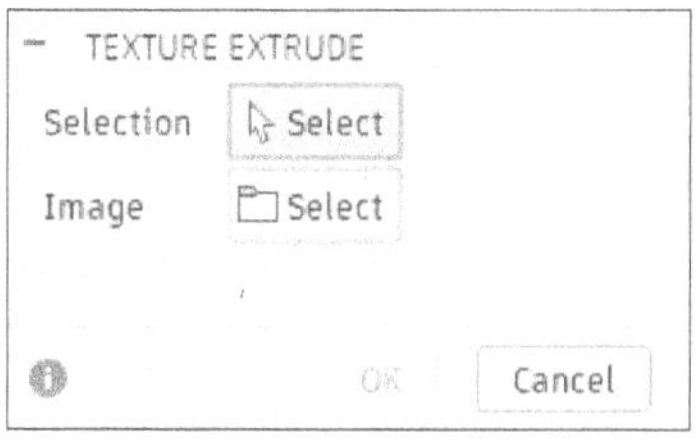

Figure-68. TEXTURE EXTRUDE dialog box

- The **Select** button of **Selection** section is active by default. Select desired mesh body or faces on which the texture is to be added; refer to Figure-69.

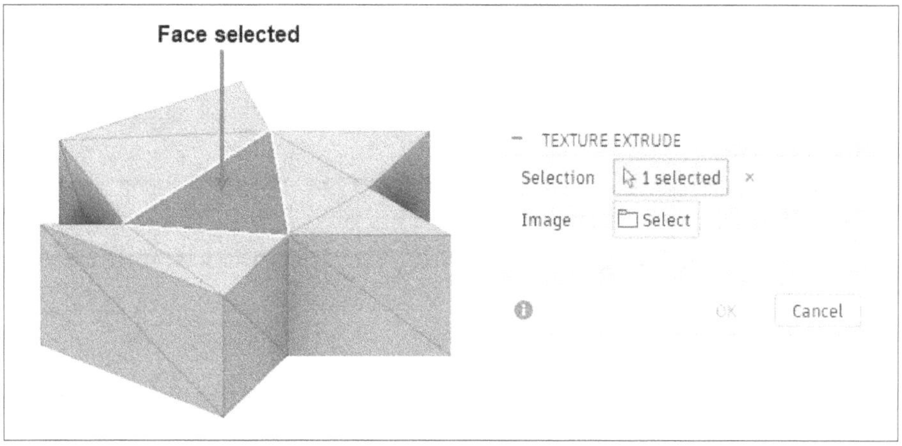

Figure-69. Face selected for texture extrude

- Click on the **Select** button of **Image** section, the **Insert** dialog box will be displayed to insert the image as discussed earlier. The image will be inserted and the updated dialog box will be displayed; refer to Figure-70.

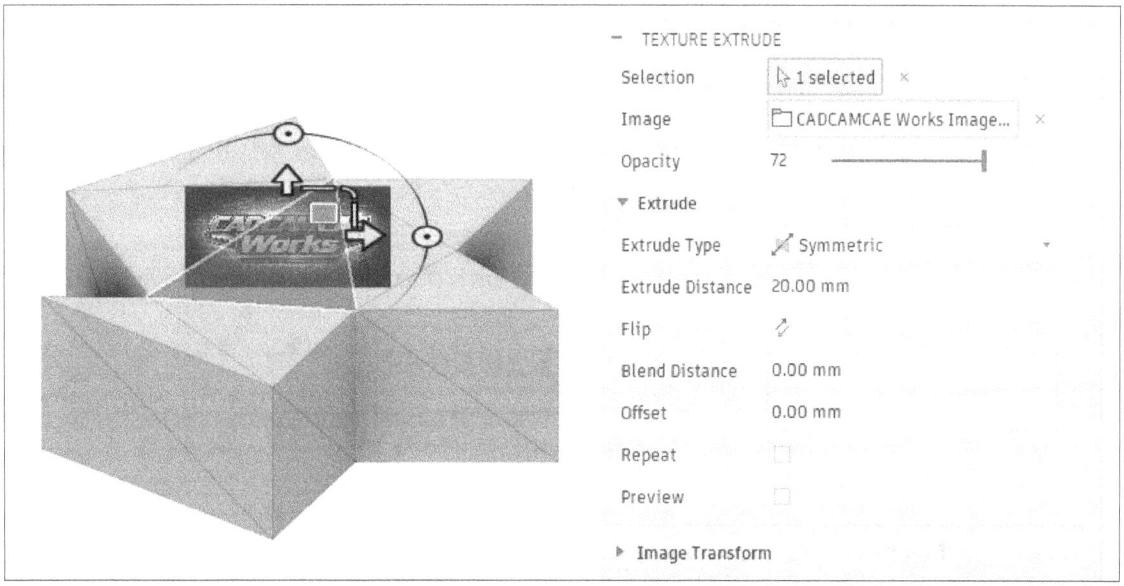

Figure-70. Image inserted with updated dialog box

- Set desired opacity of the image in the **Opacity** edit box or by using the slider.
- The options in **Extrude** and **Image Transform** rollouts have been discussed earlier.
- After specifying desired parameters, click on **OK** button from the dialog box. The surface texture will be added to the mesh body.

PRACTICAL

Create the mesh model as shown in Figure-71.

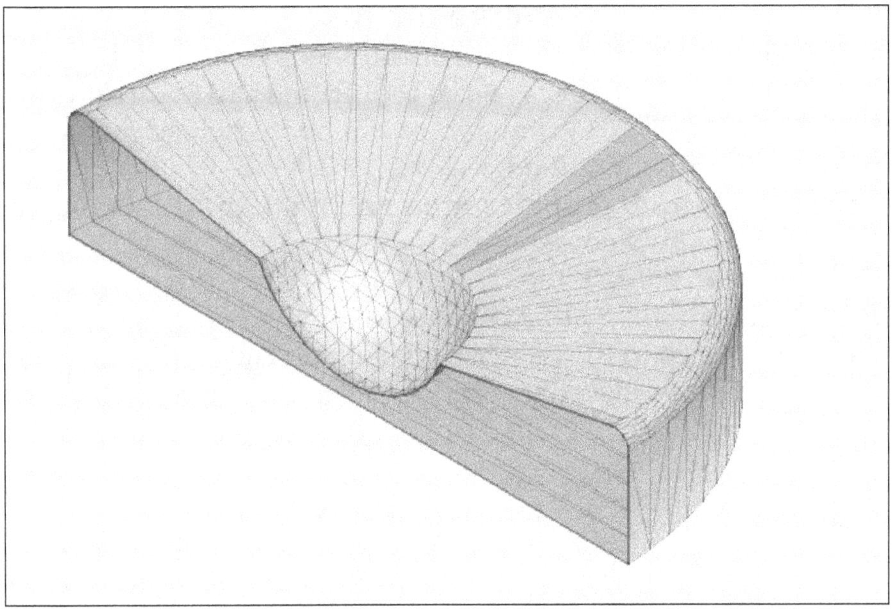

Figure-71. Final model

Converting model into mesh

Before modifying the mesh file, you need to convert the model into mesh file.

- Create or open the model of this practical in the **MODEL Workspace**. The file is available in the resource kit of this book.
- Click on the **Tessellate** tool from **CREATE** drop-down in **MESH** tab of **Ribbon**. The **TESSELLATE** dialog box will be displayed.
- The **Select** button of **Body** section is active by default. Select the model to convert it into mesh model and set the parameters to low refinement as shown in Figure-72.

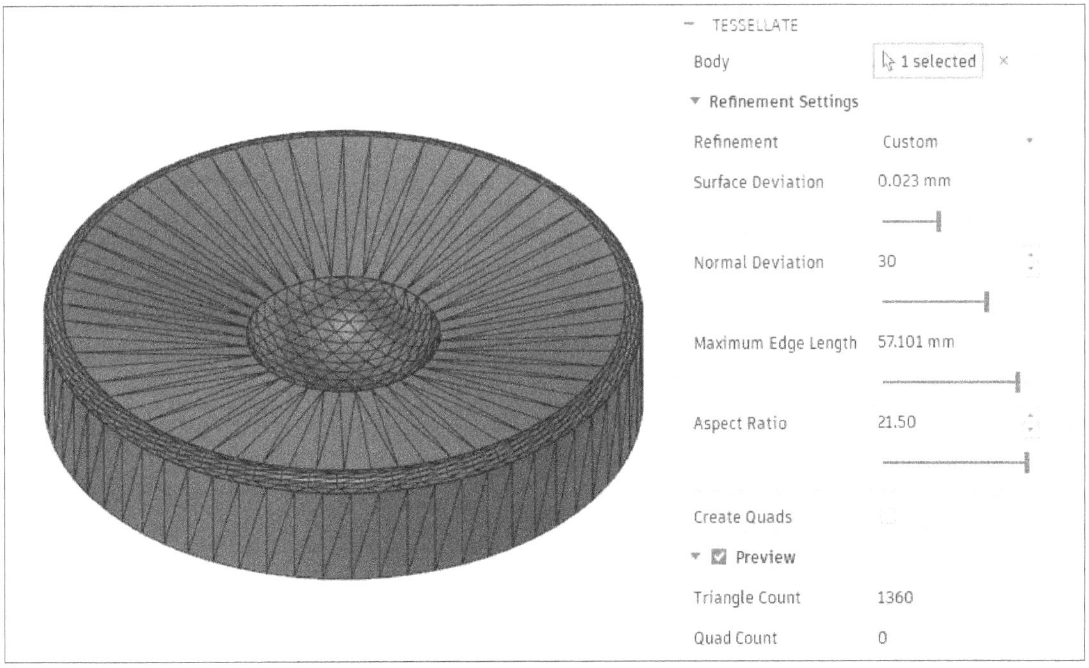

Figure-72. Specifying parameters for creating mesh file

- After specifying the parameters, click on the **OK** button from **BREP TO MESH** dialog box. The mesh body will be created and displayed on the **MESH** workspace.

Reverse the face

- The options to reverse normals of individual faces are available in Direct Editing environment. Click on the **Direct Edit** tool from **MODIFY** drop-down in the **MESH** tab of **Ribbon**. The **DIRECT EDIT** dialog box will be displayed and you will be asked to select mesh body to be modified.
- Select the mesh body from graphics area and click on the **OK** button. The direct editing environment will become active.
- Click on the **Reverse Normal** tool from **MODIFY** drop-down in the **Toolbar**. The **REVERSE NORMAL** dialog box will be displayed.
- Select the faces as shown in Figure-73 and click on the **OK** button. The selected face will be reversed. You can also use window selection for selecting multiple faces.

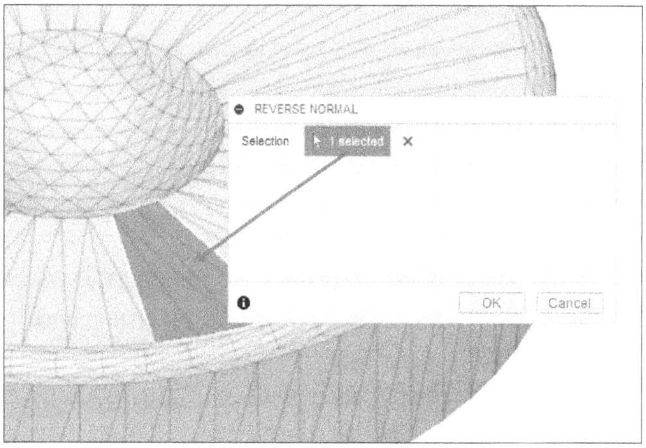

Figure-73. Selection for reverse normal

Plane Cut

- Click on the **Plane Cut** tool from **MODIFY** drop-down in the **Toolbar**. The **PLANE CUT** dialog box will be displayed.
- The **Select** button of **Body** section is active by default. You need to select the model for plane cut. Click on the model to select.
- Click on the **Select** button of **Cut Plane** section and select the **YZ** plane to cut the body; refer to Figure-74.

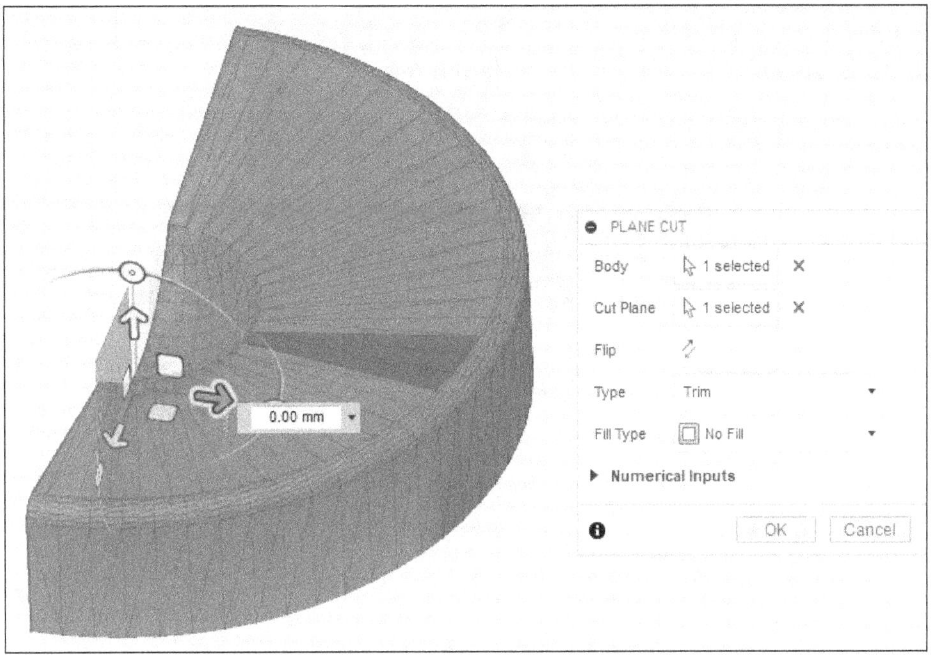

Figure-74. Selecting plane for plane cut

- Specify the parameters as shown in above figure and click on the **OK** button from **PLANE CUT** dialog box.
- After following all the steps discussed above, the model will be displayed as shown in Figure-75.

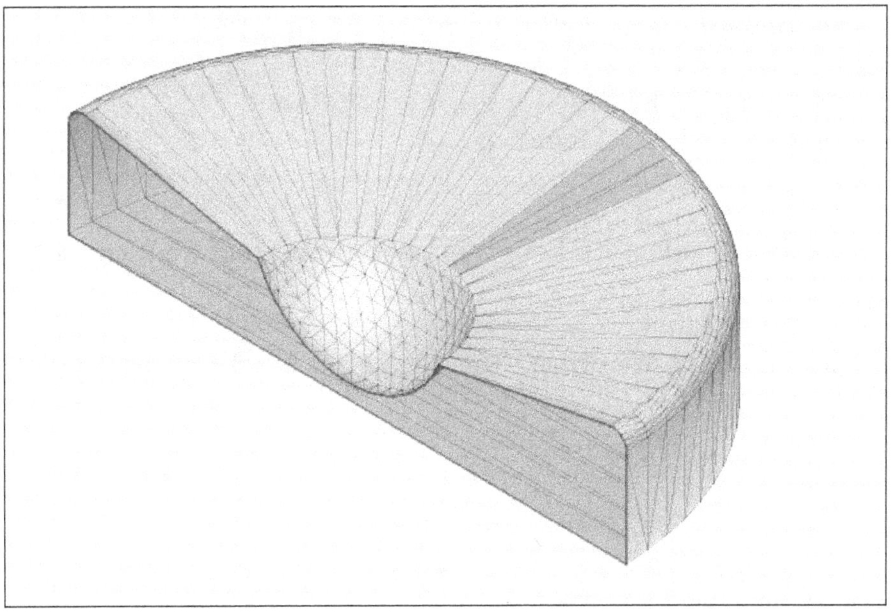
Figure-75. Final model

PRACTICE

Create the model as displayed in the Figure-76.

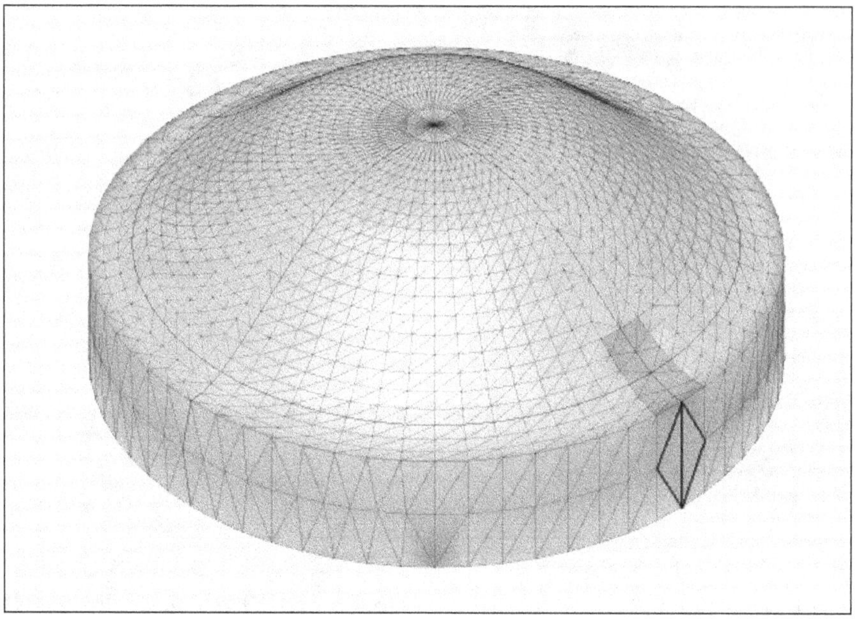

Figure-76. Practice 1

SELF ASSESSMENT

Q1. Which of the following are included in a mesh model?

a. Vertices
b. Edges
c. Faces
d. Surfaces
e. Hole features
f. Sketches

Q2. In Mesh workspace, selection brush is used instead of window selection to select elements. (T/F)

Q3. Which of the following is not an object created by BRep method?

a. Sheetmetal model
b. Surface model
c. Solid model
d. Mesh model

Q4. In Autodesk Fusion, mesh model is combination of only triangulated faces. (T/F)

Q5. Which of the following tool is used to automatically fill all the holes and cuts in the selected mesh body?

a. Erase and Fill
b. Make Closed Mesh
c. Reduce
d. Remesh

Q6. Where can the tools to create mesh objects be found in the DESIGN workspace?

A. PREPARE tab of Ribbon
B. MESH tab of Ribbon
C. MODIFY tab of Ribbon
D. ANALYZE tab of Ribbon

Q7. What type of files can be inserted using the Insert Mesh tool?

A. .OBJ and .STL
B. .CAD and .STEP
C. .BRep and .IGES
D. .FBX and .3DS

Q8. Which button allows you to modify the orientation of a mesh model when using the Insert Mesh tool?

A. Select from my computer
B. Orientation Handles
C. Rotate
D. Modify

Q9. What is the purpose of the Tessellate tool in the MESH workspace?

A. To insert a mesh file
B. To convert a solid body into a mesh body
C. To repair errors in a mesh body
D. To create mesh section sketches

Q10. Which option in the Tessellate tool allows you to manually set the refinement of the mesh?

A. High
B. Medium
C. Custom
D. Low

Q11. What does the Create Mesh Section Sketch tool generate?

A. A new mesh feature
B. A boundary sketch of the mesh body intersecting a plane
C. A repaired version of the mesh body
D. A tessellated mesh body

Q12. What does the Create Base Mesh Feature tool create?

A. An empty mesh feature
B. A detailed analysis of the mesh
C. A solid model
D. A refined mesh

Q13. What is the function of the Repair tool in the MESH workspace?

A. To refine triangular faces of the mesh
B. To insert a mesh body
C. To perform operations like stitching, closing holes, and wrapping
D. To combine multiple face groups

Q14. Which Repair option in the MESH workspace preserves sharp edges during rebuilding?

A. Fast
B. Preserve Sharp Edges
C. Accurate
D. Blocky

Q15. What does the Generate Face Groups tool do?

A. Combines face groups into one
B. Creates new face groups based on normal angles
C. Converts solid bodies into mesh bodies
D. Repairs errors in face groups

Q16. What does the Remesh tool refine?

A. Tolerances of mesh bodies
B. Selected mesh faces or bodies to form regular triangular faces
C. Density of triangular faces
D. Shape preservation of the mesh body

Q17. What does the Reduce tool do to the mesh?

A. Combines multiple face groups
B. Reduces the number of faces while maintaining shape
C. Creates new sections in the mesh body
D. Repairs internal errors in the mesh

Q18. Which Type option in the Reduce tool is used to merge faces within maximum deviation?

A. Proportion
B. Face Count
C. Adaptive
D. Tolerance

Q19. What is the function of the Plane Cut tool in the MODIFY drop-down?

A. Combines two or more face groups
B. Splits the selected mesh body using a plane
C. Reduces the number of mesh faces
D. Repairs triangular faces

Q20. What is the primary purpose of the Shell tool in a mesh body?

A. To combine mesh bodies
B. To apply thickness and scoop out material
C. To convert mesh to solid
D. To smooth out uneven regions

Q21. Which check box should you select to keep the original bodies after performing a Combine operation?

A. Preview
B. Keep Tools
C. New Component
D. Multiple Bodies

Q22. What does the Smoothness slider control in the Smooth tool?

A. Mesh size
B. Degree of smoothing
C. Brush size
D. Scale factor

Q23. What is the Reverse Normal tool used for?

A. Converting mesh to solid
B. Smoothing uneven regions
C. Flipping the normal direction of selected faces
D. Scaling mesh bodies

Q24. What does the Select Face Groups option in the Separate tool allow you to do?

A. Create separate mesh bodies from all face groups
B. Select specific faces to convert into individual mesh bodies
C. Apply uniform scaling
D. Preview combined bodies

Q25. Which option in the Scale Mesh tool uniformly scales the mesh in all directions?

A. Non Uniform
B. Parametric
C. Uniform
D. Prismatic

Q26. What is required to activate the Organic option in the Convert Mesh tool?

A. Use of the Erase and Fill tool
B. Activation of the Product Design Extension
C. Enabling the Direct Edit mode
D. Selecting the Uniform option

Q27. What does the Brush Size slider in the Direct Edit tool define?

A. Degree of smoothing
B. Range of selected entities near the cursor
C. Scale factor for scaling mesh
D. Density of the erased area

Q28. Which tool is used to create a new face group from selected faces?

A. Separate
B. Create Face Group
C. Erase and Fill
D. Shell

Q29. Which option in the Erase and Fill tool uses the minimum number of faces to fill the selected hole?

A. Smooth
B. Uniform
C. Minimal
D. Scale

Q30. Which tool is used to convert a model into a mesh file?

A. Tessellate
B. Plane Cut
C. Direct Edit
D. Reverse Normal

Q31. What is the final step in performing a Plane Cut operation?

A. Selecting the Cut Plane section
B. Specifying the YZ plane
C. Clicking OK from the PLANE CUT dialog box
D. Activating the Direct Edit environment

Q32. What is the default reference point for scaling when using the Scale Mesh tool?

A. The origin of the model
B. The centroid of the body
C. The YZ plane
D. A manually selected point

Q33. Which scale type allows you to specify different scaling factors for X, Y, and Z directions?

A. Uniform
B. Non Uniform
C. Prismatic
D. Organic

Q34. What happens when you select the Parametric option in the Convert Mesh tool?

A. The model's history is discarded
B. The mesh is converted into a T-spline solid
C. The parametric relationship of the model is preserved
D. The faces are merged into a single face

Q35. Which option in the Convert Mesh tool is part of the Product Design Extension?

A. Faceted
B. Prismatic
C. Organic
D. Base Feature

Q36. In the Direct Edit mode, what is the primary purpose of the Brush Size slider?

A. To set the smoothing level
B. To define the density of the erased region
C. To control the range of entity selection near the cursor
D. To specify scale factors for scaling operations

Q37. What is the main purpose of the Plane Cut tool?

A. To smooth out uneven mesh regions
B. To create separate mesh bodies
C. To cut the body along a specified plane
D. To scale the mesh uniformly

Q38. What does the Density slider in the Erase and Fill tool control?

A. The size of the smoothed region
B. The weight of the mesh after filling
C. The number of triangles used to fill the hole
D. The scaling factor for X, Y, and Z directions

Q39. What is the primary function of the Create Face Group tool?

A. To delete unwanted faces
B. To merge multiple face groups
C. To group selected faces into a new face group
D. To fill holes in a mesh body

Q40. What is the purpose of the Tessellate tool?

A. To scale the mesh body
B. To convert a model into a mesh file
C. To reverse the normals of selected faces
D. To delete selected faces

For Student Notes

Chapter 15

Manufacturing

Topics Covered

The major topics covered in this chapter are:

- ***New Setup***
- ***Milling Machine Setup***
- ***Turning Machine Setup***
- ***Milling and Turning Tools***
- ***Creating new Mill and Turning tool***

INTRODUCTION

CAM stands for Computer Aided Manufacturing. CAM is a mode where you can convert the 3D model into a machine readable program codes used for the manufacturing process (usually G code). Some of the common manufacturing processes that are studied under CAM are Milling, Turning, Drilling, and Laser Cutting. In the CAM workspace of Autodesk Fusion, you will be able to generate high-quality toolpaths within minutes. Depending on the Fusion version, you can create high quality 2D, 3D, 5-Axis milling, and turning toolpaths for high speed machining (HSM). You can also generate toolpaths for laser cutting machines and additive manufacturing.

STARTING WITH MANUFACTURE WORKSPACE

The tools in **MANUFACTURE** workspace are used to generate toolpaths for all types of manufacturing processes. The procedure to start **MANUFACTURE** workspace is discussed next.

- Click on the **MANUFACTURE** option from the **Change Workspace** drop-down while in any workspace; refer to Figure-1. The **MANUFACTURE** workspace will be displayed; refer to Figure-2.

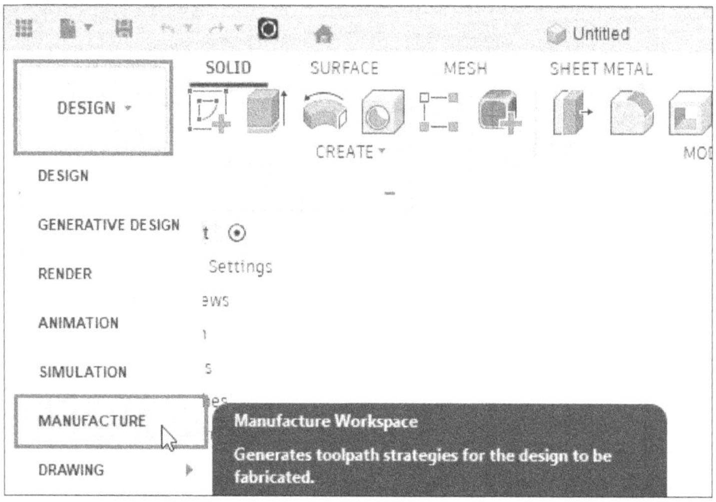

Figure-1. MANUFACTURE workspace option

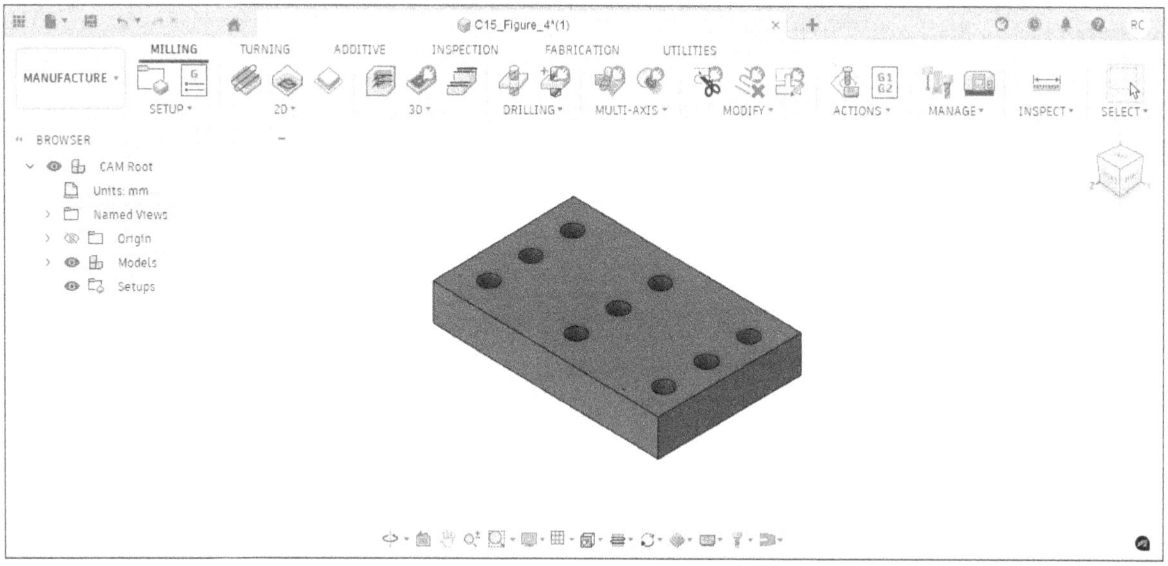

Figure-2. MANUFACTURE Workspace

JOB SETUP

In this section, we will discuss the procedure of setting up the work piece and create the required material stock for machining process. Job setup lets you define your stock for machining and machine type to be used like Milling or Turning. Stock is the workpiece (piece of raw material) from which the final product will be produced after machining. The shape and size of stock depends upon the final model which is to be created by machining.

New Setup

Before starting any machining project, you need to define a job setup to tell Autodesk Fusion that the toolpaths will be generated for Milling machine, Turning machine, or any other supported machine. You also need to set zero location to be used as machining coordinates origin. A machining coordinate origin acts as 0,0,0 coordinate for defining other locations of the part. This location is manually set in the CNC machines by moving cutting tool to desired location. You can also define any fixture component for machining. A fixture is generally used to hold the workpiece in desired orientation. The procedure to setup the workpiece is discussed next.

- Click on the **Setup** tool from **SETUP** drop-down; refer to Figure-3. The **SETUP** dialog box will be displayed along with the workpiece; refer to Figure-4.

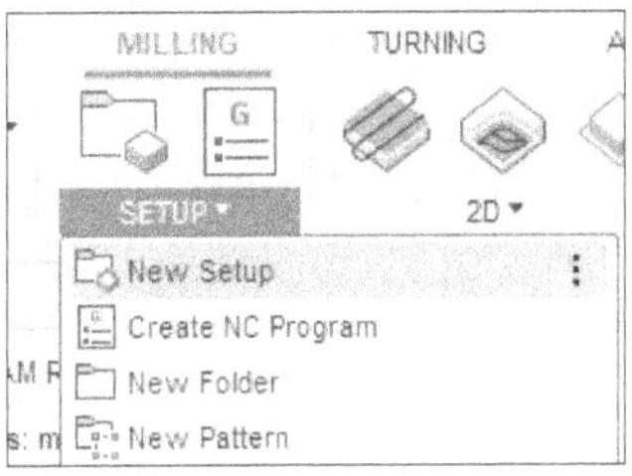

Figure-3. New Setup tool

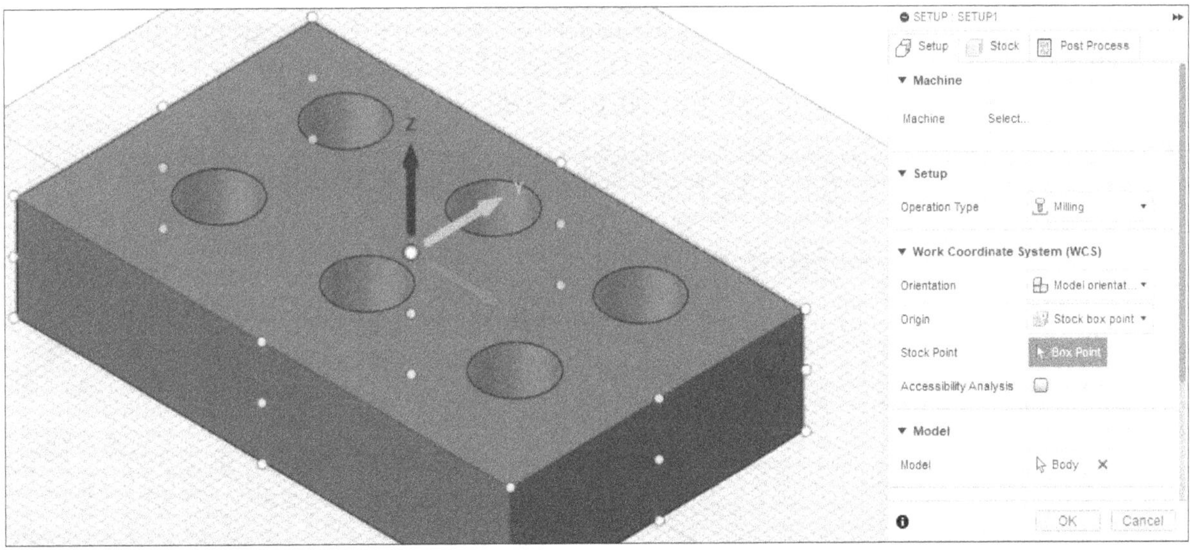

Figure-4. SETUP dialog box

Setting a Milling Machine

The options in **Machine** node of **SETUP** dialog box deals with set up of machines. Depending on your requirement, you can select a machine or you can add a new entry of your machine in dialog box. First we will discuss the procedure of setting a milling machine and later, we will discuss the procedure of setting a turning machine.

Setup

- Click on the **Select** button in the **Machine** section of the dialog box to select predefined machine or specify machine related parameters. The **Machine Library** dialog box will be displayed; refer to Figure-5.

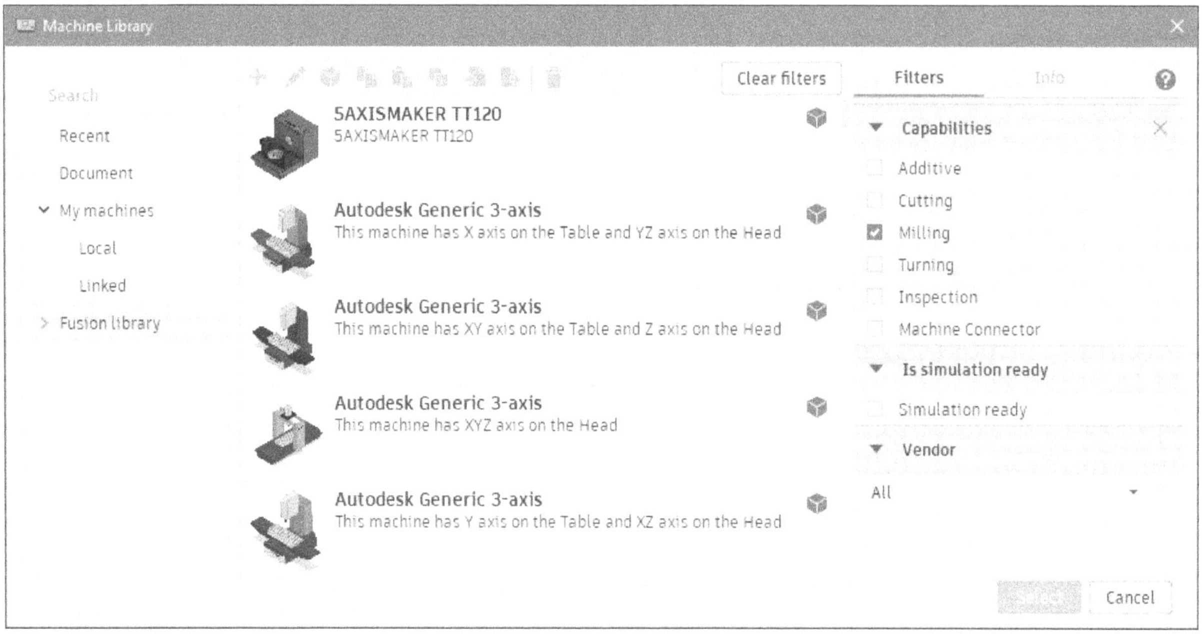

Figure-5. Machine Library dialog box

- Select desired check box(es) from the **Capabilities** node in the right of dialog box to define which type of machine you want to use. By default, the **Milling** check box is selected so predefined set of milling machines is displayed.
- Select the **Simulation ready** check box to display only those machines which have prototype model of machine for performing real-time simulation of machining.
- If you want to search desired machine using name of vendor (maker of machine) then select desired manufacturer from drop-down in the **Vendor** node.
- Select desired machine from the dialog box. The information about machine will be displayed in the **Info** tab of dialog box; refer to Figure-6.

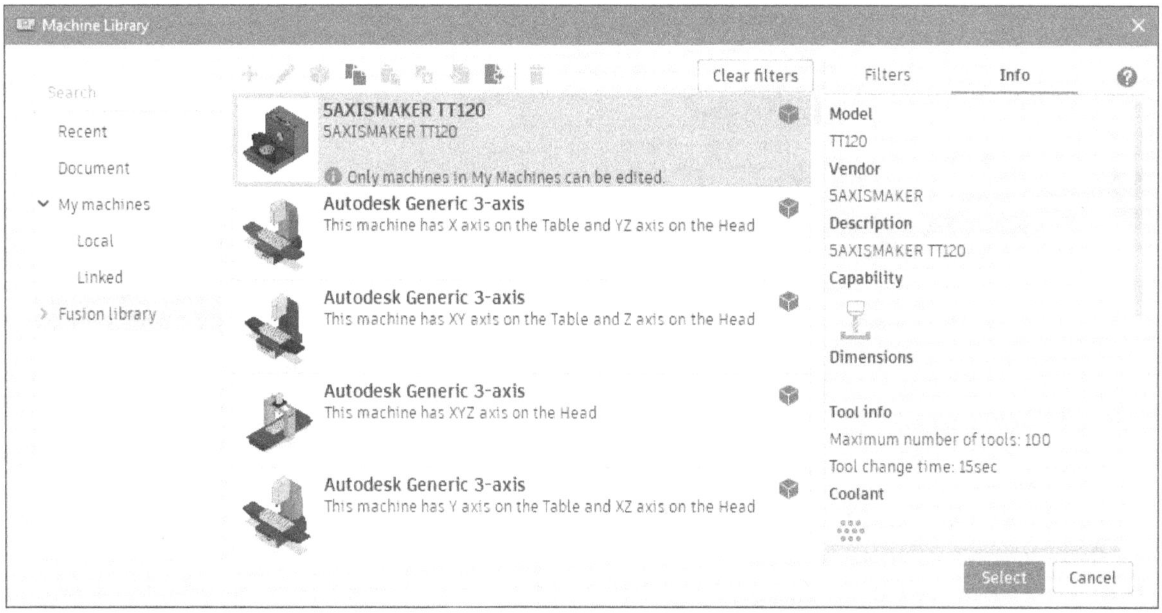

Figure-6. Info about machine

- Select the machine from list and click on the **Select** button. If you are using the machine for first time and it is not available in your local drive then **Download Machine Model** dialog box will be displayed; refer to Figure-7. Click on the **Download Model** button and save the file in desired location. The **Install Machine Connector** dialog box will be displayed if available for your CNC machine and you will be asked to install machine connector. (We have selected **HAAS VR-9** machine, in our case). Machine connector allows to connect with machine directly. Click on the Yes button if you want to run connector. Set desired location to download files and save it. The **Machine Tool Connector** dialog box will be displayed; refer to Figure-8.

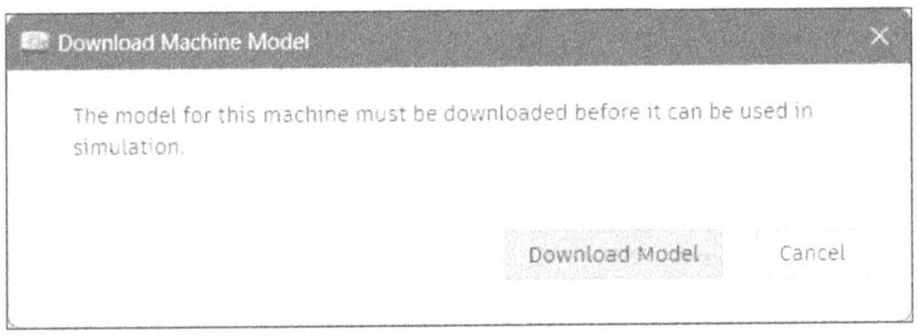

Figure-7. Download Machine Model dialog box

Figure-8. Machine Tool Connector dialog box

- You can edit a machine if it is available in the **Local** section of **My machines** node in the **Machine Library** dialog box. If you want to edit the machine then select it from **My machines** category and click on the **Select** button from the dialog box and then click on the **Edit** button from the **Machine** section of **SETUP** dialog box to modify the parameters of the selected machine. The **Machine Definition** dialog box will be displayed; refer to Figure-9. Note that you can only modify machine definitions which are created by user. You cannot modify machine definitions predefined by Autodesk.

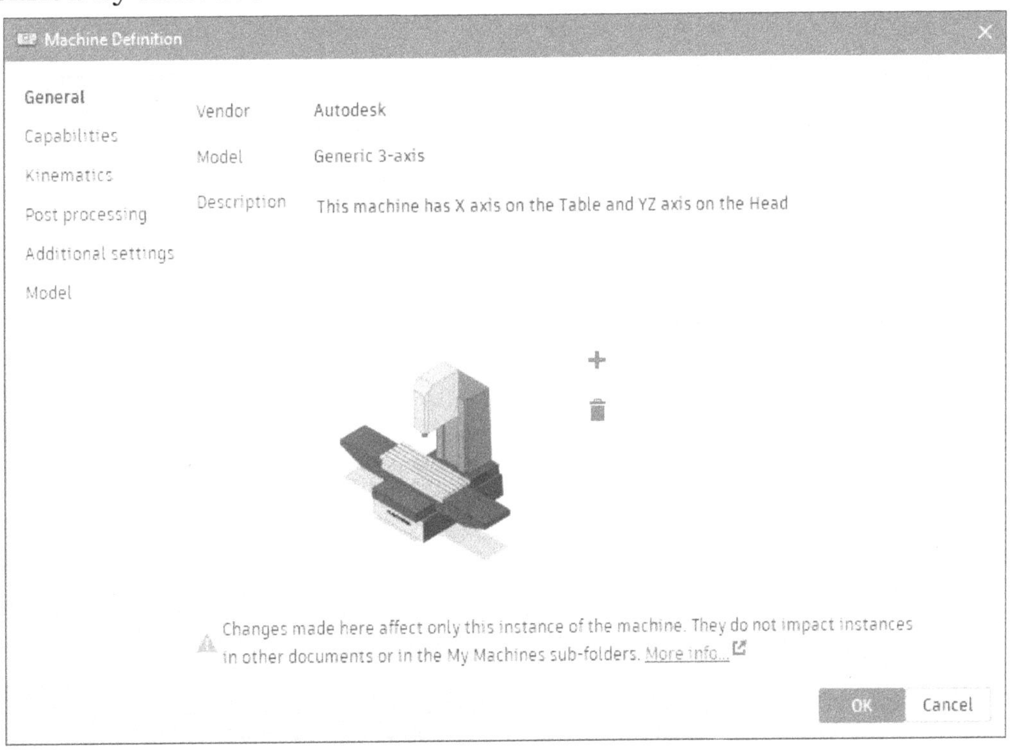

Figure-9. Machine Definition dialog box

- To create a user defined machine definition, select **Local** option from **My machines** node in the **Machine Library** dialog box. The **Create new** button will be activated in the top area of the dialog box. Click on the button, a list box will be displayed to define the type of machine to be created; refer to Figure-10. Select desired option from the list. In our case, we have selected **Milling** option. On doing so, the **Machine Definition** dialog box will be displayed. Various options of this dialog box are discussed next.

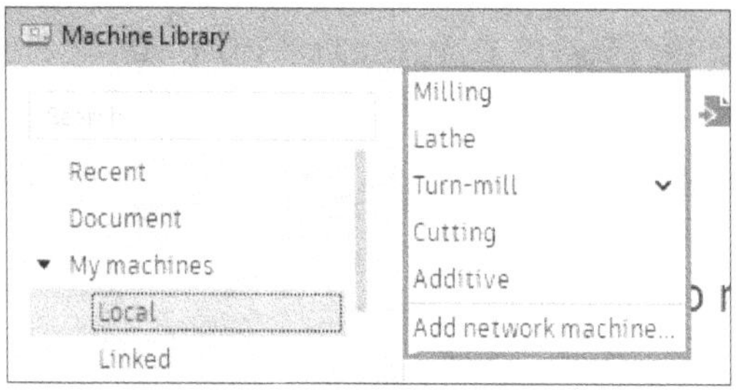

Figure-10. List for new machine types

General Parameters

- Specify name of manufacturer, model name, description of machine, and thumbnails of the machine in respective sections of the dialog box.

Capabilities Parameters

- Click on the **Capabilities** option from left area in the **Machine Definition** dialog box to define the capabilities of selected machine. The options will be displayed as shown in Figure-11.

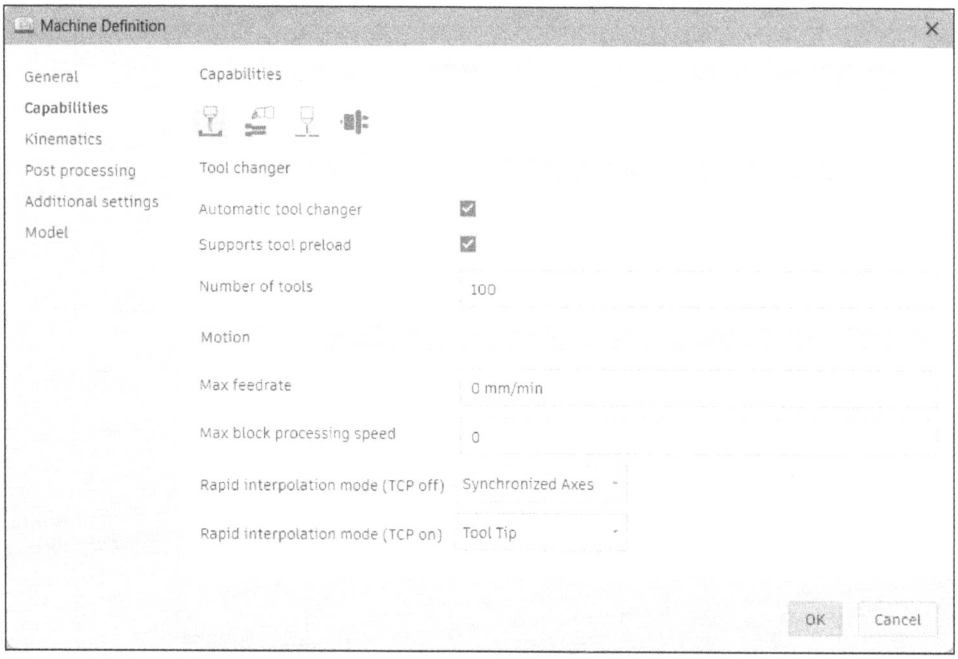

Figure-11. Capabilities page

- Select desired buttons from the **Capabilities** section to define whether your machine is capable of performing milling, turning, cutting, and machine connector operations.
- Select the **Automatic tool changer** check box if your machine supports automatic change of tool. If there is no automatic changer in your machine then you should keep this check box clear.

- Select the **Supports tool preload** check box if your machine supports staging function for tool changer.
- Specify the maximum number of tools that can be installed in your machine in the **Number of tools** edit box.
- Specify desired value in the **Max feedrate** edit box to define the maximum linear speed at which cutting tool can move while performing cutting operation.
- Specify the maximum number of blocks that can be executed per second by machine in the **Max block processing speed** edit box.

Kinematics Parameters

- Select the **Kinematics** option from the left area in the dialog box. The options will be displayed as shown in Figure-12.

Figure-12. Kinematics option

- You can drag the components of machines in the tree on this page to define their position in the machine. For example, if your machine supports motion along X and Y axes using table while your tool head can move along Z axis then your tree should display as shown in Figure-13.

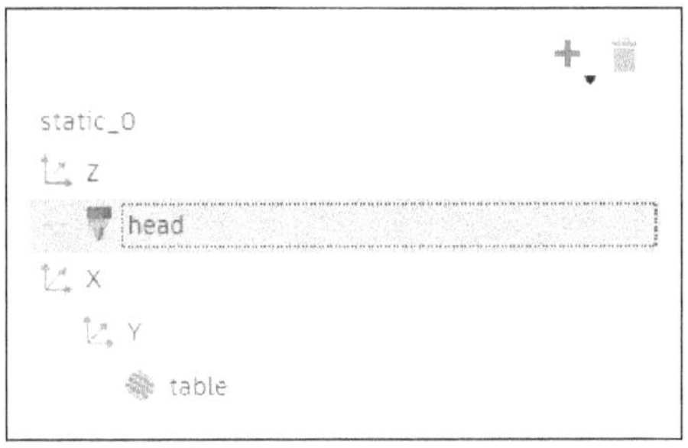

Figure-13. Tree for machine

- Click on the **Add part** button to add a new component to the machine.
- Select the component from tree to define related parameters like for X, Y, and Z axes, you can define limits of motion.

Post Processing Parameters

- Click on the **Post processing** option from the left area to define post processor being used for generating cnc program. The options will be displayed as shown in Figure-14.

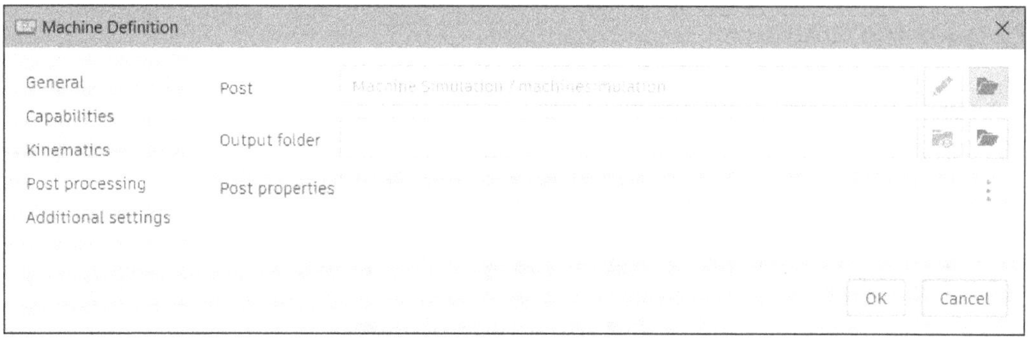

Figure-14. Post processing options

- Click on the **Open** button next to **Post** edit box for selecting a new post processor for the machine. The **Post Library** dialog box will be displayed; refer to Figure-15. Select desired post processor from the list and click on the **Select** button. The **Copy post processor to My Posts?** dialog box will be displayed. Set desired location to locally save the post processor file.

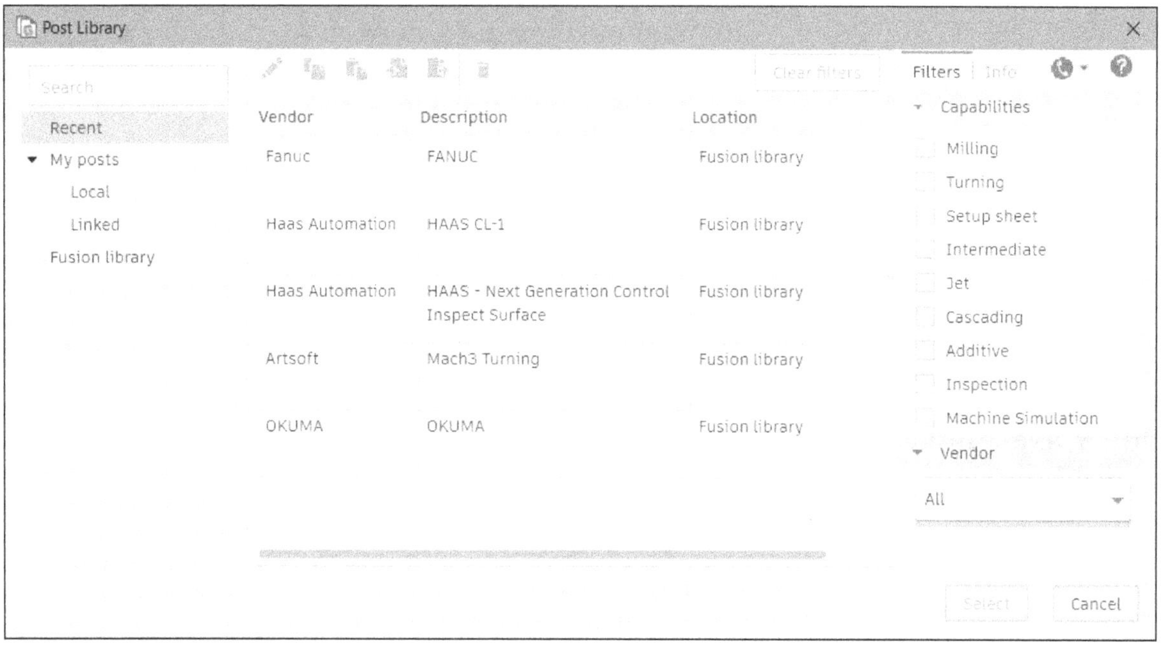

Figure-15. Post Library dialog box

- Click on the **Open** button next to **Output folder** edit box for defining the location where you can save the output of post processor.

Additional Settings Parameters

- Select the **Additional settings** option from the left area to define advanced parameters like tool change time and feedrate ratio for operations.
- Click on the **OK** button from the **Machine Definition** dialog box. After setting machine definition, click on the **Select** button from **Machine Library** dialog box to select desired machine.

Note: The options of **Machine Configuration** dialog box have been discussed later in this book.

Operation Type

- Select the **Milling** option from the **Operation Type** drop-down in **Setup** section of **Setup** tab in the **SETUP** dialog box for setting up a milling operation. Note that if you have not defined machine then you need to select desired option from **Operation Type** drop-down but if you have selected a machine in the **Machine** section of the dialog box then this option will be selected automatically in the **Operation Type** drop-down based on type of the machine.

Setting Work Coordinate System

- Select **Model Orientation** option in **Orientation** section from **Work Coordinate System (WCS)** to set the orientation of coordinate system based on key points of workpiece for machining.
- Select the **Select Z axis/plane & X axis** option from the **Orientation** section of **Work Coordinate System (WCS)** node to select the Z axis and X axis for setting the orientation of workpiece; refer to Figure-16. The updated **WCS** section will be displayed along with axis or face selection on part; refer to Figure-17. By default, **Z Axis** selection button is active and you are asked to select a reference to define direction of Z axis. Select desired face or edge. You will be asked to select direction reference for X axis. Select desired face or edge. If you want to flip direction of axes then select the **Flip Z Axis** and/or **Flip X Axis** check boxes.

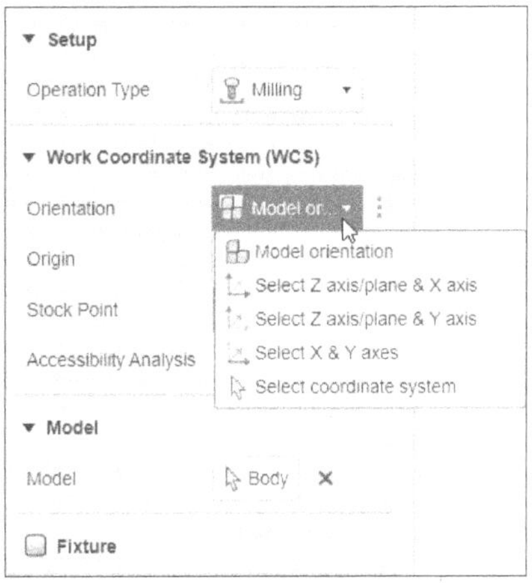

Figure-16. Orientation

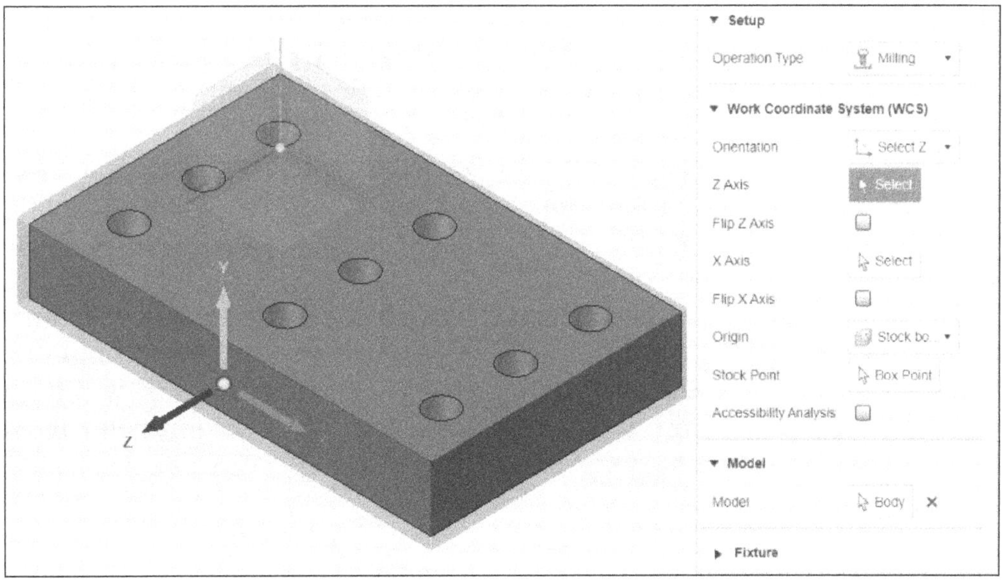

Figure-17. Updated WCS section of dialog box

- Select the **Select Z axis/plane & Y axis** option from the **Orientation** section of the **Work Coordinate System (WCS)** node to select references for defining orientation of Z axis and Y axis of WCS (Work Coordinate System). Click on the **Z Axis** button from **Work Coordinate System (WCS)** section and click on desired axis or plane from **Origin** node in the **Browser** to define the Z axis. The Z axis should be perpendicular to machining plane. Select the **Flip Z Axis** check box to flip the selected direction of Z axis at 180 degree. The **X Axis** button is active by default. Click on the axis or plane to define the X axis; refer to Figure-18. The X axis will be defined perpendicular to the selected plane. Select the **Flip X Axis** check box to flip the selected direction of X axis at 180 degree.

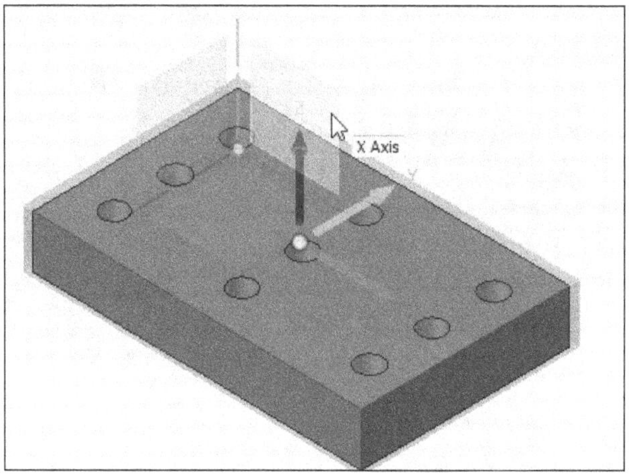

Figure-18. Defining X axis

- Select the **Select X & Y axes** option from the **Orientation** section of **Work Coordinate System (WCS)** node to select references for defining orientation of X axis and Y axis of WCS. Select desired faces or edges as discussed earlier.
- Select the **Select Coordinate System** option from **Orientation** section of **Work Coordinate System (WCS)** node to use a user defined coordinate system in the model to set the orientation of WCS.
- Select **Model Origin** option from the **Origin** drop-down of the **Work Coordinate System (WCS)** node to use World Coordinate System (WCS) origin of the current model as Work Coordinate System origin. Note that this drop-down is not available when the **Select coordinate system** option is selected in the **Orientation** drop-down of the dialog box.
- Select the **Selected point** option from the **Origin** drop-down to select a vertex or key point of model for defining WCS origin. Click on desired vertex or key point of an edge to define WCS origin.
- Select the **Model box point** option of the **Origin** drop-down from **Work Coordinate System (WCS)** section to define a point for WCS origin by selecting a point on the model bounding box. The **Model Point** selection button for **Stock Point** section is active by default. Click at desired box point of model to define WCS origin.
- Select the **Stock box point** option of the **Origin** drop-down from the **Work Coordinate System (WCS)** section to define WCS origin by selecting a point on the stock bounding box. The **Stock Point** button of **Origin** section will be activated. Click on the stock point from workpiece to define WCS origin; refer to Figure-19.
- Select the **Accessibility Analysis** check box to also perform accessibility analysis to check for undercuts.

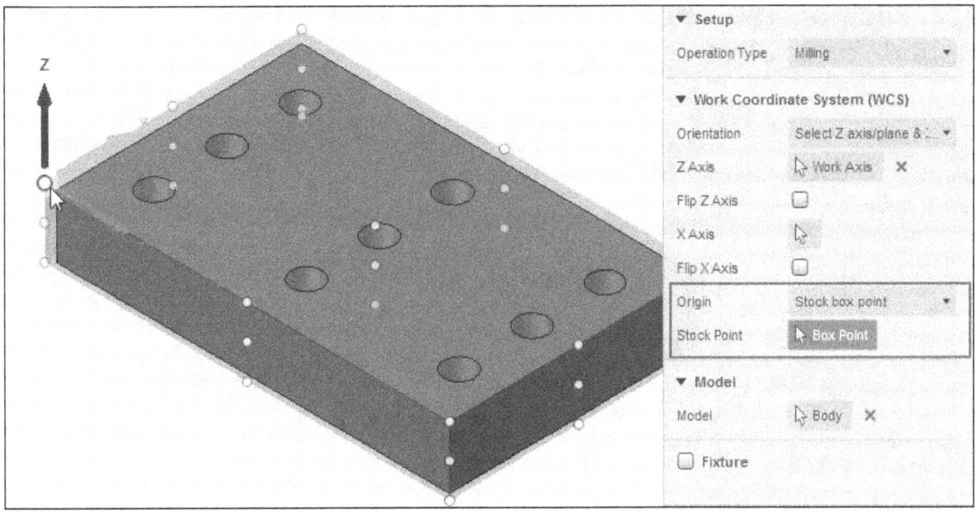

Figure-19. Defining stock box point

Model Body Selection

- If there is only one model in the drawing area then it will be considered as machining model for generating toolpaths and will be active by default in the **Model** section of dialog box.
- If there are multiple solid bodies in the drawing area then it is recommended to select required model for machining process by selecting the **Body** selection button from **Model** node and select desired body.

Fixture Selection

- Select the **Fixture** check box from the **SETUP** dialog box to define fixture for the workpiece. A fixture is used to hold workpiece in desired orientation.
- The **Fixture** selection button is active by default on selecting the **Fixture** check box. You need to select the component/body to be defined as fixture; refer to Figure-20. Note that components defined as fixture will be avoided by tool while cutting.

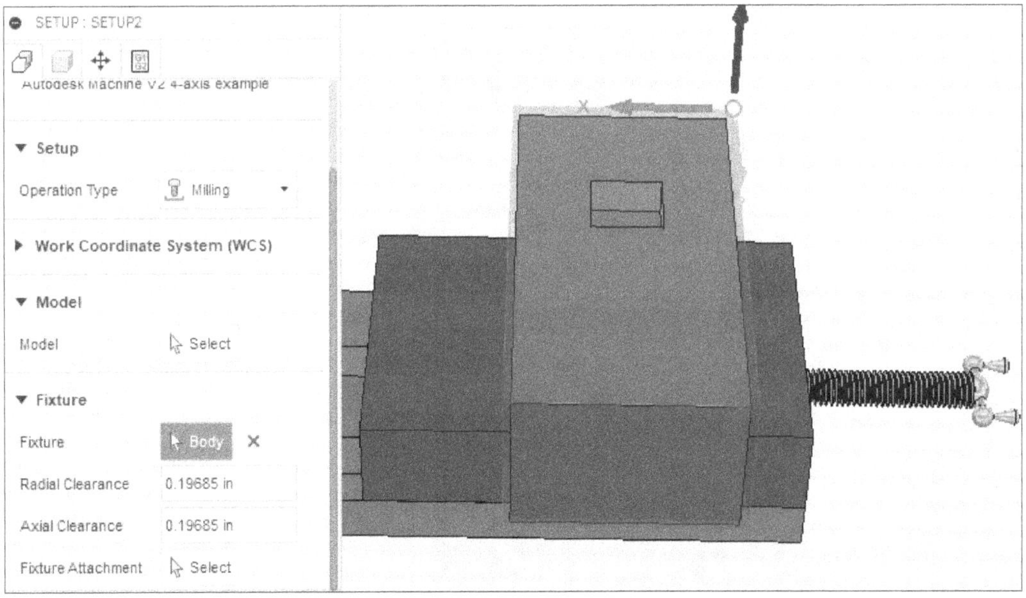

Figure-20. Selecting Fixture

- Similarly, click on the selection button for the **Fixture Attachment** section in **Fixture** node and select desired attachment body.

Stock tab

- Click on the **Stock** tab of **SETUP** dialog box to define the workpiece dimensions. The **Stock** tab will be displayed; refer to Figure-21.

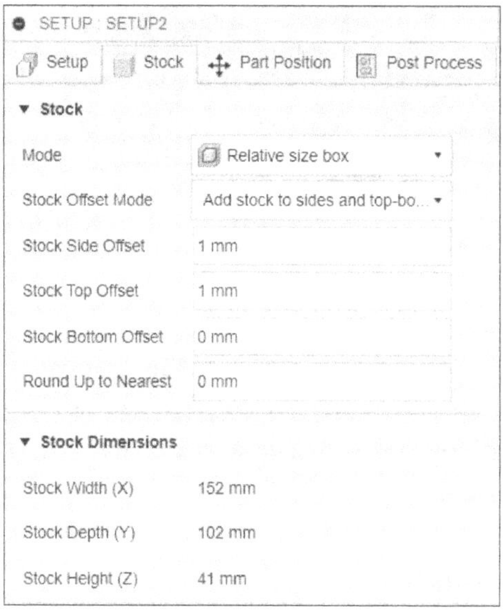

Figure-21. Stock tab

Fixed size box

- Select the **Fixed size box** option from the **Mode** drop-down in the **Stock** tab to create a rectangular stock body of defined parameter. The updated **Stock** tab will be displayed; refer to Figure-22.

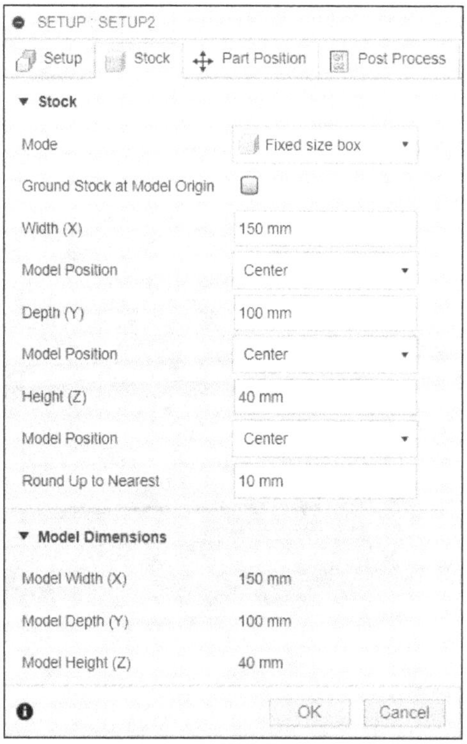

Figure-22. Fixed size box options

- Select the **Ground Stock at Model Origin** check box to place the origin of stock at origin of machining model. (Machining model is the final part design to be achieved after performing machining). Note that on selecting this check box, you will be able to define only offset distances along X, Y, and Z axes for positioning stock on the model.
- Click in the **Width (X)** edit box and specify the width of stock body.
- Select the **Offset from left side (-X)** option of **Model Position** drop-down from **Stock** section to offset the stock to the left side of model along X axis of WCS.
- Click in the **Offset** edit box and enter desired value; refer to Figure-23.

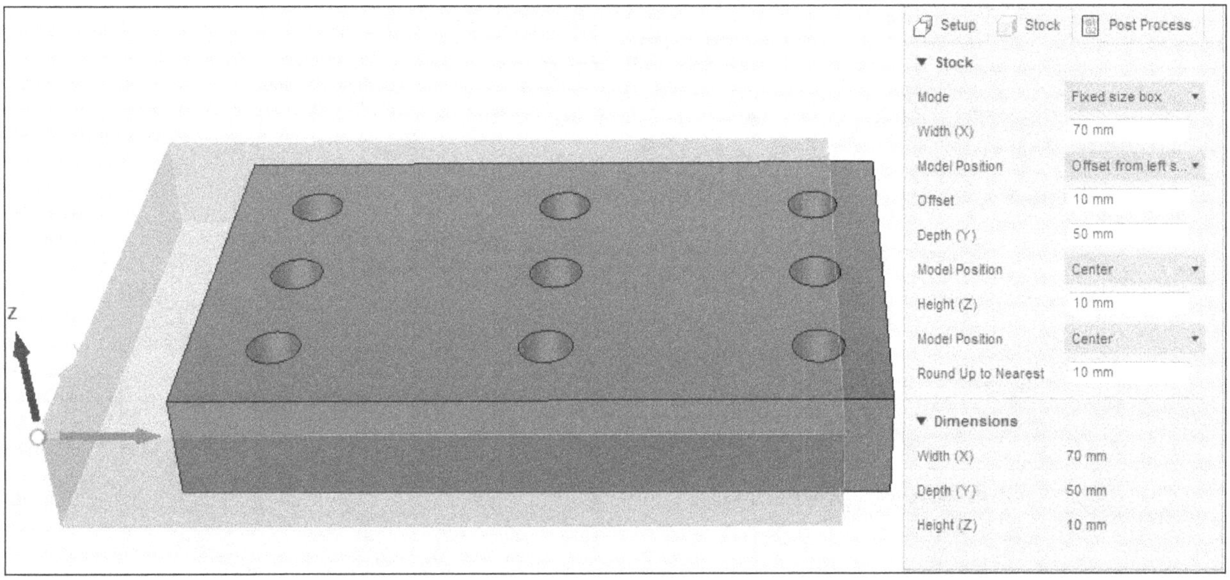

Figure-23. Offset from left side

- Select **Center** option of **Model Position** drop-down from **Stock** section to place the stock on the center of model.
- Select the **Offset from right side (+X)** option of **Model Position** drop-down from **Stock** section to offset the stock to the right side of model.
- Click in the **Offset** edit box and enter the required value. In our case, we are selecting the **Center** option.
- Click in the **Depth (Y)** edit box and enter the required depth of the stock.
- Click in the **Height (Z)** edit box and enter the required height of stock.
- Click in the **Round Up to Nearest** edit box and enter the value of increment/ decrement to be performed in stock size when you click on the spinner buttons to increase or decrease stock size in the dialog box.

Relative Size Box

- Select the **Relative size box** option from **Mode** drop-down in **Stock** tab to create a rectangular stock body larger than the main model by specifying offset distance values. The updated **SETUP** dialog box will be displayed; refer to Figure-24.
- Select the **No additional stock** option of **Stock Offset Mode** drop-down from **Stock** section to create a stock equal to size of the model.
- Select the **Add stock to the sides and top-bottom** option of **Stock Offset Mode** drop-down to create stock of specified amount for all sides of model except top and bottom of model. For Top and Bottom, you can specify different values. Specify the respective values in the **Stock Side Offset**, **Stock Top Offset**, and **Stock Bottom Offset** edit boxes.

- Select the **Add stock to all sides** option of **Stock Offset Mode** drop-down if you want to specify different offset values for different directions of model for creating stock; refer to Figure-25. Click in the offset edit boxes and specify the values as desired.

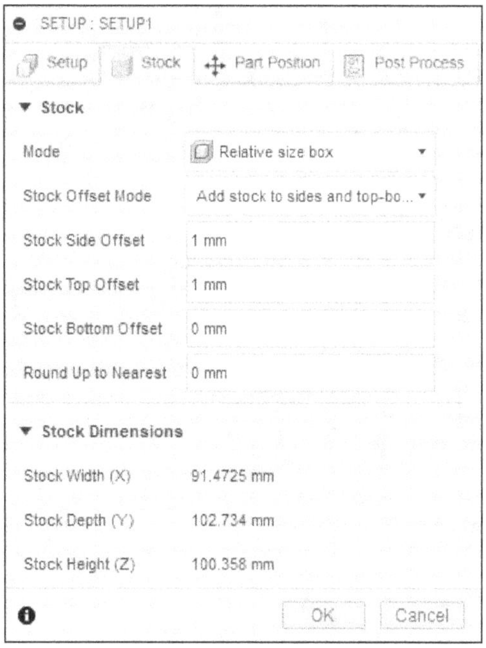

Figure-24. Relative size box option

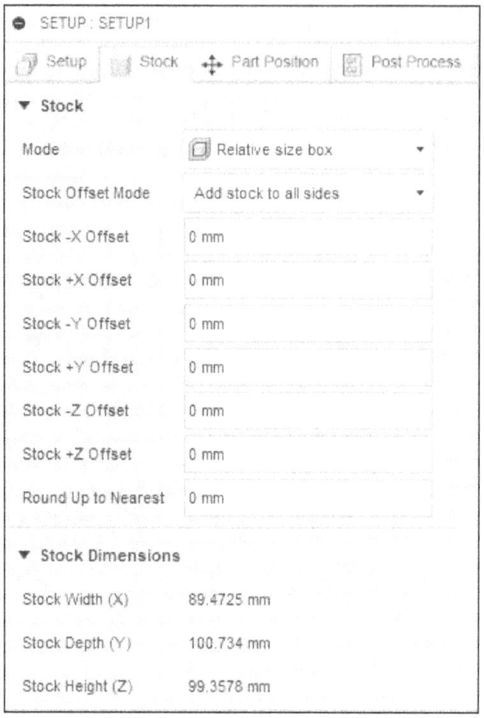

Figure-25. Add stock to all sides mode

Fixed size cylinder

- Select the **Fixed size cylinder** option of **Mode** drop-down from **Stock** section to create a fixed size cylinder stock body. The updated **SETUP** dialog box will be displayed; refer to Figure-26.

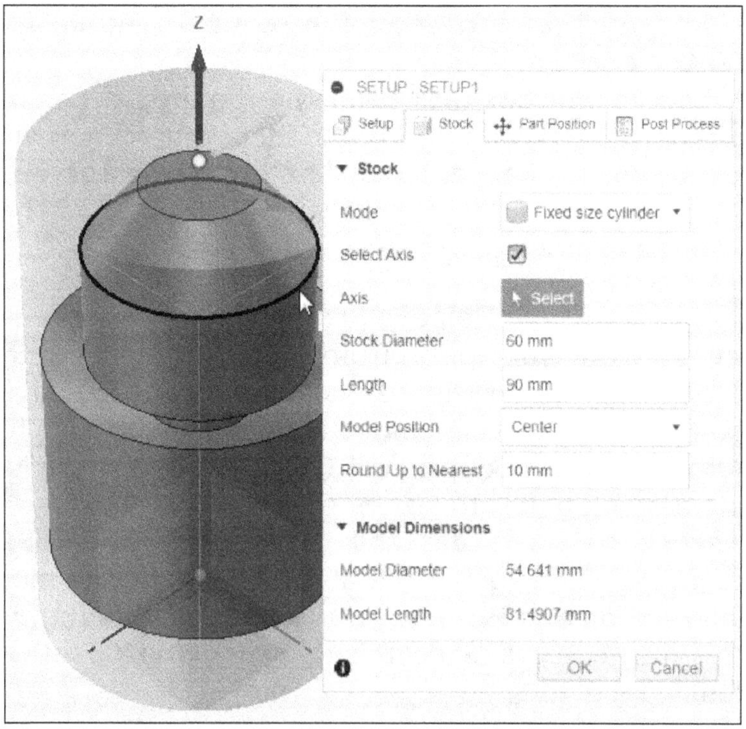

Figure-26. Selecting axis

- The **Axis** button of **Setup** section is active by default. Select the axis from model to be used as center axis of cylindrical stock; refer to Figure-26.
- Click in the **Stock Diameter** edit box from the **Stock** section and enter desired diameter of stock.
- Click in the **Length** edit box and enter desired length value for stock.

Relative size cylinder

- Select the **Relative size cylinder** option from **Mode** drop-down of **Stock** section to create cylindrical stock body of specified offset value. Here, offset values will act as thickness over the main model. The updated **SETUP** dialog box will be displayed; refer to Figure-27.

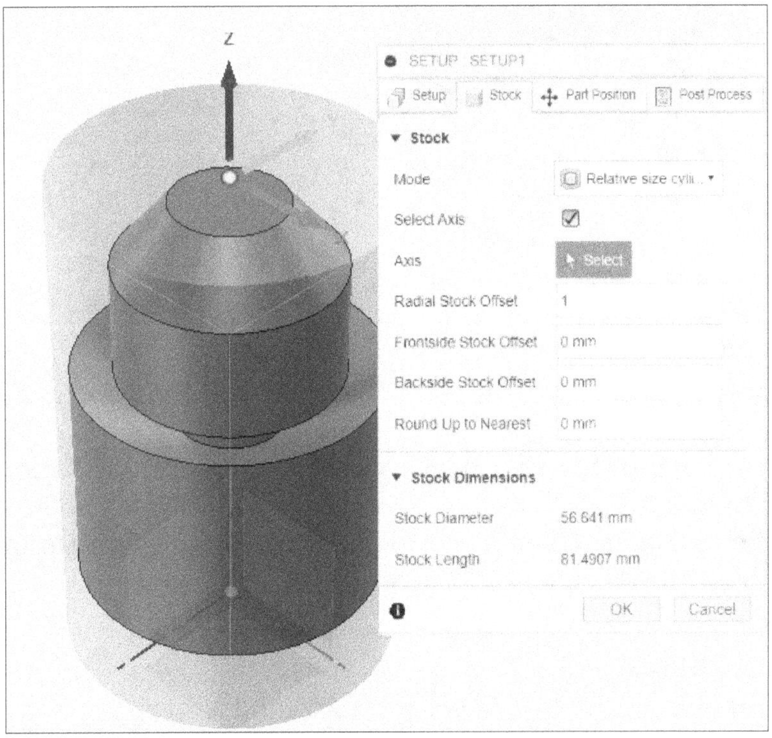

Figure-27. Relative size cylinder option

- The **Axis** button is active by default. Click on the axis from model to use as center axis of stock cylinder.
- Click in the **Radial Stock Offset** edit box and specify desired value to define thickness of stock in radial direction.
- Click in the **Frontside Stock Offset** edit box and specify thickness of stock on the top side of cylindrical stock.
- Click in the **Backside Stock Offset** edit box and specify thickness of stock on the bottom side of cylindrical stock.
- Click in the **Round Up to Nearest** edit box and specify multiple value to which size of stock will be rounded. For example if stock bars are available in multiple of 5 mm then you need to specify 5 mm in the **Round Up to Nearest** edit box.

Fixed size tube

- Select the **Fixed size tube** option of **Mode** drop-down from **Stock** section to create a tube stock body of fixed size. A tube is similar to cylinder with a through hole. The updated **SETUP** dialog box will be displayed; refer to Figure-28.

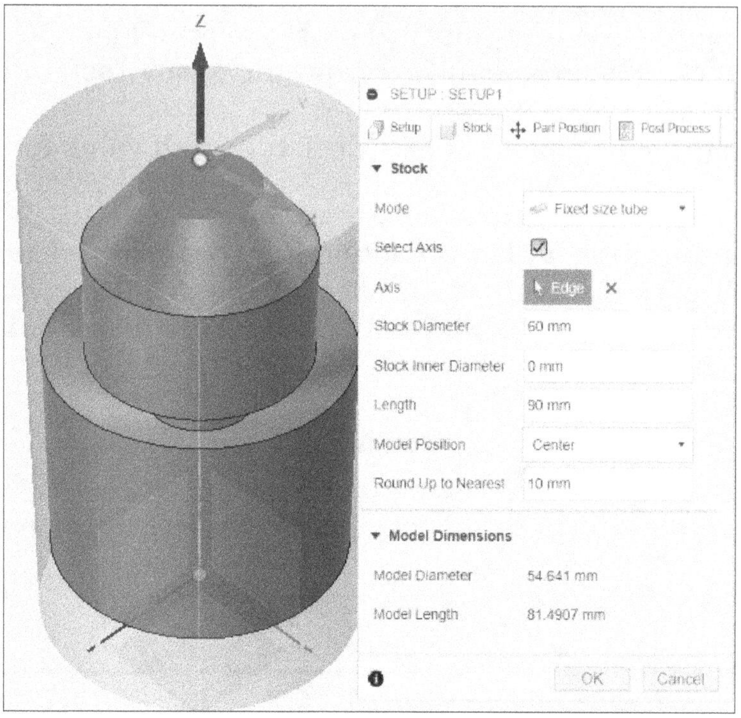

Figure-28. Fixed size tube option

- The **Axis** button is active by default. Click on the axis from model to select as center axis of tube.
- Click in the **Stock Diameter** edit box from **Stock** section and specify desired value for diameter of stock.
- Click in the **Stock Inner Diameter** edit box and specify value for inner diameter (hole diameter) of stock; refer to Figure-29.

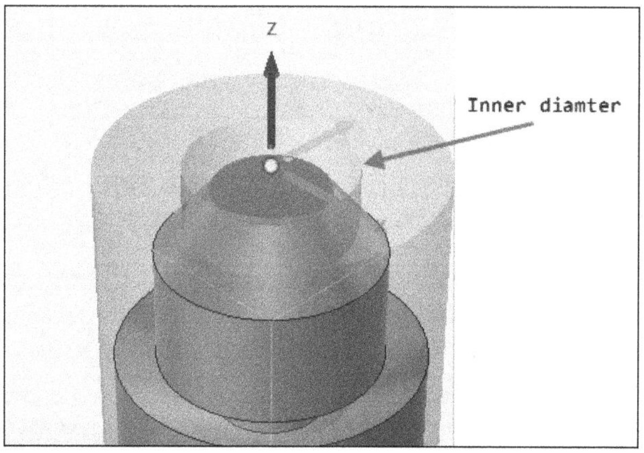

Figure-29. Inner diameter

- Click in the **Length** edit box and specify desired length of stock tube.
- Select the **Offset from front** option from **Model Position** drop-down of **Stock** section to move the stock to top side of model by value specified in **Offset** edit box; refer to Figure-30.

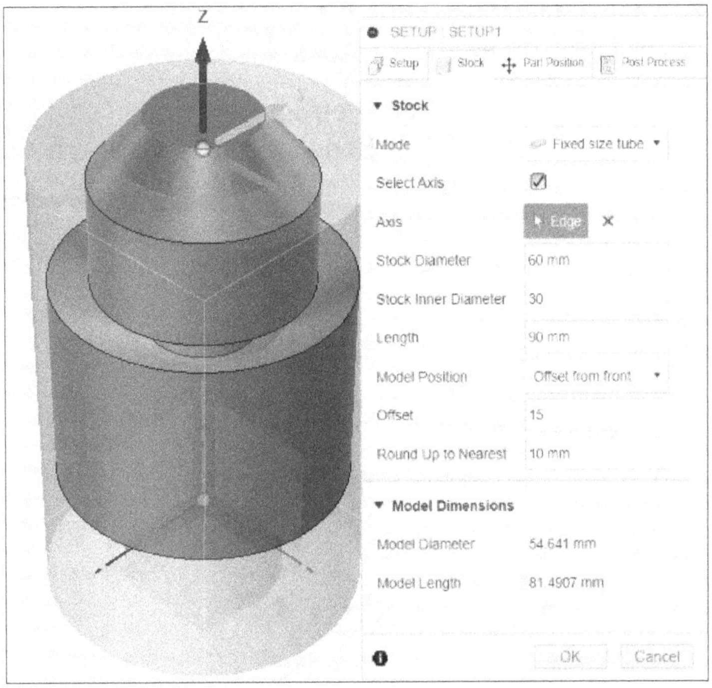

Figure-30. Offset from front option

- Click in the **Offset** edit box and specify desired value to move stock.
- Select the **Center** option of **Model Position** drop-down from **Stock** section to place the stock at the center of model.
- Select the **Offset from back** option from the **Model Position** drop-down of the **Stock** section to move the stock to bottom side of model.

Relative size tube

- Select the **Relative size tube** option from the **Mode** drop-down in the **Stock** section to create stock of specified thickness with respect to main model. The updated **SETUP** dialog box will be displayed; refer to Figure-31.

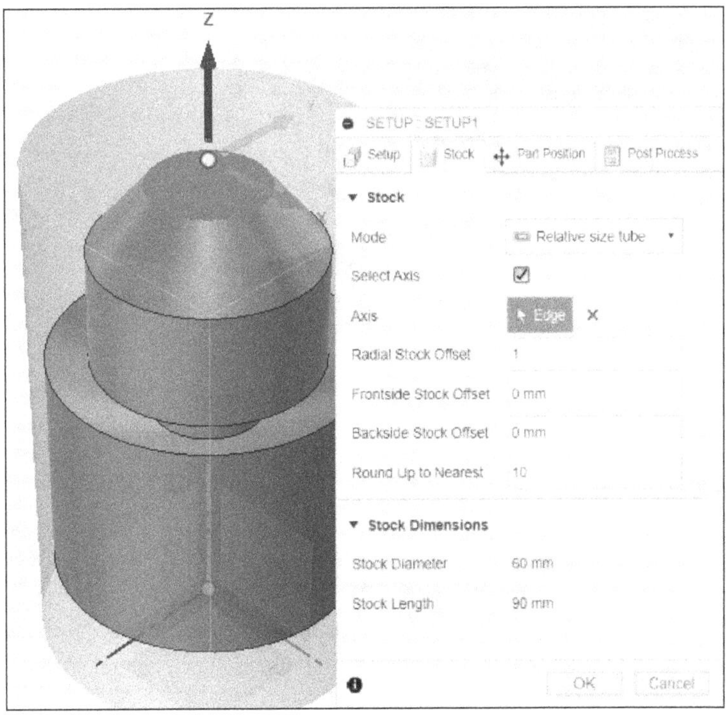

Figure-31. Relative size tube

- The edit boxes of the **Relative size tube** are same as discussed in the **Relative size cylinder** option of this tool.

From solid

- Select the **From solid** option of the **Mode** drop-down from the **Stock** section to create a stock by selecting a solid body from multi-body part or from a part file in an assembly. The updated **SETUP** dialog box will be displayed; refer to Figure-32.

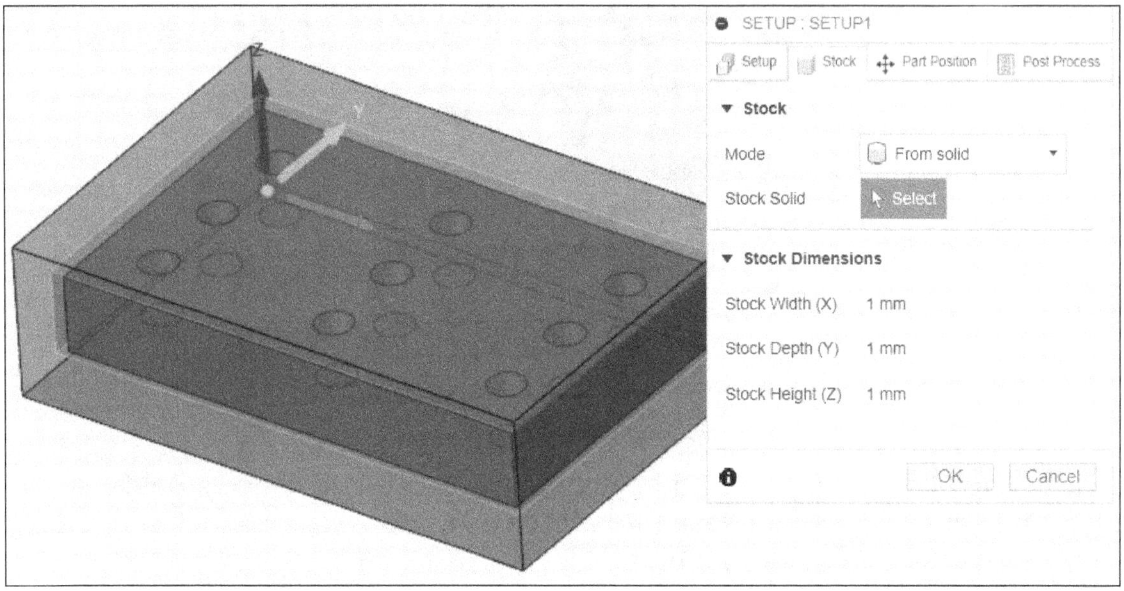

Figure-32. From solid option

- Click on the **Select** button of **Stock Solid** section and click on the body to be used as stock; refer to Figure-33.

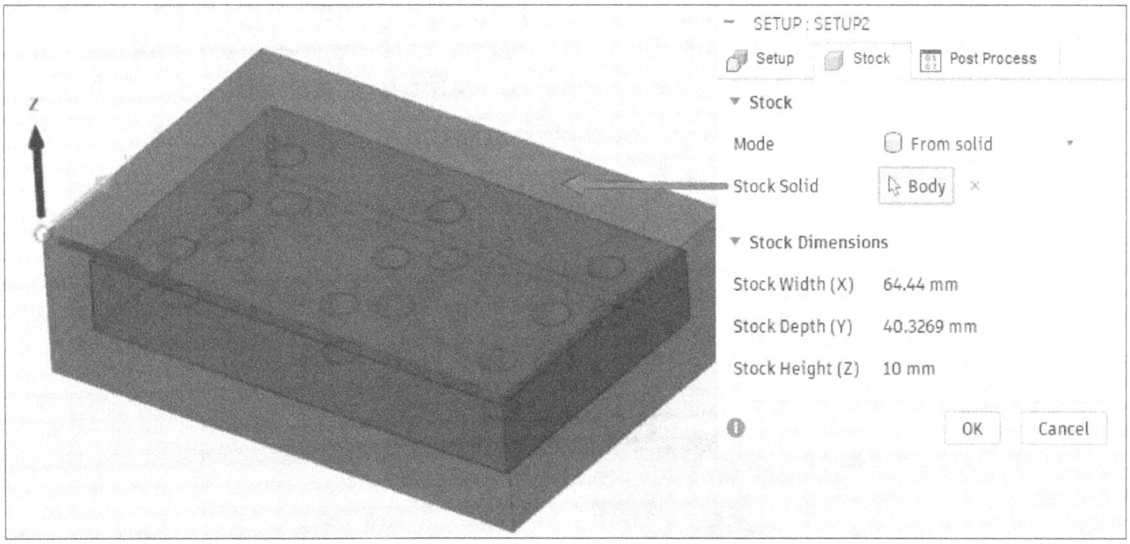

Figure-33. Selection of body for stock

- Click on the **Dimensions** node of **Stock** tab from **SETUP** dialog box to check the exact dimensions of the stock.

From preceding setup

- Select the **From preceding setup** option from the **Mode** drop-down in **Stock** section to create stock based on workpiece left after performing previous operations; refer to Figure-34.

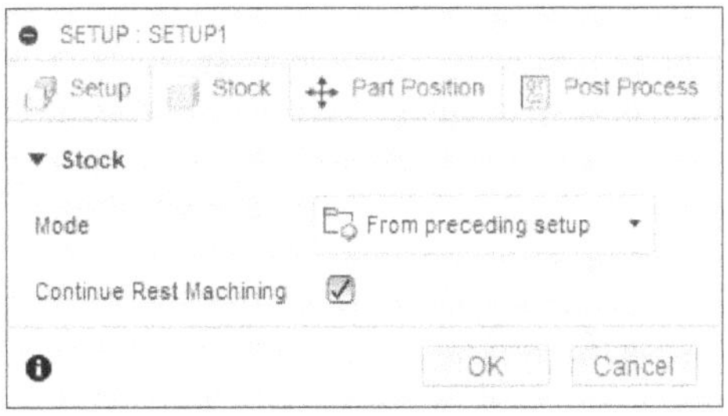

Figure-34. From preceding setup option

- Select the **Continue Rest Machining** check box if you want to perform rest machining operations based on earlier performed operations. In this way, setup will recognize what operations have been performed and what should be performed.

Part Position Tab

- The **Part Position** tab is available when you have selected an Autodesk supported machine in **Setup** tab in the dialog box. Click on the **Part Position** tab from the **SETUP** dialog box to set position of workpiece on the table of selected machine; refer to Figure-35.

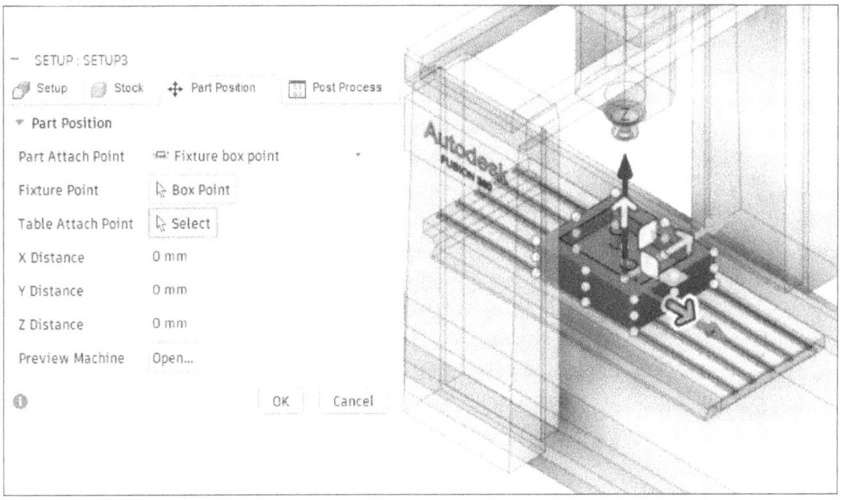

Figure-35. Part Position tab

- You can set the position of workpiece on table in the same way as discussed earlier for creating stock.
- Click on the **Open** button from **Preview Machine** section, the **PREVIEW MACHINE MOVEMENTS** dialog box will be displayed; refer to Figure-36 enabling the movement of the axes in the machine to visually verify whether the machine can reach all areas of the part without collisions or not.
- Specify desired parameters in the dialog box and click on **Close** button.

Figure-36. PREVIEW MACHINE MOVEMENTS dialog box

Post Process tab

- Click on the **Post Process** tab from **SETUP** dialog box to define post processing parameters. The **Post Process** tab will be displayed; refer to Figure-37. Post processing is the step at which CNC program generated by software is modified to suit specific machine.

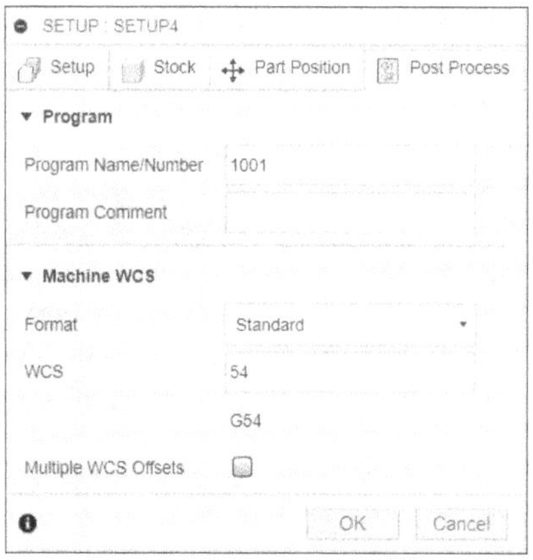

Figure-37. Post Process tab

- Click in the **Program Name/Number** edit box of the **Post Process** tab from the **SETUP** dialog box to define NC program name/number. This number is output at the start of NC program at the "0" number line. It is also used as storage name on the CNC controller storage.
- Click in the **Program Comment** edit box and enter desired comment to be added with the program. The comment text will not be read by CNC control but it will be displayed in program and machine display.
- Select the **Standard** option from the **Format** drop-down to use standard format for specifying WCS (G54, G55, G56, and so on). Select the **Extended** option from the drop-down to use extended format which follows the format G154 P54, G154 P55, and so on.
- Specify the code to be used for defining WCS offset in the **WCS Offset** edit box. The output in the NC program is generally produced by G54 through G59 codes.
- Select the **Multiple WCS Offsets** check box if you want to create multiple WCS offset values for tool wear compensations. Specify desired value in the **Number of Instances** edit box to define number of WCS offsets to be created. Specify desired value in the **WCS Offset Increment** edit box to define number of duplicate WCS Offsets to be created. Note that you can still change the values.

- The **Operation Order** drop-down below the **Multiple WCS Offsets** check box is used to specify the order of individual operations. Select the **Preserve Order** option from the **Operation Order** drop-down to machine operations by the order in which they are selected. Select the **Order by Operation** option from **Operation Order** drop-down to perform machining by the order in which operations are created. Select the **Order by tool** option from the **Operation Order** drop-down to perform machining of operations in the order of cutting tools used by them. So, if there are two cutting tools used in overall machining then first operations with tool number 1 will be performed then operation with tool number 2 will be performed.
- After specifying desired parameters, click on the **OK** button from the **SETUP** dialog box. The **Setup1** will be added in **Browser**; refer to Figure-38.
- If you want to edit the earlier created stock or setup parameter then right-click on respective **Setup** option from the **Setups** node of **BROWSER** and click on **Edit** button from marking menu/shortcut menu; refer to Figure-39. The **SETUP** dialog box will be displayed as discussed earlier.

Figure-38. Setup1 in BROWSER

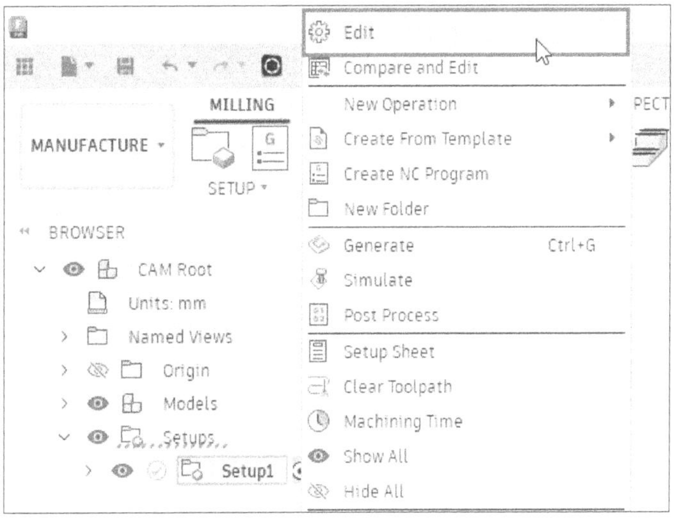

Figure-39. Edit stock

Turning Machine Setup

In this section, we will discuss the procedure of setting machine for **Turning** operation. The procedure is discussed next.

- Click on the **Turning or mill/turn** option from **Operation Type** drop-down in **SETUP** dialog box. The options used in turning process will be displayed along with the model; refer to Figure-40. You can also select a turning machine by using **Select** button in **Machine** section of this dialog box. The procedure is same as discussed for milling machine.

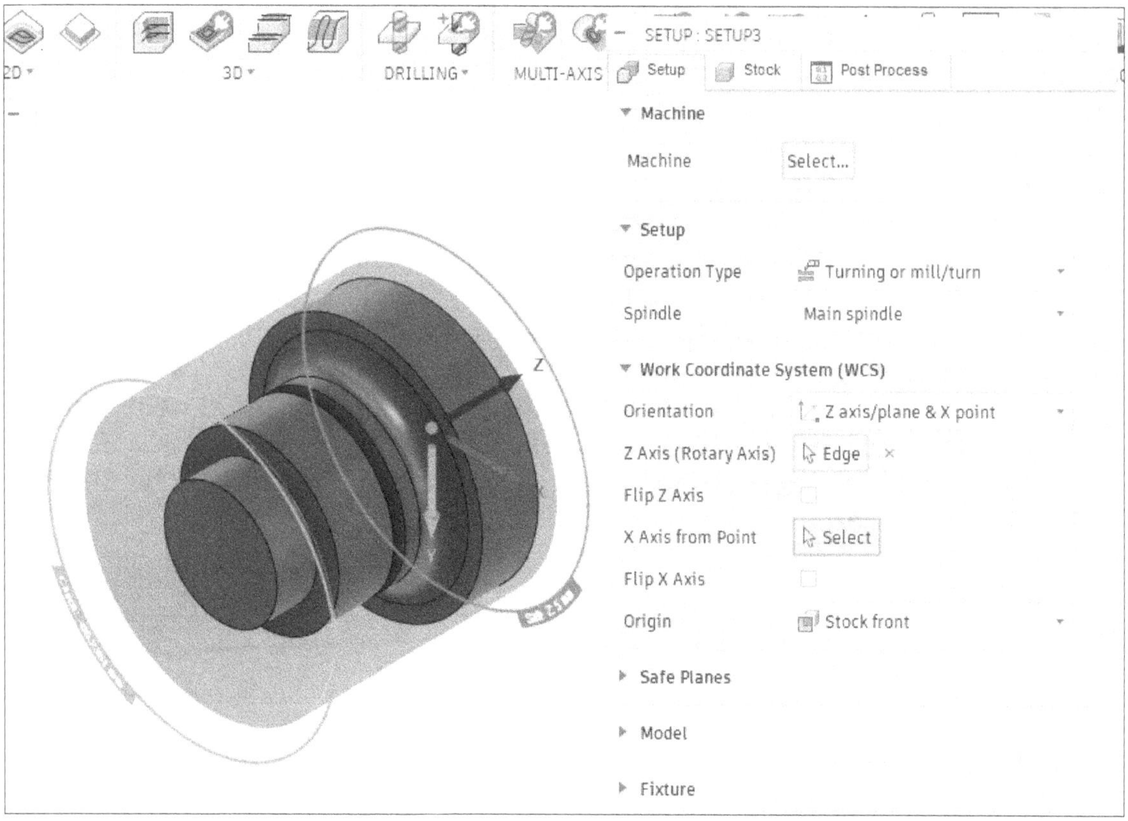

Figure-40. Turning or mill turn option

- Select **Main spindle** or **Subspindle** option from **Spindle** drop-down in **Setup** section to specify the spindle to be used if your machine has two spindles.
- Click on the **Z Axis (Rotary Axis)** button of **Work Coordinate System (WCS)** section from **SETUP** dialog box and select a reference for Z axis as desired; refer to Figure-41.

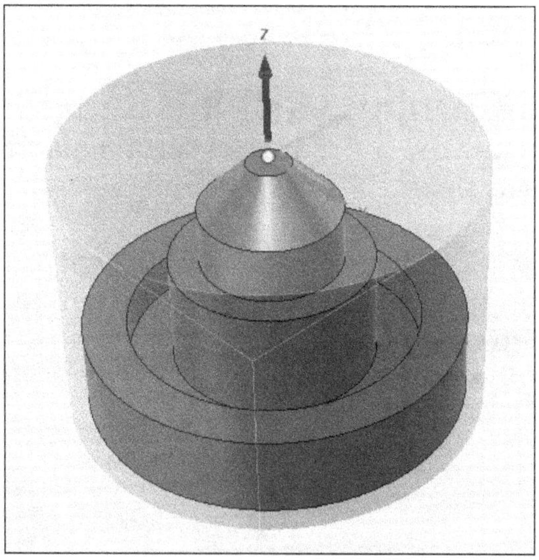

Figure-41. Selecting Z axis for turning

- Select the **Flip Z Axis** check box to flip selected direction of Z axis by 180 degree.
- The **X Axis from Point** button is active by default. Click on the axis or plane to define the X axis.
- Select the **Flip X Axis** check box to flip selected direction of X axis by 180 degree.

- The **Origin** drop-down will define where zero position will be located on the part. Click on the **Origin** drop-down from **Work Coordinate System (WCS)**section and select desired option to set origin point of WCS.
- Click in the **Safe Z Reference** drop-down and select desired reference for safe Z position where tool should move after making cutting passes.
- Click in the **Offset** edit box of **Safe Z** node in the dialog box and specify the distance of safe Z location from selected reference. Similarly, define safe zone based on the chuck reference in respective drop-down and edit box.
- Select the **Spun Profile** check box of **Model** section from **Setup** tab to generate profile for turning. If you are going to mill-turn a part which has irregular surface then you should select this check box to avoid accident; refer to Figure-42.

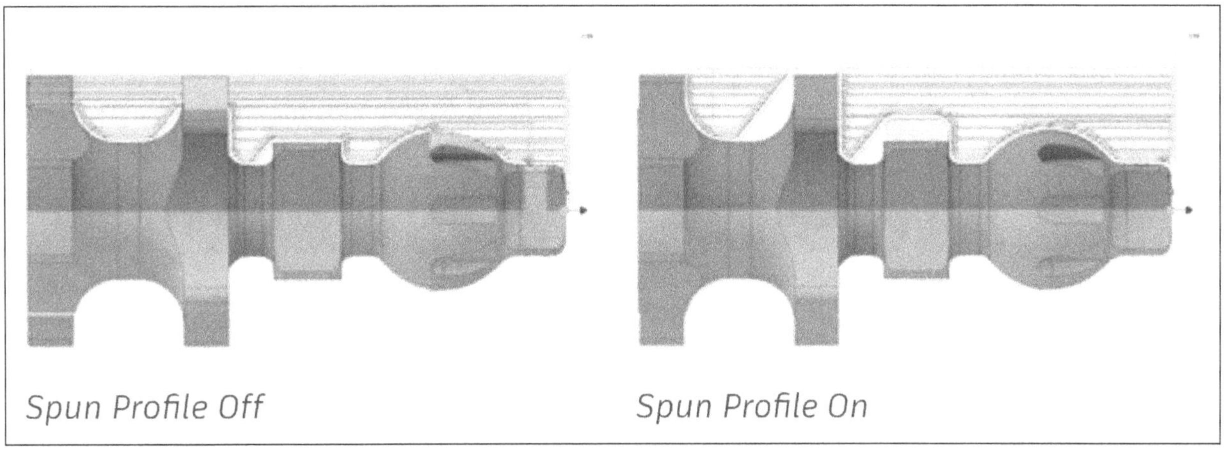

Figure-42. Spun profile option

- Click in the **Spun Profile Tolerance** edit box of **Model** section and specify desired value of tolerance up to which profile can deviate from the model boundaries.
- Select desired reference for defining position of chuck from the **Chuck reference** drop-down.
- Click in the **Offset** edit box of the **Chuck** node and specify desired value of distance at which chuck should be placed from the selected reference.

The options of **Stock** and **Post Process** tab have been discussed earlier in **Milling** section. For turning operations, the program and machine WCS options are displayed in **Post Process** tab; refer to Figure-43.

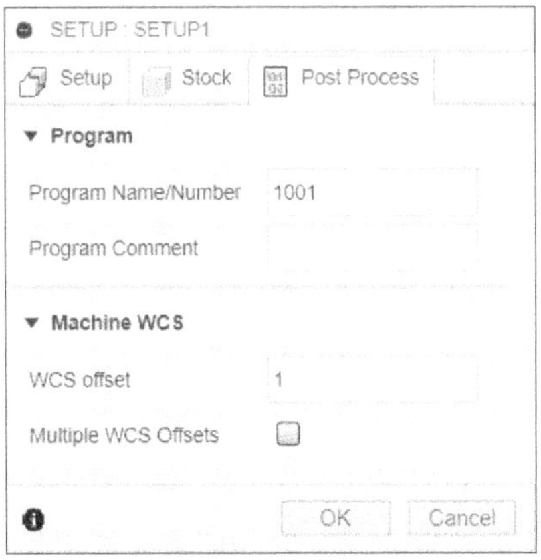

Figure-43. Post Process tab for turning

- After specifying the parameters, click on the **OK** button from the **SETUP** dialog box to complete the process of creating stock and defining machine parameters.

Cutting Machine Setup

In this section, we will discuss the procedure of setting up a cutting machine. This machine can be water jet machine, laser/plasma cutting machine, and so on. The procedure is discussed next.

- Select the **Cutting** option from **Operation Type** drop-down of the **SETUP** dialog box. The options used in cutting process will be displayed; refer to Figure-44.

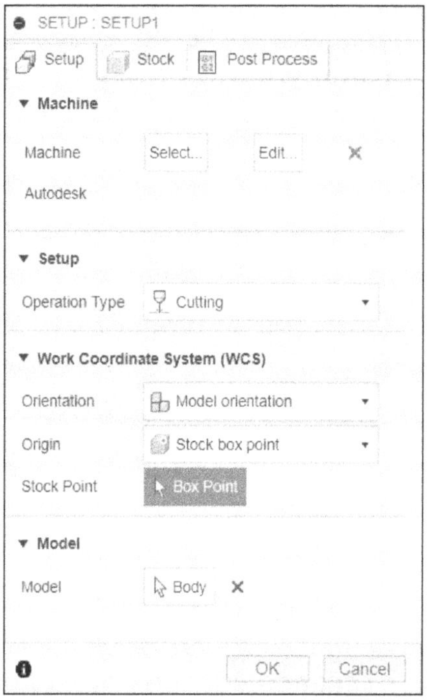

Figure-44. SETUP dialog box for Cutting operation

- Set the orientation and zero point for cutting operation in the **SETUP** dialog box.
- The other options in the dialog box have been discussed earlier.
- After specifying the parameters, click on the **OK** button from the **SETUP** dialog box.

Additive Manufacturing Machine Setup

In this section, we will setup a 3D printing machine. The procedure is given next.

- Select an additive manufacturing machine by using the **Select** button from the **Machine** node in the **SETUP** dialog box (like Aconity3D). The options will be displayed as shown in Figure-45.

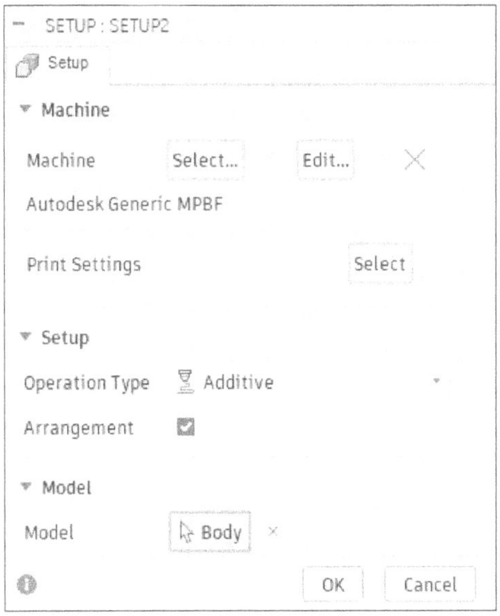

Figure-45. SETUP dialog box for additive manufacturing

- Make sure the **Additive** option is selected in the **Operation Type** drop-down of **Setup** node.
- Click on the **Select** button of **Print Settings** area from the dialog box to define material and 3D printing parameters. The **Print Setting Library** dialog box will be displayed; refer to Figure-46.

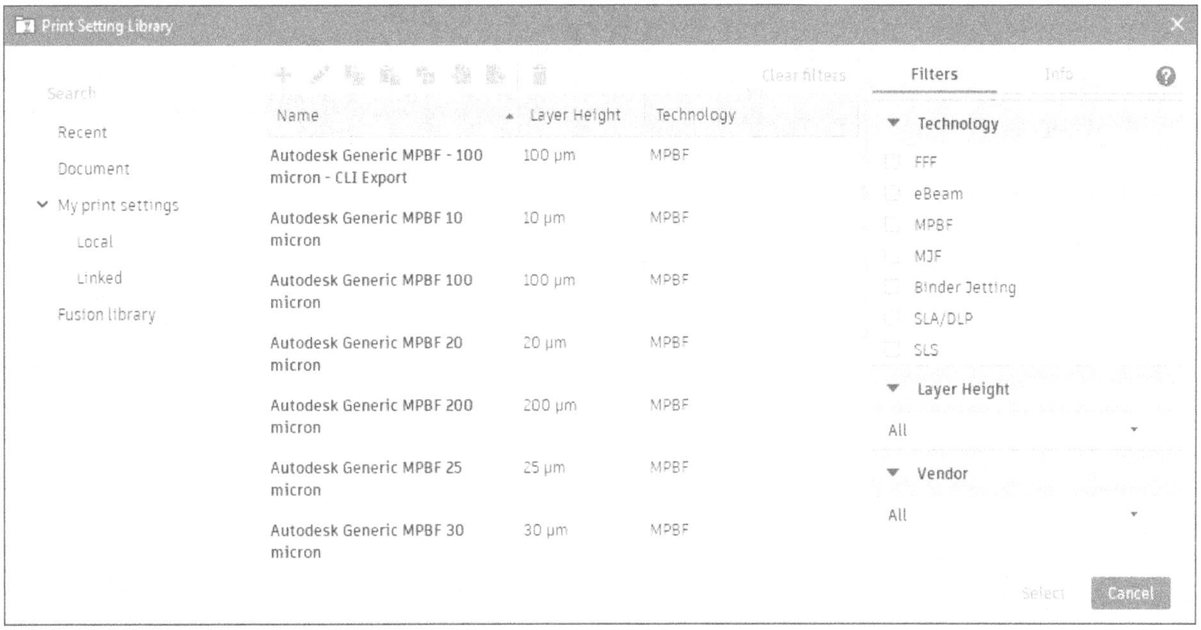

Figure-46. Print Setting Library dialog box

- Select desired printing setting from the list and click on the **Select** button from the dialog box.
- Select the **Arrangement** check box to automatically place all the parts on the machine bed. Other options in this dialog box have been discussed earlier.
- After specifying the parameters, click on the **OK** button from **SETUP** dialog box. The setup will be created. You will learn about additive manufacturing later in the book.

CREATING MANUFACTURING MODEL

The **Create Manufacturing Model** tool is used to create a copy of the main model. You can use/edit this copy of main model called manufacturing model as desired without affecting the main model. There is generally a need of removing features from the model to be 3D printed like holes, chamfers, and so on. Using this tool, ensures that your main model is not modified. The procedure to use this tool is given next.

- Click on the **Create Manufacturing Model** tool from the **SETUP** drop-down in the **MILLING** tab of the **Ribbon**. The copy of main model will be created and added in the **Manufacturing Models** node in **BROWSER**; refer to Figure-47.

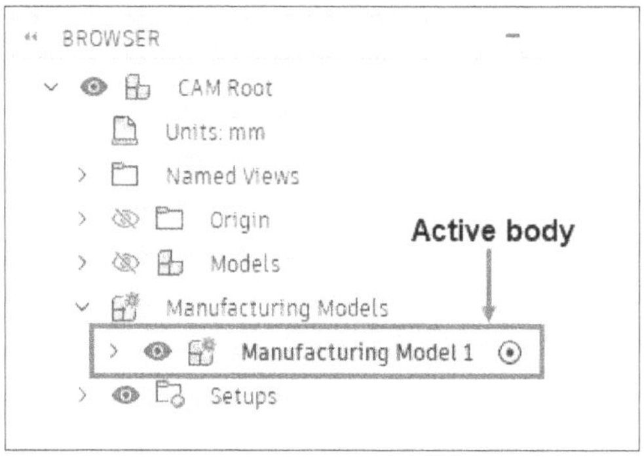

Figure-47. Manufacturing model created

TOOL SELECTION

Before proceeding towards the tools used to generate 2D and 3D path, you need to know various types of tools used in machining and their selection criteria. For this we will discuss the **Select Tool** dialog box; refer to Figure-48.

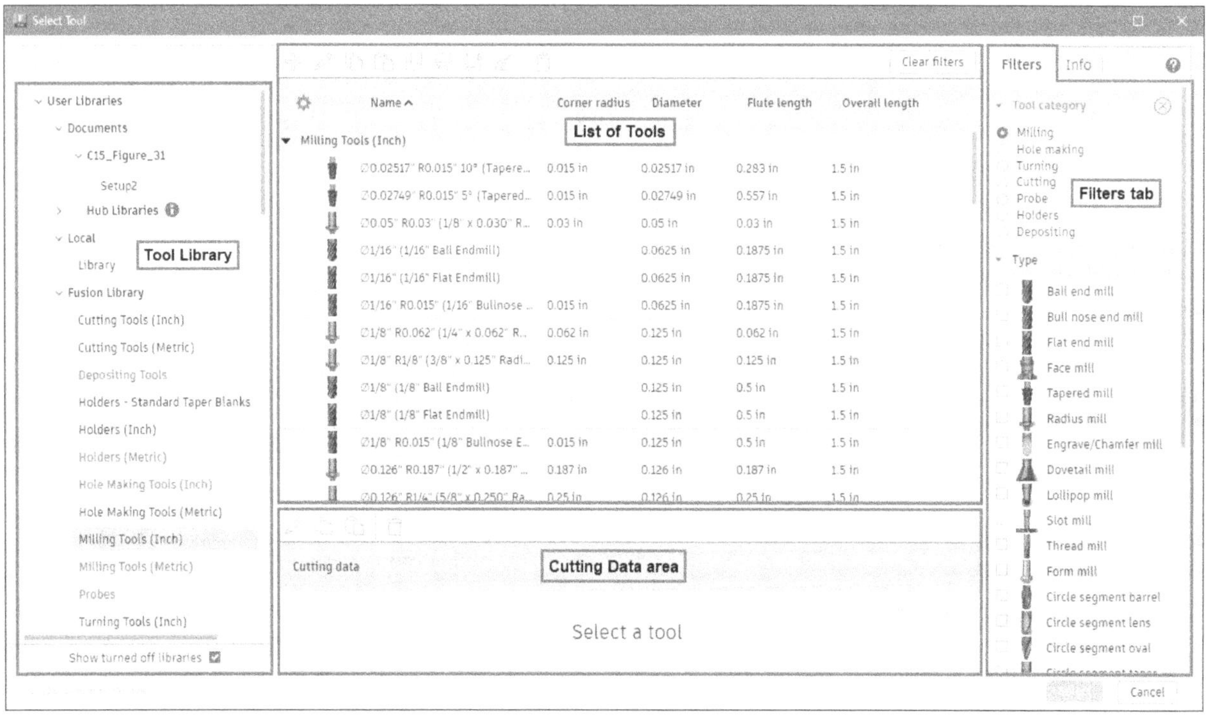

Figure-48. Select Tool dialog box

To display this dialog box, click on the **2D Adaptive Clearing** tool from the **2D** drop-down of **MILLING** tab in the **Ribbon**. A dialog box will be displayed. Click on the **Select** button from **Tool** section in the **Tool** node of the dialog box. The **Select Tool** dialog box will be displayed. You can also display a similar dialog box by clicking on the **Tool Library** tool from **MANAGE** drop-down in the **MILLING** tab of the **Ribbon**; refer to Figure-49. Note that in this chapter, we will discuss about cutting tools only. In next chapter, we will discuss the toolpaths.

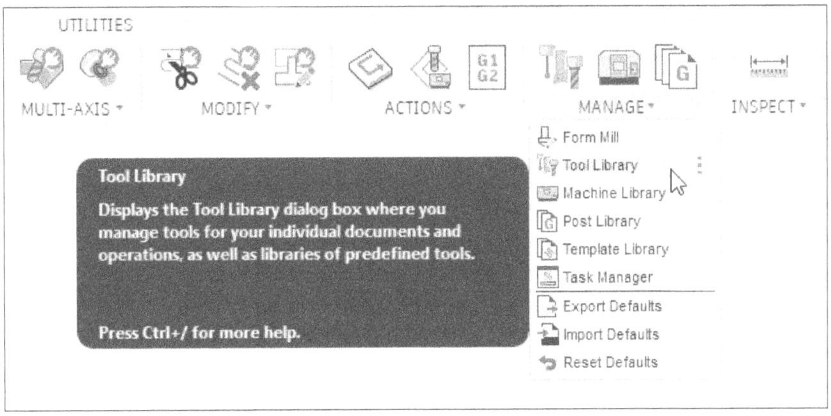

Figure-49. Tool Library tool

- Select desired category of tool from the **Tool Library** area at the left in the dialog box. List of cutting tools will be displayed.
- Select desired radio button from the **Filters** tab at the right in the dialog box to filter list of cutting tools; refer to Figure-50. On selecting a radio button, various options to further filter the list of tools will be displayed in the **Filters** tab.

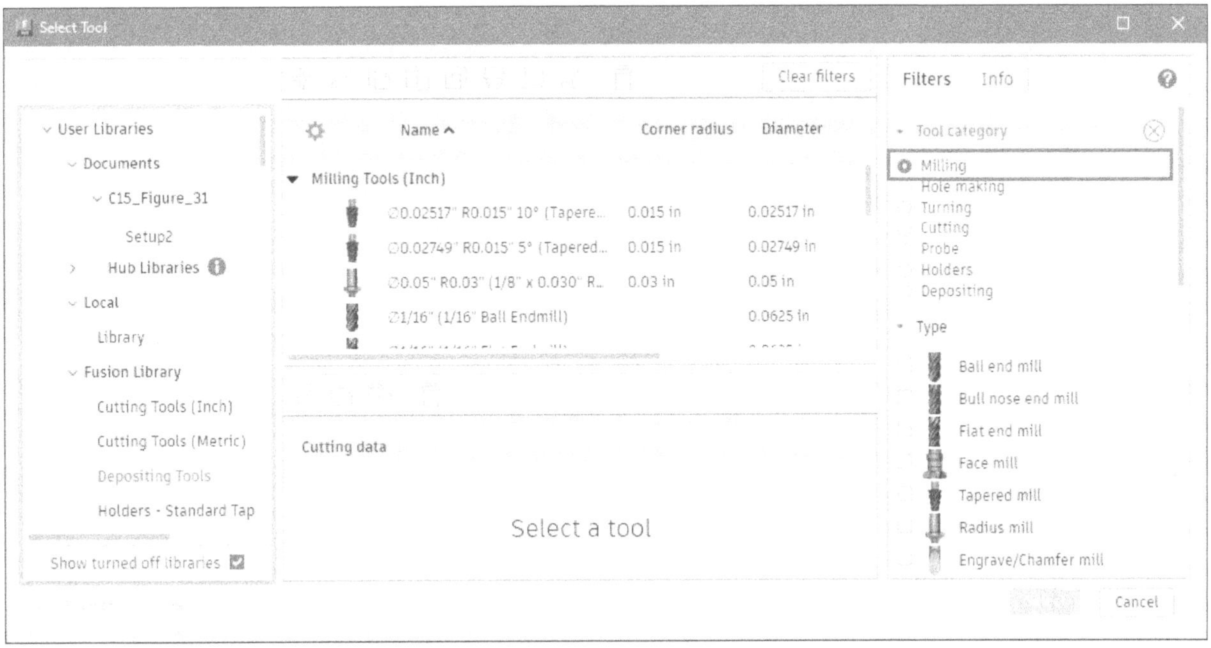

Figure-50. Applying filters to cutting tool list

- Select desired check box from **Type** rollout in the **Filters** tab to define type of cutting tool. For example, select the **Ball end mill** check box to display only ball end mill cutting tools in the list. You can select multiple check box to display tools of multiple types.
- Expand the **Diameter** node and select desired operator to be used for specifying diameter range for cutting tools; refer to Figure-51.

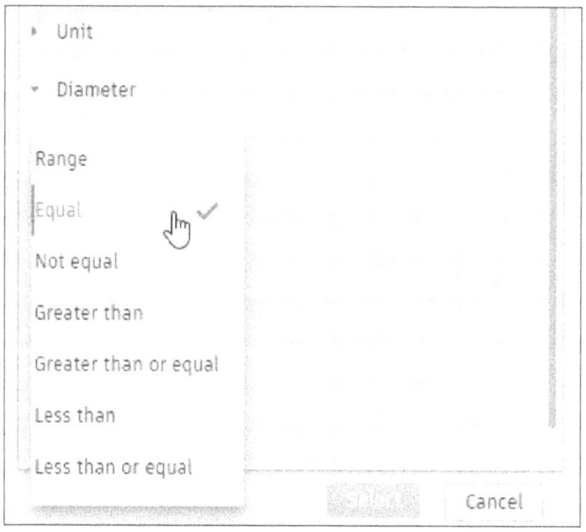

Figure-51. Operators for defining diameter range

- Select desired operator and specify related value in the edit box below it. For example, we have selected **Greater than** operator and specified value as **8 mm** so all the cutting tools which have diameter greater than 8 will be displayed; refer to Figure-52. Note that after specifying value in the edit box, you need to press **TAB** or click in the empty area of screen to update list of tools.

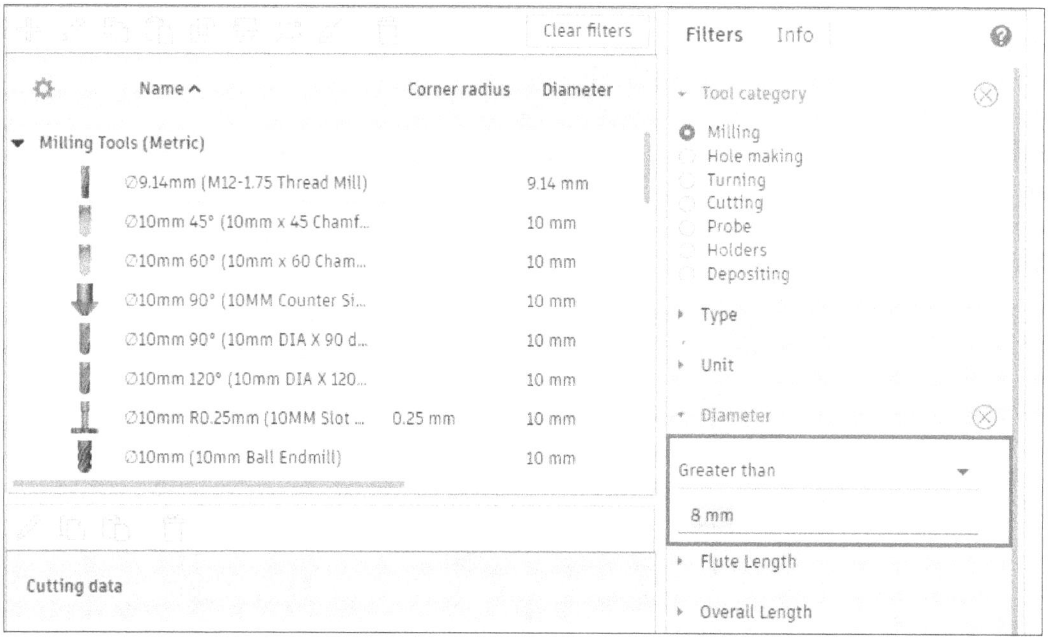

Figure-52. Filtering list of cutting tools

- Similarly, expand other rollouts in the **Filters** tab and specify related parameters to further filter list of cutting tools.
- Select desired cutting tool from the list. Information about the tool will be displayed in the **Info** tab of the dialog box and available cutting data will be displayed in the **Cutting data** area of the dialog box; refer to Figure-53.
- After selecting desired cutting tool, click on the **Select** button from the dialog box.

To check properties of selected tool, click on the **View** tool from **Toolbar** in the cutting tools list area of dialog box; refer to Figure-54. The **Select Tool** dialog box will be displayed with information of selected cutting tool; refer to Figure-55.

Figure-53. Information displayed about cutting tool

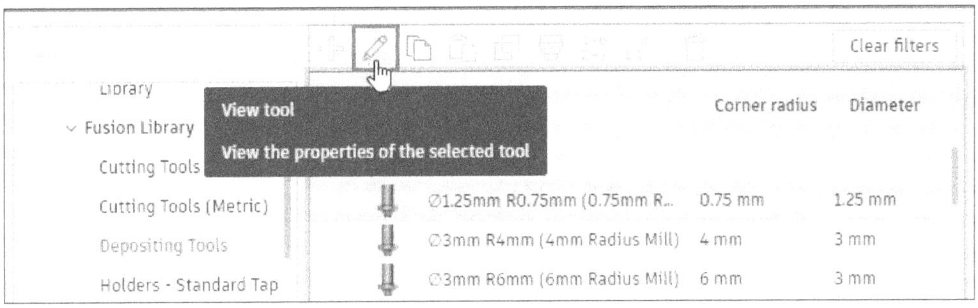

Figure-54. View tool

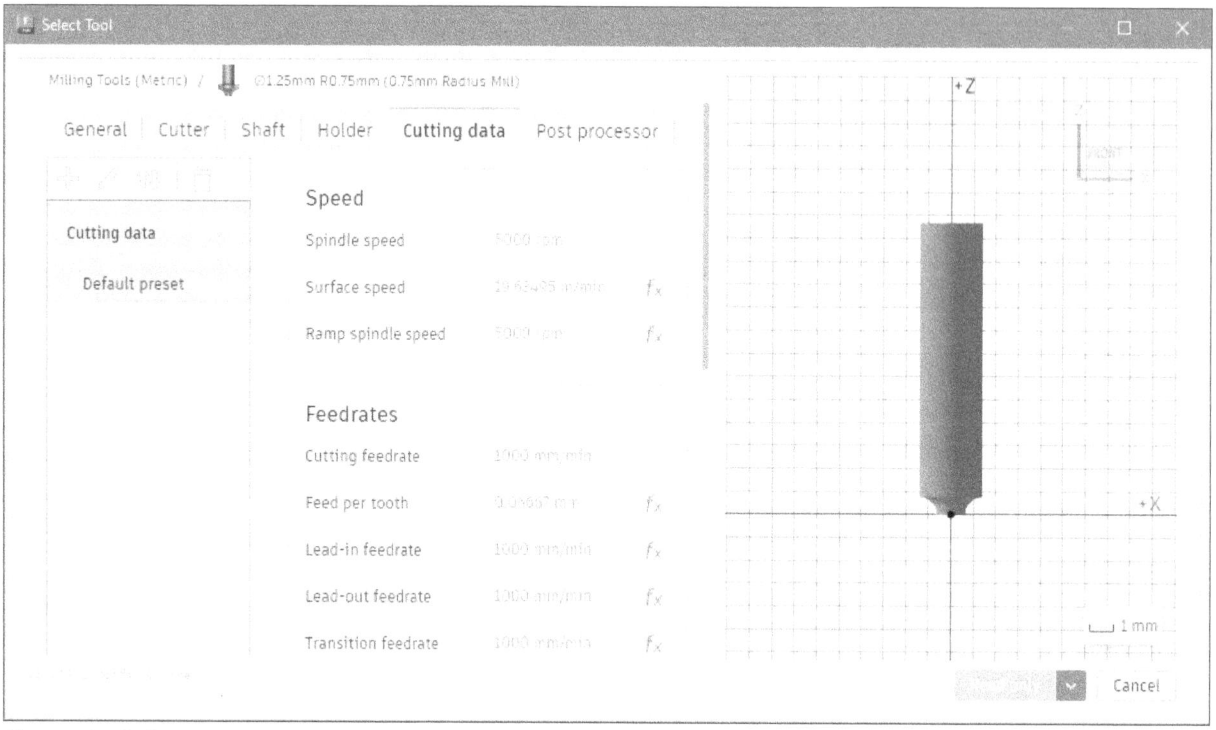

Figure-55. Information about cutting tool

TOOLS USED IN CNC MILLING AND TURNING

The tools used in CNC machines are made of cemented carbide, High Speed Steel, Tungsten Alloys, Ceramics, and many other hard materials. The shapes and sizes of tools used in Milling machines and Lathe machines are different from each other. These tools are discussed next.

Milling Tools

There are various type of milling tools for different applications. These tools are discussed next.

End Mill

End mills are used for producing precision shapes and holes on a Milling or Turning machine. The correct selection and use of end milling cutters is paramount with either machining centers or lathes. End mills are available in a variety of design styles and materials; refer to Figure-56.

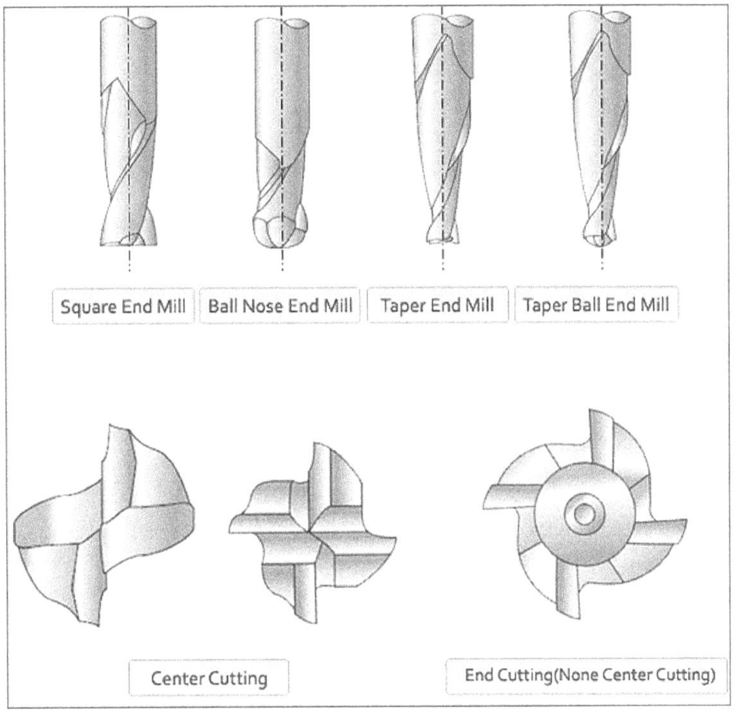

Figure-56. End Mill tool types

Titanium coated end mills are available for extended tool life requirements. The successful application of end milling depends on how well the tool is held (supported) by the tool holder. To achieve best results, an end mill must be mounted concentric in a tool holder. The end mill can be selected for the following basic processes:

FACE MILLING - For small face areas, of relatively shallow depth of cut. The surface finish produced can be 'scratchy".
KEYWAY PRODUCTION - Normally two separate end mills are required to produce a quality keyway.
WOODRUFF KEYWAYS - Normally produced with a single cutter, in a straight plunge operation.
SPECIALTY CUTTING - Includes milling of tapered surfaces, "T" shaped slots & dovetail production.
FINISH PROFILING - To finish the inside/outside shape on a part with a parallel side wall.
CAVITY DIE WORK - Generally involves plunging and finish cutting of pockets in die steel. Cavity work requires the production of three dimensional shapes. A Ball type end mill is used for the finishing cutter with this application.

Roughing End Mills, also known as ripping cutters or hoggers, are designed to remove large amounts of metal quickly and more efficiently than standard end mills; refer to Figure-57. Coarse tooth roughing end mills remove large chips for heavy cuts, deep slotting and rapid stock removal on low to medium carbon steel and alloy steel prior to a finishing application. Fine tooth roughing end mills remove less material but the pressure is distributed over many more teeth, for longer tool life and a smoother finish on high temperature alloys and stainless steel.

Figure-57. Roughing End Mill

Bull Nose Mill

Bull nose mill look alike end mill but they have radius at the corners. Using this tool, you can cut round corners in the die or mold steels. Shape of bull nose mill tool is given in Figure-58.

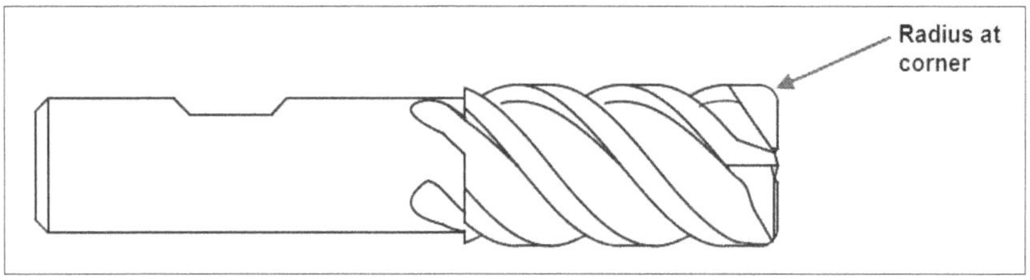

Figure-58. Bull Nose Mill cutter

Ball Nose Mill

Ball nose cutters or ball end mills has the end shape hemispherical; refer to Figure-56. They are ideal for machining 3-dimensional contoured shapes in machining centres, for example in moulds and dies. They are sometimes called ball mills in shop-floor slang. They are also used to add a radius between perpendicular faces to reduce stress concentrations.

Face Mill

The Face mill tool or face mill cutter is used to remove material from the face of workpiece and make it flat; refer to Figure-59.

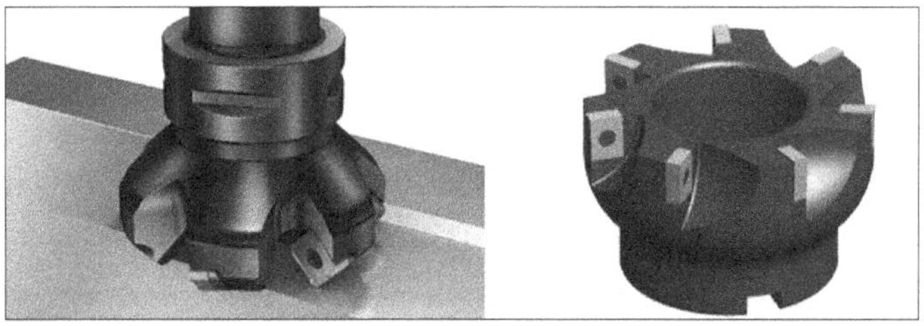

Figure-59. Face milling tool

Radius Mill and Chamfer Mill

The Radius mill tool is used to apply round (fillet) at the edges of the part. The Chamfer mill tool is used to apply chamfer at the edges of the part. Figure-60 shows the radius mill tool and chamfer mill tool.

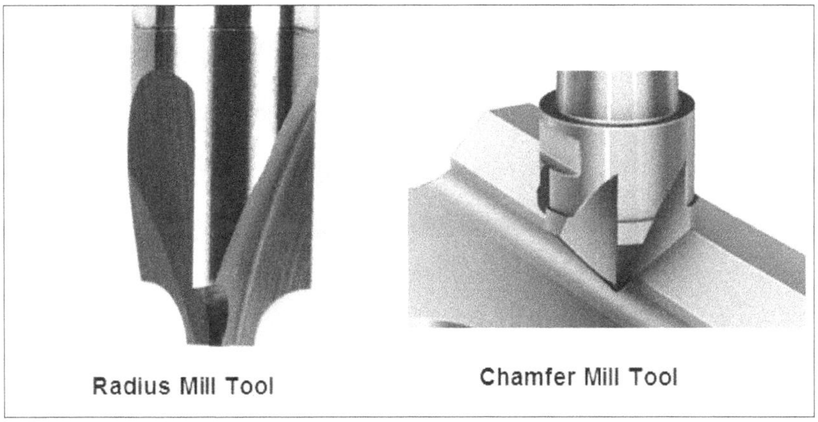

Figure-60. Radius mill and Chamfer mill tool

Slot Mill

The Slot mill tool is used to create slot or groove in the part metal. Figure-61 shows the shape of slot mill tool.

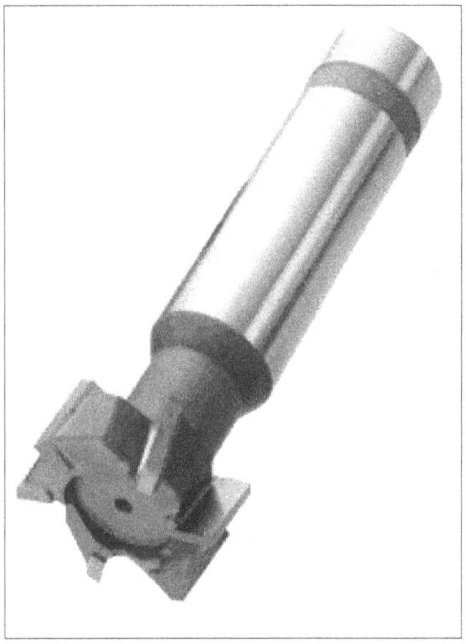

Figure-61. Slot Mill tool

Taper Mill

In CNC machining, taper end mills are used in many industries for a large number of applications, such as walls with draft or clearance angle, tool and die work, mold work, even for reaming holes to make them conical. There are mainly two types of taper mills, Taper End Mill and Taper Ball Mill; refer to Figure-56.

Dove Mill

Dove mill or Dovetail cutters are designed for cutting dovetails in a wide variety of materials. Dovetail cutters can also be used for chamfering or milling angles on the bottom surface of a part. Dovetail cutters are available in a wide variety of diameters and in 15, 45, and 60 degree angles; refer to Figure-62.

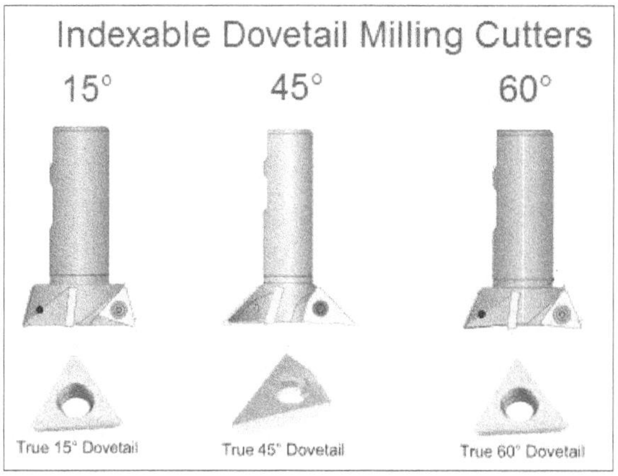

Figure-62. Dovetail milling cutters

Lollipop Mill

The Lollipop mill tool is used to cut round slot or undercuts in workpiece. Some tool suppliers use a name Undercut mill tool in place of Lollipop mill in their catalog. The shape of lollipop mill tool is given in Figure-63.

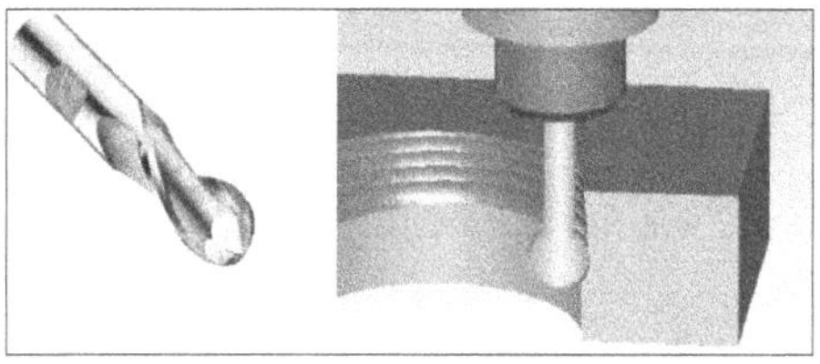

Figure-63. Lollipop mill tool

Engrave Mill

The Engrave mill tool is used to perform engraving on the surface of workpiece. Engraving has always been an art and it is also true for CNC machinist. You can find various shapes of engraving tool that are single flute or multi-flute; refer to Figure-64. You can use ball mill/end mill for engraving or you can use specialized engrave mill tool for engraving. This all depends on your requirement. If you want to perform engraving on softer materials or plastics then it is better to use ball end mill but if you want an artistic shade on the surface then use the respective engrave mill tool. Keep a note of maximum depth and spindle speed mentioned by your engrave mill tool supplier.

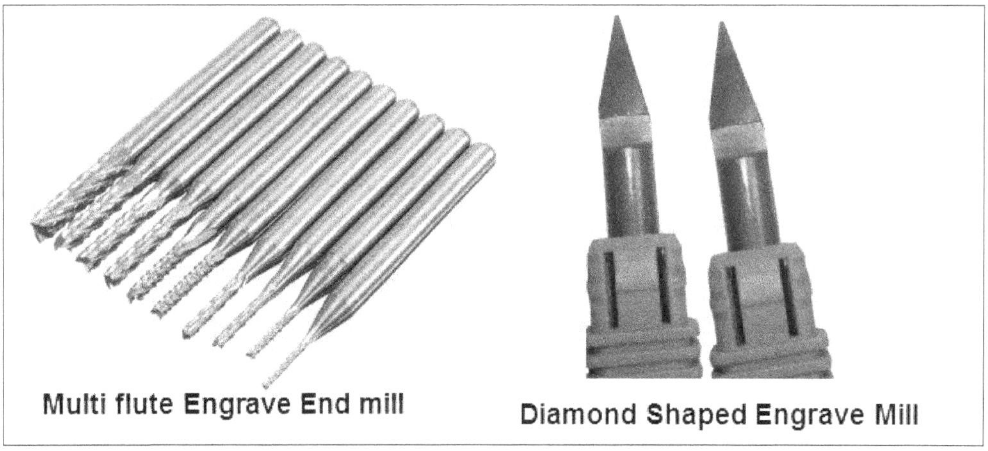

Figure-64. Engrave mill tools

Thread Mill

The Thread mill tool is used to generate internal or external threads in the workpiece. The most common question here is if we have Taps to create thread then why is there need of Thread mill tool. The answer is less machining time on CNC, tool cost saving, more parts per tool, and better thread finish. Now, you will ask why to use tapping. The answer is low machine cost. Figure-65 shows thread mill tools.

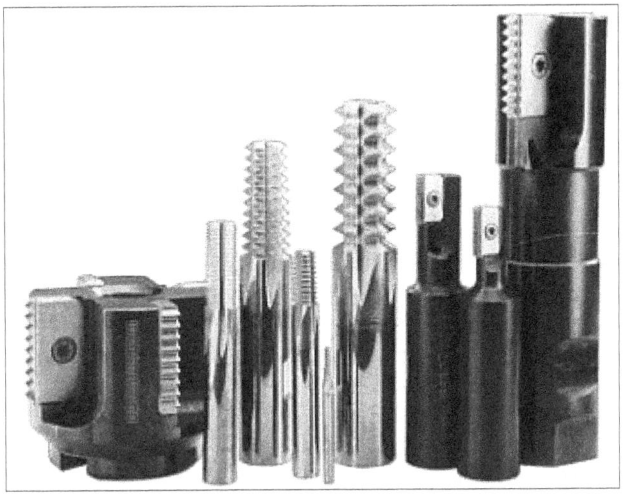

Figure-65. Thread Mill

Barrel Mill

Barrel Mill tool is the tool recently being highly used in machining turbine/impeller blades and other 5-axis milling operations. Barrel Mill has conical shape with radius at its end; refer to Figure-66. Note that earlier Ball mill tools were used for irregular surface contouring but Barrel Mill tools give much better surface finish so they are high in demand for 5-axis milling now a days.

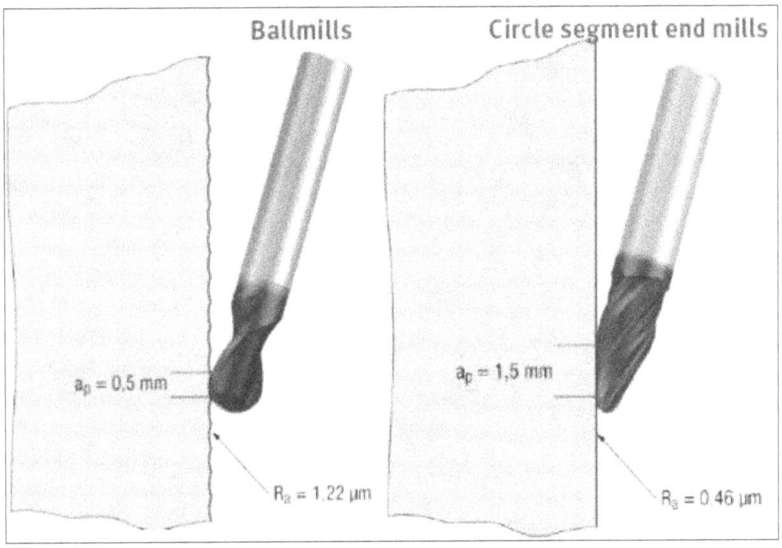

Figure-66. Barrel Mill versus Ball Mill Tool

Drill Bit

Drill bit is used to make a hole in the workpiece. The hole shape depends on the shape of drill bit. Drill bits for various purposes are shown in Figure-67. Note that drill is the machine or holder in which drill bit is installed to make cylindrical holes. There are mainly four categories of drill bit; Twist drill bit, Step drill bit, Unibit (or conical bit), and Hole Saw bit (Refer to Figure-68). Twist drill bits are used for drilling holes in wood, metal, plastic and other materials. For soft materials- the point angle is 90 degree, for hard materials- the point angle is 150 degree, and general purpose twist drill bits have angle of 150 degree at end point. The Step drill bits are used to make counter bore or countersunk holes. The Unibits are generally used for drilling holes in sheetmetal but they can also be used for drilling plastic, plywood, aluminium, and thin steel sheets. One unibit can give holes of different sizes. The Hole saw bit is used to cut a large hole from the workpiece. They remove material only from the edge of the hole, cutting out an intact disc of material, unlike many drills which remove all material in the interior of the hole. They can be used to make large holes in wood, sheet metal, and other materials.

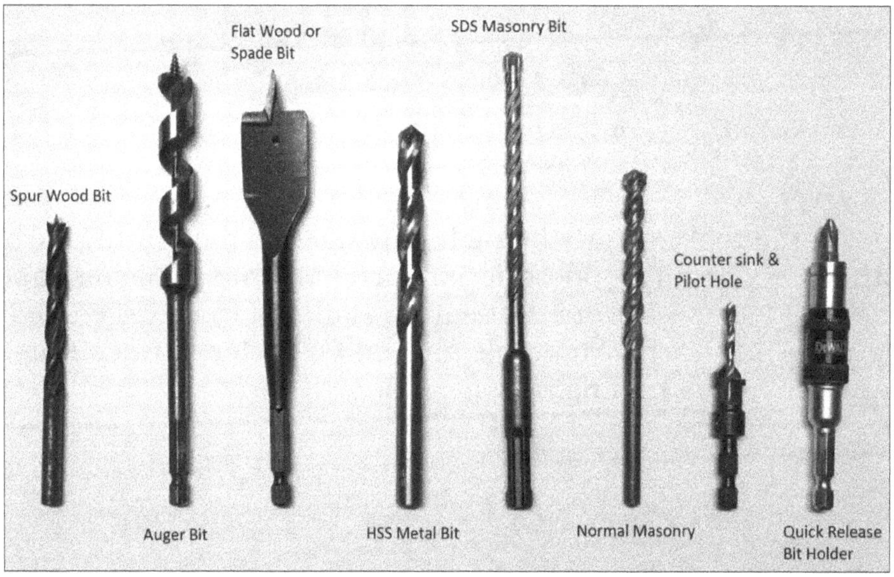

Figure-67. Drill Bits of different types

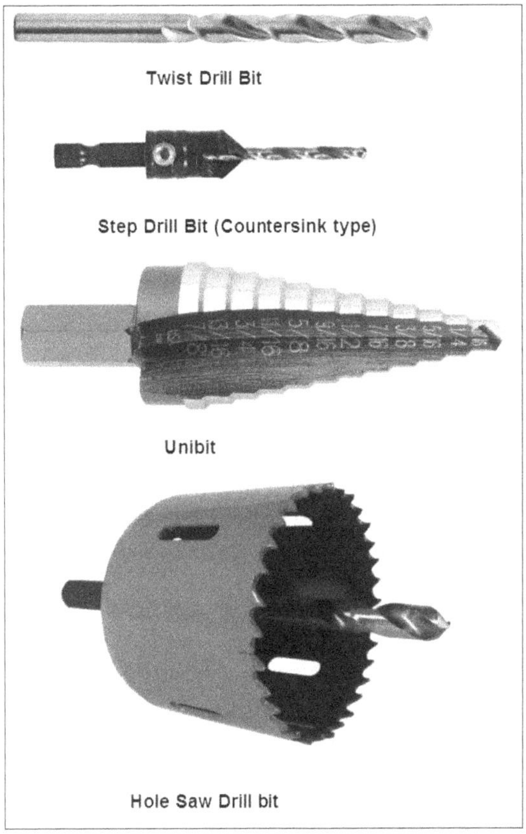

Figure-68. Types of drill bits

Reamer

Reamer is a tool similar to drill bit but its purpose is to finish the hole or increase the size of hole precisely. Figure-69 shows the shape of a reamer.

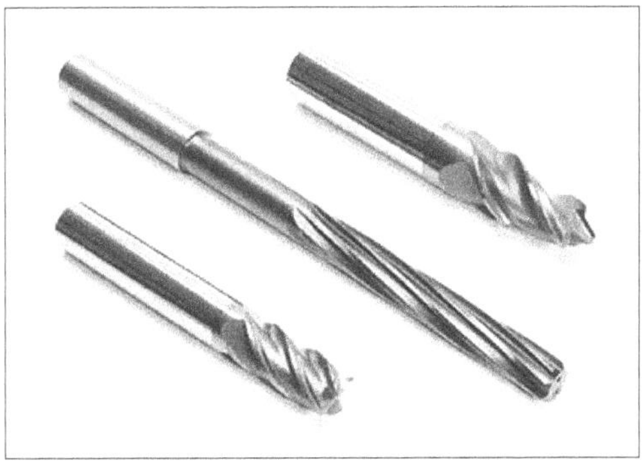

Figure-69. Reamer tool

Bore Bar

Bore Bar or Boring Bar is used to increase the size of hole; refer to Figure-70. One common question is why to use bore bar if we can perform reaming or why to perform reaming when we have bore bar. The answer is accuracy. A reamer does not give tight tolerance in location but gives good finish in hole diameter. A bore bar gives tight tolerance in location but takes more time to machine hole as compared to reamer. The decision to choose the process is on machinist. If you need a highly accurate hole then perform drilling, then boring, and then reaming to get best result.

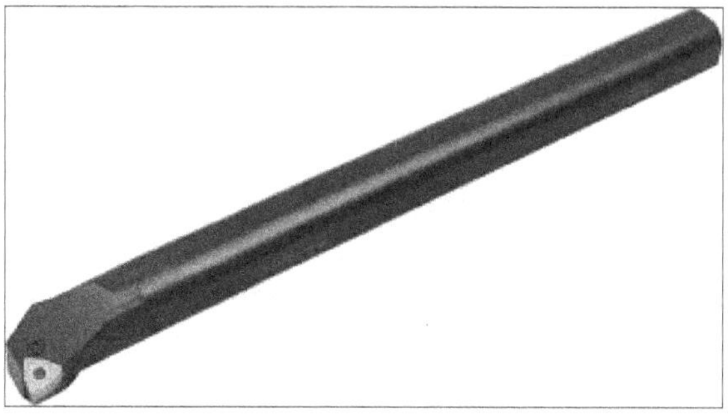

Figure-70. Boring Bar

Lathe Tools or Turning Tools

The tools used in CNC lathe machines use a different nomenclature. In CNC lathe machines, we use insert for cutting material. The Insert Holder and Inserts have a special nomenclature scheme to define their shapes. First, we will discuss the nomenclature of Insert holder and then we will discuss the nomenclature of Inserts.

Insert Holders

Turning holder names follow an ISO nomenclature standard. If you are working on a CNC shop floor with lathes, knowing the ISO nomenclature is a must. The name looks complicated, but is actually very easy to interpret; refer to Figure-71.

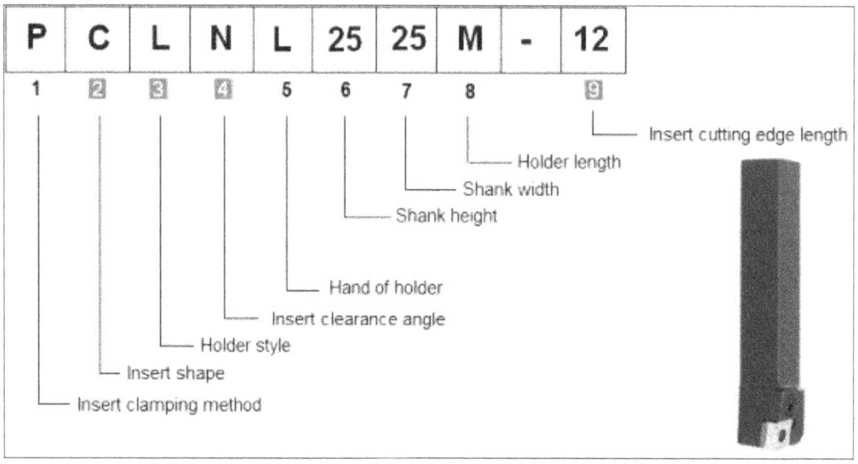

Figure-71. CNC Lathe Insert Holder nomenclature

When selecting a holder for an application, you mainly have to concentrate on the numbers marked in red in the above nomenclature. The others are decided automatically (e.g. the shank width and height are decided by the machine), or require less effort. In Figure-72, the rows with the question mark indicate the parameters that require the decision by machinist based on job.

	Parameter		How is this decided ?
1	Insert clamping method		Select based on cutting forces. Top clamping is the most sturdy, screw clamping the least.
2	Insert shape	?	Decided by the contour that you want to turn.
3	Holder style	?	Decided by the contour that you want to turn.
4	Insert clearance angle	?	Positive / Negative, based on application.
5	Hand of holder		Decided based on whether you want to cut towards the chuck or away from the chuck, and on turret position - turret front / rear
6	Shank height		Decided by holder size.
7	Shank width		Decided by machine.
8	Holder length		Decided by machine.
9	Insert cutting edge length	?	Decided based on depth of cut you want to use.

Figure-72. CNC Lathe Insert Holder nomenclature parameters

Figure-73 and Figure-74 show the options available for each of the parameters.

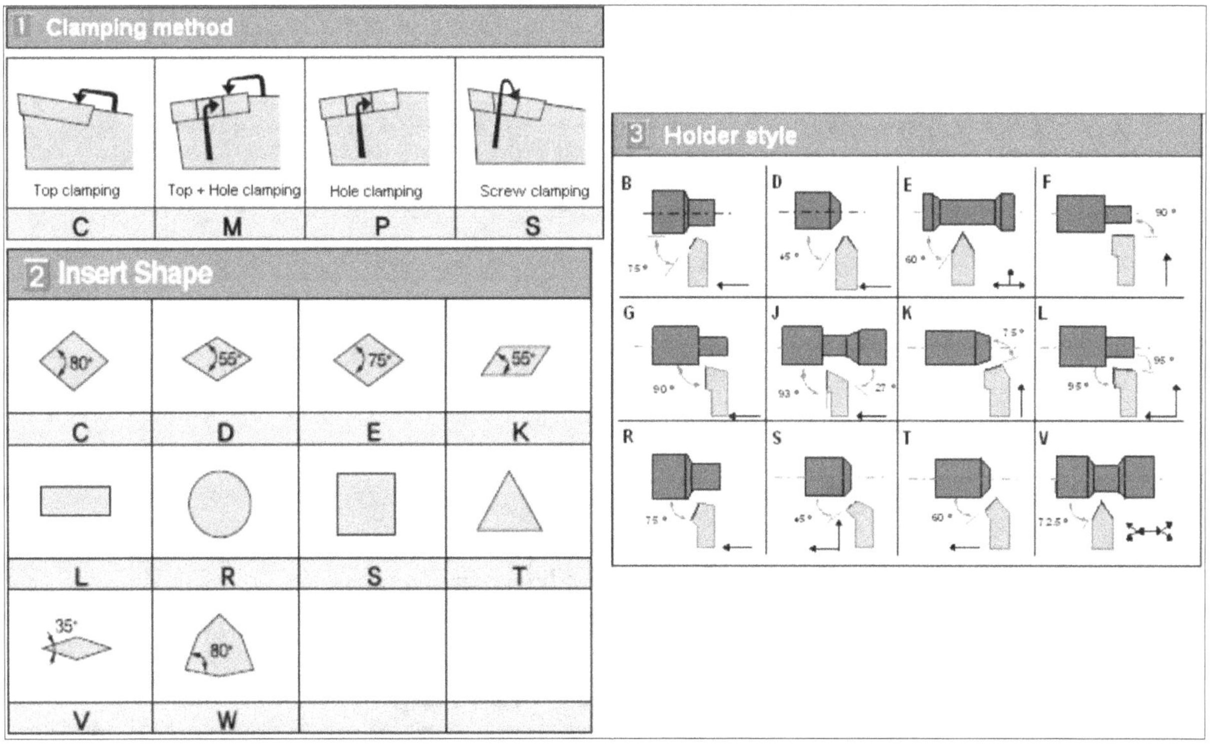

Figure-73. Clamping Method and Insert Shapes

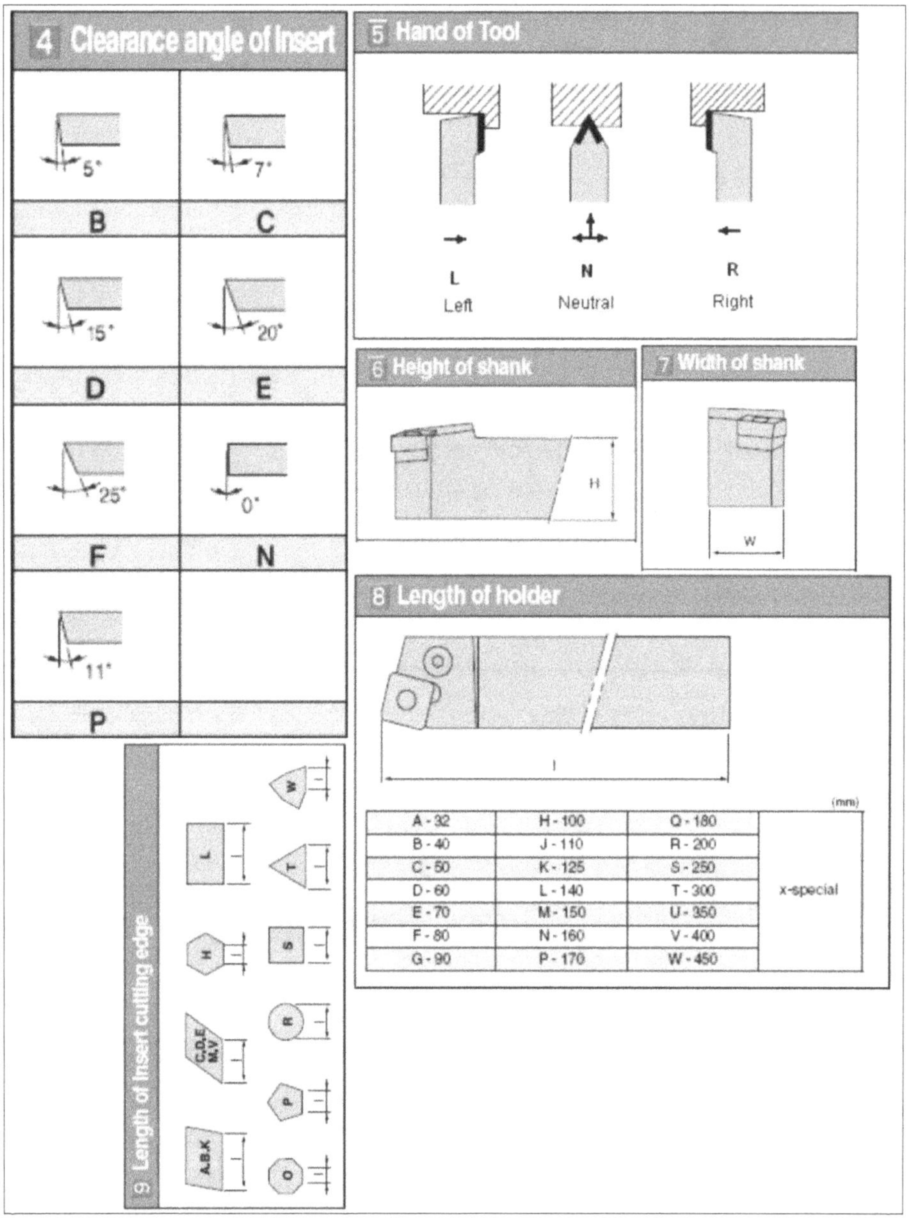

Figure-74. Insert Holder Parameters

CNC Lathe Insert Nomenclature

General CNC Insert name is given as

C	N	M	G	12	04	08
1	2	3	4	5	6	7

Meaning of each box in nomenclature is given next.

1 = Turning Insert Shape

The first letter in general turning insert nomenclature tells us about the general turning insert shape, turning inserts shape codes are like C, D, K, R, S, T, V, W. Most of these codes surely express the turning insert shape like

C = C Shape Turning Insert
D = D Shape Turning Insert

K = K Shape Turning Insert
R = Round Turning Insert
S = Square Turning Insert
T = Triangle Turning Insert
V = V Shape Turning Insert
W = W Shape Turning Insert

Figure-75 shows the turning inserts shapes.

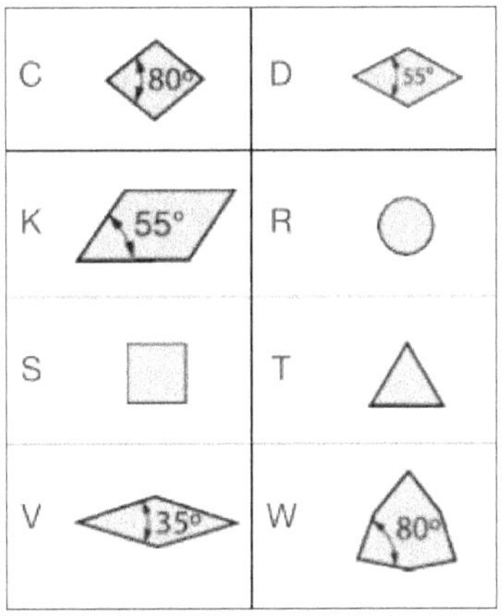

Figure-75. Turning Insert Shapes

The general turning insert shape play a very important role when we choose an insert for machining. Not every turning insert with one shape can be replaced with the other for a machining operation. As C, D, and W type turning inserts are normally used for roughing or rough machining.

2 = Turning Insert Clearance Angle

The second letter in general turning insert nomenclature tells us about the turning insert clearance angle.

The clearance angle for a turning insert is shown in Figure-76.

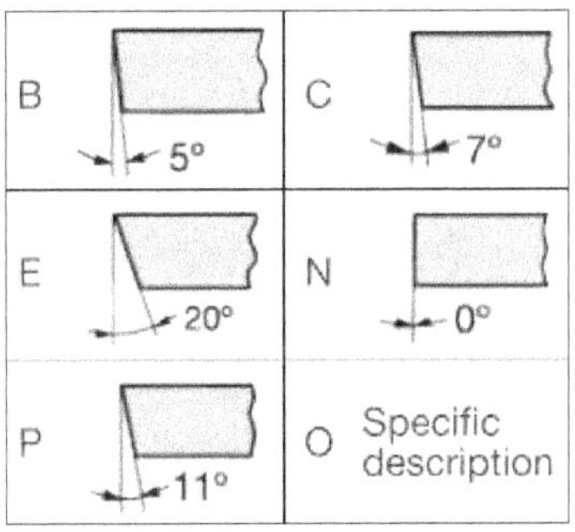

Figure-76. Turning insert clearance angle

Turning insert clearance angle plays a big role while choosing an insert for internal machining or boring small components, because if not properly chosen the insert bottom corner might rub with the component which will give poor machining. On the other hand, a turning insert with 0° clearance angle is mostly used for rough machining.

3 = Turning Insert Tolerances

The third letter of general turning insert nomenclature tells us about the turning insert tolerances. Figure-77 shows the tolerance chart.

Code Letter	Cornerpoint (inches)	Thickness (inches)	Inscribed Circle (in)	Cornerpoint (mm)	Thickness (mm)	Inscribed Circle (mm)
A	.0002"	.001"	.001"	.005mm	.025mm	.025mm
C	.0005"	.001"	.001"	.013mm	.025mm	.025mm
E	.001"	.001"	.001"	.025mm	.025mm	.025mm
F	.0002"	.001"	.0005"	.005mm	.025mm	.013mm
G	.001"	.005"	.001"	.025mm	.13mm	.025mm
H	.0005"	.001"	.0005"	.013mm	.025mm	.013mm
J	.002"	.001"	.002-.005"	.005mm	.025mm	.05-.13mm
K	.0005"	.001"	.002-.005"	.013mm	.025mm	.05-.13mm
L	.001"	.001"	.002-.005"	.025mm	.025mm	.05-.13mm
M	.002-.005"	.005"	.002-.005"	.05-.13mm	.13mm	.05-.15mm
U	.005-.012"	.005"	.005-.010"	.06-.25mm	.13mm	.08-.25mm

Figure-77. Insert tolerance chart

4 = Turning Insert Type

The fourth letter of general turning insert nomenclature tells us about the turning insert hole shape and chip breaker type; refer to Figure-78.

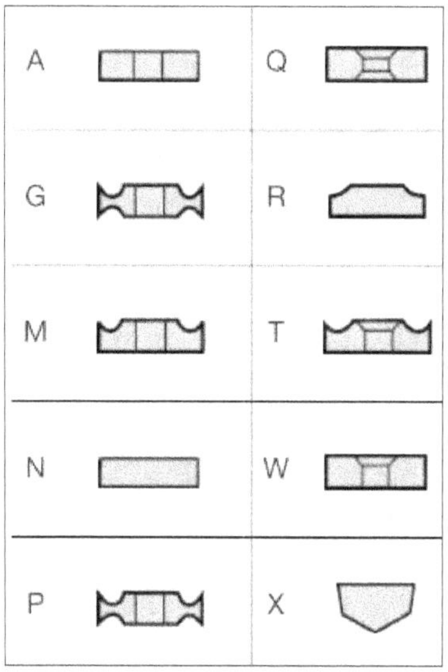

Figure-78. Turning Insert hole shape and chip breaker

5 = Turning Insert Size

This numeric value of general turning insert tells us the cutting edge length of the turning insert; refer to Figure-79.

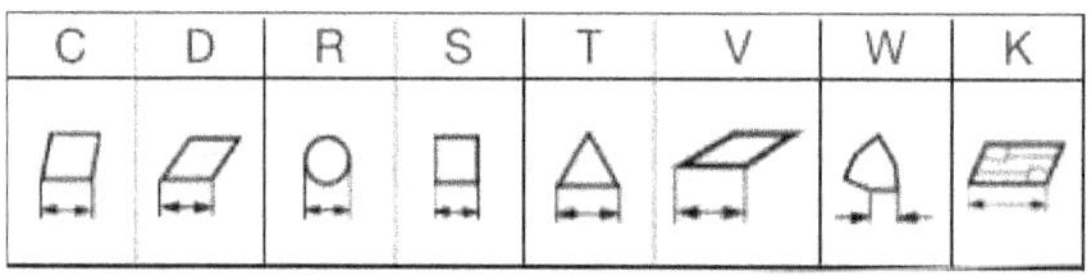

Figure-79. Turning Insert Cutting Edge Length

6 = Turning Insert Thickness

This numeric value of general turning insert tells us about the thickness of the turning insert.

7 = Turning Insert Nose Radius

This numeric value of general turning insert tells us about the nose radius of the turning insert.

Code	=	Radius Value
04	=	0.4
08	=	0.8
12	=	1.2
16	=	1.6

You can learn more about machining tools from your tool supplier manual.

TOOL LIBRARY

Tool Library is used to create and manage cutting tools used in Fusion. Click on the **Tool Library** tool from **MANAGE** drop-down in **MILLING** tab of the **Ribbon**. The **Tool Library** dialog box will be displayed; refer to Figure-80. The process to create a new tool is discussed next.

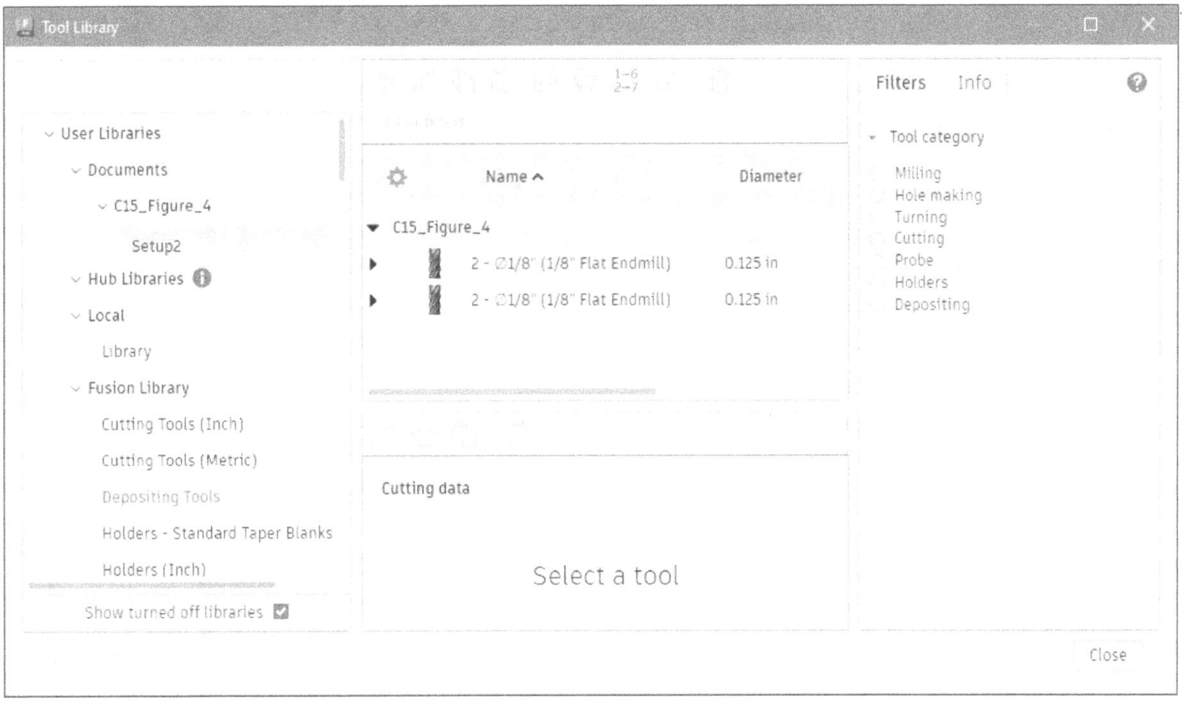

Figure-80. Tool Library dialog box

Creating a New Mill Tool

You have learned to use an already available tool of the library but what if the tool is not available in library. The procedure to create a new mill tool is discussed next.

- Select the **Library** option from the **Local** node in the **Tool Library** area at the left in the dialog box and click on the **New** tool from **Toolbar** in **Cutting Tools list** area of the dialog box. The **New tool** page will be displayed as shown in Figure-81.

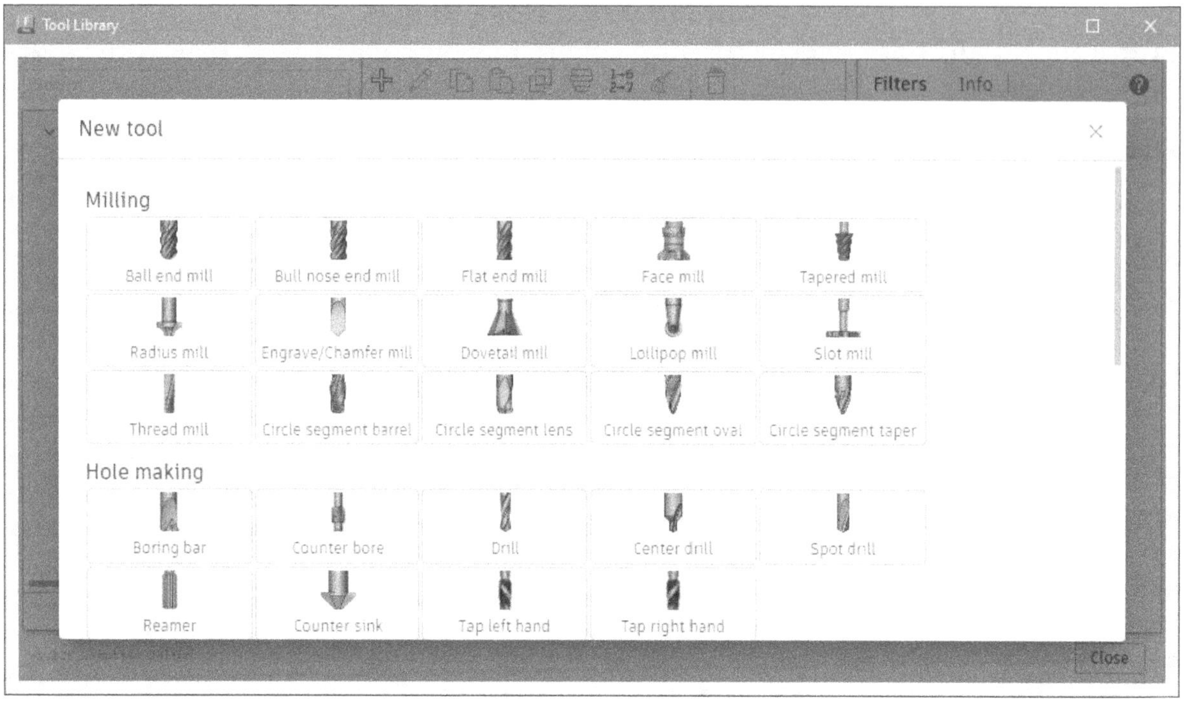

Figure-81. New tool page

- Select desired button from the page to create respective type of cutting tool. In our case, we have selected **Ball end mill** button. The **Tool Library** dialog box will be displayed with options related to selected tool type; refer to Figure-82.

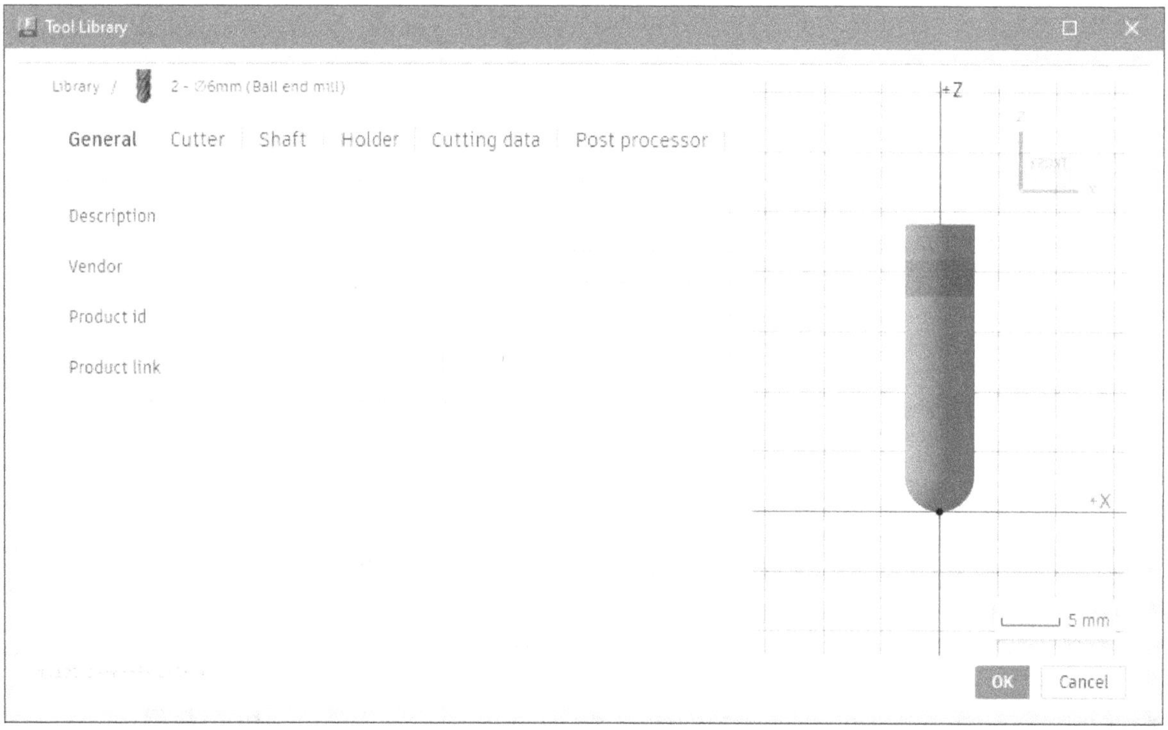

Figure-82. Tool Library dialog box

- Specify desired parameters in the edit boxes of **General** tab in the dialog box like description of tool, name of vendor, and so on.
- Click on the **Cutter** tab in the dialog box. The options will be displayed as shown in Figure-83.

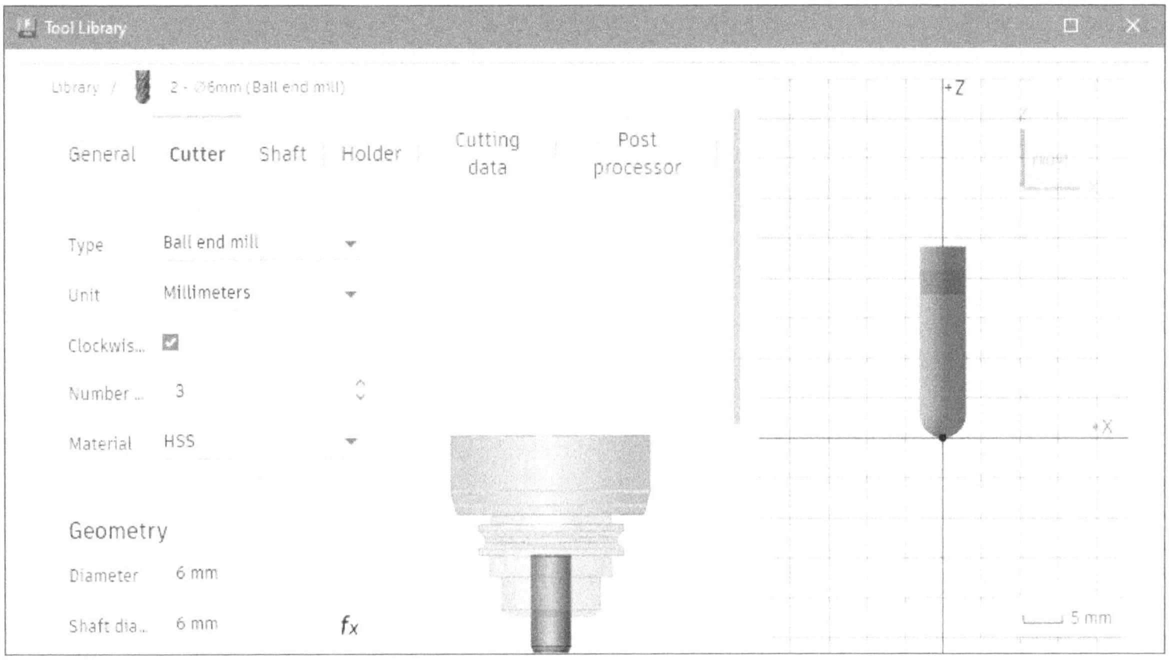

Figure-83. Cutter tab in Tool Library dialog box

- Click on the **Type** drop-down from **Cutter** tab of **Tool Library** dialog box and select desired type of cutting tool if you want to change the tool type. Preview of the selected tool type will be displayed in graphics section of dialog box.
- Click on the **Unit** drop-down from the **Cutter** tab and select desired unit type.
- Select the **Clockwise spindle rotation** check box to set the rotation of spindle to clockwise direction.
- Click in the **Number of flutes** edit box and specify desired value to define number of cutting flutes in the tool.
- Click on the **Material** drop-down and select desired material used for cutting tool.
- Click in the **Diameter** edit box of the **Geometry** section and specify the diameter of cutting tool.
- Click in the **Overall length** edit box to specify total length of cutting tool.
- Click in the **Shaft diameter** edit box of the **Geometry** section and specify the diameter of shaft.
- Similarly, click in the other edit boxes and specify desired parameters in **Geometry** section of **Cutter** tab.
- Click on the **Shaft** tab from the **Tool Library** dialog box. The **Shaft** tab will be displayed; refer to Figure-84.

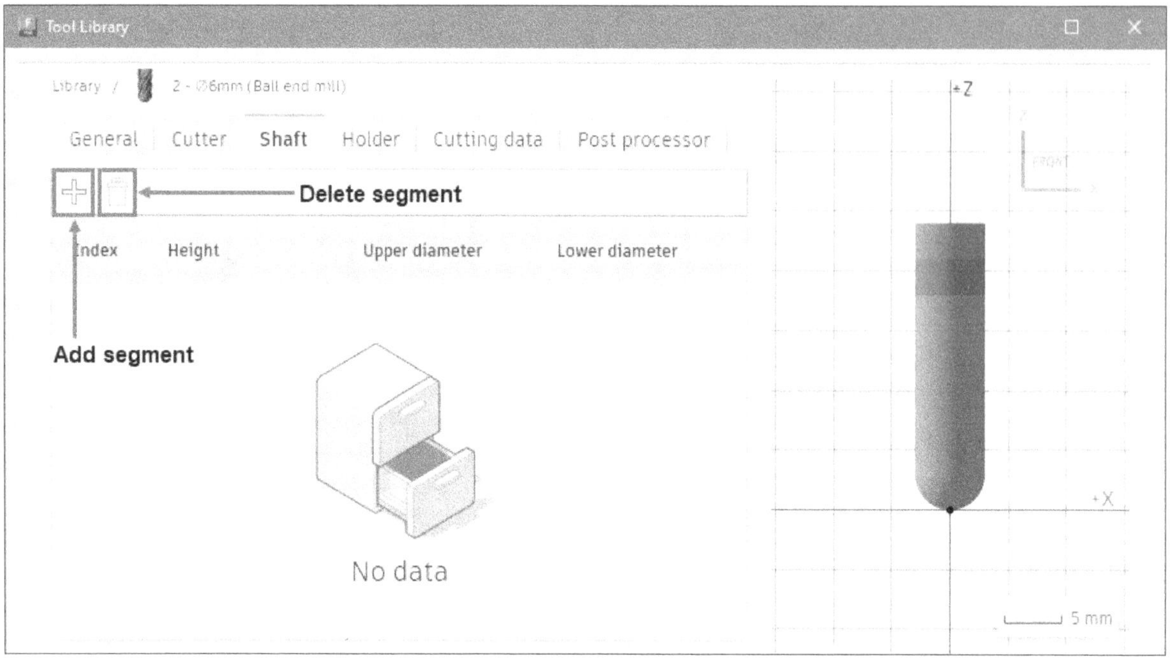

Figure-84. Shaft tab of Tool Library dialog box

- To add the shaft, click on the **Add segment** button and if you want to delete the created shaft then click on the **Delete segment** button from **Shaft** tab.
- After clicking on the **Add segment** button, double-click in the edit boxes for shaft parameter to set the shaft shape and size. Preview of the shaft will be displayed on the right in the dialog box; refer to Figure-85.

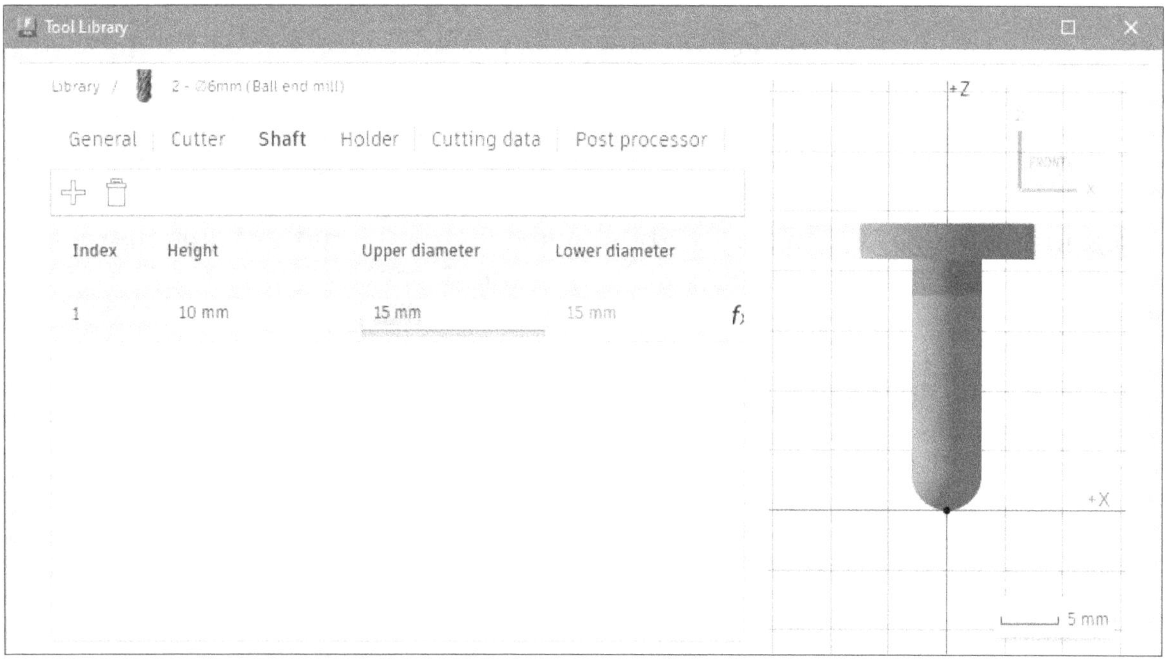

Figure-85. Editing the value of shaft

- If you want to delete a segment of shaft then select the shaft from list and click on the **Delete segment** button.
- Click on the **Holder** tab from the **Tool Library** dialog box to select desired tool holder. The **Holder** tab will be displayed; refer to Figure-86.

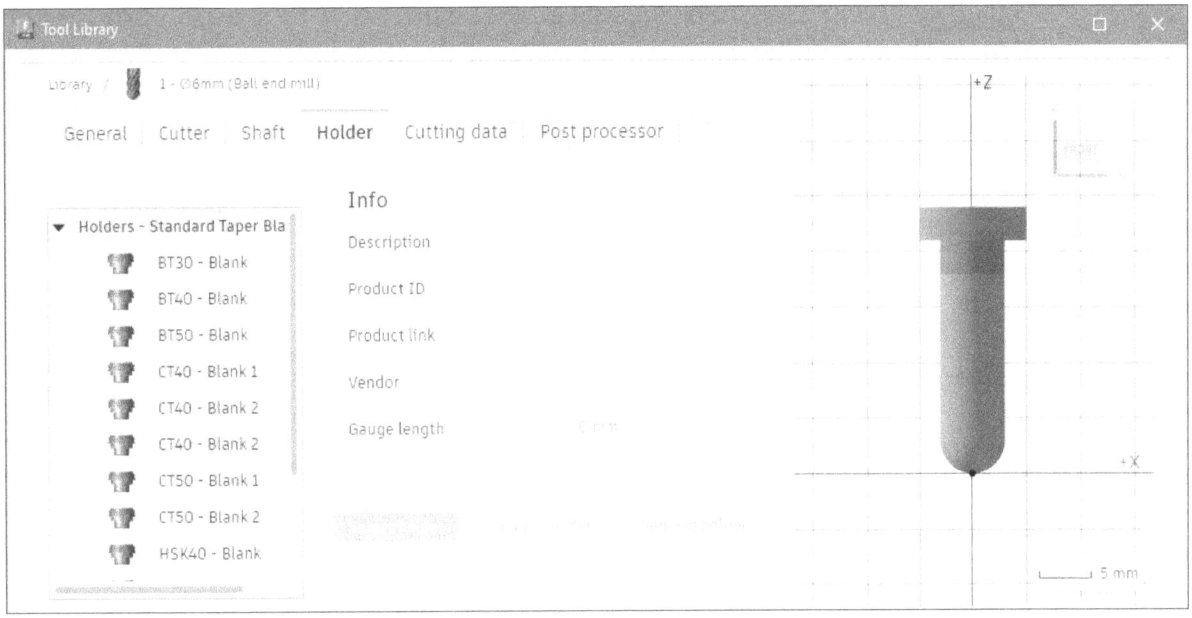

Figure-86. Holder tab

- Select desired holder from the list at the left in the dialog box and click on the **Select holder** button from the **Holder** tab to use selected holder. Preview of tool holder will be displayed. Specify desired parameters in the **Info** area of the dialog box.
- Click on the **Cutting data** tab of the **Tool Library** dialog box to set the feed and speed of cutting tool. Options in the **Cutting data** tab will be displayed as shown in Figure-87. You can use multiple cutting data presets for different materials using the **Add preset** button at the left in the dialog box.

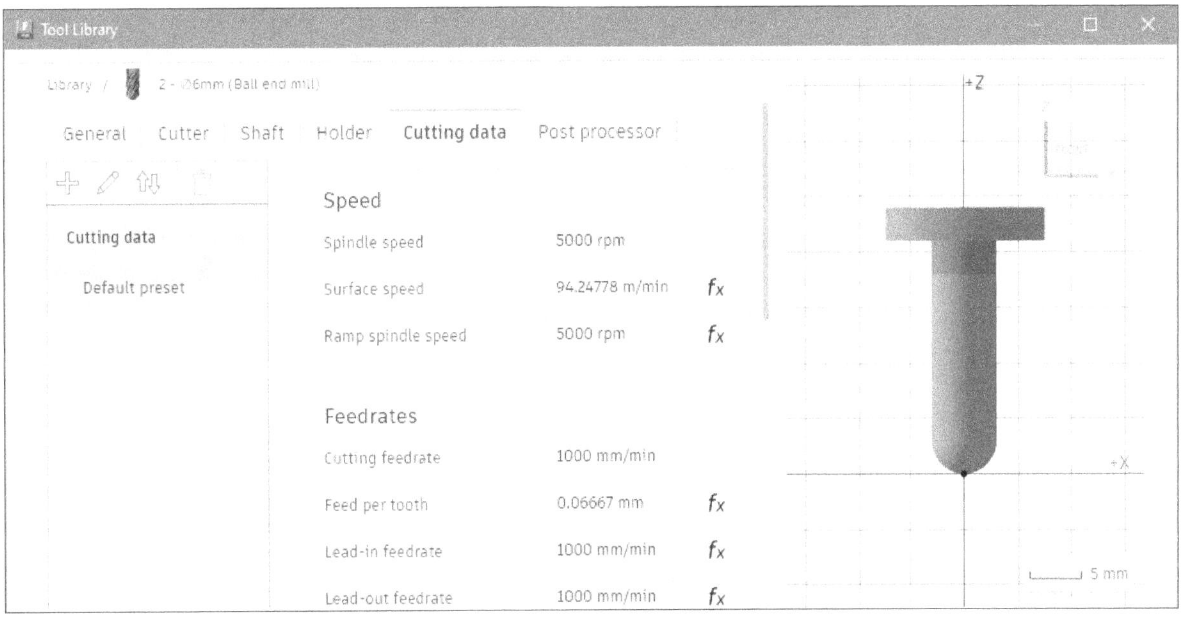

Figure-87. Cutting data tab

- Click in the **Spindle speed** edit box to define rotational speed at which cutting tool will be rotating while machining.
- Click in the **Surface speed** edit box to define surface speed at tools cutting edge. Note that the **Spindle speed** and **Surface speed** parameters are inter-related by formula "Surface speed = Π x D x RPM". Here, D is diameter of tool and RPM is the Spindle speed.

- Specify desired value in the **Ramp spindle speed** edit box to define spindle speed when cutting tool is moving in ramp motion while cutting.
- Specify desired value in the **Cutting feedrate** edit box to define speed at which tool will move on the path while cutting material.
- Specify desired value in the **Feed per tooth** edit box if you want to define cutting speed in terms of tool movement per tooth. Note that the value in this edit box is generated automatically based on value specified in **Cutting feedrate** edit box by relation "Feed per tooth = Cutting feedrate/(Spindle speed x Number of flutes in cutting tool).
- Specify desired values in the **Lead-in feedrate** and **Lead-out feedrate** edit boxes to specify at what speed the cutting tool will enter and exit the workpiece, respectively.
- Specify desired value in the **Transition feedrate** edit box to define speed at which cutting tool moves from one lead out pass to next lead in pass.
- Specify desired value in the **Ramp feedrate** edit box to define the cutting feedrate when cutting tool(s) is moving in a ramp motion. Ramp motion is generated in toolpath when cutting tool moves up or down in the workpiece while cutting.
- Specify desired value in the **Plunge feedrate** edit box of **Vertical feedrates** section in the dialog box to define vertical movement speed of tool when entering the workpiece. Similarly, you can specify value in **Plunge feed per revolution** edit box to define feed rate with respect to revolution of cutting tool and other parameters in the page.
- Select **Use Stepdown** and **Use Stepover** check boxes from **Passes and linking** section to use specified values of stepdown and stepover overriding operation parameter.
- Select desired option from the **Coolant** drop-down to define how coolant will be sprayed on the work piece while performing cutting operations.
- Click in the **Post processor** tab of **Tool Library** dialog box to specify the post processor related values of NC machining. The **Post processor** tab will be displayed; refer to Figure-88.

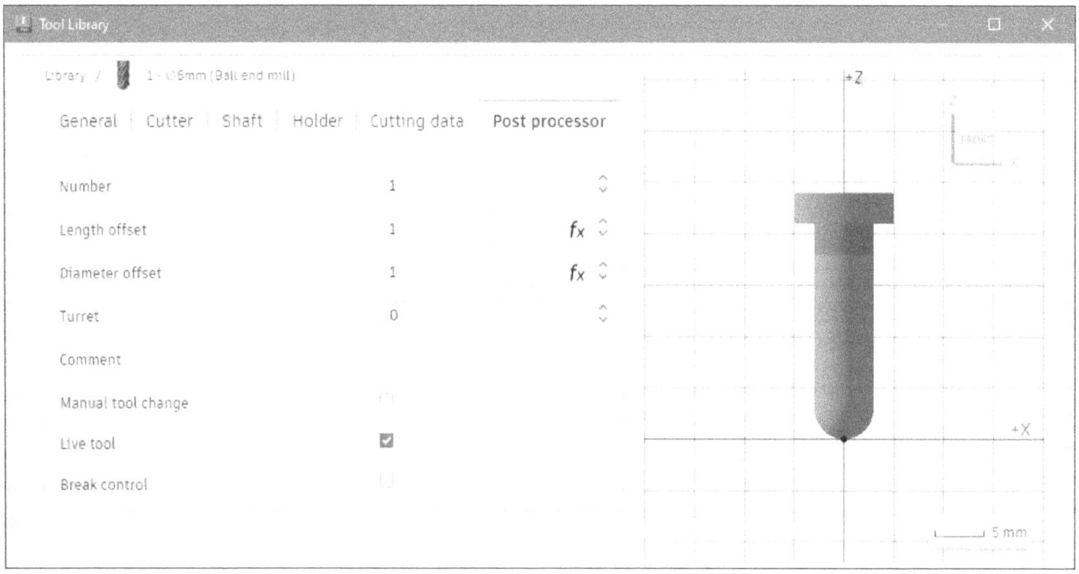

Figure-88. Post processor tab

- The parameters in this tab are used to define compensation for tool wear while machining. Note that due to repetitive cutting cycles, the cutting edges/tips of tools wear and cause lesser depth of cuts over the period of time for same toolpaths. To compensate that we add values specified in offsets of post processor to cutting operation movement for extending depths.
- Click in the **Number** edit box and specify the tool number for which you want to define parameters.
- Click in the **Length offset** edit box and define length offset number to be associated with the current tool number.
- Click in the **Diameter offset** edit box and define diameter offset number to be associated with the current tool number.
- Click in the **Turret** edit box and specify the turret number to be used for defining parameters related to cutting tools. A turret is generally a big round mechanism that holds multiple different cutting tools in the machine indexed by tool numbers. Some machines can have multiple turrets but commonly you will find a single turret in the machine.
- Click in the **Comment** edit box to associate a text comment with current selected tool. This comment tells the properties of current tool in output file. Note that the comments do not take any role in cutting operations and are provided only for information of users.
- Select **Manual tool change** check box to force manual change of cutting tool by user after each operation even in an automatic machine.
- Select the **Live tool** check box to tell the machine that current tool is a live (active) cutting tool. If this check box is not selected then current tool will not be used for cutting operations and will be considered as empty slot in turret.
- Select the **Break control** check box to check whether cutting tool is in good condition or not. Make sure your machine and post processor support this function before selecting this check box.
- After specifying all the parameters, click on the **OK** button. The mill tool will be created and added in the tools list.

Creating New Tool Library

A tool library is an organized collection cutting tools. You can create a new tool library specific to your products in your industry. To create a new library, right-click on **Local** node and select the **New library** tool from the shortcut menu. You will be asked to specify name for new library; refer to Figure-89. Specify desired name for new library and press **ENTER**. The library will be created. Note that if you select a library and create a new tool then new tool will be part of selected library.

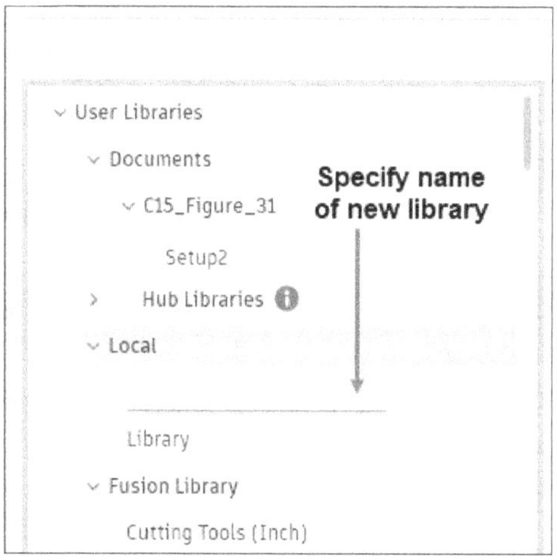

Figure-89. New library added

You can use the **Rename** tool in **Toolbar** of the dialog box after selecting a user defined library in the dialog box to change the name of the library. Using the **Duplicate library** tool, you can create a duplicate copy of selected user defined library.

Importing Libraries

The **Import libraries** tool is used to include one or more tool libraries from selected data files. The procedure to use this tool is given next.

- Right-click on the **Local** node at the left in the dialog box and select the **Import libraries** tool from the shortcut menu. The **Open File(s)** dialog box will be displayed; refer to Figure-90.

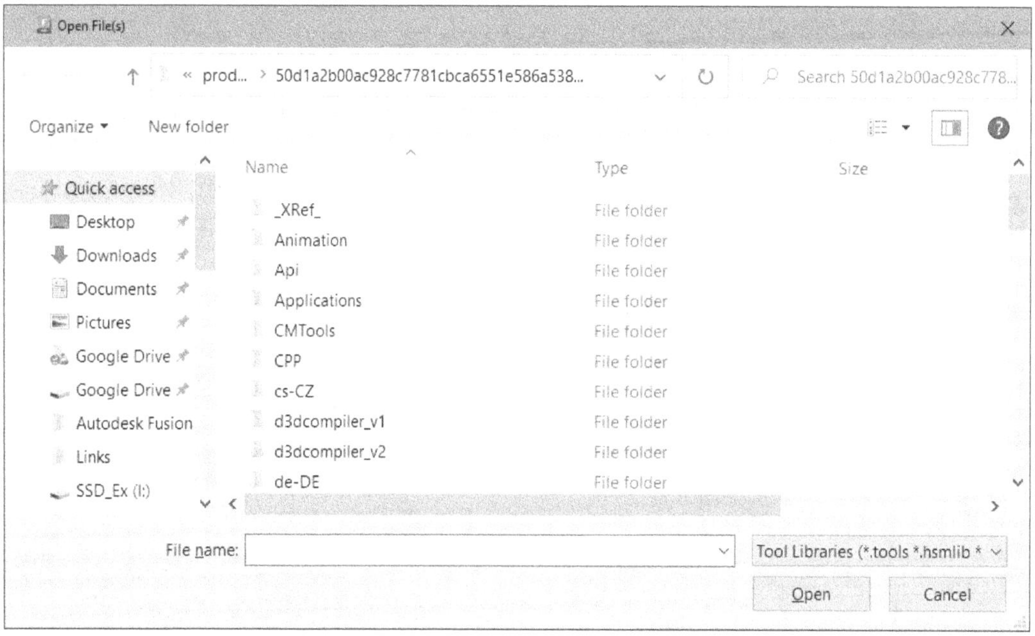

Figure-90. Open Files dialog box

- Select desired files to import library data stored in them. You can select multiple files while holding the **CTRL** key. Make sure the files are in supported formats (*.tools, *.hsmlib, *.json, and *.tsv).
- After selecting files, click on the **Open** button. The imported libraries will be added in the dialog box.

Exporting Tool Library

The **Export library** tool is used to export selected tool library data in a file. The procedure to use this tool is given next.

- Click on the **Export library** tool from the right-click shortcut menu after selecting a library from left area in the dialog box. The **Save File** dialog box will be displayed as shown in Figure-91.
- Specify desired name of file in the **File name** edit box at the bottom in the dialog box.
- Click in the **Save as type** drop-down and select desired format in which the file will be saved.

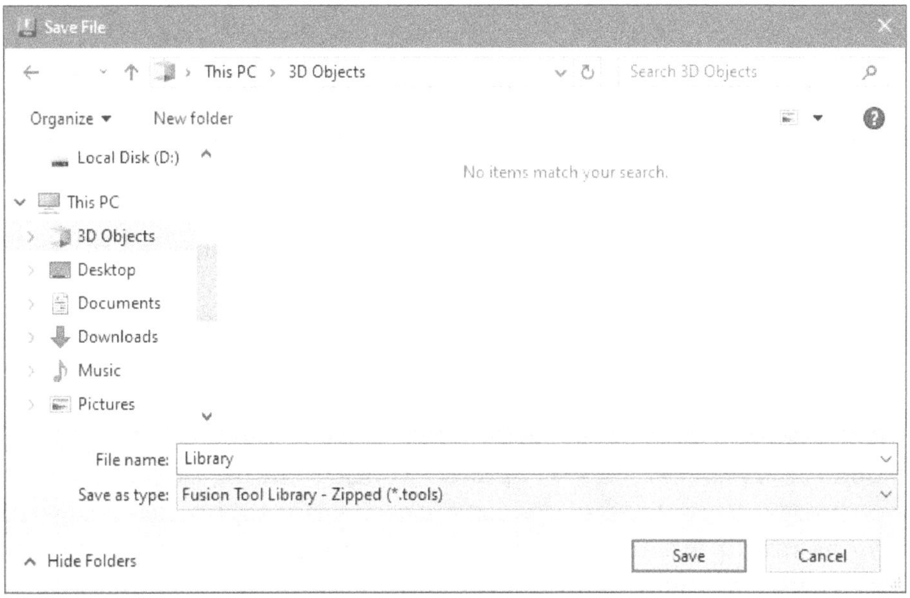

Figure-91. Save File dialog box

- You can move to desired directory by using common Operation System functions. After setting desired parameters, click on the **Save** button. The file will be exported to specified directory.

Renumbering Tools of a Library

The **Renumber tools** tool is used to change the numbering of cutting tools in selected library by specified increment value. The procedure to use this tool is given next.

- Select the user defined library whose tool numbers are to be changed from the left area in the dialog box and click on the **Renumber tools** tool from the **Toolbar** in the **Tool Library** dialog box. The **Renumber tools** page will be displayed in the dialog box; refer to Figure-92.

Figure-92. Renumber tools page

- Click in the **Start from** edit box and specify the starting number to be applied to first tool in the library.
- Click in the **Increment by** edit box and specify the increment value to be added in current tool number to get next tool number in the library. For example, if you have set increment value as 2 and first tool number is 1 then next tool number will be 3, up next will be 5, and so on.
- Select the **Update diameter offset**, **Update length offset**, and **Update compensation offset** check boxes to update respective offsets based on new tool numbers.
- After setting desired parameters, click on the **Renumber** button from the page. The tool numbers will change accordingly.

The **Delete library** tool in the **Toolbar** of **Tool Library** dialog box is used to delete selected user defined tool library. Similarly, you can use the tools in **Toolbar** of Cutting tools list area of the dialog box to manage cutting tools.

Creating New Holder

In this section, we will discuss about the procedure of creating new tool holder. The procedure is discussed next.

- Select the library in which you want to add new tool holder and click on the **New tool** button from the **Toolbar** in the **Tool Library** dialog box. The **New tool** page will be displayed in the dialog box as discussed earlier.
- Scroll down and click on the **Holder** button from the **Holders** section of the page. The **Tool Library** dialog box will be displayed; refer to Figure-93.

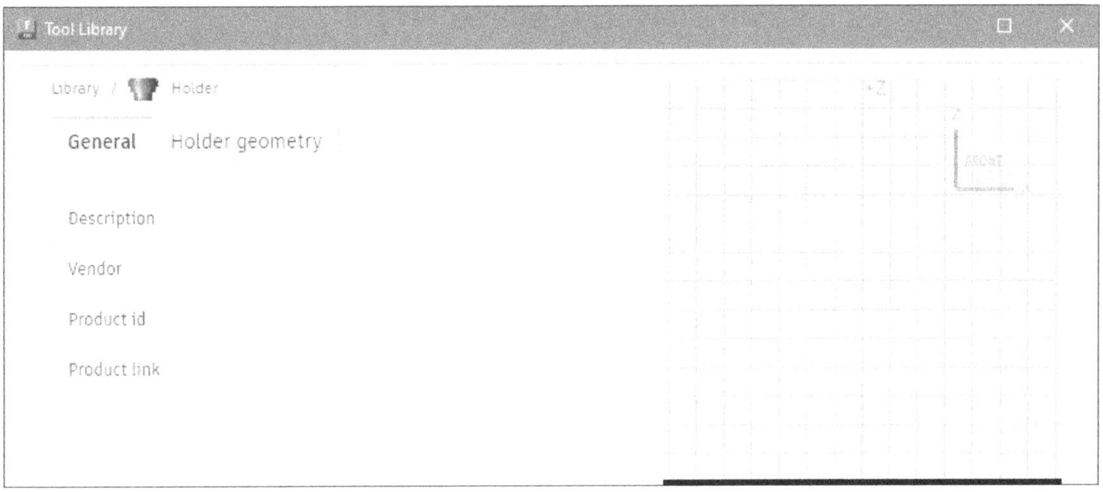

Figure-93. Tool Library dialog box for creating holder

- Click in the edit boxes of **General** tab from **Tool Library** dialog box and specify the information of holder as desired.
- Click on the **Holder geometry** tab from **Tool Library** dialog box to view or change the geometry of holder; refer to Figure-94.
- Click on the **Add segment** button from the dialog box to add desired segment in tool holder. The procedure is same as discussed earlier while creating new tool.
- To change a parameter, click in the respective edit box and specify desired value. The holder in graphic window will be updated; refer to Figure-95.

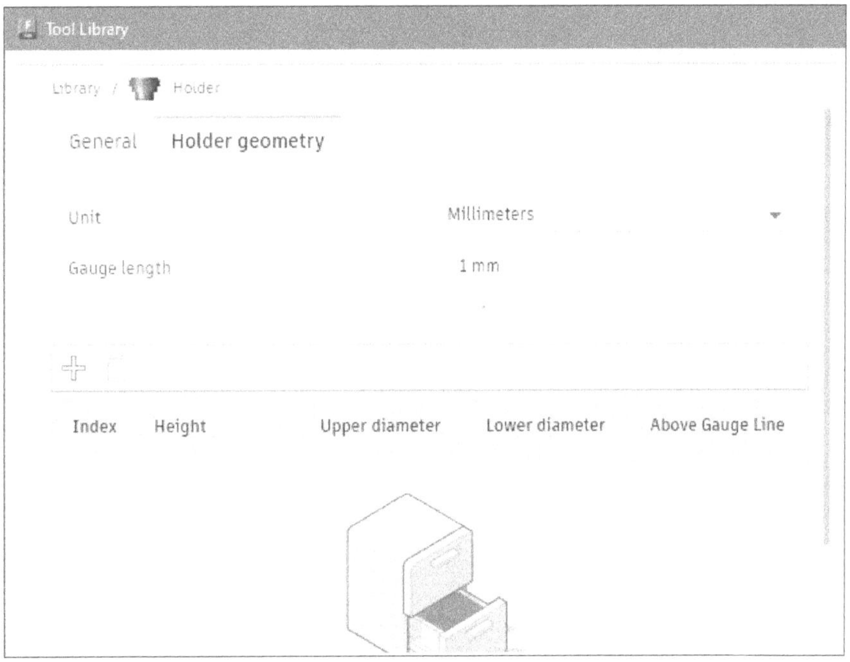

Figure-94. Holder geometry tab of Tool Library dialog box

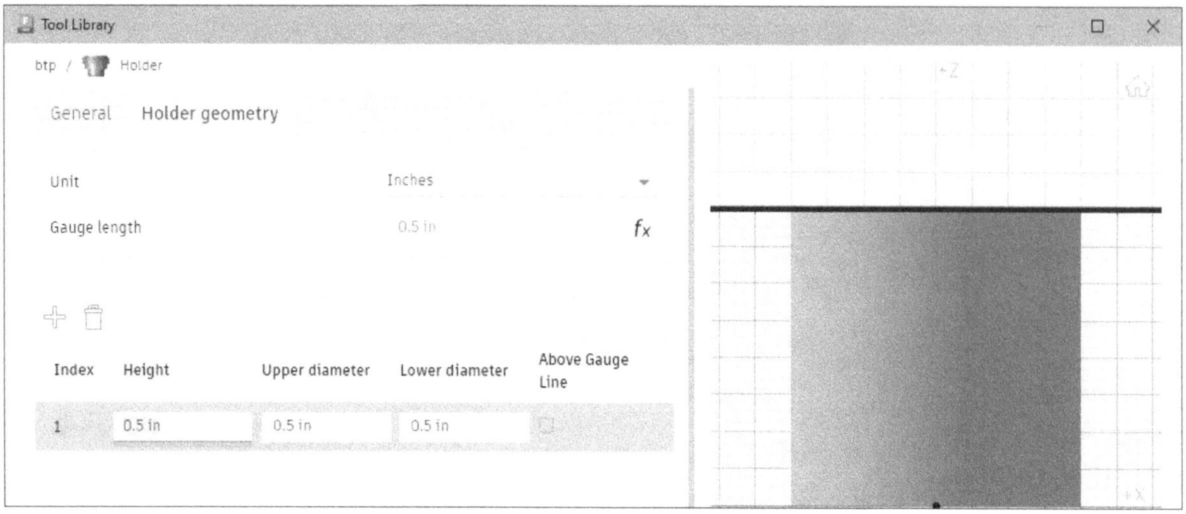

Figure-95. Preview of tool holder

- After specifying the parameter, click on the **OK** button from **Tool Library** dialog box. The created tool holder will be displayed in **Tool Library** dialog box.

Creating New Turning tool

In this section, we will discuss about the procedure of creating a new turning tool. The procedure is discussed next.

- Select the library in which you want to add new turning tool and click on the **New tool** button from the **Toolbar** in the **Tool Library** dialog box. The **New tool** page will be displayed in the dialog box as discussed earlier.
- Click on desired button from the **Turning** section of the page. Respective options will be displayed in the **Tool Library** dialog box; refer to Figure-96 (in case of turning general button selected).

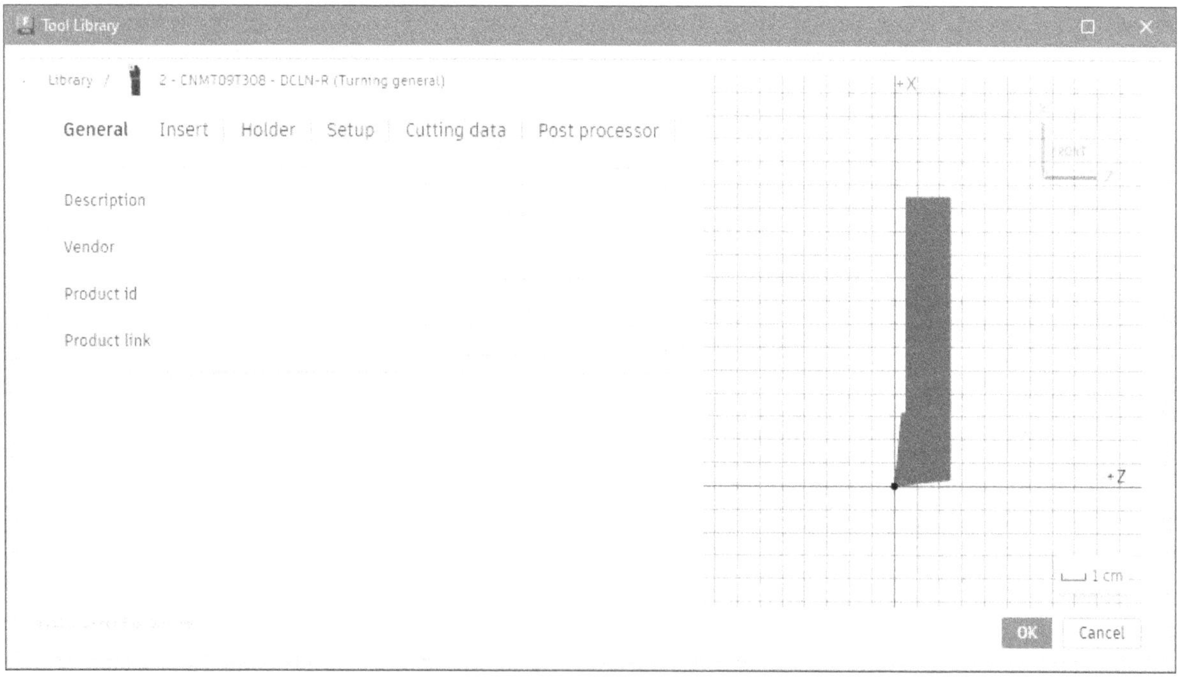

Figure-96. General tab in Tool Library dialog box

- Specify desired parameters in the **General** tab of the dialog box.

- Click on the **Insert** tab from the dialog box to specify parameters related to cutting tool insert used in turning tool. The dialog box will be displayed as shown in Figure-97.

Figure-97. Insert tab in Tool Library dialog box

- Click in the **ISO code** edit box to specify desired ISO code of cutting tool insert from your Tool Manufacturer's manual. All the parameters in the dialog box will be modified accordingly. You can also specify parameters in the other edit boxes of dialog box and value in ISO code edit box will be modified accordingly.
- Click in the **Shape** drop-down and select desired shape for tool insert. Preview of the cutting tool insert will be displayed; refer to Figure-98.

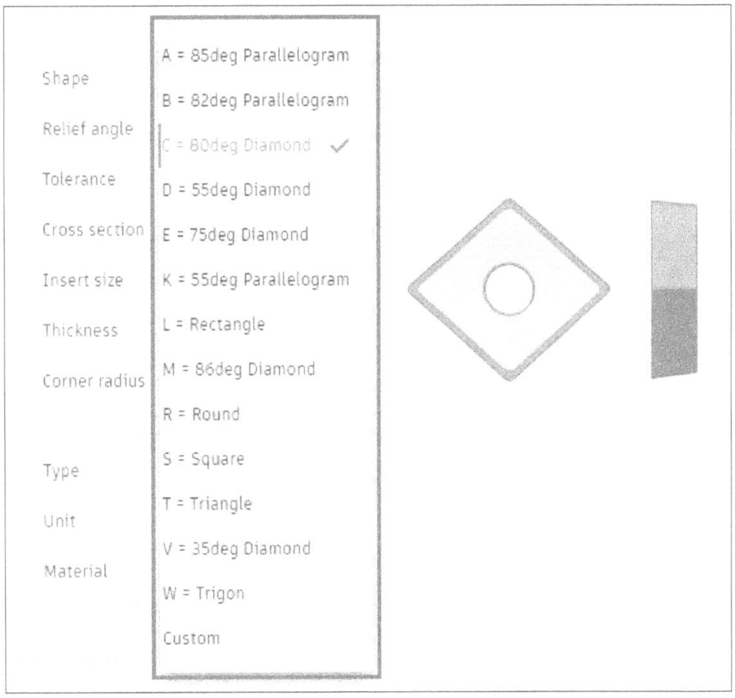

Figure-98. Preview of tool insert

- Click in the **Relief angle** drop-down and specify the slope angle to be applied on the side face of insert for breaking chips while cutting.
- Click in the **Tolerance** drop-down and select desired option to define tolerance in tool insert size.

- Click in the **Cross section** drop-down to define cross-sectional shape of the cutting tool inserts.
- Click in the **Insert size** drop-down to define size of cutting tool insert.
- Click in the **Thickness** drop-down to define thickness of cutting tool insert.
- Click in the **Corner radius** drop-down to define radius at the corners of tool insert.
- Select desired option from the **Type** drop-down to define the type of cutting insert to be created.
- Similarly, set the other parameters for turning tool in **Insert** tab.
- Specify desired parameter in the **Holder** tab of **Tool Library** dialog box as discussed earlier.
- Click in the **Setup** tab from the **Tool Library** dialog box to setup the tool. The **Setup** tab will be displayed; refer to Figure-99.
- The four arrows keys are used to define the orientation of the cutting tool in turret. This orientation defines which side of tool holder will be used for cutting. Click on the upper key to orient the tool's tip upward, left key to orient the tool to left side, right key to orient the tool to right side, and down key to orient the tool's tip downward. If you want to orient the tool at specified angle then click in the **Orientation** edit box and specify the angle.
- Click in the **Compensation** drop-down from **Setup** tab and select desired option to define where tool wear compensation will be applied.
- Select the **Clockwise spindle rotation** check box from **Spindle Rotation** section to set the rotation direction of spindle as clockwise.
- Set the parameters in other tabs of **Tool Library** dialog box as discussed earlier and click on the **OK** button. The new turning tool will be created and displayed in the **Tool Library** dialog box.

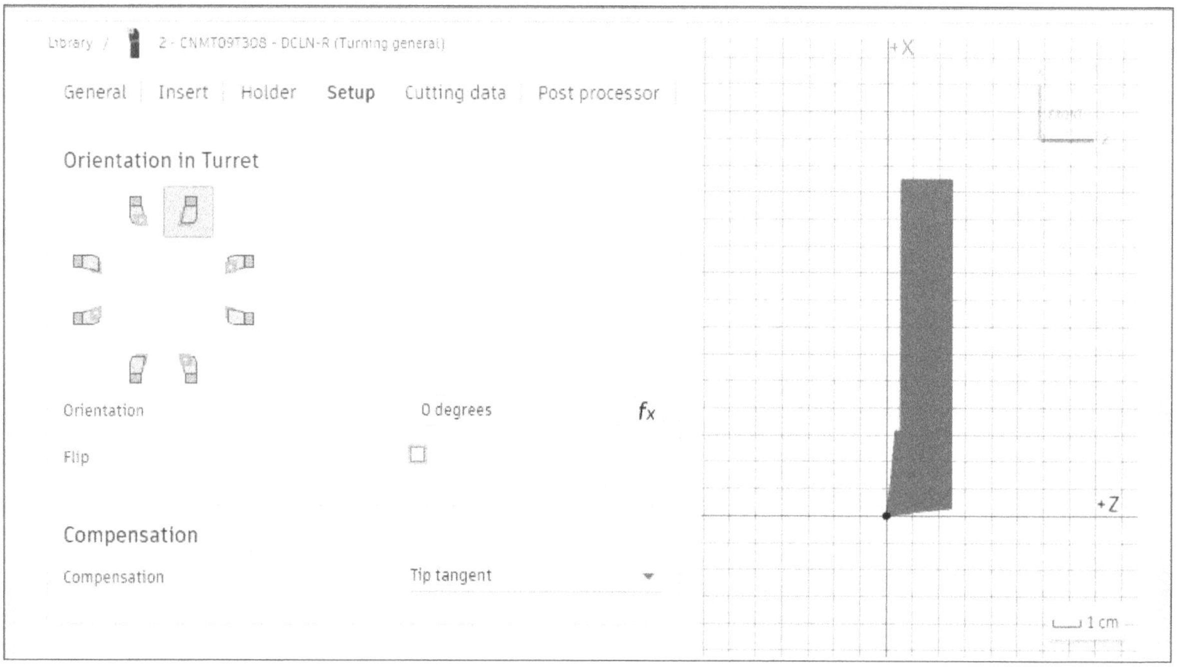

Figure-99. Setup tab for turning

Creating new tool for Waterjet/ Plasma Cutter/ Laser Cutter

In this section, we will discuss about the procedure of creating the Waterjet/Plasma Cutter/Laser Cutter tool. The procedure is discussed next.

- Select the library in which you want to add new turning tool and click on the **New tool** button from the **Toolbar** in the **Tool Library** dialog box. The **New tool** page will be displayed in the dialog box as discussed earlier.
- Click on desired button from the **Cutting** section of the page. Respective options will be displayed in the **Tool Library** dialog box; refer to Figure-100 (In case of waterjet).

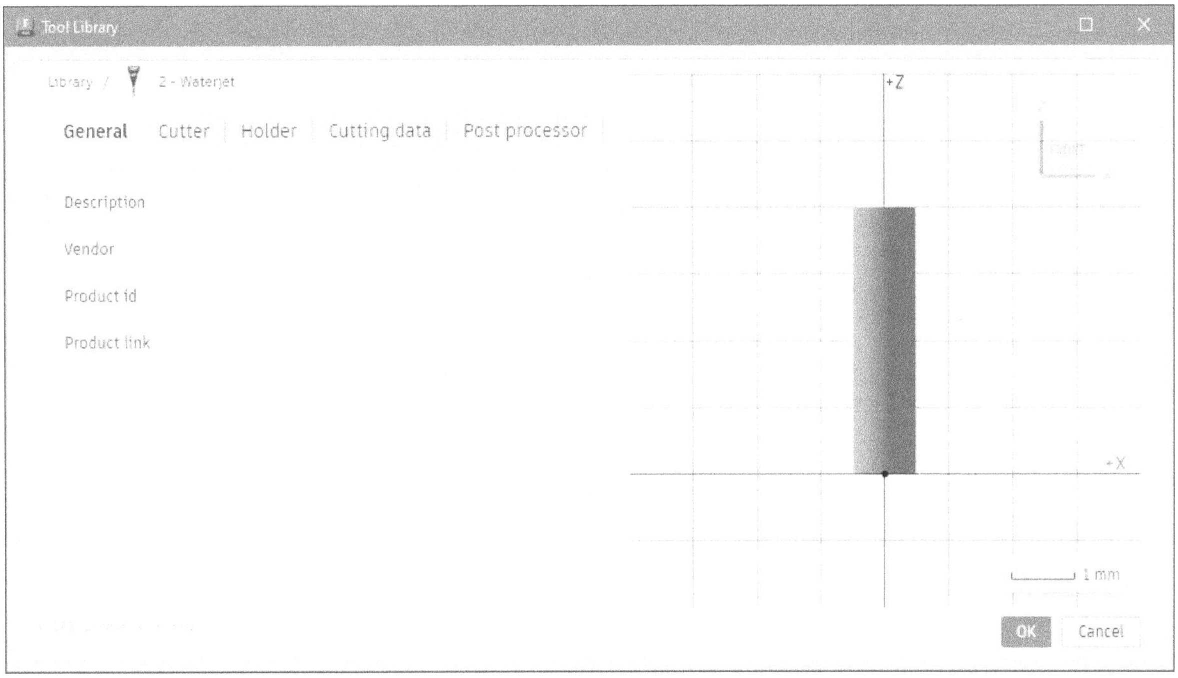

Figure-100. Tool Library dialog box for waterjet

- The options of the **Tool Library** dialog box are similar as discussed earlier in **Creating New Mill tool** section of this chapter.
- After specifying the parameters, click on the **OK** button from the **Tool Library** dialog box. The created tool will be displayed in **Tool Library** dialog box.
- After creating desired tools, click on the **Close** button from the dialog box.

MACHINE LIBRARY

The **Machine Library** tool is used to create and manage machines used in Fusion CAM. Click on the **Machine Library** tool from the **MANAGE** drop-down in the **MILLING** tab of the **Ribbon**. The **Machine Library** dialog box will be displayed; refer to Figure-101.

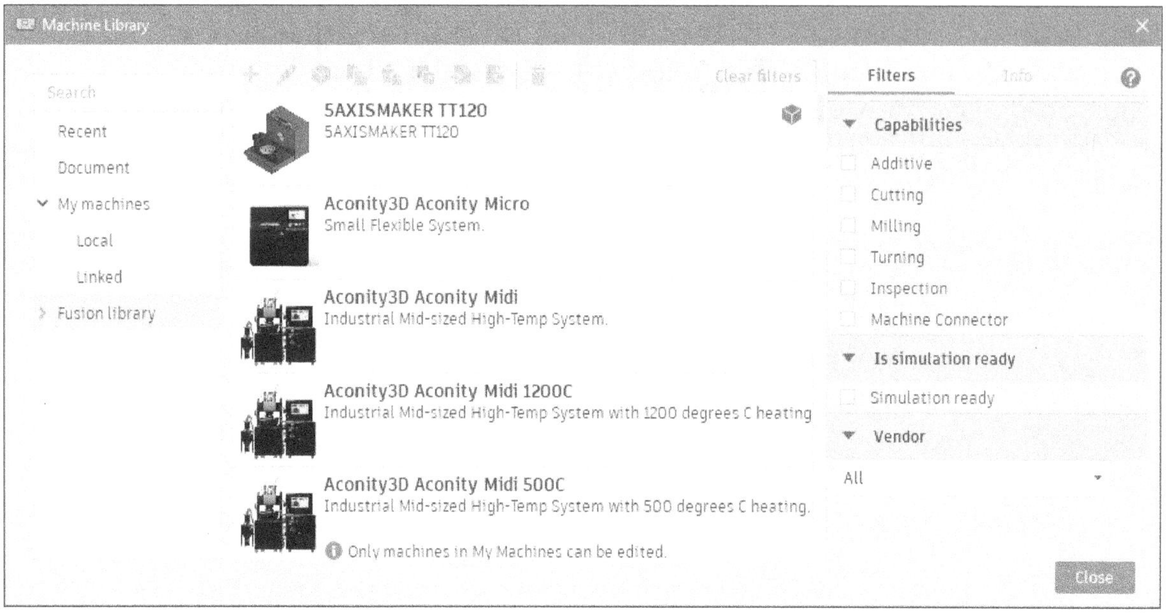

Figure-101. Machine Library dialog box

Creating a New Machine

The **Create new** tool in the **Toolbar** of the **Machine Library** dialog box is used to create a new machine of desired type. The procedure to use this tool is given next.

- Select the **Local** option in the **My machines** node from left area of the **Machine Library** dialog box and click on the **Create new** tool from the **Toolbar**. A flyout will be displayed with list of machines that can be created; refer to Figure-102.

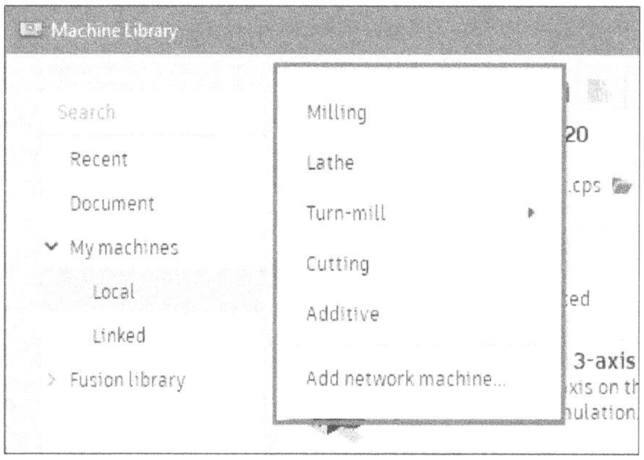

Figure-102. Create new flyout

- Select desired option from the flyout (**Milling** option in our case). The **Machine Definition** dialog box will be displayed. Most of the options of the dialog box has been discussed earlier. Rest of the options are discussed next.
- Select the **Kinematics** option from the left area of the dialog box and select X option from the tree to define parameters related to linear motion of tool and workpiece along X axis. The options will be displayed as shown in Figure-103.

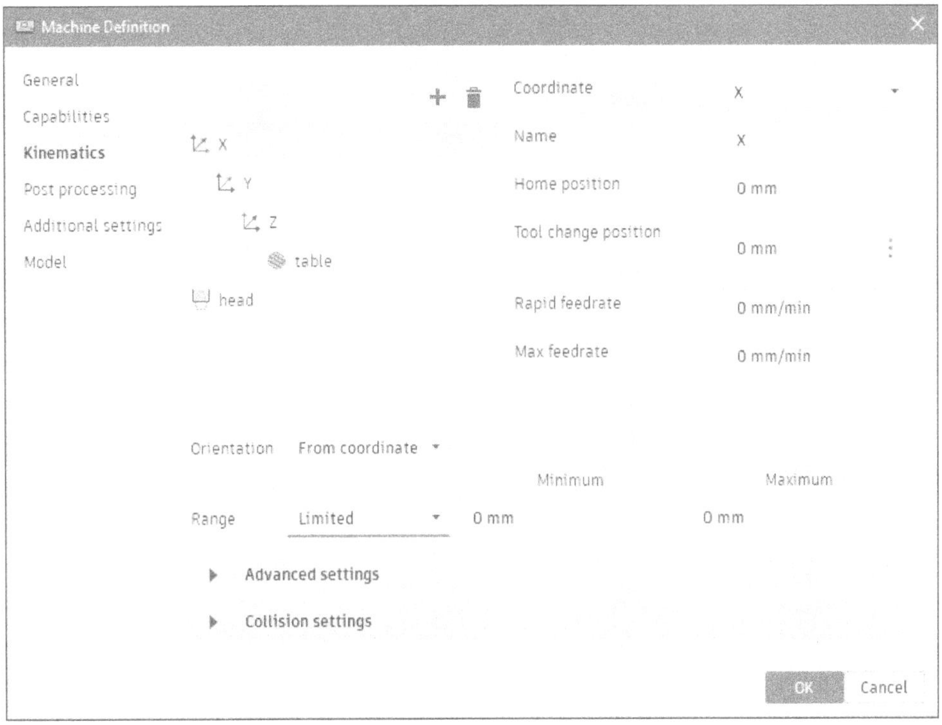

Figure-103. X Linear Kinematics options

- Specify desired text in the **Name** edit box to apply a custom name to the X axis. For example, you can write a custom name as "large base side" to identify x axis where larger side of model will be placed on machine bed.
- Click in the **Home Position** edit box to specify start position for cutting tool along X axis.
- Specify desired value in the **Rapid Feedrate** edit box to define the maximum speed up to which cutting tool can move for non-cutting passes toolpath.
- Specify desired value in the **Max Feedrate** edit box to define the maximum speed up to which cutting tool can move for cutting passes in toolpath.
- Select desired option from the **Orientation** drop-down to define the reference by which X axis of machine will be decided.
- Select Limited option from the **Range** drop-down and specify desired values in the **Minimum** and **Maximum** edit boxes for **Range** to define the minimum and maximum distance from origin within which the cutting tool can move in machine.
- Specify desired value in the **Resolution** edit box to define maximum allowed deviation (tolerance) in tool movement along X axis. Note that when a tool moves from 0 to 10 mm then it is not exact 10 mm position and there is some amount of error in that position like 10.004 or 9.9995. Using the value defined for resolution, we notify the user about accuracy of movements along X axis.
- Similarly, you can specify parameters for **Y** and **Z** options of the dialog box. Note that you can drag and drop options in the **Kinematics** node to desired location for defining order of respective components in the machine.
- If you want to add a rotary axis in the machine then select the component from tree to which you want to add rotary axis and select the **Rotary axis** option from the New part drop-down; refer to Figure-104. A new rotary axis will be added in the **Kinematics** node after selected option; refer to Figure-105. These option are similar to linear axis options discussed earlier with only difference being degree in place of mm. Figure-106 shows how rotary axes are generally placed in a 5 axis milling machine.

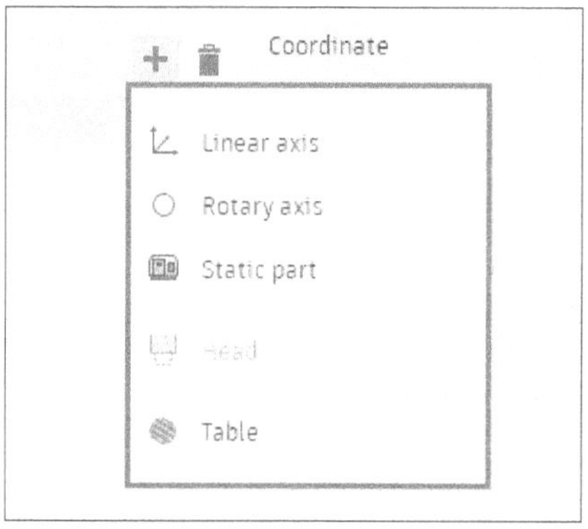

Figure-104. Add rotaty axis option

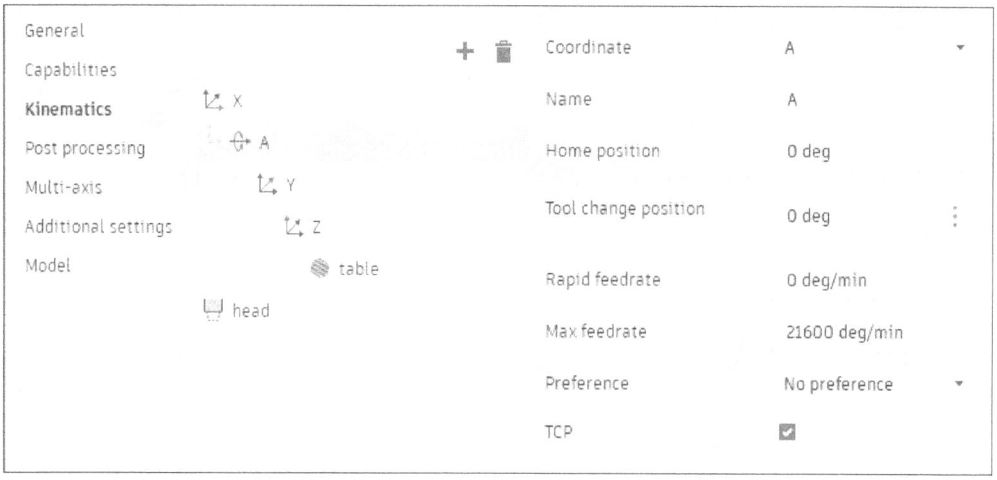

Figure-105. Rotary axis added to machine

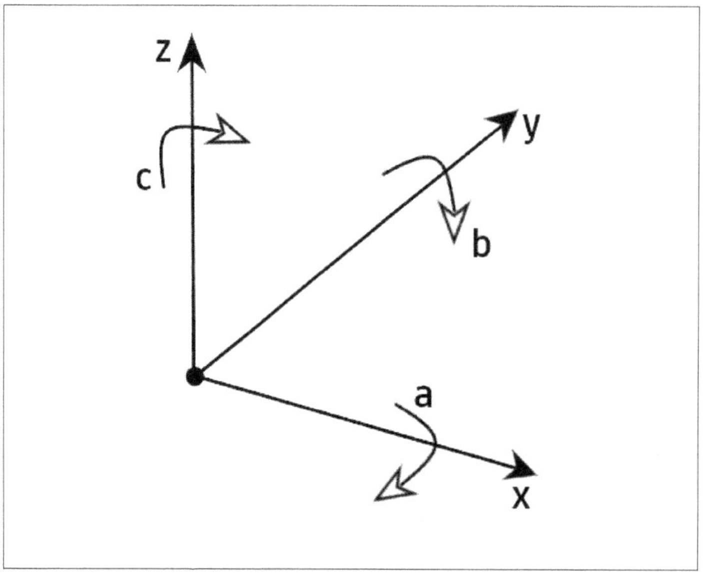

Figure-106. Rotary axes in Milling machine

- Select the **head** option from the tree to define parameters related to spindle of machine. The options will be displayed as shown in Figure-107.

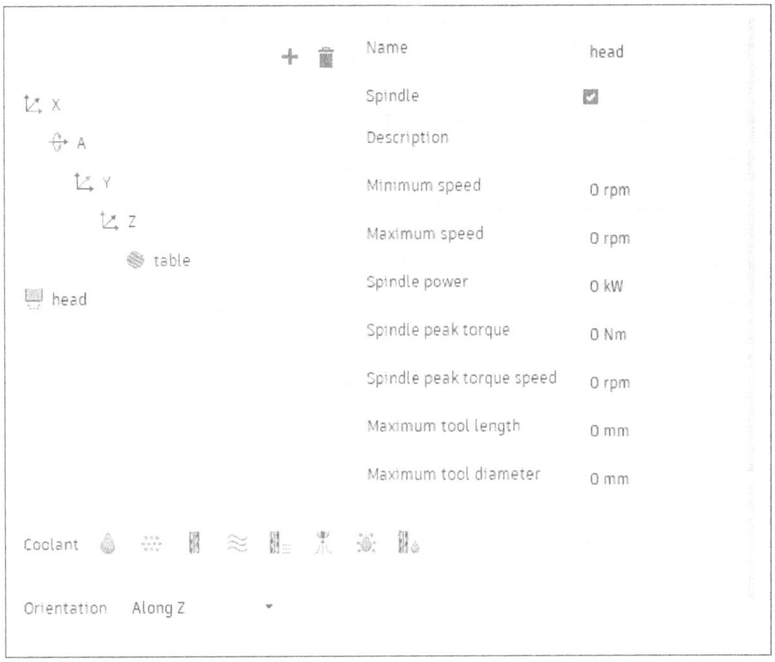

Figure-107. Spindle page

- Specify desired name for the head component of machine in the **Name** edit box.
- Specify desired text in the **Description** edit box to define user description of spindle.
- Specify desired values in the **Minimum speed** and **Maximum speed** edit boxes for **Spindle Speed** to define range within which spindle can rotate in the machine.
- Specify desired values in the **Maximum tool length** and **Maximum tool diameter** edit boxes to define maximum tool length and diameter upto which your spindle can support the tool.
- Select desired toggle buttons from the **Coolant** section to define how coolant will be dispensed by the machine.
- Select desired option from the **Orientation** drop-down to define the axis along which the head of machine will be oriented.
- If you have specified rotational axis for the machine then the **Multi-axis** option will be active at the left in the dialog box. Select this option to define multi axis milling parameters; refer to Figure-108.

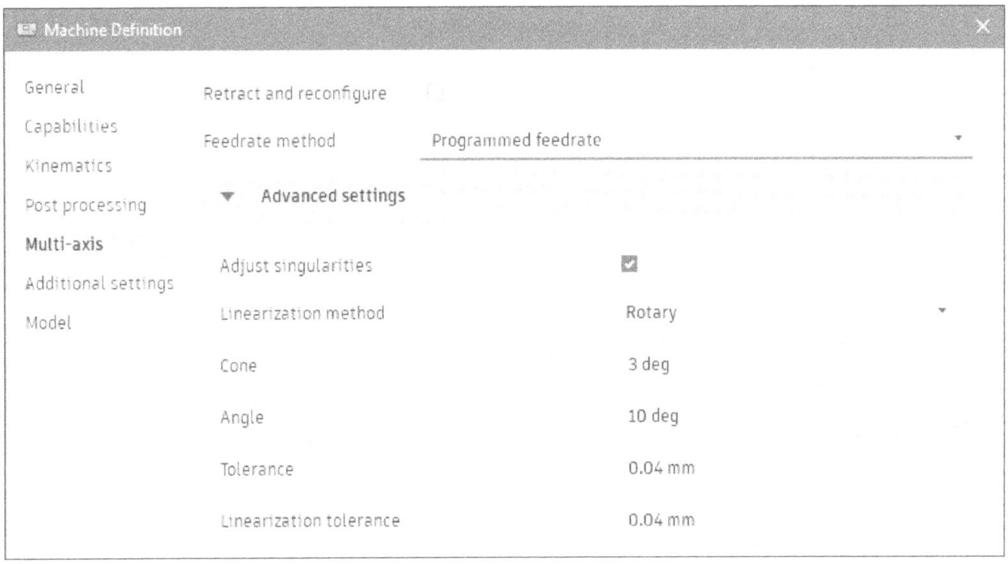

Figure-108. Multi-Axis page

- Select desired option from the **Feedrate method** drop-down to define how feedrate will be applied for multiaxis toolpaths. Select the **Programmed feedrate** option from the drop-down to specify the feedrate using program code. Select the **Inverse time (seconds)** option from the drop-down to specify cutting feedrate in terms of time in seconds required to perform the operation. Similarly, select the **Inverse time (minutes)** option from the drop-down to specify cutting feedrate in terms of time in minutes required to perform the operation. Note that you need to specify adequate time for operation to avoid over speeding of cutting tool which can cause accident. Select the **Degrees per minute standard** option from the drop-down to apply feedrate in Degree Per Minute value. Select the **Degrees per minute combination** option to use combination of both Degree Per Minute and Inch Per Minute values for defining feedrate.
- Select the **Retract and Reconfigure** check box from the page to allow backward movement of cutting tool during multi-axis cutting operation. The options for retraction and plunge feedrate will be displayed; refer to Figure-109. Select the **Use virtual tool tip** check box to output position of virtual tool for rotary axis of head.
- Specify desired values in the **X**, **Y**, and **Z** edit boxes of **Stock expansion** option to define the offset distance for stock in X, Y, and Z directions to be avoided by tool during retraction.
- Specify desired value in the **Safe retract distance** edit box to define length of retraction moves along tool axis.
- Specify desired values in the **Safe retract feedrate** and **Safe plunge feedrate** edit boxes to define the rate at which head will retract and plunge in workpiece, respectively.
- Select the **Adjust at Singularities** check box to adjust axis of cutting tool during simultaneous multi-axis operation for minimum deviation from main toolpath. If this check box is not selected then cutting tool will have to move a larger rotation for performing cuts which are perpendicular to current tool axis. In simple words, selecting this check box will allow tilting of cutting tool for performing multi-axis operations.

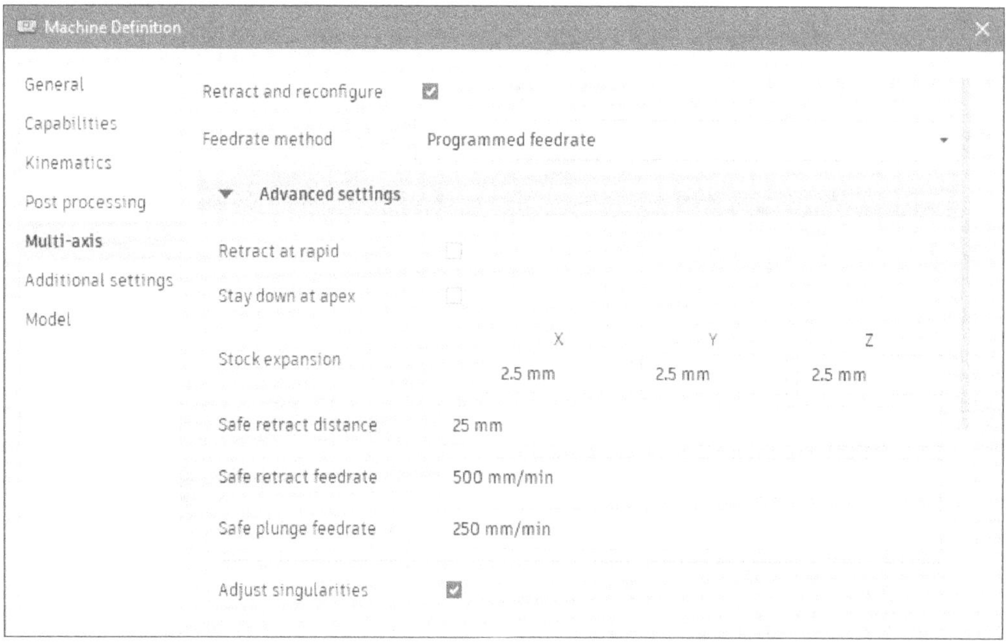

Figure-109. Retract options

- Select the **Linear** option from the **Linearization Method** drop-down to convert simultaneous multi-axis movements to linear movements within specified tolerance value specified in **Linearization Tolerance** edit box. Select the **Rotary** option from the **Linearization Method** drop-down to convert rotary multi-axis movements to curves following the circumference of cylindrical/revolved features.
- Specify desired value in the **Cone** edit box to define angular range for the cutting tool axis near the singularity point of toolpath where the adjustments of singularities will be performed. In simple words, this is the range within which the cutting tool will tilt for performing simultaneous multi-axis operations.
- Specify desired value in the **Angle** edit box to define minimum angular delta movement that cutting tool should move before singularity adjustment will be applied in toolpath.
- Specify desired value in the **Tolerance** edit box to define maximum deviation allowed from path for singularity adjustments.
- Select the **Machining Time** option from the left area in the dialog box to define
- Click on the **OK** button from the dialog box to create machine with specified configuration.

Editing A User-Defined Machine

To edit a user-defined machine, select the machine from the list of machines and click on the **Edit selected** button from **Toolbar** in the dialog box. The **Machine Configuration** dialog box will be displayed. The options of this dialog box have been discussed earlier.
You can use other buttons in **Toolbar** of the **Machine Library** dialog box as discussed earlier. After setting desired parameters, click on the **Close** button from the dialog box to exit.

PRACTICAL

Create stock of the model shown in Figure-110 and create required milling tool.

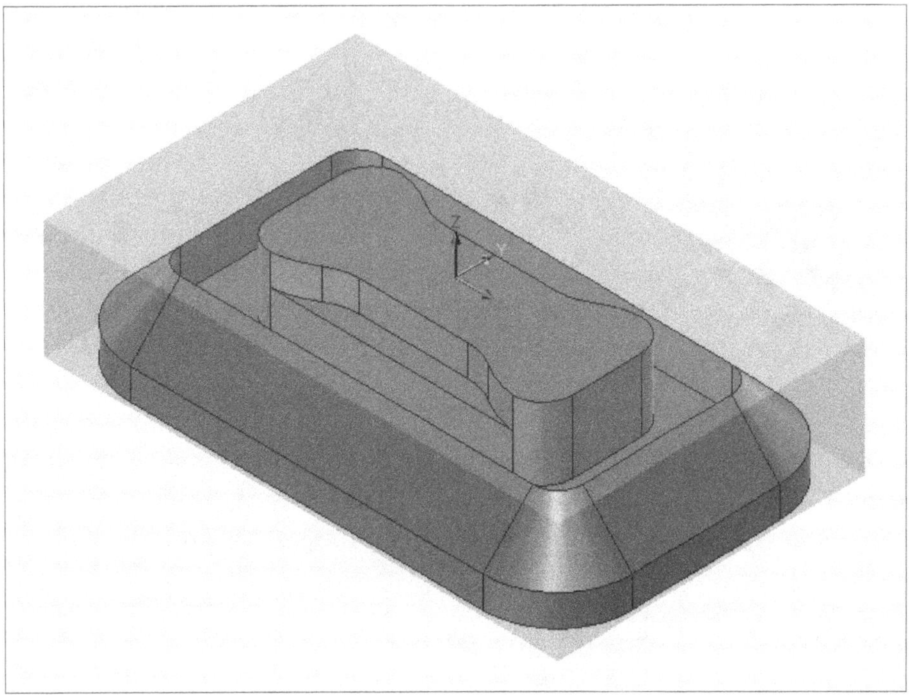

Figure-110. Practical 1

Opening Model in CAM

- Create and save the part in **DESIGN** workspace for this practical. The part file is also available in Chapter 15 folder of **Autodesk Fusion** resource kit, so you can open it from there instead of creating.
- Click on the **MANUFACTURE** option from **Change workspace** drop-down. The model will be displayed in the **MANUFACTURE** workspace; refer to Figure-111.

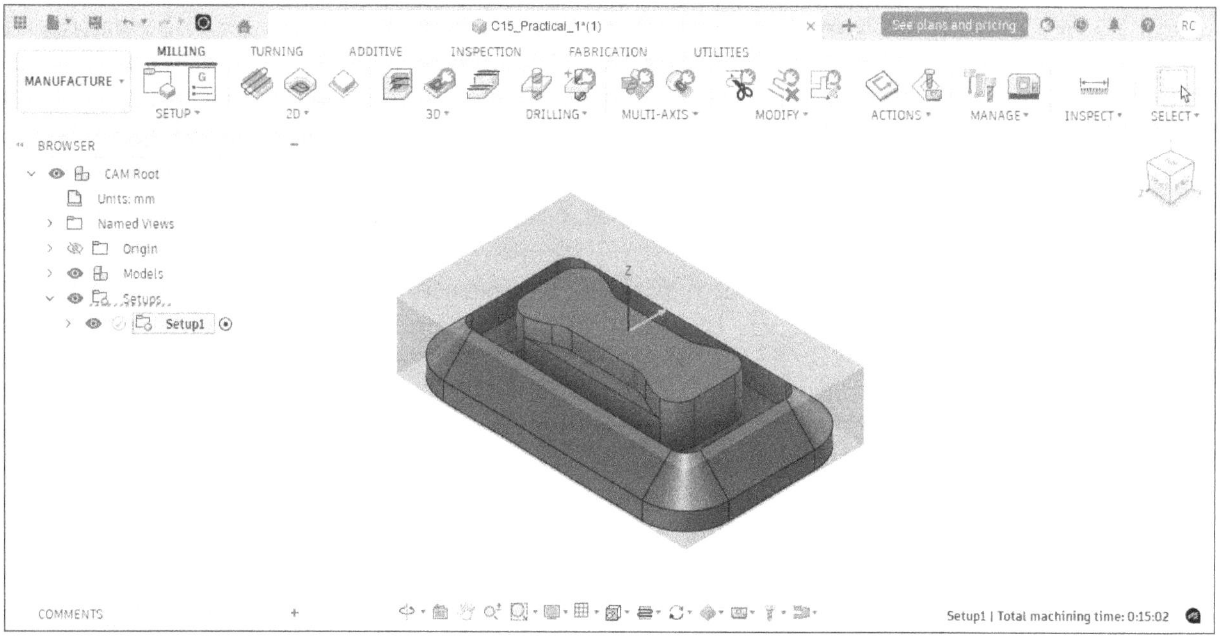

Figure-111. Model displayed in MANUFACTURE workspace

Creating Setup

- Click on the **New Setup** tool of **SETUP** drop-down from **Toolbar**. The **SETUP** dialog box will be displayed along with the setup; refer to Figure-112.

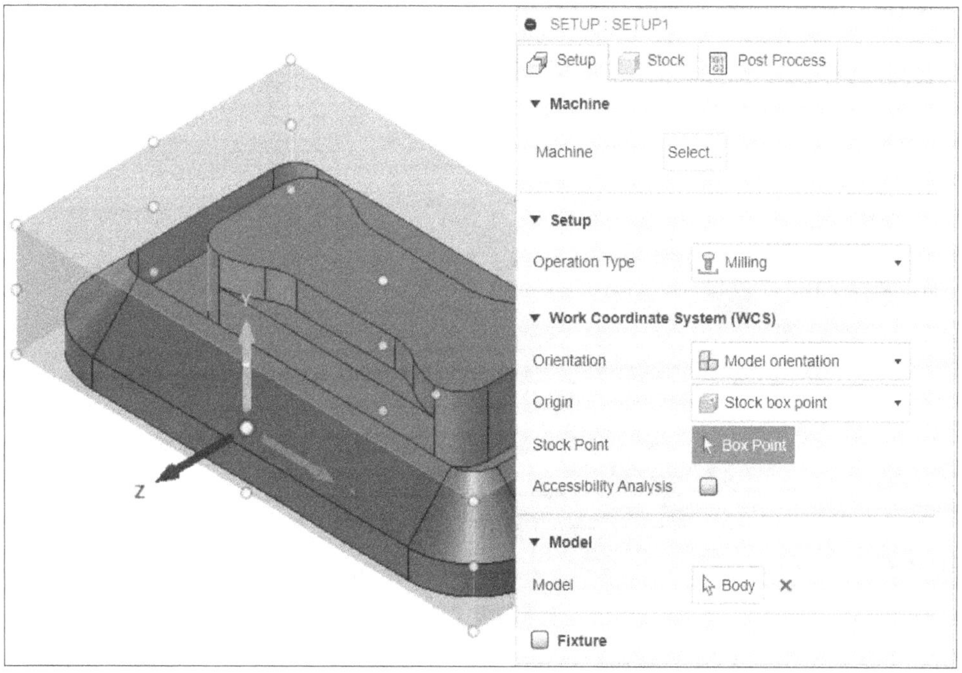

Figure-112. SETUP dialog box along with model

- Select the **Milling** option from the **Operation Type** drop-down in the **Setup** tab to specify the type of operation as milling.

- Select the **Select Z axis/plane & X axis** option from the **Orientation** drop-down of **Setup** tab and select the Z-axis for milling; refer to Figure-113. Note that you can select any desired face/edge to define Z axis for setup.

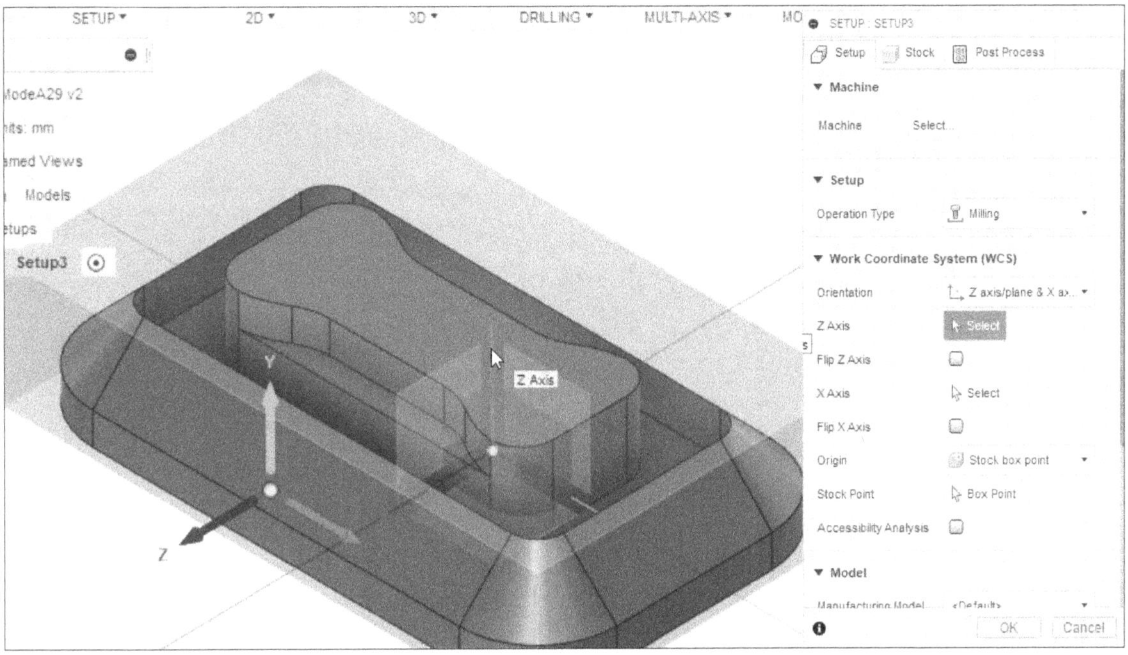

Figure-113. Selecting Z axis for milling

- The selection button of **X Axis** option is active by default. Select the X axis of WCS to select as X axis or select desired edge of model to define X axis direction.
- Click on the **Box Point** selection button for **Stock Point** option in **SETUP** tab and select the box point as displayed in the Figure-114.

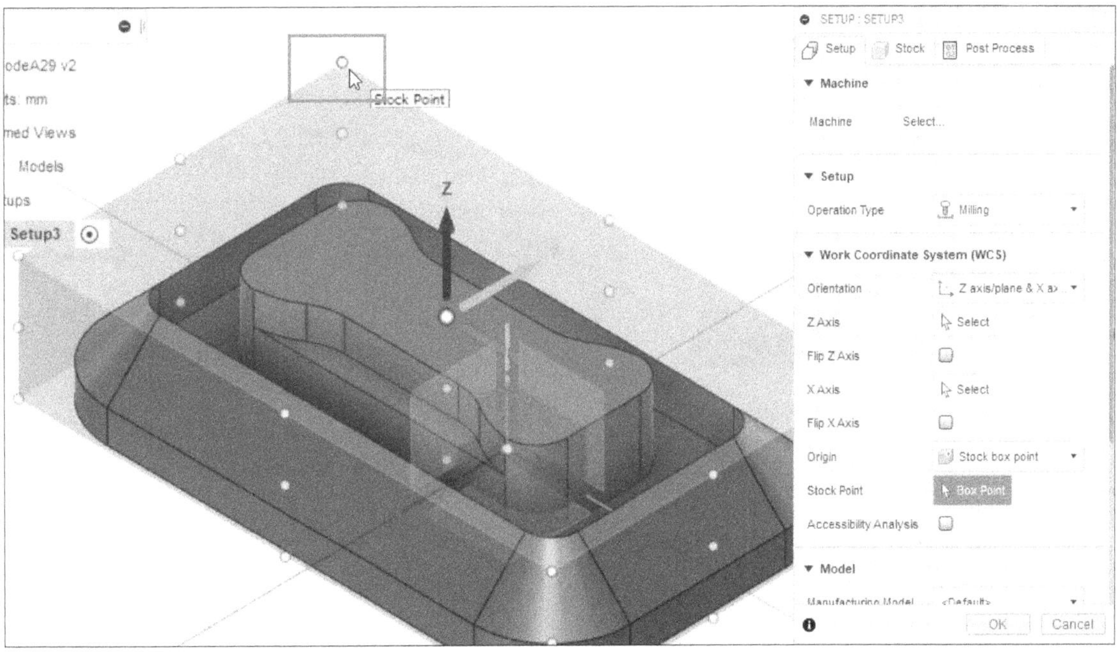

Figure-114. Selecting stock point

- Select the **Stock** tab at the top in the dialog box to define stock related parameters.
- Select the **Relative Size Box** option from the **Mode** drop-down in **Stock** tab and enter the parameters as shown in Figure-115.

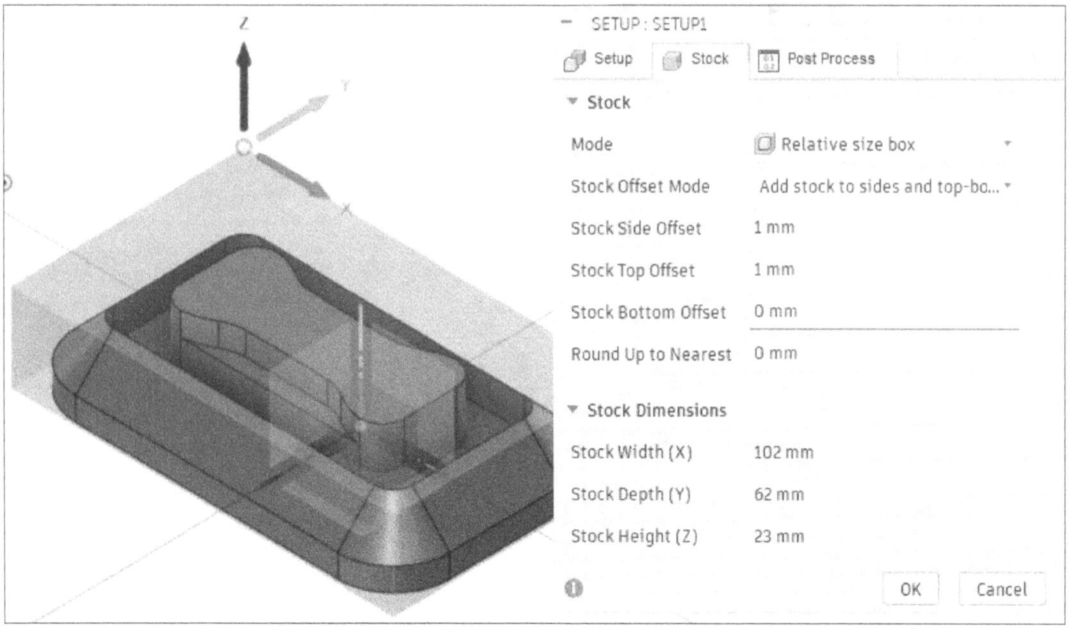

Figure-115. Specifying the parameters for creating stock

- After specifying the parameters in **SETUP** dialog box, click on the **OK** button from **SETUP** dialog box. The stock of model will be created.

Creating a new Milling tool

- Before creating a new tool, you need to know the inner and outer dimension of the model like height of pocket, radius, etc. Use the **Measure** tool in **INSPECT** drop-down of **Toolbar** to find out parameters.
- Click on the **Tool Library** tool from **MANAGE** drop-down in the **Toolbar**. The **Tool Library** dialog box will be displayed.
- Click on the **New Tool** button of **Tool Library** dialog box; refer to Figure-116. The **New Tool** page will be displayed in the dialog box.

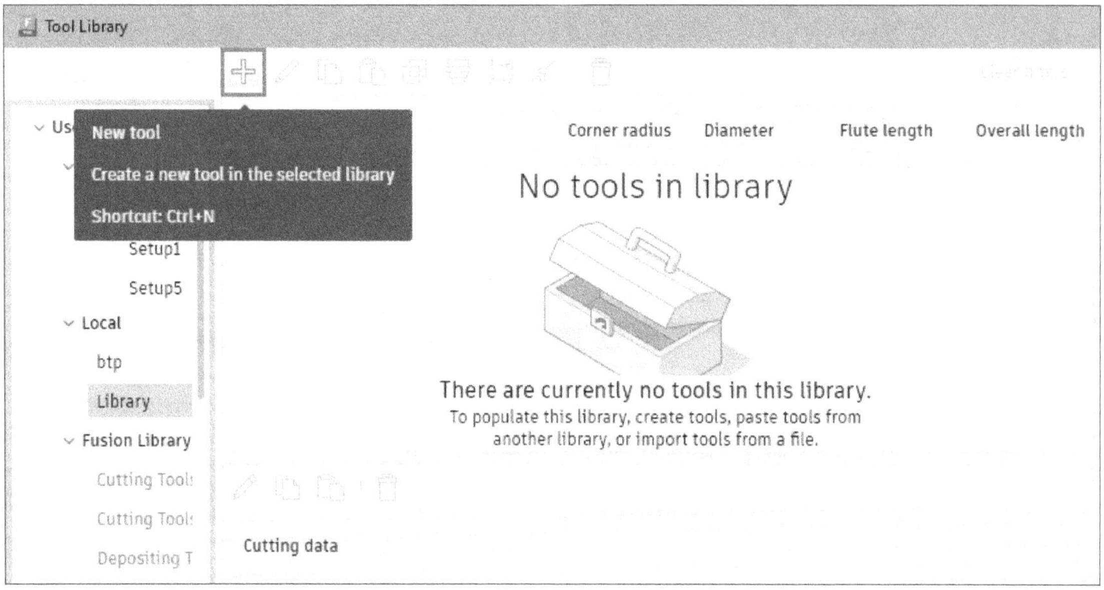

Figure-116. Creating new mill tool

- Select the **Flat end mill** button from the page. The **Tool Library** dialog box will be displayed.

- Specify desired parameters in the **General** and **Cutter** tab of **Tool Library** dialog box; refer to Figure-117.

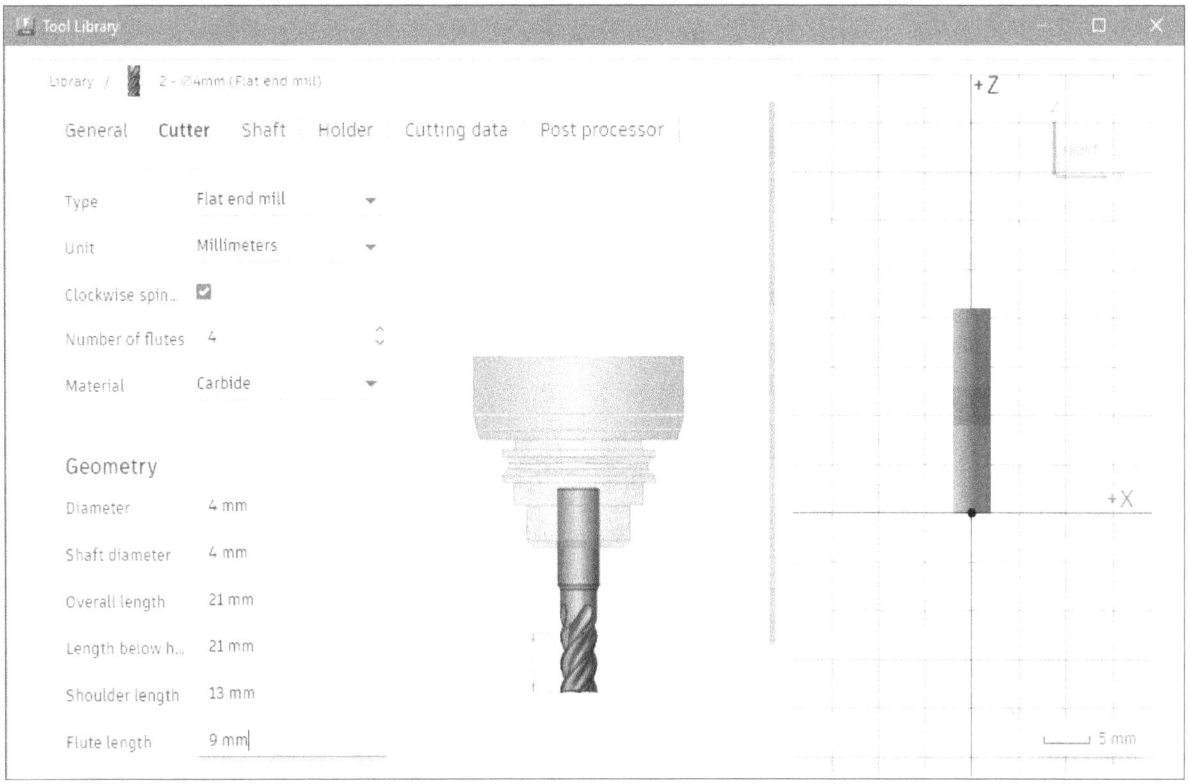

Figure-117. Cutter tab

- Select the **Shaft** tab of the **Tool Library** dialog box and specify the parameters as shown in Figure-118.

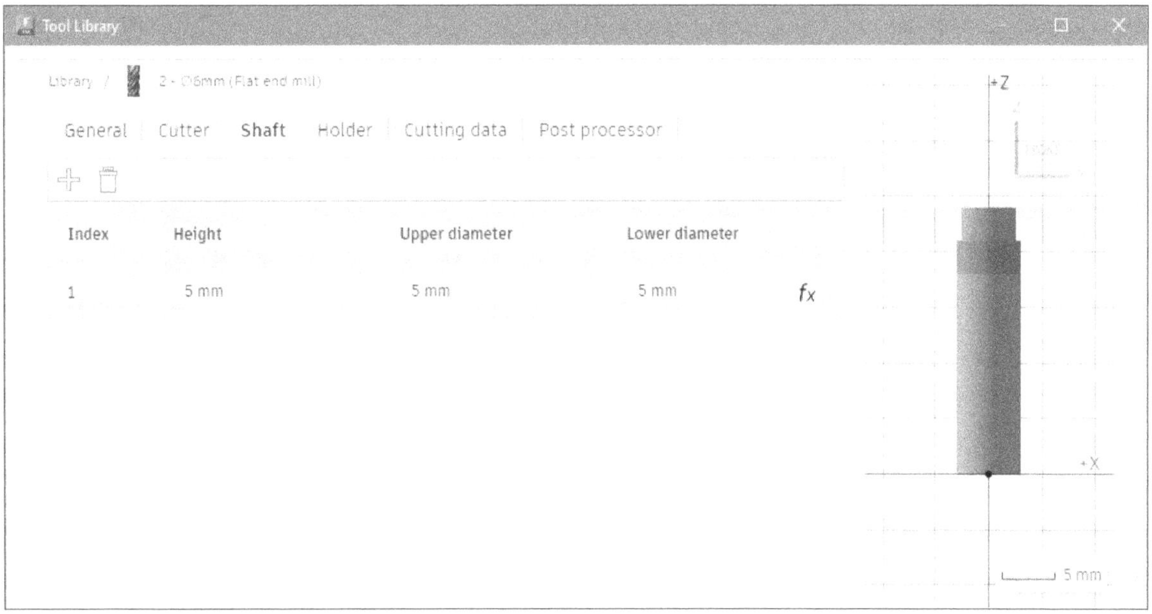

Figure-118. Shaft tab

- Select the **Holder** tab of **Tool Library** dialog box to select desired holder.
- Select desired tool holder from the list box at the left in the dialog box and click on the **Select Holder** button from the **Holder** tab. The selected holder will be displayed as shown in Figure-119.

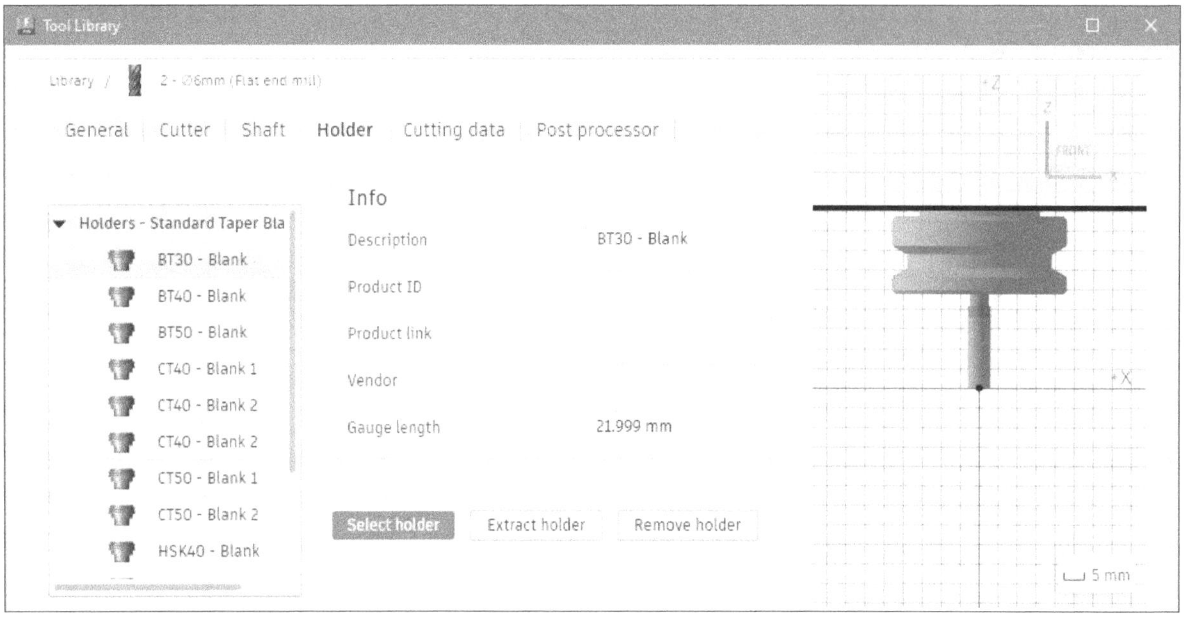

Figure-119. Selecting holder

- Click on the **Cutting data** tab of the **Tool Library** dialog box and specify the parameters as shown in Figure-120.

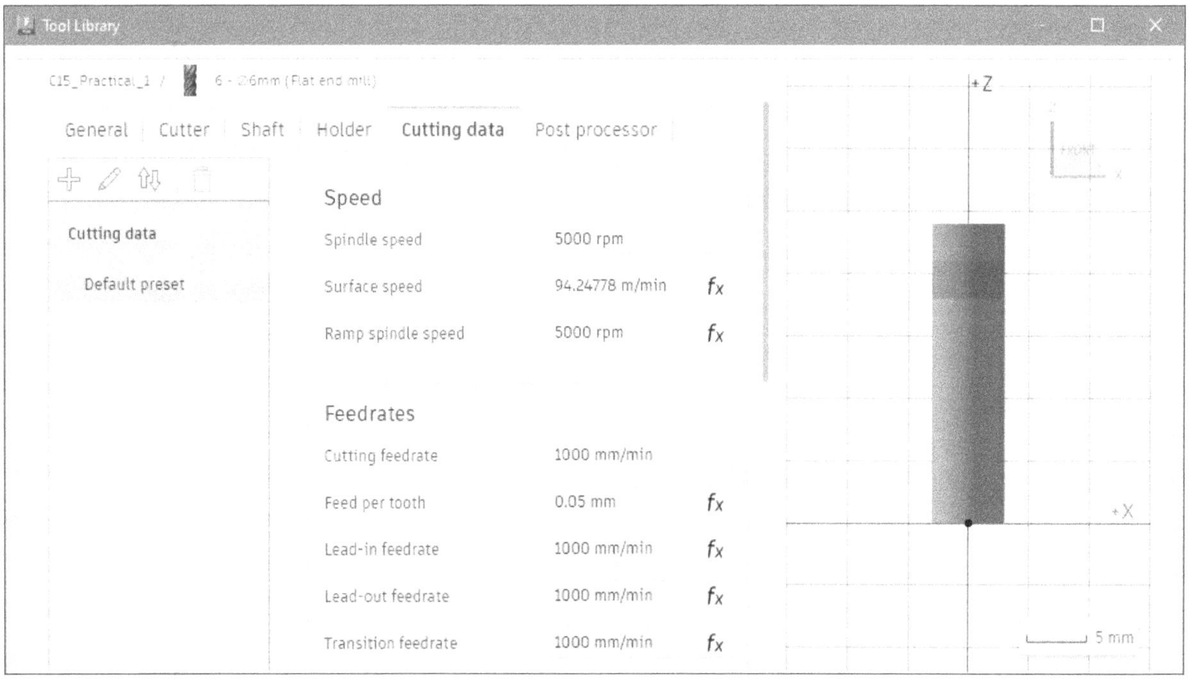

Figure-120. Specifying parameters in Cutting data tab

- After specifying the parameters, click on the **OK** button from **Tool Library** dialog box. The tool will be created and displayed in the tool library. Click on the **Close** button to exit dialog box.

PRACTICAL 2

Create the stock for lathe machining as shown in Figure-121.

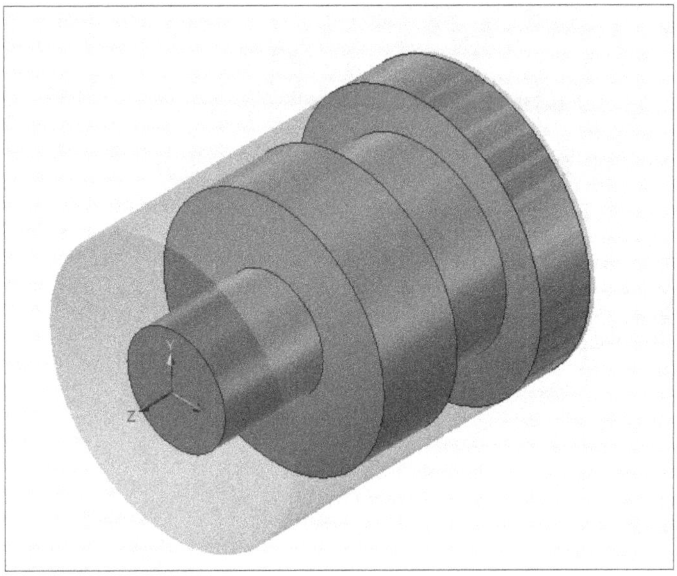

Figure-121. Practical 2

Adding model in CAM Workspace

- Create and save desired part in **DESIGN** workspace. The part file is also available in the current chapter folder of **Autodesk Fusion Resources**.
- Click on the **MANUFACTURE** option from **Change workspace** drop-down. The model will be displayed in the **MANUFACTURE** workspace; refer to Figure-122.

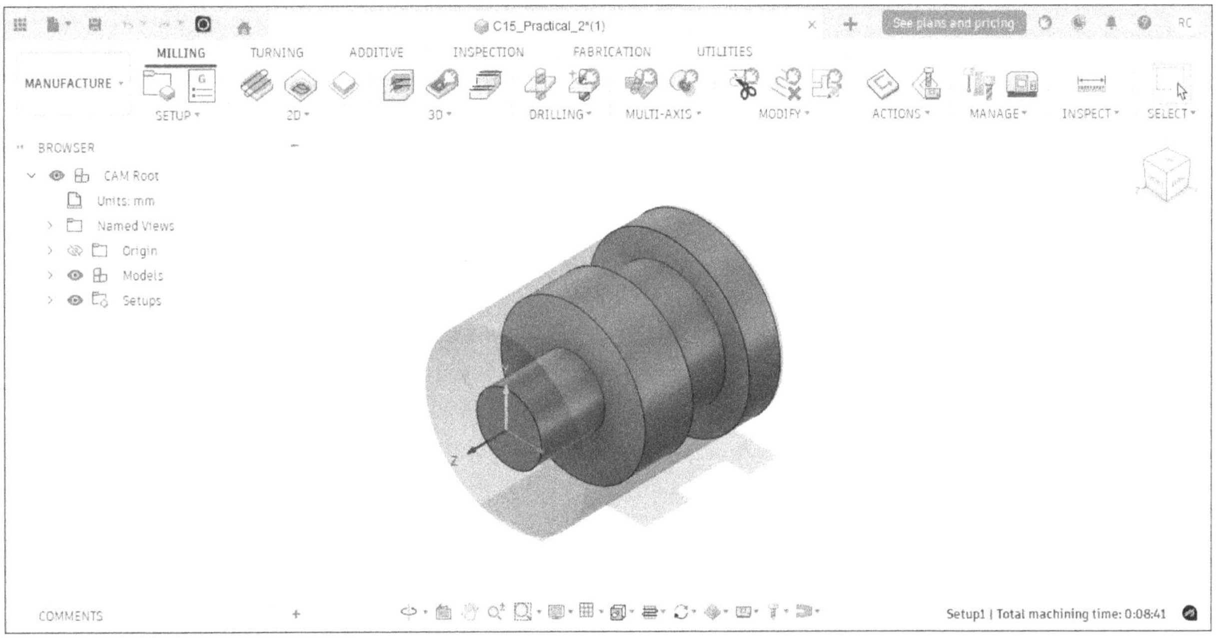

Figure-122. Model in MANUFACTURE workspace

Creating Setup

- Click on the **New Setup** tool of **SETUP** drop-down from **Toolbar**. The **SETUP** dialog box will be displayed along with the stock of model; refer to Figure-123.

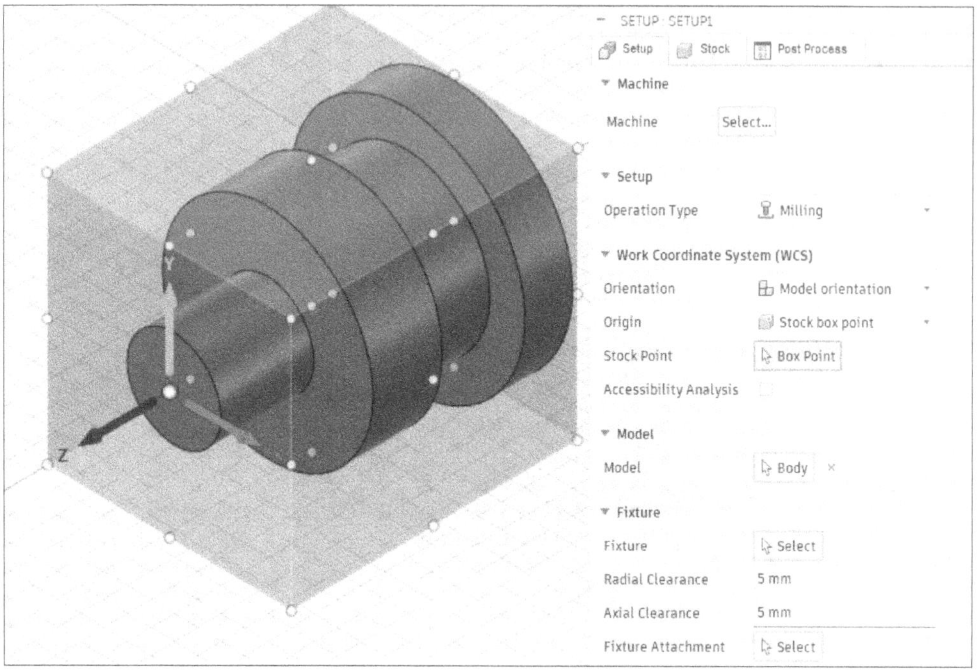

Figure-123. Model along with SETUP dialog box

- Select the **Turning or mill/turn** option from the **Operation Type** drop-down in the **Setup** tab to specify the machining type.
- The **Selection** button of **Z Axis(Rotary Axis)** option is active by default. Select the edge as displayed in Figure-124.

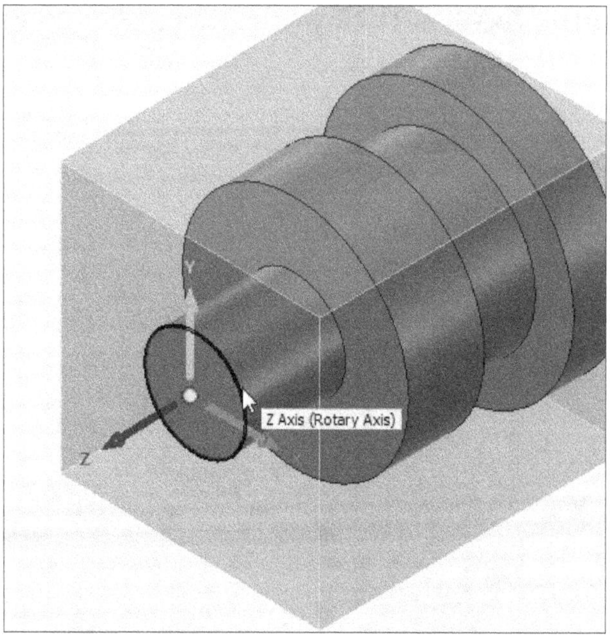

Figure-124. Selecting Z axis

- Click on the **Stock** tab of **SETUP** dialog box and specify the parameters as shown in Figure-125.

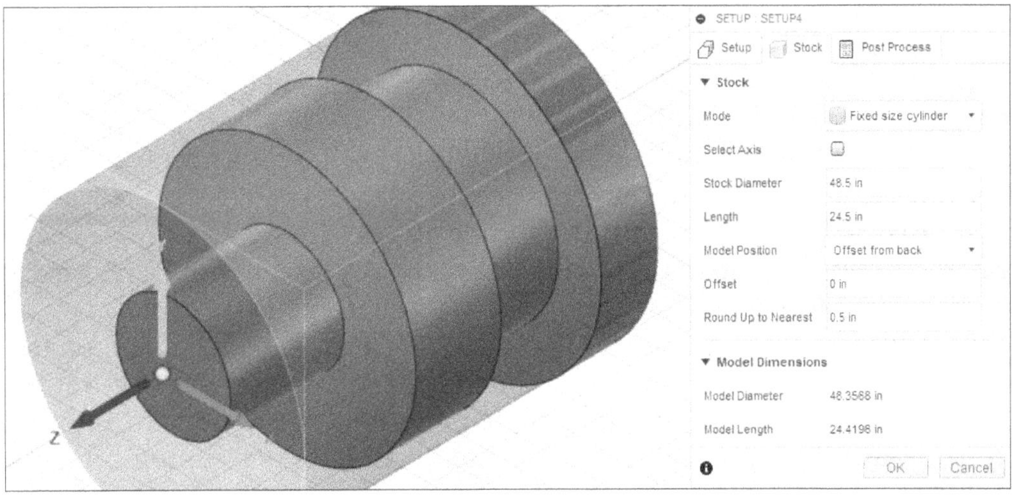

Figure-125. Specifying parameters in stock tab

- Click in the **Post Process** tab of **SETUP** dialog box and specify the parameters as shown in Figure-126.

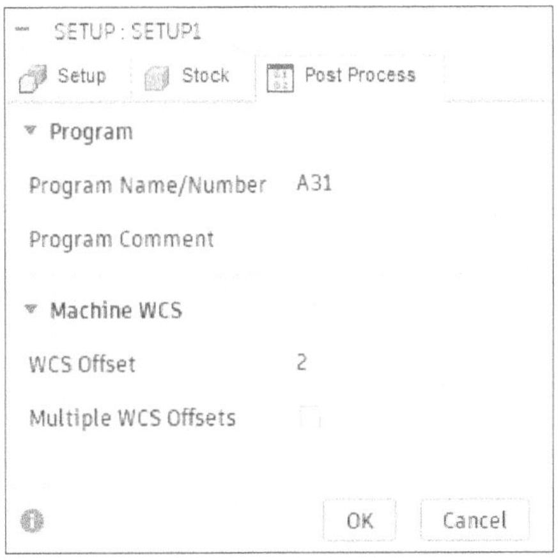

Figure-126. Post Process tab for turning

- After specifying the parameters, click on the **OK** button from **SETUP** dialog box. The stock will be created and displayed with the model; refer to Figure-127.

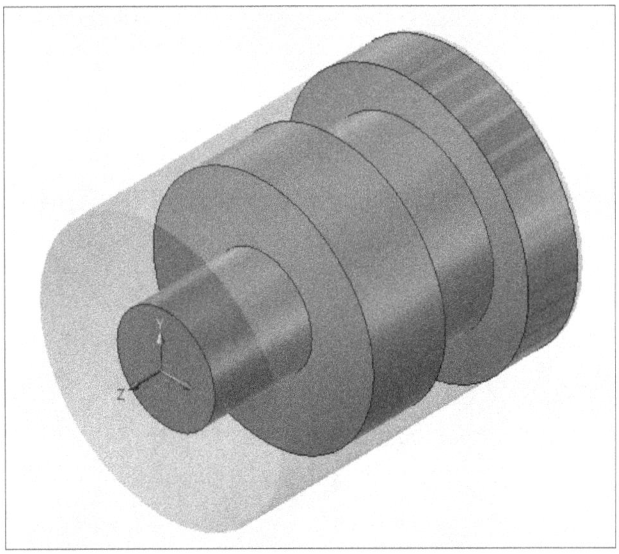

Figure-127. Stock created

Creating new Turning tool

- Before creating a new tool, you need to know the dimensions of slot, radius of part, length of part, etc. Use the **Measure** tool in **INSPECT** drop-down to find out various parameters.
- Click on the **Tool Library** tool of **MANAGE** drop-down from **Toolbar**. The **Tool Library** dialog box will be displayed.
- Select the **Library** option from the left area in the dialog box and click on the **New Tool** button from the **Toolbar** in the **Tool Library** dialog box. The **New Tool** page will be displayed in the dialog box.
- Select the **Turning general** button from the **Turning** section of the page. The **Tool Library** dialog box will be displayed for specifying parameters of new tool.
- Specify the **Description** of tool as **Roughing** tool in the **General** tab of dialog box.
- Specify the parameters in **Insert** tab from **Tool Library** dialog box as shown in Figure-128.

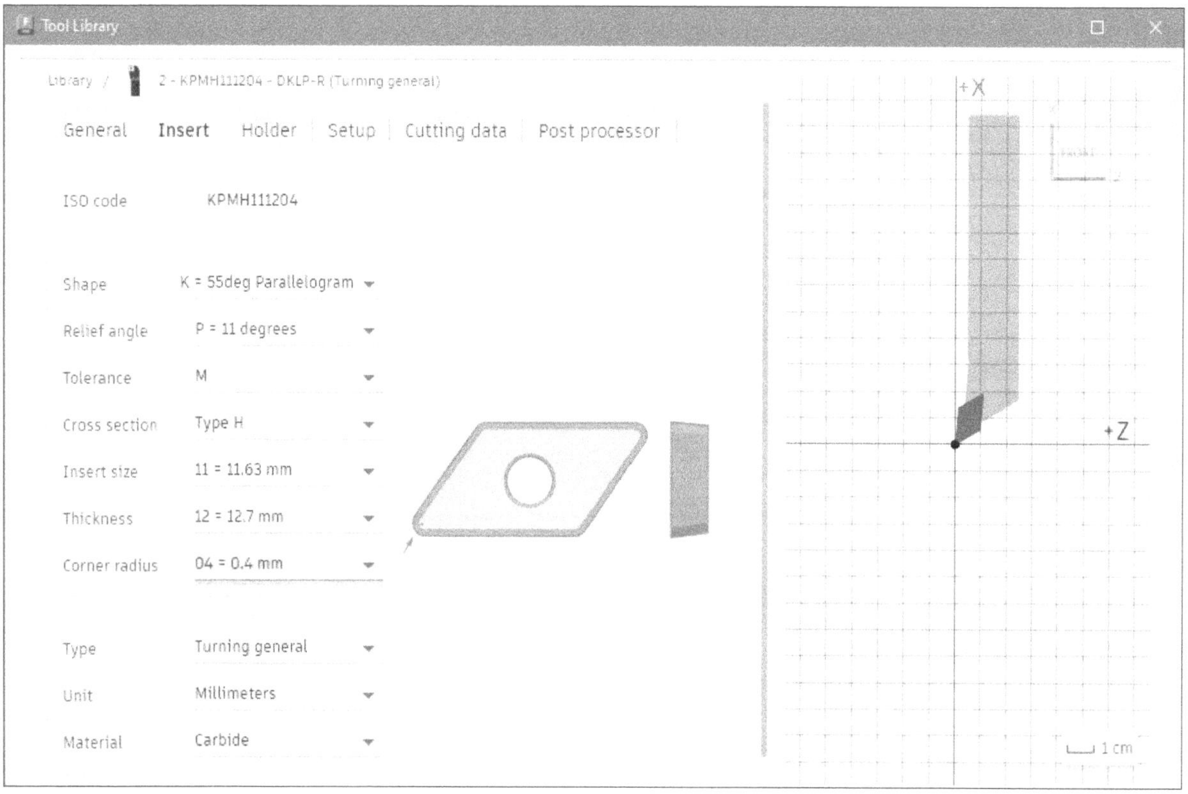

Figure-128. Insert tab

- Click on the **Holder** tab of **Tool Library** dialog box and specify the parameters as shown in Figure-129.

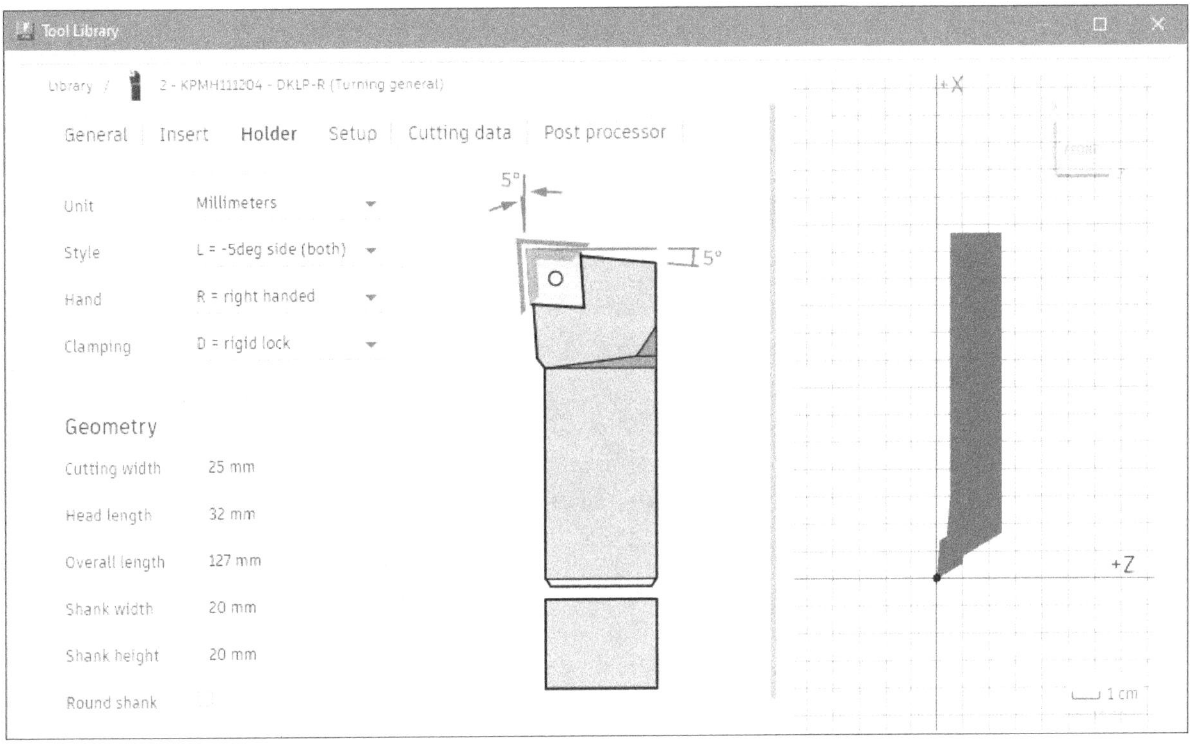

Figure-129. Holder tab

- Click on the **Cutting data** tab of **Tool Library** dialog box and specify the parameters as shown in Figure-130.

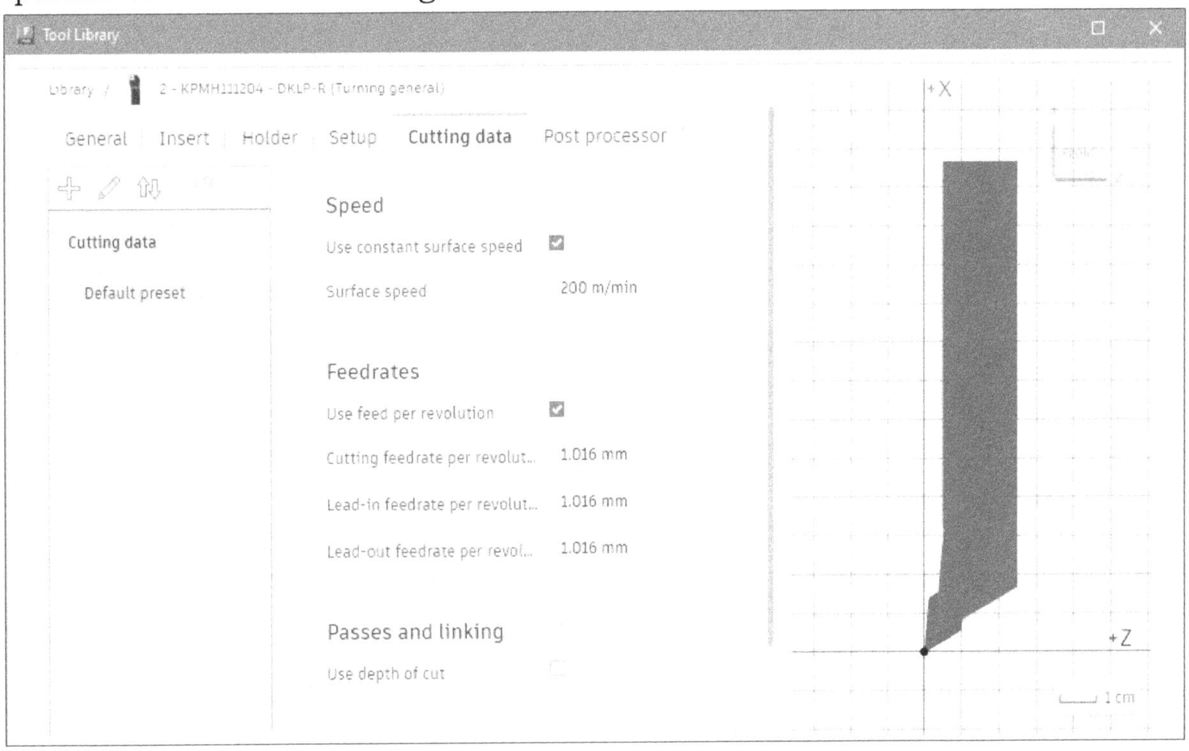

Figure-130. Cutting data tab

- After specifying the parameters, click on the **OK** button from **Tool Library** dialog box. The tool will be created and displayed in the tool library. Click on the **Close** button to exit the dialog box.

PRACTICE

Create the stock of given part; refer to Figure-131.

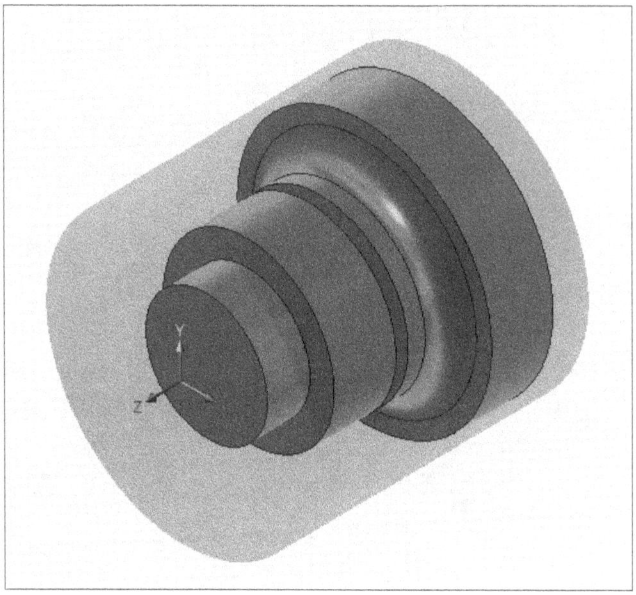

Figure-131. Practice

SELF ASSESSMENT

Q1. Which of the following workspace is used to generate toolpaths for NC programs?

a. DESIGN
b. ANIMATION
c. SIMULATION
d. MANUFACTURE

Q2. The **New Setup** tool in **SETUP** panel can be used to prepare model for additive manufacturing. (T/F)

Q3. If the workpiece provided for machining your part has an irregular shape then which of the following stock mode should be used?

a. Relative size cylinder
b. Fixed size box
c. From Part
d. Fixed size tube

Q4. Generally, in NC programming, G54 through G59 codes are used to define work coordinate system offsets. (T/F)

Q5. Which of the following cutting tools can be used for pocket milling?

a. Spot Drill
b. Thread
c. Dovetail
d. Radius

Q6. Engrave mill tool is used to apply chamfer at the edges of part. (T/F)

Q7. What is the primary function of the MANUFACTURE workspace in Autodesk Fusion?
A. Designing 3D models
B. Generating toolpaths for manufacturing processes
C. Creating electrical circuit designs
D. Simulating fluid dynamics

Q8. What is the purpose of the Job Setup in the MANUFACTURE workspace?
A. To create a 3D model of the final product
B. To define stock and machine type for machining
C. To analyze the thermal properties of materials
D. To simulate manufacturing defects

Q9. What is the zero location in a machining coordinate system used for?
A. As a visual reference for tool placement
B. As the origin (0,0,0) for defining other part locations
C. For displaying the material's thermal expansion rate
D. For verifying the tool's cutting speed

Q10. How can you select a predefined machine for machining operations?
A. By clicking on the Select button in the Machine section of the Setup dialog box
B. By defining the machine manually in the General Parameters section
C. By entering the machine's specifications in the Capabilities Parameters section
D. By selecting the Automatic tool changer option

Q11. Which check box should you select to display only machines with real-time simulation capability?
A. Supports tool preload
B. Automatic tool changer
C. Simulation ready
D. Kinematics ready

Q12. What is the purpose of the Machine Definition dialog box?
A. To create CNC toolpaths
B. To modify parameters of a selected machine
C. To add custom stock dimensions
D. To simulate the machining process

Q13. In the Capabilities Parameters section, which option allows you to specify the number of tools a machine can hold?
A. Max feedrate
B. Max block processing speed
C. Number of tools
D. Tool preload

Q14. What does the Orientation section of the Work Coordinate System (WCS) allow you to define?
A. The machine's maximum feedrate
B. The position and orientation of the workpiece
C. The type of stock material
D. The fixture attachments

Q15. Which option in the Stock tab lets you create a stock body larger than the model by specifying offset values?
A. Fixed size box
B. Relative size box
C. Add stock to all sides
D. Offset from left side (-X)

Q16. What happens when you select the Accessibility Analysis check box in the Setup dialog box?
A. The machining process is optimized for speed
B. Undercut areas are analyzed for accessibility
C. Stock dimensions are automatically adjusted
D. The coordinate system origin is recalibrated

Q17. How can the origin of the Work Coordinate System (WCS) be defined using the model's bounding box?
A. By selecting the Stock box point option
B. By selecting the Model box point option
C. By selecting the Selected point option
D. By selecting the Ground stock at model origin check box

Q18. What is the purpose of selecting the Fixture check box in the Setup dialog box?
A. To define the type of stock material
B. To create toolpaths for machining
C. To define components that hold the workpiece in place
D. To modify the machining model's dimensions

Q19. Which option in the Mode drop-down of the Stock section is used to create a fixed size cylinder stock body?
A. Relative size cylinder
B. Fixed size tube
C. Fixed size cylinder
D. From solid

Q20. What must you do after selecting the Fixed size cylinder option to define the diameter of the stock?
A. Enter the value in the Radial Stock Offset edit box.
B. Enter the value in the Stock Diameter edit box.
C. Enter the value in the Length edit box.
D. Select the Axis button.

Q21. Which option is used to create a cylindrical stock body with a specified offset value acting as thickness?
A. Fixed size cylinder
B. Relative size cylinder
C. Fixed size tube
D. From preceding setup

Q22. In the Relative size cylinder option, which edit box specifies the thickness of stock in the radial direction?
A. Frontside Stock Offset
B. Backside Stock Offset
C. Radial Stock Offset
D. Round Up to Nearest

Q23. What does the Round Up to Nearest edit box do in the Relative size cylinder option?
A. Specifies the minimum thickness of the stock.
B. Rounds up the stock size to the nearest specified multiple.
C. Specifies the length of the cylinder.
D. Sets the axis for the cylinder.

Q24. What is the key characteristic of the Fixed size tube option?
A. It creates a cylinder without a through hole.
B. It creates a tube with a fixed inner diameter.
C. It specifies thickness using offset values.
D. It uses the radial stock offset for length specification.

Q25. Which Model Position option moves the stock to the bottom side of the model?
A. Offset from front
B. Center
C. Offset from back
D. Offset from middle

Q26. How do you create a stock based on a previously performed operation?
A. Use the From solid option.
B. Use the From preceding setup option.
C. Use the Fixed size cylinder option.
D. Use the Relative size cylinder option.

Q27. Which tab allows you to set the position of the workpiece on a machine table?
A. Stock tab
B. Setup tab
C. Part Position tab
D. Post Process tab

Q28. What does the Preserve Order option in the Operation Order drop-down do?
A. It preserves the toolpaths created for the operation.
B. It performs machining in the order tools are used.
C. It performs machining in the order operations are created.
D. It performs machining in the order operations are selected.

Q29. Which checkbox in the Post Process tab allows the creation of multiple WCS offsets for tool wear compensation?
A. Continue Rest Machining
B. Spun Profile Smoothing
C. Multiple WCS Offsets
D. Arrangement

Q30. In the Turning Machine Setup, which checkbox flips the direction of the Z axis by 180 degrees?
A. Flip Z Axis
B. Flip X Axis
C. Safe Z Reference
D. Spun Profile

Q31. What is the purpose of the Spun Profile checkbox in the Turning Machine Setup?
A. To create multiple offsets for stock thickness.
B. To generate a profile for turning irregular surfaces.
C. To position the chuck accurately.
D. To define the axis for the setup.

Q32. Which option in the SETUP dialog box is selected for additive manufacturing machines?
A. Additive
B. Cutting
C. Milling
D. Turning

Q33. Which tool is used to create a copy of the main model for manufacturing purposes?
A. Create Manufacturing Model
B. Setup Model Tool
C. Tool Library
D. Adaptive Clearing

Q34. What does the Filters tab in the Select Tool dialog box allow you to do?
A. Save tools for future use.
B. Select a machine for operation.
C. Filter the list of cutting tools.
D. Adjust the tool diameter.

Q35. Which rollout in the Filters tab helps define the type of cutting tool?
A. Diameter
B. Type
C. Filters
D. Cutting Data

Q36. What does the View tool in the cutting tools list area allow you to do?
A. Display the filters applied.
B. View the cutting path of a tool.
C. Check properties of the selected tool.
D. Edit the main model parameters.

Q37. Where are cutting tools displayed after selecting a category in the Tool Library?
A. In the Filters tab
B. In the Info tab
C. In the left area of the dialog box
D. In the Cutting data area

Q38. What does the Spun Profile Tolerance edit box specify in the Turning Machine Setup?
A. Tolerance for cutting depth.
B. Tolerance for chuck position.
C. Maximum deviation of profile from boundaries.
D. Offset value for the chuck reference.

Q39. Which material is NOT mentioned as being used for CNC tools?
A. Cemented Carbide
B. High-Speed Steel
C. Plastic
D. Ceramics

Q40. What type of milling tool is designed for creating precision shapes and holes?
A. Slot Mill
B. End Mill
C. Bull Nose Mill
D. Taper Mill

Q41. Which end milling process is used for finishing three-dimensional shapes in die steel?
A. Keyway Production
B. Specialty Cutting
C. Cavity Die Work
D. Finish Profiling

Q42. What is a primary characteristic of a Bull Nose Mill?
A. Hemispherical End
B. Radius at Corners
C. Straight Plunge Operation
D. Fillet Application

Q43. Which tool is recommended for machining 3-dimensional contoured shapes?
A. Slot Mill
B. Face Mill
C. Ball Nose Mill
D. Dove Mill

Q44. What is the main purpose of a Face Mill tool?
A. Cutting dovetails
B. Engraving on workpieces
C. Flattening the face of workpieces
D. Creating slots or grooves

Q45. The Taper End Mill is commonly used for which purpose?
A. Creating rounded corners
B. Milling large flat surfaces
C. Walls with draft or clearance angle
D. Engraving on the surface

Q46. What does a Dove Mill specialize in cutting?
A. Chamfers
B. Dovetails
C. Undercuts
D. Slots

Q47. What is another name for the Lollipop Mill tool in some catalogs?
A. Slot Mill
B. Undercut Mill
C. Engrave Mill
D. Barrel Mill

Q48. Which tool is ideal for creating threads on a workpiece?
A. Reamer
B. Taper Mill
C. Thread Mill
D. Bore Bar

Q49. Barrel Mill tools are most commonly used in which type of operation?
A. 2-axis milling
B. 5-axis milling
C. Straight plunge cutting
D. Creating keyways

Q50. What is the purpose of a Reamer tool?
A. Cutting dovetails
B. Finishing or enlarging holes precisely
C. Creating cylindrical holes
D. Engraving designs

Chapter 16

Generating Milling Toolpaths - 1

Topics Covered

The major topics covered in this chapter are:

- ***2D Pocket Toolpath***
- ***2D Contour Toolpath***
- ***Trace Toolpath***
- ***Bore Toolpath***
- ***Engrave Toolpath***
- ***Adaptive Clearing Toolpath***
- ***Parallel Toolpath***
- ***Contour Toolpath***
- ***Horizontal Toolpath***
- ***Scallop Toolpath***

GENERATING 2D TOOLPATHS

In previous chapter, you have learned the procedure of creating stock for a given model and selecting/creating cutting tools to perform machining operations. In this chapter, you will learn to create 2D Milling toolpaths using tools available in the **2D** drop-down of **MILLING** tab in the **Toolbar**.

2D Adaptive Clearing Toolpath

The **2D Adaptive Clearing** tool is used to create a machining operation on the part which uses the adaptive path as per the parts curvature to avoid abrupt direction changes. This tool path is generally used as roughing toolpath for removing large amount of stock from the workpiece. The procedure to use this tool is discussed next.

- Click on the **2D Adaptive Clearing** tool from **2D** drop-down in the **Toolbar**; refer to Figure-1. The **2D ADAPTIVE** dialog box will be displayed; refer to Figure-2.

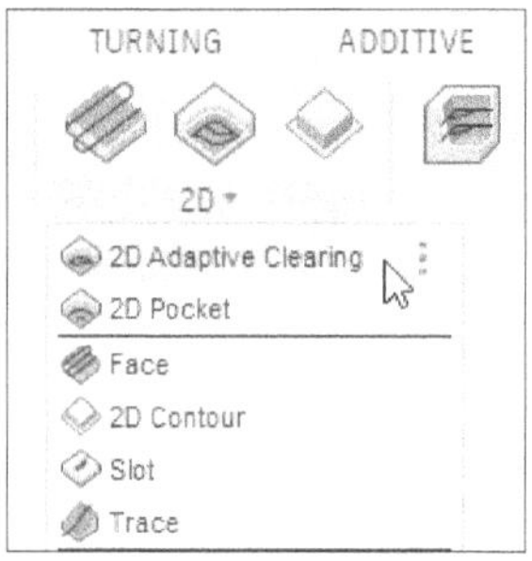

Figure-1. 2D Adaptive Clearing tool

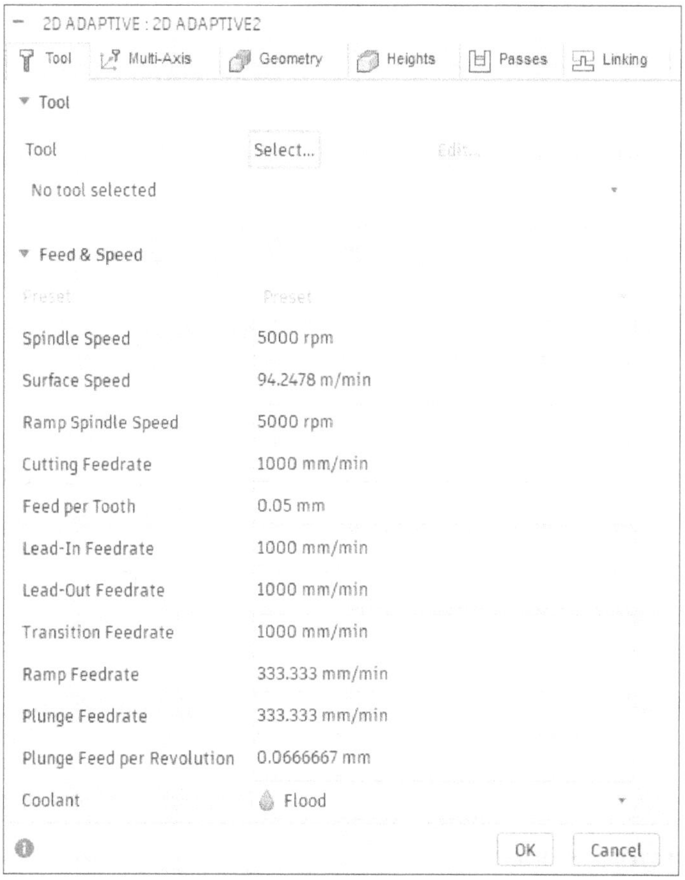

Figure-2. 2D ADAPTIVE dialog box

- Click on the **Select** button from **Tool** section in the dialog box. The **Select Tool** dialog box will be displayed.
- Select the **Milling Tools - Metric** option from the **Fusion Library** node at the left in the dialog box and select **10 mm Flat Endmill** cutting tool from the dialog box; refer to Figure-3. Click on the **Select** button from the dialog box to use this tool for machining.

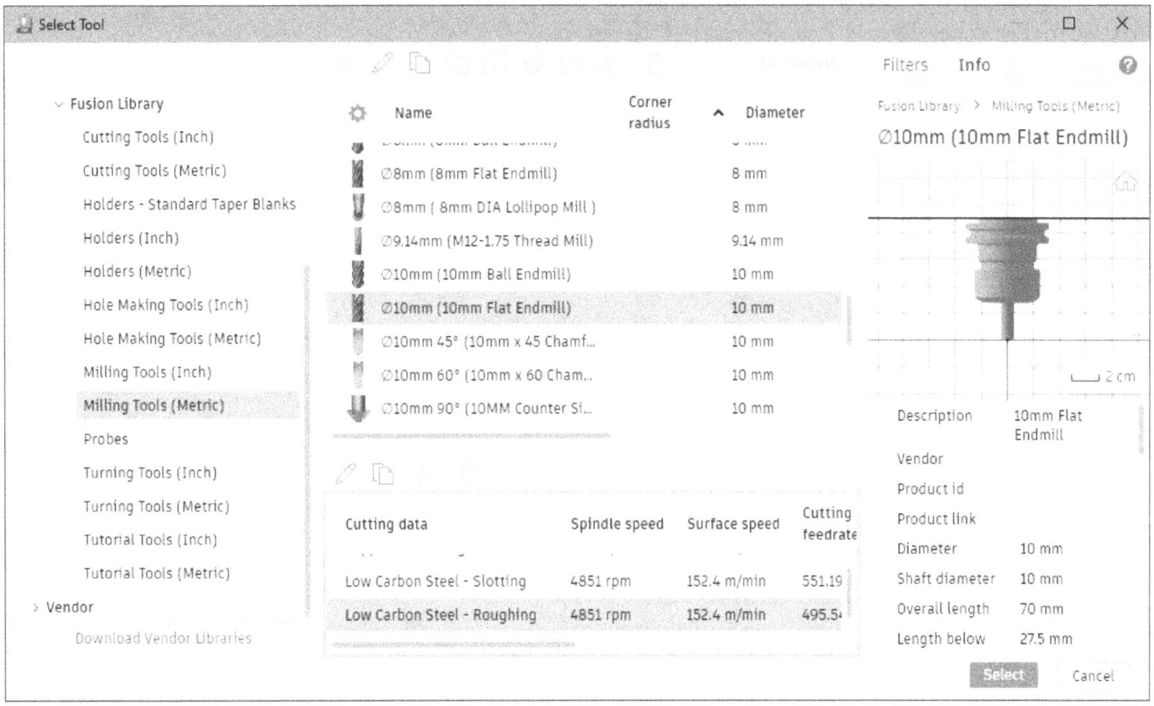

Figure-3. Tool selected with cutting strategy

- Select desired option from the **Preset** drop-down to specify cutting parameters related to respective material. For example, if you want to rough machine a low carbon steel work piece then select the **Low Carbon Steel - Roughing** option from the **Preset** drop-down; refer to Figure-4.

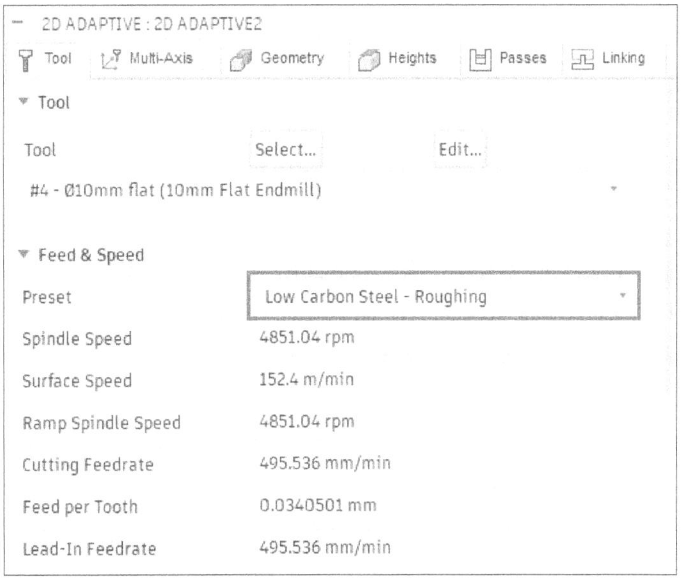

Figure-4. Preset selected

- Select desired option from the **Coolant** drop-down to define how coolant will be sprayed on the work piece while performing cutting operations.
- You can specify desired parameters in the edit boxes of the **Feed & Speed** section if you do not want to use presets.

Geometry Tab

The options in the **Geometry** tab are used to define the geometry to be machined by cutting tool. The procedure is discussed next.

- Click on the **Geometry** tab from the **2D ADAPTIVE** dialog box. The options in dialog box will be displayed as shown in Figure-5.

Figure-5. Geometry tab of 2D ADAPTIVE dialog box

- Click on the **Geometry Selections** button in the **Geometry** section of the dialog box. The options will be displayed as shown in Figure-6 to define how geometry for creating toolpath will be selected.

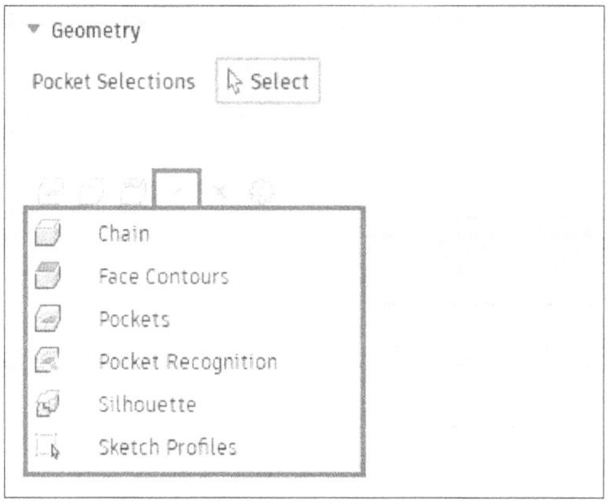

Figure-6. Geometry Selections drop-down

- Select the **Pocket recognition** option from the **Geometry Selections** drop-down if you want the software to automatically recognize pockets in selected body. The **POCKET RECOGNITION** dialog box will be displayed; refer to Figure-7.

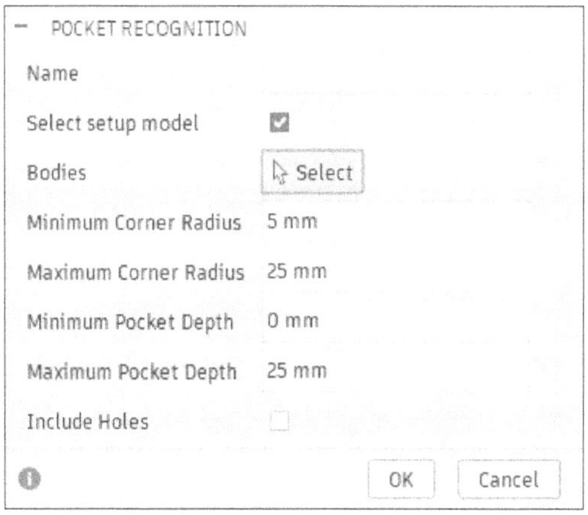

Figure-7. POCKET RECOGNITION dialog box

- Specify desired name of the pocket in the **Name** edit box of the dialog box.
- Specify the maximum and minimum parameters for corner radius and pocket depth upto which pockets will be recognized.

- Select the **Include Holes** check box if you want to recognize holes as pockets for machining. Click on the **OK** button to apply selection.
- If you do not want to use automatic recognition of pockets then select the **Pockets** option from **Geometry Selections** drop-down in the dialog box. The **Pockets** dialog box will be displayed as shown in Figure-8.

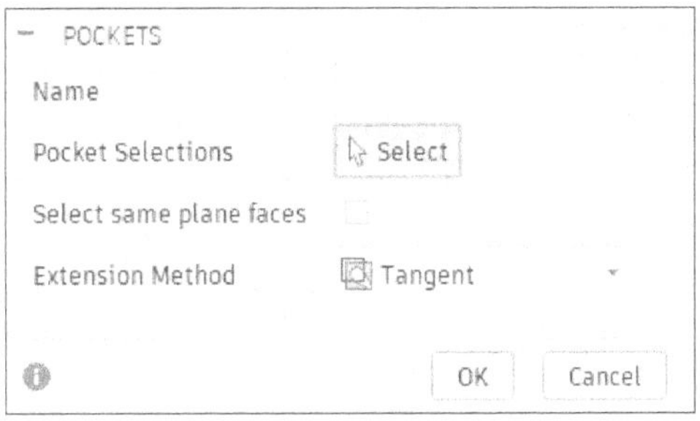

Figure-8. POCKETS dialog box

- The **Select** selection button of **Pocket Selections** section in **Geometry** node is active by default. Click on the geometries of model to be machined as shown in Figure-9. Note that selected geometries are pockets with closed chain of curves; refer to Figure-10.

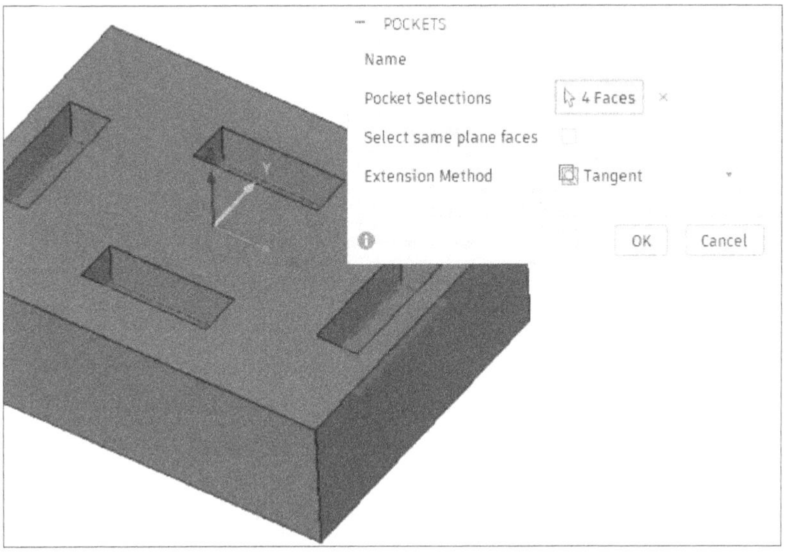

Figure-9. Faces selected for pockets

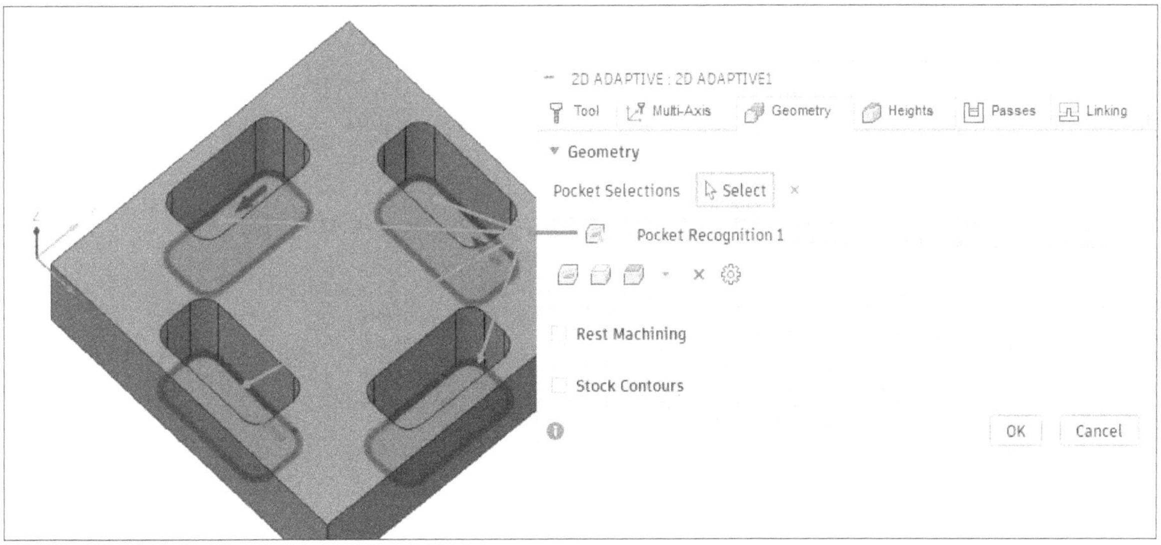

Figure-10. Selected geometry for 2D adaptive

- Select the **Select same plane faces** check box to select the pocket chains on same plane.
- Select desired option from the **Extension Method** drop-down to define method to be used for extending profile of selected pocket geometries. Select the **Tangent** option from the drop-down to extend geometry tangentially if possible/needed. Select the **Closest boundary** option if you want to extend selected geometries in direction closest to boundary of model/workpiece. Select the **Parallel** option from the drop-down to extend selected geometry chains in such a way that the extended length of geometries are parallel to each other till they intersect with boundary; refer to Figure-11. Note that extension of geometries is possible only for open pocket sections. Click on the **OK** button from the dialog box to apply selection.

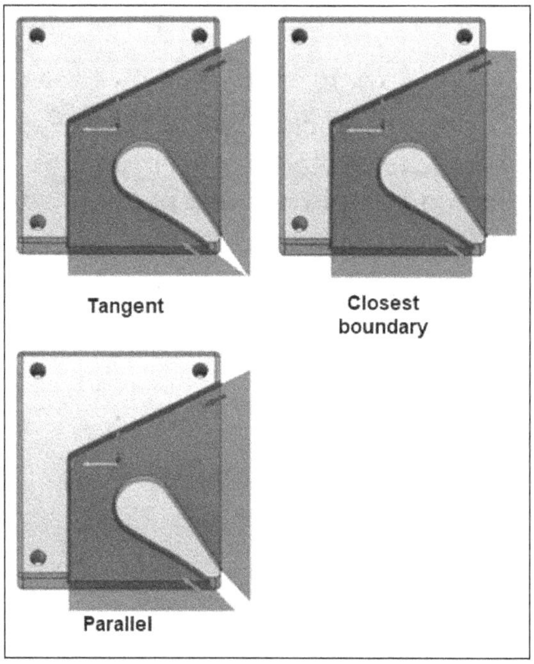

Figure-11. Extension methods

- Select the **Chain** option from **Geometry Selections** drop-down of **Geometry** section in dialog box to use selected edges as boundary for pocket. The **CHAIN** dialog box will be displayed; refer to Figure-12. Select the **Closed chain** button from the **Mode** area in dialog box to select closed loop of selected edge. Select the **Open chain** button from the **Mode** area to select each edge of the loop individually. Select the **Reverse** check box to flip the cutting direction; refer to Figure-13. Click on the **OK** button to apply geometry selection.

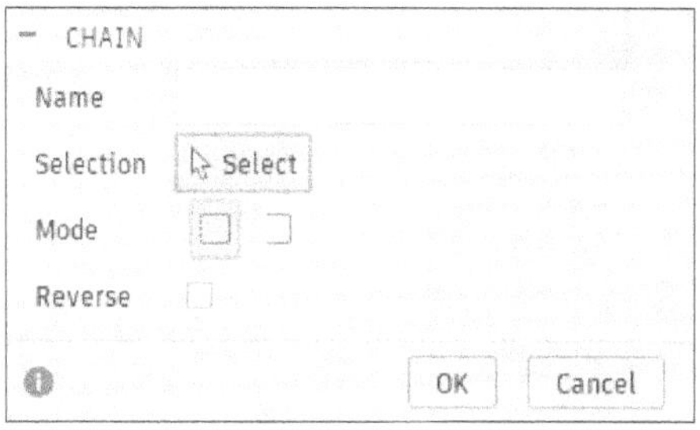

Figure-12. CHAIN dialog box

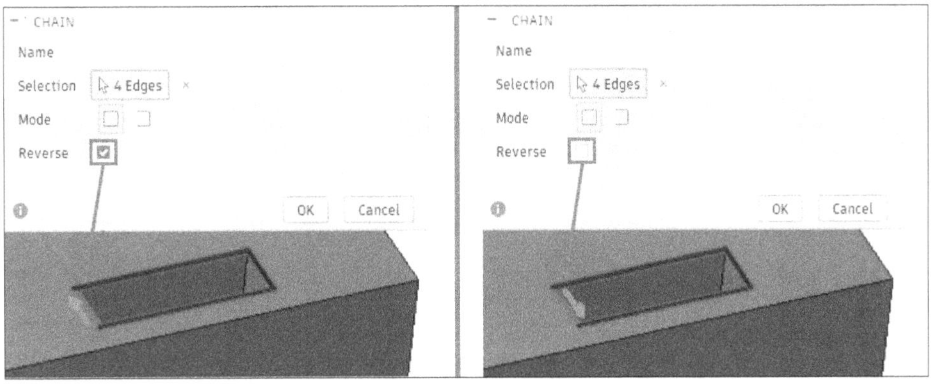

Figure-13. Reverse direction in chain selection

- Similarly, you can use other options of **Geometry Selections** drop-down in the **Geometry** section of **2D ADAPTIVE** dialog box like **Face Contours** option to select face boundaries, **Silhouette** option to select surface boundaries, and **Sketch Profiles** option to select sketched outlines.
- Select the **Stock Contours** check box of **Geometry** tab from **2D ADAPTIVE** dialog box to specify the boundaries of stock. After selecting this check box, select the edges to be defined as boundaries of the stock, the cutting tool will not perform cutting moves outside this boundary although it can move in/out of the boundaries for non-cutting moves. This option is not useful if you are machining closed pockets. Use this option to define boundaries for an open pocket; refer to Figure-14.

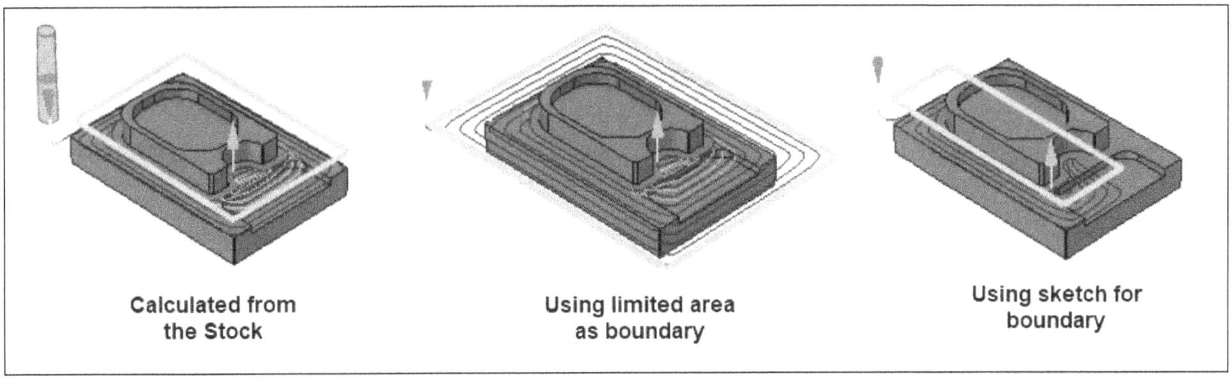

Figure-14. Stock contour selections

- Select the **Rest Machining** check box of the **Geometry** tab from the dialog box to machine only left over material from previous tool. Specify the tool diameter and corner radius of previous tool in the respective edit boxes of **Rest Machining** node for rest machining.

Heights

The **Heights** tab of the **2D ADAPTIVE** dialog box is used to set height of different planes for standard tool movement. The procedure to define these heights are discussed next.

- Click on the **Heights** tab of the **2D ADAPTIVE** dialog box. The **Heights** tab will be displayed along with preview of planes in modeling area; refer to Figure-15.

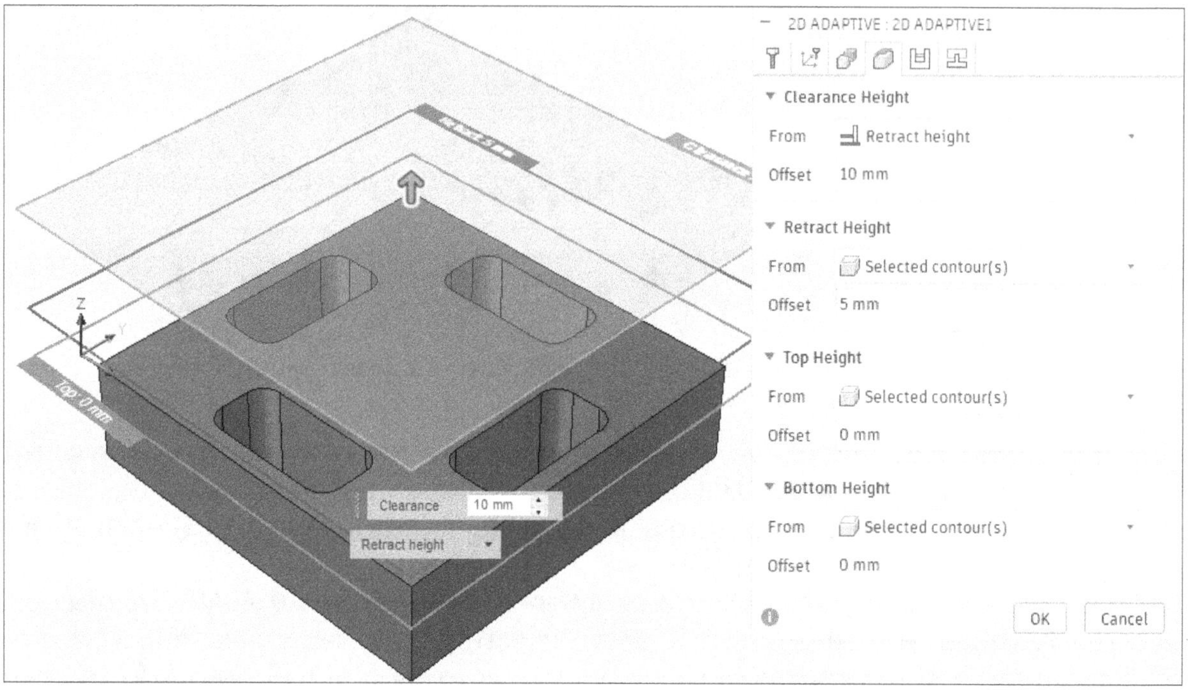

Figure-15. Heights tab

- The clearance height is the distance between tool and workpiece at which the tool rapidly moves before the start of machining process. Click in the **From** drop-down of **Clearance Height** section in **Heights** tab and select desired reference from which clearance height will be measured.
- Click in the **Offset** edit box of **Clearance Height** section and specify the value of distance by which clearance will be away from the selected reference.
- The Retract height is the distance at which cutting tool will move upward after a cutting pass and before performing next cutting pass. The Retract height should be set above the Feed Height and Top of workpiece.
- Click in the **From** drop-down from the **Retract Height** section of the **Heights** tab and select desired reference type to be used for defining retract plane.
- Click in the **Offset** edit box of the **Retract Height** section and specify the distance value of retract height from selected reference.
- The Top height is the term used to define the top level of the cut. Click in the **From** drop-down from the **Top Height** section of the **Heights** tab and select desired option.
- Click in the **Offset** edit box from the **Top Height** section and specify height from selected reference.
- The **Bottom Height** is the term used to define the depth of the cut in a workpiece. If it is not defined in the dialog box then system will automatically assume the stock depth.
- Click in the **From** drop-down from the **Bottom Height** section in **Heights** tab and select desired option.
- Click in the **Offset** edit box from the **Bottom Height** section and specify the distance from selected reference for bottom height.

Passes

The options in **Passes** tab are used to define various parameters related to cutting and non-cutting passes of tool. If you are getting chunks of material left after machining or there is stock left in some area of the workpiece then options in this tab are responsible for the problem. These options are discussed next.

Passes Options

- Click in the **Passes** tab of **2D ADAPTIVE** dialog box. The options of the tab will be displayed as shown in Figure-16.

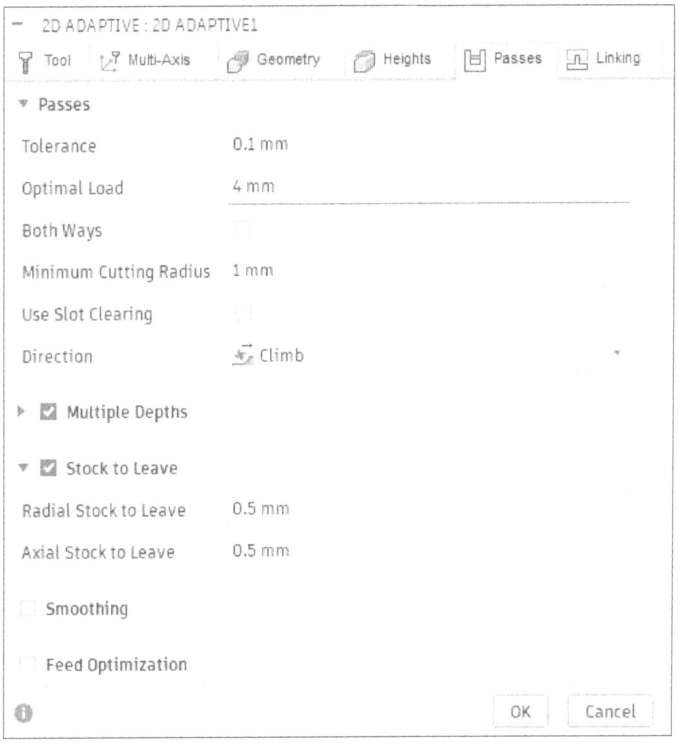

Figure-16. Passes tab

- Click in the **Tolerance** edit box of the **Passes** section from the **Passes** tab and enter desired value of deviation allowed between linear representation of curve and their original form while cutting. A very low value of tolerance can increase processing time or make the tool path impossible to cut by your tool if you are using a roughing tool.
- Click in the **Optimal Load** edit box of the **Passes** section from the **Passes** tab and enter desired value to specify the amount of engagement the adaptive strategies should maintain while cutting. This is the amount of material being removed in one cutting pass while tool is in same XY plane. The Optimal load parameter is directly linked with tool diameter and strength.
- Select the **Both Ways** check box to allow cutting during both forward and return motion of tool. Note that using this option can increase the load on tool and workpiece so you should select it cautiously and only for soft materials. On selecting this check box, the **Optimal Load Other Way** and **Other Way Feedrate** edit boxes will be displayed below the check box. Specify lower values of optimal load and feedrate in these edit boxes to reduce chances of accident.
- Click in the **Minimum Cutting Radius** edit box and specify desired value of minimum cutting radius that can be achieved while machining. If a corner on workpiece has fillet value lower than specified value then it will be ignored while machining.
- Select the **Use Slot Clearing** check box to start cutting from the middle of slot with plunge entry and continue a spiral motion for rest of the pocket; refer to Figure-17.

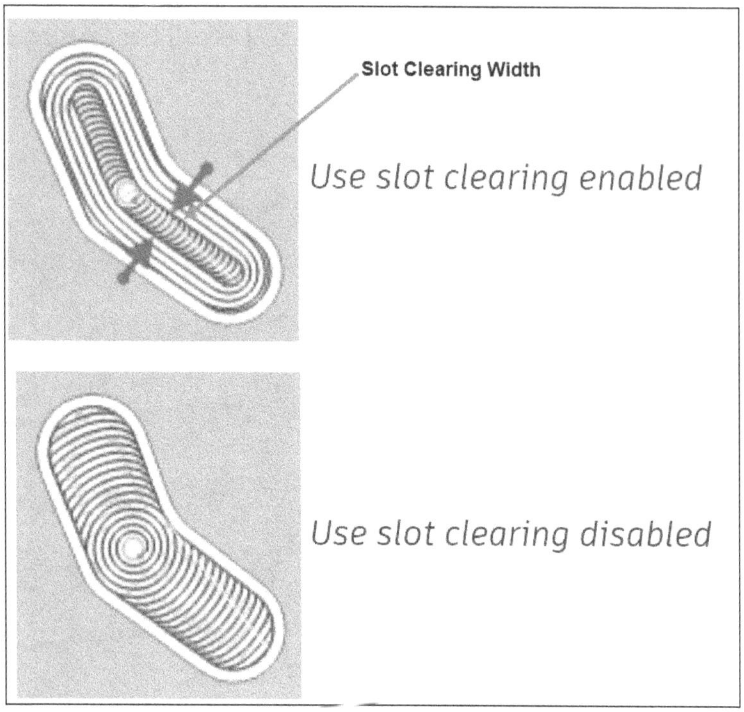

Figure-17. Slot clearing

- Click in the **Slot Clearing Width** edit box and specify desired value for width of slot. Once tool has performed machining in the slot, it will return to spiral motion of cutting near the walls of pockets.
- Select the **Conventional** option from the **Direction** drop-down of the **Passes** section to set the material removal process by conventional milling. In **Conventional** milling, the cutting process is performed in opposite direction of tool movement which causes the tool to scoop up the material; refer to Figure-18. The cutting process starts at zero thickness and increases up to maximum.
- Select the **Climb** option from the **Direction** drop-down in the **Passes** section to specify the material removal process by climb milling. In climb milling, the cutting process starts by machining maximum thickness and then decreases to zero.

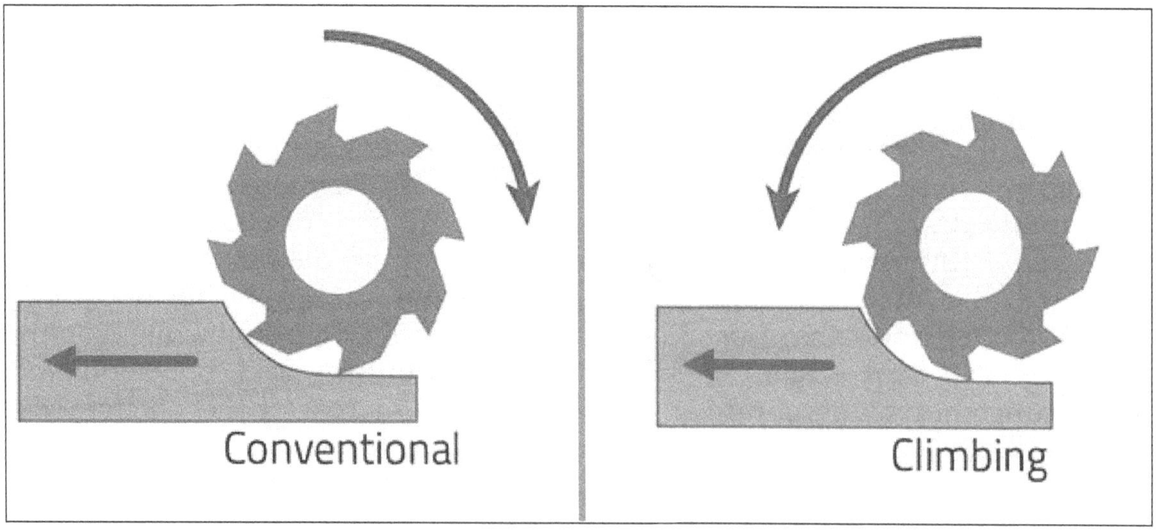

Figure-18. Conventional and climb machining

Multiple Depth Options

- Select the **Multiple Depths** check box from **Passes** tab to cut the material in multiple depths instead of cutting in one go. Note that every cutting tool has a length range by which tool can not perform cutting. When the **Multiple Depths** check box is not selected then the tool will cut only up to the depth allowed by its cutting length.
- Click in the **Maximum Roughing Stepdown** edit box and specify the maximum value of step-down distance between two roughing depths. Stepdown is the vertical distance between two cutting passes.
- Select the **Order By Depth** check box to sequence machining of pockets based on their depths. If this check box is selected then all the pockets will be machined at same level simultaneously.
- Select the **Order By Area** check box to sequence machining by pockets based on their areas. If this check box is selected then one pocket will be machined before moving to the next.

Stock To Leave Options

- Select the **Stock to leave** check box from the **Passes** tab to define the amount of stock to leave on the workpiece after roughing. This stock will be removed in finishing pass.
- Click in the **Radial Stock to Leave** edit box of the **Stock to Leave** section and specify the value of stock to remain around cylindrical faces of the part or side walls of the pockets after current operation.
- Click in the **Axial Stock to Leave** edit box of the **Stock to Leave** section and specify the value of stock to remain at the bottom flat surface/face of pocket after current operation.

Smoothing Options

- Select the **Smoothing** check box from the **Passes** tab to smoothen the toolpath by removing excessive points and fitting arcs within specified tolerance. Selecting this check box can reduce the size of G-codes as it will convert multiple connected lines into arcs wherever possible and similarly, multiple consecutive points will be converted into a line.
- Click in the **Smoothing Tolerance** edit box of the **Smoothing** section and specify desired value of tolerance.

Feed Optimization Options

- Select the **Feed Optimization** check box of the **Passes** tab to specify reduced feed at corners and curves. Note that the feed optimization options will not be available if the **Both Ways** check box is selected in the dialog box.
- Click in the **Maximum Directional Change** check box of **Feed Optimization** section and specify the maximum value of angle change allowed toolpath before feed rate is changed automatically to lower value.
- Click in the **Reduced Feed Radius** edit box and specify the value of minimum radius allowed for movement before the feed is reduced.
- Click in the **Reduced Feed Distance** edit box and specify the value for distance when approaching to a corner at which reduced feed rate will be applied.
- Click in the **Reduced Feedrate** edit box and specify the value of slower feed rate to be used when the tool is moving in X direction while cutting material.

- Select the **Only Inner Corners** check box from the **Feed Optimization** section to reduce the feed rate at inner corners.

Multi-Axis

The options of **Multi-Axis** tab are used to define whether you want to create 3 axis toolpath or wrap (4-axis and 5-axis) toolpath; refer to Figure-19. The options in this tab are discussed next.

Figure-19. Multi-Axis tab

- Select the **3-axis** button from the **Machine Type** section to perform 3 axis milling using X, Y, and Z axes. Select the **Wrap** button from the **Machine Type** section to create a wrap toolpath around selected cylindrical face. After selecting this option, select the cylindrical face; refer to Figure-20. Specify desired value in the **Offset** edit box to increase/decrease the diameter of wrap cylinder for generating toolpath.

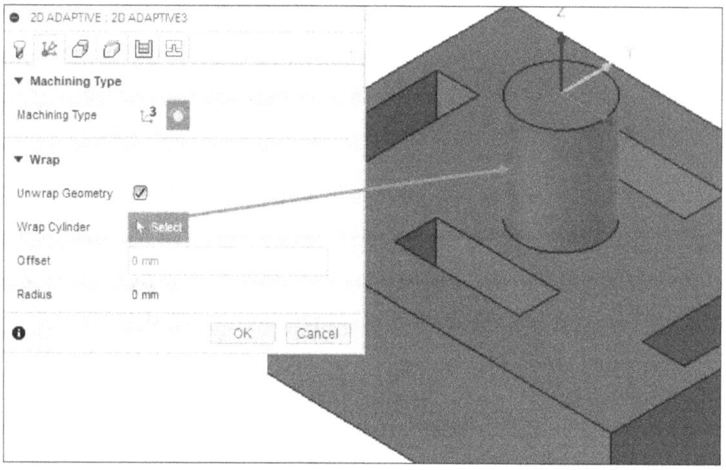

Figure-20. Wrap machining options

Linking

The options of the **Linking** tab are used to define, how toolpath passes should be linked in different directions. The procedure to use these options is discussed next.

- Click on the **Linking** tab from the **2D ADAPTIVE** dialog box. The options of the **Linking** tab will be displayed; refer to Figure-21.

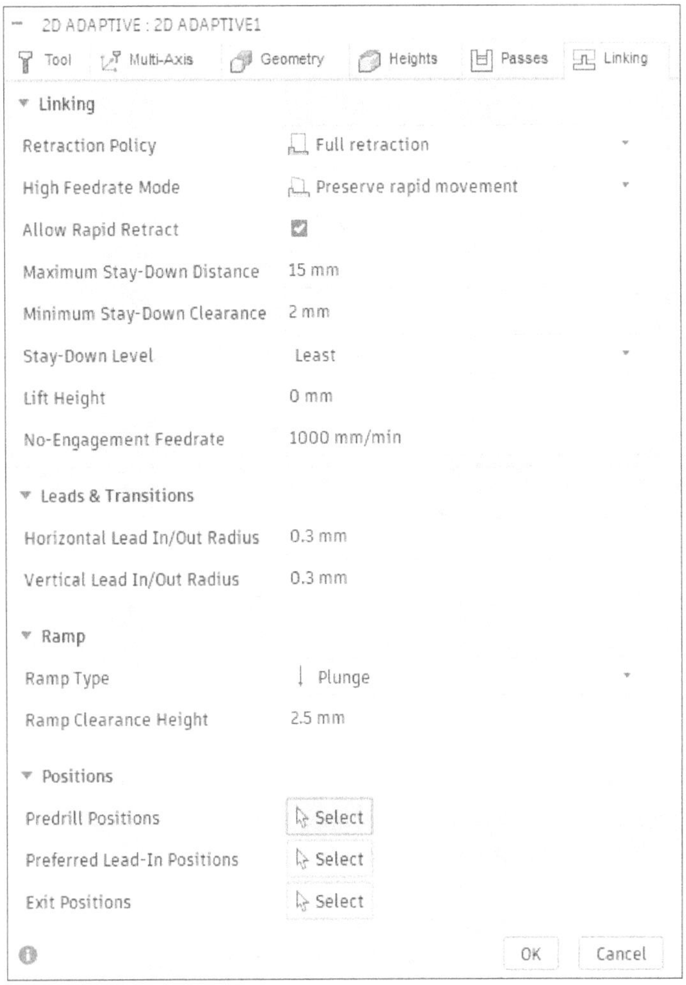

Figure-21. Linking tab

Linking Options

- Select the **Full retraction** option from the **Retraction Policy** drop-down to retract the tool up to retract height at the end of cutting pass before moving to the start of next machining pass.
- Select **Minimum retraction** option of **Retraction Policy** drop-down to move the tool up to the minimum retraction height from one cutting pass to other pass where the tool clears the work piece.
- The **High Feedrate Mode** drop-down is used to specify the tool rapid movements which should be output as true rapid movement. Click on the **High Feedrate Mode** drop-down and select desired option to define in which direction the rapid movement of tool will be retained during operation. Note that rapid movements are those in which tool does not perform any cutting operation and moves at full high feed rate to desired location.
- Select the **Allow Rapid Retract** check box from the **Linking** tab to perform the retracts as rapid movements. Clear the **Allow Rapid Retract** check box to force retract at lead-out feed rate.
- Click in the **Maximum Stay-Down Distance** edit box and specify maximum value of distance between different cutting passes up to which the tool stays down and does not retract. If there are more retractions in toolpath than expected then you should increase this value.

- Click in the **Minimum Stay-Down Clearance** edit box and specify minimum radial clearance distance value up to which cutting tool stay down.
- Click in the **Stay-Down Level** drop-down of the **Linking** section and select desired option to control how much the tool will try to stay down around obstacles during cutting process.
- Click in the **Lift Height** edit box and specify value of lift distance during reposition moves of the tool. You should specify this value to avoid cutting tool colliding with leftover stock on workpiece after cutting pass; refer to Figure-22.

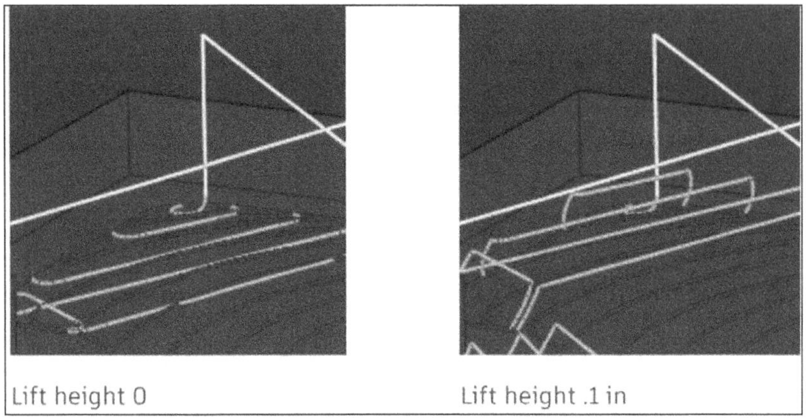

Figure-22. Lift height option effect

- Click in the **No-Engagement Feedrate** edit box of **Linking** section to specify the feedrate used for rapid movements where the tool is not in engagement with the material of workpiece during cutting pass.

Leads and Transitions

- The options of the **Leads & Transitions** section of the **Linking** tab is used to specify how leads and transitions should be generated at the time of tool entering or exiting the material.
- Click in the **Horizontal Lead In/Out Radius** edit box and specify the value of radius required for horizontal entry/exit.
- Click in the **Vertical Lead In/Out Radius** edit box and specify the value of radius required for vertical entry/exit.

Ramp Options

- The options in the **Ramps** section of **Linking** tab are used to define how cutting tool will enter into the material during its first cutting pass.
- Hover the cursor on the options of the **Ramp Type** drop-down, the explanation of these options will be displayed on the screen. Select desired option from the drop-down and specify related parameters.

Position Options

- The options of the **Positions** section in the **Linking** tab are used to specify the tool entry point and predrill positions if required.
- The **Select** selection button of **Predrill Positions** section is active by default. Click on the point in workpiece where drill has been done earlier so that the cutting tool can enter the material.
- Click on the **Select** selection button of **Preferred Lead-In Positions** section and click on the geometry near the location of workpiece where you want to enter the tool. Similarly, you can specify the exit point on workpiece for the toolpath.

- After specifying the parameter for **2D ADAPTIVE** dialog box, click on the **OK** button. The toolpath will be created and displayed on the workpiece; refer to Figure-23.

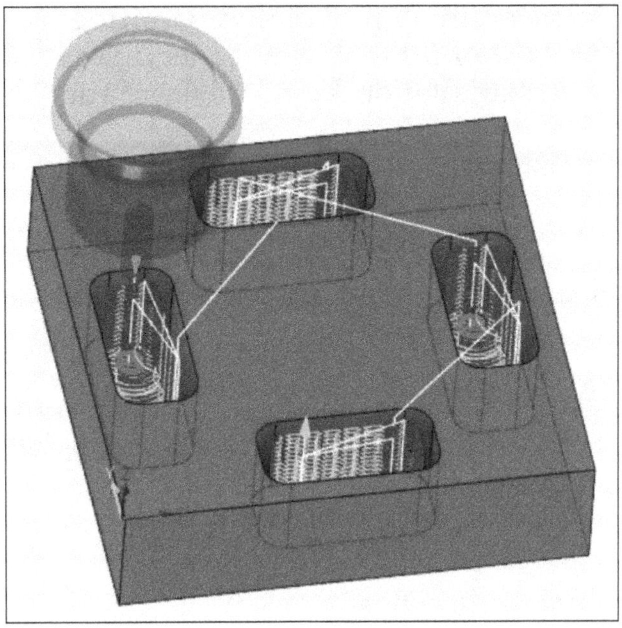

Figure-23. Toolpath created by adaptive clearing

- The option of the created toolpath will be added in **BROWSER**. Right-click on the toolpath. A shortcut menu will be displayed; refer to Figure-24.

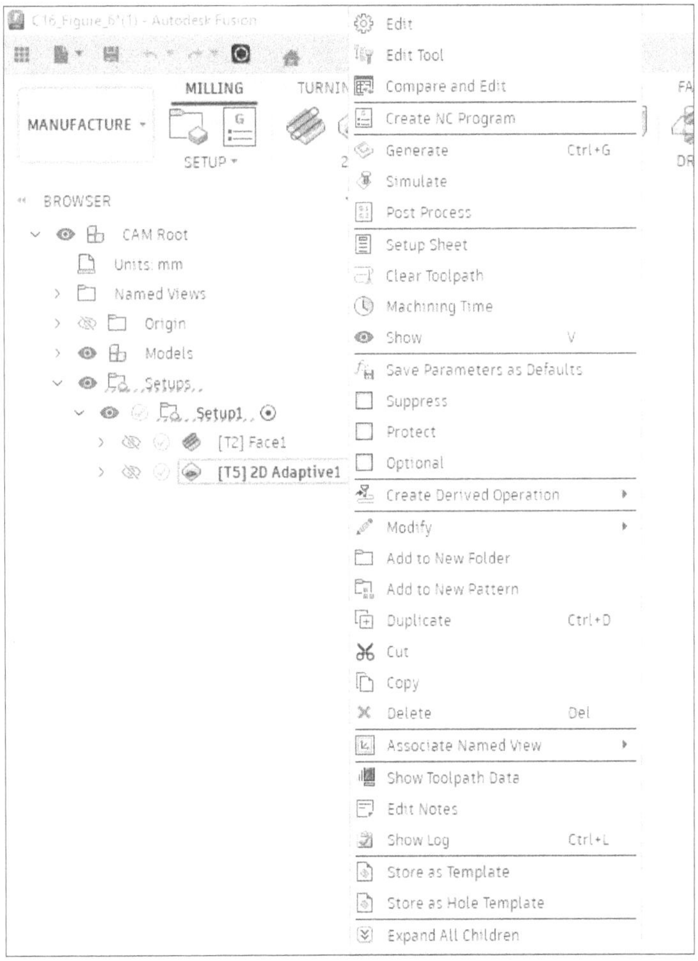

Figure-24. Shortcut menu

- If you want to edit the parameters then click on the **Edit** button from shortcut menu. The dialog box will be displayed for selected toolpath.
- If you want to check the animation of material cutting by selected toolpath then click on the **Simulate** button from shortcut menu. The **SIMULATE** dialog box will be displayed along with simulation keys. Click on the **Play** or **Pause** button as required.
- The other tools of this shortcut menu will be discussed later.

2D POCKET

The **2D Pocket** tool is used to remove material from pockets in the model. The procedure to use this tool is discussed next.

- Click on the **2D Pocket** tool from the **2D** drop-down in **MILLING** tab of **Toolbar**; refer to Figure-25. The **2D POCKET** dialog box will be displayed; refer to Figure-26.

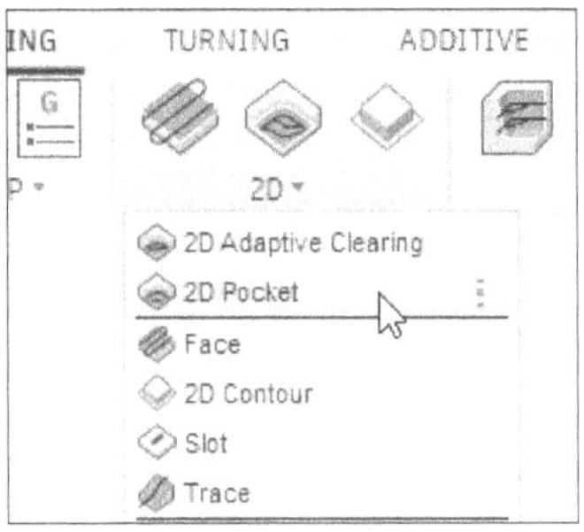

Figure-25. 2D Pocket tool

Figure-26. 2D POCKET dialog box

- Click on the **Select** button of **Tool** section. The **Select Tool** dialog box will be displayed.
- Click on desired tool from the dialog box and click on the **OK** button from **Select Tool** dialog box. The tool will be selected and displayed in **Tool** section of **2D POCKET** dialog box.
- Click on the **Geometry** tab of **2D POCKET** dialog box. The **Geometry** tab will be displayed.
- The **Select** button of **Pocket Selections** section from **Geometry** tab is active by default. Click on the surface/edge of the model to select; refer to Figure-27.

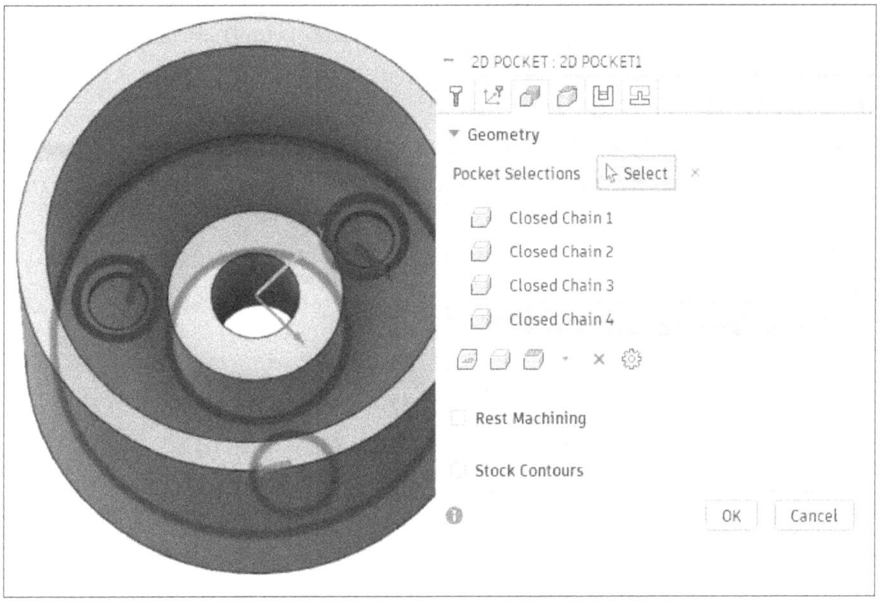

Figure-27. Pocket selections of model

- Select desired option from the **Sideways Compensation** drop-down of the **Passes** section in **Passes** tab to define the motion of tool with respect to walls.
- Select the **Preserve Order** check box if you want to machine the part in same sequence as they were selected.
- Select the **Both Ways** check box to machine both forward and backward.
- Select the **Use Morphed Spiral Machining** check box from the dialog box to perform smoother machining.
- Select the **Allow Stepover Cusps** check box if you want to allow cusps being formed at corners while cutting material. Selecting this option decreases the machining time.
- Select the **Finishing Passes** check box from **Passes** tab if you want to perform finishing pass. The options related to finishing passes will be displayed in the dialog box; refer to Figure-28.

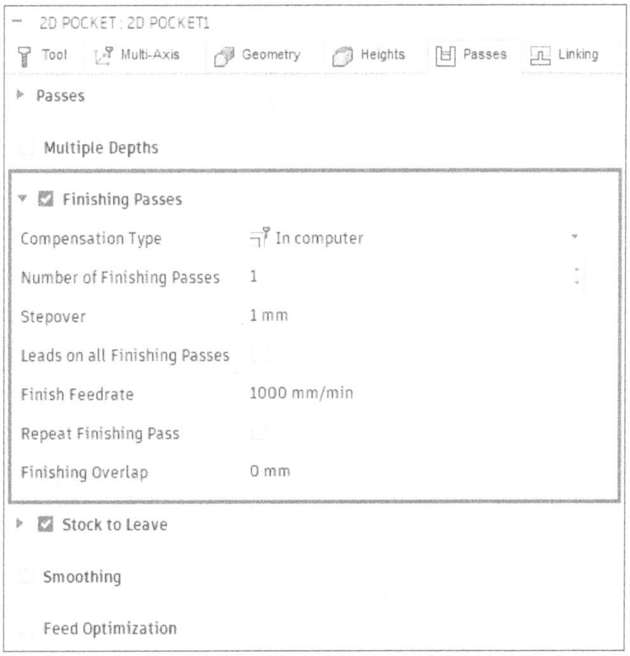

Figure-28. Finishing pass options

- Specify the total number of finishing passes to be performed in the **Number of Finishing Passes** edit box to get better finish of the model. Generally, 2 finishing passes are performed to get better finish.
- Specify desired value in the **Stepover** edit box to define the distance by which tool will move left or right in the cutting plane to perform next cutting pass.
- Select the **Leads on all Finishing Passes** check box to apply full length of lead in and lead out to finishing passes.
- Click in the **Finish Feedrate** edit box to specify movement speed by which cutting tool will move for performing finishing operation.
- Select the **Repeat Finishing Pass** check box to repeat the finish operation once more when 0 stock left.
- For machining multiple depth pockets, the **Multiple Depths** check box should be selected from **Passes** tab. The other parameters have been discussed earlier in this chapter.
- After specifying the parameters, click on the **OK** button from **2D POCKET** dialog box. The toolpath will be generated and displayed; refer to Figure-29.

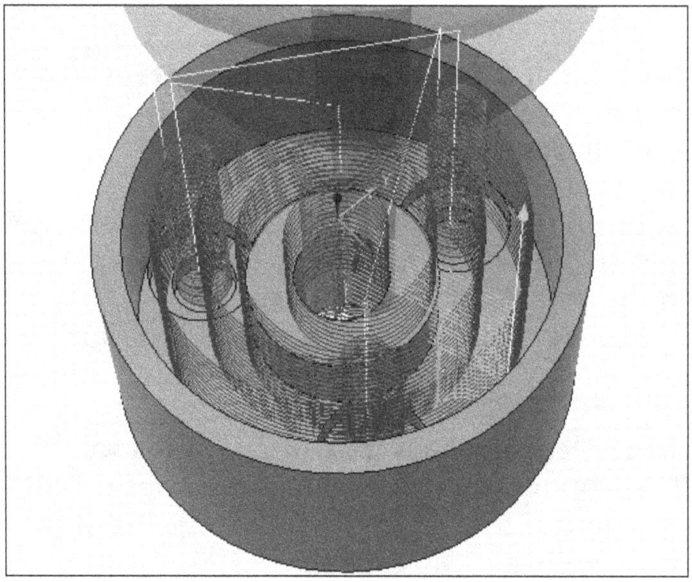

Figure-29. Created toolpath for 2D Pocket

Face

The **Face** tool is used to remove material from the top face of the workpiece. In any machining sequence, this is generally the first toolpath to be generated for flat head workpiece. The procedure to use this tool is discussed next.

- Click on the **Face** tool of **2D** drop-down from **Toolbar**; refer to Figure-30. The **FACE** dialog box will be displayed; refer to Figure-31.

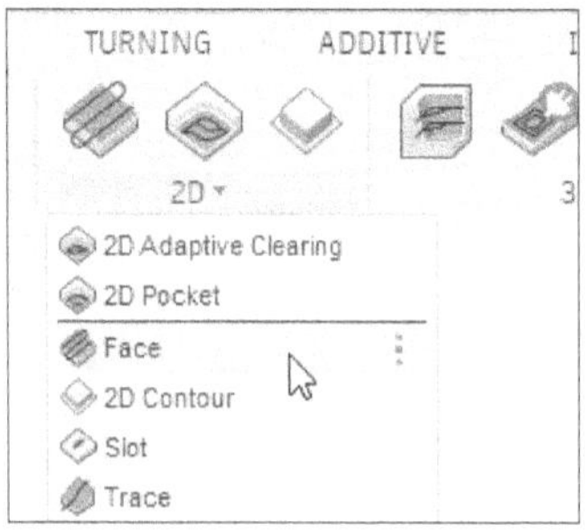

Figure-30. Face tool

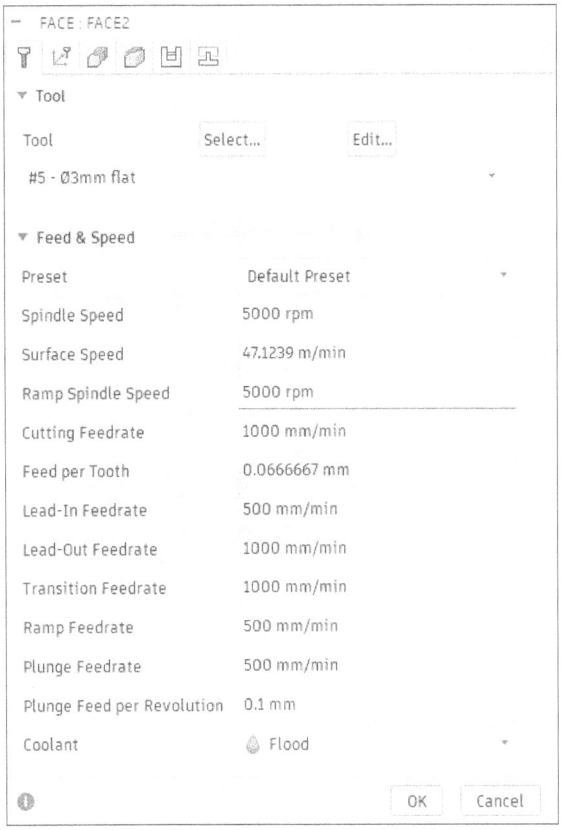

Figure-31. FACE dialog box

- Click on the **Select** button from **Tool** tab and select desired face mill tool for facing operation according to your model from **Select Tool** dialog box. Generally, we use flat end mill or face mill cutting tools for this operation.
- Click on the **Geometry** tab of **FACE** dialog box and select the **Chain** button from the **Stock Contours** section of the dialog box. The **CHAIN** dialog box will be displayed and **Select** selection button of the dialog box will be active by default asking you to select the boundary of workpiece. Click on the outer edge of the model; refer to Figure-32.

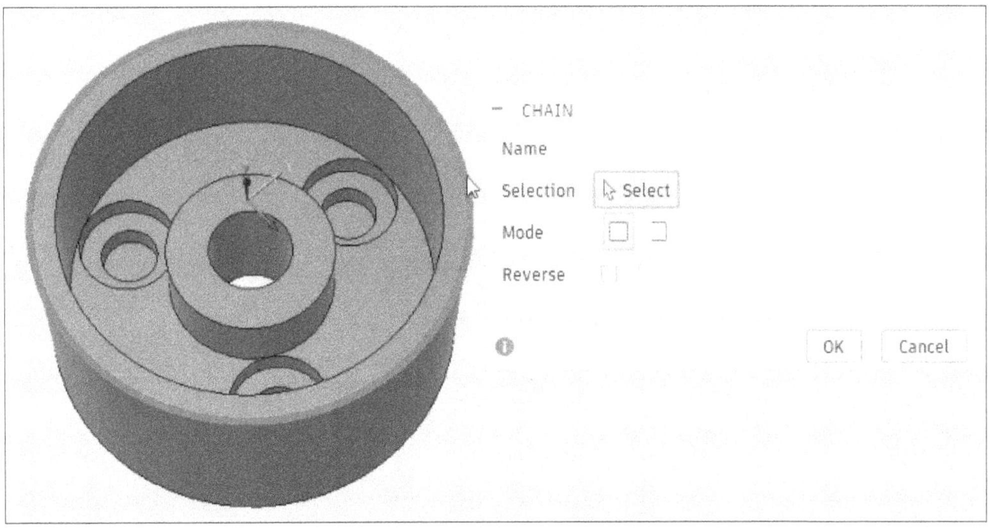

Figure-32. Selection for FACE dialog box

- Select the **Use Chip Thinning** check box from **Passes** tab of dialog box to make tool roll while cutting so that chips formed are thin.

- The other options of the dialog box have been discussed earlier. After specifying the parameters, click on the **OK** button from the **FACE** dialog box. The toolpath will be generated and displayed on workpiece; refer to Figure-33.

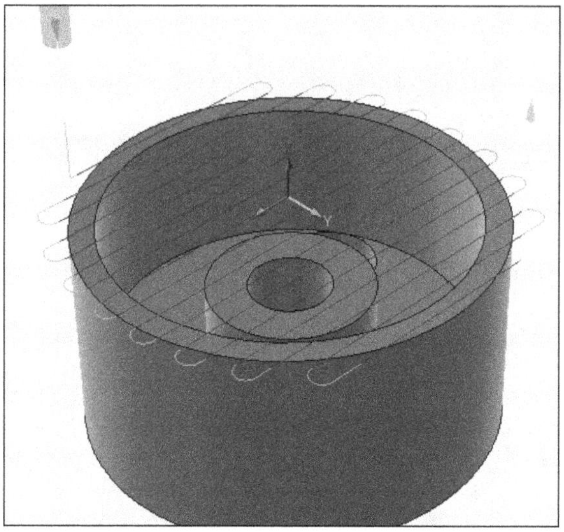

Figure-33. Created toolpath for facing

- Right-click on the recently created **Face** toolpath and click on the **Simulate** button to check the animation of facing operation.

2D Contour

The **2D Contour** tool is used to remove material by following the contour of the model. This tool is generally used to remove the material from outer/inner walls of the selected workpiece. You can use this toolpath for path roughing and finishing. The procedure to use this tool is discussed next.

- Click on the **2D Contour** tool from the **2D** drop-down of the **Toolbar**; refer to Figure-34. The **2D CONTOUR** dialog box will be displayed; refer to Figure-35.

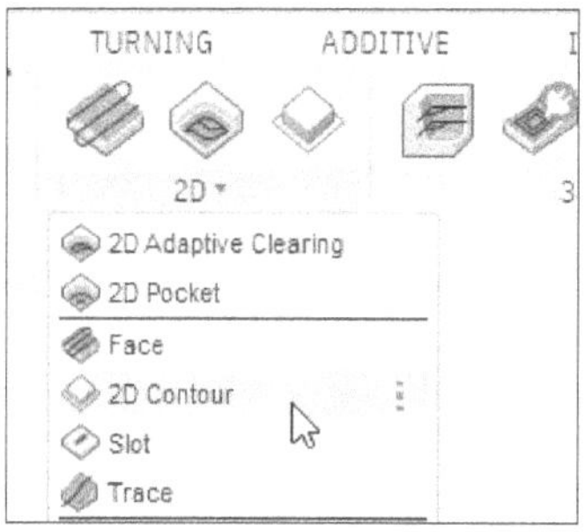

Figure-34. 2D Contour tool

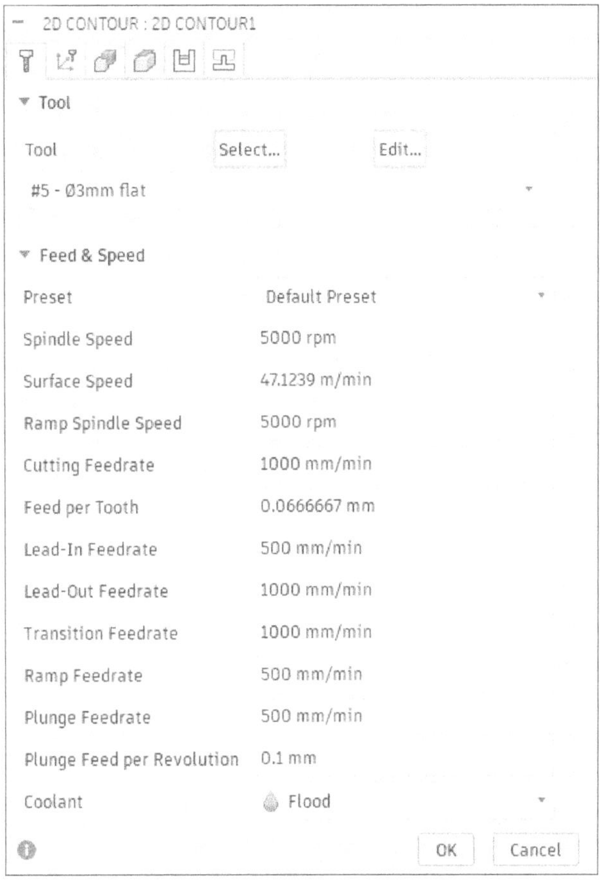

Figure-35. 2D CONTOUR dialog box

- Click on the **Select** button from the **Tool** tab of the **2D CONTOUR** dialog box and select the required tool according to your model from **Select Tool** dialog box.
- Click on the **Geometry** tab of **2D CONTOUR** dialog box. The **Geometry** tab will be displayed and the **Select** button of **Contour Selection** section will be active by default. Click on the boundary edges of the model to select; refer to Figure-36.

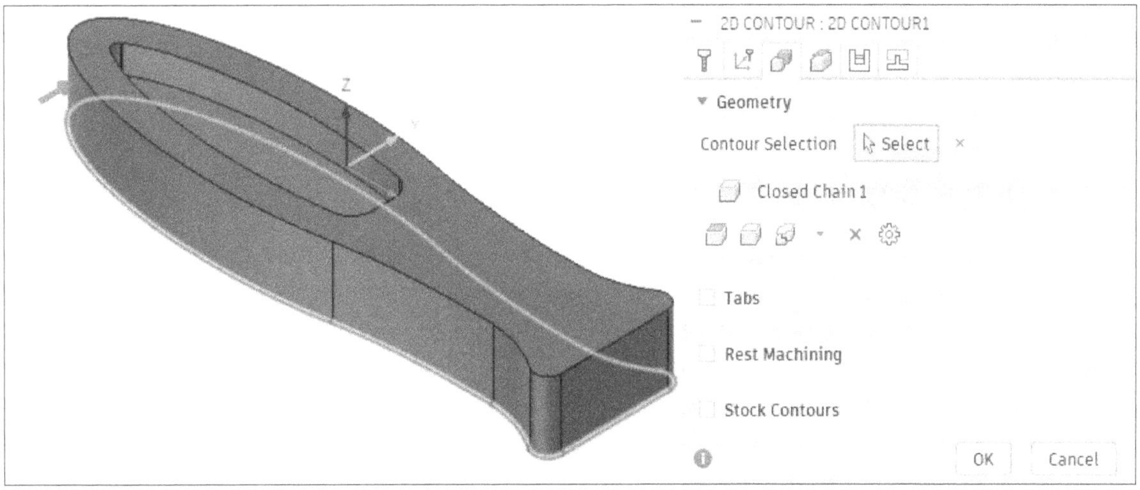

Figure-36. Selection of edge for contour

Tabs

The **Tabs** check box is used to define parameters for holding the workpiece when you are cutting a part from sheet. This option is generally used when you are working on a sheet and after operation the part will be detached from this sheet. When you use this option, cutting tool will leave small amount of stock in the form of tabs to hold the workpiece after machining. The procedure is discussed next.

- Click on the **Tabs** check box to enable options related to tab.
- Select desired shape of tab from **Tab Shape** drop-down. You can select rectangular or triangular shapes for creating tab.
- Click in the **Tab Width** edit box and specify the value of width of tab.
- Click in the **Tab Height** edit box and specify the value of height of tab.
- Select the **By distance** option from the **Tab Positioning** drop-down of **Tabs** section to position the tab around the workpiece by specified distance; refer to Figure-37.

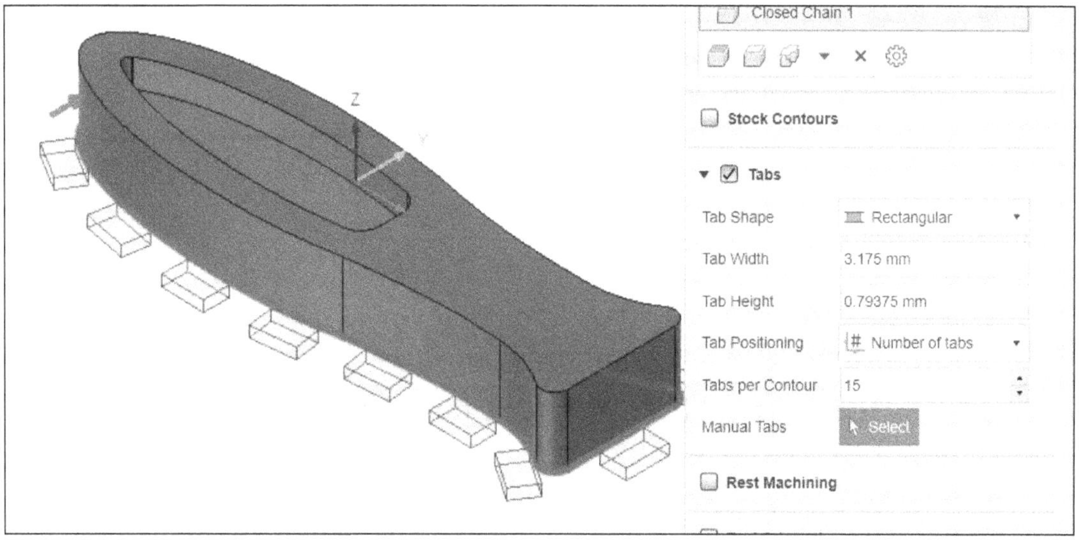

Figure-37. Tab positioning by distance

- You can also create tabs manually by selecting points on the edge. To do so, select the **Number of tabs** option from the **Tab Positioning** drop-down and select points on model edge; refer to Figure-38.

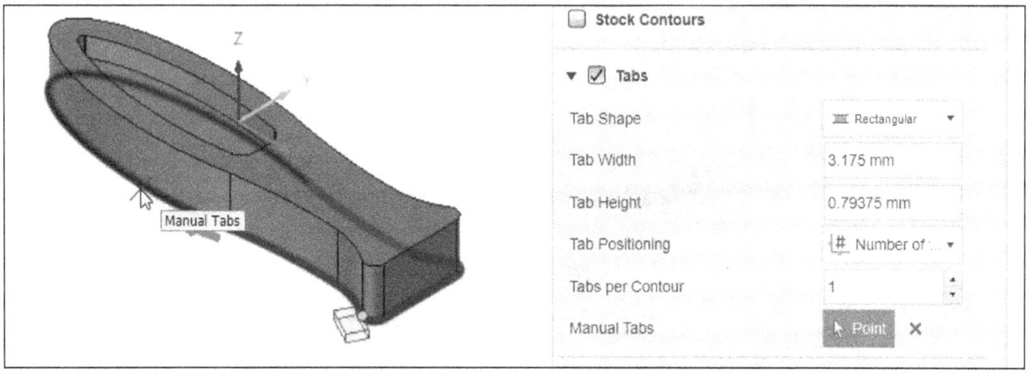

Figure-38. Positioning by points

- The other options of this dialog box are same as discussed earlier.
- After specifying the parameters, click on the **OK** button from the **2D CONTOUR** dialog box. The toolpath will be generated and displayed on the model; refer to Figure-39.

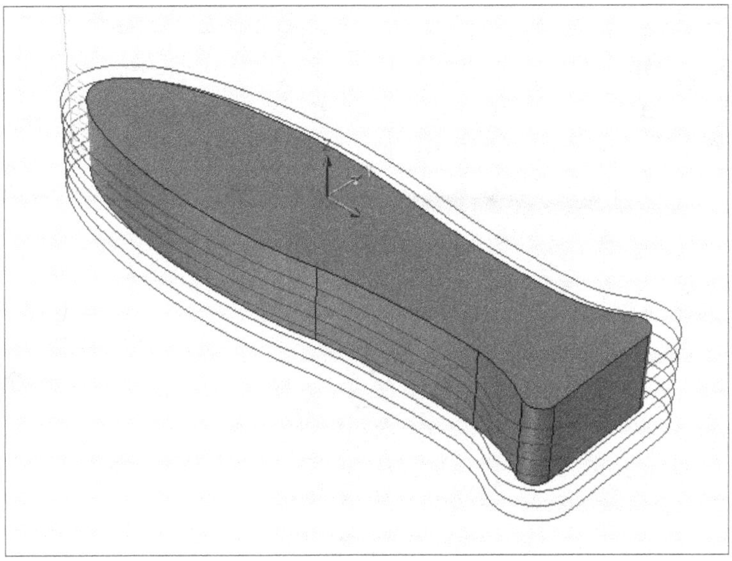

Figure-39. Created toolpath for solid

Slot

The **Slot** tool is used to remove material from model in slot pattern. Note that this slot milling is governed in 2D plane so the depth of cut need to be specified explicitly. Note that the Slot toolpath follows centerline/curve of the slot feature for cutting passes. The slot features must be created using the Slot creation tools in Design workspace of Autodesk Fusion. The procedure to use this tool is discussed next.

- Click on the **Slot** tool from the **2D** drop-down in the **Toolbar**; refer to Figure-40. The **SLOT** dialog box will be displayed; refer to Figure-41.

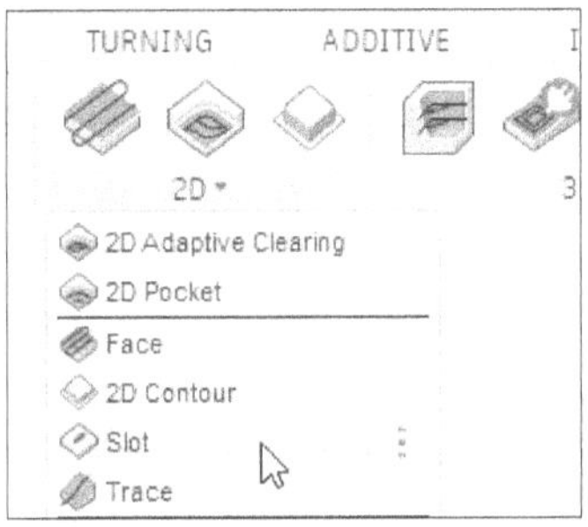

Figure-40. Slot tool

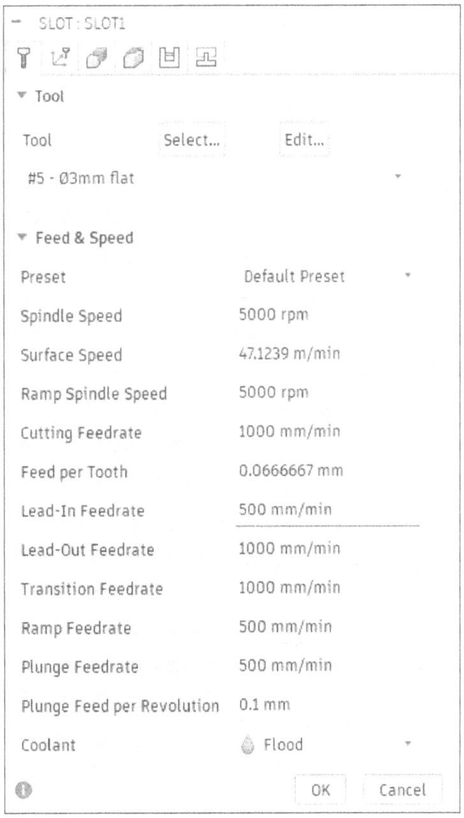

Figure-41. SLOT dialog box

- Click on the **Select** button from **Tool** tab of the **SLOT** dialog box. The **Select Tool** dialog box will be displayed. Select the tool as required.
- Click on the **Geometry** tab of **SLOT** dialog box. The **Geometry** tab will be displayed and the selection button for **Pocket Selections** option will be active by default.
- Select the curve chains for the slot; refer to Figure-42.

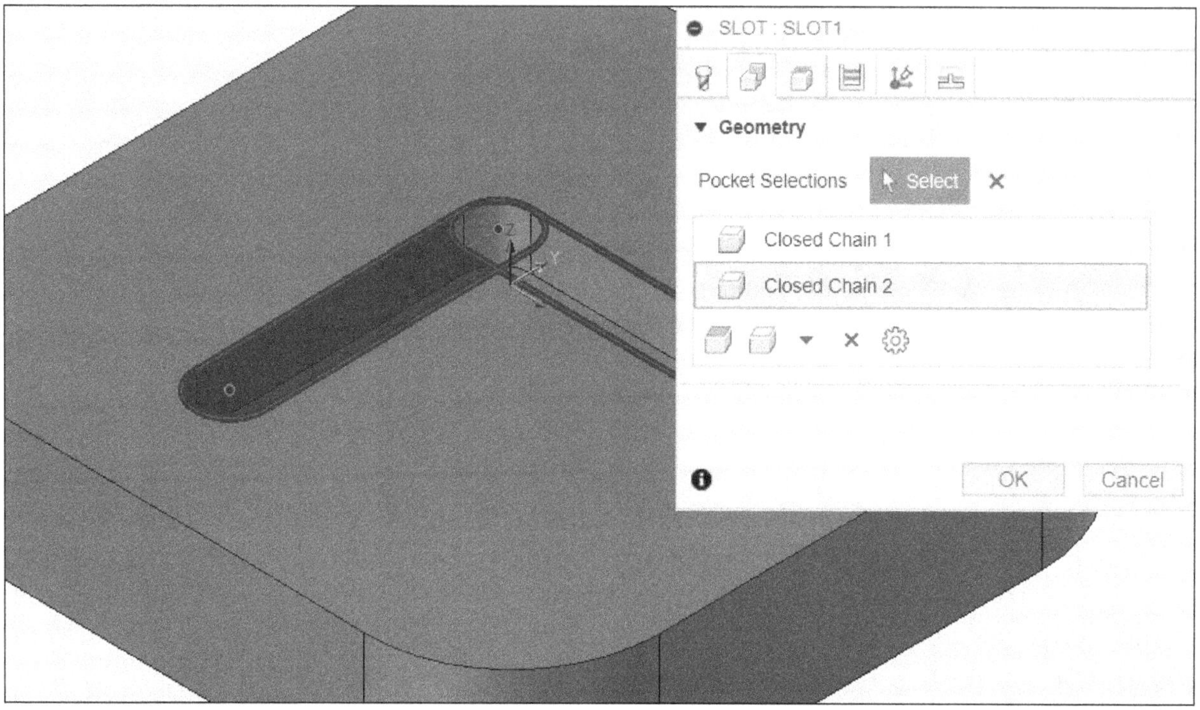

Figure-42. Selection for slot

- Select desired option from the **Ramp Type** drop-down in **Linking** tab of the dialog box. In our case, we have applied **Plunge** option of **Ramp Type** drop-down from **Linking** tab for better generation of toolpath as tool entry is not available.
- Specify desired parameters for ramp if asked based on selected option. The other options of this dialog box have been discussed earlier.
- After specifying the parameters, click on the **OK** button from the **SLOT** dialog box. The toolpath will be generated and displayed on the model; refer to Figure-43.

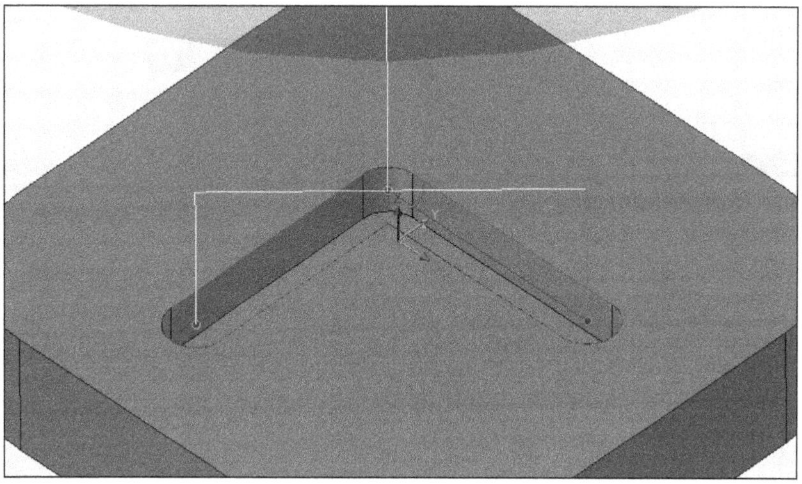

Figure-43. Generated toolpath for slot

Note that the main difference between pocket toolpaths and slot toolpaths in Autodesk Fusion is that Pocket toolpaths can machine any regular and irregular slots whereas the Slot toolpaths can machine only regular slots created in Autodesk Fusion. A pocket toolpath is fine when you are using end mill or other similar cutting tools but if you have a slot cutter with size equal to width of slot then slot toolpaths should be used.

Trace

The **Trace** tool is used to create toolpath which follows selected curves. If you want to machine a sketch curve up to specified depth then this toolpath is the right selection. Note that there is not need of cut feature to exist in the model when using this toolpath, as depth of cut is explicitly specified. The procedure to use this tool is discussed next.

- Click on the **Trace** tool of **2D** drop-down from **Toolbar**; refer to Figure-44. The **TRACE** dialog box will be displayed; refer to Figure-45.

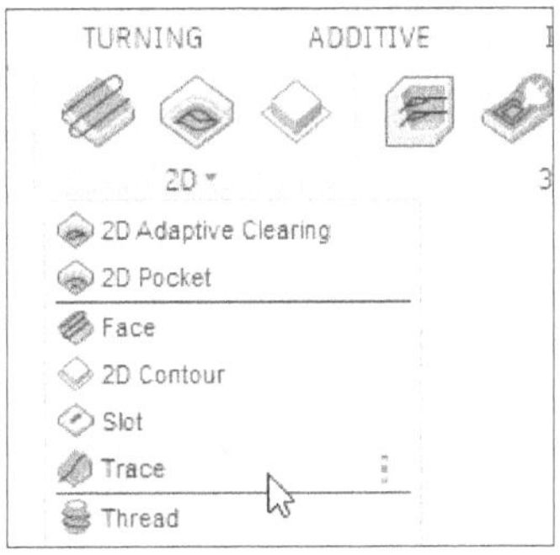

Figure-44. Trace tool

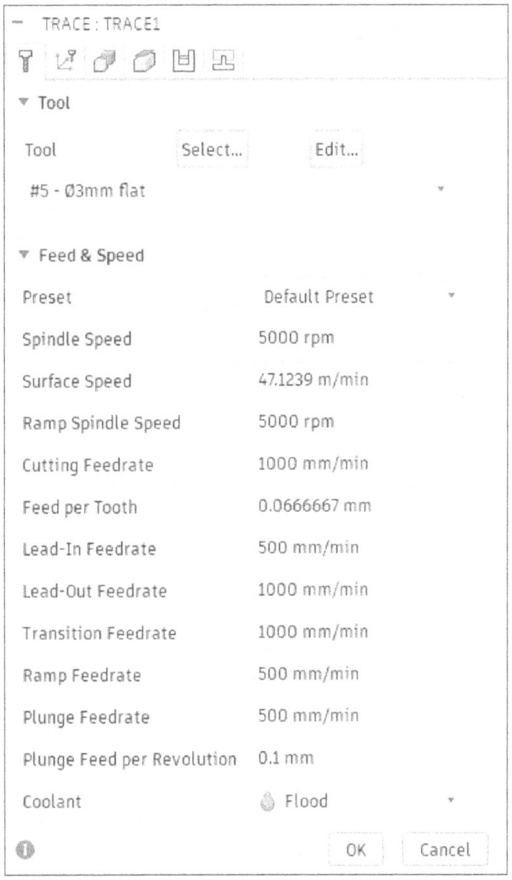

Figure-45. TRACE dialog box

- Click on the **Select** button of **Tool** tab from **TRACE** dialog box. The **Select Tool** dialog box will be displayed. Select the tool as required.
- Click on the **Geometry** tab of **TRACE** dialog box. The **Geometry** tab will be displayed and you will be asked to select curve chains to be machined.
- The selection button of **Curve Selections** section of **Geometry** tab is active by default. Select the geometry for trace; refer to Figure-46. You can also select sketch curves for this toolpath.

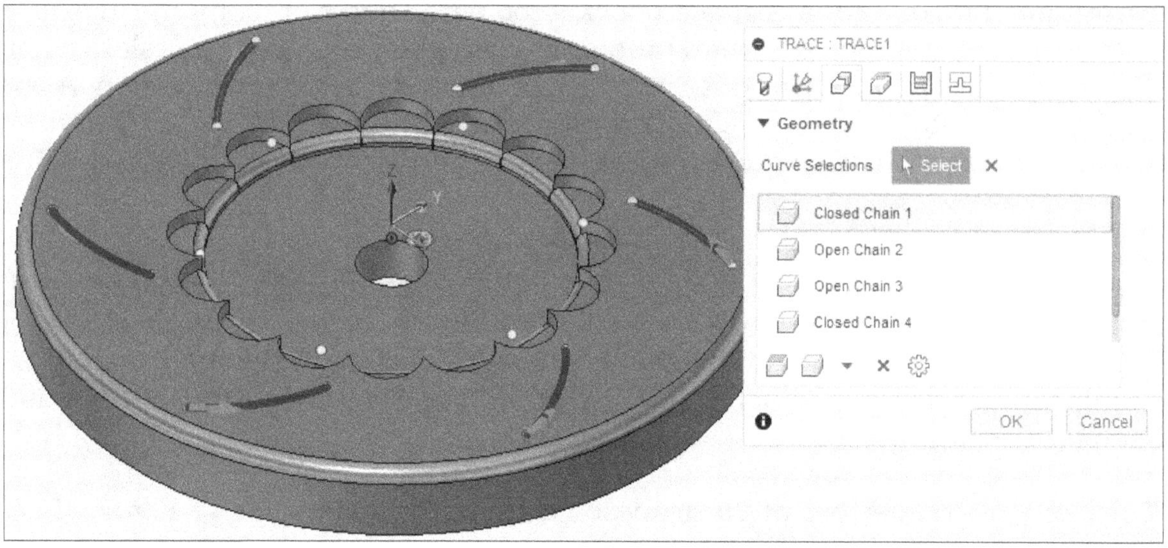

Figure-46. Selection of geometry for trace

- Click on the **Passes** tab of **TRACE** dialog box. The **Passes** tab will be displayed; refer to Figure-47.

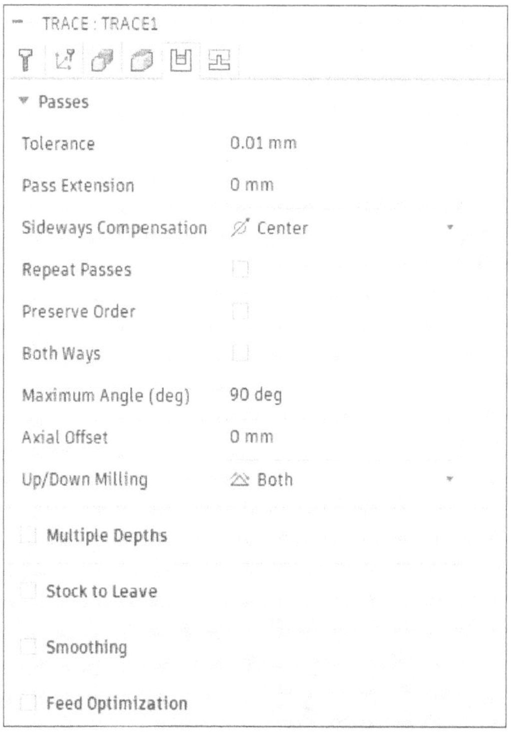

Figure-47. Passes tab of TRACE dialog box

- Click in the **Pass Extension** edit box and enter the value of distance by which the toolpath along length will be extended.
- Select the **Repeat Passes** check box from the **Passes** tab to perform an additional finishing pass with zero stock for better finish.
- Select the **Preserve Order** check box from the **Passes** tab to specify that the geometry machined in the order in which they are selected.
- Select the **Both Ways** check box from the **Passes** tab to use the climb and conventional machining for open profile of the selected geometry.
- Click in the **Maximum Angle (deg)** edit box and specify maximum plunge angle for machining. Plunge angle is the angle at which cutting tool will enter workpiece while cutting.

- Click on the **Bore** tool from the **2D** drop-down in the **Toolbar**; refer to Figure-55. The **BORE** dialog box will be displayed; refer to Figure-56.

Figure-55. Bore tool

Figure-56. BORE dialog box

- Click on the **Select** button from the **Tool** tab in the **BORE** dialog box. The **Select Tool** dialog box will be displayed. Select the tool as required.
- Click on the **Geometry** tab in **BORE** dialog box. The **Geometry** tab will be displayed and the selection button for **Circular Face Selections** option in **Geometry** tab will be active by default. You need to click on the circular faces of holes which were drilled earlier and you want to perform finish operation on those holes; refer to Figure-57.

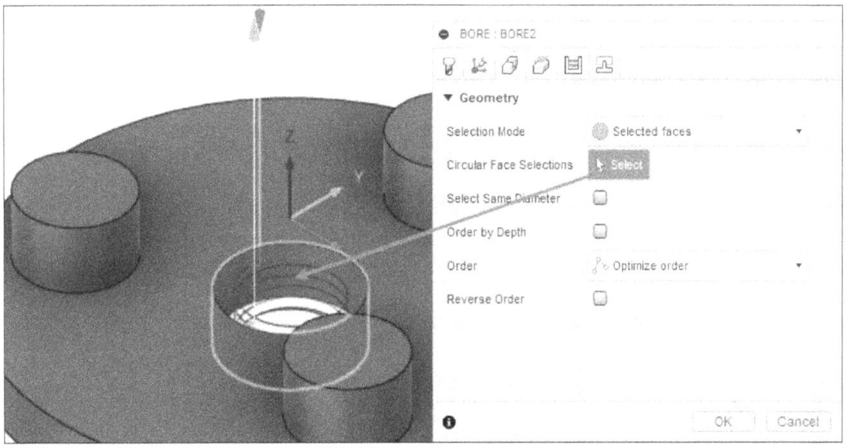

Figure-57. Selecting circular Face for bore

- The other options of the dialog box have been discussed earlier.
- After specifying the parameter, click on the **OK** button from the **BORE** dialog box. The toolpath will be generated and displayed on the model.

Circular

The **Circular** tool is used for milling circular or round pocket/boss features. This tool is useful when you want to derive height and depth of toolpath from selected cylindrical feature. The feature can be a circular pocket as well as a cylindrical island. The procedure to use this tool is discussed next.

- Click on the **Circular** tool from **2D** drop-down in the **Toolbar**; refer to Figure-58. The **CIRCULAR** dialog box will be displayed; refer to Figure-59.

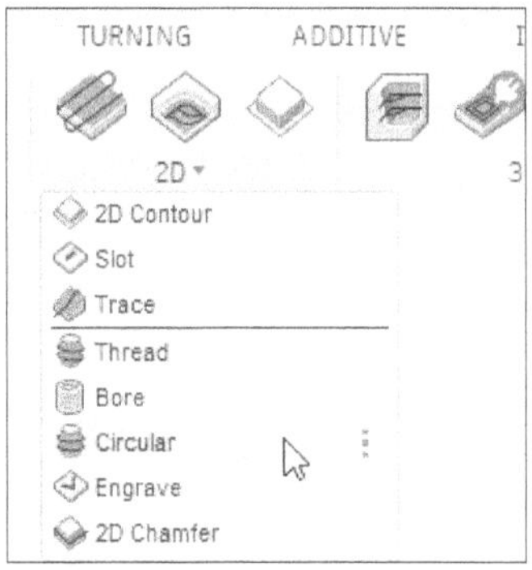

Figure-58. Circular tool

Figure-59. CIRCULAR dialog box

- Click on the **Select** button from **Tool** tab in the **CIRCULAR** dialog box. The **Select Tool** dialog box will be displayed. Select the cutting tool as required.
- Click on the **Geometry** tab in the **CIRCULAR** dialog box. The **Geometry** tab will be displayed. The **Select** button for **Circular Face Selections** option in **Geometry** tab will be active by default.
- Click on the circular face in the model to select it; refer to Figure-60.

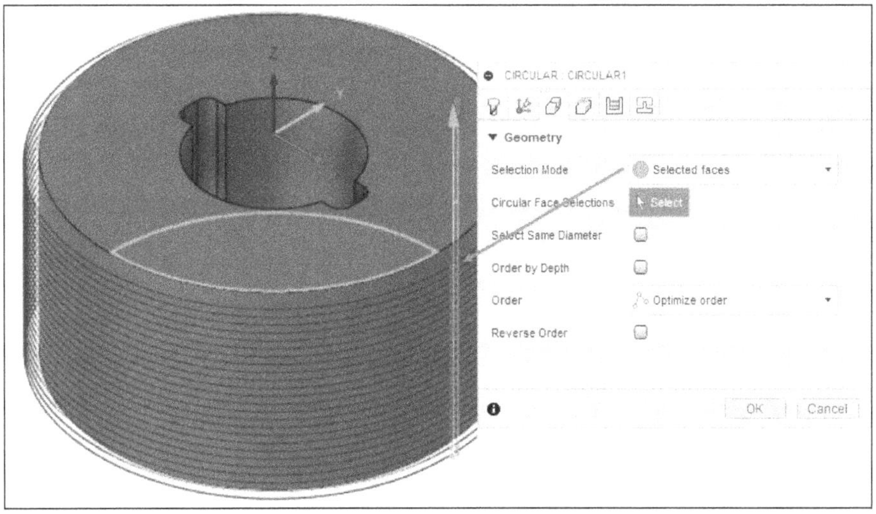

Figure-60. Selecting face for Circular tool

- The other options of the dialog box have been discussed earlier. After specifying the parameters, click on the **OK** button from the **CIRCULAR** dialog box. The toolpath will be generated and displayed on the model.

Engrave

The **Engrave** tool is used to perform artistic machining on the workpiece like creating logos. This tool is also used to print text on the press dies. The procedure to use this tool is discussed next.

- Click on the **Engrave** tool from the **2D** drop-down in the **Toolbar**; refer to Figure-61. The **ENGRAVE** dialog box will be displayed; refer to Figure-62.

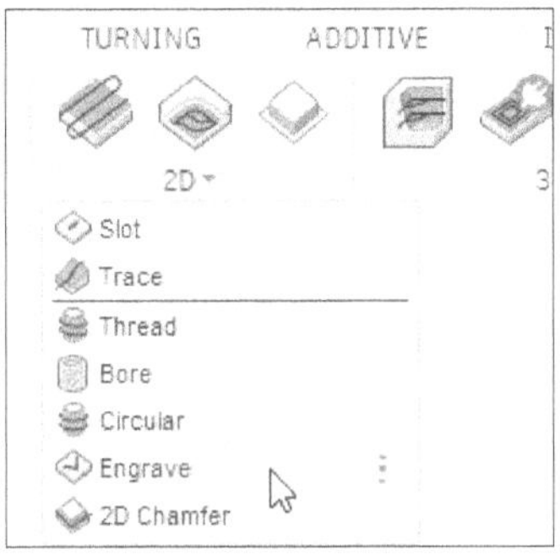

Figure-61. Engrave tool

Figure-62. ENGRAVE dialog box

- Click on the **Select** button from **Tool** tab in **ENGRAVE** dialog box. The **Select Tool** dialog box will be displayed. Select the tool as required preferably a tapered cutting tool.
- Click on the **Geometry** tab of the **ENGRAVE** dialog box. The options of **Geometry** tab will be displayed and the selection button for **Contour Selection** option in **Geometry** tab will be active by default. You need to select the curves to be engraved; refer to Figure-63.

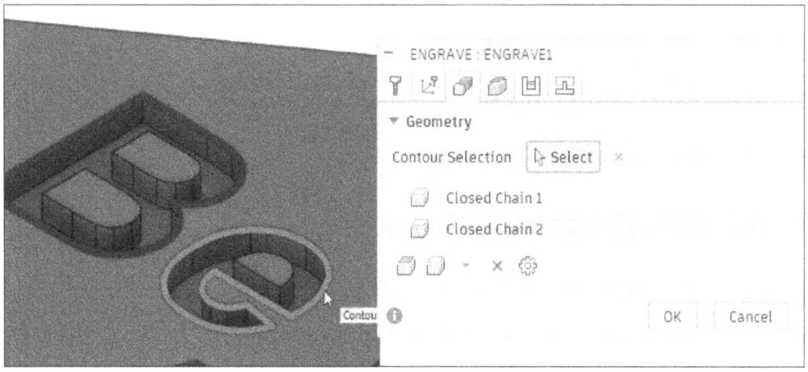

Figure-63. Contour selection for engraving

Note that sometimes people confuse in engrave and emboss features. Engraving is achieved when pockets of desired shape are created in the workpiece whereas embossing is achieved when islands of desired shapes are created in the workpiece.

- Click on the **Passes** tab and specify desired value in the **Sharp Corner Angle** edit box to define the maximum value of angle between edges at corner up to which corners will be cleared during machining. Note that in general, cutting tool creates sharp corners in engraving toolpaths.
- The other options of the dialog box are same as discussed earlier. After specifying the parameters, click on the **OK** button from **ENGRAVE** dialog box to complete the process. The toolpath will be generated and displayed on the model; refer to Figure-64.

Figure-64. Generated toolpath for engrave

2D Chamfer

The **2D Chamfer** tool is used to create chamfer profile on the edge of model. The procedure to use this tool is discussed next.

- Click on the **2D Chamfer** tool from **2D** drop-down in **Toolbar**; refer to Figure-65. The **2D CHAMFER** dialog box will be displayed; refer to Figure-66.

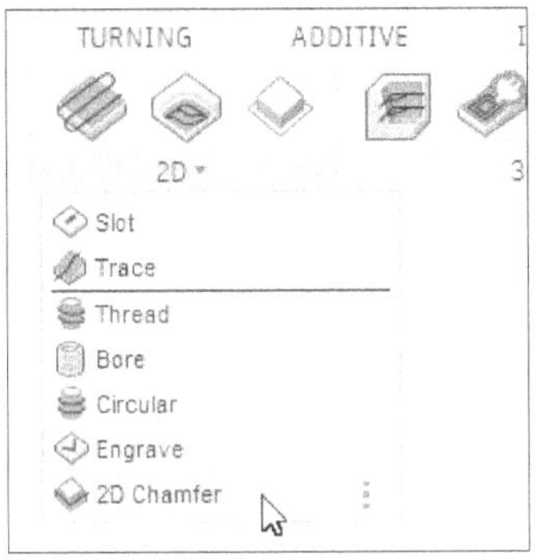

Figure-65. 2D Chamfer tool

Figure-66. 2D CHAMFER dialog box

- Click on the **Select** button of **Tool** tab from **2D CHAMFER** dialog box. The **Select Tool** dialog box will be displayed. Select the tool as required.
- Click on the **Geometry** tab of **2D CHAMFER** dialog box. The **Geometry** tab will be displayed.
- The **Nothing** button of **Contour Selection** section from **Geometry** tab is active by default. You need to select the edge for creating chamfer; refer to Figure-67.

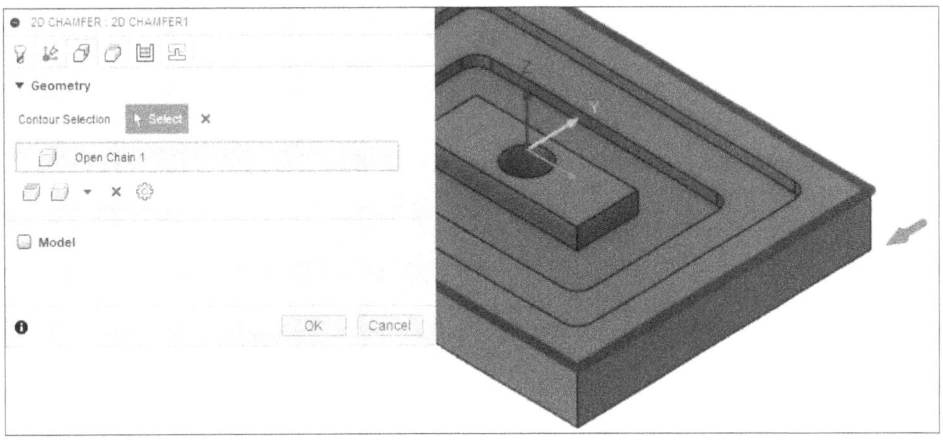

Figure-67. Selection of edge for chamfer

- Click in the **Passes** tab from **2D CHAMFER** dialog box. The options of **Passes** tab will be displayed; refer to Figure-68.

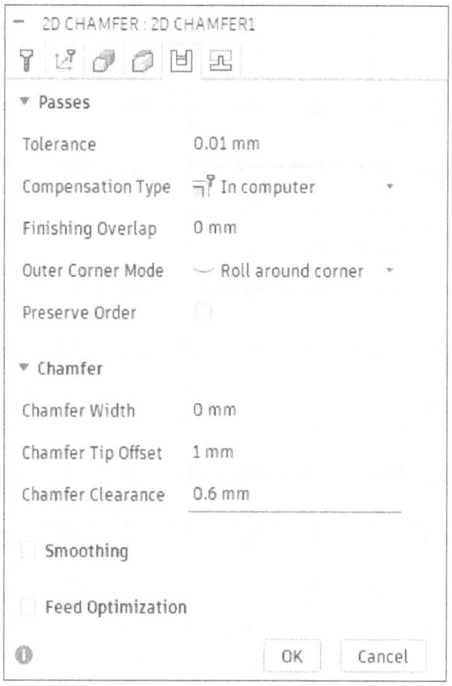

Figure-68. Passes tab of 2D CHAMFER dialog box

- Select desired option from the **Outer Corner Mode** drop-down to define whether you want to create sharp corner or roll around the corner.
- Click in the **Chamfer Width** edit box of **Chamfer** section from **Passes** tab and specify the value of width of chamfer.
- Click in the **Chamfer Tip Offset** edit box of **Chamfer** section from **Passes** tab and specify the value of tip offset so that cut is not made from the tip but from the approximate middle of cutting edge of tool.
- Click in the **Chamfer Clearance** edit box of **Chamfer** section and enter the value of clearance from near by walls to avoid collision.
- The other options of the dialog box are same as discussed earlier.
- After specifying the parameters, click on the **OK** button from the **2D CHAMFER** dialog box. The toolpath will be generated and displayed on the model; refer to Figure-69.

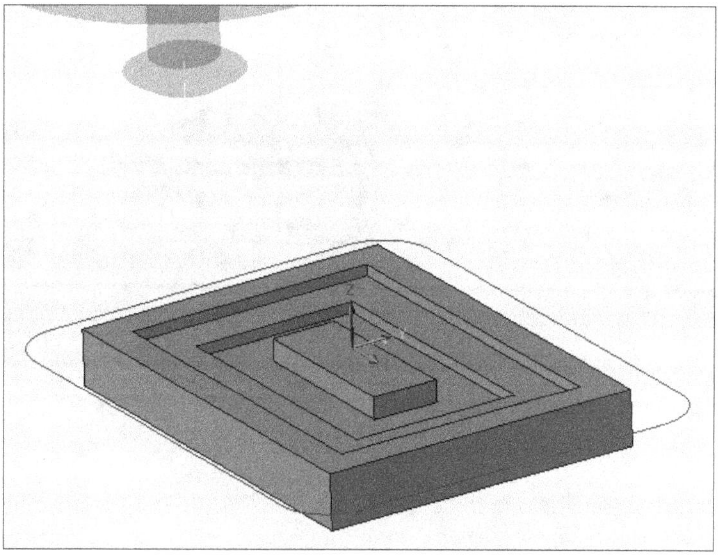

Figure-69. Toolpath generated for chamfer

Note that when you hover cursor on a toolpath in **BROWSER** then preview of toolpath is displayed in modeling area; refer to Figure-70 but when you select a toolpath from **BROWSER** then preview of material removed from stock is displayed; refer to Figure-71.

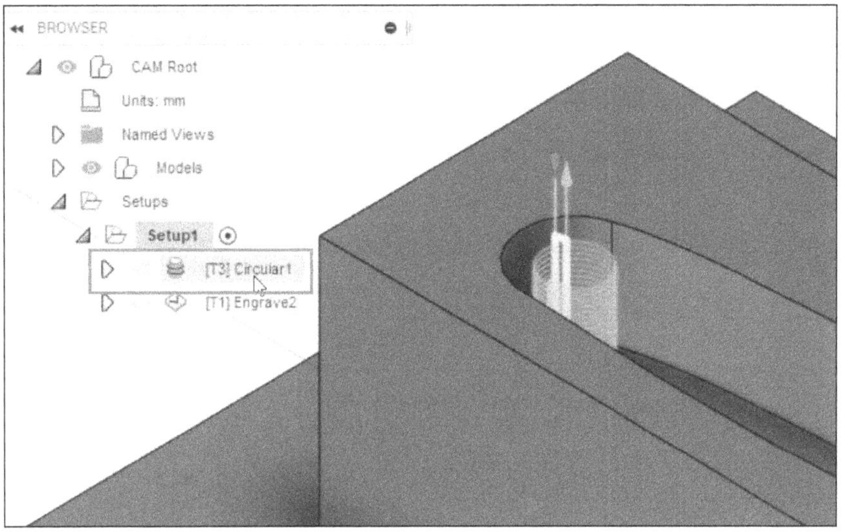

Figure-70. Hovering cursor on toolpath

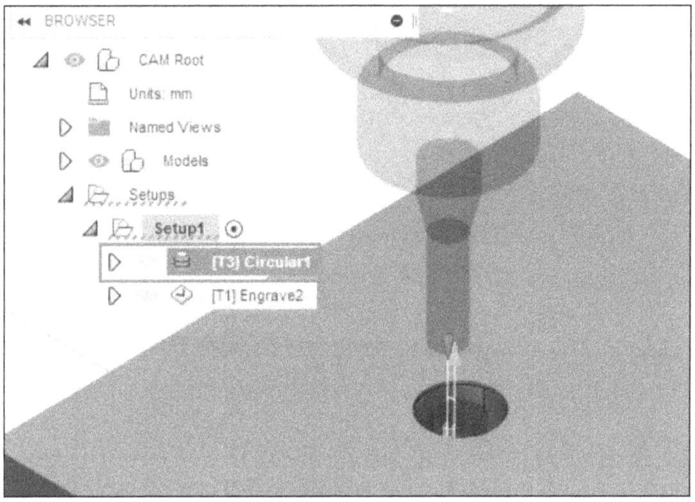

Figure-71. On selecting a toolpath

GENERATING 3D TOOLPATH

Till now, we have discussed the procedure of generating 2D Toolpaths. In this section, we will discuss the tools used for generating 3D Toolpaths. 3D toolpaths enable simultaneous movement of tool in horizontal and vertical direction whereas in 2D toolpaths, the cutting tool performs all the cutting operations in current XY plane and then moves up/down in Z direction.

Adaptive Clearing Toolpath

The **Adaptive Clearing** tool is used to remove the material in bulk from workpiece. It is generally a roughing process. It uses an advanced strategy of milling motion so that there is less load on the tool. This tool is similar to **2D Adaptive Clearing** tool but with operation scope in 3D. The procedure to use this tool is discussed next.

- Click on the **Adaptive Clearing** tool from the **3D** drop-down of **MILLING** tab in the **Toolbar**; refer to Figure-72. The **ADAPTIVE** dialog box will be displayed; refer to Figure-73.

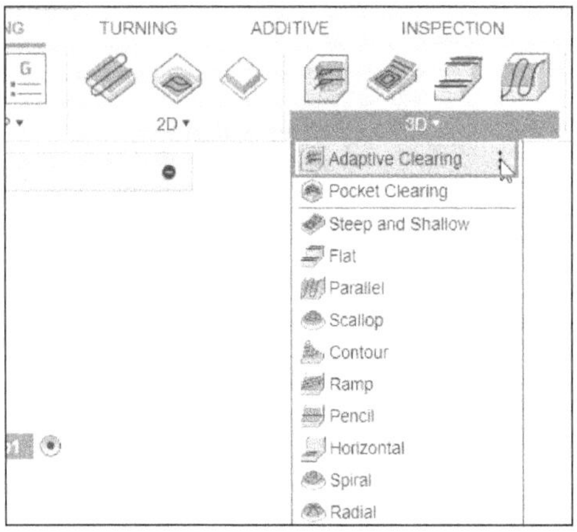

Figure-72. Adaptive Clearing tool

Figure-73. ADAPTIVE dialog box

- Click on the **Select** button of **Tool** tab from **ADAPTIVE** dialog box. The **Select Tool** dialog box will be displayed. Select the tool as required (generally, an end mill or ball/bull mill).
- Select the **Shaft & Holder** check box of **Tool** tab from **ADAPTIVE** dialog box to specify how the shaft and holder of the tool will avoid possible collisions with stock or workpiece.
- Click in the **Shaft and Holder Mode** drop-down of **Shaft and Holder** section from **Tool** tab and select desired option to define motion for avoiding collision. Select the **Pull away** option from the drop-down to create a toolpath away from the workpiece by specified shaft clearance distance. On selecting this option, the **Use Shaft** check box and **Shaft Clearance** edit boxes will become available. Select the **Use Shaft** check box to use length of tool shaft as safe distance away from workpiece while creating the toolpath. Specify desired value in the **Shaft Clearance** edit box to define extended length after shaft length to be avoided from workpiece surfaces. Select the **Detect tool length** option from the drop-down to use total length of cutting tool as safe distance of tool holder from workpiece for creating toolpath. Select the **Fail on collision** option from the drop-down to abort machining toolpath at the event of possible collision between tool holder and workpiece. Select the **Trimmed** option from the drop-down to create trimmed toolpaths at the points of possible collision of tool holder with workpiece. Figure-74 shows various available strategies.

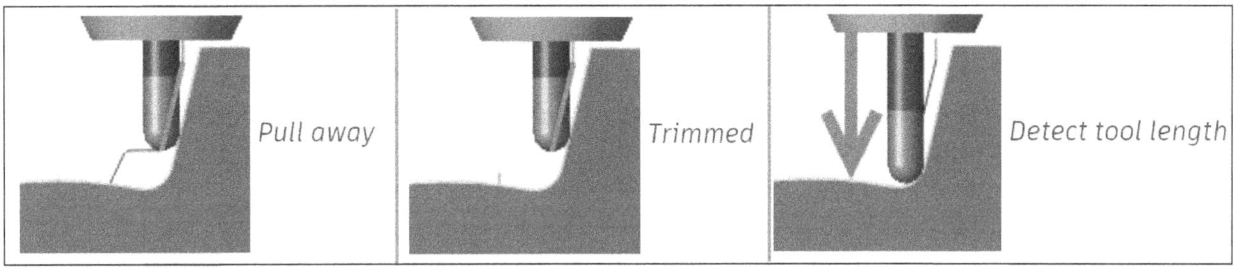

Figure-74. Holder avoidance strategies

- Select the **Use Holder** check box of the **Shaft & Holder** node to use holder of selected cutting tool in the toolpath calculation to avoid collisions along with shaft length.
- Click in the **Holder Clearance** edit box of **Shaft & Holder** node and specify desired value of tool clearance to keep the holder away from the part.

Geometry

- Click on the **Geometry** tab of **ADAPTIVE** dialog box. The options will be displayed as shown in Figure-75.

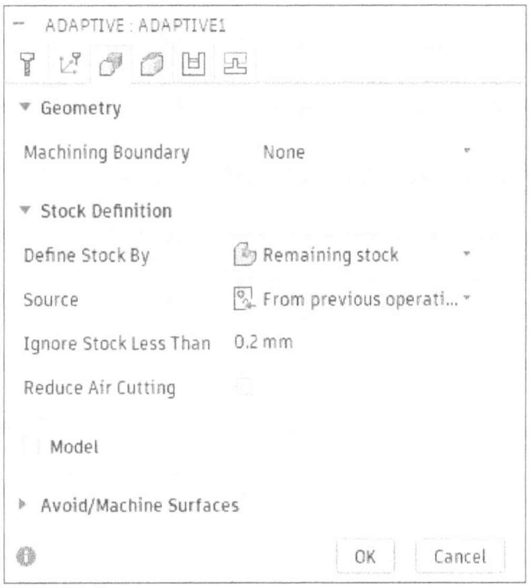

Figure-75. Geometry tab of ADAPTIVE dialog box

- Select the **None** option in the **Machining Boundary** drop-down of **Geometry** tab to machine all the stock without limitation. Note that the **None** option is not available for all machining strategies.
- Select the **Bounding Box** option in the **Machining Boundary** drop-down from **Geometry** tab to generate toolpath within boundaries of the part viewed from the WCS.
- Select the **Silhouette** option in the **Machining Boundary** drop-down from **Geometry** tab to machine the toolpath within boundary defined by projection of part on machining plane. Note that on selecting this option, the curvature of part will also be taken into account while calculation stock for machining.
- Select the **Selection** option in the **Machining Boundary** drop-down from **Geometry** tab to machine the toolpath within a region bound by selected boundary curves. Note that on selecting this option, you will be asked to select curve chains.
- You can specify the position of tool with respect to boundary chain while cutting by using the options in **Tool Containment** drop-down.

- Specify desired value in the **Additional Offset** edit box to expand the containment boundary by respective distance in all directions.
- If the **Remaining stock** option is selected in the **Define Stock By** drop-down then select the **From previous operation(s)** option from the **Source** drop-down to specify uses all the toolpath in the current setup to identify remaining unmachined region. Select **From file** option from the drop-down to specify a binary STL file that represent unmachined region. Select **From setup stock** option from the drop-down to specify use the stock defined in the setup to identify remaining region.
- Select the **Stock Contours** Selections button from the **Geometry** tab to select the side walls of model to be face machined. The **Nothing** button for **Stock Selection** option will be active by default and you will be asked to select the boundary chain (perimeter curves); refer to Figure-76. Select desired curve chains from the model.

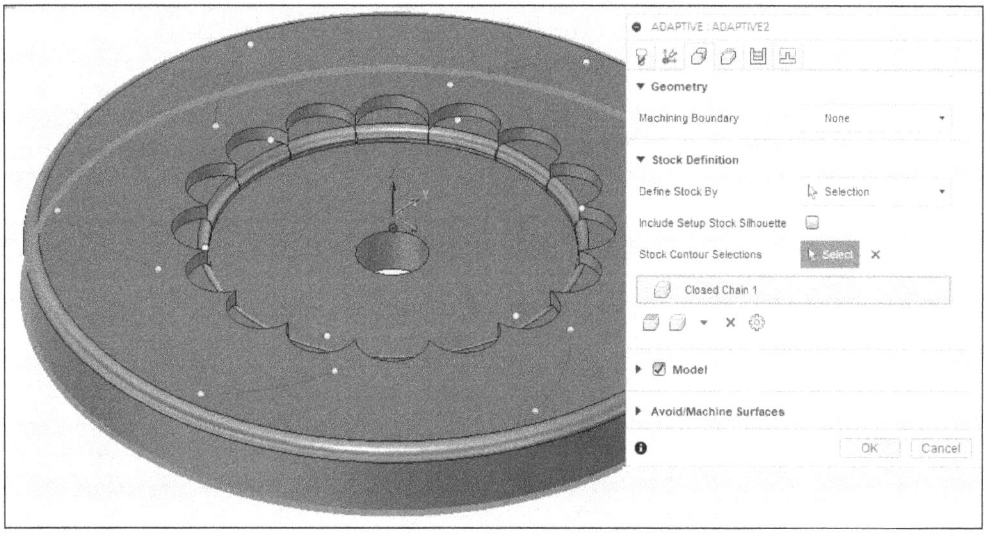

Figure-76. Selection of geometry

- Specify desired value in the **Ignore Stock Less Than** edit box to define the amount of stock below which stock will be ignored when machining.
- Select the **Reduce Air Cutting** check box to limit open area moves of cutting tool when machining.

Passes

- Click on the **Passes** tab of the **ADAPTIVE** dialog box. The options of **Passes** tab will be displayed; refer to Figure-77.

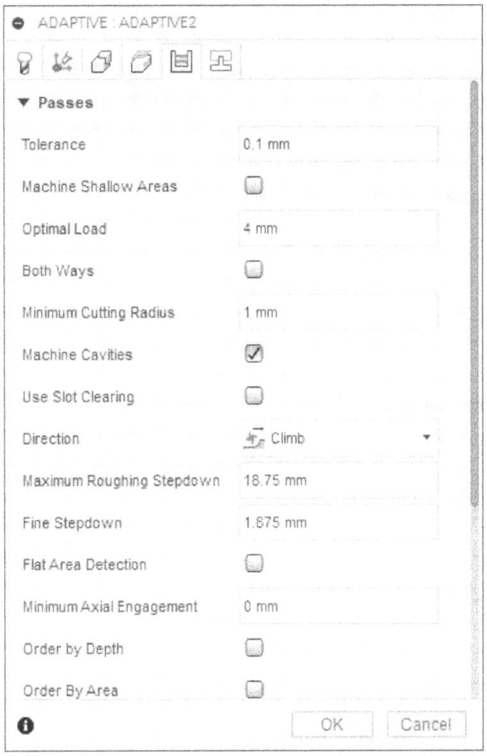

Figure-77. Passes tab of ADAPTIVE dialog box

- Click in the **Tolerance** edit box of the **Passes** tab and specify the value of tolerance for curves of model.
- Select the **Machine Shallow Areas** check box of the **Passes** tab to remove excessive cusps from the shallow areas of Z-level. After selecting check box, specify desired parameters in the **Minimum Shallow Stepdown** and **Maximum Shallow Stepover** edit boxes to define minimum vertical downward movement and maximum horizontal (left/right) movement while cutting shallow areas, respectively.
- Click in the **Optimal Load** edit box of the **Passes** tab and specify the value of engagement (stepover) between cutting tool and stock which is allowed by adaptive strategies. Note that stepover can increase/decrease based on optimum load on cutting tool.
- Select the **Both Ways** check box from the drop-down to machine stock when cutting tool is moving upward as well as downward. Set the related parameters as discussed earlier.
- Click in the **Minimum Cutting Radius** edit box of the **Passes** tab and specify the value of minimum radius that can be cut using this toolpath.
- Select the **Machine Cavities** check box of **Passes** tab to machine the pockets of the model.
- Select the **Use Slot Clearing** check box of **Passes** tab to start pocket clearing with a slot at its middle before continuing with a spiral motion towards the pocket walls.
- Select the **Fillets** check box of the **Passes** tab and specify the value of fillet radius.
- The other options of the dialog box are same as discussed earlier.
- After specifying the parameters, click on the **OK** button from **ADAPTIVE** dialog box. The toolpath will be generated and displayed on the model; refer to Figure-78.

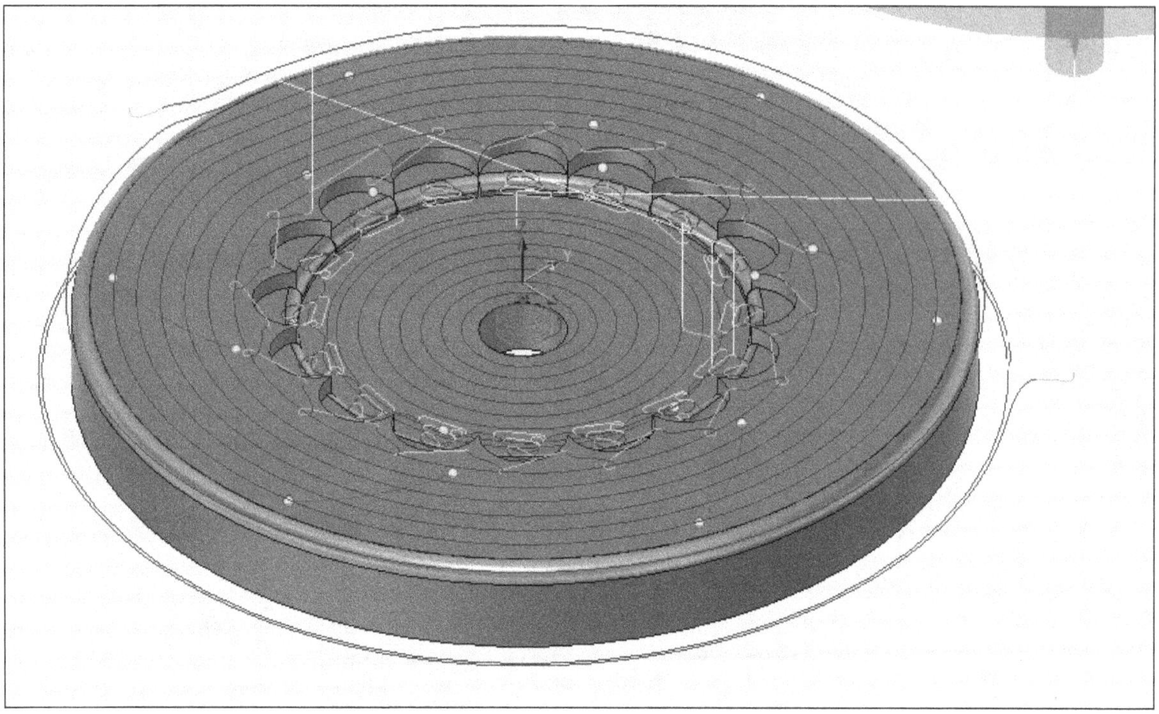

Figure-78. Generated toolpath of adaptive clearing

Pocket Clearing Toolpath

The **Pocket Clearing** tool is mainly used for clearing large quantity of stock material from pockets of the model. Note that in this toolpath, the cutting tool can move simultaneously along all three axes in 3D space. The procedure to use this tool is discussed next.

- Click on the **Pocket Clearing** tool from the **3D** drop-down in the **Toolbar**; refer to Figure-79. The **POCKET** dialog box will be displayed; refer to Figure-80.

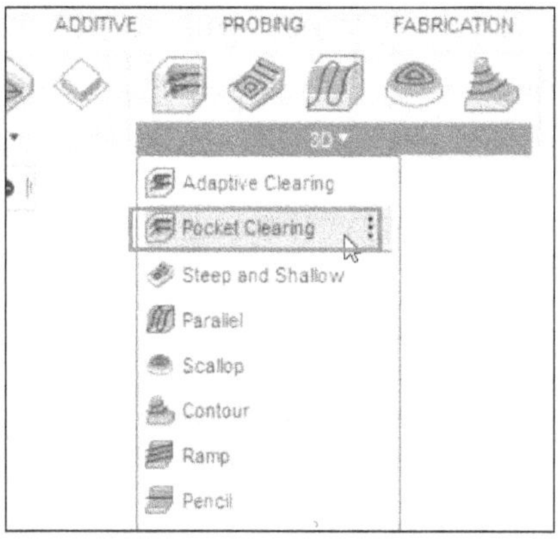

Figure-79. Pocket Clearing tool

- Click on the **Select** button of **Tool** tab from **POCKET** dialog box. The **Select Tool** dialog box will be displayed. Select the tool as required.
- The options of this dialog box are same as discussed earlier.
- After specifying the parameters, click on the **OK** button from **POCKET** dialog box. The toolpath will be generated and displayed on the model; refer to Figure-81.

Figure-80. POCKET dialog box

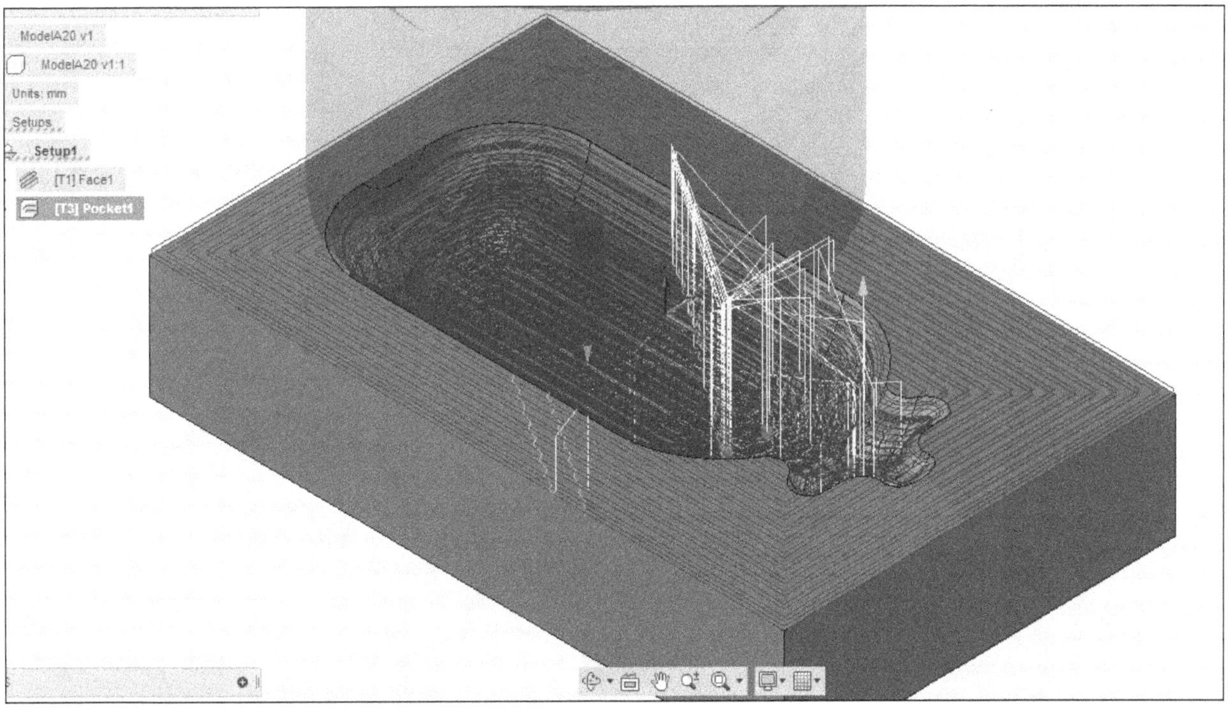

Figure-81. Generated toolpath for pocket

Steep and Shallow Toolpath

As the name suggests, this tool is used to create toolpath for machining steep and shallow areas of part based on specified angle threshold. When the area to be machined is steep then contour passes are used and when the area is shallow then parallel/scallop passes are used for machining. Note that this tool is part of Machining extension. The procedure to use this tool is given next.

- Click on the **Steep and Shallow** tool from the **3D** drop-down in the **Toolbar**; refer to Figure-82. If you are activating this tool for the first time then **Machining Extension** information box will be displayed; refer to Figure-83. Click on the **Access Options** button from the information box. The **Extension Manager** will be displayed.

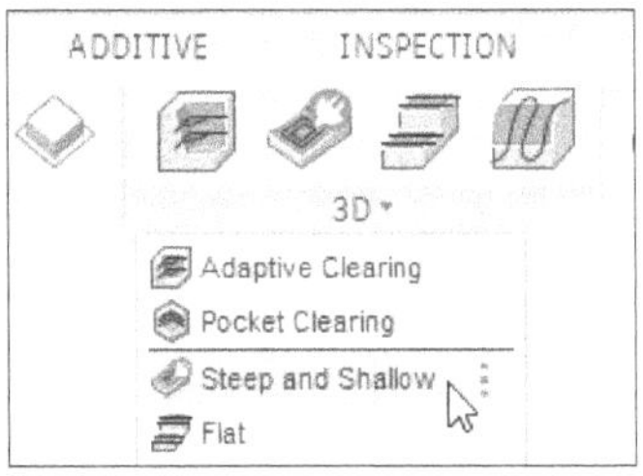

Figure-82. Steep and Shallow tool

Figure-83. Machining Extension info box

- Click on the **Start Access** button from the **Extension Manager**. For educational edition, the **Machining Extension** will be activated for free. Click on the **Close** button from the **Extension Manager** to exit. The tools of machining extension will become available.
- Click on the **Steep and Shallow** tool again from **Ribbon**. The **STEEP AND SHALLOW** dialog box will be displayed refer to Figure-84.

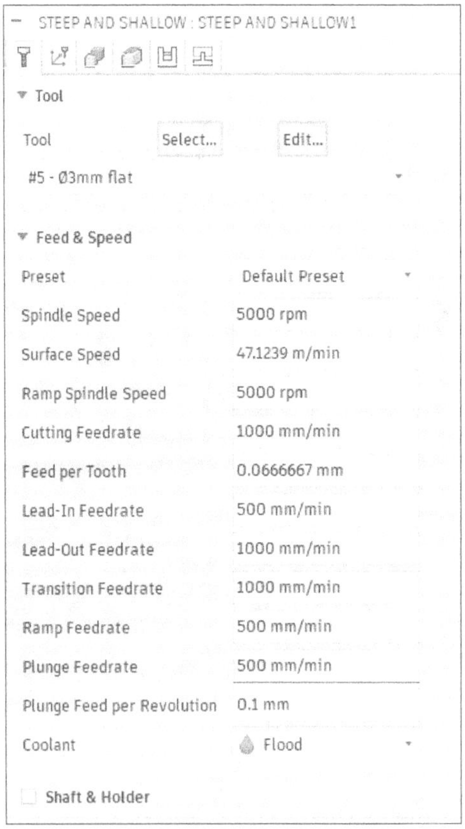

Figure-84. STEEP AND SHALLOW dialog box

- Specify desired parameters in **Tool**, **Geometry**, **Heights**, and **Linking** tabs of dialog box as discussed earlier. Click on the **Passes** tab. The options will be displayed as shown in Figure-85.

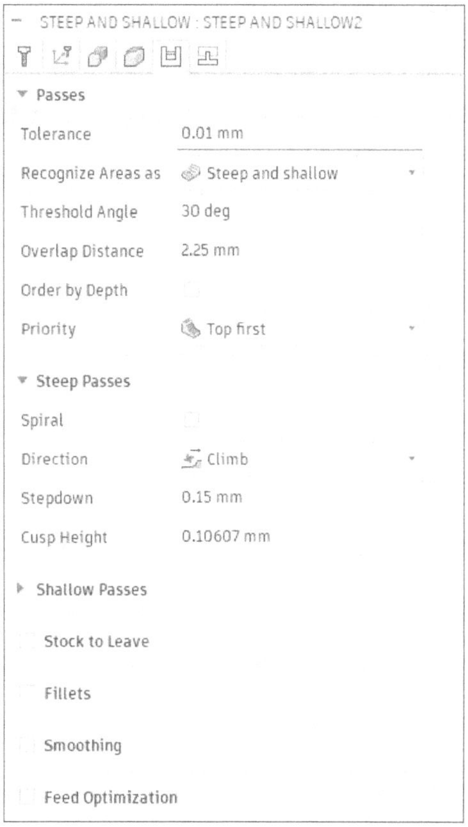

Figure-85. Passes tab of STEEP AND SHALLOW dialog box

- Select desired option from the **Recognize Areas as** drop-down to define whether selected areas are to be considered as steep faces, shallow faces, or combination of both.
- If the **Steep and shallow** option is selected in the **Recognize Areas as** drop-down then specify desired value of angle in **Threshold Angle** edit box. The areas which have slope angle larger than this value with respect to horizontal line will be counted as shallow areas and below this value will be counted as steep areas.
- The value specified in **Overlap Distance** edit box is distance past the threshold angle line which will act as transitional area for blending steep and shallow areas.
- Select the **Spiral** check box from the **Steep Passes** section to create continuous spiral toolpath for steep sections of the model; refer to Figure-86.

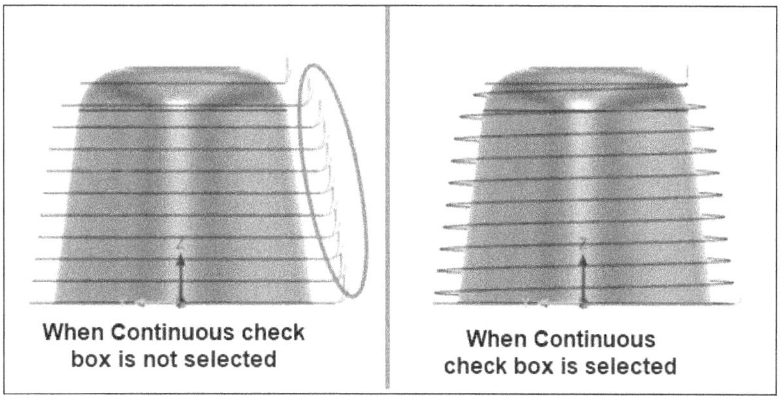

Figure-86. Steep continuous toolpaths

- Select desired option from the **Type** drop-down of **Shallow Passes** section to define whether you want to use parallel or scallop toolpaths for shallow areas.
- Select the **Smooth Offsets** check box to replace sharp corners with rounds in the steep corners of the model.
- Select the **Remove Cusps at Junctions** check box to create centerline toolpaths at corners to machine areas generally left untouched by cutting tool.
- Click on the **Multi-Axis** tab in the dialog box to define general parameters for using Multi-axis machining. Select the **5-axis** option from the **Machining Type** drop-down, the options in dialog box will be displayed as shown in Figure-87.

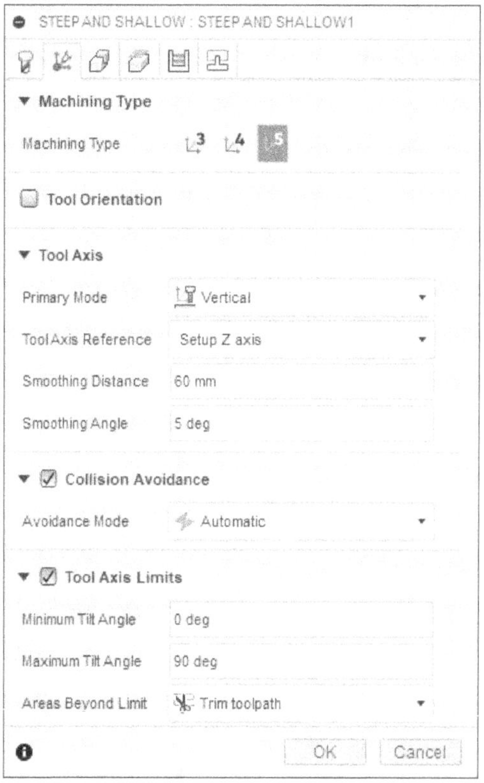

Figure-87. Multi-Axis tab

- Select desired option from the **Primary Mode** drop-down to define which axes are to be used for multi-axis machining.
- Specify desired value in the **Smoothing Distance** edit box to define minimum distance at which the cutting tool will tilt in Multi-Axis machine to create smooth surface. Similarly, you can specify the maximum tilt angle allowed for smoothening surface during machining in **Smoothing Angle** edit box.
- Select the **Collision Avoidance** check box to allow tilting of cutting tool for avoiding collision with stock.
- Select the **Tool Axis Limits** check box to define maximum tilting limits for cutting tool in Multi-axis milling machines.
- Set the other parameters as discussed earlier and click on the **OK** button from the dialog box. The toolpath will be generated; refer to Figure-88.

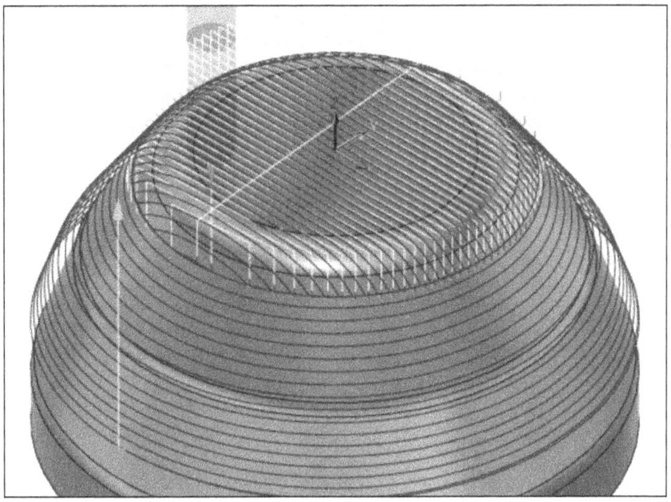

Figure-88. Steep and Shallow toolpath

Flat Toolpath

The **Flat** tool is used to create finishing toolpath for removing material from flat regions on the model surface. This toolpath automatically recognizes the flat regions on model. The procedure to create flat toolpath is given next.

- Click on the **Flat** tool from the **3D** drop-down in **MILLING** tab of the **Ribbon**. The **Flat** dialog box will be displayed.
- Select desired cutting tool and set desired parameters in the **Tool** page of dialog box as discussed earlier.
- Select the **Avoid/Machine Surfaces** check box from the **Geometry** tab of the dialog box to define the regions on model to be machined/avoided. The selection button of **Surfaces** will be active; refer to Figure-89.
- Select desired faces to be avoided by flat toolpath. Note that if **Machine** option is selected in the **Mode** drop-down then selected faces will be machined and rest of the surfaces will be avoided from machining.
- Click on the **Passes** tab to define parameters of cutting passes; refer to Figure-90.
- Select the **Pocket** option from the **Type** drop-down to machine complex circular flat faces of the model. This option will generate spiral cutting passes. The **Optimize Open Pockets** and **Spiral** check boxes will be displayed. Select the **Optimize Open Pockets** check box to shape the cutting passes similar to boundaries of cutting passes. Select the **Spiral** check box to create continuous spiral cutting passes.
- Select the **Parallel** option from the **Type** drop-down to machine flat surfaces using straight line cutting passes in rectangular fashion. The other options of the dialog box have been discussed earlier.
- Select the **Profile** option from the **Type** drop-down to use profile of selected face/surface when generating toolpath.
- Click on the **OK** button from the dialog box to create the toolpath; refer to Figure-91.

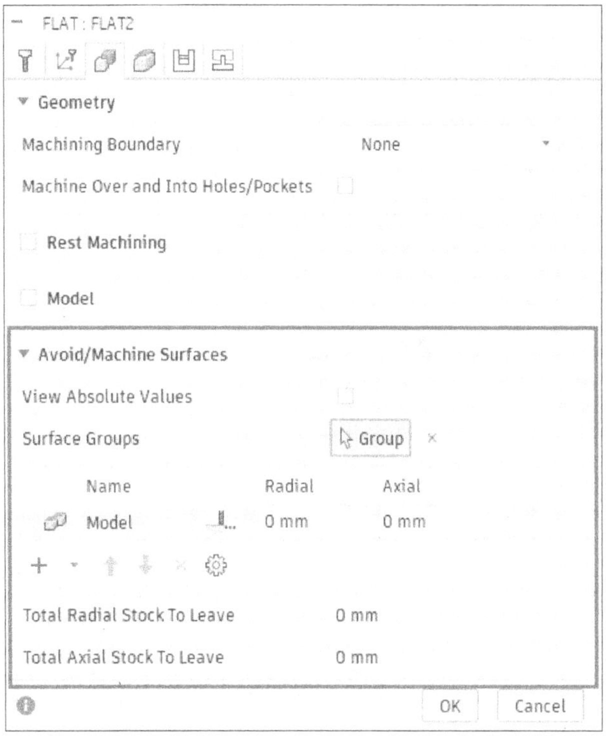

Figure-89. Avoid Machine Surfaces option

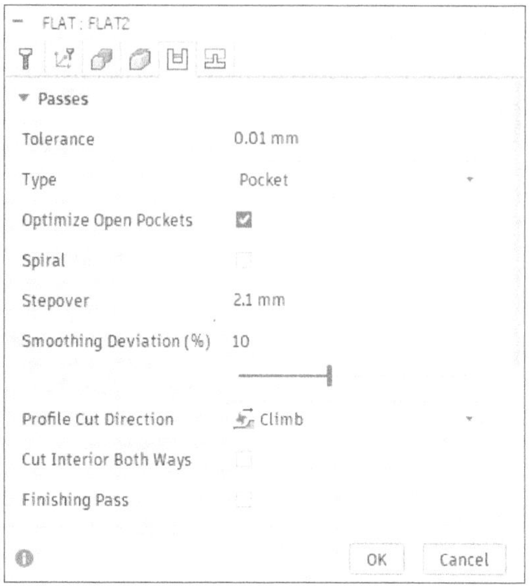

Figure-90. Passes tab of Flat dialog box

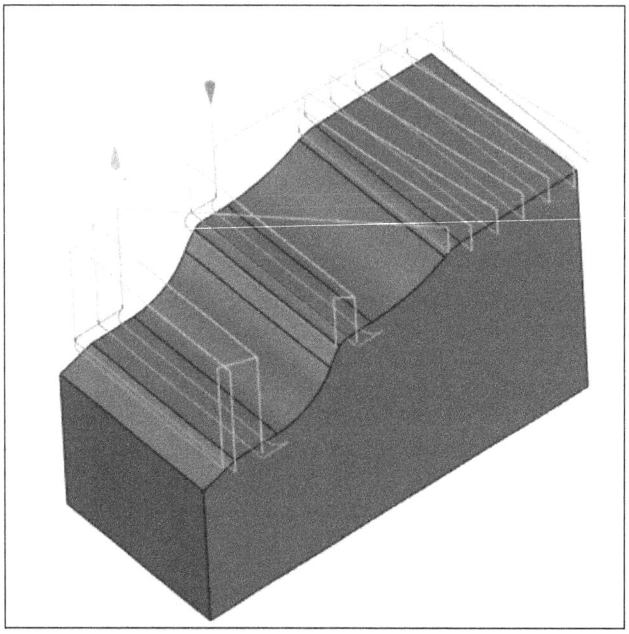

Figure-91. Flat toolpath

Parallel Toolpath

The **Parallel** tool is used mainly as finishing strategies. This toolpath is used when parallel cutting passes are needed to machine the workpiece. This toolpath is useful for machining shallow areas. The procedure to use this tool is discussed next.

- Click on the **Parallel** tool from the **3D** drop-down in the **Toolbar**; refer to Figure-92. The **PARALLEL** dialog box will be displayed; refer to Figure-93.
- Click on the **Select** button in the **Tool** tab from the **PARALLEL** dialog box. The **Select Tool** dialog box will be displayed. Select the tool as required.

- Click on the **Geometry** tab of the **PARALLEL** dialog box. The **Geometry** tab will be displayed; refer to Figure-94.

Figure-92. Parallel tool

Figure-93. PARALLEL dialog box

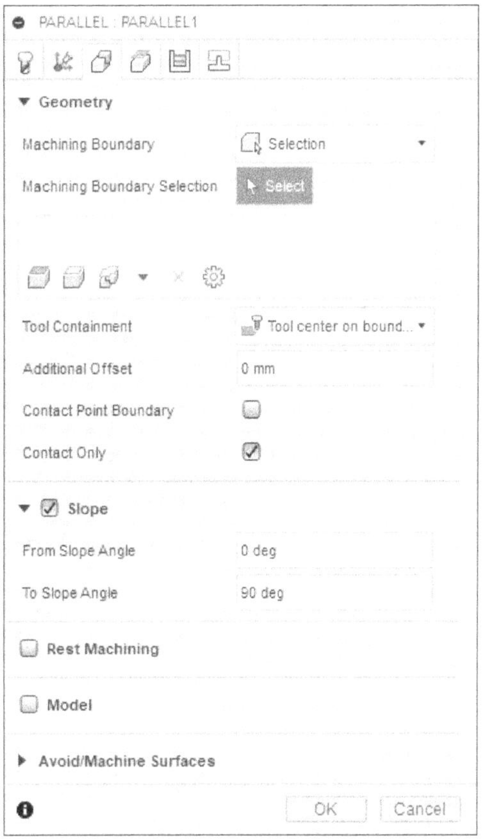

Figure-94. Geometry tab of PARALLEL dialog box

- Select the **Contact Point Boundary** check box of **Geometry** section to extend the boundary limits of toolpath where the tool actually touches the surface of model rather than the tool center location while cutting.
- Select the **Contact Only** check box of **Geometry** section to not generate the toolpath on the model where the tool is not in contact with the machining surface. You should select this check box to avoid creating toolpaths over openings (like holes) in the model.
- Select the **Slope** check box of **Geometry** tab to specify the range of slope within which the faces of part will be considered for machining.
- Click in the **From Slope Angle** edit box of **Slope** check box and specify the angle value greater than 0 degree to define starting angle of slope confinement. Only area equal to or more than this value will be machined.

- Click in the **To Slope Angle** edit box of **Slope** check box and specify the value less than 90 degree to define end angle for slope confinement. Only area equal to or less than this value will be machined.
- Select the **Avoid/Machine Surfaces** arrow button of the **Geometry** tab to define surfaces which will be avoided or machined within a specified distance.
- Select the **View Absolute Values** check box from the **Geometry** tab to changes the values displayed in the table to absolute values.
- Select the **Avoid surface** option from **Action** drop-down in table to avoid selected surfaces and select the **Machine surface** option from drop-down to machine selected surfaces. Click on the **Select** button of **Surface Groups** option and select the surfaces to be avoided or machined. Similarly, you can use other options of **Action** drop-down.
- Specify desired values in the edit boxes of the table to define clearance near avoid/touch surfaces. The other options of the dialog box are same as discussed earlier.
- After specifying the parameters, click on the **OK** button from **PARALLEL** dialog box. The toolpath will be generated and displayed on the model; refer to Figure-95.

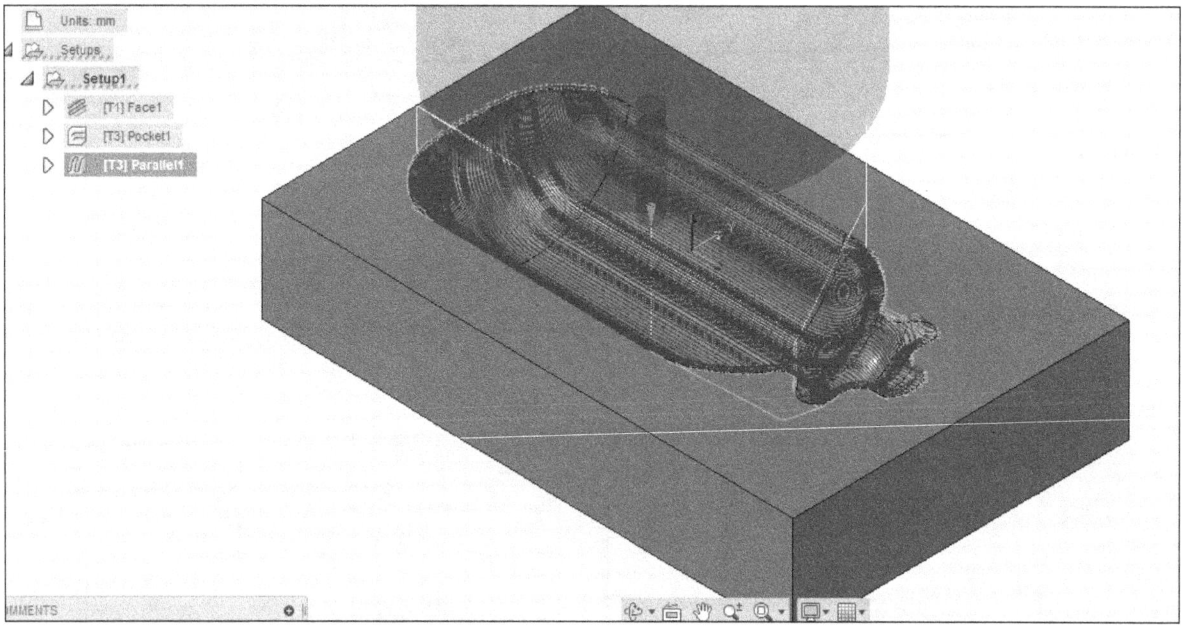

Figure-95. The generated toolpath for parallel

Scallop

The **Scallop** tool is used to finish round faces of the model with slopes. This tool can also be used to machine fillets. Although, you can use the scallop toolpath for performing roughing operations, this toolpath is generally used after Contour and Parallel toolpaths for performing finishing operation. The procedure to use this tool is discussed next.

- Click on the **Scallop** tool from the **3D** drop-down in the **Toolbar**; refer to Figure-96. The **SCALLOP** dialog box will be displayed; refer to Figure-97.
- Click on the **Select** button of **Tool** tab from **SCALLOP** dialog box. The **Select Tool** dialog box will be displayed. Select the tool as desired.
- Click on the **Passes** tab of **SCALLOP** dialog box. The **Passes** tab will be displayed; refer to Figure-98.

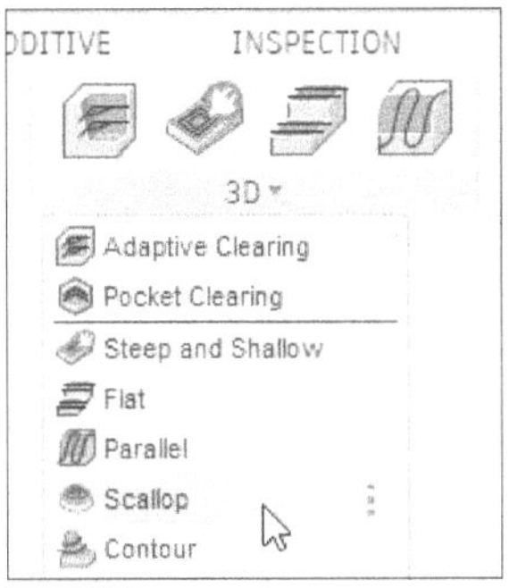

Figure-96. Scallop tool

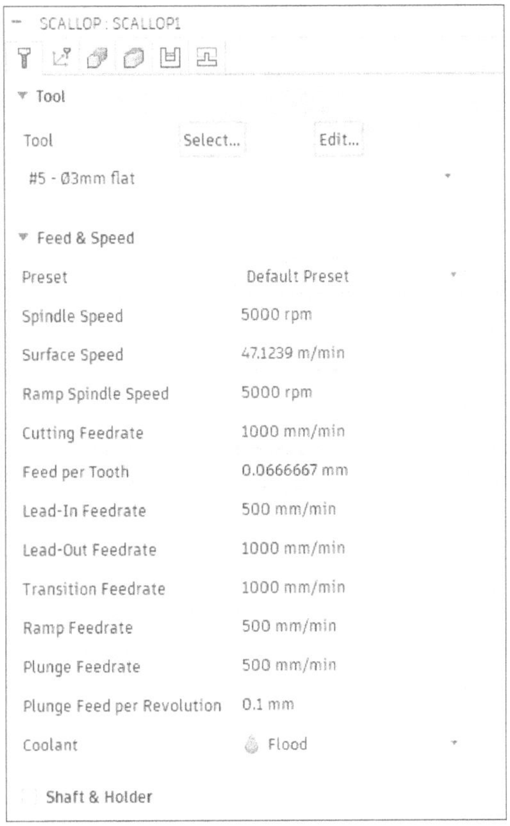

Figure-97. SCALLOP dialog box

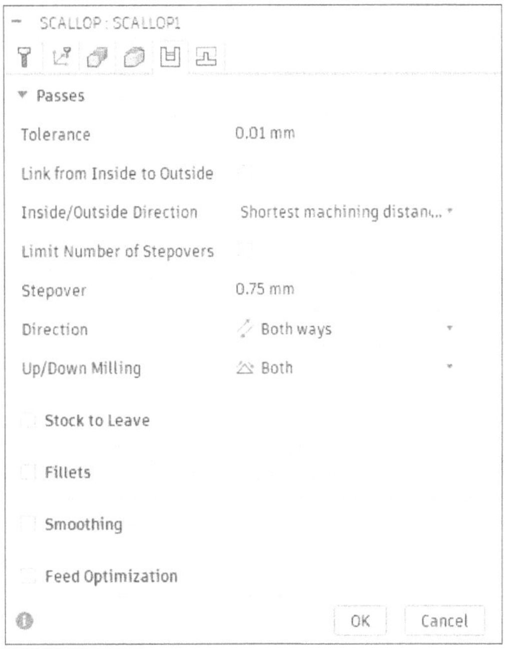

Figure-98. Passes tab of SCALLOP dialog box

- Select the **Link from Inside to Outside** check box of the **SCALLOP** dialog box to specify that linking should be done by moving from inside passes to outside passes in toolpath.
- Click in the **Inside/Outside Direction** drop-down of **Passes** tab and select desired option to define how cutting will progress on surface.
- Select the **Limit Number of Stepovers** check box in **Passes** tab to limit the number of steps that can be created to finish surface of model for given stepover distance.
- The other options of the dialog box are same as discussed earlier.
- After specifying the parameters, click on the **OK** button from the **SCALLOP** dialog box. The generated toolpath will be displayed on the model; refer Figure-99.

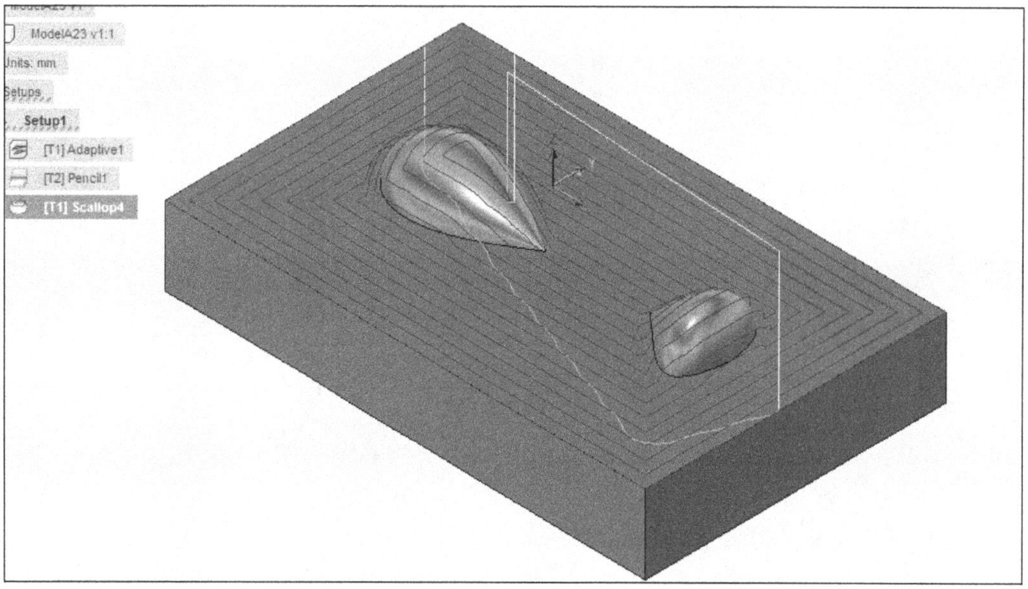

Figure-99. Generated toolpath of scallop tool

Contour

The **Contour** tool is generally used for finishing steep walls. This tool can be used for machining vertical walls. The procedure to use this tool is discussed next.

- Click on the **Contour** tool from the **3D** drop-down in the **Toolbar**; refer to Figure-100. The **CONTOUR** dialog box will be displayed; refer to Figure-101.

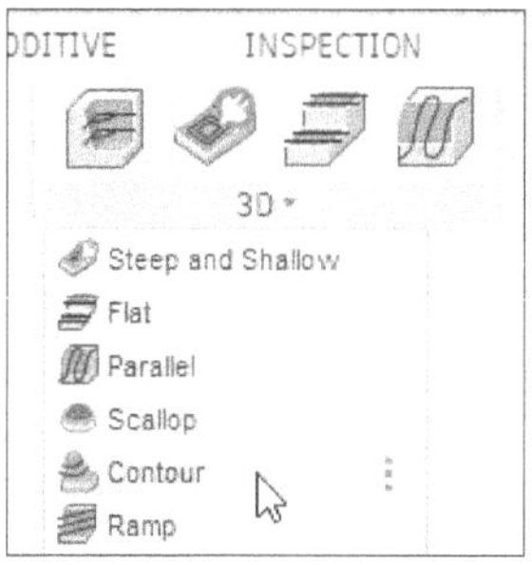

Figure-100. Contour tool

Figure-101. CONTOUR dialog box

- Click on the **Select** button of **Tool** tab in the **POCKET** dialog box. The **Select Tool** dialog box will be displayed. Select the tool as required, generally a ball end mill.
- Click on the **Multiaxis** tab of the **CONTOUR** dialog box and select 5-axis option from **Machining Type** drop-down to perform multi-axis machining.
- Select the **Collision Avoidance** check box to define method for avoiding collision of cutting tool with stock or other machining objects.
- Select the **Tool Axes Limits** check box to define range of tool tilt for multi-axis machining; refer to Figure-102.

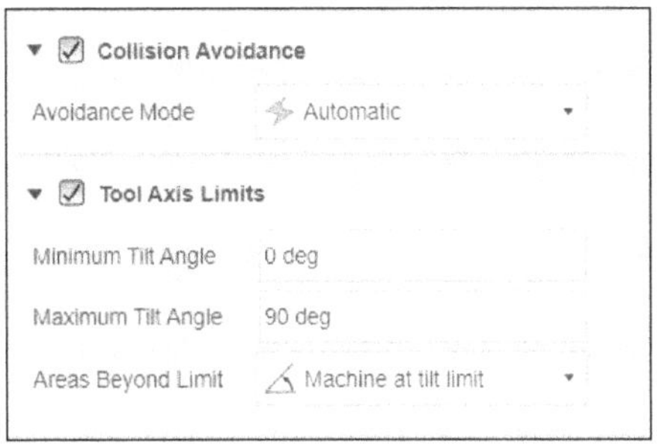

Figure-102. Multi-Axis tab of CONTOUR dialog box

- Click in the **Minimum Tilt** edit box of **Multi-Axis** tab and specify the minimum allowed tilt with respect to operation tool axis.
- Click in the **Maximum Tilt** edit box of **Multi-Axis** tab and specify the maximum allowed tilt with respect to operation tool axis.
- Select desired option from the **Areas Beyond Limit** drop-down to define how areas outside selected limit will be treated. Select the **Trim toolpath** option from the drop-down to cut extra portion of toolpath where tilting beyond limits is required. Select the **Machine at tilt limit** option from the drop-down to machine workpiece at maximum tilt limit even if specified tool tilt is more than maximum limit.
- The other options of the dialog box are same as discussed earlier.
- After specifying the parameters, click on the **OK** button from **CONTOUR** dialog box. The toolpath will be generated and displayed on the model; refer to Figure-103.

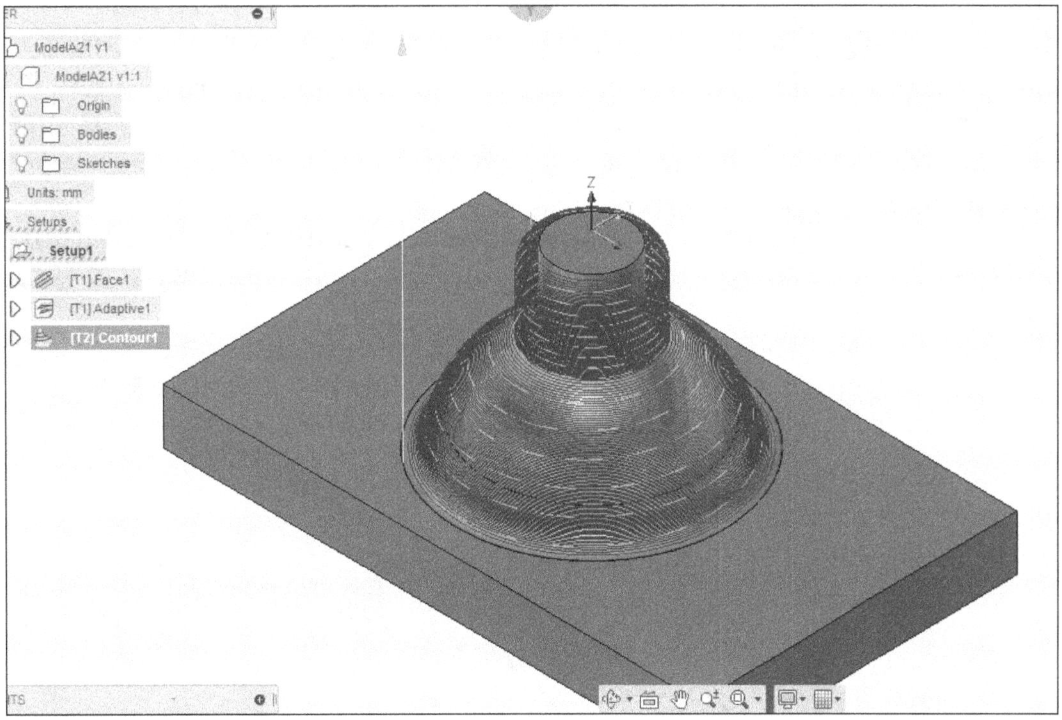

Figure-103. The generated toolpath for Contour tool

Ramp

The **Ramp** tool is used to create a finishing operation meant for machining step areas similar to Contour tool. The procedure to use this tool is discussed next.

- Click on the **Ramp** tool from **3D** drop-down in the **Toolbar**; refer to Figure-104. The **RAMP** dialog box will be displayed; refer to Figure-105.

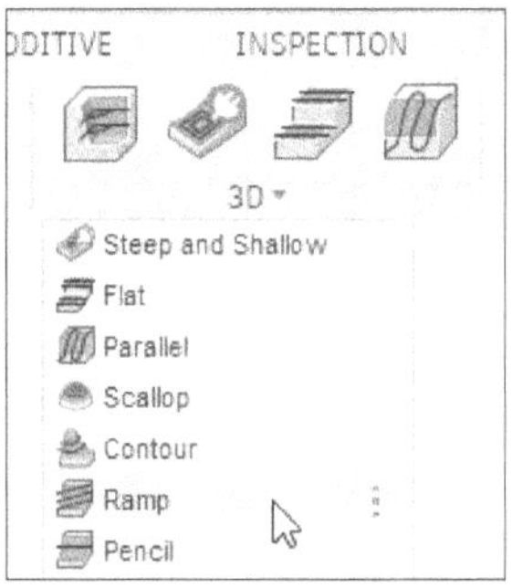

Figure-104. Ramp tool

Figure-105. RAMP dialog box

- Click on the **Select** button of **Tool** tab from **RAMP** dialog box. The **Select Tool** dialog box will be displayed. Select the tool as required (generally a ball end mill).
- Click on the **Passes** tab in the dialog box and select the **Flat Area Detection** check box to detect flat areas in the selected model faces and respond with suitable cutting strategy.
- Select the **Order Bottom-Up** check box in **Passes** tab to generate contour cutting passes for the ramp starting from minimum Z value to maximum Z value of the selected model.
- The other options of the dialog box have been discussed earlier.
- After specifying the parameters, click on the **OK** button from the **RAMP** dialog box. The generated toolpath will be displayed on the model; refer to Figure-106.

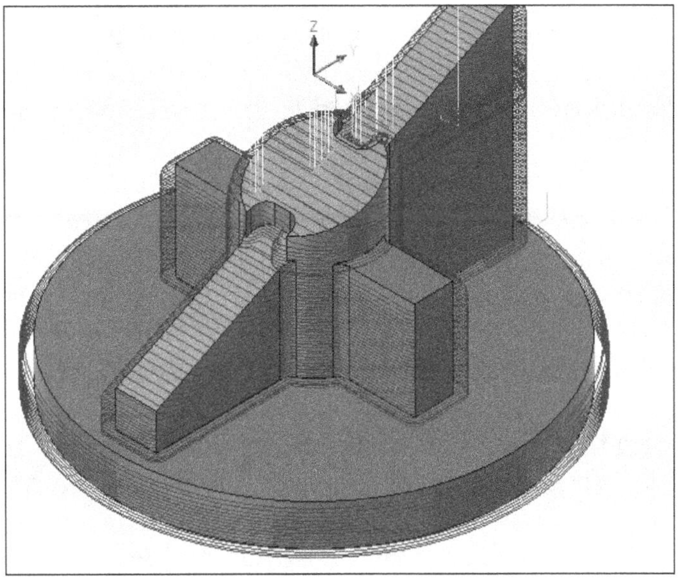

Figure-106. Generated toolpath for Ramp tool

Pencil

The **Pencil** tool is used to create toolpaths along sharp internal corners with small radii tool. This tool is generally used to remove material where no other toolpath can work. After performing finishing operation, create this toolpath for cleaning. The procedure to use this tool is discussed next.

- Click on the **Pencil** tool from **3D** drop-down in the **Toolbar**; refer to Figure-107. The **PENCIL** dialog box will be displayed; refer to Figure-108.

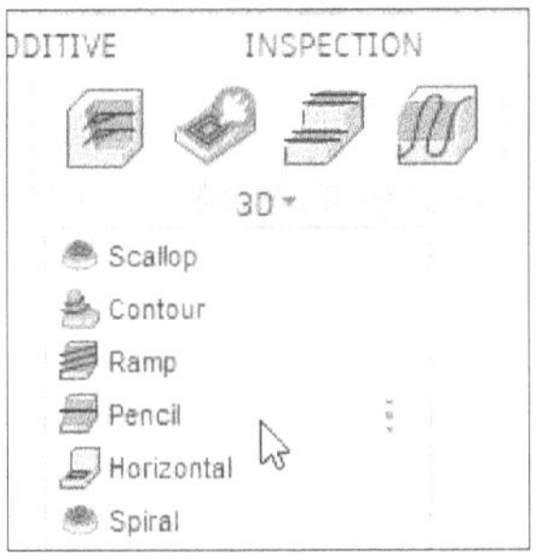

Figure-107. Pencil tool

Figure-108. PENCIL dialog box

- Click on the **Select** button in **Tool** tab from **PENCIL** dialog box. The **Select Tool** dialog box will be displayed. Select the tool as required.
- Click on the **Passes** tab and specify desired value in the **Overthickness** edit box to define additional thickness to be applied to the cutting tool for machining corner fillets.
- Specify desired value in the **Bitangency Angle** edit box to define angular span in which cutting tool touches the workpiece while cutting. A higher value means more tool area for cutting.
- The other options of the dialog box have been discussed earlier.
- After specifying the parameters, click on the **OK** button from **PENCIL** dialog box. The generated toolpath will be displayed on the model; refer to Figure-109.

Note: The Pencil toolpaths and Trace toolpaths look similar in operation but the difference between the two is their field of operation. Trace toolpaths can be assumed as 2D version of pencil toolpaths. While pencil toolpaths generate simultaneous 3 axis movements, the Trace toolpaths generate XY movements for removing material on one plane and then move upward/downward for next cutting plane.

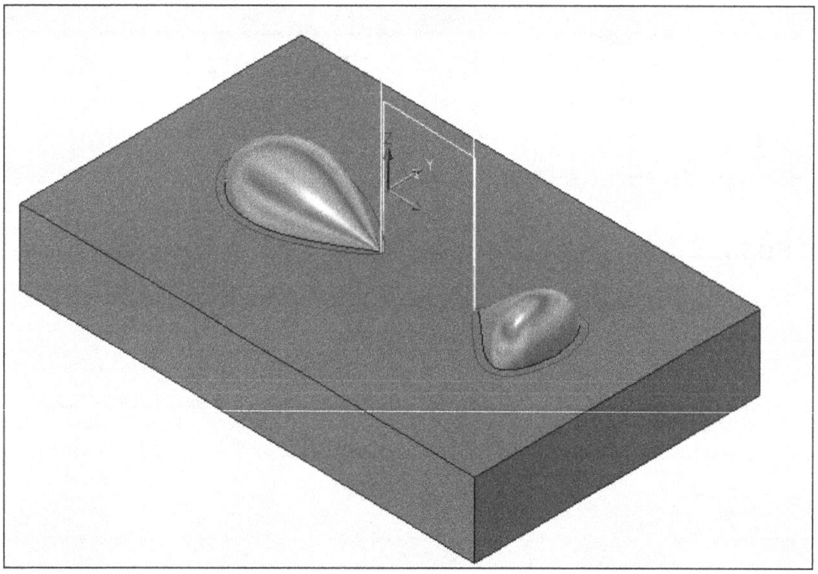

Figure-109. The generated toolpath for Pencil tool

Horizontal

The **Horizontal** tool is used for machining flat surfaces of model which are surrounded by other features. Horizontal toolpaths are generally used in collaboration with ramp toolpaths for finishing models having multiple steep walls. The procedure to use this tool is discussed next.

- Click on the **Horizontal** tool from the **3D** drop-down in the **Toolbar**; refer to Figure-110. The **HORIZONTAL** dialog box will be displayed; refer to Figure-111.

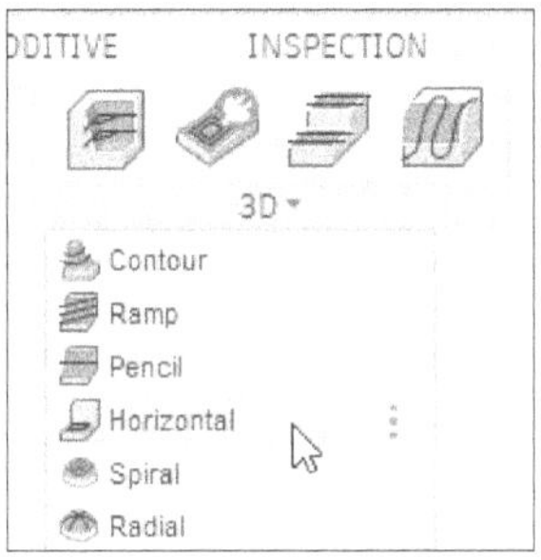

Figure-110. Horizontal tool

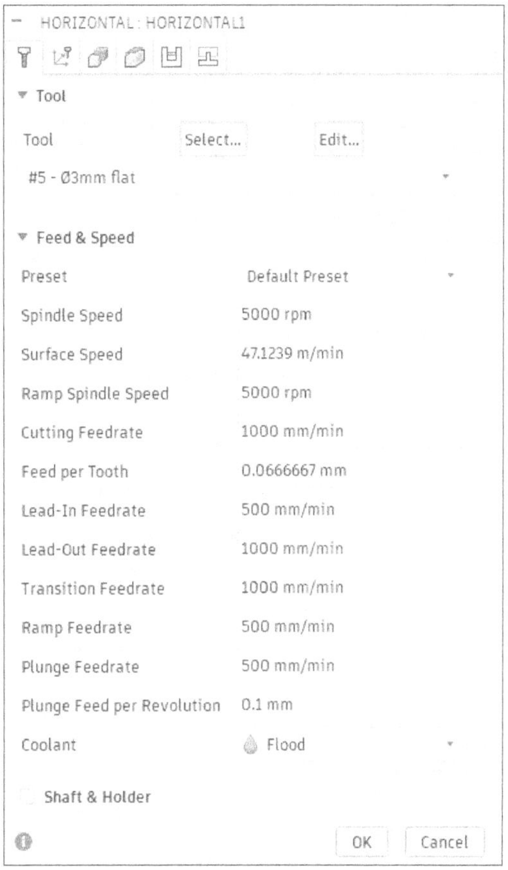

Figure-111. HORIZONTAL dialog box

- Click on the **Select** button from the **Tool** tab in the **HORIZONTAL** dialog box. The **Select Tool** dialog box will be displayed. Select the tool as required.
- Select the **Use Morphed Spiral Machining** check box in the **Passes** tab of the dialog box to generate constant spiral move toolpaths when machining flat pockets. Using this option keeps load on cutting tool in check.
- The other options of the dialog box are same as discussed earlier. After specifying the parameters, click on the **OK** button from the **HORIZONTAL** dialog box. The generated toolpath will be displayed on the model; refer to Figure-112.

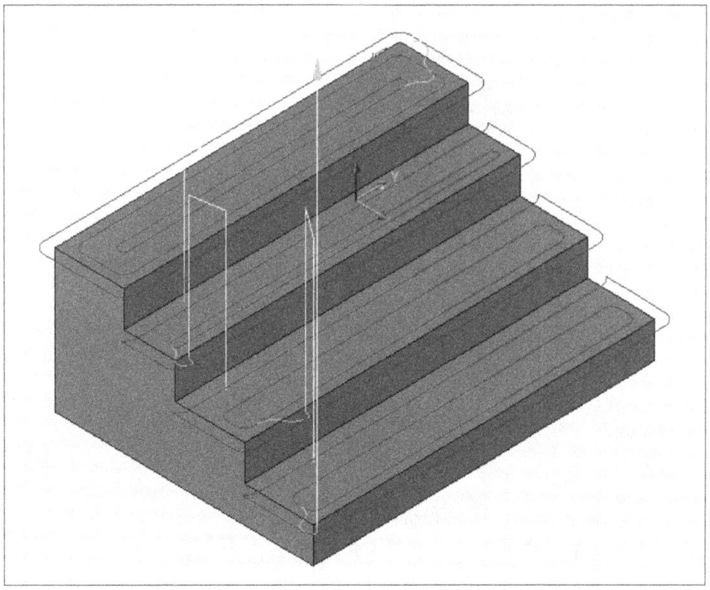
Figure-112. The generated toolpath for Horizontal tool

PRACTICAL

Generate the toolpath of the given model shown in Figure-113 using 2D Toolpath tools.

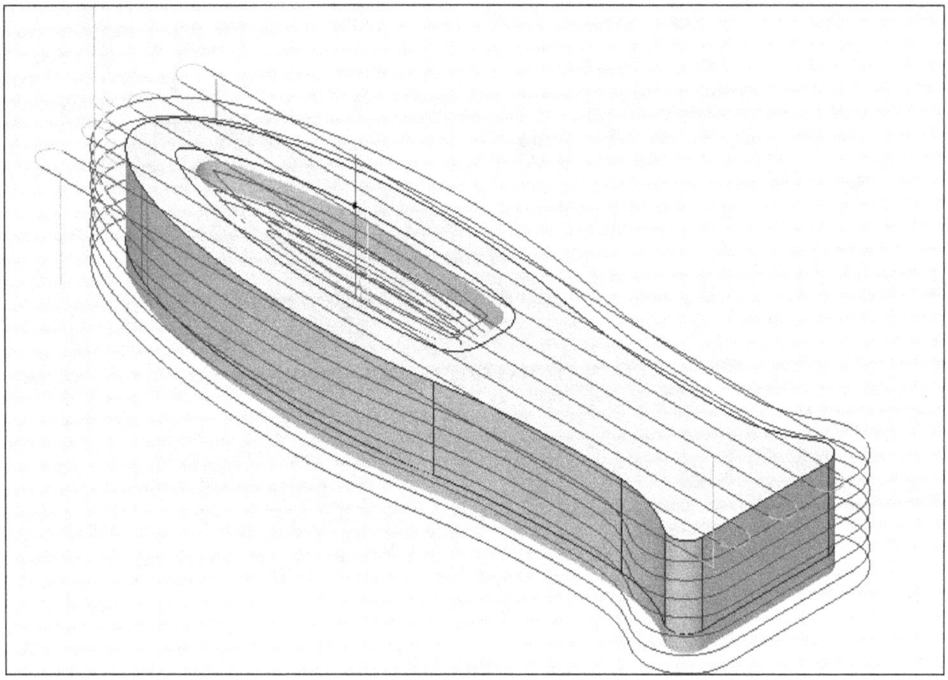

Figure-113. Practical

Adding Model to CAM

- Create and save the part in **DESIGN** workspace. The part file is available in the respective chapter folder of **Autodesk Fusion Black Book Resources**.
- Select the **MANUFACTURE** option from the **Workspace** drop-down. The model will be displayed in the **MANUFACTURE** workspace; refer to Figure-114.

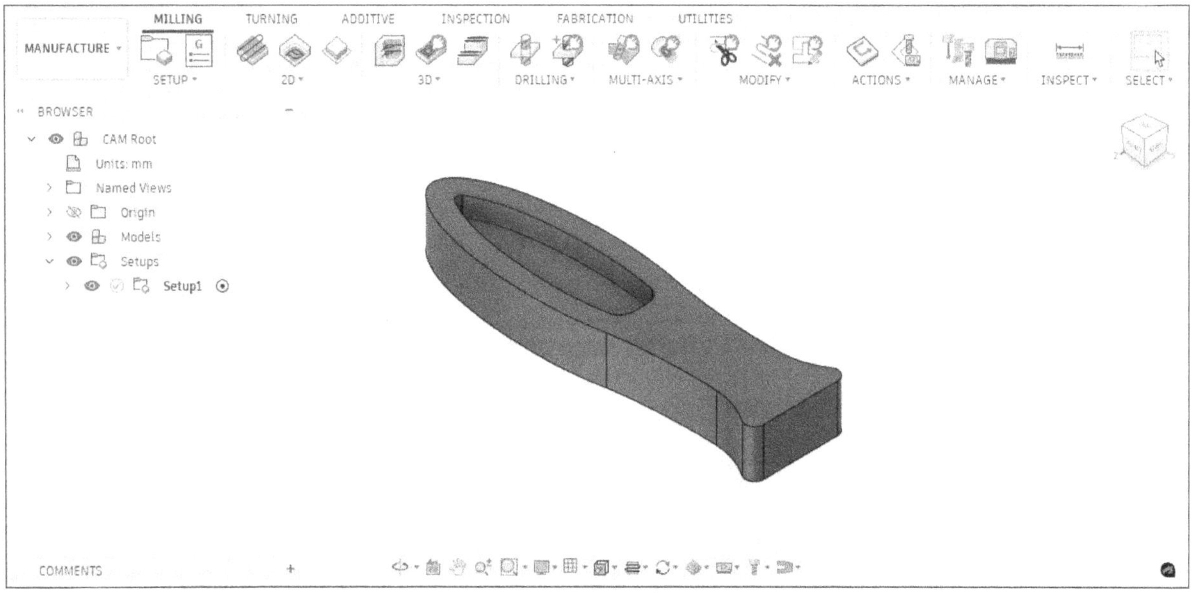

Figure-114. Practical

Creating Stock

- Click on the **New Setup** tool from the **SETUP** drop-down in the **Toolbar**. The **SETUP** dialog box will be displayed along with the stock of model.

- Click on the **Setup** tab of the **SETUP** dialog box and specify the parameters as displayed in Figure-115.

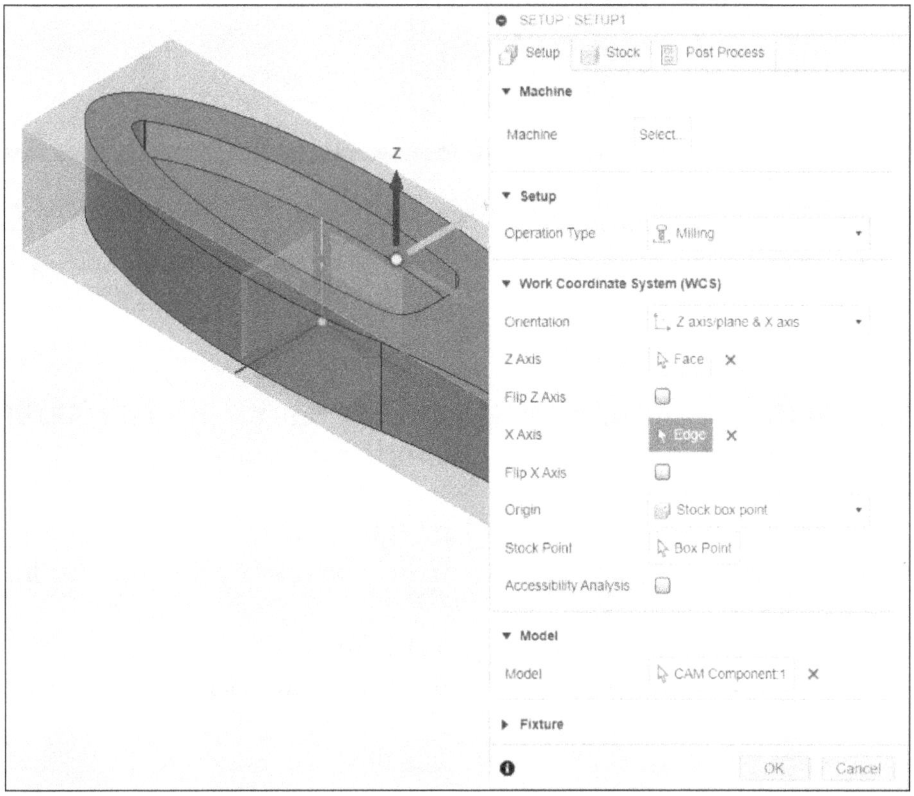

Figure-115. Setup tab of SETUP dialog

- Click on the **Stock** tab of **SETUP** dialog box and enter the parameters as displayed in Figure-116.

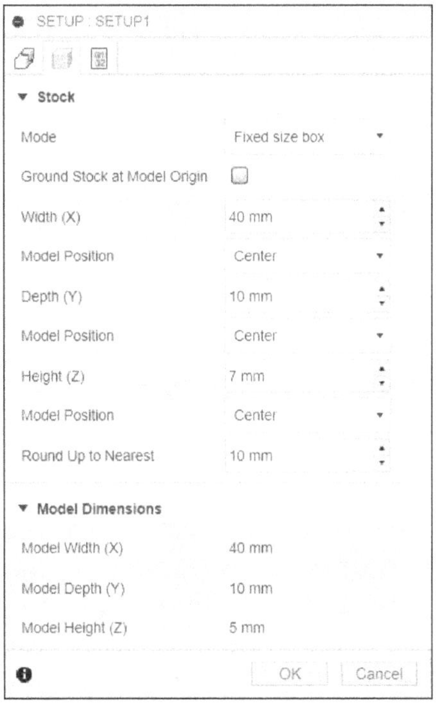

Figure-116. Stock tab of practical

- Click on the **Post Process** tab of **SETUP** dialog box and specify the parameters as displayed in Figure-117.

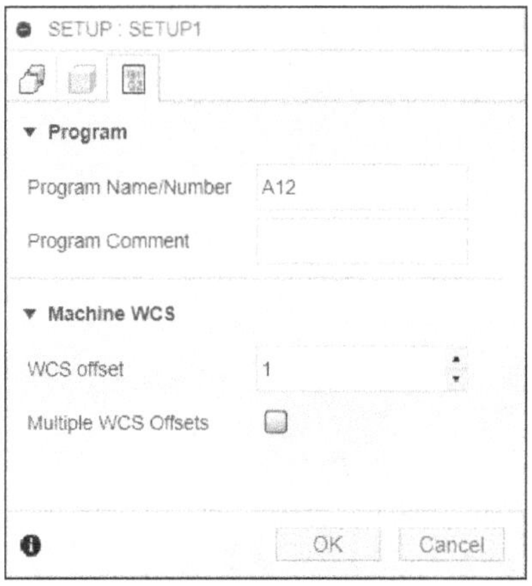

Figure-117. Post Process tab of SETUP dialog box

- After specifying the parameters, click on the **OK** button from the **SETUP** dialog box. The stock will be created and displayed on the model.

Generating Face toolpath

- Click on the **Face** tool of **2D** drop-down from **Toolbar**. The **FACE** dialog box will be displayed.
- Click on the **Select** button for **Tool** option from **Tool** tab and select the tool from **Select Tool** dialog box as displayed; refer to Figure-118.

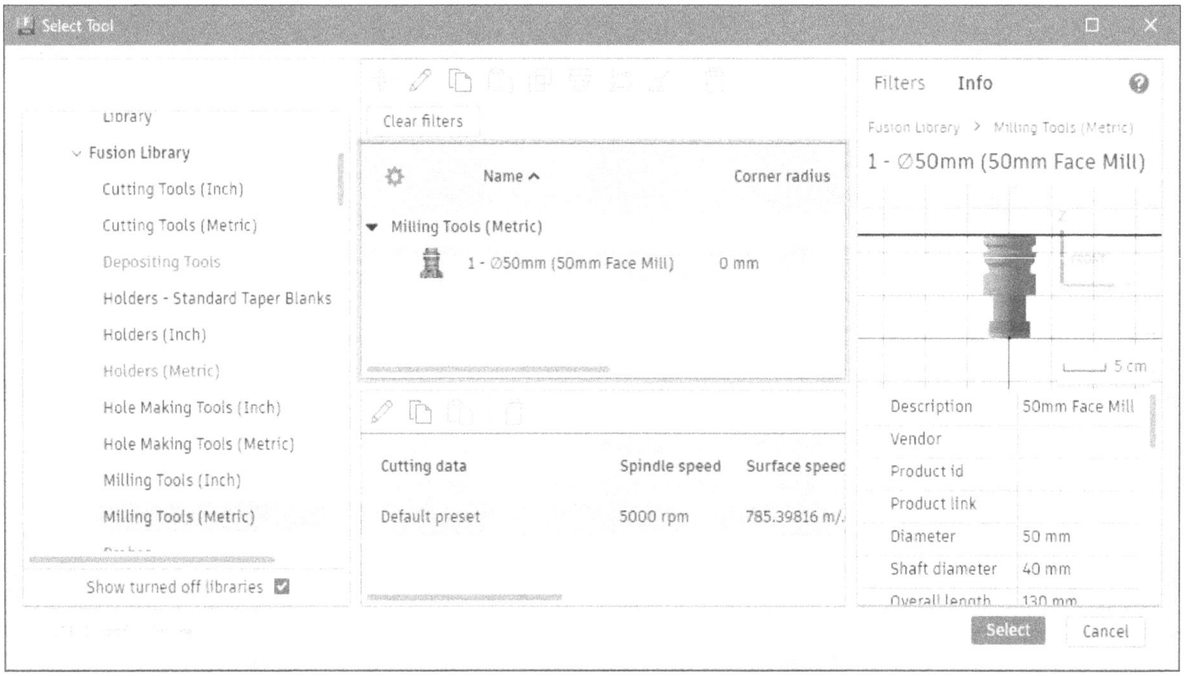

Figure-118. Selecting tool for facing

- After selecting the tool, click on the **OK** button from **Select Tool** dialog box. The tool will be selected for machining.
- Specify the parameters of **Tool** tab as displayed in Figure-119.
- Click in the **Passes** tab of the **FACE** dialog box, select the reference face to define cutting direction, and specify the parameters as displayed in Figure-120.

Figure-119. Specifying parameters in Tool tab

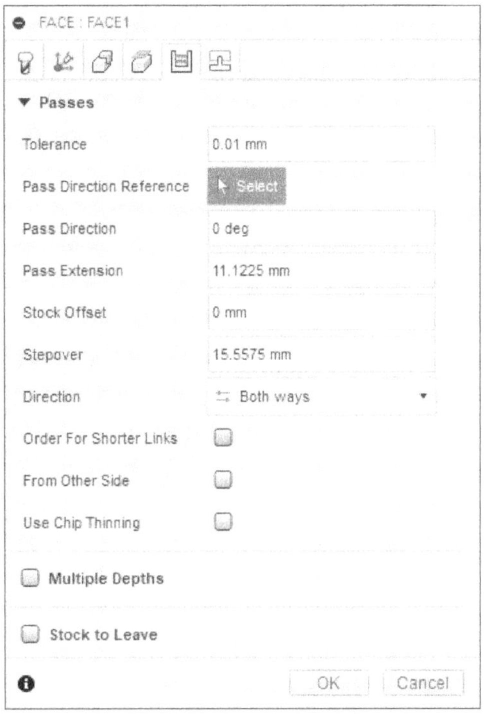

Figure-120. Passes tab of Face dialog box

- Click on the **Linking** tab of **FACE** dialog box and specify the parameters as displayed in Figure-121.

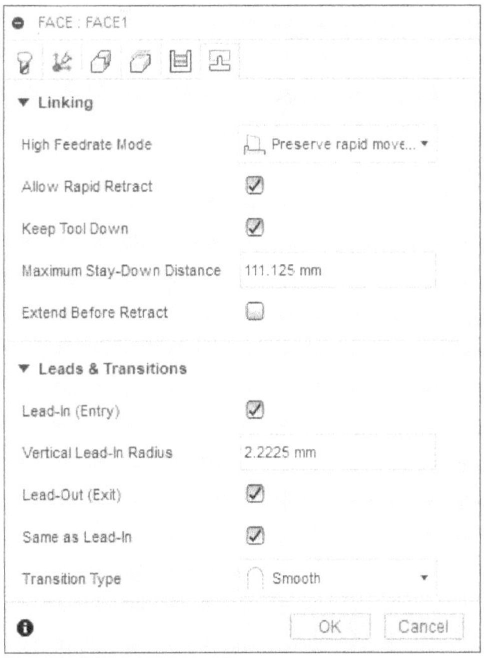

Figure-121. Linking Tab of FACE dialog box

- After specifying the parameters, click on the **OK** button from **FACE** dialog box. The toolpath will be generated and displayed on the model; refer to Figure-122.

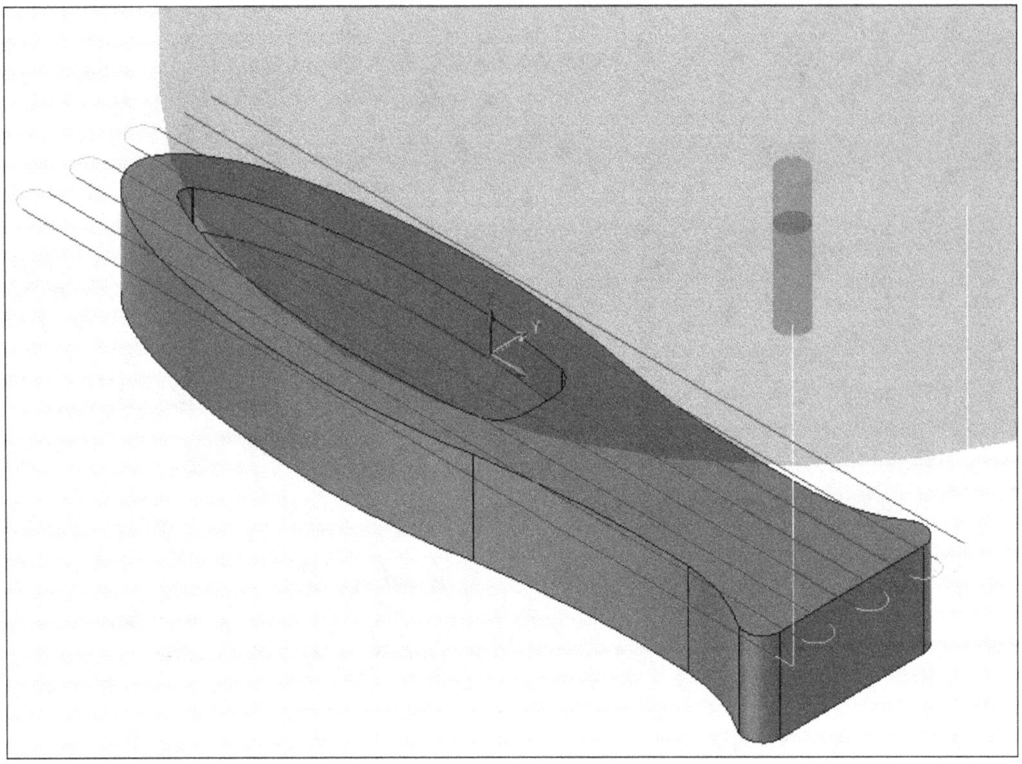

Figure-122. Created Face toolpath

Creating 2D Contour toolpath

- Click on the **2D Contour** tool from the **2D** drop-down in **Toolbar**. The **2D CONTOUR** dialog box will be displayed.
- Click on the **Select** button of **Tool** option from **Tool** tab and select the tool from **Select Tool** dialog box as displayed in Figure-123.

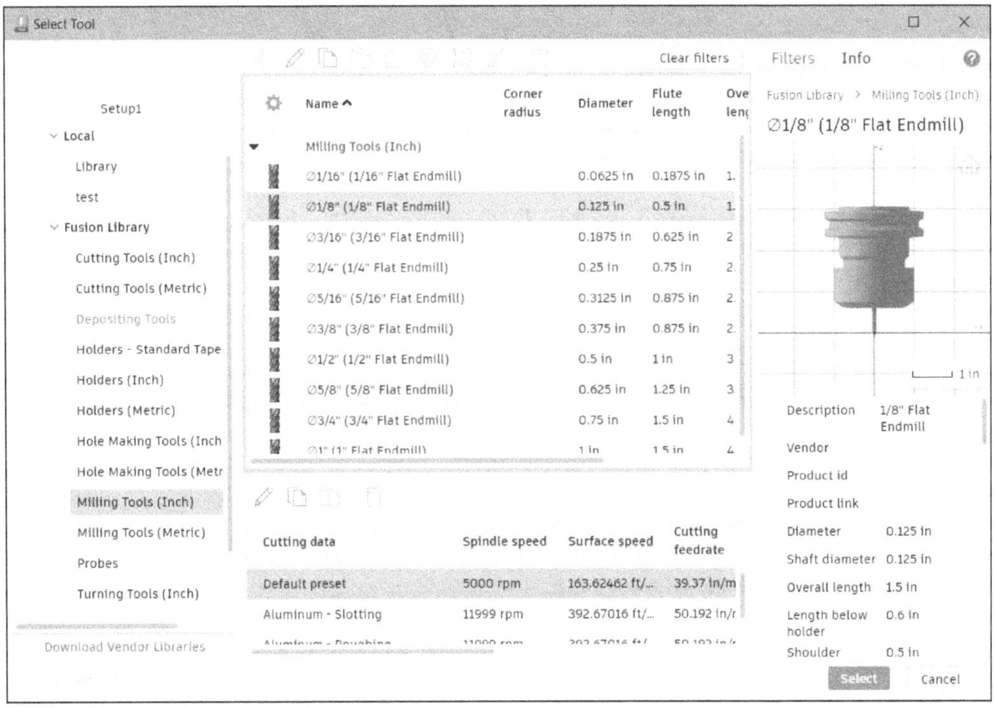

Figure-123. Selecting tool for 2D Contour

- After selecting desired cutting tool, click on the **OK** button from **Select Tool** dialog box.
- Click on the **Geometry** tab of the **2D CONTOUR** dialog box and specify the parameters as displayed in Figure-124.

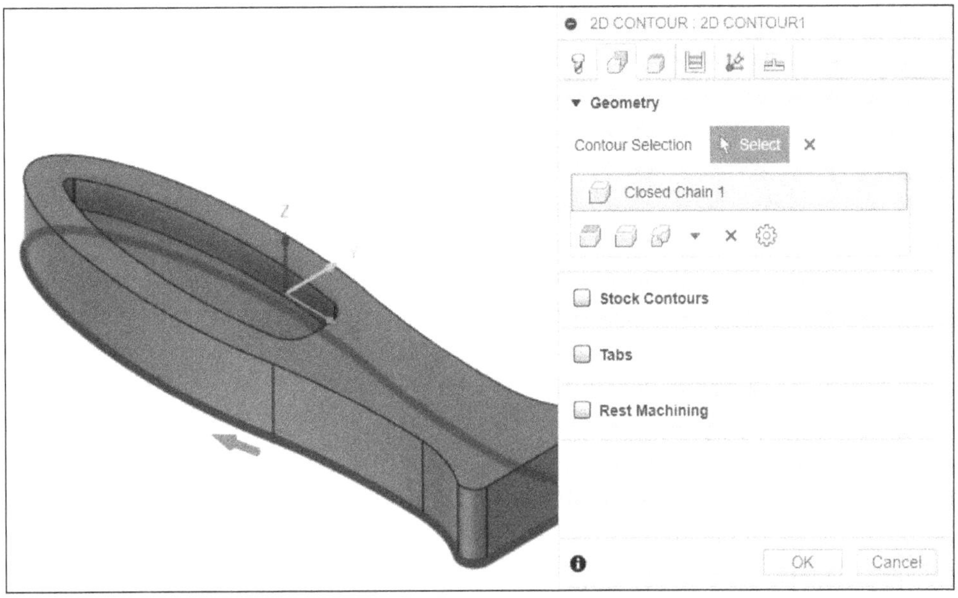

Figure-124. Geometry tab of 2D Contour

- Click in the **Passes** tab of **2D CONTOUR** dialog box and specify the parameters of **Passes** and **Multiple Depths** sections as displayed in Figure-125.
- Click on the **Linking** tab of **2D CONTOUR** dialog box and specify the parameters as displayed in Figure-126.

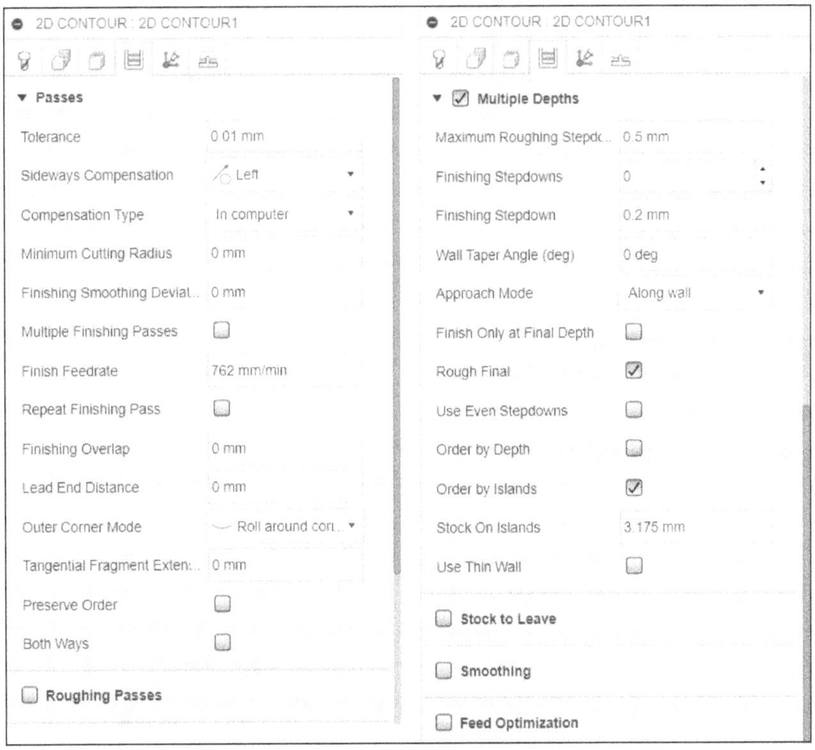

Figure-125. Passes tab of 2D CONTOUR dialog box

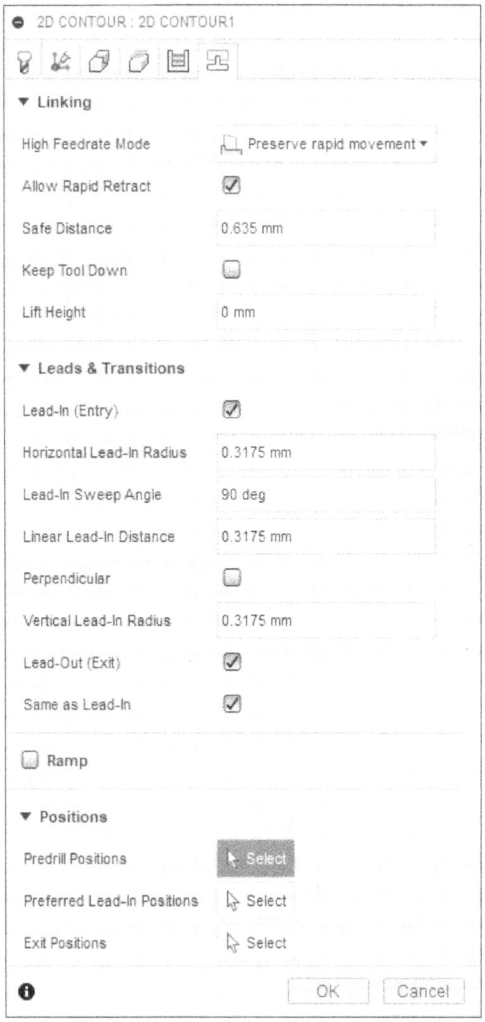

Figure-126. Linking tab of 2D CONTOUR dialog box

- After specifying the parameters, click on the **OK** button from **2D CONTOUR** dialog box. The toolpath will be generated and displayed on the model; refer to Figure-127.

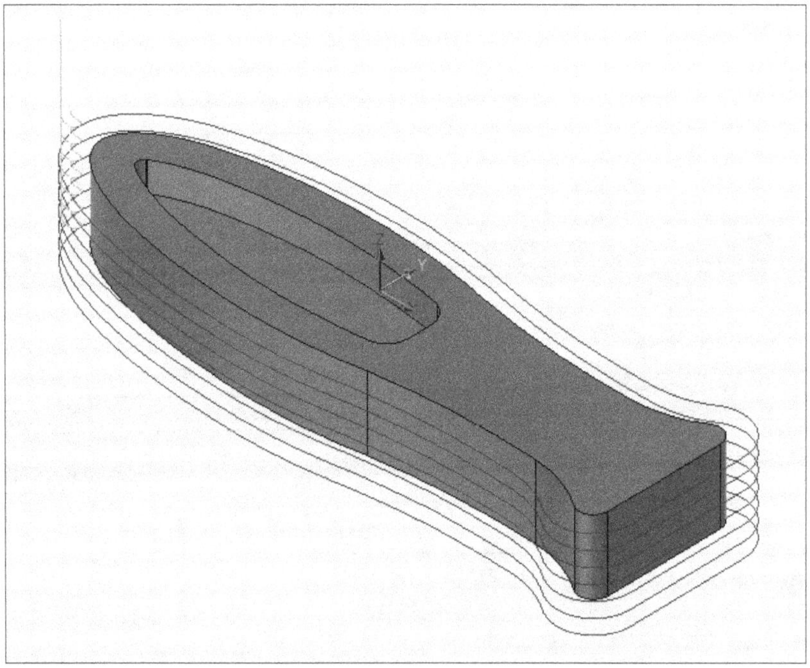

Figure-127. Generated toolpath for 2D Contour tool

Generating Pocket toolpath

- Click on the **2D Pocket** tool of **2D** drop-down from **Toolbar**. The **2D POCKET** dialog box will be displayed.
- Click on the **Select** button of **Tool** option from **Tool** tab and select the tool from **Select Tool** dialog box as displayed in Figure-128.

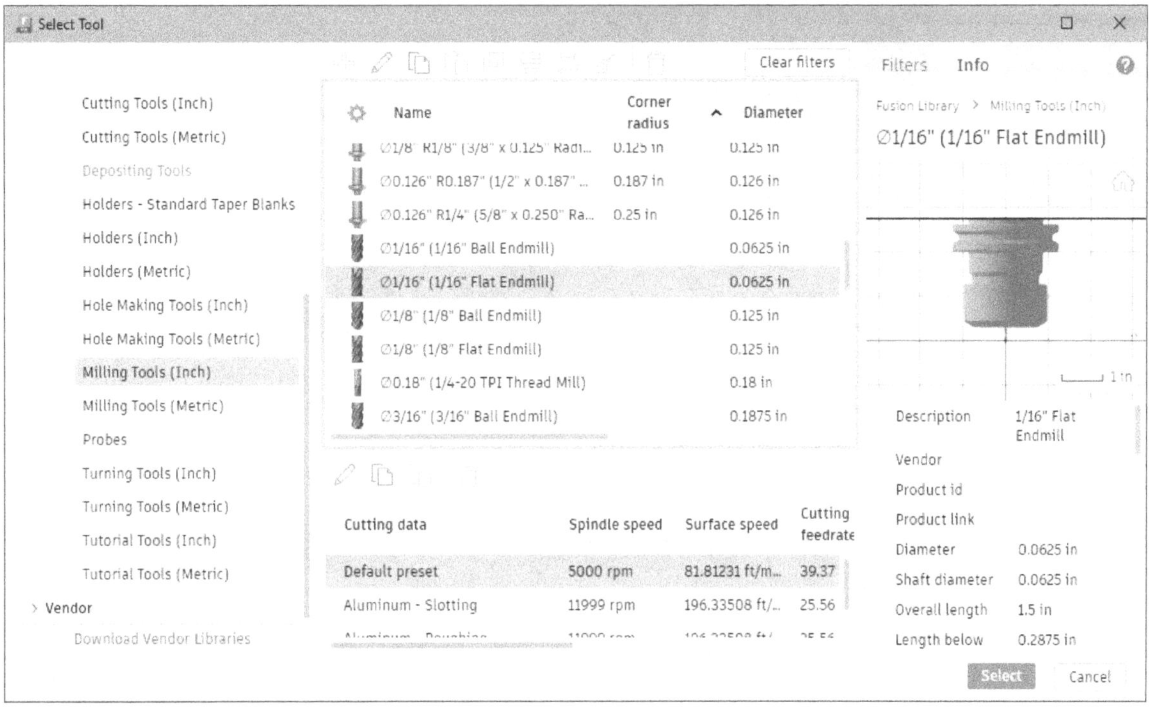

Figure-128. Selecting tool for pocket

- Specify the parameters of **Tool** tab as shown in Figure-129.

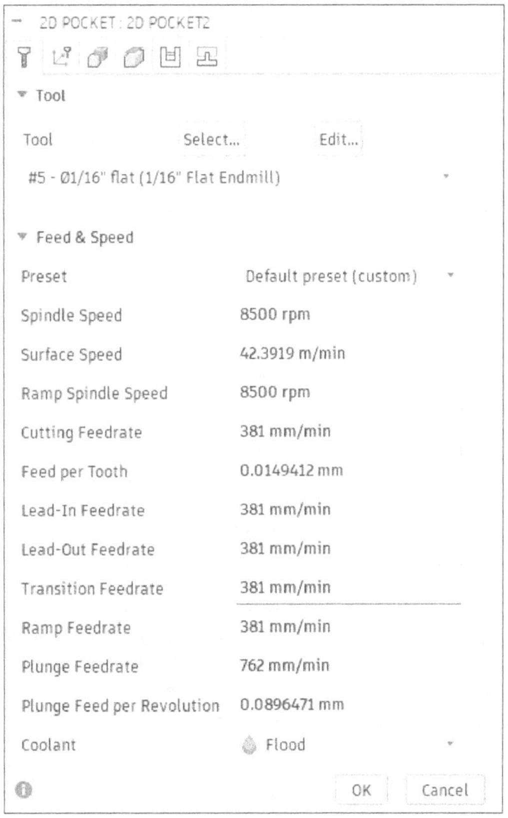

Figure-129. Specifying parameters in 2D POCKET Tool tab

- Click on the **Geometry** tab of **2D POCKET** dialog box and specify the parameters as shown in Figure-130.

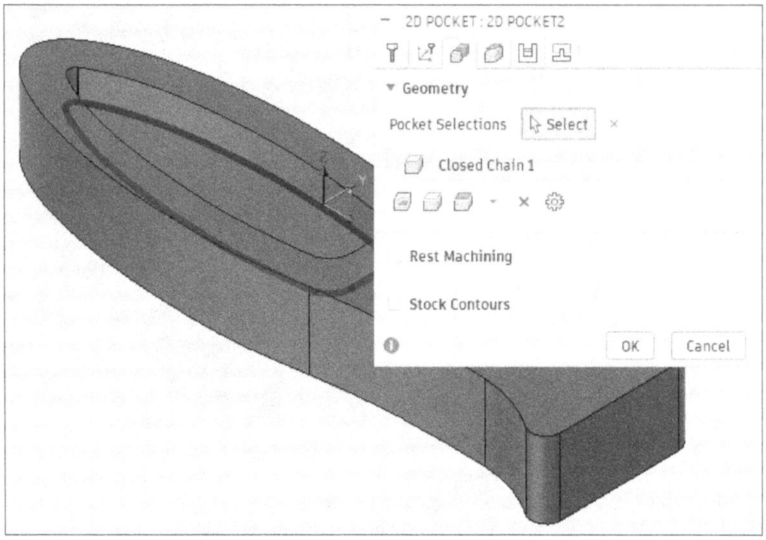

Figure-130. Geometry tab of 2D POCKET dialog box

- Click in the **Passes** tab of **2D POCKET** dialog box and specify the parameters as shown in Figure-131.
- Click in the **Linking** tab of **2D POCKET** dialog box and specify the parameters as shown in Figure-132.

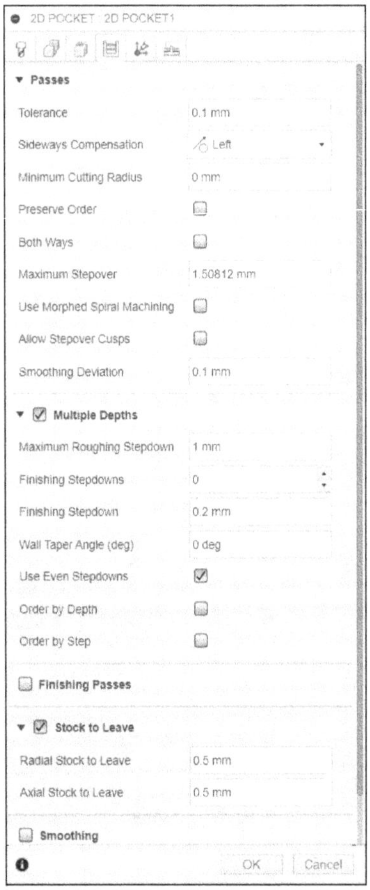

Figure-131. Passes tab of 2D POCKET dialog box

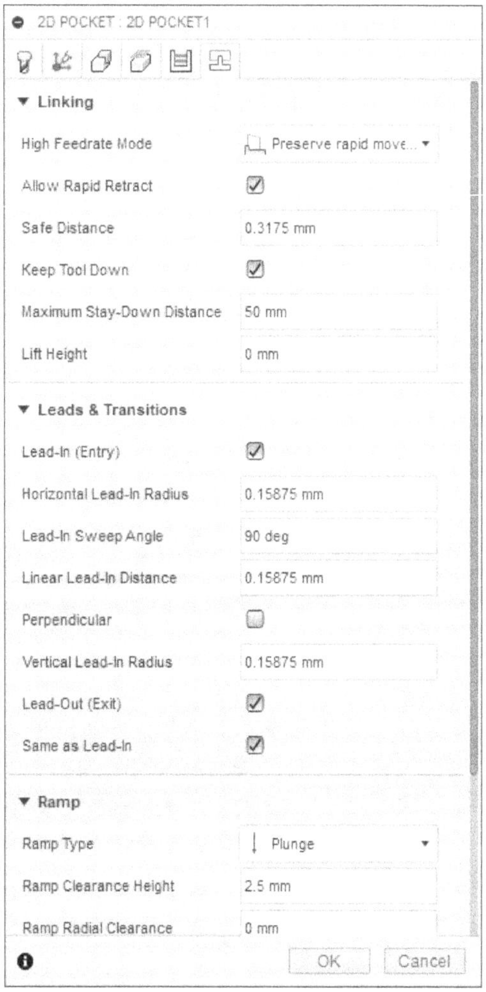

Figure-132. Linking Tab of 2D POCKET dialog box

- After specifying the parameters, click on the **OK** button from **2D POCKET** dialog box. The toolpath will be generated and displayed on the model; refer to Figure-133.
- After creating the required operations for a model, we need to simulate the generated toolpath.

Simulating the toolpath

- Select the **Setup1** option from **BROWSER** and right-click on it. A shortcut menu will be displayed.
- Click on the **Simulate** tool from shortcut menu. The **SIMULATE** dialog box will be displayed along with simulation keys; refer to Figure-134.

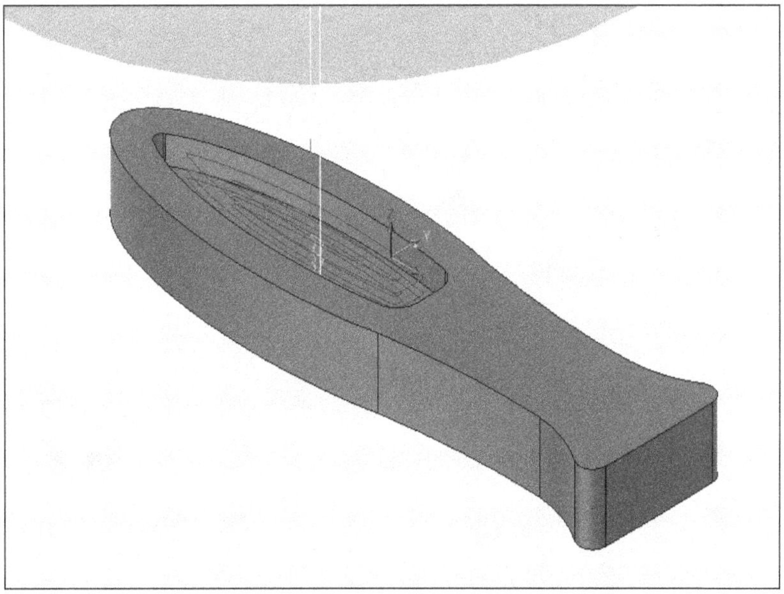

Figure-133. Generated toolpath of pocket

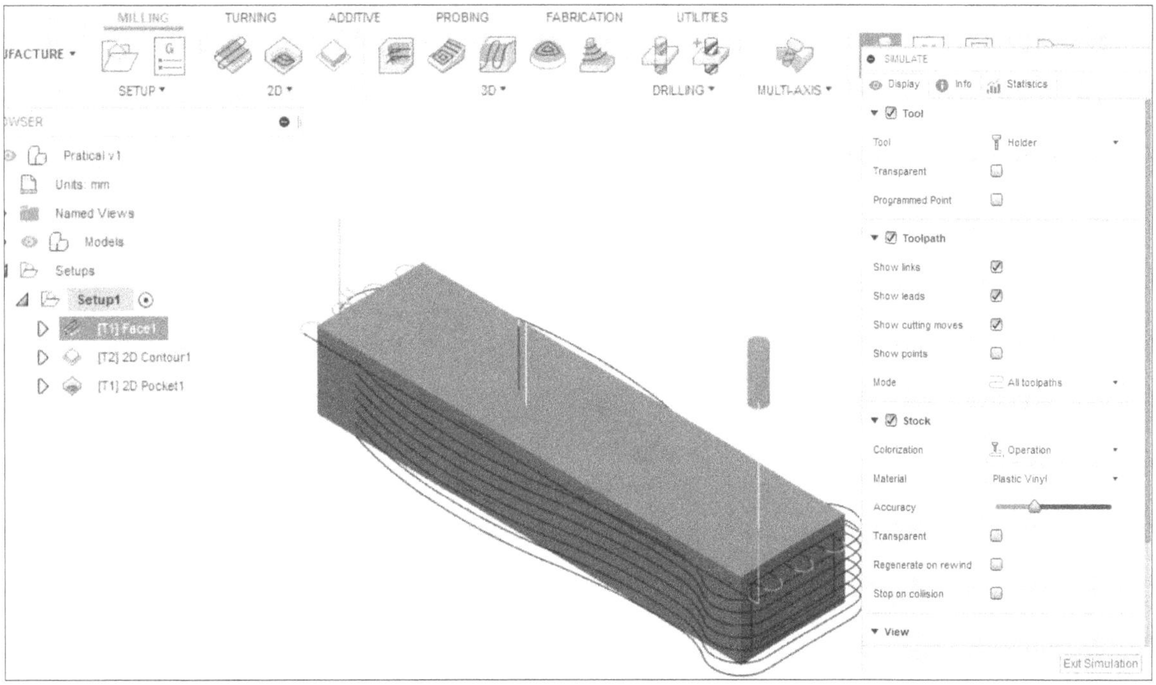

Figure-134. Simulating the model

- Click on the **Play** button to view the simulation process. One by one, all generated toolpaths will be applied to the model and at the end of simulation, the part will display along with toolpaths on the model; refer to Figure-135. Note that till now, only roughing toolpaths have been created. Create the finishing toolpaths as discussed earlier.

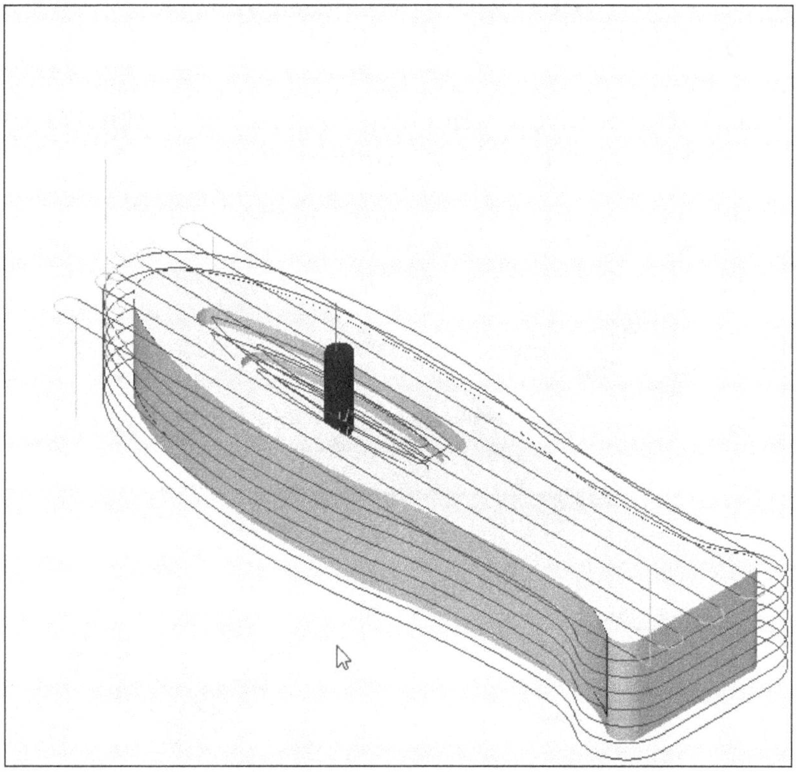

Figure-135. Running simulation process

PRACTICE 1

Machine the stock of diameter as 55 mm and length as 12 mm to create the part as shown in Figure-136. The part file of this model is available in the respective folder of **Autodesk Fusion Black Book Resources**.

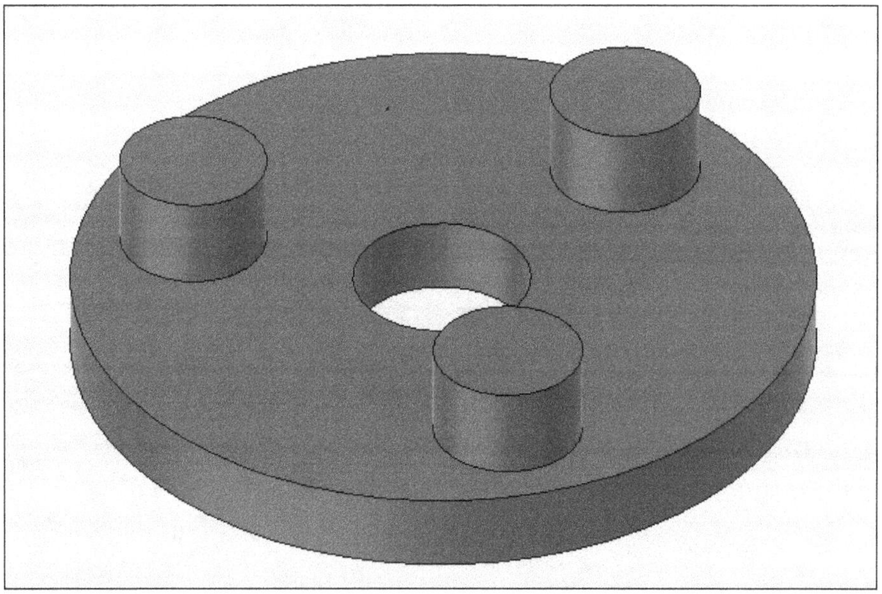

Figure-136. Practice 1

PRACTICE 2

Machine the stock of diameter as 55 mm and length as 8 mm to create the part as shown in Figure-137.

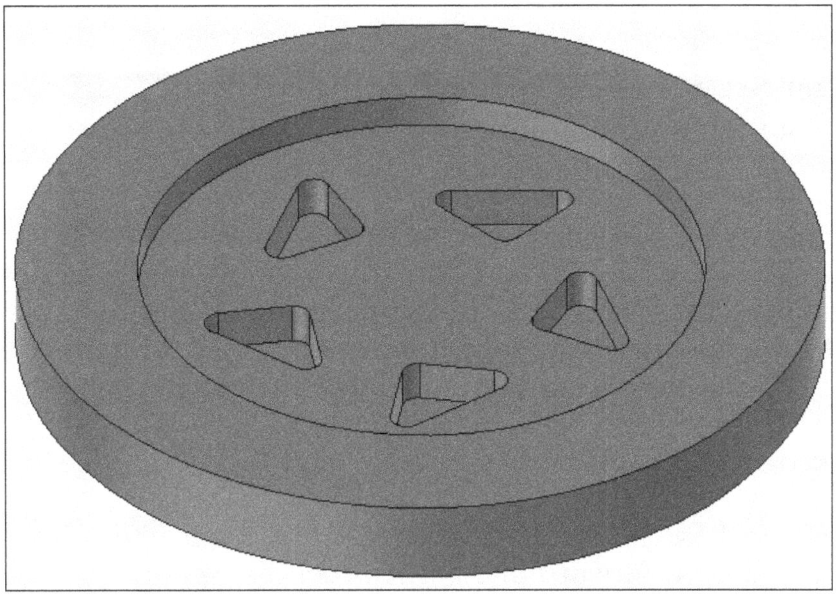

Figure-137. Practice 2

SELF ASSESSMENT

Q1. What is the primary purpose of the 2D Adaptive Clearing toolpath?
A. To create finishing passes on a workpiece
B. To remove a large amount of stock using an adaptive path
C. To drill holes automatically in a workpiece
D. To perform engraving operations

Q2. Which cutting tool is selected for machining in the 2D Adaptive Clearing operation?
A. 12 mm Ball Endmill
B. 10 mm Flat Endmill
C. 8 mm Tapered Endmill
D. 6 mm Chamfer Endmill

Q3. What is the function of the Pocket Recognition option in the Geometry tab?
A. It allows users to manually select pockets
B. It automatically recognizes pockets in the selected body
C. It extends the profile of the selected pocket geometries
D. It adjusts the tool orientation for better pocket machining

Q4. Which option should be selected to extend pocket geometries tangentially?
A. Closest boundary
B. Parallel
C. Tangent
D. Perpendicular

Q5. What does the Heights tab control in the 2D Adaptive Clearing toolpath?
A. The speed of the cutting tool
B. The coolant flow during machining
C. The height levels for tool movement
D. The tool diameter selection

Q6. Which parameter defines the top level of the cut in the Heights tab?
A. Clearance height
B. Retract height
C. Top height
D. Bottom height

Q7. What is the purpose of the Optimal Load parameter in the Passes tab?
A. It determines the maximum stepdown between two cutting depths
B. It defines the minimum cutting radius allowed in machining
C. It specifies the material engagement level during cutting
D. It sets the feedrate for rapid movements

Q8. What happens when the Both Ways check box is selected in the Passes tab?
A. Cutting occurs in both forward and return tool motions
B. The tool moves in only one direction
C. Cutting speed is reduced automatically
D. The toolpath avoids corners with small radii

Q9. Why is the Stock to Leave option used in the Passes tab?
A. To prevent cutting beyond the selected geometry
B. To leave a specified amount of stock for a finishing pass
C. To optimize feed rates in sharp corners
D. To control the coolant application

Q10. What is the purpose of the Smoothing option in the Passes tab?
A. To increase toolpath processing time
B. To reduce the size of G-code by fitting arcs within tolerance
C. To allow cutting tools to move more aggressively
D. To extend pocket geometries automatically

Q11. Which check box in the Feed Optimization section allows reducing feed rate only at inner corners?
A. Maximum Directional Change
B. Reduced Feed Radius
C. Reduced Feedrate
D. Only Inner Corners

Q12. What is the function of the Multi-Axis tab in the 2D Adaptive Clearing toolpath?
A. It determines coolant settings
B. It allows selection of 3-axis or multi-axis machining
C. It controls toolpath retraction height
D. It specifies cutting feed rates

Q13. Which Retraction Policy should be used to minimize tool retractions between passes?
A. Full retraction
B. Minimum retraction
C. Rapid retract
D. No retraction

Q14. What does the Ramp Type option in the Linking tab control?
A. The retraction height of the tool
B. The coolant application during machining
C. The method used for tool entry into the material
D. The optimal load value for cutting

Q15. What happens when the Simulate option is selected from the shortcut menu?
A. The selected toolpath is deleted
B. The animation of material cutting is displayed
C. The toolpath is regenerated with new parameters
D. The machine setup is changed

Q16. What is the primary function of the 2D Pocket tool?
A) To create internal and external threads
B) To remove material from pockets in the model
C) To create toolpaths following selected curves
D) To remove material from the top face of the workpiece

Q17. Where can you find the 2D Pocket tool in the software?
A) Under the Threading tab
B) In the 2D drop-down under the MILLING tab
C) In the 3D toolpath section
D) Under the Geometry section

Q18. What is the purpose of selecting the "Both Ways" checkbox in the 2D Pocket tool?
A) To machine both forward and backward
B) To allow multiple depth cuts
C) To create a multi-start thread
D) To define a slot pattern

Q19. What is the recommended number of finishing passes for a better finish?
A) 1
B) 2
C) 3
D) 4

Q20. What does the "Use Morphed Spiral Machining" option do?
A) Creates external threads
B) Performs a smoother machining operation
C) Adds tabs to the workpiece
D) Removes excess material from the top face

Q21. Which tool is generally the first to be used in a machining sequence for a flat head workpiece?
A) 2D Contour
B) Face
C) Slot
D) Trace

Q22. What is the function of the Chain button in the FACE dialog box?
A) To specify depth of cut
B) To select the boundary of the workpiece
C) To create tabs for holding the workpiece
D) To define a slot pattern

Q23. What is the purpose of the Tabs checkbox in the 2D Contour tool?
A) To hold the workpiece while cutting a part from a sheet
B) To create external threads
C) To enable multi-start threading
D) To select the pocket geometry

Q24. How can tabs be positioned around a workpiece?
A) By using the By Distance option
B) By selecting the Both Ways checkbox
C) By enabling the Use Morphed Spiral Machining option
D) By selecting the Preserve Order checkbox

Q25. What is the main difference between pocket toolpaths and slot toolpaths?
A) Pocket toolpaths machine only regular slots, while slot toolpaths can machine any slot
B) Slot toolpaths machine only regular slots, while pocket toolpaths can machine any slot
C) Both tools perform the same operation
D) Slot toolpaths are only used for threading

Q26. What is the primary function of the Trace tool?
A) To create toolpaths that follow selected curves
B) To remove material from pockets
C) To create threads
D) To machine multiple depths

Q27. What does the "Repeat Passes" checkbox in the Trace tool do?
A) Enables multi-start threading
B) Performs an additional finishing pass with zero stock
C) Creates lead-in and lead-out paths
D) Machines both forward and backward

Q28. What does the Thread tool allow you to do?
A) Remove material from a pocket
B) Follow selected curves for cutting
C) Create internal and external threads
D) Create toolpaths for slot milling

Q29. What does selecting the "Right Handed" option in the Thread tool do?
A) Creates a right-handed thread direction
B) Machines forward and backward
C) Adds tabs to the workpiece
D) Enables pocket machining

Q30. What is the function of the "Lead To Center" checkbox in the Thread tool?
A) To move the tool to the center of the selected chain for threading
B) To create a smooth finish
C) To add additional finishing passes
D) To create tabs manually

Q31. What is the primary function of the Bore tool?
A) To create external threads
B) To increase the diameter of a hole in tight tolerance
C) To engrave text on a workpiece
D) To remove material in bulk from the workpiece

Q32. Where can you find the Bore tool in the software?
A) Under the Engrave tab
B) In the 2D drop-down in the Toolbar
C) Under the Threading tools section
D) In the 3D toolpath tab

Q33. What needs to be selected in the Geometry tab when using the Bore tool?
A) Rectangular faces
B) Circular faces of holes
C) Edges of a chamfer
D) Text for engraving

Q34. What is the Circular tool primarily used for?
A) Milling circular or round pocket/boss features
B) Engraving artistic designs
C) Creating chamfers on sharp edges
D) Removing excess material from the model

Q35. Which of the following features can be machined using the Circular tool?
A) Only circular pockets
B) Only cylindrical islands
C) Both circular pockets and cylindrical islands
D) Only external threads

Q36. What is the purpose of the Engrave tool?
A) To increase hole diameters
B) To perform artistic machining on the workpiece
C) To create chamfer profiles
D) To remove bulk material from a workpiece

Q37. What type of tool is generally recommended for engraving?
A) End mill
B) Tapered cutting tool
C) Threading tool
D) Face mill

Q38. What is the key difference between engraving and embossing?
A) Engraving creates raised patterns, embossing creates recessed patterns
B) Engraving removes material to create recessed patterns, embossing creates raised patterns
C) Both engraving and embossing remove material
D) Engraving is only used for text, embossing is used for logos

Q39. What does the Sharp Corner Angle parameter in the Engrave tool define?
A) The minimum allowable cutting depth
B) The maximum angle between edges for clearing sharp corners
C) The tool offset from the edge
D) The tool diameter

Q40. What is the primary function of the 2D Chamfer tool?
A) To create external threads
B) To engrave logos on a press die
C) To create chamfer profiles on model edges
D) To remove material from a pocket

Q41. What must be selected in the Geometry tab when using the 2D Chamfer tool?
A) Circular faces
B) The edges where the chamfer is to be created
C) Engraving curves
D) Cylindrical bosses

Q42. What does the Chamfer Width edit box define?
A) The angle of the chamfer
B) The width of the chamfer cut
C) The depth of the chamfer cut
D) The feed rate for chamfering

Q43. What happens when you hover the cursor over a toolpath in the Browser?
A) The preview of toolpath is displayed in the modeling area
B) The preview of material removed from stock is displayed
C) The toolpath is automatically generated
D) The toolpath is deleted

Q44. What is the main difference between 2D and 3D toolpaths?
A) 2D toolpaths move the tool in the XY plane only, while 3D toolpaths allow movement in XY and Z simultaneously
B) 3D toolpaths can only be used for engraving
C) 2D toolpaths are used for roughing, and 3D toolpaths are used for finishing
D) There is no difference between 2D and 3D toolpaths

Q45. What is the function of the Adaptive Clearing tool?
A) To create external threads
B) To remove material in bulk using advanced milling motion
C) To engrave artistic features
D) To machine sharp chamfer edges

Q46. Which type of tool is typically used with the Adaptive Clearing tool?
A) Tapered cutting tool
B) Ball/bull mill or end mill
C) Threading tool
D) Face mill

Q47. What is the purpose of the Shaft & Holder checkbox in the Adaptive Clearing tool?
A) To define the toolpath based on the holder's shape
B) To enable multi-directional machining
C) To create a chamfer on sharp edges
D) To increase the diameter of a hole

Q48. What happens when you select the "Fail on collision" option in the Shaft & Holder mode?
A) The toolpath is adjusted to avoid collisions
B) The machining toolpath is aborted if a collision is detected
C) The tool moves upward to clear material
D) The toolpath continues regardless of collision risk

Q49. What does selecting the "Machine Shallow Areas" checkbox in the Passes tab do?
A) Ensures pockets are cut to full depth
B) Removes excessive cusps from shallow areas of Z-level
C) Enables high-speed engraving
D) Limits tool movement to a single axis

Q50. What is the main purpose of the Pocket Clearing toolpath?
A) To engrave text onto a workpiece
B) To clear large quantities of stock material from pockets
C) To create external threads
D) To mill circular bosses

For Student Notes

Chapter 17

Generating Milling Toolpaths - 2

Topics Covered

The major topics covered in this chapter are:

- ***Spiral Toolpath***
- ***Radial Toolpath***
- ***Morphed Spiral Toolpath***
- ***Project Toolpath***
- ***Swarf Toolpath***
- ***Multi-Axis Contour Toolpath***
- ***Drilling Toolpath***

3D TOOLPATHS

In previous chapter, we have worked on 2D toolpaths and some 3D toolpaths available in **Toolbar**. In this chapter, we will discuss rest of the 3D toolpaths. Later, we will also work on multi-axis toolpaths and drilling operations.

Spiral

The spiral toolpath is used to cut material in spiral fashion. This toolpath is useful when you need to finish faces of cylindrical objects like shown in Figure-1. The procedure to use this tool is discussed next.

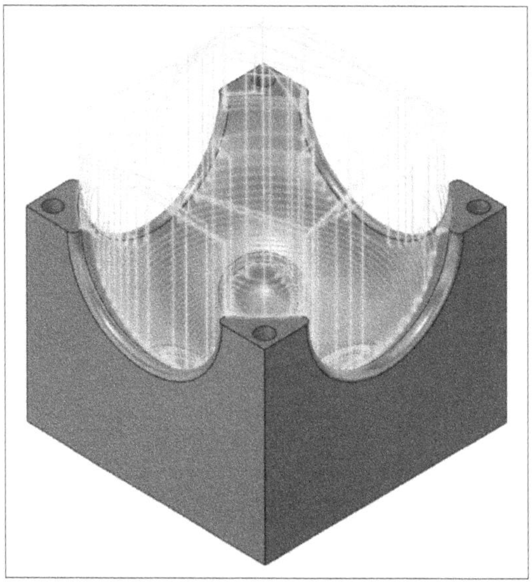

Figure-1. Spiral toolpath

- Click on the **Spiral** tool from **3D** drop-down in the **Toolbar**; refer to Figure-2. The **SPIRAL** dialog box will be displayed; refer to Figure-3.

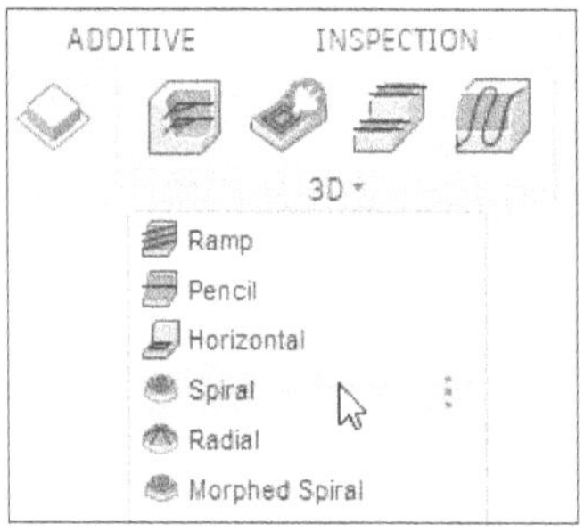

Figure-2. Spiral tool

Figure-3. SPIRAL dialog box

- Click on the **Select** button of **Tool** section from **Tool** tab. The **Select Tool** dialog box will be displayed. Select desired tool generally, an end mill or ball mill.
- Click on the **Geometry** tab in the dialog box and select desired point to be used as center for toolpath.
- Click on the **Passes** tab of **SPIRAL** dialog box. The options will be displayed as shown in Figure-4.

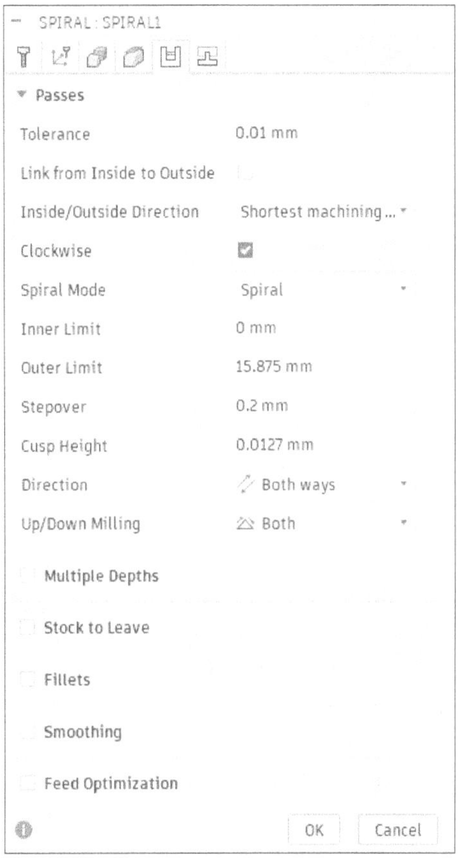

Figure-4. Passes tab of SPIRAL dialog box

- Select the **Clockwise** check box of **Passes** tab to set the direction of spiral to clockwise.
- Select the **Spiral** option from **Spiral Mode** drop-down to create a spiral toolpath which starts from the center and ends at the outermost boundary.
- Select the **Spiral with circles** option from **Spiral Mode** drop-down to create a circular toolpath at the minimum and maximum radius. This toolpath will only be created if the minimum radius is larger than zero and maximum radius is smaller than the radius of regulation boundary.
- Select the **Concentric circles** option from **Spiral Mode** drop-down to create a concentric circle toolpath; refer to Figure-5.

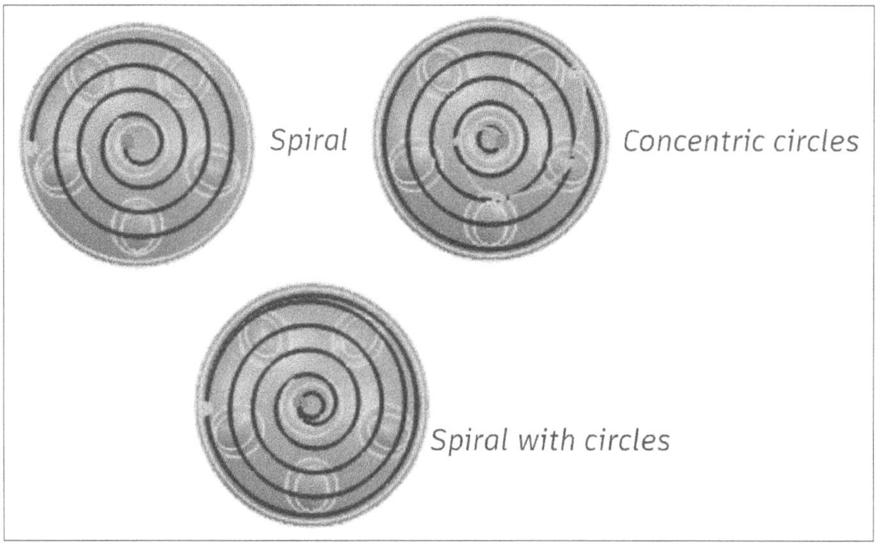

Figure-5. Spiral modes

- Click in the **Inner Limit** edit box of **Passes** tab to set the minimum inner radius. If no inner limit is specified then spiral toolpath will start from center of the selected circular face.
- Click in the **Outer Limit** edit box of **Passes** tab to set the maximum outer radius. If outer limit is not specified then spiral toolpath will extend up to the outer edge of selected circular face.
- Click in the **Stepover** edit box of **Passes** tab and specify distance between two consecutive cutting passes.
- Specify desired value in the **Cusp Height** edit box to automatically determine the value of stepover based on height of cusps. Cusp is the thin wall of material left by cutting tool during two consecutive cutting passes based on stepover.
- The other options of the dialog box are same as discussed earlier. After specifying the parameters, click on the **OK** button from **SPIRAL** dialog box. The toolpath will be generated and displayed on the model; refer to Figure-6

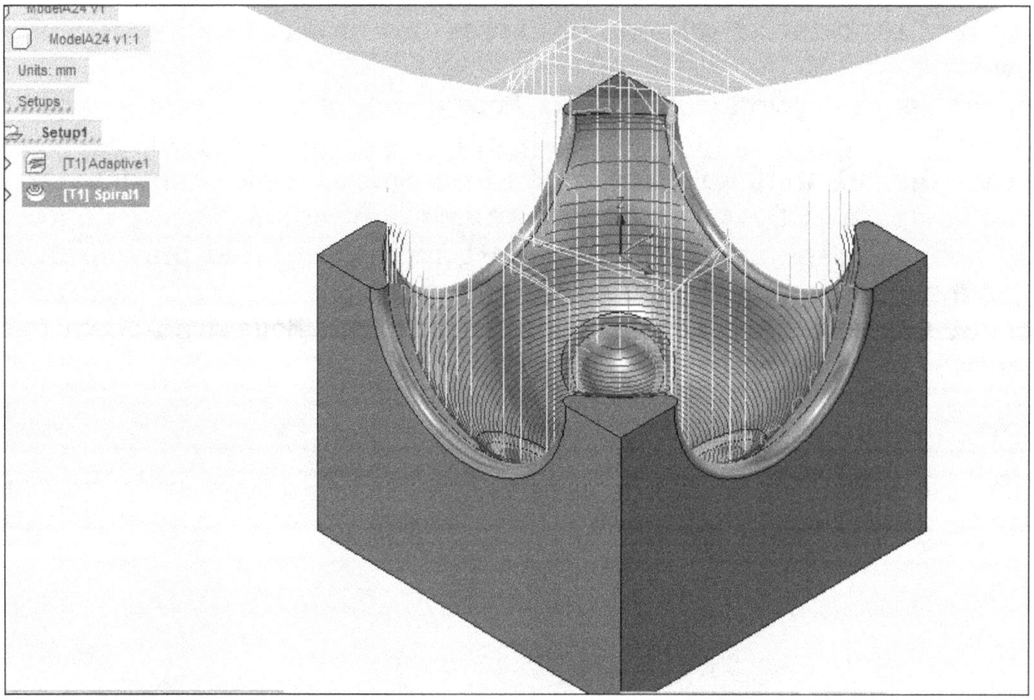

Figure-6. Toolpath generated for Spiral tool

Radial

The **Radial** tool is used to create toolpath along the radii of an arc. The toolpath created by radial is similar to the spokes of wheel which are then projected down on the surface. Note that Radial and Spiral both the toolpaths are used to machine round shallow parts. The difference between two toolpaths is their direction of cutting. In case of Radial toolpaths, the cutting passes will be straight lines connecting the center with outer edge. When we go deep in metallurgy of parts, these two toolpaths can generate different grain patterns on surface of the same part. The procedure to use Radial tool is discussed next.

- Click on the **Radial** tool of **3D** drop-down from **Toolbar**; refer to Figure-7. The **RADIAL** dialog box will be displayed; refer to Figure-8.
- Click on the **Select** button of **Tool** section from **Tool** tab. The **Select Tool** dialog box will be displayed. Select the required tool.
- Click on the **Geometry** tab in the dialog box and select desired point to be used as center for toolpath.
- Click on the **Passes** tab of **RADIAL** dialog box. The options will be displayed as shown in Figure-9.
- Click in the **Angular Step** edit box of **Passes** tab and specify the angular value of distance between two consecutive radial passes.
- Click in the **Angle From** edit box of **Passes** tab and specify the value of radial angle measured from the X-axis from where first cutting pass will be generated.
- Click in the **Angle To** edit box of **Passes** tab and specify the radial angle measured from the X-axis up to which the cutting passes can be generated.
- The other options of the dialog box are same as discussed earlier.
- After specifying the parameters, click on the **OK** button from **RADIAL** dialog box. The toolpath will be generated and displayed on the model; refer to Figure-10.

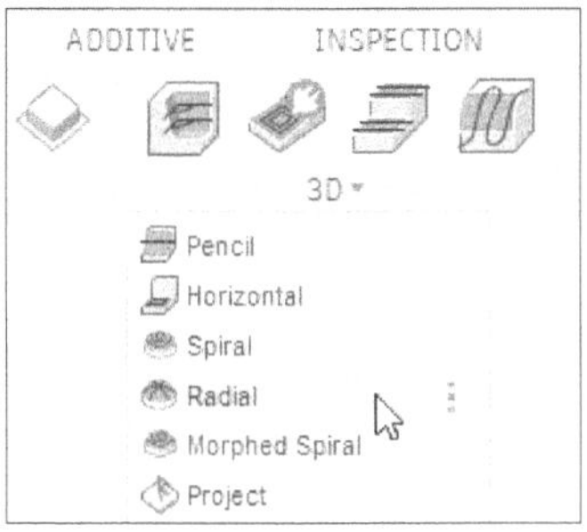

Figure-7. Radial tool

Figure-8. RADIAL dialog box

Figure-9. Passes tab of RADIAL dialog box

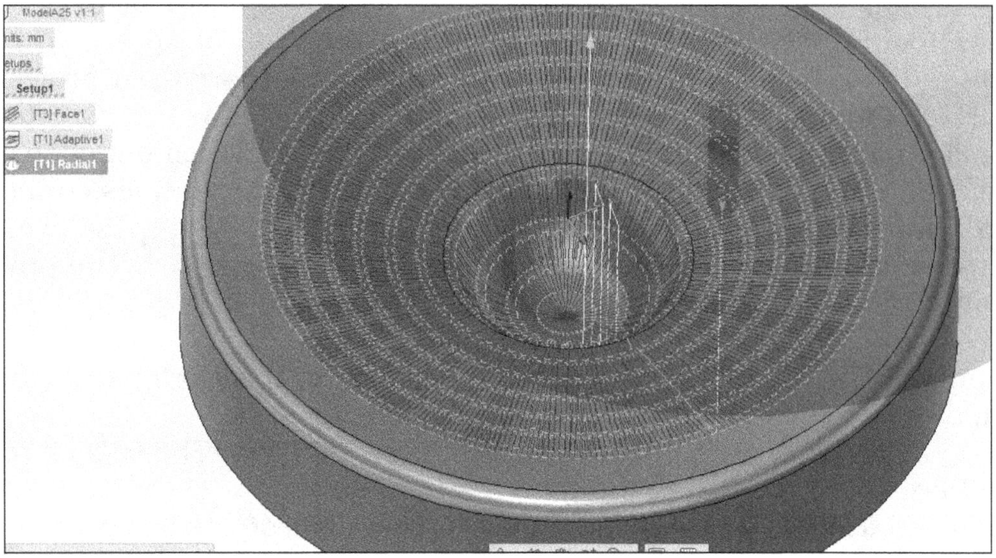

Figure-10. Toolpath generated for Radial tool

Morphed Spiral

The **Morphed Spiral** tool is mainly used to create toolpath of free-form surfaces. In this toolpath, spiral cutting passes are generated following the surface curvature within specified boundaries. The procedure to use this tool is discussed next.

- Click on the **Morphed Spiral** tool of **3D** drop-down from **Toolbar**; refer to Figure-11. The **MORPHED SPIRAL** dialog box will be displayed; refer to Figure-12.

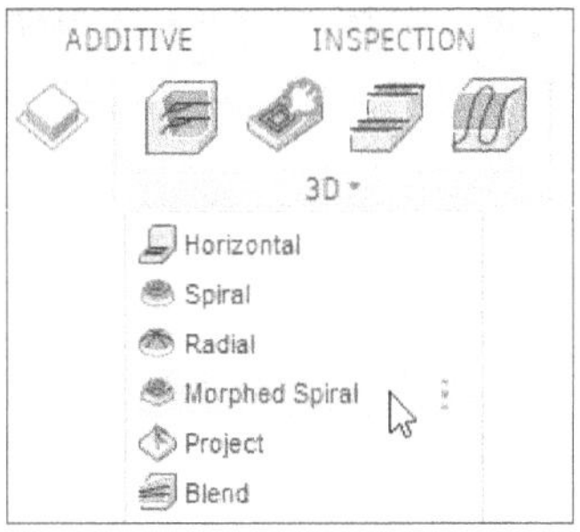

Figure-11. Morphed Spiral tool

Figure-12. MORPHED SPIRAL dialog box

- Click on the **Select** button of **Tool** section from **Tool** tab. The **Select Tool** dialog box will be displayed. Select the required tool, generally a ball end mill.
- Click on the **Geometry** tab and select the boundary curve to be used as containment boundary for toolpaths. If no chain is selected then by default, bounding box of stock is used as boundary of toolpaths.
- The other options of the dialog box are same as discussed earlier. After specifying the parameters, click on the **OK** button from **MORPHED Spiral** dialog box. The toolpath will be created and displayed on the model; refer to Figure-13.

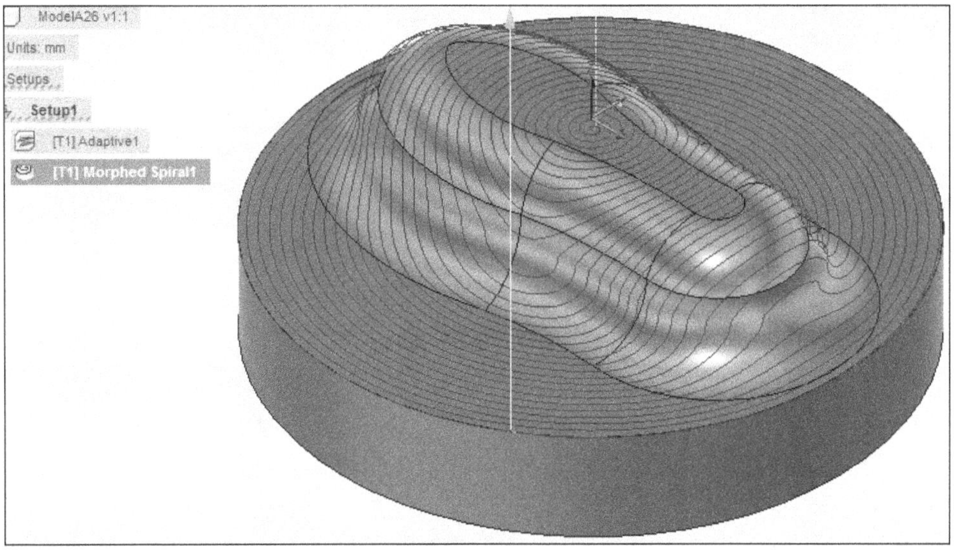

Figure-13. Generated toolpath for Morphed Spiral tool

Project

The **Project** tool is used to create a toolpath along the selected contour. The contour will be machined with the center of the tool. Note that Project toolpaths work similar to Engrave toolpaths discussed earlier. The only difference is number of dimensions in which toolpaths are generated. Engrave toolpaths are 2 dimensional whereas project toolpaths are 3 dimensional which means if you have an irregular surface on which engraving of selected curves is to be performed then you should use Project toolpaths. The procedure to use this tool is discussed next.

- Click on the **Project** tool of **3D** drop-down from **Toolbar**; refer to Figure-14. The **PROJECT** dialog box will be displayed; refer to Figure-15.
- Click on the **Select** button of **Tool** section from **Tool** tab. The **Select Tool** dialog box will be displayed. Select desired tool, generally a tapered mill.
- Click on **Geometry** tab in the dialog box and select desired curve from the model which is to be engraved. Note that there is no need of curves to be placed directly on the face of model. Make sure that projection of curves fall on the face of model where curves are to be engraved; refer to Figure-16.

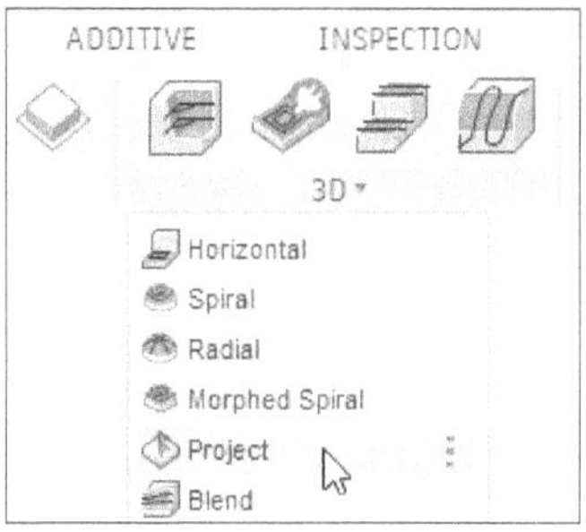

Figure-14. Project tool

Figure-15. PROJECT dialog box

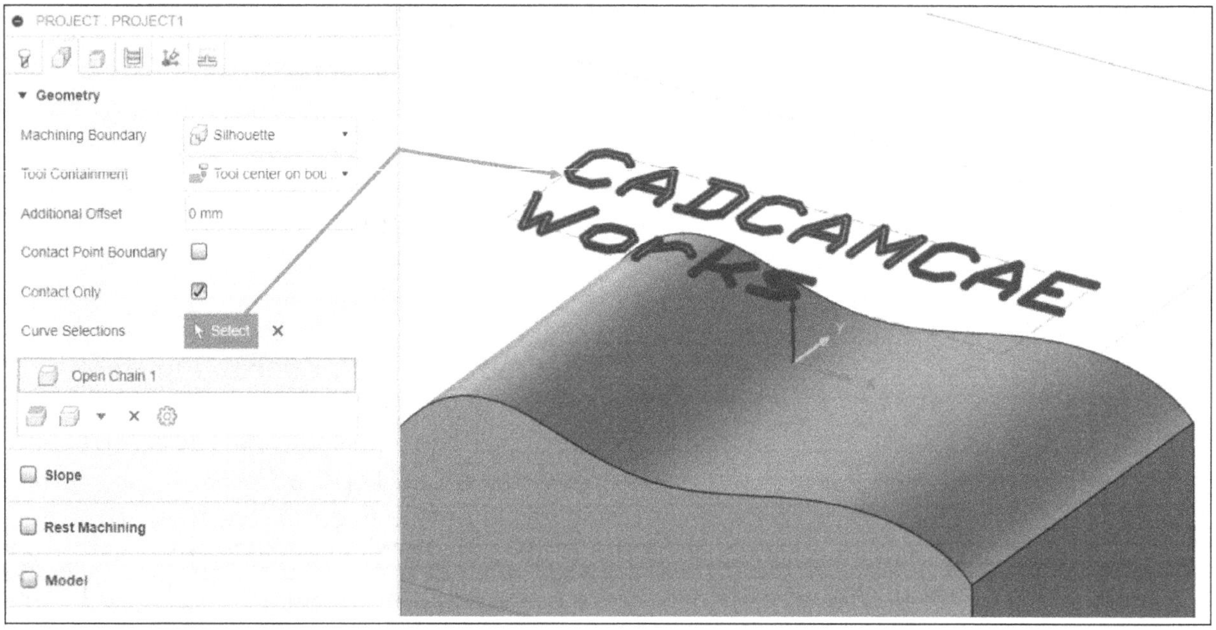

Figure-16. Curve chain selected

- The other options of the dialog box are same as discussed earlier. After specifying the parameter, click on the **OK** button from **PROJECT** dialog box. The toolpath will be generated and displayed on the model; refer to Figure-17.

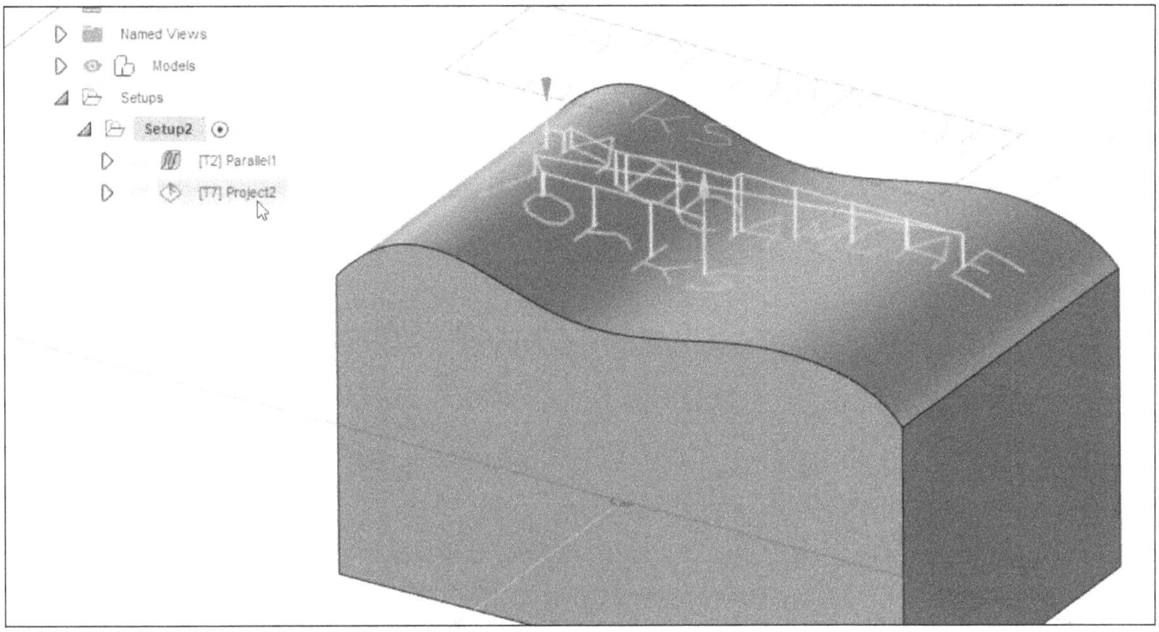

Figure-17. Generated toolpath for Project tool

Blend

The **Blend** tool is used to create toolpath for finishing shallow areas between two selected contours with uniform direction of cutting passes. The procedure to use this tool is given next.

- Click on the **Blend** tool from the **3D** drop-down in **Toolbar**. The **BLEND** dialog box will be displayed.
- Select a ball end mill or other similar tool that can machine curved surfaces using the options in the **Tool** tab.
- Click on the **Geometry** tab to define geometry selection for the toolpath. The options will be displayed as shown in Figure-18.

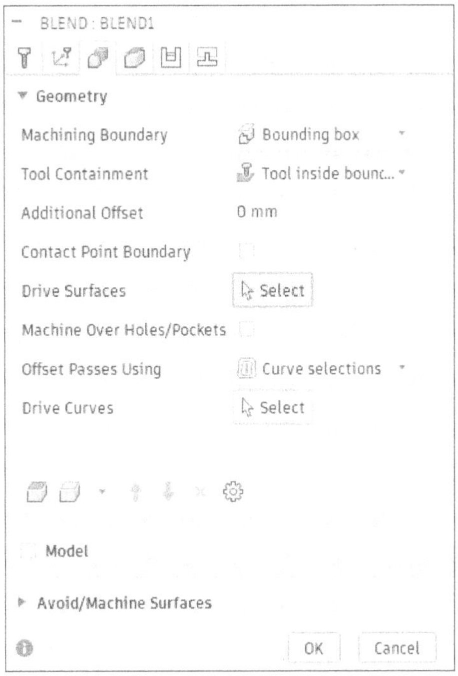

Figure-18. Geometry tab of BLEND dialog box

- By default, the **Select** button of **Drive Surfaces** is active. Select the face/surface of model on which you want to perform machining.
- Select **Machine Over Holes/Pockets** check box to create patch surfaces that enable toolpaths to move over holes or pockets, improving surface finish.
- Select desired option from **Offset Passes Using** drop-down to offset each pass of the toolpath.
- Select the **Drive Curves** selection button from the dialog box and select the two curves at boundary of face/surface to define direction of toolpath; refer to Figure-19.

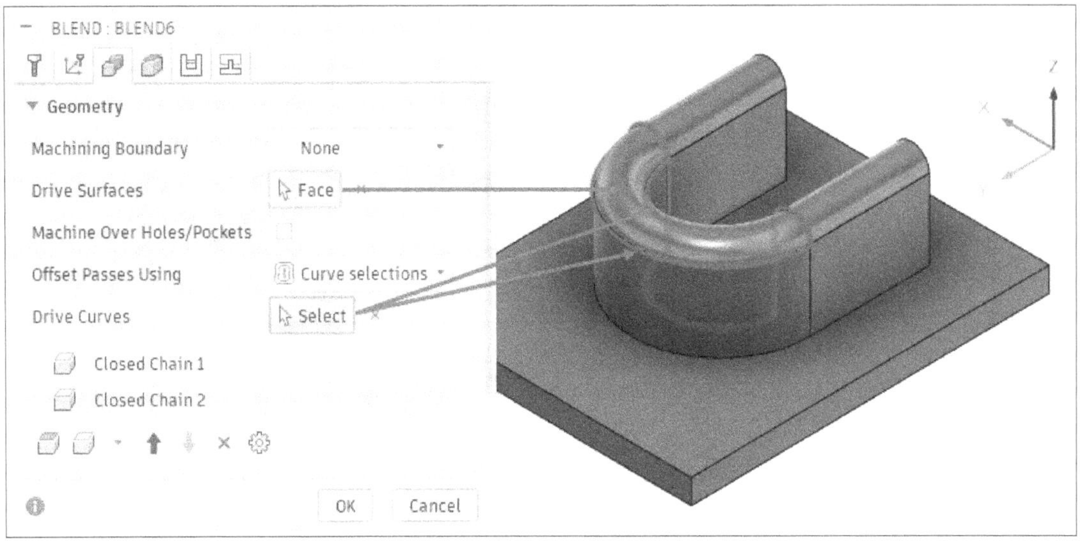

Figure-19. Selection for blend toolpath

- Set the other parameters as discussed earlier and click on the **OK** button. The toolpath will be created; refer to Figure-20.

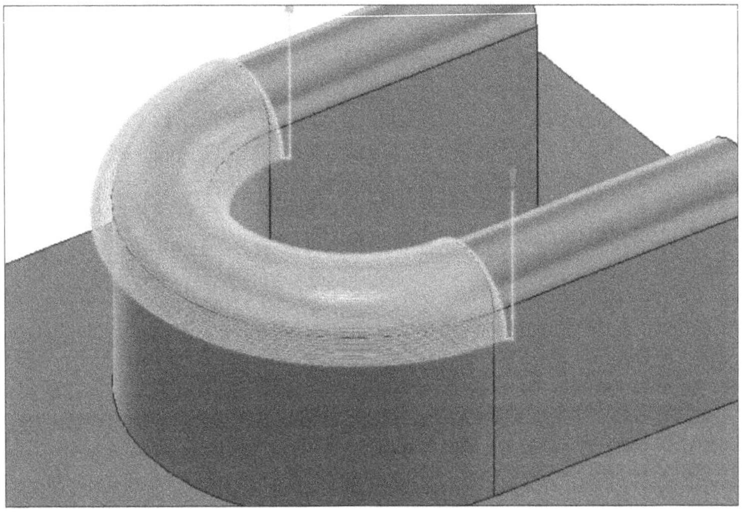

Figure-20. Blend toolpath

Morph

The **Morph** tool is used to create the toolpath for machining shallow areas between selected contour. The morph toolpaths look similar to flowlines or parallel toolpaths but the main difference is containment boundaries. In morph toolpaths, cutting tool enters from one of the open side and exits from the other side while avoiding selected contours. The procedure to use this tool is discussed next.

- Click on the **Morph** tool of **3D** drop-down from **Toolbar**; refer to Figure-21. The **MORPH** dialog box will be displayed; refer to Figure-22.

Figure-21. Morph tool

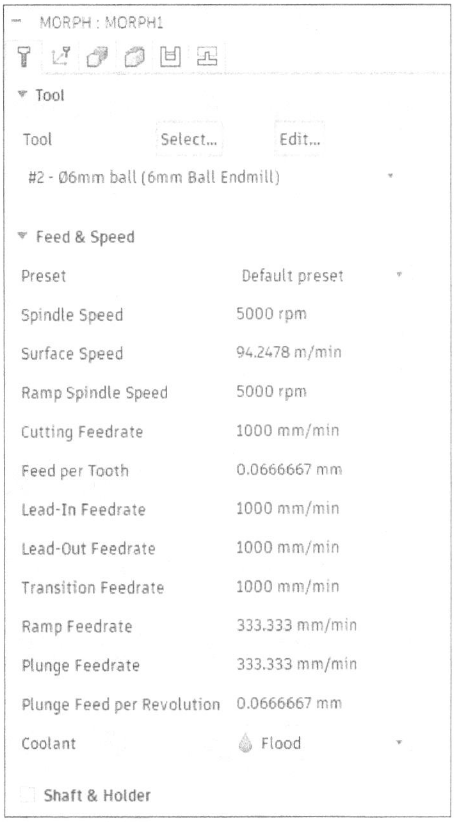

Figure-22. MORPH dialog box

- Click on the **Select** button of **Tool** section from **Tool** tab. The **Select Tool** dialog box will be displayed. Select the required tool, generally a ball or bull nose end mill.
- Select the curve to be used as containment boundaries for toolpath from the model; refer to Figure-23.

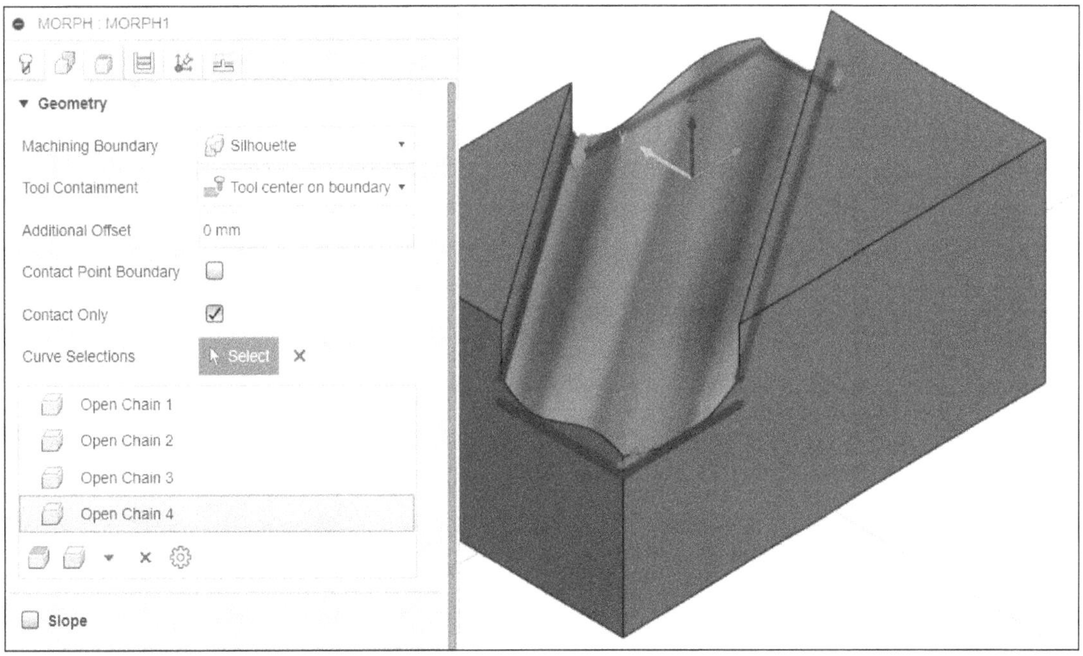

Figure-23. Curves selected for morph toolpath

- Select desired option from the **Morph Mode** drop-down in the **Passes** tab of dialog box to define how direction of toolpath will be decided. Select the **Simple** option to create linear movements of tool from one curve chain side to another. Select the **Closest** option from drop-down to make cutting tool jump to nearest point in another side while cutting. Note that sometimes selecting **Closest** option can cause unmachined areas of model. Use this option when all the chain sides are equal.
- The options of the dialog box are same as discussed earlier.
- After specifying the various parameters, click on the **OK** button from the **MORPH** dialog box. The toolpath will be generated and displayed on the model; refer to Figure-24.

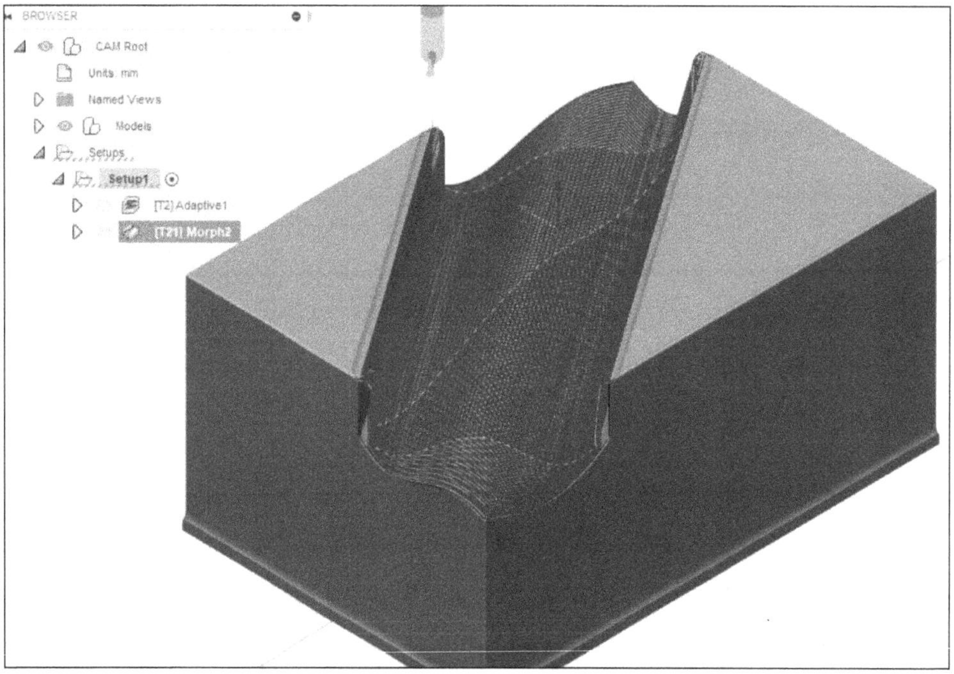

Figure-24. Toolpath generated for Morph tool

Creating Flow Toolpath

The Flow toolpath is used to machine irregular surfaces of the model by following isocurves of the model. By default, the flow toolpaths are 3D toolpaths but you can also activate the multi-axes mode if tilting of tool axis is required. Using this toolpath offers a better finish of 3D surfaces. The procedure to create this toolpath is given next.

- Click on the **Flow** tool from the **3D** drop-down in the **Ribbon**. The **Flow** dialog box will be displayed; refer to Figure-25.

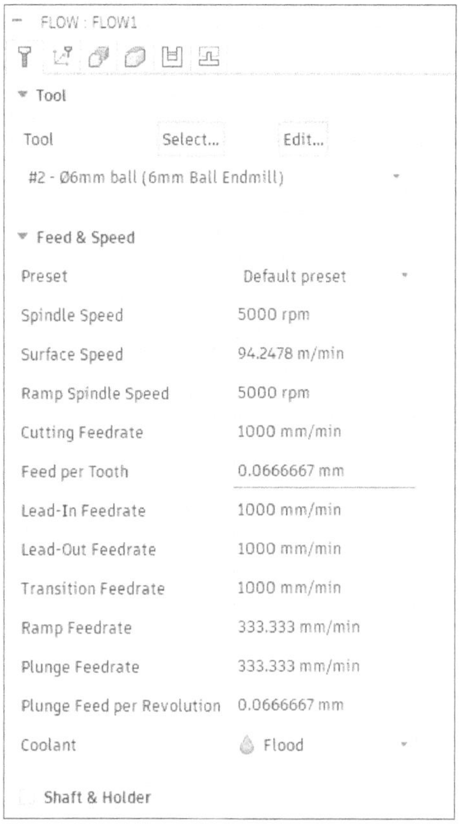

Figure-25. Flow dialog box

- Click on the **Select** button and select desired fillet tool, generally a ball end mill. Specify desired feed and speed parameters.
- Click on the **Geometry** tab and select the round faces on which you want to apply flow toolpath; refer to Figure-26.

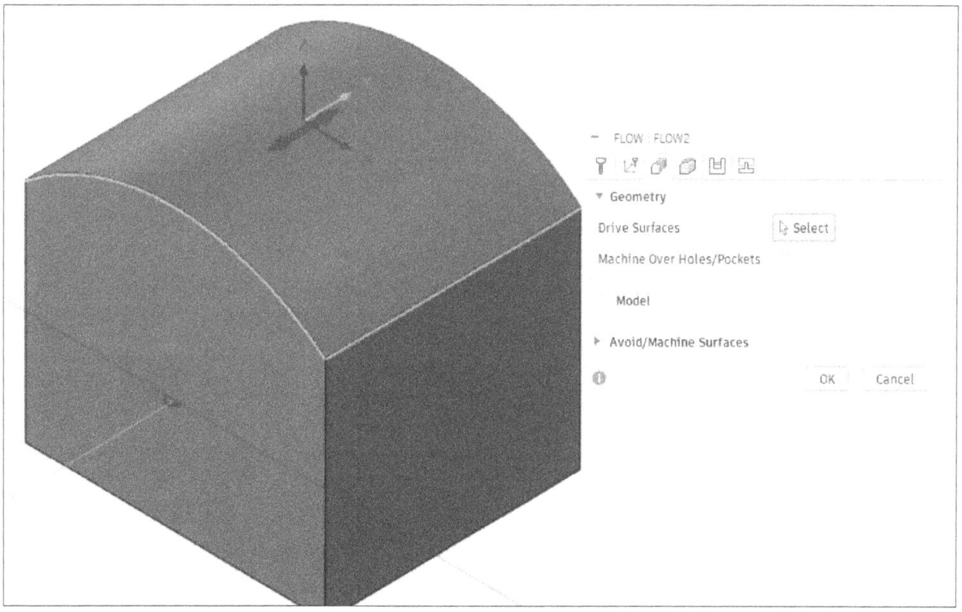

Figure-26. Faces selected for flow toolpath

- Click on the **Passes** tab in the dialog box. The options will be displayed as shown in Figure-27.

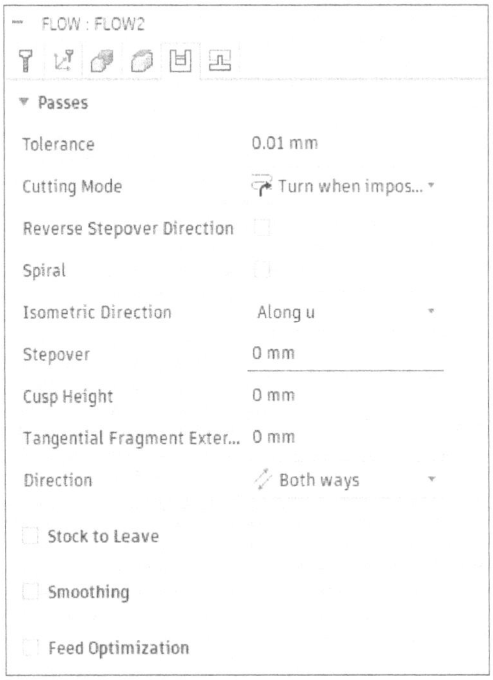

Figure-27. Passes tab for Flow dialog box

- Select the **Along u** option from **Isometric Direction** drop-down if you want the flow lines along X axis while cutting. Select the **Along v** option from the drop-down if you want the flow lines along Y axis while cutting. Note that the selected flow direction will be displayed on the model by two headed arrow on the face of model; refer to Figure-26.
- Specify desired value of **Number of Stepovers** edit box to increase the finishing steps of cut. Note that cutting tool will perform only specified number of cutting passes so make sure to input a high value for better finish.
- Click on **Multi-Axis** tab in the dialog box and select the **5-axis** button to allow tilting of tool/workpiece bed to create multi-axis toolpath.
- Specify other parameters as discussed earlier and click on the **OK** button. The toolpath will be created; refer to Figure-28.

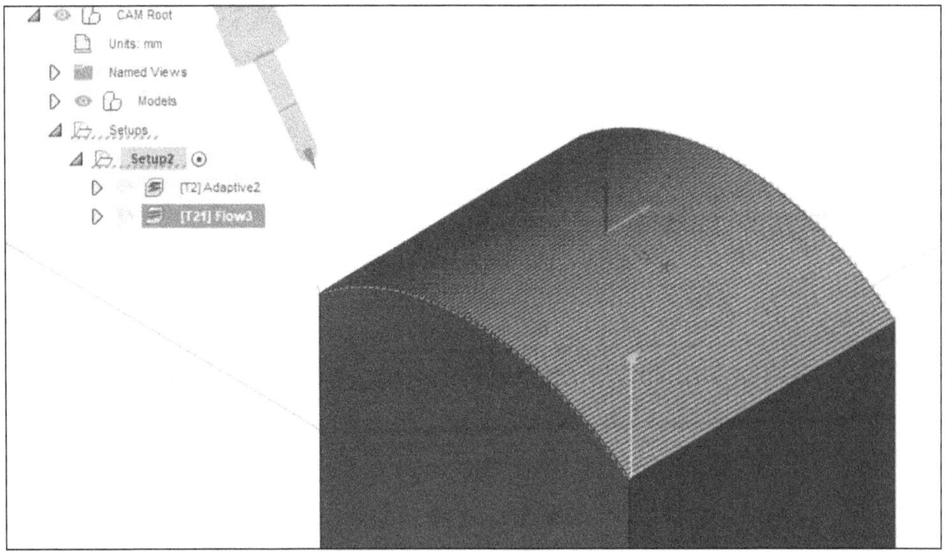

Figure-28. Flow toolpath created

Creating Corner Toolpath

The Corner toolpath is used to machine the areas formed at intersection of steep and shallow faces of the part. Note that this toolpath is used for finishing passes after roughing operation has been performed. The procedure to create this toolpath is given next.

- After perform roughing and finishing operations on the part, click on the **Corner** tool from the **3D** drop-down in the **MILLING** tab of the **Ribbon**. The **CORNER** dialog box will be displayed; refer to Figure-29.
- Click on the **Select** button from the **Tool** tab and select a tool (preferably ball end mill) of diameter lower than tools earlier used for machining operation because corner toolpath is generally used as rest machining finish toolpath.
- Click on the **Geometry** tab in the dialog box to define the geometry to be machined. The options will be displayed as shown in Figure-30.

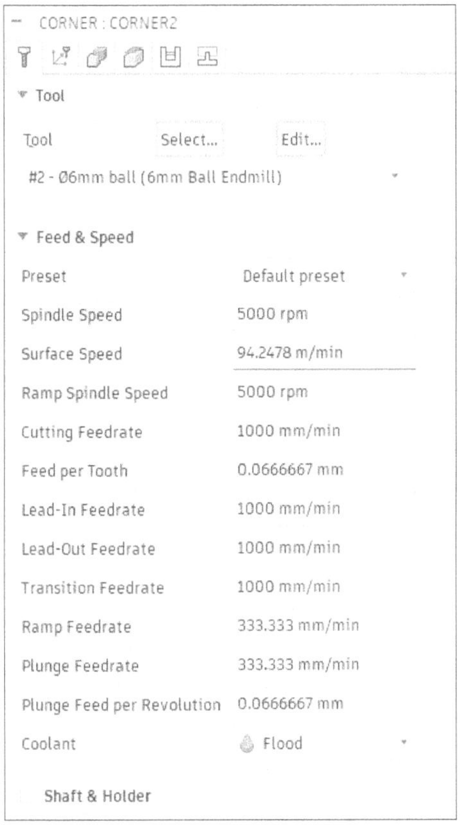

Figure-29. CORNER dialog box

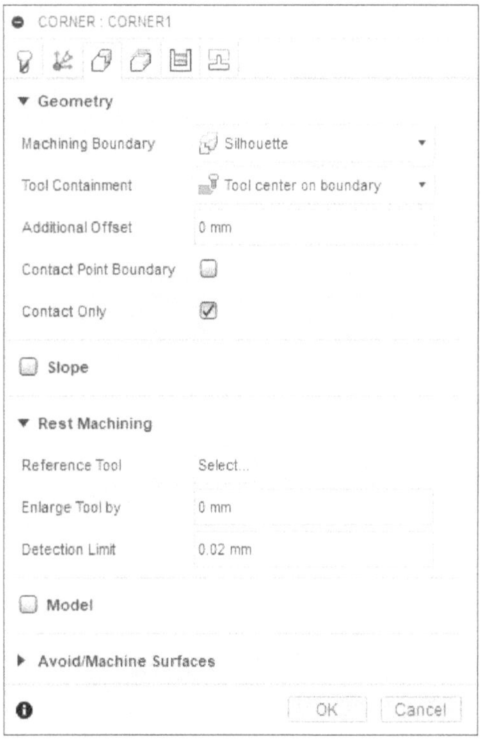

Figure-30. Geometry tab in CORNER dialog box

- Click on the **Select** button for **Reference Tool** option in the **Rest Machining** section of the dialog box and select the cutting tool using which you have performed previous operations.
- Click on the **Passes** tab to define parameters related to cutting passes. The options will be displayed as shown in Figure-31.
- Specify desired value in **Threshold Angle** edit box to define angle limit against horizontal plane above which faces will be considered steep and below which faces will be considered shallow.
- Select desired option from the **Priority** drop-down to define whether toolpath will start from top in selected geometry or it will start by machining steep faces.

- Select desired option from the **Type** drop-down in the **Steep Passes** section of the dialog box to define the direction in which cutting passes will be generated for steep faces. Select the **Along with maximum stepover** option from the **Type** drop-down to create toolpath following direction the cutting passes of previous toolpaths with maximum step over value as per rest material cutting passes. In this case step over will automatically increase in wide area of material and decrease in narrow areas of material in stock. Select the **Along with constant stepover** option from drop-down to maintain fixed stepover value irrespective of material conditions on stock. Select the **Across** option from the drop-down to create cutting passes crossing the previous rest machining cutting passes. Select the **None** option from the drop-down if you do not want to create steep cutting passes.

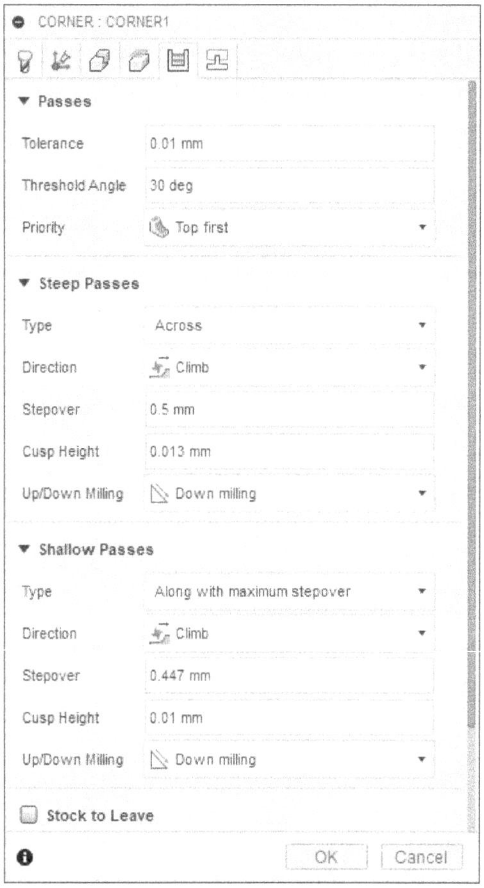

Figure-31. Passes tab in CORNER dialog box

- Similarly, you can set other options in the dialog box. After setting desired parameters, click on the **OK** button to create the toolpath. The toolpath will be created; refer to Figure-32.

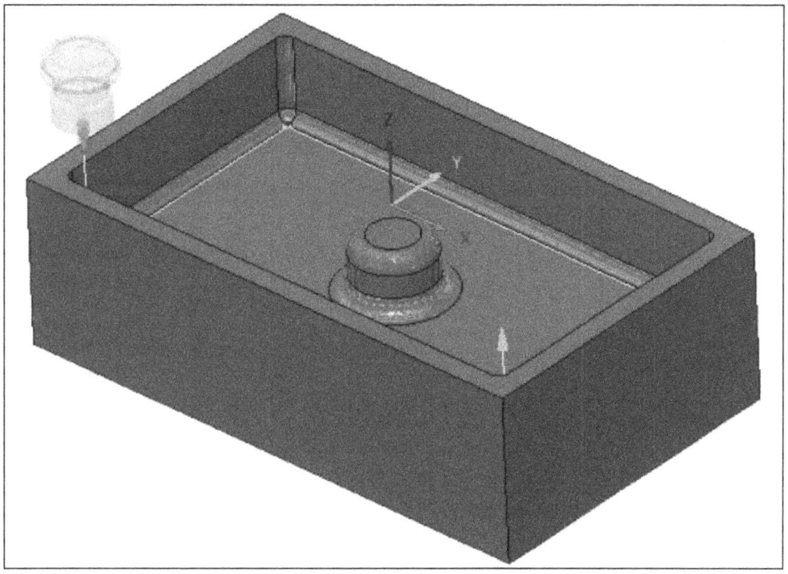

Figure-32. Corner toolpath

Creating Deburr Toolpath

The Deburr toolpath is used to remove material from sharp corners and edges of the part. This is a finishing toolpath generally used after performing rest of the finishing toolpaths. The procedure to create this toolpath is given next.

- Click on the **Deburr** tool from the **3D** drop-down in the **MILLING** tab of the **Ribbon**. The **DEBURR** dialog box will be displayed; refer to Figure-33.
- Select the **Geometry** tab from the dialog box to define geometry selection for the toolpath. The options will be displayed as shown in Figure-34.

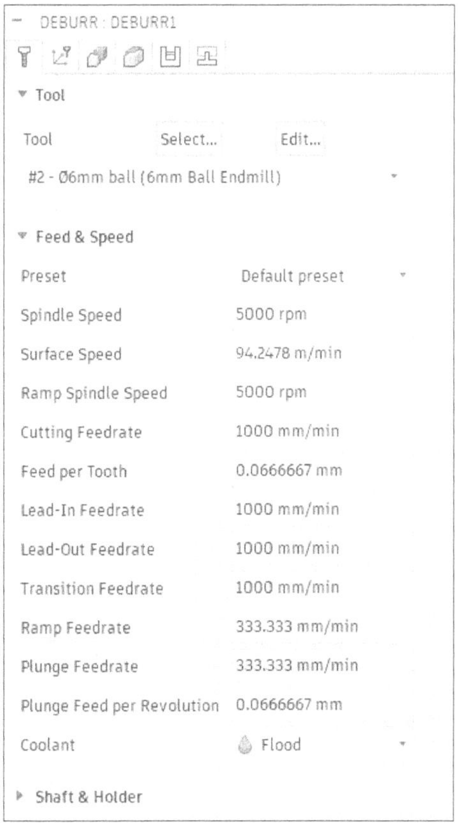

Figure-33. DEBURR dialog box

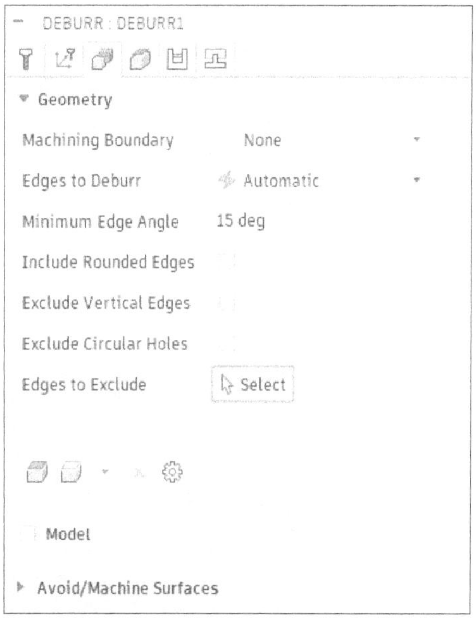

Figure-34. Geometry tab of DEBURR dialog box

- Select the **Selection** option from the **Machining Boundary** drop-down if you want to manually define machining boundary. Select the **None** option from drop-down to let software automatically decide machining boundary based on stock.
- Select the **Automatic** option from the **Edges to Deburr** drop-down to let software automatically identify sharp edges in the stock. The options to exclude selected edges from deburring toolpath will be displayed at the bottom in **Geometry** section of dialog box. Select the **Selection** option from the drop-down to manually select the edges to be deburred. The options to select edges will be displayed in the **Geometry** section.
- Click on the **Passes** tab from the dialog box to define deburring toolpath parameters. The options will be displayed as shown in Figure-35.

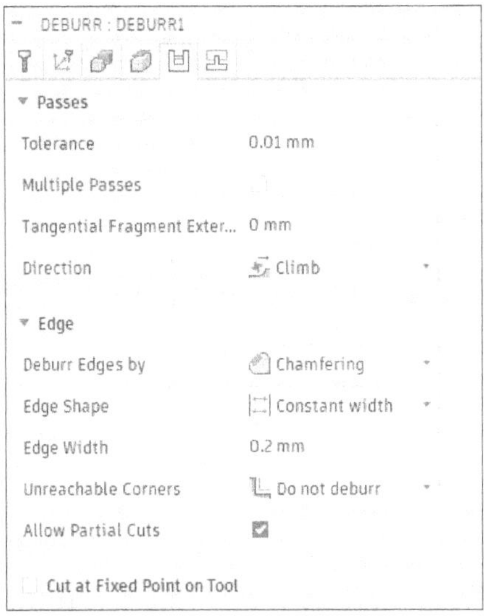

Figure-35. Passes tab of DEBURR dialog box

- Select the **Chamfering** option from the **Deburr Edges** by drop-down to create chamfers on sharp edges based on parameters specified below the drop-down. Select the **Filleting** option from the **Deburr Edges** by drop-down to create fillets (rounds) on sharp edges.
- Set the other parameters as discussed earlier and click on the **OK** button from dialog box to create the toolpath; refer to Figure-36.

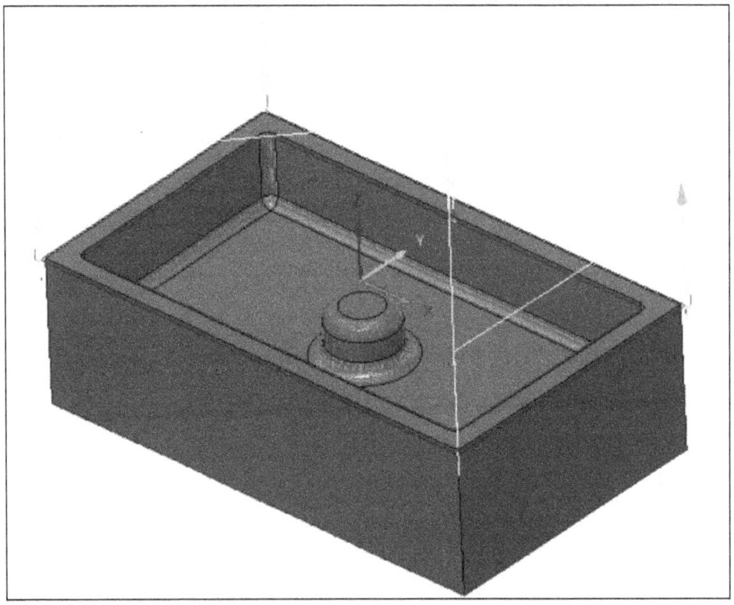

Figure-36. Deburr toolpath

Creating Geodesic Toolpath

The Geodesic toolpath is combination of Scallop and Blend toolpaths earlier discussed. This toolpath is used for finishing. The major difference between using those toolpaths and geodesic toolpath is that geodesic toolpath uses surface instead of curve chains to perform machining. Selecting surface as reference for cutting toolpath allows to create perfect harmony between cutting passes and curvature of surface of the part. The procedure to create geodesic toolpath is given next.

- After performing all the roughing operations and pre-required finishing operations, click on the **Geodesic** tool from the **3D** drop-down in the **MILLING** tab of the **Ribbon**. The **GEODESIC** dialog box will be displayed.
- Select desired cutting tool from the **Tool** tab in the dialog box (preferably Ball End Mill) as discussed earlier.
- Select the **Geometry** tab in the dialog box to define geometry to be machined by the toolpath. The options in the dialog box will be displayed; refer to Figure-37.

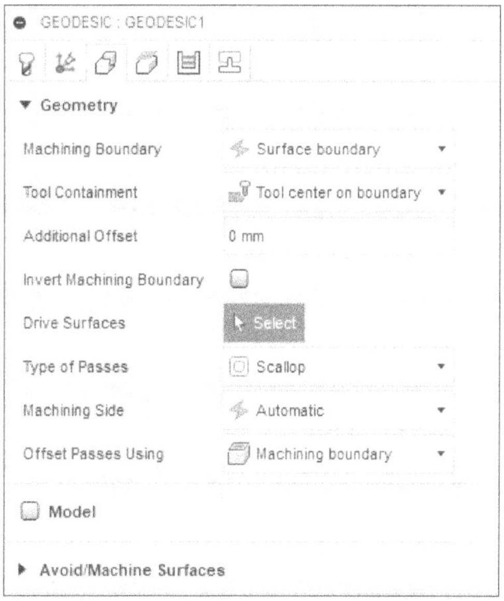

Figure-37. Geometry tab in GEODESIC dialog box

- Select the **Surface boundary** option from the **Machining Boundary** drop-down to use selected surface edges as confinement reference for toolpath. Selected surface will also be used as drive surface which means toolpaths will be offset replica of selected surface. Select the **Silhouette boundary** option from the drop-down to use boundaries of selected surface (when looked from Z axis) as confinement outline for toolpath. Select the **Selection and silhouette** option from the drop-down to manually specify machining boundary along with drive surface. Select the **Selection** option from the drop-down to confine toolpath to selected geometry.
- If the **Silhouette boundary** option is selected in the **Machining Boundary** drop-down then the **Silhouette Defined For** drop-down will be displayed; refer to Figure-38. Select the **Tool contact on outer edges** option from the drop-down to allow tool to cut from outside of outer edge of containment boundary. This will make cutting tool to remove some extra material which is near the outer edge of containment boundary. Select the **Top of Vertical walls** option from the drop-down to make the cutting tool move from top on outer edge of containment boundary. Select the **Bottom of vertical walls** option from the drop-down to allow tool to reach bottom edges of the vertical walls in the stock; refer to Figure-39.

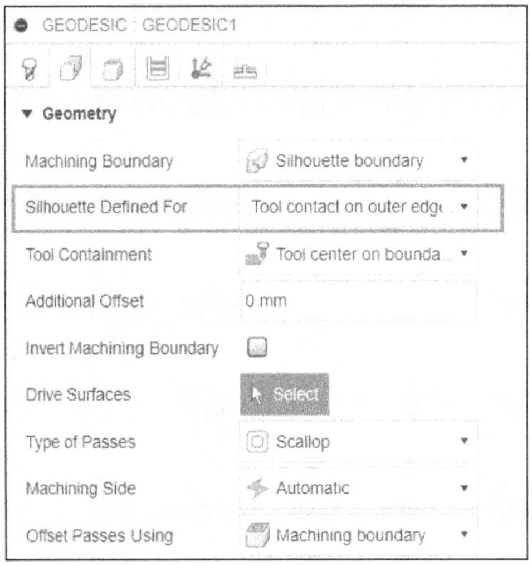

Figure-38. Silhouette Defined For drop-down

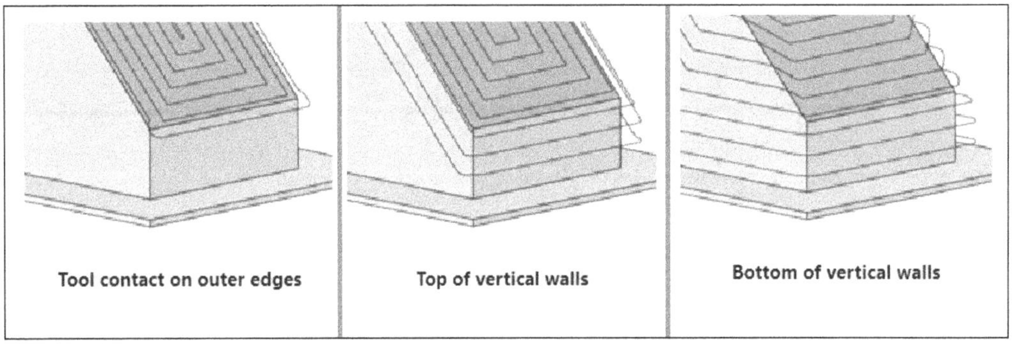

Figure-39. Silhouette Defined For drop-down options

- Select desired option from the **Tool Containment** drop-down to define whether cutting tool will move inside the boundary, outside the boundary, and tool centered on the boundary outline.
- Specify desired value in the **Additional Offset** edit box to provide extension to toolpaths at boundaries. A negative value in this edit box will reduce the toolpaths at boundaries.
- Select the **Invert Machining Boundary** check box to switch from machining steep faces to shallow faces.
- Click on the **Select** button for **Drive Surfaces** from the dialog box and select the surface(s) of the model to be machined.
- Select the **Scallop** option from the **Type of Passes** drop-down to machine shallow areas in a pocket type region. Select the **Blend** option from the **Type of Passes** drop-down to create toolpath which blends two boundary curves using offset cutting passes; refer to Figure-40.
- Select desired option from the **Machining Side** drop-down to define whether tool will be on left side of cutting passes or right side of cutting passes when performing machining.
- Select desired option from the **Offset Passes Using** drop-down to define how direction and orientation of cutting passes will be set. Select the **Machining Boundary** option from the drop-down to offset edges of the boundary reference selected in the **Machining Boundary** drop-down. Note that system will generate a combined curvature of machining boundary outlines to define offset cutting passes in this case.

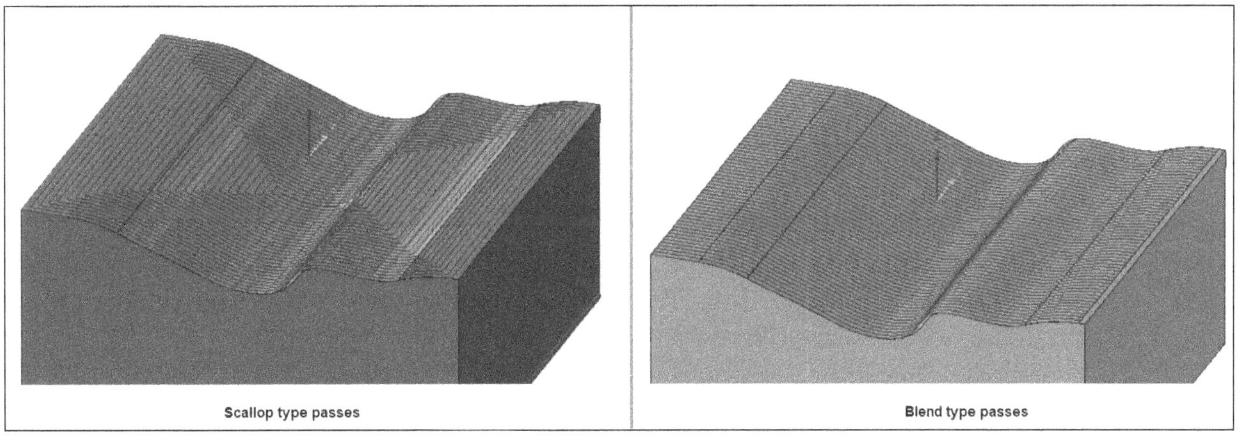

Figure-40. Type of passes for geodesic toolpath

- Select the **Surface Boundary** option from the **Offset Passes Using** drop-down to use outer edges of selected surfaces as reference for offsetting cutting passes. Select the **Circle at center** from the drop-down to move the tool to center of selected surfaces and then move outward for creating cutting passes in circular motion. Select the **Curve selections** option from the drop-down if you want to manually specify reference curves to be used offsetting cutting passes. Select the **Line at center** option from the drop-down to create a line cutting pass at center of selected surfaces and this line is offset to create toolpaths.
- Select the **Tool Orientation** check box and expand the section to modify parameters related to cutting tool orientation during machining. The options will be displayed as shown in Figure-41.

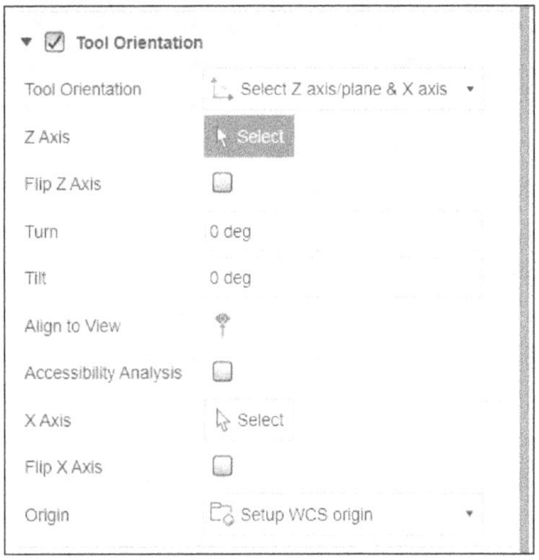

Figure-41. Tool orientation for Geodesic toolpath

- Select the **Accessibility Analysis** check box to check the areas that are not accessible by current cutting tool. All the accessible areas will be shown in green color and inaccessible areas will be shown in red color. Note that these red areas can be undercuts or areas where cutting tool size cannot reach and you will need smaller diameter tool to perform machining.
- Specify the other parameters as discussed earlier and click on the **OK** button. The toolpath will be generated.

MULTI-AXIS TOOLPATH

Till now, we have discussed the procedure of creating 2D and 3D toolpath. In this section, we will discuss the procedure of creating multi-axis toolpaths which are used to machine complex 3D shapes.

Creating Rotary Pocket Toolpath

The Rotary Pocket toolpath is used to machine grooves in rotary parts that generally need 4th axis as well for machining. The procedure to create this toolpath is given next.

- Click on the **Rotary Pocket** tool from the **MULTI-AXIS** drop-down in the **MILLING** tab of the **Ribbon**. The **ROTARY POCKET** dialog box will be displayed; refer to Figure-42.
- Select desired cutting from the **Tool** tab as discussed earlier.
- Click on the **Geometry** tab in the dialog box to define stock geometry to be machined. The options will be displayed as shown in Figure-43.

Figure-42. ROTARY POCKET dialog box

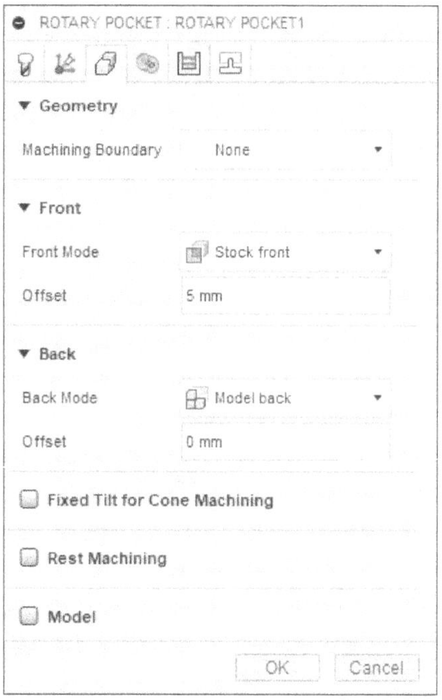

Figure-43. Geometry tab of ROTARY POCKET dialog box

- Select the **None** option from the **Machining Boundary** drop-down to machine the full stock. Select the **Selection** option from the drop-down if you want to manually specify the boundary of stock to be machined.
- Set desired options in the **Front Mode** and **Back Mode** drop-downs of **Geometry** tab to define front side of stock and back side of stock.
- Select the **Fixed Tilt for Cone Machining** check box to set the tool tilt at a specified fixed angle for machining undercuts.
- Click on the **Passes** tab to define parameters related to cutting passes. The options will be displayed as shown in Figure-44.

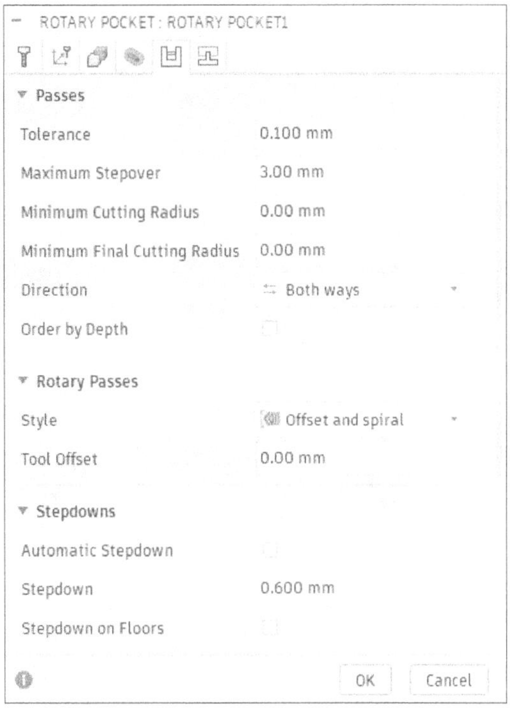

Figure-44. Passes tab in ROTARY POCKET dialog box

- Select desired option from the **Rotary Axis** drop-down in **Rotary Axis** section of **Multi-Axis** tab in dialog box to define axis to be used for defining stock orientation on machine.
- Select desired option from the **Style** drop-down to define whether you want to create only offset cutting passes or you want to include spiral cutting passes along with offset cutting passes depending on geometry.
- Select the **Exclude Small Areas** check box if you do not want to machine small areas which have gap less than percentage of diameter specified in the **Threshold as % of Tool Diameter** edit box.
- Select the **Machine Over Gaps** check box if you want to continue machining over small gaps rather creating linking moves which increase total machining time. On selecting this check box, the **Max Gap Size** edit box will be displayed to specify the size of gap for which cutting pass will continue. If the gap is larger than specified value then linking pass will be created.
- Set the other parameters in dialog box as discussed earlier and click on the **OK** button to create the toolpath; refer to Figure-45.

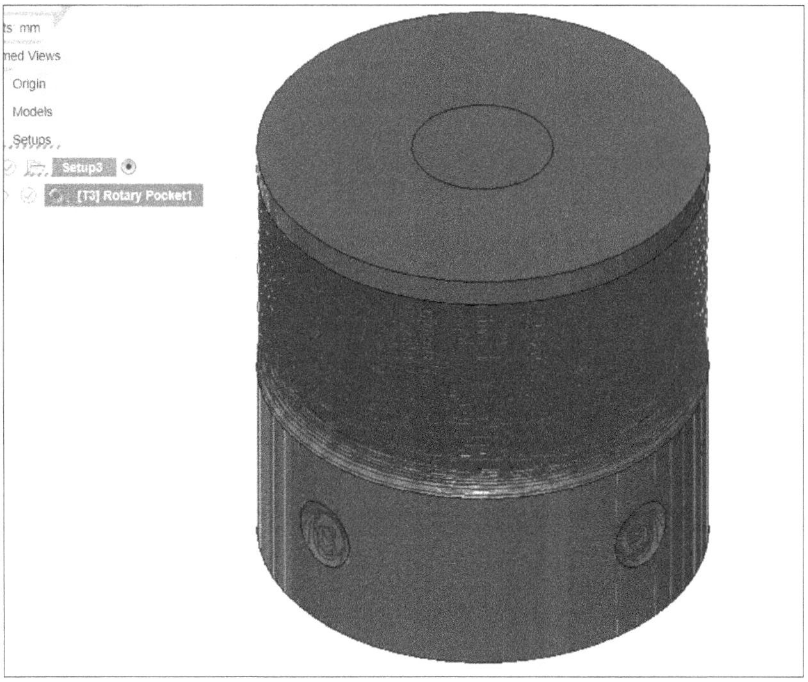

Figure-45. Rotary pocket toolpath

Creating Swarf Toolpath

Swarf is a multi-axis toolpath which is used for side cutting of model. It is used for milling the beveled edges and tapered walls. The procedure to create this toolpath is discussed next.

- Click on the **Swarf** tool of **MULTI-AXIS** drop-down from **Toolbar**; refer to Figure-46. The **SWARF** dialog box will be displayed; refer to Figure-47.

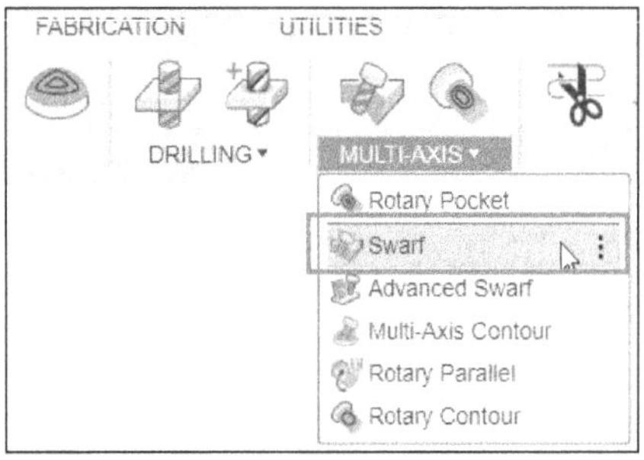

Figure-46. Swarf tool

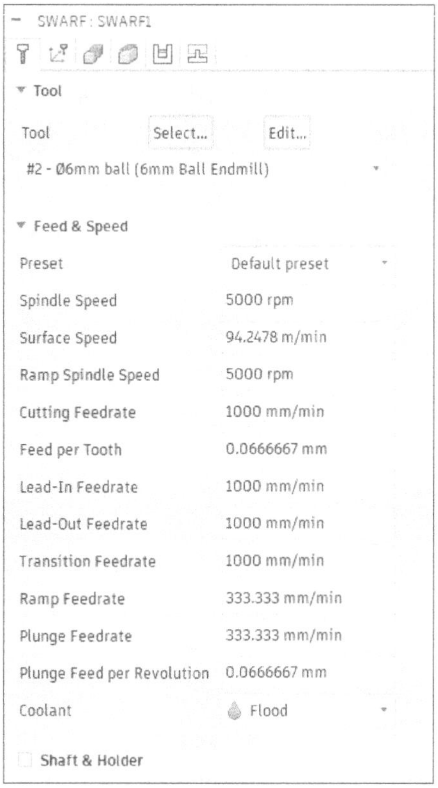

Figure-47. SWARF dialog box

- Click on the **Select** button of **Tool** section from **Tool** tab. The **Select Tool** dialog box will be displayed. Select desired tool generally, a ball end mill.

Geometry

- Click on the **Geometry** tab of **SWARF** dialog box. The **Geometry** tab will be displayed; refer to Figure-48.

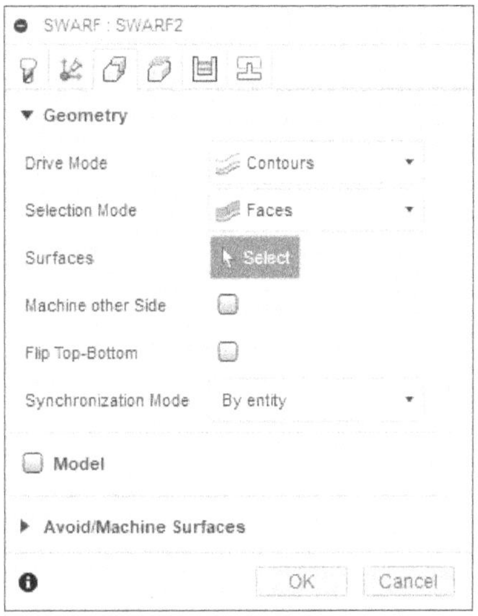

Figure-48. Geometry tab of SWARF dialog box

- Select the **Contours** option from **Drive Mode** drop-down to use boundary chains of selected face of model as driving element for cutting toolpaths. Driving element is the reference surface which defines direction and orientation of cutting passes.
- Select the **Surfaces** option from **Drive Mode** drop-down to use selected surfaces of the model as driving element for cutting toolpaths.
- Select **Faces** option from **Selection Mode** drop-down to select continuous faces from model which are to be machined.
- Select **Contour pairs** option from **Selection Mode** drop-down to select the upper and lower edge chains from the tapered face to be machined.
- Select **Manual** option from **Selection Mode** drop-down to select individual surfaces to be machined from the model.
- The **Select** button of **Surfaces** or **Geometry** section (depending on option selected in **Selection Mode** drop-down) is active by default. You need to select the face, edges, or contours as desired.
- Select the **Machine other Side** check box of **Geometry** section to force the toolpath to be created on the other side of selected contour.
- Select the **Flip Top-Bottom** check box of **Geometry** section to change the direction of tool by switching the lower and upper contour. This option will only be applied when **Contours pairs** option is not selected in the **Select Mode** drop-down.
- Click in the **Synchronization Mode** drop-down from **Geometry** tab and select desired option if **Contours** option is selected in the **Drive Mode** drop-down. The option specified in this drop-down defines how two consecutive cutting passes are related to each other.

Passes

- Click on the **Passes** tab of the **SWARF** dialog box. The options of **Passes** tab will be displayed; refer to Figure-49.

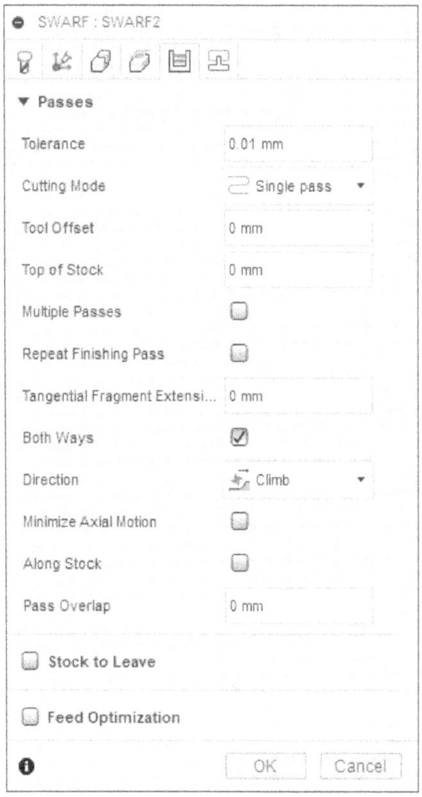

Figure-49. Passes tab of SWARF dialog box

- Click on the **Cutting Mode** drop-down of **Passes** tab and select the required option to specify the pattern in which cutting passes will be created; refer to Figure-50.

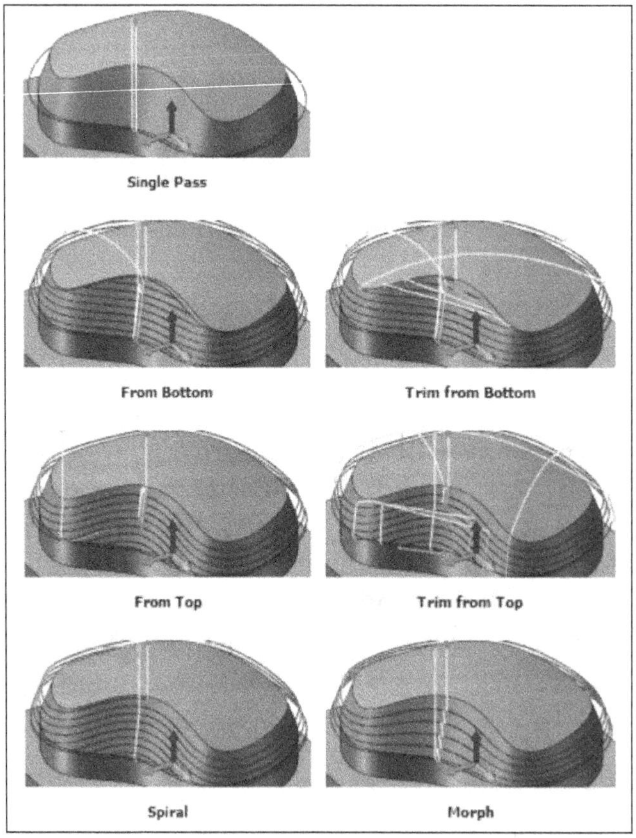

Figure-50. Cutting mode options

- Click in the **Tool Offset** edit box of **Passes** tab and enter the value of tool offset along the tool axis relative to the bottom guide curve. The cutting tool will be away from face of model by specified value.
- Click in the **Top of Stock** edit box of **Passes** tab to specify the overall thickness of the stock.
- Select the **Repeat Finishing Passes** check box of **Passes** tab to perform an additional finishing pass with zero stock.
- Specify desired value in the **Tangential Fragment Extension Distance** edit box of **Passes** tab to extends the cut tangentially at both ends of the pass.
- Select the **Minimize axial Motion** check box of **Passes** tab to minimize the motion of tool.
- Select the **Along Stock** check box of **Passes** tab to move the tool along stock for machining.
- Click in the **Pass Overlap** edit box of **Passes** tab and enter the value of distance to extend machining for a closed pass.
- Click on the **Maximum Fan Distance** edit box of **Multi-Axis** tab and specify maximum distance up to which the tool axis can fan out. As the toolpath moves from one surface to another, there can be a change in the ruling direction causing the tool axis to move. This is called fanning.
- Click in the **Maximum Segment Length** edit box of **Multi-Axis** tab and specify the value of maximum length for a single segment to be generated for toolpath.
- Click in the **Maximum Tool Axis Sweep** edit box of **Multi-Axis** tab and specify the maximum angle up to which the tool can deviate about its axis while cutting.
- The other options of the dialog box are same as discussed earlier. After specifying desired parameters, click on the **OK** button from **SWARF** dialog box. The toolpath will be generated and displayed on the model; refer to Figure-51.

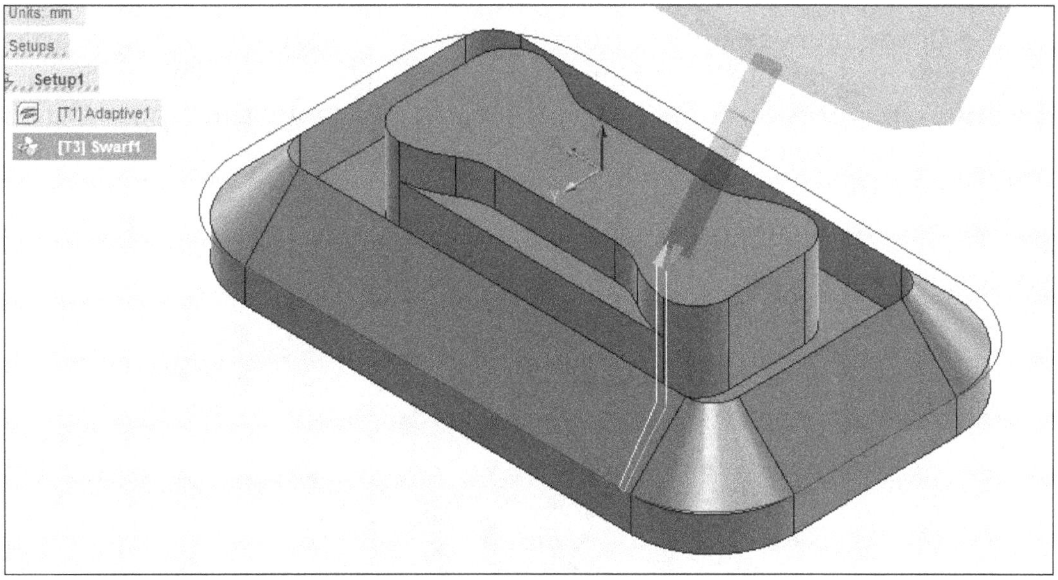

Figure-51. Toolpath generated for Swarf tool

Creating Advanced Swarf Toolpath

The Advanced Swarf toolpath is used to perform swarf milling with precise control on clearance and orientation of cutting tool. The procedure to use this tool is given next.

- Click on the **Advanced Swarf** tool from the **MULTI-AXIS** drop-down in the **MILLING** tab of the **Ribbon**. The **ADVANCED SWARF** dialog box will be displayed; refer to Figure-52.

- Select desired cutting tool from the **Tool** tab in the dialog box as discussed earlier.
- Select the **Geometry** tab from the dialog box to define the geometry to be machined; refer to Figure-53.

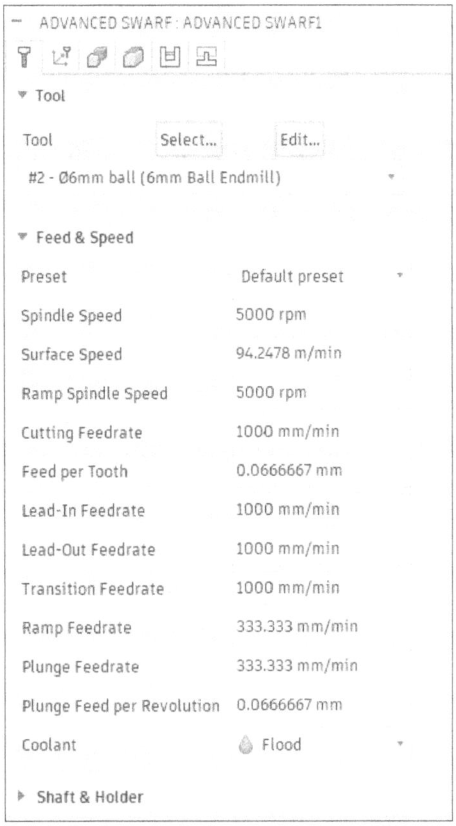

Figure-52. ADVANCED SWARF dialog box

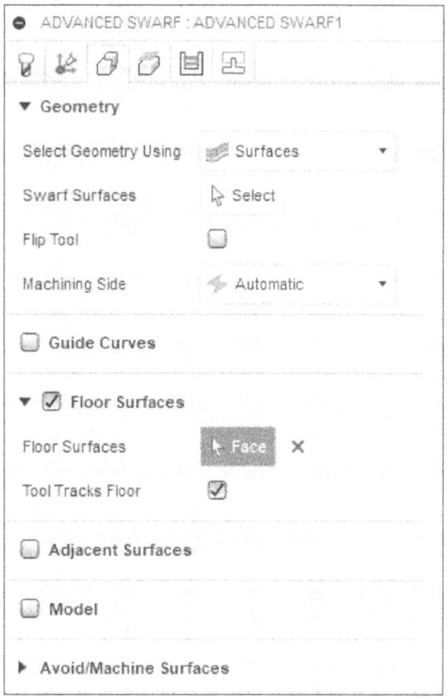

Figure-53. Geometry tab of ADVANCED SWARF dialog box

- Select the **Guide curves** option from the **Select Geometry Using** drop-down in the **Geometry** section of the dialog box to use selected curves as reference for machining. On selecting this option, selection boxes for the Upper Guide Curve and Lower Guide Curve will be displayed. Select the upper curve and lower curve of model; refer to Figure-54.

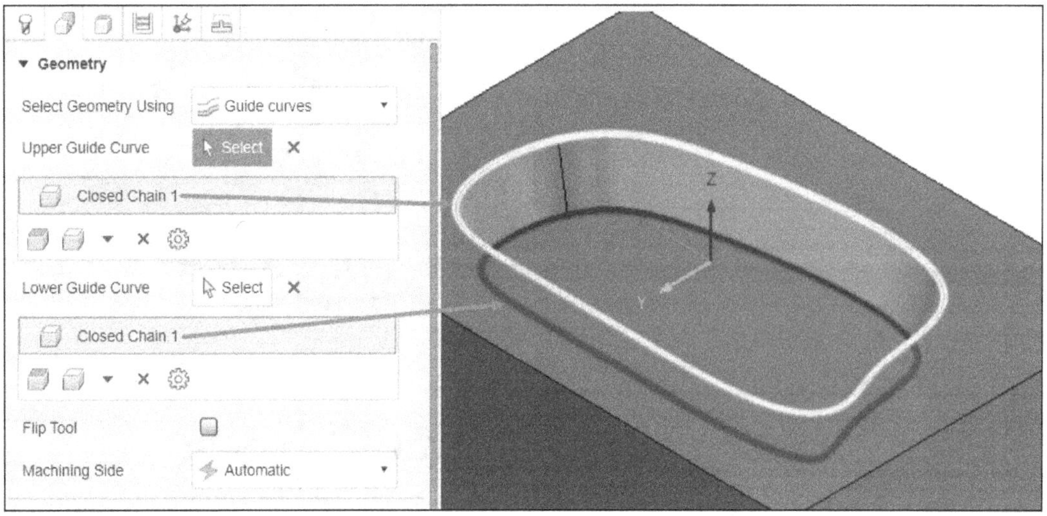

Figure-54. Curves selected for advanced swarf

- Select the **Surfaces** option from the **Select Geometry Using** drop-down to select face/surface for swarf machining; refer to Figure-55.

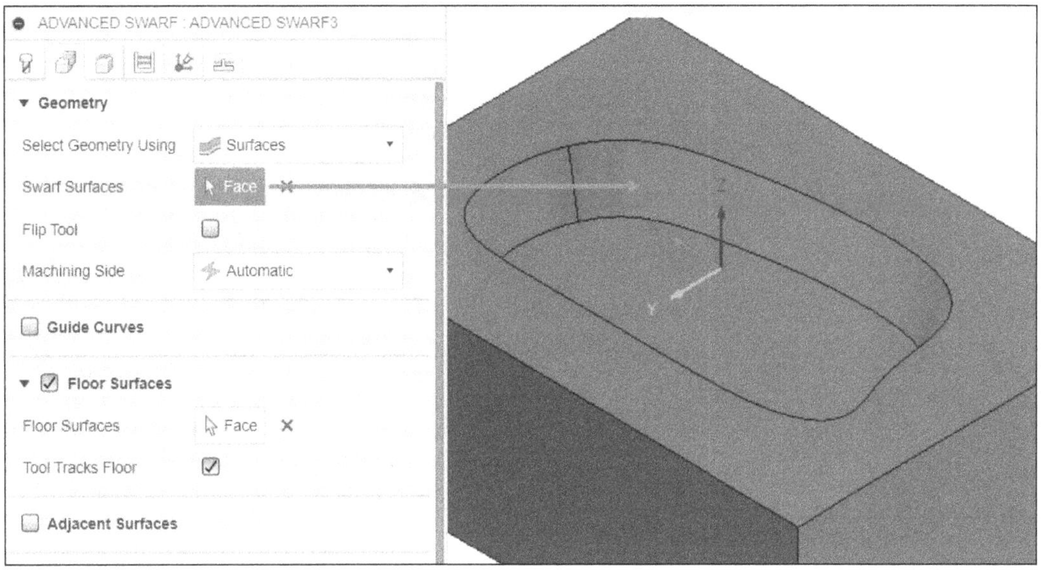

Figure-55. Face selection for swarf milling

- Select the **Guide Curves** check box to define direction references for upper guide curve and lower guide curve.
- Select the **Floor Surfaces** check box to manually define the floor face of the part upto which tool can go when machining. Select the **Tool Tracks Floor** check box to make the cutting tool follow curvature of selected floor face.
- Select the **Adjacent Surfaces** check box to select nearby surfaces for same clearance will be applied which is defined for swarf surfaces.
- Select the **Heights** tab from the dialog box to define safe distance at which cutting tool will move during machining operation to avoid accidental contact with stock or machine components.
- Click on the **Passes** tab to define parameters related to cutting passes. Select the **Automatic** option from the **Tool Axis on Extensions** drop-down to create an extension curve tangentially joining upper and lower guide curves to which cutting tool will be aligned. Select the **Align to edges** option from the drop-down to create an extension line joining upper and lower guide curves such that cutting tool is aligned to the edges of the surface.
- Specify desired values in **Start Extension** and **End Extension** edit boxes to define extension lengths for cutting passes at the start and end, respectively.
- Click on the **Multi-Axis** tab from the dialog box to define parameters related to 5-axis milling. Select the **Minimize Rotary Motion** check box to stop the machine from making large C-axis rotations.
- Select the **Manual Synchronization** check box to manually select sketched lines which will be used for alignment of cutting tool when tool reaches them while performing machining.
- Set the other parameters as discussed earlier and click on the **OK** button from the dialog box to create the toolpath; refer to Figure-56.

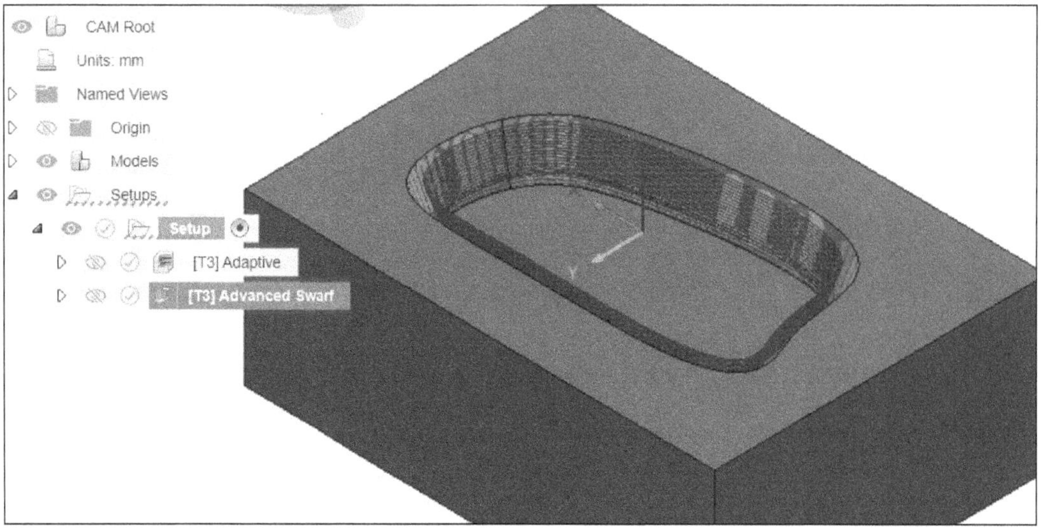

Figure-56. Advanced swarf toolpath example

Creating Multi-Axis Contour Toolpath

The **Multi-Axis Contour** tool is used for machining curves with the help of 5-Axis machining. These curves lie on the face of a model forming different 3D curvatures. The procedure to use this tool is discussed next.

- Click on the **Multi-Axis Contour** tool of the **MULTI-AXIS** drop-down from the **Toolbar**; refer to Figure-57. The **MULTI-AXIS CONTOUR** dialog box will be displayed; refer to Figure-58.

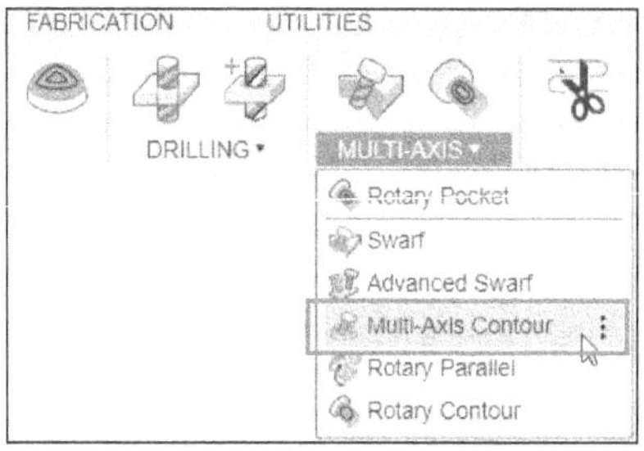

Figure-57. Multi-Axis Contour tool

- Click on the **Select** button of the **Tool** section from the **Tool** tab. The **Select Tool** dialog box will be displayed. Select desired tool, generally a ball end mill.
- Click on the curve of the model to be machined. You can select more than 1 curves for machining.
- Click on the **Passes** tab of **MULTI-AXIS CONTOUR** dialog box. The **Passes** tab will be displayed; refer to Figure-59.
- Click on the **Cutting Mode** drop-down from **MULTI-AXIS CONTOUR** dialog box and select desired option to specify the method for machining along a specific contact path. If the cutting tool cannot move at a certain point of geometry then based on option selected in this drop-down, cutting passes will be created. If **Trim impossible** option is selected in the drop-down then cutting tool will stop at impossible point in toolpath and move to next cutting pass. If **Fail when impossible** option is selected then toolpath will fail. If **Turn when impossible** option is selected then cutting tool will turn to location where it can continue the toolpath.
- Click on the **Multi-Axis** tab to specify parameters for tilting of tool and select the **5-axis** option from the **Machining Type** drop-down if not selected.

Figure-58. MULTI-AXIS CONTOUR dialog box

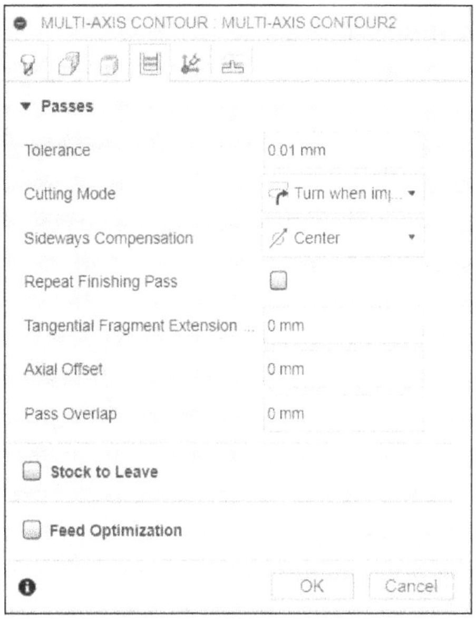

Figure-59. Passes tab of MULTI-AXIS CONTOUR dialog box

- Select desired option from the **Primary Mode** drop-down to how tool can tilt while machining. Select the **Vertical** option from the drop-down to use selected vertical axis for orienting cutting tool. Select the **Lead and lean** option from the drop-down to define tilt angles for cutting tool in XZ and YZ planes. Selecting this option allows to apply a compound tilt angle that can be used to avoid collision and reduce tool wear at single point of cutting tool. Select the **From point** option from the drop-down to use distance and angle from a selected point as reference for tool tilt. Select the **To point** option from the drop-down to tilt the cutting tool at specified angle toward selected point. Select the **From Curve** option from the drop-down to use selected curve as starting reference for tilting cutting tool. Select the **To Curve** option from the drop-down to use selected curve as placement reference of cutting tip of tool.
- Select the **Override Tilt Angle** check box to specify preferred angle which software will try to maintain while cutting.
- Select the **Collision Avoidance** check box to tilt cutting tool as per selected reference so that collision with machine components and stock is avoided.
- Select the **Tool Axis Limits** check box to specify minimum and maximum tool tilt limit. Click in the **Minimum Tilt Angle** edit box and specify the minimum value of tilting allowed from the selected operation tool axis. Click in the **Maximum Tilt Angle** edit box and specify the maximum value of tilting allowed from the selected operation tool axis.
- The other options of the dialog box are same as discussed earlier. After specifying the parameter, click on the **OK** button from **MULTI-AXIS CONTOUR** dialog box. The toolpath will be generated and displayed on the model; refer to Figure-60.

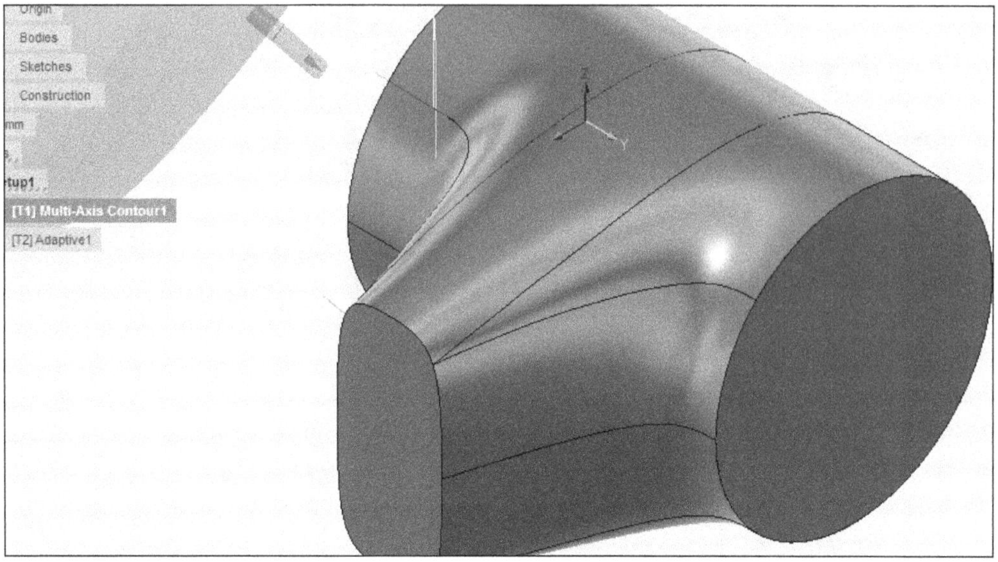

Figure-60. Generated toolpath for Multi-Axis Contour tool

Creating Multi-Axis Rotary Parallel Toolpath

The multi-axis rotary parallel toolpath is created to machine objects with rotary axis using parallel cutting passes. The procedure to create this toolpath is given next.

- Click on the **Rotary Parallel** tool from the **MULTI-AXIS** drop-down in the **MILLING** tab of the **Ribbon**. The **ROTARY PARALLEL** dialog box will be displayed; refer to Figure-61.

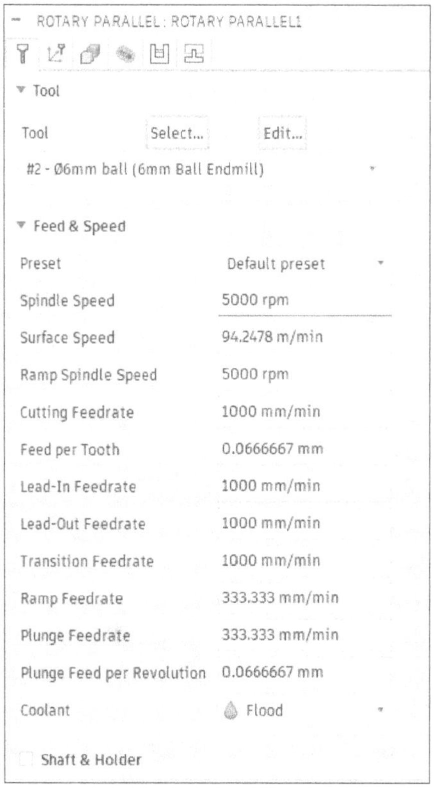

Figure-61. ROTARY PARALLEL dialog box

- Select desired cutting tool and specify cutting feed parameters in the **Tool** tab of dialog box as discussed earlier.

- Click on the **Passes** tab and select desired option from the **Style** drop-down to define pattern for rotary cutting passes. Select the **Spiral** option to generate spiral cutting passes, select the **Line** option to create linear cutting passes, or select the **Circular** option to create concentric circular toolpaths; refer to Figure-62.

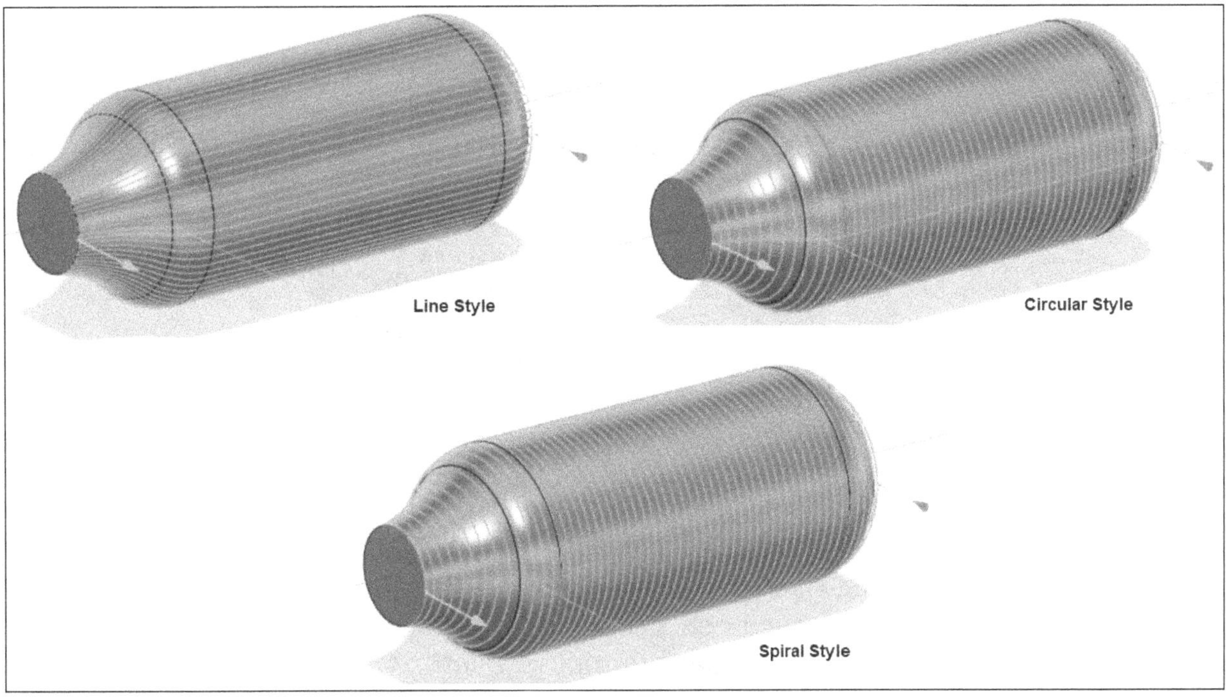

Figure-62. Rotary toolpath styles

- Specify other parameters as discussed earlier in the dialog box and click on the **OK** button. The multi-axis toolpath will be generated.

Creating Multi-Axis Rotary Contour Toolpath

The multi-axis rotary contour toolpath is used to machine steep walls of parts with rotary axis. The procedure to create this toolpath is given next.

- Click on the **Rotary Contour** tool from the **MULTI-AXIS** drop-down in the **MILLING** tab of **Ribbon**. The **ROTARY CONTOUR** dialog box will be displayed.
- Select desired cutting tool from the **Tool** tab in the dialog box.
- Click on the **Multi-Axis** tab in the dialog box and select desired option from the **Rotary Axis** drop-down to define axis direction for stock; refer to Figure-63.

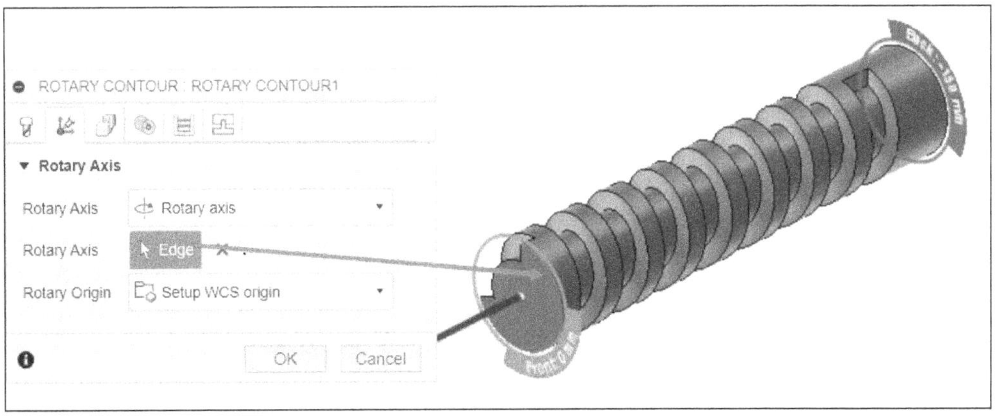

Figure-63. Defining rotary contour axis

- Set the other parameters as discussed earlier and click on the **OK** button from the dialog box. The toolpath will be created; refer to Figure-64.

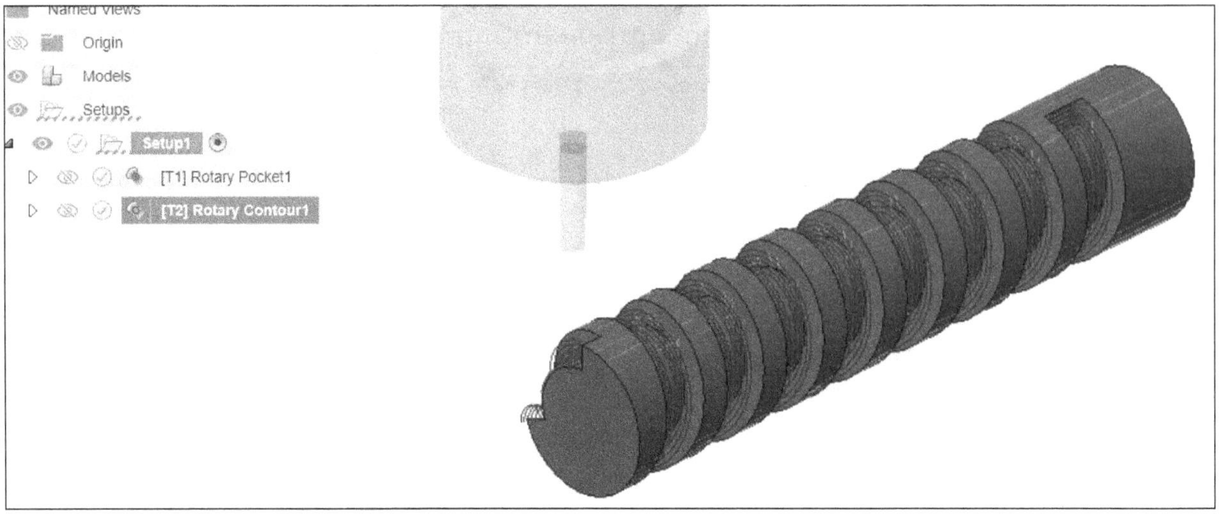

Figure-64. Rotary contour toolpath created

Creating Multi-Axis Finishing Toolpath

The **Multi-Axis Finishing** tool is used to generate finishing toolpath for parts with irregular geometries which have been previously rough machined by various multi-axis toolpaths. The procedure to use this tool is given next.

- Click on the **Multi-Axis Finishing** tool from the **MULTI-AXIS** drop-down in the **Toolbar**. The **MULTI-AXIS FINISHING** dialog box will be displayed.
- Select the **Passes** tab from the dialog box and specify desired value of stepover in the **Stepover** edit box for defining gap between two consecutive cutting passes; refer to Figure-65.

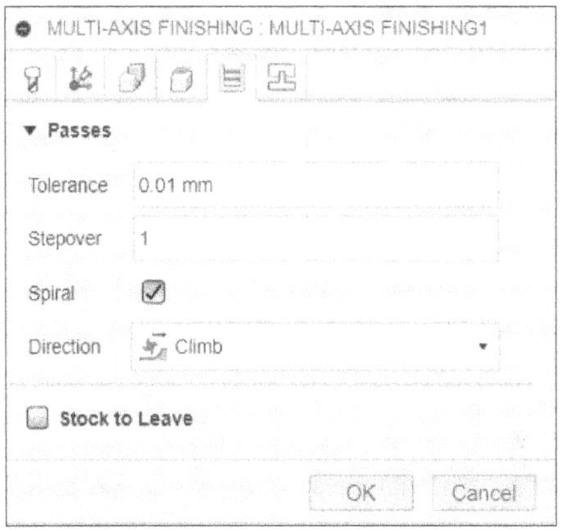

Figure-65. MULTI-AXIS FINISHING dialog box

- Select the **Spiral** check box to make the cutting passes progress in spiral shape.
- Click on the **Geometry** tab in the dialog box and select the **Floor** option from the **Areas to Machine** drop-down if you want to use selected floor surface as reference for generating toolpath. Select the **Wall** option from the drop-down if you want to use selected wall surface as reference for the toolpath. (We are using the Floor option in our case.) Select the geometry reference after selecting desired option; refer to Figure-66.

- Set the other parameters as discussed earlier and click on the **OK** button to generate the toolpath; refer to Figure-67. Note that you may need to use ball end mill for this toolpath.

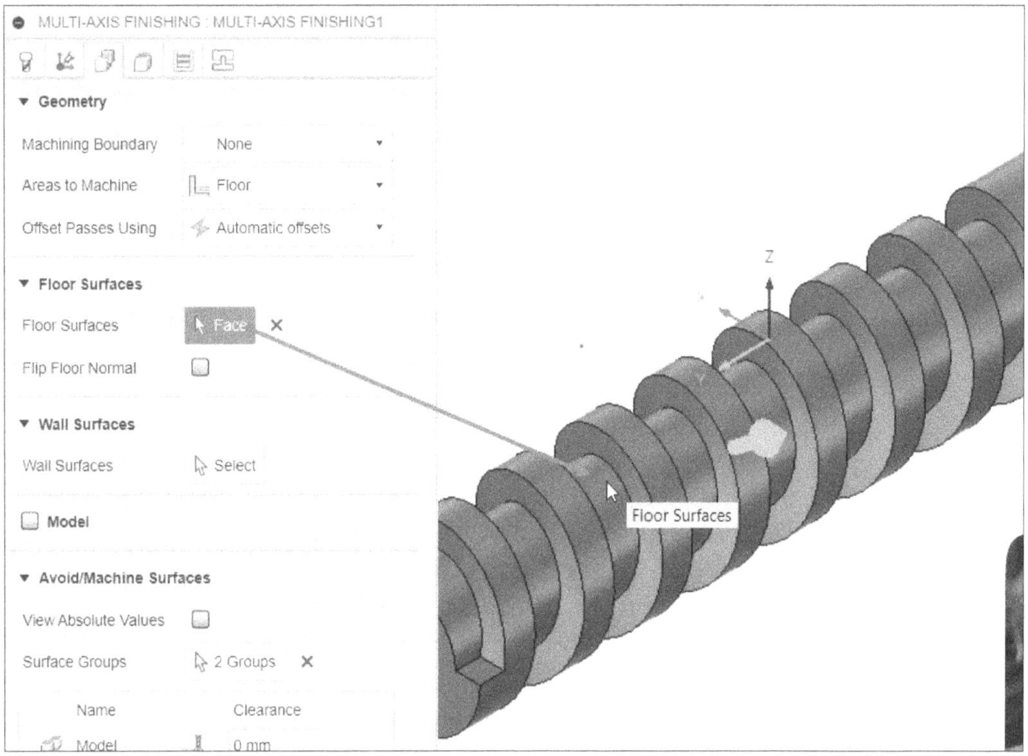

Figure-66. Selecting face for finishing toolpath

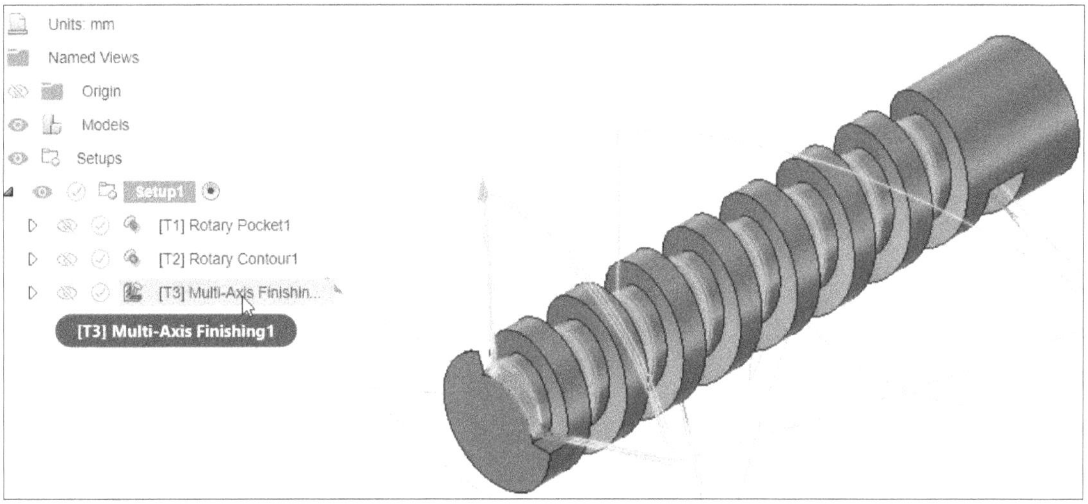

Figure-67. Multi-Axis Finishing toolpath

CREATING DRILL TOOLPATH

The **Drill** tool is used to perform drilling at the specified locations. The procedure to use this tool is discussed next.

- Click on the **Drill** tool from the **DRILLING** panel in the **Toolbar**; refer to Figure-68. The **DRILL** dialog box will be displayed; refer to Figure-69.

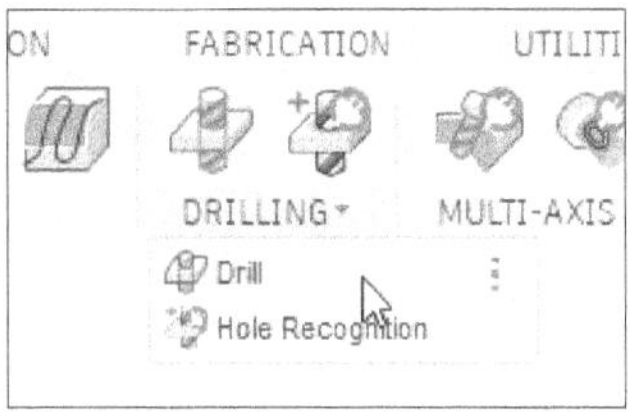

Figure-68. Drill tool

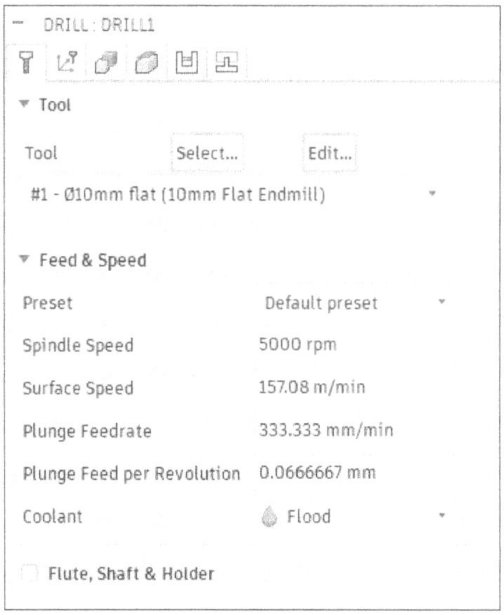

Figure-69. DRILL dialog box

- Click on the **Select** button of **Tool** section from **Tool** tab. The **Select Tool** dialog box will be displayed. Select required drill tool for drilling. Note that you can also select boring, threading, tapping, reaming, and probe tool if you are going to perform related operation.

Geometry

- Click on the **Geometry** tab of **DRILL** dialog box. The **Geometry** tab will be displayed; refer to Figure-70.

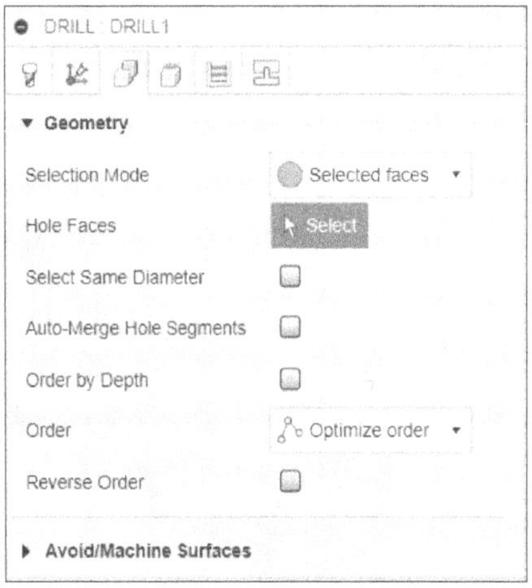

Figure-70. Geometry tab of DRILL dialog box

- Select the **Selected faces** option from **Selection Mode** drop-down to select faces of hole from model for drilling. Select the **Selected points** option from **Selection Mode** drop-down to select points of holes for drilling. Select the **Diameter range** option from drop-down if you want to select all the holes inside specified maximum & minimum diameter range.
- The **Select** button for **Hole Faces/Hole Points/Containment Boundary** section (based on your selection in **Selection Mode** drop-down) of **Geometry** tab is active by default. Click on desired geometries from the model; refer to Figure-71.

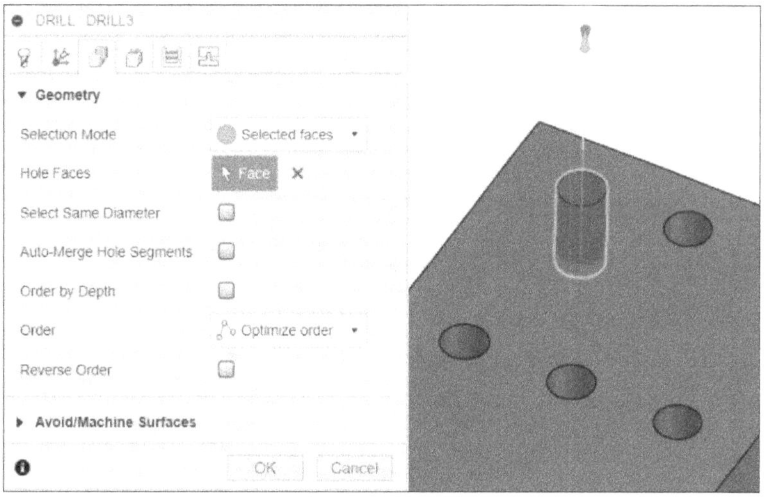

Figure-71. Selection of face for creating hole

- Select the **Select Same Diameter** check box of **Geometry** tab to select the hole of same diameter.
- Select the **Auto-Merge Hole Segments** check box of **Geometry** tab to include the neighboring segments automatically while drilling a hole with multiple segments.
- Select the **Order by Depth** check box of **Geometry** tab to controls the sorting of holes depending on their Z height.
- Select the **Optimize Order** option from the **Order** drop-down to optimize the order of drilling holes.
- Select desired option from the **Order** drop-down to define order of drilling holes.

Cycle

- Click on the **Cycle** tab of **DRILL** dialog box. The options will be displayed; refer to Figure-72.

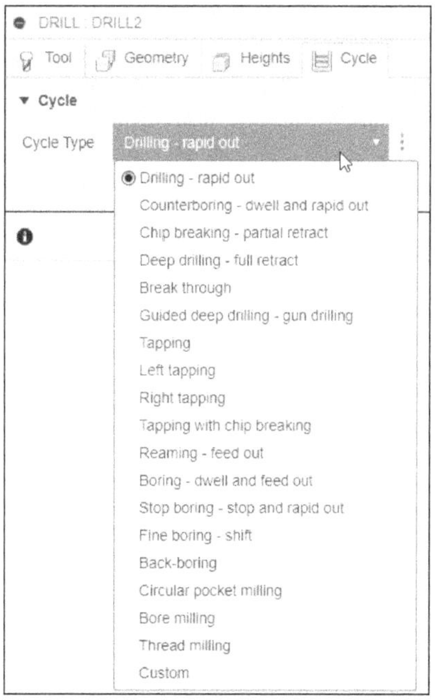

Figure-72. Cycle tab of DRILL dialog box

- Click in the **Cycle Type** drop-down of **Cycle** tab and select desired option.
- The other options of the dialog box are same as discussed earlier.

- After specifying the parameters, click on the **OK** button from **DRILL** dialog box. The toolpath will be generated and displayed on the model; refer to Figure-73.

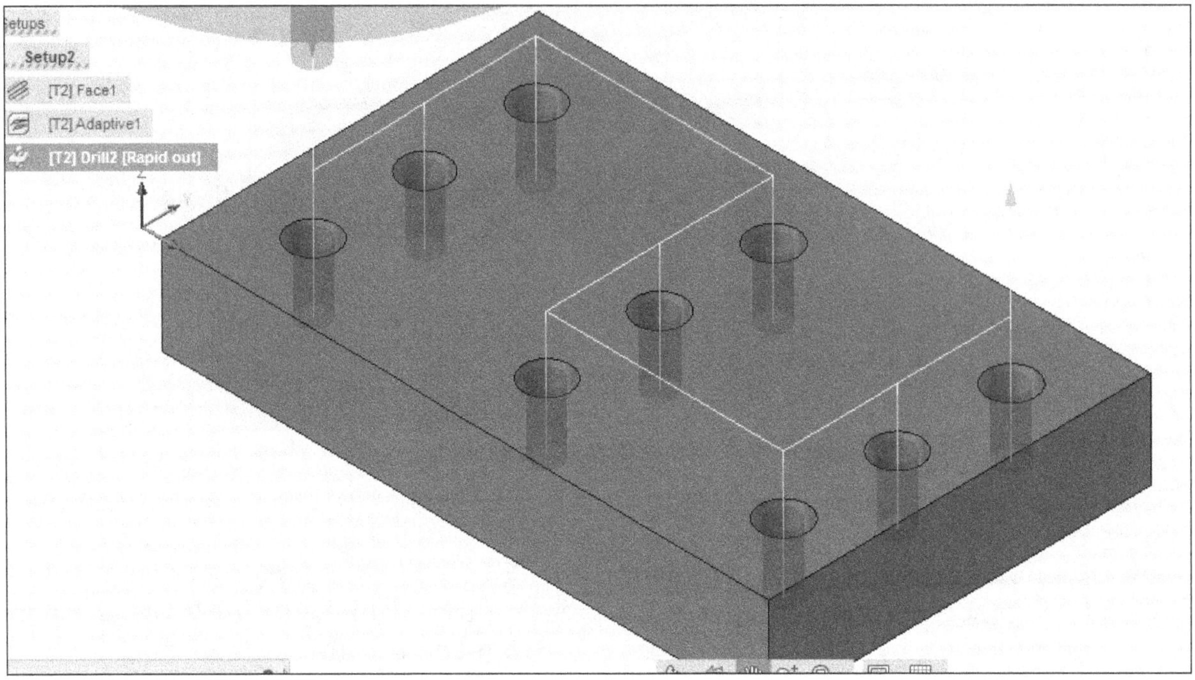

Figure-73. Toolpath generated for drill

TOOLPATH BY HOLE RECOGNITION

The **Hole Recognition** tool is used to create toolpath for drilling holes automatically based on recognized holes. The procedure to create toolpath is given next.

- Click on the **Hole Recognition** tool from the **DRILLING** drop-down in the **MILLING** tab of **Toolbar**. The **Hole Recognition** dialog box will be displayed with all the holes selected; refer to Figure-74.

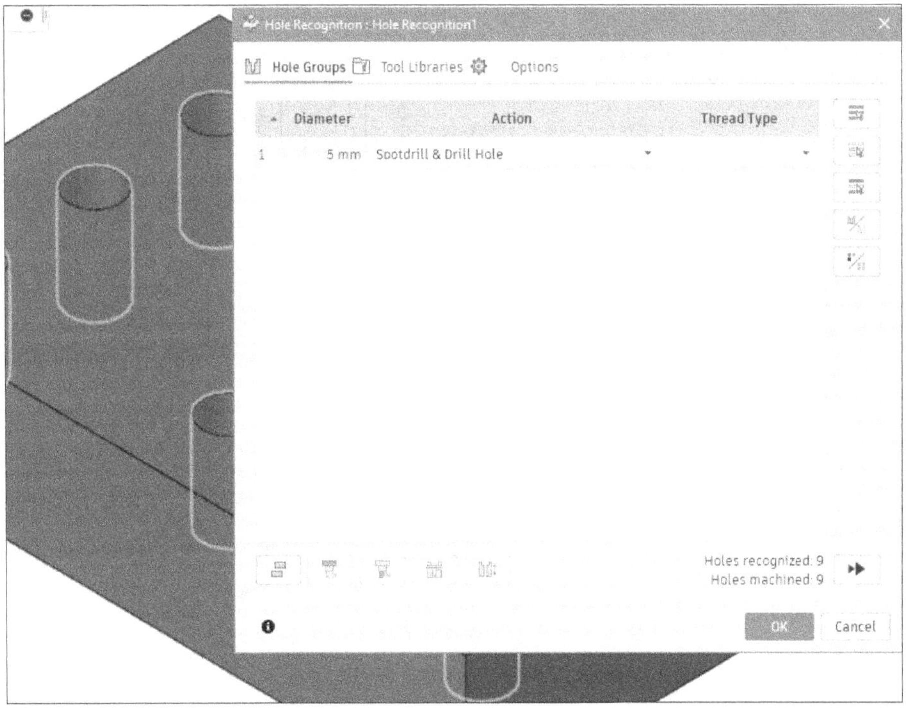

Figure-74. Hole Recognition dialog box

- Select desired tool type from the drop-down in the **Action** column of **Hole Groups** tab in the dialog box like Simple Drill, Spot Drill, and so on.
- Click on the **Tool Libraries** tab in the dialog box and select check boxes for tools you want to use for drilling.
- Click on the **Options** tab in the dialog box. The options will be displayed as shown in Figure-75.

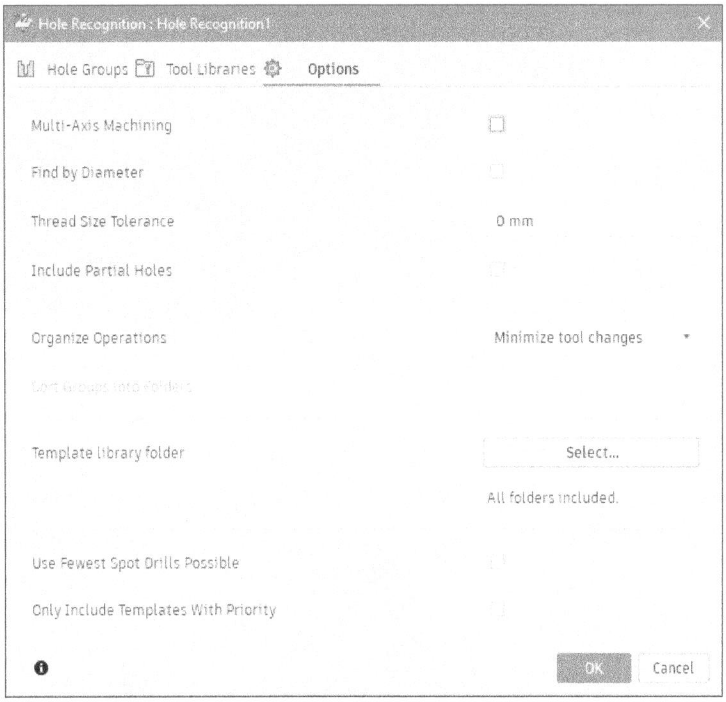

Figure-75. Options tab in Hole Recognition dialog box

- Select the **Multi-Axis Machining** check box if you do not want to limit search for holes to current active plane and perform multi axis machining.
- Select the **Find by Diameter** check box and specify maximum diameter up to which you want to search for the holes.
- Specify desired value in the **Thread Size Tolerance** edit box to define the thread deviation range within which threading tools can be used to machine threads in holes.
- Select the **Include Partial Holes** check box to include holes in multiple segments and partial sections.
- Select the **Minimize tool changes** option from the **Organize Operations** drop-down if you want selected cutting tool to complete all operations before the next tool is selected. Select the **Group by size** option from the drop-down if you want to complete all operations on first hole and then move to another hole. On selecting this option, the **Sort Groups into Folders** check box will become active. Select the check box to sort groups based on hole sizes.
- Click on the **Select** button for **Template library folder** option from the dialog box. The **Template Library** dialog box will be displayed. Select desired library to be used for templates and click on the **Select folder** dialog box.
- Select the **Use Fewest Spot Drills Possible** check box to use single spot drill for all the holes.
- Select **Only Include Templates With Priority** check box to filter the hole templates.
- After setting desired parameters, click on the **OK** button from the dialog box. The toolpaths will be created automatically; refer to Figure-76.

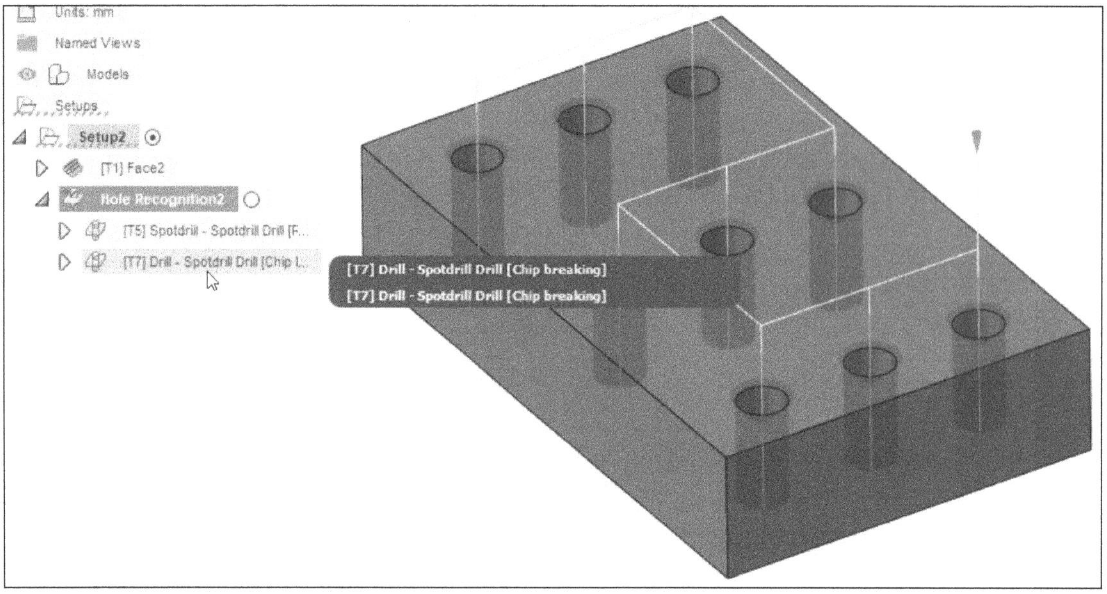

Figure-76. Toolpaths created for drilling

PRACTICAL

Create CAM program of the given model using 3D and 2D toolpaths; refer to Figure-77.

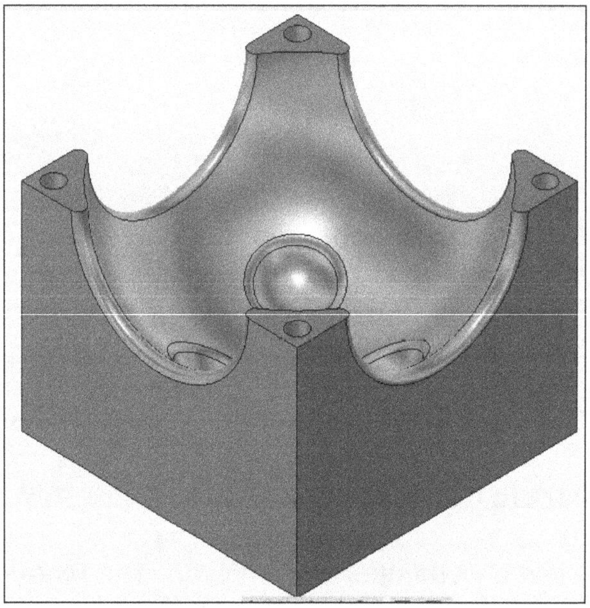

Figure-77. Practical 1

Adding Model to MANUFACTURE

- Create and save the part in **MANUFACTURE** workspace. The part file is available in the respective chapter folder of **Autodesk Fusion Black Book** resources.
- Click on the **MANUFACTURE** workspace from **Workspace** drop-down. The model will be displayed in the **MANUFACTURE** workspace.

Creating Stock

- Click on the **New Setup** tool of **SETUP** drop-down from **Toolbar**. The **SETUP** dialog box will be displayed along with the stock of model.
- Specify the parameters of **Setup** tab, **Stock** tab, and **Post Process** tab of **SETUP** dialog box as shown in Figure-78.

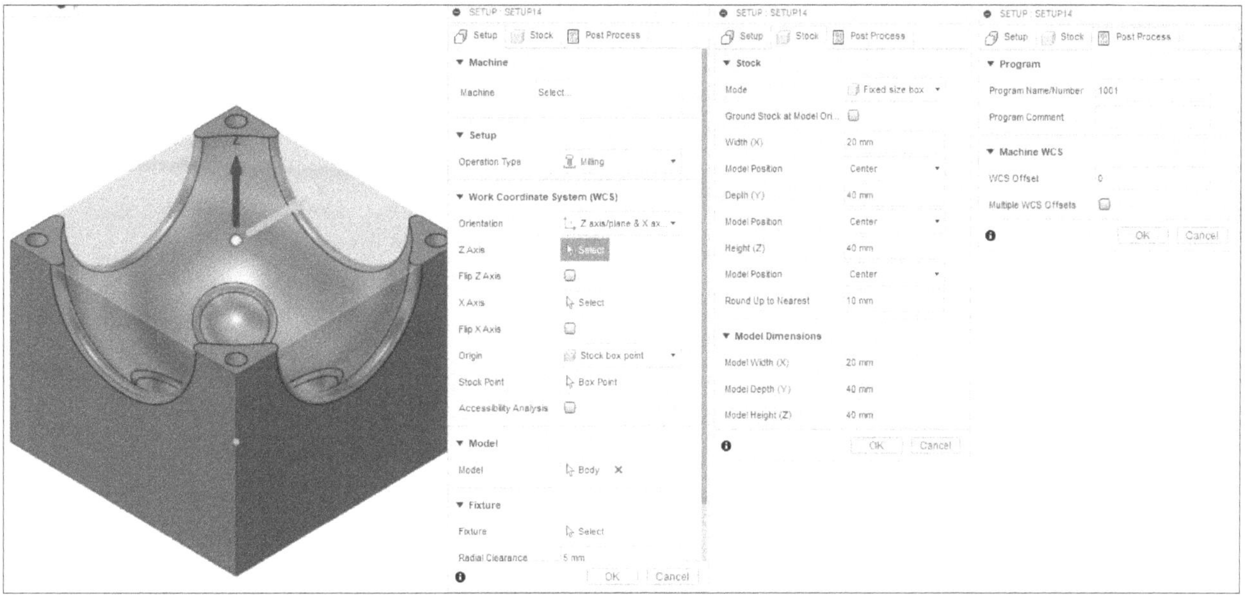

Figure-78. Specifying parameters for stock

- After specifying the parameters, click on the **OK** button from **SETUP** dialog box. The stock will be created and displayed on the model.

Generating Adaptive Clearing Toolpath

- Click on the **Adaptive Clearing** tool of **3D** drop-down from **Toolbar**. The **ADAPTIVE** dialog box will be displayed.
- Click on the **Select** button of **Tool** tab and select the tool from the record list of **Select Tool** dialog box as shown in Figure-79.

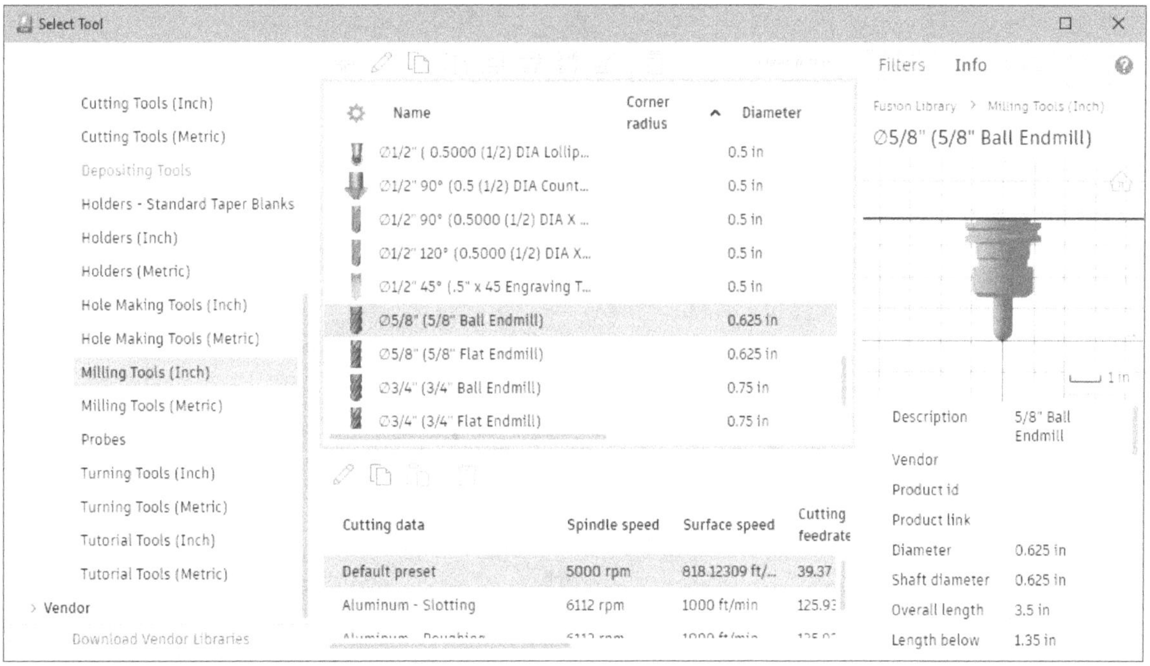

Figure-79. Selecting tool for adaptive clearing

- If the tool is not available in the list then create a new ball mill tool. After selecting the tool, click on the **OK** button from **Select Tool** dialog box. The tool will be added in the **ADAPTIVE** dialog box.
- Specify the parameters of **Geometry** tab, **Passes** tab, and **Linking** tab of **ADAPTIVE** dialog box; refer to Figure-80.

Figure-80. Parameters of Adaptive dialog box

- After specifying the parameters, click on the **OK** button from **ADAPTIVE** dialog box. The toolpath will be generated and displayed on the model; refer to Figure-81.

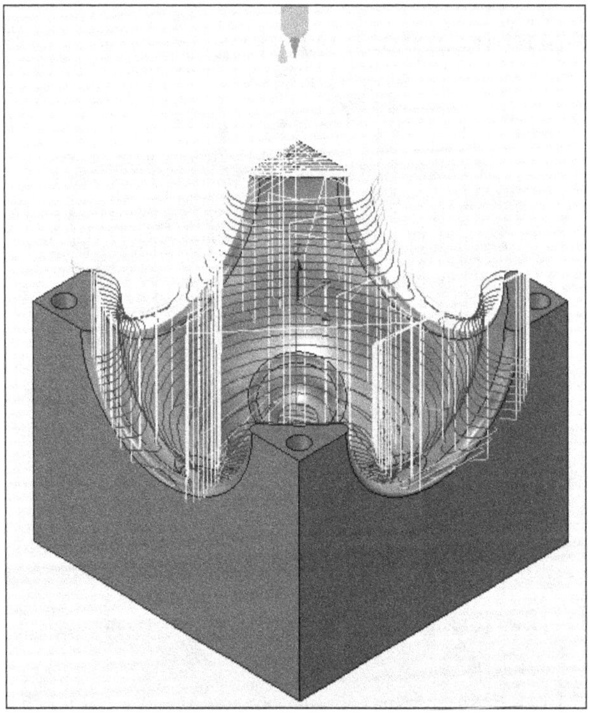

Figure-81. Toolpath of adaptive clearing

Generating Spiral Toolpath

- Click on the **Spiral** tool of **3D** drop-down from **Toolbar**. The **SPIRAL** dialog box will be displayed.
- Click on the **Select** button of **Tool** tab and select the tool from the record list of **Select Tool** dialog box as shown in Figure-82.

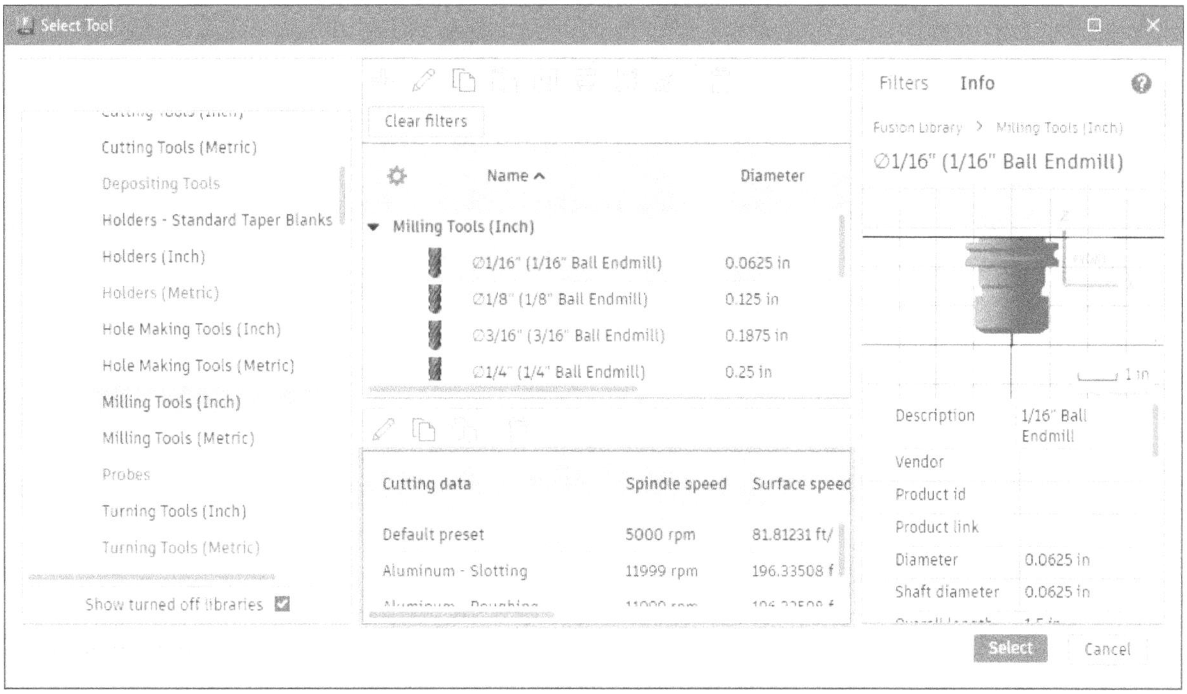

Figure-82. Selecting tool for spiral

- Specify the parameters of **Geometry** tab, **Passes** tab, and **Linking** tab of **SPIRAL** dialog box; refer to Figure-83.

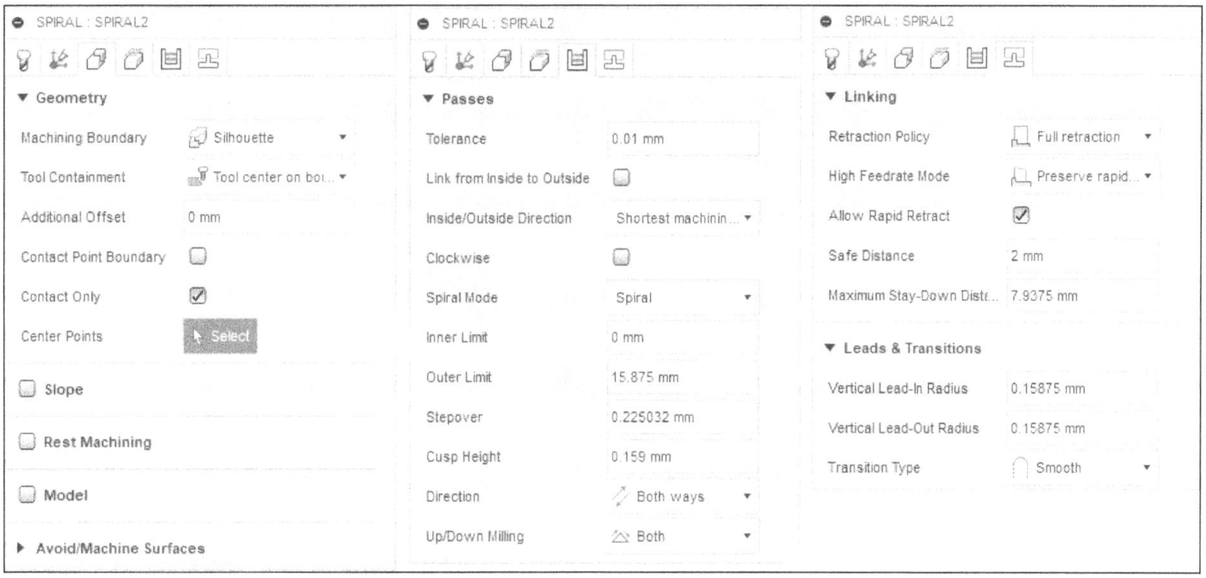

Figure-83. Specifying parameters for spiral

Generating Scallop Toolpath

- Click on the **Scallop** tool of **3D** drop-down from **Toolbar**. The **SCALLOP** dialog box will be displayed.
- Click on the **Select** button of **Tool** section and select the tool which is selected in last operation from **Select Tool** dialog box.
- Specify the parameters of **Tool** tab, **Geometry** tab, **Passes** tab, and **Linking** tab as shown in Figure-84.

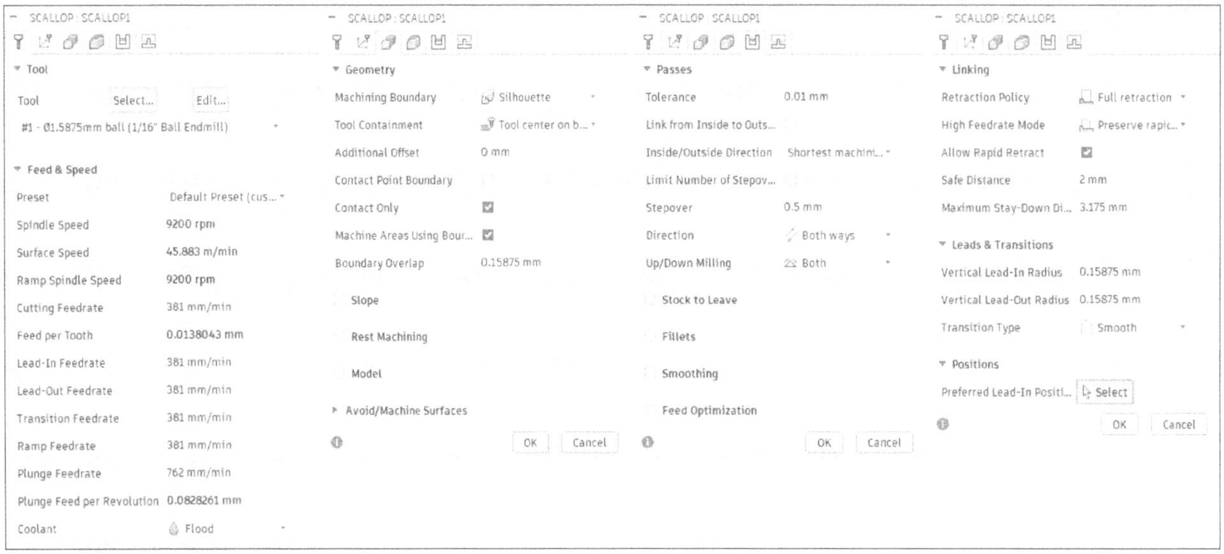

Figure-84. Parameters for Scallop tool

- After specifying the parameters, click on the **OK** button from the **SCALLOP** dialog box. The toolpath will be created and displayed on the model; refer to Figure-85.

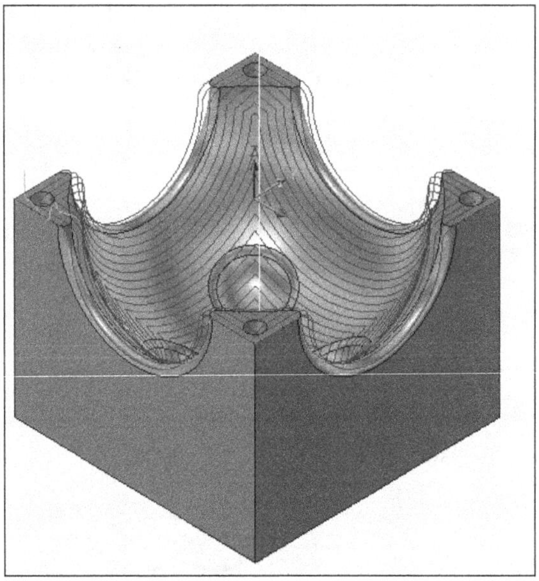

Figure-85. Toolpath generated for scallop

Generating Radial Toolpath

- Click on the **Radial** tool of **3D** drop-down from **Toolbar**. The **RADIAL** dialog box will be displayed.
- Click on the **Select** button of **Tool** section and select the tool which is selected in last operation from **Select Tool** dialog box.
- Click on the **Geometry** tab of the **RADIAL** dialog box. The **Geometry** tab will be displayed.
- Click on the **Machining Boundary** drop-down and select the **Selection** option.
- The **Select** button of **Machining Boundary** section is active by default. You need to select the chain for machining; refer to Figure-86.

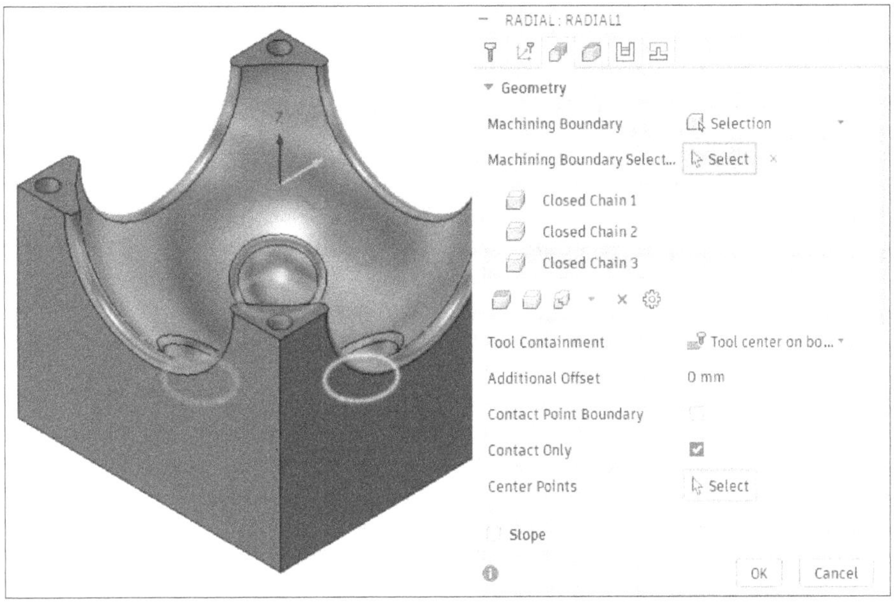

Figure-86. Selecting chains for machining

- Specify the parameters of **Passes** tab and **Linking** tab as displayed in Figure-87.

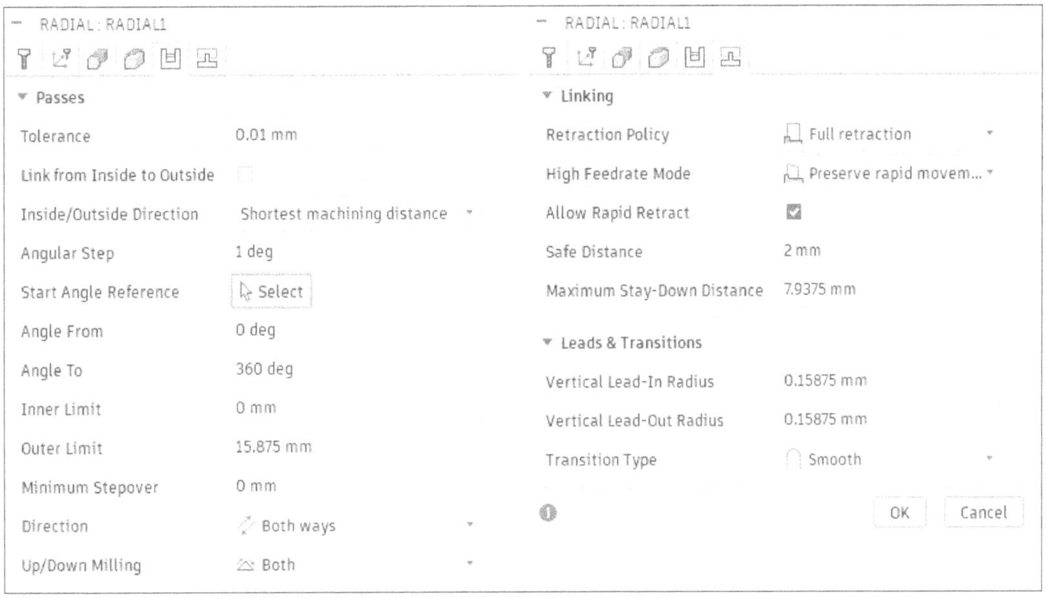

Figure-87. Parameters for Radial dialog box

- After specifying the parameters, click on the **OK** button from **RADIAL** dialog box. The toolpath will be created and displayed on the model; refer to Figure-88.

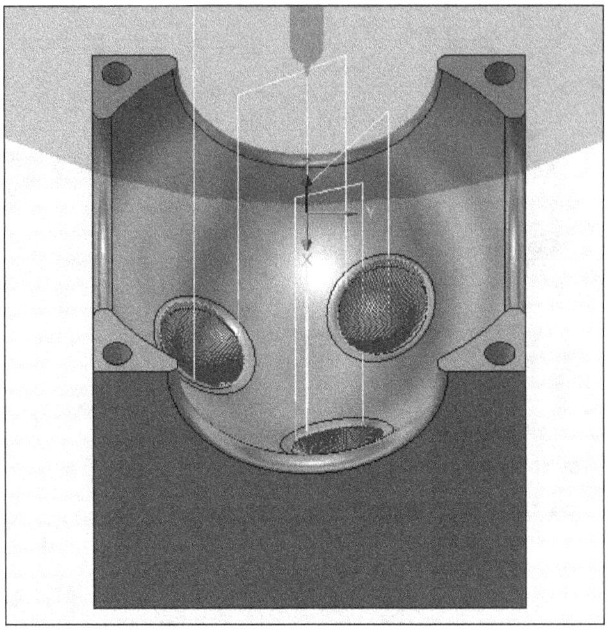

Figure-88. Toolpath generated for Radial tool

Generating Drill Toolpath

- Click on the **Drill** tool from **Toolbar**. The **DRILL** dialog box will be displayed.
- Click on the **Select** button of **Tool** section and select the tool from **Select Tool** dialog box as displayed in Figure-89.

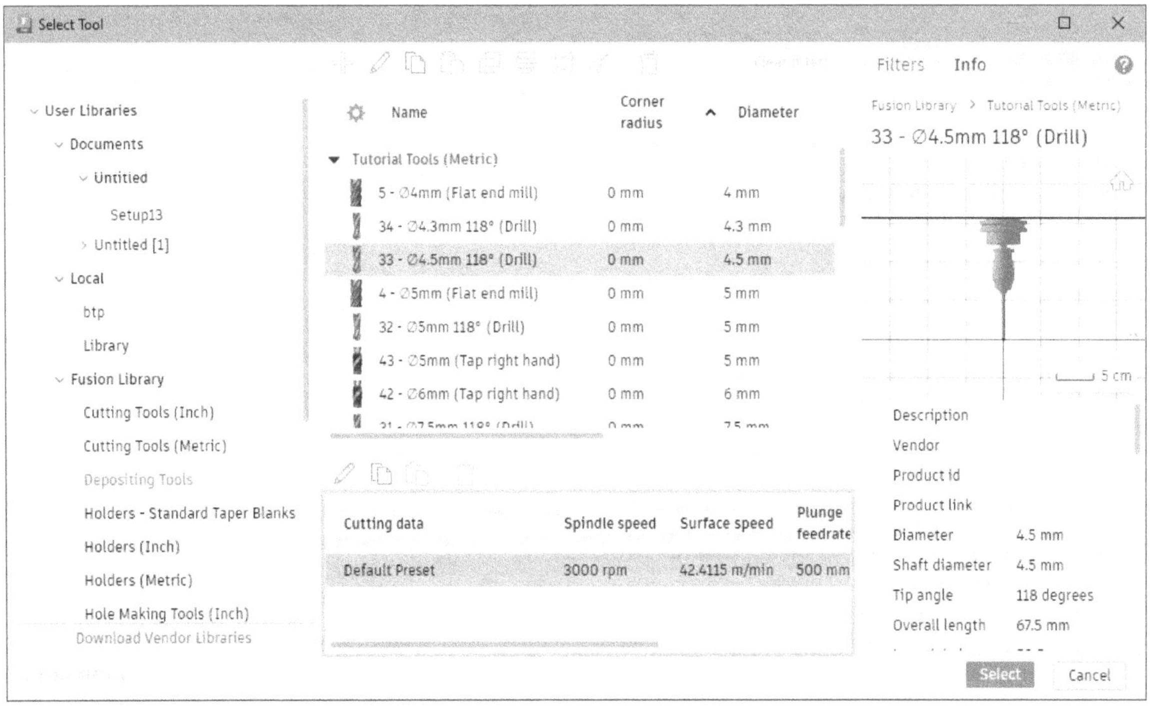

Figure-89. Selection of tool for drill

- After selecting the tool for drill, click on the **OK** button from **Select Tool** dialog box. The tool will be added in the **DRILL** dialog box.
- Specify the parameters of **Geometry** tab from **DRILL** dialog box as displayed in Figure-90. Select the round face of one of the hole.

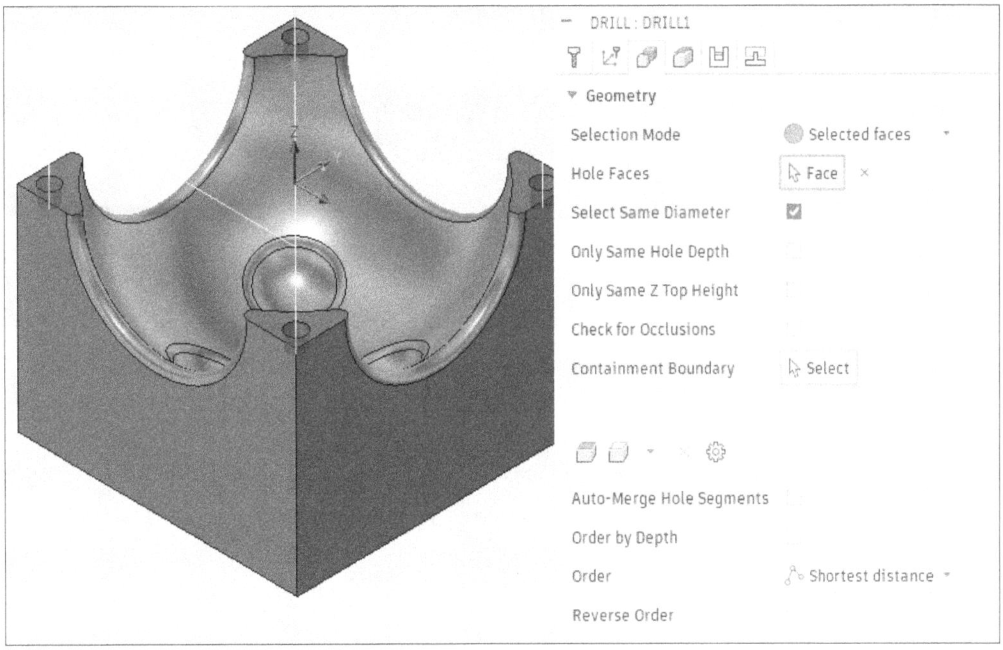

Figure-90. Specifying Geometry tab of DRILL dialog box

- After specifying the parameters, click on the **OK** button from **DRILL** dialog box. The toolpath will be generated and displayed on the model; refer to Figure-91.

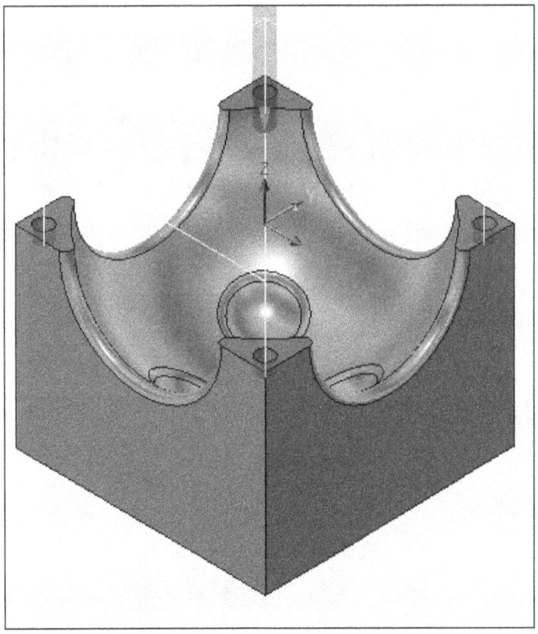

Figure-91. Generated toolpath for Drill tool

- Till now, we have applied the tools to create the required toolpath. Now, we will simulate the whole process to check whether the generated toolpath is working properly or there is a collision of tool with stock.
- Click on the **Simulate** button from shortcut menu of **Setup1** option in the **BROWSER**. The **SIMULATE** dialog box will be displayed.
- Specify the parameters of **SIMULATE** dialog box as required and click on the **Play** button. The simulation of machining process will be displayed; refer to Figure-92. Make sure to create finishing toolpaths as discussed earlier.

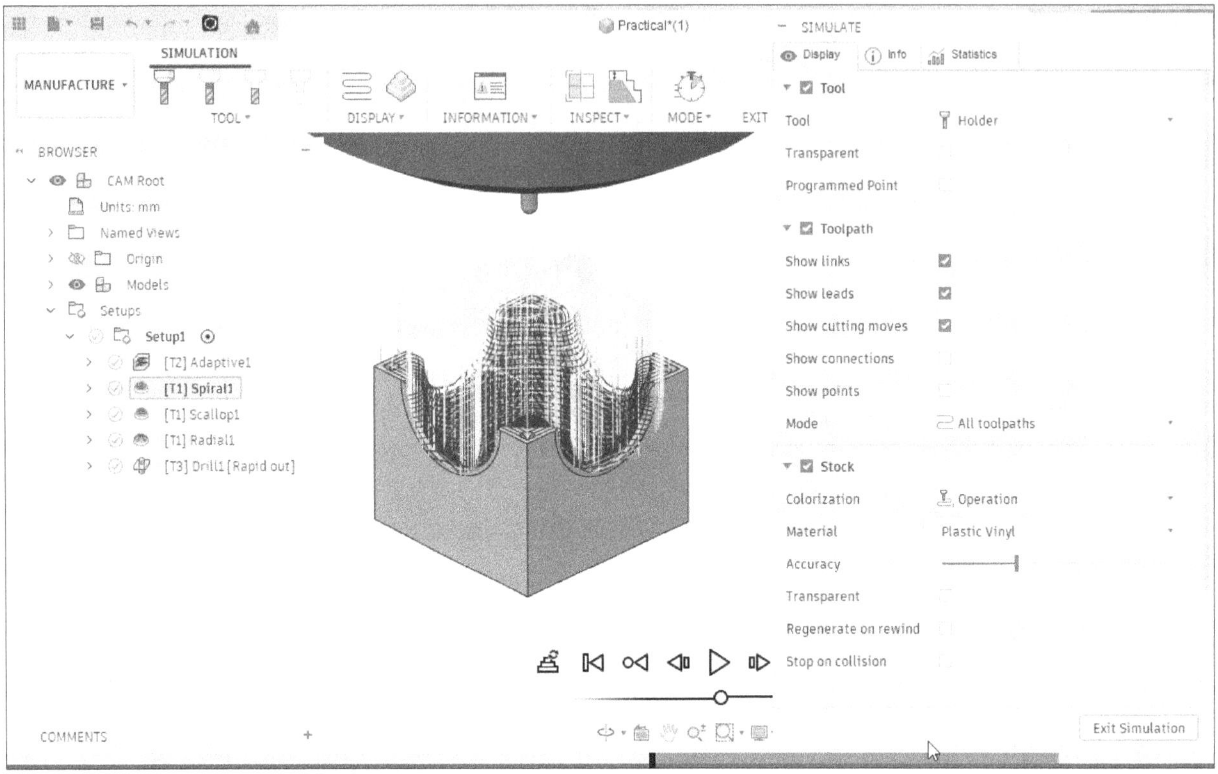

Figure-92. Simulating the generated toolpath

PRACTICE 1

Machine the stock of length as 148 mm, width as 52 mm, and height as 21 mm to create the part as shown in Figure-93. The part file of this model is available in respective folder of **Autodesk Fusion Black Book Resources**.

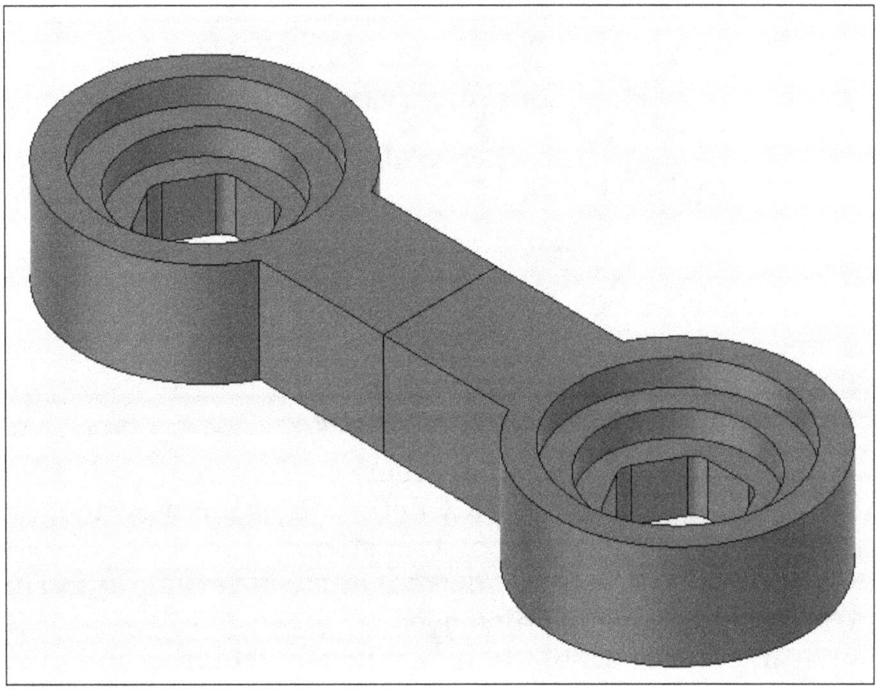

Figure-93. Practice 1

PRACTICE 2

Machine the stock of length as 102 mm, width as 62 mm, and height as 23 mm to create the part as shown in Figure-94. The part file of this model is available in respective folder of **Autodesk Fusion Black Book Resources**.

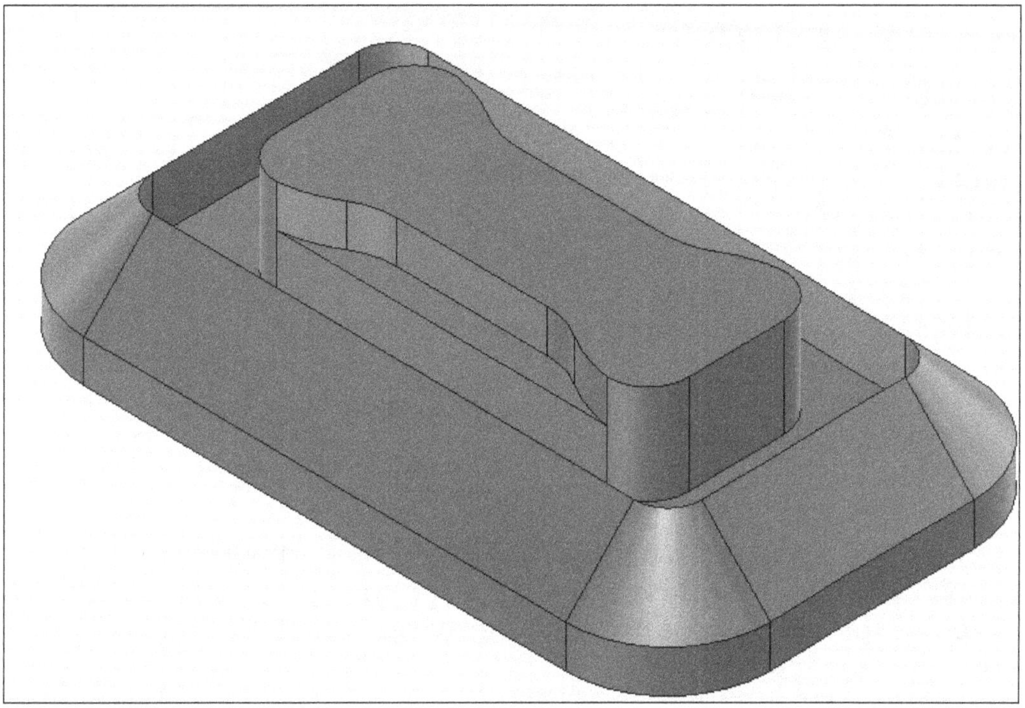

Figure-94. Practice 2

PRACTICE 3

Machine the stock of stock diameter as 80 mm, thickness as 7 mm, and align stock to the center of the part as shown in Figure-95. The part file of this model is available in the respective folder of **Autodesk Fusion Black Book Resources**.

Figure-95. Practice 3

Self Assessment

Q1. What is the primary purpose of the Spiral toolpath?
A) To create a toolpath along the radii of an arc
B) To cut material in a spiral fashion
C) To engrave 2D contours
D) To create multi-axis toolpaths

Q2. Which tool is generally used with the Spiral toolpath?
A) Tapered mill
B) Fillet tool
C) End mill or ball mill
D) Face mill

Q3. What does selecting the "Spiral with circles" option do?
A) Creates a spiral toolpath from center to outermost boundary
B) Creates a circular toolpath at minimum and maximum radius
C) Generates radial toolpaths
D) Engraves text on a cylindrical surface

Q4. What is the difference between Spiral and Radial toolpaths?
A) Spiral toolpaths follow isocurves, while Radial toolpaths follow X-axis
B) Spiral toolpaths are used only for engraving, while Radial toolpaths are for machining
C) Spiral toolpaths cut in a continuous spiral, while Radial toolpaths are straight lines from center to outer edge
D) There is no difference between them

Q5. What does the Morphed Spiral toolpath follow when cutting?
A) Straight lines
B) Surface curvature within specified boundaries
C) Engraved contours
D) Radial angles

Q6. What is the main use of the Project tool?
A) To create a toolpath along a selected contour
B) To cut in a spiral fashion
C) To generate radial toolpaths
D) To machine free-form surfaces

Q7. How does the Blend toolpath work?
A) By creating toolpaths along the spokes of a wheel
B) By engraving on cylindrical faces
C) By creating uniform cutting passes between two selected contours
D) By creating radial toolpaths

Q8. What is the key characteristic of the Morph toolpath?
A) It machines between selected contours while avoiding them
B) It only works with a tapered mill
C) It engraves curves directly on the face of a model
D) It creates a toolpath based on angular step values

Q9. What is the default behavior of the Flow toolpath?
A) It engraves 2D contours
B) It creates toolpaths for machining irregular surfaces following isocurves
C) It generates only radial toolpaths
D) It only cuts in a single direction

Q10. What happens when the Multi-Axis option is enabled in the Flow toolpath?
A) It forces the toolpath to follow isocurves
B) It allows tilting of the tool/workpiece bed
C) It restricts movement to a single axis
D) It enables radial toolpath generation

Q11. What is the primary purpose of the Corner toolpath?
A) Rough machining of sharp corners
B) Finishing steep and shallow intersection areas
C) Engraving text on part surfaces
D) Creating chamfers on sharp edges

Q12. Which type of tool is recommended for the Corner toolpath?
A) Face mill
B) Tapered mill
C) Ball end mill
D) Fillet tool

Q13. What does the Reference Tool option in the Rest Machining section specify?
A) The new tool to be used for corner finishing
B) The cutting tool used in previous operations
C) The maximum step-over value
D) The material hardness for cutting

Q14. What parameter defines the limit for steep and shallow faces in the Corner toolpath?
A) Step-over percentage
B) Threshold Angle
C) Tool diameter
D) Feed rate

Q15. What does selecting the "Along with maximum stepover" option do?
A) Maintains a fixed step-over throughout machining
B) Adjusts step-over dynamically based on material width
C) Cuts only in a single pass
D) Ignores rest machining areas

Q16. What is the purpose of the Deburr toolpath?
A) Rough cutting of stock material
B) Removing material from sharp corners and edges
C) Creating pockets in the part
D) Drilling holes in a part

Q17. What happens when the "Automatic" option is selected in the Edges to Deburr drop-down?
A) The user must manually select sharp edges
B) The software automatically identifies sharp edges
C) The software removes all edges from machining
D) The toolpath is applied to all faces

Q18. What does selecting the "Chamfering" option in the Deburr Edges by drop-down do?
A) Creates fillets on edges
B) Removes sharp edges by creating chamfers
C) Extends toolpaths beyond the edge
D) Increases tool diameter dynamically

Q19. What is the key difference between the Geodesic toolpath and Scallop or Blend toolpaths?
A) Geodesic toolpath uses surface instead of curve chains
B) Geodesic toolpath is used only for engraving
C) Geodesic toolpath follows only X and Y axes
D) Geodesic toolpath ignores curvature of the surface

Q20. What happens when the "Silhouette Boundary" option is selected in the Machining Boundary drop-down?
A) The toolpath is confined to the selected surface edges
B) The software ignores all surface boundaries
C) The software machines the entire part
D) The toolpath is restricted to the X-axis

Q21. What is the purpose of the "Invert Machining Boundary" check box in the Geodesic toolpath settings?
A) Switches from machining steep faces to shallow faces
B) Enables undercut machining
C) Changes tool orientation
D) Ignores boundary constraints

Q22. What does selecting "Blend" from the Type of Passes drop-down do?
A) Uses boundary curves to generate offset cutting passes
B) Creates a spiral toolpath
C) Follows isocurves for cutting
D) Generates only linear passes

Q23. What does the "Tool Containment" option control in the Geodesic toolpath?
A) Whether the tool moves inside, outside, or centered on the boundary
B) The maximum tool speed
C) The spindle rotation direction
D) The cutting depth

Q24. What does the Rotary Pocket toolpath require for machining?
A) A 4th axis
B) A ball end mill only
C) A specific feed rate
D) Only 2D toolpaths

Q25. What does selecting the "None" option in the Machining Boundary drop-down for Rotary Pocket toolpath do?
A) Machines the full stock
B) Requires manual selection of machining boundary
C) Ignores rotary axis settings
D) Prevents tool movement

Q26. What does the "Machine Over Gaps" option do in the Rotary Pocket toolpath?
A) Allows machining to continue over small gaps
B) Prevents machining over any gaps
C) Increases tool diameter automatically
D) Reduces spindle speed

Q27. What is the primary function of the Swarf toolpath?
A) Side cutting of beveled edges and tapered walls
B) Creating circular pockets
C) Drilling deep holes
D) Rough machining of stock material

Q28. What does selecting "Contours" in the Drive Mode drop-down of the Swarf toolpath do?
A) Uses boundary chains of selected faces as reference for toolpaths
B) Ignores all toolpath constraints
C) Forces toolpaths to be radial
D) Prevents multi-axis movements

Q29. What does the "Machine Other Side" check box do in the Swarf toolpath?
A) Forces the toolpath to be created on the other side of the selected contour
B) Disables side milling
C) Prevents steep angle machining
D) Restricts the tool to only vertical cuts

Q30. What is the function of the "Maximum Fan Distance" option in the Swarf toolpath?
A) Defines the maximum distance the tool axis can fan out
B) Controls the spindle speed
C) Sets the cutting feed rate
D) Adjusts the maximum depth of cut

Q31. What is the primary purpose of the Advanced Swarf toolpath?
A. To create helical drilling operations
B. To perform swarf milling with precise control on clearance and orientation
C. To generate a simple 2D contour path
D. To perform lathe operations

Q32. Which tab should be selected to define the geometry to be machined in the Advanced Swarf tool?
A. Tool tab
B. Geometry tab
C. Heights tab
D. Multi-Axis tab

Q33. What does selecting the "Guide Curves" option allow in the Advanced Swarf toolpath?
A. Use selected curves as reference for machining
B. Select adjacent surfaces for clearance
C. Define cutting speeds and feed rates
D. Specify the minimum and maximum tilt angles

Q34. What is the function of the "Tool Tracks Floor" check box in the Advanced Swarf toolpath?
A. Stops the tool from cutting at impossible points
B. Allows the tool to follow the curvature of the selected floor face
C. Enables drilling at multiple depths
D. Defines the height for safe tool movement

Q35. In the Multi-Axis Contour toolpath, what is the role of the "Trim impossible" option?
A. Stops the toolpath completely when encountering an impossible area
B. Ignores impossible points and moves to the next pass
C. Forces the tool to continue cutting regardless of geometry
D. Creates a backup toolpath in case of failure

Q36. Which option from the Primary Mode drop-down in Multi-Axis Contour helps in reducing tool wear?
A. Vertical
B. Lead and lean
C. From point
D. To point

Q37. What does the "Override Tilt Angle" check box do in the Multi-Axis Contour toolpath?
A. Forces the tool to always tilt to a fixed angle
B. Automatically adjusts tool tilt based on stock height
C. Allows users to specify a preferred angle for cutting
D. Prevents any tilting of the cutting tool

Q38. Which option in the Multi-Axis Rotary Parallel toolpath creates concentric cutting passes?
A. Spiral
B. Line
C. Circular
D. Random

Q39. The Multi-Axis Rotary Contour toolpath is specifically used for machining which type of surfaces?
A. Flat surfaces
B. Steep walls
C. Horizontal planes
D. Complex pockets

FOR STUDENT NOTES

Chapter 18

Generating Turning and Cutting Toolpaths

Topics Covered

The major topics covered in this chapter are:

- ***Turning Profile***
- ***Turning Face***
- ***Turning Chamfer***
- ***Turning Thread***
- ***Turning Groove***
- ***Cutting Toolpaths***

GENERATING TURNING TOOLPATH

Till now, you have learned the procedure of creating milling toolpaths with the help of various tools. In this section, you will learn about the tools used for creating Turning toolpaths. **You need to open a cylindrical part for turning in Autodesk Fusion and create a machine setup of Turning machine as discussed earlier** in Chapter 15 before working on this chapter. The tools to generate turning toolpaths are available in the **TURNING** tab of the **Ribbon**; refer to Figure-1.

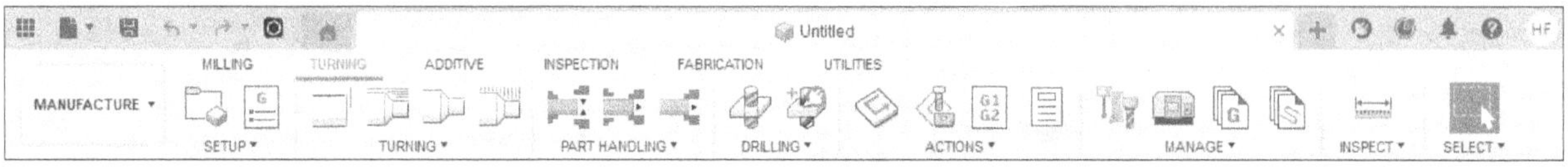

Figure-1. TURNING tab

Turning Face

The **Turning Face** tool is used for machining the front face of the part. The turning face toolpath is generally the first toolpath created for machining on CNC Turn machine. The procedure to use this tool is discussed next.

- Click on the **Turning Face** tool of **TURNING** drop-down from **Toolbar**; refer to Figure-2. The **FACE** dialog box will be displayed; refer to Figure-3.

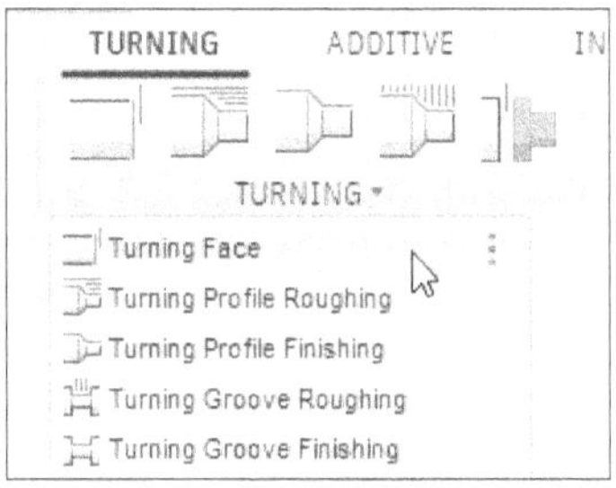

Figure-2. Turning Face tool

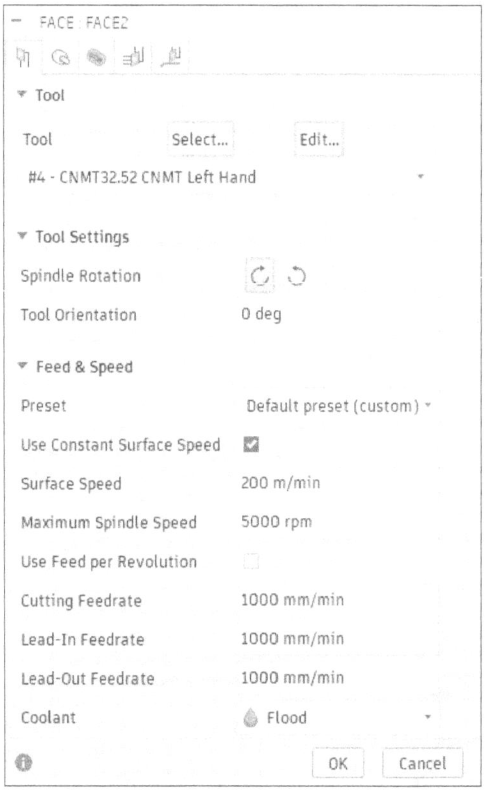

Figure-3. FACE dialog box

- Click in the **Select** selection button from **Tool** section. The **Select Tool** dialog box will be displayed. Select desired tool and click on **OK** button. The tool will be added in the **FACE** dialog box.
- Click in the **Tool Orientation** edit box from the **Tool Settings** section and specify the angular value to orient the tool as required on the tool post of machine.
- The other options of this dialog box have been discussed in next topic of this chapter.

- After specifying the parameters, click on the **OK** button from **FACE** dialog box. The toolpath will be generated and displayed on the model; refer to Figure-4.

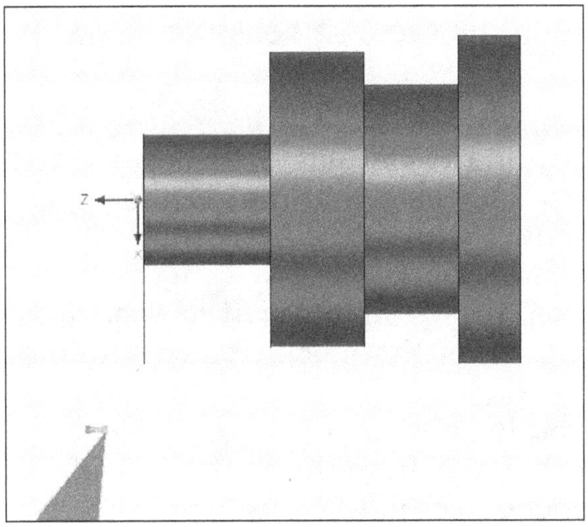

Figure-4. Toolpath generated for facing

Turning Profile Roughing

The **Turning Profile Roughing** tool is used for roughing the profile of model using various tools. The procedure to use this tool is discussed next.

- Click on the **Turning Profile Roughing** tool of **TURNING** drop-down from **Toolbar**; refer to Figure-5. The **PROFILE ROUGHING** dialog box will be displayed; refer to Figure-6.

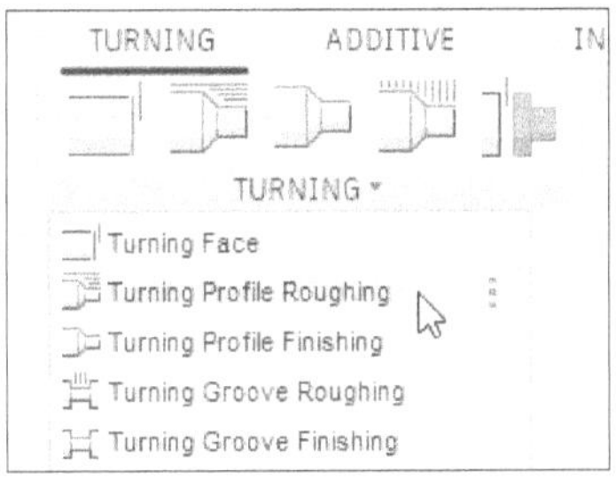

Figure-5. Turning Profile Roughing tool

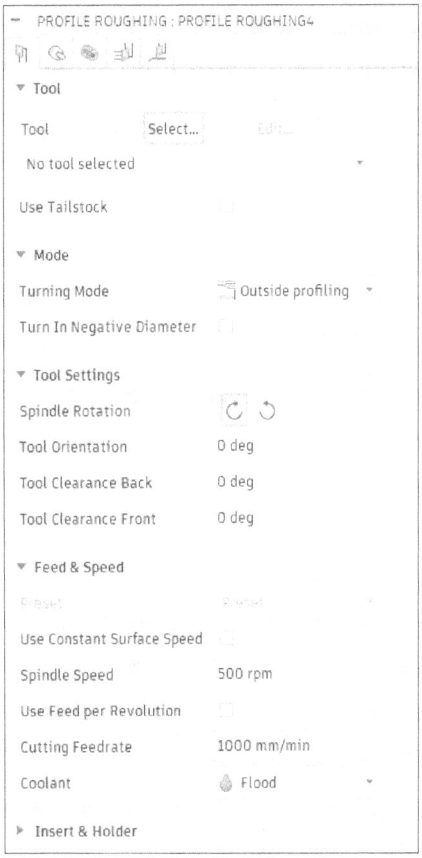

Figure-6. PROFILE ROUGHING dialog box

- Click in the **Select** button of **Tool** section from **Tool** tab. The **Select Tool** dialog box will be displayed. Select desired tool for profiling and click on the **OK** button. Note that the shape and size of cutting tool depends on shape and size of model. The tool will be added in the **PROFILE ROUGHING** dialog box.

Tool

- Select desired option from the **Coolant** drop-down of the **Tool** section.
- Select the **Use Tailstock** check box of **Tool** tab to apply support to the part to be machined. When you have a long part for turning then you should use tail stock to support the other end of part.
- Select the **Outside profiling** option of **Turning Mode** drop-down from **Mode** section to retract the tool outside of the stock and machine axially depending on the direction setting.
- Select the **Inside Profiling** option of **Turning Mode** drop-down from **Mode** section to approach or retract the tool from the center-line of part and machines radially depending on the direction setting.
- Set desired angle values in the edit boxes of **Tool Settings** section to define orientation of the cutting tool.
- Select desired option from the **Preset** drop-down of the **Feed & Seed** section.
- Select the **Use Constant Surface Speed** check box of **Feed & Speed** section from **Tool** tab to automatically adjust the spindle speed for maintaining a constant surface speed between tool and the workpiece.
- Click in the **Surface Speed** edit box of **Feed & Speed** section to specify the value of spindle speed expressed as the speed of the tool on the surface.
- Click in the **Maximum Spindle Speed** edit box of **Feed & Speed** section and specify the value of maximum allowed spindle speed when using constant surface speed.
- Select the **Use Feed Per Revolution** check box of **Feed & Speed** section to automatically adjust the feed rate based on the RPM of the spindle to maintain a constant chip load.
- Click in the **Cutting Feed Per Revolution** edit box of **Feed & Speed** section and specify the distance of tool advancement into the material for each 360 degree rotation of spindle when the tool is fully engaged.

Geometry

- Click on the **Geometry** tab of **PROFILE** dialog box. The **Geometry** tab will be displayed; refer to Figure-7.
- Select the **Model** check box of **Geometry** tab to manually select a model contour for machining. The **Select** button of **Model Contour** section will be active by default. You need to click on the contour of model to be used as profile for cutting. You can generally use **Sketch Profiles** option to select earlier created sketch profiles for machining.
- Select desired option from **Front Mode** drop-down and define the reference for front confinement region. Confinement region is an imaginary space within which machining of part will be done.
- Click in the **Offset** edit box of **Front** section in **Geometry** tab and specify the value to define offset distance for front confinement plane from selected reference in the **Front Mode** drop-down. You can specify positive as well as negative values.
- Select desired option from the **Tool Limit** drop-down to define the touch point of cutting tool for generating toolpath.

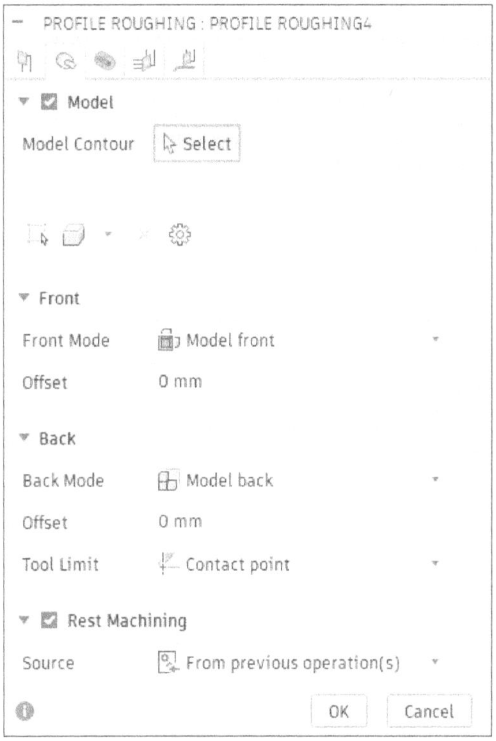

Figure-7. Geometry tab of PROFILE ROUGHING dialog box

- Specify desired value in **Tangential Extension** edit box to increase length of toolpath at the front confinement section.
- Similarly, specify parameters for back plane of confinement region.
- Select the **Groove Suppression** check box and select faces of grooves if you want to avoid machining grooves in this toolpath.
- Select the **Rest Machining** check box of **Geometry** tab to specify that only stock left after the previous operations should be machined.
- Click in the **Source** drop-down of **Rest Machining** section and select desired option to specify the source from which the rest machining stock should be calculated.

Radii

- Click on the **Radii** tab of **PROFILE** dialog box. The options of **Radii** tab will be displayed for defining clearance radius, outer radius, and inner radius of part; refer to Figure-8.
- Click in the **From** drop-down of **Clearance** section and select desired reference for clearance location where tool will move after cutting pass.
- Select the **Stock OD** check box from the **Clearance** section to specify the use only the stock outer diameter.
- Select the **Model OD** check box from the **Clearance** section to specify the use only the model outer diameter.
- Click in the **Offset** edit box of **Clearance** section and specify desired value to increase clearance radius with respect to selected reference.
- Click in the **From** drop-down of **Outer Radius** section and select desired reference for defining outer diameter of part.
- Click in the **Offset** edit box of **Outer Radius** section and specify desired value to increase outer radius with respect to selected reference.
- Click in the **From** drop-down of **Inner Radius** section and select desired reference for inner diameter of part.

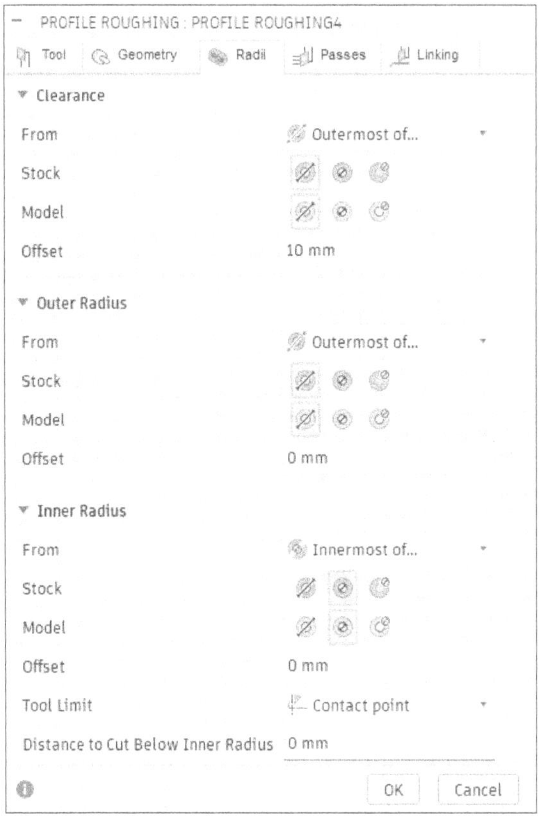

Figure-8. Radii tab of PROFILE ROUGHING dialog box

- Click in the **Offset** edit box of **Inner Radius** section and enter desired value.
- Select desired option from the **Tool Limit** drop-down to define the reference to be used as limiting point for creating toolpath.
- Click in the **Distance to Cut Below Inner Radius** edit box and specify the value of distance up to which the cutting tool should continue cutting when the tool has reached centerline of part during parting or facing operations.

Passes

- Click on the **Passes** tab of **PROFILE** dialog box to specify number of cutting passes to be created and their direction. The options of **Passes** tab will be displayed as shown in Figure-9.
- Select desired option of **Cycle** drop-down from the **Cycle and Direction** section to define how tool will retract and come back for next cutting pass. Select the **Horizontal passes**, **Vertical passes**, or **Back cutting** option to create cutting passes oriented in respective direction.
- Select the **Front to back** option of **Direction** drop-down from **Cycle and Direction** section to cut from the front side of the stock towards the back side when **Horizontal passes** or **Vertical passes** option is selected in **Cycle** drop-down.
- Select the **Back to Front** option of **Direction** drop-down from **Cycle and Direction** section to cut the material of stock from back side towards the front side when **Horizontal passes** or **Vertical passes** option is selected in **Cycle** drop-down.
- Select the **Both Ways** option of **Direction** drop-down from **Cycle and Direction** section to cut the stock in both forward and backward direction.
- Click in the **Grooving** drop-down from **Cycle and Direction** section and select desired option to define which type of grooving is allowed while cutting.

- Click in the **Tolerance** edit box of **Passes** tab and enter the value of tolerance for each cutting pass.

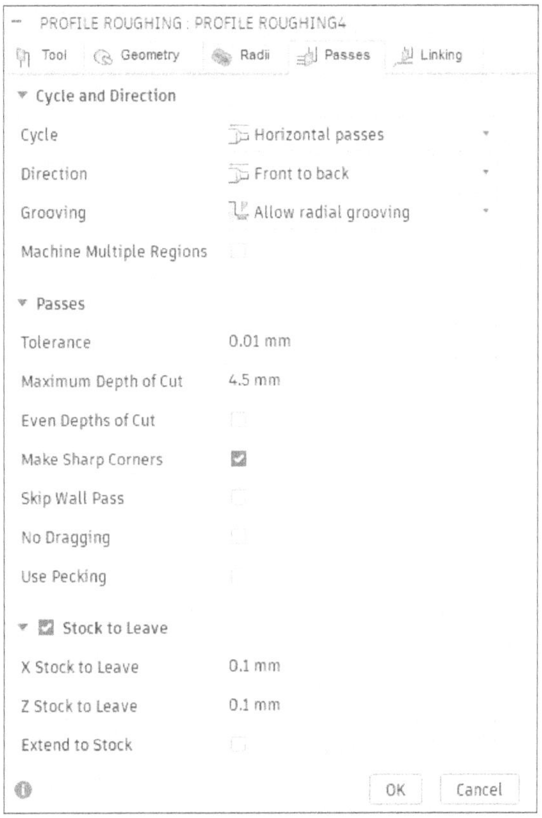

Figure-9. Passes tab of PROFILE ROUGHING dialog box

- Specify the maximum depth of cut allowed for each cutting pass in the **Maximum Depth of Cut** edit box.
- Select the **Even Depths of Cut** check box to keep depth amount same for each cuts.
- Select the **Make Sharp Corners** check box of **Passes** tab to specify that sharp corners must be created at the corners and edges if radius is not specified.
- Select the **Skip Wall Pass** check box if you do not wall to machine walls of part.
- Select the **Use Pecking** check box to use multiple retractions along its path when tool is cutting material so that long chips are not formed while cutting. Specify related depth and retraction value for pecking in respective edit boxes below the **Use Pecking** check box.
- Specify desired values of material to be left for finishing toolpath in the edit boxes of **Stock to Leave** section of the dialog box.
- Select the **Extend to Stock** check box to extend toolpaths beyond the part surface until it reaches the boundaries of stock.

Linking

Click on the **Linking** tab of **PROFILE ROUGHING** dialog box to define how cutting passes will be connected in the toolpath. The options of **Linking** tab will be displayed; refer to Figure-10.

Figure-10. Linking Tab of PROFILE ROUGHING dialog box

- Select desired option from the **High Feedrate Mode** drop-down of the **Linking** section to define when to use G01 code of rapid feed move and when to use G00 code of rapid retraction move if there is not cutting operation involved in the current step. Select the **Always use high feed** option when there are chances of collision at maximum rapid move speed and specify desired speed in the **High Feedrate Mode** edit box.
- Select the **Rapid to Next Cutting Depth** check box to specify the rapid linking move to the next depth of cut.
- Set desired options in **Approach Z** and **Retract Z** drop-downs of the **Approach & Retract** section to define the respective safe Z locations. After cutting passes, tool will move to this location.
- Select the **Override Setup Safe Z** check box if you want to override default reference for Safe Z location and specify related offset distance.
- Specify desired values in the **Z Clearance** and **X Clearance** edit boxes of **Clearance** section to define distance in Z and X direction from the part up to which the cutting tool can reach after performing cutting pass.
- Select the **Angled Entry** check box if you want the cutting tool to enter stock from specified angle with respect to positive Z axis. After selecting the check box, specify desired entry angle value in the **Entry Angle** edit box. Click in the **Entry Clearance** edit box to define distance from the stock at which cutting tool will start moving in cutting feed mode. Click in the **Entry Feed per Revolution** edit box and specify the feed rate at which cutting tool will move while entering the stock.
- Specify desired value of retraction distance for cutting pass in the **Retract Distance** edit box.
- The other options of the dialog box are same as discussed earlier in the book.
- After specifying the parameter, click on the **OK** button from the **PROFILE ROUGHING** dialog box. The toolpath will be generated and displayed on the part; refer to Figure-11.

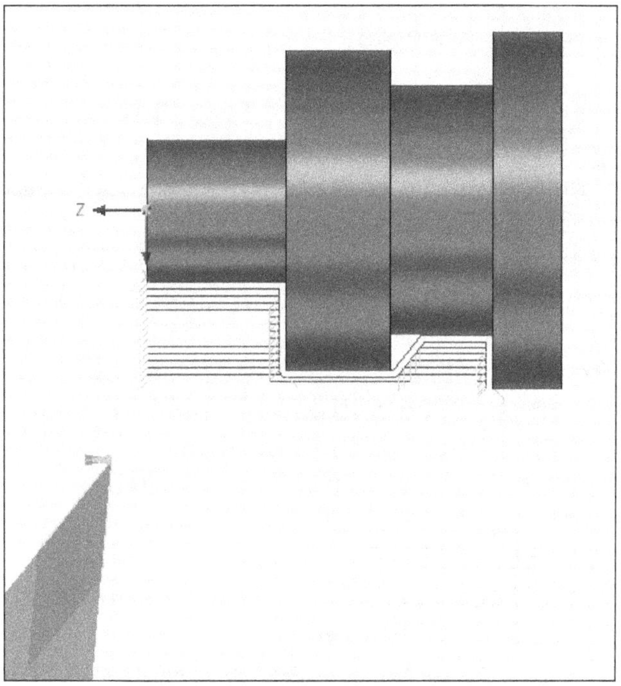

Figure-11. Generated toolpath for Turning Profile tool

Turning Profile Finishing

The **Turning Profile Finishing** tool is used to generate toolpath for performing finishing operation on the stock left by previous roughing operations. The procedure to use this tool is discussed next.

- Click on the **Turning Profile Finishing** tool from the **TURNING** drop-down in the **TURNING** tab of **Toolbar**. The **PROFILE FINISHING** dialog box will be displayed as shown in Figure-12.

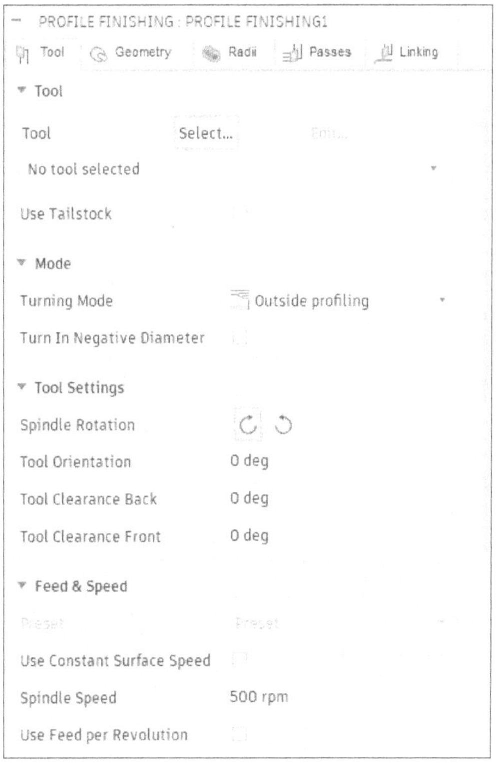

Figure-12. PROFILE FINISHING dialog box

Most of the options in this dialog box are same as discussed for **PROFILE ROUGHING** dialog box. The options which have not been discussed earlier are discussed next.

- Click in the **Tool Orientation** edit box of **Tool Settings** section in the **Tool** tab and specify the angular value by which cutting tool will be oriented on the tool post. This option is used when your lathe turret has a programmable B-Axis. This option is useful for cutting the stock corners of part.
- Click in the **Tool Clearance Back** edit box of **Tool Settings** section and specify the angular value which is added to the tool angle for providing clearance behind the cutting edge.
- Click in the **Tool Clearance Front** edit box of **Tool Settings** section and specify the angular value which is added to the tool angle for providing clearance in front of the cutting edge. Depending on the condition of your cutting tool insert, you can increase this value to use more portion of cutting tool insert for cutting.
- Select desired option from the **Preset** drop-down of the **Feed & Seed** section to use predefined cutting parameters.
- Select **Use Constant Surface Feed** check box to change the RPM of the spindle based on the current cutting diameter.
- Specify desired values in the **Surface Speed** and **Maximum Spindle Speed** edit boxes.
- Select the **Use Feed per Revolution** check box to specify feedrate in mm per revolution of spindle. Note that on selecting this check box, the **Cutting Feedrate**, **Lead-in Feedrate**, and **Lead-Out Feedrate** edit boxes will be converted to **Cutting Feed per Revolution**, **Lead-In Feed per Revolution** and **Lead-Out Feed per Revolution** edit boxes, respectively.
- Click in the **Lead-In feed per Revolution** edit box of **Feed & Speed** section and specify the feed rate of tool in cutting mode before the tool approaches and initially enters the material.
- Click in the **Lead-Out feed per Revolution** edit box of **Feed & Speed** section and specify the feedrate of tool in cutting mode when the tool exists the material.
- Select the **Spring Pass** check box from the **Passes** section of **Passes** tab in the dialog box to create additional finishing pass with zero stock thickness for better finish.
- Select the **No Dragging** check box from the **Passes** section of **Passes** tab in the dialog box to allow changing of tool position when cutting direction is switched between axial and radial. In this way, less drag (stress) is applied on the tool while cutting.
- Specify desired values for no drag parameters: **No Drag Limit**, **No Drag Clearance**, **No Drag Overlap** in their respective edit boxes. The **No Drag Limit** parameter is used to specify the minimum angle after which no drag mode will activate. The **No Drag Clearance** parameter is used to specify the distance from model face at which cutting tool will retract and switch to no drag mode. The **No Drag Overlap** parameter is used to specify overlapping distance of last cut before retracting to activate no drag mode; refer to Figure-13.

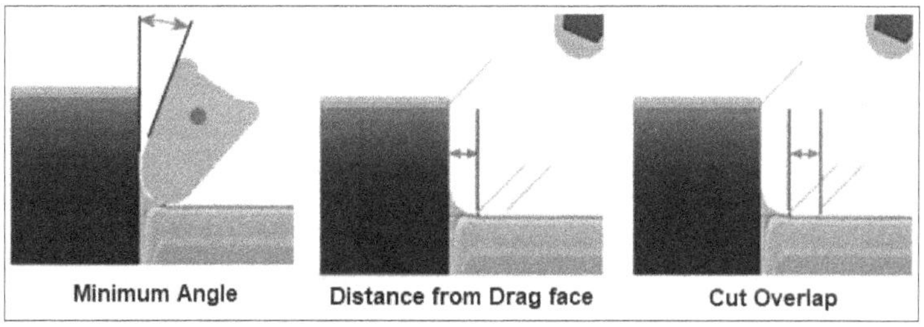

Figure-13. No Drag parameters

- Select **Machine Undercuts** check box from the **Passes** section to allow the tool to enter areas where it previously wouldn't have been able to because of under cuts areas.
- Specify desired parameters in **Leads & Transitions** section of **Linking** tab in the dialog box to define how cutting tool will enter the workpiece in first cutting pass and how tool will exit in last cutting pass.
- Specify the other parameters as discussed earlier and click on the **OK** button from the dialog box to generate the toolpath.

Turning Adaptive Roughing

The **Turning Adaptive Roughing** tool is used to remove bulk of the material from the part. The procedure to use this tool is given next.

- Click on the **Turning Adaptive Roughing** tool from the **TURNING** drop-down of **Toolbar**. The **ADAPTIVE ROUGHING** dialog box will be displayed; refer to Figure-14.

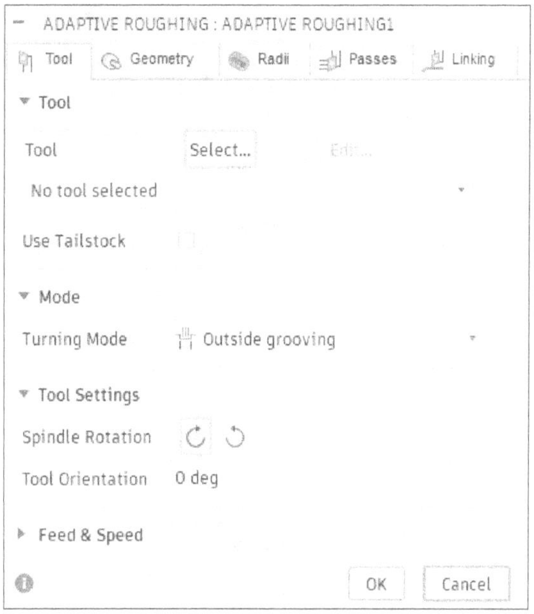

Figure-14. ADAPTIVE ROUGHING dialog box

- Select desired groove or button cutting tool for this toolpath.
- Select the **Groove Suppression** check box from the **Geometry** tab of dialog box if you want to define the faces/surfaces to be excluded during the toolpath generation; refer to Figure-15.

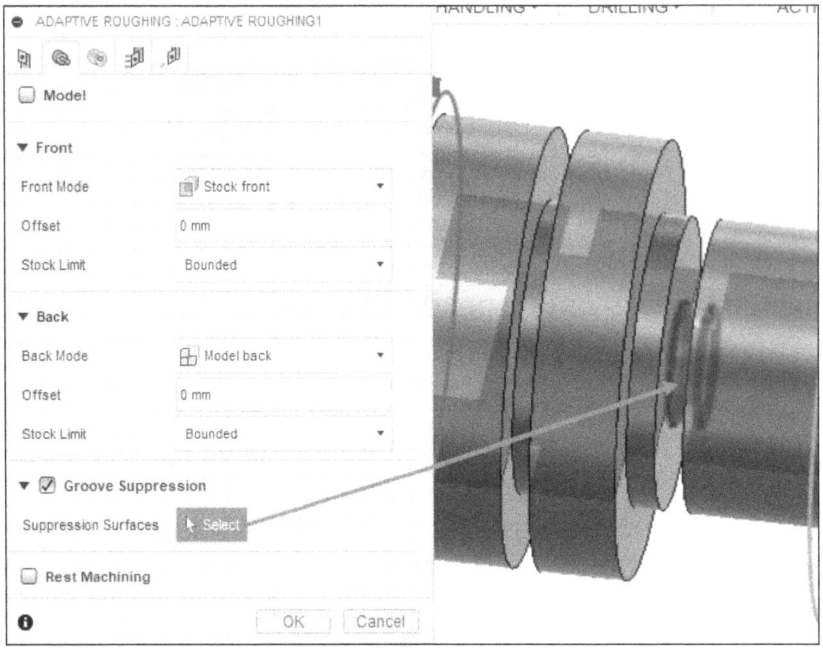

Figure-15. Face selected for groove suppression

- Set the parameters as discussed earlier and click on the **OK** button. The toolpath will be created; refer to Figure-16.

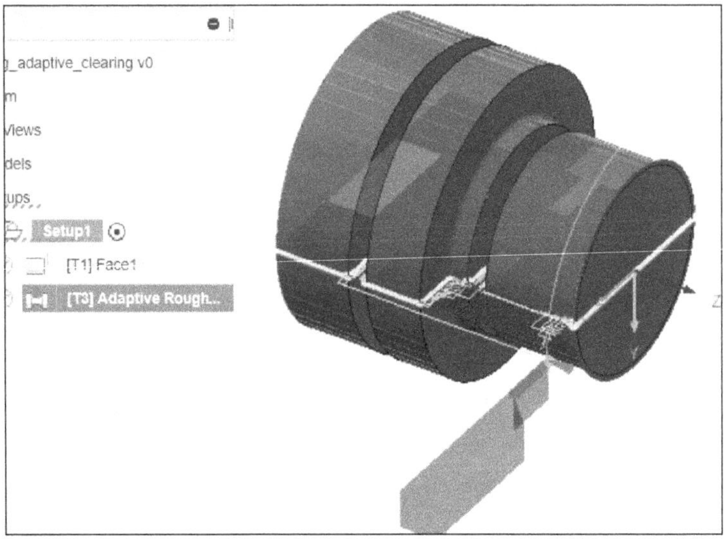

Figure-16. Adaptive roughing toolpath

Turning Groove

The **Turning Groove** tool is used for roughing and finishing strategy to create groove cuts in the model. The procedure to use this tool is discussed next.

- Click on the **Turning Groove** tool of **TURNING** drop-down from **Toolbar**; refer to Figure-17. The **GROOVE** dialog box will be displayed; refer to Figure-18.

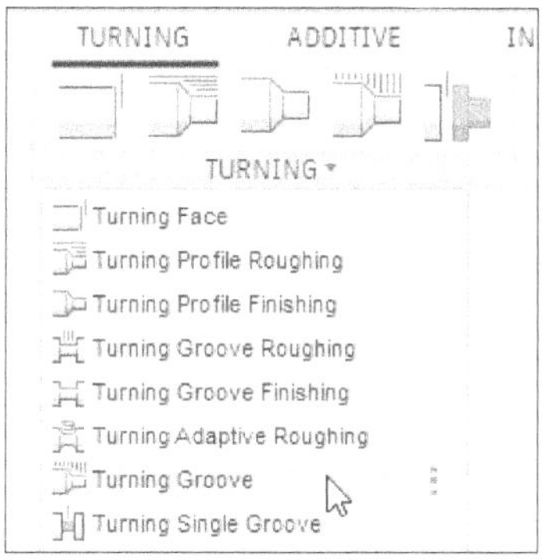

Figure-17. Turning Groove tool

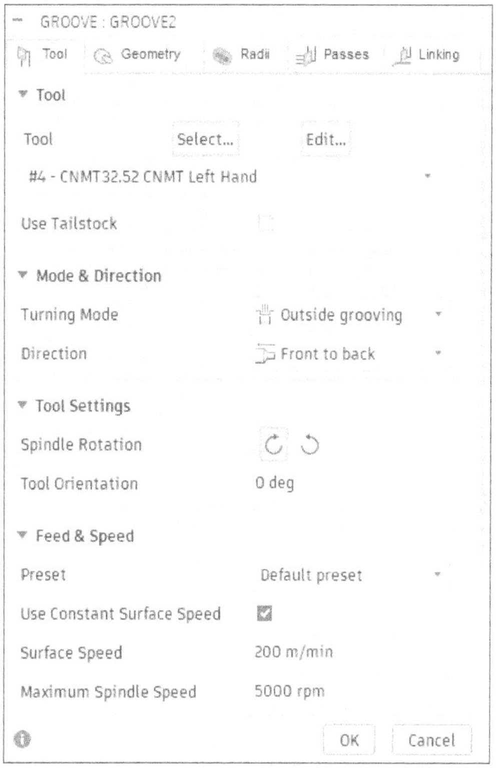

Figure-18. GROOVE dialog box

- Click in the **Select** button of **Tool** section. The **Select Tool** dialog box will be displayed. Select desired tool, generally an ID groove turning or OD groove turning tool and click on **OK** button. The tool will be added in the **GROOVE** dialog box.
- Click in the **Turning Mode** drop-down of **Mode & Direction** section from the **TOOL** tab and select desired option according to your turning strategy. If you want to create groove on outer diameter of part then select the **Outside grooving** option and if you want to create groove in the inner diameter of part then select the **Inside grooving** option.
- Click in the **Direction** drop-down of **Mode & Direction** section and select desired option to define in which direction the cutting passes will be generated.
- Select desired option from the **Preset** drop-down to set cutting speed and feed rates predefined in tool library for selected cutting tool.
- Click in the **Geometry** tab in the dialog box and set the containment region of groove as shown in Figure-19.

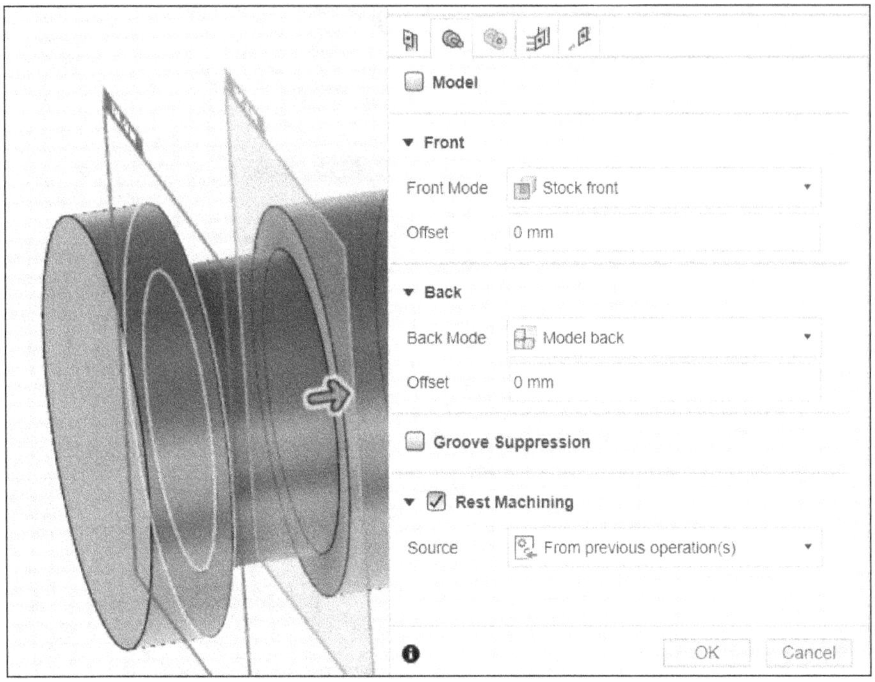

Figure-19. Selection of face for grooving

Passes tab

- Click on the **Passes** tab of the **GROOVE** dialog box. The **Passes** tab will be displayed; refer to Figure-20.

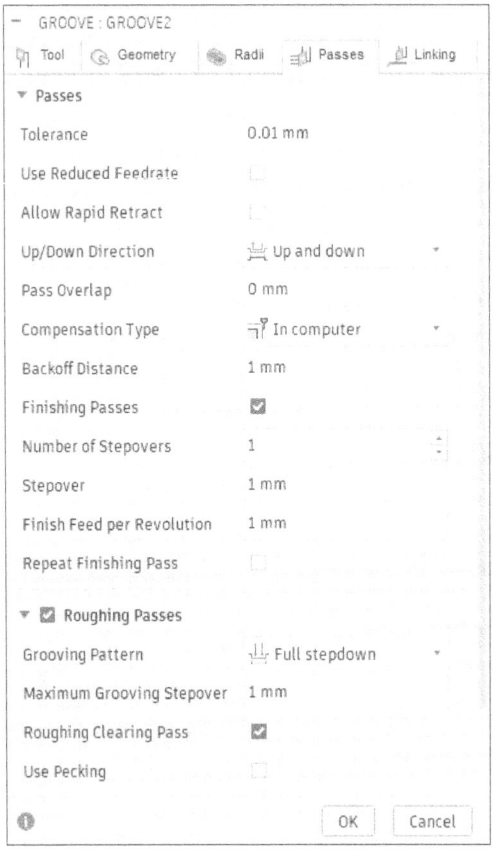

Figure-20. Passes tab of GROOVE dialog box

- Click in the **Tolerance** edit box of **Passes** tab and specify the value of tolerance allowed for linearizing toolpath curves.

- Select the **Use Reduced Feedrate** check box of **Passes** tab to reduce the feedrate when creating groove cuts along the X-Axis.
- Select the **Allow Rapid Retract** check box to retract the tool at clearance plane with maximum retraction speed.
- Click in the **Up/Down Direction** drop-down of **Passes** tab and select desired option to control the direction of finishing passes.
- Click in the **Pass Overlap** edit box of **Passes** tab to specify the overlap distance used for finishing pass split due to only up and only down machining directions.
- Click in the **Compensation Type** drop-down of **Passes** tab and select desired compensation type.
- Click in the **Backoff Distance** edit box of the **Passes** tab and specify the distance to move back at cutting feed rate from the stock before retracting at rapid rate.
- Select the **Finishing Passes** check box of the **Passes** tab to remove the material from stock using secondary finishing operation. This option is only available when **Roughing pass** check box is selected in this tab.
- Click in the **Number of Stepovers** check box of **Passes** tab and specify the value of number of finishing stepovers to be applied.
- Click in the **Stepover** edit box of **Passes** tab and specify the value of distance between two consecutive cutting passes.
- Click in the **Finish Feed per revolution** edit box of **Passes** tab and specify the value of feed rate used for final finishing pass.
- Select the **Repeat Finishing Pass** check box of **Passes** tab to perform an additional finishing pass with zero stock.
- Select **Roughing Passes** check box to enable roughing of the part before running finishing passes.
- Select the **Full stepdown** option of **Grooving Pattern** drop-down from **Passes** tab to remove the stock material radially, before moving along the spindle axis to remove material.
- Select the **Partial stepdown** option of **Grooving Pattern** drop-down to remove all the material along the spindle axis before starting to remove the material at the next depth which is specified by the **Maximum Groove Stepdown** value. The **Maximum Groove Stepdown** edit box is displayed when **Partial stepdown** option is selected in the **Grooving Pattern** drop-down.
- Select the **Sideways with Partial Stepdown** option of **Grooving Pattern** drop-down to remove the material from groove by moving cutting tool side by side. Due to this strategy, the tool life is increased and it results in smaller chips formation.
- Select the **Roughing Clearing Pass** check box to cut the cusps left by the initial roughing passes.
- Select the **Use Pecking** check box of **Passes** tab to cut the material by specified pecking depth using pecking force with the help of cutting tool. After performing one cutting pass, the tool then retracts along its path by the specified pecking retract distance.
- The other tools of the dialog box are same as discussed earlier. After specifying the parameters, click on the **OK** button from the **GROOVE** dialog box. The toolpath will be generated and displayed on the model; refer to Figure-21.

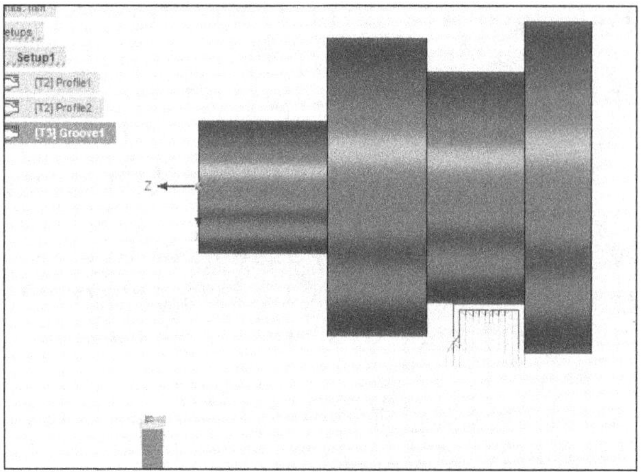

Figure-21. Generated toolpath Groove tool

Turning Groove Finishing

The **Turning Groove Finishing** tool is used to perform finishing of earlier rough machined grooves. The procedure to use this tool is given next.

- Click on the **Turning Groove Finishing** tool from the **TURNING** drop-down of the **Ribbon**. The **GROOVE FINISHING** dialog box will be displayed; refer to Figure-22.

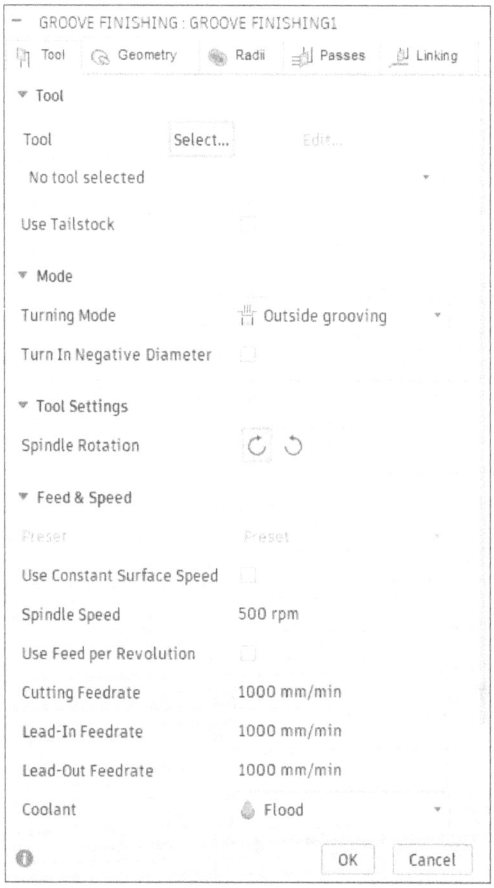

Figure-22. GROOVE FINISHING dialog box

- Select the turning groove cutting tool suitable for finishing operation from the **Tool** tab of dialog box.
- Select desired option from the **Turning Mode** drop-down to define whether you want to perform outside grooving, inside grooving, or face grooving.

- Click on the **Passes** tab of the dialog box to define parameters related to cutting passes. The options will be displayed as shown in Figure-23.

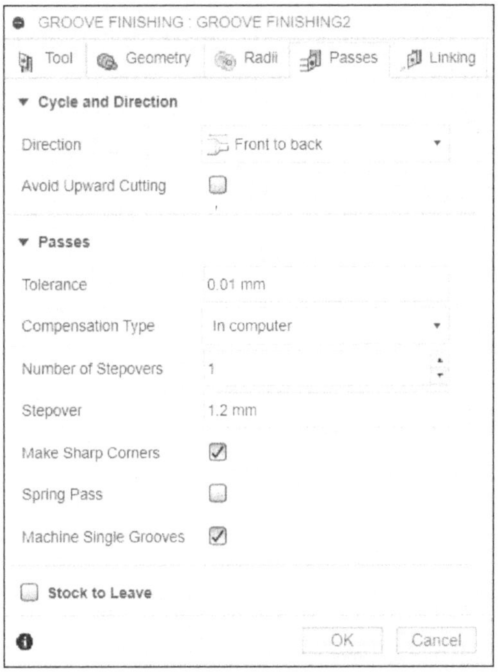

Figure-23. Passes tab of GROOVE FINISHING dialog box

- Select desired option from the **Direction** drop-down to define the direction in which cutting operation can be performed.
- Select the **Avoid Upward Cutting** check box to make sure no upward cutting is performed which can cause shear forces on the tool.
- Select the **Spring Pass** check box to perform additional finishing operation with 0 stock left.
- Set the other parameters as discussed earlier and click on the **OK** button to generate toolpath; refer to Figure-24.

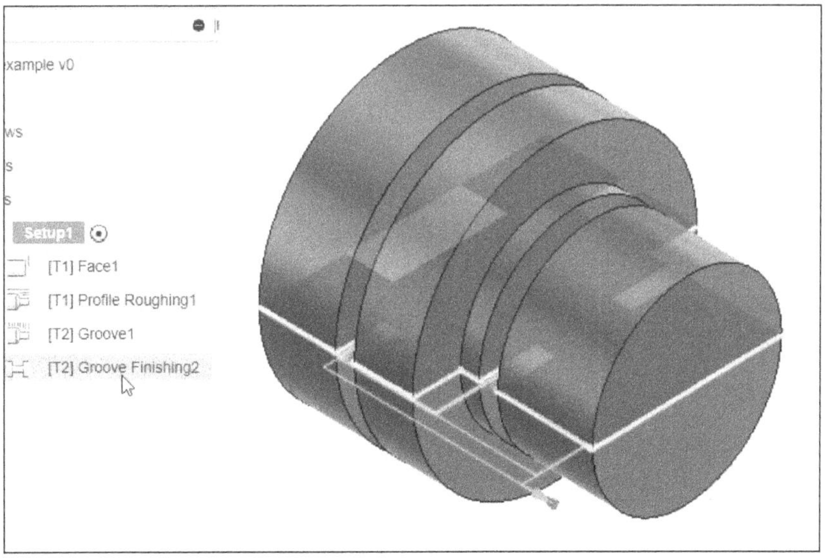

Figure-24. Groove finishing toolpath

Similarly, you can use the **Turning Groove Roughing** tool from the **TURNING** panel in the **Ribbon**.

Turning Single Groove

The **Turning Single Groove** tool is used for machining groove at selected position only. This tool will create a groove equal to the width of the tool. This is perfect for making a clearance groove behind the thread. The procedure to use this tool is discussed next.

- Click on the **Turning Single Groove** tool of the **TURNING** drop-down from **Toolbar**; refer to Figure-25. The **SINGLE GROOVE** dialog box will be displayed; refer to Figure-26.

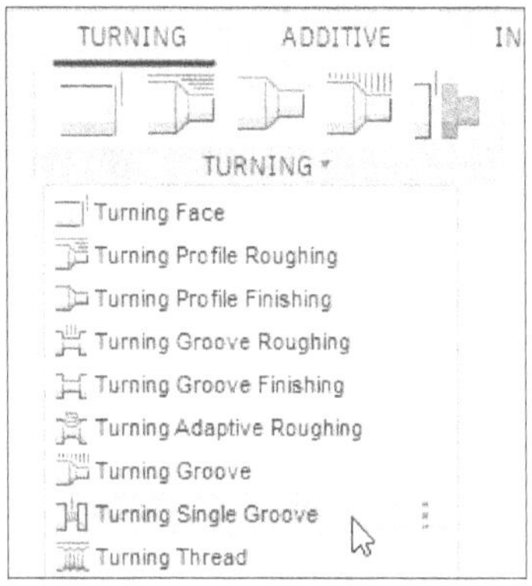

Figure-25. Turning Single Groove tool

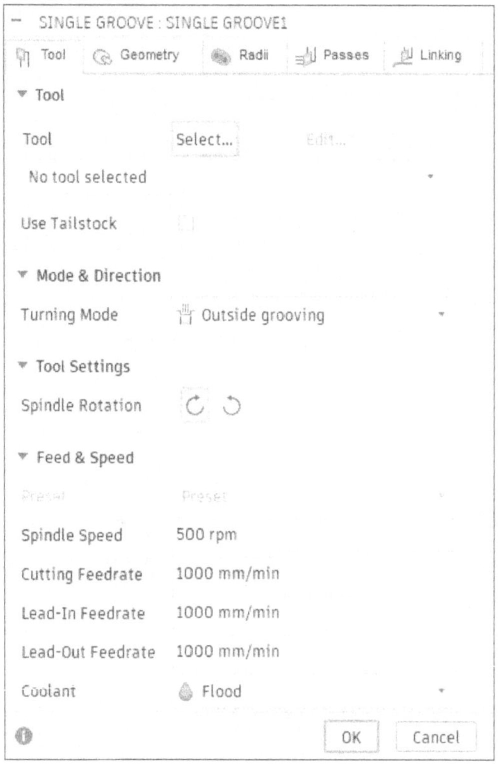

Figure-26. SINGLE GROOVE dialog box

- Click on the **Select** button of **Tool** section. The **Select Tool** dialog box will be displayed. Select desired tool, generally a grooving tool and click on **OK** button. The tool will be added in the **SINGLE GROOVE** dialog box.

Geometry

- Click on the **Geometry** tab of **SINGLE GROOVE** dialog box. The options tab will be displayed; refer to Figure-27. The **Nothing** button of **Groove Positions** section of **Geometry** tab will be active by default and you will be asked to select edge of the groove to be machined.

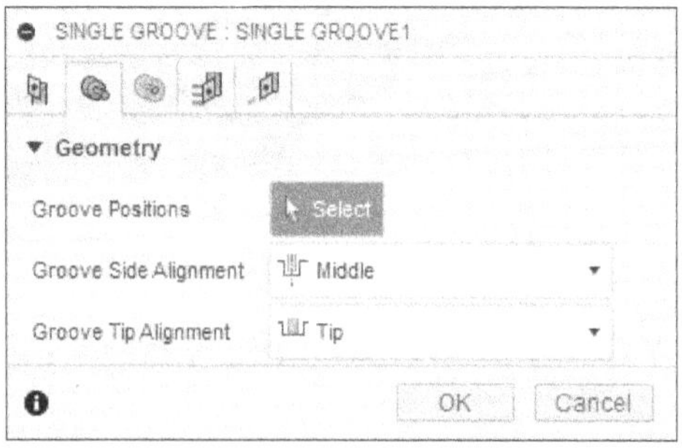

Figure-27. Geometry tab of SINGLE GROOVE dialog box

- Select desired edge of the model for groove machining.
- Click on the **Groove Side Alignment** drop-down of **Geometry** section and select desired option for alignment of tools side edge.
- Click on the **Groove Tip Alignment** drop-down of **Geometry** section and select desired option for alignment of tool tip.
- Select the **Dwell Before Retract** check box in **Passes** tab of dialog box to give a pause of specified seconds before grooving tool comes out of the workpiece after cutting. Specify desired dwell time (in seconds) in the **Dwelling Period** edit box.
- Select the **Allow Rapid Retract** check box if you want to use G00 code for retraction of tool. By default, rapid feed rate is used for retraction.
- The other options of the dialog box are same as discussed earlier. After specifying various parameters, click on the **OK** button from the **SINGLE GROOVE** dialog box. The toolpath will be generated and displayed on the model; refer to Figure-28.

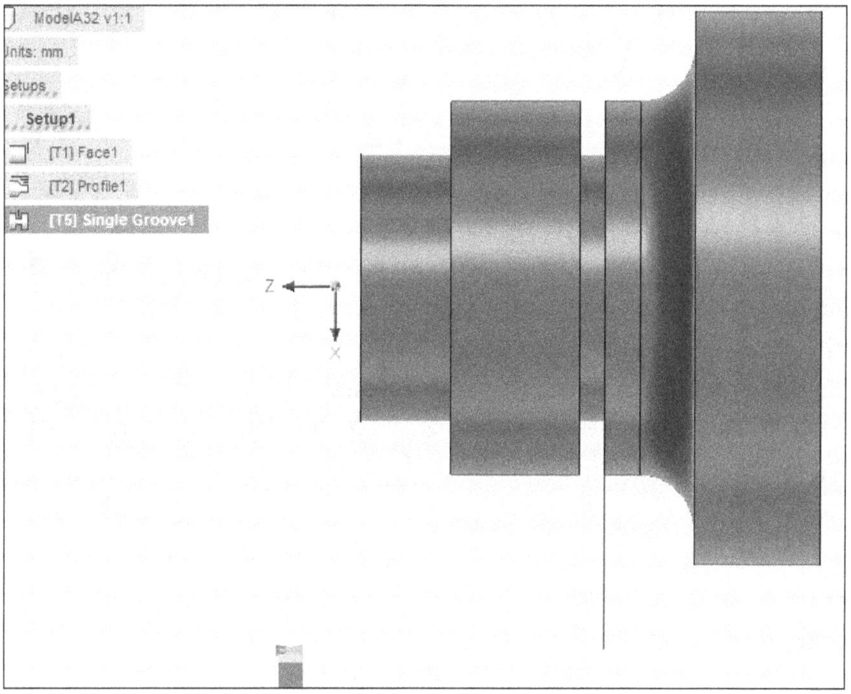

Figure-28. Toolpath generated for Single Groove tool

Turning Thread

The **Turning Thread** tool is used to cut threads on cylindrical and conical surfaces. The procedure to use this tool is discussed next.

- Click on the **Turning Thread** tool of **TURNING** drop-down from **Toolbar**; refer to Figure-29. The **THREAD** dialog box will be displayed; refer to Figure-30.

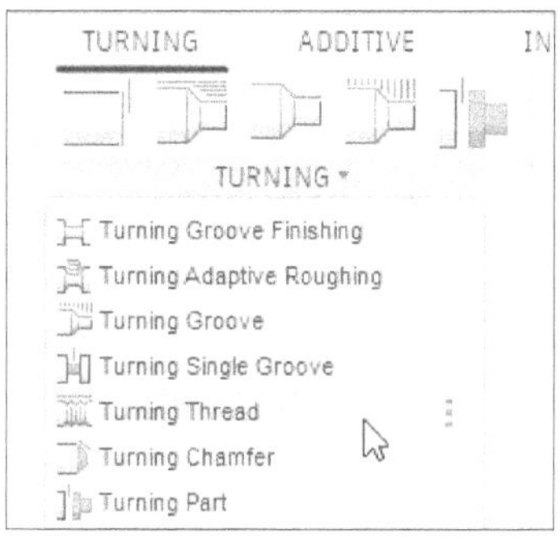

Figure-29. Turning Thread tool

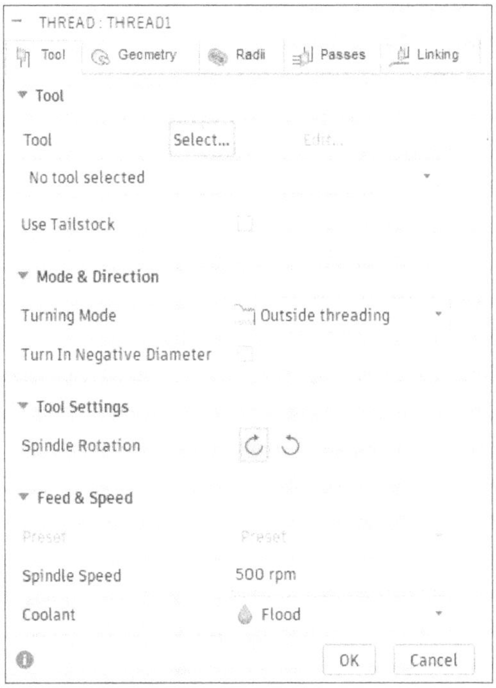

Figure-30. THREAD dialog box

- Click on the **Select** button of **Tool** section. The **Select Tool** dialog box will be displayed. Select desired tool and click on **OK** button. The tool will be added in the **THREAD** dialog box.
- Click on the **Select** button for **Thread Faces** section from the **Geometry** tab and select the round faces on which you want to machine threads; refer to Figure-31.

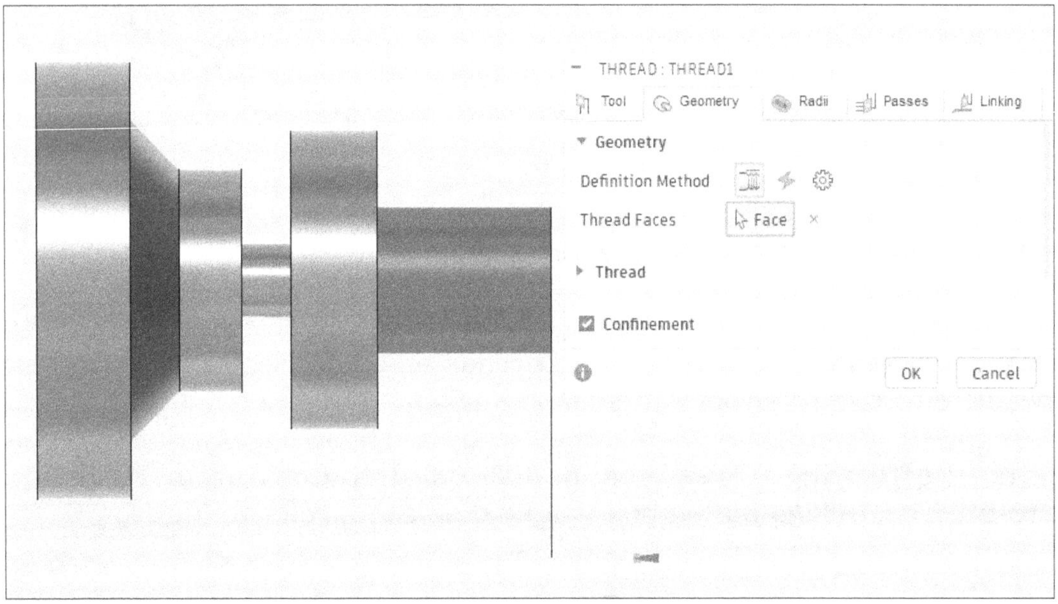

Figure-31. Selection of Face for thread

Passes

- Click on the **Passes** tab of **THREAD** dialog box. The **Passes** tab will be displayed; refer to Figure-32.

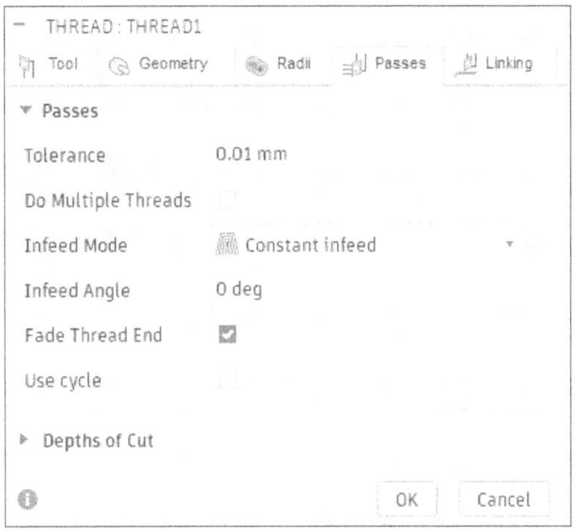

Figure-32. Passes tab of THREAD dialog box

- Click on the **Threading Hand** drop-down of **Passes** tab and select desired threading direction.
- Click in the **Thread Depth** edit box of **Passes** tab and specify desired value to define the depth of thread.
- Click in the **Thread Pitch** edit box of **Passes** tab and specify the value of thread pitch (distance between two consecutive strands of thread).
- Select the **Do Multiple Threads** check box of **Passes** tab to create multi-start threads and specify number of threads to be created.
- Click in the **Number of Threads** edit box of **Passes** tab and specify desired value to define the number of thread leads.
- Click in the **Infeed Mode** drop-down of **Passes** tab and select the required option.
- Click in the **Infeed Angle** edit box of **Passes** tab and specify angular infeed value at which cutting tool will move while cutting.
- Select the **Fade Thread End** check box of **Passes** tab to fade out the thread at the end. This fading helps easy assembly of fasteners.
- Select the **Use cycle** check box of **Passes** tab to request output as canned cycle.
- Click in the **First Pass** edit box from the **Depths and Cut** section to specify desired size of first step-down.
- Click in the **Number of Stepdowns** edit box of **Passes** tab and specify desired number of step downs to be performed for achieving desired depth.
- Select the **Spring Pass** check box from **Depths of Cut** section of **Passes** tab to perform the final finishing pass twice to remove stock left due to tool deflection.
- The other options of the dialog box were discussed earlier.
- After specifying the parameters, click on the **OK** button from the **THREAD** dialog box. The toolpath will be generated and displayed on the model; refer to Figure-33.

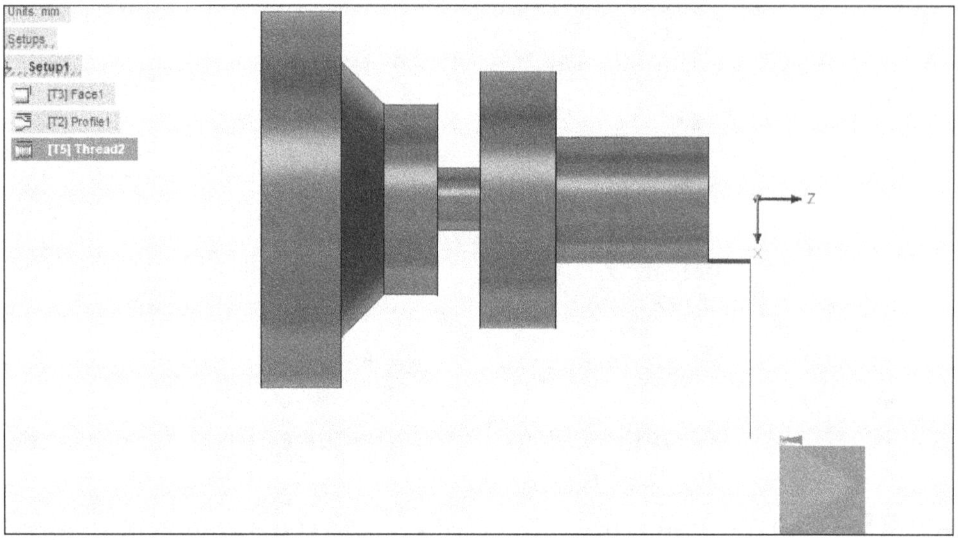

Figure-33. Toolpath generated for thread tool

- After simulating the thread toolpath, the model will be displayed as shown in Figure-34.

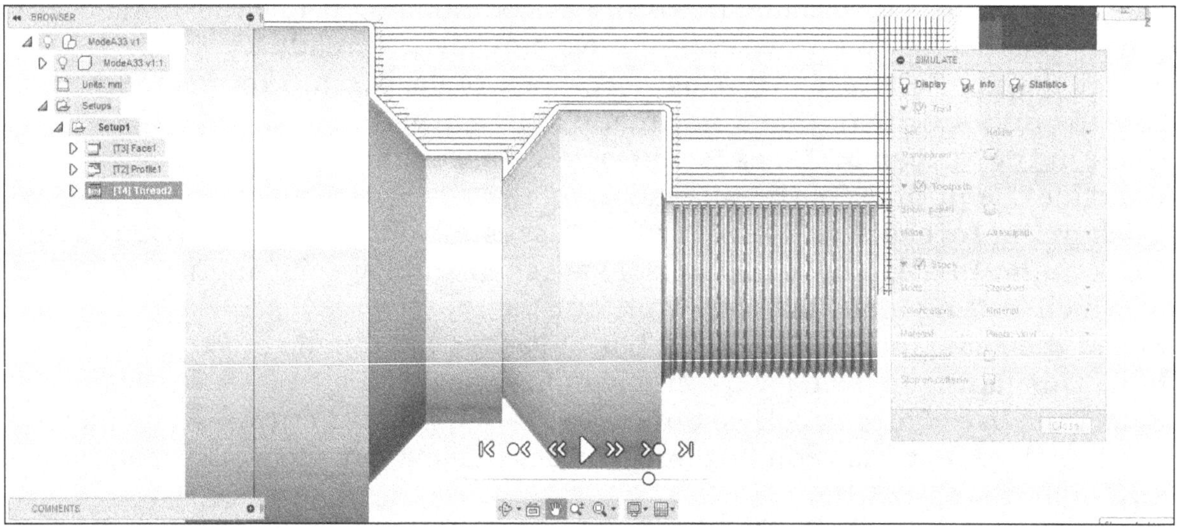

Figure-34. Simulating thread toolpath

Turning Chamfer

The **Turning Chamfer** tool is used to create toolpath for chamfering sharp corners of the model that have not been created in the design. The procedure to use this tool is discussed next.

- Click on the **Turning Chamfer** tool of **TURNING** drop-down from the **Toolbar**; refer to Figure-35. The **CHAMFER** dialog box will be displayed; refer to Figure-36.

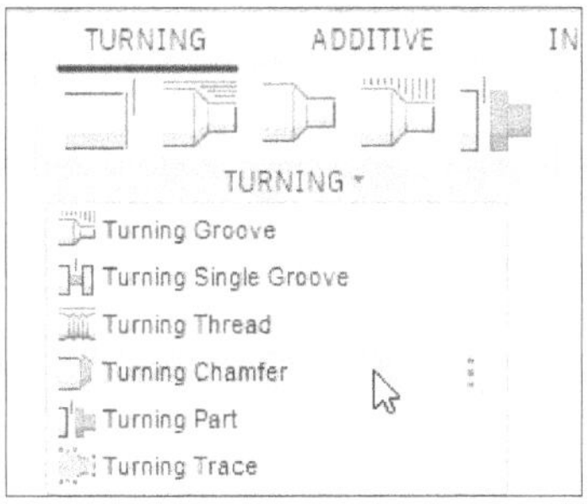

Figure-35. Turning Chamfer tool

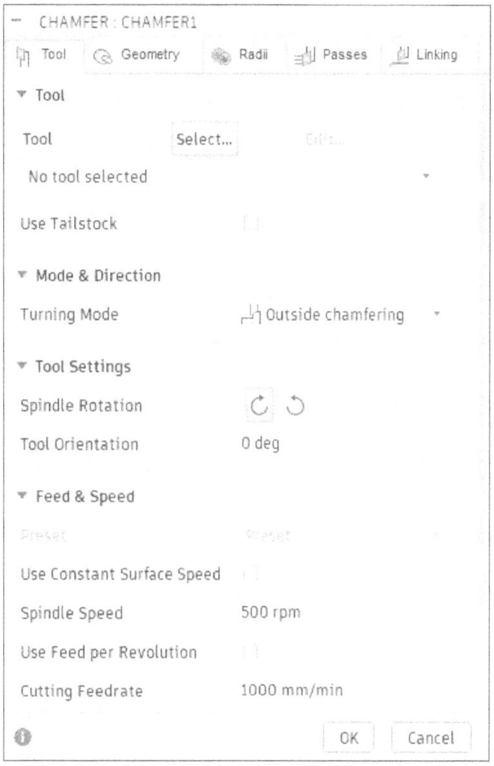

Figure-36. CHAMFER dialog box

- Click on the **Select** button of **Tool** section. The **Select Tool** dialog box will be displayed. Select the required tool and click on **OK** button. The tool will be added in the **CHAMFER** dialog box.
- Click on the **Turning Mode** drop-down of **Mode & Direction** section from **Tool** tab and select desired option to define cutting direction of chamfer.
- Click in the **Tool Orientation** edit box of **Tool Settings** section from **Tool** tab and specify desired angle value to orient the tool.

Geometry

- Click in the **Geometry** tab of **CHAMFER** dialog box. The options will be displayed as shown in Figure-37.

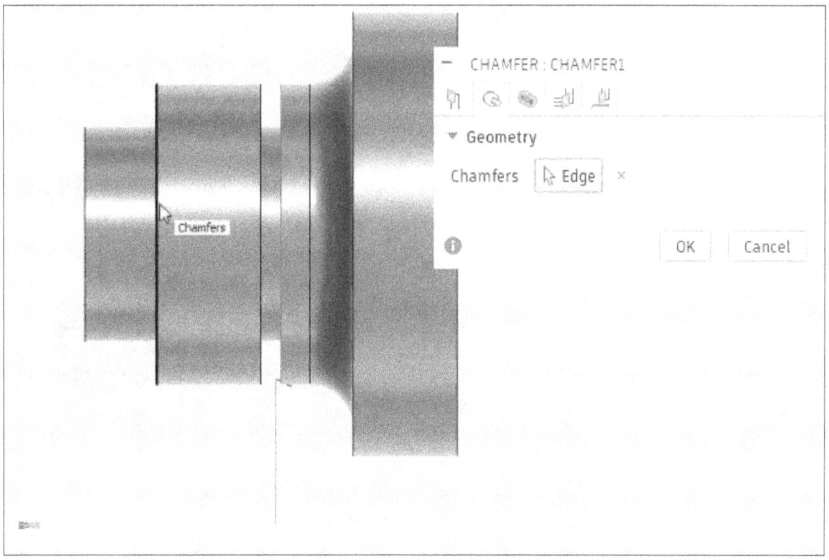

Figure-37. Geometry tab of CHAMFER dialog box

- The **Select** button of **Chamfers** section is active by default. Select the edges from model on which you want to apply chamfer.

Passes

- Click on the **Passes** tab of **CHAMFER** dialog box. The **Passes** tab will be displayed; refer to Figure-38.

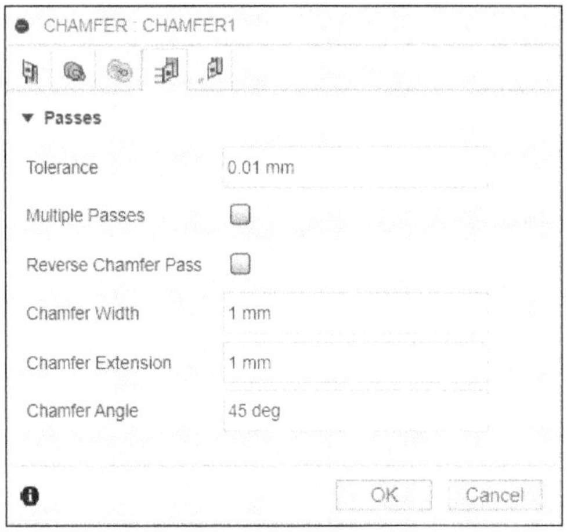

Figure-38. Passes tab of CHAMFER dialog box

- Select the **Reverse Chamfer Pass** check box to reverse the cutting direction while creating chamfer.
- Click in the **Chamfer Width** edit box of **Passes** tab and specify the value of width of chamfer.
- Click in the **Chamfer Extension** edit box of **Passes** tab and specify the value by which the chamfer cutting pass will be extended.
- Click in the **Chamfer Angle** edit box of **Passes** tab and specify the angle value of chamfer measured from the Z-Axis.
- The other options of the dialog box are same as discussed earlier in the book. After specifying the parameters, click on the **OK** button from **CHAMFER** dialog box. The toolpath will be generated and displayed on the model; refer to Figure-39.

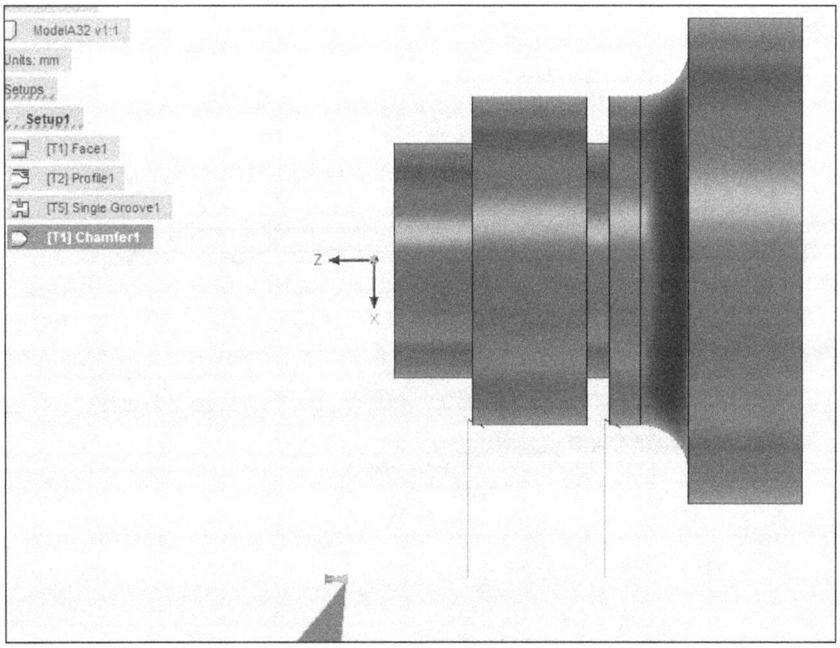

Figure-39. The generated toolpath for Chamfer tool

Turning Part

The **Turning Part** tool is used to cut off the part from the bar. This process is also known as cut off operation. The procedure to use this tool is discussed next.

- Click on the **Turning Part** tool of **TURNING** drop-down from **Toolbar**; refer to Figure-40. The **PART** dialog box will be displayed; refer to Figure-41.

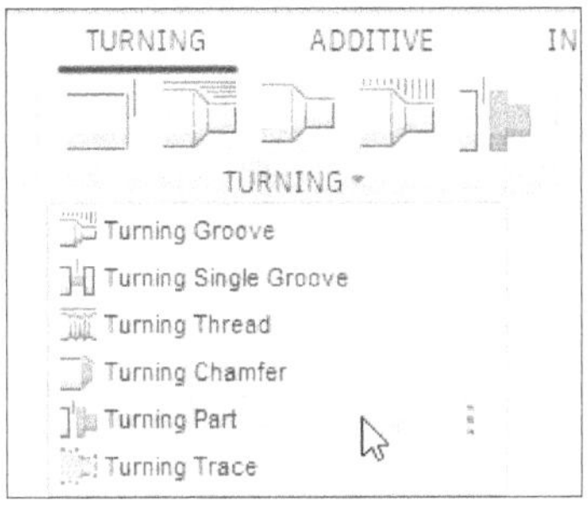

Figure-40. Turning Part tool

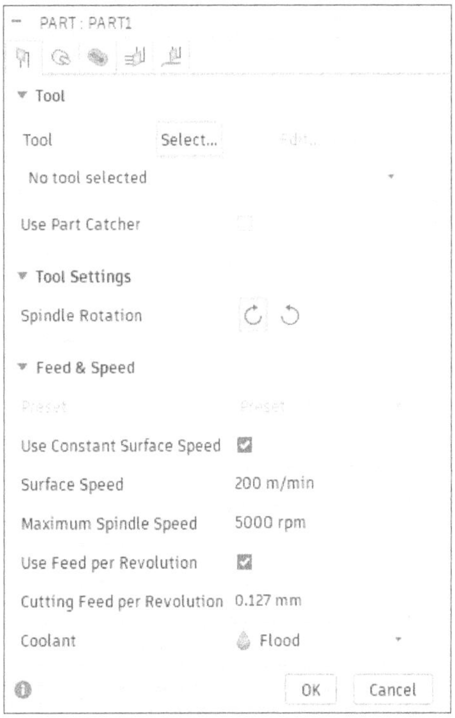

Figure-41. PART dialog box

- Click on the **Select** button from **Tool** section. The **Select Tool** dialog box will be displayed. Select desired tool and click on **OK** button. The tool will be added in the **PART** dialog box.
- Select the **Use Part Catcher** check box to use gripper arm/part catcher for removing part from chuck. Make sure your machine has part catcher installed and your machine control system supports the codes.
- Select the **Edge Break** check box from the **Geometry** tab in the dialog box to define how edges will be conditioned while parting; refer to Figure-42.

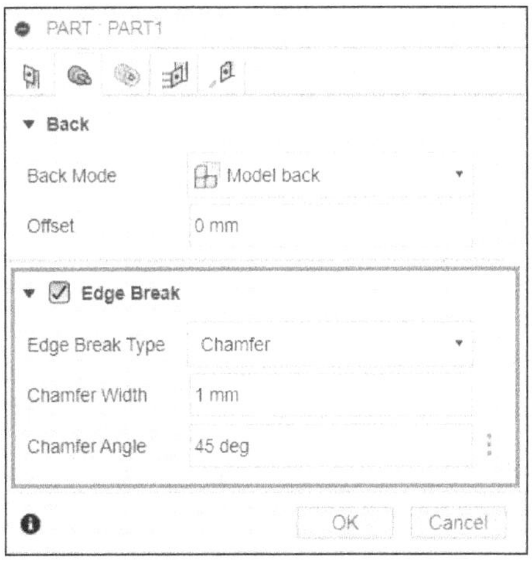

Figure-42. Edge Break options

- Select the **Chamfer** option from the **Edge Break Type** drop-down to create chamfer at the outer edge before cut off. Select the **Fillet** option from the **Edge Break Type** drop-down to create round at the outer edge before cut off. Specify the parameters related to the selected option in the edit boxes of **Edge Break** section.
- The other options of the dialog box are same as discussed earlier. After specifying the parameters, click on the **OK** button from the **PART** dialog box. The toolpath will be generated and displayed on the model; refer to Figure-43.

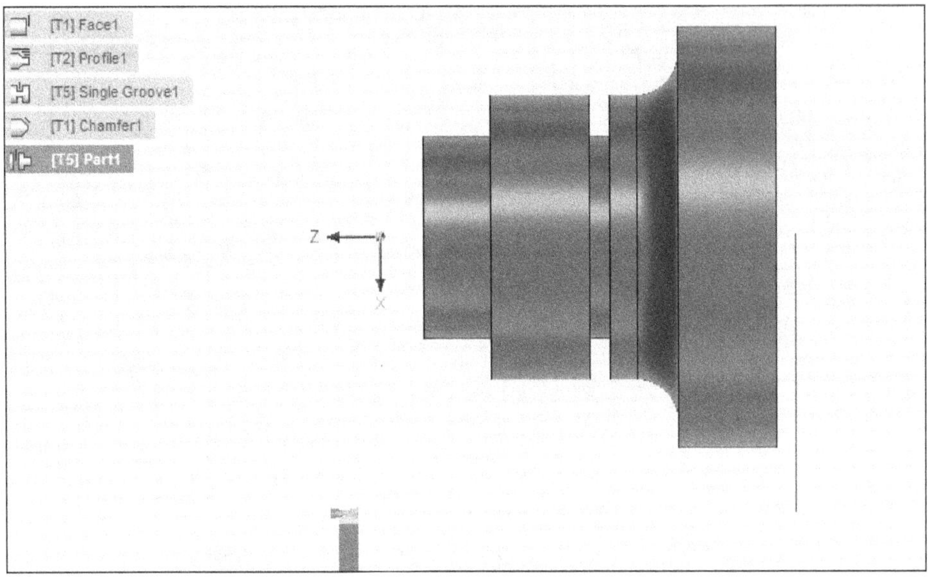

Figure-43. Generated toolpath for Turning Path tool

Sub-Spindle Grab

The **Subspindle Grab** tool is used to transfer stock from one chuck to another (Sub-spindle). This tool is useful when you want to machine back side of part after machining the front side. The procedure to use this tool is discussed next.

- Click on the **Subspindle Grab** tool of **PART HANDLING** drop-down in **Toolbar**; refer to Figure-44. The **SUBSPINDLE GRAB** dialog box will be displayed; refer to Figure-45

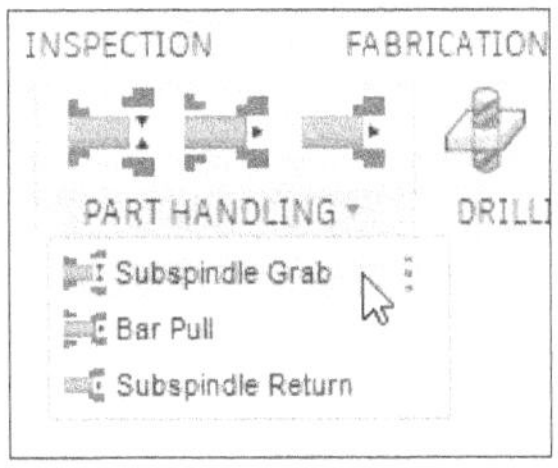

Figure-44. Subspindle Grab tool

Figure-45. SUBSPINDLE GRAB dialog box

- Click in the **Feed Plane Mode** drop-down of **Feed Plane** section and select desired option to specify the feed plane at which transfer will occur.
- Click in the **Offset** edit box of **Feed Plane** section and specify the offset distance from feed plane.
- Click in the **Grab Plane Mode** drop-down from **Grab Plane** section and select desired option to specify the chuck plane.
- Click in the **Offset** edit box of **Grab Plane** section and specify the offset distance from selected chuck plane.
- Click in the **Feedrate** edit box of **Feed & Speed** section from **SUBSPINDLE GRAB** dialog box and specify the value of feed rate at which chuck will move for stock transfer.
- Select the **Stop Spindle During Grab** check box of **Feed & Speed** section to keep spindle stopped during stock transfer operations. If this check box is not selected then you can specify rotation speed of spindle during stock transfer.
- Click in the **Spindle Speed** edit box of **Feed & Speed** section and specify the spindle speed given in rotation per minute to apply during rotation.
- Click in the **Dwelling Period** edit box of **Feed & Speed** section and specify the time for the operation to dwell (waiting period).
- Select the **Use Part Catcher** check box of **Feed & Speed** section to activate part catcher, if available.
- Click on the **OK** button from the dialog box. The operation will be created and displayed in the **BROWSER**. Note that there is no simulation for this operation in the software. Only NC codes are generated for this operation based on selected machine post processor.

Bar Pull

The **Bar Pull** tool is used to pull the stock from the main spindle using the sub-spindle. It generates an M code for this operation without creating a toolpath. The procedure to use this tool is discussed next.

- Click on the **Bar Pull** tool from the **PART HANDLING** drop-down in **Toolbar**; refer to Figure-46. The **BAR PULL** dialog box will be displayed; refer to Figure-47.

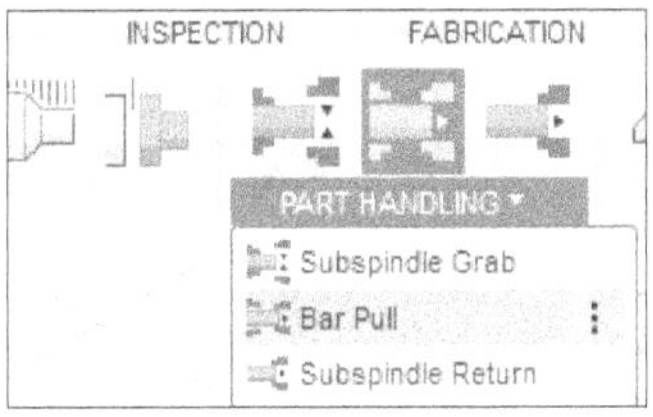

Figure-46. Bar Pull tool

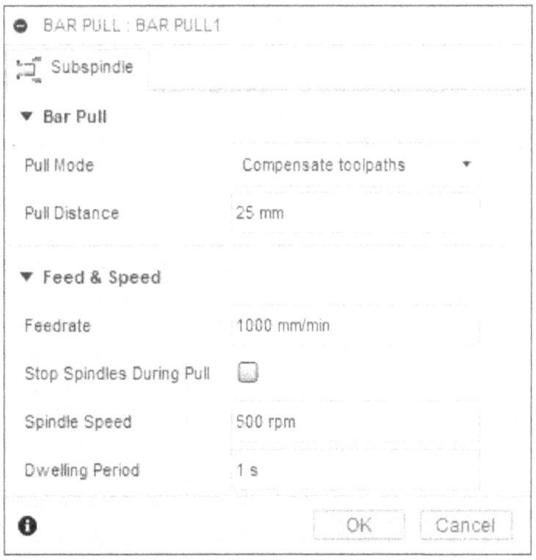

Figure-47. BAR PULL dialog box

- Click in the **Pull Mode** drop-down of **Bar Pull** section and select desired option to determine how the coordinate for the shifted part will be calculated.

- Click in the **Pull Distance** edit box of **Bar Pull** section to specify how far the sub-spindle moves from the Grab plane to pull the bar out of the spindle.
- Click in the **WCS OFFSET** edit box of **WCS Offset** section and specify desired value of coordinate system after the pull.
- Click in the **Feedrate** edit box of **Feed & Speed** section from **SUBSPINDLE GRAB** dialog box and specify the value of feed rate at which chuck will move for stock transfer.
- Select the **Stop Spindle During Grab** check box of **Feed & Speed** section to keep spindle stopped during stock transfer operations. If this check box is not selected then you can specify rotation speed of spindle during stock transfer.
- Click in the **Spindle Speed** edit box of **Feed & Speed** section and specify the spindle speed given in rotation per minute to apply during rotation.
- Click in the **Dwelling Period** edit box of **Feed & Speed** section and specify the time for the operation to dwell (waiting period).
- After specifying the parameters, click on the **OK** button from the dialog box. The operation will be created and displayed in the **BROWSER**; refer to Figure-48.

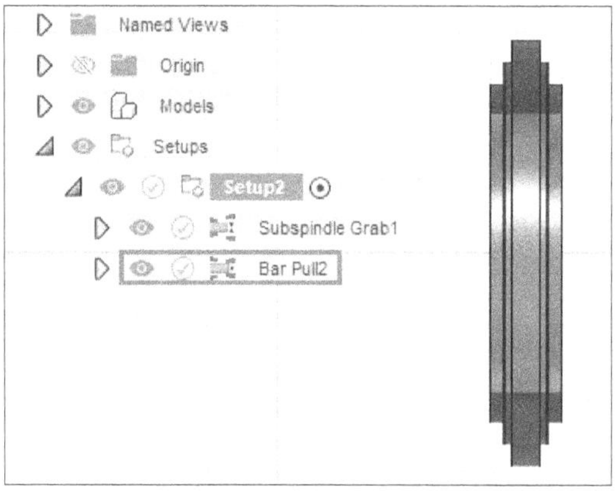

Figure-48. Bar pull created

Subspindle Return

The **Subspindle Return** tool is used for automatic stock return from secondary chuck to main chuck. No toolpath is associated with the strategy. The procedure to use this tool is discussed next.

- Click on the **Subspindle Return** tool of the **PART HANDLING** drop-down from **Toolbar**; refer to Figure-49. The **SUBSPINDLE RETURN** dialog box will be displayed; refer to Figure-50.

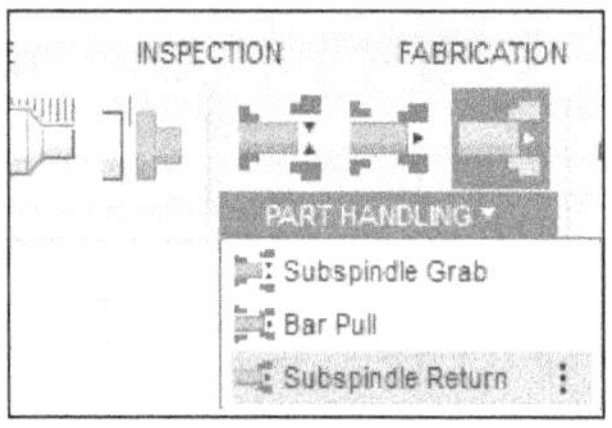

Figure-49. Turning Secondary Spindle Return tool

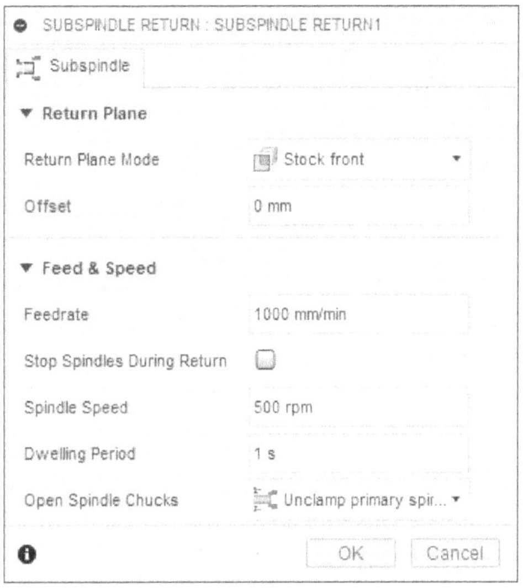

Figure-50. SECONDARY SPINDLE RETURN dialog box

- Click in the **Return Plane Mode** drop-down from the **Return Plane** section and select desired option to specify the return plane.
- Click in the **Offset** edit box of the **Return Plane** section and specify offset distance from selected reference for return plane.
- Click in the **Feedrate** edit box of the **Feed & Speed** section from **SUBSPINDLE RETURN** dialog box and specify desired value of feedrate.
- Select the **Stop Spindles During Return** check box of **Feed & Speed** section to keep spindle stopped during operations.
- Click in the **Spindle Speed** edit box of **Feed & Speed** section and specify the value of spindle speed in rpm for each machining operation.
- Click in the **Dwelling Period** edit box of **Feed & Speed** section and specify time for the operation to pause.
- Click on the **Open Spindle Chucks** drop-down of **Feed & Speed** section and select desired option to choose which spindle chucks to open before returning the secondary spindle to original position; refer to Figure-51.

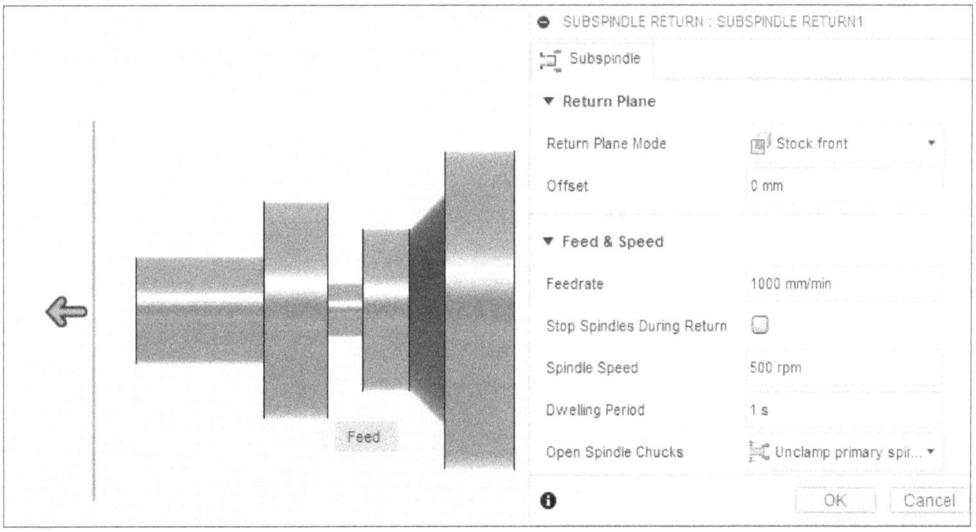

Figure-51. Subspindle Return options

- After specifying the parameters, click on the **OK** button from the **SUBSPINDLE RETURN** dialog box. The operation will be added in the **BROWSER**.

GENERATING CUTTING TOOLPATHS

Till now, you have learned the procedure to use turning toolpaths and milling toolpaths. In this section, we will discuss the procedure of generating toolpaths for 2D profile cutting using machines like water jet, laser, and plasma cutters.

Cutting

The **2D Profile** tool is used to create toolpaths for cutting 2D Profile of the stock with the help of Laser machine, Plasma cutters, and Water jet machines. The procedure to use this tool is discussed next.

- Click on the **2D Profile** tool from the **CUTTING** panel in the **FABRICATION** tab of **Toolbar**; refer to Figure-52. The **2D PROFILE** dialog box will be displayed; refer to Figure-53.

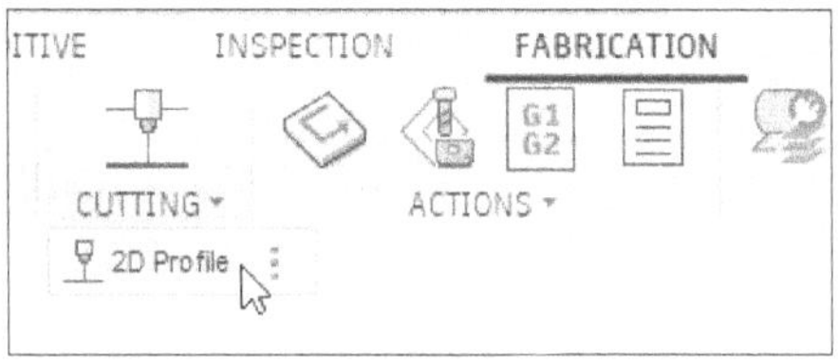

Figure-52. 2D Profile tool

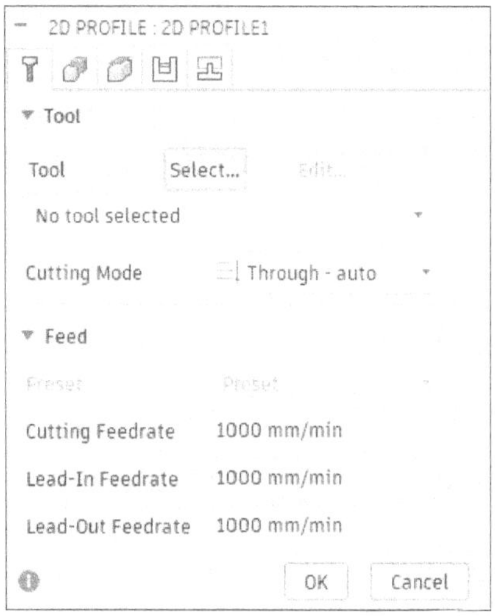

Figure-53. 2D PROFILE dialog box

- Click on the selection button for **Tool** section. The **Select Tool** dialog box will be displayed. Select desired tool for cutting (waterjet, laser cutting, or plasma cutter) and click on **OK** button. The tool will be added in the **2D PROFILE** dialog box.
- Click on the **Cutting Mode** drop-down of **Tool** section and select desired option to set the appropriate cutting quality. In some machines, there are internal quality tables to set the value.

Geometry

- Click on the **Geometry** tab of **2D PROFILE** dialog box. The options will be displayed as shown in Figure-54.

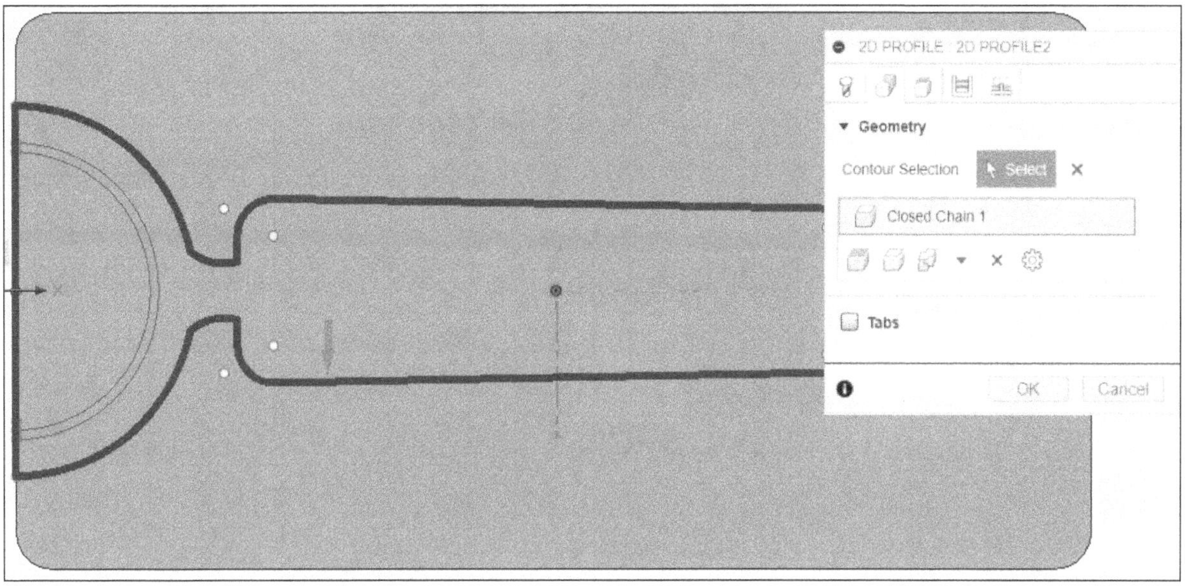

Figure-54. Geometry Tab of 2D PROFILE dialog box

- The **Select** button of **Contour Selection** section is active by default. You need to click on the curve contours from the model or sketches from **BROWSER** to be cut.
- Select the **Tabs** check box to use tabs for supporting workpiece and holding it during cutting operation. The options will be displayed as shown in Figure-55.

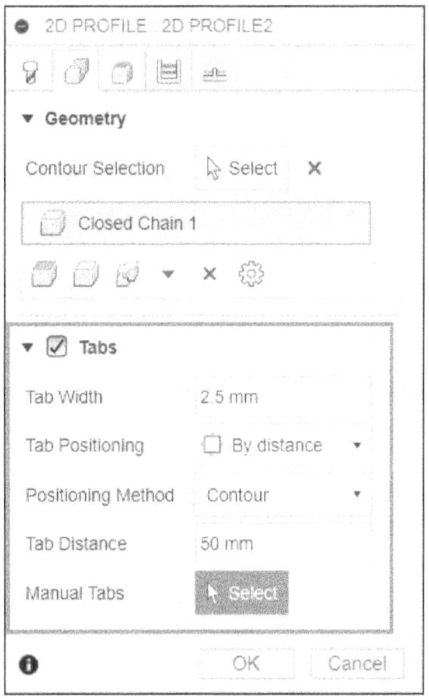

Figure-55. Tabs parameters

- Set the width of tab in the **Tab Width** edit box.
- Select the **By distance** option from the **Tab Positioning** drop-down to define distance between two consecutive tabs. Select the **Number of tabs** option from the drop-down to define number of tabs along the contour.
- Select the **Select** button for **Manual Tabs** option from the dialog box and click on the contour of profile to manually add supporting tabs.
- Set the other parameters as discussed earlier.

Linking

- Click on the **Linking** tab of **2D PROFILE** dialog box. The options will be displayed as shown in Figure-56.

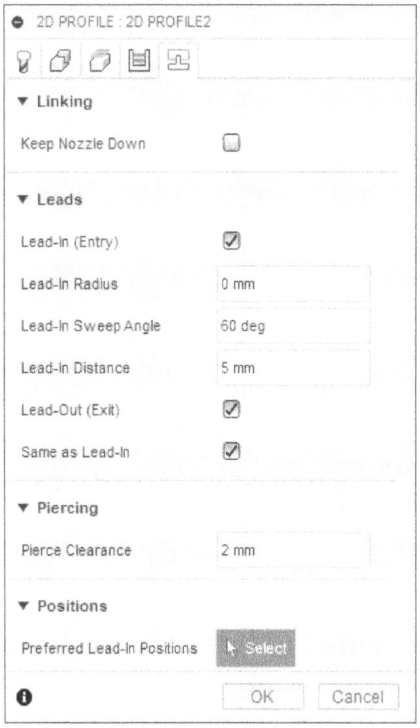

Figure-56. Linking Tab of 2D PROFILE dialog box

- Select the **Keep Nozzle Down** check box of **Linking** tab to avoid retracts and avoid previously cut areas. Set desired parameters in **Linking** section which are displayed on selecting the **Keep Nozzle Down** check box as discussed earlier.
- Select the **Lead-In (Entry)** check box of **Leads** section to enable a contour blend while entering workpiece.
- Click in the **Lead-In Radius** edit box of **Leads** section and specify the value to define the radius for lead in moves.
- Click in the **Lead-In Sweep Angle** edit box of **Leads** section and specify the value to define the sweep angle of the lead-in arc.
- Click in the **Lead-In Distance** edit box of **Leads** section and specify the value to define length of the linear lead-in move.
- Select the **Lead-Out (Exit)** check box of **Linking** tab to enable a contour blend while exiting the workpiece after operation.
- Select the **Same as Lead-In** check box of **Linking** tab to set the lead-out values identical to lead-in values as specified earlier.
- Click in the **Pierce Clearance** edit box of **Piercing** section and specify the value to distance away from the part edge to start the cut.
- The **Select** button for **Preferred Lead-In Positions** option from **Positions** section is active by default. You need to click on the point from model to define tool entry location.
- The other options of the dialog box are same as discussed earlier. After specifying the parameters, click on the **OK** button from the **2D PROFILE** dialog box. The toolpath will be generated and displayed on the model; refer to Figure-57.

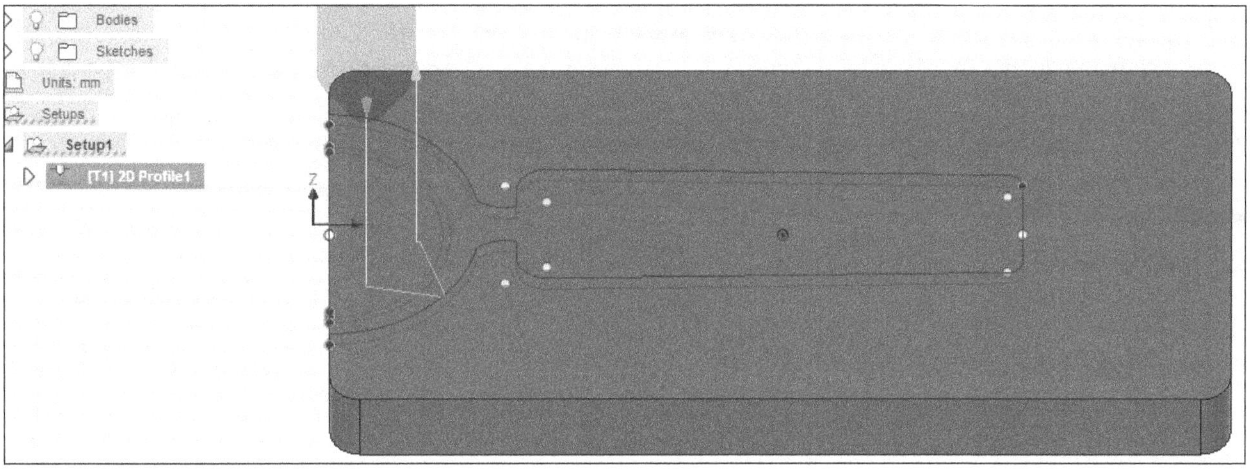

Figure-57. Generated toolpath for Cutting tool

NESTING

Nesting is the process of arranging multiple components on a manufacturing bed to simultaneously manufacture them via processes like machining, sheetmetal bending-punching, plastic molding, and so on. The nesting tools are available as **Manufacturing** extension for Autodesk Fusion which has been discussed earlier.

Selecting Source Model for Manufacturing

The **Component Sources** tool is used to select source model to be used for operations like nesting, cutting, and so on. The procedure to use this tool is given next.

- Click on the **Component Sources** tool from the **SOURCES** drop-down in the **FABRICATION** tab of the **Ribbon** after opening a model (sheetmetal model in our case). The **Component Sources** dialog box will be displayed; refer to Figure-58.

Figure-58. Component Sources dialog box

- By default, the component in graphics area is selected in the dialog box. To add another component, click on the **Add** button (+) from the dialog box if you are working on multiple components model. The **Select Sources** dialog box will be displayed.
- Select the **Override Nest QTY** check box to manually specify number of components that can be placed on manufacturing bed.
- Select the **Override Nest Material** check box to manually define material for the workpiece.
- Select desired model from the dialog box and click on the **Select** button. The component will be added in the dialog box.
- Set the priority of components to define which component will be given preference when nesting in the **Priority** edit box. The default value of priority is 100. A higher value means lower priority. When space is limited on sheet then model with lower priority value will be given preference in filling the space.
- In the **Component Grain** edit box of **Nest** section in dialog box, you can specify the angle at which component will be oriented on the sheet.
- Select the **Bind** check box to fix the rotation to the components. On selecting this check box, options below it will be deactivated. Clear this check box to allow free orientation of components in nesting.
- Select the **Pre-Kit** check box to place components in mirror orientation if possible to save space on the machine bed.
- Select desired rotate check boxes to define reference angles at which components can be oriented when performing nesting.
- Specify desired value in the **Deviation** edit box to define the tolerance within which rotation can be performed. Similarly, specify angle value in **Increment** edit box to define the angle by which rotation will increase or decrease when placing components for nesting.
- Click on the **OK** button from the dialog box to apply changes.

Creating Nest Study

The nest study is created to find out best possible layout of multiple components in the sheet. The **Create Nest Study** tool is used to create nest layout of components. The procedure to use this tool is given next.

- Click on the **Create Nest Study** tool from the **NEST** drop-down in the **FABRICATION** tab of the **Ribbon**. The **CREATE NEST STUDY** dialog box will be displayed; refer to Figure-59.

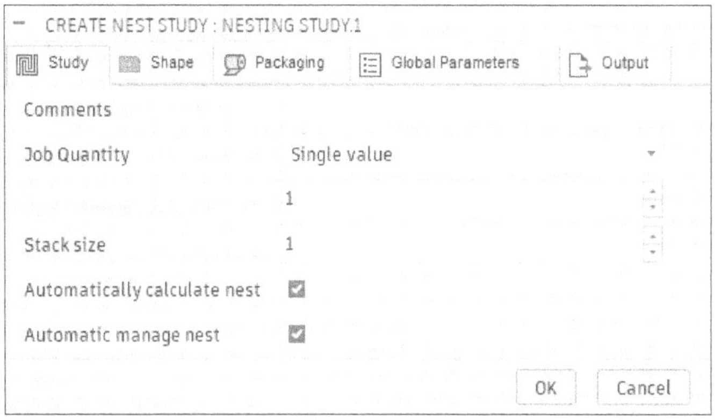

Figure-59. CREATE NEST STUDY dialog box

- Specify desired value in the **Comments** edit box to type user defined comments.
- Select the **Single value** option from the **Job Quantity** drop-down if you want to create same number of copies of various components in the sheet. Select the **Multi-value** option from the drop-down to set different numbers for various components; refer to Figure-60.

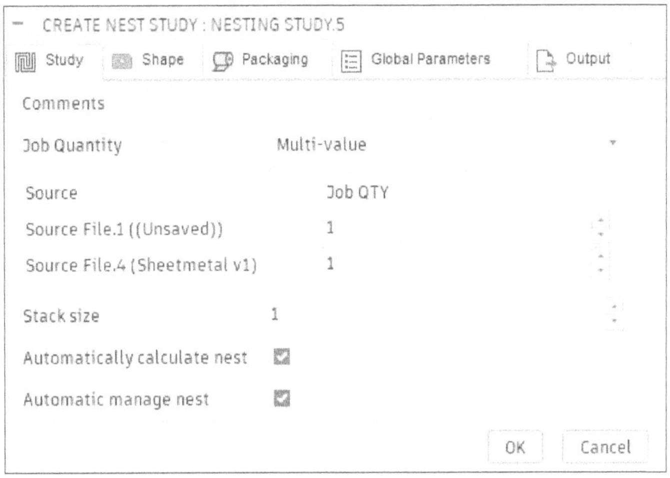

Figure-60. Setting number of components

- Set the number of workpiece sheets in stack to be created by nesting in the **Stack size** edit box.
- Select the **Automatically calculate nest** check box to automatically generate nest setup and add it into browser. If this check box is not selected then you will need to manually generate the nest using **BROWSER** options.
- Select the **Automatic manage nest** check box to allow modifications of nest based on modifications in source models.

Shape Tab Options

The options in the **Shape** tab are used to define which models are to be included in the nest; refer to Figure-61. Select check boxes of models to be included.

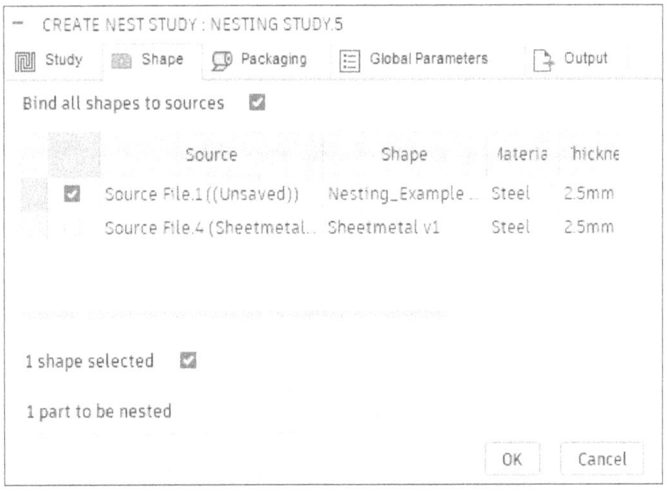

Figure-61. Shape tab

Packaging Tab Options

The options in the **Packaging** tab are used to check the number of sheets and sheet sizes selected for workpiece; refer to Figure-62. Packaging can be managed using the **Process Material Library** tool which will be discussed later.

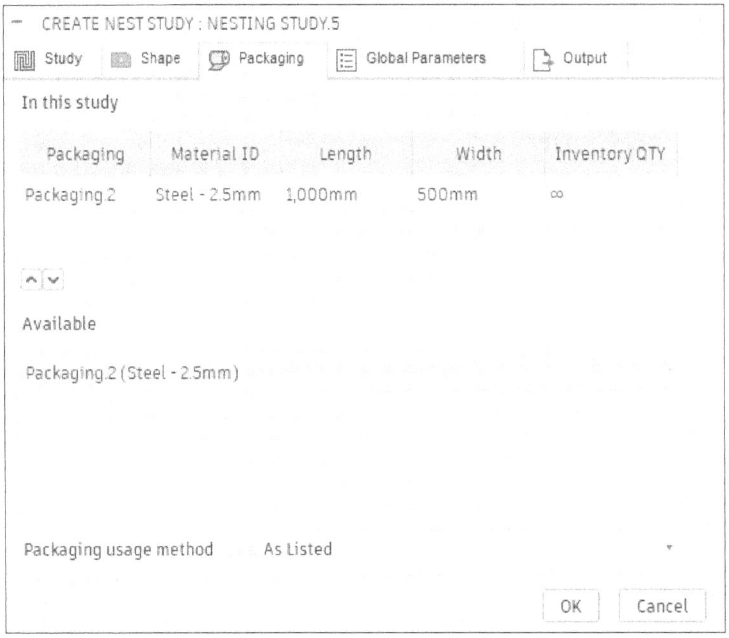

Figure-62. Packaging tab

Global Parameters Tab Options

Select the **Global Parameters** tab from the dialog box to define various parameters related to starting position, computation time, and so on; refer to Figure-63.

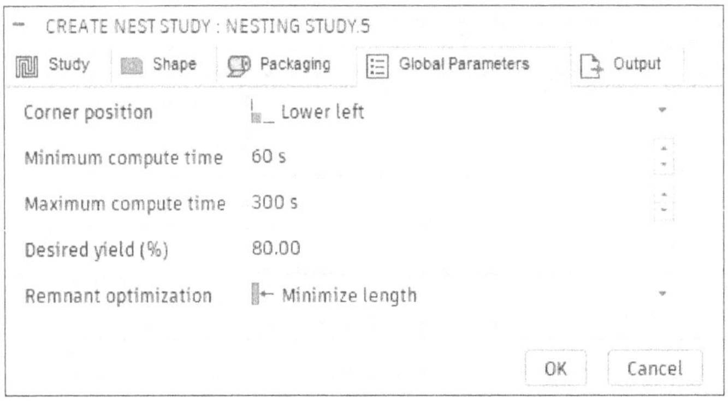

Figure-63. Global Parameters tab

- Select desired option from the **Corner position** drop-down to define the location where system will start placing the components in sheet.
- Set desired time values in the **Minimum compute time** and **Maximum compute time** edit boxes.
- Specify desired value in **Desired yield (%)** edit box to define minimum percentage of sheet area to be filled by components so that the nest can be deemed acceptable.
- Select desired option from the **Remnant optimization** drop-down to define optimization goal when placing components in sheet.

Output Tab Options

- Select the **Create manufacturing model** check box to automatically create manufacturing model using nest generated.
- Select the **Include stock** check box to include stock when placing components in the nest.
- Click on the **OK** button from the dialog box to generate nest; refer to Figure-64.

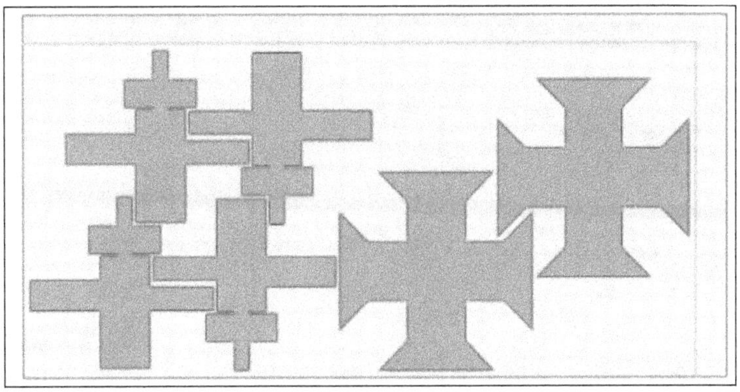

Figure-64. Flat patterns nested on a sheet

Defining Process Material Library

The **Process Material Library** tool is used to create and manage packaging as well as material for nesting study. The procedure to use this tool is given next.

- Click on the **Process Material Library** tool from the **MANAGE** drop-down in the **FABRICATION** tab of the **Ribbon**. The **Process Material Library** dialog box will be displayed; refer to Figure-65.

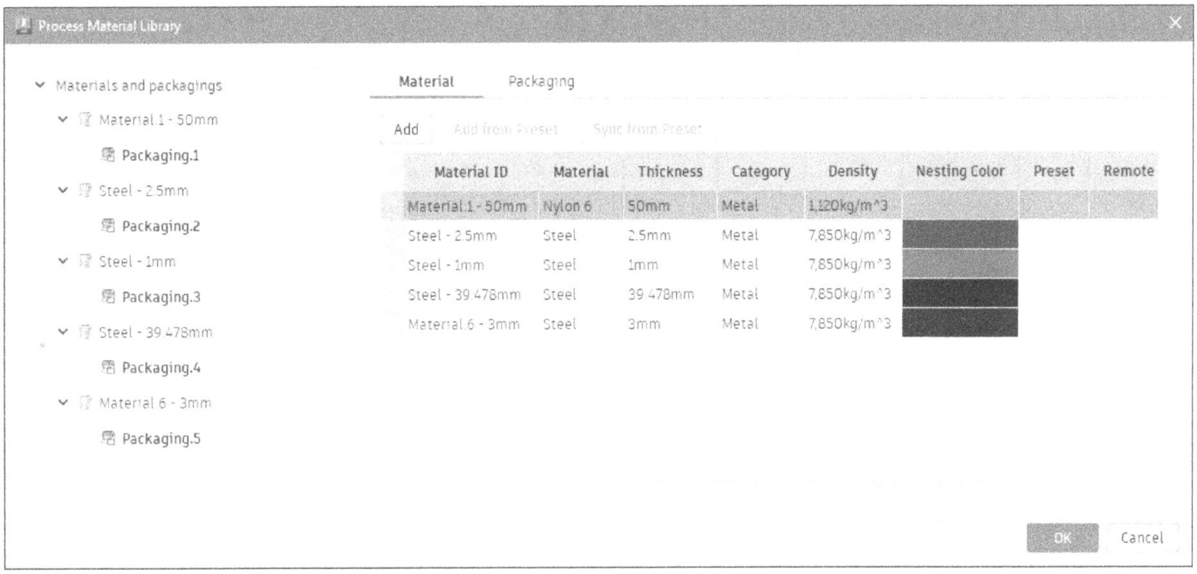

Figure-65. Process Material Library dialog box

- Click on the **Add** button from the **Material** tab at the right in the dialog box to add a new packaging material. The new material will be added in the list.
- Select the new material from left in the dialog box. The parameters related to material will be displayed; refer to Figure-66.
- Specify desired parameters in the **General** tab to define material parameters like material name, thickness, density of material, color, and so on.
- Click on the **Packaging** tab in the right area of dialog box to define name, size, shape, and cost of packaging; refer to Figure-67.
- Click on the **Nesting** tab in the dialog box to define available orientations and positions for nesting.
- Click on the **OK** button from the dialog box to create material and packaging.

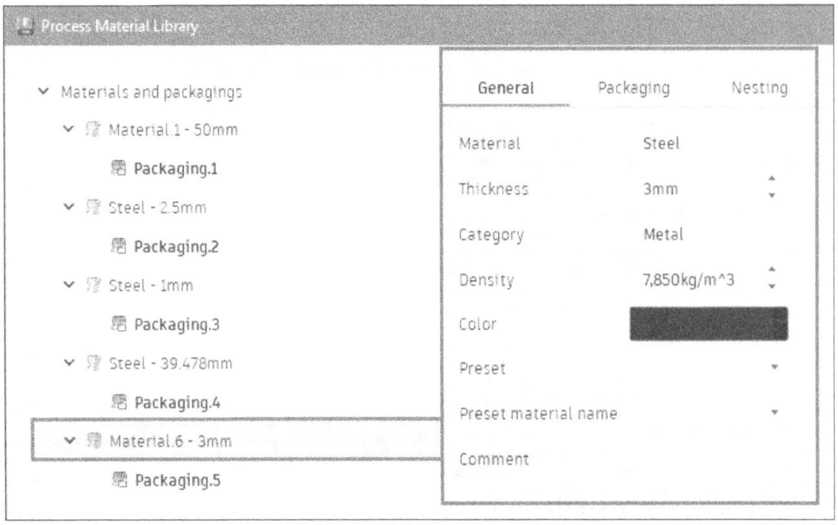

Figure-66. Material parameters

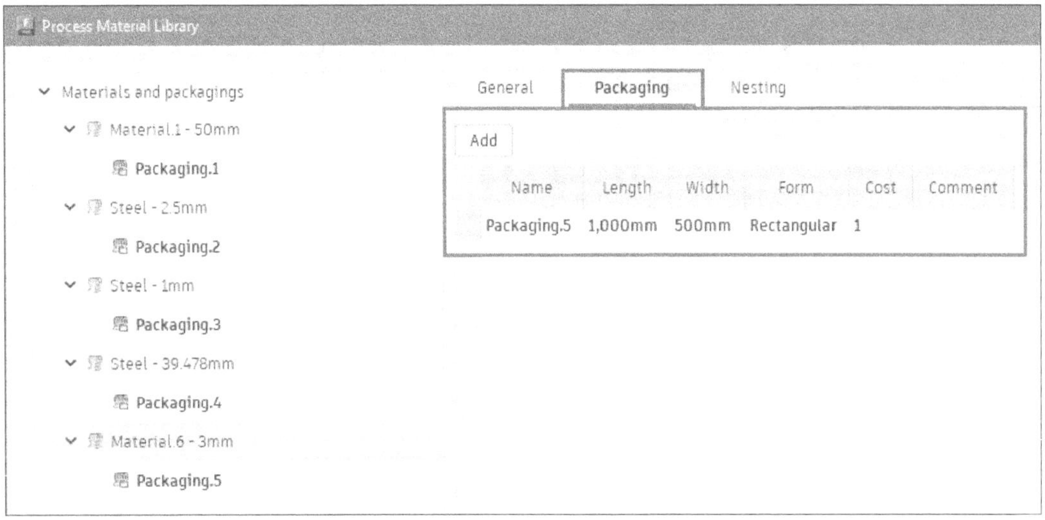

Figure-67. Packaging tab

PRACTICAL

Generate the toolpaths of the given model shown in Figure-68 using Turning tools.

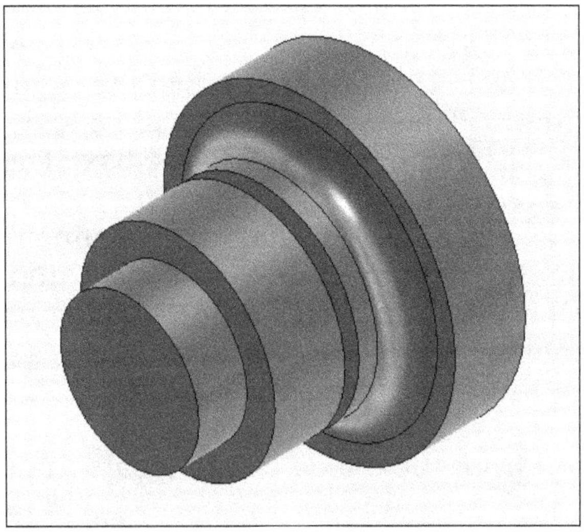

Figure-68. Practical

Adding Model to CAM

- Create and save the part in **DESIGN** workspace. The part file is available in respective chapter folder of **Autodesk Fusion Black Book Resources** folder.
- Select the **MANUFACTURE** option from **Workspace** drop-down. The model will be displayed in the **MANUFACTURE** workspace.

Creating Stock

- Click on the **New Setup** tool of **SETUP** drop-down from **Toolbar**. The **SETUP** dialog box will be displayed along with the stock of model.
- Specify the parameters of **Setup** tab and **Stock** tab of **SETUP** dialog box to create the stock; refer to Figure-69.

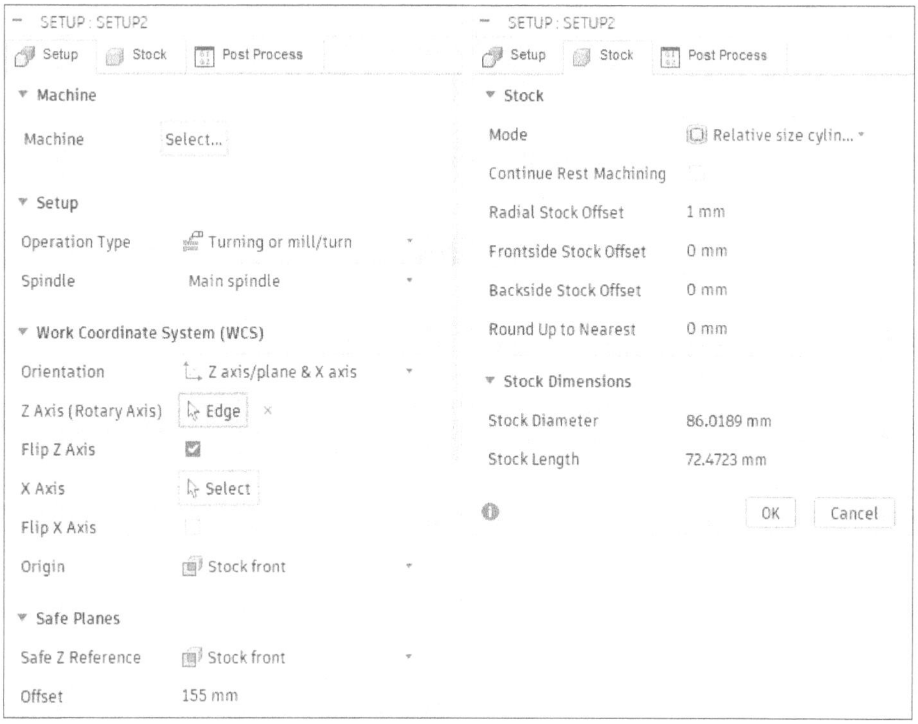

Figure-69. Specifying parameters for SETUP dialog box

- After specifying the parameters of **SETUP** dialog box, click on the **OK** button. The stock will be created and displayed on the model; refer to Figure-70.

Figure-70. Created stock for practical

Generating Face Toolpath

- Click on the **Turning Face** tool of **TURNING** drop-down from **Toolbar**. The **FACE** dialog box will be displayed.
- Click on the **Select** button for **Tool** section and select the facing tool from **Select Tool** dialog box as displayed in Figure-71.

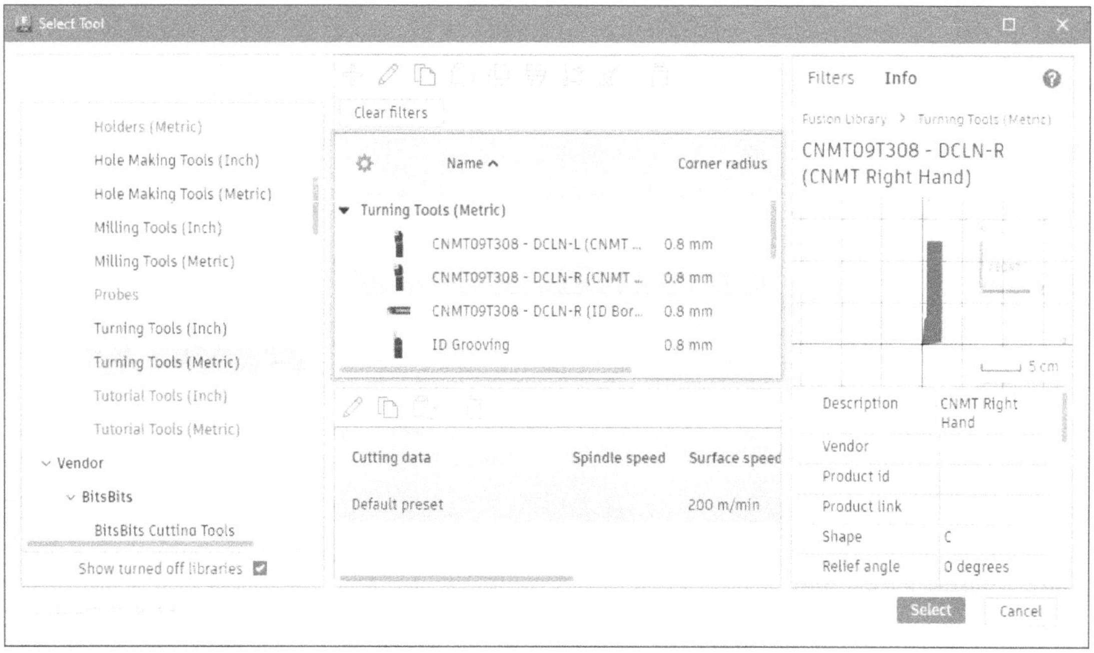

Figure-71. Selecting tool for turning

- After selecting the tool, click on the **OK** button from **Select Tool** dialog box. The tool will be added in the **Face** dialog box.
- Specify the parameters of **Tool** tab, **Geometry** tab, **Passes** tab, and **Linking** tab of **FACE** dialog box as shown in Figure-72.
- After specifying the parameters, click on the **OK** button from the **FACE** dialog box to generate the toolpath. The toolpath will be generated and displayed on the model.

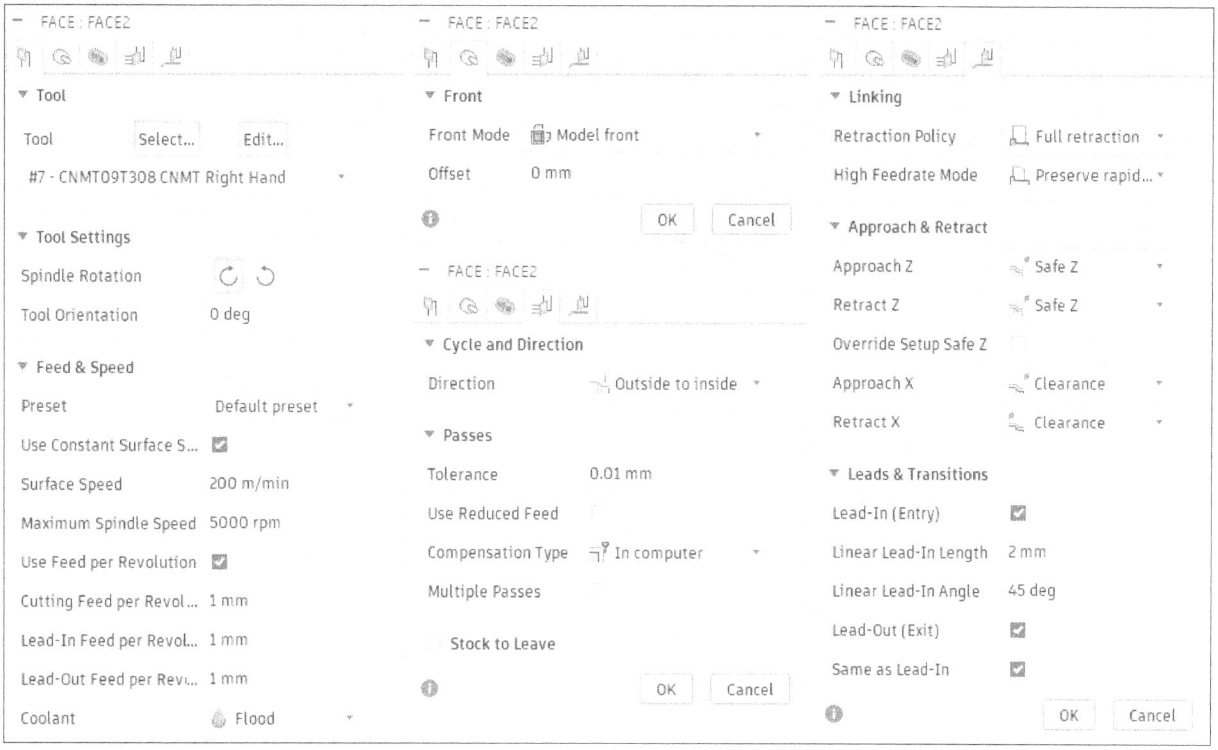

Figure-72. Specifying the parameters of FACE dialog box

Generating Turning Profile Roughing Toolpath

- Click on the **Turning Profile Roughing** tool of **TURNING** drop-down from **Toolbar**. The **PROFILE ROUGHING** dialog box will be displayed.
- Click on the **Select** button of **Tool** section and select the required tool from **Select Tool** dialog box.
- Specify the parameters of **Tool** tab, **Geometry** tab, **Passes** tab, and **Linking** tab of **PROFILE** dialog box as shown in Figure-73.

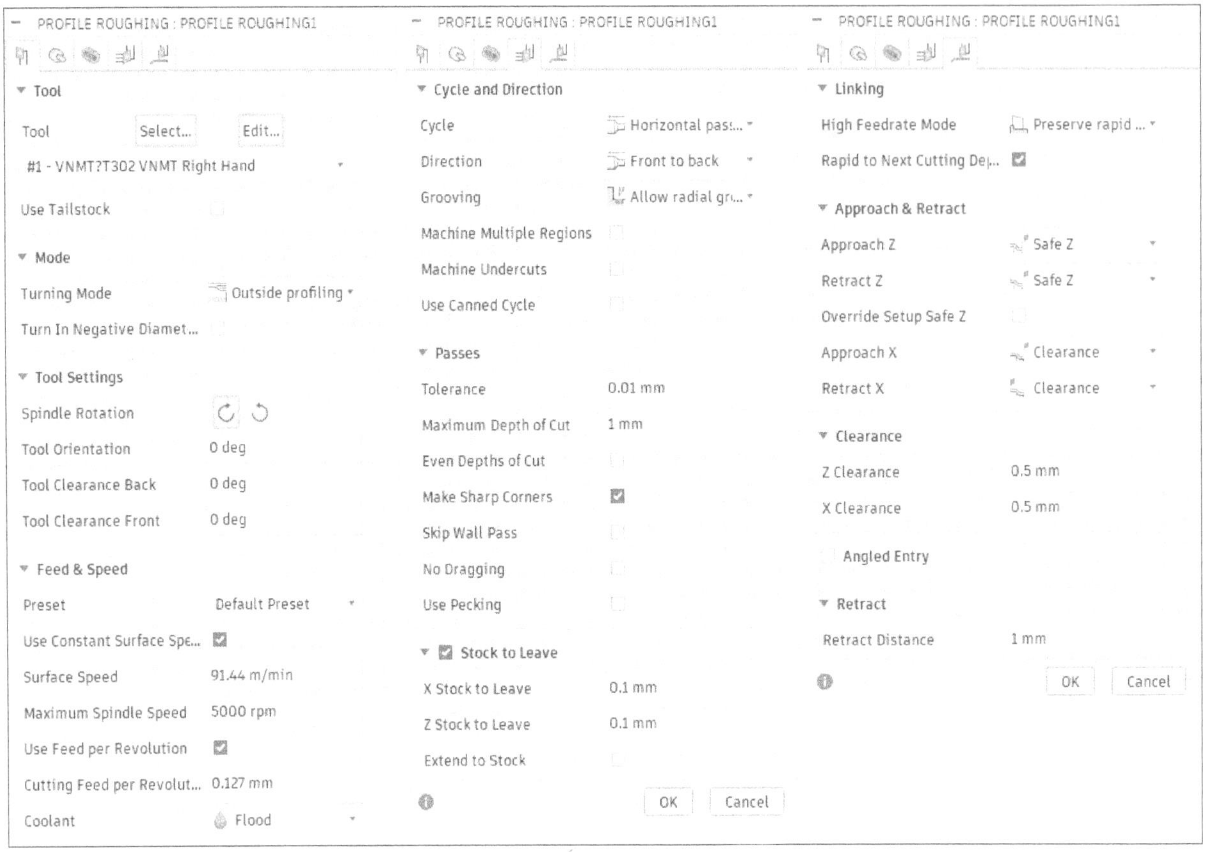

Figure-73. Specifying parameters for PROFILE dialog box

- After specifying the parameters, click on the **OK** button from **PROFILE** dialog box. The toolpath will be generated and displayed on the model; refer to Figure-74.

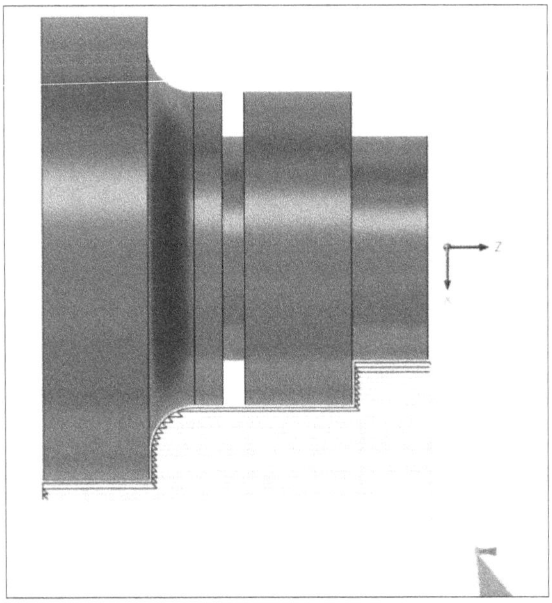

Figure-74. Generated toolpath of profile tool

Generating Turning Profile Finishing Toolpath

- Click on the **Turning Profile Finishing** tool of **TURNING** drop-down from **Toolbar**. The **PROFILE FINISHING** dialog box will be displayed.
- Click on the **Select** button of **Tool** section and select the required tool from **Select Tool** dialog box.

- Specify the parameters of **Tool** tab, **Geometry** tab, **Passes** tab, and **Linking** tab of **PROFILE** dialog box as shown in Figure-75.

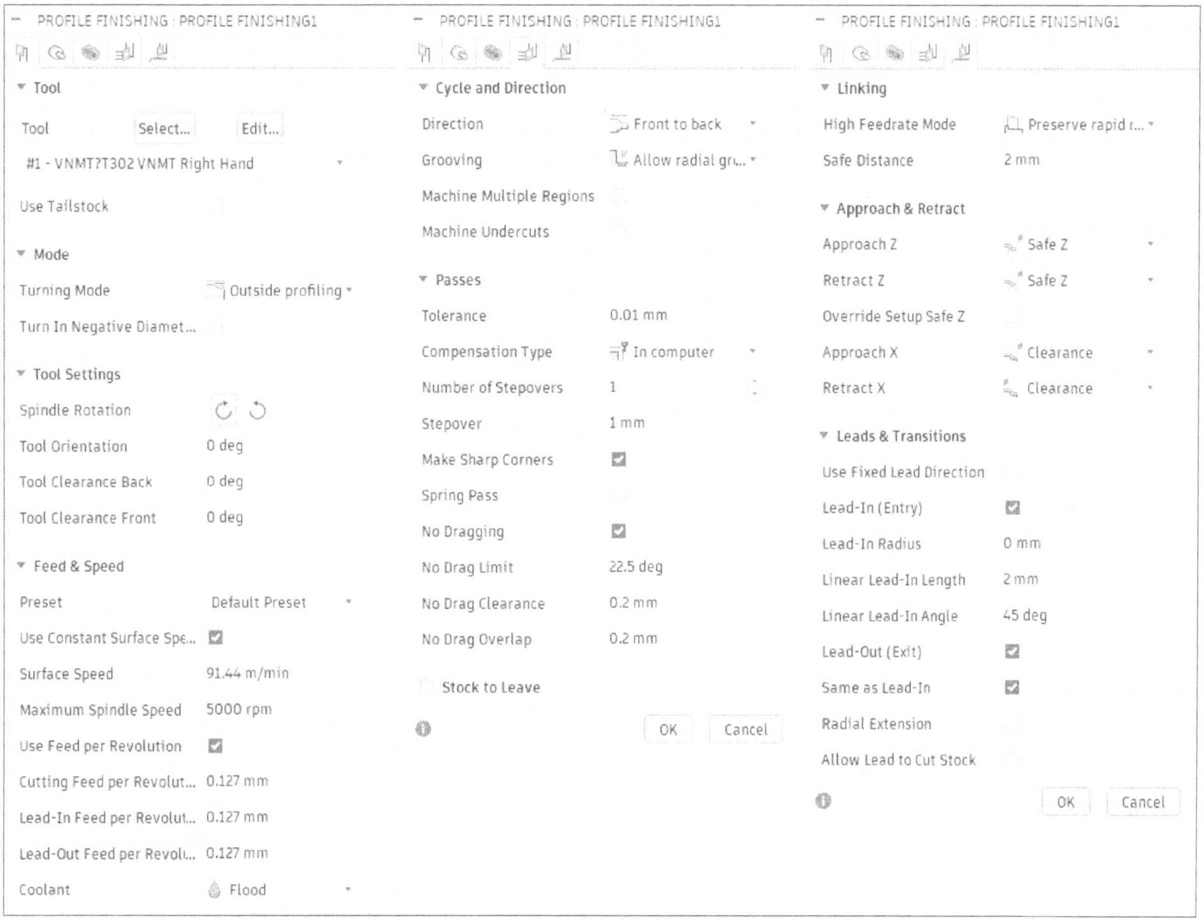

Figure-75. Parameters for Profile Finishing

- After setting the parameters, click on the **OK** button from the dialog box. The finishing toolpath for profile will be created.

Generating Turning Single Groove Toolpath

- Click on the **Turning Single Groove** tool of **TURNING** drop-down from **Toolbar**. The **SINGLE GROOVE** dialog box will be displayed.
- Click on the **Select** button of **Tool** option and select an OD groove square tool of insert thickness **4 mm** from **Select Tool** dialog box.
- Specify the parameters of **Tool** tab, **Geometry** tab, **Passes** tab and **Linking** tab of **PROFILE** dialog box as shown in Figure-76.

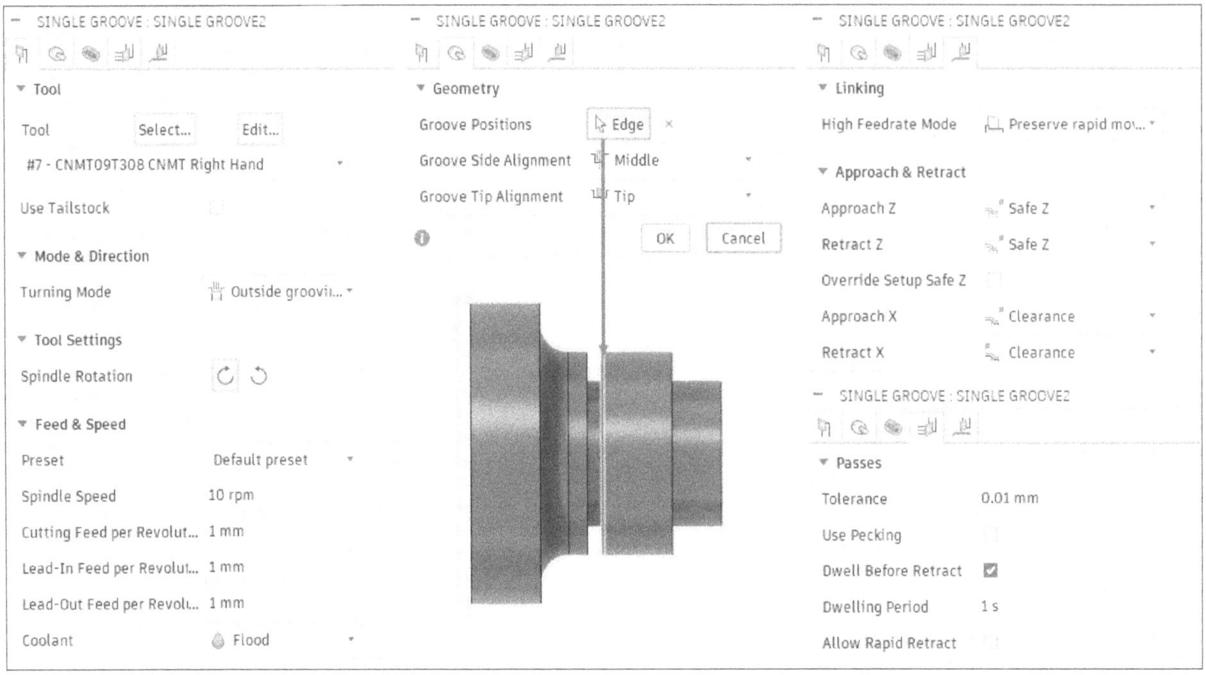

Figure-76. Specifying parameters for SINGLE GROOVE dialog box

- After specifying the parameters, click on the **OK** button from **SINGLE GROOVE** dialog box. The toolpath will be generated and displayed on the model; refer to Figure-77

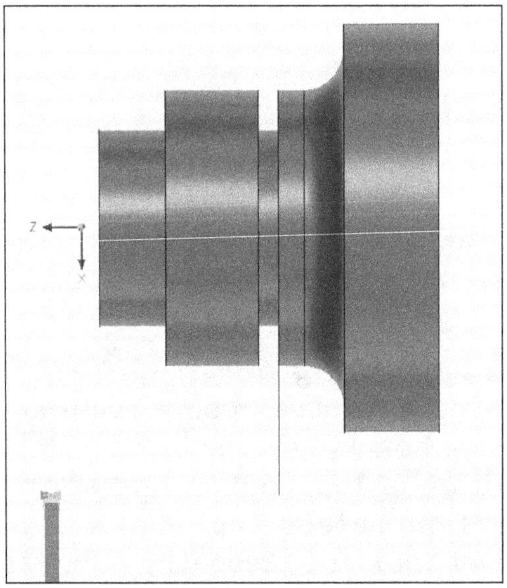

Figure-77. Generated toolpath for single groove

Generating Turning Part Toolpath

- Click on the **Turning Part** tool from **TURNING** drop-down in **Toolbar**. The **PART** dialog box will be displayed.
- Click on the **Select** button of **Tool** section from **PART** dialog box and select the grooving tool of parameters shown in Figure-78.

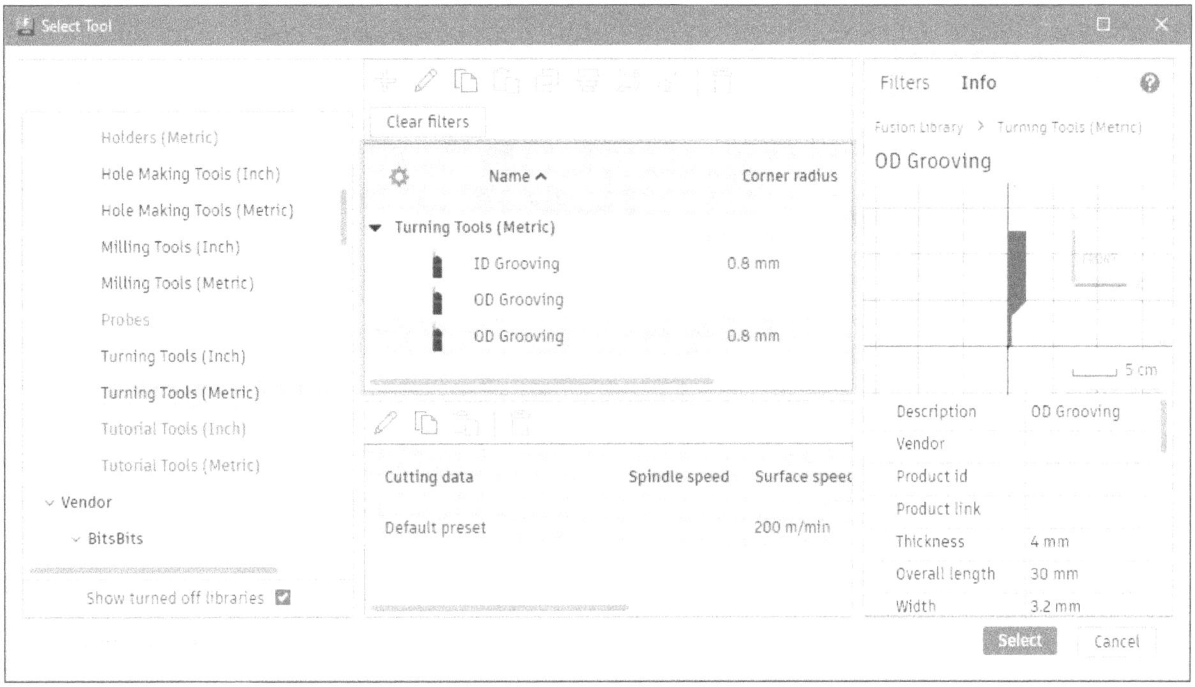

Figure-78. Selecting tool for part

- After selecting the tool of parameters displayed above, click on the **Select** button from **Select Tool** dialog box. The tool will be added in the **PART** dialog box.
- Specify the parameter of **Tool** tab, **Passes** tab, and **Linking** tab of **PART** dialog box as displayed in Figure-79.

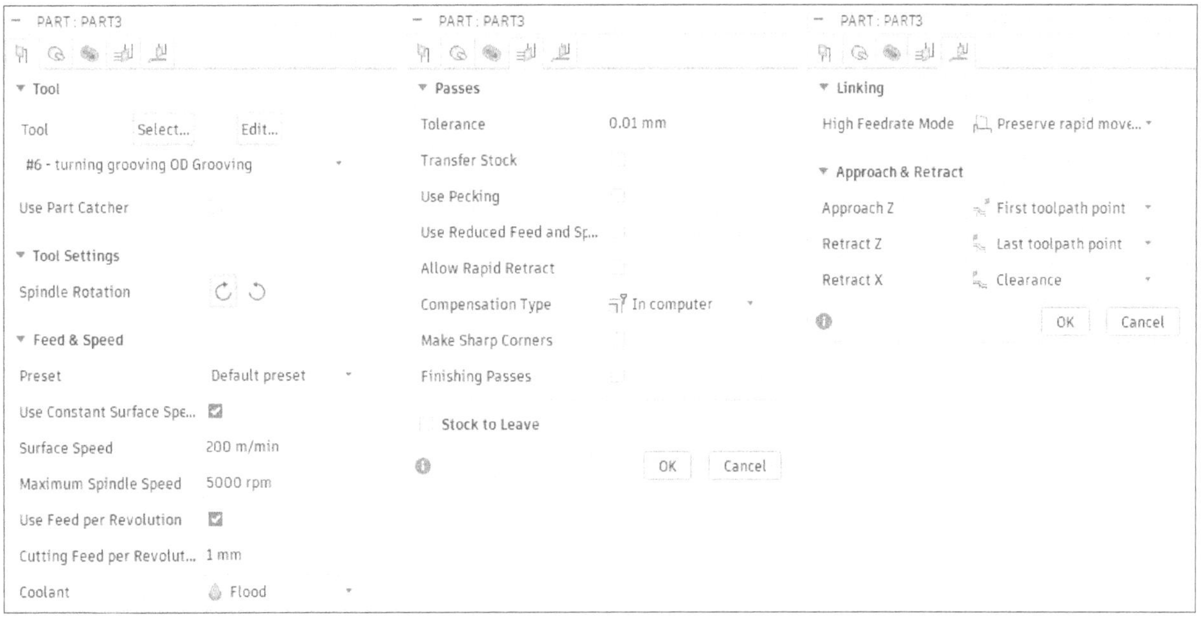

Figure-79. Specifying the parameters of PART dialog box

- After specifying the parameters, click on the **OK** button from **PART** dialog box. The toolpath will be generated and displayed on the model; refer to Figure-80.

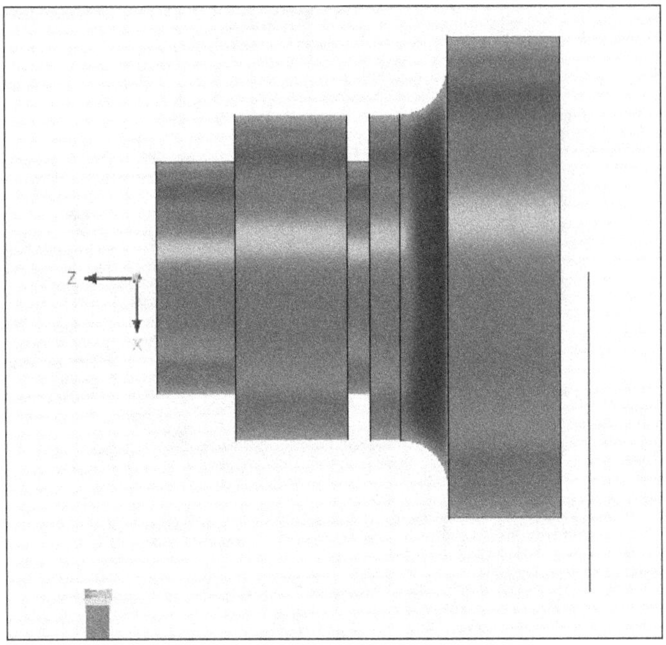

Figure-80. Generated toolpath of Part tool

Simulating the Toolpath

- Right-click on the **Setup1** option from **BROWSER** and click on the **Simulate** tool from the shortcut menu. The **SIMULATE** dialog box will be displayed along with the model.
- Use the simulation keys to play the machining animation to check the errors occurred while machining process; refer to Figure-81.

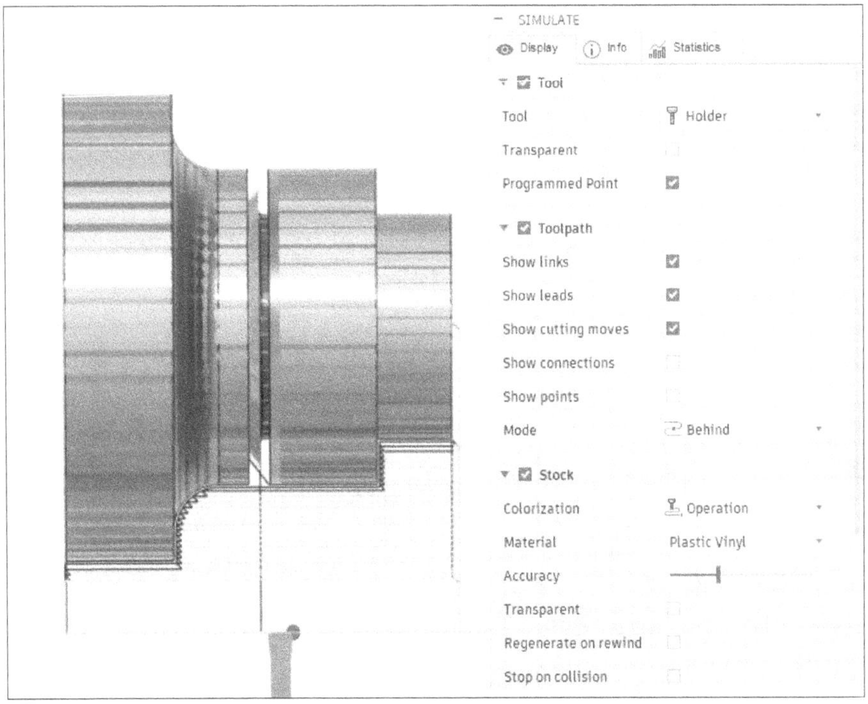

Figure-81. Simulation process

PRACTICE 1

Machine the stock of diameter as 50 mm and length as 62 mm to create the part as shown in Figure-82. The part file of this model is available in the respective folder of **Autodesk Fusion Black Book Resources**.

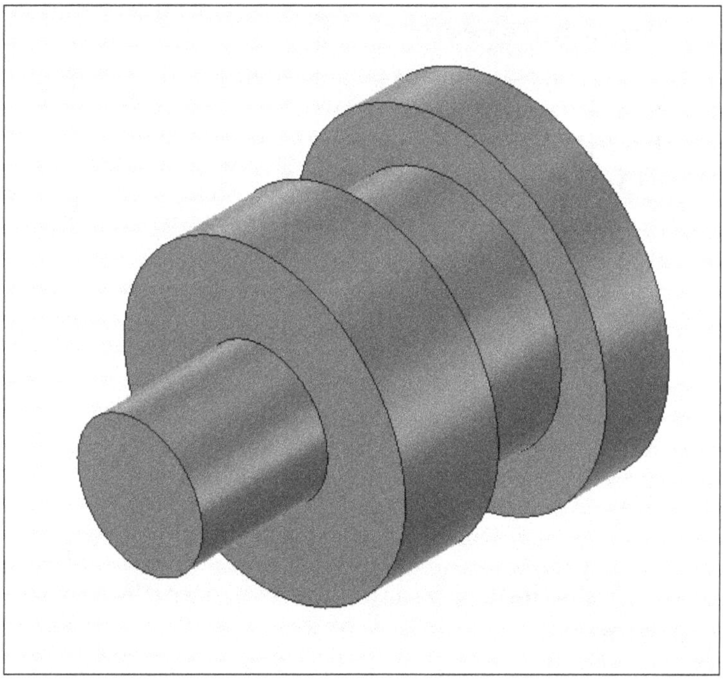

Figure-82. Practice 1

PRACTICE 2

Machine the stock of diameter as 80 mm and length as 130 mm to create the part as shown in Figure-83. The part file of this model is available in the respective folder of **Autodesk Fusion Black Book Resources**.

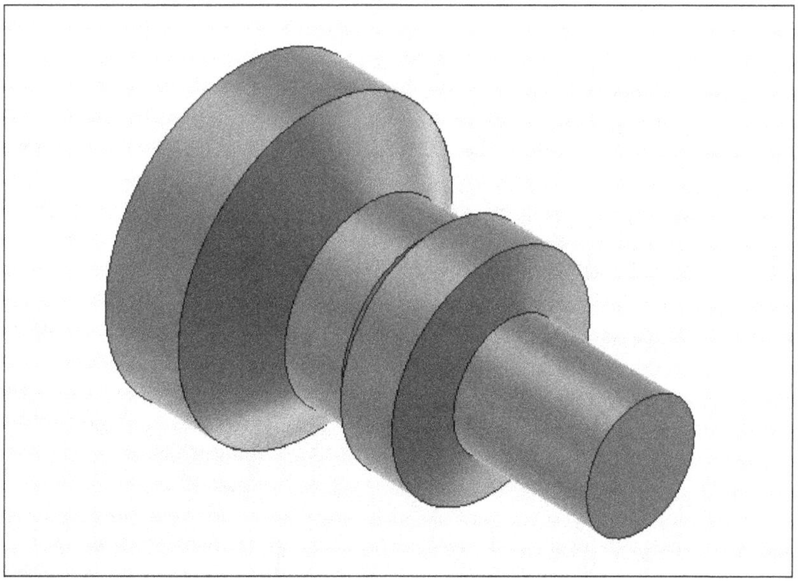

Figure-83. Practice 2

SELF ASSESSMENT

Q1. What is the primary purpose of the Turning Face tool?
A. Roughing the model profile
B. Machining the front face of the part
C. Cutting grooves in the model
D. Removing material from bulk parts

Q2. What is the first step in using the Turning Face tool?
A. Select a tool from the PROFILE dialog box
B. Set the tool orientation
C. Click on the Turning Face tool in the TURNING drop-down
D. Generate the toolpath

Q3. Which section allows you to define the orientation of the tool in the Turning Face tool?
A. Feed & Speed section
B. Tool Settings section
C. Geometry tab
D. Mode section

Q4. What option should be selected in the Turning Profile Roughing tool to support a long part during turning?
A. Outside profiling
B. Use Tailstock
C. Groove Suppression
D. Rest Machining

Q5. In the Radii tab, which option specifies the use of the model's outer diameter?
A. Model OD
B. Stock OD
C. Clearance Offset
D. Tangential Extension

Q6. In the Passes tab of the PROFILE dialog box, what is the function of the "Use Pecking" option?
A. To define sharp corners during cutting
B. To specify retractions during cutting to prevent long chips
C. To allow grooving in the toolpath
D. To adjust the feed rate

Q7. Which tab in the PROFILE dialog box is used to connect cutting passes in the toolpath?
A. Radii tab
B. Linking tab
C. Geometry tab
D. Passes tab

Q8. What feature in the Turning Profile Finishing tool ensures better finishing with zero stock thickness?
A. No Dragging
B. Spring Pass
C. Constant Surface Speed
D. Machine Undercuts

Q9. In the Turning Adaptive Roughing tool, what does the Groove Suppression option do?
A. It increases the clearance radius for the tool
B. It excludes specific faces or surfaces during toolpath generation
C. It suppresses the spindle speed
D. It reduces feed rates for grooves

Q10. What type of tool is generally selected for the Turning Groove operation?
A. ID or OD groove turning tool
B. Profiling tool
C. Roughing tool
D. Adaptive cutting tool

Q11: Which of the following actions can be performed in the Passes tab of the GROOVE dialog box?
A. Specifying thread pitch
B. Selecting compensation type
C. Activating Use Pecking option
D. Selecting chamfer tool

Q12: What is the purpose of the "Allow Rapid Retract" checkbox in the Passes tab?
A. To reduce feedrate when cutting along the X-Axis
B. To retract the tool with maximum retraction speed
C. To apply chamfer cuts before finishing
D. To repeat the finishing pass

Q13: Which checkbox must be selected in the Passes tab to allow roughing of the part before finishing passes?
A. Finishing Passes
B. Roughing Clearing Pass
C. Use Reduced Feedrate
D. Roughing Passes

Q14: What does selecting the "Fade Thread End" checkbox in the THREAD dialog box do?
A. It creates multi-start threads.
B. It adjusts the thread pitch.
C. It ensures easy assembly of fasteners.
D. It performs additional finishing passes.

Q15: In the SINGLE GROOVE dialog box, what does the "Dwell Before Retract" check box achieve?
A. It specifies the retraction distance.
B. It pauses before retracting the tool.
C. It increases cutting speed.
D. It defines groove tip alignment.

Q16: What is the use of the "Reverse Chamfer Pass" check box in the CHAMFER dialog box?
A. To apply multiple chamfer passes
B. To reverse cutting direction while chamfering
C. To specify chamfer extension value
D. To create thread chamfers

Q17: What is the primary function of the Subspindle Grab tool?
A. Machining back sides of parts
B. Generating thread toolpaths
C. Cutting material radially
D. Performing chamfer operations

Q18: In the THREAD dialog box, what does the "Do Multiple Threads" checkbox enable?
A. It allows fading of thread ends.
B. It creates multi-start threads.
C. It specifies thread depth.
D. It repeats finishing passes.

Q19: What is the primary function of the Bar Pull tool?
A. To create toolpaths for 2D cutting
B. To return stock to the main spindle
C. To draw stock from the main spindle
D. To define the nesting process

Q20: Where can you find the Bar Pull tool in the toolbar?
A. CUTTING panel
B. PART HANDLING drop-down
C. FABRICATION tab
D. NEST drop-down

Q21: In the Bar Pull dialog box, what is defined in the Pull Distance edit box?
A. The feed rate of the spindle
B. The distance the subspindle moves from the Grab plane
C. The offset distance of the return plane
D. The dwell time for operations

Q22: What does the Subspindle Return tool accomplish?
A. Generates a toolpath for cutting operations
B. Automates stock return from secondary chuck to main chuck
C. Specifies the offset distance for stock movement
D. Creates nesting studies for manufacturing

Q23: Which option in the Subspindle Feed & Speed section specifies the spindle speed in rpm?
A. Offset
B. Feedrate
C. Spindle Speed
D. Dwelling Period

Q24: What is the purpose of the 2D Profile tool?
A. To create toolpaths for turning operations
B. To arrange components on a manufacturing bed
C. To cut 2D profiles of stock using laser, plasma, or water jet
D. To define the spindle speeds for cutting

Q25: What parameter is defined in the Lead-In Sweep Angle edit box of the 2D PROFILE Linking tab?
A. The sweep angle of the lead-in arc
B. The distance between tabs
C. The radius for lead-in moves
D. The cutting quality of the machine

Q26: What does the Nesting process achieve?
A. Cuts the stock into precise dimensions
B. Arranges multiple components on a manufacturing bed
C. Creates toolpaths for turning operations
D. Defines the offset distances for spindles

Q27: In the Component Sources dialog box, what happens when you select the Bind check box?
A. Rotation of components is fixed
B. Material override options are enabled
C. Components are mirrored for better arrangement
D. Additional sources are allowed

Q28: What does the Priority edit box in the Nest section specify?
A. The material for nesting components
B. The angle for component orientation
C. The priority for filling space on the sheet
D. The cutting quality of the tool

Q29: Which tab in the CREATE NEST STUDY dialog box defines the starting position for nesting?
A. Packaging
B. Global Parameters
C. Shape
D. Output

Q30: What is the purpose of the Process Material Library tool?
A. To define stock dimensions
B. To manage materials and packaging for nesting studies
C. To define spindle speeds and feed rates
D. To create toolpaths for turning operations

Q31: How do you create stock for a model in the MANUFACTURE workspace?
A. Use the Turning Profile Roughing tool
B. Select the 2D Profile tool
C. Click on the New Setup tool in the SETUP drop-down
D. Use the Bar Pull tool

Q32: Which tool is used to create a toolpath for facing operations?
A. Turning Profile Roughing
B. Turning Face
C. Bar Pull
D. Subspindle Return

Q33. What is the first step to generate a Turning Profile Finishing toolpath?
A. Click on the Turning Single Groove tool
B. Click on the Turning Profile Finishing tool
C. Select the Turning Part tool
D. Open the Simulate tool

Q34. In the PROFILE FINISHING dialog box, what button is clicked to select the required tool?
A. Add
B. Select
C. OK
D. Cancel

Q35. After setting parameters in the PROFILE FINISHING dialog box, what is the outcome?
A. The toolpath will be displayed in the SIMULATE dialog box
B. A roughing toolpath will be generated
C. The finishing toolpath for profile will be created
D. Errors in machining will be corrected

Q36. What type of tool is selected in the SINGLE GROOVE dialog box?
A. ID groove square tool of insert thickness 4 mm
B. OD groove square tool of insert thickness 4 mm
C. OD groove square tool of insert thickness 2 mm
D. ID groove square tool of insert thickness 2 mm

Q37. Which of the following is required to generate a Turning Part toolpath?
A. Simulate the machining process
B. Select a grooving tool with specified parameters
C. Open the SINGLE GROOVE dialog box
D. Enable the PROFILE FINISHING tool

Q38. What does the simulation feature allow you to do in the machining process?
A. Automatically create finishing toolpaths
B. Display errors in machining processes
C. Generate multiple toolpaths simultaneously
D. Display roughing and finishing toolpaths together

FOR STUDENT NOTES

For Student Notes

Chapter 19

Probing, Additive Manufacturing, and Miscellaneous CAM Tools

Topics Covered

The major topics covered in this chapter are:

- ***New Folder***
- ***New Pattern***
- ***Probing***
- ***Inspecting Surface***
- ***Simulating***
- ***Generate Toolpath and Clear Toolpath***
- ***Machining Time, Tool Library, and Task Manager***
- ***Post Process***
- ***Creating Form Mill tool***

INTRODUCTION

Till now, you have learned the procedures of generating Milling and Turning toolpaths. In this chapter, you will learn some of the other tools used to organize and manipulate the toolpaths.

NEW FOLDER

The **New Folder** tool is used for creating a folder to combine similar operations in a group. The procedure to use this tool is discussed next.

- Select the operations from **BROWSER** by holding **CTRL** key and right-click on any of the selected operations. A shortcut menu will be displayed; refer to Figure-1.

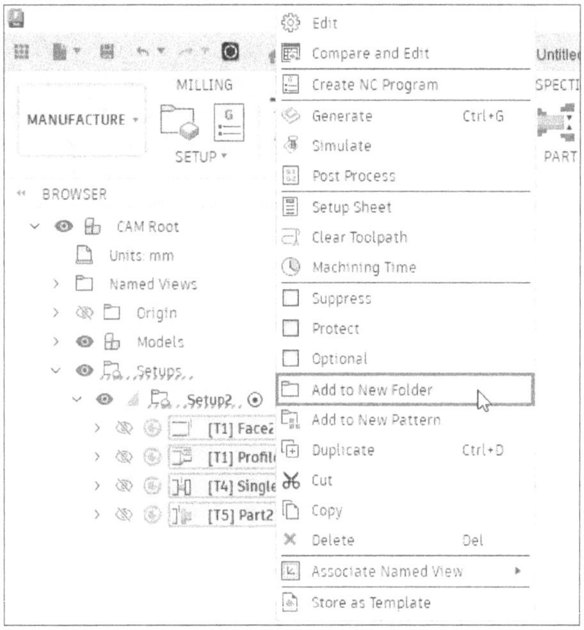

Figure-1. Add to New Folder tool

- Click on the **Add to New Folder** button from the menu. The selected operations will be added in a new folder. The folder will be displayed in the **BROWSER** with the name as **Folder**; refer to Figure-2.

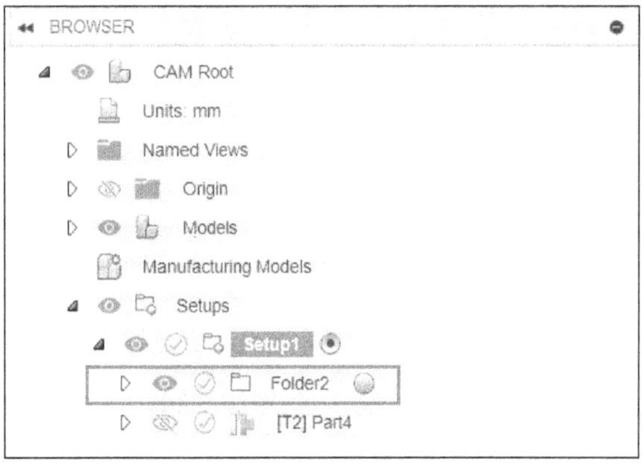

Figure-2. Operations moved in a folder

- If you want to rename the newly created folder then double-click on the folder with a pause between the clicks and specify desired name.

There is an another method for creating the folder which is discussed next.

- Click on the **New Folder** tool from **SETUP** drop-down in **Toolbar**; refer to Figure-3. The folder will be created in the **BROWSER**.

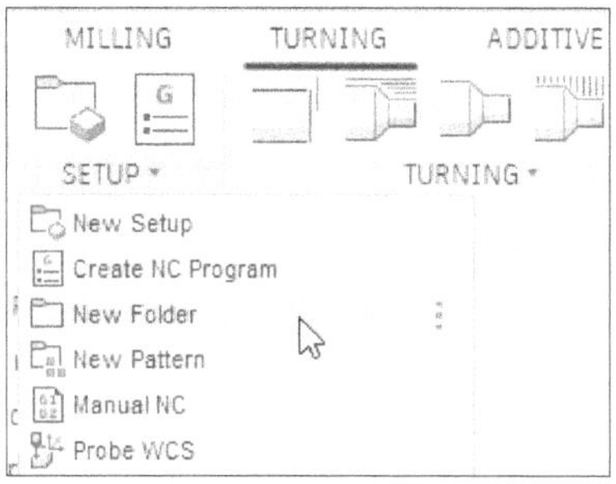

Figure-3. New Folder tool

- Select the operations while holding the **CTRL** key from **BROWSER** and drag the operations into newly created folder. The operations will be added in the created folder.

NEW PATTERN

The **New Pattern** tool is used for duplicating generated toolpath on the same model in **Linear**, **Circular**, **Mirror**, **Component**, and **Duplicate** pattern. The use of **New Pattern** tool can speed up your entire programming process since all changes to a pattern take effect immediately and no toolpath has to be updated. The procedure to use this tool is discussed next.

- Right-click on the operation(s) that you want to pattern. The shortcut menu will be displayed; refer to Figure-4.
- Click on the **Add to New Pattern** tool from the displayed menu. The **FOLDER : PATTERN** dialog box will be displayed; refer to Figure-5.

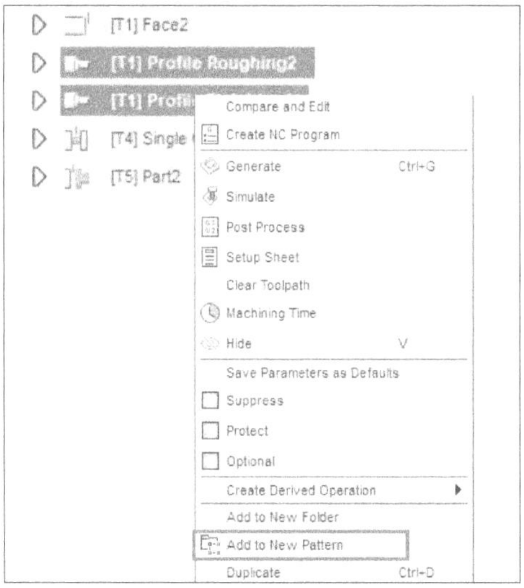

Figure-4. Add to New Pattern tool

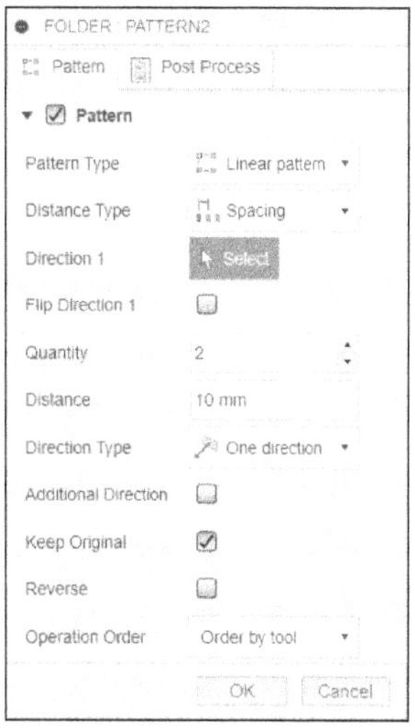

Figure-5. FOLDER PATTERN dialog box

Linear Pattern

In this section, you will learn the procedure of creating linear pattern.

- Select the **Liner pattern** option from **Pattern Type** drop-down in **FOLDER : PATTERN** dialog box for creating linear pattern.

- Select the **Spacing** option from the **Distance Type** drop-down to gap between two consecutive instances of the pattern. Select the **Extent** option from the drop-down to define total distance span within which specified pattern instances will be created.
- The selection button for **Direction 1** section of **Pattern** tab is active by default. You need to click on the edge or face from model to define the direction in which instances of pattern will be created.
- Select the **Flip Direction 1** check box of **Pattern** tab to flip the direction of pattern along selected edge or face.
- Click in the **Quantity** edit box and specify number of instances to be created.
- Click in the **Distance** edit box of **Pattern** tab and specify the value of distance between two consecutive instances of the pattern or total span of pattern depending on option earlier selected in the **Distance Type** drop-down.
- Select the **Additional Direction** check box of **Pattern** tab to use an additional direction for creating the pattern. The options to create instances in direction 2 will be displayed.
- Select the **Keep Original** check box of **Pattern** tab to keep the original toolpaths as well after creating new pattern.
- Select the **Preserve order** option from **Operation Order** drop-down in **Pattern** tab to machine all operations in each instance of the pattern before moving to the next instance.
- Select **Order by operation** option of **Operation Order** drop-down from **Pattern** tab to machine all occurrences of same operation in all instances of the pattern before moving to the next operation.
- Select **Order by tool** option of **Operation Order** drop-down from **Pattern** tab to machine all operations in the pattern that use the current tool before changing tools.
- Select the **Reverse** check box to reverse the order of cutting operations in pattern.
- The other tools of the drop-down are same as discussed earlier in this book. After specifying the parameters, click on the **OK** button from **FOLDER : PATTERN** dialog box; refer to Figure-6. The pattern will be created and displayed in the **BROWSER**.

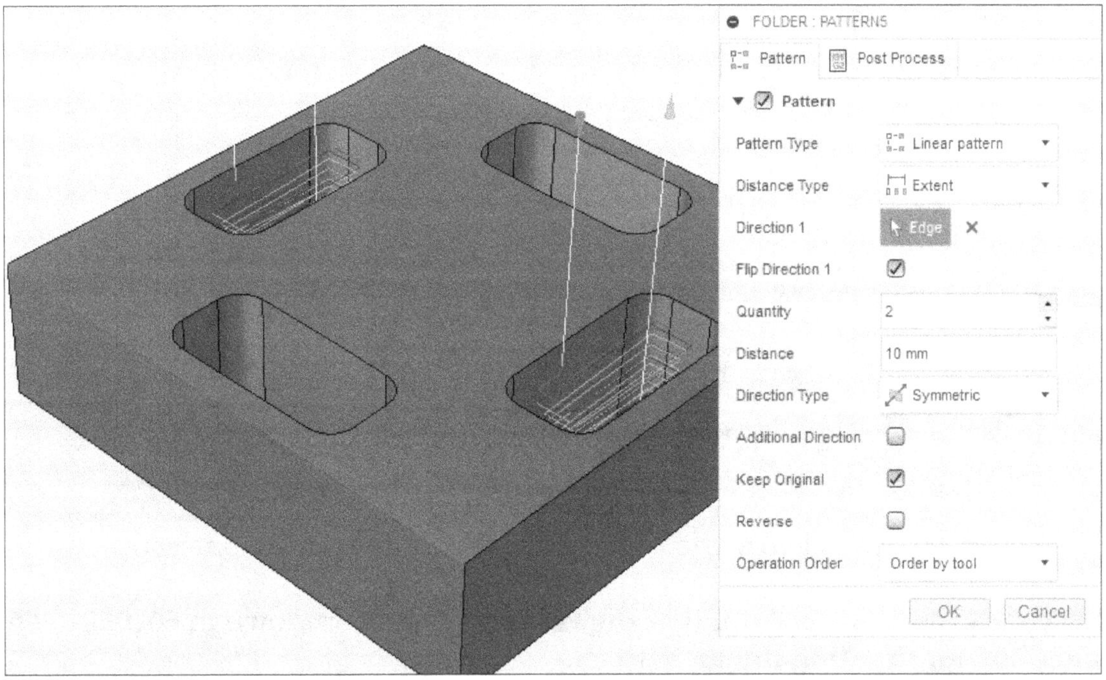

Figure-6. Applied linear pattern

Circular Pattern

In this section, you will learn the procedure of creating the circular pattern.

- Select the **Circular Pattern** option of **Pattern Type** drop-down from **FOLDER : PATTERN** dialog box for creating circular pattern; refer to Figure-7.

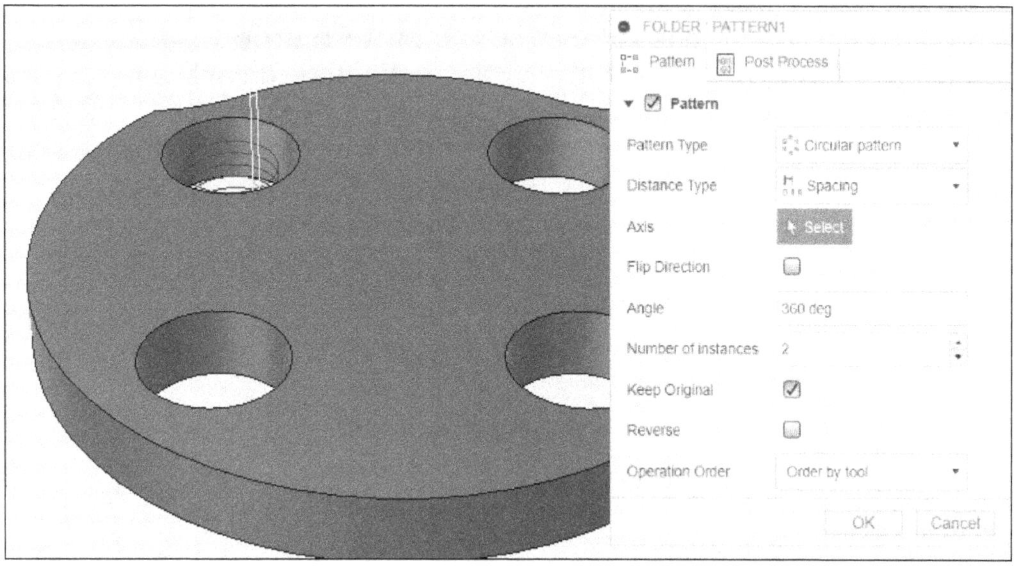

Figure-7. Circular pattern option

- Select the **Extent** option from the **Distance Type** drop-down to specify total span of circular pattern. Select the **Spacing** option from drop-down if you want to specify distance between two instances of pattern.
- The selection button of **Axis** section in **Pattern** tab is active by default. You need to click on the axis or edge from model to define center axis of pattern; refer to Figure-8.

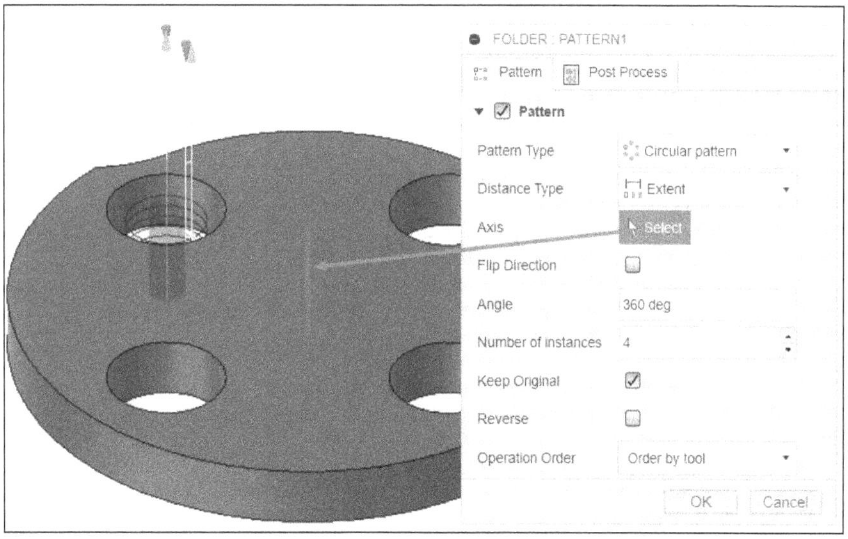

Figure-8. Selecting axis for pattern

- If you want to select the axis from default coordinate system then make it visible from **BROWSER** and select desired axis.
- Select the **Flip Direction** check box of **Pattern** tab to flip the direction of selected edge or axis.
- Click in the **Angle** edit box of **Pattern** tab and specify total angle in which all the instances of pattern will be created.

- Click in the **Number of instances** edit box of **Pattern** tab and specify the value to define number of instances to be created in circular pattern.
- Select the **Equal spacing** check box of **Pattern** tab to equally distribute the instances of selected pattern within total span of specified angle.
- Select the **Keep Original** check box of **Pattern** tab to keep the original toolpaths as well after creating new pattern.
- Select the **Reverse** check box to reverse the pattern order.
- The other tools of the drop-down are same as discussed earlier in this book. After specifying the parameters, click on the **OK** button from **FOLDER : PATTERN** dialog box; refer to Figure-9. The preview of pattern will be created and displayed on the model.

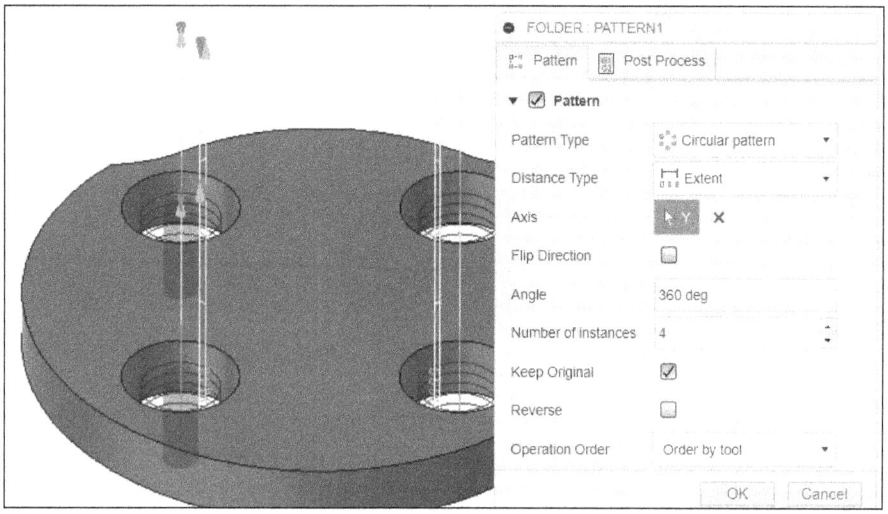

Figure-9. Preview of circular pattern

Mirror Pattern

In this section, you will learn the procedure of creating the mirror pattern.

- Select the **Mirror Pattern** option from **Pattern Type** drop-down in **FOLDER : PATTERN** dialog box for creating mirror copy of selected operation; refer to Figure-10.

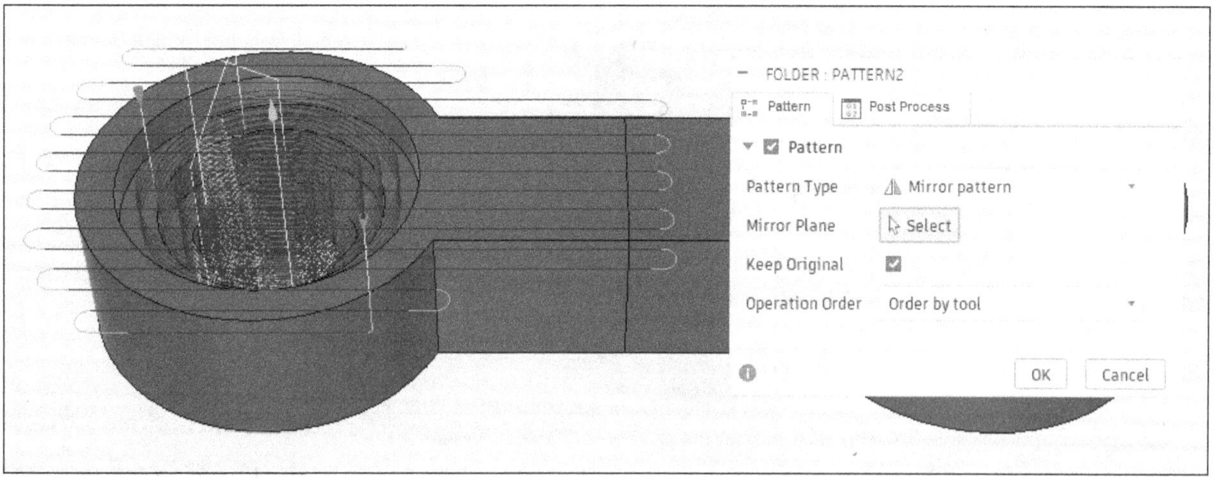

Figure-10. Mirror pattern option

- The selection button of the **Mirror Plane** section in **Pattern** tab is active by default. You need to click on the plane or face from model to select.
- The other options of the dialog box are same as discussed earlier.

- After specifying the parameters, click on the **OK** button from the **FOLDER : PATTERN** dialog box; refer to Figure-11. The preview of pattern will be created and displayed on the model.

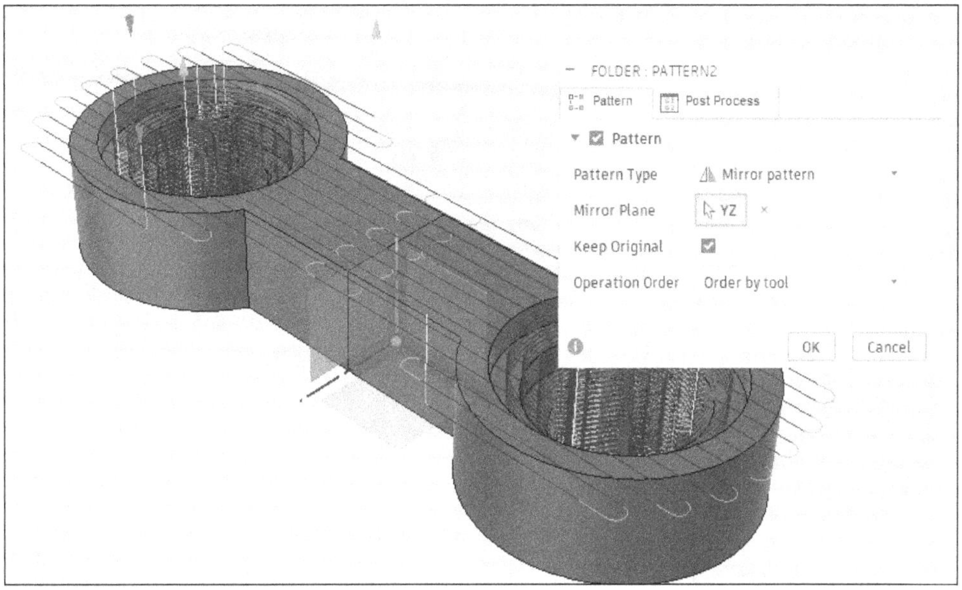

Figure-11. Completed mirror pattern

Duplicate Pattern

In this section, you will learn the procedure of creating duplicate copy of selected operations.

- Click on the **Duplication Pattern** option from **Pattern Type** drop-down in the **FOLDER : PATTERN** dialog box for creating duplicate pattern; refer to Figure-12.

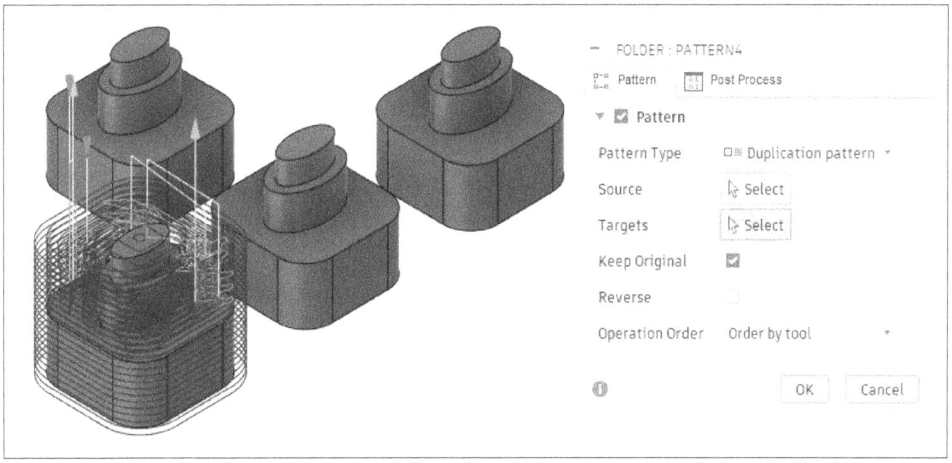

Figure-12. Duplication pattern option

- The selection button for **Source** section in **Pattern** tab is active by default. You need to click on the point from model to be defined as source point for duplicating.
- The selection button for **Targets** section in **Pattern** tab is active by default. You need to click on the target points on the model where duplicate copy of toolpath will be created.
- The other options of the dialog box have been discussed earlier. After specifying the parameters, click on the **OK** button from **FOLDER : PATTERN** dialog box; refer to Figure-13. The preview of duplicate pattern will be created and displayed on the model.

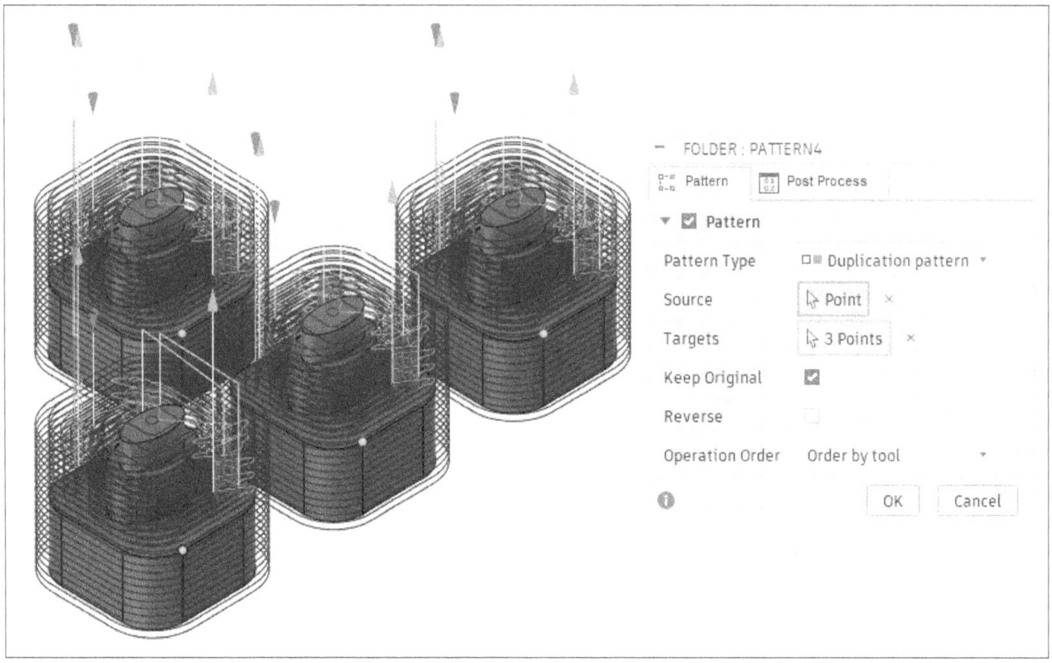

Figure-13. Selecting target body

Component Pattern

The component pattern is used to pattern the toolpaths created for one component onto the other component. Note that to use this pattern, you must have more than one components individually setup for machining in assembly. The procedure to use this option is given next.

- Select the **Component pattern** option from the **Pattern Type** drop-down in the dialog box. The **FOLDER : PATTERN** dialog box will be displayed as shown in Figure-14.

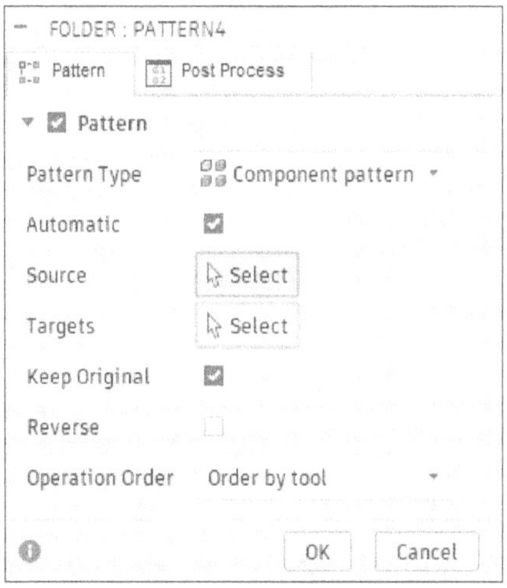

Figure-14. Component Pattern option

- Clear the **Automatic** check box if you do not want to automatically select targets based on selected source components.
- Click on selection button of **Source** option and select the component from where you want to copy the toolpaths.
- Click on the selection button of **Targets** option and select the components on which you want to paste the duplicate copies of toolpaths; refer to Figure-15.

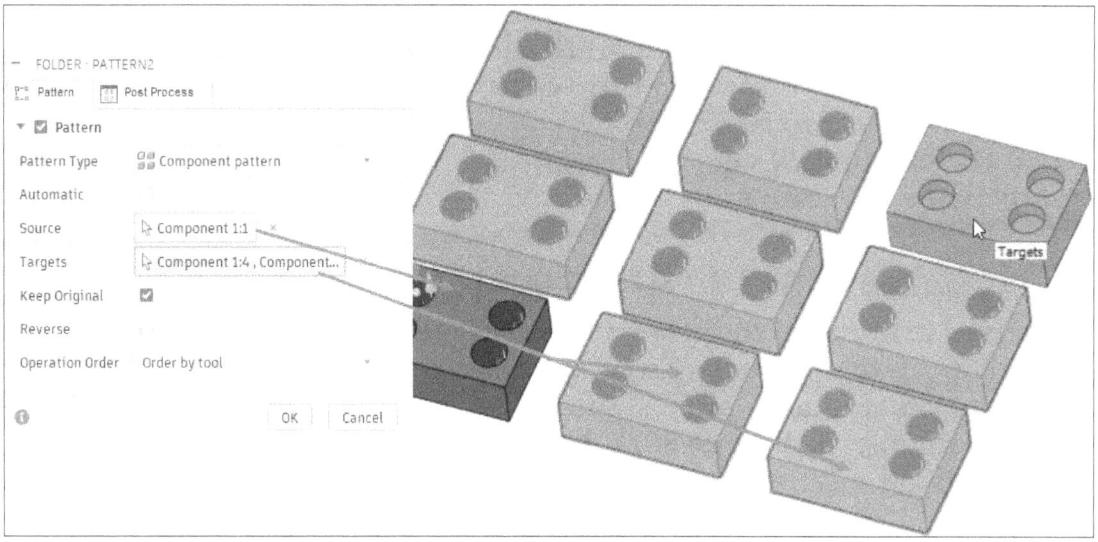

Figure-15. Components selected for pattern

- After specifying desired parameters, click on the **OK** button from the dialog box.

Manual NC

The **Manual NC** tool is used to insert special manual NC entries in the **CAM BROWSER**. The procedure to use this tool is discussed next.

- Click on the **Manual NC** tool from **SETUP** drop-down in **Toolbar**; refer to Figure-16. The **MANUAL NC** dialog box will be displayed; refer to Figure-17.

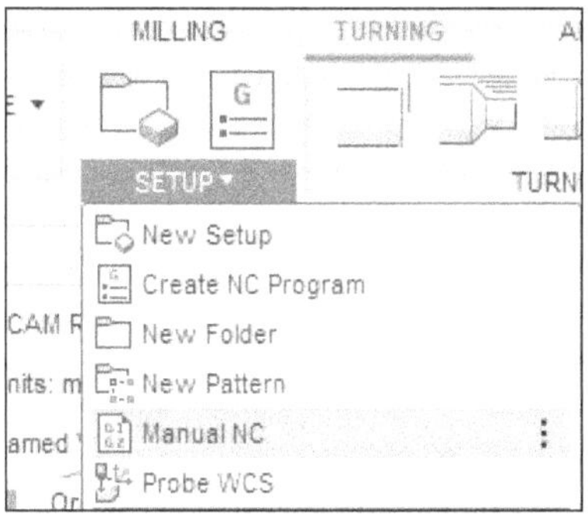

Figure-16. Manual NC tool

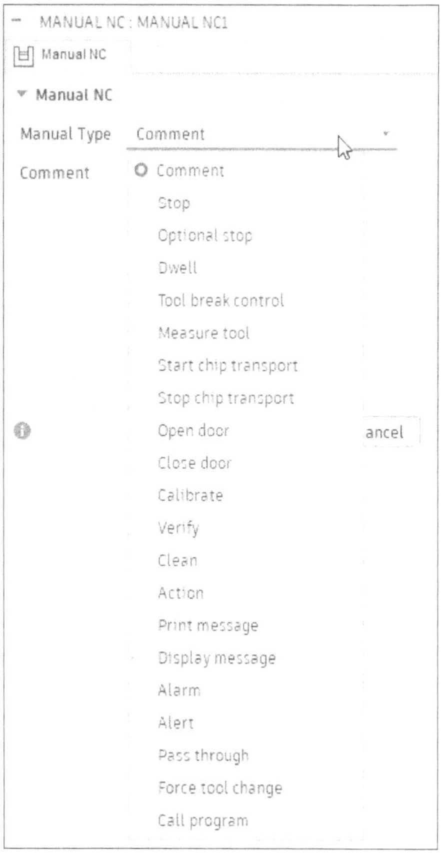

Figure-17. MANUAL NC dialog box

- Click in the **Manual Type** drop-down from **MANUAL NC** dialog box and select desired option to specify the type of manual NC operation to be inserted in toolpath.
- Click in the edit box below the drop-down and specify desired text/code to be output during post processing.
- Click on the **OK** button from the dialog box. The manual nc code will be added in the **SETUP** node of **BROWSER**.

PROBING

Probing is used to measure the geometry of object by sensing various points of object using different types of probes. There are various types of probes like mechanical probes, optical probes, laser probes, and so on. The tools to create NC program for probing are available in the **INSPECTION** tab of **Toolbar**; refer to Figure-18. Various tools in this tab are discussed next.

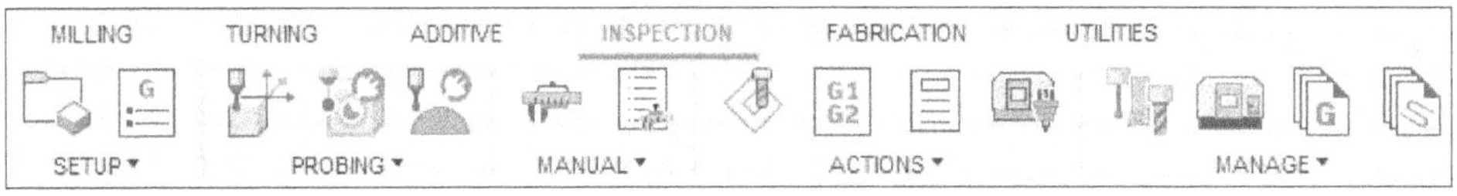

Figure-18. PROBING tab

WCS Probe

The **Probe WCS** tool is used to output NC codes for the probing cycles of your CMM (Coordinate Measuring Machine). The procedure to use this tool is discussed next.

- Click on the **Probe WCS** tool from **SETUP** drop-down in **Toolbar**; refer to Figure-19. The **PROBE WCS** dialog box will be displayed; refer to Figure-20.

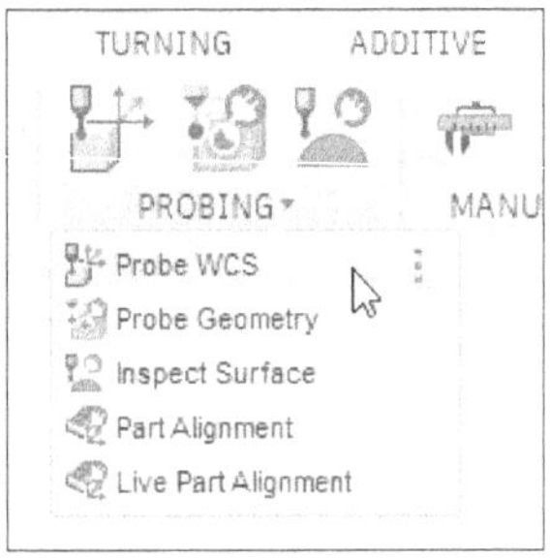

Figure-19. Probe WCS tool

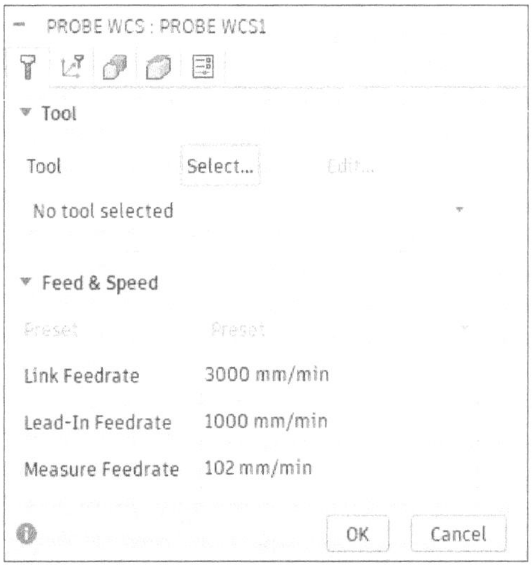

Figure-20. PROBE WCS dialog box

- Click on the **Select** button from **Tool** section in **Tool** tab. The **Select Tool** dialog box will be displayed; refer to Figure-21.

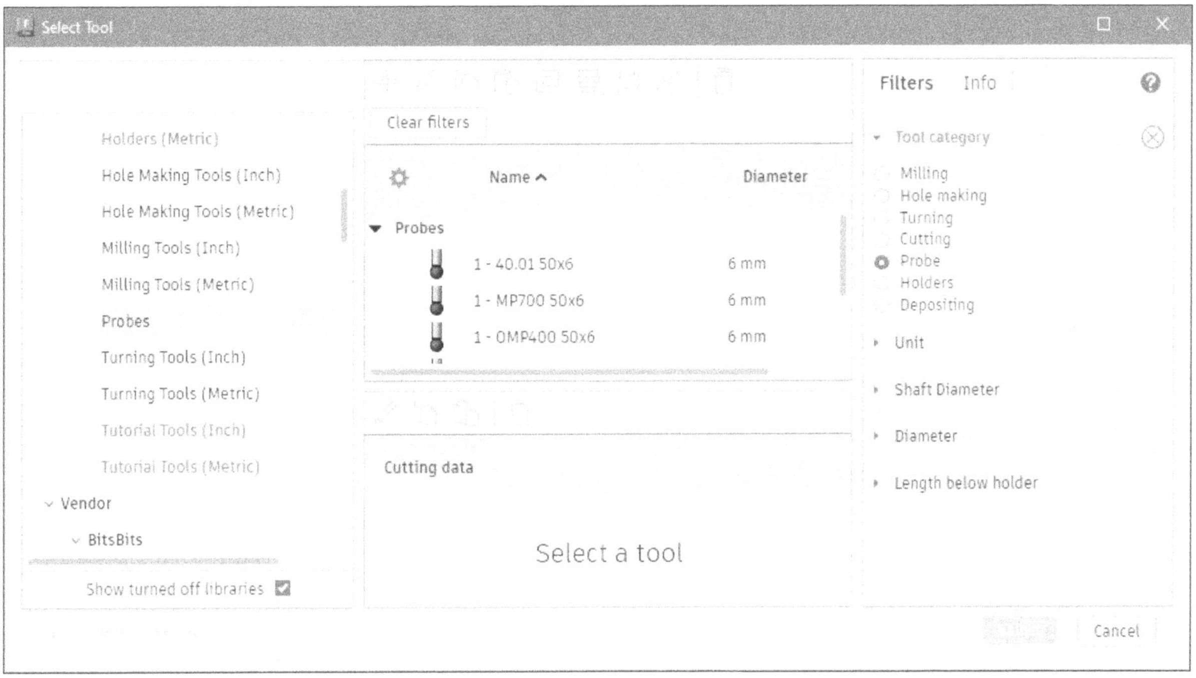

Figure-21. Select Tool dialog box for selecting probe tool

- Select desired probing tool from the table and click on the **Select** button from **Select Tool** dialog box.
- Specify desired lead-in feed rate for the probe in the **Lead-In Feedrate** edit box.

Geometry

- Click on the **Geometry** tab of **PROBE WCS** dialog box. The options will be displayed as shown in Figure-22.

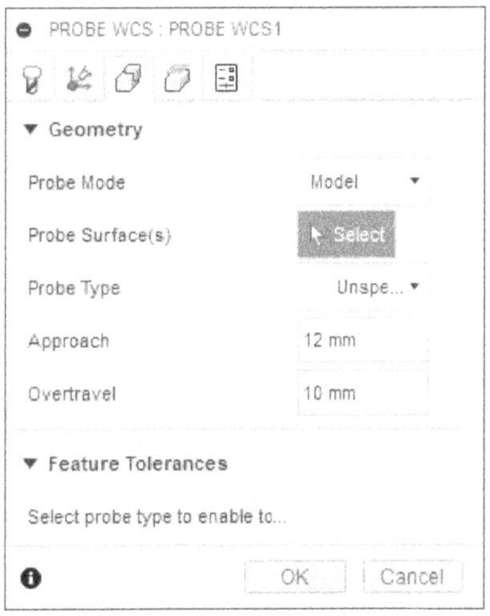

Figure-22. Geometry tab of WCS PROBE dialog box

- Click in the **Probe Mode** drop-down of **Geometry** tab from **PROBE WCS** dialog box and select desired option to define whether you want to probe part/model or stock.
- The **Select** button of **Probe Surface(s)** section of **Geometry** tab is active by default. You need to click on the face of model/stock to be checked by probe; refer to Figure-23.

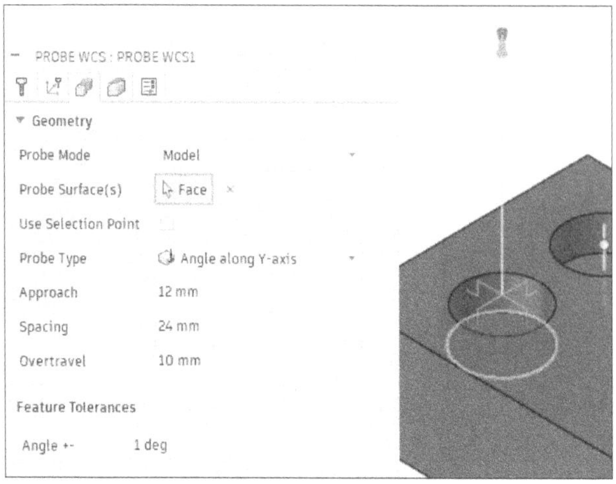

Figure-23. Selected face for probing

- Select desired option from the **Probe Type** drop-down to define what type of probe operation you want to create. If you have selected the **Z surface** option from the drop-down then the **Use Selected Point** check box will be displayed. Select this check box if you want to use selected point as reference for probing on the surface. Similarly, you can set parameters for other types as well; refer to Figure-24.

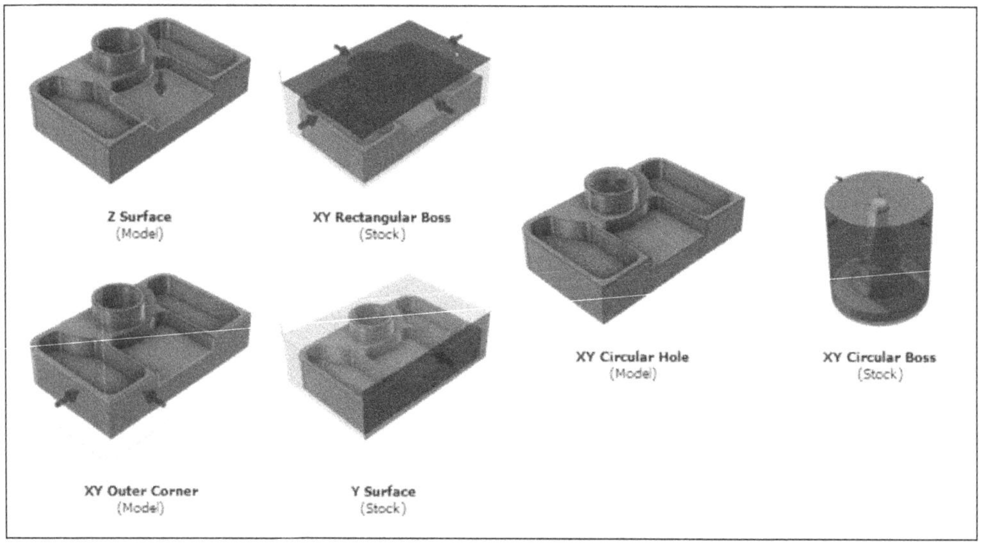

Figure-24. Probe Type options

- Specify desired value of approach distance and over travel of probe in respective edit boxes of the dialog box. The approach distance is the distance of selected point from where probe starts to measure. The over travel distance is the distance from selected point up to which the probe can move past selected point while measuring.
- Specify desired tolerance values for position and size in respective edit boxes of the **Tolerances** section in the dialog box.
- Click on the **Actions** tab of dialog box and select check boxes for actions to be displayed as messages in case of measurement error.
- The other options of the dialog box have been discussed earlier in this book. After specifying the parameters, click on the **OK** button from **PROBE WCS** dialog box. The operation will be created and displayed in the **BROWSER**.

The **Probing Geometry** tool works in the same way as **Probe WCS** tool.

Inspecting Surface

The **Inspect Surface** tool is used to probe multiple points of selected surface by using a machine. The procedure to use this tool is given next.

- Click on the **Inspect Surface** tool from the **PROBING** panel in the **INSPECTION** tab of **Toolbar**. The **INSPECT** dialog box will be displayed; refer to Figure-25.

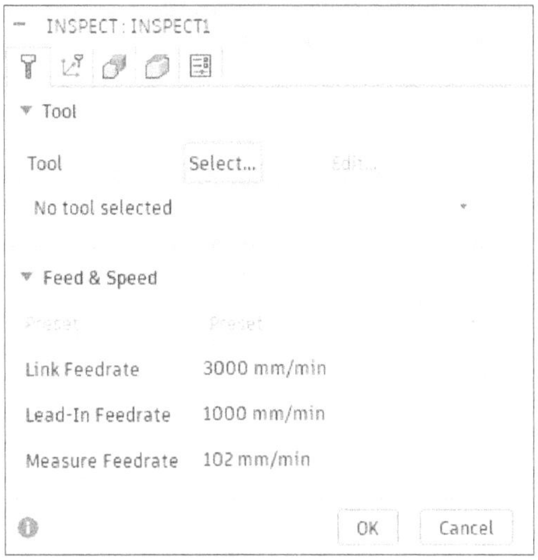

Figure-25. INSPECT dialog box

- Select desired probing tool and specify feed/speed parameters in the **Tool** tab of dialog box.
- Click on the **Multi-Axis** tab of dialog box and select the **Tool Orientation** check box to override the tool orientation defined in the setup.
- Click on the **Geometry** tab of dialog box and click on the surface at desired locations to specify inspection points to be measured.
- Click on the **Actions** tab and select the **Point Out of Position** check box to define what will happen when measured feature is out of position.
- Set the other parameters as discussed earlier and click on the **OK** button from the dialog box.

Part Alignment

The **Part Alignment** tool is used to realign the part in desired orientation for performing measurement of coordinates. The procedure to use this tool is given next.

- Click on the **Part Alignment** tool from the **PROBING** drop-down in **INSPECTION** tab of the **Ribbon**. The **PART ALIGNMENT** dialog box will be displayed; refer to Figure-26.

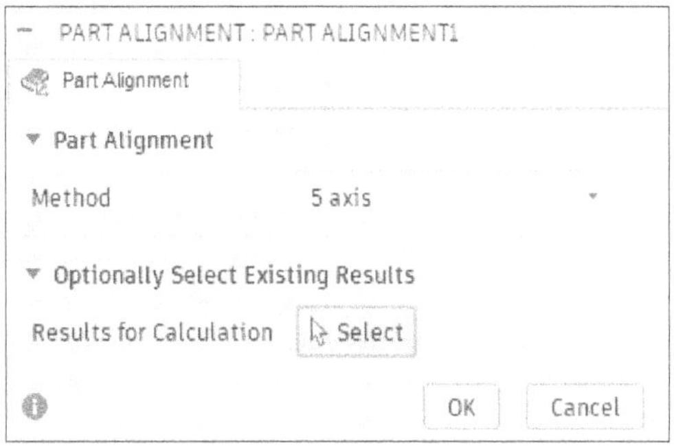

Figure-26. PART ALIGNMENT dialog box

- Select desired option from the **Method** drop-down to define number of axes about which model can be aligned.
- Click on the **OK** button from the dialog box to activate alignment mode. The **PART ALIGNMENT** tab will be displayed in the **Ribbon**; refer to Figure-27.

Figure-27. PART ALIGNMENT tab

Creating Surface Inspection Feature

- Click on the **Inspect Surface** tool from **INSPECT SURFACE** panel in the **PART ALIGNMENT** tab of the **Ribbon**. The **INSPECT** dialog box will be displayed; refer to Figure-28.

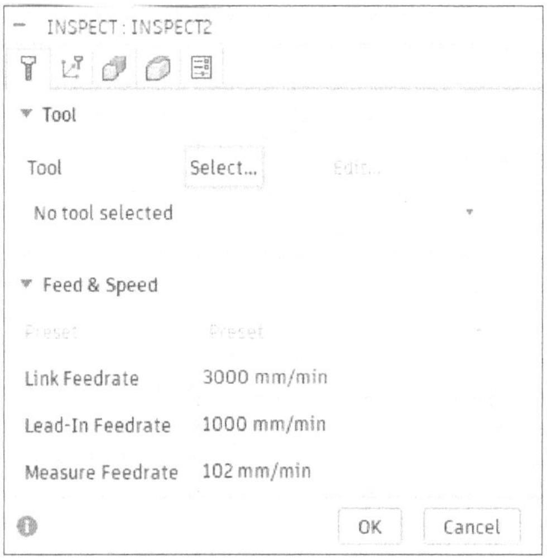

Figure-28. INSPECT dialog box

- Click on the **Select** button for **Tool** section from **Tool** tab and select desired probe tool.
- Specify desired values of feedrates in the edit boxes of the dialog box.
- Click on the **Geometry** tab in the dialog box. The options to define geometries to be measured will be displayed.
- Click at desired points of the model which are to be measured; refer to Figure-29.

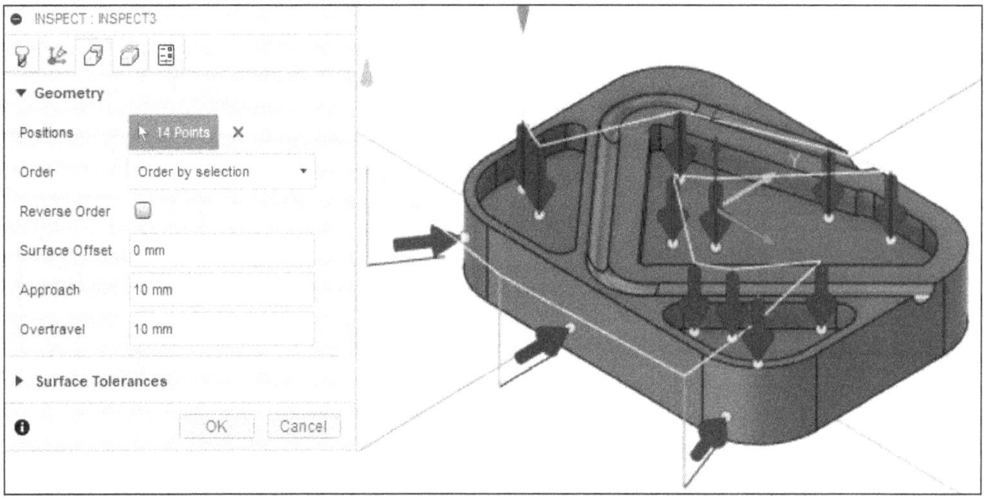

Figure-29. Points to be measured

- Set the other parameters as discussed earlier and click on the **OK** button from the dialog box.

Posting NC Program for Alignment

The **Post For Alignment** tool is used to generate NC program of inspection toolpath for alignment. The procedure to use this tool is given next.

- Click on the **Post For Alignment** tool from **POST FOR ALIGNMENT** drop-down in the **PART ALIGNMENT** tab of the **Ribbon**. The **NC Program** dialog box will be displayed; refer to Figure-30.

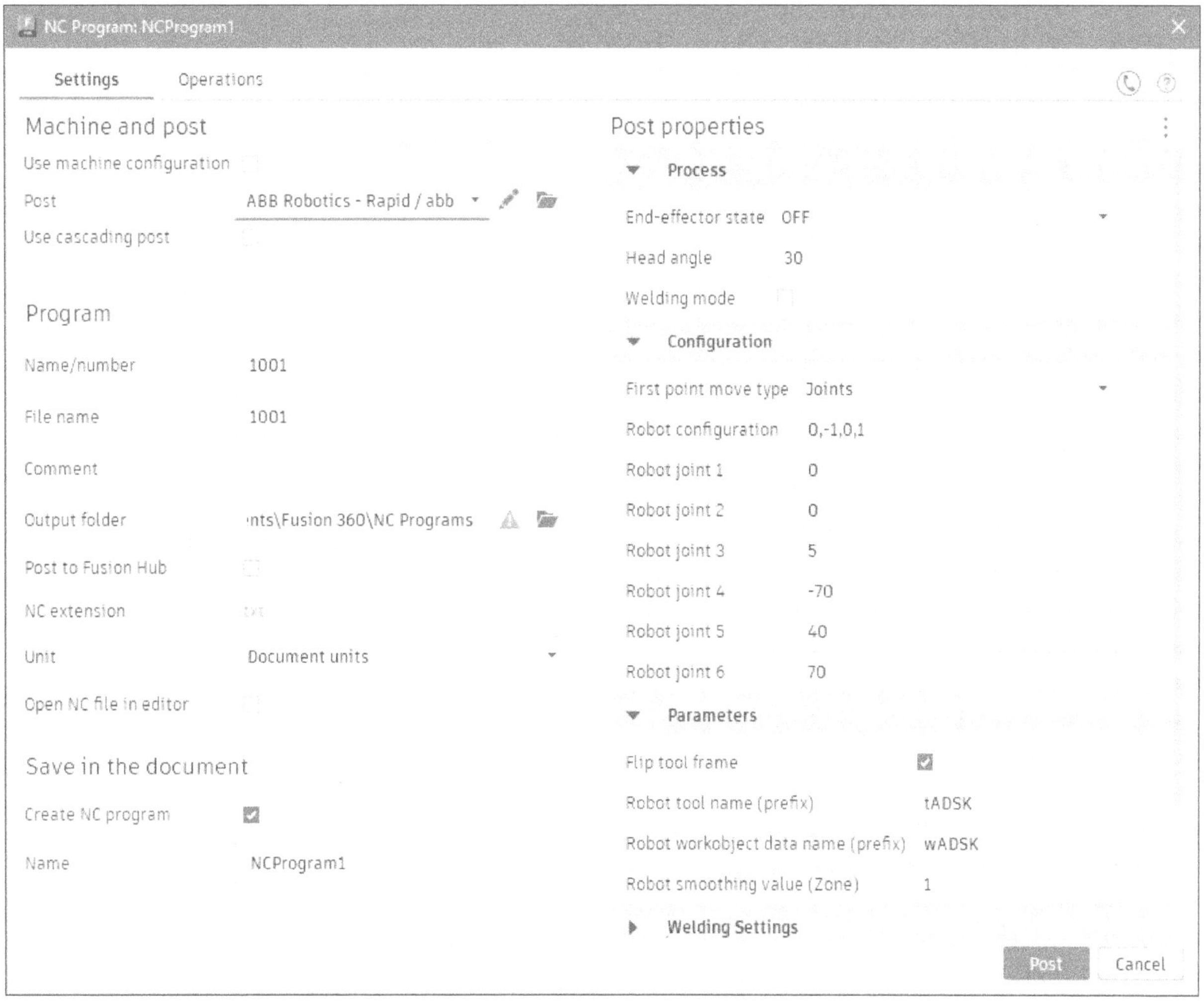

Figure-30. NC Program dialog box

- Select the **Use machine configuration** check box to use machine configuration available in the Machine library.
- Select desired post processor from the **Post** drop-down to generate NC program for probing.
- Select the **Use cascading post** check box to generate additional nc program based on selected secondary post processor. After selecting this check box, you can select secondary post processor from **Cascade** field in the dialog box.
- Specify desired text values in the **Name/number**, **File name**, and **Comment** edit boxes to define program name/number and comments to be displayed in the output file.
- Click on the **Browse** button for the **Output Folder** edit box and specify the location where you want to save the output file generated.

- Select the **Post to Fusion Hub** check box and specify location of shared folder if you want to share the output file with your colleagues using Autodesk Fusion Team app.
- The **NC extension** edit box shows the format in which output file will be generated.
- Select desired option from the **Unit** drop-down to define unit system to be used for generating tool movements in the output file.
- Select the **Create NC program** check box to specify an NC program entry should be created in the browser after post processing.
- Click in the **Name** edit box and specify desired name of the NC program.
- Specify the parameter as desired in the **Post properties** section of the dialog box based on post processor selected by you.
- Click on the **Operations** tab in the dialog box to include/exclude inspection toolpaths in the output file; refer to Figure-31.

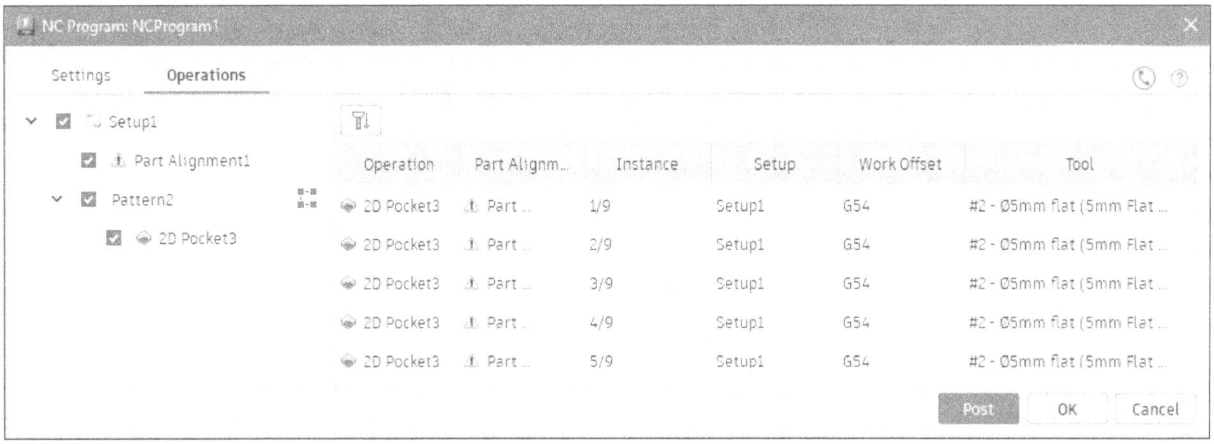

Figure-31. Operations tab

- Select check boxes from the left area in the dialog box to define inspection operations to be included in the output file.
- After setting desired parameters, click on the **Post** button. The output file will be generated.

Select the **Show Part Alignment Information** and **Show Results** tools to display respective results in the drawing area.

You can post the output file with alignment using the **Post For Live Alignment** tool from the **POST** drop-down in the **Ribbon**. The procedure is same as discussed earlier.

After performing desired operations, click on the **Exit Part Alignment** tool from the **EXIT ALIGNMENT** panel in the **Ribbon** to exit the alignment mode.

Importing Inspection Results

Once you have generated the inspection NC program, upload it on machine and check for the coordinates. If you have not done it yet then a red cross mark is displayed before **Part Alignment** feature in **BROWSER**; refer to Figure-32. The **Import Inspection Results** tool is used to import result files generated by CMM machine and project them on the model in Autodesk Fusion. The procedure to use this tool is given next.

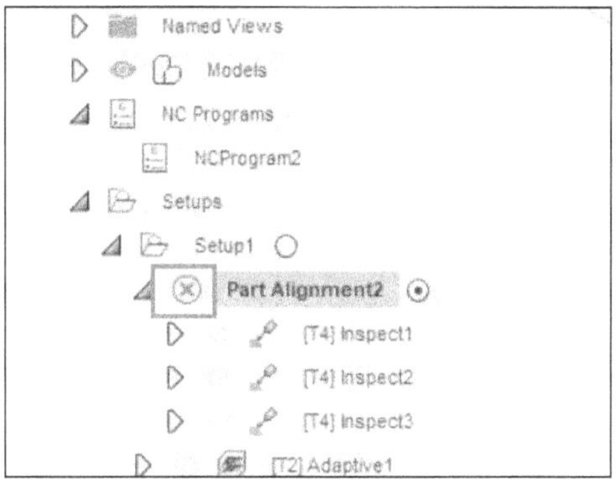

Figure-32. Cross mark for alignment feature

- Click on the **Import Inspection Results** tool from **ACTIONS** drop-down in the **INSPECTION** tab of the **Ribbon**. The **IMPORT INSPECTION RESULTS** dialog box will be displayed; refer to Figure-33.

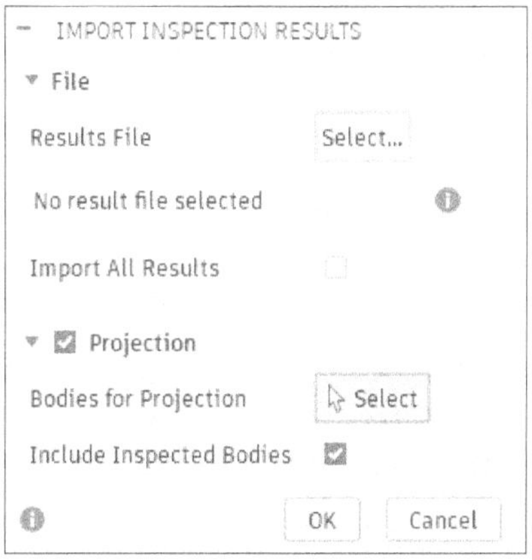

Figure-33. IMPORT INSPECTION RESULTS dialog box

- Select the model on which result points will be projected.
- Click on the **Select** button for **Results File** option and select the file generated by CMM machine after inspection.
- After selecting inspection file, click on the **OK** button from the dialog box. The projected results will be displayed on model along with a green mark before **Part Alignment** feature in the **BROWSER** showing that results have been calculated.

MANUAL INSPECTION REPORT

The tools to create and manage manual inspection reports are available in the **MANUAL** drop-down of **INSPECTION** tab in the **Ribbon**; refer to Figure-34. Using these tools, you can generate inspection report for various features of the model like diameter of holes, length of sides, and so on to be inspected physically using the measuring instruments. The tools in this drop-down are discussed next.

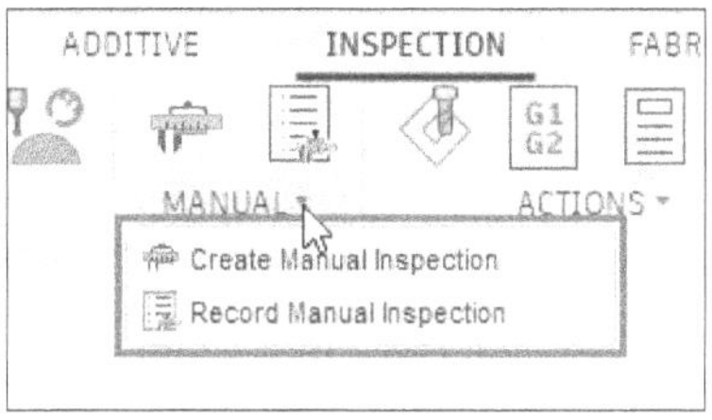

Figure-34. MANUAL drop-down

Creating Manual Inspection Report

The **Create Manual Inspection** tool is used to create a manual inspection report for measuring various features of model using physical instruments. The procedure to use this tool is given next.

- Click on the **Create Manual Inspection** tool from **MANUAL** drop-down in the **INSPECTION** tab of the **Ribbon**. The **CREATE MANUAL INSPECTION** dialog box will be displayed; refer to Figure-35.

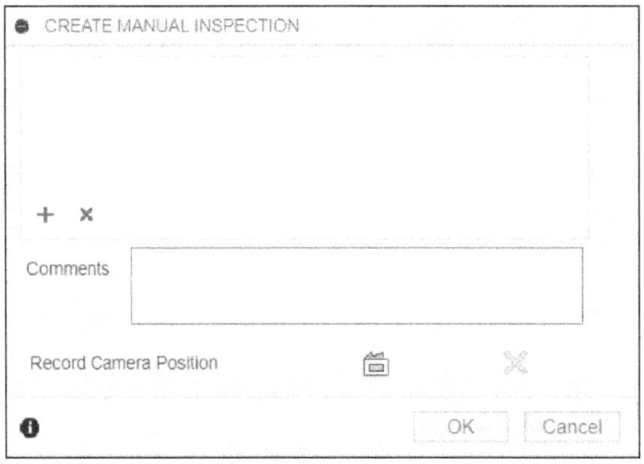

Figure-35. CREATE MANUAL INSPECTION dialog box

- Select two face to measure the distance between them using an instrument; refer to Figure-36.
- Specify desired text in the **Name** edit box to define name of the dimension.
- Specify desired values in the **Upper Tolerance** and **Lower Tolerance** edit boxes to define range within which the dimension should be measured from the part.
- Click in the **Comments** edit box to provide user notes for measuring current dimension.
- Click on the **+** button to add next dimension for inspection. You can repeat these steps to add desired number of dimensions in inspection sheet.

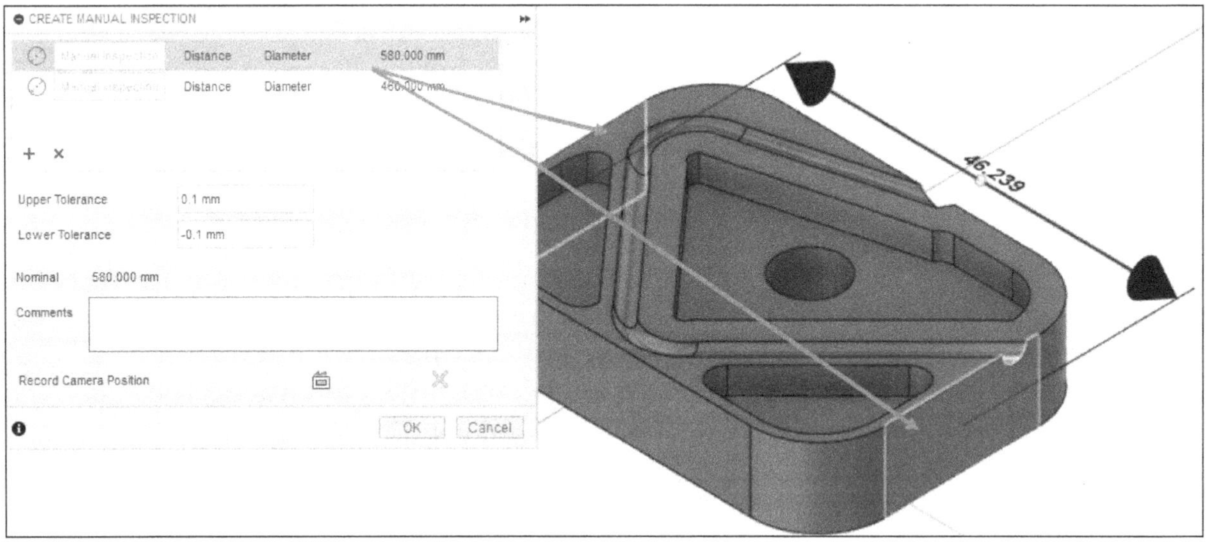

Figure-36. Faces selected for measuring distance

- Click on the **Record Camera Position** button to take a snapshot of the model in current position and orientation. This snapshot will be saved in canvas mode.
- After setting desired parameters, click on the **OK** button from the dialog box. The inspection dimensions will be added in the **Manual Inspection** node; refer to Figure-37.

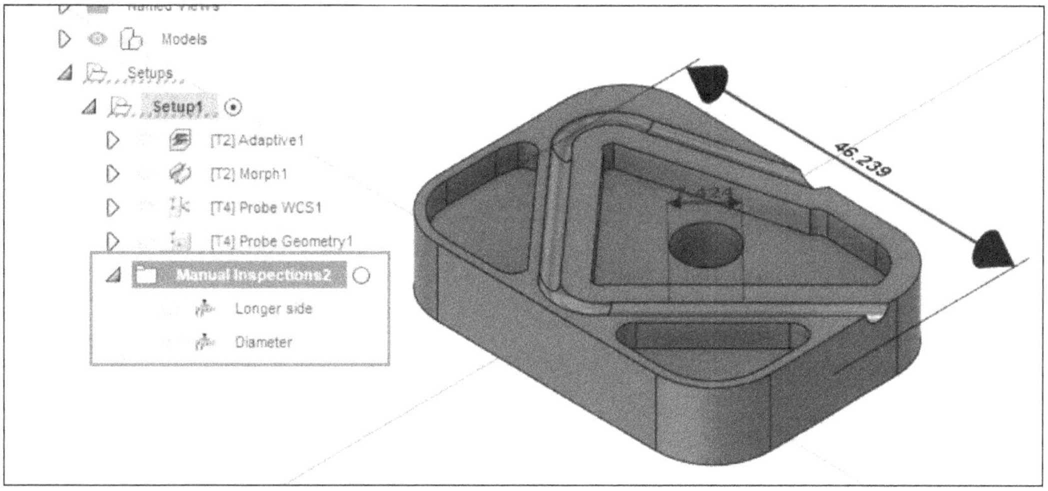

Figure-37. Inspection dimensions added

Recording Manual Inspections

The **Record Manual Inspection** tool is used to record measurements performed on the part in inspection report. The procedure to use this tool is given next.

- Select the inspection dimension to be recorded from the **Manual Inspection** node in the **BROWSER** and click on the **Record Manual Inspection** tool from the **MANUAL** drop-down in the **INSPECTION** tab of the **Ribbon**; refer to Figure-38. The **RECORD MANUAL INSPECTION** dialog box will be displayed; refer to Figure-39.

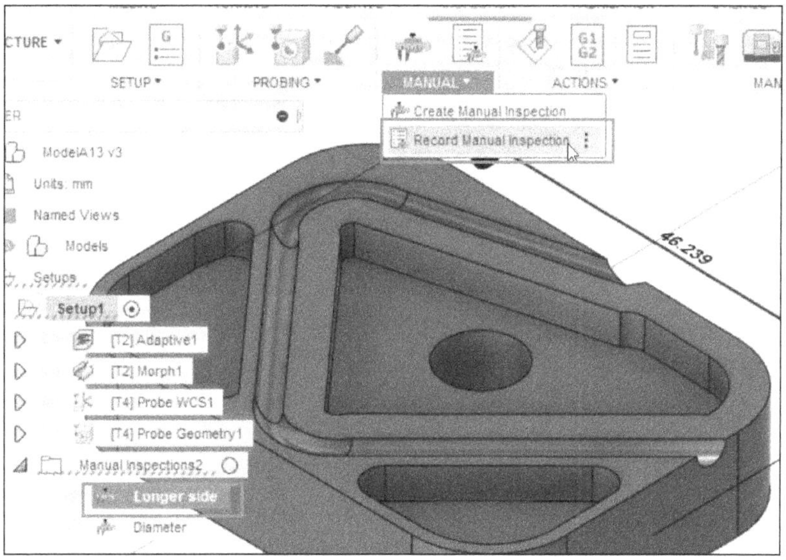

Figure-38. Selecting dimension for recording

Note that you can select multiple dimensions from the **BROWSER** for recording while holding the **CTRL** key.

- Specify the value you get by physically measuring the part in the **Measured** edit box. The deviation from mean value and amount of error will be displayed in the respective fields of the dialog box. After specifying desired parameters, click on the **OK** button from the dialog box to exit.
- If the measured values are within tolerance range then dimensions will be displayed in green color otherwise they will be displayed in orange color; refer to Figure-40.

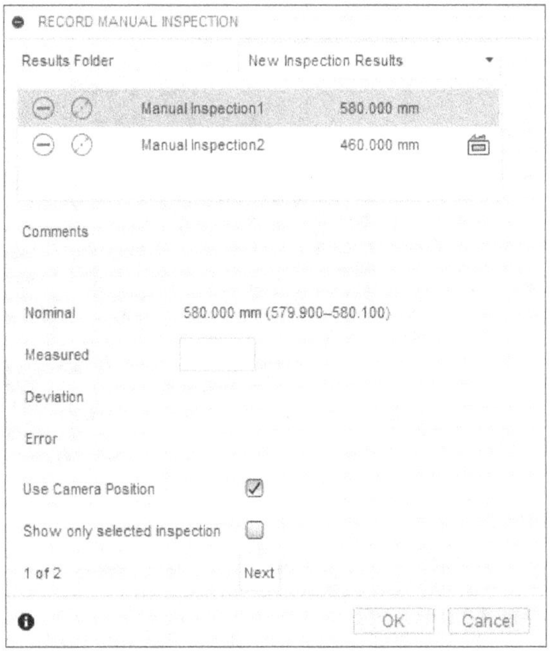

Figure-39. RECORD MANUAL INSPECTION dialog box

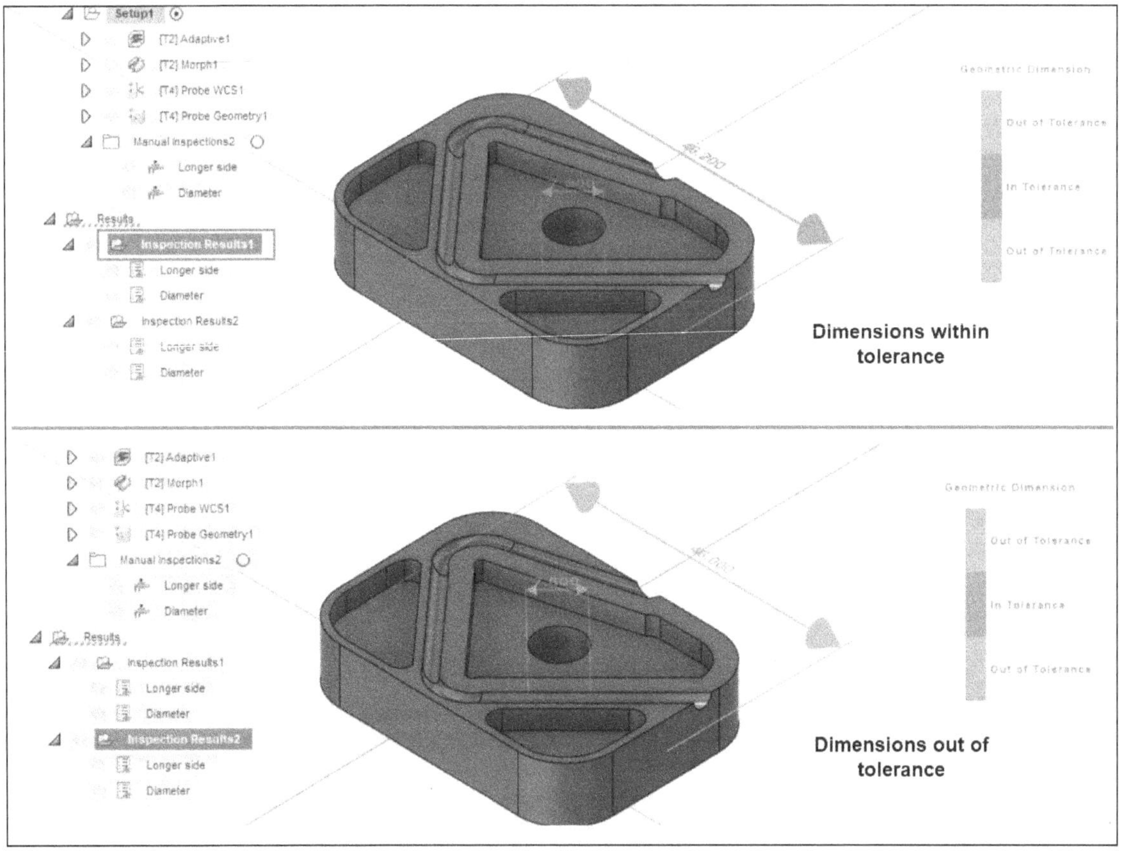

Figure-40. Inspection results

Generating/Regenerating Toolpaths

The **Generate** tool in **ACTIONS** drop-down of **INSPECTION** tab in **Ribbon** is used to generate/regenerate toolpaths after performing modifications. To use this tool, select the toolpaths to be regenerated from the **BROWSER** and click on the **Generate** tool. You can also use **Generate** option from right-click shortcut menu on selected operation to regenerate it. The procedure to generate toolpath is discussed next.

- Click on the operation for which you want to regenerate the toolpath from **Browser Tree**.
- Click on the **Generate** tool from **ACTIONS** drop-down in the **Toolbar**; refer to Figure-41.
- You can also select the **Generate** tool from shortcut menu; refer to Figure-42.

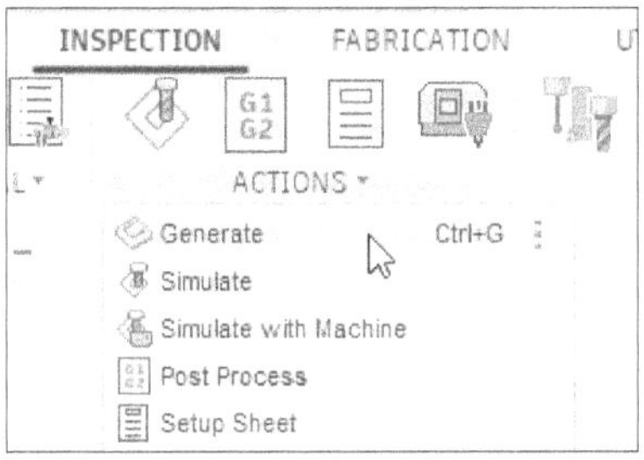

Figure-41. Generate tool

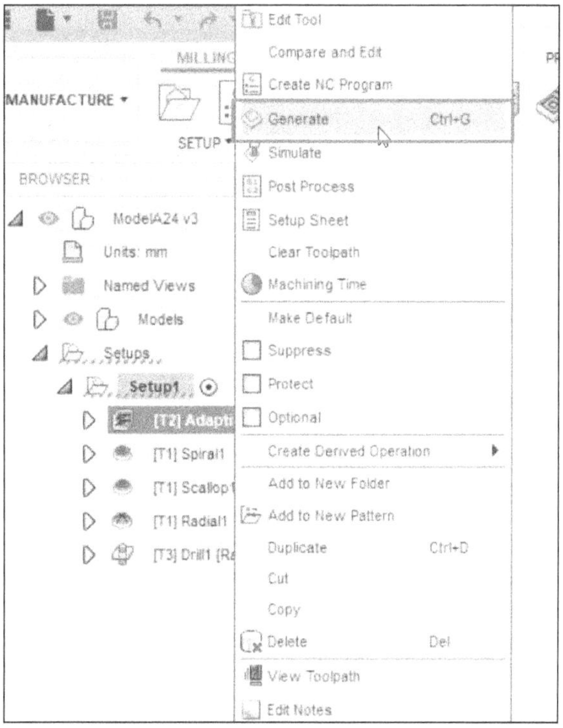

Figure-42. Selecting Generate tool from Shortcut menu

- The toolpath will be regenerated and displayed in **BROWSER**; refer to Figure-43.

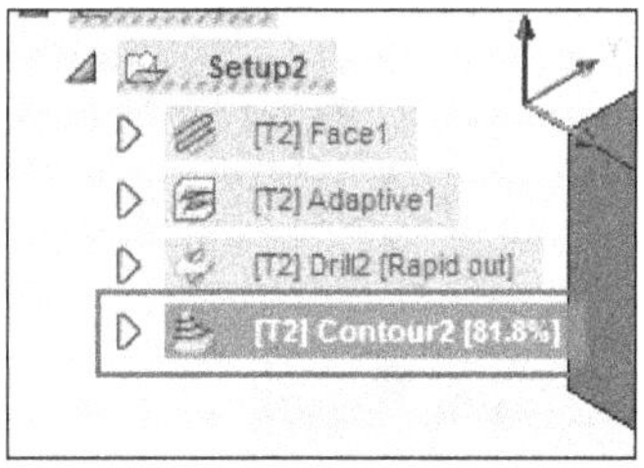

Figure-43. Regenerating toolpath

Simulate

The **Simulate** tool is used to review and simulate the created probing toolpaths. You can also use the **Simulate with Machine** tool to perform machining simulation when a machine has been define in setup. The procedure to use this tool is discussed next.

- Click on the **Simulate** tool from **ACTIONS** drop-down in the **Toolbar**; refer to Figure-44. The **SIMULATE** dialog box will be displayed along with model and simulation keys; refer to Figure-45.

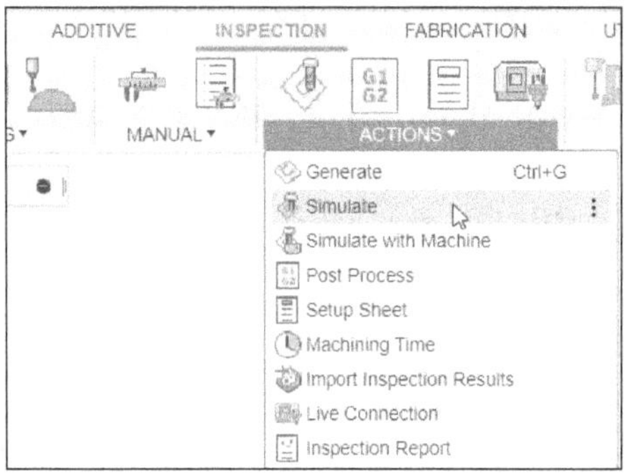

Figure-44. Simulate tool

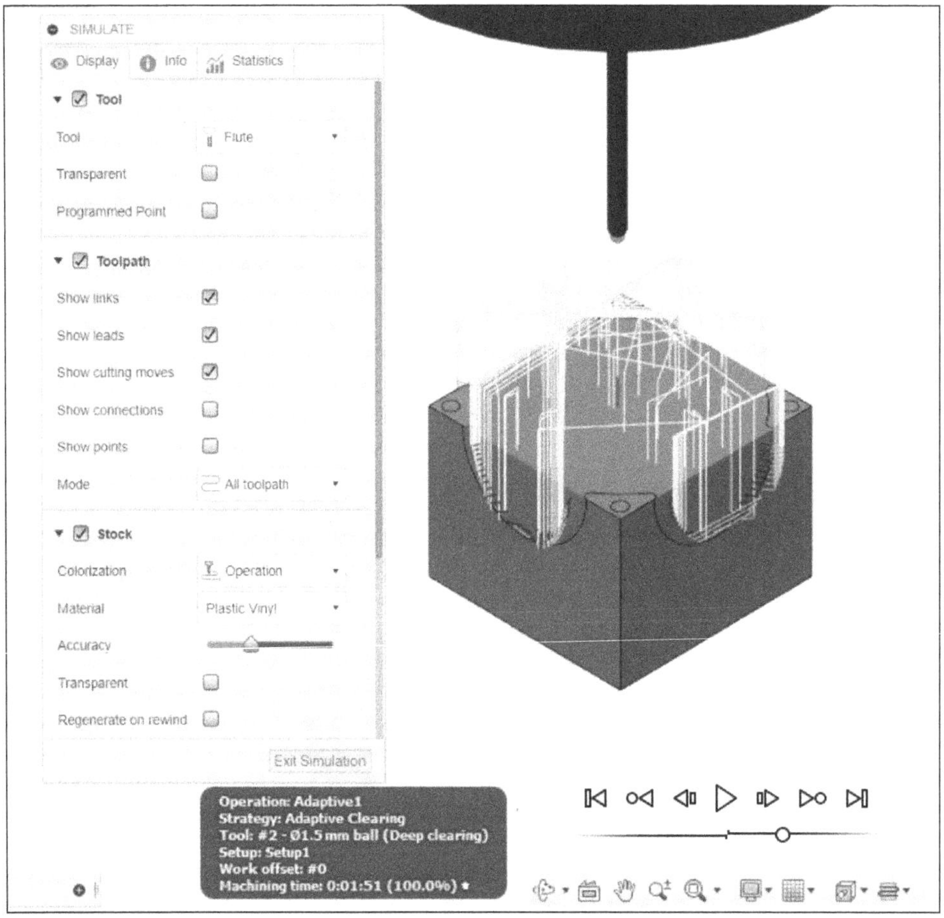

Figure-45. SIMULATE dialog box along with simulation keys

- There is also another way to select **Simulate** tool. Right-click on specific operation or setup from **BROWSER**. A shortcut menu will be displayed; refer to Figure-46. Click on the **Simulate** tool from the menu. The **SIMULATE** dialog box will be displayed.

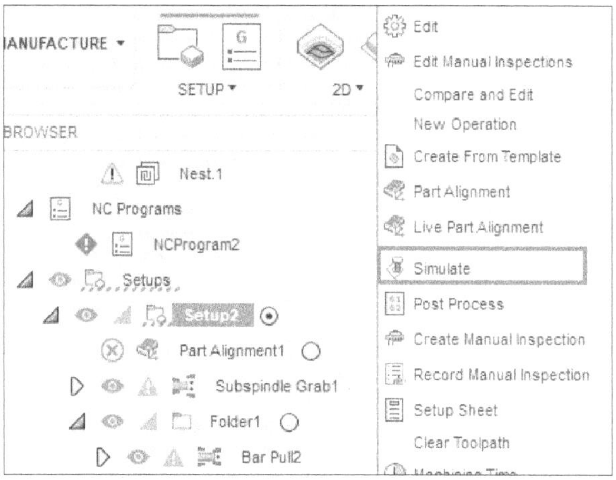

Figure-46. Simulate tool from marking menu

Display tab

- Select the **Tool** check box of **Display** tab from **SIMULATE** dialog box to view the tool and holder while machining animation process.
- Click on the **Tool** drop-down of **Display** tab and select the required option to tell software that which segment of the tool to show while machining.
- Select the **Transparent** check box of **Display** tab to make the tool transparent.
- Select the **Programmed Point** check box to display the points where changes occur in toolpath like change in toolpath curve, change in feed & speed, and so on.
- Select the **Toolpath** check box of **Display** tab to display the toolpath on the model. Clear the **Toolpath** check box to hide the toolpath.
- Select the **Show links** check box from the **Toolpath** node to show link passes joining cutting passes.
- Select the **Show leads** check box from the **Toolpath** node to show exit and entry passes.
- Select the **Show cutting moves** check box from the **Toolpath** node to display cutting passes in the simulation.
- Select the **Show connections** check box to display connecting moves between two different cutting operations using same cutting tool.
- Select the **Show Points** check box of **Toolpath** node to display the points of toolpath on the model. Clear the **Show Points** check box to hide the points.
- Click in the **Mode** drop-down of **Toolpath** node from **Display** tab and select desired option to show the toolpath of the specific part.
- Select the **Stock** check box of **Display** tab to view the stock on the part. Clear the check box to hide the stock from part.
- Click in the **Colorization** drop-down of **Stock** node to select desired option to specify how the stock should be colorized.
- Click in the **Material** drop-down of **Stock** node to specify the material used for visualization.
- Select the **Transparent** check box of **Stock** node to display the stock of model as transparent.
- Select the **Regenerate on rewind** check box from the **Stock** node to display stock again when rewinding the simulation.
- Select the **Stop on collision** option of **Stock** tab to stop the tool on collision with stock of model. When the tool or holder collides with stock then it shows red sign in the animation bar; refer to Figure-47.

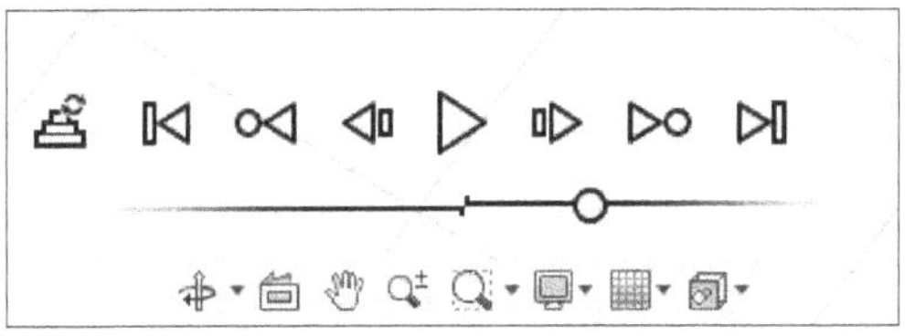

Figure-47. Holder collision with stock

- Select desired option from the **Viewpoint** drop-down in the **View** section of dialog box to define what will be viewpoint for simulation. Select the **Model** option if you want to fix the model and allow movements of machine & cutting tool. Select the **Tool** option from the drop-down if you want the cutting tool to be fixed and other elements allowed to move. Select the **Rotate Stock** option from the drop-down to allow rotation of stock with movements of cutting tool and machine.

Info tab

- Click on the **Info** tab of **SIMULATE** dialog box. The **Info** tab will be displayed; refer to Figure-48.

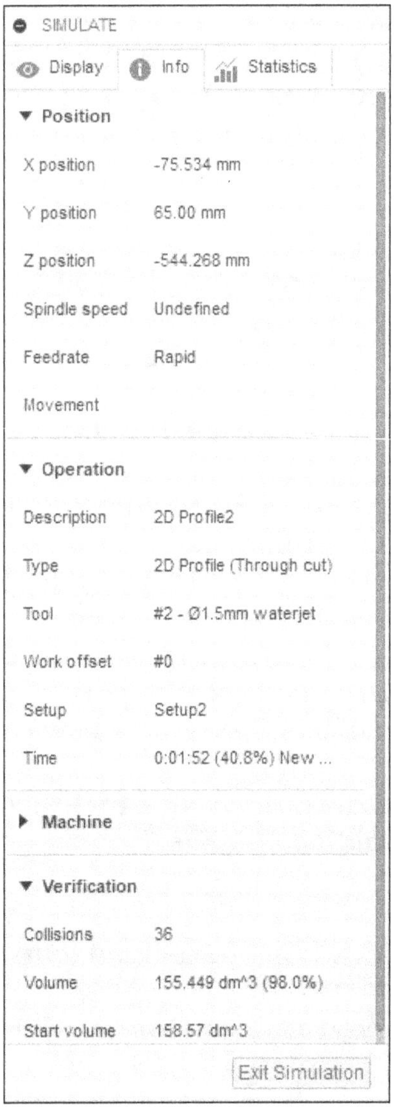

Figure-48. Info tab of SIMULATE dialog box

- In the **Info** tab, the information related to stock, operation, spindle speed, volume, cursor position, and so on will be displayed.

Statistics

- Click on the **Statistics** tab of **SIMULATE** dialog box. The **Statistics** tab will be displayed; refer to Figure-49.

Figure-49. Statistics tab

- In the **Statistics** tab, the information like Machining time, Machining distance, Operations, and Tool change will be displayed.

Simulation Keys

The simulation keys are used to watch the animation of stock removal; refer to Figure-50.

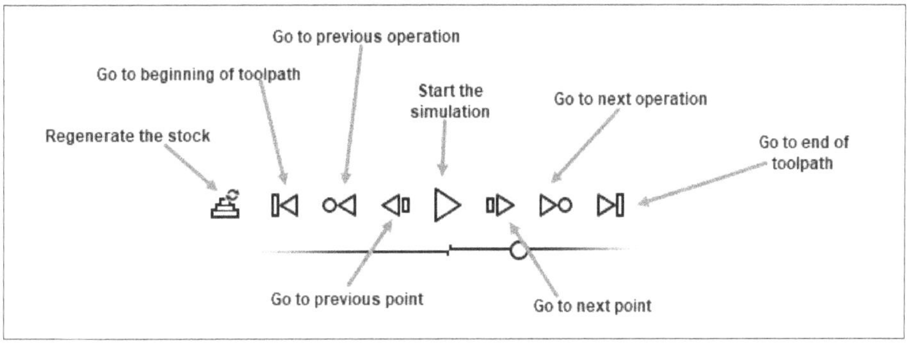

Figure-50. Simulation keys

Post Process

The **Post Process** tool is used to convert the machine-independent cutter location data into machine-specific NC code that can be run directly on CNC machines. The procedure to use this tool is discussed next.

- Click on the **Post Process** tool from **ACTIONS** tab in the **Toolbar**; refer to Figure-51. The **NC Program** dialog box will be displayed; refer to Figure-52.

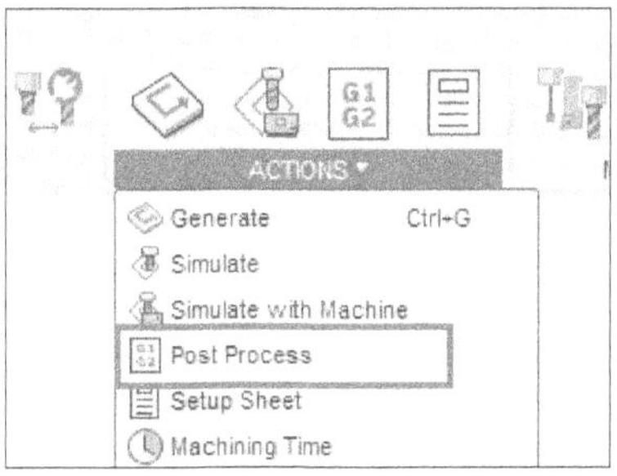

Figure-51. Post Process tool

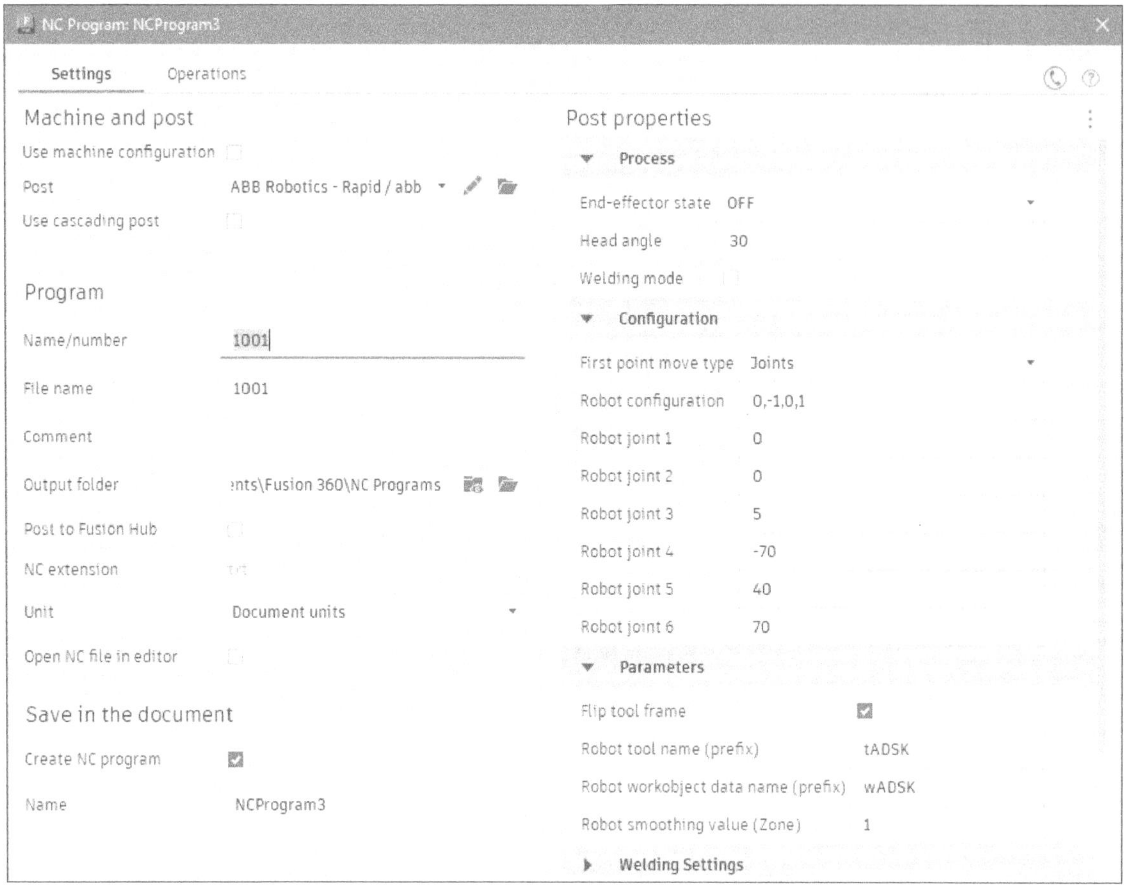

Figure-52. NC Program dialog box

- Set the parameters as discussed earlier and select the **Open NC file in editor** check box of **Post Process** dialog box to open the output NC file in editor.
- After specifying the parameters, click on the **Post** button from **Post Process** dialog box. You will be asked to download Visual Studio Code application. Download the application and install it. If the application as already been installed then the output program will be displayed; refer to Figure-53.

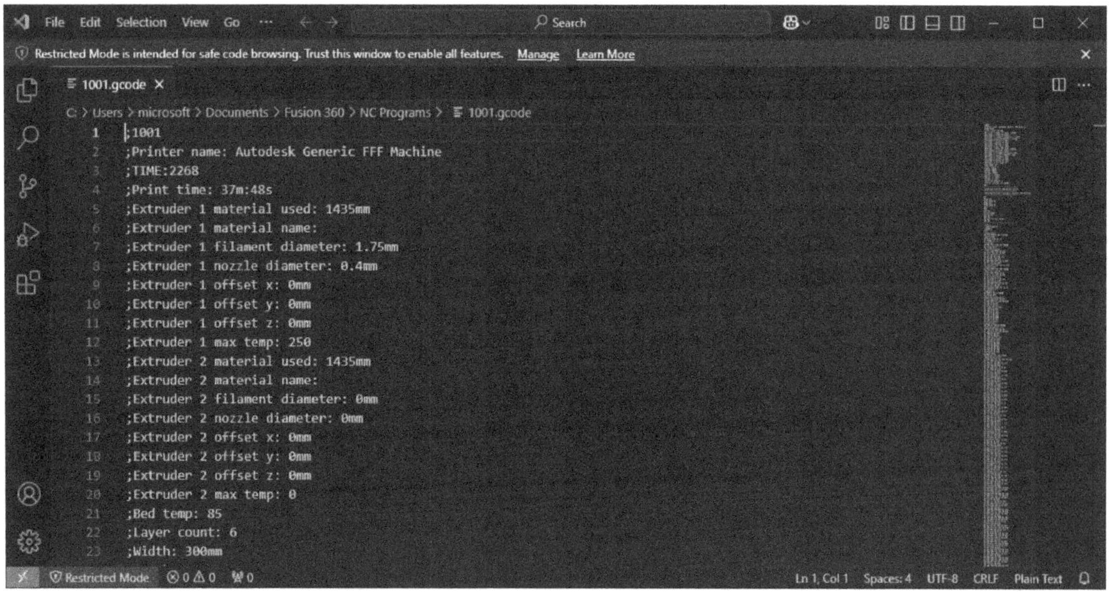

Figure-53. Visual Studio Code application window

- You can edit the codes as required by using the options of the editor.

Setup Sheet

The **Setup Sheet** tool is used to generate an overview for the NC program operator. Setup sheet provides the data related to stock, tool data, work piece position, and machine statistics. Before creating the setup sheet, you need to be sure that desired setup is selected from the **BROWSER**.

If you are on a network and the operator has access to a PC on the shop floor, you can save the setup sheet to a folder that the operator can access. This will save paper and ensure the operator always has access to the most current setup information. The default **Setup Sheet** can be viewed in any standard web browser. The procedure to use this tool is discussed next.

- Click on the **Setup Sheet** tool of **ACTIONS** panel from **Toolbar**; refer to Figure-54. The **Save** dialog box will be displayed; refer to Figure-55.

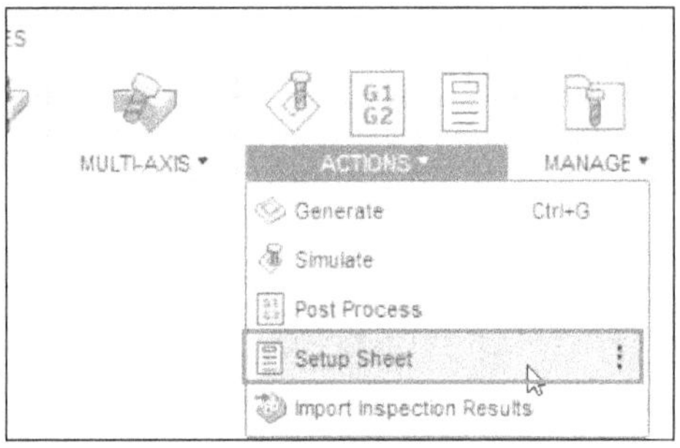

Figure-54. Setup Sheet tool

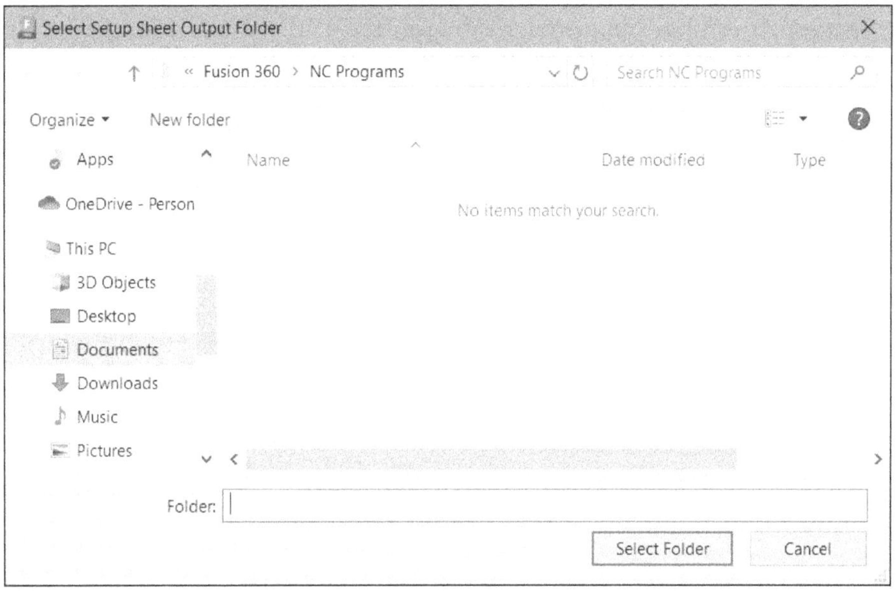

Figure-55. Setup Sheet dialog box

- Set the location folder as desired and click on the **Save** button. The setup sheet will be created and displayed in **Setup Sheet** window; refer to Figure-56.
- Click on the **Print** button from top right corner to print the sheet on paper. Click on the **Close** button (X) to exit.

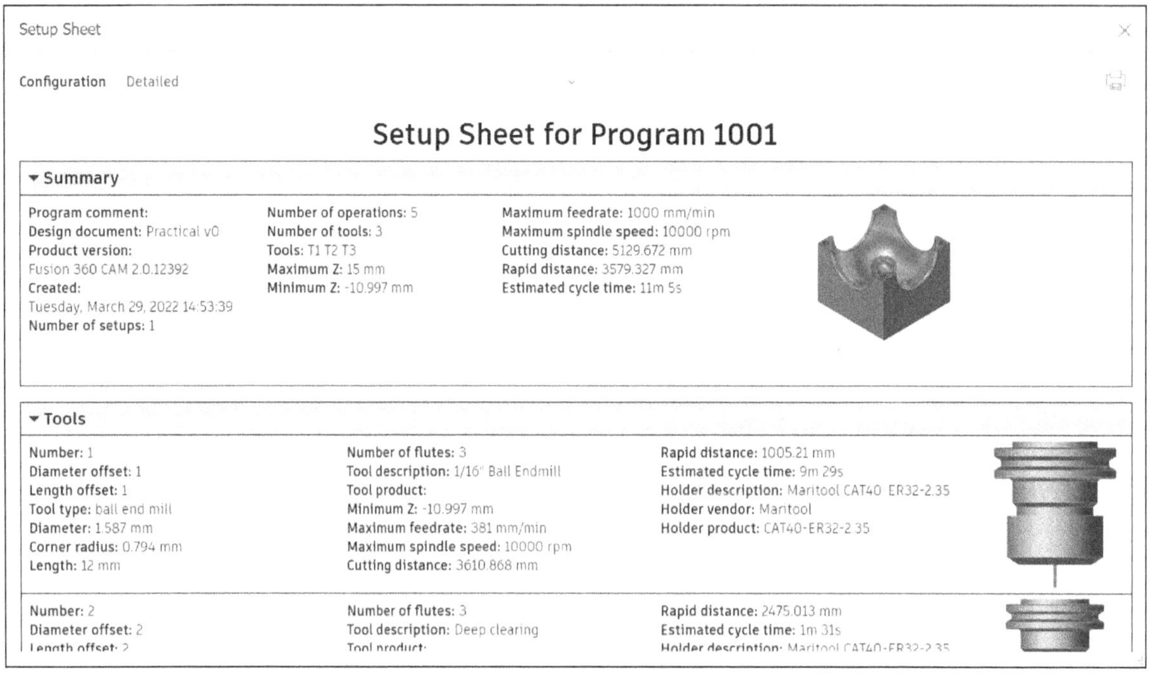

Figure-56. Created setup sheet

Importing Inspection Results

The **Import Inspection Results** tool in **ACTIONS** drop-down of **INSPECTION** tab in **Ribbon** is used to load inspection report generated by CMM machine after measuring the part. You can also project the measured points on the model in drawing area to compare the results. The procedure to use this tool has been discussed earlier.

Saving Inspection Report

The **Inspection Report** tool is used to generate PDF file of inspection result report generated by CMM or manually specified. The procedure to use this tool is given next.

- Click on the **Inspection Report** tool from **ACTIONS** drop-down in the **INSPECTION** tab of the **Ribbon** after selecting inspection results node; refer to Figure-57. The **Select Inspection Report Save Location** dialog box will be displayed; refer to Figure-58 (if you are offline).

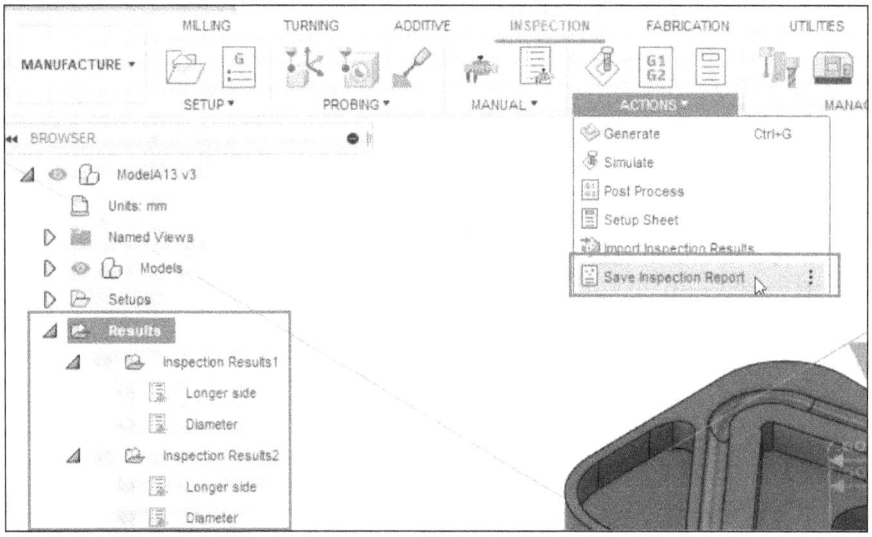

Figure-57. Save Inspection Report tool

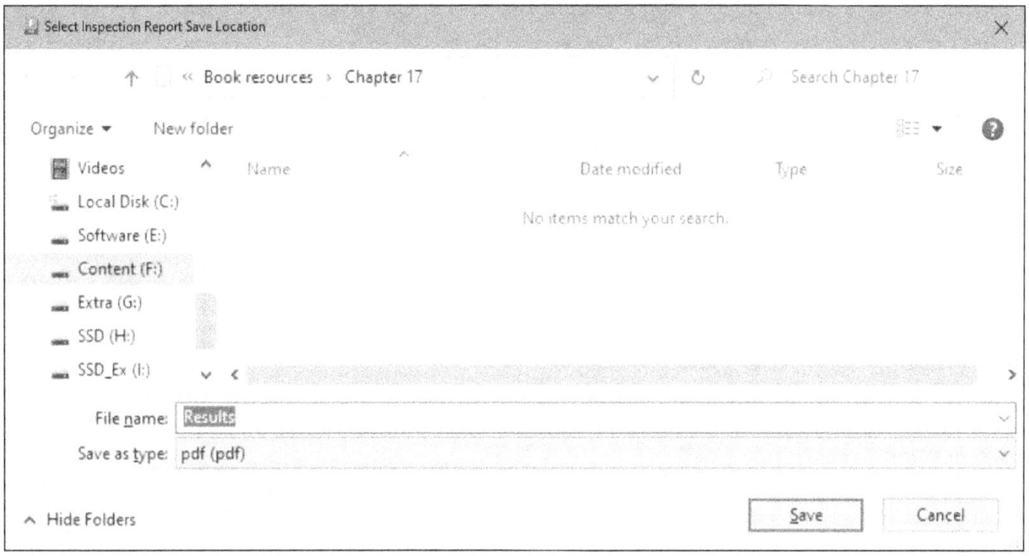

Figure-58. Select Inspection Report Save Location dialog box

- Specify desired name for file in the **File name** edit box and click on the **Save** button. The report file will be saved in specified location. You can open this file using PDF processor; refer to Figure-59.

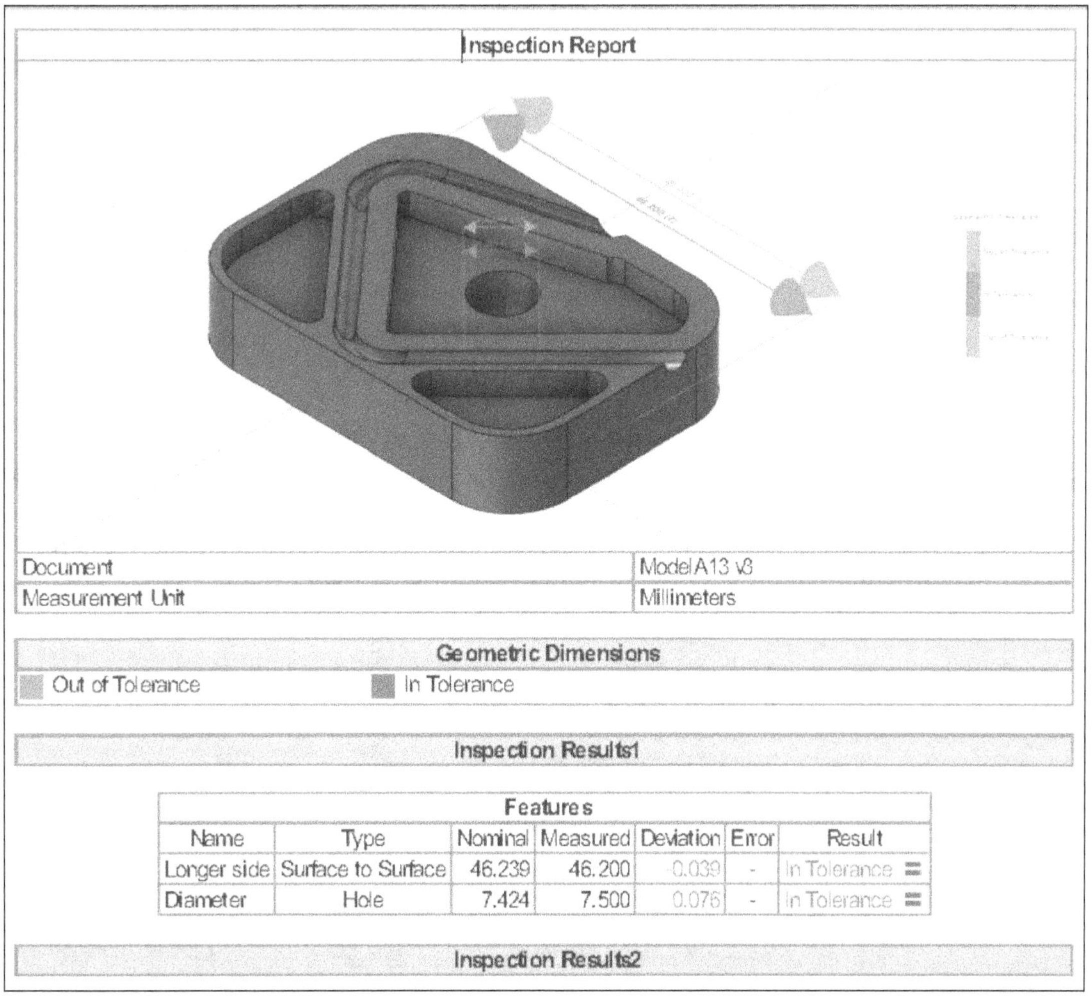
Inspection Report

Document	Model A13 v3
Measurement Unit	Millimeters

Geometric Dimensions

Out of Tolerance   In Tolerance

Inspection Results1

Features

Name	Type	Nominal	Measured	Deviation	Error	Result
Longer side	Surface to Surface	46.239	46.200	-0.039	-	In Tolerance
Diameter	Hole	7.424	7.500	0.076	-	In Tolerance

Inspection Results2

Figure-59. Inspection report generated

TOOLPATH SHORTCUT MENU

On selecting a toolpath from **BROWSER** and right-clicking on it, a shortcut menu will be displayed; refer to Figure-60. Most of the options are same as available in the **Ribbon**. Rest of the options in shortcut menu are discussed next.

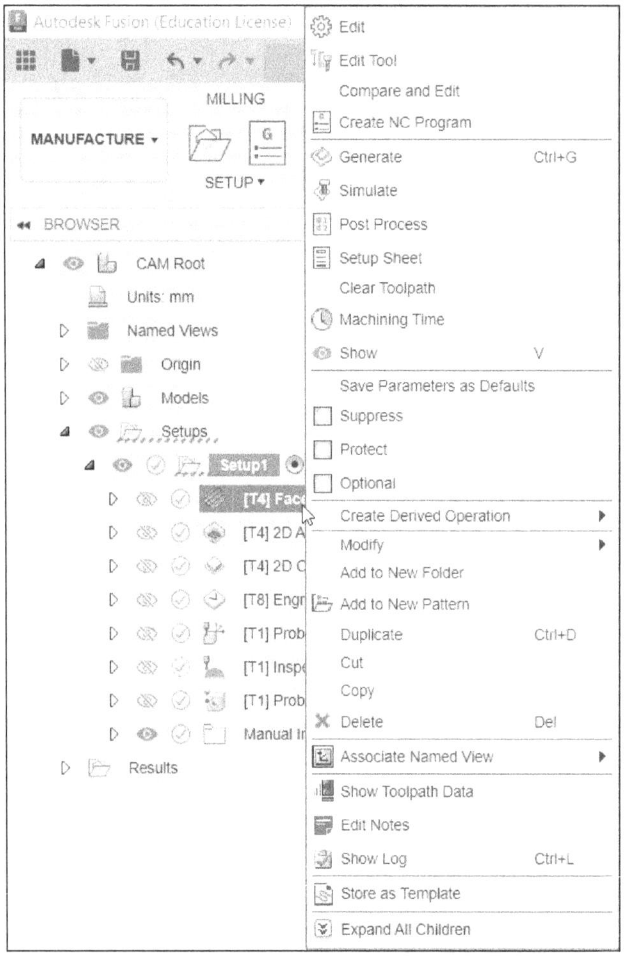

Figure-60. Shortcut menu for toolpaths

Clear Toolpath

The **Clear toolpath** tool is used to clear the toolpath of the selected operation. The procedure to use this tool is discussed next.

- Right-click on the required operation from **BROWSER** and select the **Clear Toolpath** tool from shortcut menu; refer to Figure-61.

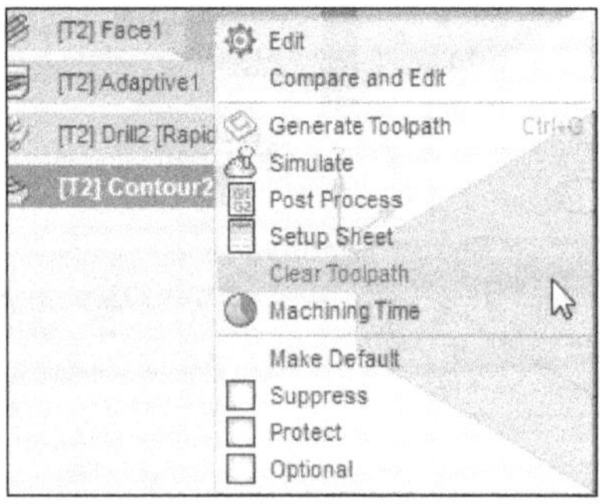

Figure-61. Clear Toolpath tool

- The tool path of selected operation will be deleted. If you want to display this toolpath then right-click again on it and select the **Generate Toolpath** option.

Machining Time

The **Machining Time** tool is used to measure and calculate the machining time for a selected operation with a high accuracy. The procedure to use this tool is discussed next.

- Right-click on the required operation from **BROWSER** and select the **Machining Time** option from shortcut menu; refer to Figure-62.

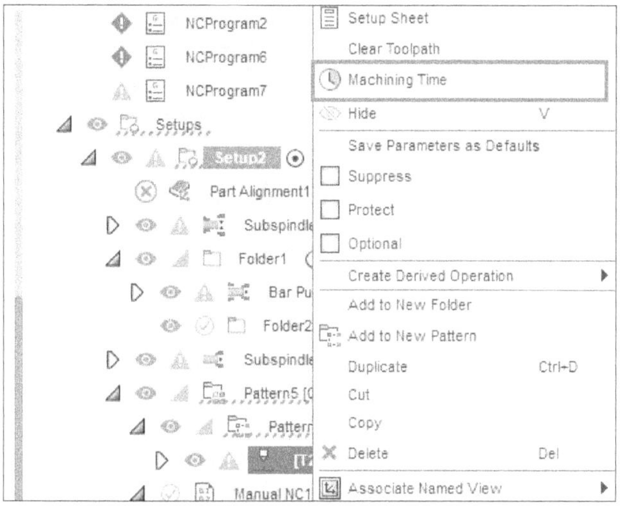

Figure-62. Machining Time tool

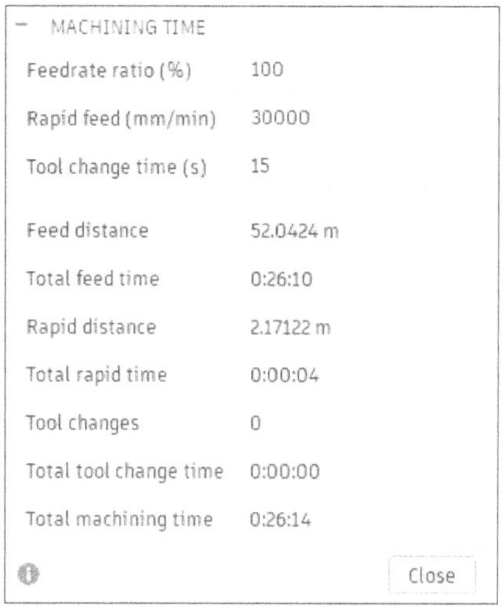

Figure-63. MACHINING TIME dialog box

- Click in the **Feedrate ratio(%)** edit box of **MACHINING TIME** dialog box and specify desired value of feed rate in percentage to check how machining time will change.
- Click in the **Rapid Feed(mm/min)** edit box of **MACHINING TIME** dialog box and specify desired value to check change in machining time.
- Click in the **Tool change Time(s)** edit box of **MACHINING TIME** dialog box and specify desired value to check change in machining time.
- In the **MACHINING TIME** dialog box, you can also check other information related to operation.

Setting Default for Toolpaths

Using the **Save Parameters as Defaults** option in shortcut menu for selected operation, you can make parameters of selected operation default for other similar operations. The procedure to use this option is given next.

- Select the operation which you want to use for setting default parameters from the **Setup** node in **BROWSER** and right-click on it. A shortcut menu will be displayed.
- Select the **Save Parameters as Defaults** option from the shortcut menu; refer to Figure-64. The **Save the current parameters as defaults** information box will be displayed; refer to Figure-65.

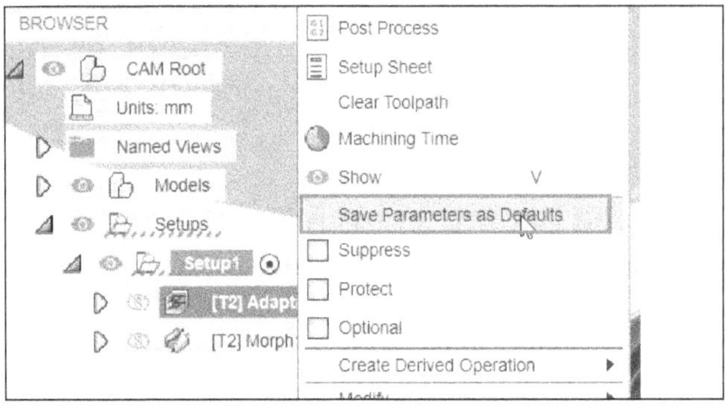

Figure-64. Save Parameters as Defaults option

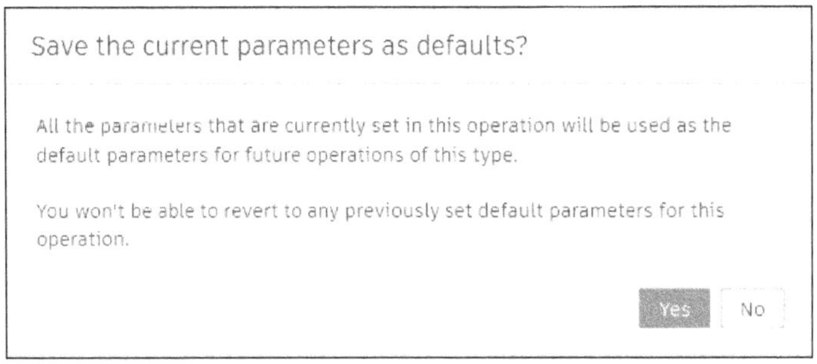

Figure-65. Save the current parameters as defaults information box

- Click on the **Yes** button from the information box to apply defaults. For example, if you have selected an adaptive toolpath to make it default then parameters in all the other adaptive toolpaths of current file will be changed according to selected adaptive toolpath.

Suppressing Toolpaths

The **Suppress** check box of shortcut menu is used to make selected toolpath inactive in the setup. Note that on suppressing a toolpath, the stock will be modified as well because effects of suppressed toolpath will be removed from stock. If you want to reactivate the suppressed toolpath then right-click on it and clear the **Suppress** check box.

Protecting Toolpaths

The **Protect** check box of shortcut menu is used to make selected toolpath protected so that accidentally no changes are made in the toolpath. Note that on selecting this check box, a lock sign will be added before toolpath in **BROWSER**; refer to Figure-66.

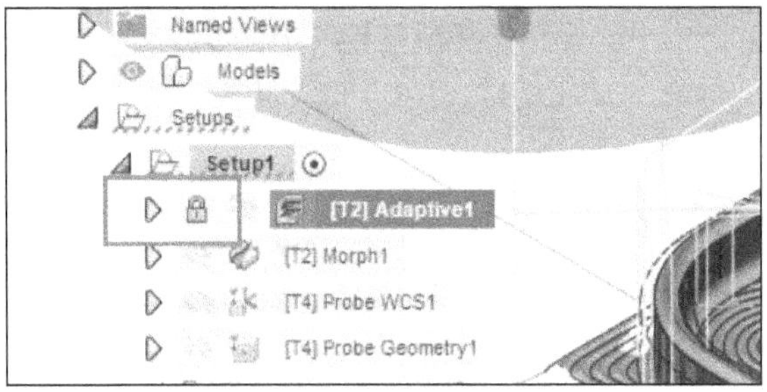

Figure-66. Lock icon for toolpath

Optional Toolpath

The **Optional** check box of shortcut menu is used to mark selected toolpath as optional so that user on machine can include or skip toolpaths from the machining setup.

Creating Derived Operation

The options in the **Create Derived Operation** cascading menu are used to create cutting operation which use parameters specified in earlier created operations. Note that selected faces, cutting tools, and cutting parameters of earlier created operation will be applied on derived operations. For example, you have performed an Adaptive Clearing operation earlier for roughing pockets and now you want to perform finishing operation then you can select Pocket Clearing operation from **Create Derived Operation** cascading menu of shortcut menu; refer to Figure-67.

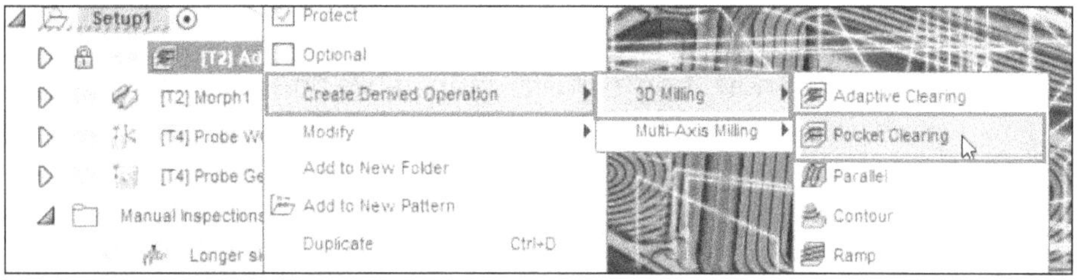

Figure-67. Creating derived operation

Viewing Toolpath Data

The **Show Toolpath Data** option in right-click shortcut menu of an operation is used to check movements of cutting tool in terms of coordinates with feed rate and spindle speed; refer to Figure-68. After checking parameters, click on the **Close** button to exit the information box.

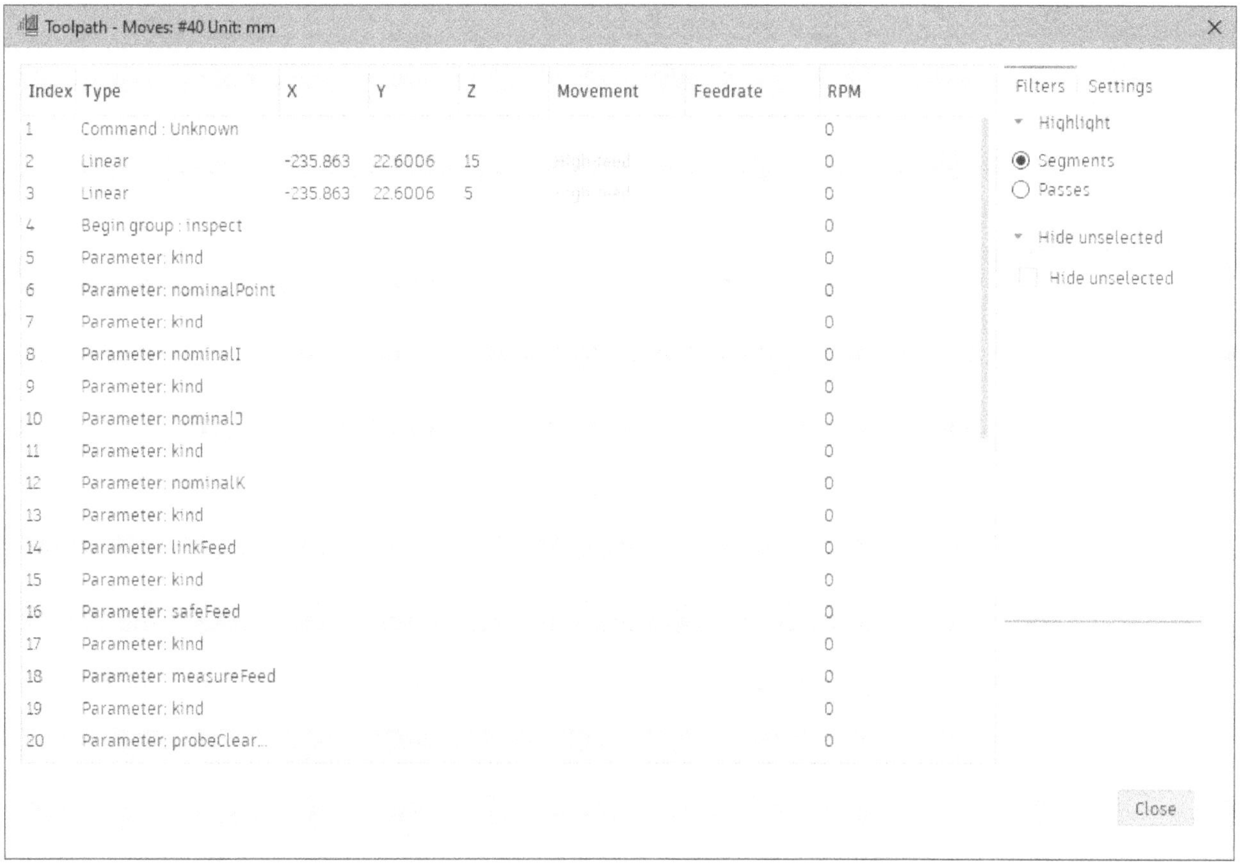

Figure-68. Toolpath information box

Editing Notes of an Operation

The **Edit Notes** option for selected operation is used to create user defined notes for the operation. On selecting **Edit Notes** option from the shortcut menu, the **EDIT NOTES** dialog box will be displayed; refer to Figure-69.

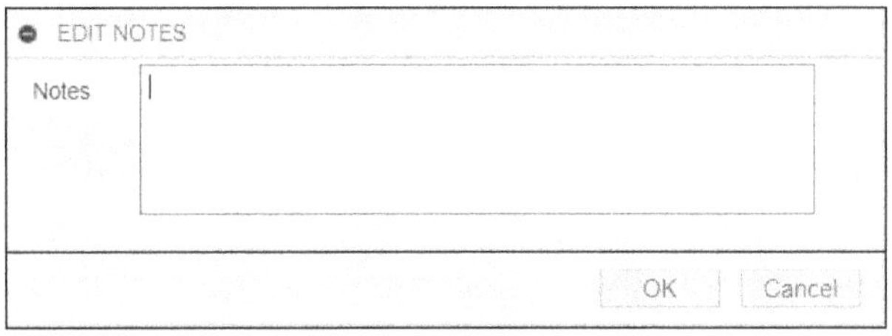

Figure-69. Notes for Adaptive dialog box

Specify desired text comments in the edit box of dialog box and click on the **OK** button.

Similarly, you can use the **Show Log** option from the shortcut menu to check log of events related to selected operation; refer to Figure-70.

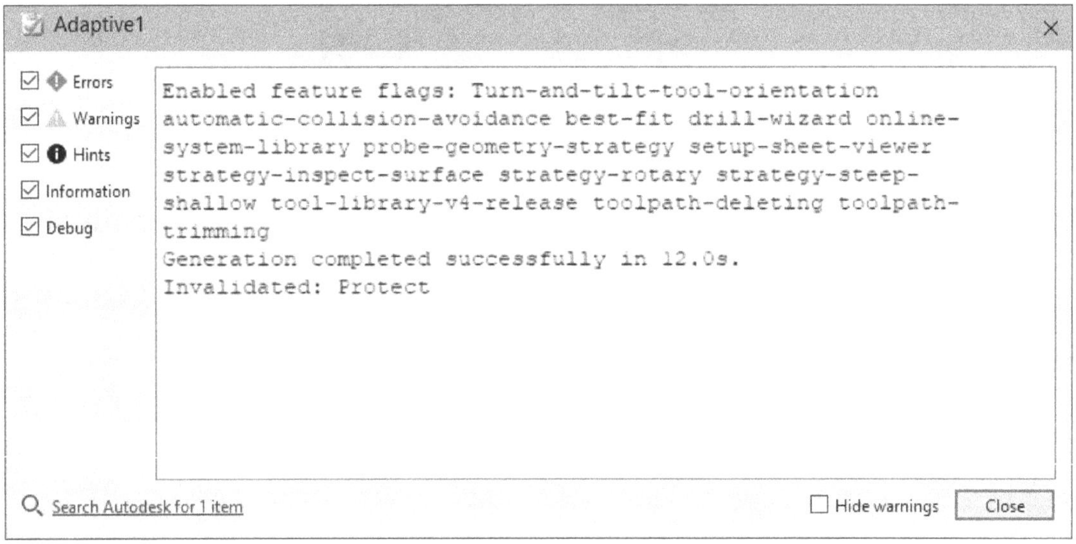

Figure-70. Tool operation log

Creating Form Mill Tool

The **Form Mill** tool in **MANAGE** drop-down is used to create a milling tool of desired shape. The procedure to use this tool is given next.

- Click on the **Form Mill** tool from the **MANAGE** drop-down in **INSPECTION** tab of the **Toolbar**. The **FORM MILL** dialog box will be displayed; refer to Figure-71.

Figure-71. FORM MILL dialog box

- Select desired sketch profile, axis, and cutting point of the tool; refer to Figure-72.

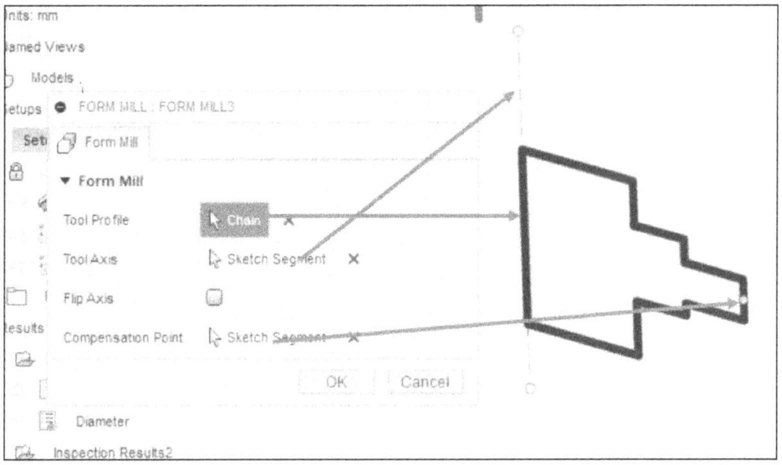

Figure-72. Selection for form tool

- Select the **Flip Axis** check box if you want to reverse the orientation of tool.
- Click on the **OK** button from the dialog box. The new tool will be added in the **Tool Library** dialog box; refer to Figure-73.

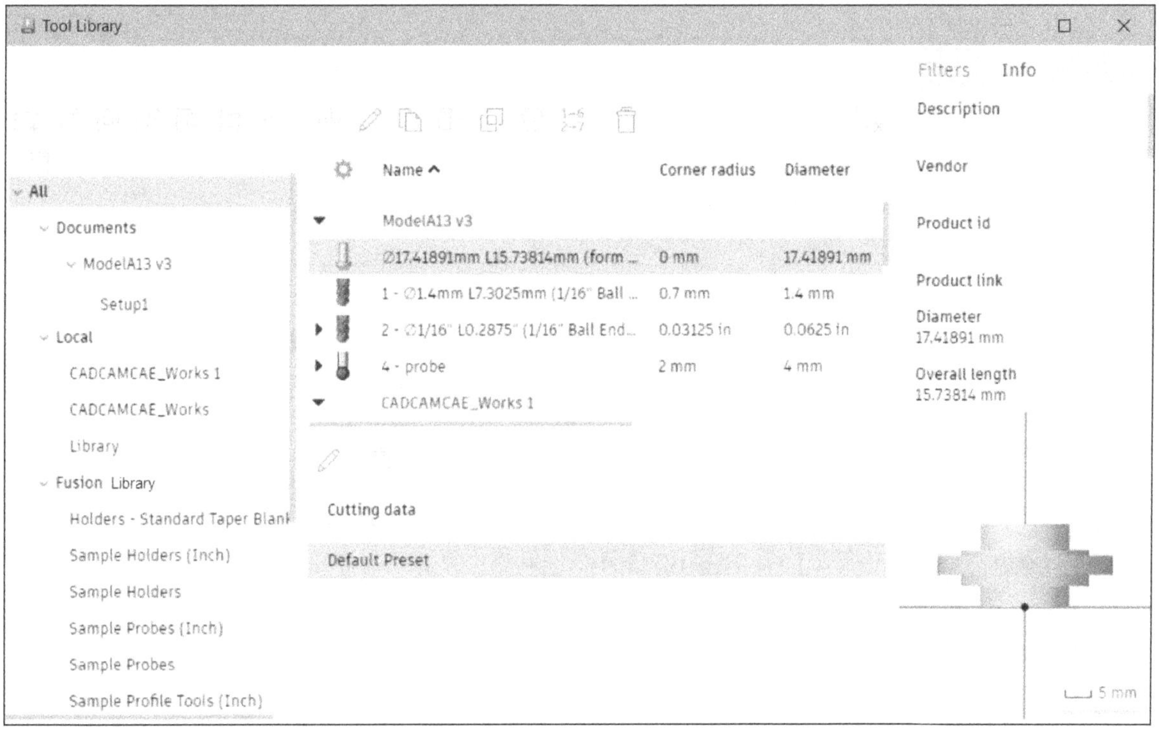

Figure-73. New form tool added in the CAM Tool Library dialog box

Tool Library

The **Tool Library** tool displays the **Tool Library** dialog box where you manage all the tools like milling, lathe, and cutting tools for your individual documents and operations, as well as libraries of predefined tools.

- Click on the **Tool Library** tool of **MANAGE** drop-down from **Toolbar**. The **Tool Library** dialog box will be displayed.
- View or modify the tool as required from the **Tool Library** dialog box. You can also perform common copy-paste functions in the library. The options of this dialog box have been discussed earlier.

Template Library

The **Template Library** tool is used to create and manage templates defined for performing set of specified operations. The procedure to use this tool is given next.

- Click on the **Template Library** tool from the **MANAGE** drop-down in the **INSPECTION** tab of the **Ribbon**. The **Template Library** dialog box will be displayed; refer to Figure-74.

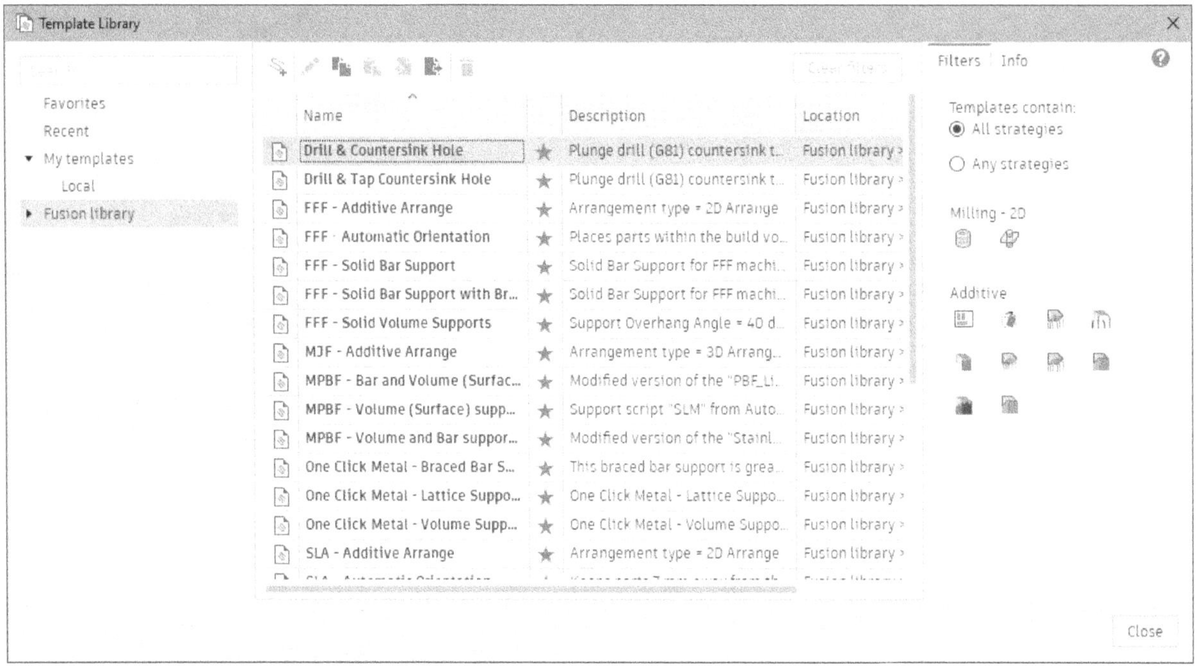

Figure-74. Template Library dialog box

- Select desired strategy from the list and click on the **Use selected template** button from the toolbar in the dialog box. The toolpaths will be added in the **BROWSER**.
- If you want to create a new template using toolpaths then select all the toolpaths to be used for creating template from **BROWSER** and right-click on any of them. A shortcut menu will be displayed.
- Select the **Store as Template** option from the shortcut menu. The **Store as template** dialog box will be displayed; refer to Figure-75.

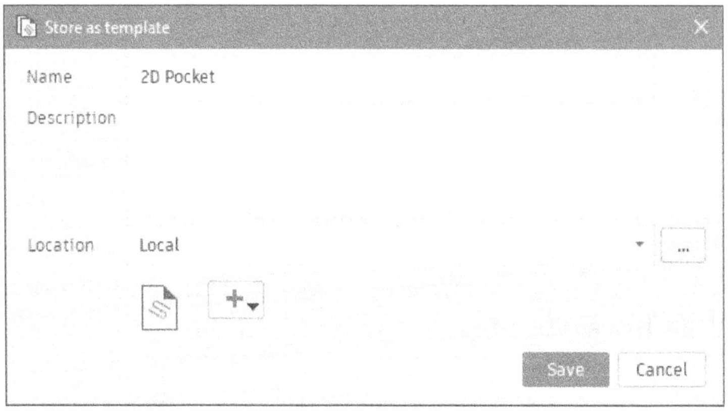

Figure-75. Store as template dialog box

- Specify desired description in the **Description** edit box.
- Click on the **Browse** button for **Location** option to define location for template. The **Template Library** dialog box will be displayed.

- Select the **Local** folder in **My templates** node from left area in the dialog box and click on the **Select folder** button. The **Store as template** dialog box will be displayed again.
- Click on the **Save** button from the dialog box to save the template.

Task Manager

The **Task Manager** tool is used for controlling toolpath generation. CAM allows you to continue working inside Fusion while generating toolpaths in the background. The main interface for controlling toolpath generation is the **CAM Task Manager**.

- Click on the **Task Manager** tool of **MANAGE** drop-down from **Toolbar**; refer to Figure-76. The **CAM Task Manager** dialog box will be displayed; refer to Figure-77.

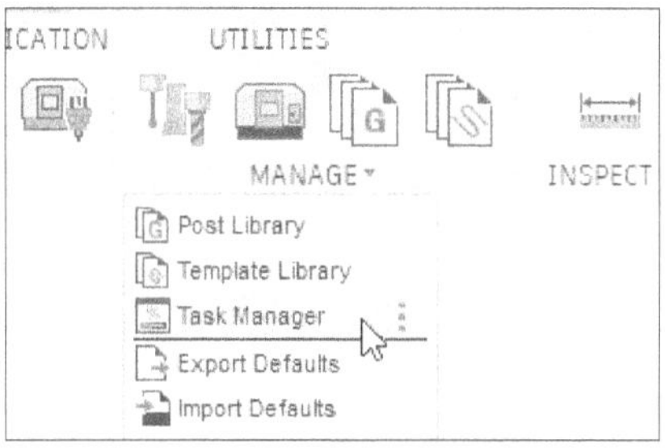

Figure-76. Task Manager tool

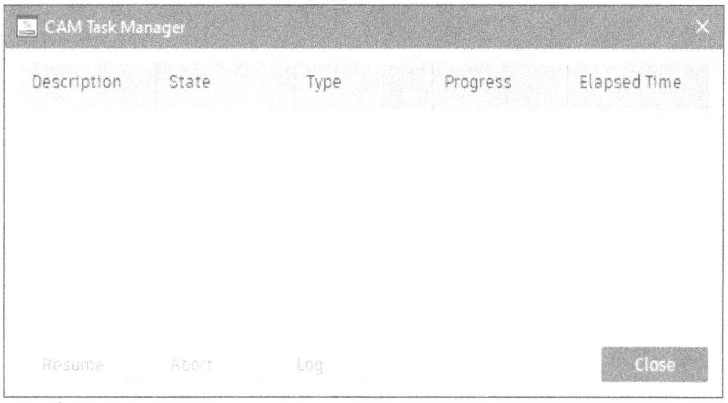

Figure-77. CAM Task Manager dialog box

- Now, generate a toolpath of any operation and you can see the progress in the **CAM Task Manager**; refer to Figure-78.

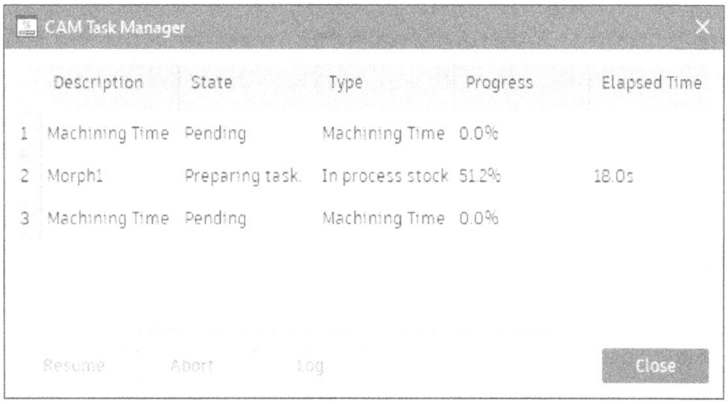

Figure-78. Running multiple operations simultaneously

Select the **Export Defaults** tool from the **MANAGE** drop-down in the **Toolbar** to export all the defaults settings of current manufacturing setup to a file.

Select the **Import Defaults** tool from the **MANAGE** drop-down in the **Toolbar** to import settings of manufacturing setup from a file.

Select the **Reset Defaults** tool from the **MANAGE** drop-down in the **Toolbar** to reset settings of current machining setup.

ADDITIVE MANUFACTURING

Additive manufacturing is a separate extension of Autodesk Fusion Manufacture workspace. You need to purchase it using credits from the **Extension Manager** dialog box. So, make sure you have access to this extension. The procedure to activate tools for additive manufacturing has been discussed earlier.

- Click on the **New Setup** tool from the **SETUP** drop-down in the **Toolbar** of **MANUFACTURE** workspace. The **SETUP** dialog box will be displayed as discussed earlier.
- Select the **Additive** option from the **Operation Type** drop-down in the **Setup** tab of dialog box. The options will be displayed as shown in Figure-79.

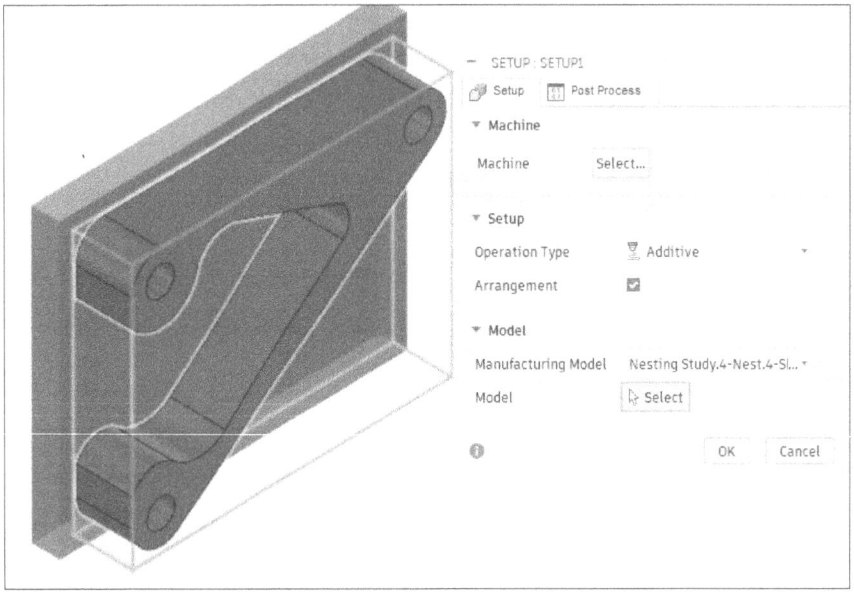

Figure-79. Options for Additive operation setup

- Click on the **Select** button for **Machine** section and select desired machine for 3D printing (Additive Manufacturing machine).
- On selecting the machine, the **Print Settings** section will be displayed in the dialog box; refer to Figure-80. Click on the **Select** button for this section. The **Print Setting Library** dialog box will be displayed; refer to Figure-81. Select desired material and nozzle from the list and click on the **Select** button. Print settings will be applied.

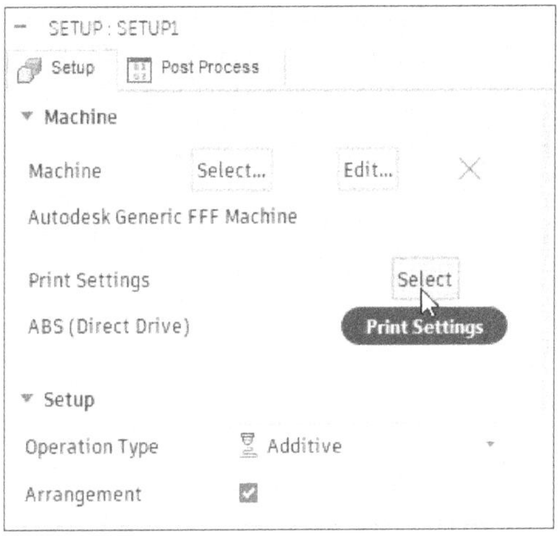

Figure-80. Print Settings option

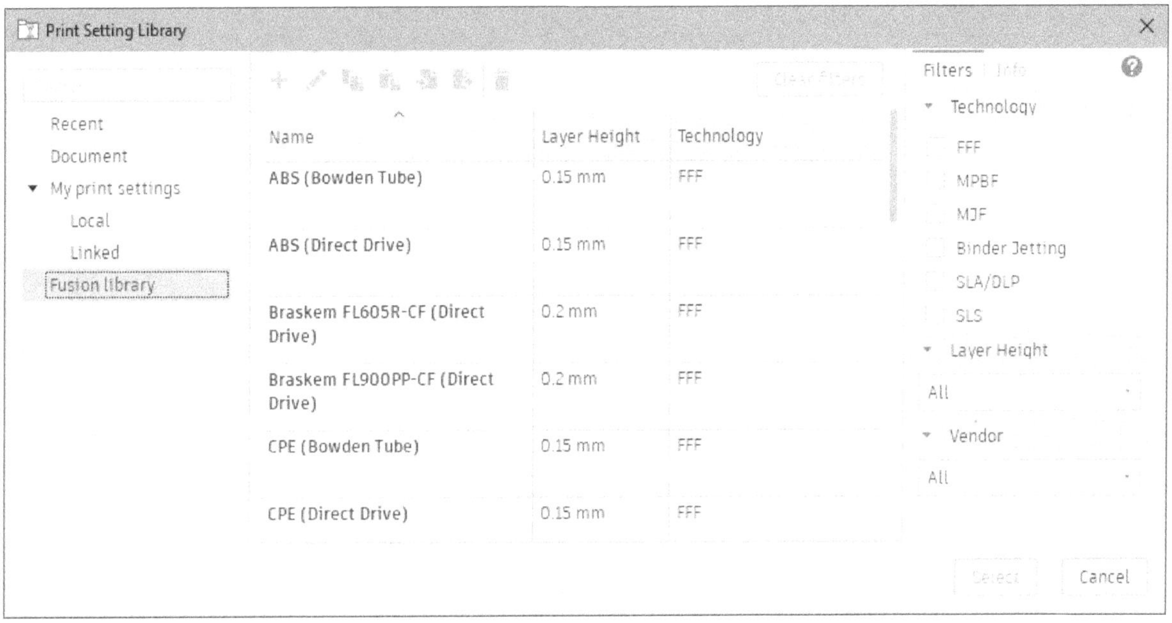

Figure-81. Print Setting Library dialog box

- Click on the **OK** button from the **SETUP** dialog box to apply operation setup.

Now, click on the **ADDITIVE** tab in the **Toolbar**. The options for additive manufacturing will be displayed; refer to Figure-82.

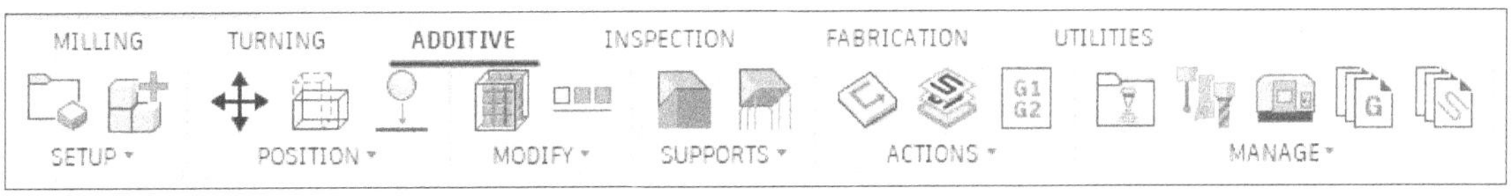

Figure-82. ADDITIVE tab in toolbar

Most of the tools in this tab have been discussed earlier like Move, Task Manager, Measure, and so on. Rest of the tools are discussed next.

Minimize Build Height

The **Minimize Build Height** tool is used to orient the part in such a way that it occupies minimum height on the machine bed and more parts can be 3D printed on bed stacked one over another, if needed. The procedure to use this tool is given next.

- Click on the **Minimize Build Height** tool from the **POSITION** drop-down in the **ADDITIVE** tab of **Toolbar**. The **MINIMIZE BUILD HEIGHT** dialog box will be displayed; refer to Figure-83.

Figure-83. MINIMIZE BUILD HEIGHT dialog box

- Select the component/components for 3D printing, specify desired value of clearance from platform in the **Platform Clearance** edit box, and click on the **OK** button. The part will be oriented; refer to Figure-84.

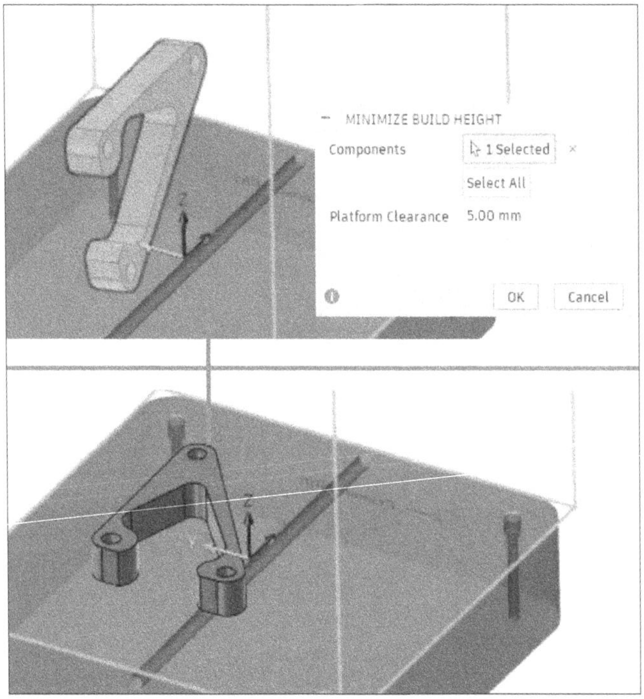

Figure-84. Setting orientation based on minimum build height

Automatic Orientation

The **Automatic Orientation** tool is used to place parts on the machine bed based on manufacturing requirements like minimum support structures and minimum build height parameters. The procedure to use this tool is given next.

- Click on the **Automatic Orientation** tool from the **POSITION** drop-down in the **ADDITIVE** tab of **Toolbar**. The **AUTOMATIC ORIENTATION** dialog box will be displayed; refer to Figure-85.

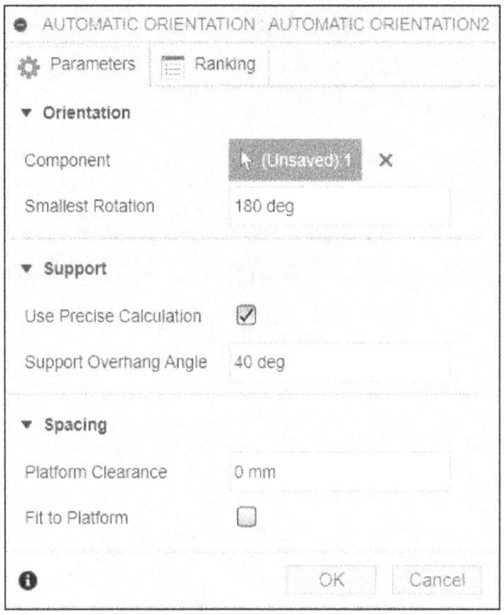

Figure-85. AUTOMATIC ORIENTATION dialog box

- Select desired object to be reoriented.
- Click in the **Smallest Rotation** edit box and specify the minimum rotation with respect to original orientation within which automatic orientation will work for finding most suitable orientation of model.
- Select the **Use Precise Calculation** check box from the dialog box to use precise calculations for defining volume of support structures.
- Specify desired value in the **Support Overhang Angle** edit box to define support angle for down-facing surfaces.
- Click in the **Platform Clearance** edit box and specify distance from the base bed that should be maintained while 3D printing.
- Select the **Fit to Platform** check box to automatically fit workpiece instance(s) on the machine bed.
- Specify desired values in the **Frame Width** and **Ceiling Clearance** edit boxes to define horizontal and vertical distances of edges of printed part from frame boundaries, respectively.
- Click on the **Ranking** tab and select the ranking for various parameters to be considered based on priority level for deciding orientation of model; refer to Figure-86. For example, if you want to set minimum part height as priority then select the **Very high** option from the **Part Height** drop-down in the dialog box.

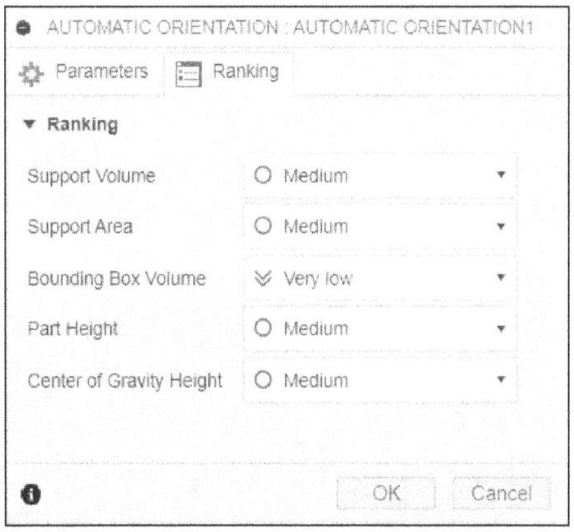

Figure-86. Ranking tab

- After setting desired parameters, click on the **OK** button from the dialog box after setting desired parameters.

Placing Parts on Platform

The **Place parts on platform** tool is used to place parts directly on platform or at some clearance distance from the platform. The procedure to use this tool is given next.

- Click on the **Place parts on platform** tool from the **POSITION** drop-down in the **ADDITIVE** tab of **Toolbar**. The **PLACE PARTS ON PLATFORM** dialog box will be displayed; refer to Figure-87.

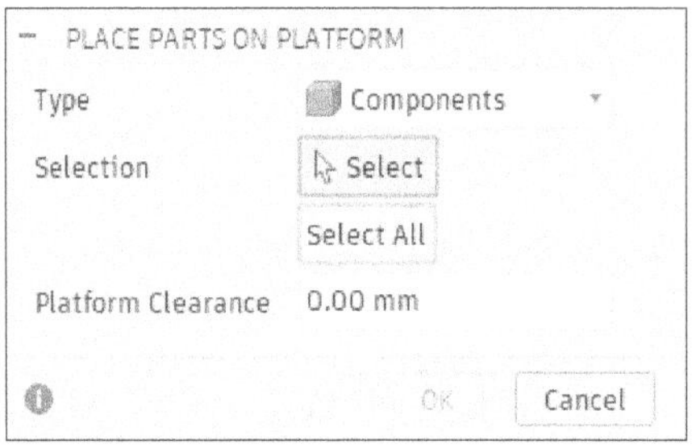

Figure-87. PLACE PARTS ON PLATFORM dialog box

- If you select the **Flat Face** option from the **Type** drop-down then you can select the face to be directly placed on the platform.
- Select desired part and specify parameters as discussed earlier.
- After specifying parameters, click on the **OK** button.

Collision Detection

The **Collision Detection** tool is used to check whether two components on machine bed are interfering. The procedure to use this tool is given next.

- Click on the **Collision Detection** tool from the **POSITION** drop-down in the **ADDITIVE** tab of **Toolbar**. The **COLLISION DETECTION** dialog box will be displayed; refer to Figure-88.

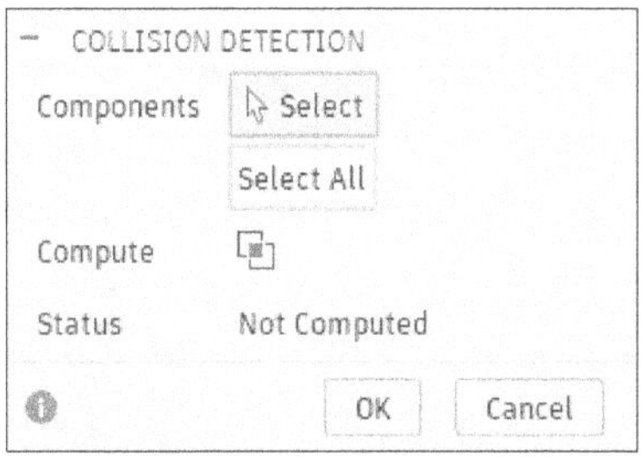

Figure-88. COLLISION DETECTION dialog box

- Select the components whose interference is to be checked and click on the **Compute** button. The status will be displayed. Click on the **OK** button to exit the dialog box.

Editing Print Settings

To modify the print settings of your 3D printer, right-click on the print material from **Setup** node; refer to Figure-89. A shortcut menu will be displayed. Select the **Edit** option from shortcut menu. The **Print Setting Editor** dialog box will be displayed; refer to Figure-90. Note that the options in this dialog box are different for different materials and printing processes. The options displayed in our case are for FFF (fused filament fabrication) printing process with ABS Plastic material.

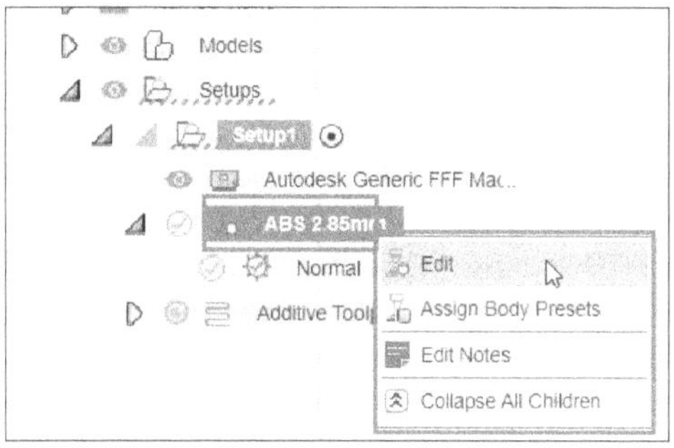

Figure-89. Shortcut menu for Print Settings

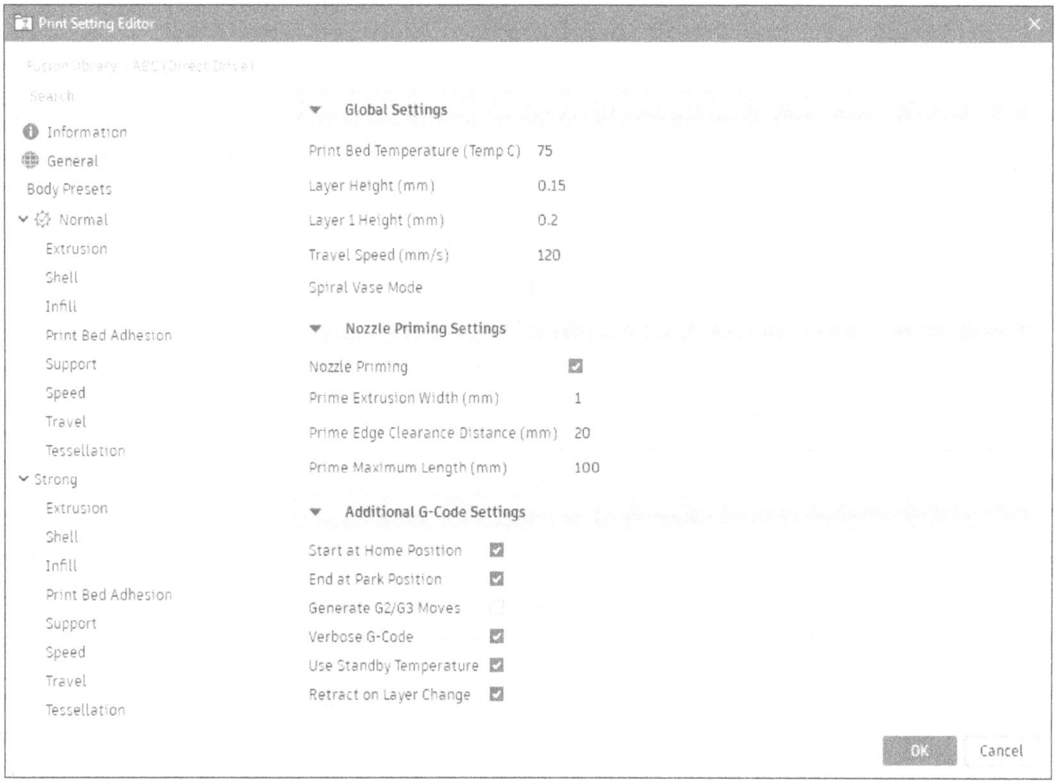

Figure-90. Print Setting Editor dialog box

Various options in this dialog box (for FFF 3D printing) are discussed next.

General Parameters

Click on the **General** option from the top left area in the dialog box to define basic parameters like height of each layer, bed temperature, nozzle speed, and so on. Various parameters of this tab are discussed next.

- Click in the **Filament Diameter (mm)** edit box to define the diameter of your filament being used for 3D Printing.
- Click in the **Print Bed Temperature (Temp C)** edit box to define temperature of heat bed in degree Celsius at which the material will be kept hot, so that bottom layers of 3D print stick properly with bed and material is soft enough to allow upcoming material layers to stick properly.
- Click in the **Layer Height (mm)** edit box and specify height of each layer while 3D printing.
- Select the **Spiral Vase Mode** check box to 3D print outer boundaries of part first and then move inwards while maintaining continuity in printing.

- Specify desired value in the **Layer 1 Height (mm)** edit box to define height of first layer of 3D print.
- Specify desired value in the **Travel Speed (mm/s)** edit box to define speed at which nozzle will move when extrusion is not occurring.
- Select the **Nozzle Priming** check box if you want to extrude some material before starting to 3D print the model so that there is a smooth flow of material through nozzle. After selecting this check box, specify desired values of filament width and clearance distance for priming in respective edit boxes of **Nozzle Priming Settings** section.
- Specify desired parameters in the **Additional G-Code Settings** section to define additional G-Codes to be added in 3D Printing NC program.
- Select the **Start at Home Position** check box to move the nozzle at home position before starting the 3D print process.
- Select the **End at Park Position** check box to move nozzle to specified park position after completing the 3D print process.
- Select the **Generate G2/G3 Moves** check box to allow circular moves along with linear moves.
- Select the **Verbose G-Code** check box to allow comments in NC program along with G-codes.
- Select the **Use Standby Temperature** check box to set temperature for extruder when extrusion is not happening during 3D print process.
- Select the **Retract on Layer Change** check box to retract nozzle to retraction plane before moving to print next layer.

Extrusion Parameters

Click on the **Extrusion** option from desired body presets at the left in the dialog box to define speed and temperature of material in the extruder of 3D printer while generating the part; refer to Figure-91. Various options of this tab are discussed next.

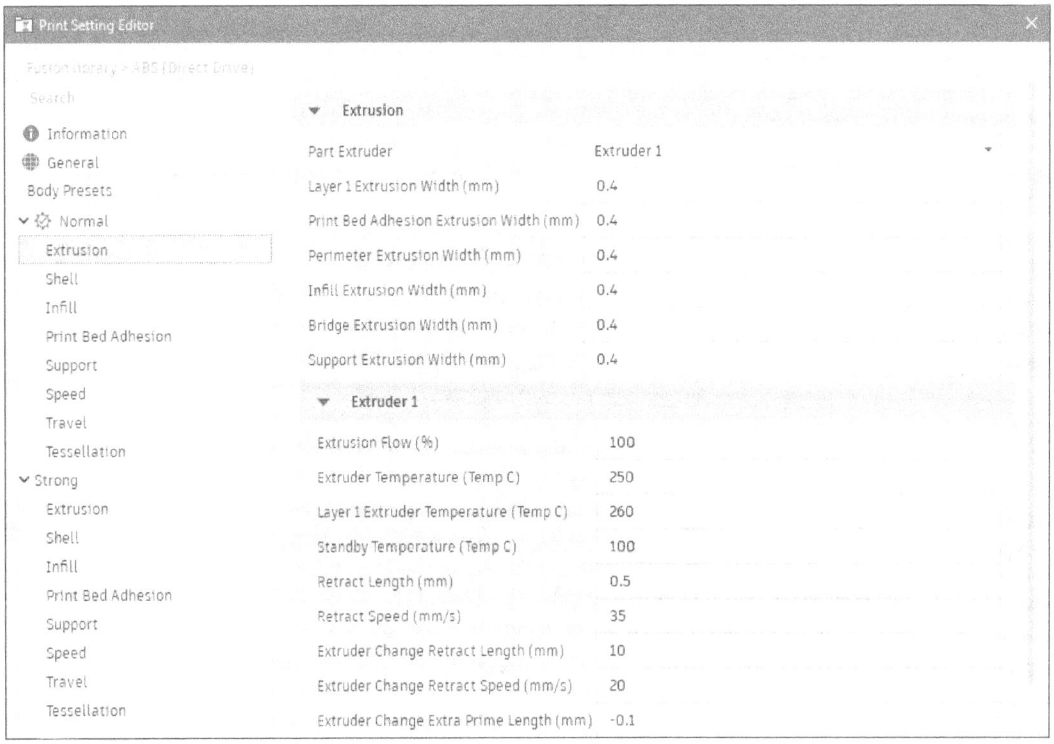

Figure-91. Extrusion tab

- Your machine can support more than one extruder for 3D printing. If that is the case then select the extruder whose parameters are to be defined in the **Part Extruder** drop-down at the top in the page.
- Specify desired values of extrusion widths for general extrusion, extrusion at boundaries, **Layer 1 Extrusion Width (mm)**, **Print Bed Adhesion Extrusion Width (mm)**, **Perimeter Extrusion Width**, **Infill extrusion**, **Support extrusion**, and **Bridge extrusion** in respective edit boxes of **Extrusion** section in the dialog box.
- Click in the **Extrusion Flow (%)** edit box and specify the percentage of material to be used for 3D printing in terms of total material stores in extruder.
- Specify desired value in the **Extruder Temperatures (Temp C)** edit box to define temperature of material in extruder. This should be equal to melting point of material used for creating 3D print.
- Specify desired value in the **Standby Temperature (Temp C)**edit box to define temperature of bed on which model will be created.
- Specify desired value of length of extrusion to be created before shutting off the extrusion in the **Retract Length (mm)** edit box.
- Specify desired value of speed at which extrusion will be performed for retract length in the **Retract Speed (mm/s)** edit box.
- Specify desired value in **Extruder Change Retract Length (mm)** edit box to define length of retraction before changing the extruder.
- Similarly, specify retraction speed to be applied when changing the extruder in **Extruder Change Retract Speed (mm/s)** edit box.
- Specify the amount of extra length to be extruded after extruder change in the **Extruder Change Extra Prime Length (mm)** edit box.

Shell Parameters

Select the **Shell** option from the left in the dialog box to define properties of layers by which 3D print model is generated; refer to Figure-92. These options are discussed next.

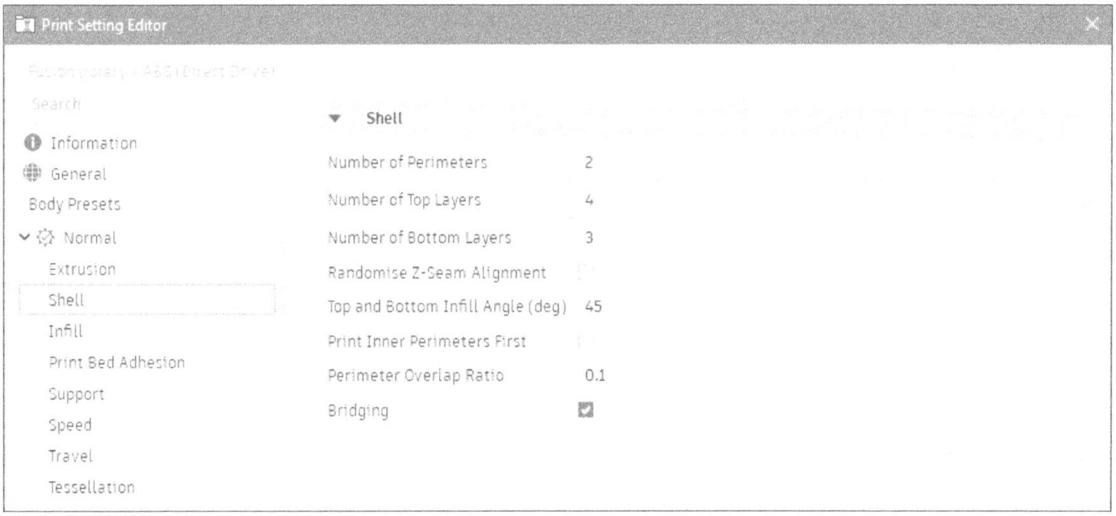

Figure-92. Shell tab

- Specify desired value in **Number of Perimeters** edit box to define boundary beads created on the bed before printing the features of model. This ensures firm base for features to be 3D printed.
- Specify desired value in **Number of Top Layers** edit box to define number of top layers to be created by solid infill on 3D printed model.

- Specify desired value in **Number of Bottom Layers** edit box to define number of layers to be created at the bottom of 3D print with solid infill.
- Select the **Randomise Z-Seam Alignment** check box to set start points of various layers at locations distributed all over between the layers so that there is no zipper seam pattern created in the model.
- Specify desired value in the **Top and Bottom Infill Angle (deg)** edit box to define the angle at which exposed infill will be created.
- Select the **Print Inner Perimeters First** check box to print inner most layer of perimeter beads first.
- Specify desired value in **Perimeter Overlap Ratio** edit box to define the amount of overlap between two consecutive perimeter beads.
- Specify desired value in the **Perimeter Overlap Ratio** edit box to define the amount of material of printed model that will overlap with innermost perimeter bead.
- Select the **Bridging** check box to bridge overhanging regions and stretch infill over them.

Infill Parameters

Select the **Infill** option from the left area in the dialog box to define parameters related to how material will be filled in various areas of model; refer to Figure-93. The options in this tab are discussed next.

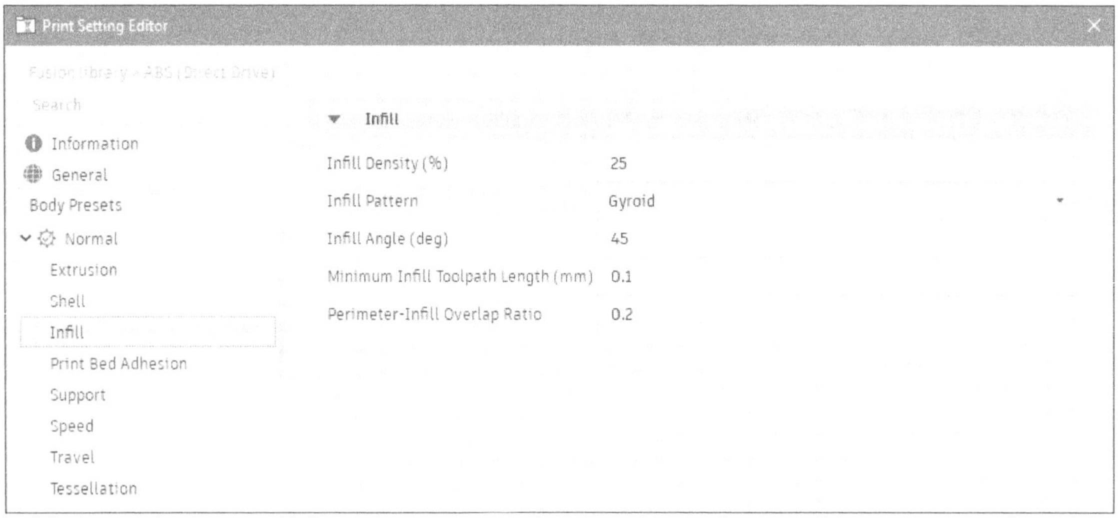

Figure-93. Infill tab

- Specify desired value in the **Infill Density (%)** edit box to define material density for non-exposed regions in the model.
- Select desired option from the **Infill Pattern** drop-down to define the pattern in which nozzle will move while filling material to 3D print. Some common infill patterns are shown in Figure-94.

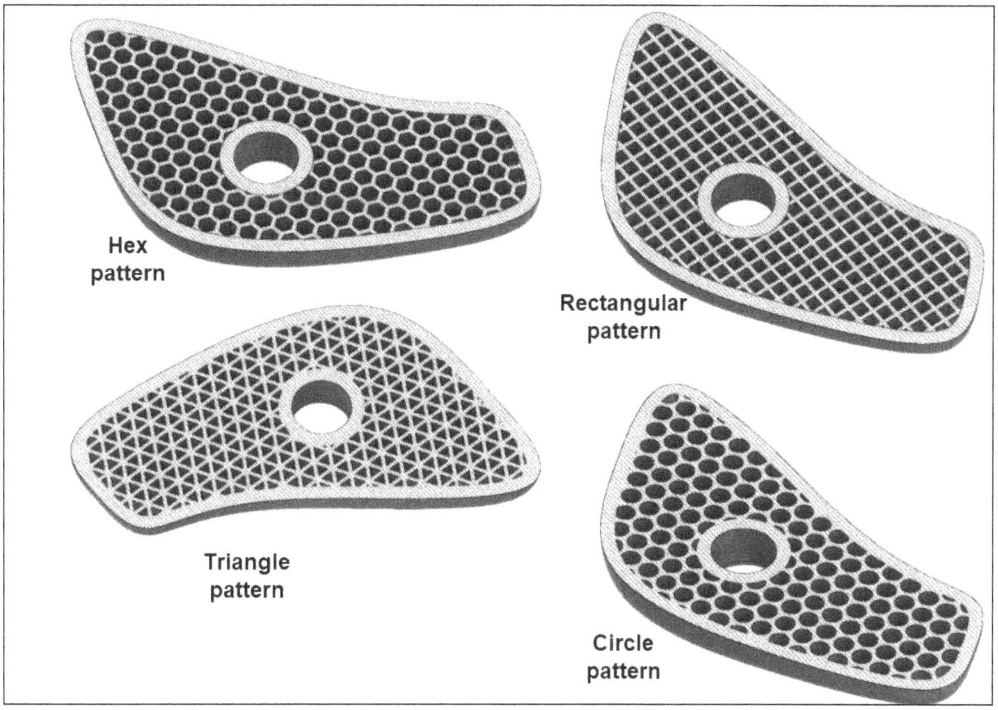

Figure-94. Common infill patterns

- Specify desired angle in the **Infill Angle (deg)** edit box to specify the sets the angle of the infill used to print the internal structure of the part.
- Specify desired value in the **Minimum Infill Toolpath Length (mm)** edit box to specify the length up to which material filling will be performed if the gap is less than specified value then it will be skipped.
- Specify desired value in the **Perimeter- Infill Overlap Ratio** edit box to define faction of filament width that will overlap between innermost perimeter and infill.

Print Bed Adhesion Parameters

The options in the **Print Bed Adhesion** section are used to define parameters for printing side walls of the model; refer to Figure-95. The options of this page are discussed next.

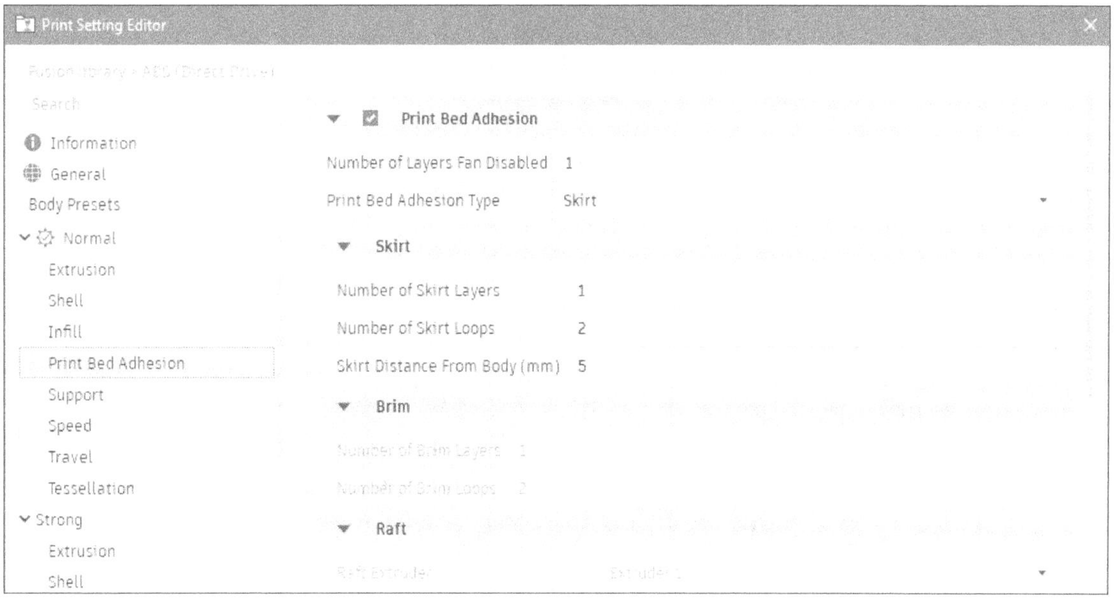

Figure-95. Print Bed Adhesion tab

- Specify desired value in the **Number of Layers Fan Disabled** edit box to define the number of layers up to which cooling fan will not be active in the machine.
- Select desired option from the **Print Bed Adhesion type** drop-down to define which method of adhesion will be used.
- Select the **Skirt** option from the **Print Bed Adhesion type** drop-down to create single line of filament around the model just to prime the nozzle before printing actual model. Specify the related parameters like distance of skirt from model, number of skirt layers, and so on in the edit boxes of **Skirt** section.
- Select the **Brim** option from the **Print Bed Adhesion type** drop-down to create flat layers of extruded material at the base of part so that the part adhesion is good to the base plate. It is generally used to bind edges of the model to the base plate. After selecting this check box, specify the related parameters in edit boxes of **Brim** section.
- Select the **Raft** option from the **Print Bed Adhesion type** drop-down to apply a thick sturdy layer of material below the part so that lesser heat goes to the model from base plate allowing the part to cool down efficiently during 3D printing. After selecting this check box, specify the related parameters as discussed earlier in the **Raft** section of dialog box.

Support Parameters

Click on the **Support** option from the left in dialog box to define parameters related to support structures. The support structures are created when the part has free falling sections in it; refer to Figure-96. Specify the parameters for support like number of support bottom layers, top layers, infill density of support structure, and so on in the page.

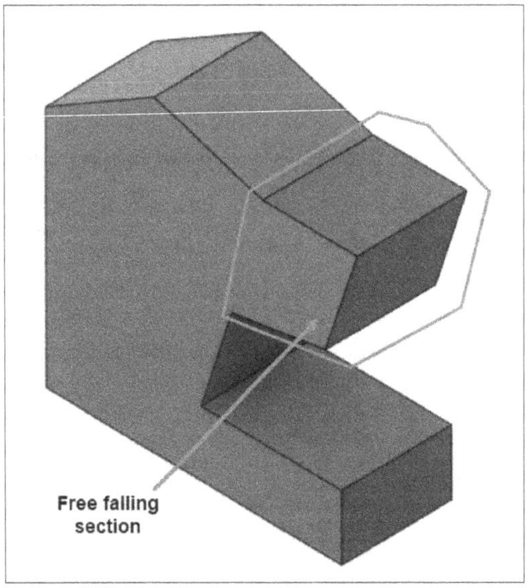

Figure-96. Free falling section of part

Speed Parameters

Select the **Speed** option from the left area in the dialog box to define nozzle speed when performing different operations like infill, internal parameter, external parameter, support creation, and so on. Deciding speed for various operations is a hit and trial task. A higher nozzle speed will cause voids in the model not providing enough material whereas a lower speed will cause extra dumping of material.

Travel Parameters

Select the **Travel** option from the left in the dialog box to define parameters related to movement of nozzle in Z direction (vertical direction) while 3D printing.

Tessellation Parameters

Select the **Tessellation** option from the left area in the dialog box to define the accuracy up to which the model will be 3D printed as compared to original 3D model.

Similarly, you can specify parameters for **Strong** body preset. After setting desired parameters, click on the **OK** button from the dialog box to apply settings.

Creating Support Structures

The tools in **SUPPORTS** drop-down of **Ribbon** (refer to Figure-97) are used to create support structures in the model so that complex free falling sections can be created in the model by 3D printing. These tools will be displayed on selecting **Autodesk Generic MPBF** machine from **Machine Library** dialog box. Various tools in this drop-down are discussed next.

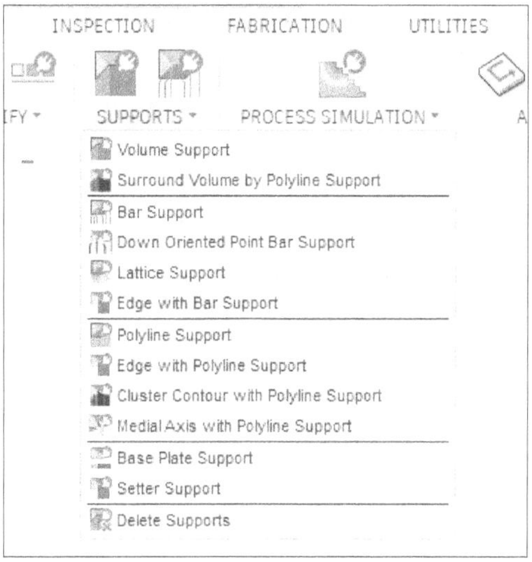

Figure-97. SUPPORTS drop-down

Creating Volume Support

The **Volume Support** tool is used to create solid large support structure as base for complex models. This type of support is useful when bottom of part is irregular and complex. The procedure to use this tool is given next.

- Click on the **Volume Support** tool from **SUPPORTS** drop-down in the **ADDITIVE** tab of the **Ribbon**. The **VOLUME SUPPORT** dialog box will be displayed; refer to Figure-98.

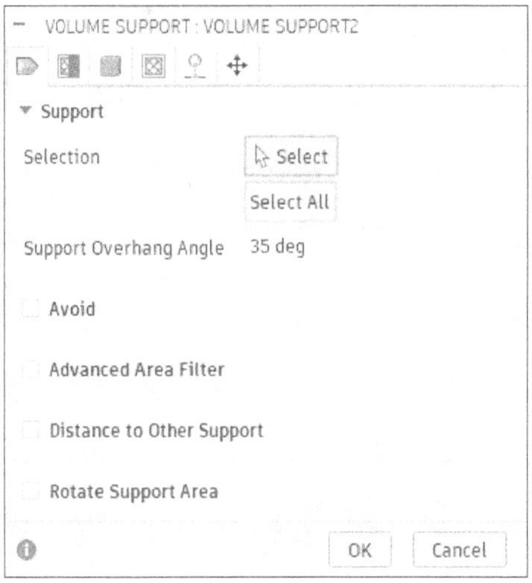

Figure-98. VOLUME SUPPORT dialog box

- By default, the selection button for **Selection** section is active. Select the model to be 3D printed from the graphics area.
- Specify desired value in the **Support Overhang Angle** edit box to define the angle at which support's top faces will be inclined for down facing surfaces of model. Note that angle is measured with respect to horizontal plane.
- Select the **Avoid** check box to define segment/section of model to be avoided when creating support structure.
- If you do not want to select the faces individually and want to use a window selection then you can use the options in **Advanced Area Filter** section of the dialog box to refine your selection of faces.
- Select the **Distance to Other Support** check box to define the gap between two support structures in case of multiple support structure creation.
- Select the **Rotate Support Area** check box to allow the detected support area to be rotated.
- Click on the **General** tab in the dialog box to define general shape of volume support structures; refer to Figure-99.

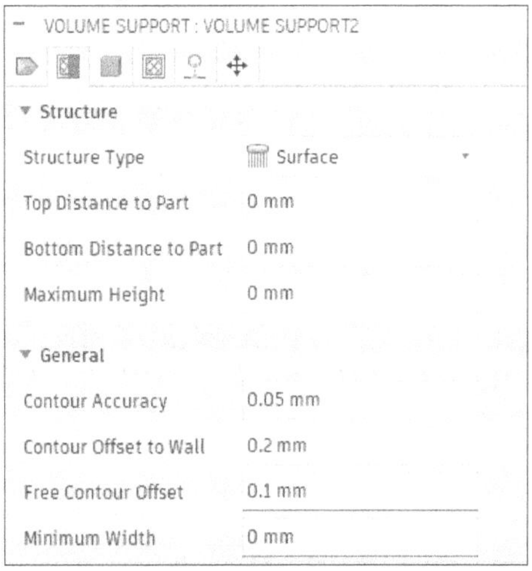

Figure-99. General tab in VOLUME SUPPORT dialog box

- Select desired option from the **Structure Type** drop-down to define the general shape of volume support. Select the **Solid** option from the drop-down to create hollow supports encased by solid walls. If you want to create structure of wired wall, punch plate, or solid structure then select the **Surface** option from the drop-down.

- Set desired parameters in various edit boxes of the tab.
- Click on the **Volume Properties** tab to modify parameters of support structure. The options will be displayed as shown in Figure-100. Note that this tab will be displayed only when **Surface** option is selected in the **Structure Type** drop-down.

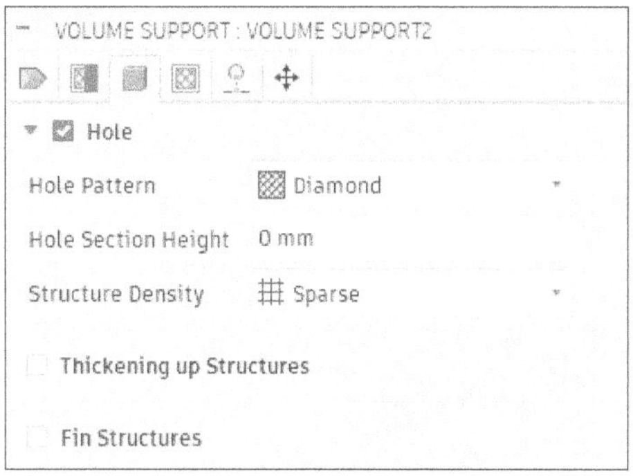

Figure-100. Volume Properties tab

- Click in the **Hole** check box and select desired option from the **Hole Pattern** drop-down to define shape and height of structure. Select desired option from the **Structure Density** drop-down to control how many holes are created in the support structure.
- Specify desired values in **Top Connections** and **Bottom Connections** edit boxes of the **Thickening up Structures** section to increase/decrease thickness of structure for top or bottom connection points of the structure. If you want to increase or decrease thickness of the main structure then specify desired value in the **Main Structure** edit box.
- Similarly, you can specify parameters for fin structure in the **Fin Structures** section of the dialog box.
- Click on the **Raster and Contour** tab in the dialog box to modify parameters related to net structure of rasters and contours. Contours are the boundary passes and rasters are the infill passes in 3D printing. The options will be displayed as shown in Figure-101.

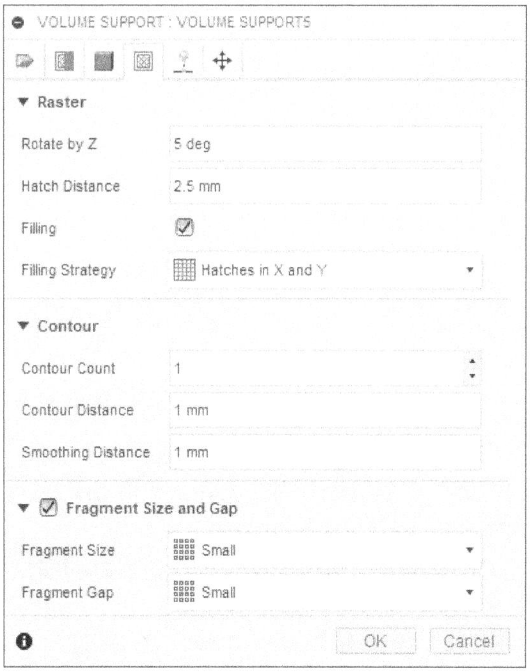

Figure-101. Raster and Contour tab

- Similarly, specify parameters related to different connection points in the **Connections** tab of dialog box.
- Click on the **OK** button from the dialog box to create support structure. Similarly, you can use the **Surround Volume by Polyline Support** tool. The **Surround Volume by Polyline Support** tool is used to apply additional polyline support after creating volume support for the model. Note that polyline supports will be added to contours of support only.
- After setting desired parameters, click on the **OK** button. The solid support structure will be created; refer to Figure-102.

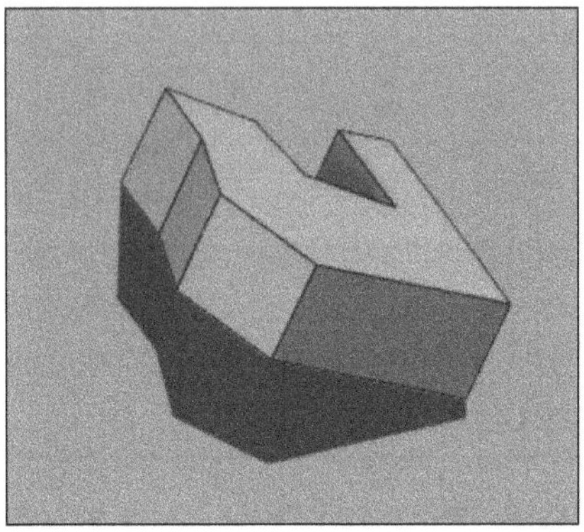

Figure-102. Volume support structure created

Creating Bar Support

The **Bar Support** tool is used to create solid bars below the face of model to provide support to model during 3D printing. The procedure to use this tool is given next.

- Click on the **Bar Support** tool from the **SUPPORTS** drop-down in the **Ribbon**. The **BAR SUPPORT** dialog box will be displayed; refer to Figure-103.

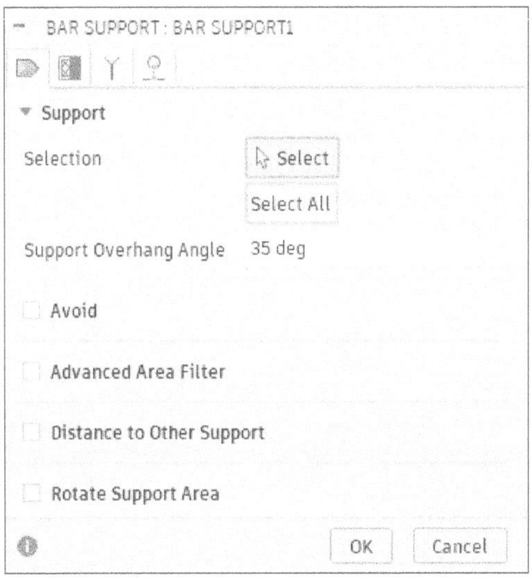

Figure-103. BAR SUPPORT dialog box

- Select the model to which you want to apply support structure and specify the parameters in the **Geometry** tab as discussed earlier.
- Click on the **General** tab in the dialog box. The options in the dialog box will be displayed as shown in Figure-104.
- Select desired option from the **Anchor Density** drop-down to define whether the support bars will be placed dense or coarse. If you want to manually define how much supporting bars will be placed then select the **Custom** option from drop-down.

- Select desired check boxes from the **Bars on Supported Model** section to define whether bars will be created on corners, along medial axis, at borders, and at down points along Z axis.

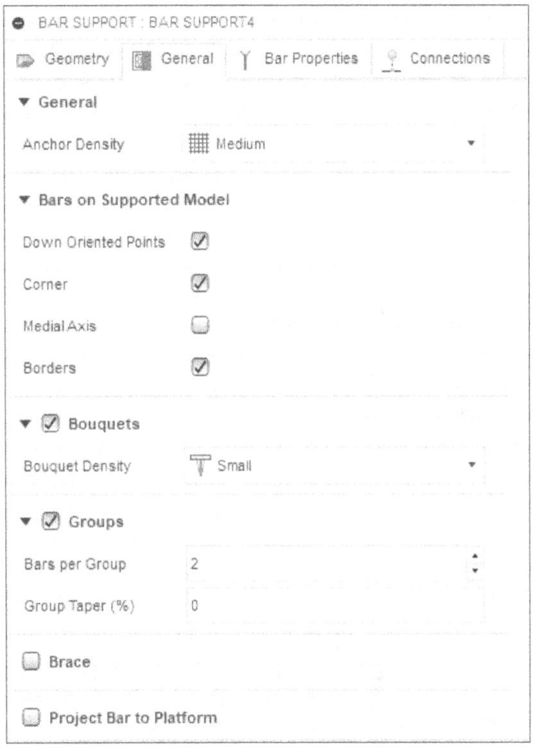

Figure-104. General tab in BAR SUPPORT dialog box

- Click in the **Bouquets** check box and select desired option from the **Bouquet Density** drop-down to define density of support tree structure to be created.
- Click in the **Groups** check box and specify desired value from the **Bars per Group** and **Group Taper (%)** respectively.
- Click in the **Brace** check box to regulate the addition of braces to the bar supports. Select desired option from the **Type** drop-down to define the arrangement of braces between bar supports. Click in the **Links per Bar** edit box to determine the number of additional bar supports that a single bar connects to using braces. Click in the **Link Angle** edit box to define the minimum angle of the braces between the bar supports. Select desired option from the **Junction Shape** drop-down to specify whether the braces are straight or curved as they connect to the bar supports. Select the **Project Bar to Platform** check box and define the angle at which support bars will be inclined. The value specified in **Maximum Projection Angle** defines the angle from vertical plane up to which inclined solid bars can be created to support the model.
- Select the **Bar Properties** tab in the dialog box to define shape and size of bars; refer to Figure-105.

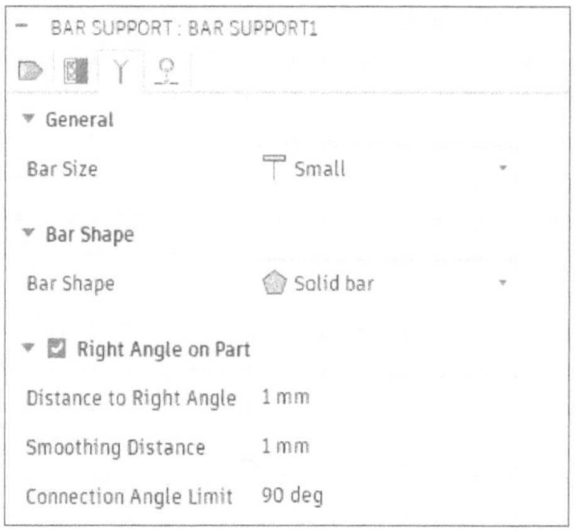

Figure-105. Bar Properties tab

- The options to define size parameters will be displayed below the drop-down in **General** section of the dialog box.
- Select desired bar shape option from the **Bar Shape** drop-down. Select the **Solid bar** option from drop-down if you want to create pentagonal section bar. If you want to create a custom bar with specified polygonal corner counts then select the **Custom solid bar** option from the drop-down and specify related parameters. Specify number of polygonal corners in **Polygon Corner Count** edit box, and specify the value of angle at **Angle at Top** edit box, set the reference direction (major axis) for oval cross-section in the **Radial Type** drop-down, and set the ratio of major axis to minor axis in percentage in **Ellipse Stretch in %** edit box. Note that ellipse stretch value can be from 100% to 200%.
- Select desired option from the **Right Angle on Part** drop-down to define how end points of support bars will connect with the model. The shape of end points define how supports will break from main model after 3D printing. Specify desired value in the **Distance to Right Angle** edit box to define the distance by which right angled support structure will start from surface of model. Specify desired value in the **Smoothing Distance** edit box to define the distance from surface of model where structure smoothening will be implemented for fine connection.
- Click on the **Connections** tab in the dialog box to define size and other parameters of support connection points; refer to Figure-106.Figure-122

Figure-106. Connections tab of BAR SUPPORT dialog box

- Click in the **Distance to Part** edit box and specify the distance between part and support.

- Select **Breakpoint** check box from the **Top Part Connection** section to determine whether the support bars should have a breakpoint at their connection to the supported surface.
- Select the **On part** option from the **Breakpoint Type** drop-down to converge faces of bar at smaller section on model; refer to Figure-107. Select the **Offsetted to Part** option to create footing between support bar and model; refer to Figure-107. Select the **Custom** option from the drop-down to create breakpoint with specified dimensions.

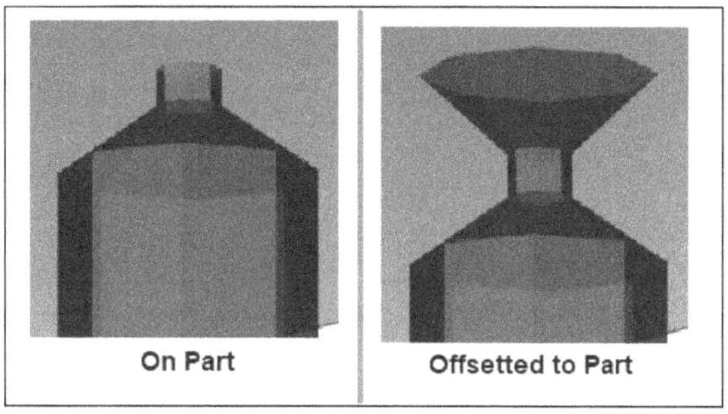

Figure-107. Breakpoints

- Select the **Pad on Platform** check box to define dimensions of thick pad created at the bottom of support bar for making support strong and sturdy; refer to Figure-108.

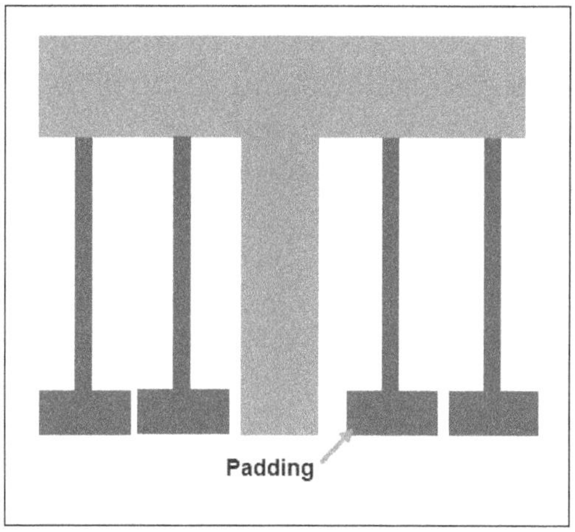

Figure-108. Padding for solid bar support

- Select the **Platform Connection** check box to define the method by which bar supports connect to the build platform. Select desired option from **Type** drop-down to regulate the connection of bar supports to the build platform. If Base plate for groups option is selected in the drop-down then click in the **Height** edit box and define the thickness of the base plate supports on the build platform. Click in the **Contour Offset** edit box to specifies the distance between the contour of the bar support group and the outer boundary of the base plate support group. Click in the **Taper Angle** edit box and specifies the angle of the taper from the base to the top of the base plate support. Select desired option from **Pattern Type** drop-down to control the grid density by setting cell size and wall thickness values for the pattern, along with the contour offset value for point connection net. If **Roots** option is selected in the **Type** drop-down then specify the number of legs, height, and diameter of base structure rods in respective edit boxes.
- Click on the **OK** button from the dialog box to create the support bars; refer to Figure-109.

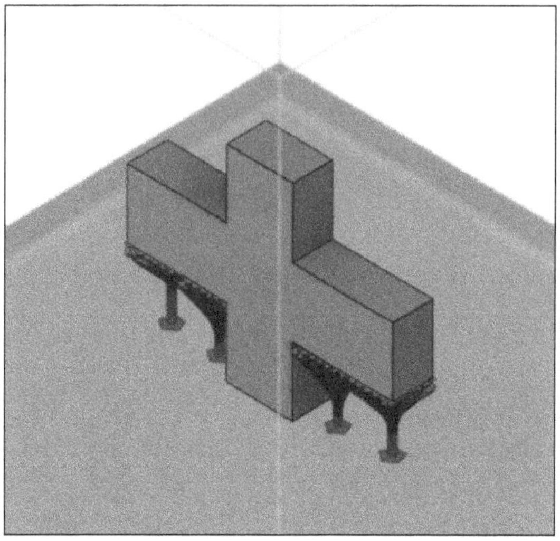

Figure-109. Solid bar supports created

You can use the **Polyline Support**, **Lattice Volume Support**, and other tools of **SUPPORTS** panel in **Toolbar** in same way as other support tools have been discussed.

The **Down Oriented Point Bar Support** tool is used to apply bar support with its pointed side on the bed.

The **Lattice Volume Support** tool is used to create supporting structure in the form of scaffolding like structures generally found in civil construction sites.

The **Edge with Bar Support** tool is used to create support at edges of the downward facing edges.

The **Polyline Support** tool is used to create supporting structures in the form of a net line structure using small diameter polyline bar.

The **Edge with Polyline Support** tool is used to add support structures to edges of steep walls of model along with polyline supports.

The **Cluster Contour with Polyline Support** tool is used to add polyline cluster near contours of polyline supports created earlier.

The **Medial Axis with Polyline Support** tool is used to create a skeleton of model support for narrow areas that could otherwise be ignored.

The **Base Plate Support** tool is used to create support between bed and bottom of part's support structures.

The **Setter Support** tool is used to create support structure at the outline of selected bodies and components.

Fill Build Volume

The **Fill Build Volume** tool is used to automatically fill free space on machine table with copies of selected object to be 3D printed. Note that you must create the setup using manufacturing model generated by using the **Create Manufacturing Model** tool in **SETUP** panel of the **Ribbon** to use this tool. The procedure to use this tool is given next.

- Click on the **Fill Build Volume** tool from the **MODIFY** drop-down in the **ADDITIVE** tab of the **Ribbon**. The **FILL BUILD VOLUME** dialog box will be displayed; refer to Figure-110.

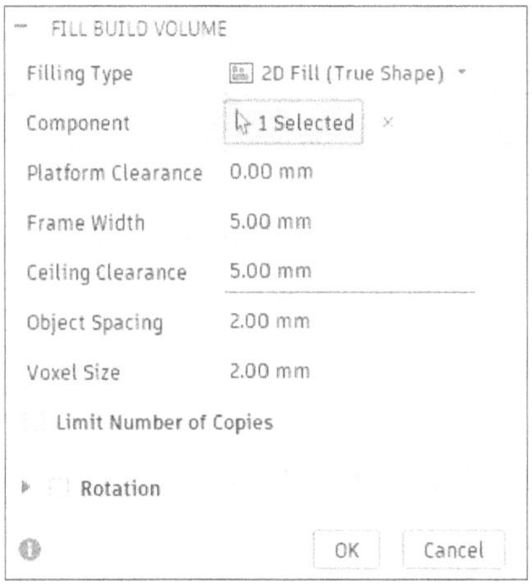

Figure-110. FILL BUILD VOLUME dialog box

- Select the model part to be duplicated on machine table for filling volume.
- Select the **2D Fill** option from the **Filling Type** drop-down to fill selected part in XY plane only. Select the **3D Fill** option from the drop-down if you want to fill along Z axis as well.
- Specify desired value in the **Platform Clearance** edit box to define gap from platform when placing the model.
- Click on the **Limit Number of Copies** check box to define the maximum number of generated copies.
- Click in the **Copies** edit box from the **Limit Number of Copies** section and specify desired value in the edit box then the number of generated copies will be restricted to the specified limit. Similarly, set the other parameters in the dialog box and click on the **OK** button. Copies of selected model will be created.

Creating Mesh Bodies from Support Structures

The **Split Supports** tool is used to create mesh body from selected support structure so that it can be modified freely using mesh editing tools. The procedure to use this tool is given next.

- Click on the **Split Supports** tool from the **MODIFY** drop-down in the **ADDITIVE** tab of the **Ribbon**. The **SPLIT SUPPORTS** dialog box will be displayed; refer to Figure-111.

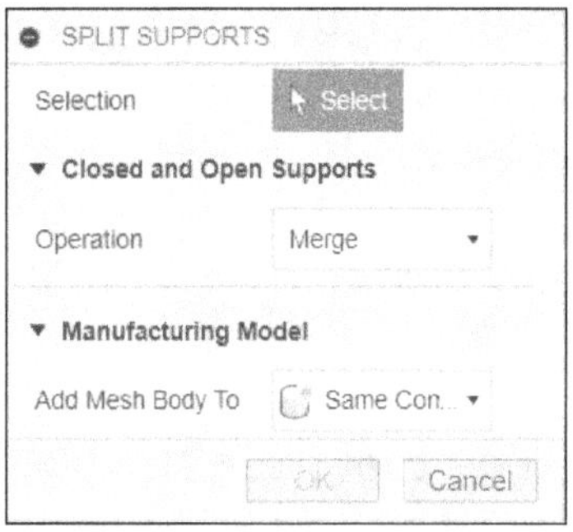

Figure-111. SPLIT SUPPORTS dialog box

- Select the supported structure model to create mesh structure object.
- Select the **Merge** option from the **Operation** drop-down if you want to combine open and closed support structure in single mesh body. Select the **Separate** option from the drop-down to create individual mesh bodies.
- Select the **Same Component** option from **Add Mesh Body To** drop-down to add newly generated mesh body to same structure model from which the mesh body has been generated. Select the **New Component** option to create a new component from generated mesh body.
- Click on the **OK** button to perform the operation.

Generating Toolpath for Additive Manufacturing

After setting desired parameters, click on the **Generate** button from the **ACTIONS** drop-down in the **ADDITIVE** tab of **Toolbar**. The toolpath will be generated and displayed in the **BROWSER**.

After creating toolpath, click on the **Simulate additive toolpath** tool from the **ACTIONS** panel and check the simulation as discussed earlier.

Using **Print Statistics** tool in **ACTIONS** drop-down, you can check the information related to 3D printing like total time required, filament length used, and so on; refer to Figure-112. Click on the **Post Process** button to post codes for machine. The procedure has been discussed later for post processing.

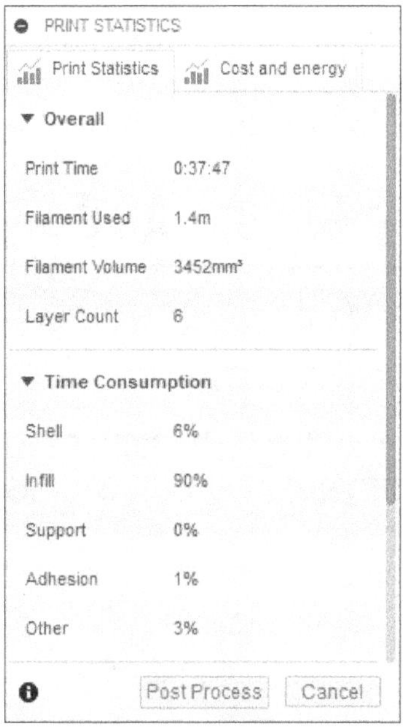

Figure-112. PRINT STATISTICS dialog box

Post Processing Additive Toolpaths

Post processing is the step in manufacturing where you generate machine readable codes for manufacturing the product. The post processing method for additive toolpaths is given next.

- Click on the **Post Process** tool from the **ACTIONS** drop-down in the **ADDITIVE** tab of the **Ribbon**. The **NC Program** dialog box will be displayed; refer to Figure-113.

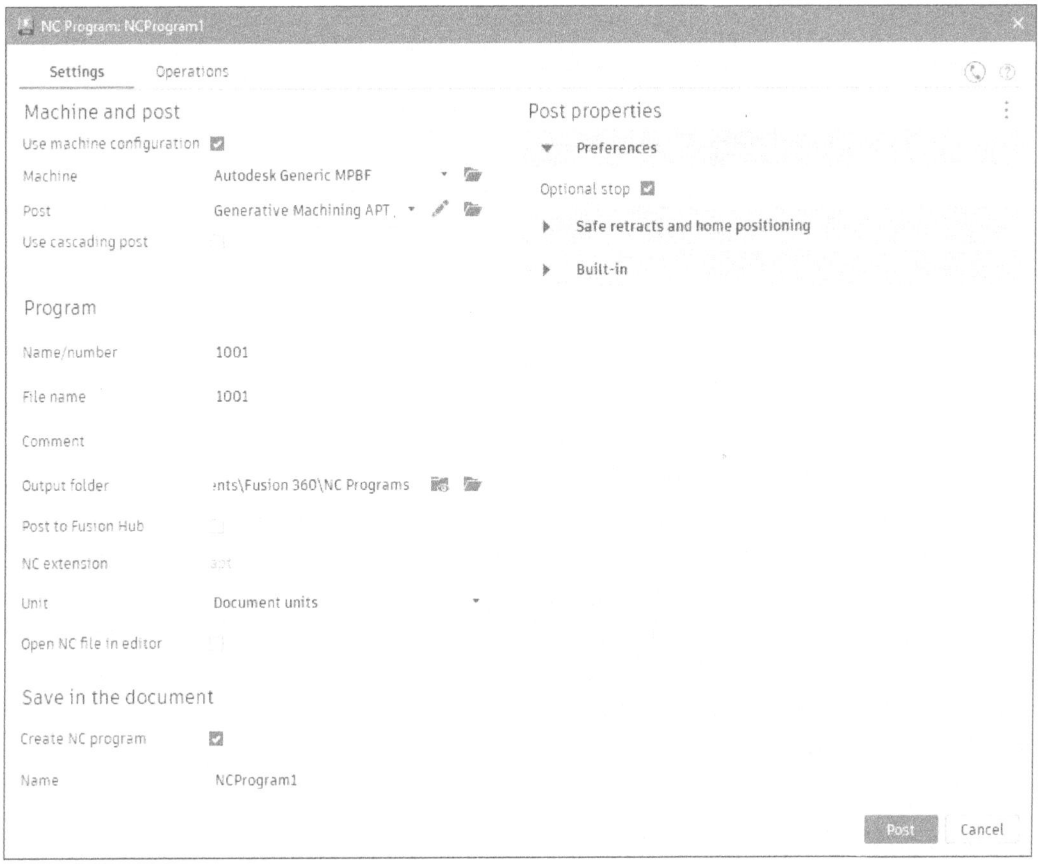

Figure-113. NC Program dialog box for additive toolpaths

- Set the parameters in **Settings** page of dialog box as discussed earlier. In the **Post properties** section of dialog box, specify temperature at different intervals, feedrates for various moves in 3D printing, and other related parameters.
- Click on the **Operations** tab in the dialog box and set check boxes for various operations to be post processed in NC code; refer to Figure-114.

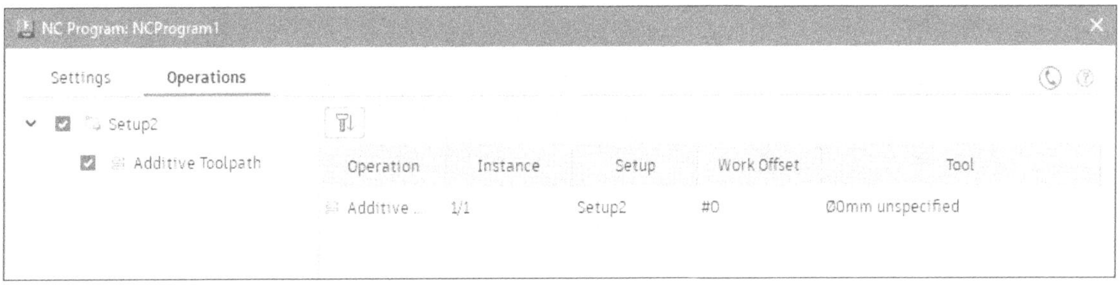

Figure-114. Operations tab in NC Program dialog box

- Specify desired parameters in the dialog box and click on the **Post** button. The NC code will be generated and displayed in the Visual Studio Code application. Save the code and close the application.

Exporting Toolpath and Printing Data

The **3MF Scene Export** tool in the **ACTIONS** panel is used to export the toolpath and printing setup for use by machines or other postprocessing software in 3mf format. The procedure to use this tool is given next.

- Click on the **3MF Scene Export** tool from the **ACTIONS** drop-down in the **ADDITIVE** tab of the **Ribbon**. The **3MF SCENE EXPORT** dialog box will be displayed; refer to Figure-115.

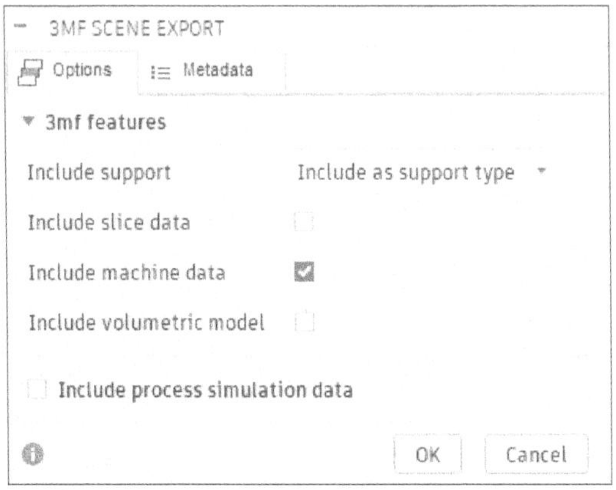

Figure-115. 3MF SCENE EXPORT dialog box

- Select check boxes from **Options** tab for features to be included in exported file apart from machining data. Select desired option from the Include support drop-down to define how support structures will be exported.
- Select **Include process simulation data** check box from the **Options** tab and specify additional information to include in the 3MF file for process simulation.
- Click on the **Metadata** tab to specify general information about product to be exported and click on the **OK** button. The dialog box to save 3mf file will be displayed; refer to Figure-116.

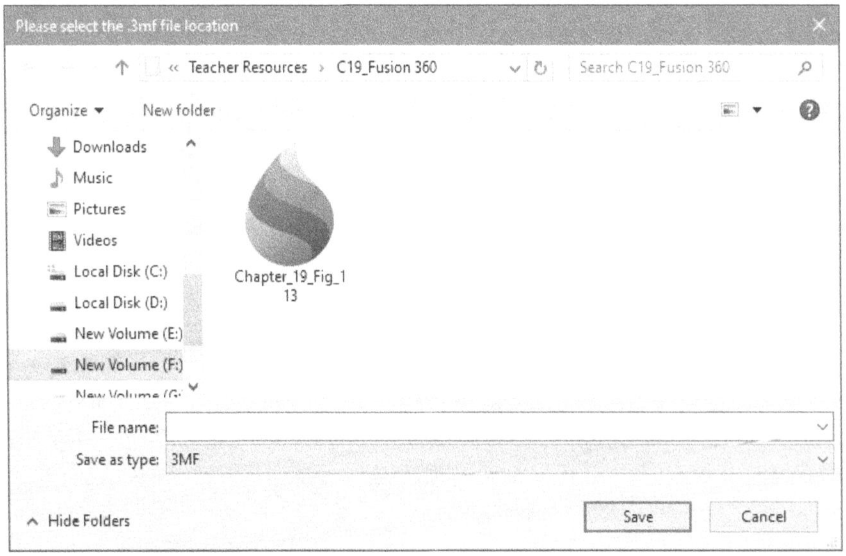

Figure-116. 3mf file location selection dialog box

- Specify name and location for file, and click on the **Save** button to save the file.

ADDITIVE BUILD EXTENSION

The general version of Autodesk Fusion allows to use only FFF type 3D printing used for manufacturing plastic parts. But if you want to 3D print metals and other materials that cannot be printed by FFF method then you can activate the Manufacturing extension as discussed earlier to use Directed Energy Deposition (DED), Metal Powder Bed Fusion (MPBF), Selective Laser Sintering (SLS), and other capable methods. In MPBF method, powder of metal is selectively melted to form layers. The tools and options related to MPBF additive manufacturing are discussed next.

Selecting an MPBF Machine

The procedure to select an MPBF machine for additive manufacturing is similar to earlier discussed procedure for selecting FFF machine. The procedure to setup MPBF machine is discussed next.

- After loading/creating a model to be 3D printed, click on the **New Setup** tool from the **SETUP** drop-down in the **ADDITIVE** tab of the **Ribbon**. The **SETUP** dialog box will be displayed as discussed earlier.
- Click on the **Select** button for **Machine** option from **Machine** section of the dialog box. The **Machine Library** dialog box will be displayed.
- Select the **Additive** check box from the **Capabilities** section and **MPBF** check box from the **Technologies** section of the dialog box. The MPBF capable machines will be displayed; refer to Figure-117.

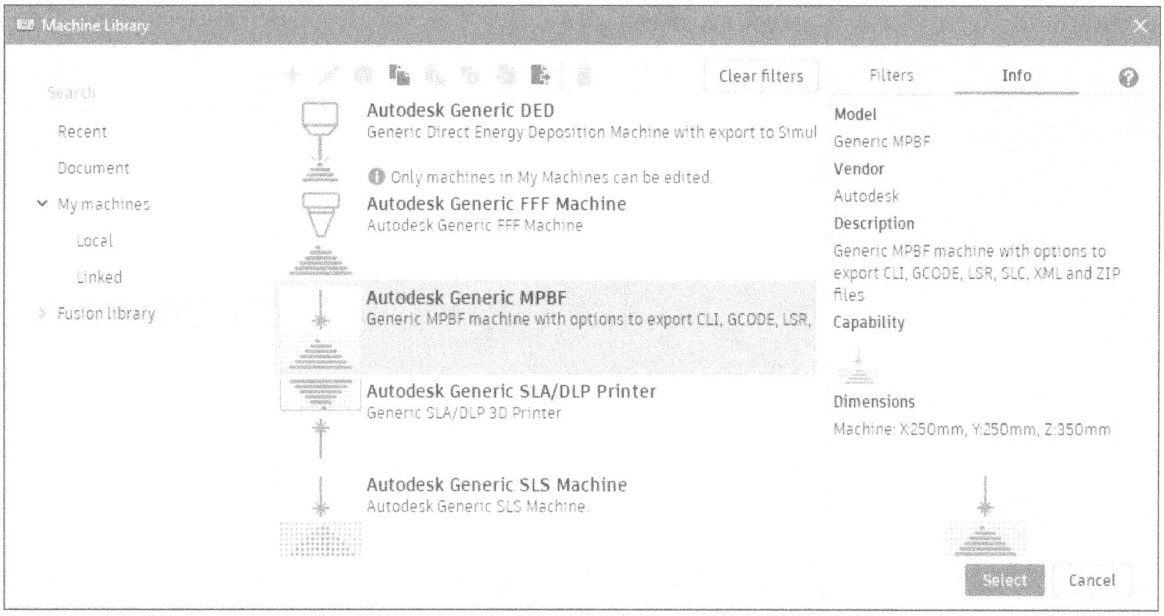

Figure-117. SLM machines

- Select desired MPBF machine from the dialog box and click on the **Select** button. The printing bed for selected machine will be displayed. Click on the **Print settings** button from the **SETUP** dialog box and select 3D printing settings related to selected machine.
- Click on the **OK** button from the dialog box. Some additional tools related to MPBF will be displayed in the **Ribbon**; refer to Figure-118.

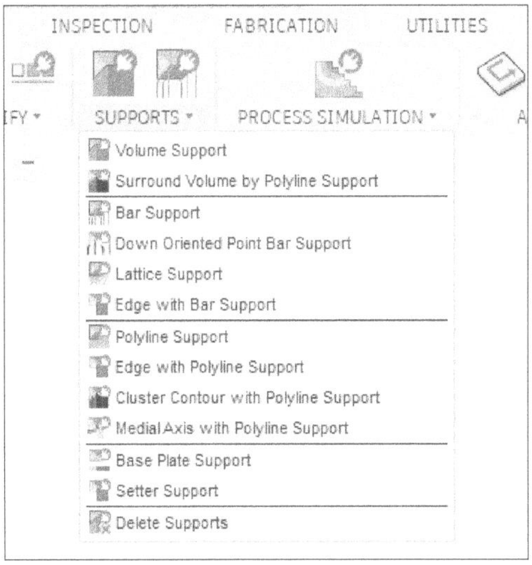

Figure-118. Tools for MPBF 3D Printing

These tools have been discussed earlier.

PERFORMING ADDITIVE MANUFACTURING SIMULATION

The tools in **PROCESS SIMULATION** drop-down are used to predict the behavior of part during additive manufacturing process for warpage and other defects. The process of perform the simulation is given next.

- Click on the **Study** tool from the **PROCESS SIMULATION** drop-down in **ADDITIVE** tab of the **Ribbon**. The **STUDY** dialog box will be displayed; refer to Figure-119.

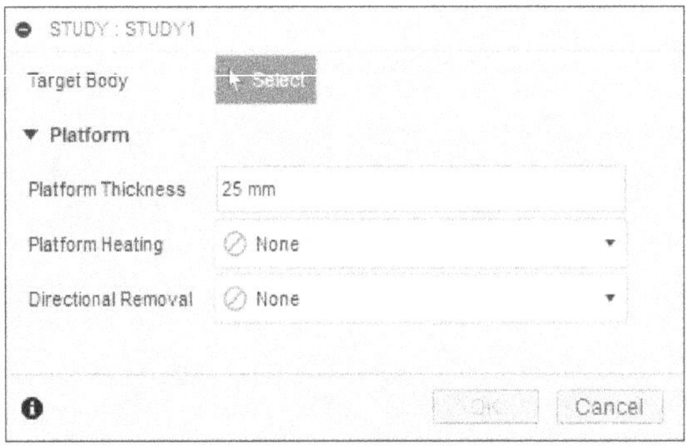

Figure-119. STUDY dialog box

- Select the model from graphics area on which you want to perform the simulation; refer to Figure-120 and click on the **OK** button from dialog box. The **SOLVE** dialog box will be displayed as shown in Figure-121.
- Click on the **Print Setting** button from the dialog box if you want to change 3D print material and related parameters.
- Click on the **Settings** button from the **Solve Accuracy** section of the dialog box to modify the parameters related to analysis. The **STUDY** dialog box will be displayed as shown in Figure-122.

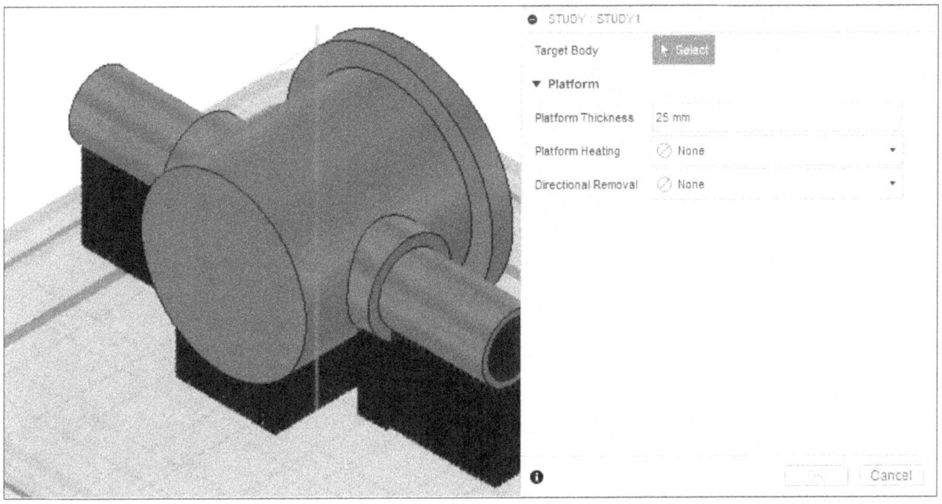

Figure-120. Body selected

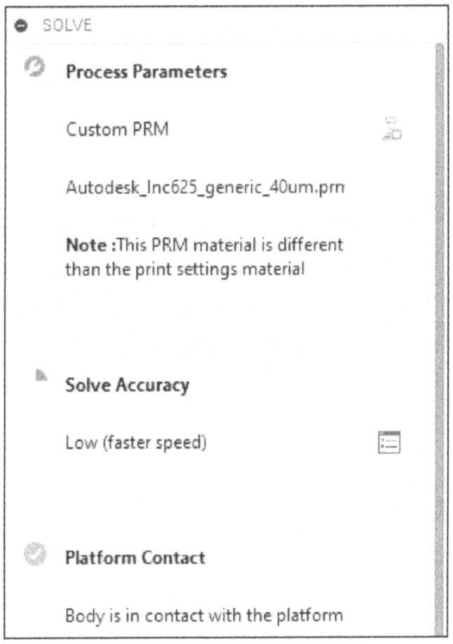

Figure-121. SOLVE dialog box

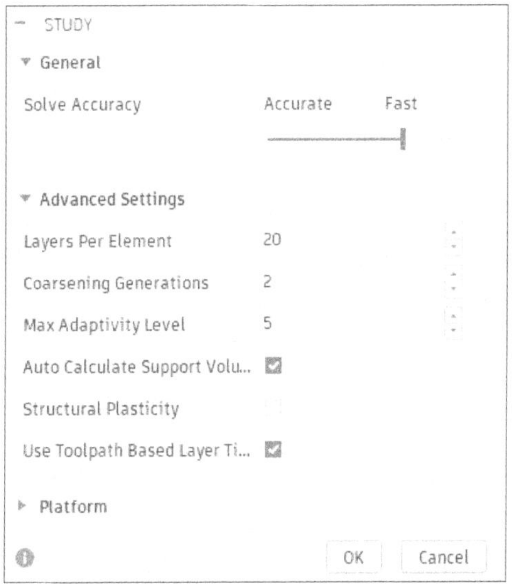

Figure-122. Settings tab of STUDY dialog box

- Use the **Solve Accuracy** slider to define whether you want to solve the analysis fast or your want to get more accurate results.
- Expand the **Advanced Settings** section and specify parameters as desired to define the accuracy of analysis. Hover the cursor on parameters in dialog box to check their usage.
- Click on the **OK** button from the dialog box to apply parameters. The **SOLVE** dialog box will be displayed again.
- Click on the **Check Mesh** button from the dialog box to generate and check mesh for study. Once the mesh generation is complete, the options will be displayed as shown in Figure-123.

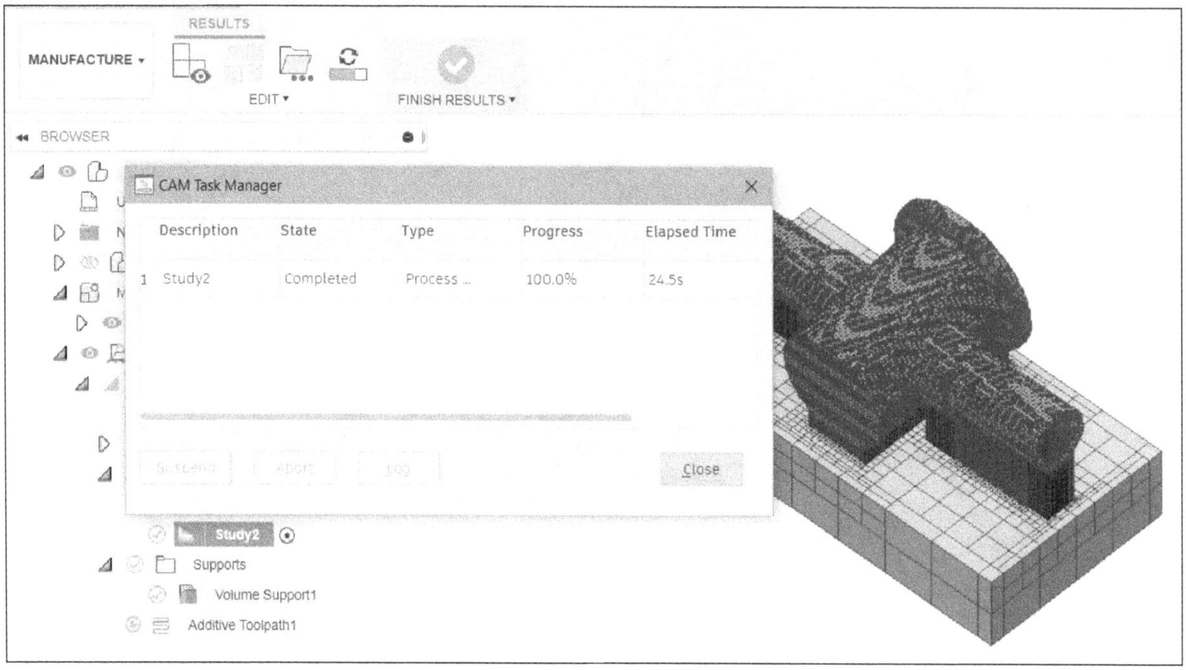

Figure-123. Mesh generated for additive manufacturing

- Click on the **Close** button from the **CAM Task Manager** to exit the dialog box.
- Click on the **Solve** tool from the **Ribbon** to perform the analysis. The results of analysis will be displayed once the solving is complete; refer to Figure-124. (Solution may take few minutes to hours depending on complexity of model).

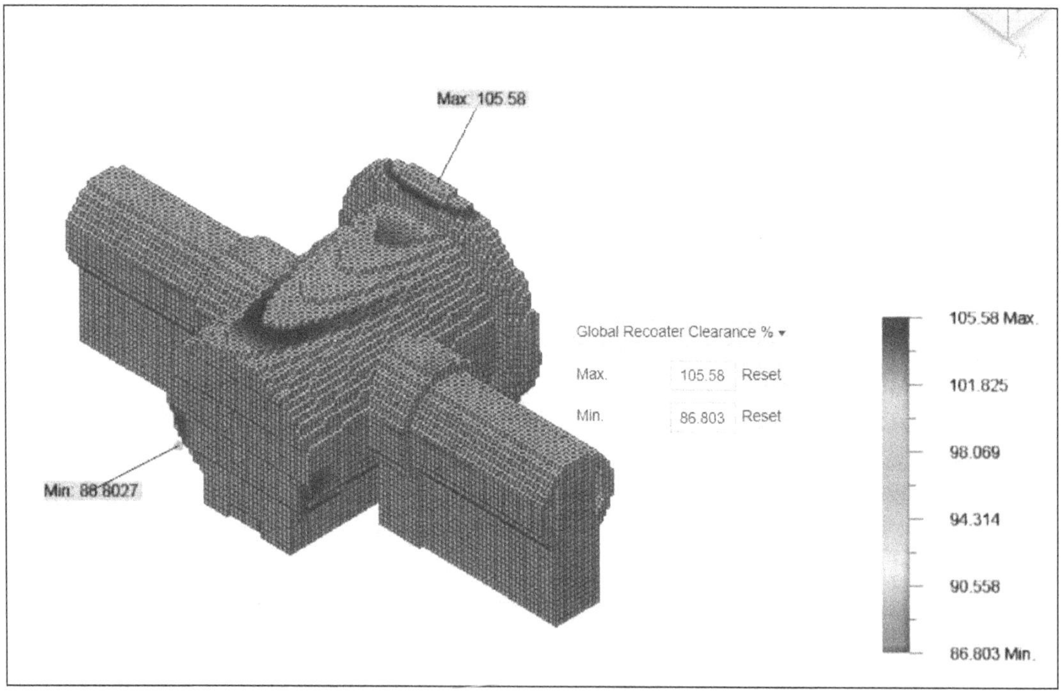

Figure-124. Solution of additive analysis

- Click on the **Finish Results** tool from **Ribbon** to exit after checking the results.

SELF- ASSESSMENT

Q1. Which of the following tools is used to group together various cutting operations?

a. Setup Sheet b. Add to New Pattern
c. Add to New Folder d. Post Process

Q2. Which of the following pattern options is used to copy all the toolpaths created on one body onto another independent body?

a. Circular Pattern b. Mirror Pattern
c. Duplicate Pattern d. Component Pattern

Q3. Which of the following NC parameters is not available for Manual NC entry?

a. Start b. Stop
c. Dwell d. Optional Stop

Q4. What is the difference between the use of **Probe WCS** tool and **Inspect Surface** tool available in **PROBING** panel of **Toolbar** in **MANUFACTURE** workspace?

Q5. The **Simulate** tool is used to check how tools cut through material in the form of an animation. (T/F)

Q6. What is the primary function of the New Folder tool?
A. To delete operations from BROWSER
B. To rename an existing operation
C. To create a folder for grouping similar operations
D. To duplicate toolpaths

Q7. How can a user rename a newly created folder?
A. Right-click and select Rename Folder
B. Double-click on the folder with a pause between clicks
C. Click on the folder and press F2
D. Open the folder properties and enter a new name

Q8. What is the purpose of the New Pattern tool?
A. To duplicate generated toolpaths in different patterns
B. To create a new folder for operations
C. To manually adjust tool orientations
D. To remove duplicate operations

Q9. In a Linear Pattern, what option determines the gap between instances?
A. Order by tool
B. Preserve order
C. Spacing
D. Flip direction

Q10. How can the direction of a Linear Pattern be flipped?
A. By selecting the Flip Direction 1 checkbox
B. By changing the operation order
C. By increasing the quantity of instances
D. By selecting Order by tool

Q11. What is the function of the Keep Original checkbox in pattern creation?
A. To delete the original toolpath after pattern creation
B. To retain the original toolpath along with the pattern
C. To enable automatic pattern generation
D. To reverse the order of pattern instances

Q12. In a Circular Pattern, what must be selected to define the center axis?
A. A plane
B. An edge or axis from the model
C. A selected point
D. A bounding box

Q13. Which option ensures equal distribution of instances in a Circular Pattern?
A. Flip Direction
B. Keep Original
C. Equal Spacing
D. Reverse Order

Q14. What does the Mirror Pattern option do?
A. Duplicates toolpaths in a linear sequence
B. Creates a flipped copy of a selected operation
C. Generates a circular repetition of toolpaths
D. Removes redundant toolpaths

Q15. Which feature of the Duplicate Pattern tool allows defining multiple locations for duplicating toolpaths?
A. Source selection
B. Flip Direction
C. Target selection
D. Spacing option

Q16. What is the purpose of the Component Pattern tool?
A. To apply toolpaths from one component to another
B. To create a mirror copy of an operation
C. To measure the geometry of an object
D. To manually adjust toolpaths

Q17. What is the function of the Manual NC tool?
A. To insert manual NC entries in the CAM BROWSER
B. To generate automated toolpaths
C. To create probe cycles for measuring parts
D. To optimize machining speeds

Q18. What type of probes can be used for Probing operations?
A. Mechanical, optical, laser
B. Thermal, hydraulic, mechanical
C. Magnetic, pneumatic, chemical
D. Electric, vacuum, ultrasonic

Q19. What is the primary function of the Probe WCS tool?
A. To measure stock dimensions
B. To create a mirror toolpath
C. To generate NC codes for probing cycles
D. To duplicate operations

Q20. In the Multi-Axis tab of the PROBE WCS dialog box, what does the Accessibility Analysis checkbox do?
A. Flips the Z-axis 180 degrees
B. Checks for areas inaccessible for the tool
C. Changes the orientation of the probing tool
D. Modifies the machining plane

Q21. Which Probe Mode option defines whether to probe the part/model or stock?
A. Tool Orientation
B. Flip Z Axis
C. Probe Mode Drop-down
D. Keep Original

Q22. What is the primary function of the Inspect Surface tool?
A. To align parts in the desired orientation.
B. To probe multiple points on a surface.
C. To simulate toolpaths.
D. To generate NC programs.

Q23. Which tab in the INSPECT dialog box allows you to specify inspection points?
A. Tool tab
B. Geometry tab
C. Actions tab
D. Multi-Axis tab

Q24. What does the Part Alignment tool primarily achieve?
A. Inspection of surface features
B. Realignment of the part for measurement
C. Creation of inspection reports
D. Toolpath simulation

Q25. What is the function of the Post For Live Alignment tool?
A. To generate an NC program for inspection toolpath alignment
B. To align parts in a specific orientation
C. To display inspection results
D. To import inspection results

Q26. How can you include/exclude inspection toolpaths in the output file while posting NC programs?
A. By selecting from the Geometry tab
B. By using the Operations tab in the dialog box
C. By modifying feed/speed parameters
D. By selecting the Simulate tool

Q27. What is indicated by a green mark before the Part Alignment feature in the BROWSER?
A. The alignment mode is active
B. The inspection file has been imported successfully
C. The part alignment tool is selected
D. The NC program is ready

Q28. What tool is used to create manual inspection reports?
A. Import Inspection Results tool
B. Simulate tool
C. Create Manual Inspection tool
D. Inspect Surface tool

Q29. In the Record Manual Inspection tool, what color indicates measured values are within the tolerance range?
A. Orange
B. Red
C. Green
D. Yellow

Q30. Which tool is used to regenerate toolpaths after modifications?
A. Inspect Surface tool
B. Generate tool
C. Post Process tool
D. Setup Sheet tool

Q31. What checkbox in the Display tab of the SIMULATE dialog box allows the tool to be transparent during simulation?
A. Show Points
B. Transparent
C. Toolpath
D. Stock

Q32. What is the purpose of the Post Process tool?
A. To generate setup sheets for CNC operators
B. To create inspection reports
C. To convert cutter location data into machine-specific NC code
D. To regenerate toolpaths

Q33. What feature of the Setup Sheet tool benefits operators on a network?
A. Generates a hard copy for operators
B. Allows saving setup sheets in shared folders
C. Ensures alignment of the part
D. Simulates toolpaths

Chapter 20

Introduction to Simulation in Fusion

Topics Covered

The major topics covered in this chapter are:

- ***Introduction.***
- ***Types of Analyses performed in Fusion.***
- ***FEA.***
- ***User Interface of Fusion Simulation.***
- ***Material Properties.***

INTRODUCTION

Simulation is the study of effects caused on an object due to real-world loading conditions. Computer Simulation is a type of simulation which uses CAD models to represent real objects and it applies various load conditions on the model to study the real-world effects. Fusion is a CAD-CAM-CAE software package. In Fusion Simulation, we apply loads on a constrained model under predefined environmental conditions and check the result (visually and/or in the form of tabular data). The types of analyses that can be performed in Autodesk Fusion are given next.

TYPES OF ANALYSES PERFORMED IN FUSION SIMULATION

Fusion Simulation performs almost all the analyses that are generally performed in Industries. These analyses and their uses are given next.

Static Analysis

This is the most common type of analysis we perform. In this analysis, loads are applied to a body due to which the body deforms and the effects of the loads are transmitted throughout the body. To absorb the effect of loads, the body generates internal forces and reactions at the supports to balance the applied external loads. These internal forces and reactions cause stress and strain in the body. Static analysis refers to the calculation of displacements, strains, and stresses under the effect of external loads, based on some assumptions. The assumptions are as follows.

- All loads are applied slowly and gradually until they reach their full magnitudes. After reaching their full magnitudes, load will remain constant (i.e. load will not vary against time).
- Linearity assumption: The relationship between loads and resulting responses is linear. For example, if you double the magnitude of loads, the response of the model (displacements, strains, and stresses) will also double. You can make linearity assumption if:

1. All materials in the model comply with Hooke's Law that is stress is directly proportional to strain.
2. The induced displacements are small enough to ignore the change in stiffness caused by loading.
3. Boundary conditions do not vary during the application of loads. Loads must be constant in magnitude, direction, and distribution. They should not change while the model is deforming.

If the above assumptions are valid for your analysis, then you can perform **Linear Static Analysis**. For example, a cantilever beam fixed at one end and force applied on other end; refer to Figure-1.

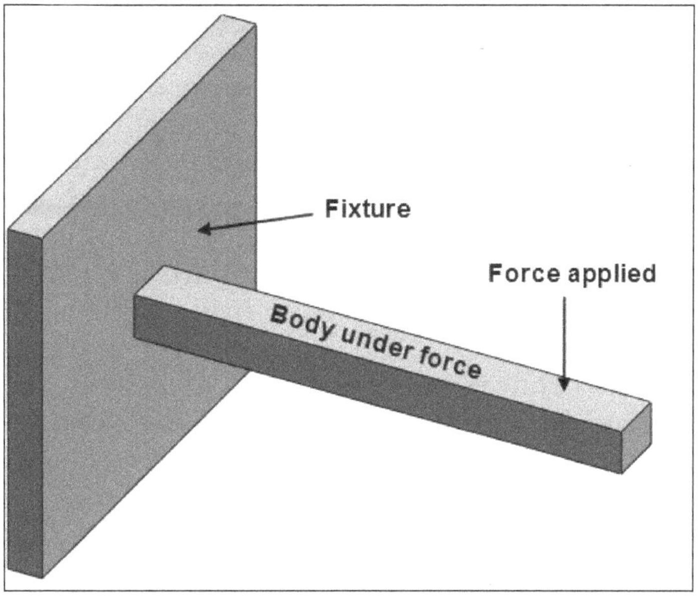

Figure-1. Linear static analysis example

Nonlinear Static Stress Analysis

If the above assumptions are not valid, then you need to perform the **Non-Linear Static analysis**. For example, force applied on an object attached with a spring; refer to Figure-2.

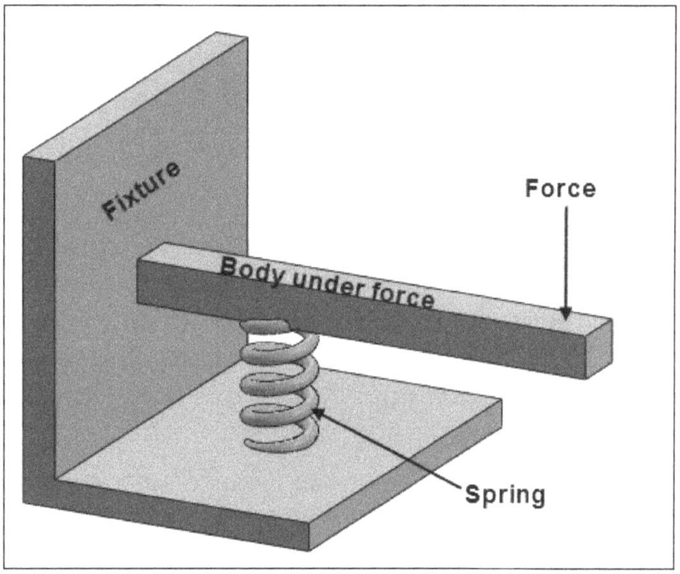

Figure-2. Non-linear static analysis example

Modal Analysis (Vibration Analysis)

By its very nature, vibration involves repetitive motion. Each occurrence of a complete motion sequence is called a "cycle." Frequency is defined as so many cycles in a given time period. "Cycles per second" or "Hertz". Individual parts have what engineers call "natural" frequencies. For example, a violin string at a certain tension will vibrate only at a set number of frequencies, that's why you can produce specific musical tones. There is a base frequency in which the entire string is going back and forth in a simple bow shape.

Harmonics and overtones occur because individual sections of the string can vibrate independently within the larger vibration. These various shapes are called "modes". The base frequency is said to vibrate in the first mode, and so on up the ladder. Each mode shape will have an associated frequency. Higher mode shapes have higher frequencies. The most disastrous kinds of consequences occur when a power-driven device such as a motor, produces a frequency at which an attached structure naturally vibrates. This event is called "resonance." If sufficient power is applied, the attached structure will be destroyed. Note that armies, which normally marched "in step," were taken out of step when crossing bridges. If the beat of the marching feet align with a natural frequency of the bridge, then it could fall down. Engineers must design in such a way that resonance does not occur during regular operation of machines. This is a major purpose of Modal Analysis. Ideally, the first mode has a frequency higher than any potential driving frequency. Frequently, resonance cannot be avoided, especially for short periods of time. For example, when a motor comes up to speed it produces a variety of frequencies. So, it may pass through a resonant frequency.

Thermal analysis

There are three mechanisms of heat transfer. These mechanisms are Conduction, Convection, and Radiation. Thermal analysis calculates the temperature distribution in a body due to some or all of these mechanisms. In all three mechanisms, heat flows from a higher-temperature medium to a lower temperature one. Heat transfer by conduction and convection requires the presence of an intervening medium while heat transfer by radiation does not.

There are two modes of heat transfer analysis.

Steady State Thermal Analysis

In this type of analysis, we are only interested in the thermal conditions of the body when it reaches thermal equilibrium, but we are not interested in the time it takes to reach this status. The temperature of each point in the model will remain unchanged until a change occurs in the system. At equilibrium, the thermal energy entering the system is equal to the thermal energy leaving it. Generally, the only material property that is needed for steady state analysis is the thermal conductivity. This type of analysis is available in Fusion.

Transient Thermal Analysis

In this type of analysis, we are interested in knowing the thermal status of the model at different instances of time. A thermos designer, for example, knows that the temperature of the fluid inside will eventually be equal to the room temperature(steady state), but designer is interested in finding out the temperature of the fluid as a function of time. In addition to the thermal conductivity, we also need to specify density, specific heat, initial temperature profile, and the period of time for which solutions are desired. Till the time of writing this book, the transient thermal analysis was not available in Fusion.

Thermal Stress Analysis

The Thermal Stress Analysis is performed to check stresses induced in part when thermal and structural loads act on the part simultaneously. Thermal Stress Analysis is important in cases where material expands or contracts due to heating or cooling of the part to certain temperature in irregular way. One example where thermal stress analysis finds its importance is two material bonded strip working in a high temperature environment.

Structural Buckling Analysis

Slender models tends to buckle under axial loading. Buckling is defined as the sudden deformation which occurs when the stored membrane (axial) energy is converted into bending energy with no change in the externally applied loads. Mathematically, when buckling occurs, the stiffness becomes singular. The Linearized buckling approach, used here, solves an eigenvalue problem to estimate the critical buckling factors and the associated buckling mode shapes.

In a laymen's language, if you press down on an empty soft drink can with your hand, not much will seem to happen. If you put the can on the floor and gradually increase the force by stepping down on it with your foot then at some point, it will suddenly squash. This sudden scrunching is known as "buckling."

Dynamic Event Simulation

The Dynamic Event Simulation analysis is used to study the effect of object velocity, initial velocity, acceleration, time dependent loads, and constraints in the design. The results of this analysis include displacements, stresses, strains, and other measurements throughout a specified time period. You can perform this analysis when you need to check the effect of throwing a phone from some height or similar cases where motion is involved.

Shape Optimization

The Shape Optimization in Fusion is not an analysis but a study to find the shape of part which utilizes minimum material but sustains the applied load up to required factor of safety.

Injection Molding Simulation

The Injection Molding Simulation is performed to check the material and time required to fill the mold. This simulation also allows you to find out quality issues, material selection, and injection locations.

Quasi-static Event Simulation

The Quasi-static Event Simulation is performed to find out static stresses and deformations in single part or multiple body assembly with nonlinear material properties. You can use this simulation when there is large deformation between contacts of simulation model.

Electronics Cooling

The Electronic Cooling simulation is performed to check whether electronic components are able to dissipate heat generated by them under natural or forced air convection.

Till this point, you have become familiar with the analyses that can be performed by using Fusion. But, do you know how the software analyze the problems. The answer is FEA.

FEA

FEA, Finite Element Analysis, is a mathematical system used to solve real-world engineering problems by simplifying them. In FEA, the model is broken into small elements and nodes. Then, distributed forces are applied on each element and node. The cumulative result of forces is calculated and displayed in results. Note that Fusion uses **Linear Tetrahedron** element with 4 nodes, Parabolic Tetrahedron element with 10 nodes and Parabolic Tetrahedron elements with Curved Edges having 10 nodes to mesh 3D solids. The **Line** element for bolt connectors (only available in Fusion Ultimate). 2D and Planar (shell) elements are not supported in Autodesk Fusion till the time we are writing this book.

As we are ready with some basic information about simulation in Fusion. Let's get started with initiating the simulation environment of Fusion.

STARTING SIMULATION IN FUSION

In Fusion, every workspace is available in a seamless manner. To start simulation in Fusion, click on the **Change Workspace** drop-down and select the **SIMULATION** option; refer to Figure-3. The **Simulation Workspace** will become active; refer to Figure-4. Also, the **New Study** dialog box will be displayed asking you to select the analysis type you want to perform.

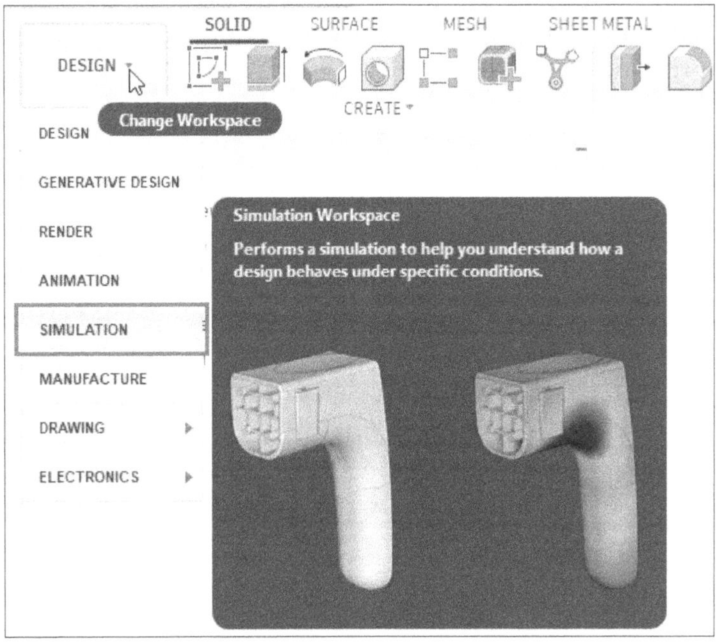

Figure-3. SIMULATION option

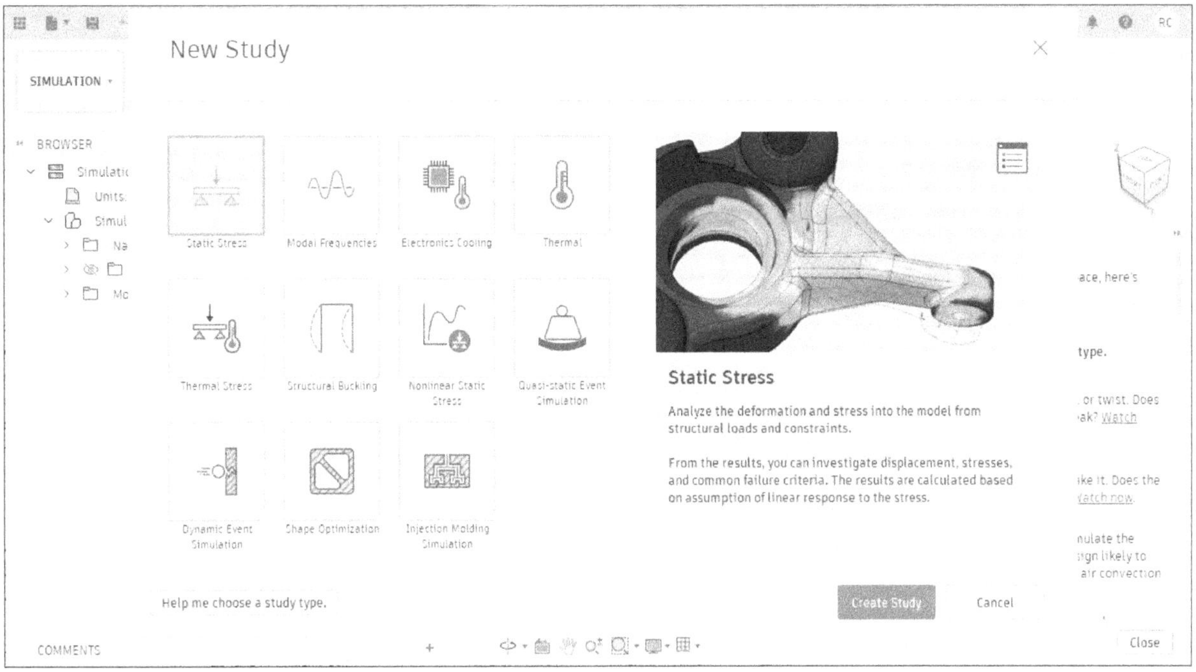

Figure-4. Simulation workspace of Fusion

PERFORMING AN ANALYSIS

The static stress analysis is performed when the load is stable and the object deforms according to Hooke's Law. The procedure to start static stress analysis is given next. You can apply the same procedure for starting other analyses too.

- Double-click on the **Static Stress** button from the **New Study** dialog box. The tools required to perform static stress analysis will be displayed in the **Toolbar**; refer to Figure-5.

Figure-5. Static stress analysis tools in toolbar

Various tools and options of **Toolbar** in Simulation environment are discussed next.

STARTING NEW SIMULATION STUDY

While you are working on an analysis and you need to start another analysis then you can do so by using the **New Simulation Study** button. The procedure is given next.

- Click on the **New Simulation Study** tool from **STUDY** panel in the **Toolbar**; refer to Figure-6. The **New Study** dialog box will be displayed as discussed earlier. You can also press **N** key from keyboard while in Simulation environment to do the same.

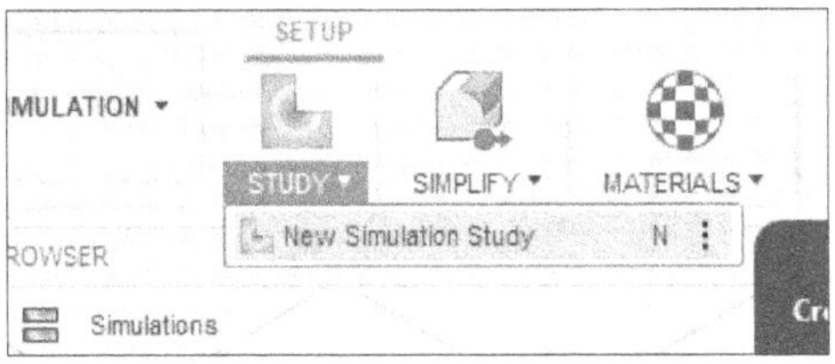

Figure-6. New Simulation Study tool

- Double-click on desired button to perform respective analysis.

SIMPLIFYING MODEL FOR ANALYSIS

Most of the parts and assemblies have features that are irrelevant to analysis. These features hardly affect the result of analysis but take too much of processing resources. Such features should be removed before performing analysis. Examples of these features can be chamfers, fillets, unnecessary components which have no role in analysis. Note that sometimes these features are important part of calculations so make sure not to remove such features. One such example can be an assembly where load is acting on chamfer so you should not remove such chamfer from model. In Autodesk Fusion, there are two ways to access tools for simplifying model; using **Simplify** button from **New Study** dialog box and using **Simplify** tool from **Toolbar** within analysis.

- Click on the **Simplify** tool from **SIMPLIFY** panel in the **Toolbar** when an analysis is already active; refer to Figure-7 or select the **Simplify** button and click on the **Simplify Model** button from the **New Study** dialog box. The **SIMPLIFY Toolbar** will be displayed; refer to Figure-8.

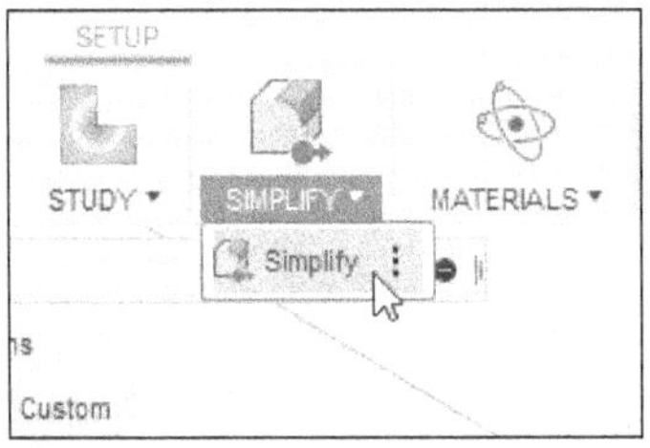

Figure-7. Simplify tool

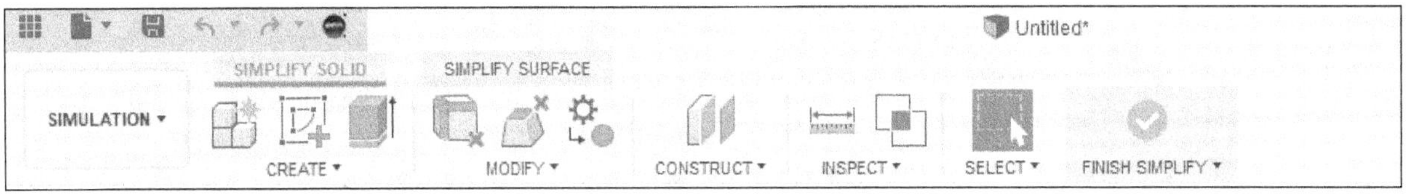

Figure-8. SIMPLIFY toolbar

If you go through various drop-downs and panels in this **Toolbar** then you will find that most of the tools are same as discussed for Modeling and Surface designing in earlier chapters. So, we will skip those tools and discuss the other tools.

Removing Features

The **Remove Features** tool is used to remove selected feature from the model in Simulation environment only. The procedure to use this tool is given next.

- Click on the **Remove Features** tool from **MODIFY** drop-down in the **SIMPLIFY** toolbar; refer to Figure-9. The **REMOVE FEATURES** dialog box will be displayed; refer to Figure-10.

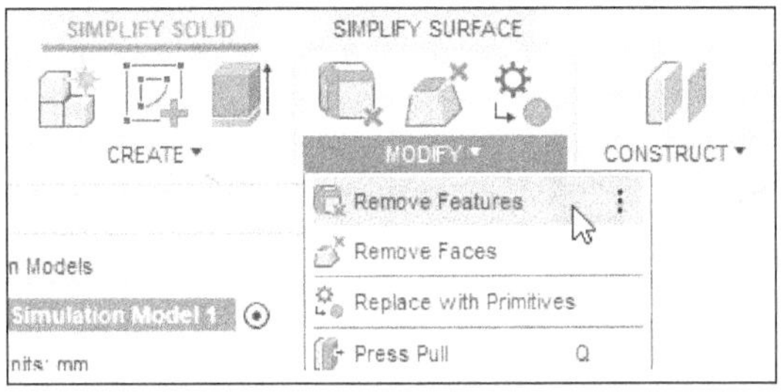

Figure-9. Remove Features tool

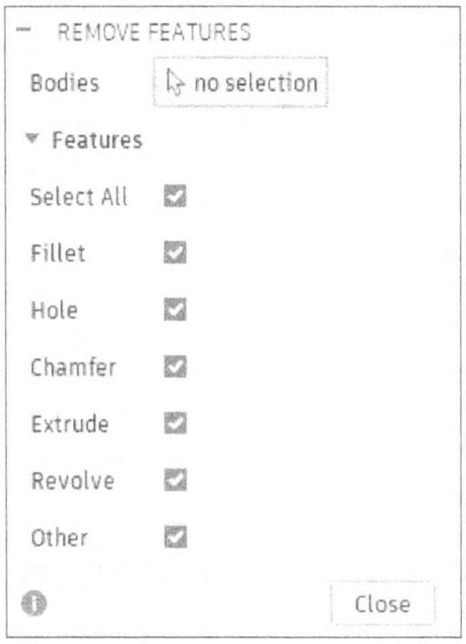

Figure-10. REMOVE FEATURES dialog box

- Select the bodies whose extra features are to be removed for performing analysis. The features being removed based on your selection in the **REMOVE FEATURES** dialog box, will be highlighted; refer to Figure-11.

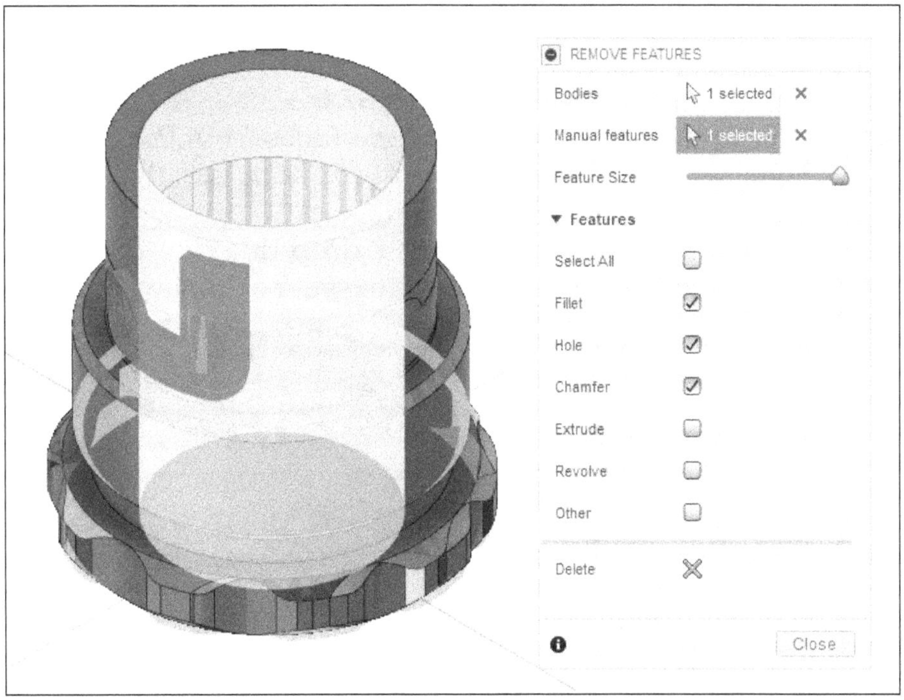

Figure-11. Features highlighted for removal

- Select desired check boxes from the dialog box to remove respective features.
- Move the **Feature Size** slider left or right to consider smaller or larger features, respectively for removal.

- Although most of the features get selected automatically based on specified conditions in the dialog box but if you want to manually add/remove the features then click on the **Select** button of **Manual features** option in the dialog box and select desired features.
- After selecting the features, click on the **Delete** button (☒) at the bottom of the dialog box and close the dialog box; refer to Figure-12.

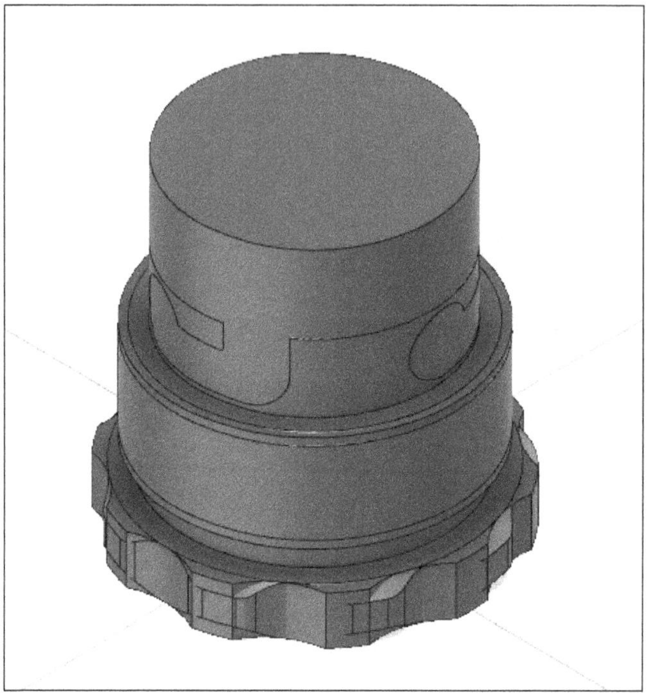

Figure-12. Selected features removed

Removing Faces

The **Remove Faces** tool is used to remove selected faces from the model and close the open sections of model automatically. The procedure to use this tool is given next.

- Click on the **Remove Faces** tool from **MODIFY** drop-down in the **SIMPLIFY** toolbar; refer to Figure-13. The **REMOVE FACES** dialog box will be displayed; refer to Figure-14.

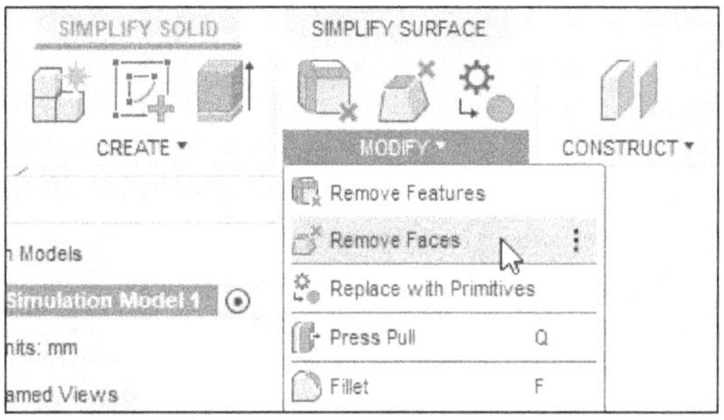

Figure-13. Remove Faces tool

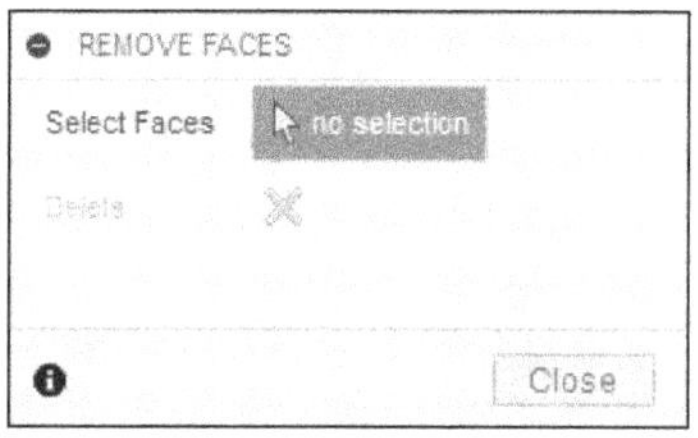

Figure-14. REMOVE FACES dialog box

- The **no selection** button of **Select Faces** section is active by default. Click on the face to be remove; refer to Figure-15.

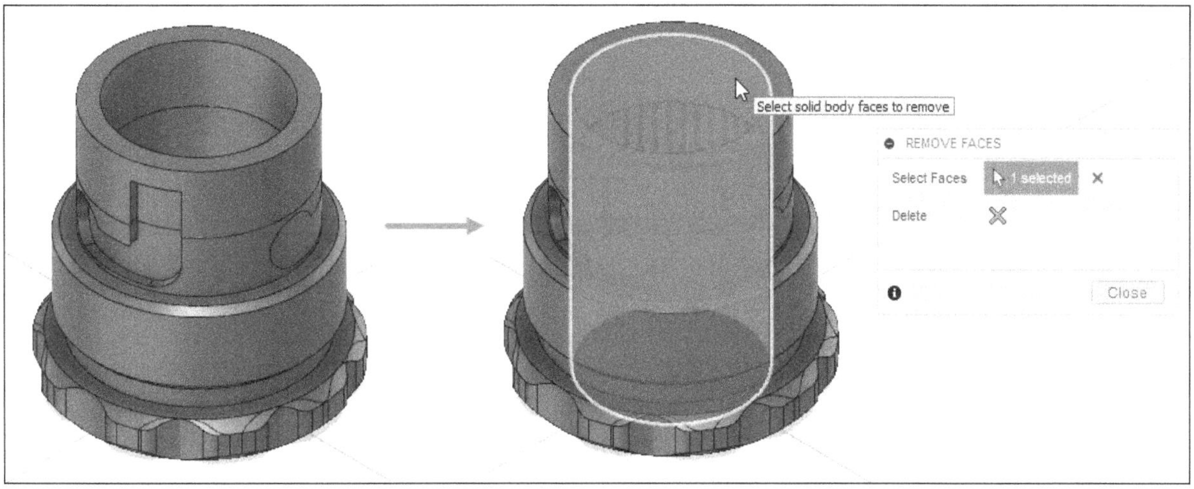

Figure-15. Selection of face to be remove

- Click on the **Delete** button from the dialog box. The selected faces will be deleted; refer to Figure-16.

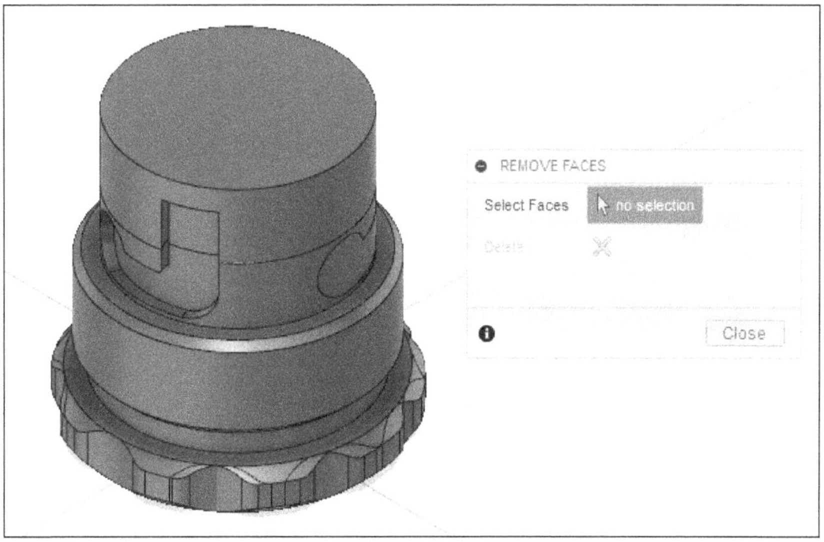

Figure-16. Selected face removed

- Click on **Close** button to exit the tool.

Replace With Primitives

The **Replace with Primitives** tool is used to replace selected body/component by primitive shapes like box, cylinder, and sphere. The procedure to use this tool is given next.

- Click on the **Replace with Primitives** tool from the **MODIFY** drop-down in the **SIMPLIFY SOLID** toolbar; refer to Figure-17. The **REPLACE WITH PRIMITIVES** dialog box will be displayed; refer to Figure-18.

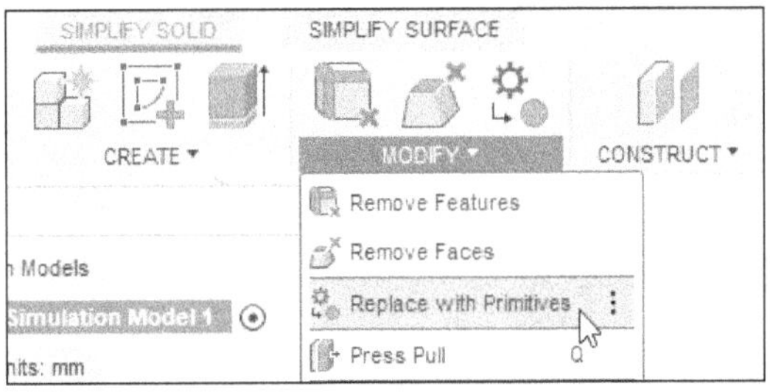

Figure-17. Replace with Primitives tool

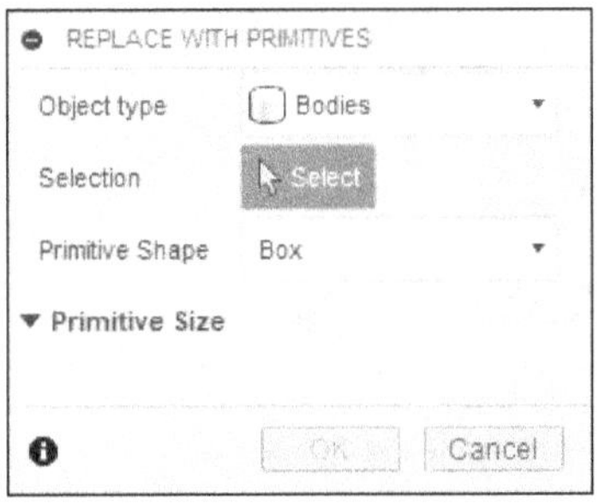

Figure-18. REPLACE WITH PRIMITIVES dialog box

- Select desired object type from the **Object type** drop-down.
- Select the **Bodies** option if you want to replace bodies with primitives and select the **Components** option if you want to replace assembly components with primitives for analysis.
- The **Select** button of **Selection** section is active by default. Click on the body/component to be selected; refer to Figure-19.

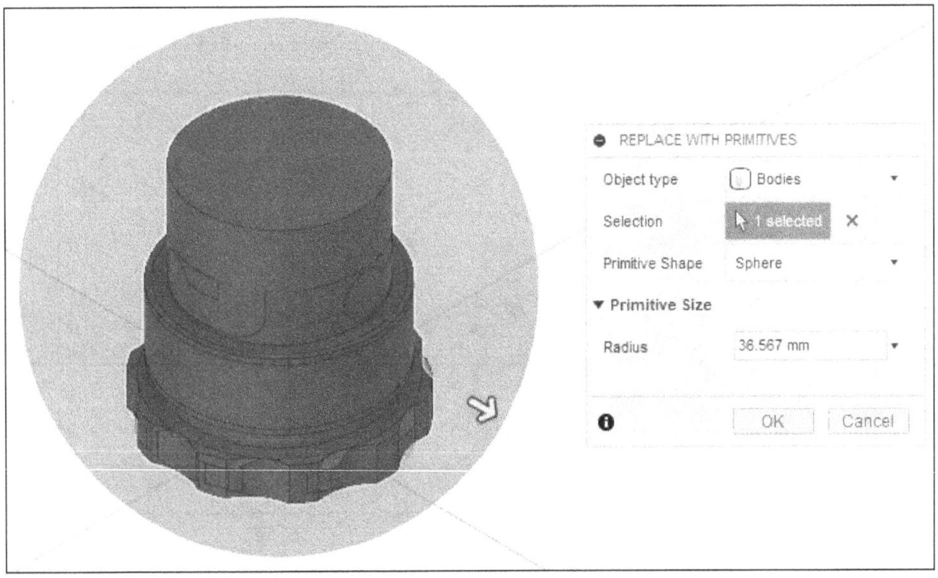

Figure-19. Selection of body to replace

- Select desired shape from **Primitive Shape** drop-down and specify the related size parameters in the edit boxes of dialog box.
- Click on the **OK** button from the dialog box to replace the body/component; refer to Figure-20.

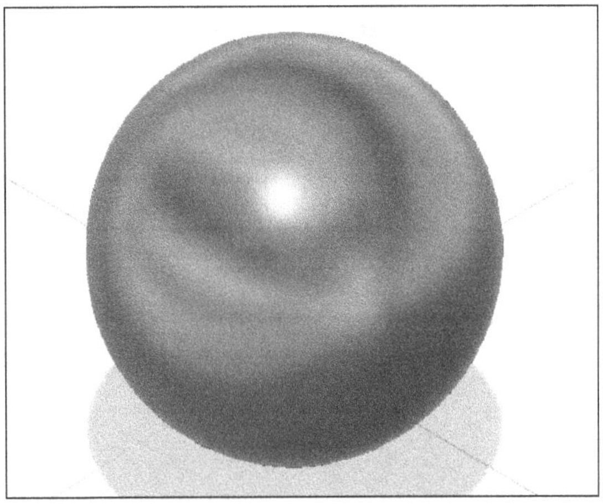

Figure-20. Selected body replaced with sphere

Similarly, you can apply simplify surfaces using the tools in **SIMPLIFY SURFACE** tab of the **Ribbon**. After performing desired simplification operations, click on the **FINISH SIMPLIFY** button from the **Toolbar** to exit Simplify mode.

STUDY MATERIAL

Study material is the material applied to model with all the physical properties so that you can check the effect of load on actual material conditions. The tools related to study material are available in the **MATERIALS** drop-down of the **Toolbar**; refer to Figure-21. These tools are discussed next.

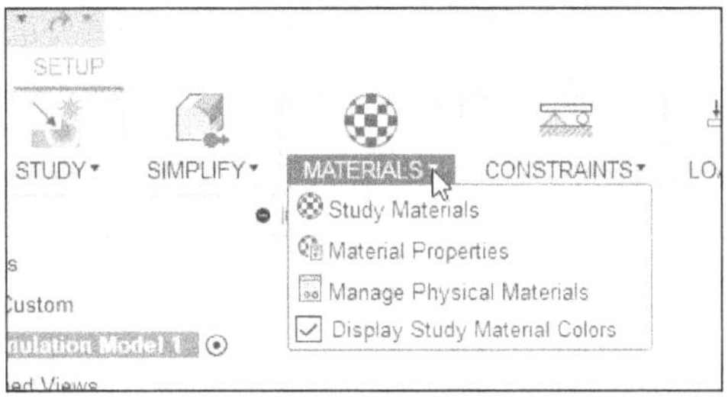

Figure-21. MATERIALS drop down

Applying Study Material

Study material is applied to assign physical properties of material to the model. The procedure to apply study material is given next.

- Click on the **Study Materials** tool from the **MATERIALS** drop-down in the **Toolbar**; refer to Figure-22. The **STUDY MATERIALS** dialog box will be displayed; refer to Figure-23.

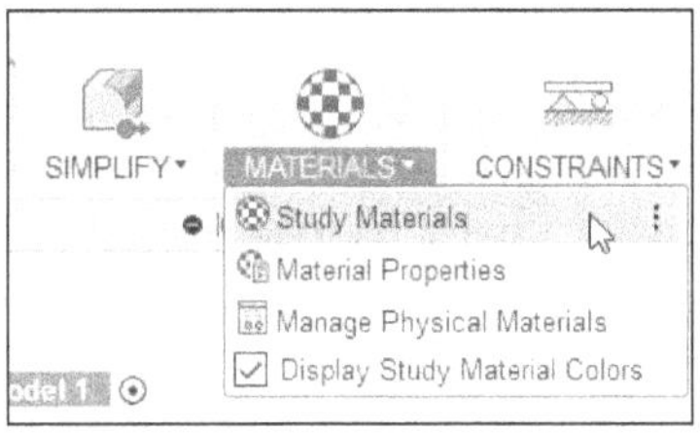

Figure-22. Study Materials tool

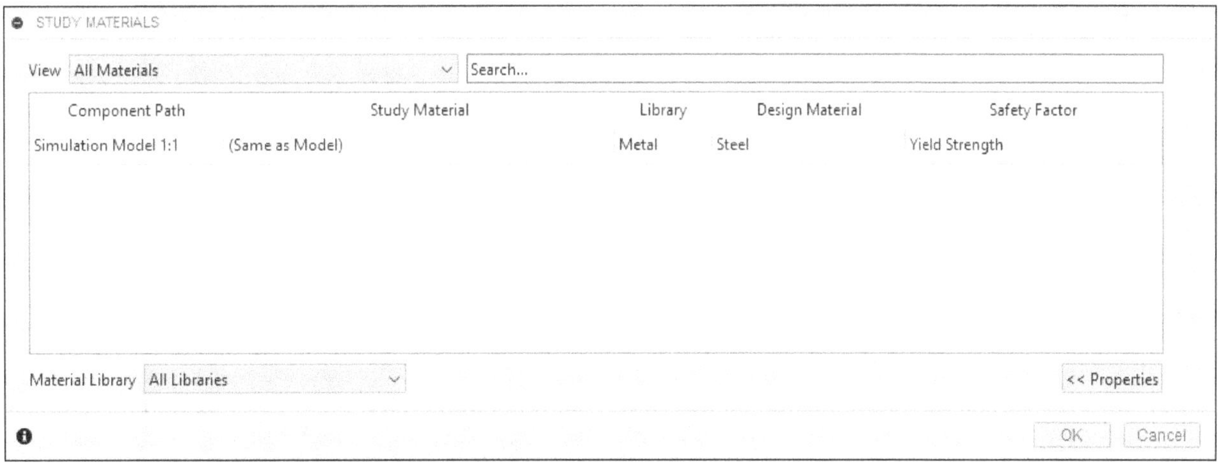

Figure-23. STUDY MATERIALS dialog box

- Click in the drop-down of **Study Materials** column in the dialog box for the current component and select desired material; refer to Figure-24.

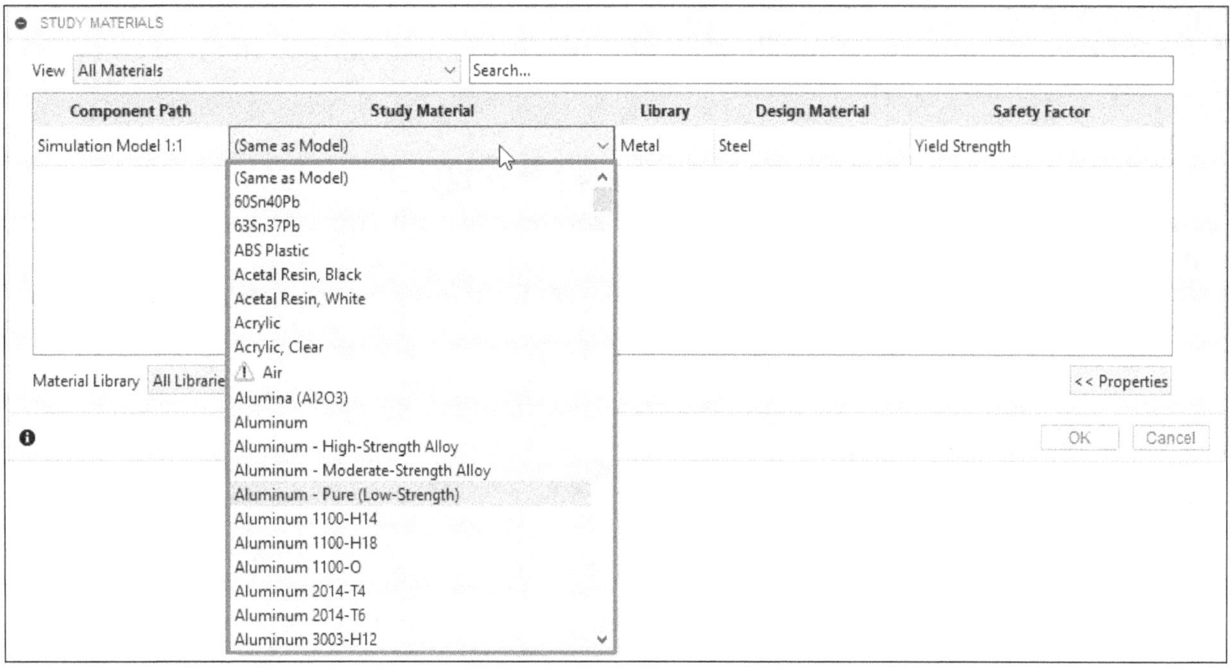

Figure-24. Study Material drop down

- Select desired safety factor criteria from the drop-down in **Safety Factor** column of the dialog box. There are two options in this drop-down; **Yield Strength** and **Ultimate Tensile Strength**. Yield Strength is the point where metal starts to permanently deform. Ultimate Tensile Strength is the point after which the metal becomes so weak that it can break. Generally, Yield Strength is used as standard for determining safety factor.
- After specifying all desired parameters, click on the **OK** button. The material will be applied.

Displaying Material Properties

All the properties of different materials in material library can be checked by using the **Material Properties** button. The procedure is discussed next.

- Click on the **Material Properties** tool from the **MATERIALS** drop-down in the **Toolbar**; refer to Figure-25. The **MATERIAL PROPERTIES** dialog box will be displayed; refer to Figure-26.

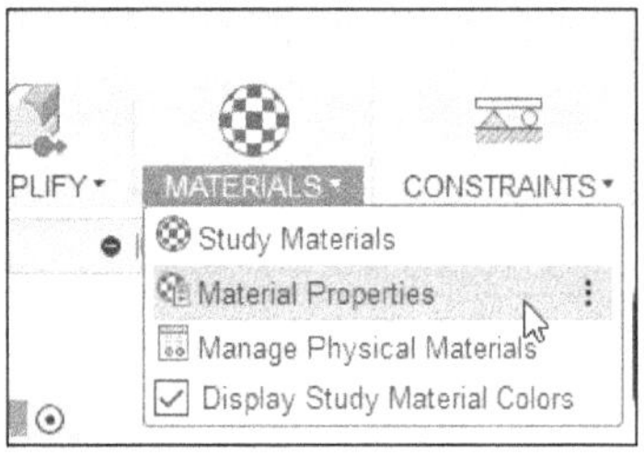

Figure-25. Material Properties tool

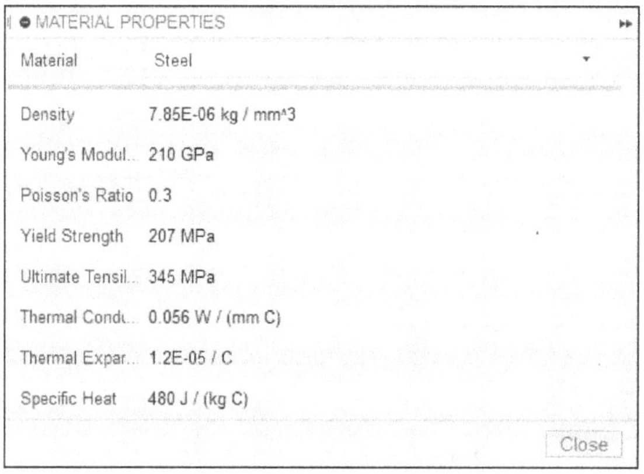

Figure-26. MATERIAL PROPERTIES dialog box

- Select the material from the **Material** drop-down at the top in the dialog box to check the material properties.
- Click on the **Close** button to exit the dialog box.

Managing Physical Material

The **Manage Physical Materials** tool is used to manage physical properties of material. If you want to edit any parameter of material before using it in analysis then you can do so by using this tool. The procedure is given next.

- Click on the **Manage Physical Materials** tool from the **MATERIALS** drop-down in the **Toolbar**; refer to Figure-27. The **Material Browser** dialog box will be displayed; refer to Figure-28.

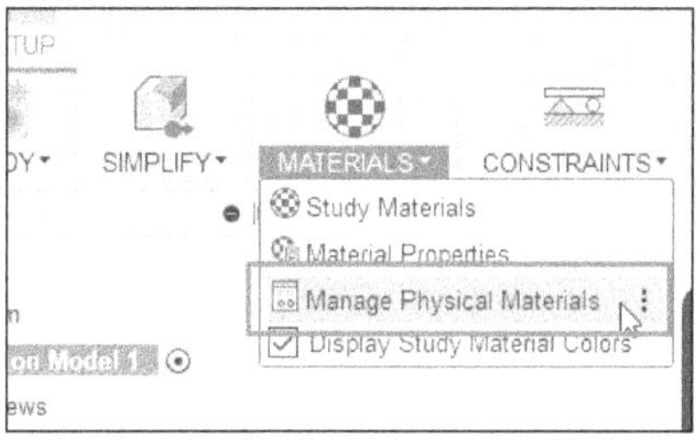

Figure-27. Manage Physical Materials tool

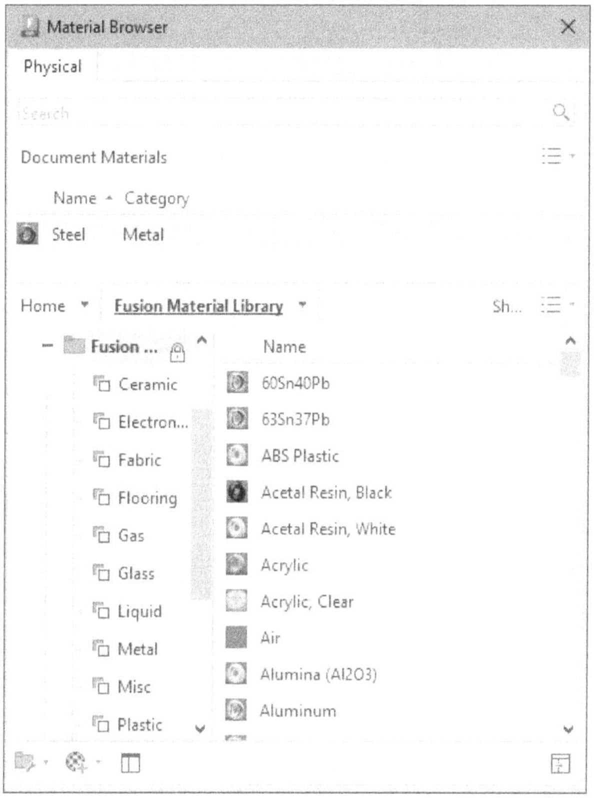

Figure-28. Material Browser dialog box

- Select desired material library and category from the left area of the **Material Browser** dialog box.
- Hover the cursor on the material that you want to edit from the right area and click on the **Adds material to favorites and displays in editor** button; refer to Figure-29. The editing options will be displayed at the right in dialog box; refer to Figure-30.

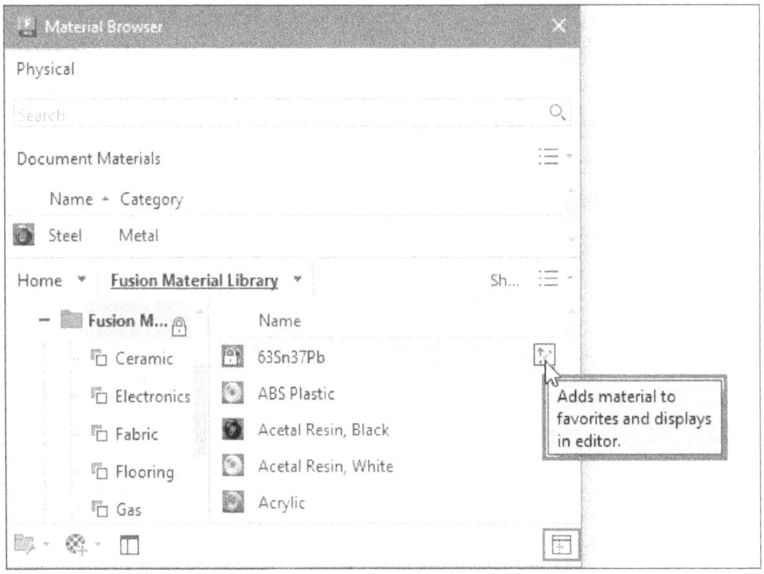

Figure-29. Adding material to edit

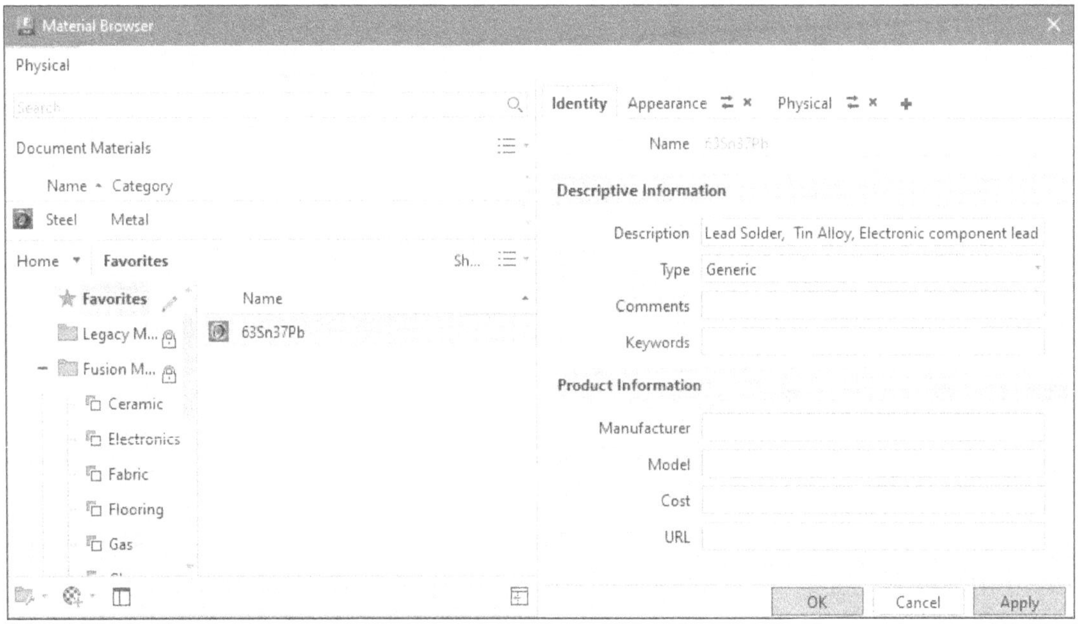

Figure-30. Material editing area

- Click at desired tab in the right area of the dialog box and specify the parameters related to material.
- Click on the **Apply** button from the right area to apply the changes and click **Cancel** button to exit editing or click on the **OK** button to apply changes and exit editing mode.
- Click on the **Close** button from top right corner to exit the **Material Browser** dialog box.

Creating New Material

If you want to create a new material then follow the procedure given next.

- Click on the **Create New Library** tool from the **Creates, opens, and edits user-defined libraries** drop-down at the bottom left corner of the **Material Browser** dialog box; refer to Figure-31. The **Create Library** dialog box will be displayed; refer to Figure-32.

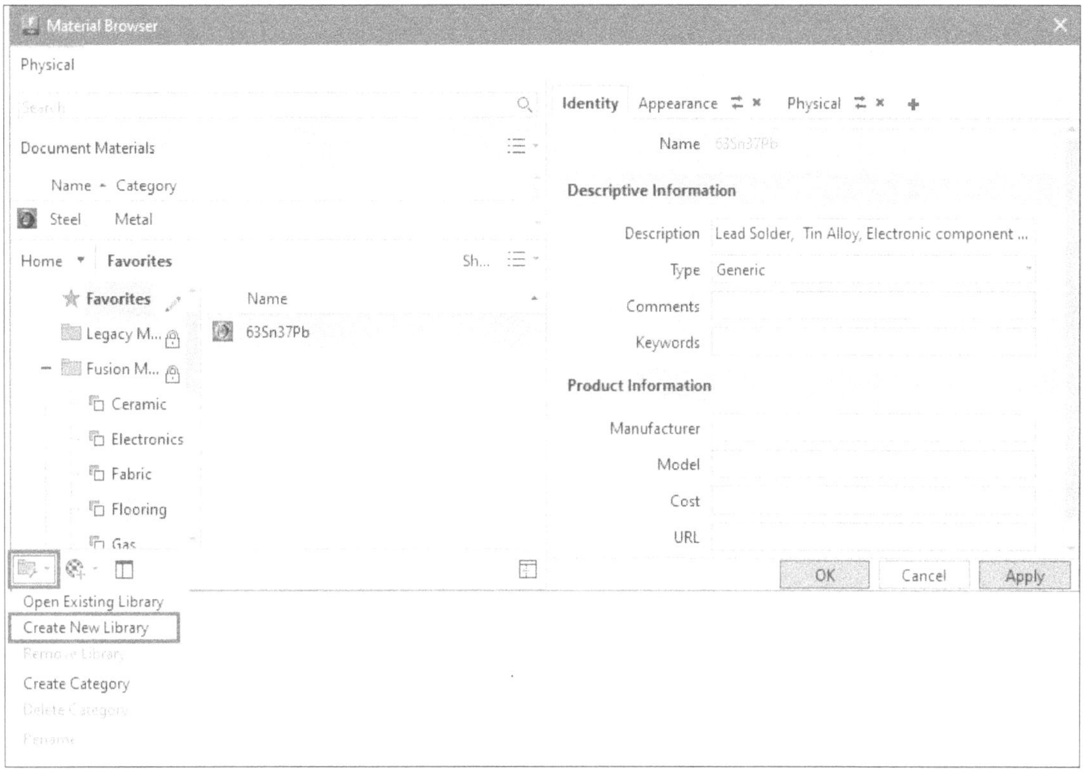

Figure-31. Create New Library tool

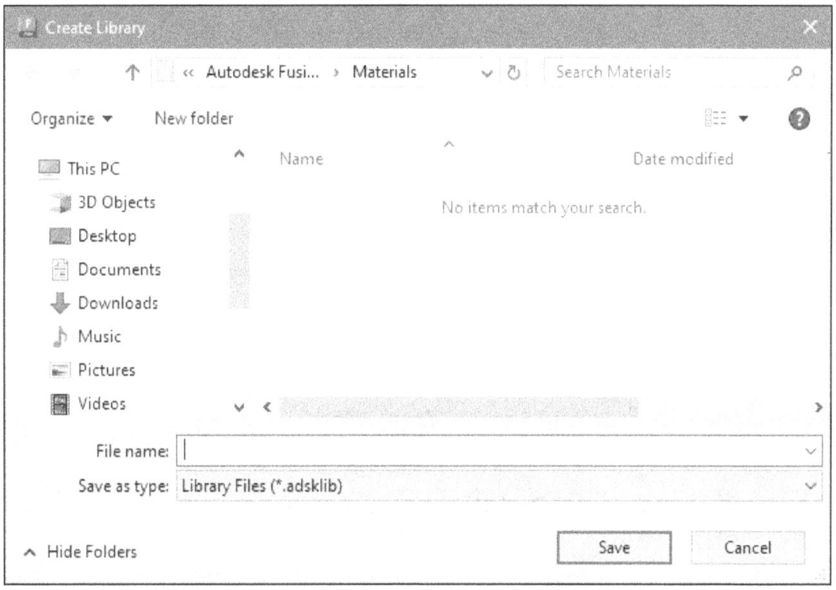

Figure-32. Create Library dialog box

- Specify desired name of the library in **File name** edit box and click on the **Save** button to save the library file at desired location. A new library will be added.
- Select the newly added library and click on the **Create Category** tool from the **Creates, opens, and edits user-defined libraries** drop-down at the bottom left corner of the **Material Browser** dialog box; refer to Figure-33. A new category will be added to the library. Right-click on the category and select **Rename** if you want to rename it as desired.

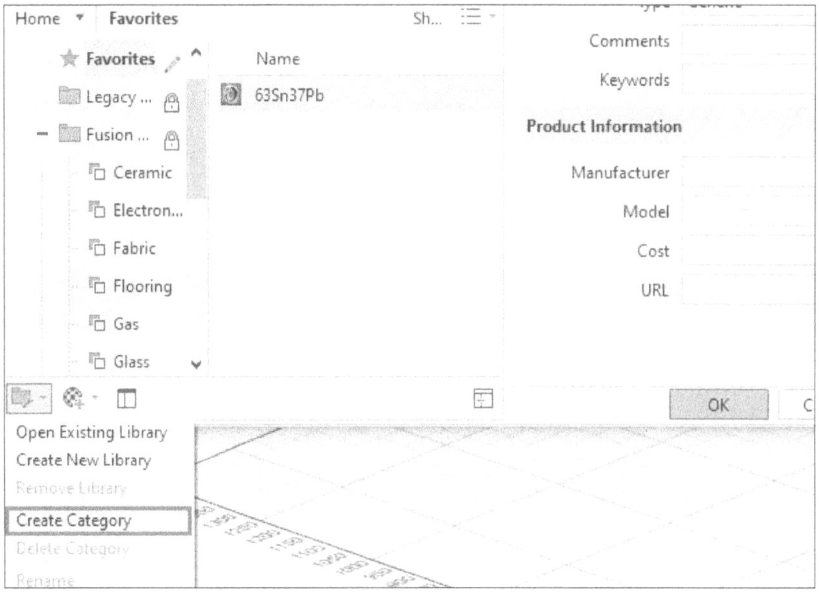

Figure-33. Create Category tool

- Click on the **Create New Material** tool from the **Creates and duplicates materials** drop-down at the bottom in the dialog box as shown in Figure-34. The **Select Material Browser** dialog box will be displayed along with editing options in the **Material Browser** dialog box; refer to Figure-35.

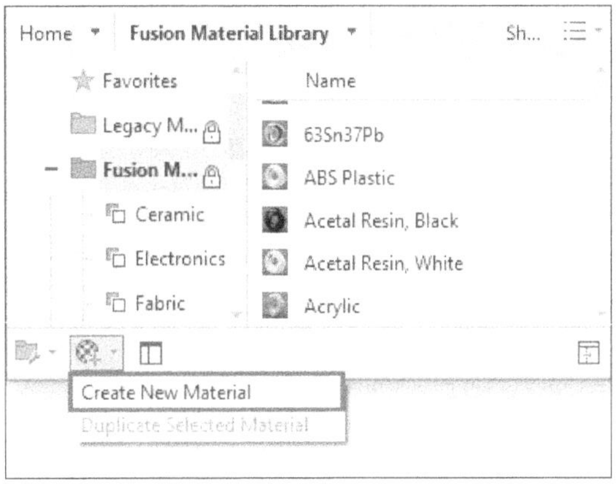

Figure-34. Create New Material tool

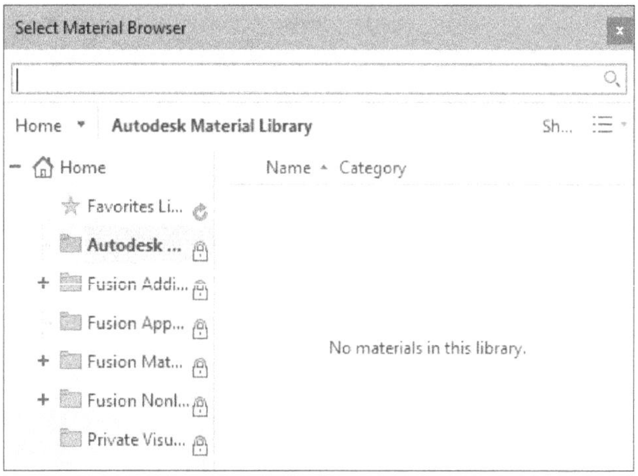

Figure-35. Select Material Browser dialog box

- Close the **Select Material Browser** dialog box and specify desired parameters of material in the right area.
- To apply physical or appearance properties to material, click on the **+** sign next to **Identity** tab in the editing area of the dialog box. A drop-down will be displayed; refer to Figure-36.

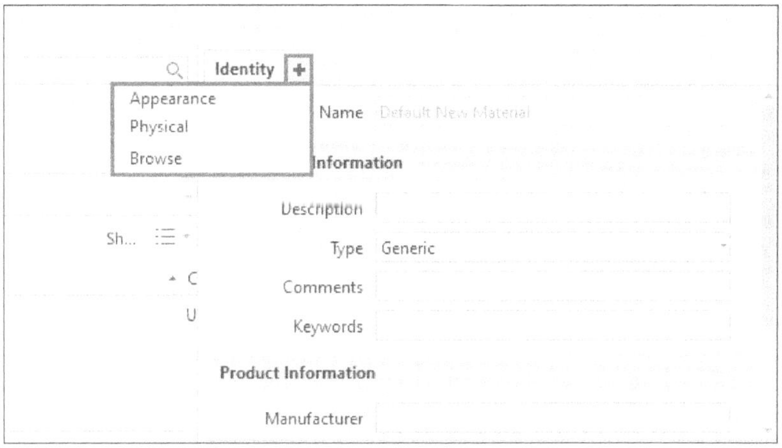

Figure-36. Adding properties of material

- Select desired option from the drop-down (like, we have selected the **Physical** option). The **Asset Browser** dialog box will be displayed; refer to Figure-37.

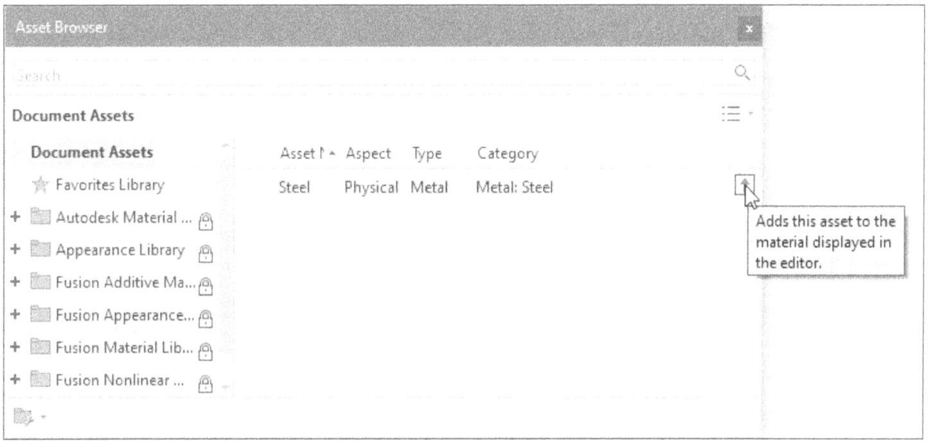

Figure-37. Asset Browser dialog box

- Click on the **Adds this asset to the material displayed in the editor** button as shown in Figure-37 to copy the physical properties of material.
- Close the **Asset Browser** dialog box. The physical properties have been assigned to the new material. Similarly, you can apply **Appearance** properties to the material.
- Click on the **Apply** button. The material will be added in the library.
- Add more materials as required and then close the dialog box. Various parameters related to material are discussed in next topic.

General Parameters of Materials in Autodesk Fusion

There are three categories in which properties of materials are defined in Autodesk Fusion: Identity, Appearance, and Physical. These categories are available as tabs in the **Material Browser** dialog box when you edit a material or create a new material; refer to Figure-38. The parameters specified in these tabs are discussed next.

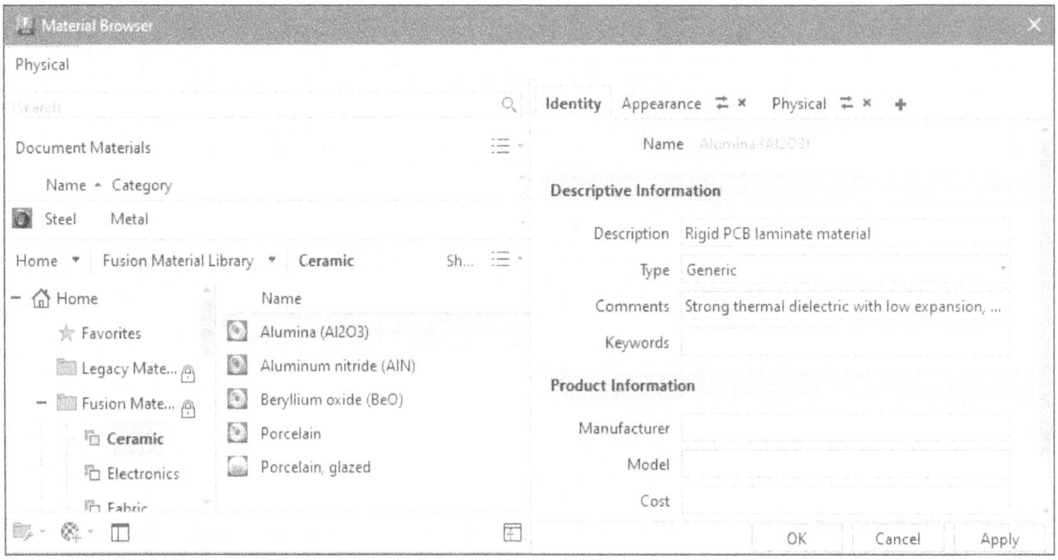

Figure-38. Categories of material properties

Identity Parameters (common for all type of materials)

The parameters of **Identity** tab are used to define description and type of material, manufacturer of material, cost of material, and other related data. These parameters are discussed next.

- Specify desired text in the **Description** edit box to add user-define description of material which can be used to identify general use of the material.
- Select desired option from the **Type** drop-down to define type of the material. Note that the type selected here will define the category in which material will be placed in Material Library.
- Specify desired text in the **Comments** edit box to define comments about the material meant to warn or notify the user of material. Like, material is fragile, material is explosive, and so on.
- Specify desired identification keywords in the **Keywords** edit box separated by comma (,) to enable fast filtering of material in the browser based on specified keywords.
- The options in **Product Information** section of this tab are used when generating reports for production or performing cost calculations. Specify desired text in the **Manufacturer** edit box to define the name of vendor from whom your organization purchases the material.
- Specify desired value in the **Model** edit box to define model number of material if provided by your manufacturer.
- Specify desired value in the **Cost** edit box to define cost of material. Note that value specified in this edit box is in the form of text which is not used for any mathematical formula.
- Specify desired value in the **URL** edit box to define website link for the material.

In Autodesk Fusion, all the materials fall into 5 categories: Metal, Transparent, Opaque, Glazing, and Layered in terms of their appearance. Any modification in appearance of material does not affect the results of analysis but they can make huge difference when generating rendered images of model discussed in Chapter 10 of this book. Some important parameters of all five categories of material appearances are discussed next.

Appearance Tab (For metal type materials)

If you are defining parameters of appearance for a metal type material then options in editing mode of **Material Browser** will be displayed as shown in Figure-39.

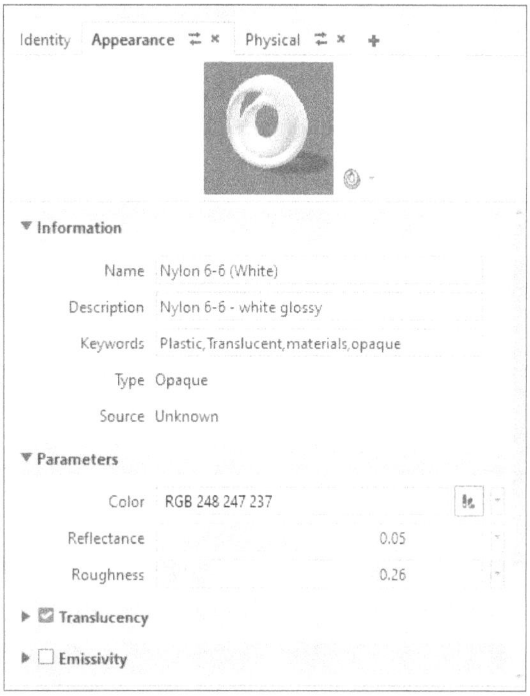

Figure-39. Appearance tab for metal type

- The options in the **Information** section of dialog box are used to define general information about the appearance of material so that user can easily identify the type of material. In this section, you need to specify Name, Description, and keywords for the material.
- The options in the **Parameters** section are used to define color and roughness of surface of material. Click in the field for **Color** option from **Parameters** section. The **Color Picker** dialog box will be displayed. Select desired color by clicking in the color board or by specifying RGB values; refer to Figure-40. After setting color, click on the **OK** button from the dialog box. Using the slider for **Roughness** option, you can define the roughness of surface of material for reflectivity. A high roughness value means less reflective surface.
- Select the **Translucency** check box to parameters that determine how freely light passes through a material. After selecting check box, set desired depth value for the free transmission of light through the material using the Depth slider. Click in the **Weight** selection box and select the preferred color for translucency. This color serves as the tint for the material. You can also choose a Pantone color using the Pantone Color Libraries button next to the Weight selection box. Select the **Emissivity** check box to enable self-illumination of the material under light. Once selected, adjust the Luminance slider to set the brightness of the emitted light in candelas per square meter. Use the Filter Color selection box to choose the color of the self-illumination.

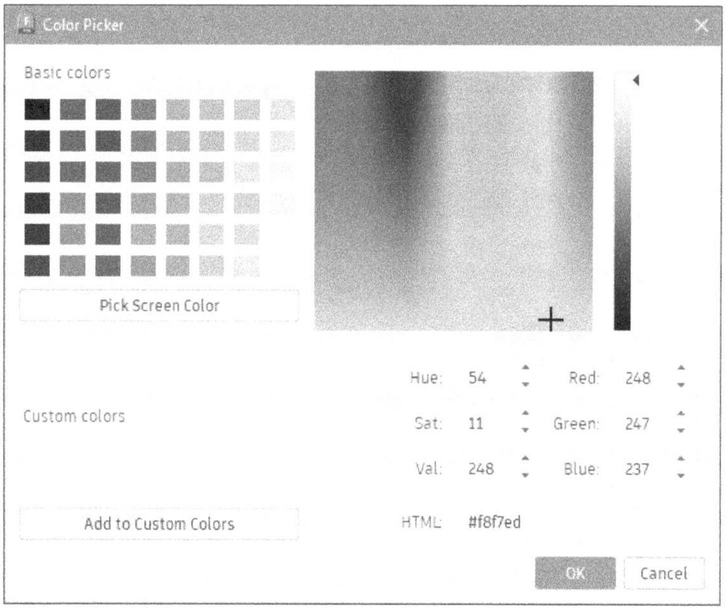

Figure-40. Color Picker dialog box

- Select the **Relief Pattern (Bump)** check box to add bumps in the texture of material. Bumps create an illusion of irregularities generally found on surfaces of real objects; refer to Figure-41. On selecting check box, the **Material Editor Open File** dialog box will be displayed and you will be asked to select an image file of bumps. Select desired image to be projected on material surface for bumps and click on the **Open** button. The appearance of material will be modified accordingly.

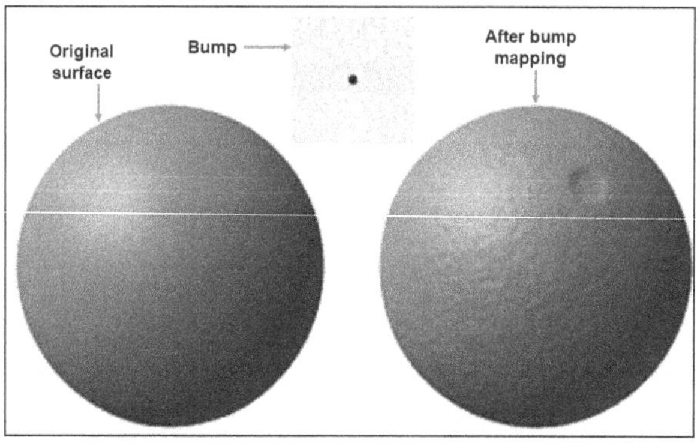

Figure-41. Bump mapping

- Select the **Cutout** check box to make net like texture of material where some portion of material will be transparent and some portion will be opaque; refer to Figure-42. After selecting check box, you need to select an image file with black area to define transparent section of texture as discussed earlier for bump mapping.
- The options in **Advanced Highlight Controls** section are used to anisotropy, orientation of anisotropy effects, highlight color, and so on. Specify desired value using slider of **Anisotropy** option to define enlargement of highlight texture in material. For example, if highlight texture is in the form of circles then anisotropy will transform them into ellipses. Specify desired value using slider of **Orientation** option to define angle at which anisotropy enlargement will occur. Specify desired value in the **Color** selection box to define color by which material will be highlighted. Generally, white color is used to give realistic highlight effect. Select desired option from the **Shape** drop-down to define how reflectivity and highlight effect of material. Select the **Long Falloff** option to produce smoother highlights and select the **Short Falloff** option to produce sharp highlights in material.

Figure-42. Cutout texture

Appearance Tab (For Opaque type materials)

If you are defining parameters of appearance for opaque type material then options in editing mode of **Material Browser** will be displayed as shown in Figure-43. Most of the options in this tab are same as discussed for metals. The other options of this tab are discussed next.

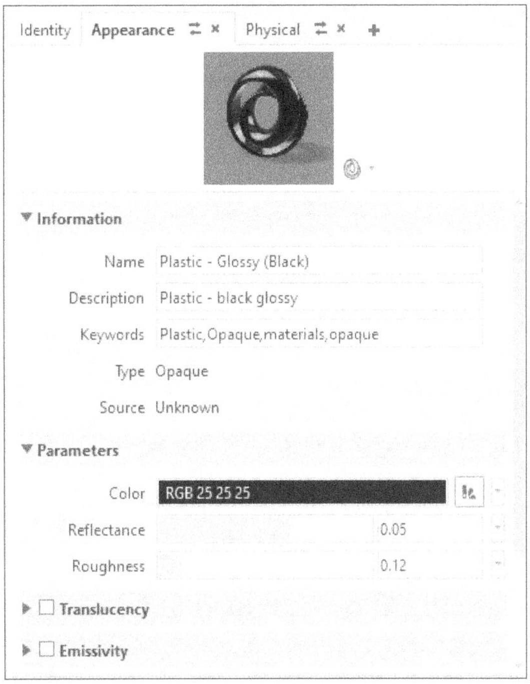

Figure-43. Appearance tab for opaque type

- Specify desired value in **Reflectance** field using slider to define amount of light that will be reflected from surface of material. Note that for opaque materials, reflection will be highest at glazing angle.

- Select the **Translucency** check box to define parameters for free transmission of light through the material. After selecting check box, specify desired value of depth up to which there will be free transmission of light through the material using **Depth** slider. Click in the **Weight** selection box and specify desired color for translucency. This color acts as tinting color for material. You can also select pantone color using **Pantone Color Libraries** button next to **Weight** selection box.
- Select the **Emissivity** check box to apply self illumination of material under light. After selecting check box, set desired value using the **Luminance** slider to define brightness of light emitting from material in candelas per meter square unit. Set desired value in **Filter Color** selection box to define color of self illuminance.

Appearance Tab (For Transparent type materials)

If you are defining parameters of appearance for transparent type material then options in editing mode of **Material Browser** will be displayed as shown in Figure-44. Most of the options in this tab are same as discussed for metals. The other options of this tab are discussed next.

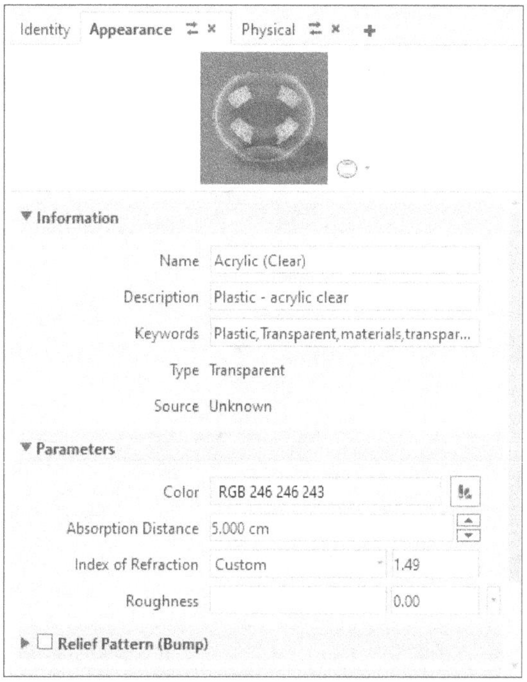

Figure-44. Appearance tab for transparent type

- Specify desired value in the **Absorption Distance** edit box to define distance up to which transmission color will reach through the model after applying transparent material.
- Select desired option from the **Index of Refraction** drop-down to define reference material to be used for defining refraction level of material. After selecting desired option, specify the value of refraction index in the edit box next to drop-down.

Appearance Tab (For Glazing type materials)

If you are defining parameters of appearance for glazing type material then options in editing mode of **Material Browser** will be displayed as shown in Figure-45. Most of the options in this tab are same as discussed for metals. The other options of this tab are discussed next.

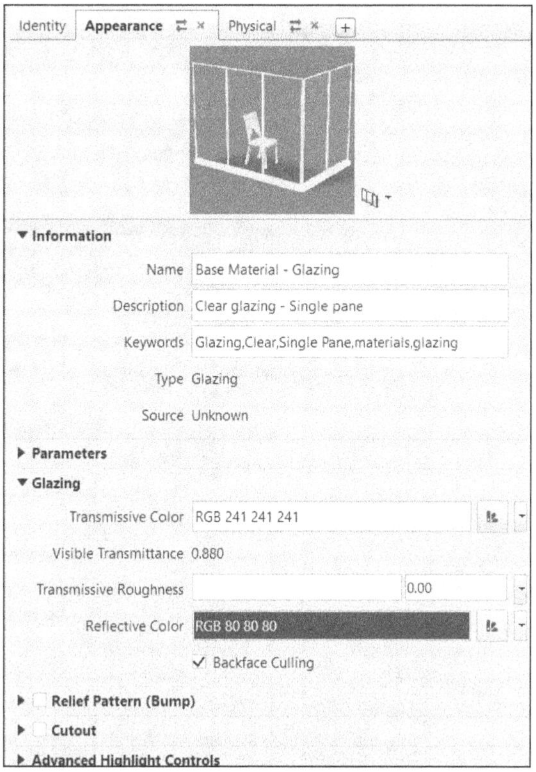

Figure-45. Appearance tab for glazing type

- Specify desired color in the **Transmissive Color** selection box of **Glazing** section to define color which will transmit through the material. Note that other colors will display material as opaque.
- Specify desired value using the **Transmissive Roughness** slider to define how much light transmission will be restricted through the material. A higher roughness value will make the material lesser transmissive.
- Set desired color in **Reflective Color** selection box to define the color which will be reflecting from the surface of objects to which material has been applied.
- Select the **Backface Culling** check box to make only front side of material reflect or transmit light. Rest of the sides of material will be completely transparent.

Appearance Tab (For Layered type materials)

If you are defining parameters of appearance for layered type material then options in editing mode of **Material Browser** will be displayed as shown in Figure-46. Most of the options in this tab are same as discussed for metals. The other options of this tab are discussed next.

- Specify desired colors for base layer, base highlight, and top coat of material. Set the other parameters as discussed earlier.

Physical Tab

The options in **Physical** tab are used to define properties that affect the physical data of material used by various simulations (analyses). Parameters like thermal conductivity, yield strength, young's modulus are some example of physical properties. On selecting this tab in editing mode of **Material Browser**, the options will be displayed as shown in Figure-47. The options in **Information** section are same as discussed earlier. The other options are discussed next.

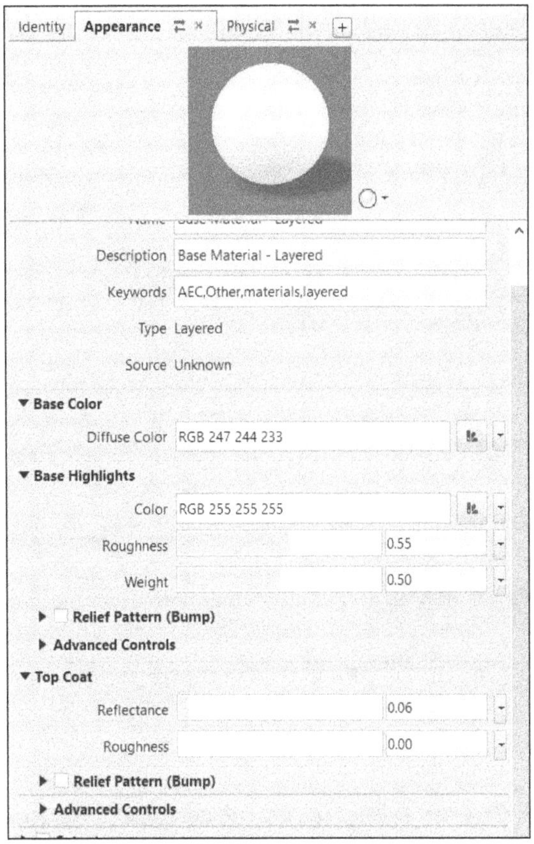

Figure-46. Appearance tab for layered type

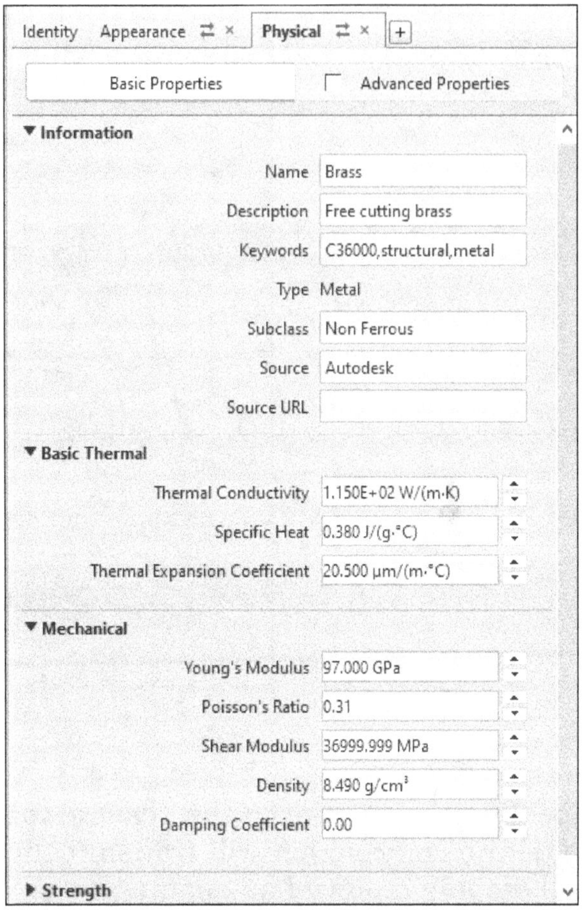

Figure-47. Physical tab for materials

Basic Properties

- The options in **Basic Thermal** section are used to define how much heat can transfer through the material and related parameters. Specify desired value in **Thermal Conductivity** edit box to define the amount of heat in **W** that can be transferred through the unit length of material at unit temperature. Specify desired value in **Specific Heat** edit box to define the amount of heat energy required by unit mass of material to raise its temperature by 1 unit. Specify desired value in the **Thermal Expansion Coefficient** edit box to define the amount of length increase in material due to unit increase in temperature.

- The options in **Mechanical** section are used to define parameters like Young's modulus, Poisson's ratio, and so on. Specify desired value in **Young's Modulus** edit box to define the amount of stress required for deformation per unit strain in the material. This parameter is also called **Modulus of elasticity** and defines relationship between stress and strain of the material. Specify desired value in **Poisson's Ratio** edit box to define relationship between compression applied on one direction of material causing expansion in other perpendicular direction. You can check the role of this parameter by compressing a rectangular piece of sponge. Specify desired value in **Shear Modulus** edit box to define amount of shear stress required for unit shear strain to occur in material. Shear forces cause objects to tilt while their base is fixed. Specify desired value in **Density** edit box to define mass of per unit volume of material. This parameter is used to determine mass of the model. Specify desired value in the **Damping Coefficient** edit box to define a ratio by which oscillations in the material are dissipated. Note that if there is no damping in a spring placed in vacuum then it will keep on oscillating forever once stretched and released. The damping coefficient of material directly affects results of Modal analysis and other frequency related analyses.
- The options in **Strength** section are used to define strength parameters of material up to which the material will be useful for mechanical applications. Specify desired value in the **Yield Strength** edit box to define the amount of stress at which permanent deformation will occur in material. Specify desired value in the **Tensile Strength** edit box to define amount of stress required to break off the material. Tensile strength is also called ultimate tensile strength and ultimate strength of material.

Advanced Properties

Select the **Advanced Properties** check box in **Physical** tab to activate advanced properties of the material and then click on the **Advanced Properties** tab. The options will be displayed as shown in Figure-48. The options in this tab define whether material is linear, non-linear, or hyper elastic. These options are discussed next.

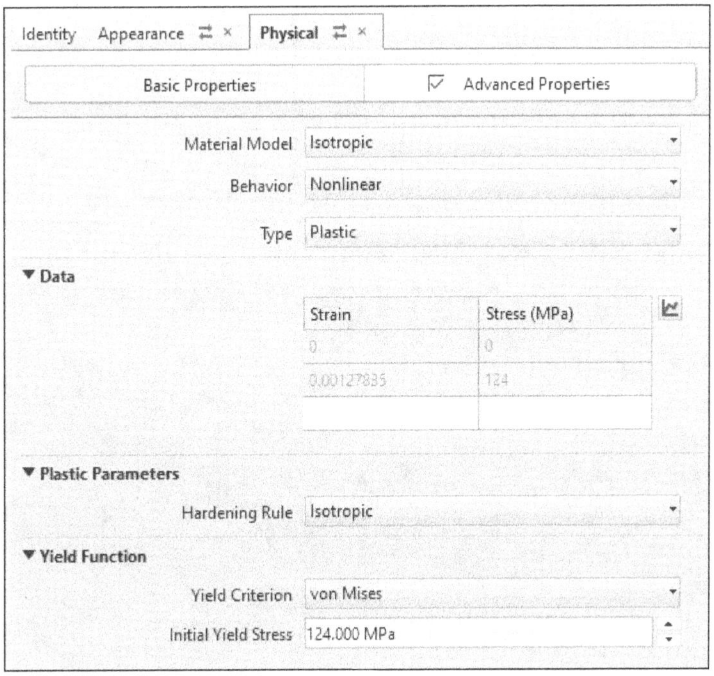

Figure-48. Advanced Properties tab

Isotropic Materials

- Select the **Isotropic** option from the **Material Model** drop-down to define that properties of the material are same in all the direction. It means you can apply 100 N load in any direction of material and it will cause same stress in the material.
- For isotropic materials, three options are available in the **Behavior** drop-down to define whether material behaves linearly to stress or it behaves non-linearly. Select the **Linear** option from the drop-down if your material follows Hooke's Law for given range of analysis loads. On selecting **Linear** option, no other parameters need to be specified. Select the **Nonlinear** option from the **Behavior** drop-down if various inner stresses cause non-linear variation in strain of material; refer to Figure-49. After selecting this option, you need to specify stress and strain data of material in the table of **Data** section. Note that non-linearity can be of three types available in **Type** drop-down which are Elastic non-linearity, Plastic non-linearity, and Elastic-Plastic (Bi-linear) non-linearity; refer to Figure-50. Select the **Elastic** option from **Type** drop-down if your material generates non linear strain for given range of stresses but returns to its original shape when load is removed. Select the **Plastic** option from the **Type** drop-down if your material has non-linear stress-strain curve and do not return to original shape after removing load. Select the **Elastic-Plastic (Bi-linear)** option if material behaves elastically up to specified yield stress value and then behaves plastically up to specified tangent modulus value. Note that Tangent Modulus is equal to Young's Modulus in elastic range of material. Specify other parameters as needed for non-linearity of material. Note that one of the cause for using Non-linear static analysis in Autodesk Fusion is non-linearity of material selected for model.

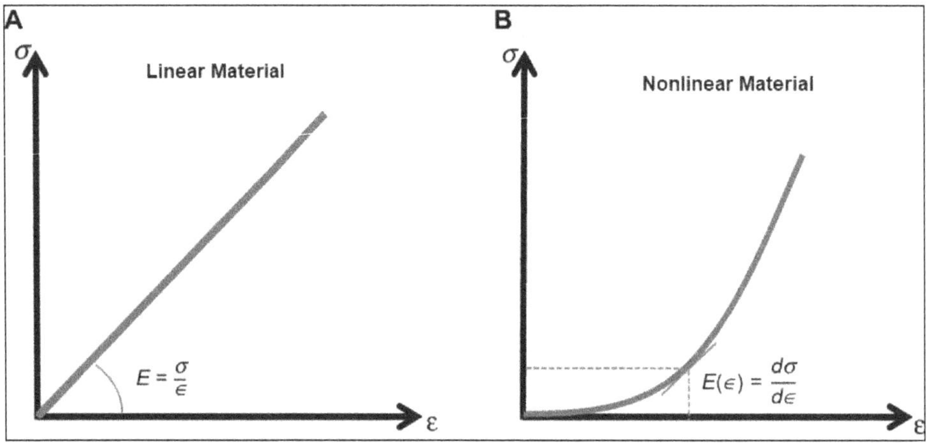

Figure-49. Linear vs non linear materials

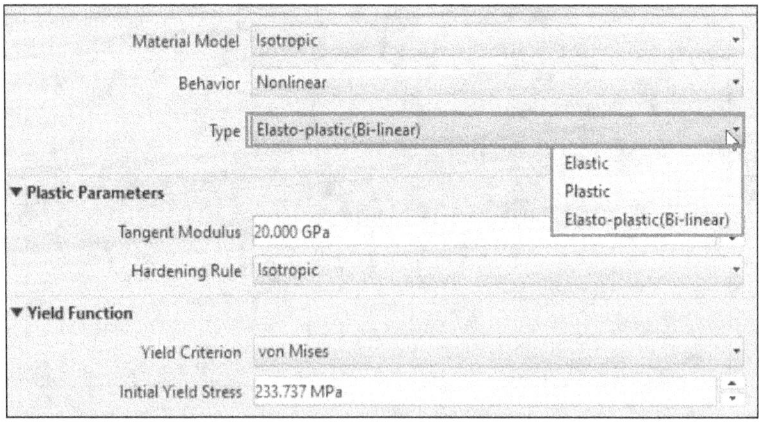

Figure-50. Nonlinearity types

- A material can be non-linear due to change in temperature as well. For such materials, select the **Temperature Dependent** option from the **Behavior** drop-down after selecting Isotropic material model option. The options in dialog box will be displayed as shown in Figure-51. Double-click in the empty fields of tables to specify the behavior of material for different temperature values.

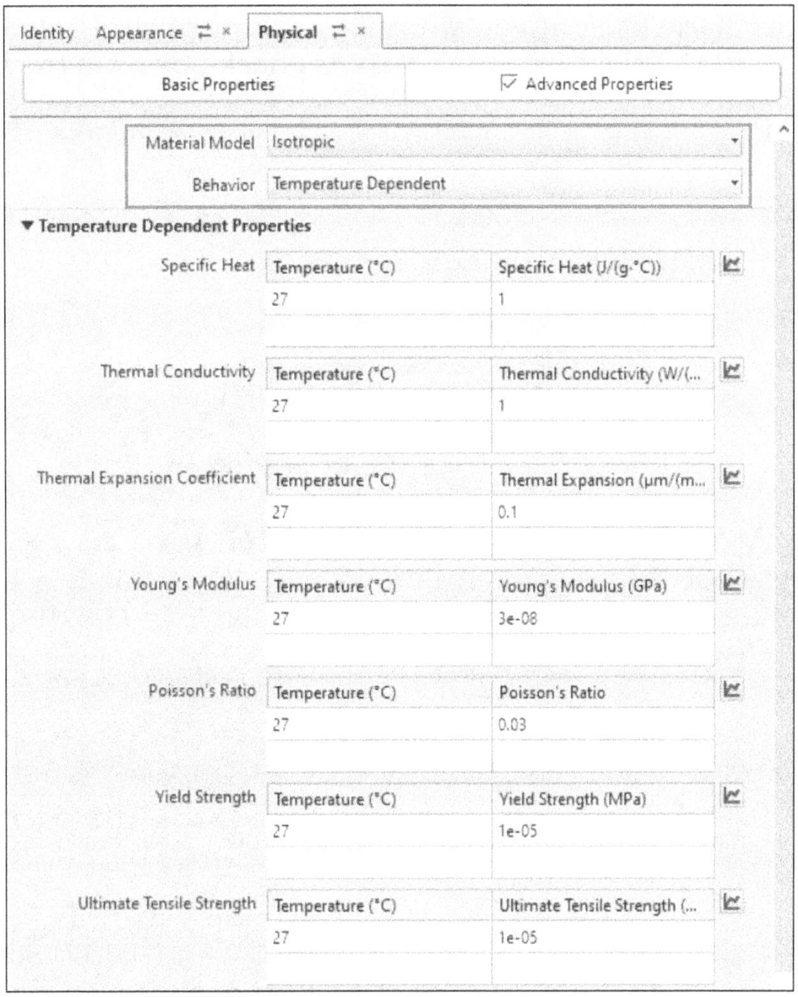

Figure-51. Temperature dependent isotropic material

- Select the **Hyperelastic** option from the **Material Model** drop-down to define that material does not follow standard stress-strain relationship. A hyperelastic material gets its stress-strain relationship from strain energy density function. More detail about this material is beyond the scope of this book but you can assume rubber like materials to be hyperelastic and follow Mooney Rivlin equation for strain less than 100% ; refer to Figure-52.

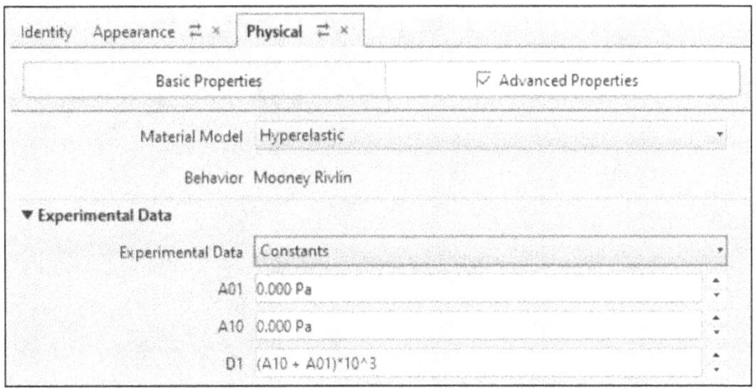

Figure-52. Hyperelastic material type

- After specify desired parameters, click on the **OK** button to apply modifications to material.

Displaying Study Material Colors

By default, appearance assigned to the part in the **Design workspace** is displayed in the **Simulation workspace**. If you want to display appearance of study material then select the **Display Study Material Colors** check box from the **MATERIALS** drop-down; refer to Figure-53.

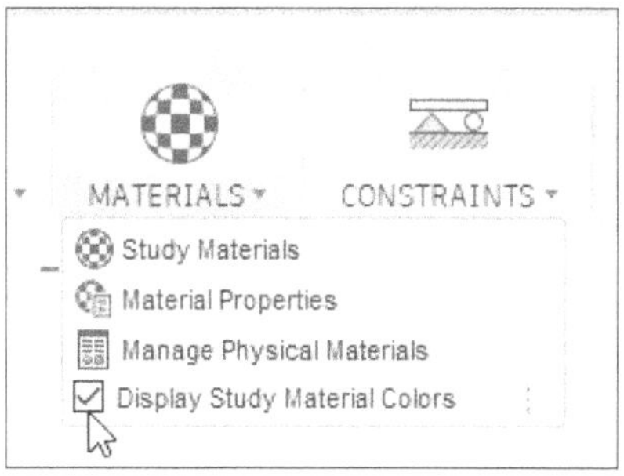

Figure-53. Display Study Material Colors check box

APPLYING CONSTRAINTS

Constraints are used to restrict motion of part when load is applied to form equilibrium. The tools to apply constraints are available in **CONSTRAINTS** drop-down in the **Toolbar**; refer to Figure-54.

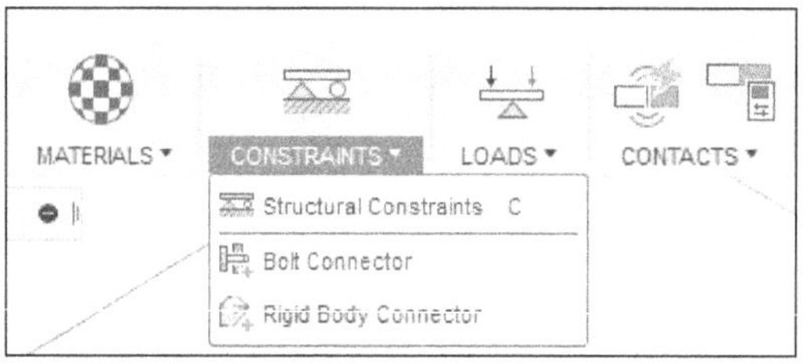

Figure-54. CONSTRAINTS drop down

The procedure to apply different type of constraints are discussed next.

Applying Structural Constraints

The structural constraints are used to apply different type of structural constraints like fixed, pin, frictionless, and so on. The procedure to apply structural constraint is given next.

- Click on the **Structural Constraints** tool from the **CONSTRAINTS** drop-down in the **Toolbar**; refer to Figure-55. The **STRUCTURAL CONSTRAINTS** dialog box will be displayed; refer to Figure-56.

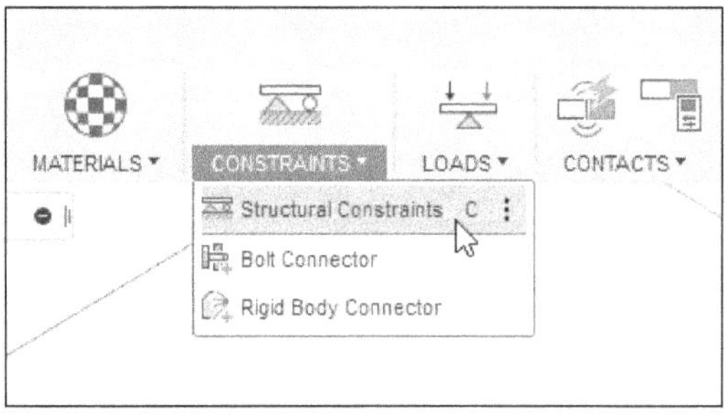

Figure-55. Structural Constraints tool

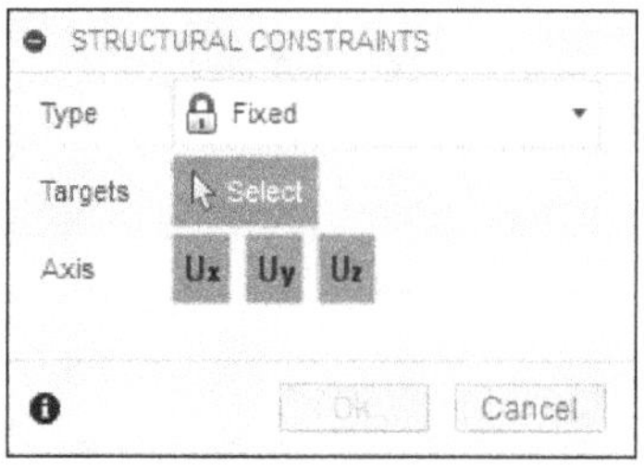

Figure-56. STRUCTURAL CONSTRAINTS dialog box

Fixed Constraint

- Select **Fixed** option from **Type** drop-down in the **STRUCTURAL CONSTRAINTS** dialog box if you want to fix selected faces/edges/vertices of the part.
- Select the face/edge/vertex that you want to be fixed.
- Select desired axis button from the **Axis** section. Like, select the **Ux** button if you want to restrict movement along X axis. By default, all the three buttons are selected and hence the movement along all the three axes is restricted. Refer to Figure-57.

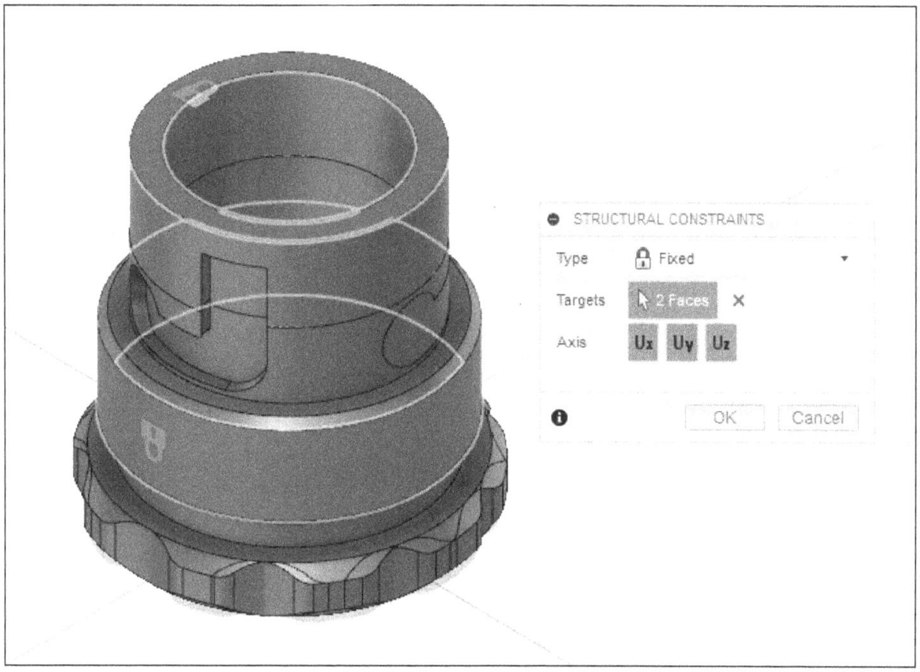

Figure-57. Faces selected for fixed constraint

- Click on the **OK** button from the dialog box to fix selected geometries.

Pin Constraint

The Pin constraint is used to restrict radial, axial, and tangential movement of a cylindrical part. The procedure to use this constraint is given next.

- Select the **Pin** option from the **Type** drop-down in the **STRUCTURAL CONSTRAINTS** dialog box. The options in the dialog box will be displayed as shown in Figure-58.

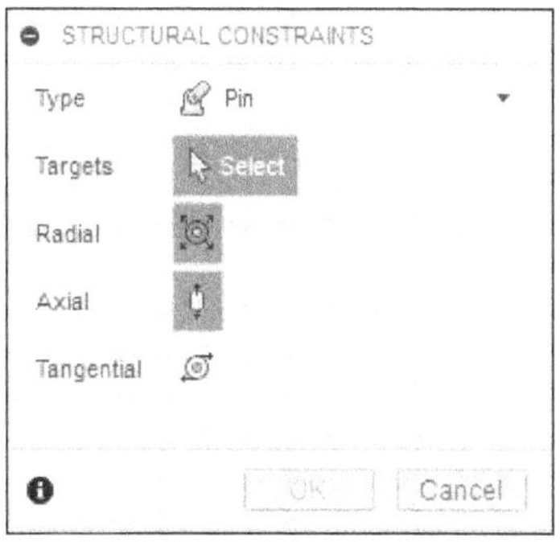

Figure-58. STRUCTURAL CONSTRAINTS dialog box with Pin option selected

- Select the cylindrical face on which you want to apply pin constraint; refer to Figure-59.

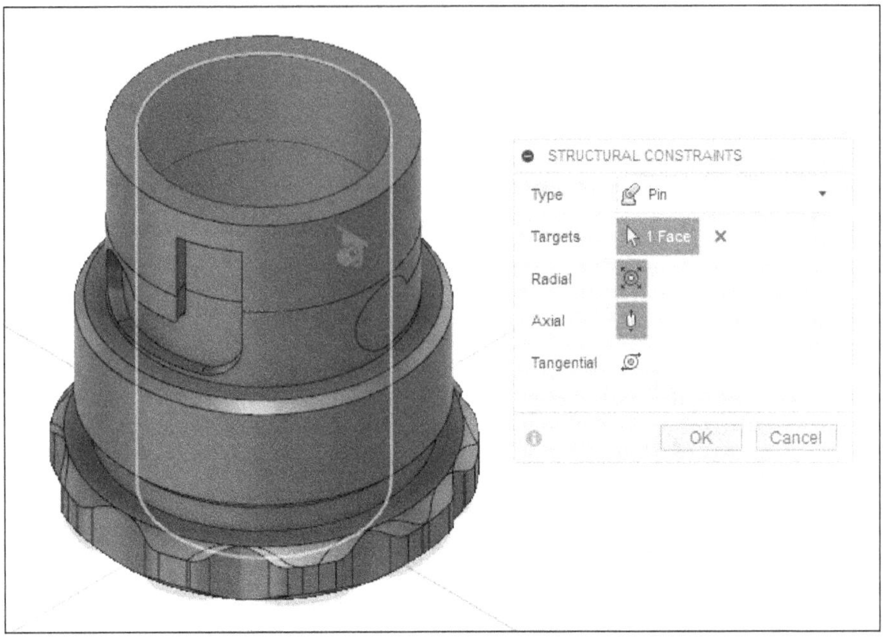

Figure-59. Face selected to apply pin constraint

- Select desired buttons to restrict the respective motion. For example, select the **Radial** button to restrict radial motion.
- Similarly, specify other parameters as required and click on the **OK** button to complete the process.

Frictionless Constraint

The Frictionless constraint is used to restrict the movement of object perpendicular to selected face. However, the object is free to move in the plane as if it is sliding on the face. The procedure to apply this constraint is given next.

- Select the **Frictionless** option from the **Type** drop-down in the **STRUCTURAL CONSTRAINTS** dialog box. The options in the dialog box will be displayed as shown in Figure-60.

Figure-60. STRUCTURAL CONSTRAINTS dialog box with Frictionless option selected

- Select desired face on which you want to apply the frictionless constraint; refer to Figure-61.

Figure-61. Face selected to apply frictionless constraint

- Click on the **OK** button to exit.

Prescribed Displacement Constraint

The **Prescribed Displacement** constraint is used to apply fixed constraint at specified displacement. The procedure to use this constraint is given next.

- Select the **Prescribed Displacement** option from **Type** drop-down in the **STRUCTURAL CONSTRAINTS** dialog box. The options in the dialog box will be displayed as shown in Figure-62 and you will be asked to select the face/edge/vertex.

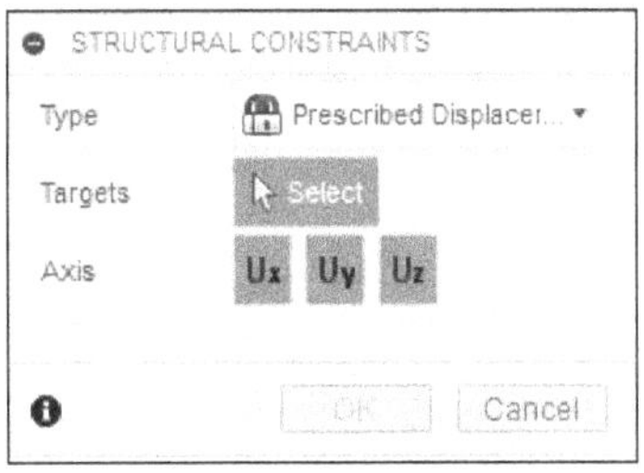

Figure-62. STRUCTURAL CONSTRAINTS dialog box with Prescribed Displacement option selected

- Select desired geometry on which you want to apply constraint. The **STRUCTURAL CONSTRAINTS** dialog box will be updated; refer to Figure-63.

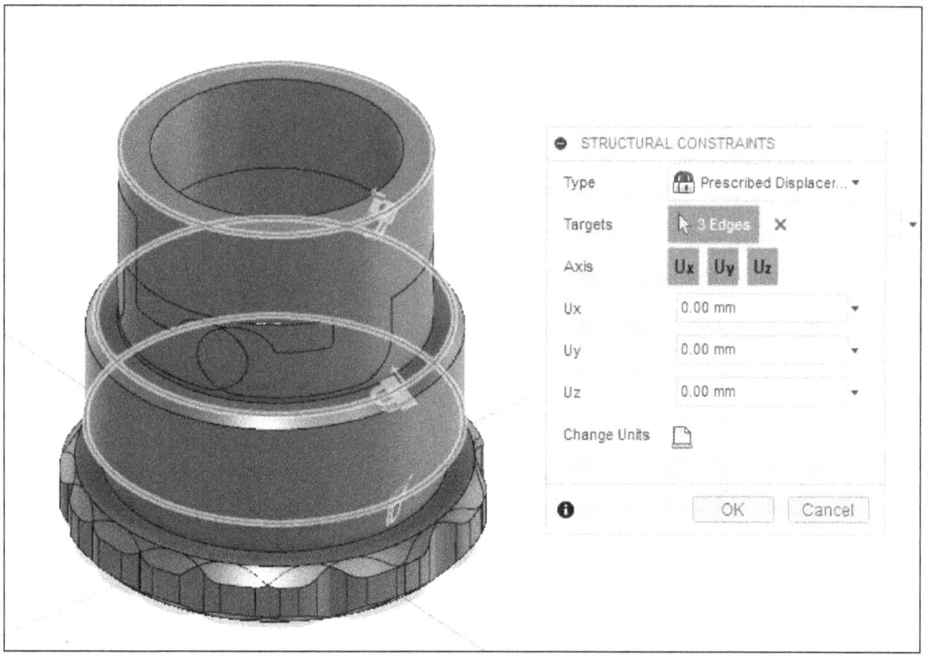

Figure-63. Edges selected to apply prescribed displacement constraint

- Specify desired parameters and click on the **OK** button to exit the tool.

Remote Constraint

The **Remote** constraint is used to apply fixed constraint linked to a remote location. The procedure to use this constraint is given next.

- Select the **Remote** option from the **Type** drop-down of the **STRUCTURAL CONSTRAINTS** dialog box and you will be asked to select faces to be constrained.
- Select desired face from the model. The options will be displayed as shown in Figure-64.

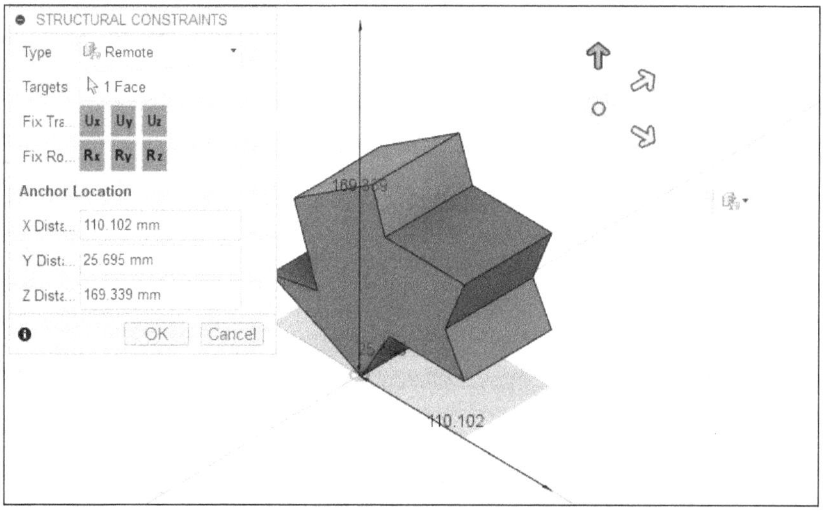

Figure-64. Remote constraint options

- Select desired buttons for **Fix Translation** and **Fix Rotation** options to constraint movements for respective translation and rotation axes.
- Click in the **X Distance**, **Y Distance**, and **Z Distance** edit boxes to define the anchor point location from where the constraint is being applied on selected face/body.
- After specifying desired parameters, click on the **OK** button from the dialog box.

Applying Bolt Connector Constraint

Bolt connector is used to apply connection similar to bolt fastener connection in assemblies. Note that bolt connector represents the nut-bolt connection or threaded nut connection mathematically. The procedure to apply bolt connector is given next.

- Click on the **Bolt Connector** tool from the **CONSTRAINTS** drop-down in the **Toolbar**; refer to Figure-65. The **BOLT CONNECTOR** dialog box will be displayed; refer to Figure-66.

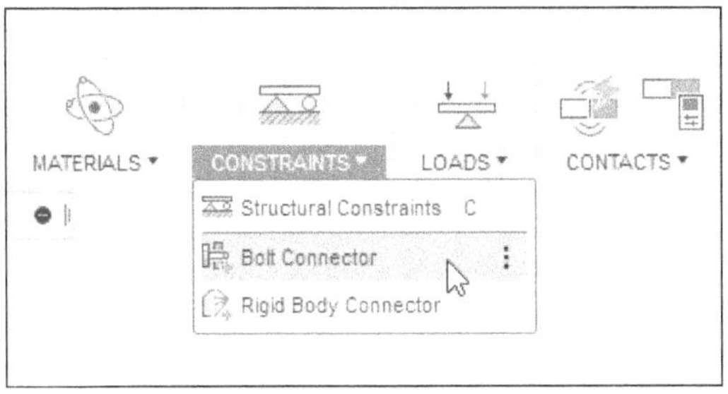

Figure-65. Bolt Connector tool

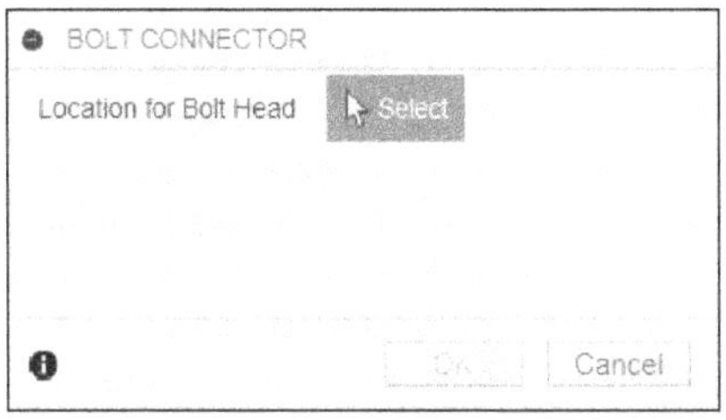

Figure-66. BOLT CONNECTOR dialog box

- The **Select** button of **Location for Bolt Head** option is active by default.
- Select the round edge of the part where you want the bolt head to be placed. The **BOLT CONNECTOR** dialog box will be updated; refer to Figure-67.

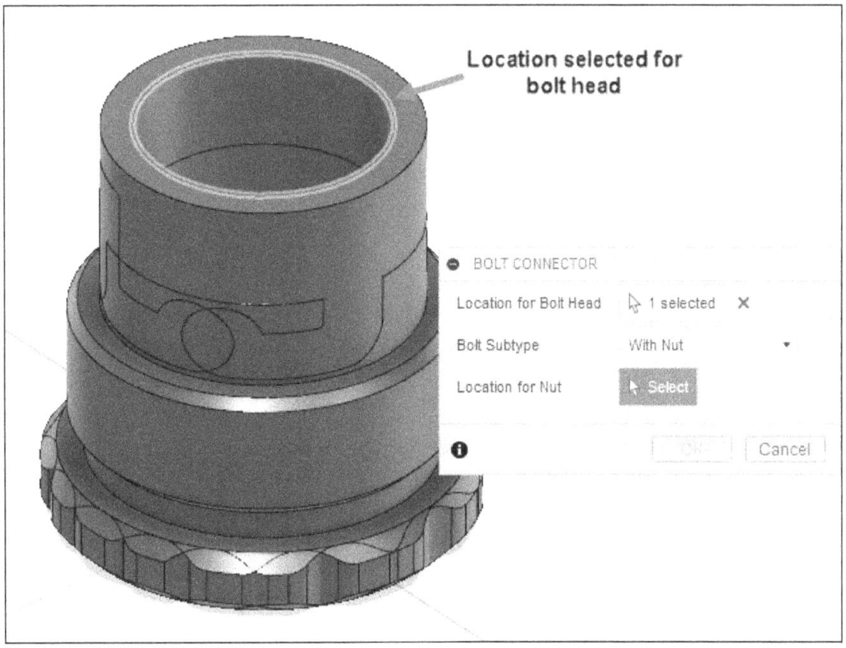

Figure-67. Updated BOLT CONNECTOR dialog box after selecting location for bolt head

Bolt Fastener with Nut

- Select the **With Nut** option from the **Bolt Subtype** drop-down if you want to create a bolt-nut fastener constraint. You will be asked to select the round edge where nut will be placed.
- Select desired edge. The **BOLT CONNECTOR** dialog box will be updated with preview of bolt-nut fastener; refer to Figure-68.
- Select the **Head Washer** and **Nut Washer** check boxes to create washers with bolt head and nut, respectively.
- Specify the parameters like bolt diameter, bolt washer, nut washer, pre-load, and so on in respective sections. Click on the **OK** button to create the constraint.

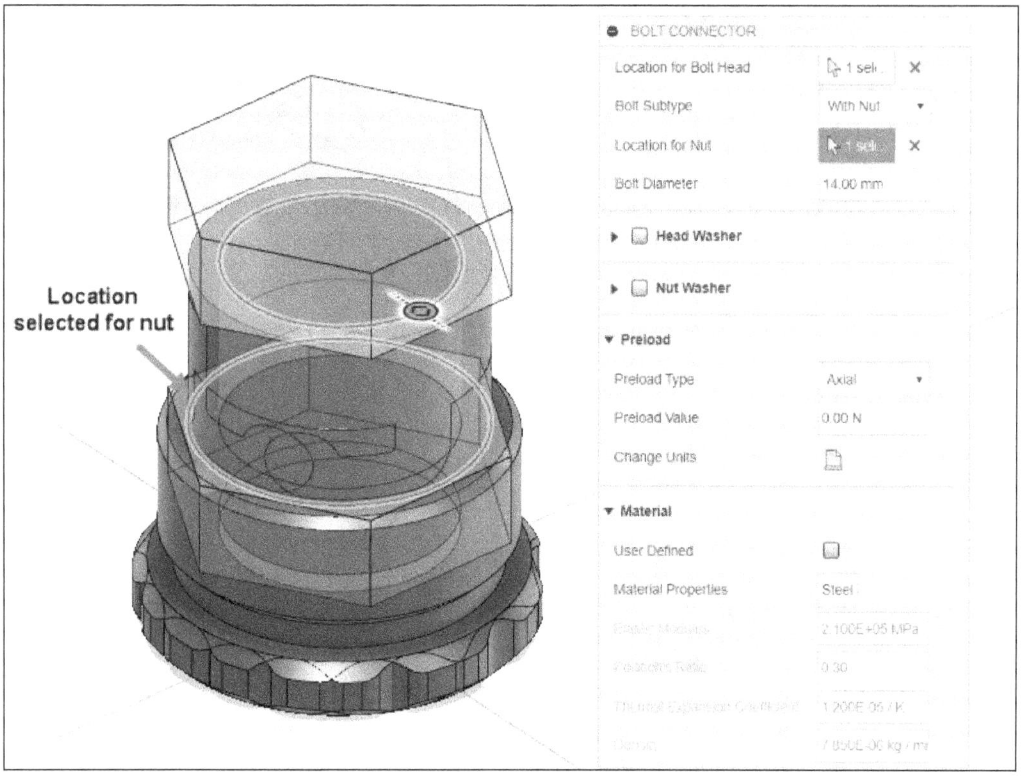

Figure-68. Preview of bolt nut fastener after selecting location for nut

Bolt with Threaded Hole

- Select the **Threaded Hole** option from the **Bolt Subtype** drop-down if you want to create threaded bolted connection. You will be asked to select face to be threaded.
- Select desired face. Preview of the bolt will be displayed; refer to Figure-69.

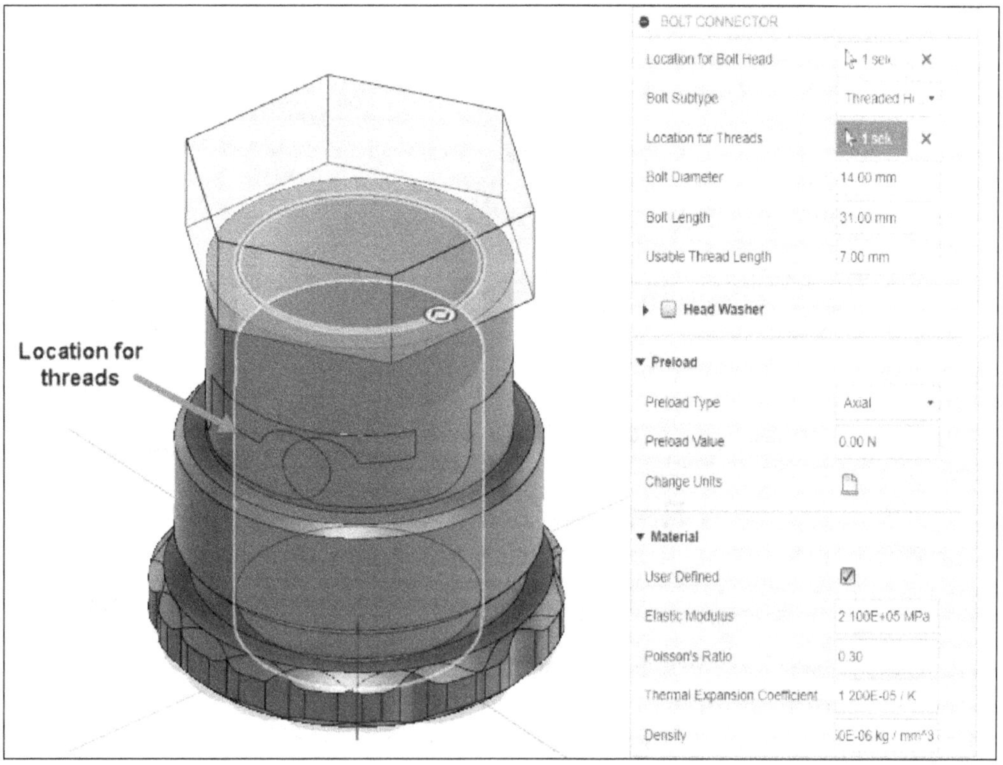

Figure-69. Preview of threaded bolt

- Set desired parameters for preloading of the nut/bolt in the **Preload** section of **PropertyManager**.
- Specify the parameters as required and click on the **OK** button to exit the tool.

Rigid Body Connector Constraint

The Rigid Body Connector constraint is used where a vertex of one component is to be rigidly connected with face, edge, or vertex of other body. The procedure to use this constraint is given next.

- Click on the **Rigid Body Connector** tool from the **CONSTRAINTS** drop-down in the **Toolbar**; refer to Figure-70. The **RIGID BODY CONNECTOR** dialog box will be displayed; refer to Figure-71.

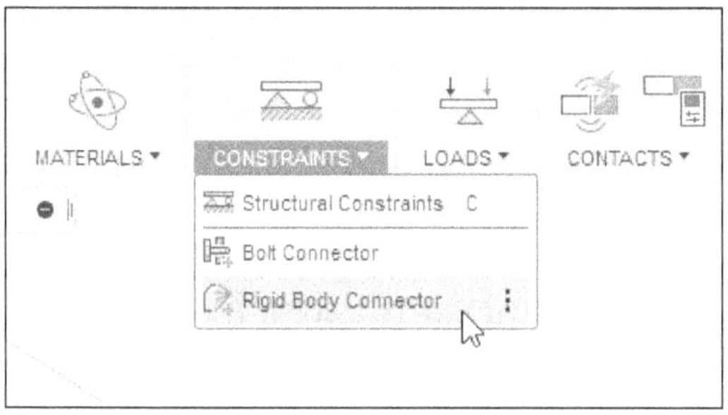

Figure-70. Rigid Body Connector tool

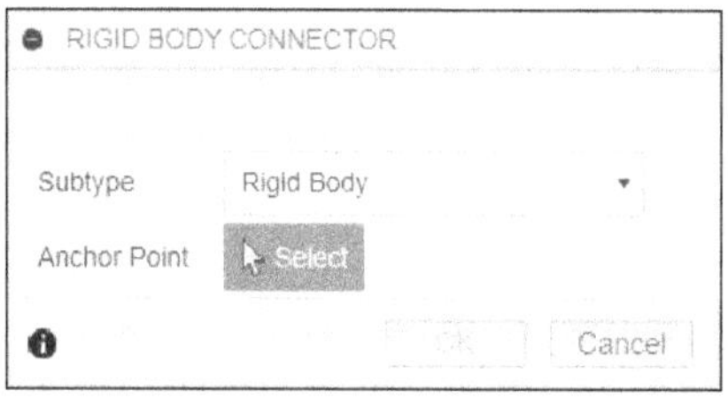

Figure-71. RIGID BODY CONNECTOR dialog box

- Select desired vertex that you want to be anchor point for connection on the first body/component. You will be asked to select dependent entities.
- Select the points/faces/edges that are dependent on the anchor point for movement; refer to Figure-72.

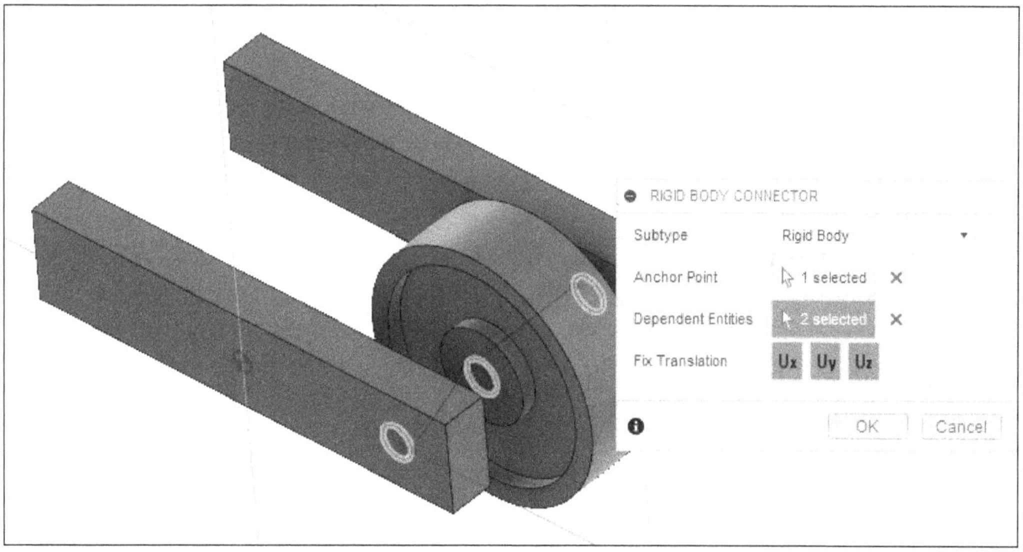

Figure-72. Rigid Body Connector constraint

- Similarly, you can use the **Interpolation** option from the **Subtype** drop-down to create rigid connection with translational and rotational constraining.

APPLYING LOADS

Loads in Fusion are the representation of forces and loads applied on the part in real world. The tools to apply loads are available in the **LOADS** drop-down in the **Toolbar**; refer to Figure-73. Various tools in this drop-down are discussed next.

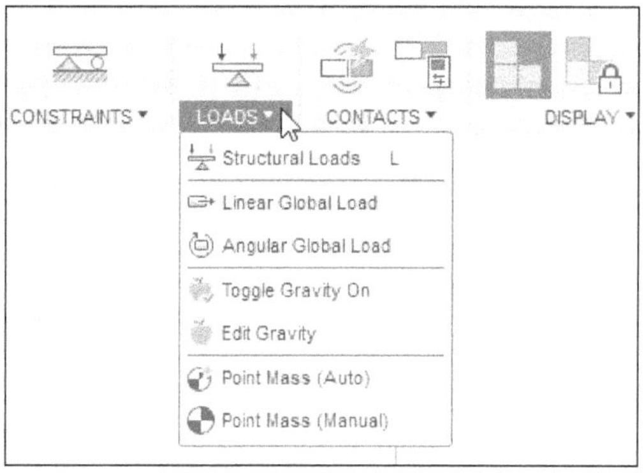

Figure-73. LOADS drop down

Applying Structural Loads

There are various structural loads that can be applied on the object like force, pressure, moment, remote force, bearing load, and hydrostatic pressure. The procedure to apply different loads are discussed next.

- Click on the **Structural Loads** tool from the **LOADS** drop-down in the **Toolbar**. The **STRUCTURAL LOADS** dialog box will be displayed; refer to Figure-74.

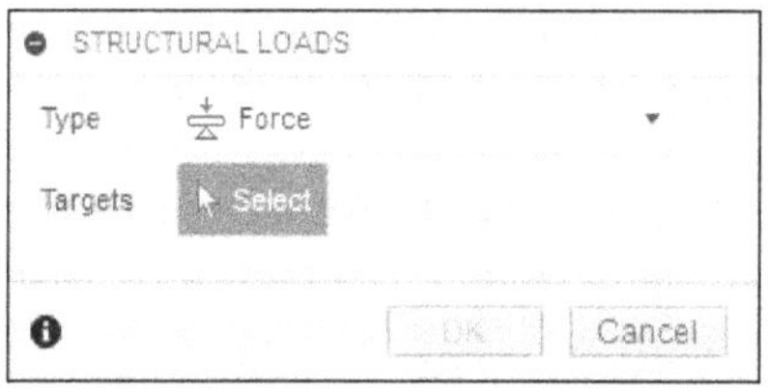

Figure-74. STRUCTURAL LOADS dialog box

Applying Force

- By default, **Force** option is selected in the **Type** drop-down of **STRUCTURAL LOADS** dialog box. If not selected by default in your case then select the **Force** option from the **Type** drop-down. You will be asked to select face/edge/point on which force is to be applied.
- Select desired face/edge/point. The options in the **STRUCTURAL LOADS** dialog box will be modified according to geometry selected; refer to Figure-75.
- Select desired **Direction Type** button from the dialog box. If you have selected the **Normal** button then force will be applied perpendicular to the selected face. You can use the **Flip** button below it to reverse direction of force; refer to Figure-76.

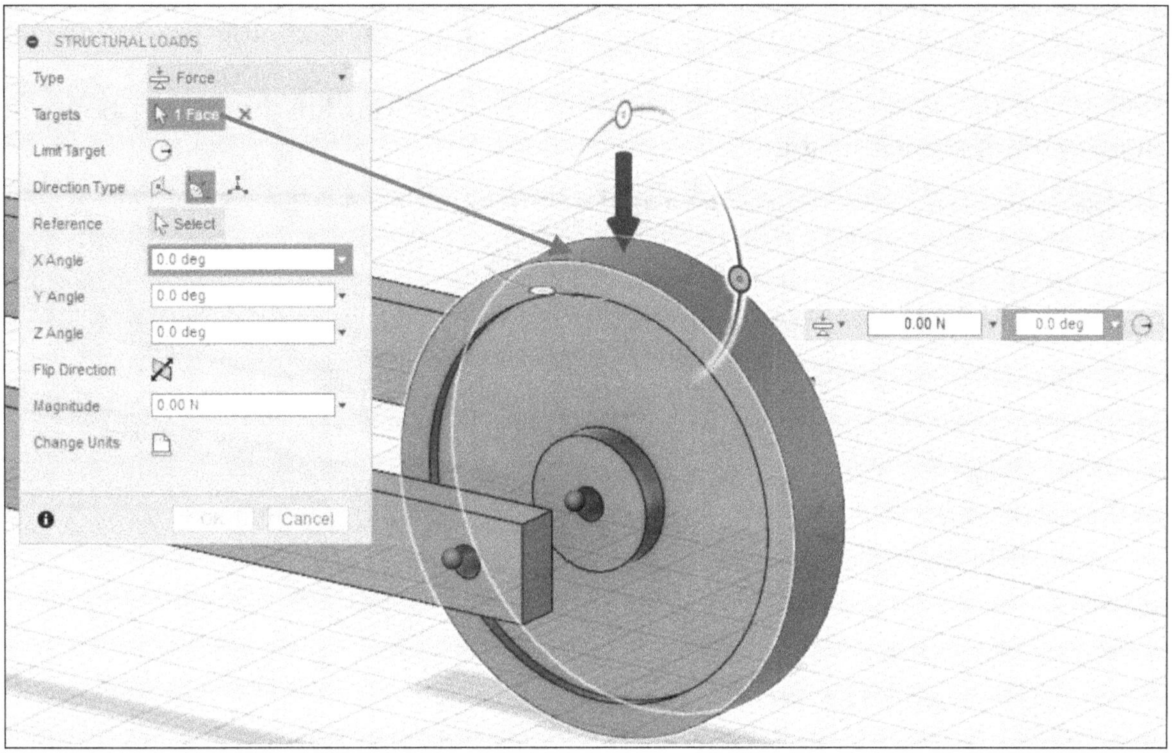

Figure-75. Face selected to apply force

- Select the **Angle (delta)** button from the **Direction Type** section of the dialog box if you want to apply force at some angle; refer to Figure-75. Specify desired angle values in the **X Angle**, **Y Angle**, and **Z Angle** edit boxes. Select the **Flip Direction** button to reverse the direction if required. Note that the **Limit Target** button is also available in the dialog box. Select this button and specify the radius range in which the force will be applied.
- Select the **Vectors** button from the **Direction Type** section if you want to specify force value along each vector direction.
- To change the unit of load, click on the **Change Units** button if you want to change the unit for load.
- Click on the **OK** button from the dialog box to apply the load.

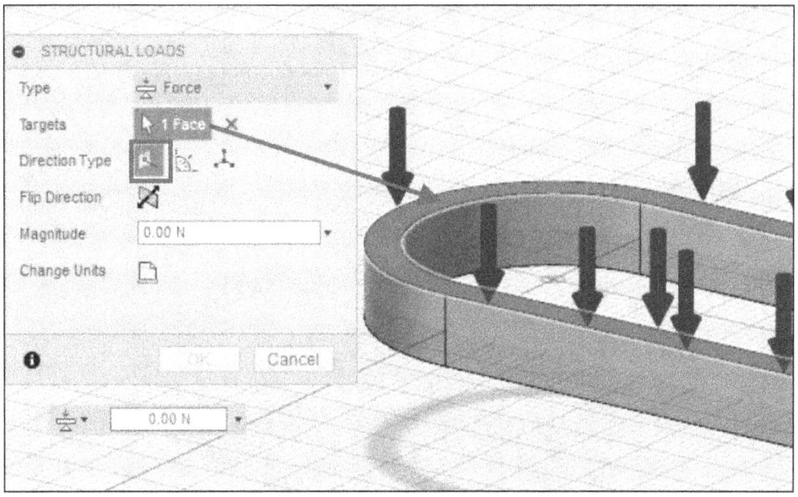

Figure-76. Force applied with Normal button selected

Applying Pressure

- Select the **Pressure** option from the **STRUCTURAL LOADS** dialog box. You will be asked to select the faces to apply pressure.
- Select the face(s) to apply pressure force. The options in the dialog box will be displayed as shown in Figure-77.

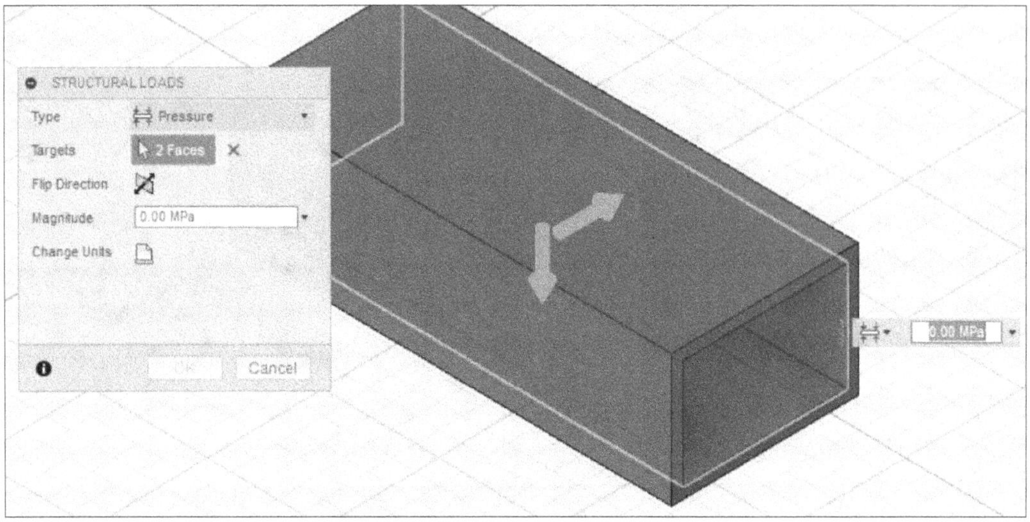

Figure-77. STRUCTURAL LOADS dialog box with pressure option

- Specify desired value of pressure in the **Magnitude** edit box. If you want to change the unit then select the **Change Units** button and specify desired value in the edit box displayed.
- Click on the **OK** button from the dialog box to apply the pressure load.

Applying Moment

- Select the **Moment** option from the **STRUCTURAL LOADS** dialog box. You will be asked to select the faces to apply moment.
- Select desired face. The options in the dialog box will be updated; refer to Figure-78.

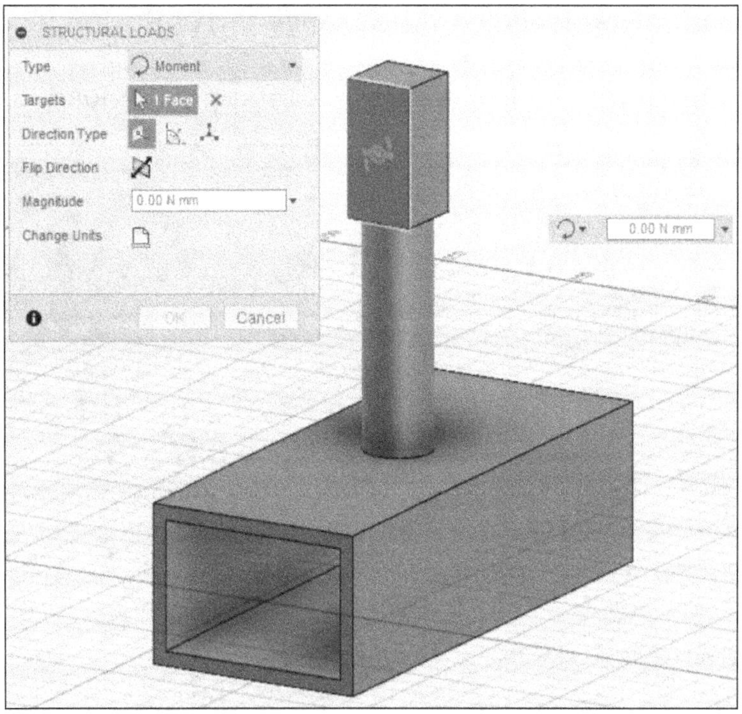

Figure-78. STRUCTURAL LOADS dialog box with moment option

- Set desired value of moment in the **Magnitude** edit box.
- Set other parameters as discussed earlier and click on the **OK** button to apply moment load.

Applying Bearing Load

Bearing load is the force exerted by bearing on round face of the part. The procedure to apply bearing load is given next.

- Select the **Bearing Load** option from the **Type** drop-down in the **STRUCTURAL LOADS** dialog box. You will be asked to select the round face on which bearing load is to be applied.
- Select desired face. The options in the dialog box will be displayed as shown in Figure-79.

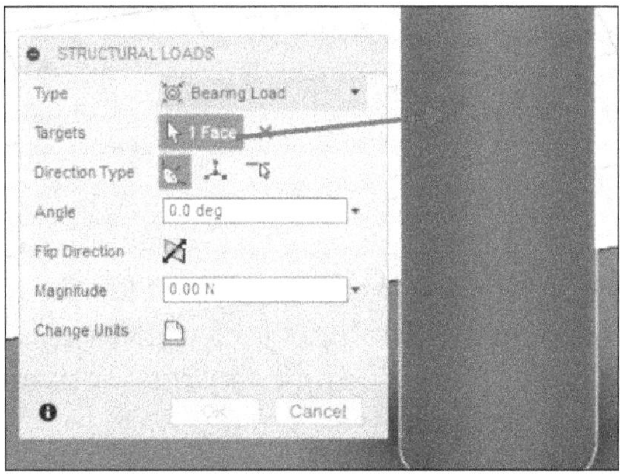

Figure-79. STRUCTURAL LOADS dialog box with Bearing Load option

- Specify desired parameters as discussed earlier. Note that bearing load is a directional force and applicable on only half of the full 360 cylindrical face.
- After specifying the parameters, click on the **OK** button to apply bearing load.

Applying Remote Force

The remote force is used to represent effect of load on selected faces which was applied at different location; refer to Figure-80. The procedure to apply load is given next.

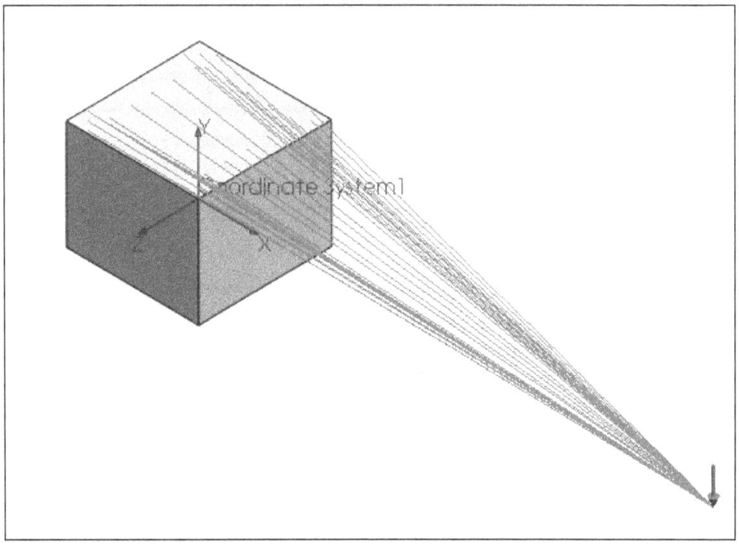

Figure-80. Remote load applied

- Select the **Remote Force** option from the **Type** drop-down in the **STRUCTURAL LOADS** dialog box. You will be asked to select a location to apply force.
- Select desired face/edge/point. The options in the dialog box will be displayed as shown in Figure-81.

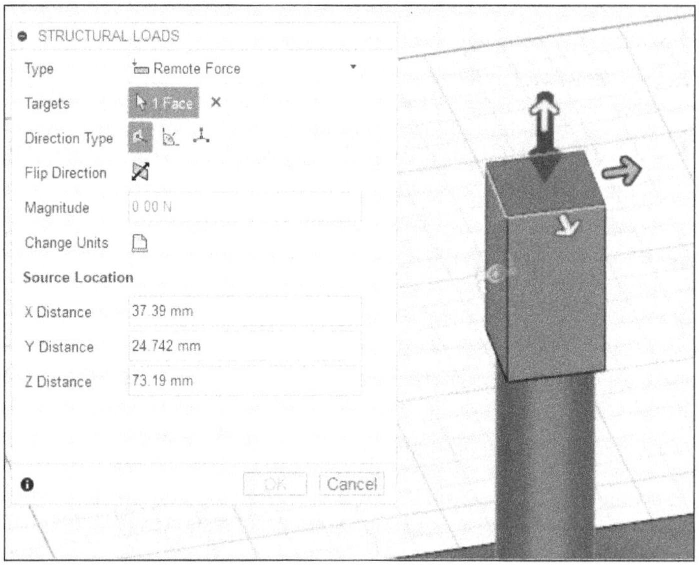

Figure-81. STRUCTURAL LOADS dialog box with Remote Force option

- Set the X, Y, and Z distances of the load location in the **X Distance**, **Y Distance**, and **Z Distance** edit boxes of the dialog box, respectively.
- Specify other parameters as discussed earlier.
- Click on the **OK** button to apply remote force.

Similarly, you can apply remote moment by using the **Remote Moment** option from the **Type** drop-down in the **STRUCTURAL LOADS** dialog box.

Applying Hydrostatic Pressure

Hydrostatic pressure is a linearly varying pressure exerted by fluid on the surface of part. This force is applicable when the part is in contact with high volume of fluid. The procedure to apply this load is given next.

- Select the **Hydrostatic Pressure** option from the **Type** drop-down in the **STRUCTURAL LOADS** dialog box. You will be asked to select the face(s) to apply hydrostatic pressure.

Note that if you are applying hydrostatic pressure for the first time then a message box will be displayed prompting you to activate gravity. Activate the gravity by clicking on the **OK** button.

- Select desired face(s). The options in the dialog box will be displayed as shown in Figure-82.

Figure-82. STRUCTURAL LOADS dialog box with Hydrostatic Pressure option

- Click on the **Select** button for **Select Surface Point** section in the dialog box and select desired point up to which the fluid is filled in the system.
- Specify desired offset value for fluid surface point in the **Offset Distance** edit box.
- Select desired fluid type from the **Fluid Type** drop-down. If you have a different fluid which is not available in drop-down then select the **Custom** option and specify the density of fluid in the **Density** edit box.
- Click on the **OK** button after specifying desired values to apply load.

Applying Linear Global Load (Acceleration)

Linear Global Load is the applied when the whole system is under acceleration like an object placed in an accelerating car. The procedure to apply linear global load is given next.

- Click on the **Linear Global Load** tool from the **LOADS** drop-down in the **Toolbar**. The **LINEAR GLOBAL LOAD** dialog box will be displayed as shown in Figure-83 and you will be asked to select a reference for acceleration direction.

Figure-83. LINEAR GLOBAL LOAD dialog box

- Select desired face/edge to specify the direction of acceleration; refer to Figure-84.

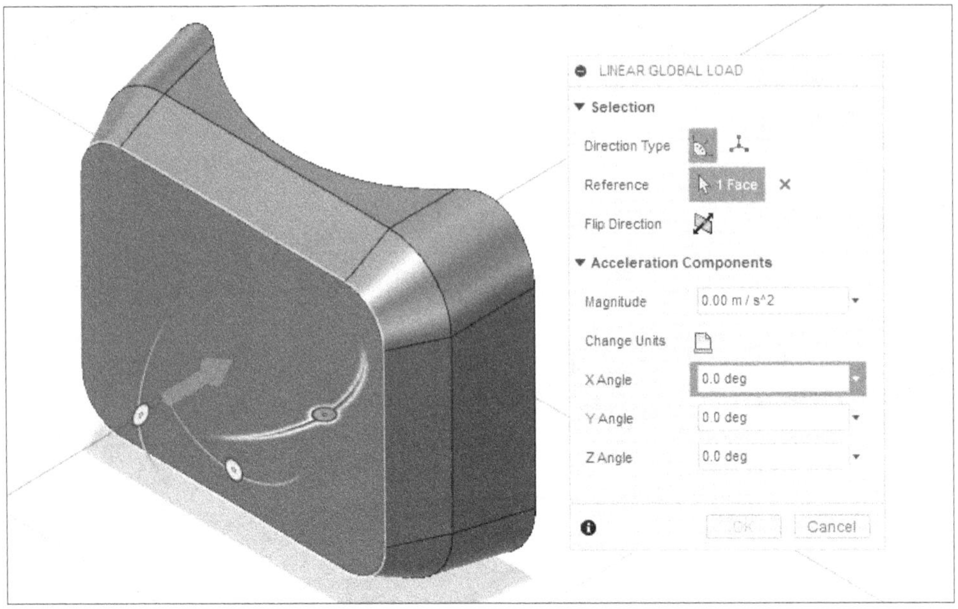

Figure-84. Selection of face for acceleration

- Specify desired value of acceleration in the **Magnitude** edit box.
- Similarly, specify desired angle values for X, Y, and Z in the **X Angle**, **Y Angle**, and **Z Angle** edit boxes.
- Specify other parameters as required and click on the **OK** button to apply the linear global load.

Applying Angular Global Load

The Angular Global Load is applied to give angular velocity or angular acceleration to the system. The procedure to apply angular global load is given next.

- Click on the **Angular Global Load** tool from the **LOADS** drop-down in the **Toolbar**. The **ANGULAR GLOBAL LOAD** dialog box will be displayed; refer to Figure-85.

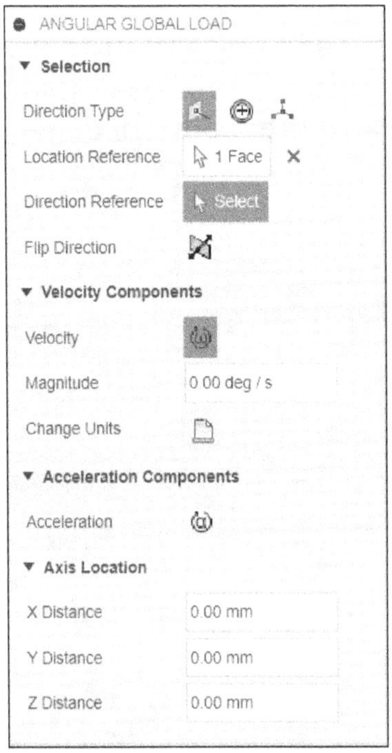

Figure-85. ANGULAR GLOBAL LOAD dialog box

- The **Select** button of **Location Reference** section is active by default. Select desired location for applying velocity or acceleration. The input boxes will be displayed to apply angular velocity and specify the location of the exerting point along X direction.
- Click on the **Select** button from the **Direction Reference** section and select the face to define axis for angular velocity/acceleration.
- Specify the other parameters as discussed earlier.
- Click on the **Acceleration** button if you want to specify the acceleration also from the **Acceleration Components** rollout in the dialog box. Specify the related parameters as discussed earlier.
- Click on the **OK** button to apply angular velocity/acceleration.

Toggling Gravity On/Off

Anyone who has passed high school should be knowing what is gravity and yet gravity is a mystery for scientists! The procedure to activate and de-activate gravity is given next.

- Click on the **Toggle Gravity On** button from the **LOADS** drop-down in the **Toolbar** if the gravity is off and you want to activate it for simulation.
- Click on the **Toggle Gravity Off** button from the **LOADS** drop-down in the **Toolbar** if the gravity is on and you want to de-activate it for simulation; refer to Figure-86.

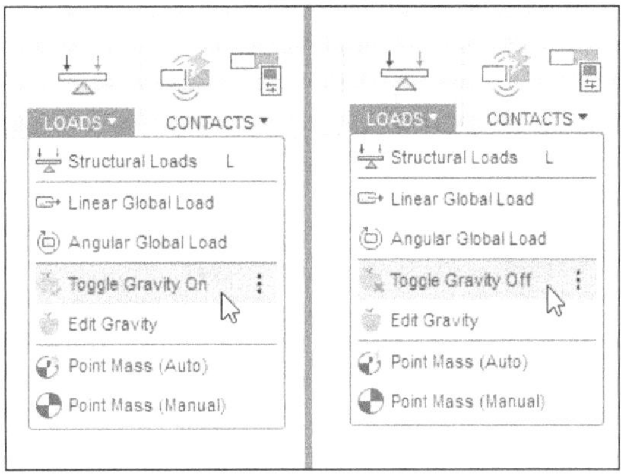

Figure-86. Toggle Gravity On or Off tool

Editing Gravity

The **Edit Gravity** tool is used to edit the value and direction of gravity acting in the simulation. The procedure is given next.

- Click on the **Edit Gravity** tool from the **LOADS** drop-down in the **Toolbar**. The **EDIT GRAVITY** dialog box will be displayed; refer to Figure-87.

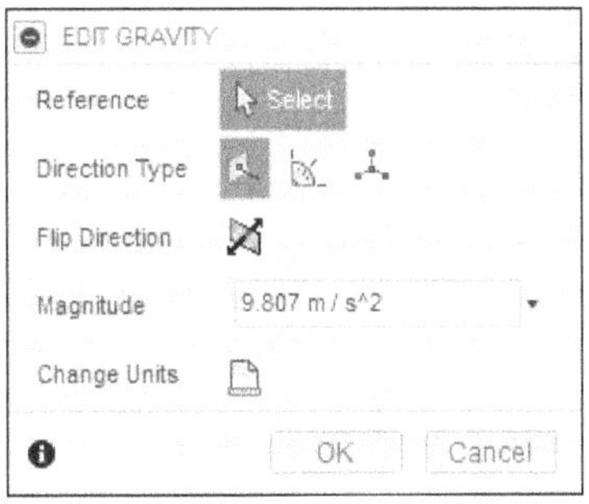

Figure-87. EDIT GRAVITY dialog box

- The **Select** button of **Reference** section is active by default. Select desired direction reference (face/edge) to specify the direction of gravity.
- Specify desired value of gravity in the **Magnitude** edit box.
- Click on the **OK** button to apply the edited Gravity.

Apply Point Mass (Auto)

The **Point Mass (Auto)** tool is used to replace the real component with a point mass. This phenomena is used to simplify simulation calculations. The procedure to use this tool is given next.

- Click on the **Point Mass (Auto)** tool from the **LOADS** drop-down in the **Toolbar**. The **POINT MASS (AUTO)** dialog box will be displayed; refer to Figure-88.

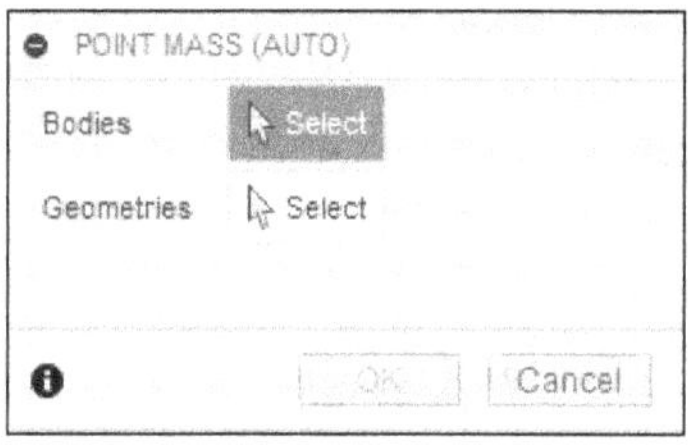

Figure-88. POINT MASS (AUTO) dialog box

- The **Select** button of **Bodies** section is active by default. Select the object that you want to be replaced by point mass.
- Click on the **Select** button for **Geometries** section and select the face on which you want to place the mass.
- Specify desired mass value in the **Mass** edit box of the dialog box; refer to Figure-89.

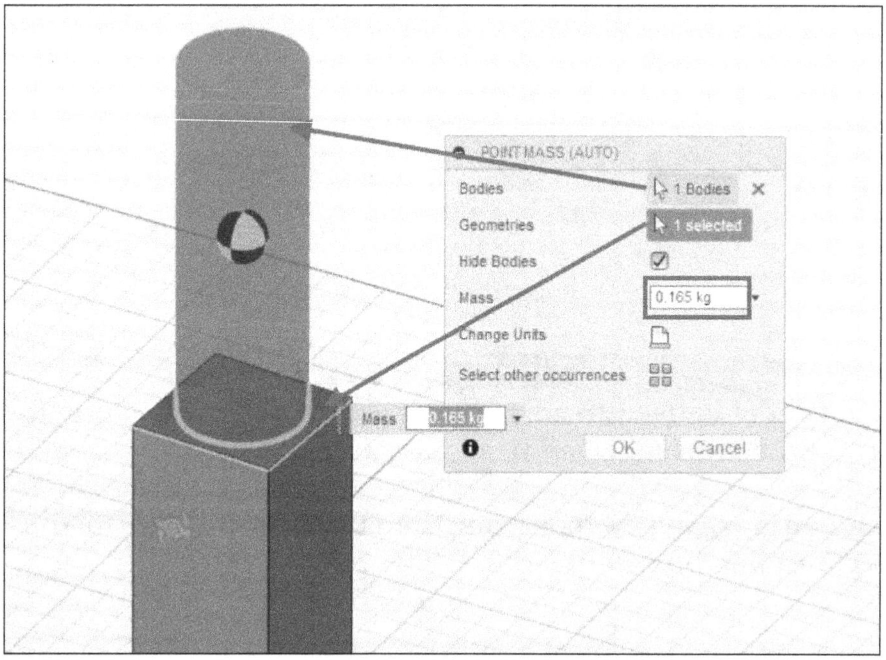

Figure-89. Specifying mass value for point mass

- Specify other parameters as required and click on the **OK** button to apply point mass.

Apply Point Mass (Manual)

The **Point Mass (Manual)** tool works in the same way as **Point Mass (Auto)**. The only difference between the two is that in case of **Point Mass (Manual)** tool, you do not need to select a body to be replaced by mass but specify the location where point mass will be placed.

APPLYING CONTACTS

Contacts are applied when there are two or more bodies/components in contact with each other and load is transferred between them during simulation. The tools to apply contacts are available in the **CONTACTS** drop-down; refer to Figure-90. These tools are discussed next.

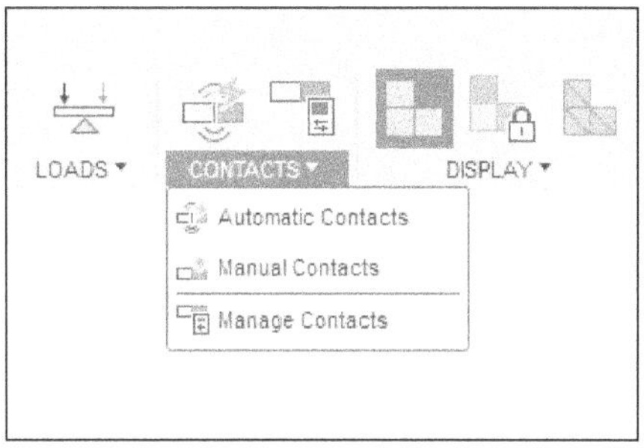

Figure-90. CONTACTS drop down

Applying Automatic Contacts

If you are performing analysis on an assembly with multiple components then applying automatic contact is a very important steps. Without applying automatic contact, you can not perform analysis of assembly in Fusion. Based on the joints applied to components and gap between the components, contacts are applied between the components automatically. The procedure to apply automatic contact is given next.

- Click on the **Automatic Contacts** tool from **CONTACTS** drop-down in the **Toolbar**. The **AUTOMATIC CONTACTS** dialog box will be displayed; refer to Figure-91.

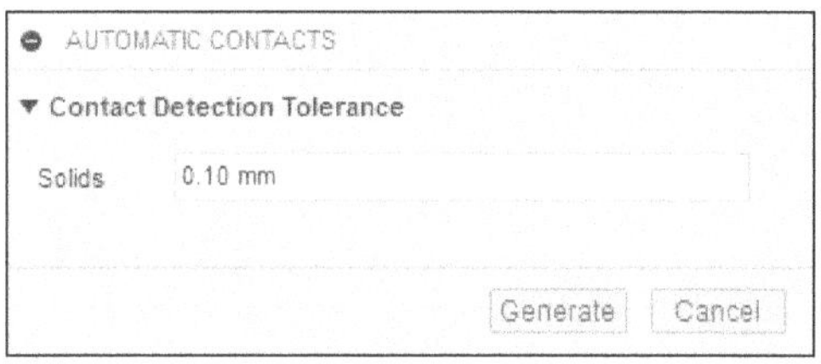

Figure-91. AUTOMATIC CONTACTS dialog box

- Specify desired value of tolerance in **Solids** edit box of the **AUTOMATIC CONTACTS** dialog box. The tolerance specified here is the maximum gap up to which the software will apply contacts. If the gap between two components is more than the specified value then Fusion will not apply any contact automatically.
- Click on the **Generate** button. The contacts will be generated automatically.

Modifying Contacts

The **Automatic Contacts** tool applies the same contact to the components in the assembly. The procedure to check and modify automatically applied contacts is given next.

- To check the automatically applied contacts, click on the **Edit** button displayed on hovering the cursor over **Contacts** node of the **BROWSER**; refer to Figure-92. The **CONTACTS MANAGER** dialog box will be displayed; refer to Figure-93. Here, you can check the contacts automatically applied.

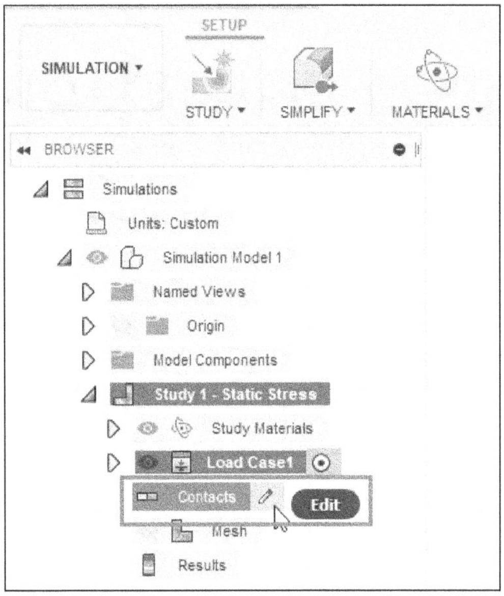

Figure-92. Contacts Edit button

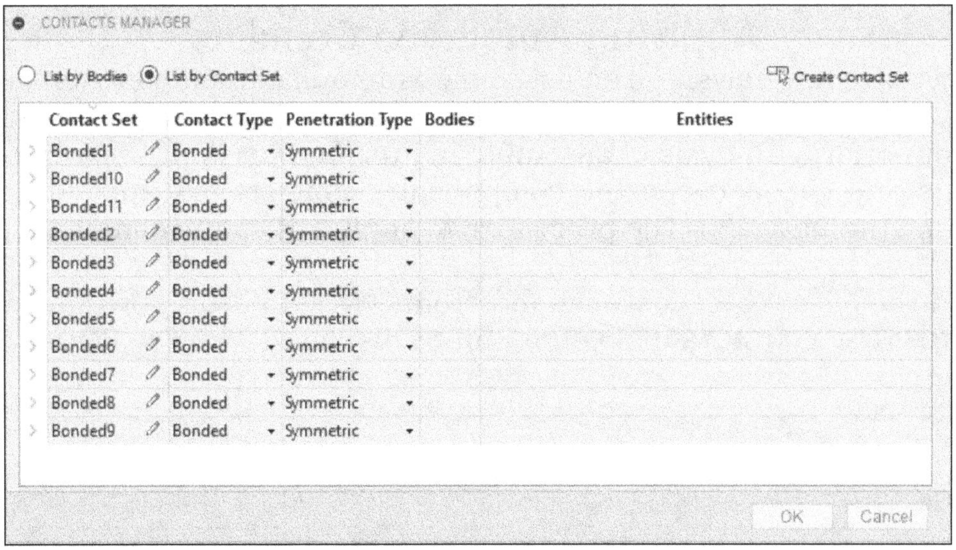

Figure-93. CONTACTS MANAGER dialog box

- Select the contact that you want to edit from the **Contact Set** column in the **CONTACTS MANAGER** dialog box. The contact will be highlighted in the model.
- To modify the contact, click in the **Contact Type** column for the selected contact. List of different available contacts will be displayed; refer to Figure-94.

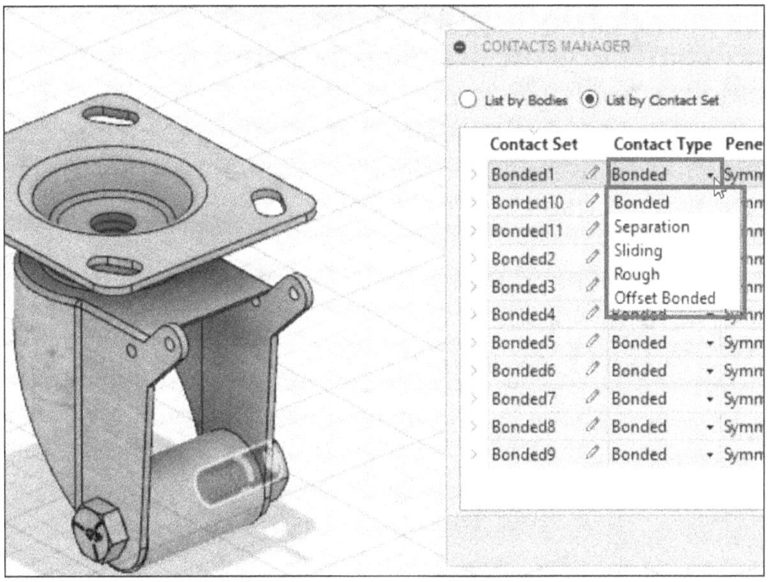

Figure-94. Contact Type list

- Select desired contact type to change. Various contact types are discussed next.

Bonded Contact Type

The bonded contact is used when there is no relative displacement between two connected solid bodies. This type of contact is used to glue together different solids of an assembly. The two surfaces that are in contact are classified as master and slave. Every node in the slave surface(slave nodes) is tied to a node in the master surface(master node) by a constraint. You will learn about master surface and slave surface in the next topic.

Separation Contact Type

The separation contact is applied when separation between parts is allowed but prohibits part penetration.

Sliding Contact Type

The sliding contact is a type of contact which allows displacement tangential to the contacting surface but no relative movement along the normal direction. This type of contact constraint is used to simulate sliding movement in the assembly. The two surfaces that are in contact are classified as master and slave. Every node in slave surface(slave nodes) is tied to a node in the master surface(master node) by this constraint.

Rough Contact Type

The rough contact is used when two parts cannot slide over each other as friction between them is very high. Note that the parts cannot penetrate in each other if this contact type is selected.

Offset Bonded Contact Type

The offset bonded contact is used when two parts are at a distance in assembly but you want them to be bonded as bonded contact type.

Applying Manual Contacts

Applying automatic contacts is the first step for performing analysis on the assembly but **Automatic Contacts** apply the same contact to all the assembly joints which can be changed by using **CONTACTS MANAGER**. But what to do if automatic contacts are not generated for required faces. The **Manual Contacts** tool is used to apply these contacts. The procedure to use this tool is given next.

- Click on the **Manual Contacts** tool from the **CONTACTS** drop-down in the **Toolbar**. The **MANUAL CONTACTS** dialog box will be displayed as shown in Figure-95. Also, you will be asked to select the primary body.

Figure-95. MANUAL CONTACTS dialog box

- The **Select** button of **Primary Body** section is active by default. Select the first body. You will be asked to select the secondary body.
- Select the second body. You will be asked to select the face/edge on the first body.
- Select desired face/edge at which the body is in contact with other body.
- Click on the **Select** button of **Selection Set 2** section in the dialog box and select the contacting face/edge on the second body. The options in the dialog box will be displayed as shown in Figure-96.

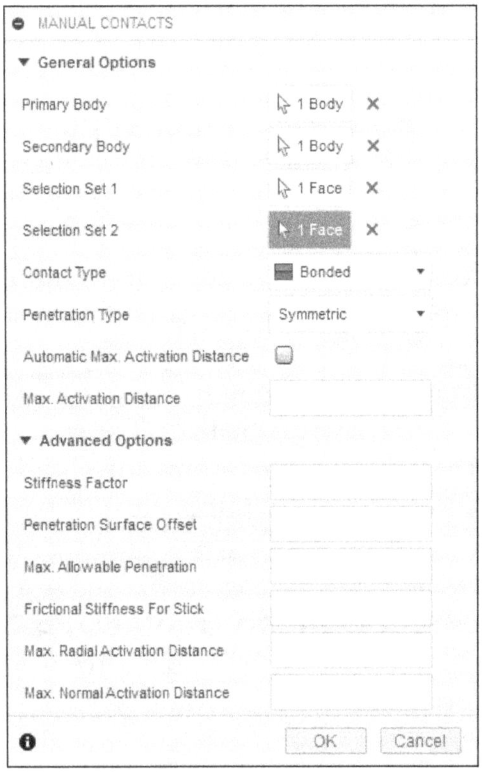

Figure-96. Options in MANUAL CONTACTS dialog box

- Select desired contact type from the **Contact Type** drop-down in the dialog box.
- Select desired option from the **Penetration Type** drop-down. If you have selected the **Symmetric** option then both master component and slave component cannot penetrate into each other. If the **Unsymmetric** option is selected then the master component can penetrate the slave component.
- Specify desired maximum activation distance in the **Max. Activation Distance** edit box. This parameter is useful when parts are not coincident and a small gap is present between them. Choose a small value to prevent conflicting contact interactions.
- Similarly, specify the other parameters as required.
- Click on the **OK** button to create the contact.

Manage Contacts Tool

The **Manage Contacts** tool in the **CONTACTS** drop-down is used to edit contacts earlier applied. On clicking this tool, the **CONTACTS MANAGER** will be displayed. The options in the **CONTACTS MANAGER** have already been discussed.

SOLVING ANALYSIS

Once you have applied all the information required to perform analysis, you need to perform a check whether you have specified the required information or not. Once the system says, it has the required information then you are good to go for analysis. The tools to perform pre-check and analysis are available in the **SOLVE** drop-down of the **Toolbar**; refer to Figure-97. These tools are discussed next.

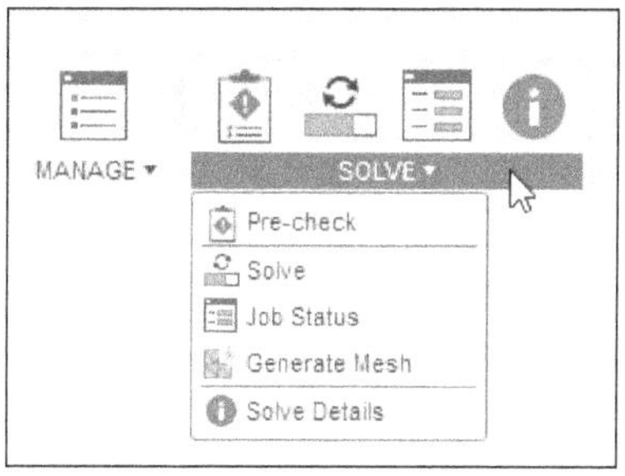

Figure-97. SOLVE drop down

Performing Pre-check

Pre-checking is an important step before performing analysis. Although, the tool will not tell you that you have specified load at wrong place or other design faults but the tool will warn you that you have not specified load, constraint, contact like parameters which need to be specified before performing analysis. The procedure to perform pre-check is given next.

- Click on the **Pre-check** tool from the **SOLVE** drop-down in the **Toolbar**. If there is any parameter left to be specified then **Cannot Solve** dialog box will be displayed; refer to Figure-98.

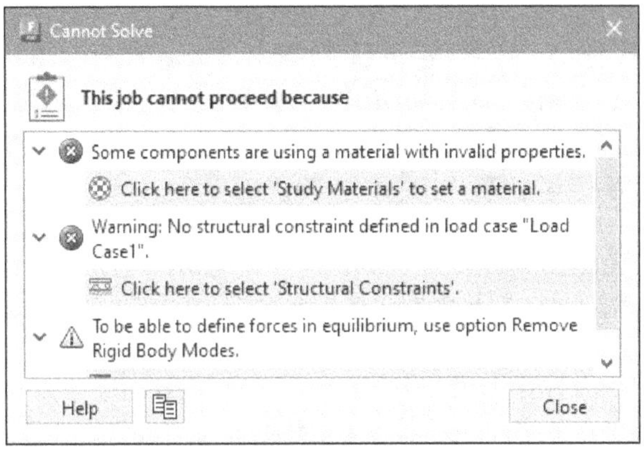

Figure-98. Cannot Solve dialog box

- Apply the parameters which are not specified. If all the parameters are specified then **Ready to Solve** dialog box will be displayed; refer to Figure-99.

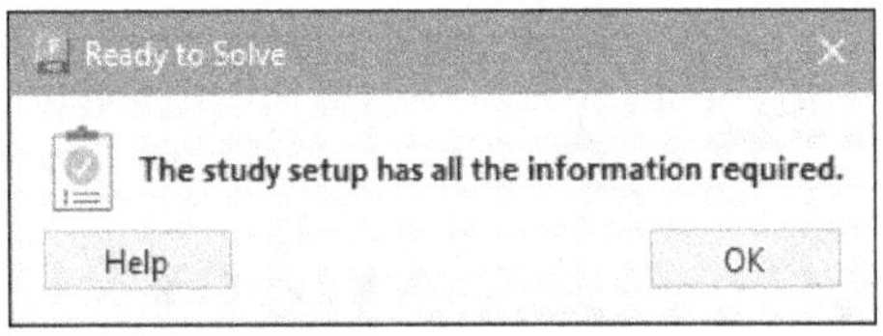

Figure-99. Ready to Solve dialog box

- Click on the **OK** button and perform meshing.

Meshing

Meshing is the base of FEM. Meshing divides the solid/shell models into elements of finite size and shape. These elements are joined at some common points called nodes. These nodes define the load transfer from one element to other element. Meshing is a very crucial step in design analysis. The automatic mesher in the software generates a mesh based on a global element size, tolerance, and local mesh control specifications. Mesh control lets you specify different sizes of elements for components, faces, edges, and vertices.
The software estimates a global element size for the model taking into consideration its volume, surface area, and other geometric details. The size of the generated mesh (number of nodes and elements) depends on the geometry and dimensions of the model, element size, mesh tolerance, mesh control, and contact specifications. In the early stages of design analysis where approximate results may suffice, you can specify a larger element size for a faster solution. For a more accurate solution, a smaller element size may be required.

Meshing generates 3D tetrahedral solid elements and 1D beam elements. A mesh consists of one type of elements unless the mixed mesh type is specified. Solid elements are naturally suitable for bulky models. Shell elements are naturally suitable for modeling thin parts (sheet metals), and beams and trusses are suitable for modeling structural members.

The procedure to create the mesh of the solid is given next.

- Click on the **Generate Mesh** tool from the **SOLVE** drop-down in the **Toolbar**. The system will start creating mesh and progress bar will be displayed. Once, the operation is complete. The mesh will be displayed; refer to Figure-100.

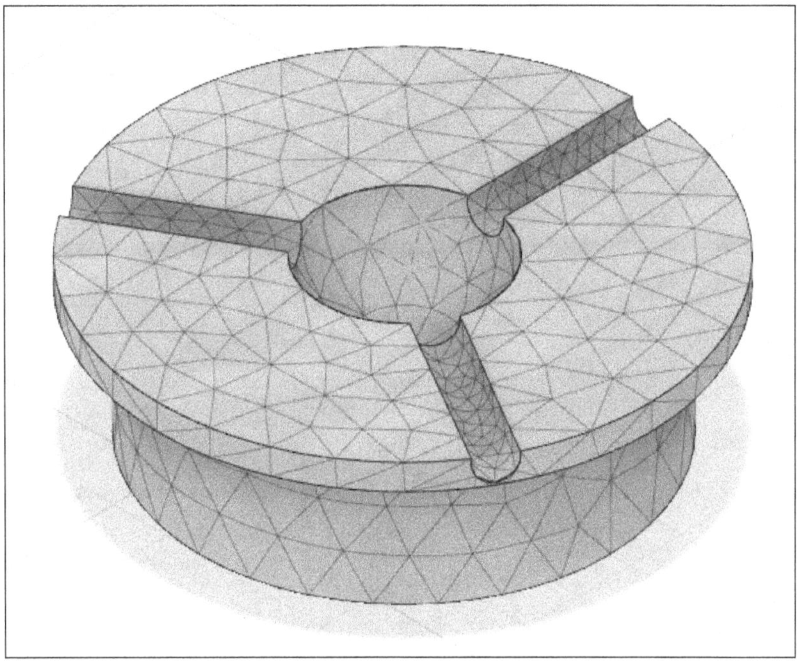

Figure-100. Mesh automatically created

- If you want to change the automatic mesh settings then click on the **Edit** button displayed on hovering the cursor over **Mesh** in the **BROWSER**; refer to Figure-101. The **Mesh Settings** dialog box will be displayed; refer to Figure-102.

Figure-101. Edit button of mesh

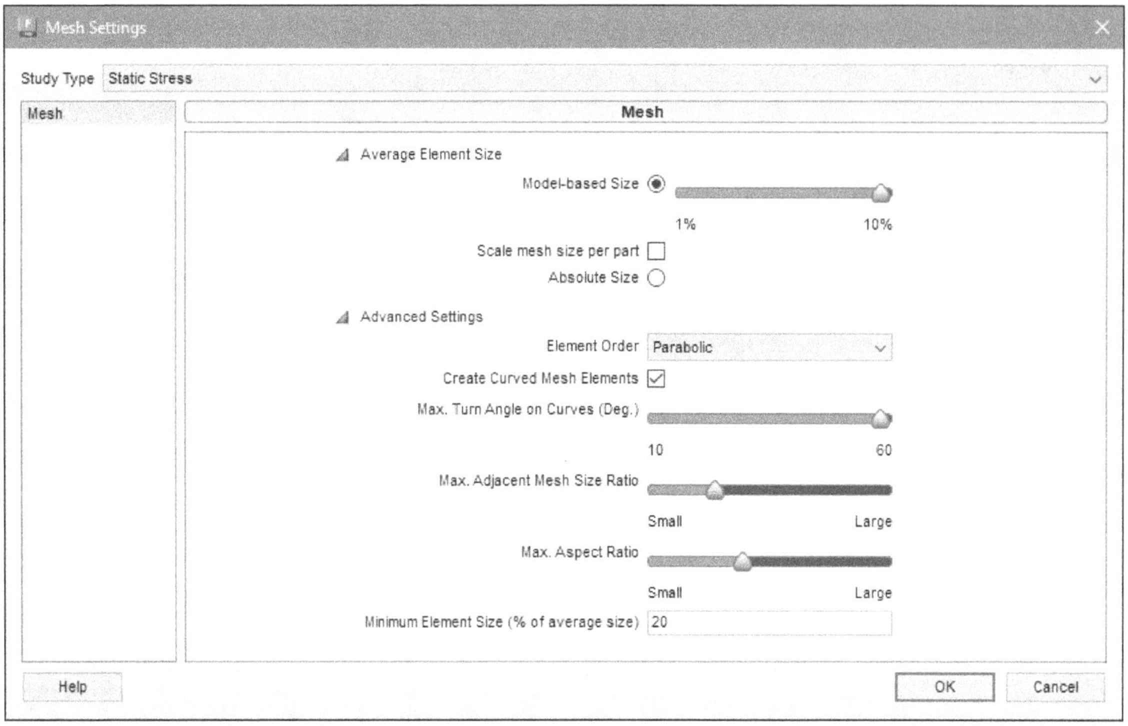

Figure-102. Mesh Settings dialog box

- Move the **Model-based Size** slider towards left to decrease the average size of mesh. Note that decreasing the size will increase the analysis solution time.
- Select the **Scale mesh size per part** check box if you want system to scale mesh size of each individual part in assembly based on its size. In other words, if there are 10 parts in assembly with different sizes then mesh elements of each part will have different size. The bigger the part size, the bigger will be mesh element size.
- If you want to specify a value to define size of all mesh elements then select the **Absolute Size** radio button and specify desired value for element size in the edit box next to it.
- Expand the **Advanced Settings** node to define advanced parameter of mesh. Select desired element order from the **Element Order** drop-down in the **Advanced Settings** node of the dialog box. Select the **Parabolic** option element order for complex parts which require higher degree of elements. For simple parts, select the **Linear** option from the drop-down.
- Select the **Create Curved Mesh Elements** check box if you want the mesh elements to follow curvature of round/curved faces of the part. Note that boundaries of mesh elements will be distorted to get curves of part.
- Similarly, specify other parameters in the **Advanced Settings** node and click on the **OK** button to apply mesh settings.

Applying Local Mesh Control

Local mesh control is used when you need to increase or decrease the size of elements in a finite area of the part. The procedure to apply local mesh control is given next.

- Click on the **Local Mesh Control** tool from the **MANAGE** drop-down in the **Toolbar**; refer to Figure-103. The **LOCAL MESH CONTROL** dialog box will be displayed; refer to Figure-104. You will be asked to select a face/edge.

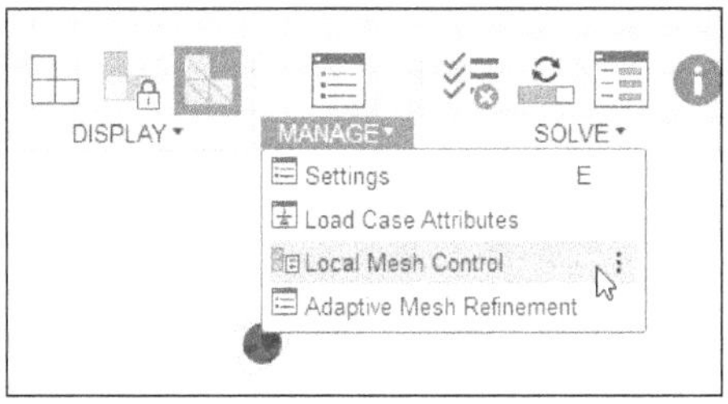

Figure-103. Local Mesh Control tool

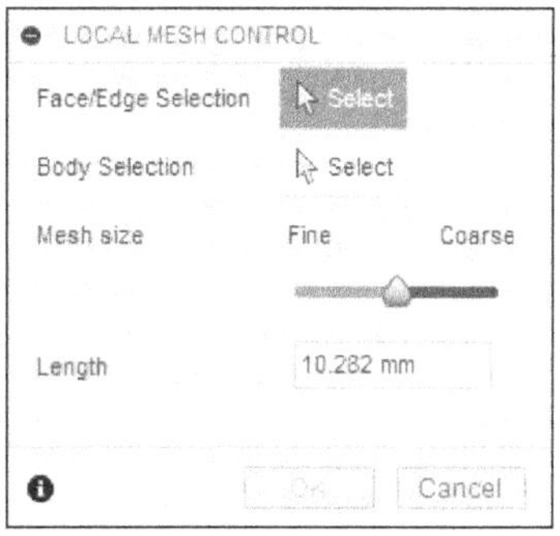

Figure-104. LOCAL MESH CONTROL dialog box

- The **Select** button of **Face/Edge Selection** section is active by default. Select the face/edge(s) for which you want to increase/decrease the element size. If you are working on an assembly then you can select the body after clicking on the **Select** button from **Body Selection** section of the dialog box.
- After selecting desired geometries, move the slider towards coarse or fine to change the mesh size.
- Click on the **OK** button to apply the change.

Note that changes in mesh will not be reflected automatically. To update mesh, right-click on the **Mesh** in the **Browser** and select the **Generate Mesh** option from the shortcut menu; refer to Figure-105.

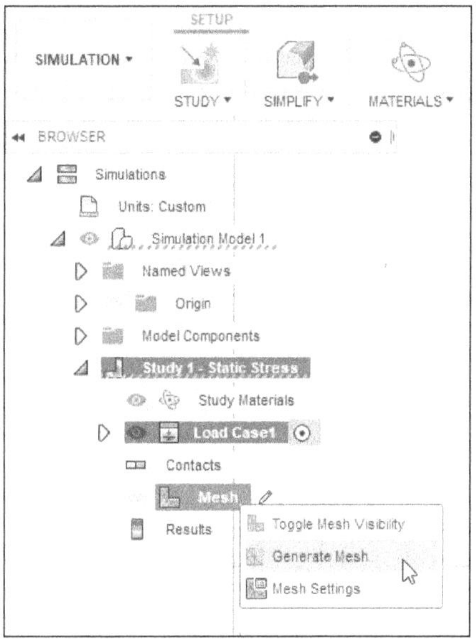

Figure-105. Generate Mesh option

Adaptive Mesh Refinement

Adaptive mesh refinement is used when dynamic refinement of mesh is required at the stress-strain locations to increase accuracy. The procedure to apply adaptive mesh refinement is given next.

- Click on the **Settings** tool from the **MANAGE** drop-down in the **Toolbar**. The **Settings** dialog box will be displayed. Click on the **Adaptive Mesh Refinement** option in the left side of the **Settings** dialog box. The **Adaptive Mesh Refinement** page will be displayed; refer to Figure-106.

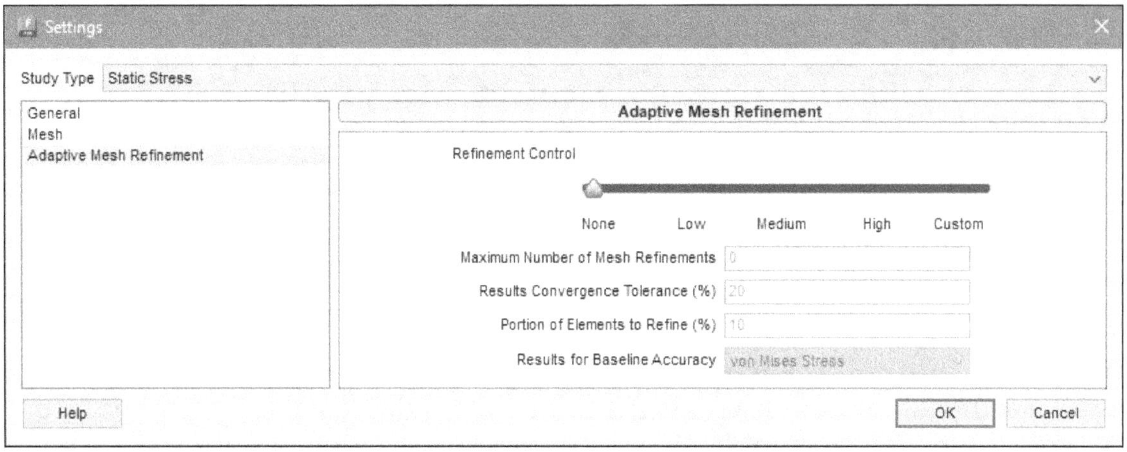

Figure-106. Adaptive Mesh Refinement page in Settings dialog box

- Move the **Refinement Control** slider towards right to increase refinement level of meshing at high stress areas.
- Click on the **OK** button to apply refinement.

Solving Analysis

Once you have specified all the parameters then it is time to solve the analysis. The procedure to do so is given next.

- Click on the **Solve** tool from the **SOLVE** drop-down in the **Toolbar**. The **Solve** dialog box will be displayed; refer to Figure-107.

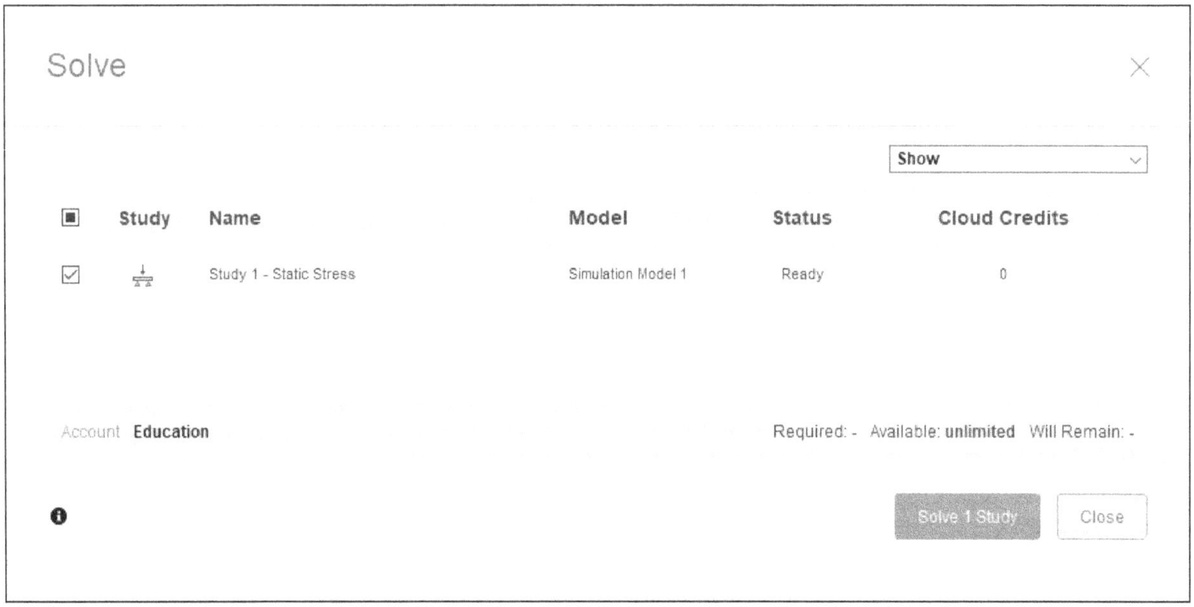

Figure-107. Solve dialog box

- Make sure **Ready** is displayed in the **Status** column for study to be performed.
- Select desired check boxes from the **Show** drop-down to display respective objects in the dialog box; refer to Figure-108.

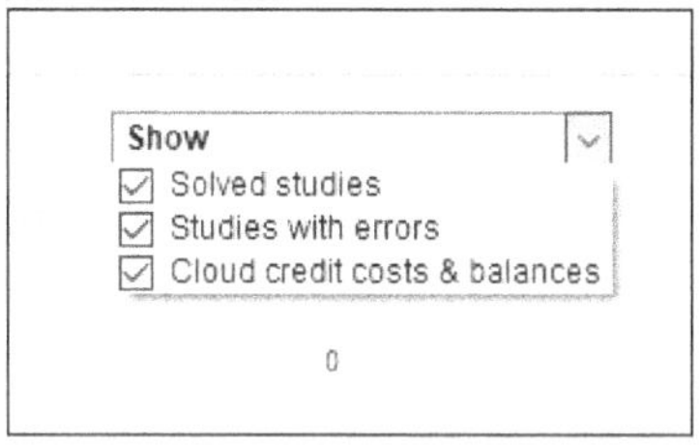

Figure-108. Show drop-down

- Click on the **Solve 1 Study** button. The **Job Status** dialog box will be displayed solving the model; refer to Figure-109.

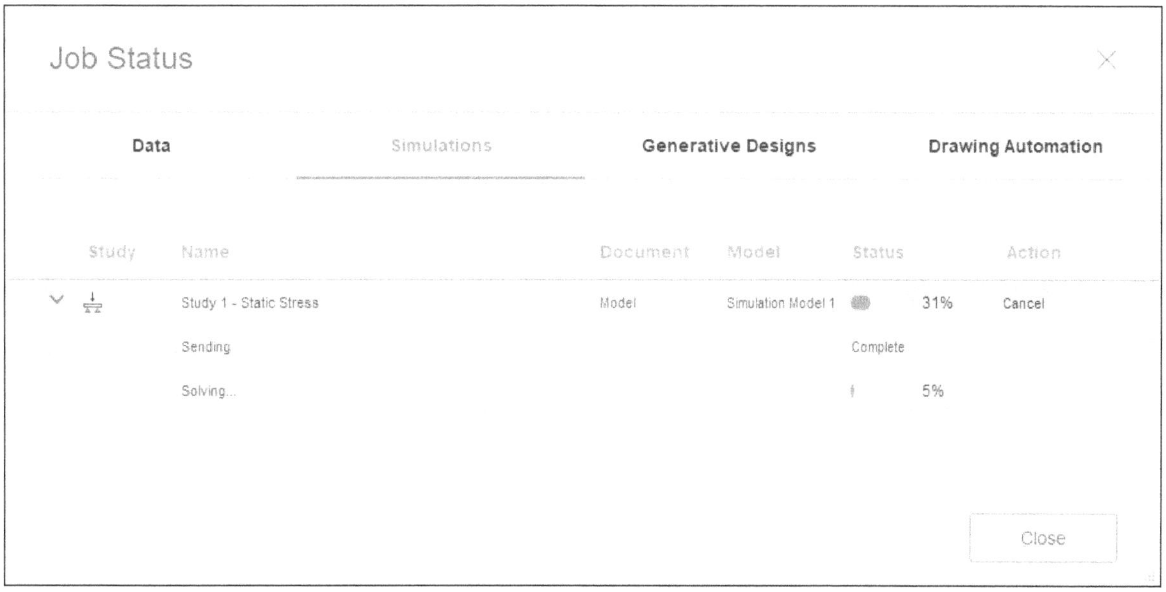

Figure-109. Job Status dialog box solving the model

- After solving the model. The **Results** option will be displayed in the **Action** section. Click on the **Results** option. The results will be displayed along with **RESULTS DETAILS** dialog box; refer to Figure-110.

Figure-110. Results displayed after solving analysis

To check the strongest areas of design, click on the **Show strongest areas of design** button from the **RESULTS DETAILS** dialog box. The strongest areas of design will be displayed; refer to Figure-111.

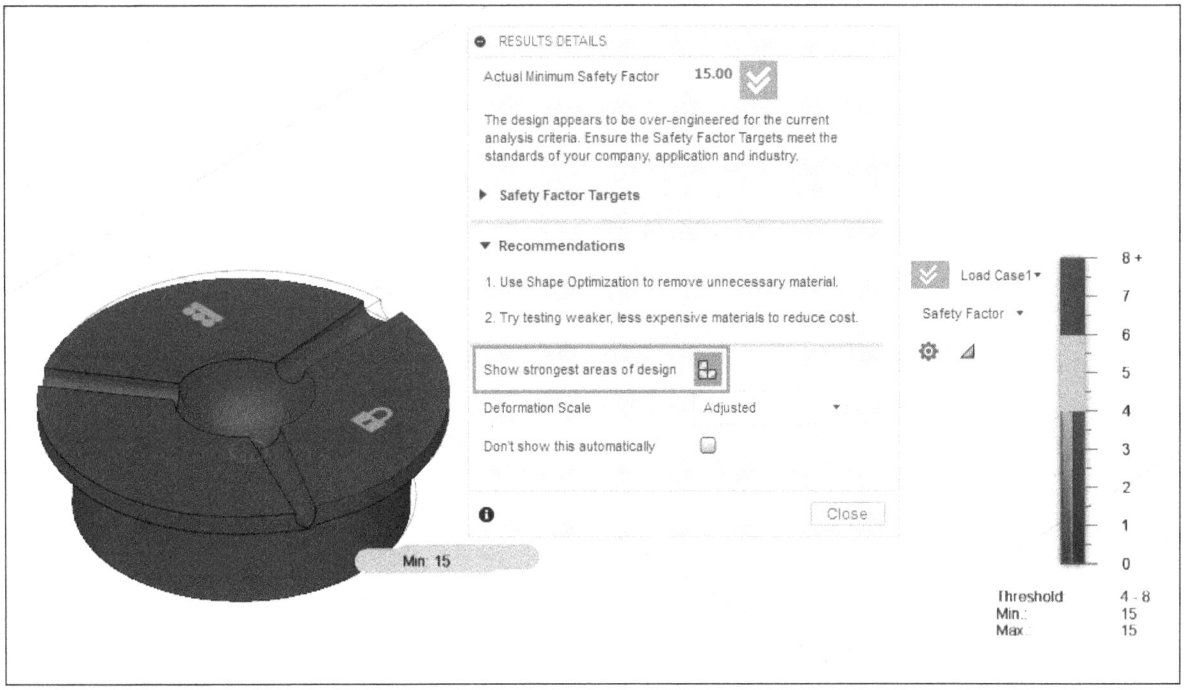

Figure-111. Strongest area results

Move the sliders on scale to change the threshold to be counted as weak area.

Preparing and Managing the Results

Once the analysis is complete, the next step is to prepare and manage the results as required. The tools to prepare results are available in the **RESULT TOOLS** drop-down from **RESULTS** tab in the **Toolbar**; refer to Figure-112. The tools in this drop-down are discussed next.

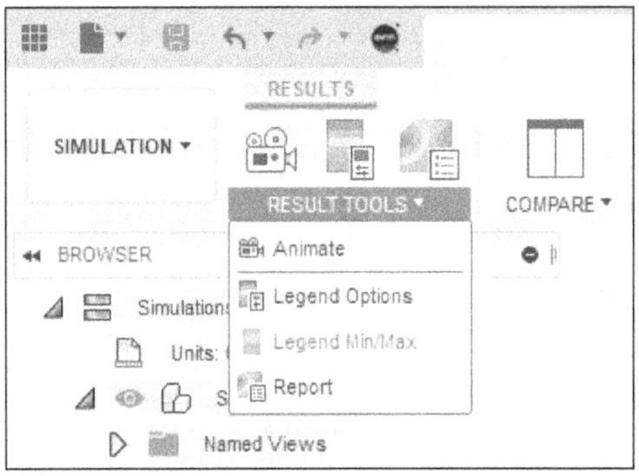

Figure-112. RESULT TOOLS drop down

Animating the Results

Animation is used to represent analysis results in dynamic motion. The procedure to animate the analysis result is given next.

- Click on the **Animate** tool from the **RESULT TOOLS** drop-down in the **Toolbar**. The **ANIMATE** dialog box will be displayed; refer to Figure-113.

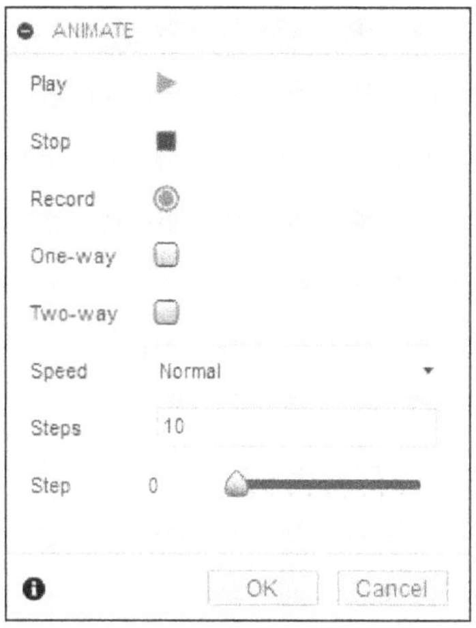

Figure-113. ANIMATE dialog box

- Select the **One-way** check box or the **Two-way** check box to repeat the animation.
- Set other parameters as required and click on the **Play** button.
- Click on the **OK** button to exit the dialog box.

Legend Options

The **Legend Options** tool is used to modify the appearance of legends displayed in the results. The procedure to use this tool is given next.

- Click on the **Legend Options** tool from the **RESULT TOOLS** drop-down in the **Toolbar**. The **LEGEND OPTIONS** dialog box will be displayed; refer to Figure-114.

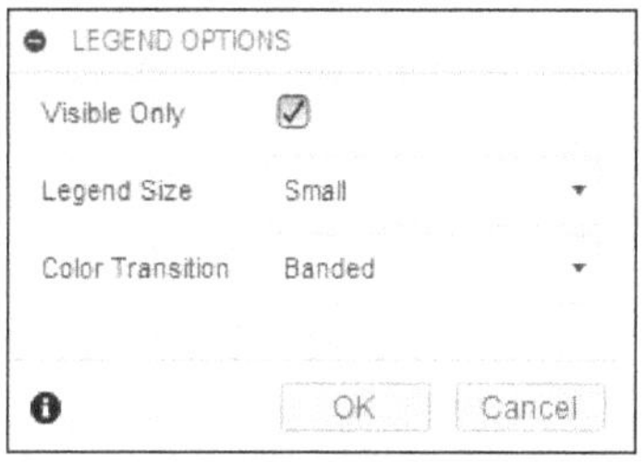

Figure-114. LEGEND OPTIONS dialog box

- Select desired legend size and color transition method from the **Legend Size** drop-down and **Color Transition** drop-down, respectively.
- Click on the **OK** button to apply changes.

Generating Reports

Once you find the analysis results as expected, it is the time to generate reports. The procedure to generate report is given next.

- Click on the **Report** tool from the **RESULT TOOLS** drop-down in the **Toolbar**. The **Report** dialog box will be displayed; refer to Figure-115.

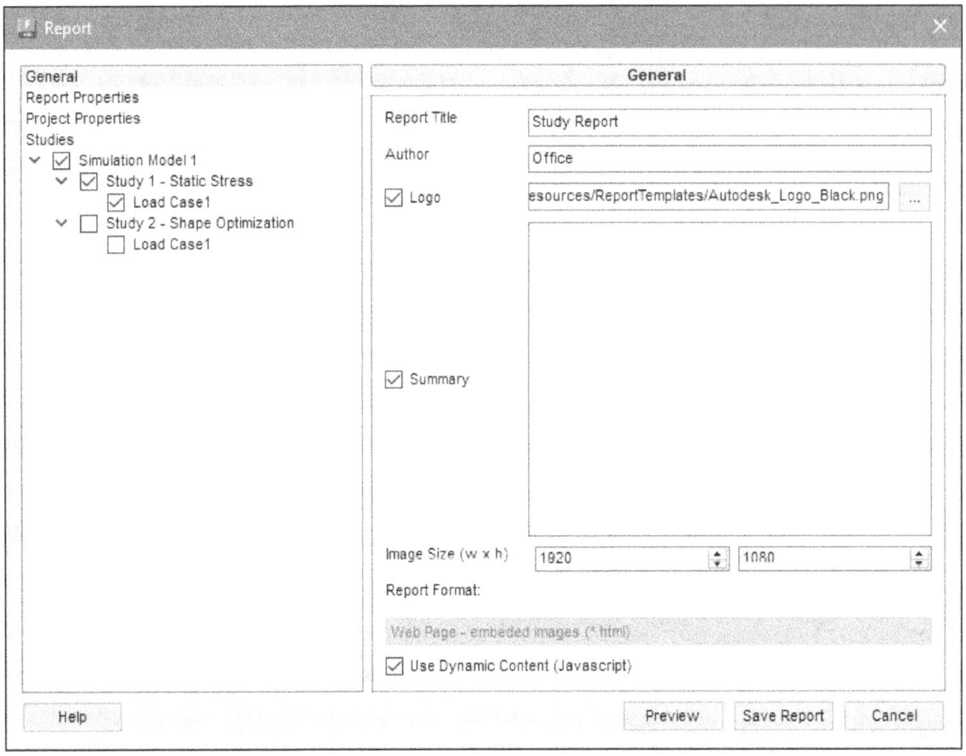

Figure-115. Report dialog box

- Click on the **Save Report** button to save the report. The **Save Report As** dialog box will be displayed; refer to Figure-116.

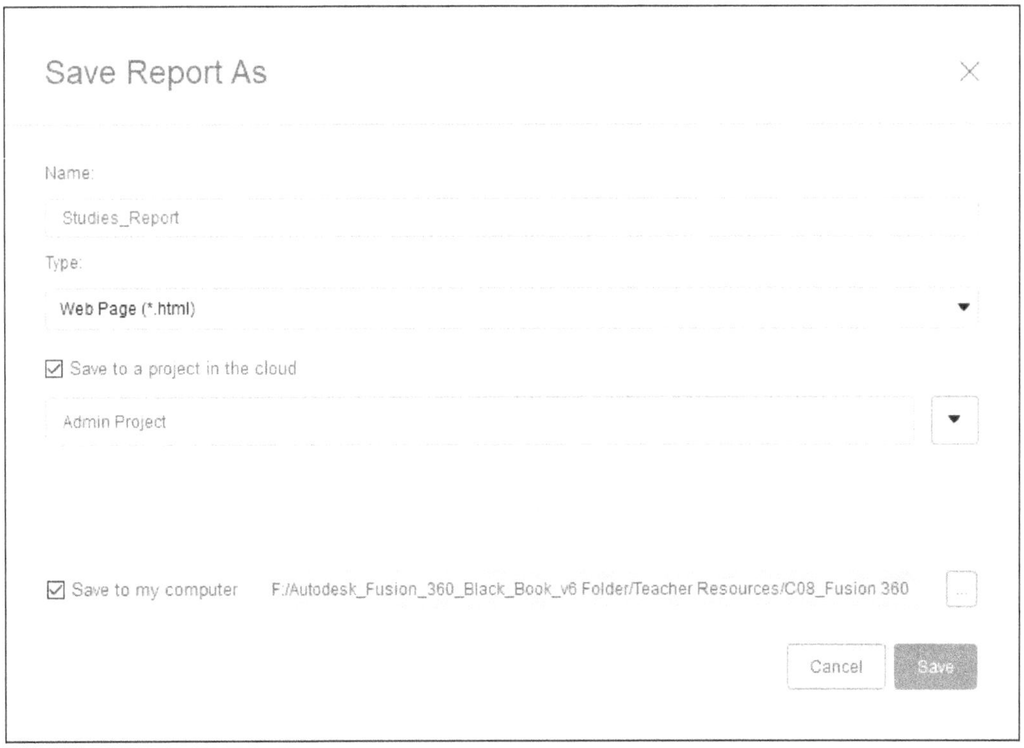

Figure-116. Save Report As dialog box

- Specify desired name of the report and click on the **Save** button. The file will be saved and displayed in the web browser.
- Or select the **Save to my computer** check box to specify desired location of file in the **Select Location** dialog box.

Comparing Results of Analyses

The **Compare** tool in **COMPARE** drop-down is used to compare results of two analyses along with parameters specified for those analyses. The procedure to use this tool is given next.

- After performing at least two analyses to be compared, click on the **Compare** tool from the **COMPARE** drop-down in the **RESULTS** tab of the **Toolbar**. The results of analyses will be displayed in two windows of application; refer to Figure-117.

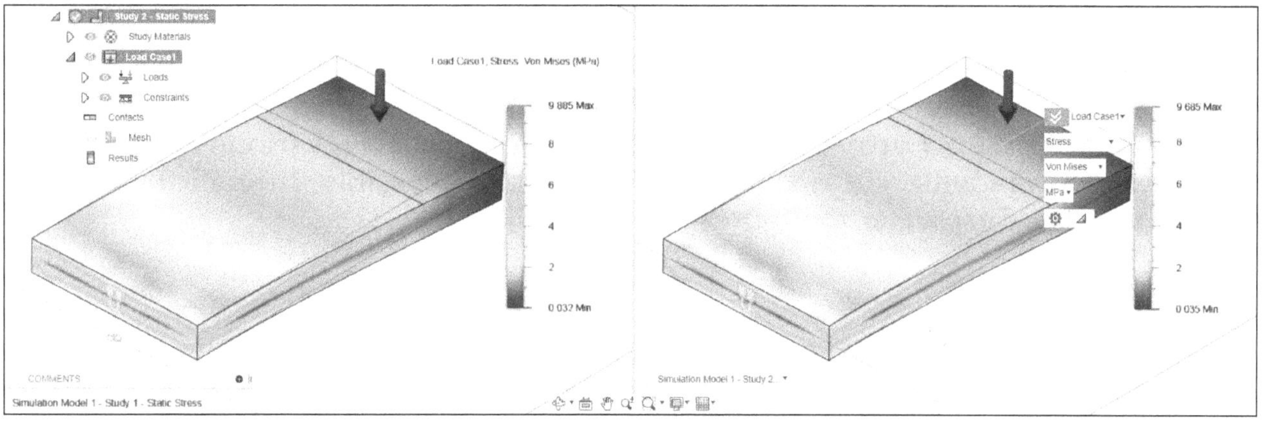

Figure-117. Comparing results

- Click on desired side in result window and set desired result parameters like select **Stress** option from result type drop-down of the legends bar; refer to Figure-118.

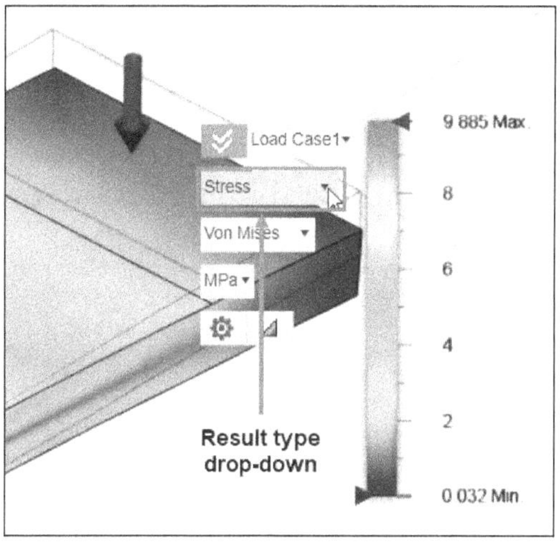

Figure-118. Result type drop-down

- Check other results as desired and click on the **Finish Compare** tool from the **FINISH COMPARE** drop-down in the **Toolbar**.

DEFORMATION drop-down

The options in the **DEFORMATION** drop-down are used to scale up or scale down the deformation caused in the part due to load in the results. By default, the deformation scale is set to **Adjusted**. To change the scale, select desired option from the **DEFORMATION** drop-down; refer to Figure-119.

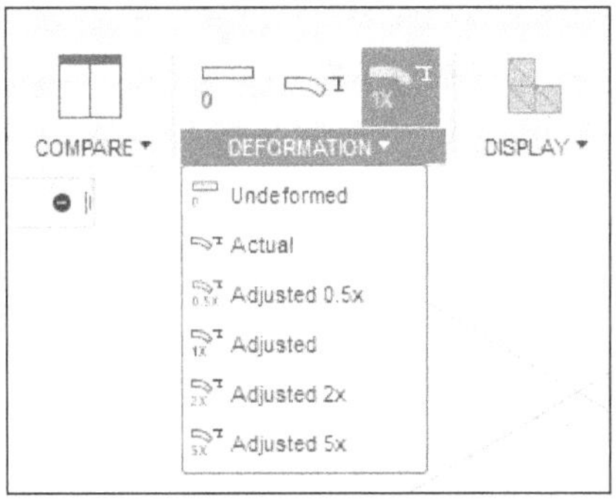

Figure-119. DEFORMATION drop down

DISPLAY Options

The options of **DISPLAY** drop-down are used to switch between various display styles of the model in results. The display commands are accessible through the **DISPLAY** panel in the **Toolbar**; refer to Figure-120.

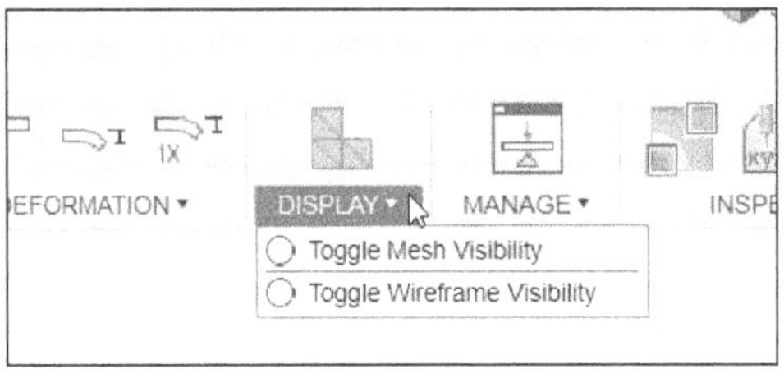

Figure-120. DISPLAY drop down

- The **Toggle Mesh Visibility** option is used to enable or disable the display of the mesh in results.
- The **Toggle Wireframe Visibility** option is used to toggle the wireframe display of the model in results.

Note that if you are not in **Results** mode then two more options are displayed in the **DISPLAY** drop-down; refer to Figure-121.

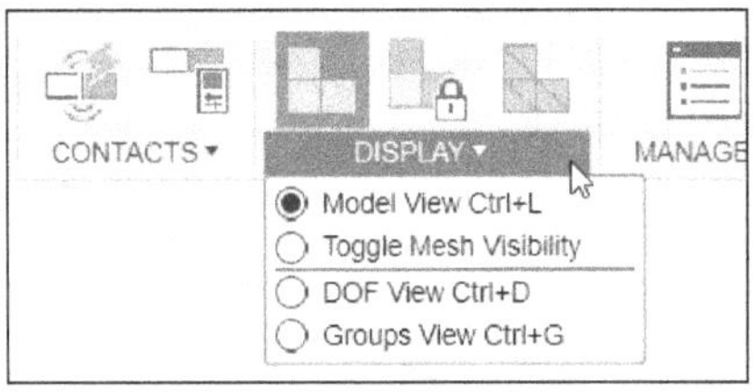

Figure-121. DISPLAY drop down

- Select the **DOF View** radio button to check whether the model is fully fixed, partially fixed, or free. The model will be displayed in respective color code; refer to Figure-122.

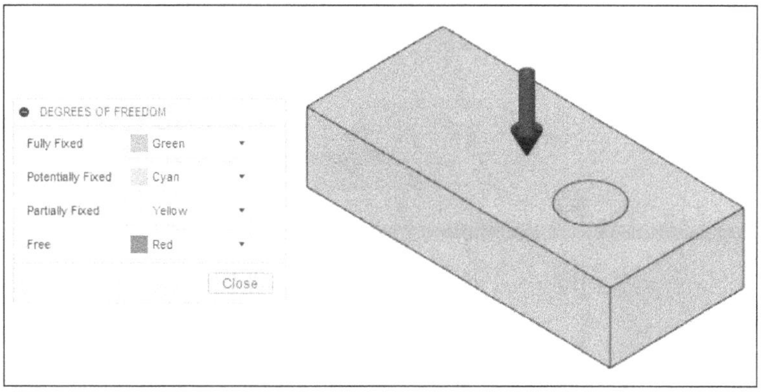

Figure-122. Degrees of freedom

- Select the **Groups View** radio button from the drop-down if you want to display components of different groups in different colors.

Load Case Attributes

The **Load Case Attributes** tool is used to check and modify loads applied in the analysis. The procedure to use this tool is given next.

- Click on the **Load Case Attributes** tool from the **MANAGE** drop-down in the **RESULTS** tab of **Toolbar**. The **LOAD CASE ATTRIBUTES** dialog box will be displayed; refer to Figure-123.

Figure-123. LOAD CASE ATTRIBUTES dialog box

- Double-click on desired parameter in the dialog box to modify. Related dialog box will be displayed. For example, double-click on **Force** parameter in the dialog box then **EDIT STRUCTURAL LOAD** dialog box will be displayed.
- After setting desired parameters, click on the **Close** button.

Inspecting Result Parameters

The options in the **INSPECT** drop-down of **RESULTS** tab are used to check various result parameters of the analysis performed on the model; refer to Figure-124. These tools are discussed next.

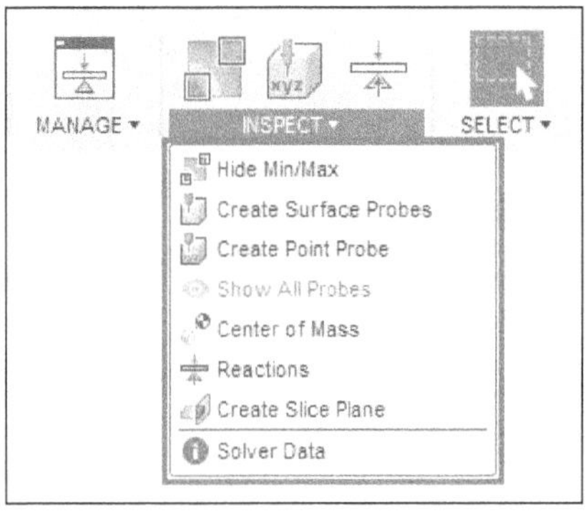

Figure-124. INSPECT drop-down

Showing/Hiding Minimum and Maximum Result Value

Select the **Show Min/Max** option from the **INSPECT** drop-down if you want to show minimum and maximum value of result parameter in the results. If the values are shown in the results and you want to hide them then select **Hide Min/Max** option.

Creating Surface Probe

The **Create Surface Probes** tool is used to check analysis results on various surface points of the model. The procedure to use this tool is given next.

- Click on the **Create Surface Probes** tool from the **INSPECT** drop-down in the **RESULTS** tab of the **Ribbon**. The **CREATE SURFACE PROBES** dialog box will be displayed and analysis result will be displayed when you hover the cursor on the surface of model; refer to Figure-125.

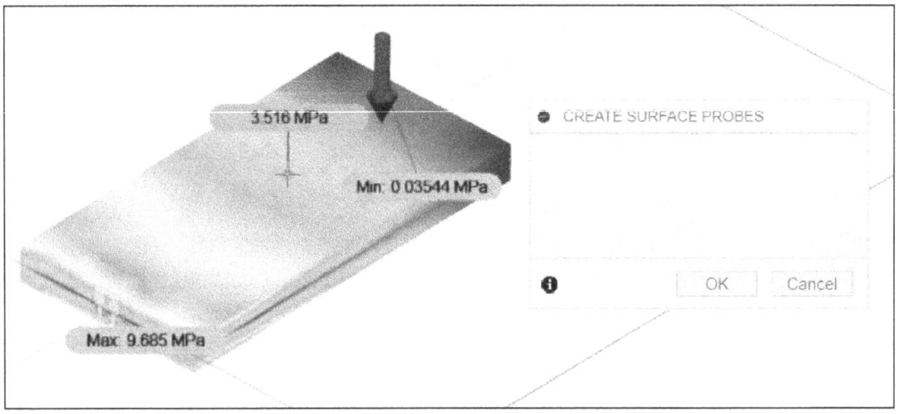

Figure-125. CREATE SURFACE PROBES dialog box

- Click at desired locations on the surface of model to check the probe results; refer to Figure-126.

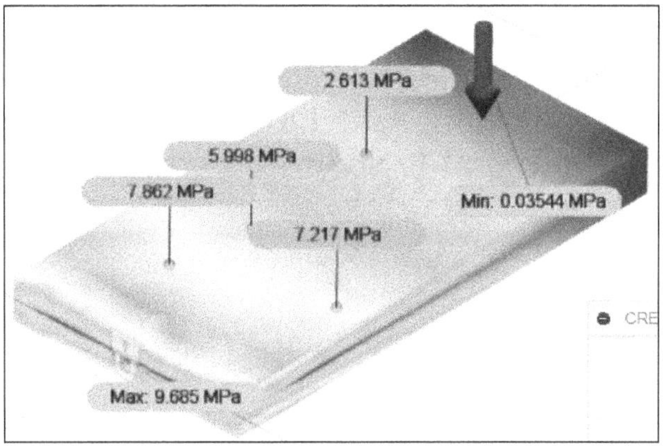

Figure-126. Surface probe results

- Click on the **OK** button from the dialog box to exit.

Creating Point Probe

The **Create Point Probe** tool is used to check analysis results at desired point (location) on the model. The procedure to use this tool is given next.

- Click on the **Create Point Probe** tool from the **INSPECT** drop-down in the **RESULTS** tab of the **Toolbar**. The **POINT PROBE** dialog box will be displayed and as you hover the cursor on the model, the result parameter will be displayed along with coordinates of the point; refer to Figure-127.

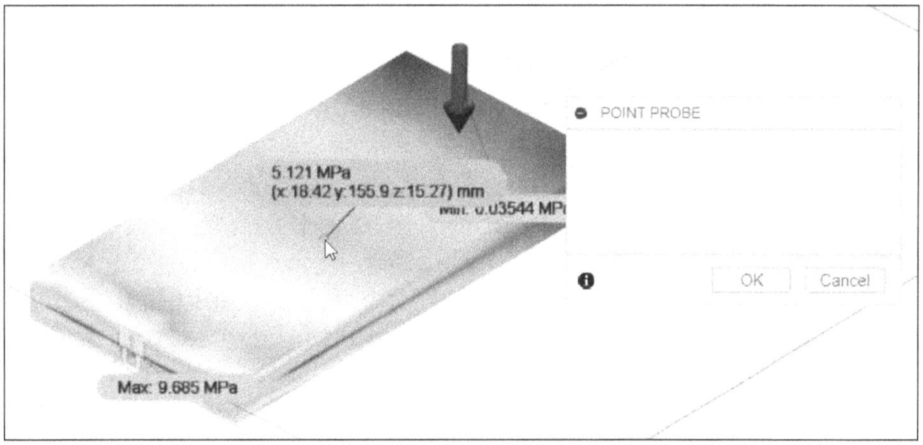

Figure-127. Result on a point

- Click at desired location to display results at selected locations and click on the **OK** button.

Hiding Probes

The **Hide All Probes** tool is used to hide all the probes displayed on the model.

Showing Probes

The **Show All Probes** tool is used to display all the probes again if hidden.

Deleting All Probes

The **Delete All Probes** tool is used to delete all the probes earlier applied on the model.

Center of Mass

The **Center of Mass** tool in **INSPECT** drop-down is used to show both displaced and un-displaced center of mass for bodies. On clicking this tool, the **CENTER OF MASS** dialog box will be displayed and you will be asked to select the bodies; refer to Figure-128. Select the body for which you want to show the center of mass; refer to Figure-129.

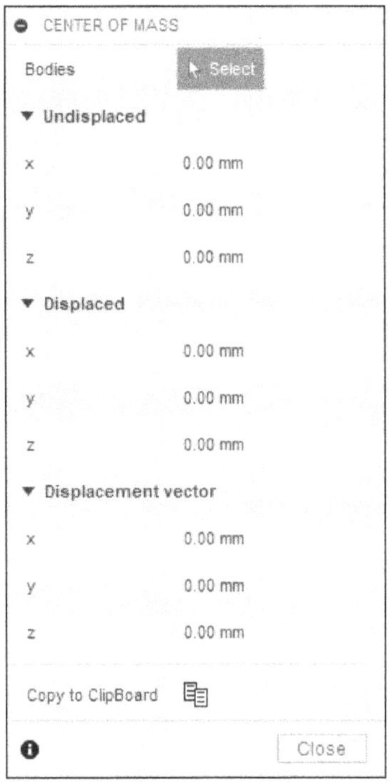

Figure-128. CENTER OF MASS dialog box

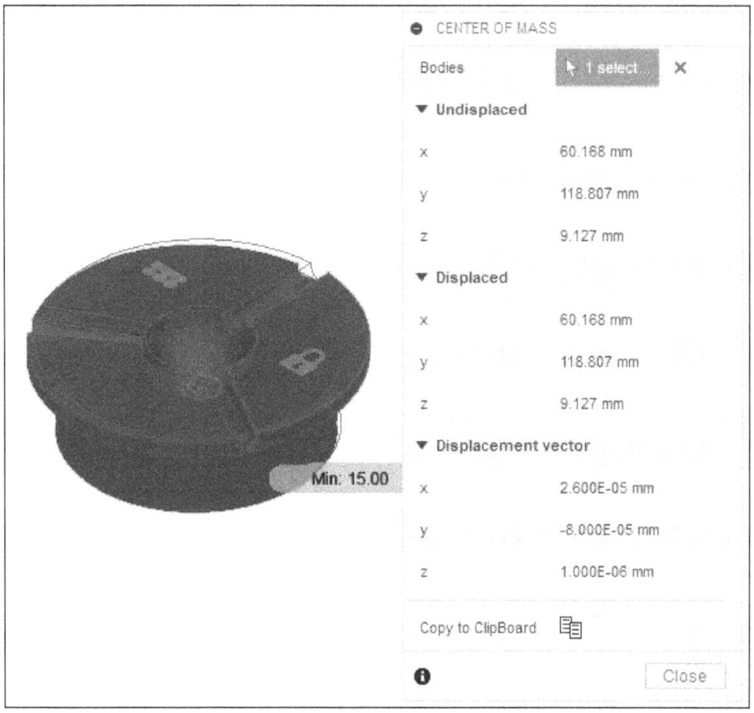

Figure-129. Body selected for center of mass

- Click on the **Close** button from the dialog box to exit.

Checking Reaction Forces and Moments

The **Reactions** tool in **INSPECT** drop-down is used to check reaction forces and moments caused in the model due to application of forces. On clicking this tool, the **REACTIONS** dialog box will be displayed and you will be asked to select faces to be checked; refer to Figure-130. Select the constrained face on which you want to check reaction forces & moments; refer to Figure-131.

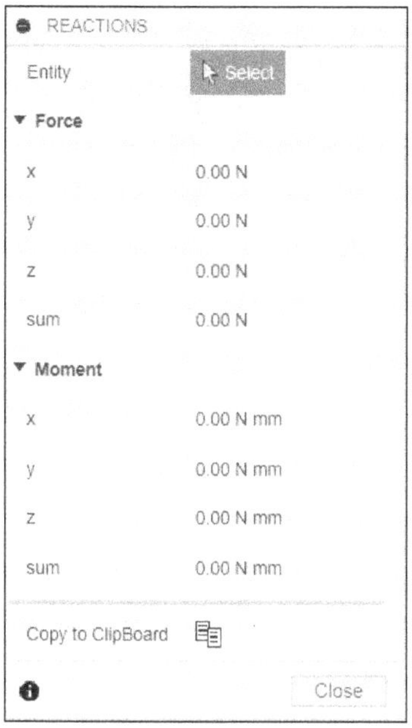

Figure-130. REACTIONS dialog box

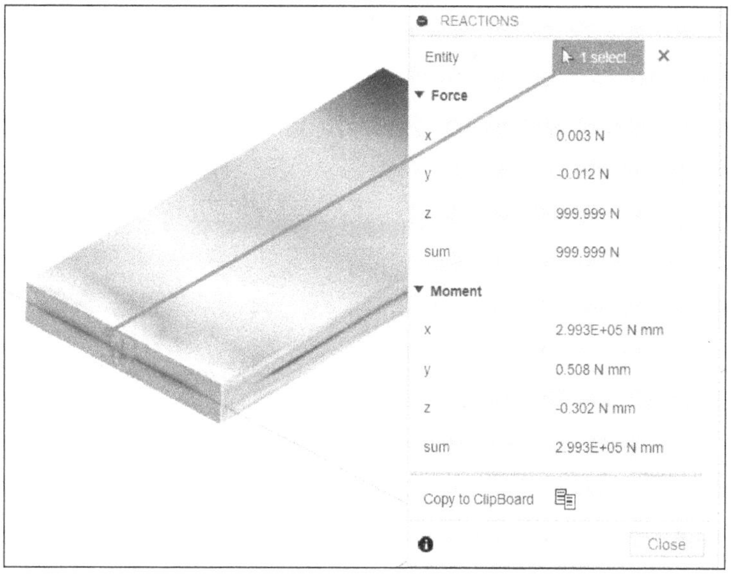

Figure-131. Face selected for reaction

- Click on the **Close** button from the dialog box to exit.

Creating Slice Plane

The **Create Slice Plane** tool is used to check result of analysis at desired level in model using clipping plane. The procedure to use this tool is given next.

- Click on the **Create Slice Plane** tool from the **INSPECT** drop-down in the **RESULTS** tab of the **Toolbar**. The **SLICE PLANE** dialog box will be displayed.
- Select desired face of the model to be used as reference for creating clipping plane. The **EDIT SLICE PLANE** dialog box will be displayed; refer to Figure-132.

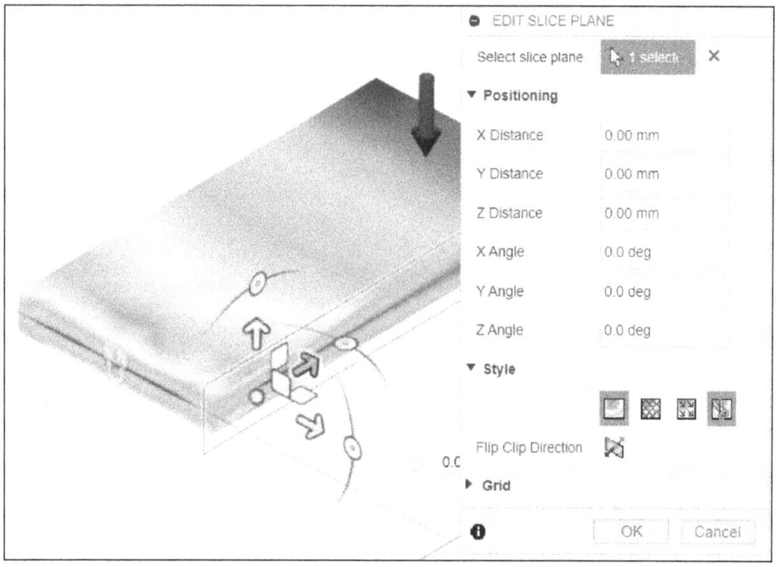

Figure-132. EDIT SLICE PLANE dialog box

- Move the slice plane to desired location using handles displayed on the model or specify desired parameters in the dialog box to set location of clipping plane.
- Using the buttons in **Style** section, you specify the style of displaying results at clipping plane.
- After setting desired parameters, click on the **OK** button from the dialog box.

Checking Solver Data

The **Solver Data** option in **INSPECT** drop-down of **RESULTS** tab is used to check solver data and solver output file; refer to Figure-133. Select the **Solver Output** option from the drop-down at the top in dialog box to check data of analysis results; refer to Figure-134.

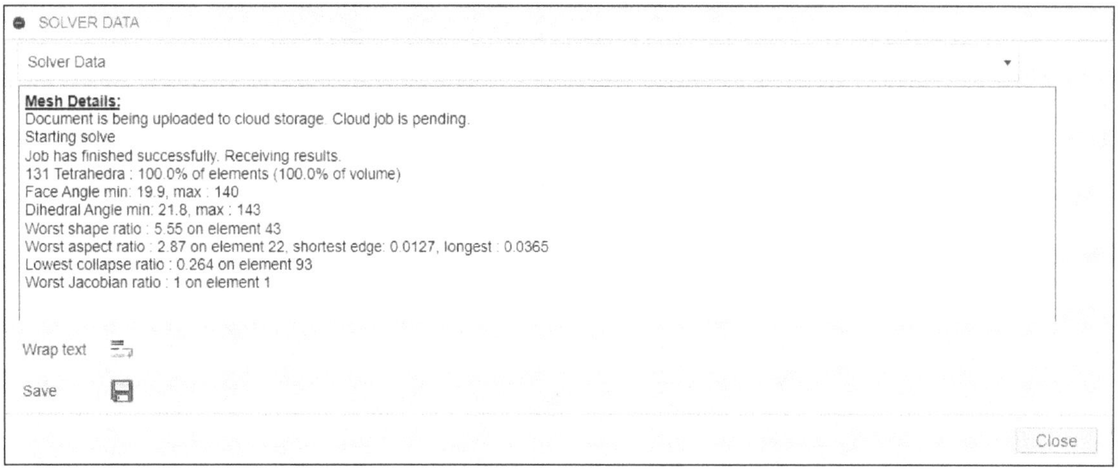

Figure-133. Solver Data dialog box Solver Data page

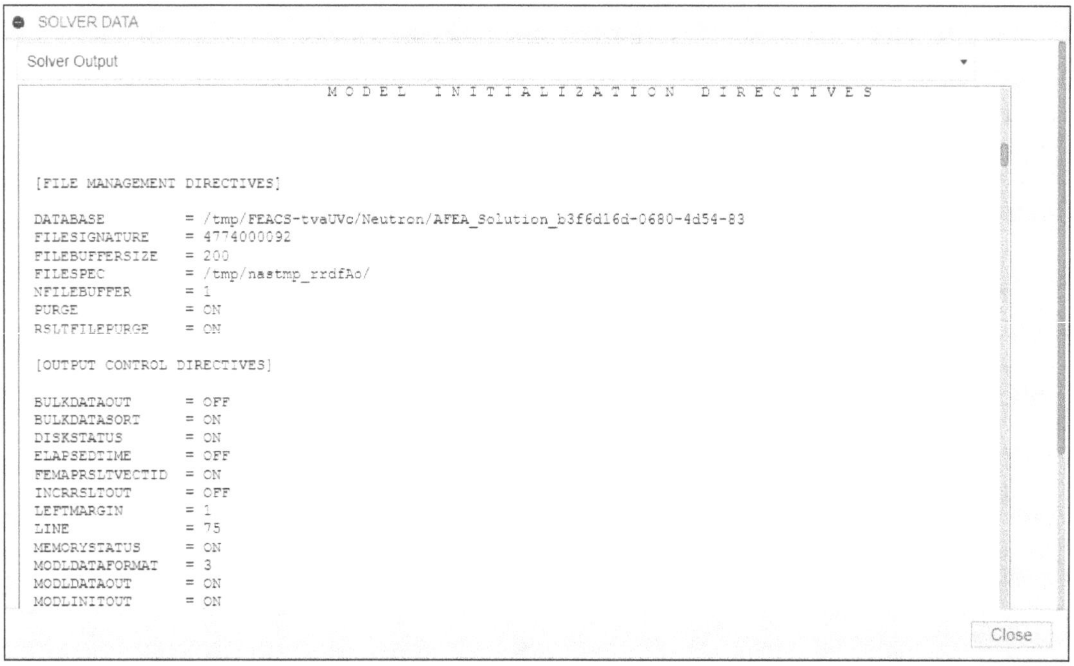

Figure-134. Solver Output page

Click on the **Save text file** button to save the output file for analyzing later.

Click on the **Finish Result** tool from the **FINISH RESULTS** drop-down in the **RESULTS** tab of **Toolbar** to exit the result mode.

EXPORTING STUDY TO ANSYS SETUP

The **Export Study to Ansys Setup** tool is used to export complete setup of analysis like geometry, loads, constraints, and so on to a **.sdz** file. The procedure to use this tool is given next.

- Click on the **Export Study to Ansys Setup** tool from the **ANSYS** drop-down in the **SETUP** tab of the **Toolbar**. The **Export to Ansys Setup** dialog box will be displayed; refer to Figure-135.

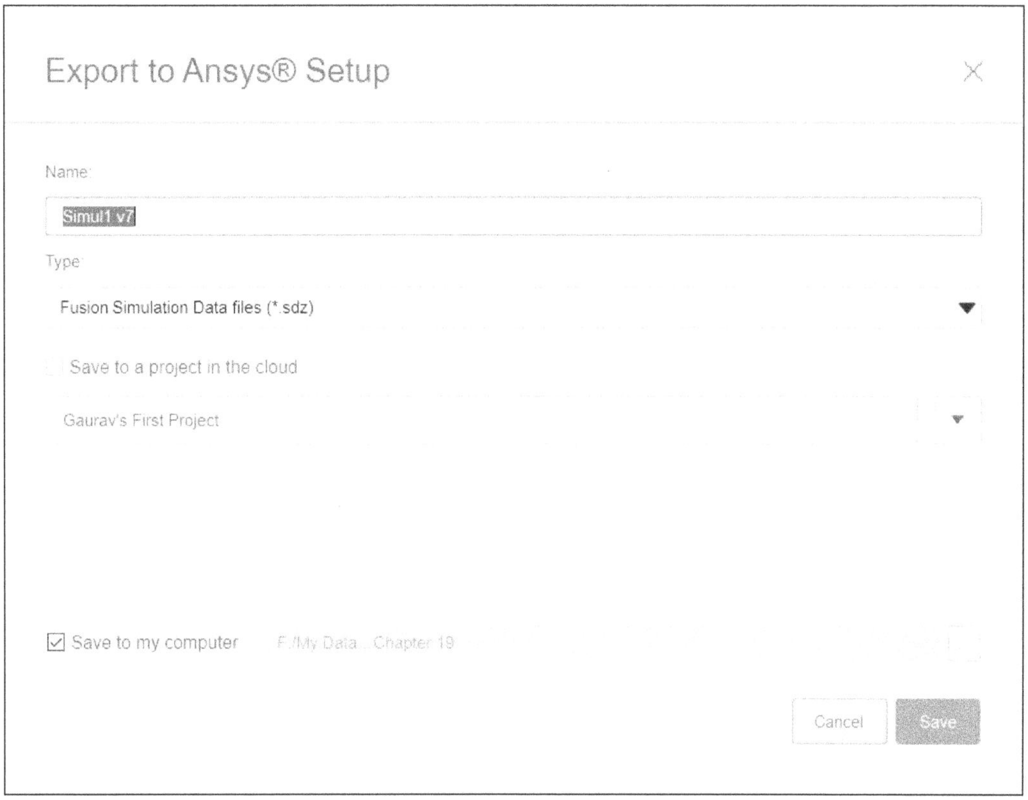

Figure-135. Export to Ansys Setup dialog box

- Specify desired value in the **Name** edit box to define name for simulation file.
- Select desired option from the **Type** drop-down to define format in which the data related to analysis will be saved.
- Select the **Save to my computer** check box to save the file at desired location in computer.
- Click on the **Save** button from the dialog box to save the file. You can later load this file in Ansys software to perform advanced analyses.

In this chapter, you have worked on a Static Stress analysis. You have also gone through the basic process of analysis in Fusion. In the next chapter, you will work through other types of analyses available in Autodesk Fusion.

SELF-ASSESSMENT

Q1. An analysis fulfills following conditions:

- All loads are applied slowly and gradually until they reach their full magnitudes. After reaching their full magnitudes, load will remain constant (i.e. load will not vary against time).
- Linearity assumption: The relationship between loads and resulting responses is linear. For example, if you double the magnitude of loads, the response of the model (displacements, strains, and stresses) will also double.

Which of the following analyses should be used to check the design?

a. Linear Static Analysis b. Non-linear Static Analysis
c. Linear Dynamic Analysis d. Buckling Analysis

Q2. What is the difference between steady state thermal analysis and transient thermal analysis?

Q3. Which of the following analyses is used to study the effect of object velocity, initial velocity, acceleration, time dependent loads, and constraints in the design in Autodesk Fusion?

a. Shape Optimization b. Structural Buckling Analysis
c. Event Simulation d. Modal Analysis

Q4. Which of the following is not an element type for 3D objects in Autodesk Fusion simulation?

a. Linear Tetrahedron b. Parabolic Tetrahedron
c. Parabolic Tetrahedron with Curved edges d. Wedge

Q5. Which of the following tools is used to apply pin constraint?

a. Structural Constraint b. Bolt Connector
c. Rigid Body Connector d. Joint Origin

Q6. A linearly varying pressure exerted by fluid on surface of a part is called ....

Q7. The **Pre-check** tool is used to check if constraint is applied on wrong face of model. (T/F)

Q8. What is the most common type of analysis performed in Fusion?
A. Thermal Analysis
B. Static Analysis
C. Modal Analysis
D. Dynamic Event Simulation

Q9. What is assumed about the loads in a static analysis?
A. They are applied suddenly and vary with time
B. They are applied gradually and remain constant
C. They fluctuate unpredictably
D. They are only applied at the boundaries

Q10. Which of the following is a condition for making the linearity assumption in static analysis?
A. The material does not follow Hooke's Law
B. Boundary conditions change during the loading
C. Displacements are small enough to ignore stiffness changes
D. Loads change in magnitude while deforming

Q11. When is Nonlinear Static Stress Analysis required?
A. When linear assumptions hold true
B. When loads remain constant
C. When assumptions of linearity do not hold
D. When boundary conditions do not change

Q12. In Modal Analysis, what does the term "mode shape" refer to?
A. The way an object deforms under thermal conditions
B. The different shapes an object takes under vibration
C. The heat distribution in a body
D. The point at which an object buckles

Q13. What phenomenon occurs when a system vibrates at its natural frequency due to external forces?
A. Harmonic distortion
B. Resonance
C. Thermal expansion
D. Modal shift

Q14. What is the primary difference between Steady State and Transient Thermal Analysis?
A. Transient analysis considers time-dependent temperature changes
B. Steady-state analysis considers time-dependent temperature changes
C. Transient analysis ignores material conductivity
D. Steady-state analysis requires initial temperature conditions

Q15. What happens in Structural Buckling Analysis?
A. A material deforms due to resonance
B. A slender model suddenly deforms under axial loading
C. An object vibrates at increasing frequencies
D. A material heats up and expands

Q16. What type of analysis is performed to determine stresses due to simultaneous thermal and structural loads?
A. Dynamic Event Simulation
B. Modal Analysis
C. Thermal Stress Analysis
D. Static Analysis

Q17. What does Shape Optimization focus on in Fusion?
A. Finding the most complex design
B. Determining the shape that uses minimum material while maintaining strength
C. Reducing thermal stress
D. Increasing resonance frequency

Q18. What is the purpose of Electronics Cooling simulation?
A. To analyze dynamic motion of electronics
B. To determine if electronic components dissipate heat effectively
C. To evaluate the structural integrity of a circuit board
D. To optimize the mechanical vibration of electronics

Q19. What is Finite Element Analysis (FEA) used for?
A. Calculating the exact mathematical solution of a structure
B. Simplifying real-world engineering problems using small elements and nodes
C. Predicting the lifespan of materials
D. Designing 3D models

Q20. In Fusion, what type of elements are used for meshing 3D solids?
A. Line and planar elements
B. Linear and parabolic tetrahedron elements
C. Shell and bolt elements
D. Hexahedral elements

Q21. What is the primary purpose of the Simulation Workspace in Fusion?
A. To create 3D models
B. To perform structural analysis on models
C. To generate manufacturing toolpaths
D. To apply color and textures to models

Q22. What is the function of the Remove Features tool in the Simulation environment?
A. To delete the entire model
B. To remove irrelevant features that do not impact analysis results
C. To add additional constraints to the model
D. To modify material properties

Q23. Why is material selection important in study material analysis?
A. It determines how the object will look
B. It ensures accurate load distribution and stress calculations
C. It allows the software to run faster
D. It reduces the number of simulation steps

Q24. What is the primary function of the Manage Physical Materials tool?
A. To create new materials
B. To manage physical properties of materials
C. To delete existing materials
D. To apply textures to materials

Q25. Where can you find the Manage Physical Materials tool in Autodesk Fusion?
A. In the FILE menu
B. In the MATERIALS drop-down in the Toolbar
C. In the RENDER tab
D. In the ASSEMBLY menu

Q26. What is the purpose of the "Adds material to favorites and displays in editor" button?
A. To delete the selected material
B. To highlight the material in the library
C. To add the material to favorites and enable editing
D. To apply the material to the model

Q27. What is the final step in editing a material's physical properties?
A. Click the Apply button and then click OK
B. Click the Save button
C. Click the Reset button
D. Click the Delete button

Q28. How do you create a new material library in Autodesk Fusion?
A. By clicking the Create New Library tool
B. By renaming an existing library
C. By exporting materials from another software
D. By copying a default library

Q29. Which tab in the Material Browser defines description, cost, and manufacturer details?
A. Appearance
B. Physical
C. Identity
D. General

Q30. How can you quickly filter materials in the Material Browser?
A. By using the Cost field
B. By entering Keywords
C. By selecting Manufacturer
D. By sorting by Color

Q31. Which of the following is NOT a material category in Autodesk Fusion?
A. Metal
B. Transparent
C. Opaque
D. Ceramic

Q32. What happens when you increase the roughness value in the Appearance tab?
A. The material becomes more reflective
B. The material becomes less reflective
C. The material changes color
D. The material becomes transparent

Q33. What does the Translucency option define in the Appearance tab?
A. The amount of heat the material can transfer
B. The free transmission of light through the material
C. The ability of material to absorb sound
D. The density of the material

Q34. What is the function of the Emissivity check box in the Appearance tab?
A. To add a glow effect to the material
B. To make the material rougher
C. To make the material translucent
D. To change the color of the material

Q35. What does the Relief Pattern (Bump) check box do?
A. Changes the base color of the material
B. Adds an illusion of surface irregularities
C. Makes the material completely transparent
D. Adjusts the reflectance of the material

Q36. How can you define the reflectivity of an opaque material?
A. By adjusting the Reflectance slider
B. By changing the material type
C. By modifying the thermal conductivity
D. By selecting a new manufacturer

Q37. What does the Index of Refraction option define in transparent materials?
A. The density of the material
B. The roughness of the material
C. The refraction level of the material
D. The emission intensity of the material

Q38. What effect does selecting the Backface Culling check box have?
A. It makes only the front side of material reflect or transmit light
B. It makes the material completely opaque
C. It reduces the material's density
D. It increases the material's reflectance

Q39. What is Young's Modulus used for in the Physical tab?
A. To define the stress required for deformation per unit strain
B. To specify the reflectivity of the material
C. To define the roughness of the material
D. To adjust the light absorption rate

Q40. What is the function of the Poisson's Ratio parameter?
A. It defines the expansion in one direction due to compression in another
B. It defines the temperature at which material melts
C. It specifies the reflectivity of a transparent material
D. It defines the density of a metal

Chapter 21

Simulation Studies in Fusion

Topics Covered

The major topics covered in this chapter are:

- ***Introduction***
- ***Nonlinear Static Stress Analysis***
- ***Modal Frequencies Analysis***
- ***Buckling Analysis***
- ***Thermal Analysis***
- ***Event Simulation***
- ***Shape Optimization***
- ***Electronics Cooling***
- ***Injection Molding Simulation***

INTRODUCTION

In previous chapter, you have learned about the basics of the analysis. In this chapter, you will learn the procedure of applying different analyses on the part.

NONLINEAR STATIC STRESS ANALYSIS

Non-linear static stress analysis is used to check the effect of load on part when three common forms of nonlinearity like material, geometric, and boundary conditions nonlinearity are applicable in analysis. The procedure to apply non-linear static stress analysis is given next.

- Click on the **New Simulation Study** button from **STUDY** drop-down in the **Toolbar**. The **New Study** dialog box will be displayed. You can also press **N** while in **Simulation** workspace to do the same.
- Double-click on the **Nonlinear Static Stress** button from the dialog box. The analysis environment will be displayed.
- Click on the **Settings** button from the **MANAGE** drop-down in the **Toolbar**; refer to Figure-1. The **Settings** dialog box will be displayed; refer to Figure-2.

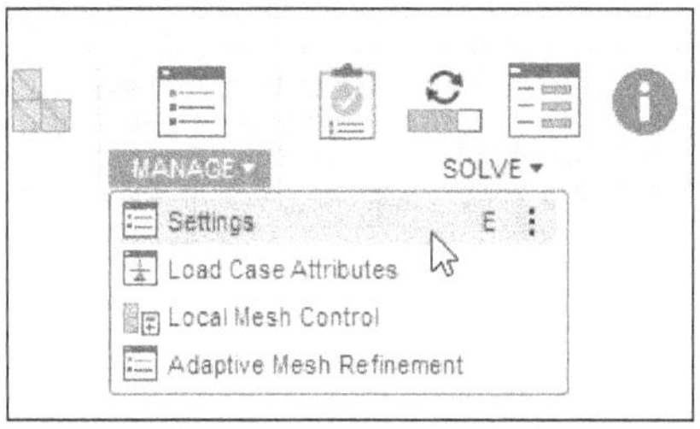

Figure-1. Settings tool

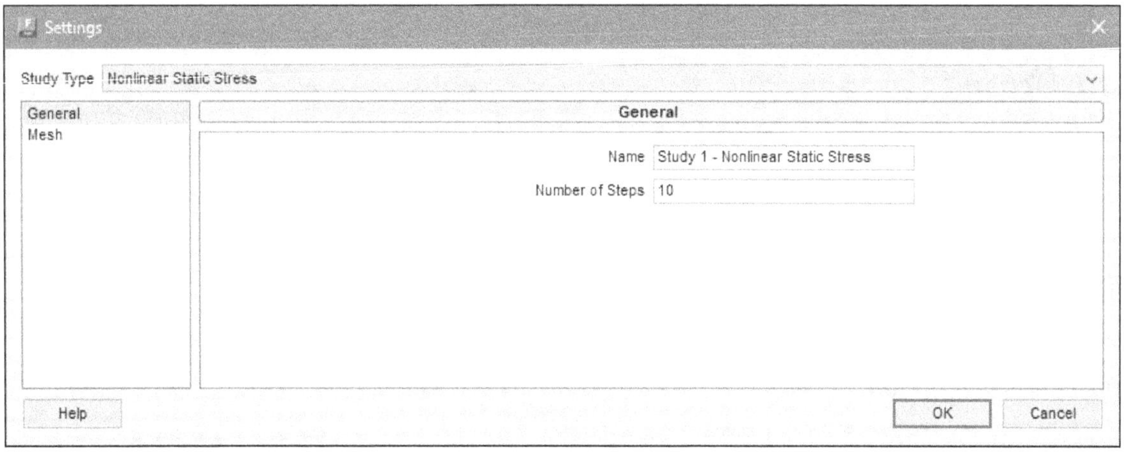

Figure-2. Settings dialog box

- In the **Number of Steps** edit box, specify desired number of steps in which the total load will be applied.
- Click on the **OK** button to apply the parameters.
- Apply the material, load, and constraint as required on the model; refer to Figure-3. Note that for nonlinear materials, you need to select **Fusion Nonlinear Material Library** option from the **Material Library** drop-down in the **STUDY MATERIALS** dialog box; refer to Figure-4.

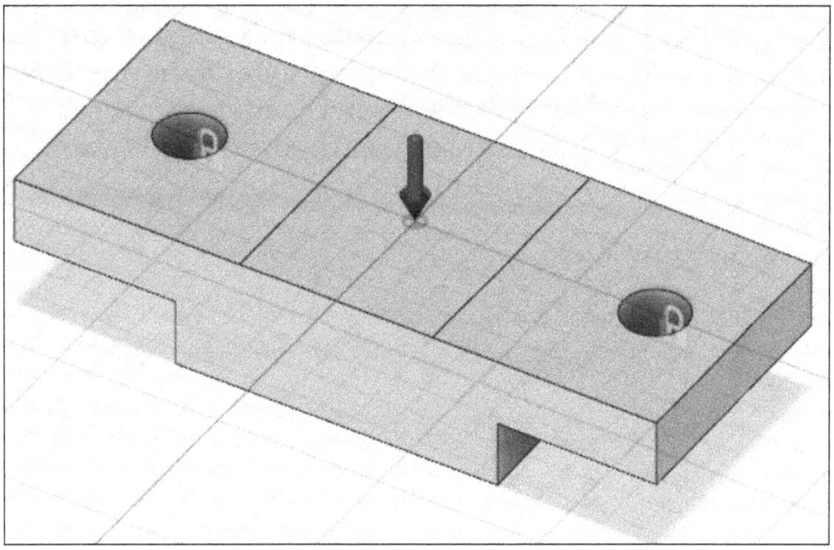

Figure-3. Load and constraint applied

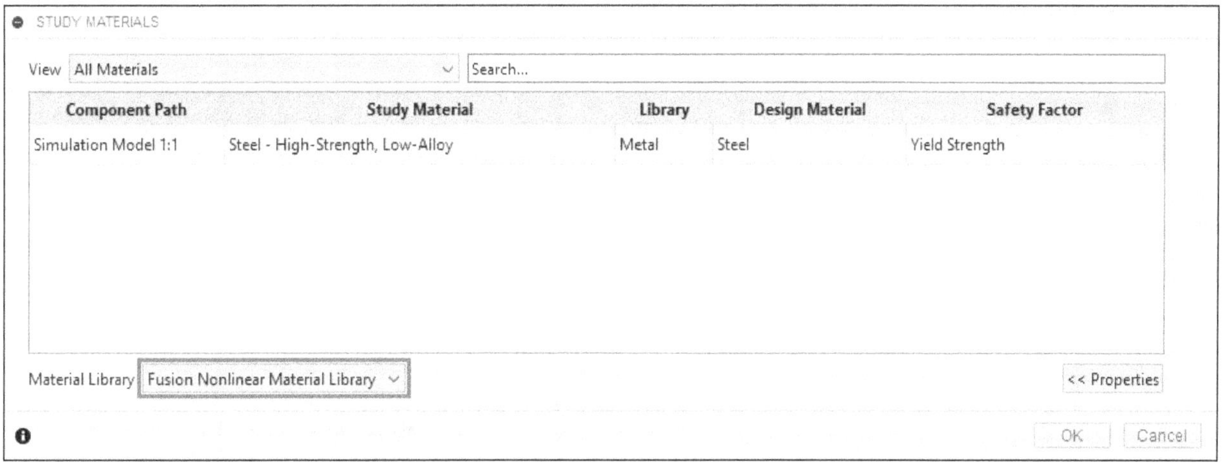

Figure-4. Non linear material library option

- Click on the **Solve** button from the **SOLVE** drop-down in the **Toolbar**. The **Solve** dialog box will be displayed.
- Click on the **Solve 1 Study** button from the dialog box. The result will be displayed on the screen; refer to Figure-5.

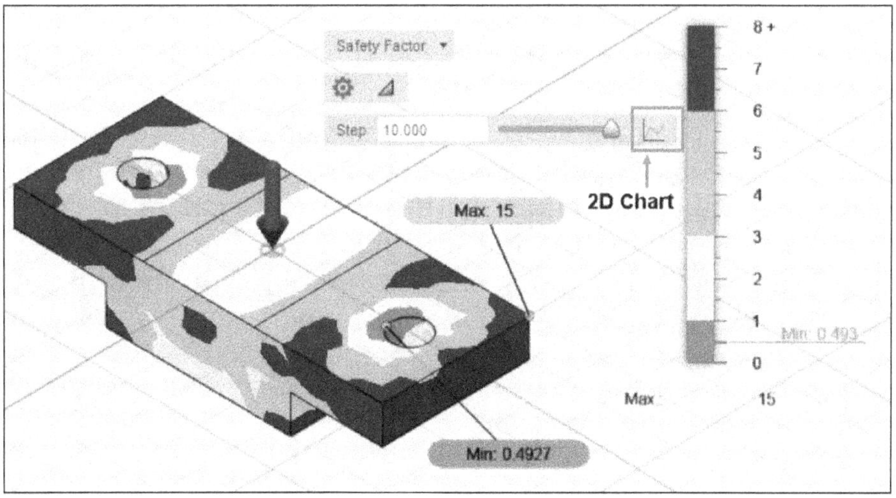

Figure-5. Result of non linear static analysis

- Click on the **2D Chart** button in the results to check the transient behavior. The **TRANSIENT RESULTS PLOT** dialog box will be displayed with the results; refer to Figure-6. Note that this plot gives insight of what is happening in the model at each time step. There can be some cases where maximum stress will be occurring at the middle of time steps and value at last time step will be minimal. If you miss such value then your part may fail in the assembly.

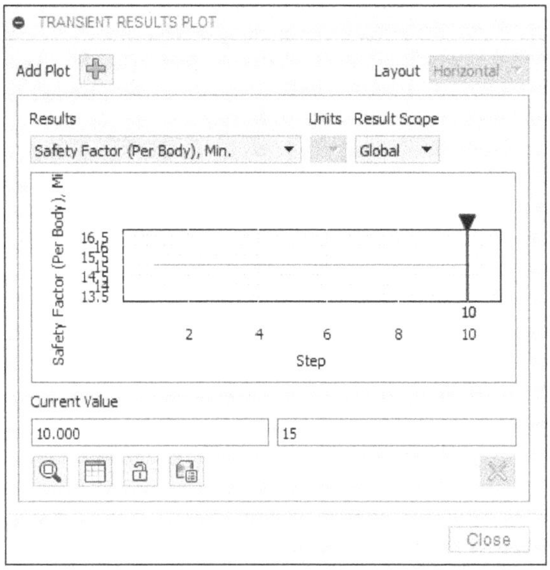

Figure-6. TRANSIENT RESULTS PLOT dialog box

- Move the slider in the graph to check the results of load at different steps. Select desired result type from the **Results** drop-down in the dialog box.

You can generate the report as discussed earlier.

STRUCTURAL BUCKLING ANALYSIS

Slender models tend to buckle under axial loading. Buckling is defined as the sudden deformation which occurs when the stored membrane (axial) energy is converted into bending energy with no change in the externally applied loads. Mathematically, when buckling occurs, the stiffness becomes singular. The Linearized buckling approach, used here, solves an eigenvalue problem to estimate the critical buckling factors and the associated buckling mode shapes.

A model can buckle in different shapes under different levels of loading. The shape the model takes while buckling is called the buckling mode shape and the loading is called the critical or buckling load. Buckling analysis calculates a number of modes as requested in the Buckling dialog. Designers are usually interested in the lowest mode (mode 1) because it is associated with the lowest critical load. When buckling is the critical design factor, calculating multiple buckling modes helps in locating the weak areas of the model. The mode shapes can help you modify the model or the support system to prevent buckling in a certain mode.

A more vigorous approach to study the behavior of models at and beyond buckling requires the use of nonlinear design analysis codes. In a laymen's language, if you press down on an empty soft drink can with your hand, not much will seem to happen. If you put the can on the floor and gradually increase the force by stepping down on it with your foot, at some point it will suddenly squash. This sudden scrunching is known as "buckling."

Models with thin parts tend to buckle under axial loading. Buckling can be defined as the sudden deformation, which occurs when the stored membrane (axial) energy is converted into bending energy with no change in the externally applied loads. Mathematically, when buckling occurs, the total stiffness matrix becomes singular.

In the normal use of most products, buckling can be catastrophic if it occurs. The failure is not one because of stress but geometric stability. Once the geometry of the part starts to deform, it can no longer support even a fraction of the force initially applied. The worst part about buckling for engineers is that buckling usually occurs at relatively low stress values for what the material can withstand. So, they have to make a separate check to see if a product or part thereof is okay with respect to buckling.

Slender structures and structures with slender parts loaded in the axial direction buckle under relatively small axial loads. Such structures may fail in buckling while their stresses are far below critical levels. For such structures, the buckling load becomes a critical design factor. Stocky structures, on the other hand, require large loads to buckle, therefore buckling analysis is usually not required.

Buckling almost always involves compression. In civil engineering, buckling is to be avoided when designing support columns, load bearing walls and sections of bridges which may flex under load. For example an I-beam may be perfectly "safe" when considering only the maximum stress, but fail disastrously if just one local spot of a flange should buckle! In mechanical engineering, designs involving thin parts in flexible structures like airplanes and automobiles are susceptible to buckling. Even though stress can be very low, buckling of local areas can cause the whole structure to collapse by a rapid series of 'propagating buckling'.

Buckling analysis calculates the smallest (critical) loading required for buckling a model. Buckling loads are associated with buckling modes. Designers are usually interested in the lowest mode because it is associated with the lowest critical load. When buckling is the critical design factor, calculating multiple buckling modes helps in locating the weak areas of the model. This may prevent the occurrence of lower buckling modes by simple modifications.

USE OF BUCKLING ANALYSIS

Slender parts and assemblies with slender components that are loaded in the axial direction buckle under relatively small axial loads. Such structures can fail due to buckling while the stresses are far below critical levels. For such structures, the buckling load becomes a critical design factor. Buckling analysis is usually not required for bulky structures as failure occurs earlier due to high stresses. The procedure to use buckling analysis in Fusion is given next.

- Open/create the part on which you want to perform buckling analysis. Click on the **New Simulation Study** button from **STUDY** drop-down in the **Toolbar**. The **New Study** dialog box will be displayed.
- Double-click on the **Structural Buckling** tool from the **New Study** dialog box. The analysis environment will be displayed.
- Apply material, constraints, loads, and other parameters as required and solve the study as discussed earlier. The results of buckling will be displayed; refer to Figure-7.

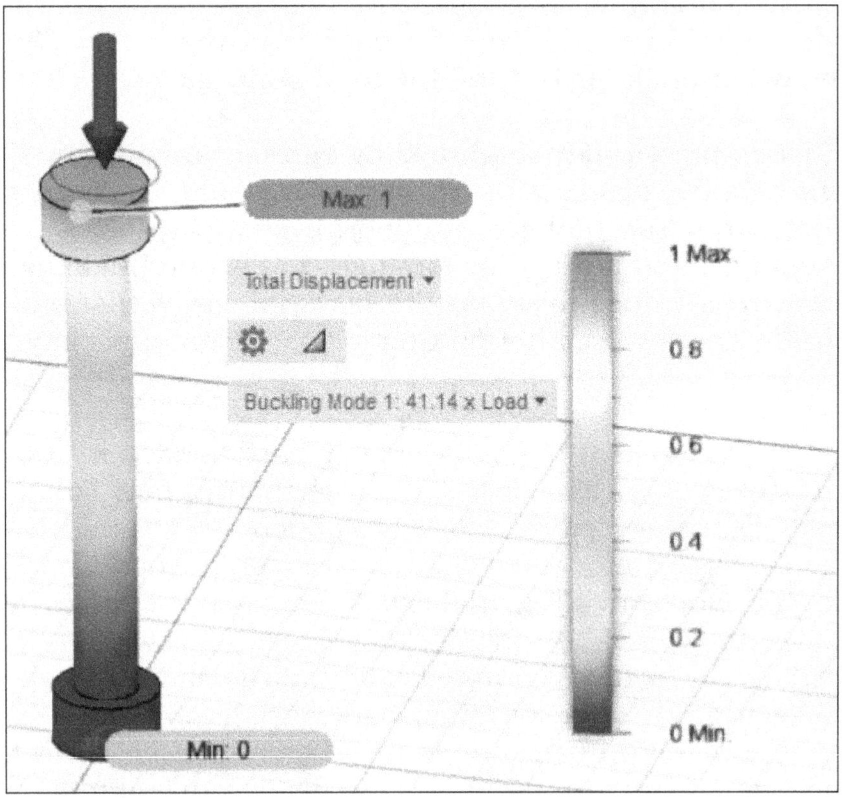

Figure-7. Result of buckling analysis

- Click in the **Buckling Mode** drop-down in the results and select desired buckling mode to check the effect; refer to Figure-8.

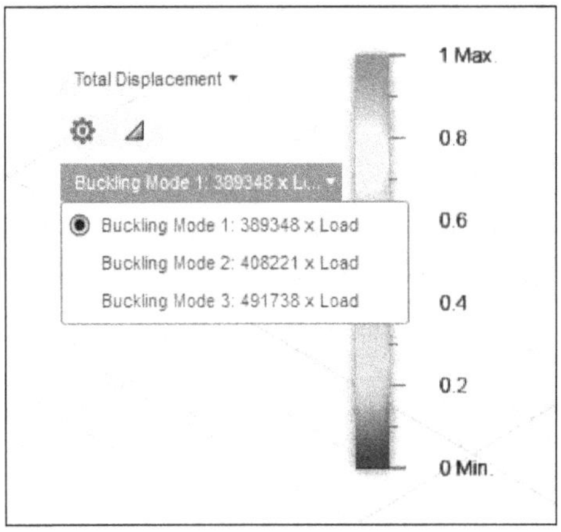

Figure-8. Buckling Mode drop down

MODAL FREQUENCIES ANALYSIS

Every structure has the tendency to vibrate at certain frequencies, called **natural or resonant frequencies**. Each natural frequency is associated with a certain shape, called **mode shape**, that the model tends to assume when vibrating at that frequency. When a structure is properly excited by a dynamic load with a frequency that coincides with one of its natural frequencies, the structure undergoes large displacements and stresses. This phenomenon is known as **Resonance**. For undamped systems, resonance theoretically causes infinite motion. **Damping**, however, puts a limit on the response of the structures due to resonant loads.

A real model has an infinite number of natural frequencies. However, a finite element model has a finite number of natural frequencies that are equal to the number of degrees of freedom considered in the model. Only the first few modes are needed for most purposes.

If your design is subjected to dynamic environments, static studies cannot be used to evaluate the response. Frequency studies can help you design vibration isolation systems by avoiding resonance in specific frequency band. They also form the basis for evaluating the response of linear dynamic systems where the response of a system to a dynamic environment is assumed to be equal to the summation of the contributions of the modes considered in the analysis.

Note that resonance is desirable in the design of some devices. For example, resonance is required in guitars and violins.

The natural frequencies and corresponding mode shapes depend on the geometry, material properties, and support conditions. The computation of natural frequencies and mode shapes is known as modal, frequency, and normal mode analysis.

When building the geometry of a model, you usually create it based on the original (undeformed) shape of the model. Some loads, like the structure's own weight, are always present and can cause considerable effects on the shape of the structure and its modal properties. In many cases, this effect can be ignored because the induced deflections are small.

Loads affect the modal characteristics of a body. In general, compressive loads decrease resonant frequencies and tensile loads increase them. This fact is easily demonstrated by changing the tension on a violin string. The higher the tension, the higher the frequency (tone).

You do not need to define any loads for a frequency study but if you do, their effect will be considered. By having evaluated natural frequencies of a structure's vibrations at the design stage, you can optimize the structure with the goal of meeting the frequency vibro-stability condition. To increase natural frequencies, you would need to add rigidity to the structure and (or) reduce its weight. For example, in the case of a slender object, the rigidity can be increased by reducing the length and increasing the thickness of the object. To reduce a part's natural frequency, you should, on the contrary, increase the weight or reduce the object's rigidity.

Note that the software also considers thermal and fluid pressure effects for frequency studies.

The procedure to perform the frequency analysis is given next.

- Open/create the part on which you want to perform modal analysis. Click on the **New Simulation Study** button from **STUDY** drop-down in the **Toolbar**. The **New Study** dialog box will be displayed.
- Double-click on the **Modal Frequencies** tool from the **New Study** dialog box. The analysis environment will be displayed.
- Click **Settings** tool from the **MANAGE** drop-down in the **Toolbar**. Select **Modal Frequencies** option from **Study Type** drop-down in the dialog box. The **Settings** dialog box for **Modal Frequencies** option will be displayed; refer to Figure-9.

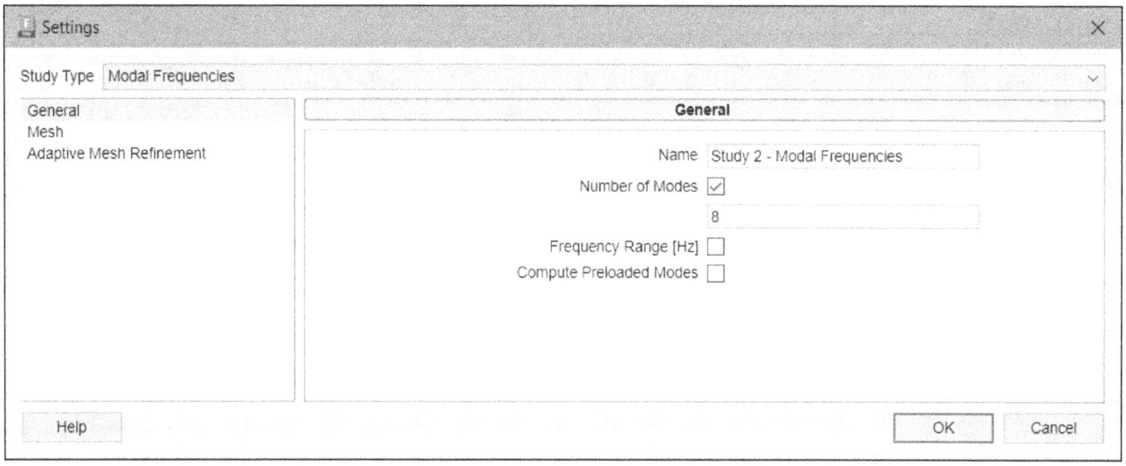

Figure-9. Settings dialog box for modal frequencies option

- Select the **Number of Modes** check box and specify the total number of frequencies that you want to test for resonance.
- Select the **Frequency Range (Hz)** check box to specify the minimum & maximum frequencies within which the natural frequencies are to be found.
- Select the **Compute Preloaded Modes** check box if you include the effect of structural loads in modal frequency analysis.
- After specifying all the parameters, click on the **OK** button.
- Apply material, constraint, load, and other parameters as required and solve the study as discussed earlier. Note that you can perform modal analysis without applying any load but if you apply a load then its effects will also be counted in the results if the **Compute Preloaded Modes** check box is selected in the **Settings** dialog box. The results of modal analysis will be displayed; refer to Figure-10.

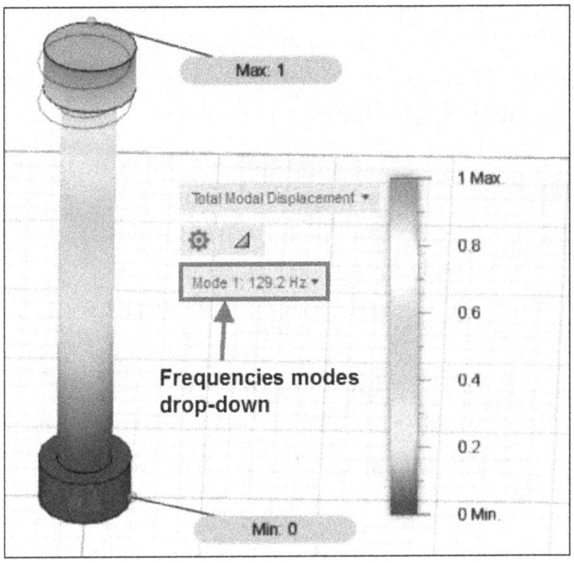

Figure-10. Frequencies drop-down

- Click on the **Mode** drop-down in **Results** area to check different natural frequencies of the model.

THERMAL ANALYSIS

Thermal analysis is a method to check the distribution of heat over a body due to applied thermal loads. Note that thermal energy is dynamic in nature and is always flowing through various mediums. There are three mechanisms by which the thermal energy flows:

- Conduction
- Convection
- Radiation

In all three mechanisms, heat energy flows from the medium with higher temperature to the medium with lower temperature. Heat transfer by conduction and convection requires the presence of an intervening medium while heat transfer by radiation does not.

The output from a thermal analysis can be given by:
1. Temperature distribution.
2. Amount of heat loss or gain.
3. Thermal gradients.
4. Thermal fluxes.

This analysis is used in many engineering industries such as automobile, piping, electronic, power generation, and so on.

Important terms related to Thermal Analysis

Before conducting thermal analysis, you should be familiar with the basic concepts and terminologies of thermal analysis. Following are some of the important terms used in thermal analysis:

Heat Transfer Modes

Whenever there is a difference in temperature between two bodies, the heat is transferred from one body to another. Basically, heat is transferred in three ways: Conduction, Convection, and Radiation.

Conduction

In conduction, the heat is transferred by interactions of atoms or molecules of the material. For example, if you heat up a metal rod at one end, the heat will be transferred to the other end by the atoms or molecules of the metal rod.

Convection

In convection, the heat is transferred by the flowing fluid. The fluid can be gas or liquid. Heating up water using an electric water heater is a good example of heat convection. In this case, water takes heat from the heater.

Radiation

In radiation, the heat is transferred in space without any matter. Radiation is the only heat transfer method that takes place in space. Heat coming from the Sun is a good example of radiation. The heat from the Sun is transferred to the earth through radiation.

Thermal Gradient

The thermal gradient is the rate of increase in temperature per unit depth in a material.

Thermal Flux

The Thermal flux is defined as the rate of heat transfer per unit cross-sectional area. It is denoted by q.

Bulk Temperature

It is the temperature of a fluid flowing outside the material. It is denoted by Tb. The Bulk temperature is used in convective heat transfer.

Film Coefficient

It is a measure of the heat transfer through an air film.

Emissivity

The Emissivity of a material is the ratio of energy radiated by the material to the energy radiated by a black body at the same temperature. Emissivity is the measure of a material's ability to absorb and radiate heat. It is denoted by e. Emissivity is a numerical value without any unit. For a perfect black body, $e = 1$. For any other material, $e < 1$.

Stefan–Boltzmann Constant

The energy radiated by a black body per unit area per unit time divided by the fourth power of the body's temperature is known as the Stefan-Boltzmann constant. It is denoted by s.

Thermal Conductivity

The thermal conductivity is the property of a material that indicates its ability to conduct heat. It is denoted by K.

Specific Heat

The specific heat is the amount of heat required per unit mass to raise the temperature of the body by one degree Celsius. It is denoted by C.

PERFORMING THERMAL ANALYSIS

- Click on the **New Simulation Study** button from **STUDY** drop-down in the **Toolbar**. The **New Study** dialog box will be displayed.
- Double-click on the **Thermal** button from the dialog box. The thermal analysis environment will be displayed.
- Apply desired material to the mode as discussed earlier.
- Click on the **Thermal Loads** tool from the **LOADS** panel in the **Toolbar**; refer to Figure-11. The **THERMAL LOADS** dialog box will be displayed; refer to Figure-12.

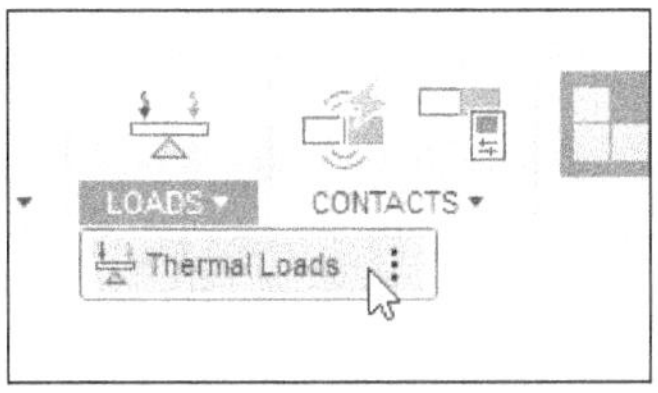

Figure-11. Thermal Loads tool

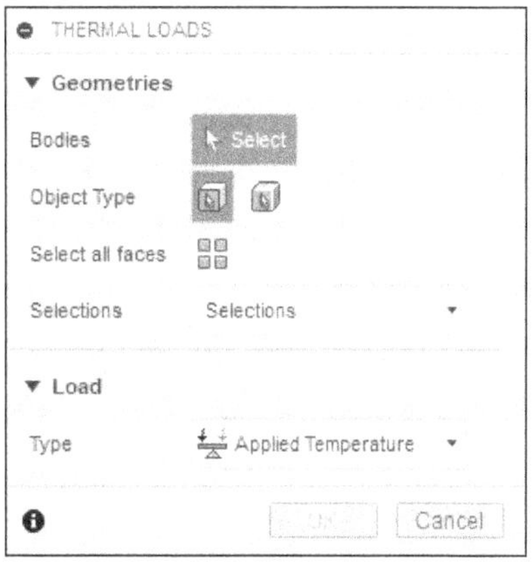

Figure-12. THERMAL LOADS dialog box

- Select desired thermal load type from the **Type** drop-down in the **Load** section of the dialog box. Select the **Applied Temperature** option from the drop-down and enter desired temperature if you want to apply a fix temperature to the selected geometry. Select the **Heat Source** option if you want to specify the amount of heat energy to be applied on selected geometry. Select the **Radiation** option if heat is transferred through radiation to the selected face. Select the **Convection** option if heat is transferred through convection. Select the **Internal Heat** option from the drop-down if heat is generated inside the model.
- Select the face/edge/vertex on which you want to apply thermal load. If you want to select a body then click on the **Bodies** button from the **Object Type** section of the dialog box and then select the body.
- Specify desired values of thermal load in edit boxes as per the option selected in the **Type** drop-down.
- Click on the **OK** button from dialog box to apply the settings.
- Specify the contacts as discussed earlier for heat flow between different components of the assembly.
- Click on the **Settings** button from the **MANAGE** drop-down in the **Toolbar**. The **Settings** dialog box will be displayed. Specify desired value of atmospheric temperature in the **Global Initial Temperature** edit box. Set the other parameters as discussed earlier. Click on the **OK** button from the dialog box to apply settings.

- After specifying all the parameters, click on the **Solve** button. The **Solve** dialog box will be displayed. Click on the **Solve Study** button in the dialog box. The results of analysis will be displayed; refer to Figure-13. You can use probes to check results at different locations as discussed earlier.

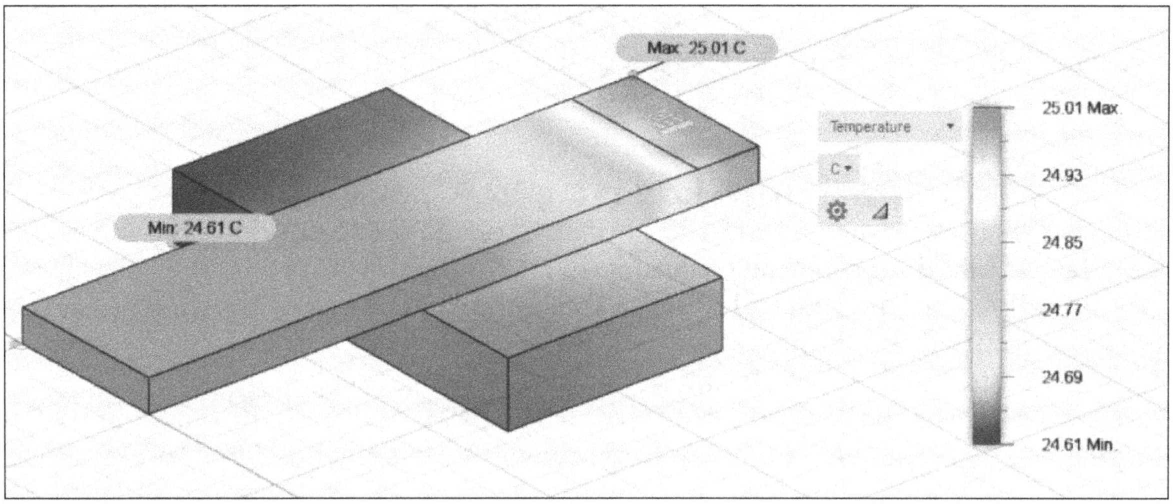

Figure-13. Result of thermal analysis

THERMAL STRESS ANALYSIS

The thermal stress analysis is used to check the effect of thermal and structural loads on the model. The procedure to perform the analysis is same as discussed earlier for thermal and stress analyses.

DYNAMIC EVENT SIMULATION

Event Simulation is used to study the effect of motion/load on different parts/bodies in model. This analysis is similar to dynamic non-linear analysis, you may have studied in engineering. In this example, we will simulate the collision of a ball on the plate. The procedure to perform event simulation is given next.

- Click on the **New Simulation Study** button from **STUDY** drop-down in the **Toolbar**. The **New Study** dialog box will be displayed. Double-click on the **Dynamic Event Simulation** button from the dialog box. The environment to solve event simulation will be displayed.
- Specify the material, constraints, and loads as applied earlier.
- Click on the **Prescribed Translation** tool from **CONSTRAINTS** drop-down in the **Toolbar**; refer to Figure-14 and specify the displacement, velocity, or acceleration of the selected body as required; refer to Figure-15.

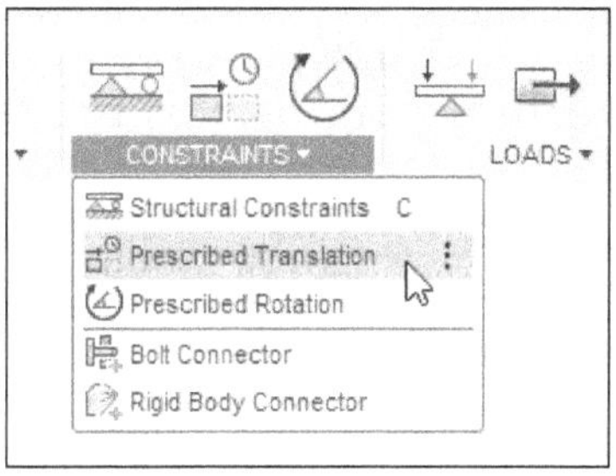

Figure-14. Prescribed Translation tool

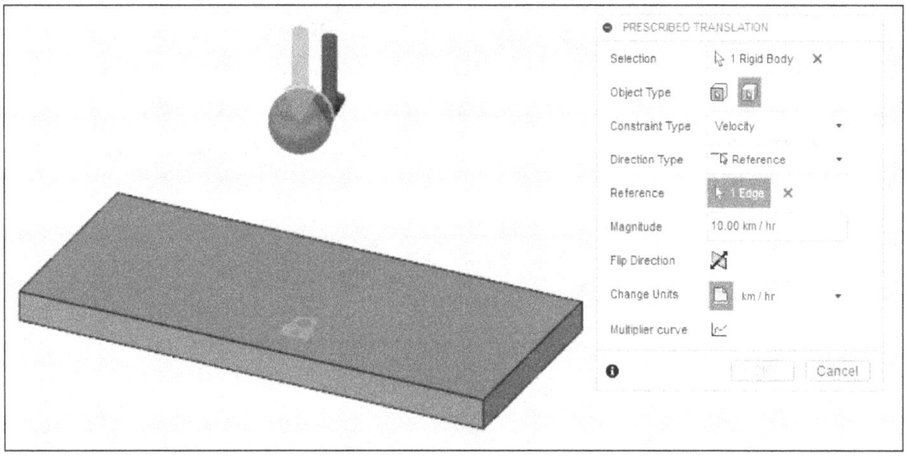

Figure-15. PRESCRIBED TRANSLATION dialog box

- Click on the **Solve** tool from **SOLVE** drop-down in the **Toolbar** and then click on the **Solve** button from the dialog box displayed. The results of analysis will be displayed. Set the slider to desired step to check the analysis result at intermediate steps.

Note that you can also use **Prescribed Rotation** tool from the **CONSTRAINTS** drop-down in **Toolbar** to apply rotation constraint to the model.

QUASI-STATIC EVENT SIMULATION

The Quasi-static Event Simulation is performed to study the large deformations in the part/assembly due to heavy loads that can change the contact conditions. The procedure to perform Quasi-static event simulation is similar to Dynamic event simulation performed earlier. Note that this study uses nonlinear behavior of material and loads in the simulation. Figure-16 shows strain result of an example quasi-static event simulation.

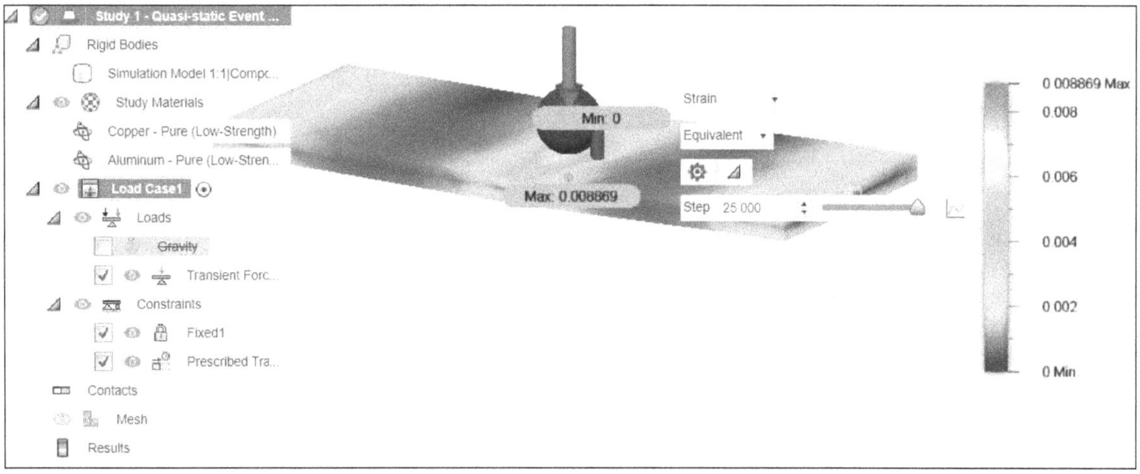

Figure-16. Example of quasi-static event simulation

SHAPE OPTIMIZATION

The Shape optimization study is used to reduce the mass of part while satisfying all the design requirements of the part. The procedure to use shape optimization is given next.

- Create/open the model on which you want to perform shape optimization study. Click on the **New Simulation Study** tool from **STUDY** drop-down in the **Toolbar**. The **New Study** dialog box will be displayed.
- Double-click on the **Shape Optimization** button from the dialog box. The environment to perform shape optimization will be displayed.
- Set the material, constraint, load, and contacts as required.

Target Body

- Click on the **Target Body** tool from **SHAPE OPTIMIZATION** drop-down in the **Toolbar** to define the body for which you want to perform optimization. The **TARGET BODY** dialog box will be displayed; refer to Figure-17.

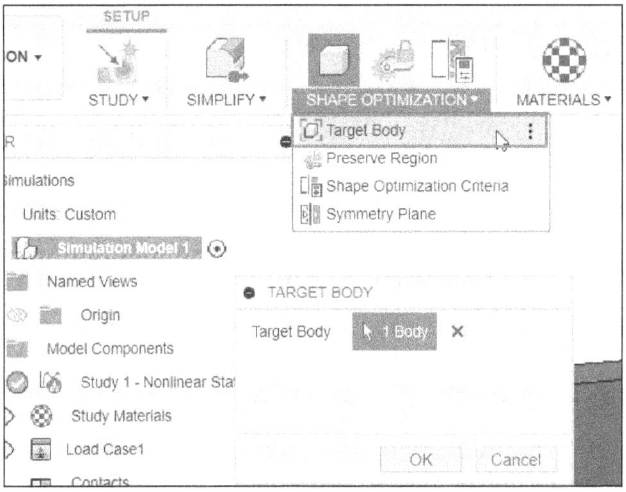

Figure-17. TARGET BODY dialog box

- Select the body to be used for performing shape optimization and click on the **OK** button from the dialog box.

Preserve Region

- Click on the **Preserve Region** tool from the **SHAPE OPTIMIZATION** drop-down in the **Toolbar**; refer to Figure-18. The **PRESERVE REGION** dialog box will be displayed; refer to Figure-19.

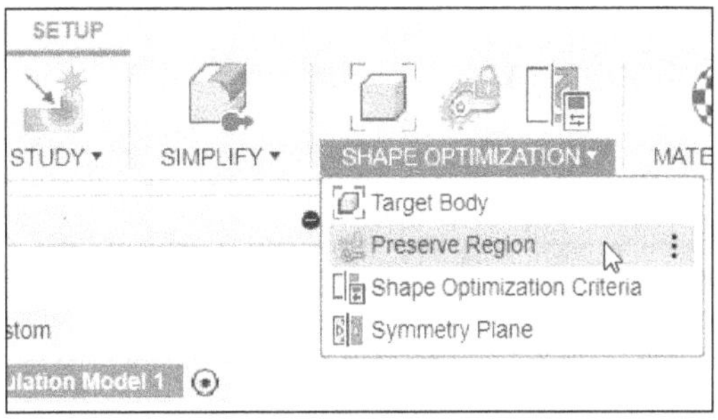

Figure-18. Preserve Region tool

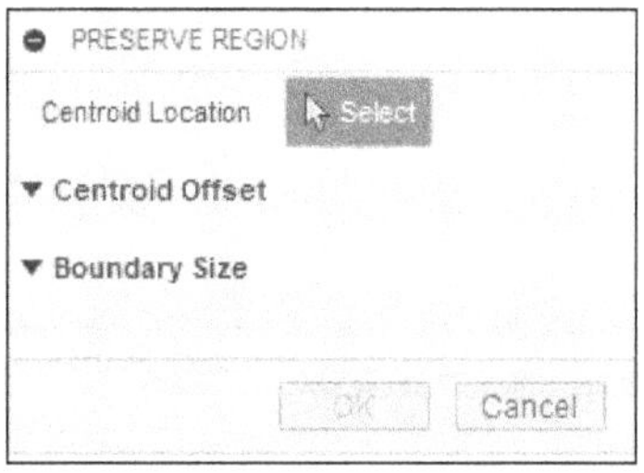

Figure-19. PRESERVE REGION dialog box

- Select the face that you want to be preserved after shape optimization. The options for preserving region based on selected faces will be displayed in the dialog box.
- Set desired options like if you have select a cylindrical face then specify the radius up to which you want to preserve the region; refer to Figure-20.
- Click on the **OK** button from the dialog box to apply the parameters.

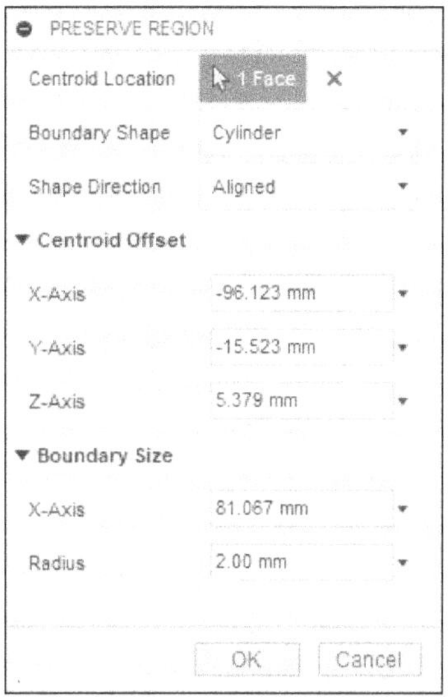

Figure-20. PRESERVE REGION dialog box with cylindrical face selected

Setting Shape Optimization criteria

- Click on the **Shape Optimization Criteria** tool from the **SHAPE OPTIMIZATION** drop-down in the **Toolbar**; refer to Figure-21. The **SHAPE OPTIMIZATION CRITERIA** dialog box will be displayed; refer to Figure-22.

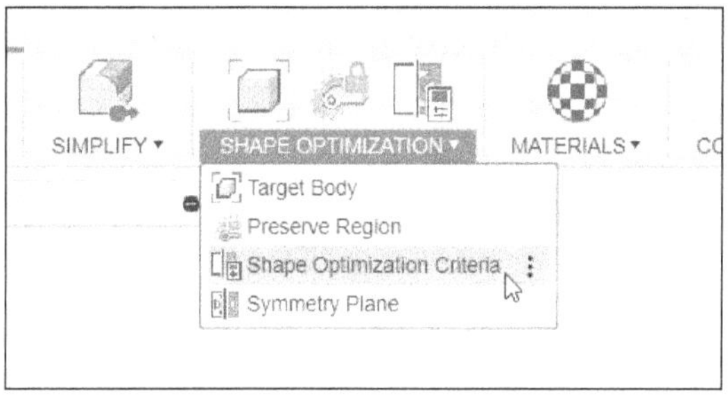

Figure-21. Shape Optimization Criteria tool

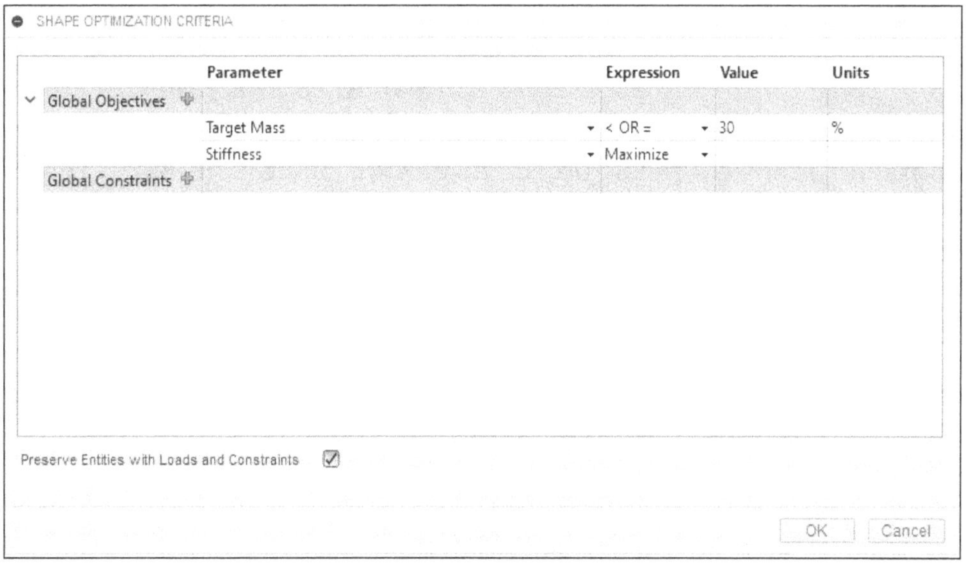

Figure-22. SHAPE OPTIMIZATION CRITERIA dialog box

- Set desired conditions in the dialog box like, Target Mass less than or equal to 40%.
- Click on the **OK** button to apply the settings.

- Create desired load and constraint conditions for the model.
- Click on the **Solve** tool from **SOLVE** drop-down in the **Toolbar**. The **Solve** dialog box will be displayed.
- Click on the **Solve** button. The result will be displayed; refer to Figure-23.

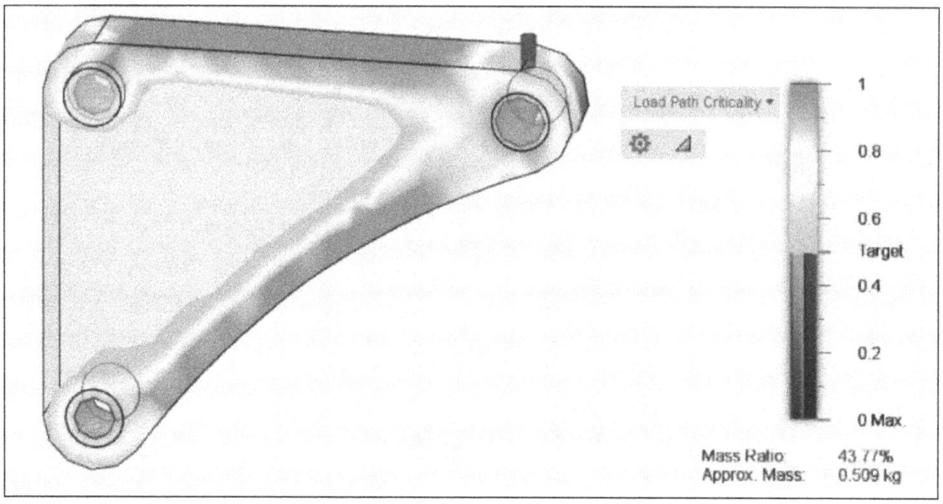

Figure-23. Result of shape optimization

Generating Mesh Body of Result

- Click on the **Promote** tool from **RESULT TOOLS** drop-down in **Toolbar**; refer to Figure-24. The **PROMOTE** dialog box will be displayed; refer to Figure-25.

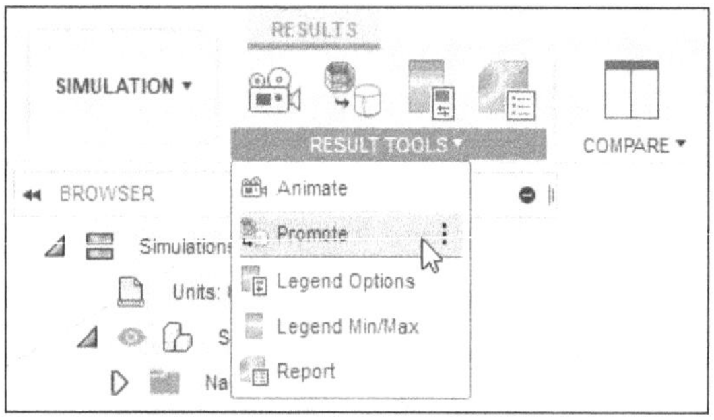

Figure-24. Promote tool

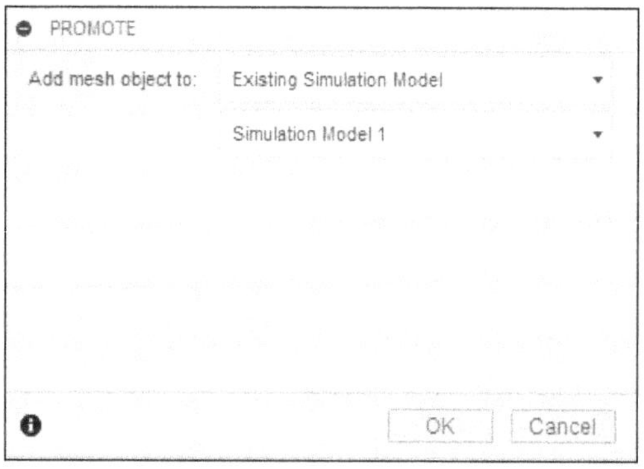

Figure-25. PROMOTE dialog box

- Select the **Design Workspace** option from the **Add mesh object to** drop-down to generate mesh model as mesh object in model. Select the **Existing Simulation Model** option from the drop-down to add the mesh object in selected simulation model. Select the **Clone Current Simulation Model** option to create a copy of simulation model with mesh body.
- Select the **Clone Studies** check box while making copy to also copy simulation study parameters.
- Click on the **OK** button from the dialog box. The mesh body will be displayed which can be used to modify the part; refer to Figure-26.

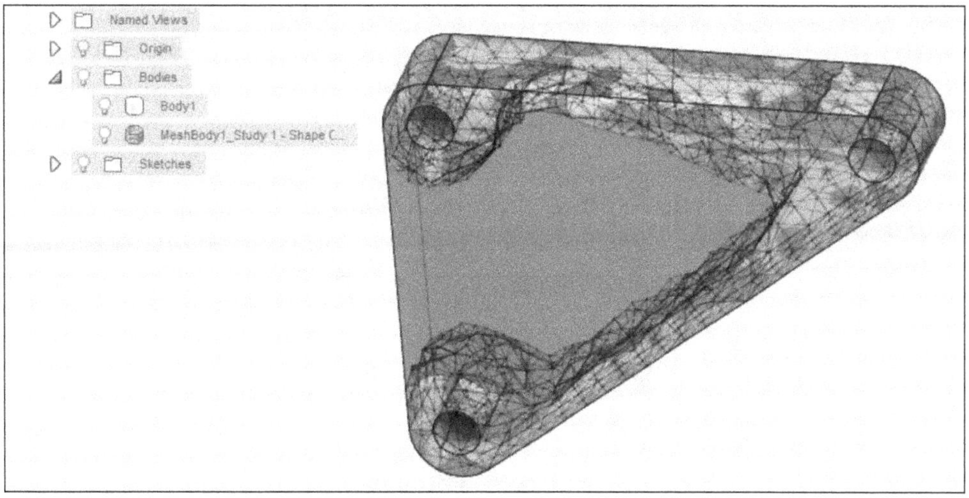

Figure-26. Mesh model generated in Model workspace

ELECTRONICS COOLING

The Electronics Cooling study is performed to check whether temperature of selected bodies exceed the specified values or not due to internal heat loads on the PCB. While writing this edition of book, the Electronics Cooling study was in Preview mode. So, you can expect more changes in this study. The procedure to perform this study is given next.

- Create/open the model on which you want to perform electronics cooling study. Click on the **New Simulation Study** tool from **STUDY** drop-down in the **Toolbar**. The **New Study** dialog box will be displayed.
- Double-click on the **Electronics Cooling** button from the dialog box. The environment to perform electronics cooling study will be displayed; refer to Figure-27.

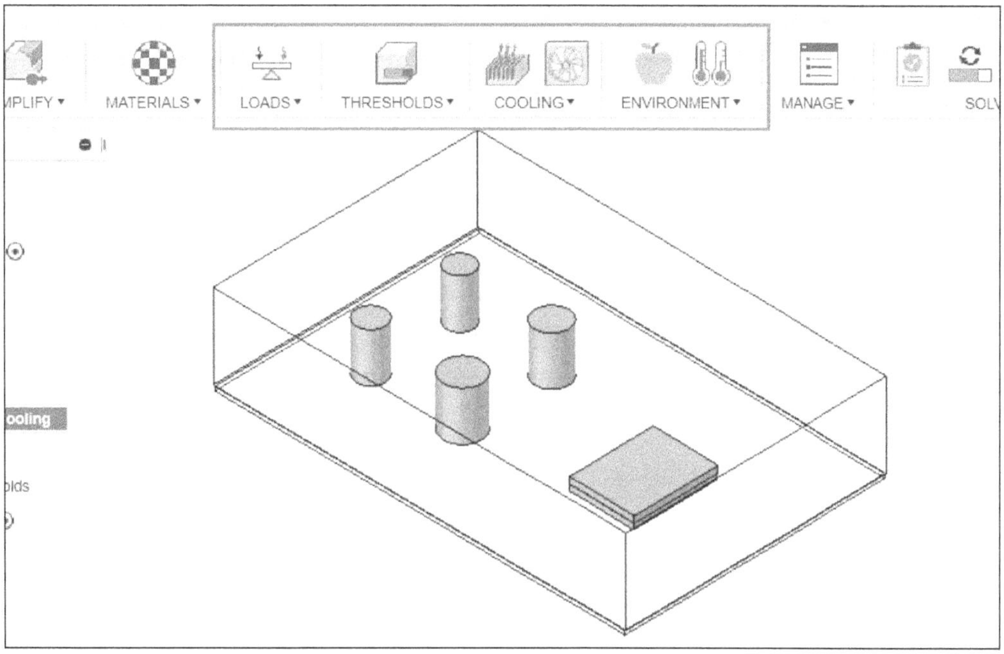

Figure-27. Tools specific to electronics cooling study

- Apply the materials as discussed earlier. Generally, PCB is made of epoxy resin with fiberglass layers.

Applying Internal Heat

Internal heat is applied to various electronics components to define how much heat is generated through the components. The procedure to apply internal heat is given next.

- Click on the **Thermal Loads** tool from the **LOADS** drop-down in the **SETUP** tab of the **Toolbar**. The **THERMAL LOADS** dialog box will be displayed; refer to Figure-28.

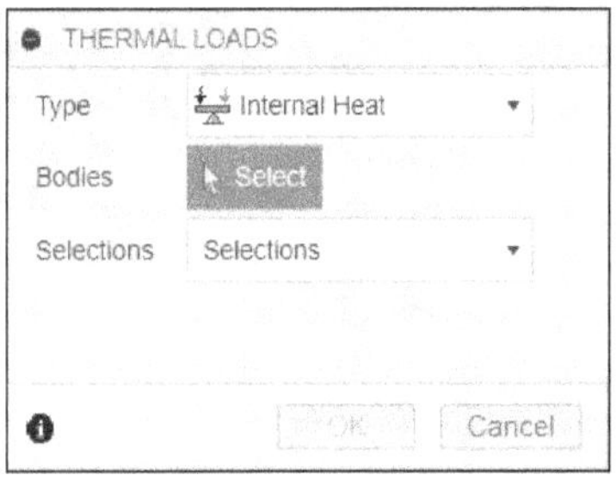

Figure-28. THERMAL LOADS dialog box

- Select all the bodies to which you want to apply thermal loads and specify desired value of heat in the **Internal Heat Value** edit box; refer to Figure-29.

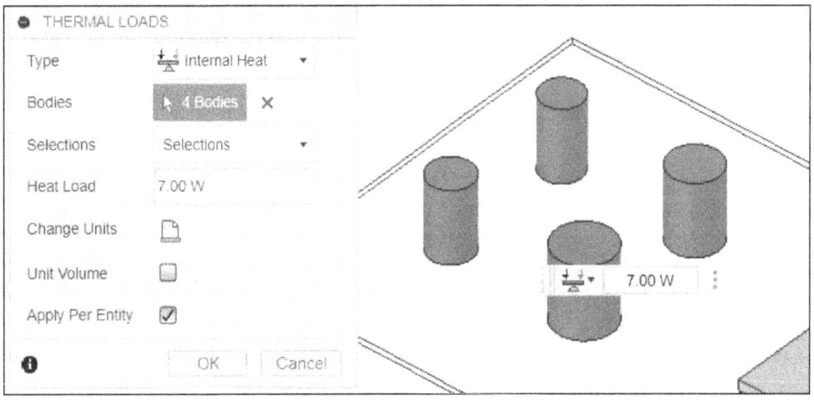

Figure-29. Applying internal heat load

- After setting desired parameters, click on the **OK** button from the dialog box. The internal heat loads will be generated.

Applying Heat Transfer

The **Heat Sink** tool is used to apply effect of a heat sink on selected body. The procedure to apply heat sink is given next.

- Click on the **Heat Sink** tool from **COOLING** drop-down in the **SETUP** tab of the **Toolbar**. The **HEAT SINK** dialog box will be displayed; refer to Figure-30.

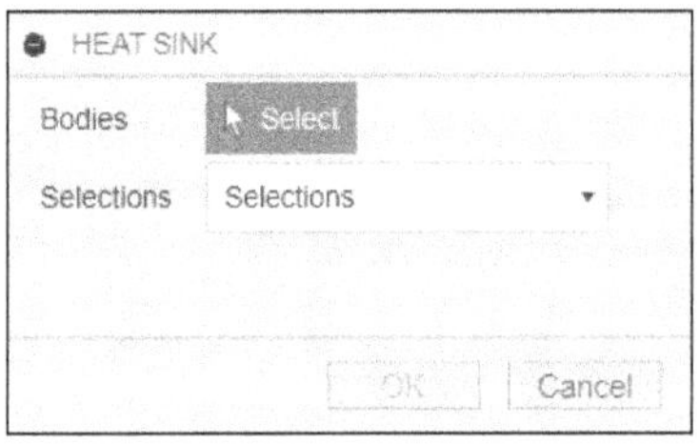

Figure-30. HEAT SINK dialog box

- Select desired body to be used as heat sink and click on the **OK** button from the dialog box.

Applying Forced Flow

The **Fan** tool is used to apply volumetric air or fluid flow to selected bodies. The procedure to apply force flow is given next.

- Click on the **Fan** tool from the **COOLING** drop-down in the **SETUP** tab of the **Toolbar**. The **FAN** dialog box will be displayed; refer to Figure-31.

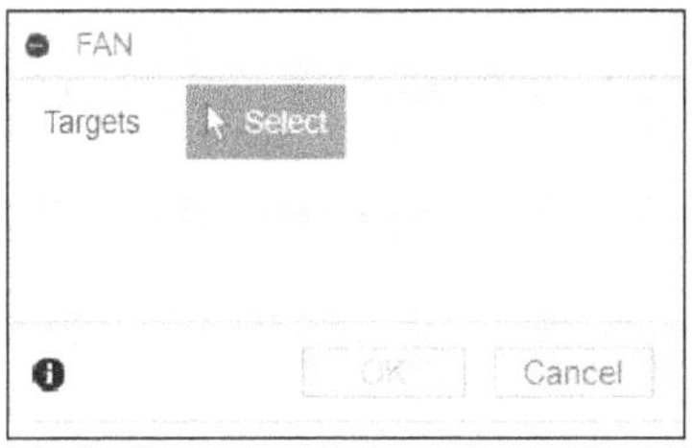

Figure-31. FAN dialog box

- Select desired body to be used as target for applying cooling fan volume; refer to Figure-32. Note that we have created a box with air material applied to it as forced flow body.

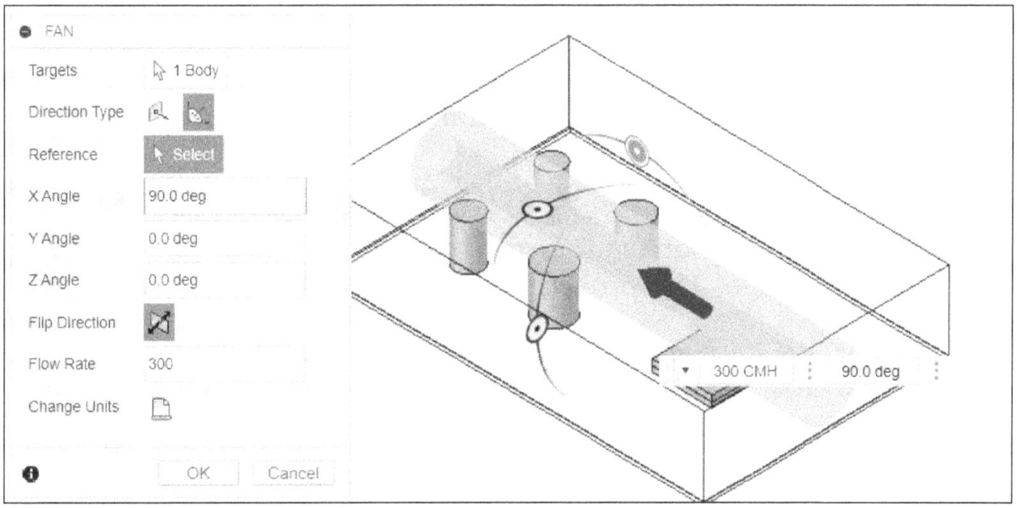

Figure-32. Applying forced flow parameters

- After setting desired parameters, click on the **OK** button from the dialog box to apply the forced flow.

Specifying Temperature Thresholds

Temperature threshold is defined as maximum safe temperature up to which selected electronic components can function properly. The procedure to specify critical temperature is given next.

- Click on the **Temperature Thresholds** tool from the **THRESHOLDS** drop-down in the **SETUP** tab of the **Ribbon**. The **TEMPERATURE THRESHOLDS** dialog box will be displayed; refer to Figure-33.

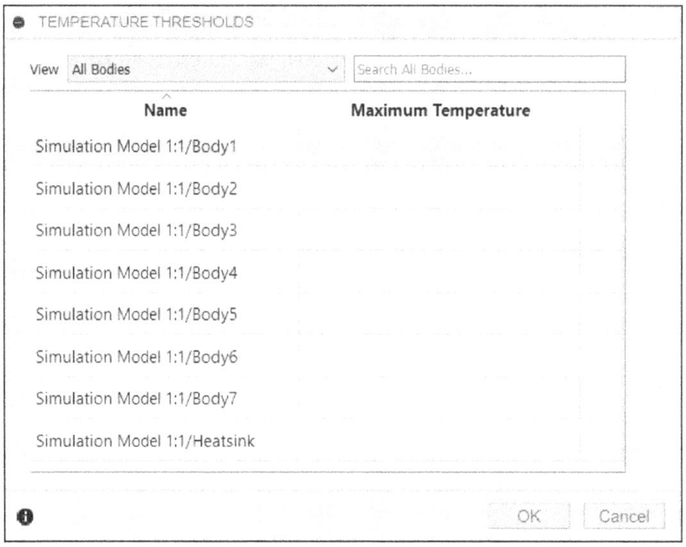

Figure-33. TEMPERATURE THRESHOLDS dialog box

- Specify desired values in the edit boxes under **Maximum Temperature** column. After setting desired parameter, click on the **OK** button from the dialog box.

After setting desired parameters, click on the **Solve** tool from the **SOLVE** drop-down in the **SETUP** tab of **Toolbar** and solve the analysis as discussed earlier.

INJECTION MOLDING SIMULATION

The injection molding simulation is performed to check whether the mold fills properly within specified time frame. The procedure to perform this analysis is given next.

- Click on the **Injection Molding Simulation** button from the **New Study** dialog box and click on the **Create Study** button; refer to Figure-34. The tools related to injection molding simulation will be displayed; refer to Figure-35.

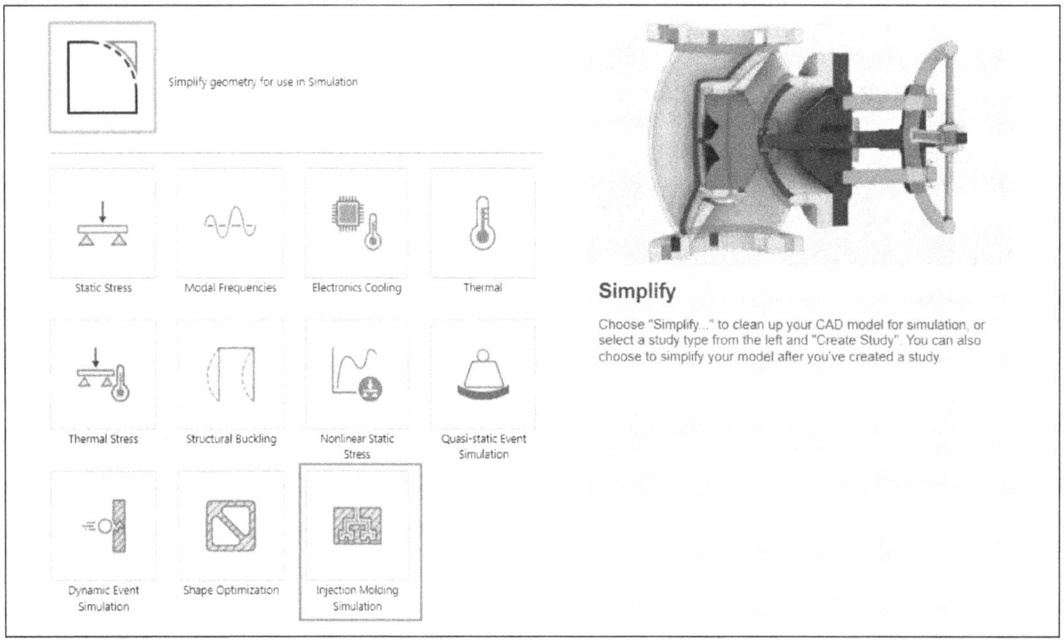

Figure-34. Injection Molding Simulation button

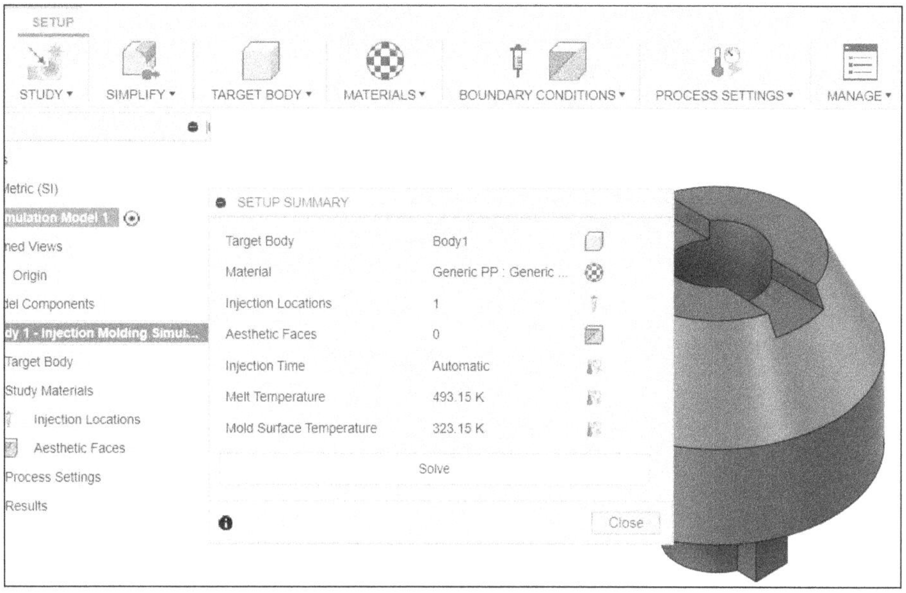

Figure-35. Interface of Injection Molding Simulation

- You can use the options in **Ribbon** as well as **SETUP SUMMARY** dialog box to define setup of injection mold simulation. Here, we will discuss the method using **SETUP SUMMARY** dialog box, you can use the tools in **Ribbon** in the same way.

Selecting Target Body

Target body is the solid body of plastic model to be manufactured using injection molding process. If there is only one body in the model then it will be selected automatically but if there are multiple bodies then you need to select desired body from graphics area. The method to select target body is given next.

- Click on the **Target Body** button from the **SETUP SUMMARY** dialog box. The **TARGET BODY** dialog box will be displayed; refer to Figure-36.

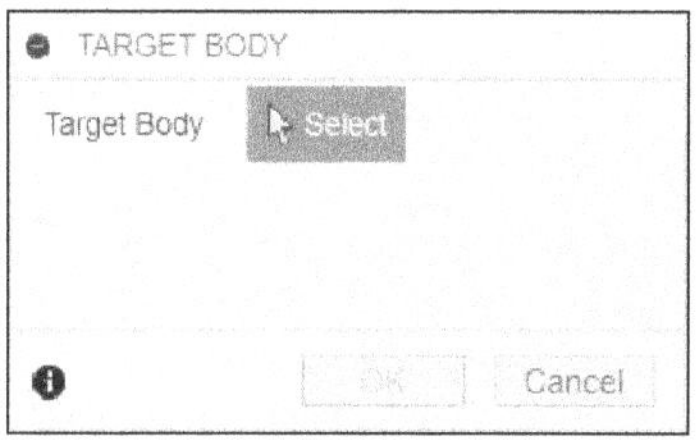

Figure-36. TARGET BODY dialog box

- Select the body to be used for simulation and click on the **OK** button from the dialog box.

Selecting Material

The material used in injection molding is generally plastic with various important parameters like shrinkage, melting temperature, thermal conductivity specified related to injection molding process. The procedure to select material is given next.

- Click on the **Study Materials** button from the **SETUP SUMMARY** dialog box or **Ribbon**. The **STUDY MATERIALS** dialog box will be displayed; refer to Figure-37.

Figure-37. STUDY MATERIALS dialog box

- Select desired material from the list and click on the **Select** button from the dialog box. The selected material will be added in the **SETUP SUMMARY** dialog box.

Defining Injection Locations

Injection location is the point on model where nozzle will start filling plastic in the mold. The procedure to define injection locations is given next.

- Click on the **Injection Locations** button from the **SETUP SUMMARY** dialog box or **Ribbon**. The **INJECTION LOCATIONS** dialog box will be displayed with default injection location selected at center of part; refer to Figure-38.

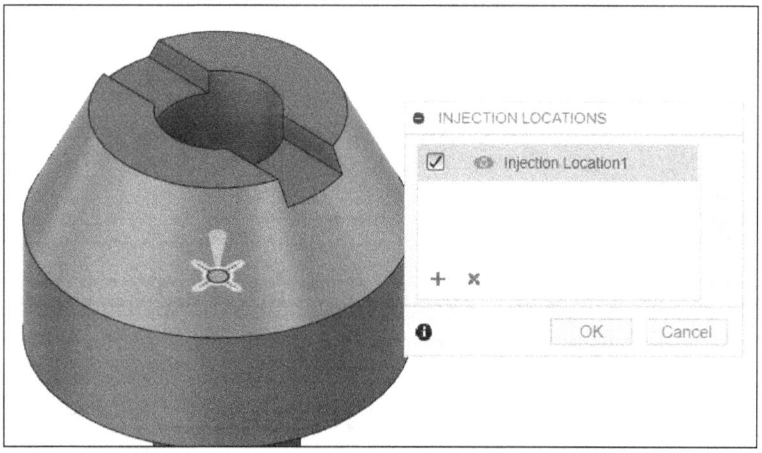

Figure-38. INJECTION LOCATIONS dialog box

- Select the injection location and click on the **Remove injection point** button from dialog box to delete selected location.
- If there is no location selected by default then click on the face of model where you want to define injection location(s); refer to Figure-39.

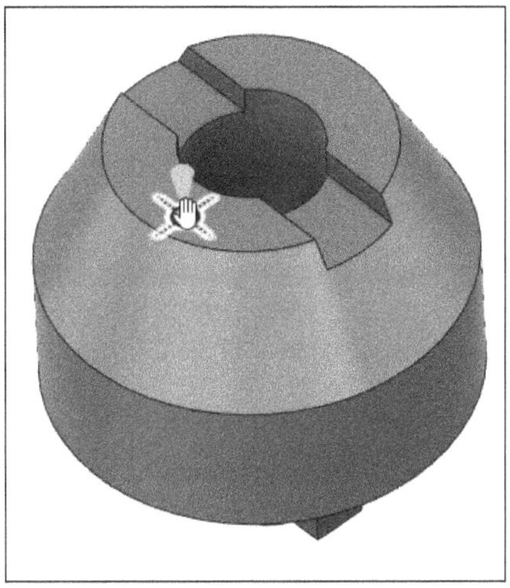

Figure-39. Defining injection location

- Click on the **Add injection point** button from the dialog box if you are not asked to define the location by default and specify desired locations.
- Click on the **OK** button from dialog box to apply the locations.

Defining Aesthetic Faces

The aesthetic faces are the faces which should be manufactured with better finish. The procedure to define aesthetic faces is given next.

- Click on the **Aesthetic Faces** button from the **SETUP SUMMARY** dialog box or **Ribbon**. The **AESTHETIC FACES** dialog box will be displayed; refer to Figure-40.

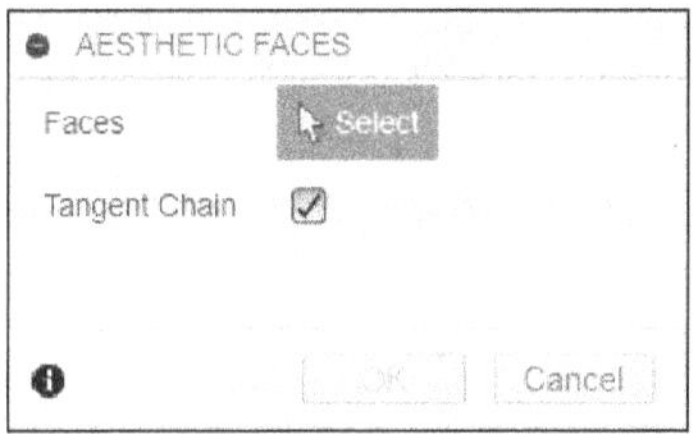

Figure-40. AESTHETIC FACES dialog box

- Select the face(s) to be defined as aesthetic faces and click on the **OK** button from the dialog box.

Defining Process Settings

The **Process Settings** tool is used to define parameters related to injection process. The procedure to define process settings is given next.

- Click on the **Process Settings** tool from the **Ribbon** or **SETUP SUMMARY** dialog box. The **PROCESS SETTINGS** dialog box will be displayed; refer to Figure-41.

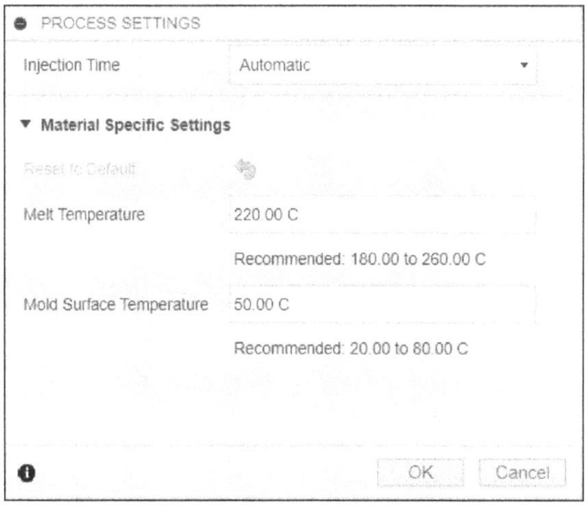

Figure-41. PROCESS SETTINGS dialog box

- Select the **Automatic** option from **Injection Time** drop-down to find out injection time automatically based on lowest injection pressure for filling the mold. Select the **Specified** option from the drop-down if you want to specify injection time and pressure will be decided automatically.
- Specify the mold material temperature and mold surface temperature in **Melt Temperature** and **Mold Surface Temperature** edit boxes, respectively in the dialog box.
- Click on the **OK** button from the dialog box to set parameters.

Checking Results of Analysis

Click on the **Solve** button from the **SETUP SUMMARY** dialog box or the **Solve** button from the **SOLVE** drop-down in the **Ribbon** after specifying parameter. The **Solve** dialog box will be displayed as discussed earlier. Click on the **Solve Study** button from the dialog box. Once the analysis is complete, the results will be displayed; refer to Figure-42. Various result options are discussed next.

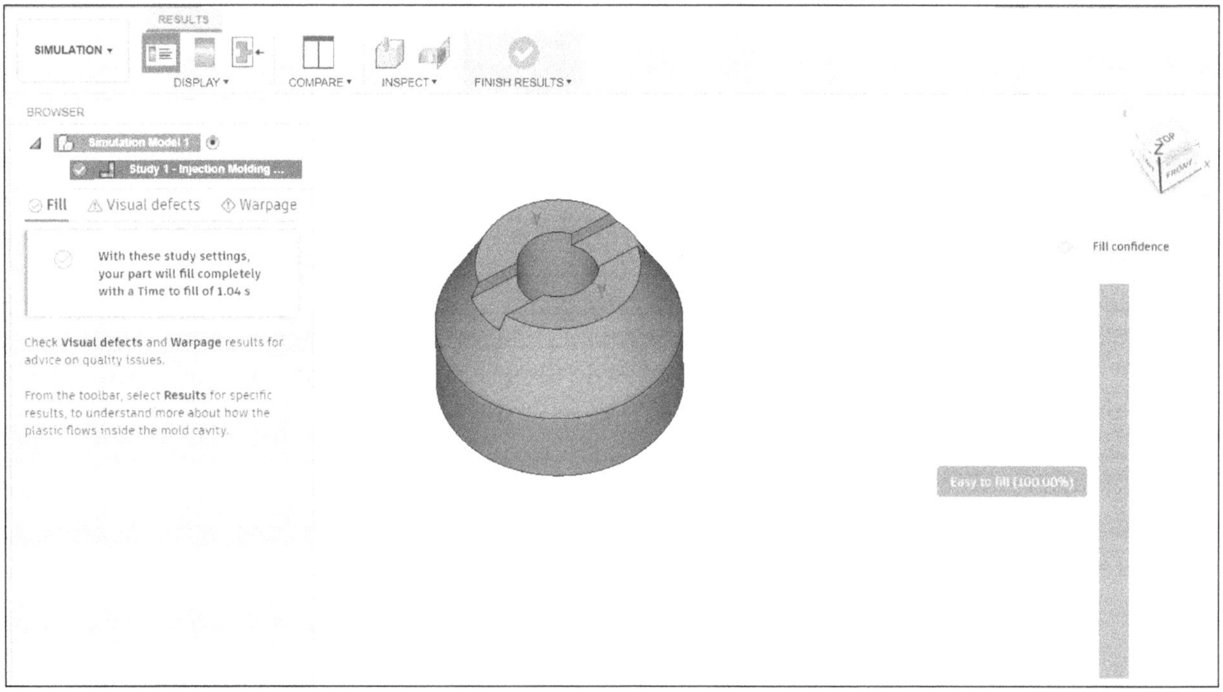

Figure-42. Injection Molding Simulation results

Guided Results

Click on the **Guided Results** tool from the **DISPLAY** drop-down of the **RESULTS** tab in **Ribbon** to check results with related help information as shown in Figure-42. Select **Fill** tab from the left area in **BROWSER** to check fill time taken by injection process to fill the mold completely. Select the **Visual defects** tab in the **BROWSER** to check defects which may occur during the injection process; refer to Figure-43. In our case, there are two types of visual defects that may occur: sink marks; refer to Figure-44 and weld lines; refer to Figure-45.

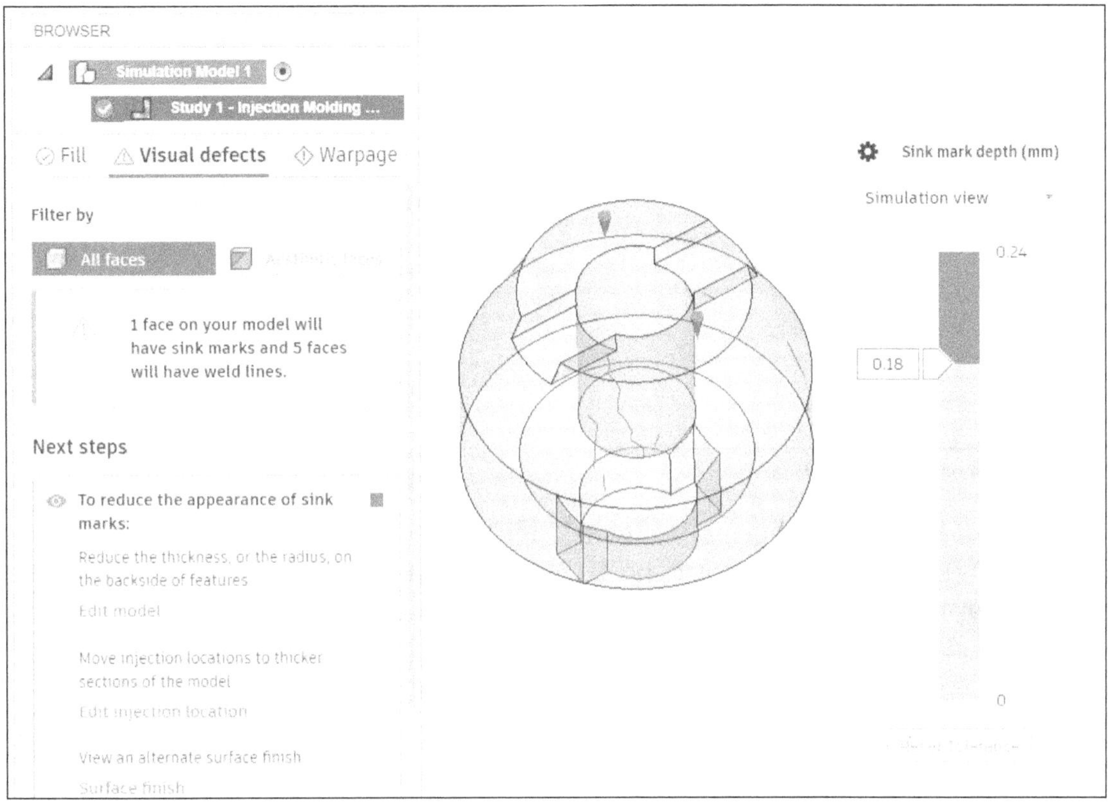

Figure-43. Visual defects tab

Figure-44. Sink marks

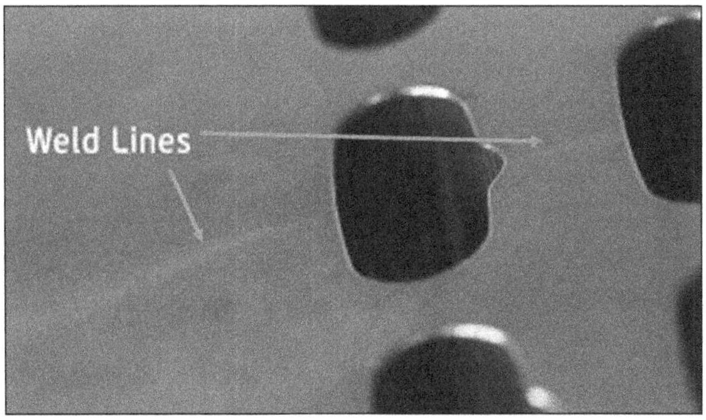

Figure-45. Weld line

Note that hints to reduce sink marks and weld lines are displayed in the **Next steps** area of the **BROWSER**. Apply respective modifications to improve quality of molded part like changing location of injection and then re-run the analysis to check whether these defects occur again.

Click on the **Warpage** tab to check if plastic deforms at sharp edges more than specified allowance; refer to Figure-46. You can apply modifications in the **Next** steps section to improve quality of mold.

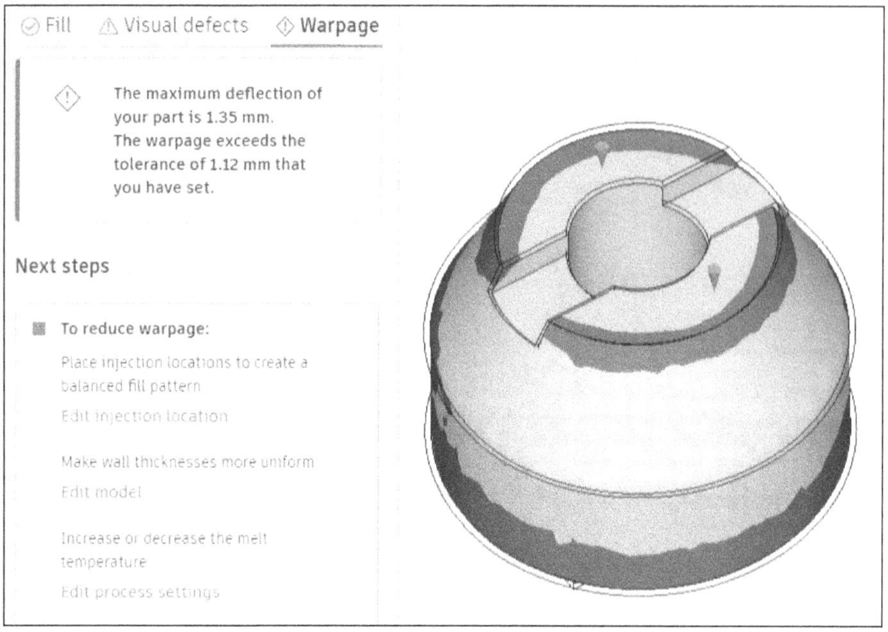

Figure-46. Warpage tab

Result Plots

Click on the **Results** button from the **DISPLAY** drop-down in the **RESULTS** tab of the **Ribbon**. The options will be displayed as shown in Figure-47. Select desired plot option from the **BROWSER** to check resulting plot.

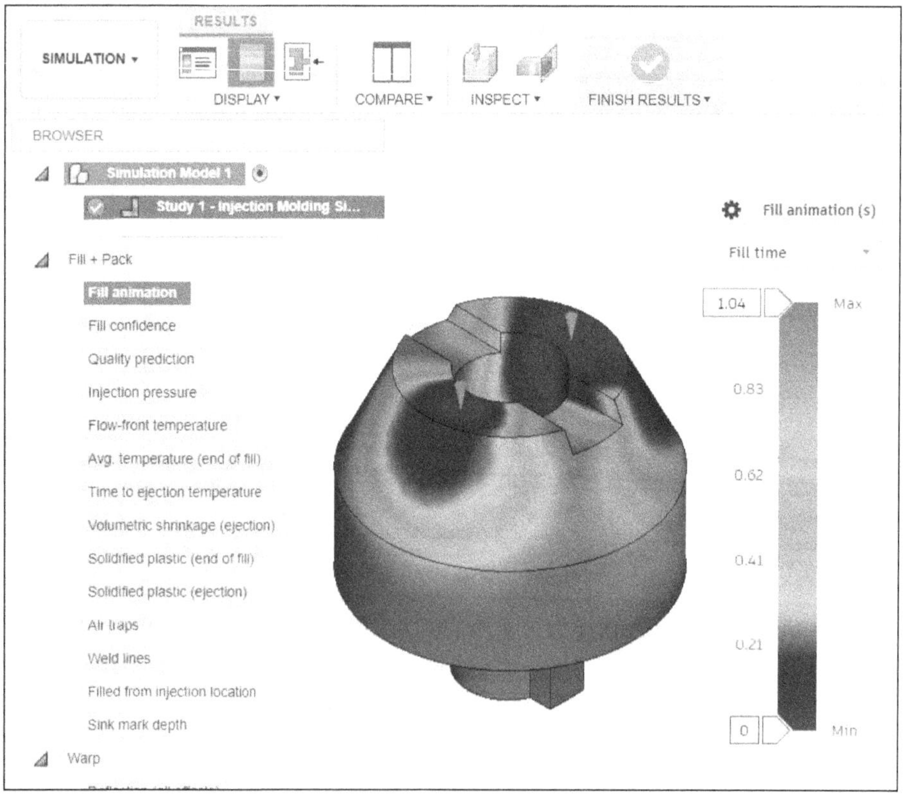

Figure-47. Results options

Molding Process Results

Click on the **Molding Process** tool from the **DISPLAY** drop-down in the **Ribbon**. The analysis results will be displayed with parameters related to molding process; refer to Figure-48.

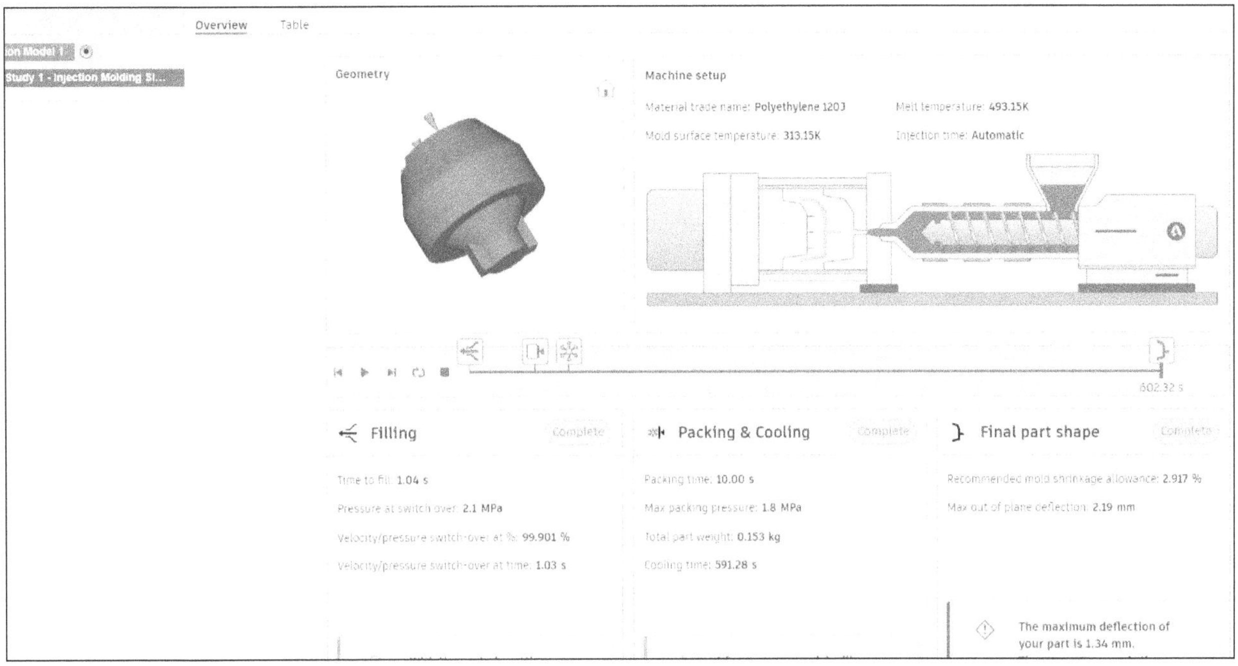

Figure-48. Molding Process results

Click on the **Play** button from dialog box to check results at various time steps. After checking results, click on the **Finish Results** tool from the **Ribbon**.

PRACTICE 1

Consider a rectangular plate with cutout. The dimensions and the boundary conditions of the plate are shown in Figure-49. It is fixed on one end and loaded on the other end. Under the given loading and constraints, plot the deformed shape. Also, determine the principal stresses and the von Mises stresses in the bracket. Thickness of the plate is 0.125 inch and material is **AISI 1020**.

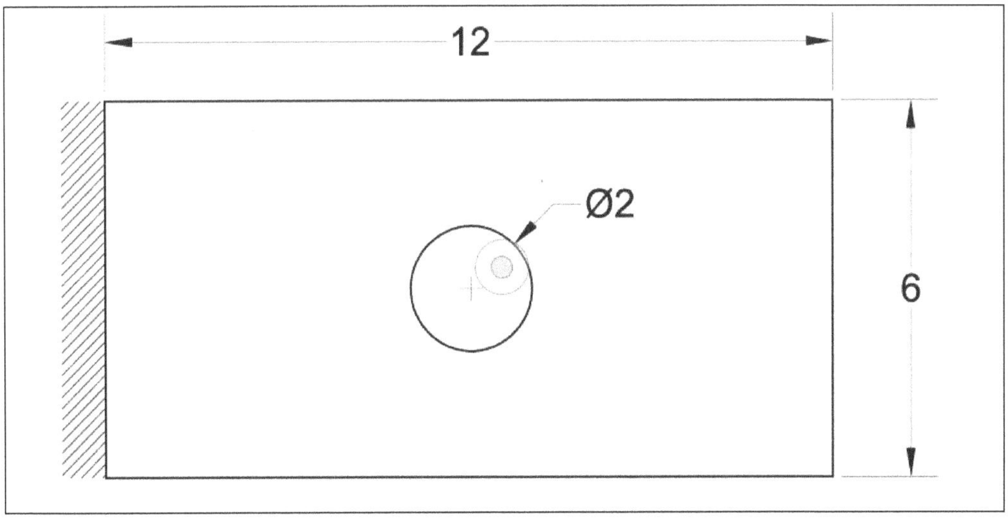

Figure-49. Drawing for Practice1

PRACTICE 2

Open the model for this exercise from the resource kit and perform the static analysis using the conditions given in Figure-50. Find out the **Factor of Safety** for the model.

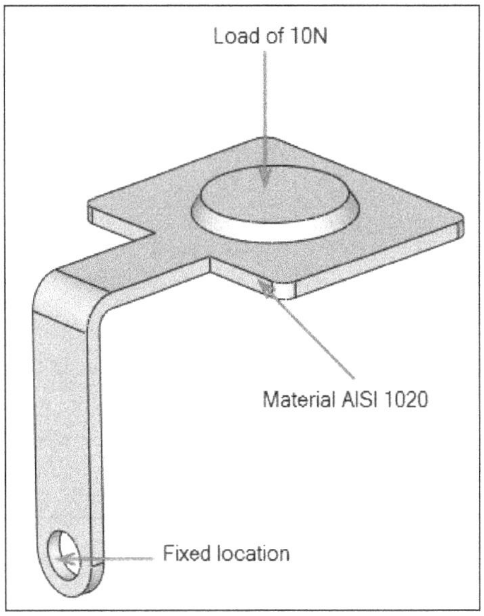

Figure-50. Model for Practice2

PRACTICE 3

Check out what happens to the fork under the conditions specified in Figure-51. Note that the material of fork is **Alloy Steel** and it is in the hands of a nasty kid. (You know kids!! they don't exert linear forces.)

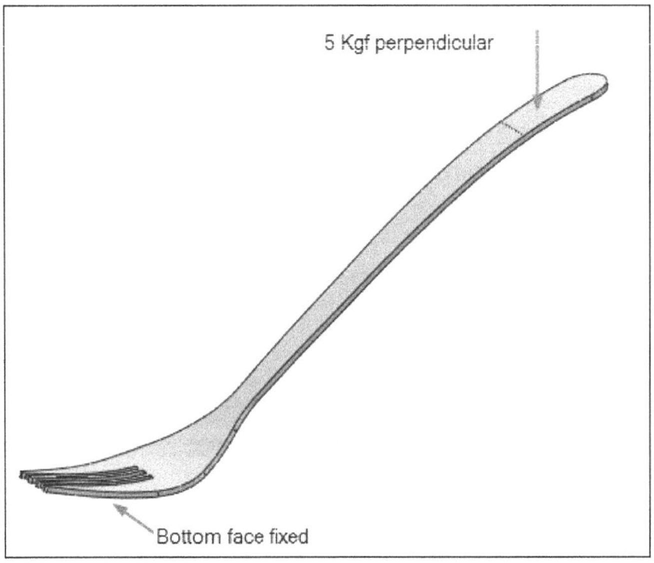

Figure-51. Model for Practice3 of Non-linear static analysis

PROBLEM 1

A metal sphere of diameter d = 35mm is initially at temperature Ti = 700 K. At t=0, the sphere is placed in a fluid environment that has properties of T∞ = 300 K and h = 50 W/m2-K. The properties of the steel are k = 35 W/m-K, ρ = 7500 kg/m3, and c = 550 J/kg-K. Find the surface temperature of the sphere after 500 seconds.

PROBLEM 2

A flanged pipe assembly; refer to Figure-52, made of plain carbon steel is subjected to both convective and conductive boundary conditions. Fluid inside the pipe is at a temperature of 130°C and has a convection coefficient of hi = 160 W/m^2-K. Air on the outside of the pipe is at 20°C and has a convection coefficient of ho = 70 W/m^2-K. The right and left ends of the pipe are at temperatures of 450°C and 80°C, respectively. There is a thermal resistance between the two flanges of 0.002 K-m^2/W. Use thermal analysis to analyze the pipe under both steady state and transient conditions.

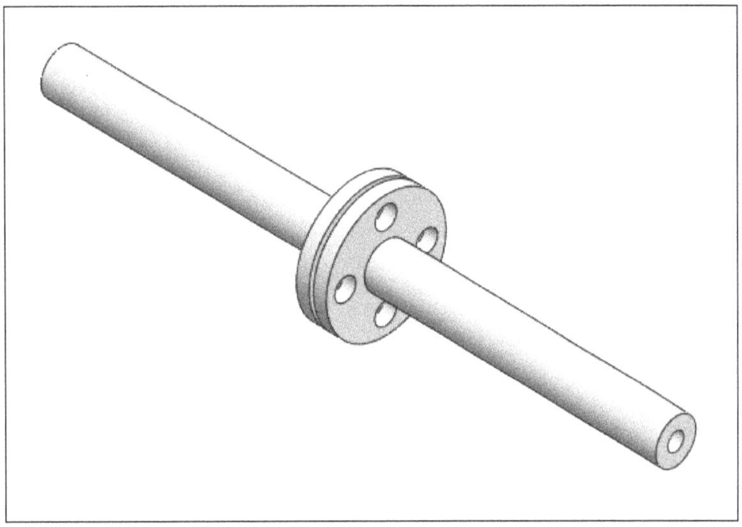

Figure-52. Flanged pipe assembly

SELF ASSESSMENT

Q1. Which of the following is not a parameter of non linearity for non-linear static analysis?

a. Material b. Geometry
c. Load d. Time

Q2. Using transient results plot, you can check the effect of load with respect to time. (T/F)

Q3. When the stored membrane (axial) energy is converted into bending energy with no change in the externally applied loads then you can perform structural buckling analysis. (T/F)

Q4. The buckling mode displays shape of model under buckling load. (T/F)

Q5. When a structure is properly excited by a dynamic load with a frequency that coincides with one of its natural frequencies, the structure undergoes large displacements and stresses. (T/F)

Q6. The phenomena by which a structure goes large deformation when excited at natural frequency is called ....

Q7. Which of the following is a parameter does not apply for structural analysis?

a. Film Coefficient
b. Pressure
c. Density
d. Force

Q8. Which of the following is a key characteristic of nonlinear structural behavior?
a) Proportionality between load and deformation
b) Material remains within the elastic limit
c) Dependence of stiffness on deformation
d) Use of only small displacement theory

Q9. What type of nonlinearity arises due to large deformations affecting equilibrium conditions?
a) Material nonlinearity
b) Geometric nonlinearity
c) Contact nonlinearity
d) Elastic linearity

Q10. In nonlinear finite element analysis, which method is commonly used for solving equilibrium equations?
a) Gaussian elimination
b) Newton-Raphson method
c) Finite difference method
d) Monte Carlo simulation

Q11. The critical buckling load of a column depends on:
a) Material density only
b) Slenderness ratio and boundary conditions
c) Load direction only
d) Temperature effects alone

Q12. Which type of buckling occurs in thin-walled structures due to localized instability?
a) Global buckling
b) Local buckling
c) Torsional buckling
d) Snap-through buckling

Q13. Euler's buckling formula is valid under which assumption?
a) Large deformations are considered
b) The material is plastic
c) The column is perfectly straight initially
d) Shear deformation is significant

Q14. Which boundary condition is used when heat flux is known at the boundary?
a) Dirichlet condition
b) Neumann condition
c) Mixed condition
d) Robin condition

Q15. Shape optimization is primarily used to:
a) Increase material cost
b) Reduce structural weight while maintaining performance
c) Ignore stress concentration effects
d) Avoid finite element analysis

Q16. The key objective function in topology optimization is typically:
a) Minimizing stress concentration
b) Maximizing compliance
c) Minimizing structural stiffness
d) Maximizing weight

Q17. In shape optimization, sensitivity analysis helps in:
a) Selecting finite element mesh
b) Determining the influence of shape changes on objective functions
c) Applying boundary conditions
d) Reducing computational cost

Q18. Which tool should be used to set shape optimization criteria?
A) Shape Optimization Tool
B) Shape Optimization Criteria Tool
C) Shape Criteria Selection Tool
D) Optimization Settings Tool

Q19. What parameter is set in the Shape Optimization Criteria dialog box?
A) Maximum stress
B) Target mass
C) Load factor
D) Heat dissipation

Q20. After setting shape optimization criteria, which tool is used to solve the analysis?
A) Simulation Tool
B) Optimize Tool
C) Solve Tool
D) Run Analysis Tool

Q21. What is the function of the Promote tool in the Result Tools drop-down?
A) Convert results into reports
B) Generate a mesh body of the result
C) Apply constraints to the model
D) Delete simulation data

Q22. When adding a mesh object, which option should be selected to create a copy of the simulation model with a mesh body?
A) Design Workspace
B) Existing Simulation Model
C) Clone Current Simulation Model
D) Clone Studies

Q23. What is the primary purpose of an Electronics Cooling study?
A) Determine electrical conductivity
B) Check temperature exceeding due to internal heat loads
C) Analyze structural deformation
D) Simulate airflow dynamics

Q24. What material is generally used for a PCB in an Electronics Cooling study?
A) Aluminum
B) Copper
C) Epoxy resin with fiberglass layers
D) Carbon fiber

Q25. Which tool is used to apply internal heat to electronic components?
A) Heat Source Tool
B) Thermal Loads Tool
C) Heat Application Tool
D) Temperature Control Tool

Q26. How is a heat sink applied in an Electronics Cooling study?
A) By selecting the Heat Sink tool from the COOLING drop-down
B) By manually specifying a cooling coefficient
C) By modifying the internal heat values
D) By changing the thermal conductivity of the material

Q27. Which tool is used to apply forced air or fluid flow for cooling?
A) Airflow Tool
B) Fan Tool
C) Cooling Flow Tool
D) Heat Dissipation Tool

Q28. What is the purpose of specifying a temperature threshold?
A) Define minimum temperature for solidification
B) Set maximum safe temperature for electronic components
C) Control environmental temperature fluctuations
D) Adjust humidity levels in the simulation

Q29. Which tool is used to specify temperature thresholds in an Electronics Cooling study?
A) Temperature Control Tool
B) Temperature Thresholds Tool
C) Thermal Regulation Tool
D) Critical Heat Tool

Q30. What is the objective of an Injection Molding Simulation?
A) Simulate mold filling within a specified time
B) Determine the best cooling rate for plastic materials
C) Optimize the placement of heat sinks
D) Reduce weight of the molded part

Q31. How is the target body selected for an injection molding simulation?
A) Automatically selected if only one body exists
B) Selected manually from a list of materials
C) Defined using external boundary conditions
D) Predefined in the study setup

Q32. Which property is NOT typically specified for injection molding materials?
A) Shrinkage
B) Melting temperature
C) Thermal conductivity
D) Electrical resistance

Q33. What is an injection location in an injection molding simulation?
A) The point where heat is applied
B) The location where the mold opens
C) The point where plastic begins filling the mold
D) The area where cooling is applied

Q34. How can aesthetic faces be defined in an injection molding study?
A) By setting surface roughness manually
B) By selecting faces using the Aesthetic Faces tool
C) By applying an external force
D) By increasing injection speed

Q35. What does the Process Settings tool allow you to define?
A) Structural optimization parameters
B) Electrical conductivity properties
C) Injection time, pressure, and mold temperature
D) Heat sink placement

Q36. Which tool provides guided results with additional help information?
A) Guided Results Tool
B) Simulation Insights Tool
C) Results Interpretation Tool
D) Study Analysis Tool

Q37. What type of defect can be identified in the Guided Results section?
A) Brittle fracture
B) Sink marks
C) Overheating
D) Material swelling

Q38. What does the Warpage tab in the results display?
A) Temperature variations across the mold
B) Deformation of plastic at sharp edges
C) Injection flow speed
D) Stress distribution in the mold

Q39. How can the molding process results be visualized over time?
A) By clicking the Process Overview tool
B) By selecting the Simulation Animation option
C) By using the Play button in the Molding Process tool
D) By manually adjusting time steps

FOR STUDENT NOTES

Chapter 22

Sheetmetal Design

Topics Covered

The major topics covered in this chapter are:

- ***Introduction to Sheet Metal***
- ***Sheetmetal Rules***
- ***Creating Flanges***
- ***Unfolding Sheetmetal Part***
- ***Convert to Sheet Metal***
- ***Flat Pattern***
- ***Exporting DXF***
- ***Practical and Practice***

INTRODUCTION

Sheet metal is used when you need a component of thickness in the range of 0.16 mm to 12.70 mm and do not require conventional cutting machines. The components that can be created by Punch-press and bending machines are designed in Sheet Metal environment. In Autodesk Fusion, the tools to design sheet metal components are available in **SHEET METAL** tab of **DESIGN** workspace; refer to Figure-1. Various tools and parameters of **SHEET METAL** tab are discussed next.

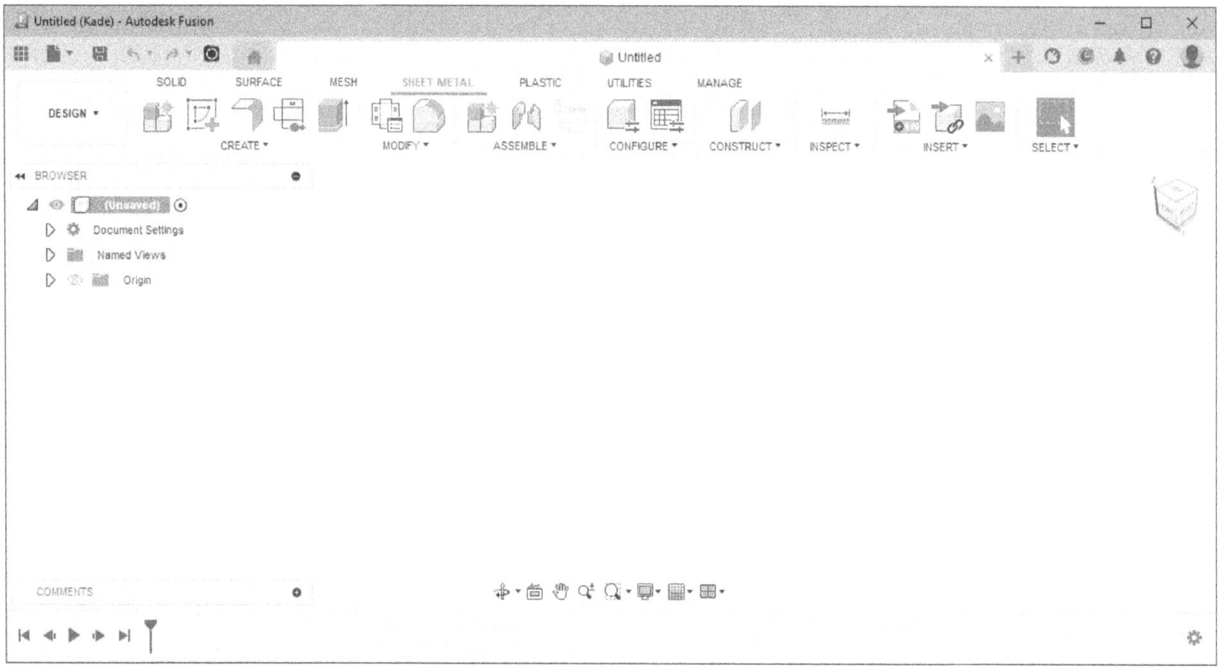

Figure-1. SHEET METAL toolbar in DESIGN Workspace

SHEET METAL RULES

The Sheet Metal rules are used to specify various parameters related to sheet metal design like bend radius, corner conditions, K Factor, thickness of sheet, and so on. The procedure to set sheet metal rules in Autodesk Fusion are discussed next.

- Click on the **Sheet Metal Rules** tool from the **MODIFY** drop-down in **Toolbar**; refer to Figure-2. The **SHEET METAL RULES** dialog box will be displayed; refer to Figure-3.

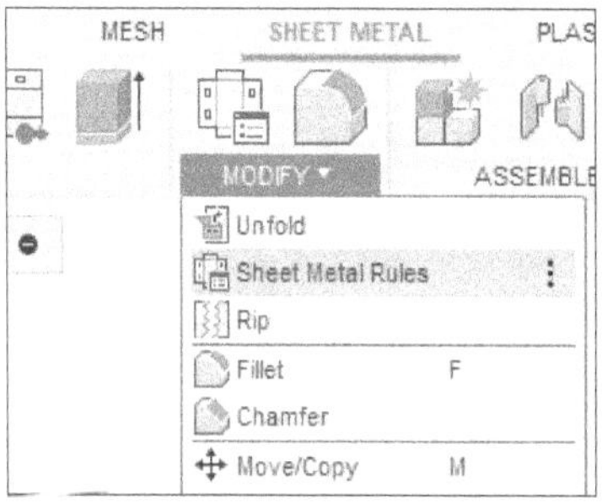

Figure-2. Sheet Metal Rules tool

- Expand desired category from the dialog box to check the parameters; refer to Figure-4.

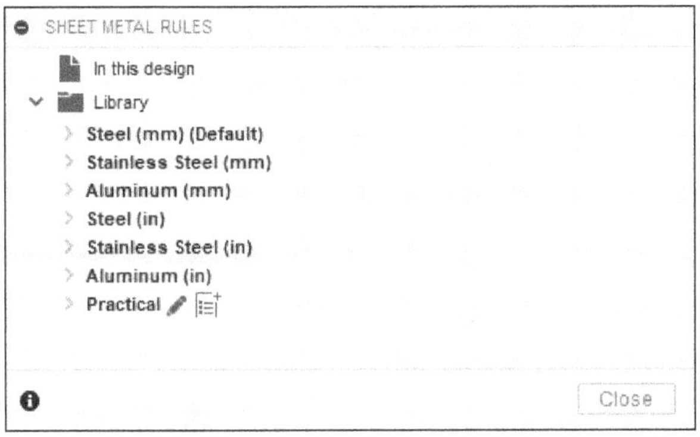

Figure-3. SHEET METAL RULES dialog box

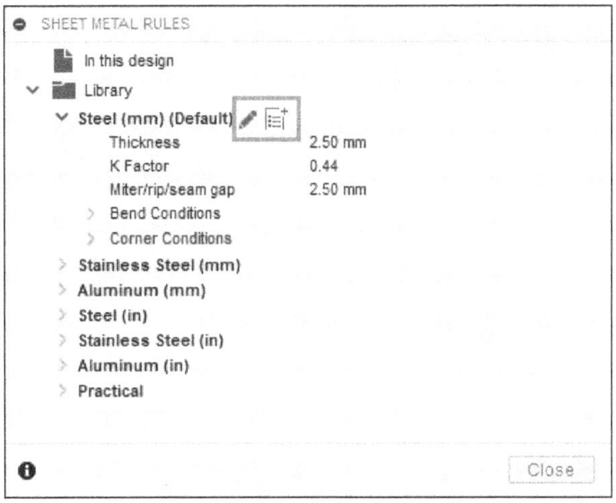

Figure-4. Properties of steel in SHEET METAL RULES dialog box

- Hover the cursor on the name of property. Two buttons will be displayed next to it as shown in Figure-4.

Modifying the rules

- Click on the **Edit Rule** button for desired sheet metal rule from **SHEET METAL RULES** dialog box; refer to Figure-5, if you want to modify the property. The **Edit Rule** dialog box will be displayed; refer to Figure-6.

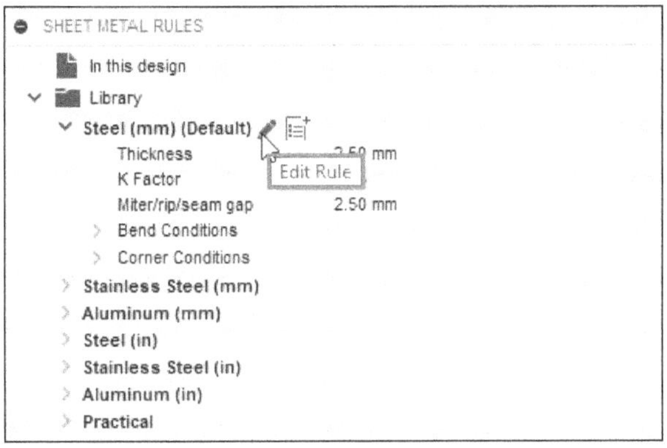

Figure-5. Edit Rule button

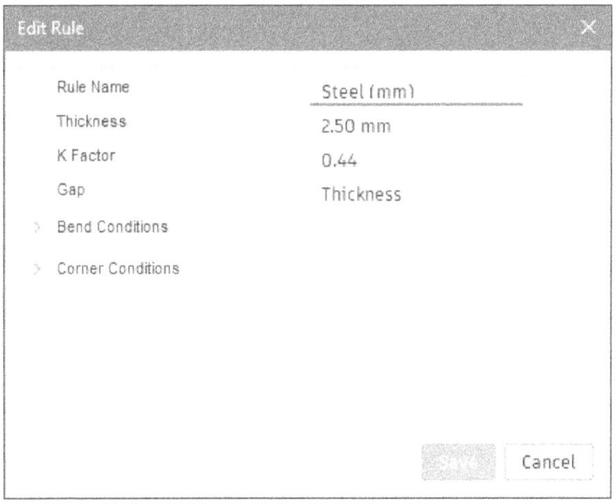

Figure-6. Edit Rule dialog box

- Specify desired name for the rule in the **Rule Name** edit box.
- Set the other parameters like sheet thickness, K factor, seam gap, etc. in their respective edit boxes.
- Click on the **Save** button after setting parameters to save the rule.

Creating New Sheet Metal Rule

- Click on the **New Rule** button from **SHEET METAL RULES** dialog box if you want to create a new sheet metal rule; refer to Figure-7. The **New Rule** dialog box will be displayed; refer to Figure-8.

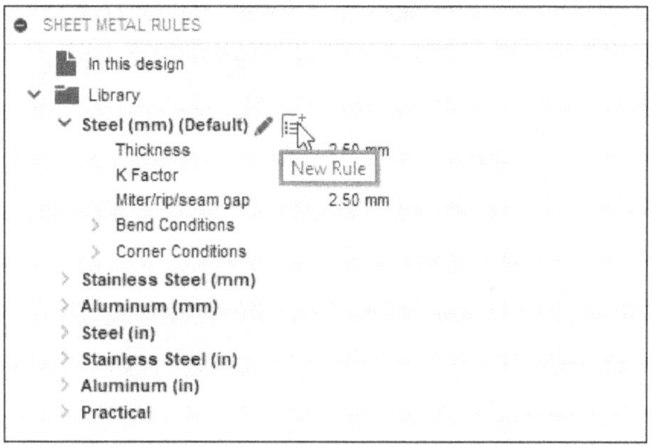

Figure-7. New Rule button

Figure-8. New Rule dialog box

- Set desired parameters as discussed earlier and click on the **Save** button to save new sheet metal rule.

CREATING FLANGES

Flanges are the building blocks of sheet metal parts. Flanges act as base and walls of sheet metal parts. The procedure to create flange is given next.

- Click on the **Flange (Base/Edge/Contour)** tool from **CREATE** drop-down in the **Toolbar**; refer to Figure-9. The **FLANGE** dialog box will be displayed; refer to Figure-10. You will be asked to select a sketch or edge to create flange.

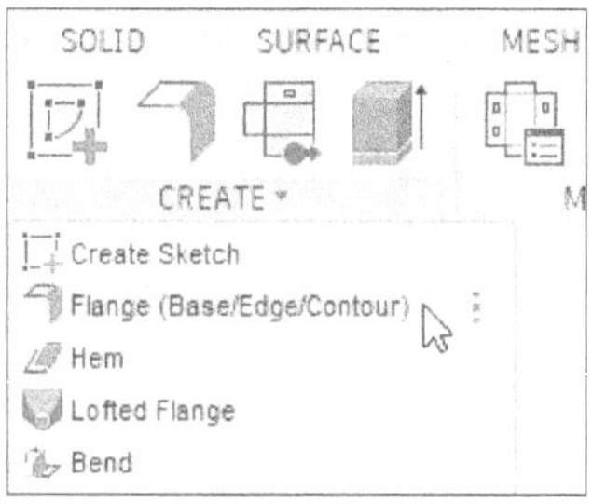

Figure-9. Flange tool

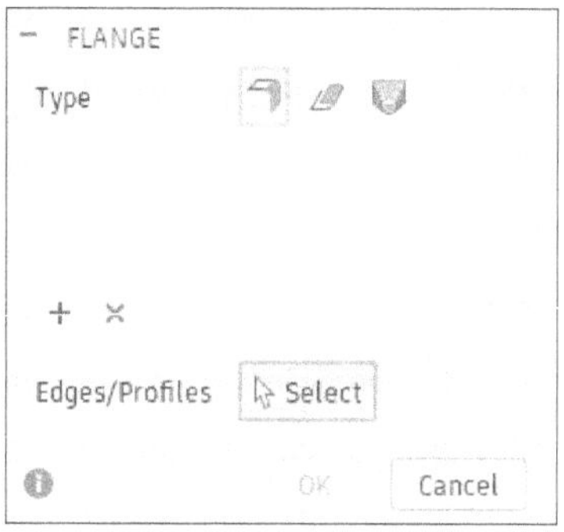

Figure-10. FLANGE dialog box

- Select desired sketch or edge. Preview of the flange will be displayed; refer to Figure-11 and Figure-12.

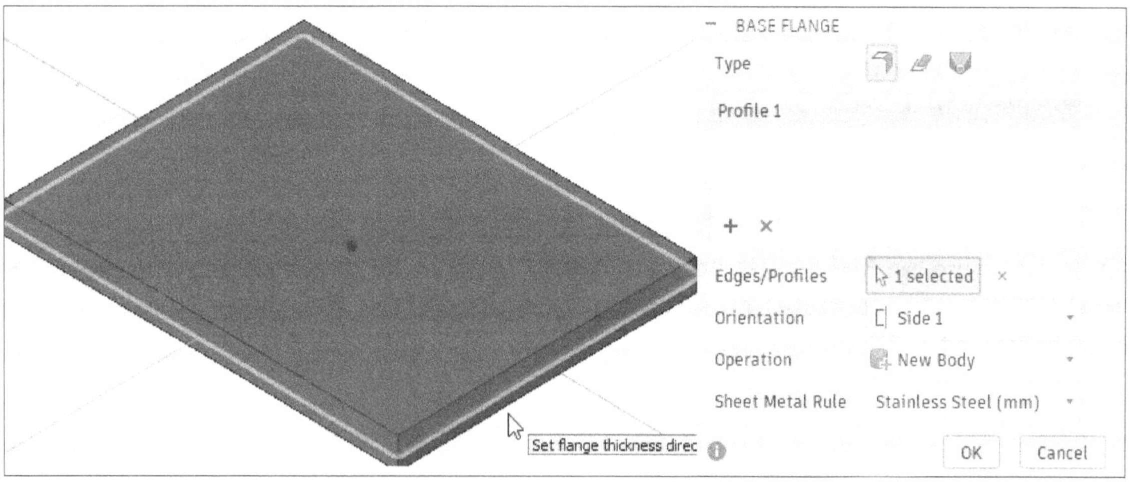

Figure-11. Preview of flange by using sketch

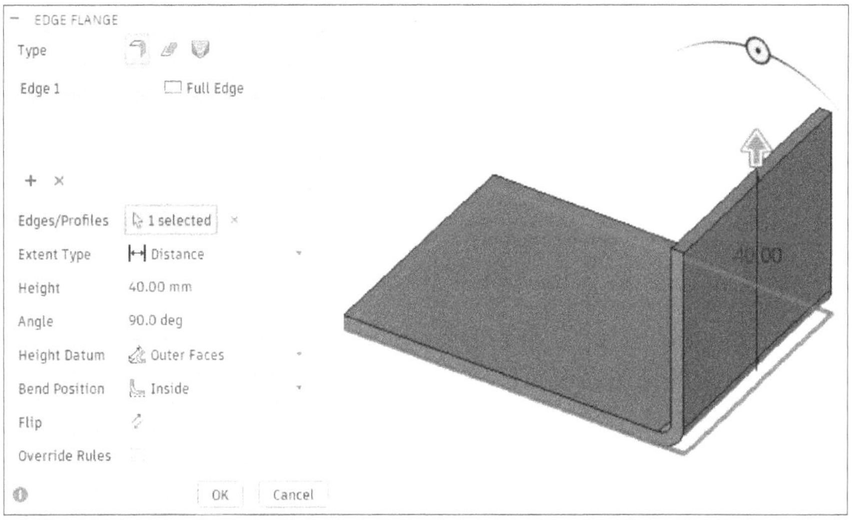

Figure-12. Preview of flange by using edge

- If you have used a closed sketch to create flange then set the thickness side in the **Orientation** drop-down.
- Select **Distance** option from **Extent Type** drop-down to extrude the flange by specifying the height of the flange. Select **To Object** option to extend the flange upto the selected face, plane, or body.
- If you have selected an edge to create flange then the options of the dialog box will be displayed as shown in Figure-12. Set desired **Height** and **Angle** values in the respective edit boxes in the dialog box.
- Select desired option from the **Height Datum** drop-down. Select the **Inner Faces** option if you want to set the height of flange from the inner face. Select the **Outer Faces** option if you want to set the height of flange from the outer face. Select the **Tangent To Bend** option if you want to set the height from the edge of bend created by flange.
- Select the **Inside** option from the **Bend Position** drop-down if you want the bend to be created starting from the inner edge of the flange. Select the **Outside** option if you want the bend to be created from outer edge of the flange. Select the **Adjacent** option if you want to create bend ahead of the outer edge of bend equal to the thickness of sheet. Select the **Tangent** option if you want the bend to start tangent to the face of the selected flange.
- To flip the direction of flange, click on the **Flip** button.
- By default, the bend rules are applied on the flange to be created but if you want to change any of the rule specific to the flange then select the **Override Rules** check box. The options below it will be displayed; refer to Figure-13.

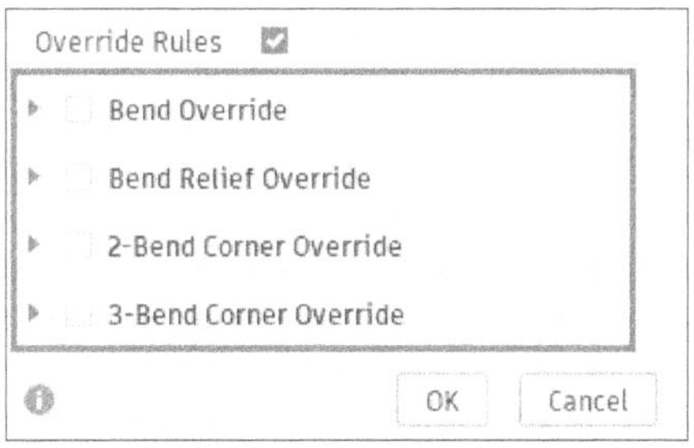

Figure-13. Override Rules options in FLANGE dialog box

- Select desired check box and change the parameter as required.
- Click on the **OK** button to create the flange.

Creating Contour Flange

Using the **Flange (Base/Edge/Contour)** tool, you can also create contour flanges. The procedure is given next.

- Create a sketch of desired shape and size for contour flange; refer to Figure-14.

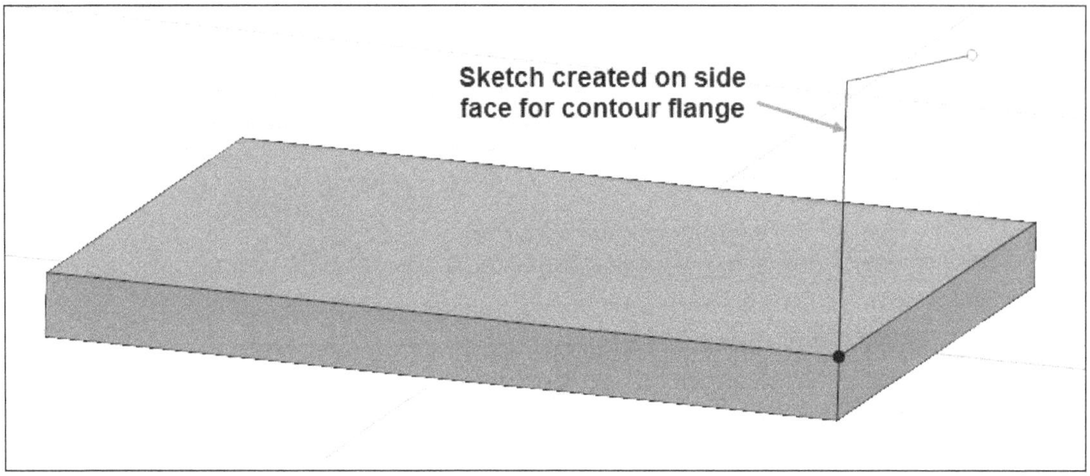

Figure-14. Sketch created for contour flange

- Click on the **Flange (Base/Edge/Contour)** tool from **CREATE** drop-down in the **Toolbar** and select the newly created sketch for creating contour flange; refer to Figure-15.

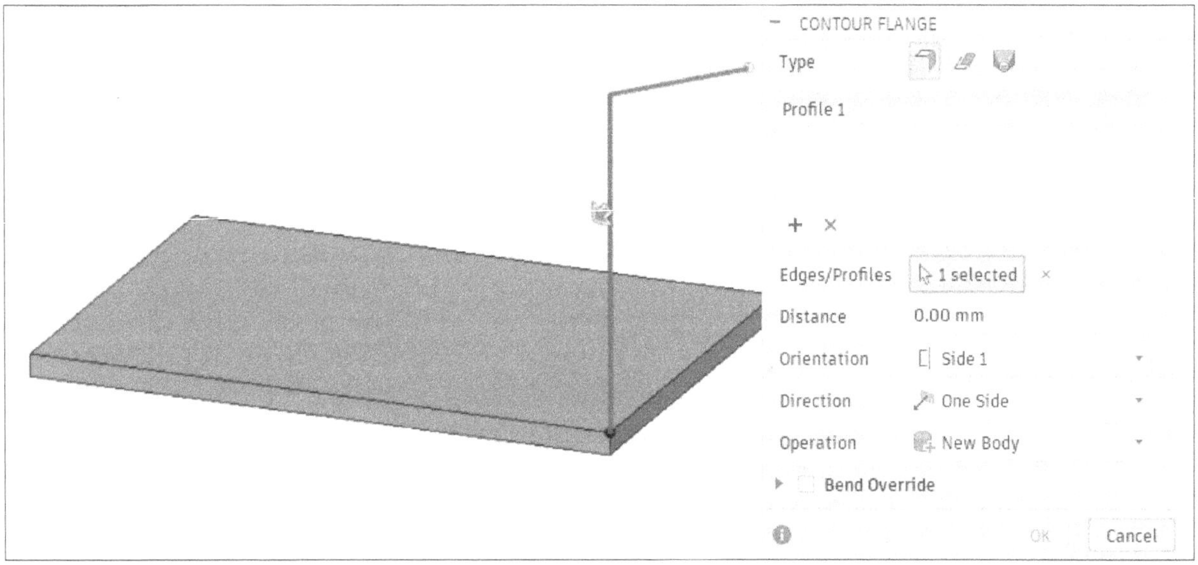

Figure-15. Sketch selected for contour flange

- Now, select all the edges one by one by clicking **Add** button from **CONTOUR FLANGE** dialog box to define shape of flange. Preview of the contour flange will be displayed; refer to Figure-16.
- Select the **Miter Corners** check box if you want to create miter cut in flanges.
- Click on the **OK** button from the dialog box to create the flanges.

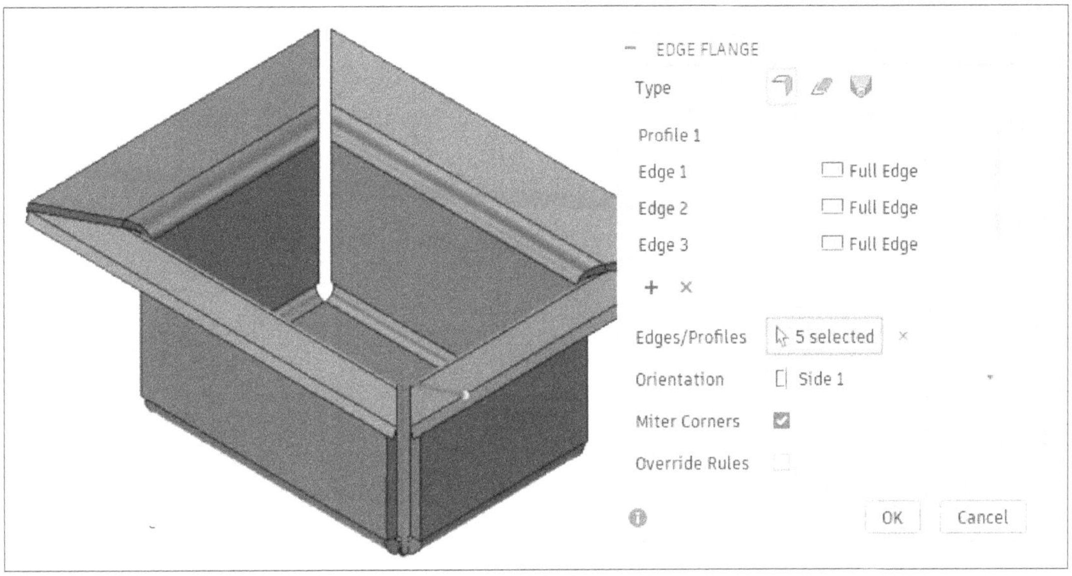

Figure-16. Preview of contour flange

Creating Hem

The **Hem** option in **FLANGE** dialog box is used to fold a sheet metal edge back onto itself. The procedure to create hem is given next.

- Click on the **Hem** button from the **FLANGE** dialog box. The options will be displayed as shown in Figure-17.

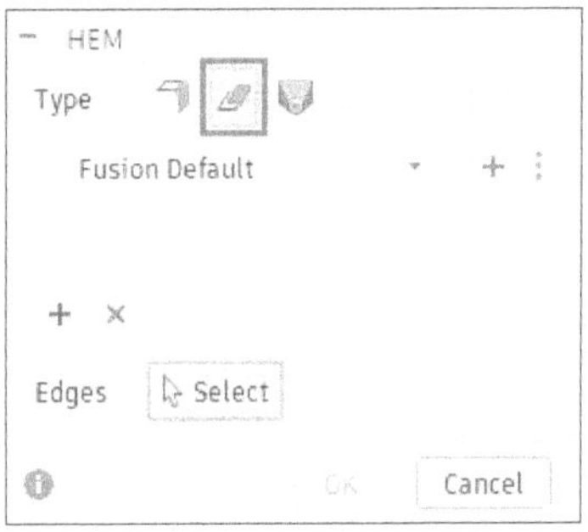

Figure-17. Hem options

- Select desired edge on the sheet metal body. Preview of hem will be displayed; refer to Figure-18.

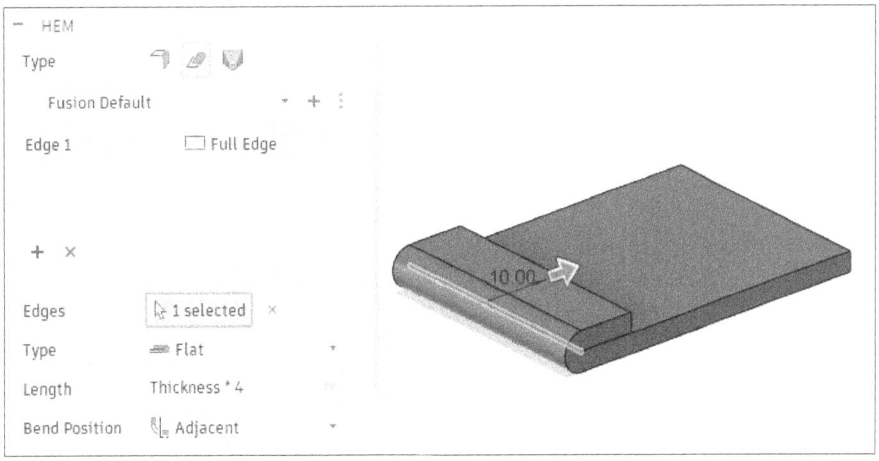

Figure-18. Preview of hem

- Select desired type of hem to be created from **Type** drop-down. Preview of all types of hem are shown in Figure-19.

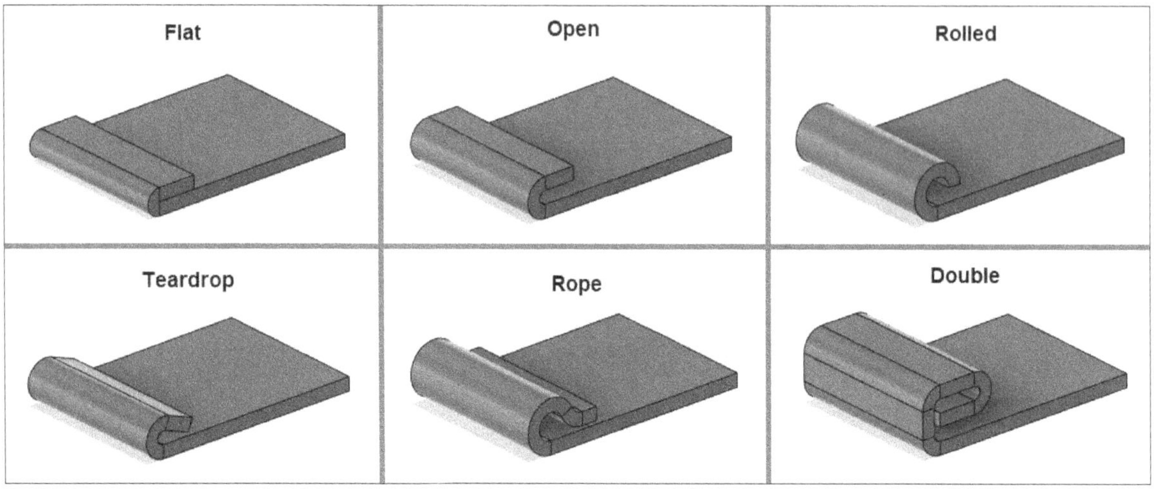

Figure-19. Preview of hem types

- Other parameters in the dialog box are same as discussed earlier.
- After specifying desired parameters, click on the **OK** button from the dialog box. The hem will be created.

Creating Lofted Flange

The **Lofted Flange** option in **FLANGE** dialog box is used to create flange by joining two profiles at specified distance. The procedure to create lofted flange is given next.

- Click on the **Lofted Flange** button from the **FLANGE** dialog box. The options will be displayed as shown in Figure-20.

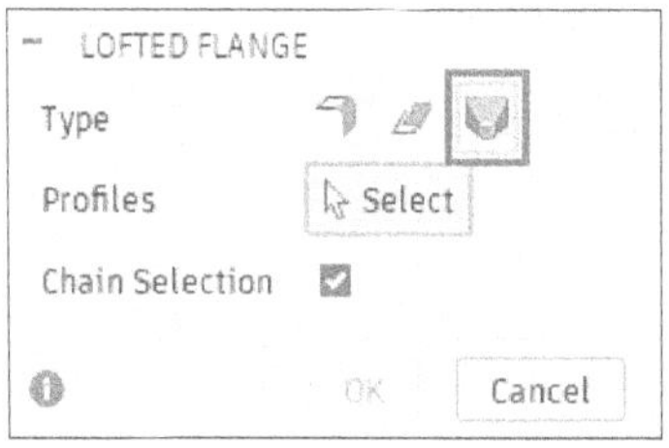

Figure-20. Lofted flange options

- Select two or more profiles. Preview of lofted flange will be displayed; refer to Figure-21.

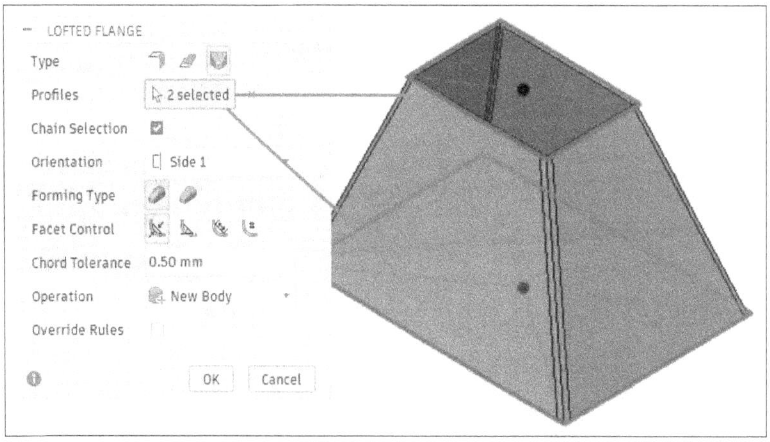

Figure-21. Selection for lofted flange

- Select the **Brake Form** button from the **Forming Type** section to create lofted flange generated by punch and die machine. Select the **Die Form** button from the **Forming Type** section to create lofted flange generated by stamping die process.
- On selecting the **Brake Form** button, the **Facet Control** options will be displayed. Select the **Chord Tolerance** button to specify maximum chord distance for determining number of facets at bends. Select the **Facet Angle** button to use facet angle as reference for determining number of facets at the bends. Select the **Facet Distance** button to specify maximum span of each facet in the bend. Select the **Facet Number** button to specify maximum number of facets that can be generated in each bend.
- Set the other parameters as discussed earlier and click on the **OK** button from the dialog box. The flange will be created; refer to Figure-22.

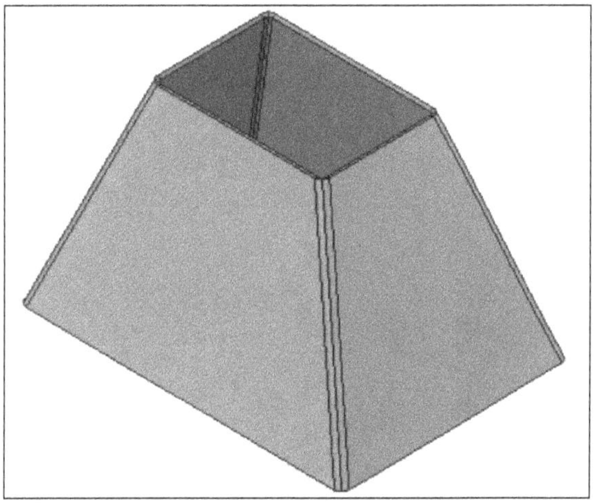

Figure-22. Lofted flange created

CREATING BEND

The **Bend** tool is used to create bend at selected line on the model. The procedure to use this tool is given next.

- Click on the **Create Sketch** tool from the **CREATE** drop-down in the **SHEET METAL** tab of the **Ribbon**. You will be asked to select a sketching plane.
- Select the face of sheet metal model on which you want to create bend line and create a line sketch joining edges of the model; refer to Figure-23.

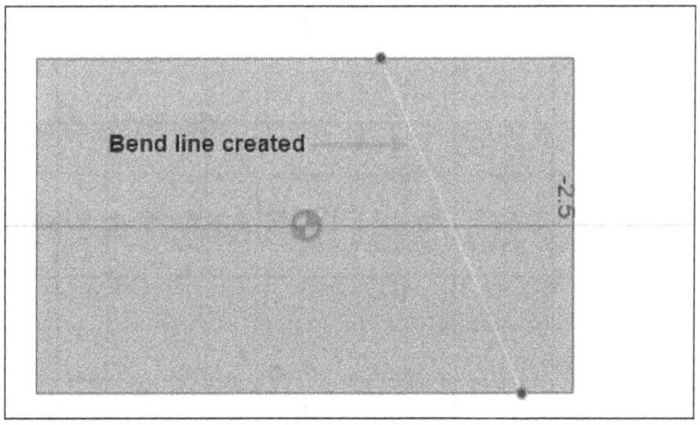

Figure-23. Bend line created

- Click on the **Bend** tool from the **CREATE** drop-down in the **SHEET METAL** tab of the **Ribbon**. The **BEND** dialog box will be displayed; refer to Figure-24.

Figure-24. BEND dialog box

- Select the side of bend line to be made stationary. You will be asked to select bend line.
- Select desired bend line (line sketch created earlier) from the model. Preview of bend will be displayed; refer to Figure-25.

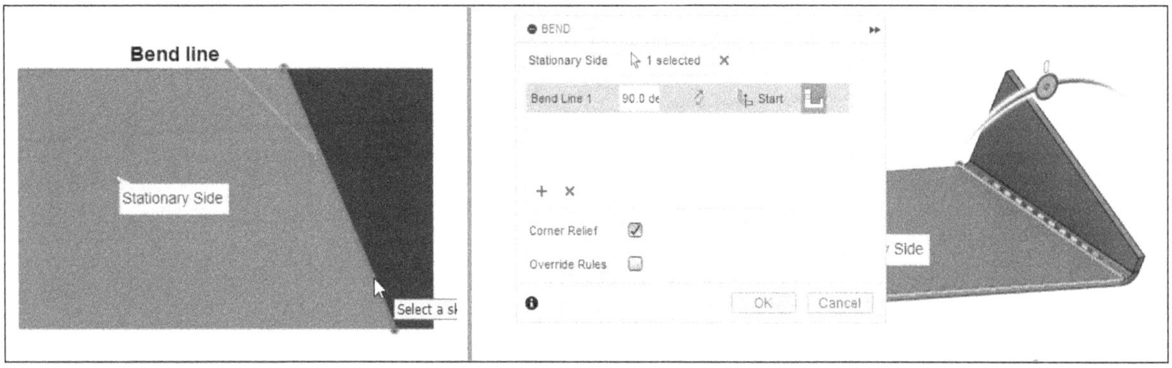

Figure-25. Creating bend

- Click in the **Bend Angle** field of the table for desired bend to modify bending angle; refer to Figure-26. Similarly, you can flip bend, define bend line position, and set bend relief on/off using the options in the table.

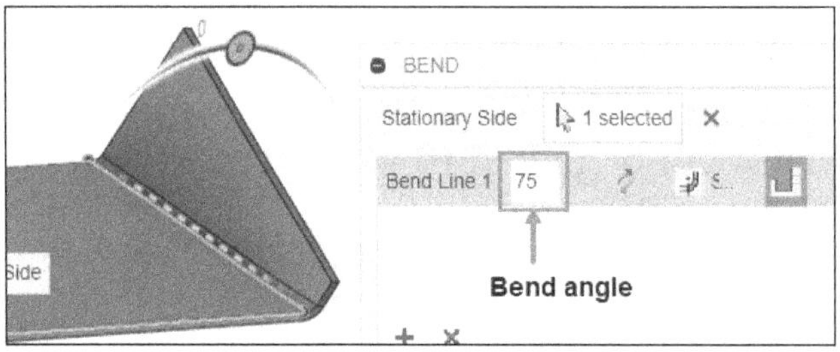

Figure-26. Bend angle specified

- After setting desired parameters, click on the **OK** button from the dialog box.

UNFOLDING SHEETMETAL PART

The **Unfold** tool is used to unbend all the selected bends of the part. The procedure to unfold is given next.

- Click on the **Unfold** tool from **MODIFY** drop-down in the **Toolbar**; refer to Figure-27. The **UNFOLD** dialog box will be displayed; refer to Figure-28.

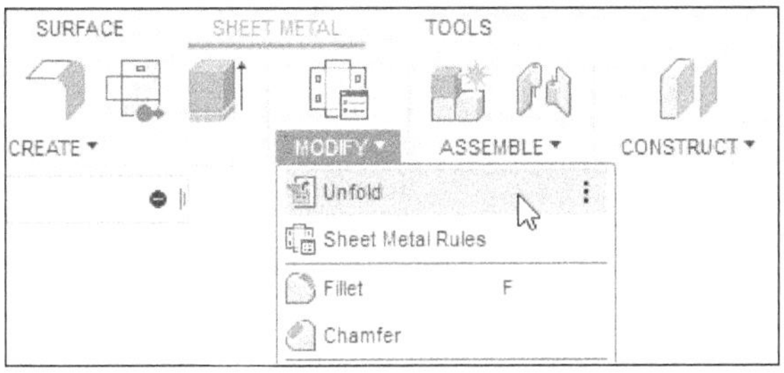

Figure-27. Unfold tool

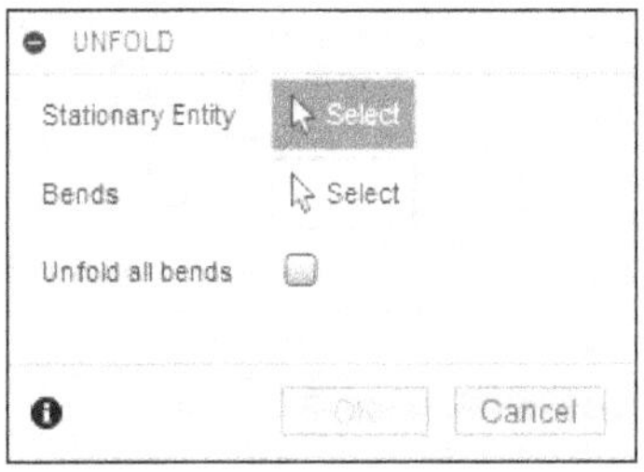

Figure-28. UNFOLD dialog box

- Select desired face to be made stationary. All the bends will be highlighted; refer to Figure-29.

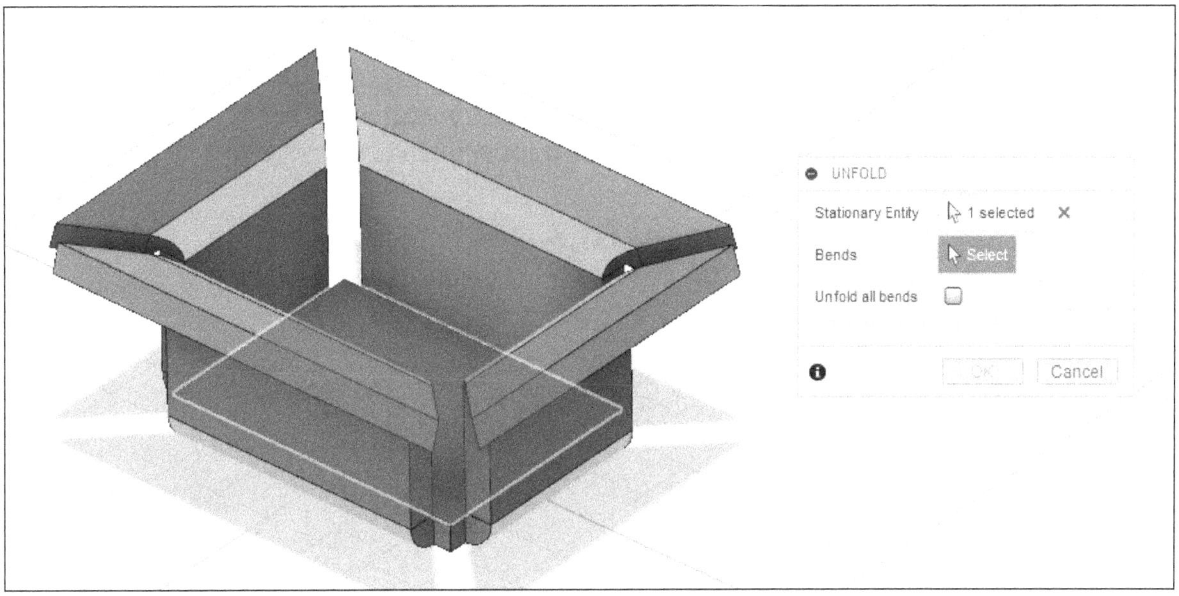

Figure-29. Bends highlighted

- Select the bends that you want to be unfolded. Preview of unfolding will be displayed; refer to Figure-30.

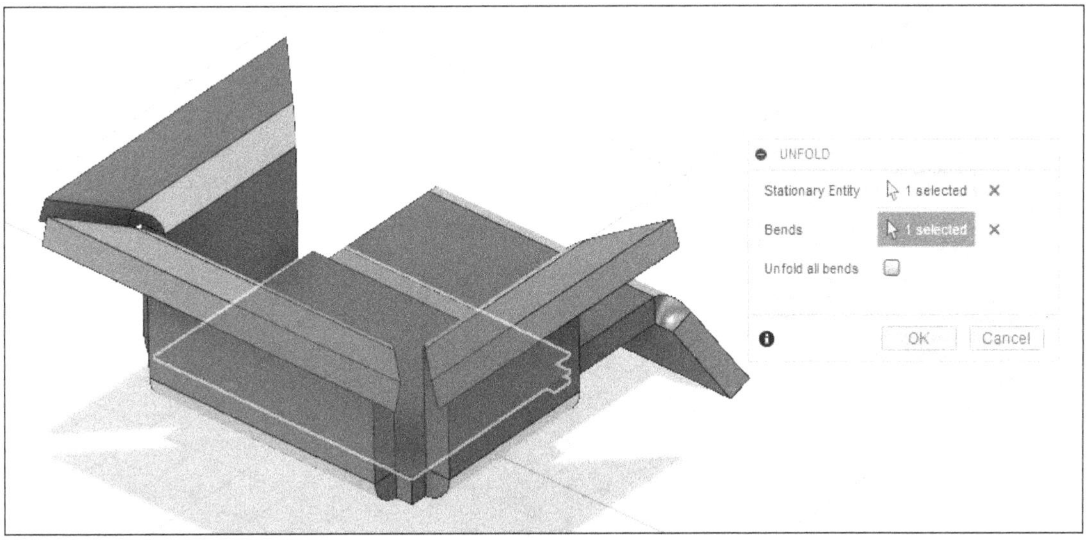

Figure-30. Preview of unfolding

- If you want to unfold all the bends then select the **Unfold all bends** check box.
- Click on the **OK** button to create the unfold feature.

Refolding Faces

The **Refold** tool is used to refold the unfolded faces. To do so, click on the **Refold** tool from **REFOLD FACES** drop-down in the **Toolbar**; refer to Figure-31. The **Refold** tool will become active when the faces have been unfolded.

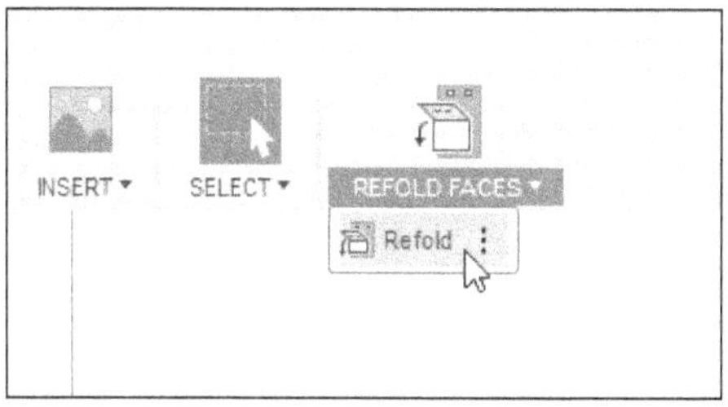

Figure-31. Refold tool

Some people may ask why to unfold and refold the faces of sheet metal parts. The answer is editing between unfolding and refolding steps. After unfolding, you can create holes or other modifications at the bend locations and then you can refold them.

Rip

The **Rip** tool is used to create a rip on a sheet metal flange or removes a face. The procedure to use this tool is discussed next.

- Click on the **Rip** tool from **MODIFY** drop-down in the **Toolbar;** refer to Figure-32. The **Rip** dialog box will be displayed; refer to Figure-33.

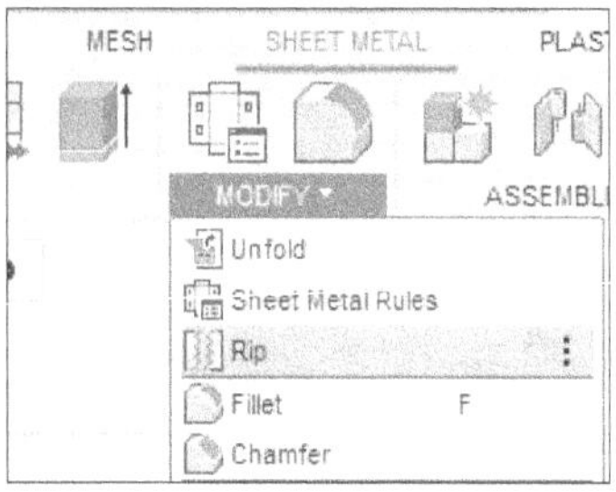

Figure-32. Rip tool

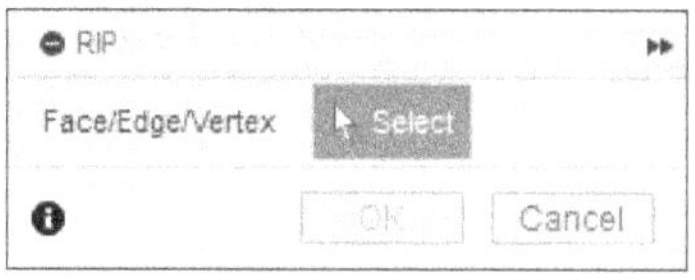

Figure-33. Rip dialog box

- Select two points on the external edges or tangentially continuing edge of the model to apply the rip feature; refer to Figure-34.

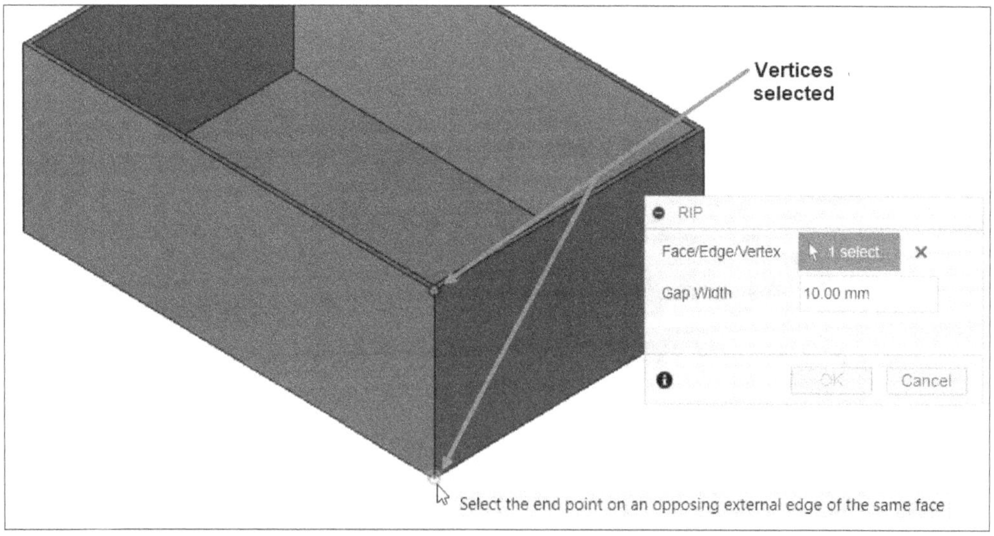

Figure-34. Selecting the point on rip

- After selecting desired geometry, specify desired values in the **Gap Width**, **Offset 1**, and **Offset 2** edit boxes.
- After specifying desired parameters, click on the **OK** button from the dialog box. The **Rip** will be created; refer to Figure-35.

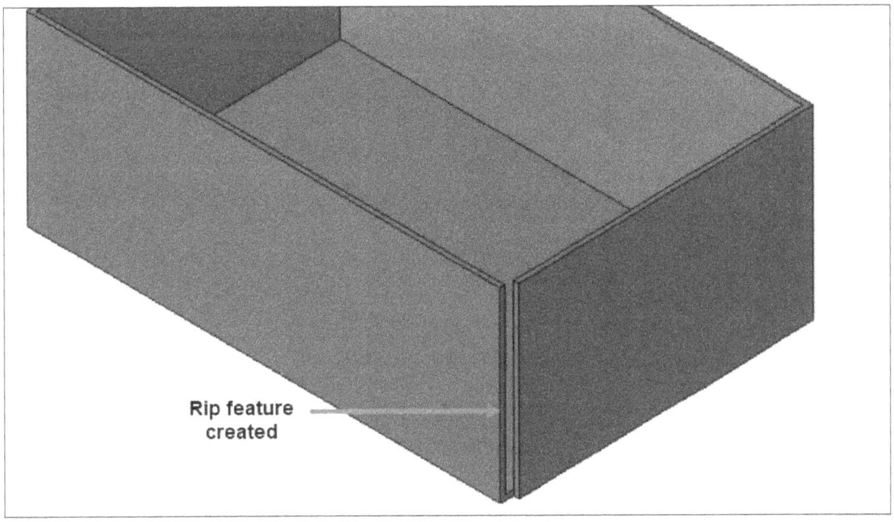

Figure-35. Rip created

CONVERT TO SHEET METAL

The **Convert to Sheet Metal** tool is used to convert a thin part into sheet metal part. The procedure to use this tool is given next.

- Click on the **Convert to Sheet Metal** tool from the **CREATE** panel in the **SHEET METAL** tab of **Toolbar**; refer to Figure-36. The **CONVERT TO SHEET METAL** dialog box will be displayed; refer to Figure-37 and you will be asked to select a thin part created as solid.

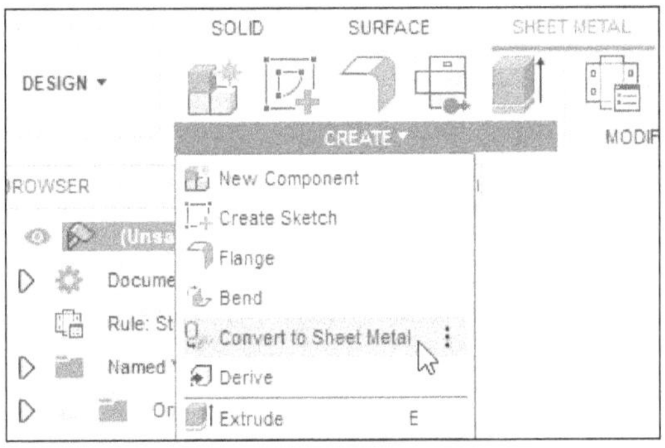

Figure-36. Convert to Sheet Metal tool

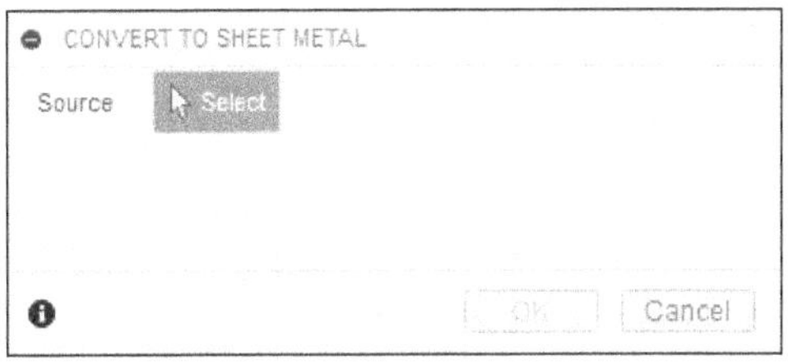

Figure-37. CONVERT TO SHEET METAL dialog box

- Click on the face of part to be converted into sheet metal. The updated **CONVERT TO SHEETMETAL** dialog box will be displayed; refer to Figure-38.

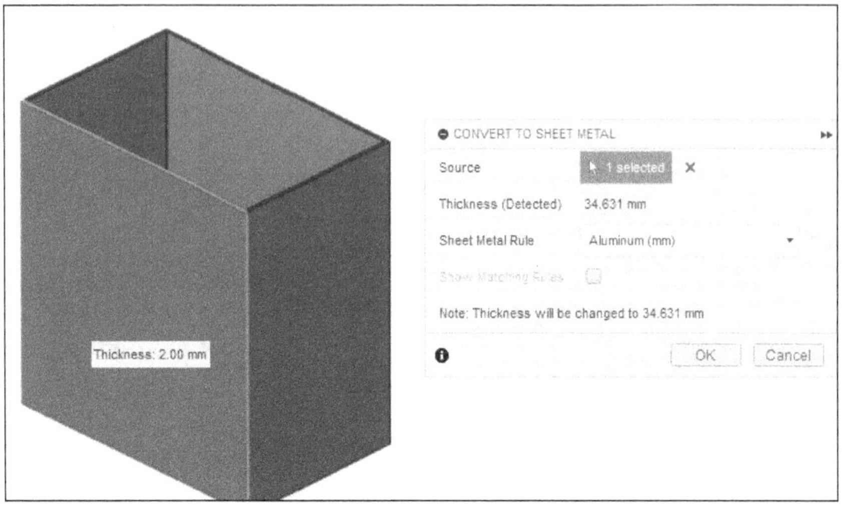

Figure-38. Updated CONVERT TO SHEET METAL dialog box

- By default, the **Show Matching Rules** check box is selected and hence only the rules that match with the model thickness are displayed. Clear this check box to select other rules.
- Click on the **OK** button from the dialog box. The part will be converted to a sheet metal part.

FLAT PATTERN

The **Create Flat Pattern** tool is used to create flat pattern using the sheet metal part so that the part can be cut from the sheet and bent to form desired product. The procedure to use this tool is given next.

- Click on the **Create Flat Pattern** tool from **CREATE** drop-down in the **Toolbar**; refer to Figure-39. The **CREATE FLAT PATTERN** dialog box will be displayed; refer to Figure-40.

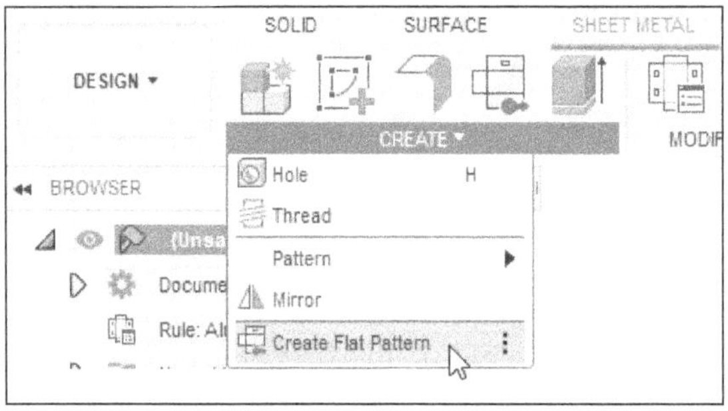

Figure-39. Create Flat Pattern tool

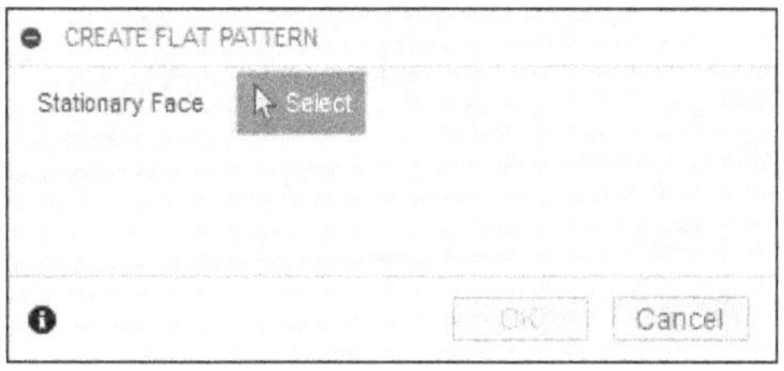

Figure-40. CREATE FLAT PATTERN dialog box

- Select the face that you want to be stationary and click on the **OK** button. The flat pattern will be created; refer to Figure-41.

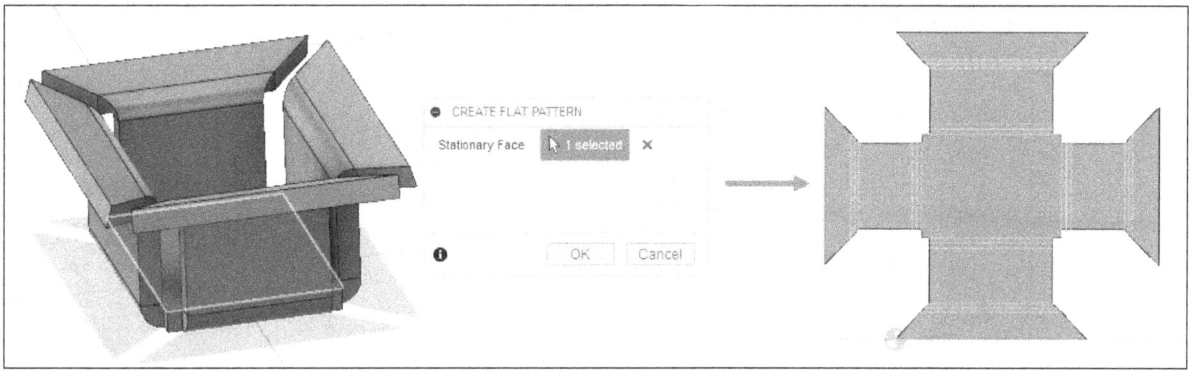

Figure-41. Flat Pattern created

EXPORTING DXF

The **Export Flat Pattern as DXF** tool is used to export the created flat pattern. The procedure is given next.

- Click on the **Export Flat Pattern as DXF** tool from **EXPORT** panel in the **Toolbar** after creating the flat pattern; refer to Figure-42. The **EXPORT FLAT PATTERN AS DXF** dialog box will be displayed; refer to Figure-43.

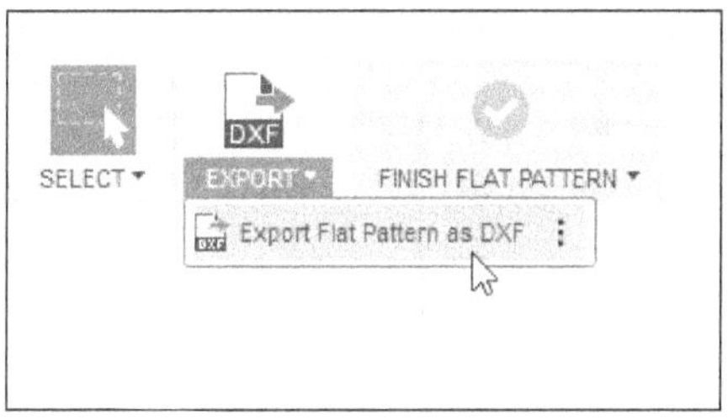

Figure-42. Export Flat Pattern as DXF tool

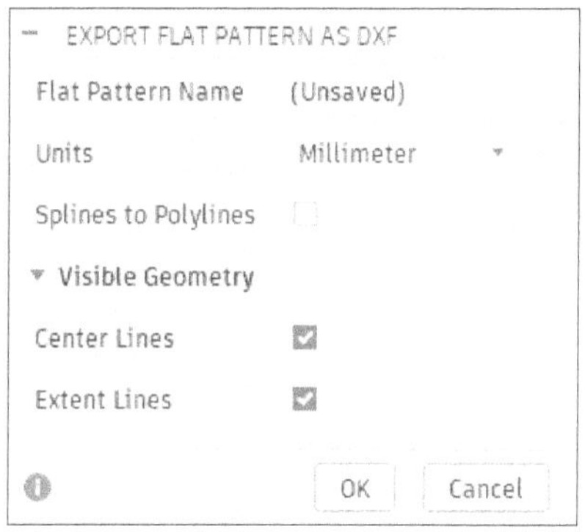

Figure-43. EXPORT FLAT PATTERN AS DXF dialog box

- Select desired unit from **Units** drop-down in which the pattern is to be exported.
- Select the **Splines to Polylines** check box if you want to convert all splines in the flat pattern to polylines. Specify the **Tolerance** value in the edit box as desired. This option is useful when your laser cutting machine do not support splines.
- Select **Center Lines** and **Extent Lines** check box from **Visible Geometry** rollout to include the bend center lines and bend extent lines, respectively.
- Click on the **OK** button from the dialog box. The **Export DXF** dialog box will be displayed; refer to Figure-44.

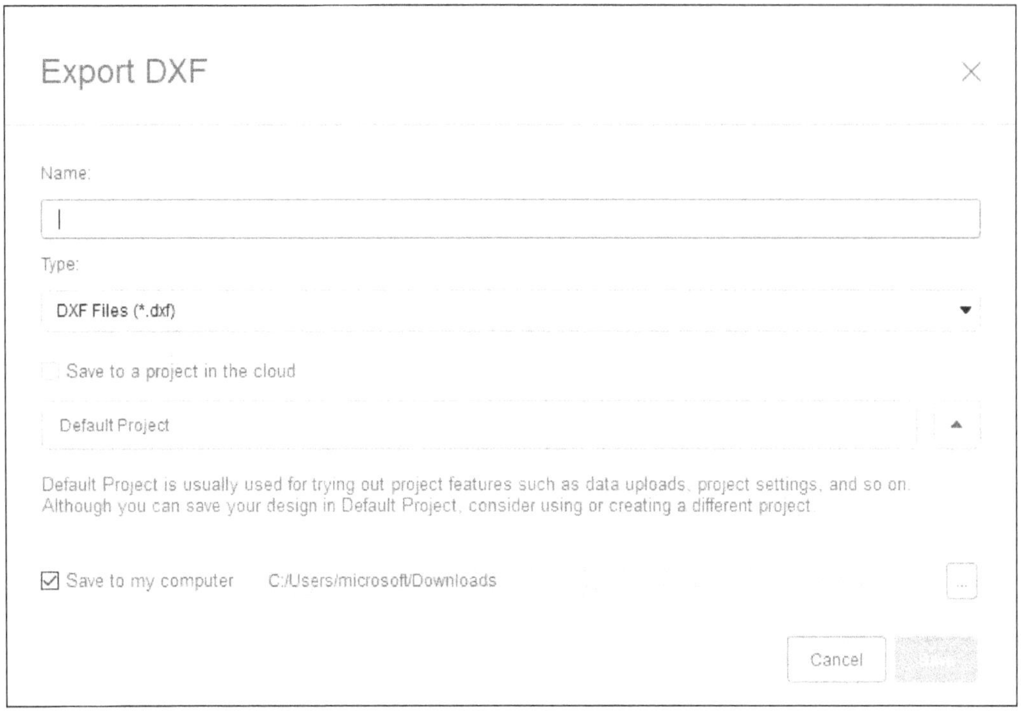

Figure-44. Export DXF dialog box

- Specify desired name of file and click on **Save** button to save the file or select **Save to my computer** check box to specify desired location of file in the **Select Location** dialog box.

PRACTICAL

Create the sheet metal model as shown in Figure-45. Dimensions are given in Figure-46. Also, create flat pattern and annotate the drawing.

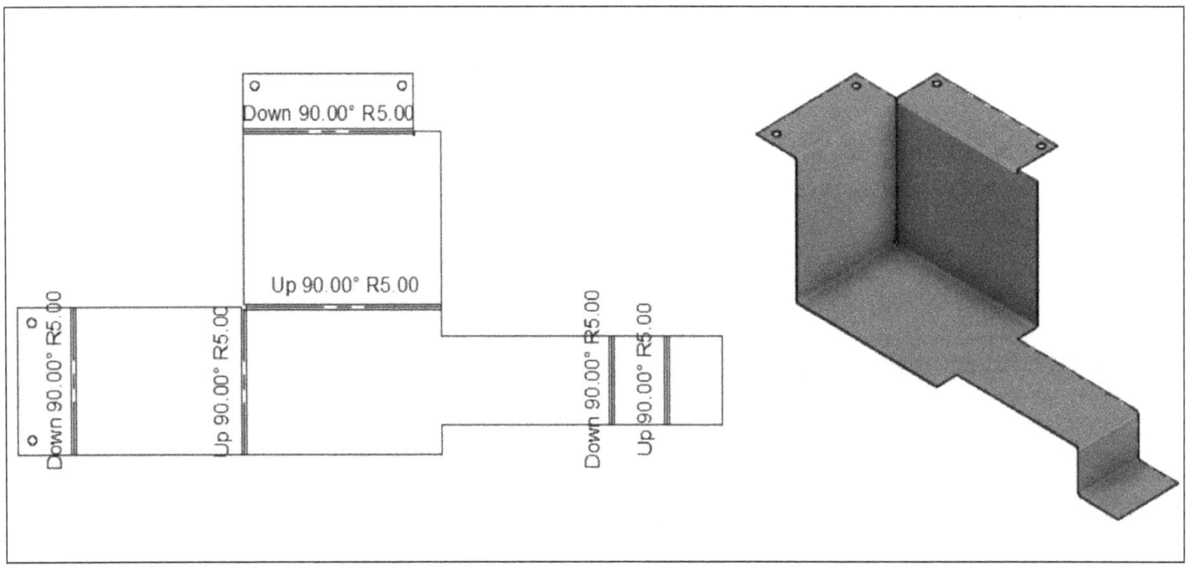

Figure-45. Sheet Metal model

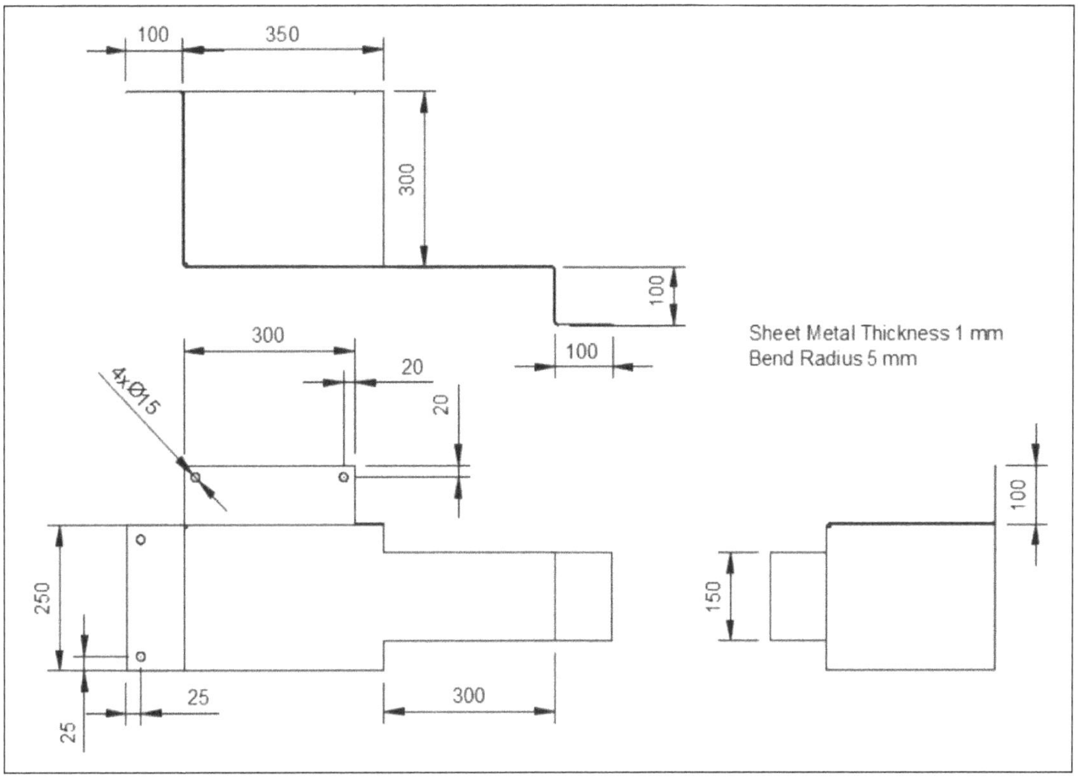

Figure-46. Dimensions for sheetmetal model

Starting Sheet Metal and Creating Base Sheet

- Start Autodesk Fusion and select the **SHEET METAL** tab in **DESIGN** workspace. The tools related to Sheet Metal design will become active.
- Click on the **Create Sketch** tool from **CREATE** drop-down in the **Toolbar** and create a sketch on the **XY** plane as shown in Figure-47.

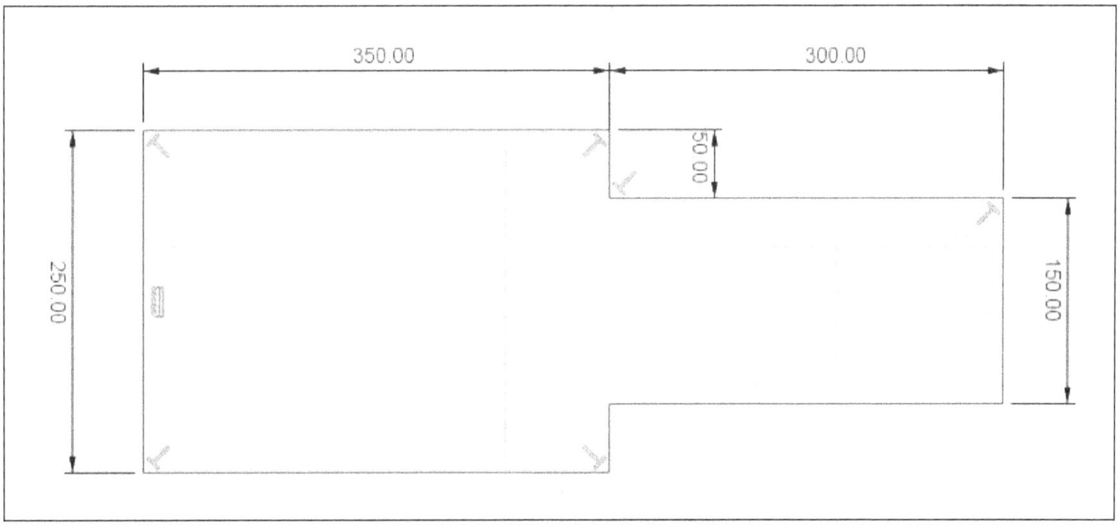

Figure-47. Sketch for Practical

- Click on the **FINISH SKETCH** tool from the **Toolbar** to exit the sketching environment.

Setting Sheet Metal Rules

- Click on the **Sheet Metal Rules** tool from **MODIFY** drop-down in the **Toolbar**. The **SHEET METAL RULES** dialog box will be displayed.

- Select any of the sheet metal rule and click on the **New Rule** button. The **New Rule** dialog box will be displayed.
- Specify the name of rule as **Practical** in the **Rule Name** edit box. Click in the **Thickness** edit box and specify the value as **1 mm**.
- Expand the **Bend Conditions** node and specify the **Bend radius** as **5 mm**.
- Click on the **Save** button and **Close** the dialog box.

Creating Flanges

- Click on the **Flange (Base/Edge/Contour)** tool from **CREATE** drop-down in the **Toolbar** and select the newly created sketch.
- Select the **Practical** option from the **Sheet Metal Rule** area of the dialog box; refer to Figure-48 and click on the **OK** button.

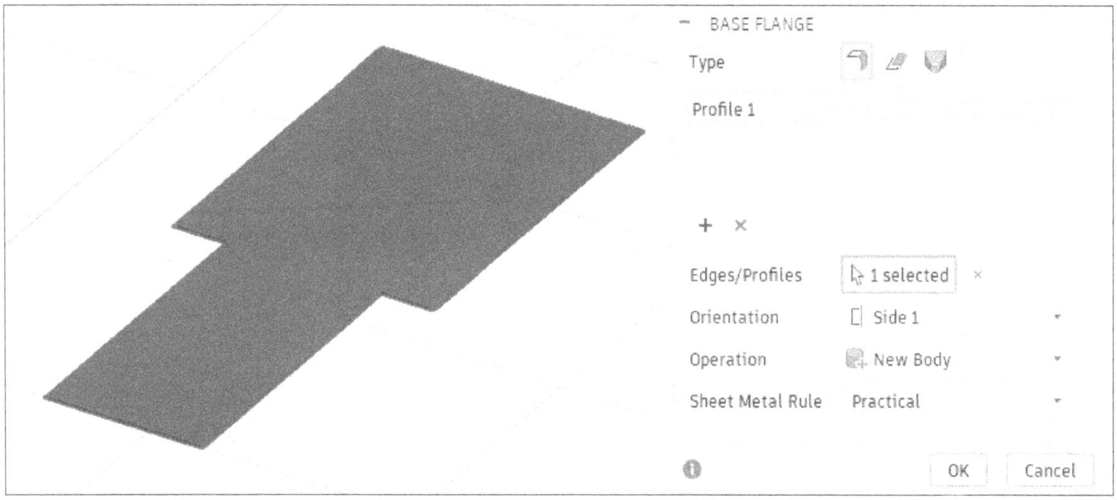

Figure-48. Practical sheet metal rule

- Click on the **Flange (Base/Edge/Contour)** tool again from **CREATE** drop-down in the **Toolbar**. Select the edges as shown in Figure-49 and specify the height as **300**.

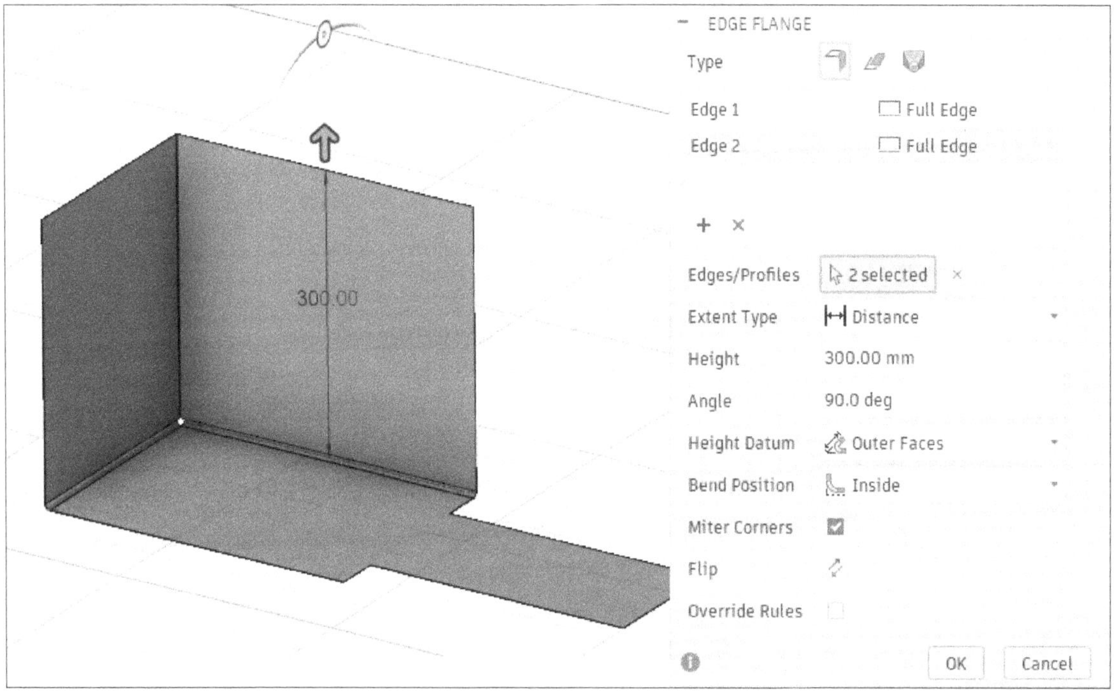

Figure-49. Edges selected for Flange

- Click on the **OK** button to create vertical flanges.
- Click again on the **Flange** tool and select the outer edges of the newly created vertical flanges.
- Set the height of flanges as **100** mm and clear the **Miter Option** check box. Preview of the flanges will be displayed; refer to Figure-50.

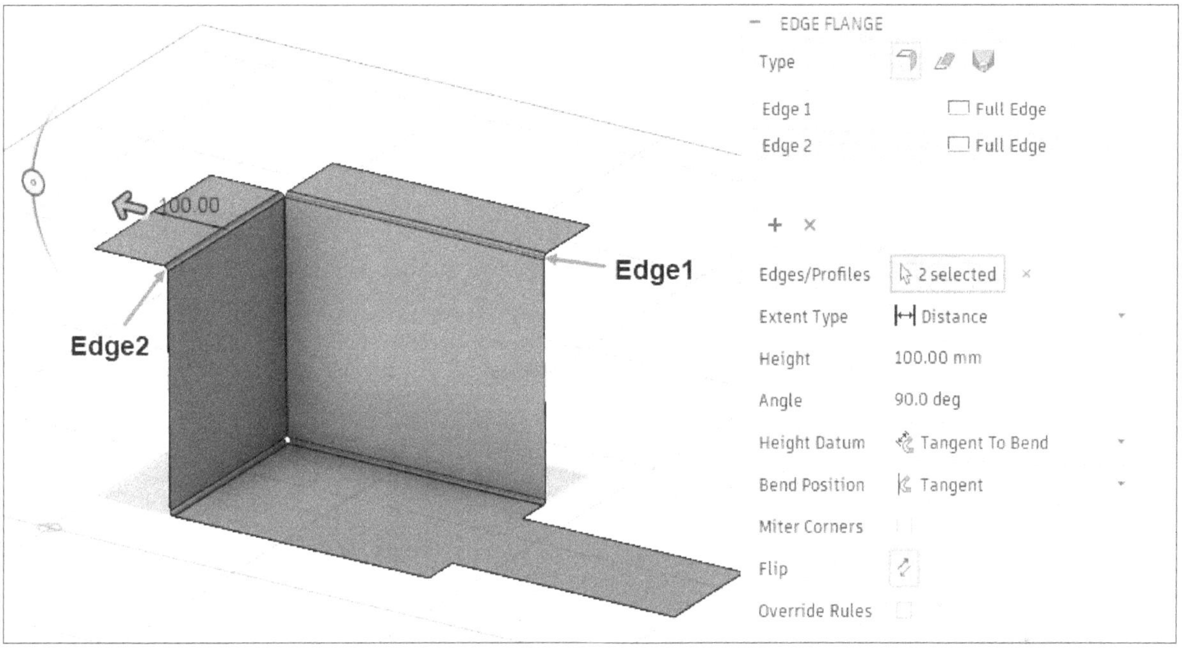

Figure-50. Preview of flanges

- Click on the **Full Edge** option of **Edge 1** in the selection box and select the **Two Offset** option. Now, you will be able to edit the length of flange.
- Move the drag handle to **50** mm backward; refer to Figure-51.

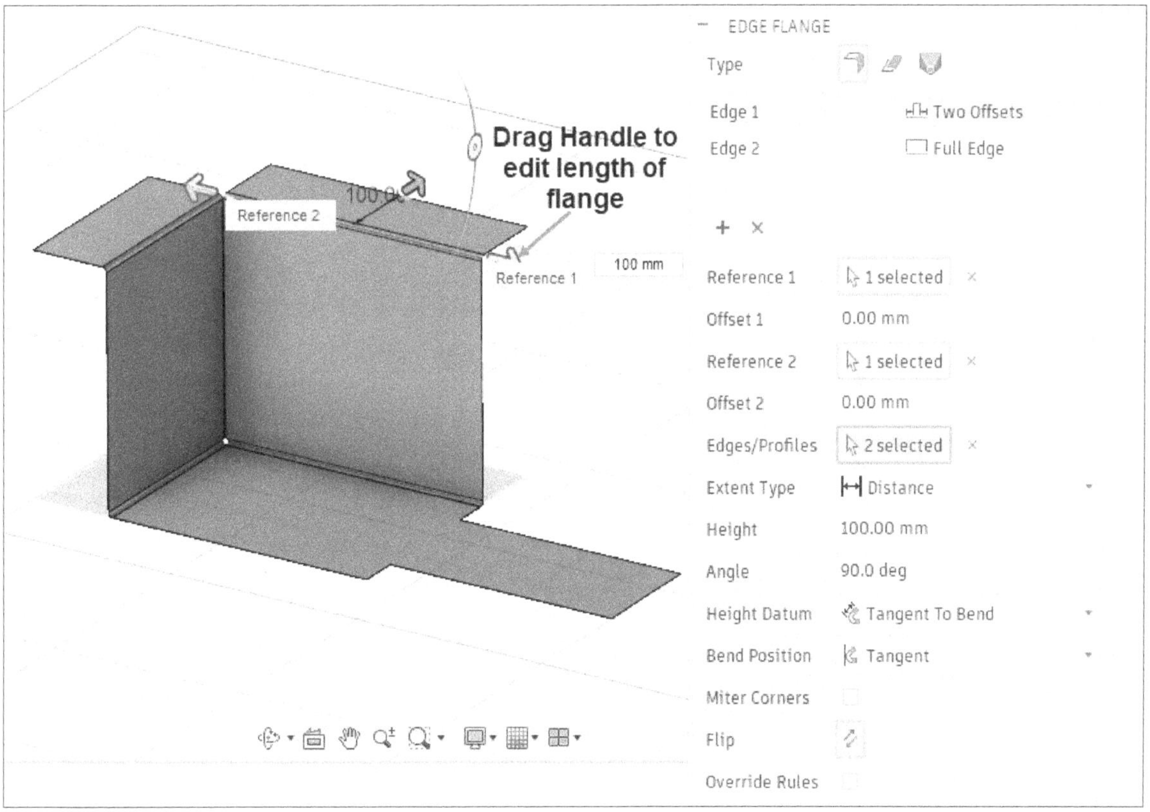

Figure-51. Editing length of flange

- Click on the **OK** button from the dialog box. Similarly, you create other flanges to form a part as shown in Figure-52.

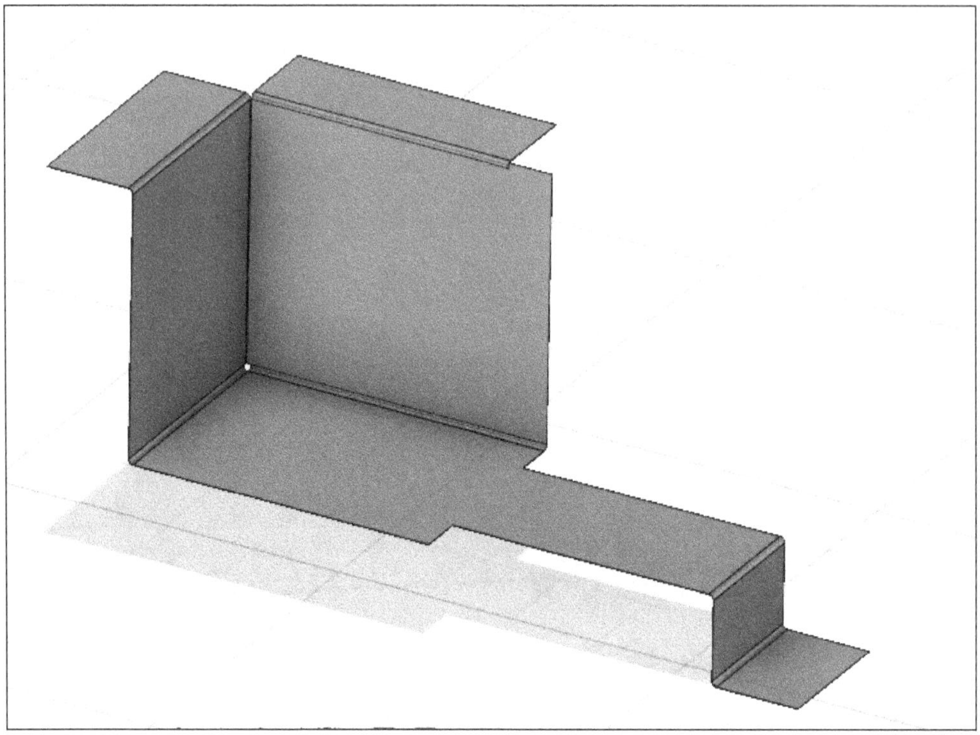

Figure-52. Flanges created

Creating Holes

- Click on the **Create Sketch** tool from **CREATE** drop-down in the **Toolbar**. You will be asked to select a face/plane.
- Select the face as shown in Figure-53. Create four points as shown in Figure-54 and exit the sketching environment.

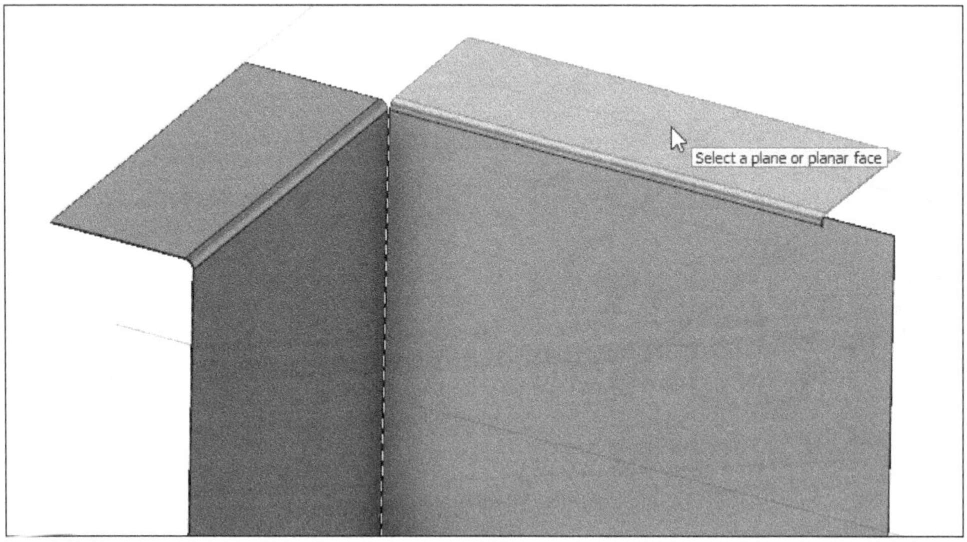

Figure-53. Face selected for sketching

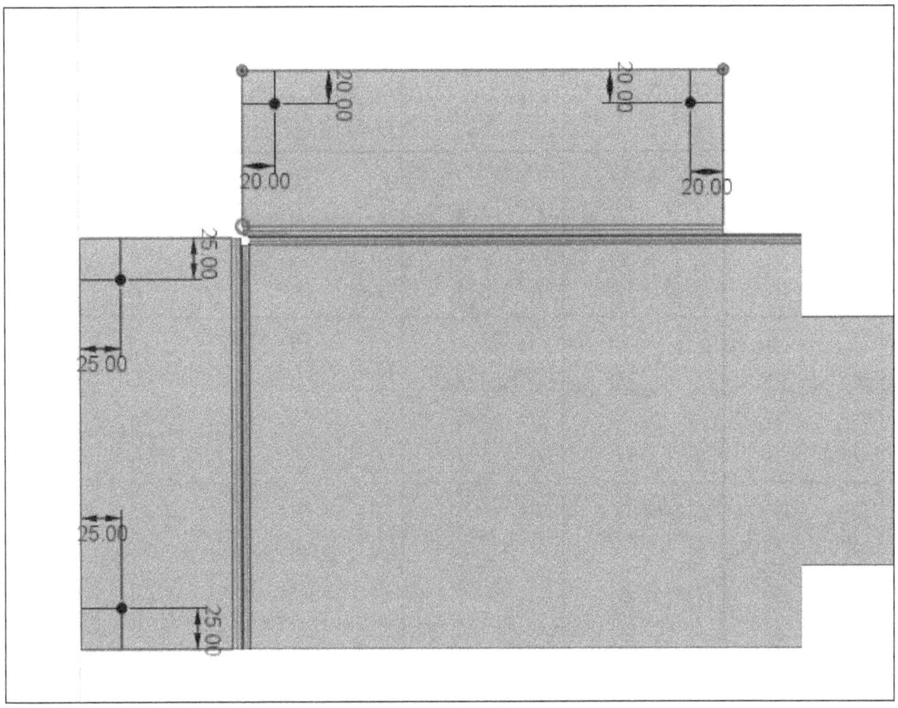

Figure-54. Points created for hole

- Click on the **Hole** tool from **CREATE** drop-down in the **Toolbar**. The **HOLE** dialog box will be displayed.
- Select the **From Sketch (Multiple Holes)** button from **Placement** section in the dialog box. You will be asked to select the sketch points.
- Select all the sketch points created earlier and specify depth as **5 mm** and diameter as **15 mm** in the respective edit boxes of the dialog box. Preview of the holes will be displayed; refer to Figure-55.

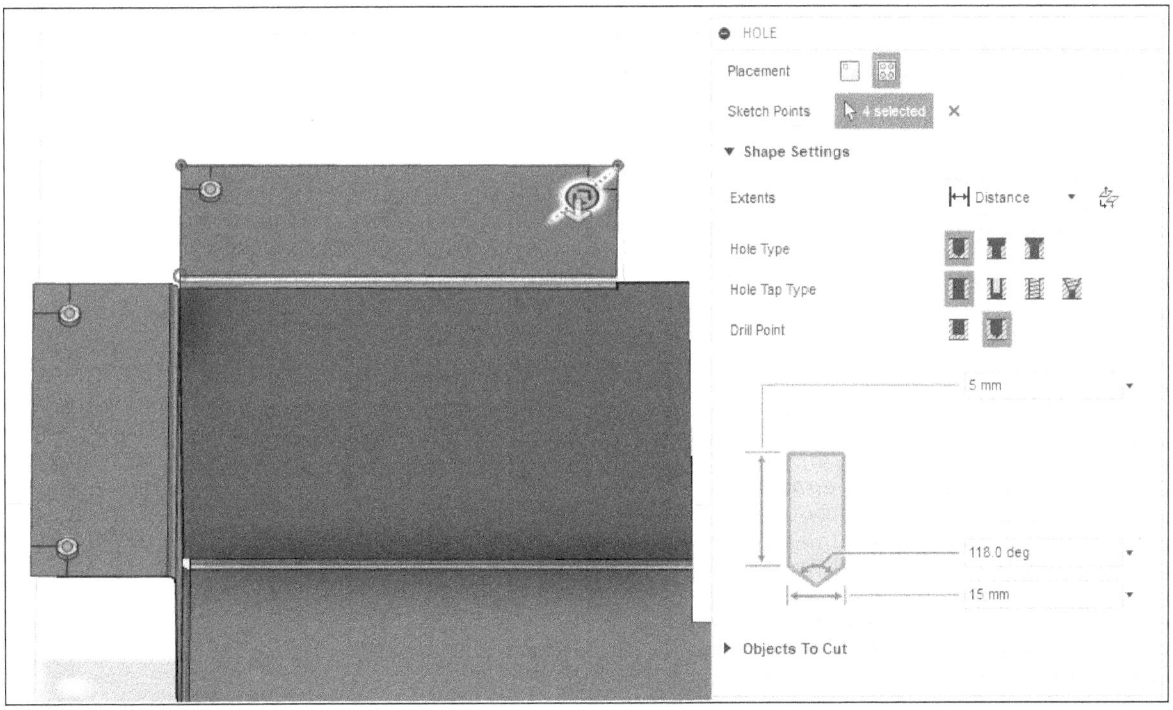

Figure-55. Preview of holes

- Click on the **OK** button from the dialog box to create the holes. The final part will be created.

- Click on the **Create Flat Pattern** tool from **CREATE** drop-down in the **Toolbar**. You will be asked to select a stationary face. Select the base flange and click on the **OK** button. The flat pattern will be displayed; refer to Figure-56.

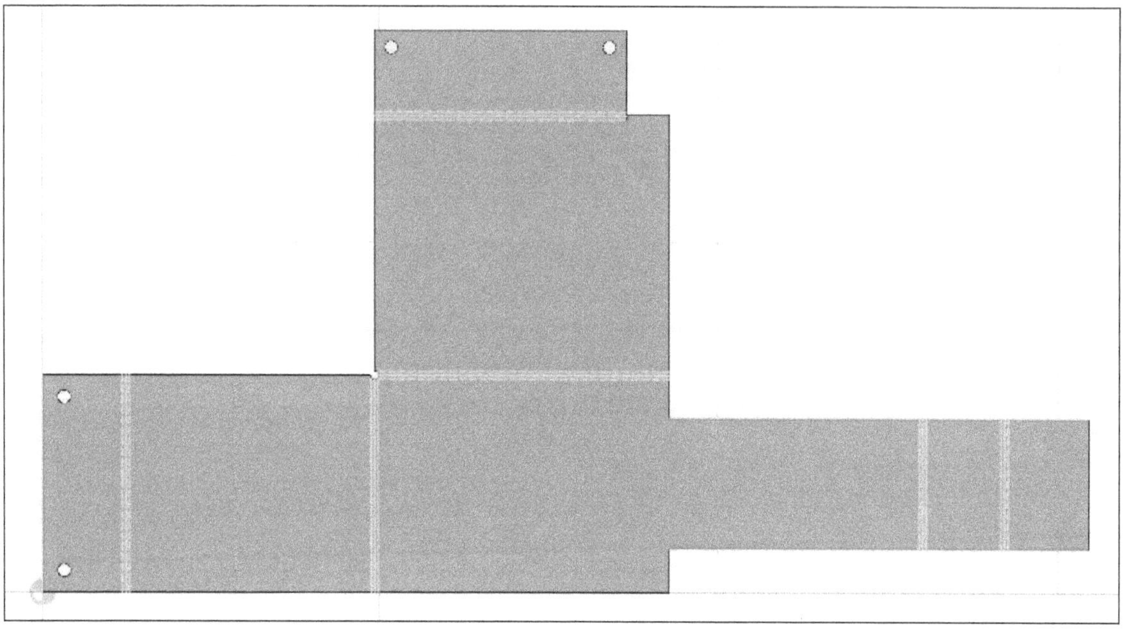

Figure-56. Flat pattern created

Creating Drawing for Flat Pattern

- Click on the **From Design** tool from **DRAWING** cascading menu in the **Change Workspace** drop-down. The **Save** dialog box will be displayed.
- Specify desired name and location and then click on the **Save** button. The **CREATE DRAWING** dialog box will be displayed.
- Set desired parameters and click on the **OK** button. You will be asked to place the drawing view.
- Set desired parameters in the **DRAWING VIEW** dialog box and place the **TOP** view of flat pattern; refer to Figure-57.

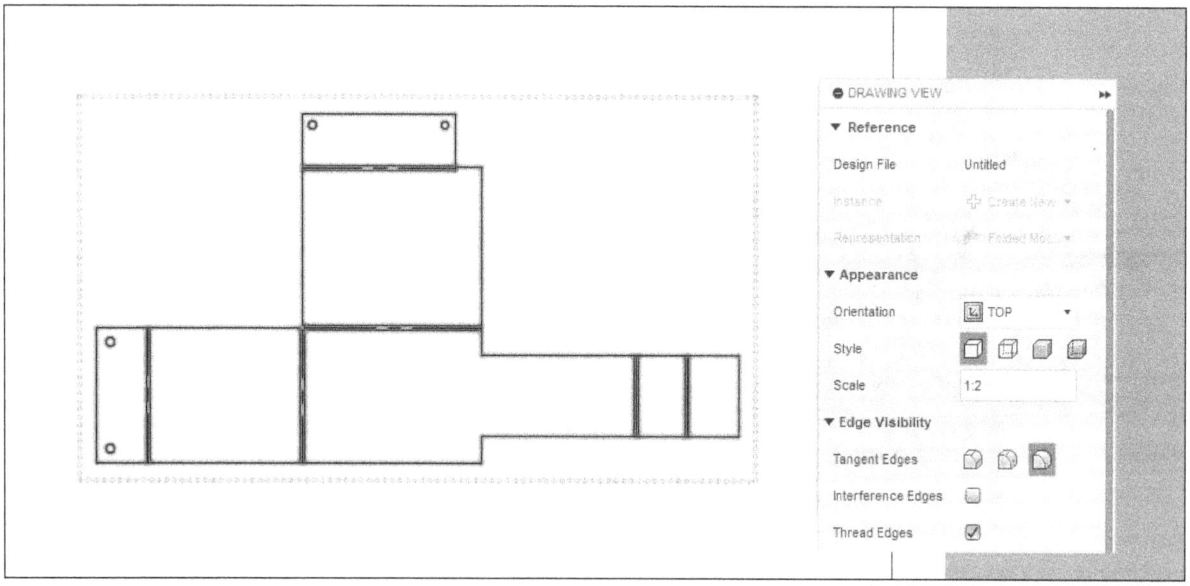

Figure-57. Flat Pattern placed in drawing

Annotating Flat Pattern in Drawing

- Click on the **Leader** tool from **TEXT** drop-down in the **Toolbar**. You will be asked to select the edges to be annotated.
- One by one, select the center lines of all the bends in the flat pattern. The annotations will be displayed as shown in Figure-58. You can also use bend identifiers with table to annotate bends in a sheet metal part.

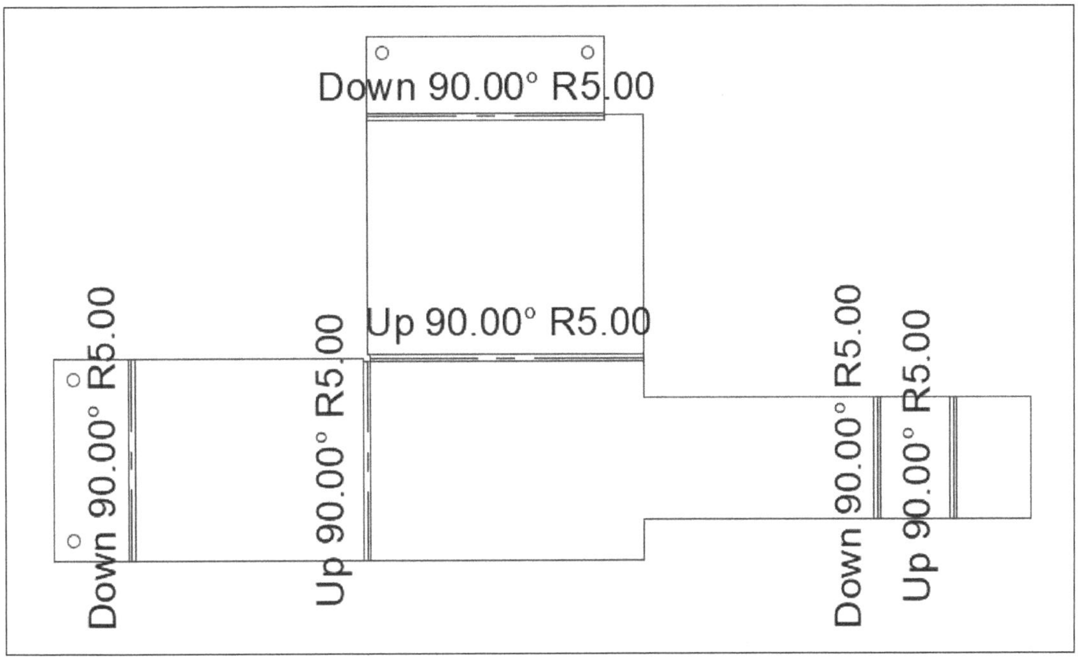

Figure-58. Annotations applied for bends

- Apply the other dimensions and create the other views as discussed earlier in the book.

PRACTICE

Create the sheet metal model as shown in Figure-59. The drawing is given in Figure-60.

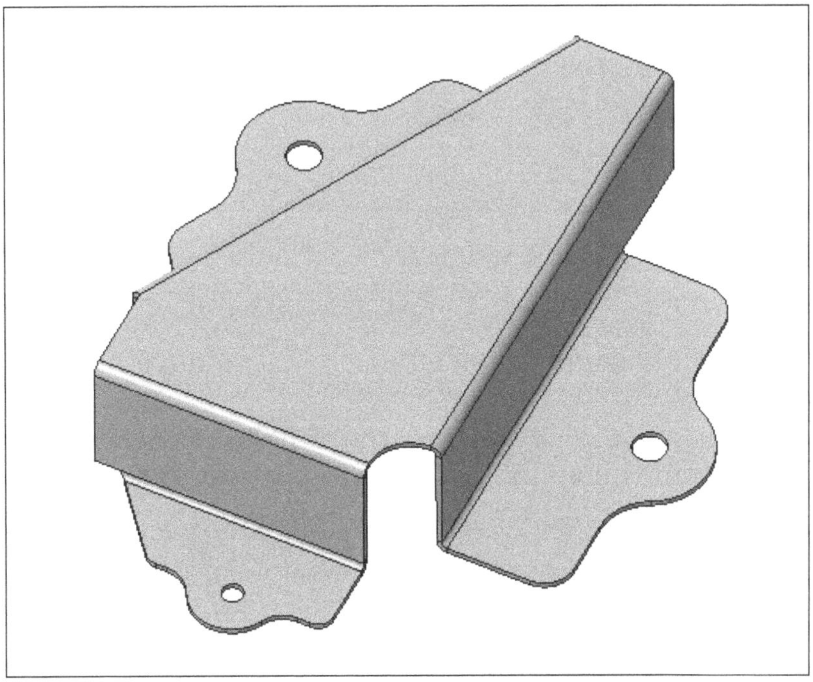

Figure-59. Model for Practice

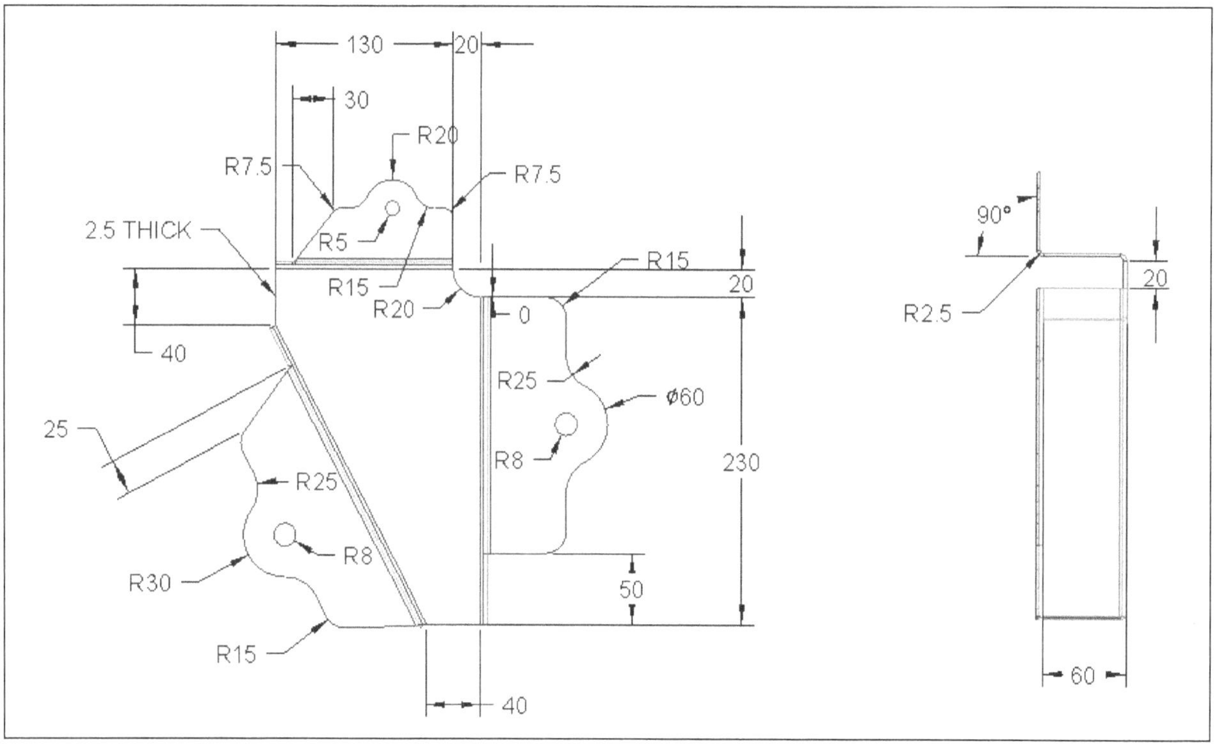

Figure-60. Drawing for Practice

SELF ASSESSMENT

Q1. In which areas, **Sheet Metal Rules** are used?

Q2. If you want to modify the property of sheet metal rule then click on the **Edit Rule** button from **SHEET METAL RULES** dialog box. T/F

Q3. Flanges act as .... and .... of sheet metal parts.

Q4. Which of the following options should be selected from **Bend Position** drop-down in the **FLANGE** dialog box to create bend ahead of the outer edge of bend equal to the thickness of sheet?

a) Adjacent
b) Outside
c) Inside
d) Tangent

Q5. The **Refold** tool will become active when the faces have been unfolded. T/F

Q6. Select the .... check box from **EXPORT FLAT PATTERN AS DXF** dialog box if you want to convert all splines in the flat pattern to polylines.

Q7. Which tool is used to set various parameters related to sheet metal design in Autodesk Fusion?
A) Flange Tool
B) Sheet Metal Rules Tool
C) Lofted Flange Tool
D) Convert to Sheet Metal Tool

Q8. What is the purpose of the Edit Rule button in the Sheet Metal Rules dialog box?
A) To delete an existing sheet metal rule
B) To create a new sheet metal rule
C) To modify an existing sheet metal rule
D) To export sheet metal rules

Q9. What does the K Factor in sheet metal rules represent?
A) The thickness of the sheet metal
B) The bend radius of the sheet metal
C) The neutral axis shift during bending
D) The seam gap between flanges

Q10. How can you create a new sheet metal rule in Autodesk Fusion?
A) By clicking on the Flange tool
B) By using the Edit Rule button
C) By clicking on the New Rule button in the Sheet Metal Rules dialog box
D) By selecting the Override Rules checkbox

Q11. What is the purpose of the Flange tool?
A) To create bends in a sheet metal part
B) To create and modify sheet metal rules
C) To convert a solid part into sheet metal
D) To create base and walls of a sheet metal part

Q12. If you use a closed sketch to create a flange, what should you set in the Orientation drop-down?
A) Thickness Side
B) Bend Position
C) Height Datum
D) Override Rules

Q13. Which option from the Height Datum drop-down sets the height of the flange from the inner face?
A) Outer Faces
B) Inner Faces
C) Tangent To Bend
D) Adjacent

Q14. What happens when you select the Inside option from the Bend Position drop-down?
A) The bend is created from the outer edge of the flange
B) The bend starts from the inner edge of the flange
C) The bend is created ahead of the outer edge of the bend
D) The bend starts tangent to the face of the selected flange

Q15. Which tool is used to create a contour flange?
A) Bend Tool
B) Lofted Flange Tool
C) Flange Tool
D) Unfold Tool

Q16. What is the purpose of the Lofted Flange option in the FLANGE dialog box?
A) To create a flange from a single edge
B) To create a flange by joining two profiles at a specified distance
C) To create a flat pattern for sheet metal
D) To create a bend along a specified line

Q17. Which forming type is used to create a lofted flange generated by a punch and die machine?
A) Die Form
B) Brake Form
C) Facet Angle
D) Convert to Sheet Metal

Q18. What does the Facet Control option "Facet Number" specify?
A) Maximum chord distance for determining facets
B) Maximum number of facets in each bend
C) Maximum span of each facet in the bend
D) The angle reference for determining facets

Q19. Which tool is used to create a bend at a selected line on a sheet metal model?
A) Flange Tool
B) Unfold Tool
C) Bend Tool
D) Convert to Sheet Metal Tool

Q20. What is the function of the Unfold tool?
A) To apply a bend relief
B) To create a bend along a selected line
C) To unbend selected bends of the part
D) To convert a solid part into sheet metal

Q21. Why would you unfold and refold sheet metal faces?
A) To delete bend rules
B) To create holes or modifications at bend locations
C) To convert a sheet metal part into a solid model
D) To change the sheet metal thickness

Q22. Which tool is used to convert a thin part into a sheet metal part?
A) Convert to Sheet Metal Tool
B) Lofted Flange Tool
C) Flange Tool
D) Bend Tool

Q23. What is the purpose of the Flat Pattern tool?
A) To create a 3D flange
B) To unfold selected bends in a part
C) To create a flat pattern for cutting and bending
D) To convert a sheet metal part into a solid part

Q24. What does the "Export Flat Pattern as DXF" tool do?
A) Creates a flat pattern
B) Saves the flat pattern as a DXF file
C) Applies bend relief to the flat pattern
D) Converts a sheet metal part into a solid model

Q25. What is the function of the Override Rules checkbox in the Flange tool?
A) To disable all bend rules
B) To apply default bend rules only
C) To allow modifying rule-specific parameters for a flange
D) To delete existing flange rules

Q26. What is the purpose of the Flip button in the Flange tool?
A) To change the thickness of the flange
B) To flip the direction of the flange
C) To delete the flange
D) To apply default bend rules

Q27. Which feature allows creating miter cuts in flanges?
A) Override Rules
B) Miter Option
C) Bend Position
D) Height Datum

Q28. What does the Brake Form button do in the Lofted Flange tool?
A) Creates a flange using stamping die process
B) Generates a lofted flange using a punch and die machine
C) Creates a flat pattern of the flange
D) Converts a solid model into a sheet metal part

Q29. What is required to create a Lofted Flange?
A) A single edge selection
B) A single face selection
C) Two or more profiles
D) A predefined bend rule

Q30. What does the Facet Distance option in Lofted Flange control?
A) The total length of the flange
B) The span of each facet in the bend
C) The number of profiles used in the lofted flange
D) The angle at which the flange bends

Q31. How is the Bend tool activated in Autodesk Fusion?
A) By selecting a bend relief option
B) By selecting a line sketch from the model
C) By clicking on an existing bend
D) By modifying the K Factor

Q32. What is the first step when using the Unfold tool?
A) Selecting the bend radius
B) Selecting a stationary face
C) Clicking the Override Rules checkbox
D) Defining a custom bend relief

Q33. Why might a user select "Unfold all bends" in the Unfold tool?
A) To apply additional bends
B) To remove all bend reliefs
C) To unfold all bends in one step
D) To create a new sheet metal rule

Q34. What must be done before using the Refold tool?
A) Select a bend relief
B) Apply a flat pattern
C) Unfold the faces
D) Convert the model to sheet metal

Q35. What is the advantage of unfolding and refolding a sheet metal part?
A) It allows adding features like holes at bend locations
B) It prevents the creation of lofted flanges
C) It disables sheet metal rules
D) It automatically converts the part into a DXF file

Q36. Which tool converts a thin solid model into a sheet metal part?
A) Flange Tool
B) Convert to Sheet Metal Tool
C) Unfold Tool
D) Sheet Metal Rules Tool

Q37. What does the "Show Matching Rules" checkbox do in the Convert to Sheet Metal tool?
A) Displays only rules matching the model thickness
B) Applies all available rules to the part
C) Enables a preview of the sheet metal part
D) Disables thickness restrictions

Q38. What is the final step in creating a flat pattern?
A) Selecting a bend relief
B) Selecting a stationary face
C) Exporting the pattern as a DXF file
D) Converting the part into a solid model

Q39. What is the purpose of exporting a flat pattern as a DXF?
A) To create a 3D extrusion
B) To modify bend relief settings
C) To generate a file for laser cutting or CNC machining
D) To convert the part into a lofted flange

Q40. Which checkbox should be selected to convert splines into polylines when exporting a DXF?
A) Show Matching Rules
B) Convert Splines to Polylines
C) Override Rules
D) Enable Facet Distance

FOR STUDENT NOTES

Chapter 23

Generative Design

Topics Covered

The major topics covered in this chapter are:

- ***Introduction to Generative Design***
- ***Generative Study Settings***
- ***Design Space Parameters***
- ***Setting Design Criteria***
- ***Running Generative Study***
- ***Exploring Generative Design Results***

INTRODUCTION

Generative Design in Autodesk Fusion is used to modify the shape of components under specified load conditions so that minimum material is used for getting same optimum results of analysis. This workspace is not available in educational edition of software and you will need either commercial trial or subscribed version of software. Following are the general features of Generative Designing in Autodesk Fusion:

- Consolidating parts by reducing the overall number of components;
- Reducing the weight of parts and components by using the least amount of material to make the element as effective as possible;
- Increasing performance by designing stronger parts and components.

Generative Design is sometimes confused with Optimization Study. Note that in optimization study, the material is removed from model to get the optimum model for given analysis but in generative design study, shape of the model is also modified as required to get optimum model. Select the **GENERATIVE DESIGN** option from the **Change Workspace** drop-down in the **Toolbar**. The **New Generative Study** dialog box will be displayed; refer to Figure-1. Click on the **Structural Component** button from dialog box and click on the **Create Study** button. The tools to perform Generative Design study for structural components will be displayed in the **Generative Design** workspace; refer to Figure-2. The procedure to switch workspace has been discussed earlier. Various tools of Generative Design workspace are discussed next.

Figure-1. New Generative Study dialog box

Note that the options to start generative design extension will be displayed if you are starting this workspace for the first time. You can start the extension as discussed earlier. The tools to perform generative design study on structural components are discussed next.

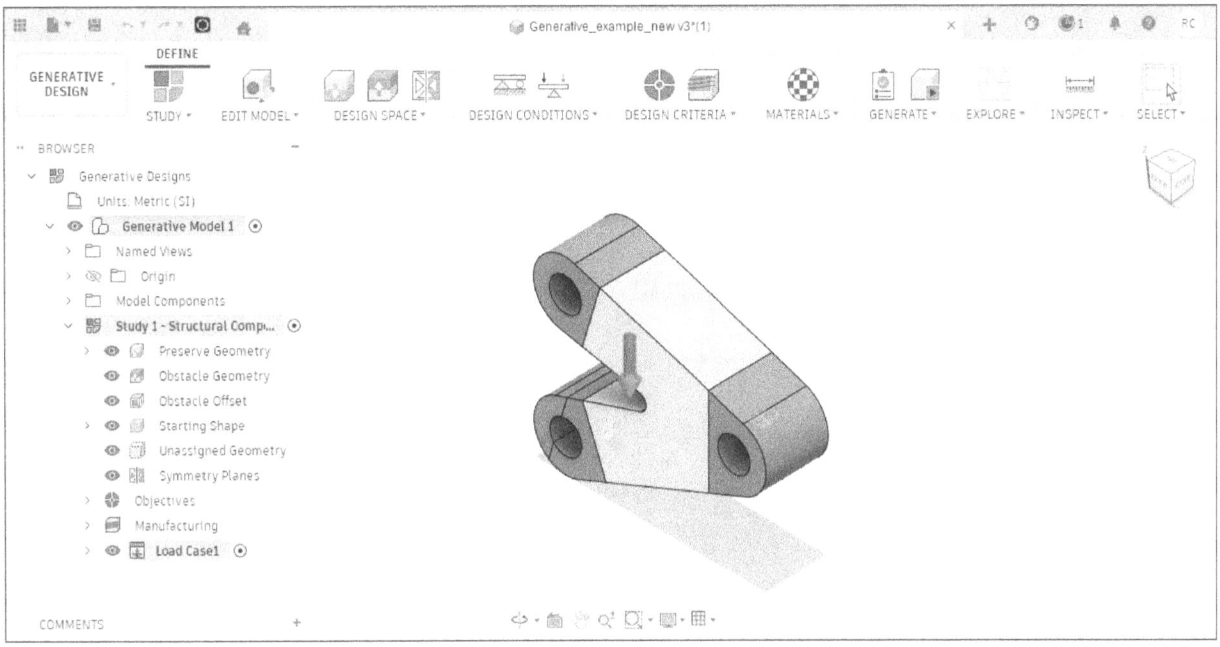

Figure-2. Generative Design workspace

WORKFLOW OF GENERATIVE DESIGN

Every analysis study follows a predefined strategy to get the result output. For Generative Design, the workflow can be summarized by Figure-3.

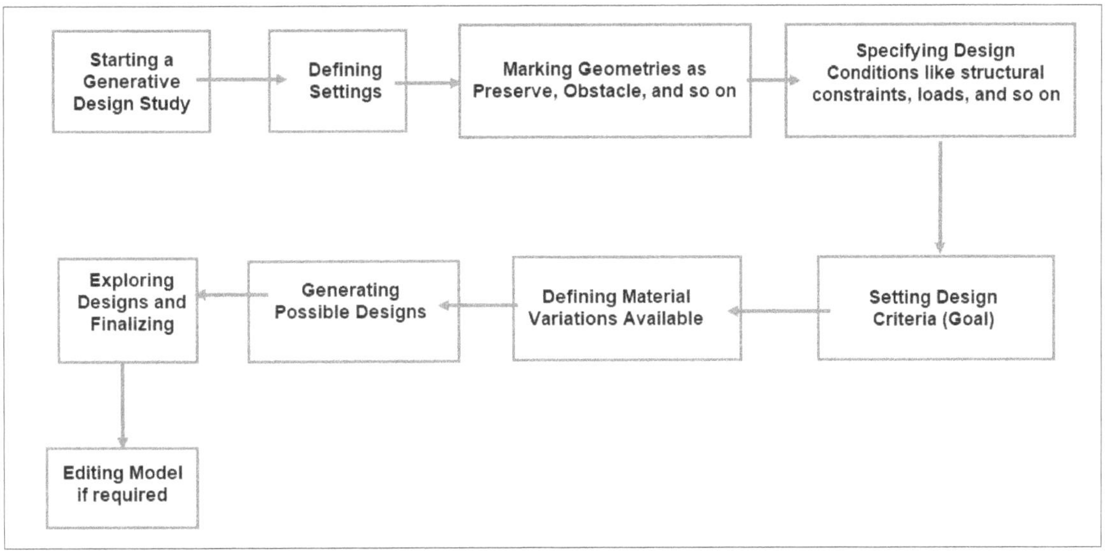

Figure-3. Workflow of Generative Design

Various tools available in Generative Design workspace are sequentially discussed next.

CREATING NEW GENERATIVE DESIGN STUDY

By default when you switch workspace to Generative Design, a generative design study is created automatically. If you want to create a new generative design study, then click on the **New Generative Study** tool from the **STUDY** drop-down in the **DEFINE** tab of **Ribbon**. A new generative design study will be added in the **BROWSER**; refer to Figure-4.

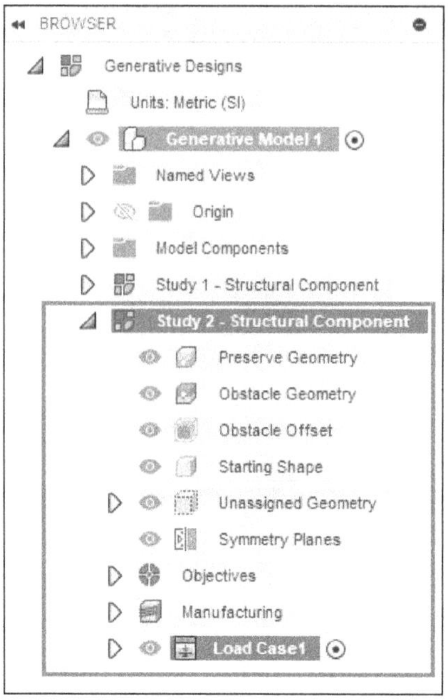

Figure-4. New generative design study

Note: If you want to change the units for generative design study then click on the **Edit** button next to **Units** in **BROWSER**; refer to Figure-5. The **Units Settings** dialog box will be displayed; refer to Figure-6. Set desired units or unit system as discussed earlier and click on the **OK** button.

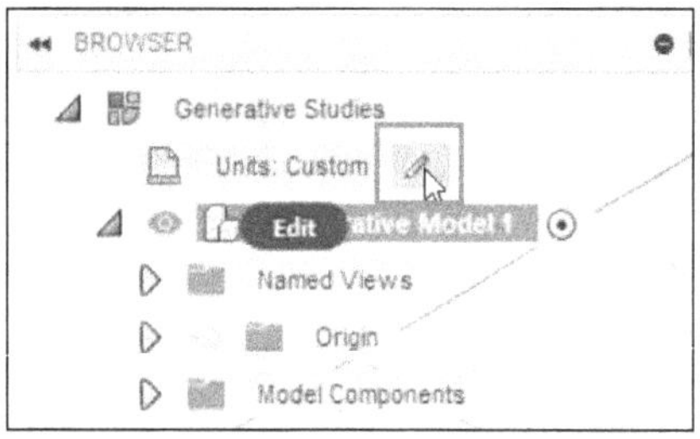

Figure-5. Edit button for Unit

Figure-6. Units Settings dialog box

DEFINING DESIGN SPACE REGIONS

By Design space, we mean categorizing the model into different regions based on whether the region can be modified, preserved, avoided, or marked as starting point for generating designs. The tools to perform these tasks are available in **DESIGN SPACE** drop-down of the **Ribbon**; refer to Figure-7. These tools are discussed next.

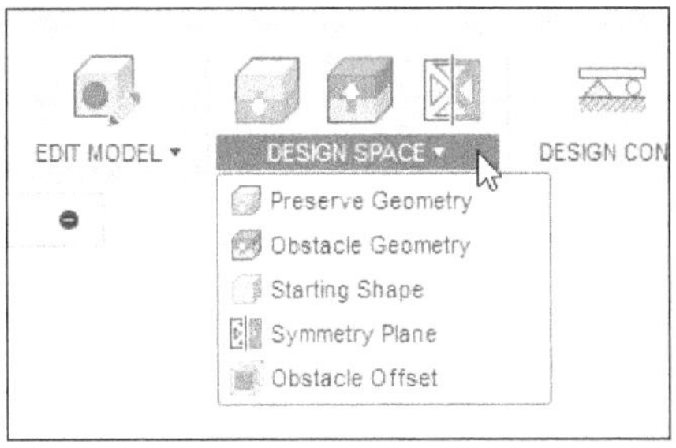

Figure-7. DESIGN SPACE drop-down

Preserving Geometry

The **Preserve Geometry** tool is used to keep selected portion of the model as it is in all variations of the model generated by study. Generally, bodies of the model which are referenced in assembly are preserved like cap of a bottle, speaker housing of a headphone, and so on. It happens because in assembly line, some components are manufactured by vendors and they fit in many models of the same product. The procedure to use this tool is given next.

- Click on the **Preserve Geometry** tool from the **DESIGN SPACE** drop-down in the **DEFINE** tab of the **Ribbon**. The **PRESERVE GEOMETRY** dialog box will be displayed; refer to Figure-8.

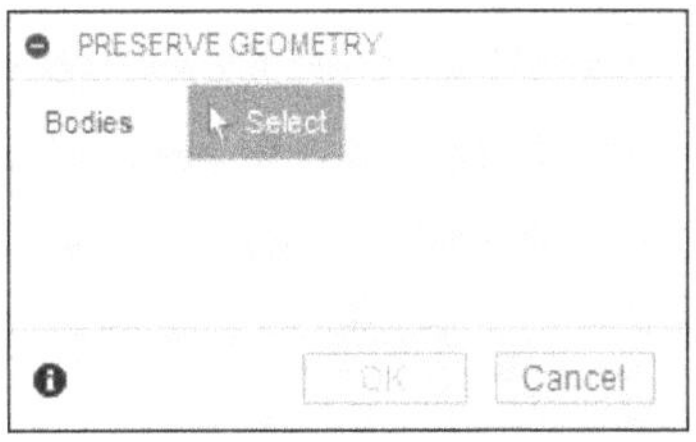

Figure-8. PRESERVE GEOMETRY dialog box

- Select the body(s) that you want to preserve in variations of model; refer to Figure-9 and click on the **OK** button. The selected bodies will be marked in green color denoting that they are preserved geometries.

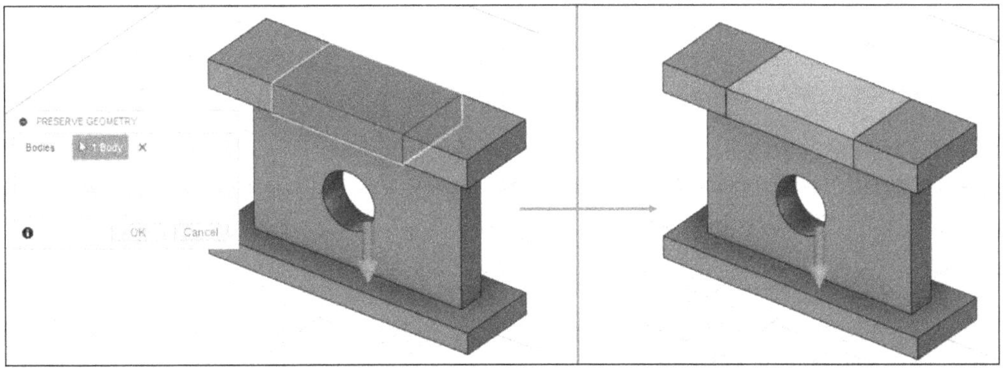

Figure-9. Preserving geometry

Note: If you have single body model and want to preserved some regions of the model then you can use **Split Body** tool of **Design** workspace discussed earlier in the book.

Obstacle Geometries

The obstacle geometries are those which cannot be modified by generative design and do not allow generative design variations to expand past them. For example, roof and floor of a car are obstacles when generating designs of car seat. A car seat cannot go below the floor and cannot go above the roof. The procedure to define obstacle geometries is given next.

- Click on the **Obstacle Geometry** tool from the **DESIGN SPACE** drop-down in the **DEFINE** tab of the **Ribbon**. The **OBSTACLE GEOMETRY** dialog box will be displayed; refer to Figure-10.

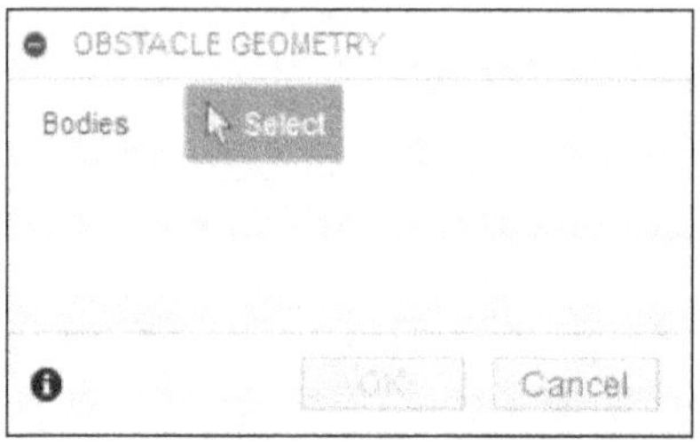

Figure-10. OBSTACLE GEOMETRY dialog box

- Select desired bodies from the model which you want to use as limiting boundaries and click on the **OK** button. Selected objects will be marked in red color denoting obstacle geometries; refer to Figure-11.

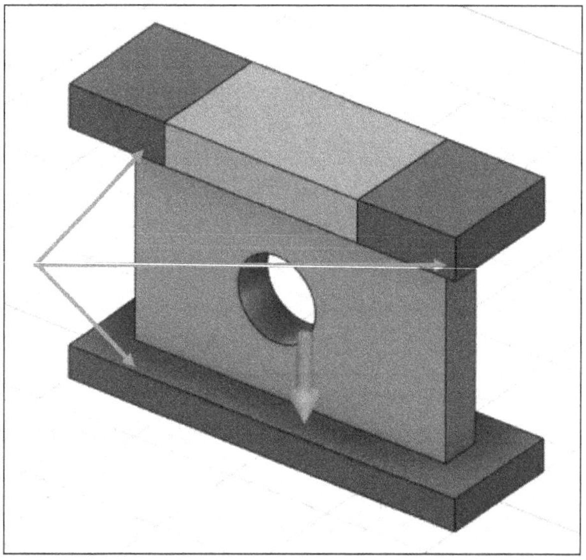

Figure-11. Obstacle geometries marked

Defining Starting Shape

The **Starting Shape** tool is used to define initial shape from which generative design outcomes will be generated. Note that it is not compulsory to select starting shape. The procedure to use this tool is given next.

- Click on the **Starting Shape** tool from the **DESIGN SHAPE** drop-down in the **DEFINE** tab of the **Ribbon**. The **STARTING SHAPE** dialog box will be displayed and you will be asked to select the body.

- Select desired body and click on the **OK** button. Selected body will be marked as starting body; refer to Figure-12. Select **Add/Remove Material** radio button from the **Options** section to permit the material to extend beyond the initial shape's boundary. Select **Remove Material** radio button to indicate an existing design or boundary that can only be reduced.

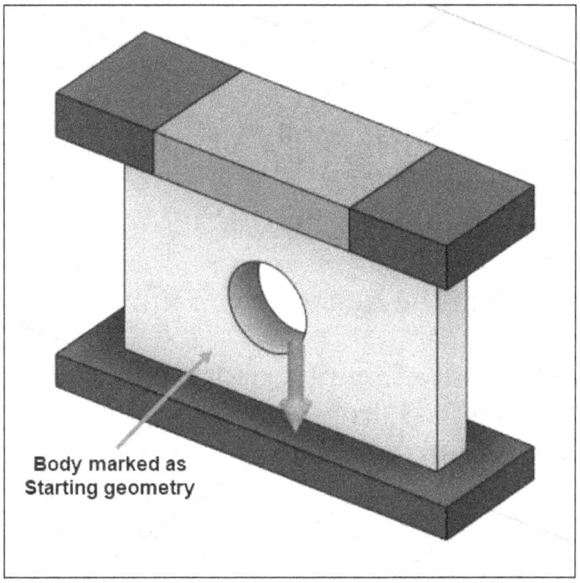

Figure-12. Marking starting body

Defining Symmetry Plane

The **Symmetry Plane** tool enable you to define a symmetry plane to generate symmetrical outcomes. Select a construction plane to define it as the symmetry plane. Using this option will reduce the processing time.

Defining Obstacle Offset

The **Obstacle Offset** tool is used to increase the size of obstacle boundaries without modifying model. The procedure to use this tool is given next.

- Click on the **Obstacle Offset** tool from the **DESIGN SPACE** drop-down in the **Toolbar**. The **OBSTACLE OFFSET** dialog box will be displayed; refer to Figure-13.

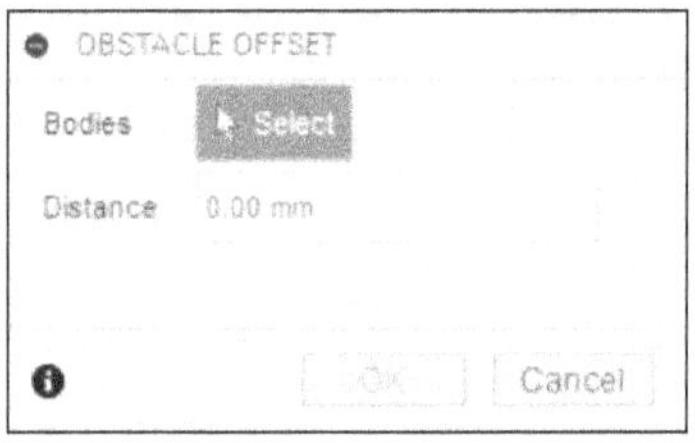

Figure-13. OBSTACLE OFFSET dialog box

- Select the obstacle bodies earlier defined from the model and set desired value by which you want to offset the size of obstacle body; refer to Figure-14.

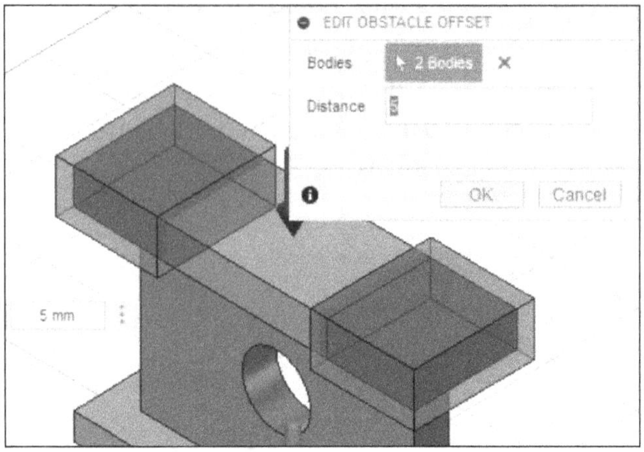

Figure-14. Obstacle offset preview

- Click on the **OK** button from the dialog box to apply offset.

After defining design space requirements, define the design conditions using tools available in the **DESIGN CONDITIONS** drop-down of **Ribbon**. The tools in this drop-down have been discussed earlier in previous chapters.

Defining Objectives for Generative Design

The **Objectives** tool in **DESIGN CRITERIA** drop-down of **Ribbon** is used to define objectives for performing generative design study. Generally, the objective of generative design study is to either reduce the mass or increase the stiffness of model but in Autodesk Fusion Generative Design, you can also specify limiting factors for design simulations like safety factor, starting modal frequency, maximum displacement allowed, and so on. The procedure to use this tool is given next.

- Click on the **Objectives** tool from the **DESIGN CRITERIA** drop-down in the **DEFINE** tab of the **Ribbon**. The **OBJECTIVES AND LIMITS** dialog box will be displayed; refer to Figure-15.
- Select the **Minimize Mass** radio button to reduce maximum possible mass while keeping model strength enough to get safety factor specified in **Safety Factor** edit box of this dialog box.
- Select the **Maximize Stiffness** radio button to increase the strength of model while keeping mass of model near the value specified in **Mass Target** edit box of this dialog box; refer to Figure-16.

Figure-15. OBJECTIVES AND LIMITS dialog box

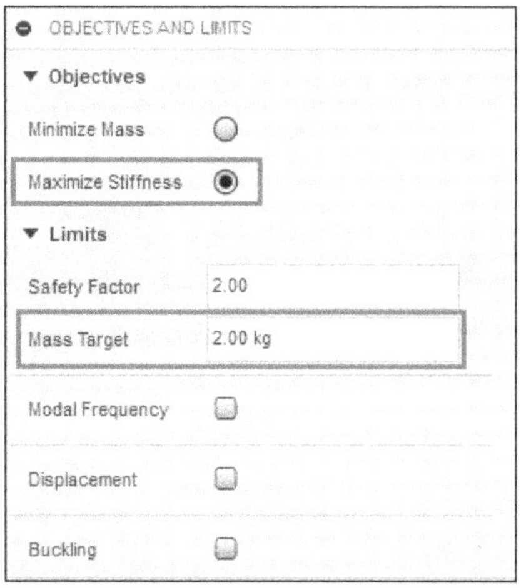

Figure-16. Mass Target edit box

- Select **Modal Frequency** check box to define the lowest frequency at which the design's response occurs.
- Select the **Displacement** check box to define the distance upto which displacement in model will be allowed in different directions.
- Select **Buckling** check box to specify the safety factor value that is sufficient to avoid buckling of the design.
- After setting desired parameters, click on the **OK** button from the dialog box.

Defining Manufacturing Criteria

The **Manufacturing** tool in **DESIGN CRITERIA** drop-down of **Ribbon** is used to define the manufacturing processes by which the model will be manufactured after generating designs. The design alternatives generated by Generative Design will be based on the manufacturing processes selected. For example, if Milling process is selected then software will make sure to include only those features in design which can be manufactured by milling. You can select multiple processes to explore design alternatives for respective processes. The procedure to use this tool is given next.

- Click on the **Manufacturing** tool from the **DESIGN CRITERIA** drop-down in the **DEFINE** tab of the **Ribbon**. The **MANUFACTURING** dialog box will be displayed; refer to Figure-17.

Figure-17. MANUFACTURING dialog box

- Select the **Unrestricted** check box to tell software that manufacturing constraints do not apply when generating different shapes. Selecting this check box is not advised when you want to generate a manufacturable model for production because giving software total freedom in generating shapes can produce design alternatives which may not be possible to manufacture using conventional machines causing the cost of production to go high.
- Select the **Additive** check box to use 3D printing for manufacturing of model. This will make software to generate designs which are manufacturable by Additive manufacturing processes. After selecting check box, define the direction in which nozzle of 3D printer will create layers. Select the **Include all directions** check box to perform manufacturing in all directions. Specify desired values in the **Overhang Angle** and **Minimum Thickness** edit boxes as discussed earlier.

- Select the **Milling** check box to use Milling as manufacturing process for producing model. By default, a 3-axis machine configuration is added in the machine list. You can add as many machining configurations as available in your machine shop. For example, if you have three machines available in your machine shop like 2.5 axis, 3-axis, and 5-axis mill machines then you can add the new configurations by using **Add new configuration** button from the **Milling** section; refer to Figure-18. Specify desired values for minimum tool diameter, tool shoulder length, and head (shaft and holder) diameter in respective edit boxes.
- Select the **2-axis Cutting** check box if you want to include laser/waterjet/plasma cutting manufacturing processes for generating designs. Note that if you have selected multiple manufacturing processes in this dialog box then designs for all selected processes will be generated separately.
- After setting desired parameters in the dialog box, click on the **OK** button from the dialog box.

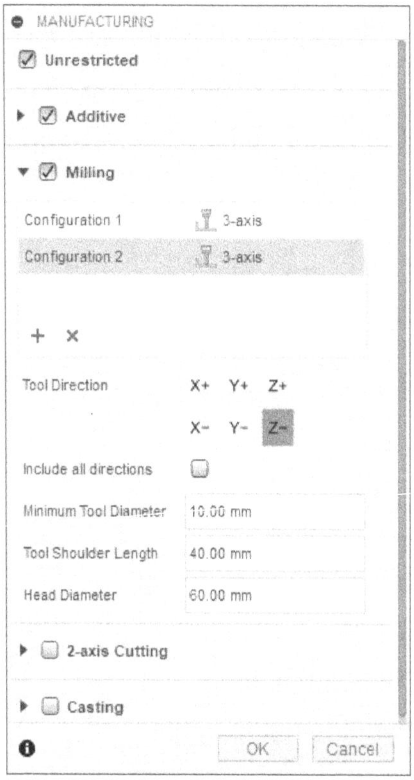

Figure-18. Adding new configurations

SELECTING STUDY MATERIALS

In Autodesk Fusion Generative Design, you can select multiple materials to check different variations of the design. Generally, material cost takes a fair share in total manufacturing cost of product. If you can find a cheaper material that fulfills all the design requirements then it will reduce the final cost of production. The procedure to select materials for design study is given next.

- Click on the **Study Materials** tool from the **MATERIALS** drop-down in the **DEFINE** tab of the **Ribbon**. The **STUDY MATERIALS** dialog box will be displayed; refer to Figure-19.

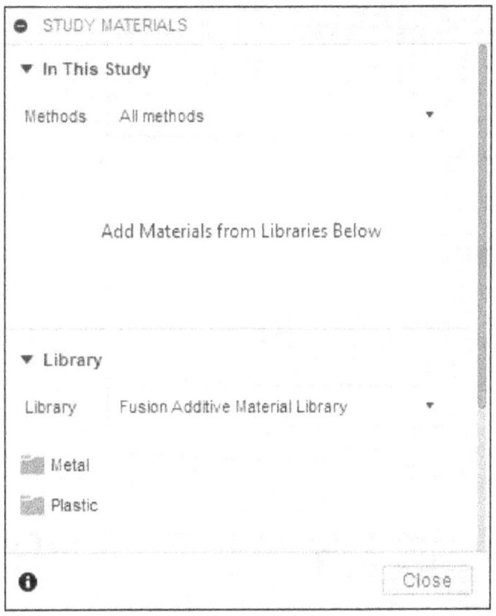

Figure-19. STUDY MATERIALS dialog box

- If you have selected additive manufacturing process along with other processes then by default, **Fusion Additive Material Library** option will be selected in the **Library** drop-down of the **Library** section in the dialog box. This happens because here, the limiting process for manufacturing is 3D printing, the other manufacturing processes can handle almost all the available materials in Fusion Material Library. So, it is advised to choose materials from additive material library only. Expand desired material folder from Library section, select the material you want to add in study, and then drag it to **In This Study** section of the dialog box; refer to Figure-20. You can add up to 7 different materials (including the material applied in design environment) in the study.
- If you want to remove a material from the list then right-click on it and select the **Delete** option from shortcut menu displayed; refer to Figure-21.

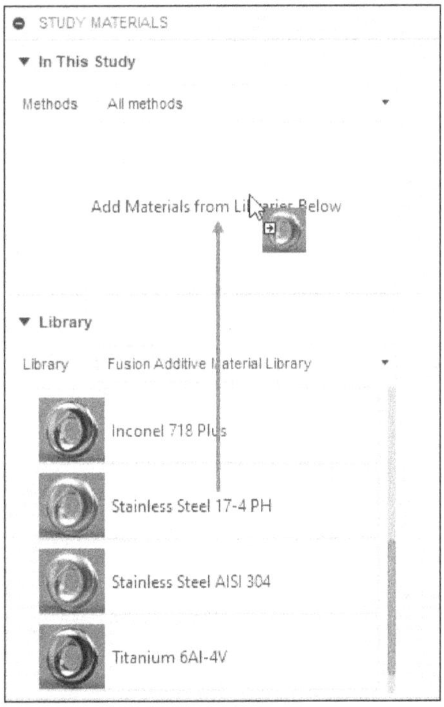

Figure-20. Adding study material

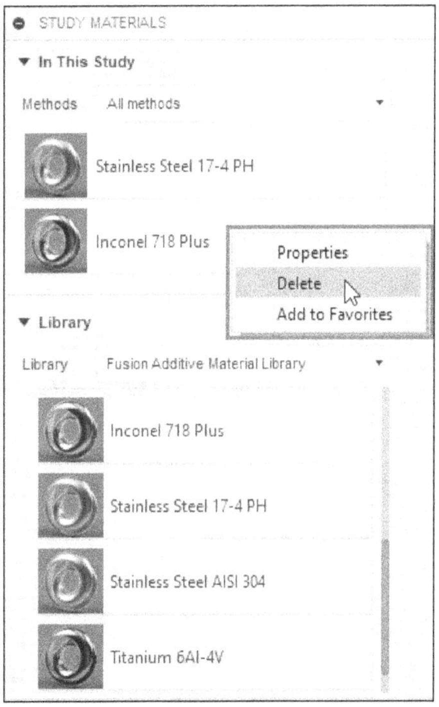

Figure-21. Removing material from list

- After adding desired materials, click on the **Close** button to exit dialog box.

PREFORMING PRE-CHECK

Click on the **Pre-check** tool from the **GENERATE** drop-down to check whether all the requirements to perform study are met or not. If everything is in place then **Ready to Generate** dialog box will be displayed; refer to Figure-22. Click on the **OK** button to exit the dialog box.

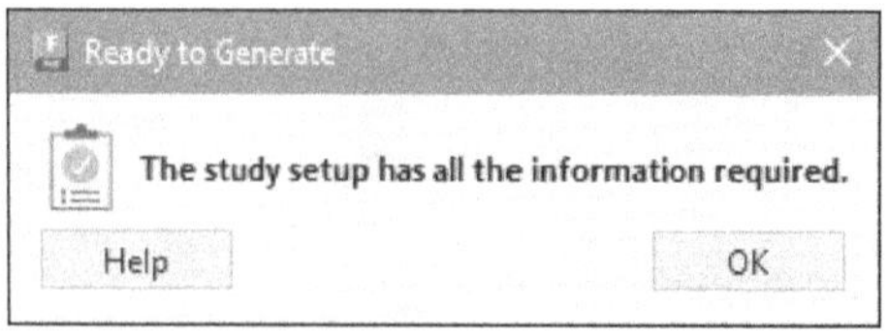

Figure-22. Ready to Generate dialog box

CHECKING PREVIEW OF GENERATIVE DESIGN

The **Previewer** tool in **GENERATE** drop-down of **Ribbon** is used to check preview of study results by solving the study setup without including manufacturing and material settings; refer to Figure-23. Previewer performs calculates locally to display result preview. This tool helps in finding which sections of model are getting modified by study. If you find unwanted areas of model being modified then you can change the setup before finally solving the study. After checking preview, click on the **Stop Previewer** tool from **GENERATE** drop-down of **Ribbon** to exit preview mode.

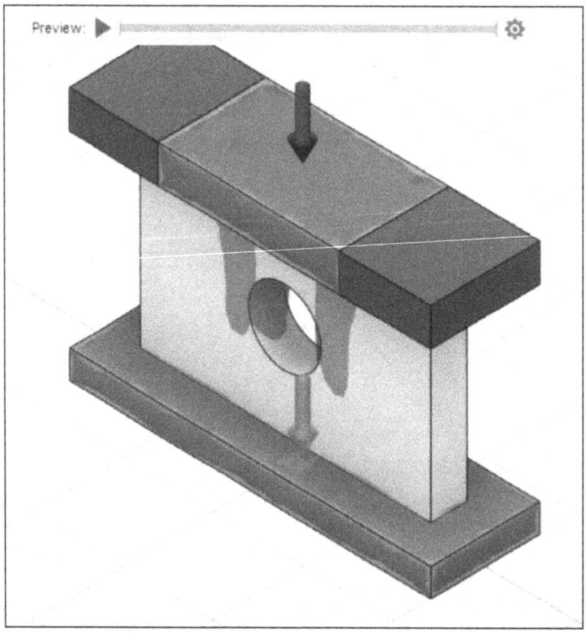

Figure-23. Preview of generative design study

STUDY SETTINGS

The study settings are used to define the scope within which study will be performed. You have learned about study settings earlier in Chapters related to Simulation. To access the settings of Generative Design study, click on the **Study Settings** tool from the **STUDY** drop-down in the **Ribbon** or press **E** from keyboard. The **Study Settings** dialog box will be displayed; refer to Figure-24. Using the **Outcomes resolution** slider, specify the smoothness level in model structure up to which you want to generate the designs. After setting desired parameter, click on the **OK** button from the dialog box.

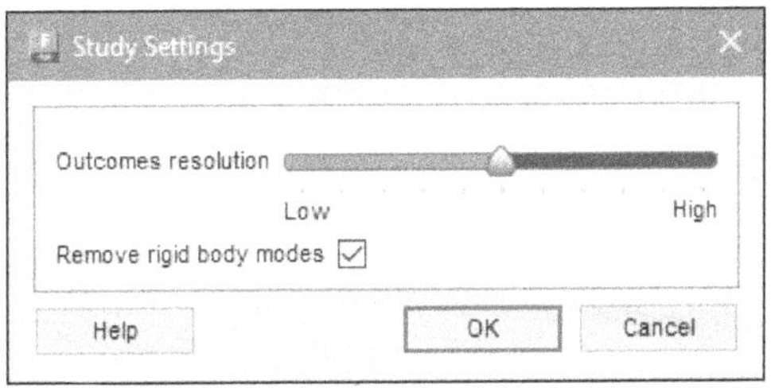

Figure-24. Study Settings dialog box

GENERATING DESIGNS

The **Generate** tool in **GENERATE** drop-down of **Ribbon** is used to solve study for getting design variations. The procedure to use this tool is given next.

- Click on the **Generate** tool in **GENERATE** drop-down of **Ribbon**. The **Generate** dialog box will be displayed similar to **Solve** dialog box discussed earlier in Simulation; refer to Figure-25.

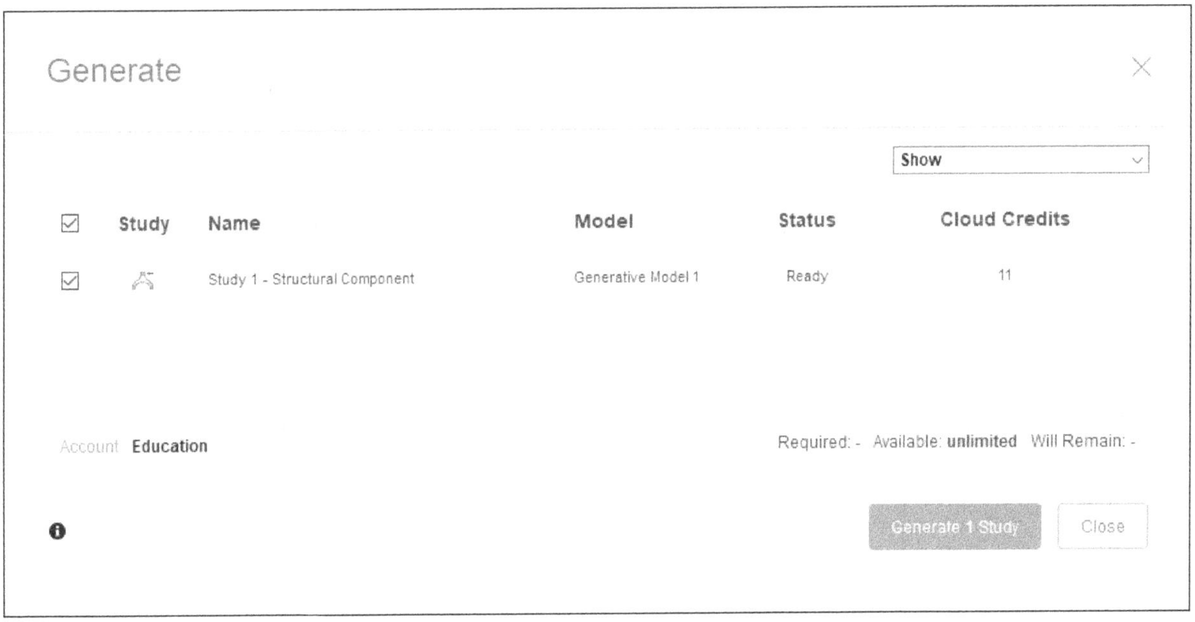

Figure-25. Generate dialog box

- Click on the **Generate Study** button from the bottom of dialog box to perform study. The status of study will be displayed in **Job Status** dialog box; refer to Figure-26. Once the study is complete, you can check the results in Explore environment displayed automatically.

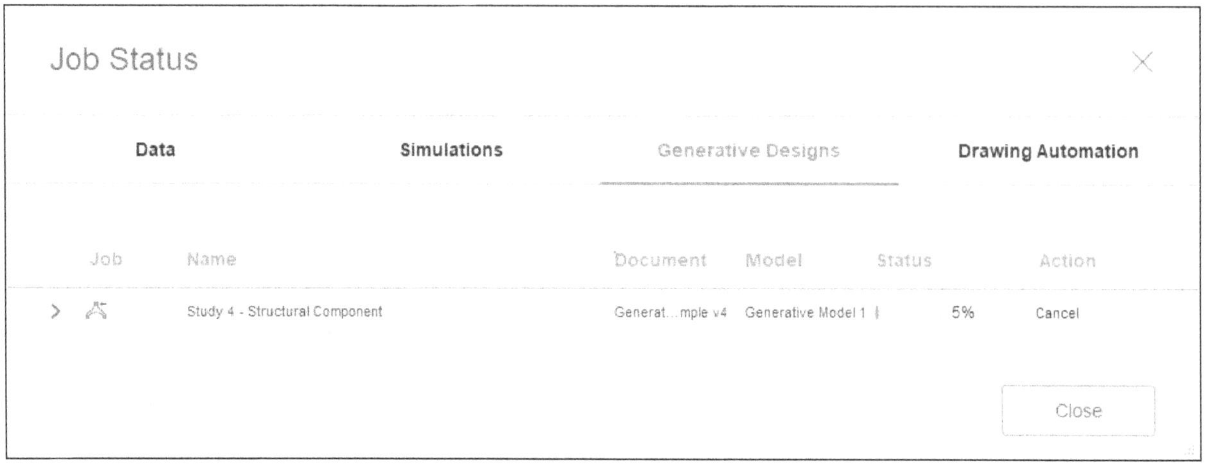

Figure-26. Job Status dialog box

- You can filter the designs based on specified criteria in **Outcome Filters** section of the application window; refer to Figure-27.

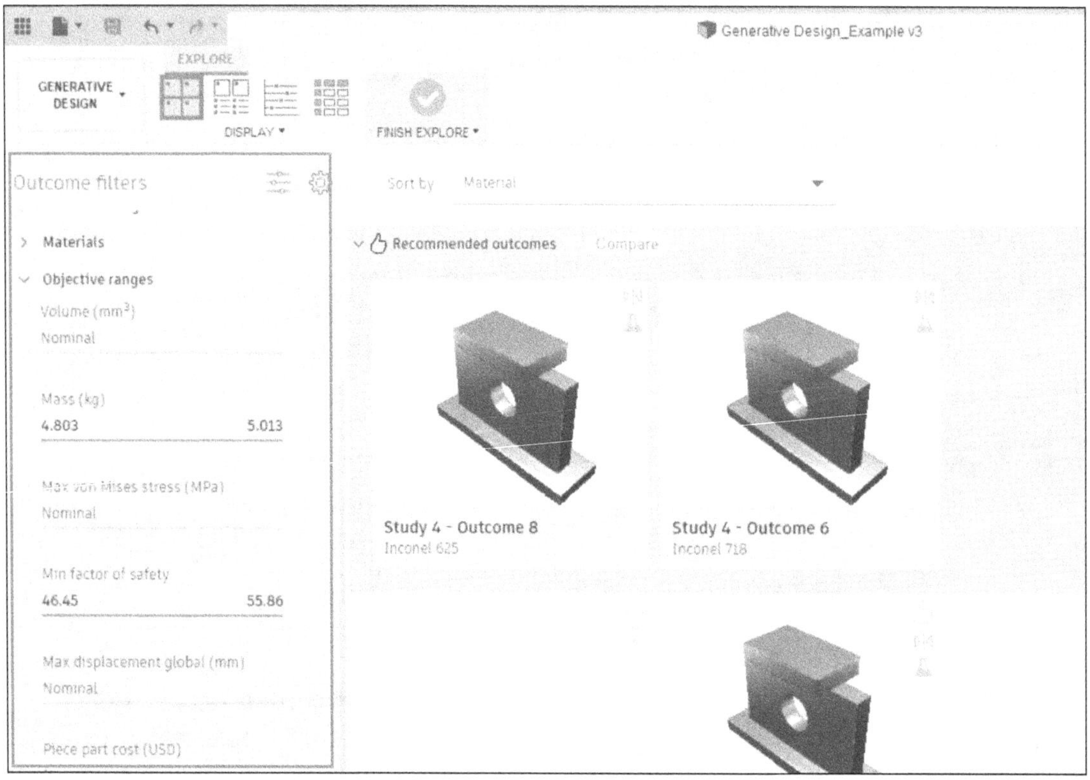

Figure-27. Outcome filters

- Double-click on desired design alternative which you find most suitable for your design. The **OUTCOME VIEW** tab will be displayed in **Ribbon** and selected design alternative will be displayed in the drawing area; refer to Figure-28.

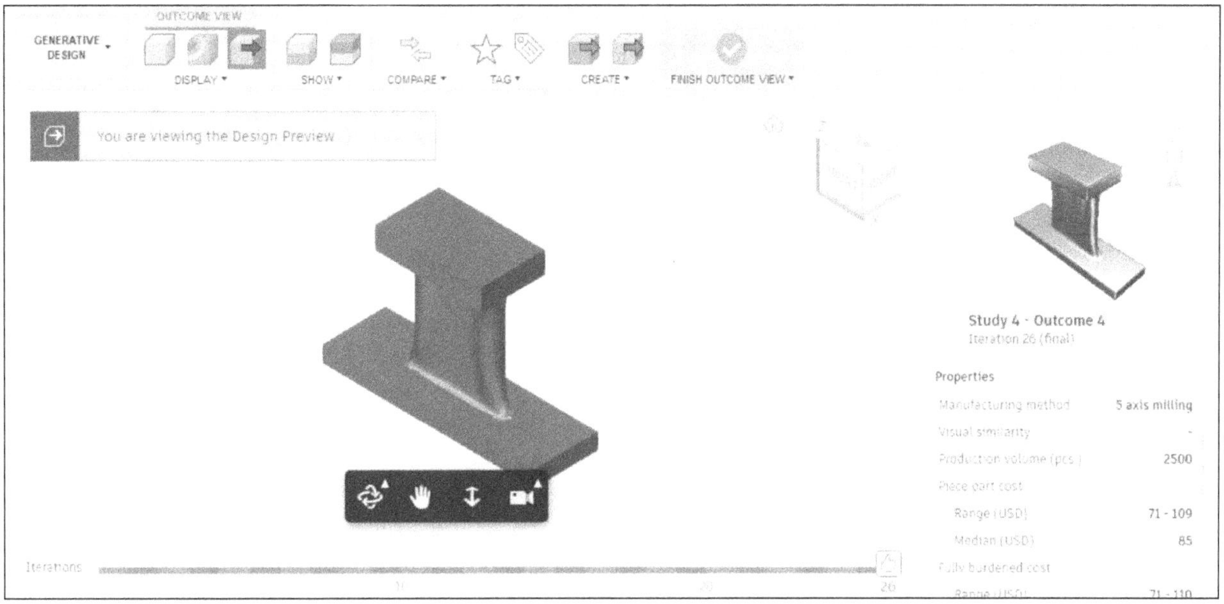

Figure-28. Outcome of Generative Design

- Check various results of outcome using the tools available in **DISPLAY** and **SHOW** drop-downs of the **Ribbon**. You can use the **Compare** tool of **COMPARE** drop-down to compare two outcomes.
- To create design from the outcome, click on the **Design from Outcome** tool from the **CREATE** drop-down in the **OUTCOME VIEW** tab of the **Ribbon**. The **Create a design from this outcome** dialog box will be displayed; refer to Figure-29.

Figure-29. Create design dialog box

- Click on the **Create design** button from the dialog box. The design model file will be generated using cloud server services and after the process is complete, model will be displayed in **DESIGN** workspace; refer to Figure-30. You can modify the design as discussed in previous chapters.

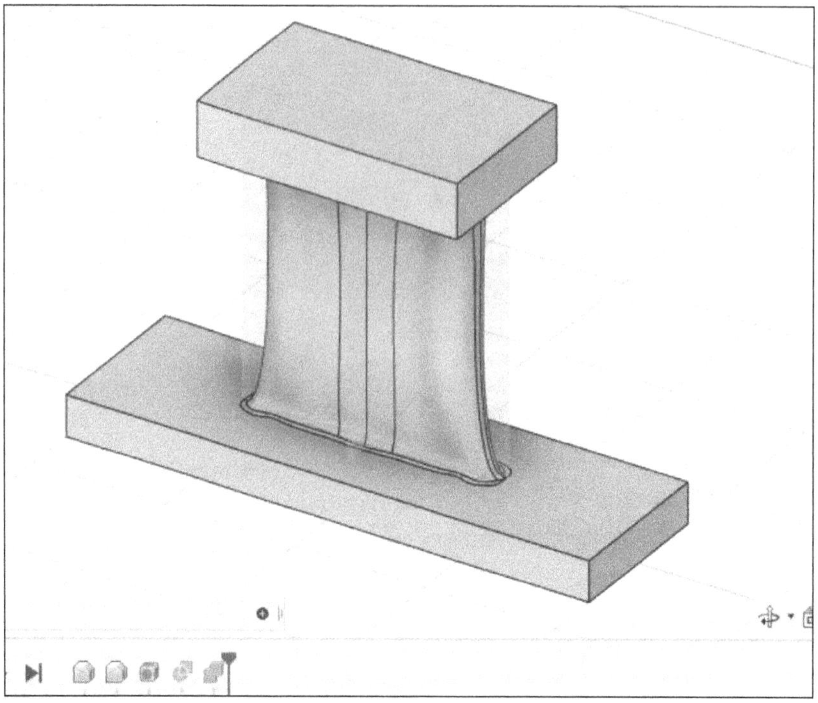

Figure-30. Design model of outcome

Similarly, you can use the **Mesh Design from Outcome** tool to generate mesh model using outcome.

SELF ASSESSMENT

Q1. What is the difference between generative design and optimization study?

Q2. Using Generative Design study, you can reduce the weight of parts and components while keeping them as effective in the assembly under loads. (T/F)

Q3. The .... tool is used to keep selected portion of the model as it is in all variations of the model generated by study.

Q4. The .... geometries are those which cannot be modified by generative design and do not allow generative design variations to expand past them.

Q5. The .... tool is used to define initial shape from which generative design outcomes will be generated.

Q6. Minimizing Mass of the model is only objective of generative design study. (T/F)

Q7. The Fluid Path Generative Study is used to create hollow geometry for fluid flow which has optimized pressure drop. (T/F)

Q8. What is the purpose of the Learning Panel in Autodesk Fusion?
A. To access interactive help on using Generative Design and other features
B. To edit the material properties of a design
C. To create new generative design studies
D. To define manufacturing constraints

Q9. What is the first step in creating a new Generative Design Study?
A. Selecting the material for the study
B. Clicking on the New Generative Study tool from the STUDY drop-down
C. Defining the symmetry plane
D. Performing a fluid path generative study

Q10. Which tool is used to define regions that must remain unchanged in all design variations?
A. Obstacle Geometry
B. Preserve Geometry
C. Starting Shape
D. Symmetry Plane

Q11. What does the Objectives tool in the DESIGN CRITERIA drop-down allow users to do?
A. Define manufacturing constraints
B. Set objectives like minimizing mass or maximizing stiffness
C. Add obstacle geometries
D. Define symmetry planes

Q12. Which manufacturing process allows 3D printing for model creation?
A. Milling
B. Additive
C. 2-axis Cutting
D. Die Casting

Q13. Which tool is used to check whether all parameters are set correctly before running a study?
A. Generate
B. Study Settings
C. Pre-Check
D. Previewer

Q14. What does the Previewer tool in GENERATE drop-down do?
A. Generates the final design
B. Checks preview of study results without manufacturing and material settings
C. Defines study materials
D. Performs fluid path generative study

Q18. What is the purpose of Generative Design in Autodesk Fusion?
A. To manually create designs for 3D printing
B. To use AI-powered algorithms to explore design possibilities
C. To create animated simulations of mechanical parts
D. To replace CAD modeling with automated sketches

Q19. What is the role of the Preserve Geometry tool in Generative Design?
A. To define areas that must be retained in all design iterations
B. To specify regions that should not be part of the final shape
C. To generate a new shape from scratch
D. To add materials to the design

Q20. In Autodesk Fusion's Generative Design workflow, what is the purpose of the Study Materials tool?
A. To specify multiple materials that the software can evaluate
B. To automatically assign the most cost-effective material
C. To limit the design to only one pre-selected material
D. To convert an existing model into a generative study

Q21. How does Obstacle Geometry affect a Generative Design study?
A. It ensures that no material is added in certain regions
B. It allows unrestricted material placement in all areas
C. It sets a boundary for the final part size
D. It optimizes material strength in specific areas

Q22. What happens if no Manufacturing Constraints are applied in a Generative Design study?
A. The design will be optimized for traditional machining
B. The software will assume additive manufacturing by default
C. The software will generate the most optimized shape without considering feasibility
D. The study will fail to generate any results

Q23. Which Symmetry Plane option should be selected when designing a mirror-image part?
A. No symmetry
B. Single-plane symmetry
C. Two-plane symmetry
D. Three-plane symmetry

Q24. What does the Minimum Thickness setting in Generative Design do?
A. Prevents thin, weak sections in the generated model
B. Increases the weight of the final part
C. Reduces computational time during study generation
D. Defines the maximum allowable thickness of the design

Q25. What is the primary advantage of using Generative Design over traditional CAD modeling?
A. It allows fully manual control over the final design
B. It generates optimized designs that minimize material usage and weight
C. It eliminates the need for engineers in the design process
D. It focuses only on aesthetics rather than function

Q26. Which tool in Autodesk Fusion allows users to analyze stress distribution in a generated design?
A. Pre-Check
B. Shape Optimization
C. Simulation
D. Flow Path Analysis

Q27. How does Load Definition affect a Generative Design study?
A. It determines where forces are applied and how the structure responds
B. It restricts the size of the generated model
C. It selects the best material for the study
D. It specifies the manufacturing process

Q28. What does Factor of Safety (FOS) represent in Generative Design results?
A. The ratio of applied stress to yield strength
B. The estimated cost of manufacturing
C. The minimum material thickness required
D. The number of iterations completed in the study

Q29. Which of the following statements about Generative Design is false?
A. It can explore multiple design alternatives automatically
B. It always generates a single final design
C. It can incorporate real-world constraints and forces
D. It allows users to specify materials and manufacturing methods

Q30. What is the purpose of the Shape Preview tool in Generative Design?
A. To generate the final design without manufacturing considerations
B. To provide a quick visualization of how the generated shape will look
C. To manually edit the generated shape
D. To compare different materials

FOR STUDENT NOTES

Index

Symbols

A

B

C

D

Q

R

V

W

X

Y

Z

Ethics of an Engineer

- Engineers shall hold paramount the safety, health and welfare of the public and shall strive to comply with the principles of sustainable development in the performance of their professional duties.
- Engineers shall perform services only in areas of their competence.
- Engineers shall issue public statements only in an objective and truthful manner.
- Engineers shall act in professional manners for each employer or client as faithful agents or trustees, and shall avoid conflicts of interest.
- Engineers shall build their professional reputation on the merit of their services and shall not compete unfairly with others.
- Engineers shall act in such a manner as to uphold and enhance the honor, integrity, and dignity of the engineering profession and shall act with zero-tolerance for bribery, fraud, and corruption.
- Engineers shall continue their professional development throughout their careers, and shall provide opportunities for the professional development of those engineers under their supervision.

OTHER BOOKS BY CADCAMCAE WORKS

Autodesk Revit 2026 Black Book
Autodesk Revit 2025 Black Book
Autodesk Revit 2024 Black Book
Autodesk Revit 2023 Black Book

Autodesk Inventor 2026 Black Book
Autodesk Inventor 2025 Black Book
Autodesk Inventor 2024 Black Book
Autodesk Inventor 2023 Black Book

Autodesk Fusion Black Book (V 2701.1.18)
Autodesk Fusion PCB Black Book (V 2701.1.18)

AutoCAD Electrical 2026 Black Book
AutoCAD Electrical 2025 Black Book
AutoCAD Electrical 2024 Black Book
AutoCAD Electrical 2023 Black Book

Basics of Autodesk Inventor Nastran 2026
Basics of Autodesk Inventor Nastran 2025

Autodesk CFD 2026 Black Book
Autodesk CFD 2024 Black Book

Tinkercad Black Book: (2nd Edition)

SolidWorks 2026 Black Book
SolidWorks 2025 Black Book
SolidWorks 2024 Black Book
SolidWorks 2023 Black Book

SolidWorks Simulation 2026 Black Book
SolidWorks Simulation 2025 Black Book
SolidWorks Simulation 2024 Black Book
SolidWorks Simulation 2023 Black Book

SolidWorks Flow Simulation 2026 Black Book
SolidWorks Flow Simulation 2025 Black Book
SolidWorks Flow Simulation 2024 Black Book

SolidWorks CAM 2026 Black Book
SolidWorks CAM 2025 Black Book
SolidWorks CAM 2024 Black Book
SolidWorks CAM 2023 Black Book

SolidWorks Electrical 2026 Black Book
SolidWorks Electrical 2025 Black Book
SolidWorks Electrical 2024 Black Book

SolidWorks Workbook 2022

Mastercam 2023 for SolidWorks Black Book
Mastercam 2022 for SolidWorks Black Book
Mastercam 2017 for SolidWorks Black Book

Mastercam 2026 Black Book
Mastercam 2025 Black Book
Mastercam 2024 Black Book
Mastercam 2023 Black Book

Creo Parametric 12.0 Black Book
Creo Parametric 11.0 Black Book
Creo Parametric 10.0 Black Book
Creo Parametric 9.0 Black Book
Creo Parametric 8.0 Black Book

Creo Manufacturing 12.0 Black Book
Creo Manufacturing 11.0 Black Book
Creo Manufacturing 10.0 Black Book
Creo Manufacturing 9.0 Black Book

ETABS V22 Black Book
ETABS V21 Black Book
ETABS V20 Black Book
ETABS V19 Black Book

FreeCAD 1.0 Black Book
FreeCAD 0.21 Black Book
FreeCAD 0.20 Black Book
FreeCAD 0.19 Black Book

LibreCAD 2.2 Black Book

Ansys Discovery 2025 Black Book

www.ingramcontent.com/pod-product-compliance
Lightning Source LLC
LaVergne TN
LVHW080524210926
848481LV00022B/2824